PHILIP'S 20

ROAD ATLA

Britain and Ireland

About Philip's maps

This atlas contains maps at different scales to get you to your destination as easily and as quickly as possible.

Route planning maps show the whole country at a glance, so you can choose the most direct route, whether on motorways or A-roads. Road numbers, junction numbers, motorway services and dual carriageways are all clearly marked.

Road maps at 3 miles to 1 inch (Scottish Highlands and Islands at 4 miles to 1 inch) show the road network in detail and mark hundreds of places of interest. The roads are colour coded according to importance. Scenic routes are highlighted and in country areas lanes over 4 metres wide are coloured yellow.

Approach maps at 1⅓ miles to 1 inch guide you through the suburbs of major cities, and give road names as well as numbers.

Town plans show the streets in the central area and mark one ways, car parks, stations and important buildings.

Philip's road maps were voted the clearest and most detailed in an independent consumer survey with 442 respondents.

Contents

II **Top 10 Tips** to avoid speeding fines

IV **Mobile speed camera sites**

X **Route planning maps** with list of restricted motorway junctions

XVI **Distance table**

1 **Key to road map pages**

2 **Road maps of Britain at 3 miles to 1 inch**

177 **Town plans and urban approach maps**

177 Aberdeen
Aberystwyth
178 Barrow-in-Furness
Bath
179 Birmingham
180 Birmingham *approaches*
182 Blackpool
Bournemouth
183 Bradford
Brighton
202 Bradford and Leeds *approaches*
184 Bristol
185 Bristol *approaches*
186 Cardiff
187 Cardiff *approaches*
188 Cambrdge
Canterbury
189 Carlisle
Cheltenham
190 Chester
Colchester
191 Coventry
Derby
192 Dorchester
Dundee
193 Durham
Exeter
194 Edinburgh
195 Edinburgh *approaches*
196 Glasgow *approaches*
198 Glasgow
199 Gloucester
Hull
200 Ipswich
Lancaster
201 Leeds
202 Leeds and Bradford *approaches*
204 Liverpool
205 Liverpool *approaches*
206 Leicester
Lincoln
207 London streets
210 London *approaches*
218 Manchester
219 Manchester *approaches*
220 Middlesbrough
Milton Keynes
221 Newport
Northampton
222 Newcastle
223 Newcastle *approaches*
224 Norwich
Nottingham
225 Nottingham *approaches*
226 Oxford
Plymouth
227 Poole
Portsmouth
228 Preston
Reading
229 Salisbury
Scarborough
230 Sheffield
231 Sheffield *approaches*
232 Shewsbury
Southampton
233 Stoke on Trent (Hanley)
Stratford-upon-Avon
234 Sunderland
Swansea
235 Swindon
Telford
236 Torquay
Winchester
237 Windsor
Wolverhampton
238 Worcester
York

239 M25 and routes into London
240 M60 and routes into Manchester and Liverpool

241 **Airport and port plans**

241 Heathrow, Gatwick, Manchester
242 Dover, Felixstowe, Portsmouth, Southampton

243 **The Channel**

243 Boulogne and Calais – town plans and approaches
244 Cross-Channel ferry map

246 **Ireland**

246 Road maps of Ireland at 10 miles to 1 inch
253 Belfast and Cork town plans
254 Derry/Londonderry and Dublin town plans
255 Index to road maps of Ireland

257 **Index to road maps of Britain**

First published in 2003 by Philip's
a division of Octopus Publishing Group Ltd
2–4 Heron Quays, London E14 4JP

www.philips-maps.co.uk

First edition 2006
Second impression 2006

Cartography by Philip's

Data for the speed cameras provided by PocketGPSWorld.com Ltd.

Information for Tourist Attractions in England supplied by the British Tourist Authority / English Tourist Board.

Information for National Parks, Areas of Outstanding Natural Beauty, National Trails and Country Parks in Wales supplied by the Countryside Council for Wales.

Information for National Parks, Areas of Outstanding Natural Beauty, National Trails and Country Parks in England supplied by the Countryside Agency.

Data for Regional Parks, Long Distance Footpaths and Country Parks in Scotland provided by Scottish Natural Heritage.

Gaelic name forms used in the Western Isles provided by Comhairle nan Eilean.

Data for the National Nature Reserves in England provided by English Nature.

Data for the National Nature Reserves in Wales provided by Countryside Council for Wales. Darparwyd data'n ymwneud â Gwarchodfeydd Natur Cenedlaethol Cymru gan Gyngor Cefn Gwlad Cymru.

Information on the location of National Nature Reserves in Scotland was provided by Scottish Natural Heritage.

Data for National Scenic Areas in Scotland provided by the Scottish Executive Office. Crown copyright material is reproduced with the permission of the Controller of HMSO and the Queen's Printer for Scotland. Licence number C02W0003960.

The maps of Ireland on pages 246 to 254 are based on Ordnance Survey Ireland by permission of the Government Permit Number 8097 © Ordnance Survey Ireland and Government of Ireland, and

ORDNANCE SURVEY® OF NORTHERN IRELAND Ordnance Survey Northern Ireland on behalf of the controller of Her Majesty's Stationery Office © Crown copyright 2006 Permit Number 60127.

The town plans of Calais and Boulogne are based on data supplied by Hachette Livre. The road mapping of Northern France was supplied by Blay-Foldex SA Copyright © Blay-Foldex SA

Printed in Italy by Rotolito

Cover photograph: Upper Lake, Killarney National Park, County Kerry 250 B3
nagelestock.com / Alamy

Photographic acknowlegements:
Cover: *nagelestock.com / Alamy* • Page II top *Mark Sykes / Alamy* • Page II bottom *South West Images Scotland / Alamy* • Page III, clockwise from top right: *Jack Sullivan / Alamy; Adrian Sherratt / Alamy; Tony Charnock / Alamy; Iain Cooper / Alamy; Simon Holdcroft / Alamy; Mike Harrington / Alamy*

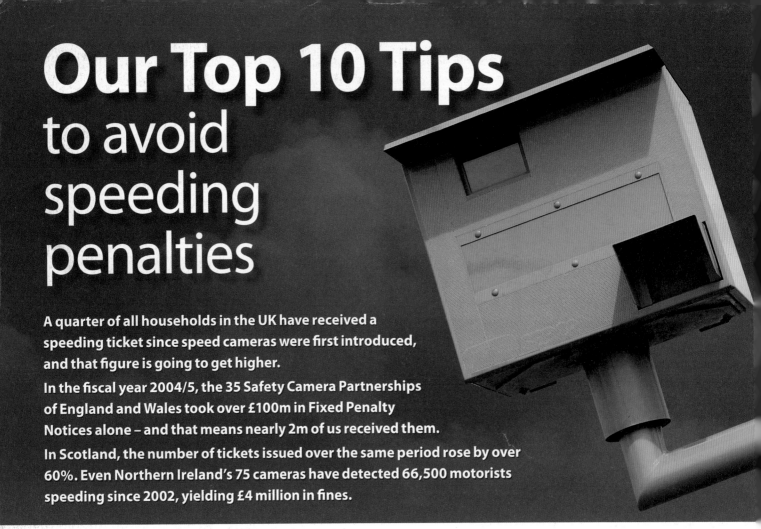

Our Top 10 Tips to avoid speeding penalties

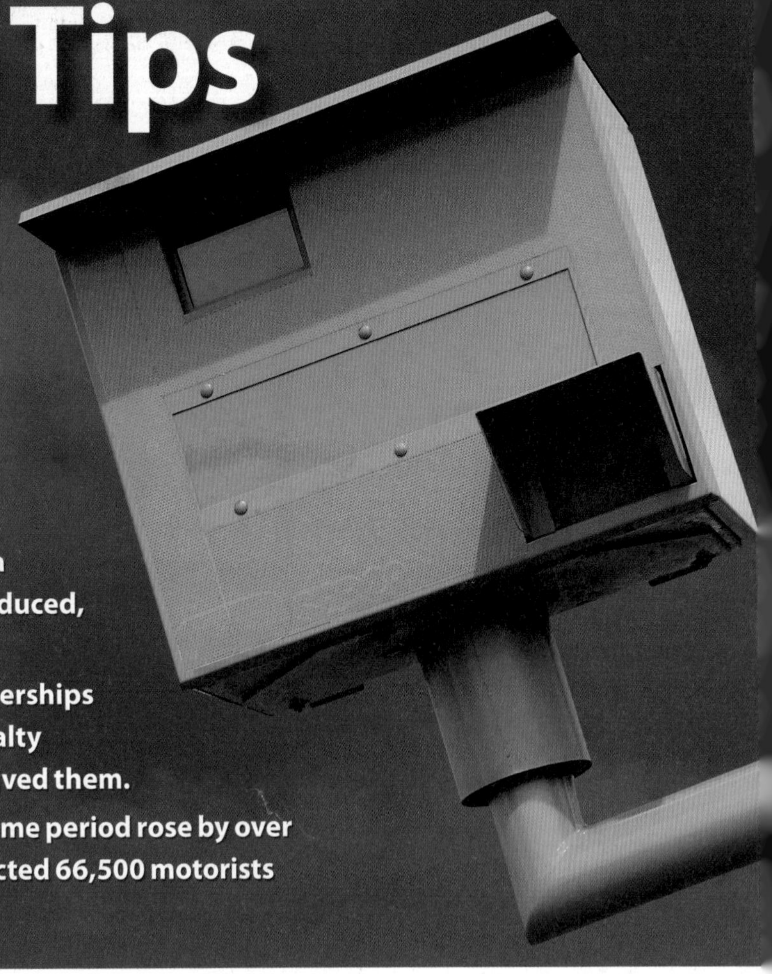

A quarter of all households in the UK have received a speeding ticket since speed cameras were first introduced, and that figure is going to get higher.

In the fiscal year 2004/5, the 35 Safety Camera Partnerships of England and Wales took over £100m in Fixed Penalty Notices alone – and that means nearly 2m of us received them.

In Scotland, the number of tickets issued over the same period rose by over 60%. Even Northern Ireland's 75 cameras have detected 66,500 motorists speeding since 2002, yielding £4 million in fines.

We asked Stephen Mesquita, speed camera expert, who last year spearheaded a national television campaign to publicise camera locations, to give his Top 10 Tips about what you can and can't do to avoid the cost of speeding fines, and keep the penalty points off your licence.

First, some facts: There are now over 3,300 fixed camera sites in the UK and about 3,400 'located' mobile sites listed on the official web sites. So the total's climbing towards 7,000 (far more than the 4,500 some websites quote).

If you are caught speeding, you can agree to pay a fixed £60 fine and get 3 points on your licence. The points normally stay on your licence for 4 years (11 if the conviction was drink- or drug-related or you failed to provide a specimen for analysis). In some cases, breaking a temporary speed limit where there are roadworks will only trigger the fine, not the endorsement. If you get 12 points on your licence within a three year period – or just 6 in your first two years as a driver – you will be banned from driving.

> ...what's left is a legacy of inconsistency...

If you go over the speed limit by too much, you'll get an automatic summons – then, at the discretion of the court, the fines will be higher and the points could go up to 6 or even a ban.

You can challenge the penalty in court. But if you lose, it's likely to prove expensive.

Let me come clean from the start. I'm in favour of speed cameras where they do genuinely stop accidents (most people are). And I'm in favour of safe driving. But what the UK has ended up with is a mess.

Originally police forces were allowed to make their own decisions, place cameras where they liked, and raise as much money as possible. Then, when the government saw how unpopular speed cameras were becoming, they backtracked. First, cameras had to be placed only at accident black spots. Then the fines had to be siphoned back into road safety via the Treasury. Now the government has decreed that new cameras are only to be used if it can be proved that they are the best way to reduce accidents. That's fine – but what's left is a legacy of inconsistency that, unless it is sorted out, will continue to baffle and upset the law-abiding motorist.

So read on – because, if this hasn't affected you yet, it may well do in the future.

1 Beware camera-infested counties

Yes, I know. It's not a very practical suggestion but there is a serious point behind it. The Safety Camera Partnerships set up in each county stress that there are strict criteria for the siting of cameras – but there seems to be a concentration of cameras in some counties which aren't necessarily the busiest or the most dangerous to drive in. Which either means that the rules aren't being consistently applied or we are still living with cameras located before the rules came into being.

England and Wales

So, if the number of fixed cameras is anything to go by, here are the Top 10 counties to avoid in England and Wales (in order of fixed camera numbers)

1 London	6 Mid and South Wales
2 Staffordshire	7 West Yorkshire
3 Lancashire	8 Derbyshire
4 West Midlands	9 Hertfordshire
5 Thames Valley	10 Devon and Cornwall

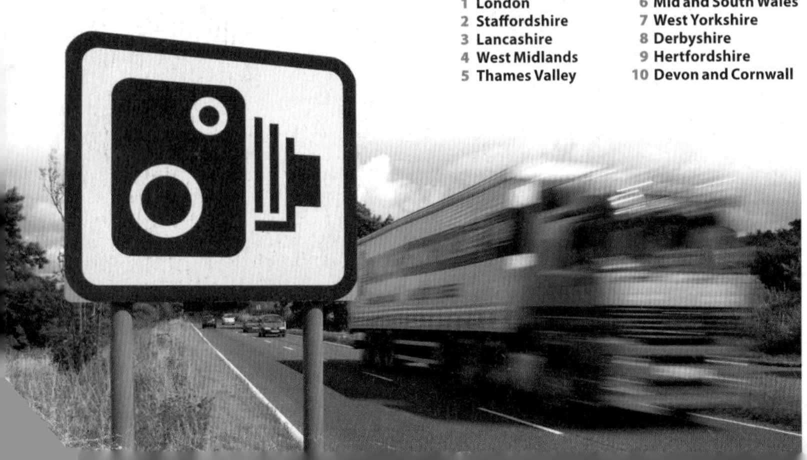

Some of those you'd expect to be in the list. Others are a surprise. There are some quite busy counties, like Hampshire and Surrey, that have less than a third of the fixed cameras of any of those in our list. That's because their Safety Camera Partnerships didn't inherit a speed-camera jungle so were able to apply the accident black spot rules from scratch.

But more to the point, which counties raised the most revenue – and were they the ones with the most fixed cameras? Here are the top 10 income generators from Fixed Penalty Notices in 2004-5 Financial Year in England and Wales:

1 London	6 Northumbria
2 Mid and South Wales	7 West Yorks
3 Thames Valley	8 Kent
4 Avon and Somerset	9 Nottinghamshire
5 Essex	10 Lancashire

You'd expect London to be top. But productivity in Northumbria, whose web site lists only around 120 fixed and mobile sites, is remarkable. Similarly, Nottinghamshire, at number 9, lists under 100 fixed cameras and no mobile sites.

> ...productivity in Northumbria is remarkable

We haven't produced a similar table for 'located' mobile sites, because it is impossible to find a consistent measure. Some counties only publicise the sites they are likely to monitor that week. Others give no mobile site information at all. Some define a mobile site with pinpoint accuracy, while others, like Fife in Scotland, simply highlight a stretch of road that could be 10 miles long. And how on earth did the inhabitants of Carmarthenshire earn a quarter of all the mobile locations in Wales? Confused by all this? So are we.

Scotland

Don't think you can escape in Scotland. There are fewer fixed cameras in the whole of Scotland than in any of the Top 5 English counties, but not surprisingly, Strathclyde and Lothian and Borders are the most camera-infested regions, with few or no fixed cameras in Highland, Fife or Dumfries and Galloway. Mobile camera sites are more evenly spread through the regions.

Ireland

In the North, there are only 4 fixed cameras and 71 mobile sites. In the Republic, there are just 3 cameras working in 20 boxes at any one time. But beware: a government report has recommended privatising speed cameras and allowing 600 of them to be operated by private operators – and not just at accident black spots. Not surprisingly, this has caused an outcry among the motoring organizations ('like shooting fish in a barrel' said one) – so watch this space.

2 Beware 30 and 40 mph limits

What are the speed limits for the majority of camera locations?

If your vision of the most common speeding ticket is the event we all see by the side of the motorway (a car stopped by the police car doing well over 70) then you're in for a surprise. The majority of speeding cameras – over 70% of both fixed and 'located' mobile cameras – are in zones where the limit is 30 to 40 mph.

Of course, mobile cameras can be anywhere. But our tip No 2 is – be especially careful of 30 and 40 mile and hour limits. Other than in London, the least guarded speed limit is 50 mph.

3 Stick to the B-Roads and Motorways

Fact: over 60% of the fixed camera sites and over 50% of the 'located' mobile sites are on A-Roads. Most of the rest are on unclassified roads – generally in towns and villages. B-Roads and Motorways are relatively unsurveyed – although the M-ways may have a lot of 'unlocated' sites.

4 Drive like a woman (it's safer)

More than 80% of all speeding penalties are given to men.

There are two types of speeder – the deliberate speeder and the accidental speeder.

If you are interested in the camera locations in this atlas so that you can break the speed limit between them, you're a deliberate speeder, and almost certainly a man. Read on. Our Top 10 Tips might make you more conscious of the chances – and consequences – of being caught.

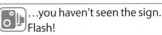

> ...you haven't seen the sign. Flash!

Who are the accidental speeders? Almost everyone at some time. We've all done it. You're in an area that you're not familiar with. It's dark. You're quite alert but you're caught up in the rush hour and the traffic is moving fast. You've gone from a 40 zone to a 30 but you haven't seen the sign. Flash!

The truth is – most of us speed both deliberately and accidentally at some stage in our driving careers. The message is – cameras are widespread and they're not very forgiving.

Speed limits (mph)	Built-up area	Single carriageway	Dual carriageway	Motorway
:ars and motorcycles	30	60	70	70
:ars towing caravans and trailers	30	50	60	60
3uses and Coaches	30	50	60	60
Goods vehicles under 7.5 tonnes	30	50	60	70 (60 if articulated or towing)
Goods vehicles over 7.5 tonnes	30	40	50	60

› if you don't want the fine or the endorsement, ›u need to concentrate as much on your speed as ›u concentrate on not having an accident.

you are a conscientious driver who feels the need › develop your skills of concentration in particular ›d defensive driving in general, then I'd recom- ›end The Institute of Advanced Motorists (IAM) tel: 20 8996 9600.

5 Know your speed limit rules

:reet lights = 30mph, unless it says otherwise. It's a orrible rule. Lots of people who should know about don't. Lots of people who do know about it would ›ke to see it changed.

dd to that the apparently arbitrary definition of 0mph and 40mph limits, and the frequency with ›hich they change, and you have a recipe for con- ›sion. Again, lots of inconsistencies to baffle the ›otorist.

...done for speeding at 31mph in a 30 mph zone

›e round white sign with a black diagonal flash ›rough it means 60 mph max, except on dual car- ›ageways and M-ways.

›ow much leeway do you have? Is it zero tolerance? it the ACPO guidelines of +10%+2mph (that's the ›ssociation of Chief Police Officers, by the way)? Or is somewhere in between? Well, the law is this – you ›n be done for speeding at 31mph in a 30 mph ›ne. As to the complicated equation, the police ›ress that guidelines are just that and they do not al- ›r the law. But they probably would admit that they ›ould be inundated if they stopped every motorist ›ho is driving a couple of mph over the limit.

›u are probably getting a bit of help from your ›eedometer. It's the clever idea of the car makers › set our speedometers 2–3mph faster than we are ›tually going. Now that so many of us have GPS in ›e car, this is getting more widely known. Now you ›ow, it might be wiser to use the extra mph as air ›etween you and a ticket.

6 Learn to tell your Gatso from your Digital Specs

ere's a concise guide to cameras. There are loads of ›fferent species, so we're only going to describe the ›ain families.

›atso – the most common ones. Generally in yel- ›w boxes, they flash you from the back and store ›ur number plate on film. As the film only has 400 ›xposures, don't assume, if you see the flash in your ›ar-view mirror, that you've been done. In fact it's ›ckoned that you have a three in four chance that ›e one you've just passed is not working.

›ruvelo – pink-eyes. The pink eye gives you an in- ›ared flash from the front, after sensors in the road ›ave registered your speed. Unlike the GATSO, which ›n't identify the driver (worth remembering if you ›ant to argue) the TRUVELO gets a mug-shot.

›igital Specs – pairs of video cameras set some ›stance apart to create a no-speeding zone between them. If your average speed over the distance exceeds the limit, you are snapped with an infrared flash. So they are much more testing for the driver. It's one thing slowing down when you see a camera, it's another thing maintaining an average speed over a distance of several miles. Still relatively rare.

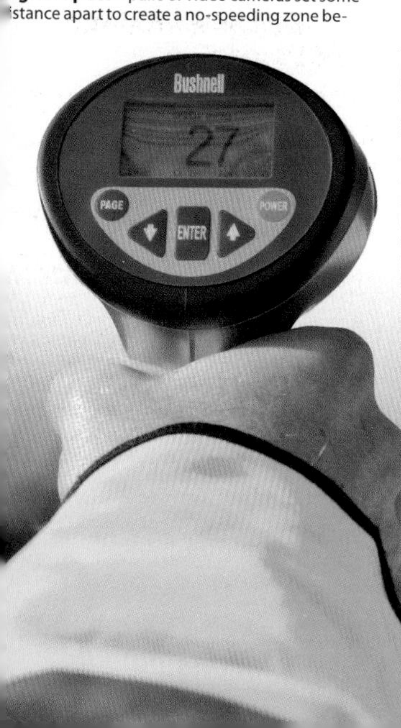

DS2s – strips in the road detect your speed and pass the information to an innocent-looking post at the side of the road. Look out for the detector van nearby, because that's what does the business.

Red light cameras – the UK total is creeping up towards 1,000. If you drive through a traffic light when it's at red, sensors in the road tell the camera to flash you.

All of the above can be detected using GPS devices for fixed cameras but not these -

Lasers – most mobile cameras are Lasers. You normally see a tripod in a van with the backdoors open and facing you; or on a motorway bridge or hand-held by the side of the road. They work – although rumour has it not in very bad weather – and they can't be detected by any of the GPS devices. If you happen to see a local villager touting a laser gun, you may get a letter asking you to drive more carefully but not a fine or penalty points.

7 Know where the cameras are

If you are serious about not getting caught speeding, there are some obvious precautions you can take before setting out.

- Check in this atlas whether there are fixed cameras on the route you are planning to take (they are marked on the map as small yellow squares)
- Check in the listings whether there are 'located' mobile sites on your route.
- Use a camera detector, such as those marketed by Road Angel, Road Pilot or Cyclops. These are perfectly legal, if expensive; they just tell you where the cameras are. Devices that detect and jam police laser detectors are about to be banned.
- Use the web sites for up-to-date information, including guidelines (but only guidelines) about where the police are locating their mobile vans each week. Each Safety Camera Partnership has a website (search for the county name followed by Safety Camera Partnership). Don't use the Department for Transport listings, which were 18 months out of date at the time we went to press.

8 If you do get a ticket, check it carefully

Even if there is film in the camera, you may not get a ticket.

A close study of the accounts of each of the Safety Camera Partnerships of England and Wales reveals a varying success in actually sending out the tickets and collecting the money. Some areas are collecting 100% of their fines. Others, particularly in the major urban areas, collect only just over 50%. The official reason is that tickets are not issued to owners of unregistered cars, foreign-registered cars and emergency vehicles being caught on camera(!). As an example, one coastal county with a lot of ferry traffic collected at 77% in 2004/5.

...tractor caught speeding at 85 mph in Wales

There's always a chance you may not get your ticket – but if you do, check it carefully. Make sure it is your car, and that you were driving at the time and place recorded. The cameras aren't perfect, and mistakes have been made. My favourite is the tractor caught speeding at 85 mph in Wales. It turned out there was a 'confusion about the number plate' – the tractor had never been to Wales and could only do a max of 26 mph.

9 Don't challenge a penalty without good reason

If you are caught speeding, you've got two choices. Pay the £60 and accept the 3 points. It's humiliating and irritating but then that's the idea. Or contest it.

From the 2004/05 Partnership accounts, about 10% of people challenge and don't pay the fixed penalty fines. Rumour is that the percentage is rising. You may get off, but if you contest a penalty and lose, you could pay a stiffer penalty.

If you do decide to fight, do as much research and get as much information about the circumstances as you can; and get as much case-study information as you can about the camera involved. The more witnesses and information you have, the more a good lawyer can build a case on your behalf.

Again, www.speed-trap.co.uk has some interesting case studies.

But don't expect success with any of these fabrications:

- Falsely nominate a fictitious person, or a real one from a foreign country, as the driver
- Nominate a person at an address that doesn't exist or at a derelict house
- Nominate a fictitious person at a real address
- Say the car was 'on a test drive' or that you don't have the name of the person who was driving it'
- Say you weren't in the area at the time – it must have been a cloned car'
- Give another registration number or change yours
- Register the car with incorrect details e.g. a wrong house number
- Say you don't know who was driving the car – 'it could have been one of several people'
- Ask your partner to pay the fixed penalty because you've already got points on your licence

These ten ingenious lies come to you courtesy of DriveSafe, who are the Greater Manchester Casualty Reduction Partnership, with the message that they know the scams to look out for, both the ones listed here and many more.

Lies can turn a simple speeding fine into something much more serious. In fact, you can be prosecuted for trying to pervert the course of justice. A criminal record can cost you much more than the £60 fixed penalty.

10 Avoid the points by going back to school

In a few counties, the police are giving drivers who are caught speeding another option. They can go on a Speed Awareness Scheme. These normally last half a day, you have to pay for them (probably more than £60) but you don't get the penalty points. So, if you like the sound of this as an option, it's worth considering.

Your alternative is to ask for your case to go forward for prosecution (see Top Tip No. 9)

And finally...

If you've got this far, you're obviously a bit of an aficionado on the subject of speeding, so I'm going to allow myself just one bit of preaching.

The 'Speed Kills' slogan has become much-used. But here are three pieces of information that certainly make me think twice about letting the needle stray over the prescribed limit:

1 Every year we kill over 3,000 of our fellow-citizens on our roads and we seriously injure 35,000. If you happen to live in a reasonable-sized town, just work that out as a percentage of the population of where you live. Road deaths have not fallen substantially since the proliferation of speed cameras – but the evidence seems to be reasonably conclusive that speed cameras reduce the number of deaths and serious injuries at the sites themselves.

2 The argument rages about whether speed is the cause of accidents or not. But that's all rather academic (isn't it?). A car that's not moving is not likely to injure someone. If the accident happens when the car is in motion, speed is at least part of the cause.

But here's the point. This is the 'if I hit a pedestrian, will I kill them?' chart ➤

So if you hit a pedestrian in a 30mph area and you're doing just 35mph (just on the 10% plus 2mph leeway) you're more than twice as likely to kill them. Not a nice thought. Maybe I should have called that the 'if I am hit by a car while on foot, will I be killed by it?' chart.

3 Every death costs us, as taxpayers, £1.5m and every serious injury £100,000. And that's doesn't take into account the human cost.

So, at the end of all this, my 11th Top 10 Tip is

11 Don't press the pedal to the metal

Above, from top:
- Portable Gatso camera • Mobile safety camera unit
- SPECS camera in Nottingham • Truvelo camera

Websites for further information

Official

Safety Camera Partnerships (use Google and put in Safety Camera Partnership plus the area you want)
- www.safetycamera.org.uk • www.dvla.gov.uk
- www.thinksafety.org.uk • www.dft.gov.uk
- www.road-safe.org

Safety pressure groups
- www.rospa.com • www.transport2000.org.uk
- www.roadpeace.org • www.brake.org.uk

Anti-camera pressure groups and web sites
- www.speed-trap.co.uk • ukgatsos.com
- www.ukspeedcameras.co.uk • www.abd.org.uk
- www.ukspeedtraps.co.uk • www.speedcam.co.uk
- www.speedcamerasuk.com

Case studies and news reports
- www.bbc.co.uk

Below The probability that a pedestrian will be killed when struck by a vehicle travelling between 20mph and 40mph

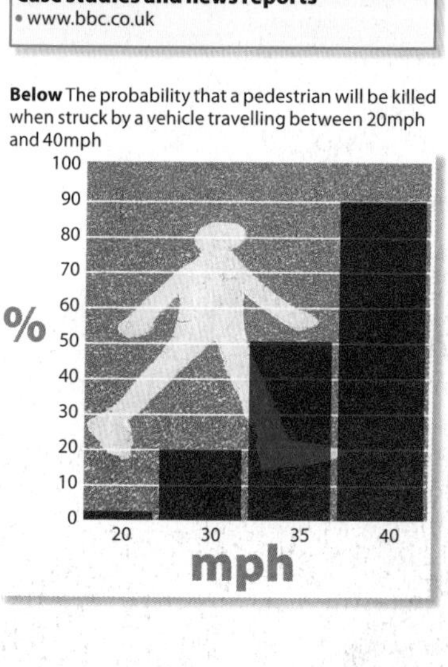

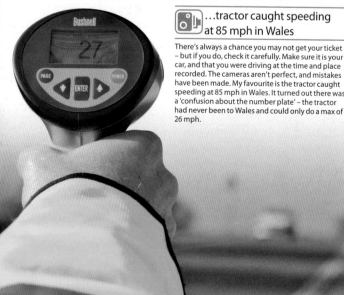

Mobile speed camera sites

The vast majority of speed cameras used on Britain's roads are operated by safety camera partnerships. This table lists the sites where each safety camera partnership may enforce speed limits through the use of mobile cameras or detectors. These are usually set up on the roadside or a bridge spanning the road and operated by a police or civilian enforcement officer. The speed limit at each site (if available) is shown in red type, followed by the approximate location in black type.

England

Avon and Somerset

Bath and North East Somerset, Bristol, North Somerset, Somerset, South Gloucestershire

M32
60 Bristol Stadium

A4
30 Bath, Newbridge Rd
30 Bristol, Anchor Rd
30 Bristol, Totterdown Bridge
50 Nr Keynsham, Keynsham Bypass jct A4175 Durley Hill
50 Portway
30 Portway, nr A4176 Bridge Valley Rd

A4/B4054
30 Bristol, Avonmouth Rd

A30
50 Cricket St Thomas
30 East Chinnock
40 Roundham
40 Yeovil, Hospital Rdbt
30 Yeovil, Sherborne Rd

A37
30 Bristol, Wells Rd (nr jct Airport Rd)
30 Bristol, Wells Rd (nr St Johns La)
60 Chilthorne Domer (east)
50 Emborough
30 Gurney Slade (north)
60 Lydford to Bristol
40 Lydford to Yeovil
60 Nr Podimore, Fosse Way, north of Podimore Rdbt
30 Shepton Mallet

A38
40 Aztec West, nr Bradley Stoke Way
30 Bathpool
40 Bedminster Down, Bridgwater Rd
40 Bristol, Bedminster Down Rd nr Bishopsworth Rd
30 Bristol, Bedminster Down Rd/West St
30 Bristol, Cheltenham Rd/Gloucester Rd, nr Cranbrook Rd
30 Bristol, Gloucester Rd nr B4052 Ashley Down Rd
30 Bristol, Stokes Croft nr Bond St
40 Churchill – Langford
40 Cross
30 East Reach/Toneway
40 Filton, Gloucester Rd (north) nr B4057 Gypsy Patch Lane
50 Heatherton Grange
40,30 North Petherton
40 Patchway, Gloucester Rd nr Highwood Rd
50 Pawlett (south)
50 Redhill
30 Rooks Bridge (east)
30 Taunton – Bridgwater
30 Taunton, Wellington Rd (inbound)
30 Taunton, Wellington Rd (outbound)
30 West Huntspill (north)

A39
30 Ashcott
30 Bilbrook
30 Bridgwater, Bath Rd
30 Bridgwater, North Broadway nr A38 Taunton Rd
30 Bridgwater, North Broadway/Broadway/Monmouth St
30 Chewton Mendip
40 Coxley nr Wells
50 Green Ore (south)
40 Horsey, Bath Rd
30 Quantock Rd
30 Walton

A46
60 Bath to Wickwar Rd
40 Dunkirk

A303
50 Buckland St Mary
50 Downhead nr Ilchester

A303/A3088
70 Cartgate Rdbt

A357
30 Templecombe

A303/A358
60 Southfields Rdbt

A358
60 Ashill
30 Donyatt
30 Henlade, nr M5 jct 25
40 Hornsbury Mill
40 Pen Elm (south)
30 Staplegrove Rd
30 Taunton Deane, Priorswood Rd
30 Taunton, Greenway Rd

A359
30 Mudford (north)

A361
30 Doulting
40 Durston
60 Frome Bypass
30 Othery
30 Pilton
30 West Pennard

A362
40 Terry Hill

A367
30 Bath, Green Park Rd
30 Bath, Bear Flat
30 Radstock, Wells Rd

A369
40 Abbots Leigh
60 Easton-in-Gordano, Martcombe Rd nr M5 jct 19

A370
30 Cleeve Village
30 Congresbury, Station Rd, Bristol Rd
30 Flax Bourton nr B3130
40 Long Ashton Bypass, Bristol End
50 West Wick, Somerset Avenue, west of M5 jct 21
30 Weston-super-Mare, Beach Rd
50 Weston-super-Mare, Herluin Way nr Winterstoke Rd
50 Weston-super-Mare, Somerset Avenue (central reservation)
50 Weston-super-Mare, Somerset Avenue, jct Moor Lane
30 Weston-super-Mare, Winterstoke Rd

A371
30 Draycott
40 Priestleigh (south)
30 Winscombe, Sidcot Lane nr jct A38,

A372
30 Aller

A378
30 Curry Rivel
40 Wrantage

A403
40 Avonmouth Docks

A420
30 Bristol, Lawrence Hill
30 Kingswood, Two Mile Hill Rd, Regent St
30 Old Market, nr Temple Way/Bond St
30 Redfield, Church Rd
30 St George, Clouds Hill Rd/Bell Hill Rd
30 Warmley, High St London Rd nr A4175 Bath Rd
60 Wick, Tog Hill

A432
30 Bristol, Fishponds Rd nr B4048 Lodge Causeway
30 Bristol, Fishponds Rd nr B4469 Royate Hill
30 Bristol, Fishponds Rd with B4469 Muller Rd
30 Bristol, Stapleton Rd nr jct A4320 Easton Way
40 Hambrook, Badminton Rd nr A4174 Avon Ring Rd
40 Kendleshire
30 Yate, Station Rd/B4059 Stover Rd

A3027
30 North St/East St

A3029
40 Bristol, Avon Bridge

A3039
30 Devonshire Rd

A3088
30 Yeovil, Lysander Rd

A3259
30 Monkton Heathfield

A4018
30 Bristol, Black Boy Hill/Whiteladies Rd
30 Bristol, Cribbs Causeway jct 17 M5
30 Bristol, Westbury Rd nr B4054 North View
30 Bristol, Whiteladies Rd into Queens Rd
30 Westbury on Trym, Falcondale Rd

A4044
30 Bristol, Temple Way/Redcliffe Way

A4081
40 Catbrain

A4162
30 Bristol, Sylvan Way/Dingle Rd/Canford Lane

A4174
50 Avon Ring Rd nr jct 1 M32
30 Bristol, Hartcliffe Way
40 Bristol, Hengrove Way/Airport Rd nr Creswicke Rd
50 Bromley Heath
50 Filton, Filton Rd/Avon Ring Rd nr Coldharbour Lane
40 Filton, Station Rd, nr Great Stoke Way

A4320
30 Bristol, at A4 Bath Rd nr Sandy Park Rd

B3124
30 Clevedon, Walton Rd

B3130
30 Nailsea, Stockway (north)/Chapel Avenue
30,40 Wraxall

B3133
30 Clevedon, Central Way

B3139
30,40 Mark Causeway
30 Chilcompton

B3140
30 Berrow, Coast Rd

B3141
30 East Huntspill

B3151
30 Compton Dundon
30 Ilchester
30 St, Somerton Rd

B3153
30 Keinton Mandeville (east Somerton)

B3170
30 Shoreditch Rd

B3440
30 Weston-super-Mare, Locking Rd/Regent St/Alexandra Parade

B4051
30 Bristol, Park Row/Perry Rd

B4054
30 Sea Mills, Shirehampton Rd

B4056
30 Bristol, Northumbria Drive/Linden Rd/Westbury Park
30 Bristol, Southmead Rd nr Pen Park Rd
30 Bristol, Southmead Rd nr Wellington Hill

B4057
30 Bristol, Crow Lane nr A4018 Passage Rd
30 Gypsy Patch Lane nr Hatchet Rd
50 Winterbourne Rd nr B4427 Gloucester Rd

B4058
30 Bristol, Frenchay Park Rd
30 Winterbourne, Winterbourne Hill/High St

B4059
30 Yate, Goose Green Way

B4060
30 Yate, Station Rd/Bowling Hill/Rounceval St

B4061
30 Thornbury, Bristol Rd

B4465
30 Mangotsfield, Broad St

B4465
30 Staple Hill, Staple Hill Rd/High St nr Forest Rd

Unclassified
30 Bristol, Bishopsworth, Whitchurch/Hareclive Rd
30 Bristol, Bishport Avenue
30 Knowle Bristol, Broadwalk
30 Bristol, Hengrove, Hawkfield Rd nr A4174 Hartcliffe Way
30 Bristol, Kingsway
30 Bristol, Long Cross, Lawrence Weston
30 Bristol, Stoke Hill/Stoke Rd nr Saville Rd, Clifton
30 Bristol, Sturminster Rd
30 Bristol, Whitchurch Lane nr Dundry Rd
30 Little Stoke, Little Stoke Lane
30 Taunton, Cheddon Rd
30 Taunton, Chestnut Drive
30 Taunton, Lisieux Way
30 Taunton, Trull Rd
50 Watergore, Harp Rd
30 Yeovil, Combe St

Bedfordshire and Luton

A5
60 Battlesden
40 Hockcliffe
60 Kensworth

A6
60 Gravenhurst, Barton Rd
30 Kempston, Ampthill Rd
30 Luton, New Bedford Rd
60 Pulloxhill, Barton Rd
60 Silsoe, Barton Rd

A421
50 Brogborough
60 Link Rd

A428
30 Bedford, Bromham Rd
30 Bedford, Goldington Rd

A505
30 Dunstable, Luton Rd
60 Leighton to Linslade Bypass

A507
30 Ridgmont, High St East
30 Ridgmont, High St West
60 Shefford, nr New Rd

A603
30 Bedford, Cardington Rd
30 Bedford, Lovell Rd
40 Willington

A1081
60 Luton, Airport Way

A4146
40 Leighton Buzzard, Billington Rd

A5120
40 Houghton Regis, Bedford Rd
30 Toddington, Station Rd

A5134
30 Kempston, High St

B530
60 Houghton Conquest

B1040
30 Biggleswade, Potton Rd

Unclassified
30 Bedford, Roff Avenue
30 Bromham, Stagsden Rd
30 Clapham, Highbury Grange
30 Cranfield, High St
30 Eaton Bray, Bower Lane
30 Flitwick, Ampthill Rd
30 Flitwick, Dunstable Rd
30 Heath and Reach, Woburn Rd
30 Leighton Buzzard, Heath Rd
30 Luton, Crawley Green Rd
30 Luton, Grange Avenue
30 Luton, Leagrave High St
30 Luton, Marsh Rd
30 Luton, Park Viaduct
30 Luton, Waller Avenue
30 Luton, Whitehorse Vale
30 Slip End, Markyate Rd

Berkshire

see Thames Valley

Bucks

see Thames Valley

Cambridgeshire

A14(E)
70 2km west of A1 Brampton Hut
70 East/Westbound

A15
30 New Fletton, London Rd

A47
60 Thorney Toll

A141
60 Clews Corner
60 Warboys
60 Wimblington/Doddington Bypass

A142
60 Soham Bypass
60 Witchford Bypass

A605
60 Elton, Bullock Rd
40 Kings Dyke

A1073
60 Eye Green, Peterborough Rd

A1123
60 Bluntisham, Needingworth Bypass

A1123
40 St Ives, Houghton Hill
40 Wiburton Village

A1307
70 Bartlow crossroads
30 Hills Rd
60 Linton Bypass

B645
40 Tilbrook Bends

Cheshire

A50
30 Grappenhall, Knutsford Rd
30 Knutsford, Manchester/Toft Rd
30 Warrington, Long Lane

A54
60 Ashton, Kelsall Rd

A56
40 Lymm, Camsley Lane

A57
40 Paddington, New Manchester Rd

A523
30 Poynton, London Rd

A532
30 Crewe, West St

A533
40 Middlewich, Booth Lane

A537
50 Macclesfield, Buxton Rd nr Wildboarclough

A5019
30 Crewe, Mill St

A5032
30 Whitby, Chester Rd

A5034
60 Mere, Mereside Rd

A5104
30 Chester, Hough Green

B5071
30 Crewe, Gresty Rd

B5078
30 Alsager, Sandbach Rd North

B5082
30 Northwich, Middlewich Rd

B5132
30 Ellesmere Port, Overpool Rd

B5463
30 Little Sutton, Station Rd

B5470
30 Macclesfield, Rainow Rd

Unclasssified
30 Burtonwood, Lumber Lane
30 Ellesmere Port, Overpool Rd
30 Fearnhead, Harpers Rd
30 Hough Green, Prescot Rd
30 Howley, Battersby Lane
40 Runcorn, Astmoor Rd
30 Runcorn, Boston Avenue
30 Runcorn, Clifton Rd
30 Runcorn, Halton Rd
30 Runcorn, Heath Rd
30 Runcorn, Northwich Rd
30 Runcorn, Warrington Rd
30 Vale Royal, Woodford Lane (St John's Drive)
30 Whitecross, Lovely Lane
30 Widnes, Birchfield Rd
30 Widnes, Hough Green Rd
30 Wilmslow, Hough Lane
40 Winsford, Bradford Rd

Cleveland

Darlington, Hartlepool, Middlesbrough, Redcar and Cleveland

A171
50 Redcar, Charltons

A172
40 Middlesbrough, Morton Rd from crossroads to St Lukes
30 Middlesbrough, Morton Rd from Longlands to St Lukes
40 Middlesbrough, Stokesley – from Guisborough Rd jct to Captain Cooks Crescent

A177
50,60 Stockton, Durham Rd

A178
30 Seaton Carew, The Front

A179
30 Hartlepool, Easington Rd/Powlett Rd

A689
50 to 40 Hartlepool, from Sappers Corner

B1380
40 Middlesbrough, from Marton Crossroads to Ormesby Rd
30 Redcar, Eston

Unclassified
30 Dormanstow, Broadway
30 Eaglescliffe, Yarm Rd
30 Hartlepool, Catcote Rd
40,30 Hartlepool, Coronation Drive
30 Hartlepool, Owton Manor Lane and Wynyard Rd
30 Hartlepool, Oxford Rd
30 Hartlepool, Raby Rd
30 Hartlepool, Throston Grange Lane
30 Hartlepool, Winterbottom Avenue
30 Middlesbrough, Acklam Rd
40 Middlesbrough, Acklam Rd from Blue Bell to the Crematorium
30 Middlesbrough, Mandale Rd
30 Middlesbrough, Ormesby Rd
30 Middlesbrough, Trimdon Avenue
30 Ormesby, Normanby Rd
30 Redcar, Bankfields Rd
30 Redcar, Carlin How
30 Redcar, Church Lane
30 Redcar, Flatts Lane
30 Redcar, Greenstones Rd
30,40 Redcar, Kirkleatham Lane
30 Redcar, Marske High St
30 Redcar, Normanby Rd
30 Redcar, Ormesby Bank
30 Redcar, Redcar Lane
30 Redcar, Redcar Rd
30 Redcar, Stanghow Rd
30 Redcar, West Dyke Rd
30 Seaton Carew, Seaton Lane
30 Seaton Carew, Station Lane
40 Stockton, Bishopton Avenue
30 Stockton, Bishopton Rd West
30 Stockton, Darlington Lane
30 Stockton, Harrogate Lane
30 Stockton, Junction Rd
30 Stockton, Thames Rd
30 Stockton, Thornaby Rd
30 Stockton, Whitehouse Rd
30 Thornaby, Acklam Rd
30 Thornaby, Cunningham Drive

Cumbria

M6
70 Brunthwaite
70 Capplerigg
70 Cowperthwaite
70 Tebay

A6
60 Garnett Bridge/Hollowgate
30 Kendal, Milnthorpe Rd
30 Kendal, Shap Rd
30 London Rd
30 Penrith, Scotland Rd
60 Thiefside

A7
60 Westlinton Crossroads

A65
30 Kendal, Burton Rd
40 Kirby Lonsdale, Devils Bridge
60 Kirkby Lonsdale, Hollin Hall to Hornsbarrow

A66
60 Brigham/Broughton to Chapel Brow
60 Crackenthorpe
60 Dubwath/Bass Lake
60 Sandford Rd Ends
60 Troutbeck/Mungrisdale
60 Warcop, Brough Hill

A69
60 Aglionby
60 Scarrow Hill

A74
70 Kendal, Floriston

A590
60 Bouth Rd Ends
60 Haverthwaite/Backbarrow
70 Heaves/Levens/Gilpin
60 Newlands

A592
30,40 Rayrigg Rd

A595
60 Broughton, Wreaks End
30 Carlisle, Wigton Rd
60 Red Dial, Greenhill Hotel
60 West Woodside/Curthwaite Jct
40 Whitehaven, Loop Rd

A596
60 Micklethwaite

A683
60 Middleton to Cautley

A685
30 Kendal, Appleby Rd

A686
60 Edenhall to Meathaw Hill

A5087
30 Ulverston

B5277
30 Grange, Lindale Rd

B5299
40 Carlisle, Dalston Rd

Unclassified
30 Carlisle, Durdar Rd/Blackwell Rd
30 Barrow in Furness, Abbey Rd
30 Barrow in Furness, Michelson Rd

Derbyshire

A6
30 Allestree
30 Alvaston to Raynesway
40 Ambergate, Matlock Rd nr Chase Rd
30 Bakewell
40 Bakewell, Buxton Rd nr Holme Lane
30 Belper
40 Darley Dale, Dale Rd North nr The Parkway
40 Darley Dale, Dale Rd North opp The Parkway
30 Derby, London Rd
30 Fairfield, Fairfield Rd nr North Rd
40 Matlock Bath to Matlock, Dale Rd nr St John's Rd
40 Matlock Bath to Matlock, Dale Rd opp No. 138
40 Rock Corner, Buxton Rd
50 Taddington to Buxton

A52
30 Derby, Ashbourne Rd
40 Mackworth

A53
30 Buxton, Station Rd o/s Railway Station
30 Buxton, Station Rd opp Railway Station

A57
30 Glossop, Dinting Vale nr Primary School
30 Glossop, Dinting Vale opp Dinting Lane
30 Glossop, High St West nr Glossop Brook Rd

A61
30 Chesterfield, Derby Rd nr Herriot Drive
30 Chesterfield, Derby Rd nr Langer Lane
50 Stretton, Main Rd nr B6014
50 Stretton, Main Rd nr Straw Lane

A444
30 Overseal, Acresford Rd nr Valley Rd
30 Overseal, Burton Rd nr Lullington Rd
30 Stanton, Woodland Rd nr Piddocks Rd
30 Stanton, Woodland Rd opp Park Rd

A511
40 Bretby, Ashby Rd East nr Greary Lane
30 Hatton, Station Rd
30 Swadlincote, Ashby Rd nr Field Lane
30 Swadlincote, Burton Rd nr Eureka Rd
30 Swadlincote, Burton Rd nr Lincoln Way
30 Swadlincote, Burton Rd nr Sandcliffe Rd
30 Swadlincote, Burton Rd nr Springfield Rd
30 Woodville, Burton Rd nr Sorrel Drive
30 Woodville, High St nr Butt Lane

A514
30 Derby, Osmaston Rd nr Keble Close
30 Derby, Osmaston Rd nr Shaftesbury St
30 Derby, Osmaston Rd opp Cotton Lane
30 Hartshorne
30 Shelton Lock, Chellaston Rd nr Shelton Drive
30 Swadlincote
40 Swadlincote to Hartshorne
30 Ticknall

A516
30 Uttoxeter, New Rd

A601
30 Derby, Abbey St

A608
30 Heanor, Church St nr Hands Rd
30 Heanor, Heanor Rd nr Peatburn Ave
30 Heanor, Mansfield Rd adj Watson Ave
30 Heanor, Mansfield Rd opp Watson Ave
30 Langley Mill, Station Rd adj Aldred's Lane
30 Smalley

A609
30 Ilkeston, Nottingham Rd opp Ashdale Rd
30 Ilkeston, Nottingham Rd opp Little Hallam Lane
30 Kilburn to Horsley Woodhouse

A610
40 Codnor Gate
40 Ripley, Nottingham Rd nr Brittain Dr

A615
60 Tansley to Wessington

A616
30 Clowne
30 Creswell

A617
40 Bramley Vale
40 Glapwell to Pleasley

A6175
30 Holmewood
30 North Wingfield

A618
30 Killamarsh, Rotherham Rd

A619
50 Barlborough, Worksop Rd nr Van Dyks Hotel
40 Brimington, Chesterfield Rd opp Lansdowne Rd
30 Brimington, Ringwood Rd nr Foljambe Rd
30 Chesterfield, Chatsworth Rd nr Chatsworth Ave
30 Chesterfield, Chatsworth Rd opp Church View
30 Chesterfield, Chatsworth Rd opp Haddon Close
30 Hollingwood, Chesterfield Rd opp Ringwood Hall
40 Mastin Moor, Worksop Rd nr Norbriggs Rd
40 Mastin Moor, Worksop Rd nr Renishaw Rd
30 Middlecroft, Chesterfield Rd nr Ringwood Ave
30 Staveley, Chesterfield Rd nr Middlecroft Rd
50 Whitwell Common, Worksop Rd opp Highwood Lane
50 Whitwell, Barlborough nr Southgate Bungalows
50 Whitwell, Clinthill Lane o/s Southgate Bungalows

A623
30 Stoney Middleton

A624
40 Hayfield, Chapel Rd nr Church
40 Hayfield, Chapel Rd nr New Mills Rd

A632
30 Bolsover
30 Bolsover, Langwith Rd
30 Calow, Top Rd o/s No.33
30 Calow, Top Rd o/s No.62
40 Duckmanton, Chesterfield Rd nr Staveley Rd
40 Duckmanton, Chesterfield Rd opp Arkwright Arms Pub
30 Langwith, Main Rd nr Langwith Drive
30 Langwith, Main Rd nr Whaley Rd
30 Matlock

A5111
40 Derby, Harvey Rd nr Cockayne St North
40 Derby, Harvey Rd nr Neilson St
40 Derby, Harvey Rd nr Wyndham St
40 Derby, Harvey Rd o/s Newsagents
40 Derby, Osmaston Park Rd nr Arkwright St

A5250
30 Derby, Burton Rd
30 Littleover, Burton Rd

A6005
30 Draycott to Breaston
30 Long Eaton, Derby Rd opp Russell St
30 Long Eaton, Nottingham Rd nr Charlton Ave
30 Long Eaton, Nottingham Rd opp Cleveland Ave
30 Spondon, Derby Rd nr Derwent Rd
30 Spondon, Derby Rd o/s Asc
30 Spondon, Nottingham Rd Angler's Lane

A6007
30 Codnor to Heanor
30 Heanor, Ilkeston Rd nr Westfield Ave
40 Ilkeston, Heanor Rd nr Broadway
40 Ilkeston, Heanor Rd nr Hospital
40 Ilkeston, Heanor Rd nr Woodside Crescent
40 Shipley, Hardy Barn o/s No.64
40 Shipley, Hassock Lane Nor nr Algrave Hall Farm
40 Shipley, Hassock Lane Sou nr Pitt Lane

A6096
30 Kirk Hallam, Ladywood Rd Godfrey Dr
30 Kirk Hallam, Ladywood Rd Goole Ave
30 Spondon, Dale Rd nr Dreyf Close
30 Spondon, Dale Rd nr Wood Rd
30 Spondon, Dale Rd opp Sandringham Dr

B5010
30 Sandiacre, Derby Rd adj Brook St
30 Sandiacre, Derby Rd adj Friesland Drive
30 Sandiacre, Derby Rd adj Woodside Rd

B5036
30 Cromford, Cromford Rd

B5353
30 Newhall, Park Rd

B6002
30 Sandiacre, Longmoor Rd nr Springfield Ave
30 Sandiacre, Longmoor Rd o No.108
30 Sandiacre, Longmoor Rd nr Queen's Drive

B6019
30 Alfreton, Mansfield Rd nr Prospect St
30 South Normanton, Mansfie Rd nr Carter Lane West
30 South Normanton, Mansfie Rd nr Storth Lane
30 South Normanton, The Common nr Market St
30 South Normanton, The Common nr The Hamlet

B6051
30 Chesterfield, Newbold Rd
30 Newbold, Newbold Rd

B6052
30 Eckington, High St nr j/w School St
30 Eckington, West St nr j/w Fanshaw Rd
30 Whittington

B6056
30 Eckington, Dronfield Rd op Ravenscar Rd
30 Marsh Lane, Main Rd nr School Lane
30 Marsh Lane, Main Rd o/s No.45

B6062
30 Chinley

B6179
30 Little Eaton
40 Lower Kilburn
50 Lower Kilburn to Little Eato
30 Ripley to Marehay

B6407
30 Shirebrook, Portland Rd ad Ashbourne St
30 Shirebrook, Portland Rd op Ashbourne St

B6540
30 Long Eaton, Tamworth Rd Charles St
30 Long Eaton, Tamworth Rd Wyvern Ave
30 Long Eaton, Tamworth Rd opp Draycott Rd
30 Long Eaton, Tamworth Rd opp No.559
30 Long Eaton, Tamworth Rd opp Shaftesbury Ave

Unclassified
30 Chaddesden, Nottingham F nr No.427 (Cemetery)
30 Chaddesden, Nottingham F nr Pentagon Island
30 Chaddesden, Nottingham F o/s No.590 (Cherry Tree)
30 Charlesworth, Long Lane
30 Chesterfield, Boythorpe Rd
30 Chesterfield, Linacre Rd
30 Chesterfield, Old Rd
30 Denby, St Lane
30 Derby, Blagraves Lane
30 Derby, Kedleston Rd
30 Derby, Stenson Rd
30 Langley Mill, Upper Dunste Rd
30 Shardlow, London Rd
40 Stenson Fields, Stenson Rd
30 Swadlincote, Hearthcote Rd

evon and ornwall

30
Chiverton Cross
Highgate (Eastbound)
Highgate Hill
Sowton
Temple

38
Bittaford Straight, Wrangaton
Deep Lane
Lee Mill, Lee Mill On-slip
Lower Clicker Tor
Smithaleigh
Smithaleigh, Smithaleigh Overbridge
Wrangaton, Bittaford Straight

39
Barras Moor
Camelford, Valley Truckle
Perranarworthal, nr Truro

361
Ashford
Barnstaple, Eastern Avenue
Knowle
Knowle (Westerland)
Wrafton

374
Ebford
Plymouth, Plymouth Rd (Inbound)
Plymouth, Plymouth Rd (Outbound)
Torpoint, Anthony Rd

376
Exmouth, Exeter Rd

377
Copplestone
Crediton, Western Rd
Exeter, Alphington Rd

379
Brixton Village
Paignton, Dartmouth Rd
Starcross
Starcross, The Strand
Teignmouth, Teignmouth Rd
Torquay, Babbacombe Rd
Yealmpton

380
Kingskerswell, Newton Rd

381
Newton Abbott, East St

385
Collaton St Mary, Totnes Rd
Totnes, Ashburton Rd

386
Chubb Tor
Plymouth, Outland Rd
Plymouth, Roborough Down
Plymouth, Tavistock Rd

388
Kelly Bray

390
Penstraze
Sticker Bypass

394
Kenneggy Downs

396
Rewe
Stoke Canon, Exeter Rd

3015
Exeter, Topsham Rd

3047
Carbis Bay
Pool, Trevenson Rd
Tuckingmill

3058
Trewoon

3064
Plymouth, St Budeaux Bypass

3075
Rosecliston

3165
Raymonds Hill, Crewkerne Rd

3174
Ottery St Mary, Barrack Rd

3183
Exeter, Heavitree Rd
Exeter, New North Rd

3212
Exeter, Dunsford Rd
Exeter, Pinhoe Rd

3213
Wrangaton Village, nr South Brent

3233
Barnstaple, Bickington Rd

3250
Plymouth, North Hill

3284
Liskey
Liskey, Perranporth
Chudleigh, Station Hill

3396
Plymouth, Milehouse Rd

nclassified
Avonwick Village
Buddle Lane, Exwick Rd
Elburton, Haye Rd
Exeter, Exwick Lane
Fraddon Village, nr Indian Queens
Goss Moor, Castle an Dinas
Honicknowle, Shakespeare Rd
Ivybridge, Exeter Rd
Monkton Village
Paignton, Colley End Rd
30 Paignton, Preston Down Rd
30 Plymouth, Beacon Park Rd
30 Plymouth, Church Hill
30 Plymouth, Devonport Rd
30 Plymouth, Eggbuckland Rd
30 Plymouth, Glen Rd
30 Plymouth, Honicknowle Lane
30 Plymouth, Honicknowle Lane (North)
30 Plymouth, Lipson Rd
30 Plymouth, Mannamead Rd
30 Plymouth, Molesworth Rd
30 Plymouth, North Prospect Rd
40 Plymouth, Novorrossiysk Rd
30 Plymouth, Pomphlett Rd
30 Plymouth, Southway Drive
30 Plymouth, St Levan Rd
30 Plymouth, Tamerton Foliot Rd
30 Plymouth, Union St
30 Plymouth, Weston Park Rd
30 Plymouth, Wolseley Rd (Both Directions)
30 Plympton, Glen Rd
30 Saltash, Callington Rd
30 St Judes, Grenville Rd

Dorset

A30
Babylon Hill
Shaftesbury, Long Cross

A35
Bakers Arms Rdbt, Lytchett Minster Rdbt j/w A350
Bere Regis nr Woodbury Cross
Bridport, Cross Dykes nr Whiteway Cross
Christchurch Bypass
Dorchester, Friary Press
Kingston Russell
Lyndhurst Rd
nr Morden Hill and Slepe
Organford
Poole, Upton Rd
Sea Rd South
Vinney Cross nr Bridport

A37
Holywell Cross
Long Ash Lane
Staggs Folly

A348
Bear Cross, Ringwood Rd

A338
Cooper Dean, Wessex Way
Bournemouth, Spur Rd

A350
Holes Bay Rd
Poole Rd
Poole, Upton Country Park to A35 j/w Creekmoor
Stourplane, Shashton Rd

A352
Wool, Dorchester Rd

A354
Dorchester Rd/Ridgeway Hill
Poole, Gravel Hill
Redlands, Dorchester Rd
Upwey, Dorchester Rd
Weymouth, Buxton Rd

B3065
Poole, Pinecliff Rd
Poole, The Avenue

B3073
West Parley, Christchurch Rd
Wimborne, Oakley Hill

B3074
Broadstone, Higher Blandford Rd

B3082
Blandford Rd nr Badbury Rings

B3092
Gillingham, Colesbrook

B3157
Limekiln Hill
Portesham
Weymouth, Chickerell Rd
Weymouth, Lanehouse Rocks Rd

B3369
Poole, Sandbanks Rd
Poole, Shore Rd

Unclassified
Blandford, Salisbury Rd
Bournemouth, Branksome Wood Rd
Bournemouth, Carbery Avenue
Bournemouth, Littledown Avenue
Bournemouth, Southbourne Overcliff Drive
Dorchester Rd (Manor Rdbt to Weymouth Hospital)
Poole, Herbert Avenue
Poole, Old Wareham Rd
Portland, Weston Rd
Staplehill, Wimborne Rd
Upton, Poole Rd

Durham

A66
Bowes Moor/Galley Bank/ Greta Bridge

A67
Conniscliffe

A167
Chester-le-St, North Lodge
Darlington, North Rd
Durham, Whitesmocks and Tollhouse Rd

A690
Crook, Low Willington to West Rd
Durham, West Rainton

A1086
Crimdon to Horden

B6188
Dipton, New Kyo to Flint Hill

B6280
Darlington, Yarm Rd

B6282
Bishop Auckland, Etherley and B6284 Ediscum Garth

B6288
Spennymoor/A167 Croxdale

Unclassifed
Darlington, McMullen Rd
Durham, Finchale Rd
Peterlee, Essington Way

Essex

A12
Braintree, Overbridge nr Kelvedon Interchange

A13
30 Castle Point, High St (Hadleigh twds London)
30 Leigh on Sea, London Rd
Southend, Bournes Green Chase
Southend, North Shoebury
Southend, Southchurch Boulevard

A113
30 Epping, High Rd

A120
Little Bentley, Pellens Corner

A121
30 Epping, High Rd
30 Loughton, Goldings Hill (j/w Monkchester Close)
Loughton, High Rd
Waltham Abbey, Farm Hill Rd
Waltham Abbey, Sewardstine Rd

A126
30 Grays, London Rd
30 Tilbury, Montreal Rd

A128
Chipping Ongar, High St
30 Ingrave/Herongate, Brentwood Rd

A129
30 Basildon, Crays Hill
Billericay, Southend Rd
Rayleigh, London Rd
30 Wickford, London Rd
Wickford, Southend Rd

A130
30 Canvey Island, Long Rd
South Benfleet, Canvey Way

A133
30 Elmstead Market, Clacton Rd

A133
Little Bentley, Colchester Rd

A134
40 Great Horkesley, Nayland Rd

A137
30 Lawford, Wignall St

A1016
30 Chelmsford, Waterhouse Lane

A1017
30 Sible Hedingham, Swan St

A1023
30 Brentwood, Chelmsford Rd
30 Brentwood, London Rd
30 Brentwood, Shenfield Rd

A1025
40 Harlow, Third Avenue

A1060
Little Hallingbury, Lower Rd

A1090
30 Purfleet, London Rd
30 Purfleet, Tank Hill Rd

A1124
30 Colchester, Lexden Rd

A1158
30 Westcliff on Sea, Southbourne Grove

A1168
30 Loughton, Rectors Lane

A1169
40 Harlow, Southern Way

A1205
40 Harlow, Second Avenue

B170
Loughton, Roding Lane
Chigwell, Chigwell Rise

B172
Theydon Bois, Coppice Row

B173
Chigwell, Lambourne Rd

B184
40 Great Easton, Snow Hill

B186
30 South Ockendon, South Rd

B1002
30 Ingatestone, High St

B1007
30 Billericay, Laindon Rd
40 Chelmsford, Stock Rd

B1007
30 Billericay, Stock Rd

B1008
30 Chelmsford, Broomfield Rd

B1013
30 Hawkwell, High Rd
30 Hawkwell, Main Rd
30 Hockley/Hawkwell, Southend Rd
Rayleigh, High Rd
30 Rayleigh, Hockley Rd

B1014
30 South Benfleet, Benfleet Rd

B1018
30 Latchingdon, The St
30 Maldon, The Causeway

B1019
30 Hatfield Peveral, Maldon Rd

B1021
Burnham on Crouch, Church Rd

B1022
30 Colchester, Maldon Rd
30 Heckfordbridge, Maldon Rd
30 Maldon, Colchester Rd
30 Tiptree Heath, Maldon Rd

B1027
30 Clacton-on-Sea, Valley Rd/Old Rd
30 St Osyth, Pump Hill
40 Wivenhoe, Brightlingsea Rd

B1028
30 Wivenhoe, Colchester Rd
30 Wivenhoe, The Avenue

B1033
30 Kirby Cross, Frinton Rd

B1335
40 South Ockendon, Stifford Rd

B1352
Harwich, Main Rd

B1383
30 Newport, London Rd
Stansted Mountfitchet, Cambridge Rd

B1389
30 Witham, Colchester Rd
30 Witham, Hatfield Rd

B1393
30 Epping, Palmers Hill

B1441
30 Clacton-on-Sea, London Rd

B1442
30 Clacton-on-Sea, Thorpe Rd

B1464
30 Bowers Gifford, London Rd

Unclassified
40 Alresford, St Osyth Rd
30 Aveley, Purfleet Rd
Aveley, Romford Rd
30 Barstable, Sandon Rd
30 Basildon, Ashlyns
40 Basildon, Cranes Farm Rd (j/w Honywood Rd)
Basildon, Crayhill Rd
30 Basildon, Felmores
Basildon, London Rd, Wickford
30 Basildon, Vange Hill Drive
30 Basildon, Whitmore Way
30 Basildon, Wickford Avenue
30 Billericay, Mountnessing Rd
30 Bowers Gifford, London Rd
30 Braintree, Coldnailhurst Avenue
30 Brentwood, Eagle Way (nr j/w Clive Rd twds Warley Rd)
30 Buckhurst Hill, Buckhurst Way/Albert Rd
30 Canvey Island, Dovervelt Rd
30 Canvey Island, Link Rd
30 Canvey Island, Thorney Bay Rd
Chadwell St Mary, Brentwood Rd
30 Chadwell St Mary, Linford Rd
30 Chadwell St Mary, Riverview
30 Chelmsford, Baddow Rd
30 Chelmsford, Chignall Rd
30 Chelmsford, Copperfield Rd
Chelmsford, Galleywood Rd
30 Chelmsford, Longstomps Avenue
30 Clacton-on-Sea, St Johns Rd
30 Clacton, Kings Parade
30 Clacton, Marine Parade East
30 Colchester, Abbots Rd
30 Colchester, Avon Way
30 Colchester, Bromley Rd
Colchester, Ipswich Rd
30 Colchester, Old Heath Rd
30 Colchester, Shrub End Rd
30 Corringham, Southend Rd
30 Corringham, Springhouse Rd
Danbury, Maldon Rd
30 Daws Heath, Daws Heath Rd
30 Eastwood, Green Lane j/w Kendal Way
30 Eastwood, Western Approaches j/w Rockall
30 Grays, Blackshots Lane
30 Grays, Lodge Lane
Grays, London Rd (nr Angel Rd)
Grays, London Rd (nr Bransons Way)
40 Harlow, Abercrombie Way, twds Southern Way
40 Harlow, Howard Way
30 Hullbridge, Coventry Hill
30 Laindon, Durham Rd
30 Laindon, Nightingales
30 Laindon, Wash Rd
Langdon Hills, High Rd
30 Leigh on Sea, Belton Way East
30 Leigh on Sea, Belton Way West
30 Leigh on Sea, Blenhelm Chase
30 Leigh on Sea, Grand Parade/ Cliff Parade
30 Leigh on Sea, Hadleigh Rd
30 Leigh on Sea, Highlands Boulevard
30 Leigh on Sea, Manchester Drive
30 Leigh on Sea, Mountdale Gardens
30 Leigh on Sea, Western Rd
30 Loughton, Alderton Hill
30 Loughton, Loughton Way
Loughton, Valley Hill
30 Maldon, Fambridge Rd
30 Maldon, Holloway Rd
30 Maldon, Mundon Rd
30 Pitsea, Rectory Rd
30 Prittlewell, Kenilworth Gardens
30 Prittlewell, Prittlewell Chase
30 Rayleigh, Bull Lane
Rayleigh, Downhall Rd
30 Rayleigh, Trinity Rd, nr Church Rd
30 Rochford, Ashingdon Rd
30 Rochford, Rectory Rd
Rush Green, St Osyth Rd
30 Shoeburyness, Ness Rd
30 South Woodham Ferrers, Hullbridge Rd
30 South Woodham Ferrers, Inchbonnie Rd
30 Southend on Sea, Lifstan Way
Southend, Bournemouth Park Rd
30 Southend, Hamstel Rd
Southend, Western Esplanade/Westcliff on Sea
30 Southend, Woodgrange Drive j/w Sandringham Rd
30 Springfield, New Bowers Way
30 Stanford le Hope, London Rd
30 Tendring, Burrs Rd, Clacton
Tendring, Harwich Rd, Wix Arch Cottages to Cansey Lane
Theydon Bois, Piercing Hill
30 Thorpe Bay, Barnstaple Rd
30 Thorpe Bay, Thorpe Hall Avenue
Waltham Abbey, Paternoster Hill
Weeley Heath, Clacton Rd
30 West Thurrock, London Rd
30 Westcliff on Sea, Chalkwell Avenue
30 Westcliff on Sea, Kings Rd
30 Wickford, Radwinter Avenue
30 Witham, Powers Hall End
30 Witham, Rickstones Rd

Gloucestershire

A38
40 Twigworth

A40
60 Andoversford
50 Churcham
60 Farmington
40 Gloucester Rd
60 Hampnett
60 Hazleton
60 Northleach
60 The Barringtons
60 Whittington Area

A46
40 Ashchurch
40 North of Nailsworth

A48
60 Stroat

A417
70 Burford Jct
40 Corse, Gloucester Rd
70 Dartley Bottom
40 Lechlade
30 Maisemore
40 North of Hartpury

A419
40 Oldends Lane to Stonehouse Court

A429
60 Nr Bourton-on-the-Water
40 Fossebridge

A430
40 Hempsted Bypass

A435
60 Colesbourne

A436
60 Jct with B4068

A4013
30 Gloucester, Princess Elizabeth Way
30 Gloucester, Princess Elizabeth Way (Arle)

A4019
50 Uckington

A4136
40 Brierley
40 Coleford, Lower Lane
40 Harrow Hill
40 Little London

A4151
40 Steam Mills

A4173
30 nr St Peters School

B4008
40 Hardwicke, Bristol Rd south of Tesco rdbt
30 Olympus Park Area, Bristol Rd
30 Stonehouse, Gloucester Rd

B4060
30 Katharine Lady Berkeley's School

B4215
50 South east of Rudford
50 South of Newent Bypass

B4221
30 Picklenash School
40 Kilcot Village

B4226
60 Speech House

B4228
30 Coleford, Old Station Way
40 Perrygrove

B4231
30 Bream, Coleford Rd

B4633
30 Cheltenham, Gloucester Rd

Unclassified
30 Gloucester, Abbeymead Avenue
30 Gloucester, Barrow Hill
30 Gloucester, Chesterton Lane
30 Gloucester, Parkend Fancy Rd
30 Gloucester, St Georges Rd
30 Gloucester, Swindon Lane
30 Gloucester, Wymans Lane
30 Lydney, Highfield Rd
40 Minchinhampton Common
30 Siddington
40 Tewkesbury, Gloucester Rd

Greater Manchester

A6
30 Devonshire, Stockport Rd
30 Heaton Chapel, Wellington Rd
30 Longsight, Stockport Rd
30 Stockport Rd (North)
30 Stockport Rd (South East)

A34
30 Birchfield Rd (North)
40 Didsbury, Kingsway (North)
40 Gatley

A49
30 Marus Bridge, Warrington Rd (South)
30 Standish, Wigan Rd (South)

A56
30 Bury, Manchester Rd (North)
30 Derby, Bury New Rd (North)
30 Shuttleworth, Whalley Rd (North)
30 White City, Chester Rd

A57
30 Godley, Mottram Rd (West)
30 Hyde Rd
30 Hyde, Manchester Rd (West)
30 West Gorton, Hyde Rd

A58
30 Ashton, Liverpool Rd (West)
30 Bamfurlong (South West), Lily Lane
30 Bury, Bolton Rd (North East)
30 Bury, Bolton Rd (South West)
40 Hunger Hill, Wigan Rd (Doyle Rd)

A62
30 Ancoats, Oldham Rd
30 Ancoats, Oldham Rd (North East)
30 Newton Heath, Oldham Rd
30 Newton Heath, Oldham Rd (North East)

A571
30 Wigan, Victoria St (South West)

A572
30 Astley, Chaddock Lane (West)
30 Lowton, Newton Rd (South)

A574
30 Leigh, Warrington Rd (South)

A576
30 Crumpsall, Middleton Rd
30 Crumpsall, Middleton Rd (South)

A579
50 Leigh, Atherleigh Way (South)

A580
70 Leigh, East Lancashire Rd

A635
40 Ardwick, Mancunian Way
Beswick, Ashton Old Rd
40 Mancunian Way (East)
30 Openshaw, Ashton Old Rd
30 Openshaw, Ashton Old Rd (East)
30 Stalybridge, Stamford St (West)

A662
30 Beswick, Ashton New Rd
30 Clayton, Ashton New Rd

A664
Blackley, Rochdale Rd
30 Collyhurst, Rochdale Rd
30 Harpurhey, Rochdale Rd
30 Rochdale Rd (Whitemoss) (North)

A665
30 Cheetham Hill Rd (Alms Hill) (North)
30 Cheetham Hill, Cheetham Hill Rd
30 Prestwich, Bury Old Rd

A667
30 Radcliffe, Ringley Rd (West)

A670
30 Hazlehurst, Mossley Rd (South West)

A5079
30 Kingsway/Slade Lane (South West)

A5103
30 Princess Rd (Greame St) (North)
40 Princess Rd (Whitchurch) (North)
40 Withington, Princess Rd
30 Edge Lane (West)

A5209
30 Almond Brook Rd (East)
30 Crow Orchard Rd

A6010
30 West Gorton, Pottery Lane

A6104
40 Higher Blackley, Victoria Avenue

A6144
30 Harboro Rd (West)
30 Warburton Lane (South West)

A6145
30 Hulton Lane (North)

B5165
30 Timperley, Park Rd

B5213
30 Flixton, Church Rd (East)
30 Flixton, Church Rd (West)
30 Urmston, Church Rd (West)

B5217
30 Seymour Grove (South)

B5218
30 Upper Chorlton Rd (South)

B5235
40 Westhoughton/Atherton Boundary

B5237
30 Bickershaw Lane (West)

B5375
30 Shevington, Miles Lane (South)

B6177
30 Mossley, Stamford Rd

B6226
30 Horwich, Chorley Old Rd

Unclassified
30 Bird Hall Lane (North) (facing south)
30 Bury, Radcliffe Rd (North East)
30 Councillor Lane (West)
30 Crumpsall, Hazelbottom Rd
30 Great Moor (Mile End), Buxton Rd (South)
30 Hazelbottom Rd (North)
30 Kings Rd (East)
30 Kings Rd (West)
30 Marple Rd Offerton (South East)
30 Queensway (South)

Hampshire and Isle of Wight

A3
70 Liphook
30 Petersfield

A27
40 Fareham (east and west bound)
30 Fareham, Portchester Rd (eastbound)
30 Fareham, Portchester Rd (westbound)
30 Fareham, The Avenue

A30
30 Blackwater
30 Hook, London Rd

A32
30 West Meon

A33
50 Basingstoke
50 Chandlers Green
50 Sherfield on Loddon
50 Southampton, Millbrook Rd (western end of Flyover to Regents Park Rd)
30 West Quay Rd

A35
50 Totton

A325
40 East Hampshire (south)
70 Farnborough, Farnborough Rd
40 Rushmoor (north)

A334/B2177
40 Wickham

A335
30 Eastleigh

A337
30 New Forest (east)
40 New Forest (west)

A338
40 New Forest (south and north bound)

A339
60 Lasham

A340
30 Basingstoke
30 Tadley

A343
30 Hurstbourne Tarrant

A3020
40 Blackwater Rd

A3024
40 Bursledon Rd
30 Northam Rd to southern river bank

A3054
30 Newport, Fairlee Rd
30 Wootton / Lushington Hill, High St

B3037/A335
30,40 Eastleigh

B3055
40 New Forest

B3395
30 Sandown, Culver Parade

Unclassified
30 Apse Heath
30 Binstead Hill
30 Brading, High St New Rd
30 East Cowes, Victoria Grove/ Adelaide Grove
30 East Cowes, York Avenue
40 Fareham, Western Way
30 Fleet, Reading Rd South
30 Newport, Staplers Rd/Long Lane
30 Portsmouth, Northern Rd (north and south bound)
40 Southampton, The Avenue (north and south bound)
30 Swanick, Swanick Lane
50 Totton / Redbridge, Redbridge Flyover

Herefordshire

see West Mercia

Hertfordshire

A41
40 Watford, North Western Avenue

A119
30 Hertford, North Rd

A411
30 Bushey, London Rd
30 Watford, Hempstead Rd

A414
40 Hemel Hempstead, St Albans Rd
40 Hertford, Hertingfordbury Rd

A505
30 Hitchin, Cambridge Rd

A600
30 Hitchin, Bedford Rd

A602
40 Hitchin, Stevenage Rd
40 Stevenage, Broadhall Way (north of j/w Valley Way)
40 Stevenage, Monkswood Way

A1000
40 Bishop's Stortford, Barnet Rd

A1057
40 Hemel Hempstead, St Albans Rd West
30 St Albans, Hatfield Rd

A1170
30 Wormley, High Rd nr Macers Lane Jct
30 Wormley, High Rd nr Slipe Lane Jct

A4125
40 South Oxhey, Sandy Lane
30 Watford, Eastbury Rd
30 Watford, Tolpits Lane by jct with Scammell Close

A4251
30 Bourne End, London Rd

A5183
30 St Albans, Frogmore Rd

A6141
30 Baldock, London Rd
60 Letchworth, Letchworth Gate

B156
30 Broxbourne, Goffs Lane

B176
30 Cheshunt, High St

B197
30 Stevenage, North Rd

B487
30 Hatching Green, Redbourn Lane
40 Hemel Hempstead, Queensway

B488
40 Tring, Icknield Way at j/w Little Tring Rd

B556
30 Potters Bar, Mutton Lane

B1004
30 Bishop's Stortford, Windhill

B1502
30 Hertford, Stansted Rd

B5378
30 Elstree, Allum Lane
40 Shenley, Shenleybury

Unclassified
30 Cheshunt, Hammond St Rd
30 Hoddesdon, Essex Rd
30 Letchworth, Pizmore Way
30 Royston, Old North Rd
30 South Oxhey, Hayling Rd
30 St Albans, Sandpit Lane
30 Stevenage, Clovelly Way 75m south of j/w Scarborough Avenue
30 Stevenage, Clovelly Way jct of Eastbourne Avenue
30 Stevenage, Grace Way (200m north of Vardon Rd)
30 Stevenage, Grace Way (200m south of Vardon Rd)
40 Stevenage, Gresley Way (nr Dene Lane Footbridge)
40 Stevenage, Gresley Way (nr Woodcock Rd Jct)
30 Watford, Radlett Rd
30 Watford, Whippendell Rd (o/s Wemco House)
30 Welwyn Garden City, Heronswood Rd
30 Welwyn Garden City, Howlands

Humberside

East Riding of Yorkshire, Hull, North East Lincolnshire, North Lincolnshire

M180
70 North Lincolnshire, West of River Trent

A18
60 North East Lincolnshire, Barton St Central

60 North East Lincolnshire, Barton St North
60 North East Lincolnshire, Barton St South
30 North Lincolnshire, Wrawby
A63
50 East Riding, Melton
40 Hull, Castle St
40 Hull, Daltry St Flyover
A161
30 Belton
A163
30 Holme on Spalding Moor
A164
30 Leconfield
A165
30 Beeford
40 East Riding, Coniston
30 Freetown Way
40 Holderness Rd
30 Skirlaugh
A180
70 Great Coates Jct
A614
40 Holme on Spalding Moor
30 Middleton on the Wolds
60 Shiptonthorpe, north of rdbt
60 Shiptonthorpe, south of the village
A1033
40 Thomas Clarkson Way
30 Thorngumbald, Main St
30 Withernsea
A1077
30 Barton
A1079
50 Barmby Moor
30 Bishop Burton
30 Hull, Beverley Rd (Desmond Ave to Riverdale Rd)
40 Hull, Beverley Rd (Sutton Rd to Mizzen Rd)
A1084
30 Brigg, Bigby High Rd
A1174
30 Dunswell
30 Woodmansey
B1206
30 Barrow, Wold Rd
B1230
40 Gilberdyke
40 Newport
B1398
40 Greetwell
Unclassified
30 Ashby, Grange Lane South
30 Ashby, Messingham Rd
30 Belton, Westgate Rd
30 Beverley, Hull Bridge Rd
30 Bilton, Main Rd
30 Bridlington, Kingsgate
30 Bridlington, Quay Rd/St John's St
30 Broughton, High St
30 Cleethorpes, Clee Rd
30 East Halton, College Rd
30 Goole, Airmyn Rd
30 Grimsby, Cromwell Rd
30 Grimsby, Great Coates Rd
30 Grimsby, Laceby Rd
30 Grimsby, Louth Rd
30 Grimsby, Waltham Rd
30 Grimsby, Weelsby Rd
30 Hessle, Beverley Rd
30 Hornsea, Rolston Rd
30 Howden, Thorpe Rd
30 Hull, Anlaby Rd
40 Hull, Boothferry Rd
30 Hull, Bricknell Avenue
30 Hull, Greenwood Avenue
30 Hull, Hall Rd
30 Hull, John Newton Way/Bude Rd
30 Hull, Leads Rd
30 Hull, Marfleet Lane
30 Hull, Marfleet Lane/Marfleet Avenue
30 Hull, Priory Rd
30 Hull, Saltshouse Rd
40 Hull, Spring Bank West
30 Hull, Wawne Rd
30 Humberston, Tetney Rd
30 Immingham, Pelham Rd
70 Laceby Bypass
30 Preston, Station Rd
30 Scunthorpe, Ashby Rd
30 Scunthorpe, Cambridge Avenue
30 Scunthorpe, Cottage Beck Rd
40 Scunthorpe, Doncaster Rd
30 Scunthorpe, Luneburg Way
40 Scunthorpe, Queensway
30 Scunthorpe, Rowland Rd
30 South Killingholme, Top Rd
30 Yaddlethorpe, Moorwell Rd

Kent and Medway

A2
70 Canterbury
60 Dover, Guston
70 Dover, Lydden
40 Medway, London Rd
A20
70,40 Dover, Dover Rd/Archcliffe
40,50 Tonbridge and Malling, London Rd
A21
70 Sevenoaks Bypass
60 Tonbridge and Malling, Castle Hill
60 Tunbridge Wells, Key's Green
A25
30 Sevenoaks, Seal Rd
A26
40 Tonbridge and Malling, Maidstone Rd
A28
40 Ashford, Ashford Rd
A224
30 Sevenoaks, Tubs Hill
A225
30 Sevenoaks, Sevenoaks Rd
A226
50 Gravesham, Rochester Rd/Gravesend Rd through Chalk
50 Gravesham, Rochester Rd/Gravesend Rd through Shorne
40 Gravesham, Rochester Rd/Gravesend Rd through Higham
A227
30 Gravesham, through Culverstone Green
40 Gravesham, through Istead Rise
30 Gravesham, through Meopham Green
A228
40 Medway, Ratcliffe Highway
A229
50 Maidstone, Bluebell Hill
40,30 Maidstone, Linton Rd/Loose Rd
30 Medway, City Way
40 Tunbridge Wells, Angley Rd (Hartley Rd)
A249
70 Maidstone, Chalky Rd/Rumstead Lane, South St
70 Swale, Chestnut St
A253
30 Thanet, Canterbury Rd West
A256
70 Dover
30 Dover, London Rd
40 Thanet, Haine Rd
A258
50 Dover, Dover Rd
A259
40 Shepway
60 Shepway, Guldeford Lane
30 Shepway, High St
A262
30 Ashford, High St
A268
30 Tunbridge Wells, Queen St
A289
50 Medway, Medway Tunnel
70 Medway, Wainscott Bypass
A290
30 Canterbury, Blean
A291
30 Canterbury, Canterbury Rd
A292
30 Ashford, Mace Lane
A2033
30 Shepway, Dover Rd
A2990
60 Canterbury, Old Thanet Way
B258
30 Dartford, Barn End Lane
B2015
40 Nettlestead Green, Maidstone Rd
B2017
30 Tunbridge Wells, Badsell Rd
B2067
60 Ashford, Ashford Rd
30 Ashford, Woodchurch Rd
B2071
30 Shepway, Littlestone Rd
B2097
30 Rochester, Maidstone Rd
B2205
30 Swale, Mill Way
Unclassified
30 Canterbury, Mickleburgh Hill
30 Canterbury, Rough Common Rd
30 Dartford, Ash Rd/Hartley Rd
30 Gravesham, Sole St
30 Medway, Beechings Way
30 Medway, Esplanade
30 Medway, Maidstone Rd
30 Medway, St End Rd
30 Medway, Walderslade Rd
30 Sevenoaks, Ash Rd/Hartley Rd
30 Swale, Lower Rd
30 Thanet, Shottendane Rd

Lancashire

A6
40 Broughton, Garstang Rd (north of M55)
30 Chorley, Bolton Rd
30 Fulwood, Garstang Rd (south of M55)
30 Fulwood, Garstang Rd, north of Blackpool Rd
30 Lancaster, Greaves Rd
50 Lancaster, Scotforth Rd nr Burrow Lane Bailrigg
30 Preston, North Rd
30 Preston, Ringway
A56
30 Colne, Albert Rd
30 Colne, Burnley Rd
30 Nelson, Leeds Rd
A59
60 Gisburn, Gisburn Rd
50 Hutton, Liverpool Rd
30 Preston, New Hall Lane
A65
40 Lancaster, Cowan Bridge
A570
40 Scarisbrick, Southport Rd, Brook House Farm
A581
40 Ulnes Walton, Southport Rd
A583+A5073
30 Blackpool, Whitegate Drive/Waterloo Rd
A583+B5266
30 Blackpool, Church St/Newton Drive
A584
30 Blackpool, Promenade
30 Lytham, West/Central Beach
30 Warton, Lytham Rd
A584+A587
30 Blackpool, Promenade/Fleetwood Rd
A587
30 Blackpool, East/North Park Drive
30 Cleveleys, Rossall Rd/Crescent East
A588
60 Pilling, Head Dyke Lane
60 Wyre, Lancaster Rd, Cockerham at Gulf Lane
A666
30 Darwen, Blackburn Rd
30 Darwen, Bolton Rd nr Cross St
30 Darwen, Duckworth St
A671
30 Read, Whalley Rd
A674
30 Cherry Tree, Preston Old Rd
A675
50 Belmont, Belmont Rd (south of village)
50 Darwen, Belmont Rd, north of Belmont Village
60 Withnell, Bolton Rd (Dole Lane to Calf Hey Bridge)
A680
40 Edenfield, Rochdalee Rd
A682
60 Barrowford, Gisburn Rd nr Moorcock Inn
30 Brierfield, Colne Rd
40 Crawshawbooth, Burnley Rd
60 Gisburn, Gisburn Rd
60 Gisburn, Long Preston Rd
A683
30 Lancaster, Morecambe Rd
A5073
30 Blackpool, Waterloo Rd
A5085
30 Lane Ends, Blackpool Rd
A5209
30 Newburgh, Course Lane/Ash Brow
A6068
50 Barrowford, Barrowford Rd
A6114
30 Burnley, Casterton Avenue
A6177
50 Haslingden, Grane Rd West of Holcombe Rd
50 Hyndburn, Haslingden Rd/Elton Rd
B5192
30 Kirkham, Preston St
B5251
30 Chorley, Pall Mall
B5254
30 Lostock Hall, Leyland Rd/Watkin Lane
30 South Ribble, Leyland Rd (north of Talbot Rd to A59 Golden Way Rdbt, Penwortham)
B5256
30 Leyland, Turpin Green Lane
B5269
40 Goosnargh, Whittingham Lane
B6231
30 Oswaldtwistle, Union Rd
Unclassified
60 Belmont, Egerton Rd
30 Blackburn, East Park Rd
30 Blackburn, Whalley Old Rd, west of Railway Bridge
30 Blackpool, Dickson Rd, Queens St to Pleasant St
30 Briercliffe, Burnley Rd
30 Darwen, Lower Eccleshill Rd
60 Galgate, Bay Horse Rd
30 Nelson, Netherfield Rd
30 Preston, Lytham Rd
30 Preston, St Georges Rd
30 St Anne's, Church Rd to Albany Rd, nr High School

Leicestershire and Rutland

A1
70 Empingham, Great North Rd
70 Stretton, Great North Rd
A5
60 Hinckley, Watling St (B578 to M69)
50 Hinckley, Watling St (M69 to A47)
70 Sharnford, Watling St (Highcross to B4114)
A6
40 Birstall, Loughborough Rd
40 Leicester, Abbey Lane
30 Leicester, London Rd (Knighton Drive)
30 Loughborough, Derby Rd
40 Oadby, Glen Rd/Harborough Rd
A47
60 Barrowden, Peterborough Rd
60 Bisbrooke, Uppingham Rd
30 Earl Shilton, Hinckley Rd
40 Houghton on the Hill, Uppingham Rd
30 Leicester, Hinckley Rd
30 Leicester, Humberstone Rd
50 Morcott, Glaston Rd
50 Skeffington, Uppingham Rd
50 Tugby, Uppingham Rd
A50
70 Hemmington to Lockington
40 Leicester/Glenfield, Groby Rd/Leicester Rd
30 Woodgate
A426
50 Dunton Bassett, Lutterworth Rd
40 Glen Parva, Leicester Rd
60 Lutterworth, Leicester Rd
60 Whetstone, Lutterworth Rd
A444
60 Fenny Drayton, Atherstone Rd
30 Twycross Village, Main St
60 Twycross, Norton Juxta
A447
60 Cadeby, Hinckley Rd
40 Ravenstone, Wash Lane
A512
30 Loughborough, Ashby Rd
40 Shepshed, Ashby Rd Central
A563
30 Leicester, Attlee Way
30 Leicester, Colchester Rd/Hungarton Boulevard
30 Leicester, Glenhills Way
40 Leicester, Krefield Way
30 Leicester, New Parks Way
A594
30 Leicester, St Georges Way
A606
60 Barnsdale, Stamford Rd
60 Leicester, Broughton/Old Dalby
60 Tinwell, Stamford Rd
A607
30 Leicester, Melton Rd
30 Melton, Norman Way
70 Thurmaston, Newark Rd
60 Waltham on the Wolds, Melton Rd
60 Waltham/Croxton Kerrial, Melton Rd
A4304
40 Market Harborough, Lubbenham Hill
A5199
30 Leicester, Welford Rd
30 Wigston, Bull Head St
30 Wigston, Leicester Rd
A5460
40 Leicester, Narborough Rd
A6004
30 Loughborough, Alan Moss Rd
A6030
30 Leicester, Wakerley Rd/Broad Avenue
A6121
30 Ketton, Stamford Rd
B568
30 Leicester, Victoria Park Rd
B581
30 Broughton Astley, Broughton Way
B582
30 Blaby, Little Glen Rd
B590
30 Hinckley, Rugby Rd
B591
60 Charley, Loughborough Rd
B676
60 Freeby, Saxby Rd
B4114
40 Enderby/Narborough, Leicester Rd/King Edward Avenue
30 Leicester, Sharnford
B4616
30 Leicester, East Park Rd
B4666
30 Hinckley, Coventry Rd
B5003
40 Norris Hill, Ashby Rd
B5366
30 Leicester, Saffron Lane
B5350
30 Loughborough, Foreset Rd
30 Loughborough, Nanpantan Rd
Unclassified
30 Barrow upon Soar, Sileby Rd
30 Blaby, Lutterworth Rd
30 Ibstock, Leicester Rd
30 Leicester, Fosse Rd South
30 Shepshed, Leicester Rd

Lincolnshire

A15
60 Ashby Lodge
60 Aswarby
A15-B1191
60 Dunsby Hollow
A16
60 Boston, Boston Tytton Lane
40 Burwell
60 Deeping Bypass
60 Grainsby to Holton-le-Clay
60 North Thoresby
A17
60 Fleet Hargate
60 Hoffleet Stow
60 Moulton Common
A52
60 Bridge End
60 Horbling and Swaton
60 Ropsley
A153
40 Billinghay
50 Tattershall
A158
50 Scremby to Candlesby
A631
60 Hemswell
60 West Rasen, Dale Bridge
B1188
30 Branston
60 Canwick, Highfield House
60 Potterhanworth

London

M11
Chadwell
M25
Egham
Elmbridge, Byfleet
Hillingdon
Hillingdon, Colnbrook
Runneymeade
Spelthorne
Wraysbury
A3
Kingston Bypass
Wandsworth, Kingston Rd
A4
Hounslow, Brentford, Great West Rd
Hounslow, Great West Rd
A5
Barnet, Hendon Broadway
Brent, Edgware Rd
A10
Enfield, Great Cambridge Rd
Hackney, Stamford Hill
A13
Barking and Dagenham, Alfreds Way
Barking and Dagenham, Ripple Rd
Dagenham, Ripple Rd
Newham, Alfreds Way
A20
Bexley, Sidcup Rd
Bromley, Sidcup Bypass
Greenwick, Sidcup Rd
A21
Lewisham, Bromley Rd
A22
Croydon, Godstone Rd
A40
City of Westminster, Westway
Ealing, Perivale
Ealing, Western Avenue
Hammersmith and Fulham, Westway
Hillingdon, Ruislip, Western Avenue
A110
Enfield, Enfield Rd
A124
Newham, Barking Rd
A205
Richmond upon Thames
Richmond upon Thames, Upper Richmond Rd West
A213
Bromley, Croydon Rd
A214
Wandsworth, Trinity Rd
A215
Croydon, Beulah Hill
A217
Croydon, Garratt Lane
A219
Hammersmith and Fulham, Scrubs Lane
A222
Bromley, Bromley Rd
A232
Sutton, Cheam Rd
A298
West Barnes, Bushey Rd
A312
Hillingdon
A315
Hounslow, High St
A406
Barking and Dagenham, Barking Relief Rd
Barnet, North Circular Rd
Redbridge, Southend Rd
A501
Camden, Euston Rd
A503
Haringey, Seven Sisters Rd
A3220
Wandsworth, Latchmere Rd
A4006
Brent, Kenton Rd
B178
Barking and Dagenham, Ballards Rd
B272
Sutton, Foresters Rd
B278
Sutton, Green Lane
B279
Sutton, Tudor Drive
Unclassified
Barnet, Oakleigh Rd South
Bexley, Abbey Rd
Bexley, Bellegrove Rd
Bexley, Erith Rd
Bexley, Farady Avenue
Bexley, King Harolds Way
Bexley, Lower Rd
Bexley, Penhill Rd
Bexley, Pickford Lane
Bexley, Well Hall Rd
Bexley, Woolwich Rd
Brent, Crest Rd
Brent, Hillside
Brent, Kingsbury Rd
Brent, Kingsbury, Fryent Way
Brent, Sudbury, Watford Rd
Brent, Wembley, Watford Rd
Brent, Woodcock Hill
Bromley, Beckenham Rd
Bromley, Burnt Ash Lane
Bromley, Crystal Palace Park Rd
Bromley, Elmers End Rd
Bromley, Main Rd
Bromley, Sevenoaks Way
Bromley, Wickham Way
City of Westminster, Great Western Rd
City of Westminster, Millbank
City of Westminster, Vauxhall Bridge Rd
Croydon, Addiscombe, Long Lane
Croydon, Brigstock Rd
Croydon, Coulsdon, Coulsdon Rd
Croydon, Coulsdon, Portnalls Rd
Croydon, Thornton Rd
Ealing, Greenford, Greenford Rd
Ealing, Horn Lane
Ealing, Lady Margaret Rd
Ealing, Ruislip Rd
Ealing, Southall, Greenford Rd
Ealing, Uxbridge Rd
Eastcote, Field End Rd
Enfield, Fore St
Forest Hill, Stanstead Rd
Forest Hill, Stanstead Rd
Greenwick, Beresford St
Greenwick, Court Rd
Greenwick, Creek Rd
Greenwick, Glenesk Rd
Greenwick, Rochester Way
Greenwick, Rochester Way
Greenwick, Woolwich Church St
Hackney, Clapton Common
Hackney, Seven Sisters Rd
Hackney, Upper Clapton Rd
Hammersmith and Fulham, Fulham Palace Rd
Hammersmith and Fulham, Uxbridge Rd
Hammersmith and Fulham, Westway
Haringey, Belmont Rd
Haringey, Bounds Green Rd
Haringey, Seven Sisters Rd
Haringey, White Hart Lane
Harrow, Alexandra Avenue
Harrow, Harrow View
Harrow, Harrow Weald, Uxbridge Rd
Harrow, Honeypot Lane
Harrow, Porlock Avenue
Harrow, Watford Rd
Havering, Chase Cross Rd
Havering, Eastern Avenue
Havering, Eastern Avenue East
Havering, Hall Lane
Havering, Hornchurch, Parkstone Avenue
Havering, Ockenden Rd
Havering, Romford, Brentwood Rd
Havering, Wingletye Lane
Hillingdon, Cowley, Cowley Rd
Hillingdon, Cowley, High Rd
Hillingdon, Harefield, Church Hill
Hillingdon, Hayes, Kingshill Avenue
Hillingdon, Hayes, Uxbridge Rd
Hillingdon, Northwood Hills, Joel St
Hillingdon, Park Rd
Hillingdon, Stockley Rd
Hillingdon, Uxbridge, Cowley Rd
Hounslow, Bedfont, Hatton Rd
Hounslow, Great West Rd
Hounslow, Hanworth, Castle Way
Hounslow, Harlington Rd West
Islington, Holloway Rd
Islington, Seven Sisters Rd
Islington, Upper St
Kensington and Chelsea, Barlby Rd
Kensington and Chelsea, Chelsea Embankment
Kensington and Chelsea, Chesterton Rd
Kensington and Chelsea, Holand Park Avenue
Kensington and Chelsea, Holland Villas Rd
Kensington and Chelsea, Kensington Park Rd
Kensington and Chelsea, Kensington Rd
Kensington and Chelsea, Ladbroke Grove
Kensington and Chelsea, Latimer Rd
Kensington and Chelsea, Royal Hospital Rd
Kensington and Chelsea, Sloane St
Kensington and Chelsea, St Helens Gardens
Kingston upon Thames, Kingston Rd
Kingston upon Thames, Manor Drive North
Kingston upon Thames, Richmond Rd
Lambeth, Atkins Rd
Lambeth, Brixton Hill
Lambeth, Brixton Rd
Lambeth, Clapham Rd
Lambeth, Herne Hill Rd
Lambeth, Kennington Park Rd
Lambeth, Kings Avenue
Lambeth, Streatham High Rd
Lewisham, Brockley Rd
Lewisham, Brownhill Rd
Lewisham, Burnt Ash Hill
Lewisham, Lee High Rd
Lewisham, Lewisham Way
Lewisham, Westwood Hill
Merton, Central Rd
Merton, Colliers Wood, High St
Merton, Hillcross Avenue
Merton, London Rd
Merton, Martin Way
Merton, Ridgway Place
Merton, West Barnes Lane
Newham, Barking Rd
Newham, Romford Rd
Newham, Royal Albert Dock, Spine Rd
Newham, Royal Docks Rd
North Dagenham, Rainham Rd
Redbridge, Hainault, Manford Way
Redbridge, Woodford Avenue
Redbridge, Woodford Rd
Richmond upon Thames, Kew Rd
Richmond upon Thames, Sixth Cross Rd
Richmond upon Thames, Uxbridge Rd
Southwark, Albany Rd
Southwark, Alleyn Park
Southwark, Brenchley Gardens
Southwark, Camberwell New Rd
Southwark, Denmark Hill
Southwark, Kennington Park Rd
Southwark, Linden Grove
Southwark, Old Kent Rd
Southwark, Peckham Rye
Southwark, Salter Rd
Southwark, Sunray Avenue
Streatham, Streatham High Rd
Sutton, Beddington Lane
Sutton, Cheam Common Rd
Sutton, Maiden Rd
Sutton, Middleton Rd
Tower Hamlets, Bow Rd
Tower Hamlets, Cambridge Heath Rd
Tower Hamlets, Homerton High Rd
Tower Hamlets, Manchester Rd
Tower Hamlets, Mile End Rd
Tower Hamlets, Upper Clapton Rd
Tower Hamlets, Westferry Rd
Waltham Forest, Chingford Rd
Waltham Forest, Hoe St
Waltham Forest, Larksall Rd
Wandsworth, Battersea Park Rd
Wandsworth, Garratt Lane
Wandsworth, Upper Richmond Rd
Woolwich, Woolwich Church St

Norfolk

A10
60 Stow Bardolph
60 Tottenhill/Watlington
A11
60 Attleborough Bypass
70 Ketteringham
70 Roundham
70 Snetterton
70 Wymondham/Bestthorpe
A12
70 Hopton
A17
60 Terrington St Clement
A47
60 East Winch
60 Emneth
60 Honington/Easton
50 Lingwood/Acle
60 Mautby/Halvergate
60 Narborough
70 Postwick
70 Pullover Rdbt
60 Scarning
60 Swaffham/Sporle
70 Terrington St John
70 Tuddenham
60 Wendling/Framsham
A140
60 Aylsham
60 Dickleburgh Moor
60 Erpingham
60 Long Stratton/Tivetshall St Mary
60 Newton Flotman
40 Newton Flotman/Saxlingham Thorpe
30 Norwich, Harford Bridge
40 Roughton village
70 Scole Bypass
60 St. Faiths
A143
60 Billingford/Brockdish
A146
60 Hales
A148
60 Bodham
60 Fakenham Bypass
40 King's Lynn, Grimston Rd
60 Pretty Corner
50 Thursford
A149
70 Caister Bypass
60 Catfield
40 Catfield/Potter Heigham
30 Hunstanton
60 Kings Lynn/Nth Runcton
60 Knights Hill
60 Little Snoring
60 Roughton (N and S Repps)
60 Sandringham
50 Wayford Bridge East
50 Wayford Bridge West/Smallburgh
A1065
60 Hilbrough
60 South Acre
60 Weeting with Broomhill
A1066
60 Rushford
60 South Lopham
40 Thetford, Mundford Rd
A1067
50 Bawdeswell
60 Morton/Attlebridge
A1075
60 Wretham (heath)
A1082
30 Sheringham
A1122
60 Swaffham/Beachamwell
A1151
60 Rackheath/Wroxham
B111
30 East Harling
B1108
30 Norwich, Earlham Rd
B1135
50 Wymondham/Wreningham
B1149
60 Horsford Woods
B1150
50 Scottow
50 Westwick
B1152
60 Orby
B1332
50 Ditchingham
Unclassified
70 Caister, High St/Norwich Rc
30 Caister, Ormesby Rd
60 Drayton, Reepham Rd
30 Shipdham, High St
30 Walton

North Yorkshire

A1
70 Catterick
A59
60 Beamsley
A64
70 Malton
A65
60 Clapham
60 Settle
Unclassified
30 Tunstall, Main St

Northants

A5
Daventry
DIRFT to County Boundary
Kilsby
Norton/Whilton Crossroads
Towcester Racecourse to A4
A6
Burton Latimer Bypass
A14
Kelmarsh
Kettering to jcts 7-10
A43
Laxton Turn to A47
Duddington
M1 jct 16 to Weedon
Mawsley to A14 jct 8
Towcester to M1 jct 15a
Towcester/Brackley
A45
Daventry/Weedon
Mereway rdbt
Northampton
Northampton/Brackmills
Stanwick to Raunds
Tiffield
A361
Byfield
Byfield to Chipping Warder
A422
Brackley, Banbury Rd
Brackley West to A43
A428
East Haddon
Great Houghton to Yardley Hastings
A508
Grafton Regis
Plough Gyratory
St Georges Avenue to Holly Lodge Rd
St Peters Way to St Georges Avenue
Stoke Bruerne to A5
Wootton Flyover to M1 jct 1
A509
Wellingborough to Isham

605
Thrapston to Warmington
511
Sherwood, Hucknall Rd
4256
Daventry
4500
Abington Park to York Rd
Great Billing to Earls Barton
Park Avenue to Booth Lane South
Weedon Rd to Duston Rd Northampton
5076
Northampton, Mere Way
Northampton, Great Billing Way South
5193
Wellingborough, London Rd
6003
Kettering to Corby
6014
Corby, Oakley Rd
569
Irchester to Rushden
nclassified
Brackmills Ind Est
Desborough to Rothwell
Kilsby, Rugby Rd
Milton Malsor
Northampton, Grange Rd
Northampton, Salthouse Rd
Northampton, Welsh Lane
Watford to West Haddon

orthumbria

ateshead, Newcastle-oon-Tyne, North Tyneside, orthumberland, South neside, Sunderland

Berwick Bypass, Dunns Jct (N)
68
Colt Crag
69
Haltwhistle Bypass
Hexham, Two Mile Cottage
167
Newcastle, Stamfordham Rd
182
Sunderland, Houghton Rd
183
Broadway, Chester Rd
186
Denton Burn, West Rd
Newcastle, City Rd at Beamish House
Newcastle, West Rd at Turret Rd
Newcastle, Westgate Rd at Elwick Row
189
Cramlington, High Pitt
Cramlington, Spine Rd
South Gosforth, Haddricks Mill Rd
191
Benton, Whitley Rd
193
Wallsend, Church Bank
194
Simonside, Newcastle Rd
196
Blackclose Bank
690
Sunderland, Durham Rd
Sunderland, Stoneygate, Houghton, Durham Rd
694
Gateshead, Rowlands Gill, Station Rd
Gateshead, Winlaton Mill (Spa Well Rd)
695
Gateshead, Crawcrook Bypass
Prudhoe Jct B6395

Belsay Village
Blaxter Cottages
Kirkwhelpiington
Otterburn Monkridge
697
Morpeth, Heighley Gate
Northumberland
1018
Sunderland, Ryhope Rd, Irene Avenue
1058
Newcastle, Jesmond Rd at Akenside Terrace
1068
Amble Ind Est
1147
Stakeford, Gordon Terrace
1171
Cramlington, Dudley Lane
1290
Sunderland, Southwick, Keir Hardie Way
1300
South Tyneside, Nook, Prince Edward Rd
6085
Newcastle, Lemington Rd
5127
Gateshead, Barley Mow, Durham Rd
1288
Gateshead, Leam Lane/A195
1296
Gateshead, Sheriffs Highway, QE Hospital
Gateshead, Sheriffs Highway, Split Crow Rd

B1298
30 South Tyneside, Boldon Colliery, New Rd
B1301
30 South Tyneside, Dean Rd (John Clay St)
30 South Tyneside, Laygate, Eglesfield Rd
B1316
30 North Tyneside, Lynn Rd
B1318
30 North Tyneside, Seaton Burn, Bridge St
B1426
30 Gateshead, Felling, Sunderland Rd
B1505
30 North Tyneside, West Moor, Great Lime Rd
B6315
30 Gateshead, High Spen, Hookergate Lane
B6317
30 Gateshead, Ryton, Main Rd
30 Gateshead, Whickham Highway
B6318
60 Whitchester, Military Rd
60 Whittington Fell, Military Rd
B6324
40 Newcastle, Stamfordham Rd southeast of Walbottle Rd
B6918
30 Newcastle, Woolssington Village
Unclassified
30 Ashington, Station Rd
30 Benton, Coach Lane
30 Gateshead, Blaydon, Shibdon Bank
30 Gateshead, Crawcrook, Greenside Rd
30 Gateshead, Felling, Watermill Lane
30 Gateshead, Whickham, Fellside Rd
30 Gateshead, Askew Rd West
30 Hebburn, Campbell Park Rd
70 Nafferton Eastbound
60 Newcastle, Dinnington Rd North Brunton Lane
40 Newcastle, West Denton Way east of Hawksley
30 North Shields, Norham Rd
30 South Tyneside, Harton Lane
40 South Tyneside, Hedworth Lane, Abingdon Way
40 Sunderland, Farringdon, North Moor Lane
40 Sunderland, North Hylton Rd, Castletown Way
30 Sunderland, Silksworth Rd, Rutland Avenue
30 Sunderland, Springwell Rd
30 Sunderland, Warwick Terrace
30 Wallsend, Battle Hill Drive
30 Whiteleas, Nevinson Avenue

Nottinghamshire

A1(T)
70 East Markham (Northbound)
A52(T)
40 Clifton Boulevard
A60
30 Carlton in Lindrick
30 Mansfield, Nottingham Rd
60 Market Warsop/Cuckney
Nottingham, Bellar Gate to Woodthorpe Drive
Nottingham, London Rd
50 Ravenshead
30 South, Nottingham
A609
30 Nottingham, Ilkeston Rd/Wollaton Rd/Russell Drive
A610
30 Nottingham, Bobbers Mill
A611
30 Annelsey, Derby Rd
30 Nottingham, Hucknall Rd
A612
30 Southwell, Nottingham Rd
A614
60 Arnold, Burnt Stump
A617
40 Mansfield, Chesterfield Rd South
A620
40 Retford, Welham Rd
A631
50 Beckingham Bypass
50 Beckingham, Flood Plain Rd
50 Beckingham, nr Wood Lane
60 Gringley to Beckingham, nr Mutton Lane
50 West of Beckingham
A6005
30 Nottingham, Castle Boulevard/Abbey Bridge/Beeston Rd
A6008
30 Nottingham, Canal St
A6130
30 Nottingham, Gregory Boulevard
30 Nottingham, Radford and Lenton Boulevards
A6200/A52
30 Nottingham, Derby Rd
B679
30 West Bridgford, Wilford Lane
B682
30 Nottingham, Sherwood Rise/Nottingham Rd/Vernon Rd
B6004
40 Arnold, Oxclose Lane
B6010
30 Giltbrook, Nottingham Rd
B6011
30 Hucknall, Annesley Rd/Nottingham Rd/Portland Rd
B6020
30 Rainworth, Kirklington Rd
B6040
30 Worksop, Retford Rd
B6166
30 Newark on Trent, Lincoln Rd/Northgate
B6326
40 Newark on Trent, London Rd
Unclassified
30 Newark, Balderton, Hawton Lane
30 Nottingham, Beechdale Rd/Wigman Rd
30 Nottingham, Bestwood Park Drive
Nottingham, Radford Boulevard/Lenton Boulevard
30 Nottingham, Ridge Way/Top Valley Drive

Oxfordshire

see Thames Valley

Shropshire

see West Mercia

Somerset

see Avon and Somerset

South Yorkshire

A18
60 Doncaster, Slay Pits to Tudworth, Epworth Rd
40 Doncaster, Carr House Rd/Leger Way
A57
40,60 Anston, Sheffield Rd/Worksop Rd
60 Rotherham, Worksop Rd
60 Sheffield, Mosborough Parkway
A60
60 Tickhill, Doncaster Rd
30,60 Tickhill, Worksop Rd
A61
30 Cutting Edge, Park Rd
30,40 Sheffield, Chesterfield Rd/Chesterfield Rd South
30,40 Sheffield, Halifax Rd
30 Sheffield, Penistone Rd
A614
60 Thorne, Selby Rd
A618
40 Wales Bar, Mansfield Rd
A628
30,40 Barnsley, Cundy Cross to Shafton Two Gates
40,60 Barnsley, Dodworth
40 Penistone, Barnsley Rd
A629
60 Barnsley, Wortley
30 Burncross, Hallwood Rd/Burncross Rd
40 Rotherham, New Wortley Rd
30,40 Rotherham, Wortley Rd/Upper Wortley Rd
A630
30,40,60 Dalton/Thrybergh, Doncaster Rd
30,40,60 Doncaster, Balby Flyover to Hill Top
40 Doncaster, Wheatley Hall Rd
40,50 Rotherham, Centenary Way
A631
40 Brinsworth, Bawtry Rd
30,40 Hellaby/Maltby, Bawtry Rd/Rotherham Rd
50 Rotherham, West Bawtry Rd
40 Wickersley/Brecks, Bawtry Rd
A633
30 Athersley South, Rotherham Rd
40 Monk Bretton, Rotherham Rd
30 Wath upon Dearne, Sandygate
30,40 Wombwell, Barnsley Rd
A635
30,40,60 Barnsley, Doncaster Rd/Saltersbrook Rd
A638
40 Doncaster, Bawtry Rd
40,50 Doncaster, Great North Rd/York Rd
A6022
30 Rotherham, Swinton
A6101
40 Sheffield, Rivelin Valley Rd
A6102
30,40 Hillsborough/Deepcar, Manchester Rd/Langsett Rd
A6109
40 Rotherham, Meadow Bank Rd
A6123
40 Rotherham, Herringthorpe Valley Rd
A6135
40 Sheffield, Ecclesfield Rd/Chapeltown Rd
B6059
30,40 Rotherham, Kiveton/Wales
B6089
40 Thorn Hill/Greasbrough, Greasbrough Rd/Greasbrough St
B6096
30 Barnsley, Wombwell to Snape Hill
B6097
30,60 Wath upon Dearne, Doncaster Rd
B6100
30 Barnsley, Ardsley Rd/Hunningley Lane
B6411
30 Thurnscoe, Houghton Rd
B6463
60 Tickhill, Stripe Rd
Unclassified
30 Armthorpe, Hatfield Lane/Mill St
30 Armthorpe, Nutwell Lane
30 Barnsley, Pogmoor Rd
30 Bolton upon Dearne, Dearne Rd
30 Doncaster, Melton Rd/Sprotbrough Rd
30 Doncaster, Urban Rd
30,60 Edlington/Warmsworth, Broomhouse Lane/Springwell Lane
40,60 Finningley, Hurst Lane
30 Grimethorpe, Brierley Rd
30,60 Rotherham, Fenton Rd
30,40 Rotherham, Haugh Rd
30 Rotherham, Kilnhurst Rd
30 Stainforth, Station Rd
40 Wath upon Dearne, Barnsley Rd
30 Wheatley, Thorne Rd

Staffordshire

A5
60 A5127 to A38 – Wall Island to Weeford Island
60 Brownhills, Watling St
60,70,60,30 btwn A34 Churchbridge and The Turf Pub Island (B4154)
50 Cannock, Watling St
50,40 from A38 to Hints Lane
70 from A461 to A5127 (Muckley Corner Island to Wall Island Lichfield/Tamworth)
60,70,60 Hanney Hay/Barracks Lane Island to Muckley Corner Island
50 M6 jct 12 to A460/A4601 Island
50,30 South Cannock, A460/A4601 to A34 Longford Island to A34 Bridgetown
60 Wall, Watling St
60 Weeford, Watling St
A34
30 Cannock North, North of Holly Lane jct to A34/B5012 rdbt
30,50,30 Cannock South to County Boundary
30 Cannock South, A34 from south of jct of A5 Walstall Rd to north of jct with Jones Lane
40 Newcastle North, from Wolstanton Rd/Dimsdale Parade west Island to Milehouse Lane/B5367
30,40 Newcastle Rd btwn Hanford Island to London Rd Bowling Club
40 Newcastle South, Barracks Rd to Stoke City Boundary
70,40 Newcastle under Lyme to Talke, btwn Wolstanton Rd/Dimsdale Parade West Island to Jct of A500
30,40 Stafford South, from A449 jct to Acton Hill Lane Jct
30 Stafford, btwn A5013 and A518
40 Stafford, Queensway
40,30 Stone Rd from jct of Longton Rd/A5035 to Handford Island/A500
40,30 Stone Rd Redhill (A513/A34) island to Lloyds Island, Eccleshall Rd
30,60 Talke, Jct A500 to Jct A5011
A38
40 Alrewas, btwn Rradley Lane and Wychnor Lane
70 btwn London Rd Lichfield and A5121 Burton
70 btwn Weeford Island and Bassetts Pole Island (Community Concern Site)
A50
30 Kidsgrove, btwn City Boundary and Oldcott Drive
30 Kidsgrove, Liverpool Rd
30 Stoke on Trent, Victoria Rd btwn Leek Rd and City Rd
A51
60 btwn Armitage Lane Rugeley and A515 nr Lichfield
30,40,60 Lichfield, from A5127 Birmingham Rd to Heath Rd
30 Lichfield, Tamworth Rd
50 Pasturefields, A51 from south of jct with Amerton Lane to south of Hoomill Lane
40,30 Rugeley North, from A51 jct with Bower Lane to island of A460 Sandy Lane and B5013 Elmore Lane
30,40 Rugeley South, from south of island of A460/Sandy Lane and B5013 Elmore Lane to Brereton Island
30 Tamworth, A51 Tamworth Rd/Dosthill Rd from south of jct with Peelers Way to jct with A51 Ascot Drive
60,40,50 Weston, btwn New Rd and 500m past Sandy Lane (going north)
A52
30 Stoke on Trent, Werrington Rd – btwn jct of B5040 to half mile east of Brookhouse Lane (Ashbank)
30,40 Stoke, Werrington Rd, btwn Brookhouse Lane and Kingsley Rd
A53
40,30,40,60 Endon, from A53 Leek New Rd from jct with Nursery Avenue to jct with Dunwood Lane
60,40,30 Longsden, from A53 jct with Dunwood Lane to A53 jct with Wallbridge Drive
A444
30 Stanton Rd – St Peters Bridge to Derbyshire boundary
A449
70,40 Coven, btwn Station Drive by Four Ashes to just before M54 island
40 Coven, Wolverhampton Rd
60,70 Gailey, btwn Rodbaston Drive and Station Drive
60 Galley, Wolverhampton Rd
40 Penkridge, Lynehill Lane to 0.5mile north of Goodstation Lane
30 Stafford, Lichfield Rd to Gravel Lane
A454
50 Trescott, Bridgenorth Rd btwn Brantley Lane and Shop Lane
A458
40,50 Gilberts Cross, btwn Six Ashes Rd, Six Ashes and Morfe Lane
A460
30 Rugeley, A460 from A51/A460 jct of Sandy Lane/Hednesford Rd to south of jct A460 Stile Cop Rd
A500
40 btwn M6 jct 16 and A34
A511
40,30 Burton North, btwn Anslow Lane to island of A5121
30 Burton South, island of A5121 to Brizlincote Lane (by Derbyshire boundary)
A518
30 Stafford, btwn M6 and Bridge St
30,40 Stafford, Riverway to Blackheath Lane
A519
40 Newcastle, Clayton Rd – from south of A519 Clayton Rd/Friars Wood and Brook Lane to rdbt on A519
A519
30 Woodseaves, btwn Moss Lane and Lodge Lane (Community Concern Site)
A520
30 Sandon Rd btwn Grange Rd and A50
30 Weston Rd – from north of the A50 to City boundary (Park Hall) through Meir and Weston Coyney
A522
50,40 Beamhurst, btwn Fole Lane and Grange Rd, nr Uttoxeter
A4601
30 Cannock, btwn A34 Walsall Rd jct to Longford Island A5
30 Old Hednesford Rd btwn jct with A5190 Lichfield Rd and jct with A460 Eastern Way
30,40 Wedges Mill, Longford Island twd jct 11 to just before Saredon Rd
A5005
Stoke on Trent, Lightwood Rd btwn A520 and A50
A5013
30 Stafford, Eccleshall Rd btwn A34 and M6
A5035
30 Trentham, Longton Rd btwn Trentham Rdbt A34 and A50 jct at Longton
A5121
30 Burton, Derby Rd
50,40,30 Burton, from Island Junction with B5108 Branston to Borough Rd
30,40 Burton, from jct with Byrkley St, Horninglow to jct with Hillfield Lane
30 Burton, Wellington Rd
A5127
30 Lichfield, Trent Valley Rd
30 Lichfield, from jct with Upper St John St towards Sthay (incs change in speed limit over railway bridge)
A5189
30 Burton, St Peters Bridge
30,40 Burton, btwn Wellington Rd jct along St Peters Bridge to Stapenhill Rd rdbt
A5190
30 Burntwood, Cannock Rd from Attwood Rd to Stockhay Lane Jct
30 Cannock, Cannock Rd
30,40,60 Cannock, from Five Ways Island to Hednesford Rd
B5027
30 Stone Rd btwn Byrds Lane and Springfield Rd
B5044
30 Silverdale, btwn Sneyd Terrace and the jct of the B5368 (Church Lane/Cemetery Rd)
B5051
30 btwn Sneyd Hill Rd and Brown Edge
30 Stoke on Trent, Ford Green Rd
B5066
30 Hilderstone, btwn B5027 and Hall Lane
60 Sandon, Sandon Rd btwn A51 and Salt Lane
30 Stafford, Sandon Rd btwn A513 and Marston Rd
B5080
30,40 Tamworth, Pennine Way btwn B5000 and Pennymoor Rd
B5404
40,30 Tamworth, from Sutton Rd to jct of A4091 (Coleshill Rd/Fazeley Rd)
30 Tamworth, Watling St btwn jct with A51 and A5
B5500
30 Audley btwn Barthomley Rd and Park Lane (Community Concern Site)
30,40 Bignall End/Bignall Hill, btwn Boons Hill Rd and Alsager Lane
Unclassified
30 Burntwood, Church Rd btwn Rugeley Rd and Farewell Lane
30 Burton on Trent, Violet Way/Beauford Rd btwn A444 and A511
30 Burton, Rosliston Rd btwn A5189 St Peters Bridge and County Boundary by Railway Bridge
30 Cannock, Pye Green Rd
30 Cedar Rd btwn Crackley Bank and B5500 Audley Rd
30 Cheadle Rd btwn Uttoxeter Rd and Quabbs Lane
40 Cresswell, Sandon Rd btwn Severley Green Rd and Uttoxeter Rd
30 Hednesford, Rawnsley Rd btwn A460 and Littleworth Rd
30,40 Leek New Rd – btwn B5049 Hanley Rd and B5051 jct with A53 at Endon
30 Oxford Rd/Chell Heath Rd btwn A527 and B5051
30 Stoke on Trent, Chell Heath Rd
30 Stoke on Trent, Dividy Rd – btwn B5039 and A52

Suffolk

A11
50 Barton Mills
Elveden
40 Elveden Cross Rds
Elveden, Chalk Hall
Worlington
A12
40 Blythburgh
Kelsale
30 Little Glemham
50 Little Glemham, North Lound
40 Marlesford
40 Melton
Saxmundham
A14
Exning
Newmarket
Rougham
A134
40 Barnham
30 Little Welnetham
Long Melford
40 Nowton
A137
30 Brantham
A140
50 Thwaite
40 Wetheringsett
A143
30 Bury St Edmunds
30 Chedburgh
40 Stanton
40 Stanton Bypass
40 Stradishall, Highpoint Prison
A144
30 Ilketshall St Lawrence
A145
40 Felixstowe, Trinity Avenue
A146
50 Barnby Bends
A1065
40 Eriswell
Mildenhall
North of RAF Lakenheath
A1071
40 Boxford
Hadleigh, Lady Lane
A1088
30 Honington
A1092
30 Cavendish
30 Clare
40 Glemsford, Skates Hill
A1101
30 Flempton
30 Mildenhall
50 Shippea Hill
A1117
30 Lowestoft, Saltwater Way
A1120
30 Stonham Aspal
A1156
30 Ipswich, Norwich Rd
A1156
40 Nacton
A1214
40 Ipswich, London Rd
A1302
30 Bury St Edmunds
A1304
Newmarket, Golf Club
A1307
40 Haverhill
B1078
30 Barking
30 Needham Market
B1106
30 Fornham
B1113
40 Bramford
B1115
40 Chilton
B1384
30 Carlton Colville
B1385
30 Corton
B1438
30 Melton Hill
B1506
40 Kentford
Moulton
Unclassified
30 Felixstowe, Grange Farm Avenue
30 Felixstowe, High Rd
30 Ipswich, Ellenbrook Rd
30 Ipswich, Foxhall Rd
30 Ipswich, Landseer Rd
30 Ipswich, Nacton Rd
30 Kesgrave, Ropes Drive

Surrey

A31
60 Hogs Back, (Central and Eastern Sections)
A308
50 Staines Bypass
Unclassified
30 Staines, Kingston Rd

Sussex

A24
30 Worthing, Broadwater Rd nr Cecilian Avenue
A27
70 Angmering, Hammerpot n/side
60 Firle, Firle Straight
70 Shoreham, Holmbush
A29
30 Aldingbourne, Westergate St/Elmcroft Place
30 Aldingbourne, Westergate St/Hook Lane
40 Bognor, Shripney Rd
A259
30 Bognor, Hotham Way
30 Brighton, Marine Parade/Eaton Place
30 Fishbourne, Main Rd
30 Saltdean, Marine Drive
A280
40 Patching
A281
30 Horsham, Guildford Rd
A283
30 Northchapel
30 Pulborough, Lower St
A285
30 Petworth, Station Rd
A2031
30 Worthing, Offington Lane/Rogate Rd
30 Worthing, Offington Lane/The Plantation
A2032
30 Worthing, Littlehampton Rd nr Little Gables
A2280
40 Eastbourne, Lottbridge Drove
B2093
30 Hastings, The Ridge
B2104
30 Hallsham, Ersham Rd
B2138
30 Fittleworth, Lower St
B2166
30 Bognor, Aldwick Rd
Unclassified
30 Bognor, Hawthorn Rd/Amberley Drive
30 Brighton, Ditching Rd/Balfour Rd
30 Brighton, Falmer Rd Woodingdean
30 Crawley, Breezhurst Drive
30 Crawley, Gatwick Rd nr Hazlewick Flyover
30 Crawley, Gossops Drive
30 Crawley, Manor Royal/Faraday Rd
30 Heathfield, Hallsham Rd
30 Horsham, Pondtall Rd/Haybarn Drive
30 Horsham, Pondtall Rd/Pondtall Close
30 Hove, New Church Rd/Wish Rd
30 Hove, Shirley Drive/Onslow Rd
30 Shirley, Shirley Drive/Shirley Rd
30 Worthing, The Boulevard

Thames Valley

Bracknell Forest, Buckinghamshire, Milton Keynes, Oxfordshire, Reading, Slough, West Berkshire, Windsor and Maidenhead, Wokingham

A5
70 Wolverton
70 Bletchley
A30(T)
30 Sunningdale, London Rd
A34
70 Radley
70 Kennington
A40
60 Cassington
70 Forest Hills
A41
70 Buckland
A44
50 Kiddington with Asterleigh
A338
50 Hungerford
A361
30 Chipping Norton, Burford Rd
60 Little Faringdon
A404
70 Little Marlow, Marlow Bypass
A413
60 Swanbourne
60 Weedon
60 Hardwick
60 Wendover Bypass
A421
70 Tingewick Bypass
60 Wavendon
A422
50 Radclive cum Chackmore
A509
70 Newport Pagnell
60 Emberton Bypass
A4074
60 Dorchester
50 Nuneham Courteney
A4095
40 Freeland, Witney Rd
A4130
60 Nuffield
40 Remenham Hill
A4155
30 Shipiake
A4260
50 Shipton on Cherwell, Banbury Rd
60 Rousham, Banbury Rd
60 Steeple Aston
B4009
50 Ewelme
B4011
60 Piddington
B4494
60 Leckhampstead
Unclassified
30 Abingdon, Drayton Rd
30 Abingdon, Oxford Rd
30 Aylesbury, Buckingham Rd
30 Aylesbury, Gatehouse Rd
30 Aylesbury, Oakfield Rd
30 Aylesbury, Tring Rd
30 Aylesbury, Walton St
30 Aylesbury, Wendover Rd
30 Barkham, Barkham Rd
60 Beenham, Bath Rd
30 Blackbird Leys, Watlington Rd
30 Bletchley, Buckingham Rd
40 Bracknell, Bagshot Rd
50 Bracknell, Nine Mile Ride
30 Bracknell, Opladen Way
30 Buckingham, Stratford Rd
50 Burnham, Bath Rd
30 Chalfont St Peter, Gravel Hill
40 Chipping Norton, London Rd
40 Curbridge, Bampton Rd
40 Denham, North Orbital Rd
30 Denham, Oxford Rd
40 Earley, 30 London Rd
30 Great Missenden, Rignall Rd
60 Hardmead, Newport Rd
30 Hazelmere, Sawpit Hill
30 High Wycombe, Holmers Farm Way
30 High Wycombe, Marlow Hill
30 High Wycombe, New Rd
30 High Wycombe, West Wycombe Rd
60 Hungerford, Bath Rd
30 Kidlington, Oxford Rd
60 Kintbury, Bath Rd
30 Long Crendon, Bicester Rd
40 Maidenhead, Braywick Rd
70 Milton Keynes, Woughton on the Green, Standing Way
30 Milton Keynes, Avebury Boulevard
30 Milton Keynes, Midsummer Boulevard

30 Milton Keynes, Silbury Boulevard
30 Monks Risborough, Aylesbury Rd
30 Oxford, Church Cowley Rd
30 Oxford, Headington Rd
30 Oxford, London Rd
30 Oxford, Windmill Rd
30 Reading, Berkeley Avenue
30 Reading, Castle Hill
30 Reading, Kings Rd
30 Reading, Park Lane
30 Reading, Vastern Rd
30 Reading, Wokingham Rd
30 Slough, Buckingham Rd
30 Slough, Cippenham Lane
40 Slough, London Rd
30 Slough, Parlaunt Rd
30 Slough, Sussex Place
60 Speen, Bath Rd
30 Stanford in the Vale, Faringdon Rd
40 Sunninghill, Brockenhurst Rd
30 Tiddington, Oxford Rd
40 Tilehurst, Bath Rd
30 Wantage, Charlton Rd
70 Winkfield, Bagshot Rd
30 Witney, Corn St
30 Wokingham, London Rd
60 Wroxton, Stratford Rd

Warwickshire

A5
50 North Warwickshire, Grendon to Hinckley
60 Rugby, Churchover
A45
50 Rugby, nr Ryton
A46
60 Stratford upon Avon, nr Snitterfield
60 Warwick, nr Stoneleigh
A47
30 Nuneaton and Bedworth, Hinckley Rd
40 Nuneaton and Bedworth, Longshoot, Nuneaton Radial Route
A422
30 Stratford upon Avon, Stratford, Alcester Rd
A423
60 Rugby, nr Marton
30 Rugby, Marton
60 Stratford upon Avon, nr Fenny Compton
60 Stratford upon Avon, South of Southam
A425
30 Stratford upon Avon, Ufton
30 Warwick, Radford Semele
A426
30 Rugby, Dunchurch Rd
60 Stratford upon Avon, nr Stockton
A428
30 Rugby, Binley Woods
60 Rugby, Church Lawford
40 Rugby, Long Lawford
A429
60 Stratford upon Avon, Stretton on Fosse
60 Stratford upon Avon, Wellesbourne
A435
40 Stratford upon Avon, Mappleborough Green
A439
50 Stratford upon Avon, Stratford to A46
A446
60 North Warwickshire, Allen End
A452
60 Warwick, Greys Mallory
60 Warwick, Heathcote
A3400
50 Stratford upon Avon, Alderminster
60 Stratford upon Avon, Little Wolford
40 Stratford upon Avon, North of Henley in Arden
50 Stratford upon Avon, Pathlow
A4091
60 North Warwickshire, Middleton
A4189
60 Stratford upon Avon, Outhill to Lower Norton
B4089
Stratford upon Avon, Alcester, Arden Rd
B4098
40 North Warwickshire, Corley, Tamworth Rd
B4100
60 Stratford upon Avon, Gaydon
B4110
60 Warwick, Bishops Tachbrook
B4112
40 Nuneaton and Bedworth, Nuneaton Radial Route, Ansley Rd
B4113
30 Nuneaton and Bedworth, Hilltop, Nuneaton Radial Route
B4114
60 North Warwickshire, Church End
30 Nuneaton and Bedworth, Ansley Common, Coleshill Rd
30 Nuneaton and Bedworth, Tuttle Hill
60 Rugby, Burton Hastings, Lutterworth Rd
B4429
40 Rugby, Ashlawn Rd
B4455
60 Rugby, Fosse Way south of Princethorpe
B5414
30 Rugby, Clifton Rd
Unclassified
30 Nuneaton and Bedworth, Donnithorne Avenue
30 Warwick, Primrose Hill

West Mercia

Herefordshire, Shropshire, Telford and Wrekin, Worcestershire

A5
60 Aston towards Oswestry
60 Aston towards Shrewsbury
60 Moreton Bridge towards Chirk
60 West Felton
A40
50 Pencraig
A41
40,60 Albrighton Bypass
60 Chetwynd
60 Prees Heath
40 Tern Hill
60 Whitchurch Bypass
A44
40 Wickhamford towards Broadway
30 Worcester, Bromyard Rd towards Bromyard
A46
50 Beckford, Cheltenham Rd
60 Evesham Bypass
A49
60 Ashton towards Leominster
60 Ashton towards Ludlow
60 Dorrington
30 Dorrington towards Shrewsbury
40 Herefordshire, Harewood End
A417
40 Ledbury, Parkway
A442
40 Crudgington
A456
30 Blakedown
30 Newnham Bridge towards Tenbury Wells
A458
40 Morville
30 Much Wenlock
30 Shrewsbury, The Mount towards Town Centre
A465
60 Allensmore
A483
30 Pant
A491
60 Bromsgrove, Sandy Lane nr Hagley
50 Bromsgrove, Stourbridge Rd
A528
30 Shrewsbury, Ellesmere Rd towards Town Centre
A4103
60 Hereford, Lumber Lane towards Lugg Bridge
60 Hereford, west of Lumber Lane towards Great Malvern
40 Newtown Cross towards Hereford
60 Ridgeway Cross towards Hereford
50 Stiffords Bridge to Storridge
50 Stiffords Bridge towards Worcester
A4104
30 Welland, Drake St
30 Welland, Marlbank Rd
A4110
30 Hereford, Three Elms Rd towards City Centre
40 Hereford, Three Elms Rd towards Leominster
A5064
30 Shrewsbury, London Rd
B4096
30 Lower Marlbrook, Old Birmingham Rd
B4211
30 Great Malvern, Church St
B4349
60 Clehonger
B4373
40 Telford, Castlefield Way
40 Telford, Wrockwardine Wood Way
B4386
30 Shropshire, Mytton Oak Rd
B4638
30 Worcester, Woodgreen Drive
B5060
40 Telford, Castle Farm Way
B5061
40 Telford, Holyhead Rd
B5062
30 Shrewsbury, Sundorne Rd
B5069
30 Shropshire, Gobowen Rd
Unclassified
30 Hadley, Britannia Way
30 Hereford, Yazor Rd
30 Newport, Wellington Rd
50 Pencraig, towards Monmouth
50 Pencraig, towards Ross on Wye
30 Redditch, Birchfield Drive
40 Redditch, Coldfield Drive
30 Redditch, Studley Rd
30 Redditch, Studley Rd towards Park Farm
30 Shrewsbury, Monkmoor Rd
30 Shropshire, Longden Rd (Rural)
30 Snedshill, Holyhead Rd
30 Telford, Britannia Way
30 Telford, Hollinsgate
40 Telford, Stafford Park 1
30 Telford, Trench Rd

West Midlands

Birmingham, Coventry, Dudley, Sandwell, Solihull, Walsall, Wolverhampton

A5
60 Brownhills, Watling St
50 Cannock, Watling St
60 Wall, Watling St
A41
40 Albrighton Bypass towards Wolverhampton
40,60 Albrighton, Albrighton Bypass towards Newport
A46
70 Stoneleigh, Kenilworth Bypass
A51
30 Lichfield, Tamworth Rd
60 Weeford, Watling St
A446
60 Allens End, London Rd
60 Bassetts Pole, London Rd
A449
40 Coven, Wolverhampton Rd
60 Gailey, Wolverhampton Rd
A4177
60 Hasley Knob, Honiley Rd
A5127
30 Lichfield, Trent Valley Rd
B4065
30 Ansty, Main Rd
B4098
40 Fillongley, Coventry Rd
60 Fillongley, Tamworth Rd
B4101
40 Tanworth, Broad Lane
B4103
30 Kenilworth, Castle Rd
30 Kenilworth, Clinton Lane
B4109
40 Bulkington, Coventry Rd
Unclassified
30 Ash Green, Royal Oak Lane
30 Ash Green, St Giles Rd
30 Ash Green, Vicarage Lane
30 Coleshill, Station Rd

West Yorkshire

A58
40 Leeds, Easterley Rd
A61
40 Leeds, Scott Hall Rd
60 Rothwell, Wakefield Rd northbound carriageway lamp post 140
40 Rothwell, Wakefield Rd southbound carriageway jct Castlefields
60 Rothwell, Wakefield Rd southbound carriageway nr Wood Lane lamp post 124
A62
30 Huddersfield, Manchester Rd
A64
40 Leeds, York Rd
A616
30 Huddersfield, Woodhead Rd
A629
50 Elland, Calderdale Way southbound carriageway north of Huddersfield Way
50 Halifax, Keighley Rd
40 Shelley, Pennistone Rd
A636
30 Wakefield, Denby Dale Rd southbound carriageway jct Cotton St
A638
50 Ossett Bypass westbound carriageway layby location lamp post 39
A638
30 Wakefield, Dewsbury Rd eastbound carriageway jct Broadway
A644
30 Mirfield, Huddersfield Rd
A646
30 Portsmouth, Burnley Rd jct Durn St
30 Todmorden, Halifax Rd jct Hallroyd Rd
A651
40 Birkenshaw, Bradford Rd
A652
30 Batley, Bradford Rd
30 Batley, Bradford Rd opp Hampson St
30 Batley, Bradford Rd opp no.253 Lucas Yard
40 Birstall, Bradford Rd
A653
40 Shaw Cross, Leeds Rd
A657
30 Shipley, Leeds Rd eastbound carriageway nr jct Cragg Rd
30 Shipley, Leeds Rd westbound carriageway jct Little Cote Farm
A6025
50 Elland, Park Wood, Elland Rd
A6038
40 Baildon, Otley Rd opp lamp post 117
B6145
30 Bradford, Greenside, Thornton Rd
30 Bradford, Thornton, Thornton Rd
B6269
40 Shipley, Cottingley Cliffe Rd westbound carriageway jct New Brighton
Unclassified
30 Huddersfield, Dalton, Long Lane o/s No.144
30 South Elmsall, Minsthorpe Lane jct Ash Grove
30 South Kirby, Minsthorpe twds A180 jct Minsthorpe Vale
60 Walton, Wetherby Rd

Wiltshire and Swindon

M4
70 approx 1.8km west of jct 15
70 approx 6.9km east of jct 15
70 at jct 15
70 approx 3km east of jct 16
70 approx 8.4km west of jct 16
70 approx 3.1km east of jct 17
70 approx 8.3km east of jct 17
A4
40 Froxfield
60 West Overton
A30
40 Fovant
60 The Pheasant
A36
60 Brickworth
60 Hanging Langford
50 Knook
30 Salisbury, Wilton Rd
60 south of Whaddon
60 Stapleford to East Clyffe
A303
50 Chicklade
60 Parsonage Down
60 Willoughby Hedge
A338
40 Bosscombe
30 nr Little Woodbury
60 nr Southgrove Copse
A342
60 Chirton to Charlton
30 Ludgershall, andover Rd
50 Lydeway
A346
60 Chiseldon Firs
60 Whitefield
A350
60 Heywood
70 Pretty Chimneys
A354
40 Coombe Bissett
A360/A344
60 Airmans Corner
A361
60 Inglesham
60 nr Blackland Turning
70 nr jct with B3101
60 nr Shepherds Shore
30 Southwick
30 Trowbridge, Frome Rd
60 west of Beckhampton
A363
30 Bradford on Avon, Trowbridge Rd
30 North Bradley, Woodmarsh
40 Trowle Common
A419
70 Cricklade
70 nr Covingham
70 Widhill
A420
60 Giddeahall to Ford
A3026
40 Ludgershall, Tidworth Rd
A3028
40 Durrington, Larkhill Rd
A3102
30 Calne, Oxford Rd
30 Lyneham
30 Melksham, Sandridge Rd
30 Wootten Bassett
A4259
50 nr Coate
40 Swindon 2, Queens Drive (nr to jct with Rushton Rd)
A4361
60 Broad Hinton
60 Uffcott Xrd
30 Wroughton, Swindon Rd
B390
60 Maddington Farm
B3105
30 Hilperton, Hill St/Marsh St
B4006
40 Swindon, Marlborough Rd
B3098
30 Bratton
B3106
30 Hilperton, Hammond Way
B3107
30 Bradford on Avon, Holt Rd
B4006
30 Stratton St Margaret, Swindon Rd
30 Swindon, Whitworth Rd
B4040
50 Leigh
B4041
30 Wootten Bassett, Station Rd
B4143
30 Swindon, Bridge End Rd
B4192
50 Liddington
B4289
40 Great Western Way nr Bruce St Bridges
B4553
40 Swindon, Tewkesbury Way
B4587
30 Swindon, Akers Way
Unclassified
30 Corsham, Park Lane
30 Swindon, Ermin St
30 Swindon, Merlin Way
30 Swindon, Moredon Rd
30 Trowbridge, Wiltshire Drive

Worcestershire

see West Mercia

Wales

Mid and South Wales

Blaenau Gwent, Bridgend, Caerphilly, Cardiff, Carmarthenshire, Merthyr Tydfil, Monmouthshire, Neath Port Talbot, Newport, Pembrokeshire, Rhondda Cynon Taff, Swansea, Torfaen, Vale of Glamorgan

M4
70 1.1km east of Jct33 where Llantrisant Rd crosses M4
70 1.5km east of Jct37
70 2km east of Jct35
70 at Jct36 overpass
70 Cherry Orchard Overbridge Jct30-32
70 Llanmartin
70 Rhiwbina Hill overpass (Jct30-32)
50 Toll Plaza
A40
60 Buckland Hall, Brecon to Abergavenny
70 from 1.2km east to 100m west of Bancyfelin Jct
70 Johnstown, Carmarthen to St Clears
60 Llanhamlac, Brecon to Abergavenny
60 Llansantffried Jct
70 Mitchel Troy
70 Monmouth, opp. Llangattock Lodge
60 Rhosmaen, Llandeilo
60 Scethrog, Brecon to Abergavenny
40 Trecastle
60 Whitemill
A40 to B4302
30 Rhosmaen, jct to N
A44
60 Forest Bends
30 Llanbadarn Fawr
60 Llanfihangel Nant Melan
60 Sweet Lamb, West of Llangurig
60 The Gwystre opp Gwystre Farm
A48
70 300m South of Bristol House Layby to Pont Abraham Rdbt
30 Baglan, Dinas Baglan
30 Belle Vue, Cardiff Rd
50 Berryhill
40 Bonvilston
40 Brocastle
30 Castleton
70 Cowbridge Bypass
40 Crosshands to Cwmgwili
70 Cwmgwili, Pontarddulais Rd Jct.to Bristol House Layby
70 from 1.7km west to 300m east of Llanddarog Jct
70 from 1.8km west to 300m east of Foelgastell Jct
70 from 700m east to 2.2km west of Nantycaws Jct
40 Langstone
30 Pontarddulais, Bolgoed Rd
30 Pontardulais, Carmarthen Rd
30 Pontardulais, Fforest Rd
30 Port Talbot, Margam Rd (Rhanallt S)
30 St Nicholas
A438
40 Three Cocks
A449
70 Llandenny
70 Llantrissent nr Usk
70 nr Coldra
A458
60 Cefn Bridge
60 Llanfair Caereinion (Neuadd Bridge)
40 Trewern
A465
60 btwn Aberbaden and Llanfoist
60 llanfoist nr Abergavenny
50 Llanelly
40 Pandy
50 Pandy (50mph area)
60 Triley Mill nr Abergavenny
A466
40 High Beech Rdbt to Old Hospital
30 Llandogo
30 Monmouth, Redbrook Rd
30 St. Arvans
30 Tintern
A467
60 Abertillery
40 Blaina
70 Danycraig, Risca
40 Warm Tum (changing from 40 to 30 soon)
A468
30 Machen Village
A469
70 Caerphilly, Lower Rhymney Valley Relief Rd
30 Tir-Y-Birth
A470
70 Abercynon (southbound)
70 at Aberfan overbridge
30 at Cilfynydd
70 at overbridge of Cilfynydd
60 Brecon to Merthyr (Storey Arms)
40 Cardiff, Manor Way
30 Erwood
60 Erwood South
40 Llandinam to Caersws Jct
40 Llandinam Village
60 Llanidloes to Llandinam
30 Llyswen
30 Newbridge on Wye
60 Newbridge to Rhayader
70 nr Taffs Well North
70 nr Taffs Well South
60 Powys, Beacons Reservoir
70 Rhydyfelin overbridge, Dynea Rd
60 South of Builth (Aberduhonw)
60 South of Builth (Abernant)
60 South of Builth (Ysgiog)
A472
30 Hafodrynys
30 Maescwmmer
60 Monkswood
30 Usk Bridge to Old Saw Mill
A473
30 Bridgend, Bryntirion Hill
30 Pencoed, Penybont Rd
A474
30 All the village of Glanaman
40 Alltwen, Graig Rd
30 Ammanford to Portamman, Heol Wallasey Jct
30 Glanffrwd Est Jct. to Garnant
30 Heol-Y-Gors
30 Neath, Penywern Rd
30 Rhyd y Fro, Commercial St
A475
40 Llanwnen
40 Lampeter, Pentrebach, County Rd
A476
30 Carmel to N at Temple Bar
40 Carmel, Stag and Pheasant
30 Ffairfach, 30 mph to the Square
30 Gorslas, Cross Hands Rdbt to the Phoenix Inn
40 Gorslas, The Gate
30 Heol Bryngwili, Cross Hands
30 Llannon, Erw Non Jct to Clos Rebecca Jct
30 Swiss Valley, Thomas Arms, Llanelli to North
30 Upper Tumble, Llannon Rd and Bethania Rd
A477
40 Bangeston to Nash Fingerpost Roadworks
30 Llanddowror
A478
30 Clunderwen
30 Llandissilio
30 Pentlepoir
A479
30 Bronllys
A482
30 Aberaeron, Lampeter Rd
30 Cwmann, North
30 Cwmann, South
30 Village of Llanwrda
A482 and A475
30 Lampeter
A483
60 Abbey Cwm Hir Jct
30 Ammanford, Tycroes to Villiers Jct
30 Ffairfach, N to Llandeilo Bridge
30 Llandeilo, Rhosmaen St
A483
50 Garthmyl, Refail Garage
60 Garthmyl, Welshpool
60 Llandrindod, Midway Bends
60 North of Crossgates
A484
40 Bronwydd Village
30 Burry Port
30 Cenarth
40 Cwmffrwd
30 Cynwyl Elfed
30 from 80m west of New Rd Jct, east to N N.C.E
40 Idole, from 200m s.w. of B4309 Jct south to N
30 Llanelli, Sandy Rd
60 Llanelli, Trostre Rdbt to Berwick Rdbt
60 Pembrey
30 Pembrey, Danybanc Jct to St Illtyds Rise Jct
40 Pentrecagel
40 Rhos
40 Saron
A485
40 Alltwalis
30 Cwmann, from the A482 Jct N
40 Llanllwwni
30 Llanybydder (North)
30 Llanybydder (South)
40 Peniel
A487
40 Approach to Llanrhystud from the south
30 Central Aberaeron
30 Central Aberystwyth
30 Ceredigion, Bow St
30 Eglwyswrw
40 Furnace
40 Llanarth
30 Llanfarian
30 Newgale
30 Newport
40 Penglais Hill/Waunfawr
40 Penparc, Trunk Rd
40 Rhydyfelin
30 Rhydypennau
30 Talybont
A489
60 Caersws Jct to Penstrowed
60 Kerry, County Rd, Glanmule Garage
40 Newtown, west of Hafren coll
60 Penstrowed to Newtown
A4042
60 Llanover
A4046
40 Ebbw Vale (nr Tesco's)
30 Ebbw Vale, College Rd
30 Waynllwyd
A4048
30 Argoed
30 Blackwood (Sunnybank)
30 Cwmfelinfach Village
30 Hollybush
30 Pontllanfraith, Blackwood Rd
A4054
30 Edwardsville, Nantddu, Tec
30 Merthyr Vale, Cardiff Rd
A4061
30 Ogmore Vale, Cemetery Rd
A4066
40 Broadway
40 Llanmiloe, Pendine
40 Pendine, Llanmiloe
30 Pendine, Marsh Rd
A4067
60 Abercraf
60 Crai
A4068
30 Cwmtwrch, Bethel Rd
30 Cwmtwrch, Heol Gleien
A4069
30 Llandovery, Broad St
30 Llangadog, East
30 Llangadog, North, Station Rd
30 Llangadog, South
30 Station Rd to the Remploy Factory
A4074
30 Milford Haven, St Lawrence Hill
A4075
30 Pembroke
A4076
30 Carew
30 Johnston
A4093
30 Glynogwr
A4102
30 Gellideg, Swansea Rd
A4106
30 Porthcawl, Newton Nottage Rd
Porthcawl, The Porthway
A4107
30 Abergwynfi, High St
A4109
Aberdulias, Main Rd
30 Crynant, Main Rd
30 Glynneath
30 Seven Sisters, Dulais Rd
A4118
60 Fairwood Common
A4119
50 Llantrisant, Mwyndy Cross
A4120
30 Aberystwyth
A4138
30 Hendy, Loughor Bridge to 40mph speed limit
40 Talyclun, from the 30mph at Hendy to the B4297 Jct
A4139
30 Pembroke
30 Pembroke Dock
30 Tenby
A4216
30 Cockett, Cockett Rd
A4221
60 Caehopkin
A4222
30 Cowbridge, Abertin Rd
30 Maendy
A4226
40 Barry, Five Mile Lane
A4233
30 Ferndale, The Parade
B4181
30 Bridgend, Coity Rd
B4223
30 Ton Pentre, Pentwyn Rd
B4235
60 Gwernesney nr Usk
B4242
30 Pontneddfechan, Gwyn Neath
B4245
30 Caldicot Bypass
30 Langstone, Magor Rd
60 Leechpool
30 Rogiet, Caldicot Rd
30 Undy
B4254
30 Penpedairheol, Pengam Rd
B4265
30 St Brides Major
B4281
30 Kenfig Hill, High St
B4282
30 Bridgend, Bridgend Rd and Castle St
30 Bryn, Measteg Rd
B4290
30 Skewen, Pen-yr-Heol and Crymlyn Rd
B4295
40 btwn Gowerton and Penclawdd
60 btwn Penclawdd and Llanrhidian
B4297
40 Bynea, Lougher Bridge Rdb to Station Rd Jct
30 Capel Hendre
30 Fforest
30 Llanedi
30 Llangennech, Cleviston Par Jct to Park Lane Jctct
30 Llwynhendy, from Capel So to the Police Station
B4301
30 Bronwydd Village
B4302
30 Talley
B4303
30 Llanelli, Dafen Rdbt to Felinfoel Rdbt
B4304
40 Llanelli, Copperworks Rdbt to Morfa Rdbt
30 Llanelli, Lower Trostre Rd Rdbt to Trostre Rd Rdbt
B4306
30 Bancffosfelen, Heol Y Banc
30 Llangendeirn
30 Pontyberem, Llanon Rd
B4308
40 Penmynydd
B4309
30 Five Roads
B4310
30 Drefach, Heol Caegwyn
40 Nangaredig, Station Rd
B4312
30 Johnstown, from the Squar to N
30 Llangain
B4314
30 Narberth
30 Pendine
B4317
30 Carway, East
30 Carway, West
30 Ponthenri, Myrtle Hill
30 Pontyberem, Heol Capel Ifa
30 Pontyberem, Station Rd
B4320
30 Hundleton
B4322
40 Pembroke Dock, Pembroke Rd
B4325
30 Neyland
B4328
30 Whitland, Trevaughan
B4333
30 Cynwyl Elfed (North)
30 Hermon
30 Newcastle Emlyn, Aber-ara
B4336
30 All the village of Llanfihang Ar Arth
30 Llandysul, Pont-tyweli
B4337
30 Llanybydder (East)
30 Llanybydder (West)
40 Talsarn
B4347
30 Newcastle Village
B4350
60 Glasbury to Hay on Wye, County Rd
B4436
40 Kittle, Pennard Rd
B4459
30,40 Pencader
B4524
30 Corntown
B4556
30 All the village of Caerbryn
30 Blaenau, Penygroes Rd

) Pengroes, Norton Rd

4560
) Beaufort, Ebbw Vale, Llangynidr Rd

4591
) High Cross, Risca Rd

4598
) Horse and Jockey nr Abergavenny
) Llancayo

4599
) Ystradgynlais

4622
0 Broadlands Link Rd

nclassified
Aberbargoed, Bedwwellty and Coedymoeth Rd Jct
0 Abercwmboi, Park View Terrace
0 Abercynon, Abercynon Rd
0 Abergavenny, Hereford Rd
0 Abergwili, Ambulance Station to the Bypass Rdbt
0 Abertillery, Gwern Berthi
0 Ammanford, Layby outside Saron Church, Saron Rd
0 Ammanford, New Rd and Pantyffynnon Rd
0 Argoed, Penylan Rd
0 Barry, Barry Rd
0 Barry, Buttrills Rd
0 Barry, Gladstone Rd
0 Barry, Holton Rd
0 Barry, Jenner Rd
0 Beddau, Bryniteg Hill
0 Beddau, Gwaunmiskin Rd
0 Betws, Betws Rd
0 Betws, Maesquarre Rd
0 Birchgrove, Birchgrove Rd
0 Bishopston, Northway
0 Brackla, Brackla Way
0 Bridgend Ind Est, Kingsway
0 Bridgend Ind Est, North Rd
0 Bridgend Ind Est, South Rd
0 Bridgend Ind Est, Western Avenue
0 Bridgend Inner Bypass
0 Bridgend, Coychurch Rd
0 Bridgend, Pen-Y-Cae Lane
30 Britton Ferry, Old Rd
30 Brynamman, Brynamman Rd
30 Brynmawr, Beaufort Hill and High St
30 Brynna, Brynna Rd
30 Caerleon, Ponthir Rd
30 Caerleon, Usk Rd
30 Caerphilly, 2 Llanbradach
30 Caerphilly, Kendon Hill
30 Caerphilly, Mountain Rd
30 Caldicot, Chepstow Rd
30 Cardiff, Circle Way E/W Llanedeyrn
30 Cardiff, Cyncoed Rd
30 Cardiff, Excalibur Drive
30 Cardiff, Heol Isaf
30 Cardiff, Leckwith Rd
30 Cardiff, Newport Rd
30 Cardiff, North Rd
30 Cardiff, Pencisely Rd
30 Cardiff, Penylan, Colchester Avenue
30 Cardiff, Rhiwbina, Heol y Deri
30 Cardiff, Rhyd-y-pennau Rd
30 Cardiff, Roath, Lake Rd East/West
30 Cardiff, Rumney, Wentloog Avenue
30 Cardiff, St Fagans Rd
30 Cardiff, Willowbrook Drive
30 Carmarthen, Lime Grove Avenue and Fountain Head Tce
30 Cefn Criwber, Cefn Rd
30 Cefn Glas, Liangewydd Rd
30 Cefn Glas, Merlin Crescent
30 Cefncoed, High St
30 Cefncoed, Vaynor Rd
30 Cefneithin
30 Ceredigion, Cardigan, North
30 Ceredigion, Llandysul Central
30 Ceredigion, New Quay Central
30 Church Village, Main Rd
30 Cilfynydd, Cilfynydd Rd
30 Clydach, Pontardawe Rd
30 Clydach, Vadre Rd
30 Cockett, Cwmbach Rd
30 Coity, Heol Spencer
60 Coldharbour, Usk to Raglan Rd
30 Cowbridge, Primrose Hill
30 Crofty, New Rd
30 Crumlin, Hafodyrynys Hill
40 Cwmbwria, Carmarthen Rd
30 Cwmgovilon
30 Cwmgwili
30 Cwmgwili, Thornhill Rd
30 Deri, New Rd
30 Derwen Fawr, Rhy-Y-Defaid Drive
30 Dinas, Dinas Rd
30 Dowlais, High St
30 Drefach, Heol Blawnhirwaun
30 Ebbw Vale, Letchworth Rd
30 Ebbw Vale, Newchurch Rd
30 Ebbw Vale, Steelworks Rd
30 Farm Shop, Pentregethin Rd
30 Felinfoel, Llethri Rd
30 Ferndale, Highfield Jct
30 Ferndale, Oakland Terrace
30 Fforest Fach, Carmarthen Rd
40 Five Mile Lane
30 Fochrie, Olgivie Terrace
30 Foelgastell
30 Forden
60 from 120m s.e. of Heol Login for 1.2km s.e. along Nantycaws Hill
40 Gelligaer, Church Rd
30 Gelli, Gelli Ind Est
30 Gelli, Gelli Rd
30 Gilwern, Cae Meldon (aka Ty Mawr Lane)
30 Gorseinon, Frampton Rd
30 Gorslas, Pengroes Rd
30 Haverfordwest, New Rd/Uzmaston Rd
30 Heath, Maescoed Rd
30 Hendreforgan, Gilfach Rd
30 Hopkinstown, Hopkinstown Rd
30 Jersey Marine, New Rd
30 Johnstown, St Clears Rd
30 Killay, Goetre Fawr Rd
30 Llanelli, Denham Avenue
30 Llanelli, Heol Goffa (from the A476 Jct to the A484 Jct)
30 Llanfihangel Ar Arth (South)
30 Llangonoed, Bridgend Rd
30 Llangyfelach, Swansea Rd
30 Llangynwyd, Bridgend Rd
30 Llanharan, Brynna Rd
30 Llanharen, Bridgend Rd
60 Llanhenock, Caerleon to Usk Rd – Apple tree farm
30 Llantrisant, Cross Inn Rd
50 Llantwit Major Bypass
30 Llantwit Major, Llanmaes Rd
30 Maesteg, Heol Ty-With
30 Maesteg, Heol-Ty-Gwyn
30 Malpas, Rowan Way
30 Merthyr Tdyfil, Brecon Rd
30 Merthyr Tdyfil, Goatmill Rd
30 Merthyr Tdyfil, Goitre Lane
30 Merthyr Tdyfil, Gumos Rd
30 Merthyr Tdyfil, Heol-Tai-Mawr
30 Merthyr Tdyfil, Heolgerrig Rd
30 Merthyr Tdyfil, Pant Rd
30 Merthyr Tdyfil, Plymouth St
30 Merthyr Tdyfil, Rocky Rd
30 Merthyr Tdyfil, The Walk
30 Milford Haven, Priory Rd
40 Milford Haven, Thornton Rd
40 Monmouth, Bend at Green Farm
30 Monmouth, Devauden Village
30 Monmouth, Dixton Rd
30 Monmouth, Hereford Rd
30 Monmouth, Magor (West)
60 Monmouth, Parkwall
30 Monmouth, Usk Bridge to Llanbadoc
30 Morriston, Caemawr Rd
30 Morriston, Clasemont Rd
30 Mount Pleasant, Cardiff Rd
30 Mountain Ash, Llanwonno Rd
30 Mountain Ash, Miskin Rd
30 Mountain Ash, New Rd
30 Nantgarw, Oxford St
30 Nash Village, West Nash Rd
30 New Tredegar, White Roase Way
30 Newbridge, Park Rd
30 Newport, Allt-Yr-Yn Avenue
30 Newport, Caerleon Rd (east of Beaufort Rd)
30 Newport, Chepstow Rd nr Abertnaw Rd
40 Newport, Chepstow Rd nr Royal Oak Hill
30 Newport, Corporation Rd
30 Newport, Lighthouse Rd
30 Newport, opp Power Station, Risca Rd
30 Newport, Rhiwderin
30 Newport, Wharf Rd
30 North Cornelly, Heol Fach
30 Pembroke, Merlins Bridge
30 Pencoed, Felindre Rd
30 Pendarren, High St
30 Pendine
30 Penrhiwceiber, 2 Penrhiwceiber Rd
40 Pentrecagel
30 Ponthir, Caerleon Rd
30 Pontllanfraith, Bryn Rd
30 Pontyclun, Cowbridge Rd
30 Pontymister, Welsh Oak PH
30 Pontymister, Welsh Oak PH
30 Pontypool, Little Mill
30 Pontypridd, The Broadway
40 Porthcawl, Bridgend Rd
30 Porthcawl, Fulmar Rd
30 Rassau, Reservoir Rd
30 Rhondda Cynon Taff, Tonteg Rd
30 Rhymney, Llys Joseph Parry (nr Farmers Arms)
30 Rhymney, Wellington Way
30 Risca, Cromwell Rd
30 Risca, Holly Rd
30 Risca, Waun Fawr Park Rd
30 Rogerstone, Pontymason Lane
30 Sandfields, Village Rd
30 Saron Village, Dyffryn Rd
30 Skewen, Burrows Rd
30 St Athan, Cowbridge Rd
30 Steynton
30 Sully, Haynes Rd
30 Sully, South Rd
30 Swansea, Fabian Way
30 Swansea, Grovesend
40 Swansea, Mumbles Rd (A4067) Sketty Lane to St Helens Sports Gr.
30 Swansea, Mynydd Newydd Rd, Caemawr Rd, Parry Rd, Vicarage Rd (Heol Ddu to Clasemont Rd)
30 Swansea, Peniel Green Rd (nr Station Rd o/s TOTAL Garage)
60 Tiers Cross
30 Ton Pentre, Maindy Rd
30 Tonteg, Church Rd
30 Tonyrefail, Gilfach Rd
30 Tonyrefail, Penrhiwfer Rd
30 Torfaen
30 Treboeth, Llangyfelach Rd
30 Tredegar, Vale Terrace
30 Trelewis, Gelligaer Rd
30 Upper Boat, Cardiff Rd
Upper Church Village, Pen yr Eglwys
30 Usk, Porthycame St
30 Vale of Glamorgan, Pen-y-turnpike Rd
30 Waungren, Pentre Rd
30 Whitland (East), Spring Gardens
30 Whitland (west)
30 Whitland, Market St
30 Whitland, North Rd
30 Wick, St Brides Rd
30 Willowtow, Gwaun Helyg Rd
30 Ynystawe, Clydach Rd
30 Ynyswdre, Heol-Yr-Ysgol
30 Ynysybwl, New Rd

North Wales

Ceredigion, Conwy, Denbighshire, Flintshire, Gwynedd, Isle of Anglesey, Powys, Wrexham

A5
30 Holyhead

A5/A5025
50 Holyhead to Llanfachraeth

A470
30,60 Conwy Valley
40,60 Dolgellau
40,60 (30 at rdbts) Llandudno to the A55
30,40,60 Tal-y-waenydd to Congl-y-wal (Blaenau)

A483/A5
60 Ruabon to Chirk

A487
30,40,50,60 Caernarfon to Dolbenmaen
30,40,60 Penmorfa to Gellilydan

A494
40,60 Bala to Glanrafon
30 Llyn Tegid, Bala
40,60 Ruthin to Llanferres

A496
30,40,60 Harlech to Llanbedr

A499
30,40,60 Pwllheli

A525
40,60 Denbigh to Ruthin
30,40,60 Llanfair Dyffryn Clwyd to Llandegla
30,60 Wrexham to Minera
30,40,60 Wrexham to Redbrook Maelor

A534
30 Holt Rd

A539
30,60 Llangollen, Mill St
30,40,60 Trevor to Erbistock

A541
30 Mold Rd
30,40,60,70 Mold to Caergwrle
30,40,60,70 Wrexham to Cefn-y-bedd

A541/525
30,40,60 St Asaph to Bodfari

A545
30,40 Menai Bridge to Beaumaris

A547
30,40,50 Colwyn Bay
30,40,60 Prestatyn to Rhuddlan
30 Rhyl, Vale Rd/Rhuddlan Rd

A548
30,40 Abergele to Kinmel Bay
30 Abergele, Dundonald Avenue
30,40,50,60,70 Gronant to Flint (Oakenholt)
30,40 Rhyl to Prestatyn

A549
30,60 Mynydd Isa to Buckley

A550/B5125
30 Hawarden

A4086
30,40,60 Cwm-y-glo to Llanrug

A4212
60 Graig Las/Tryweryn to Trawsfynydd

A4244
60 Ty Mawr to Cym-y-glo

A5025
30,40,50,60 Amlwch, Menai Bridge

A5104
30 Coed-Talon to Leeswood

A5112
30,40 Llandygai to Bangor

A5119
30,50,60 Mold to Flint

A5152
30,60 Bala
30 Chester Rd
30,40 Rhostyllen

B4545
30,40 Kingsland to Valley

B5108
30,60 Benllech

B5109
30 Llangefni

B5113
30 Colwyn Bay, Kings Rd/Kings Drive

B5115
30 Llandrillo, Llandudno Rd
30,40 Llandudno Promenade to Rhos Point

B5118
30 Rhyl Promenade

B5120
30 Prestatyn, Pendyffryn Rd

B5129
30,60 Kelsterton to Saltney Ferry

B5420
30 Menai Bridge

B5425
30,60 Llay, New Rd

B5443
30 Rossett

Unclassified
30,40,60 Johnstown
30,60 Kinmel Bay, St Asaph Avenue
30,40,60 Menai Bridge to Gwalchmai

Scotland

Dumfries and Galloway

A74(M)
70 Cogries

A7
60 Langholm

A76
Auldgirth
60 Closeburn
30 Dumfries, Glasgow Rd Gateside

A77
60 Balyett
60 Cairnryan
60 Whiteleys

A701
30 Moffat
60 Mollinburn/St Anns

A709
60 Burnside

A711
50 Beeswing
30 Kirkcudbright

A716
60 Stoneykirk

A718
60 Craichmore

B721
30 Eastriggs

Fife

A91
Deer Centre to Stratheden Jct
Guardbridge to St Andrews
Melville Lodges to St Andrews

A92
Cadham to New Inn
Cardenden Overbridge to Chapel
Cowdenbeath to Lochgelly
Crossgates to New Inn
Melville Lodges to Lindifferon
New Inn to Tay Bridge
Rathillet (south) to Easter Kinnear

A823
Dunfermline, Queensferryroad
Dunfermline, St Margaret Drive

A907
Dunfermline, Halbeath Rd

A911
Glenrothes to Leslie
Glenrothes to Milton

A914
Edenwood to Cupar
Forgan to St Michaels
Kettlebridge
New Inn to Cupar
Pitlessie to Clushford Toll

A915
Checkbar Jct to Percival Jcts

A921
Kirkcaldy, Esplanade
Kirkcaldy, High St/Path
Kirkcaldy, Rosslyn St
Kirkcaldy, St Clair St

A977
Kincardine, Fere Gait

A985
Culross (west) to C38 Valleyfield
Kincardine to Rosyth
Rosyth, Admiralty Rd
Waukmill to Brankholm

B914
Redcraigs to Greenknowes

B942
East of Collinsburgh

B980
Rosyth, Castlandhill Rd

B981
Cowdenbeath, Broad St
Gosshill to Ballingry
Kirkcaldy, Dunnikier Way

B9157
Bankhead of Pitheadle to Kirkcaldy
Orrock to East Balbairdie
Sheriff Rdbt to Kirkcaldy
White Lodge Jct to Croftgary

Unclassified
Buckhaven, Methilhaven Rd
Dunfermline, Townhill Rd
Glenrothes, Formonthills Rd
Glenrothes, Southfield Rd
Glenrothes, Woodside Way
Kirkcaldy, Hendry Rd
Leven, Glenlyon Rd
Methil, Methilhaven Rd

Lothian and Borders

East Lothian, Edinburgh, Midlothian, Scottish Borders, West Lothian

A8
40 Edinburgh, at Ratho station

A7
60 Crookston
Galashiels, Buckholmside to Bowland
30 Hawick Sandbed to Galalaw
30 Stow to Bowland

A68
30 Jedburgh
Soutra Hill

A70
30 Edinburgh, Balerno between Bridge Rd and Stewart Rd

A71
30 Breich
30 Polbeth

A72
Borders, Holylee nr Walkerburn
Castlecraig nr Blyth bridge
30 Peebles, Innerleithen Rd

A90
40 Edinburgh, Southbound from Burnshot flyover to Cammo Rd

A697
30 Greenlaw and south approach
Orange Lane
Ploughlands to Hatchednize

A697/8
30 Coldstream

A698
Ashybank
Crailinghall

A699
40 Maxton Village

A701
Blyth Bridge to Cowdenburn
30 Rachan Mill, Broughton to A72

A702
Dolphinton to Medwyn Mains

A703
30 Eddleston and approaches Leadburn to Shiplaw
30 Peebles to Milkieston
30 Peebles, Edinburgh Rd

A705
30 between Whitburn and East Whitburn

A706
30 Whitburn, Carnie Place

A720
50 Edinburgh, City Bypass, east of Gogar Rdbt

A899
50 btwn Lizzie Bryce Rdbt and Almond Interchange
50 South of Deer Park Rdbt

A6091
Melrose bypass

A6105
30 Gordon and approaches

B6374
30 Galashiels, Station Bridge to Lowood Bridge

Unclassified
30 Edinburgh, Bruntsfield place btwn Thorneybauk and Merchiston place
40 Edinburgh, Comiston Rd btwn Oxgangs Rd and Buckstone Dr
40,60 Edinburgh, Frogston Rd west btwn Mounthooly loan and Mortonhall gate
30 Edinburgh, Lower Granton Rd btwn Granton Square and Trinity Rd
30 Edinburgh, Muirhouse Parkway
40 Edinburgh, West Approach Rd btwn Morrison St Link and Dundee St
30 Edinburgh, West Granton Rd
30 Whitburn, West Main St

North East Scotland

Aberdeen, Aberdeenshire, Moray

A90
40 Aberdeen, Midstocket Rd to Whitestripes Avenue Rdbt
60 btwn bend at South of Leys and Bogbrae
60 btwn Bogbrae and north of Bridgend
70 btwn Candy and Upper Criggie
60 btwn Jct with B9032 and A98 at Fraserburgh
70 btwn Laurencekirk and north of Fourdon
70 btwn Mill of Barnes and Laurencekirk
60 btwn St Fergus and access Rd to Bilbo
70 Dundee to Aberdeen Rd at Jct with B9120 Laurencekirk
70 north of Newtonhill Jct to South of Schoolhill Rd
60 Peterhead and St Fergus, btwn A982 North Rd
60 Peterhead, btwn north of Bridgend and Blackhills
70 Portlethen to South Damhead (southbound), south of Schoolhill Rd
70 south of Schoolhill Rd, Portlethen to South Damhead (northbound)

A92
60 btwn Johnshaven and Inverbervie
60 btwn rdside of Kinneff and Mill of Uras

A93
30 Aboyne
40 at Banchory eastbound from Caravan Site
30 at Banchory westbound from Church
60 btwn Cambus O'May and Dinnet
60 btwn Dinnet to Aboyne
60 btwn Kincardine O'Neil and Haugh of Sluie

A95
30 Cornhill
60 btwn 30mph at Keith and Davoch of Grange

A96
60 btwn East Mill of Carden at B9002 Jct and north of Pitmachie
60 btwn Forgie and A98 Jct at Fochabers
60 btwn north of Pitmachie and Jct with A920 at Kirton of Culsalmond
30 Haudigain rdbt to Chapel of Stoneywood
60 Mosstodloch to Lhanbryde (East)
40 South Damhead to Midstocket Rd

A98
30 Banff
60 btwn Carnoch Farm Rd, Buckie and 30mph at Cullen
60 btwn Fochabers 30mph and Mill of Tynet
60 Buckle, btwn Mill of Tynet and Barhill Rd Jct

A941
60 btwn 30mph at Lossiemouth and 40mph at Elgin
60 btwn Clackmarras Rd and South Netherglen
60 btwn Glassgreen and Clackmarras Rd
60 from South Netherglen and Rothes

A947
60 btwn Mains of Tulloch Jct and Fyvie

A947
60 btwn Newmachar and Whiterashes

A948
60 btwn Ellon to Auchnagatt

A952
60 btwn New Leeds and Jct with A90 at Cortes

B9040
60 btwn Silver Sands Caravan Park to Jct with B9012

B9089
60 from Kinloss and crossroads at Roseisle Maltings

Unclassified
30 Aberdeen, Beach Boulevard to Links Rd
30 Aberdeen, Beach Boulevard to Wales St
30 Aberdeen, Great Northern Rd
30 Aberdeen, Great Southern Rd
30 Aberdeen, King St
30 Aberdeen, Springhill Rd
30 Aberdeen, St Machar Drive
40 Aberdeen, Wellington Rd
40 Aberdeen, West Tullos Rd

Northern Scotland

Highland, Orkney, Shetland, Western Isles

A9
Altnasleanach by Inverness
Caulmaillie, Golspie, Sutherland
Cuaich by Dalwhinnie
Daviot, by Inverness
Fearn, by Tain
North Kessock jct (both directions)
North of Dalwhinnie junction nr Dalwhinnie
South of the Mound, by Golspie

A82
Altsigh Youth Hostel, by Inverness
Drumnadrochit, Temple Pier
Invergarry Power Station
Kingshouse Hotel, Glencoe
White Corries, Rannoch Moor, Lochaber

A87
West of Bunloyne jct

A95
by Grantown on Spey, Congash
Drumuillie by Boat of Garten
North of Cromdale

A96
East Auldearn jct, by Nairn
Gollanfield, by Nairn
Nairn, West Aulderin Jct
West of Allanfearn jct, by Inverness

A99
Hempriggs, south of Wick

A834
Dingwall, nr Foddarty Bridge
Dingwall, Strathpeffer Rd

A835
Inverlael straight nr Ullapool

A939
Ferness to Grantown, Spey Rd

B9006
Sunnyside, Culloden, Inverness

Strathclyde

Argyll & Bute, East Ayrshire, East Dunbartonshire, East Renfrewshire, Glasgow, Inverclyde, North Ayrshire, North Lanarkshire, Renfrewshire, South Ayrshire, South Lanarkshire, West Dunbartonshire

M74
Abington, Jct 13 (northbound)

A70
East Tarelgin

A73
Airdrie, Carlisle Rd

A76
New Cumnock, nr Lime Rd

A78
Fairlie, Main Rd

A82
Bridge of Orchy
Milton, Dunbarton Rd

A85
west of Tyndrum

A89
Airdrie, Forrest St

A706
South of Forth

A730
Rutherglen, Blairbeth Rd

A737
Dairy, New St/Kilwinning Rd

A749
East Kilbride Rd btwn Cathkin Rd and Cairnmuir Rd

A807
Bardowie, Balmore Rd

A814
Dunbarton, Cardross Rd

A815
nr Ardkinglass

B768
Rutherglen, Burnhill St

B803
Airdrie to Glenmavis, Coatbridge Rd

B814
Duntocher Rd

B8048
Kirkintilloch, Waterside Rd

Unclassified
Bargeddie, Glasgow Rd
Barrhead, Aurs Rd
Bishopbriggs, Woodhill Rd
Clydebank, Glasgow Rd
Coatbridge, Townhead Rd
Drymen Rd/Duntocher Rd
East Kilbride, Maxwelton Rd at Kirkoswald (South)
Johnstone, Beith Rd
Neilston, Kingston Rd
Newton Mearns, Mearns Rd
Paisley, Glasgow Rd nr Newtyle Rd
Rutherglen, Glasgow Rd
Rutherglen, Mill St
Troon, Craigend Rd

Tayside

Angus, Dundee, Perth & Kinross

A9
60 Inverness to Perth Rd, nr Balnansteuartach
70 Perth to Inverness Rd, nr Inveralmond Industrial Estate
70 Stirling to Perth Rd, btwn Broom of Dalreoch and Upper Cairnie
70 Stirling to Perth Rd, Tibbermore jct

A90
40 Dundee nr Fountainbleau Drive, Forfar Rd
70 Dundee to Perth Rd, Walnut Grove to Inchyra
70 Dundee to Perth Rd, west of Longforgan village
50 Dundee, Kingsway
50 Dundee, Swallow rdbt to Strathmartine Rd rdbt

A91
60 Milnathort to Devon Bridge

A92
60 Arbroath to Montrose
30 Dundee btwn Arbroath Rd and Craigie Avenue, Greendykes Rd
40 Dundee, East Dock St

A93
60 Guildtown to Blairgowrie
60 Old Scone to Guildtown

A94
60 Scone to Coupar Angus

A822
60 Crieff to Braco

A923
60 Blairgowrie to Tullybaccart

A933
60 Colliston to Redford

A935
60 Brechin to Montrose

A972
40 Dundee, Kingsway East to Pitairlie Rd

A977
60 Kinross to Crook of Devon

B961
30 Dundee, Drumgeith Rd

B996
60 Kinross to Kelty

Unclassified
30 Dundee, Broughty Ferry Rd
30 Dundee, Charleston Drive
30 Dundee, Laird St
30 Dundee, Old Glamis Rd
30 Dundee, Perth Rd
30 Dundee, Strathmartine Rd

Northern Ireland

A1
50/60/70 Sprucefield Rdbt to Border

A2
30/40/50/60 Belfast to Bangor
40 Bangor Ring Rd

A6
60 Derry, Glenshane Rd

A8
40/60/70 Larne, Moss Rd/Pound Street

A25
30/40/60 Newry to Belleek

A26
50/60/70 Ballymoney and Balleymena, Frosses Rd

A29
60 Dungannon, Cookstown Rd

A55
30/40/50/70 Belfast, Holywood Rd to Dunseverick Avenue
30/40/50 Belfast, Malone Rd/University Rd

Unclassified
60 Antrim, Dublin Rd
40/60 Ballybogey
30/60 Ballycastle, Moyarget Rd
40 Ballymena, Galgorm Rd
30 Banbridge, Scarva Rd
30 Bangor, Donaghadee Rd
30 Belfast, Ballysillan Rd
30 Belfast, Castlereagh Rd
30 Belfast, Cliftonville Rd
30 Belfast, Crumlin Rd
30 Belfast, Falls Rd/Andersonstown Rd/Stewartstown Rd
30 Belfast, Glen Rd
50 Belfast, Milltown Rd
30 Belfast, Old Holywood Rd
40 Belfast, Saintfield Rd
30 Belfast, Springfield Rd
30 Belfast, Upper Lisburn Rd
30 Carrickfergus, Woodburn Rd
30/40/60 Carryduff, Belfast Rd
50 Carryduff, Saintfield Rd
30/40 Castlewellan, Mill Hill
30 Coleraine, Ballycastle Rd
60 Coleraine, Dunhill Rd
60 Cookstown, Drum Rd
30/40/60 Derry, Culmore Rd
30 Dundonald, Comber Rd
60 Dungannon, Ballygawley Rd
60 Dungiven, Foreglen Rd
60 Enniskillen to Derrylin Rd
60 Enniskillen to Lisbellaw
30 Enniskillen, Cornagrade Rd
30 Glengormley, Antrim Rd
40 Glengormley, Ballyclare Rd
30/40/60 Kilkeel, Newcastle Rd
30/60 Kircubbin, Portaferry Rd
30/60 Limavady, Ballyquin Rd
50 Lisburn, Knockmore Rd
30 Londonderry, Dungiven Rd
30 Londonderry, Racecourse Rd
30 Londonderry, Springtown Rd
60 Maghera, Glenshane Rd
30 Maghera, Tobermore Rd
30/60 Middletown, Armagh Rd
60 Newcastle, Dundrum Rd
30/40 Newry, Dublin Rd
40/60 Newry, Tandragee Rd
70 Newry, Warrenpoint Rd
30/40 Newtownards, Bangor Rd
40 Newtownards, Portaferry Rd
60 Omagh, Doogary to Ballygawley Rdbt
60 Omagh, Killyclougher Rd
30/60 Portadown, Armagh Rd
30/40 Portrush, Ballyreagh Rd
30 Warrenpoint, Newry Rd

Republic of Ireland

No official safety camera partnership has been established to date.

Route Planner

Roads under construction

County	Page		Road scheme	Opens
Bedfordshire	54	D2	**A421 Great Barford Bypass**	Sept. 2006
Buckinghamshire	40	E2	**M40 Junction 3 Improvement**	Feb. 2007
Buckinghamshire	40	B1	**A4146 Linslade Western Bypass**	Mar. 2007
Cambridgeshire	54	D4	**A428 Caxton Common – Hardwick**	Jul. 2007
Cambridgeshire	54	C3	**A1198 Papworth Everard Bypass**	Mar. 2007
Cornwall	4	C4	**A30 Bodmin – Indian Queens Improvement**	Jul. 2007
Cumbria	99	B8	**A66 Temple Sowerby Bypass**	Feb. 2008
Devon	20	F4	**Barnstaple Western Link Road**	Dec. 2006
Durham	101	B6	**A688 West Auckland Bypass (Stage 2)**	Aug. 2008
Gloucestershire	37	C5	**A430 Gloucester South West Bypass**	Feb. 2007
Kent	30	C3	**Sittingbourne Northern Relief Road**	Dec. 2007
Northumberland	117	F8	**A197 Pegswood Bypass**	June 2007
Powys	48	F3	**Talgarth Relief Road**	Jan. 2007
Rh. Cyn. Taff	34	E4	**A4233 Porth & Lower Rhondda Fach Relief Road**	Feb. 2007
Rutland	65	D5	**A606 Oakham Bypass**	Dec. 2006
Staffordshire	62	C4	**A51 Rugeley Bypass**	Dec. 2007
Suffolk	56	D4	**B1115 Stowmarket Relief Road**	Oct. 2008
Sunderland	111	D6	**Central Route**	Jul. 2006
Warwickshire	51	C7	**A429 Barford Bypass**	Dec. 2006
West Yorkshire	95	F6	**A63 East Leeds Link Road**	Mar. 2007
Fife	133	F8	**A876 Kincardine Bridge**	June 2008

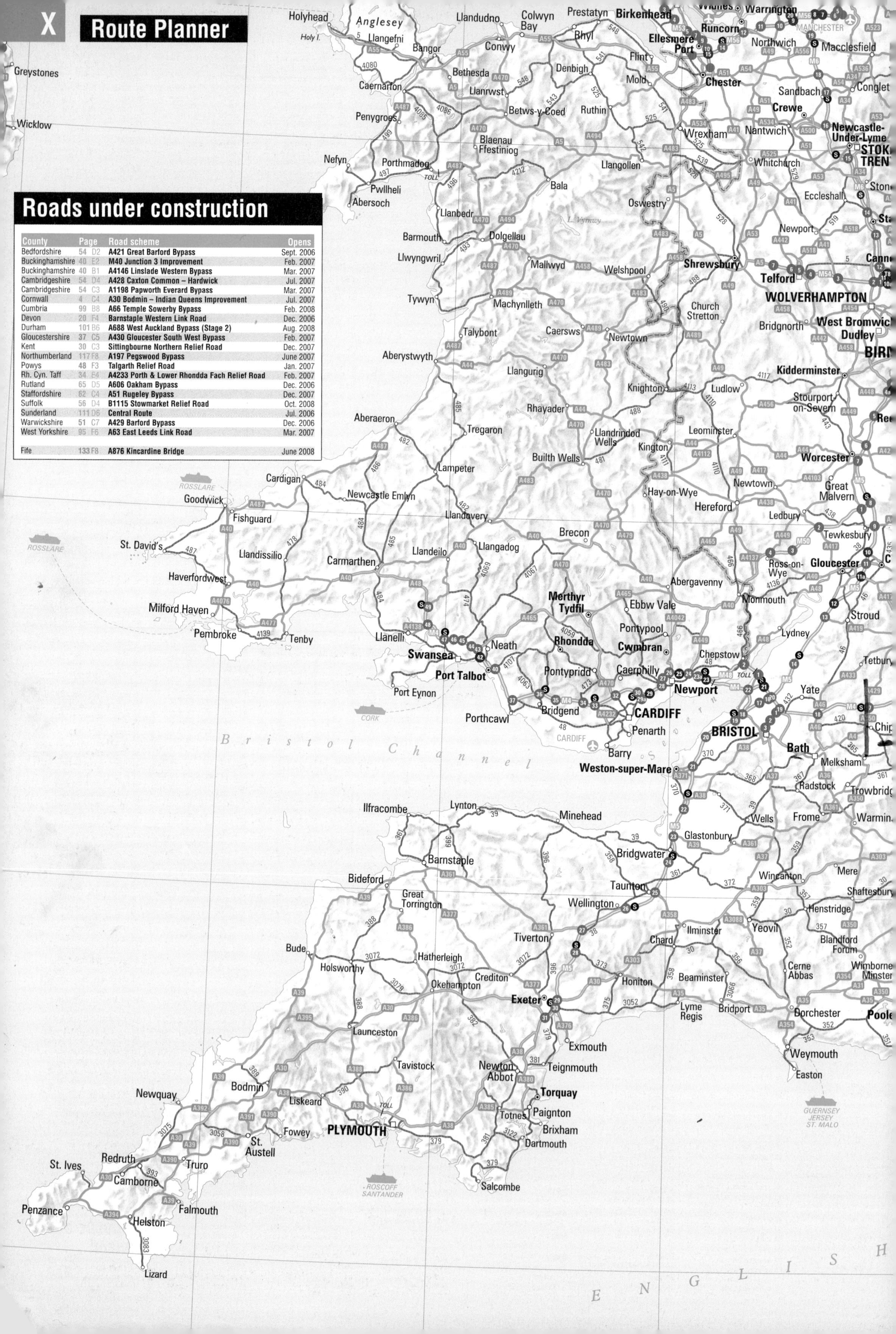

Cliftonville
Broadstairs, Tenterden.

NORTH CHANNEL
IRISH SEA
Firth of Clyde
Solway Firth
Cardigan Bay
Islay
Arran
Isle of Man
Anglesey
Lough Neagh
Strangford Lough
Port Askaig
Feolin Ferry
Bridgend
Portnahaven
Port Ellen
Tarbert
Colintraive
Dunoon
Rothesay
Gourock
Greenock
Port Glasgow
Helensburgh
Clydebank
Paisley
GLASGOW
Largs
Lochranza
Tayinloan
Brodick
Blackwaterfoot
Kilchenzie
Campbeltown
Ardrossan
Irvine
Troon
Prestwick
Ayr
Stewarton
Kilmarnock
East Kilbride
Hamilton
Kilsyth
Falkirk
Cumbernauld
Airdrie
Dunfermline
Cowdenbeath
Burntisland
North Berwick
EDINBURGH
Livingston
Haddington
Bonnyrigg
Penicuik
Leadburn
Lauder
Carnwath
Lanark
Biggar
Peebles
Galashiels
Selkirk
Hawick
Mauchline
Cumnock
Sanquhar
Moffat
Turnberry
Maybole
Dalmellington
L. Doon
Carsphairn
Thornhill
Ballantrae
Barrhill
New Galloway
Dumfries
Lockerbie
Kirkcolm
Cairnryan
Stranraer
Portpatrick
Newton Stewart
Glenluce
Wigtown
Castle Douglas
Crocketford
Dalbeattie
Kirkcudbright
Caulkerbush
Dundrennan
Drummore
Whithorn
Gretna
Longtown
Carlisle
Brampton
High Hesket
Penrith
Ballintoy
Ballycastle
Coleraine
Ballymoney
Glenariff
Glenarm
Swatragh
Ballymena
Broughshane
Larne
Magherafelt
Ballyclare
Carrickfergus
Antrim
Moneymore
Newtownabbey
Bangor
BELFAST
Newtownards
Lisburn
Saintfield
Portadown
Lurgan
Ballynahinch
Portaferry
Armagh
Banbridge
Downpatrick
Ardglass
Kilcoo
Newcastle
Newry
Warrenpoint
Annalong
Kilkeel
Cullaville
Dundalk
Ardee
Drogheda
Balbriggan
Malahide
DUBLIN
Dun Laoghaire
Bray
Greystones
Hollywood
Wicklow
Arklow
Gorey
Camolin
Bride
Ballaugh
Ramsey
Peel
Laxey
Douglas
Port Erin
Castletown
Maryport
Bothel
Cockermouth
Workington
Whitehaven
Keswick
Egremont
Ullswater
Shap
Ambleside
Windermere
Coniston
Kendal
Bootle
Whicham
Ulverston
Barrow-in-Furness
Morecambe
Heysham
Lancaster
Fleetwood
Blackpool
Lytham St. Anne's
Preston
Southport
Chorley
Ormskirk
Wigan
Kirkby
LIVERPOOL
Wallasey
Bootle
St. Helens
Widnes
Warrington
Birkenhead
Runcorn
Ellesmere Port
Northwich
Chester
Amlwch
Holyhead
Llangefni
Bangor
Llandudno
Colwyn Bay
Conwy
Prestatyn
Rhyl
Flint
Denbigh
Mold
Bethesda
Caernarfon
Llanrwst
Betws-y-Coed
Ruthin
Penygroes
Wrexham
Nantwich
Blaenau Ffestiniog
Nefyn
Porthmadog
Llangollen
Whitchurch
Pwllheli
Abersoch
Bala
Oswestry
Llanbedr
L. Vyrnwy
Barmouth
Dolgellau
Llwyngwril
Mallwyd
Welshpool
Shrewsbury
Telford
Tywyn
Machynlleth
Church
FLEETWOOD
LIVERPOOL DOUGLAS
BELFAST
DUBLIN
LIVERPOOL
LARNE
BELFAST DOUGLAS DUBLIN
DOUGLAS LIVERPOOL
TOLL
M8
M80
M9
M74
A74(M)
M6
M1
M2
M22
M50
M55
M62
M56
M53
A77
A75
A76
A702
A701
A7
A6
A66
A595
A590
A55
A5
A470
A487
A483
A458
A494
A49
A41
A1
A2
A20
A24
A25
A26
A27
A28
A29
A3
A36
N11
N2
N3
N7
N81

Restricted motorway junctions

M1	Northbound	Southbound
2	No exit	No access
4	No exit	No access
6a	No exit Access from M25 only	No access Exit to M25 only
7	No exit Access from M10 only	No access Exit to M10 only
17	No access Exit to M45 only	No exit Access from M45 only
19	No exit to A14	No access from A14
21a	No access	No exit
23a	Exit to A42 only	
24a	No exit	No access
35a	No access	No exit
43	No exit to M621 northbound	
48	No exit to A1 southbound	

M2	Eastbound	Westbound
1	Access from A2 eastbound only	Exit to A2 westbound only

M3	Eastbound	Westbound
8	No exit	No access
10	No access	No exit
13	No access to M27 eastbound	
14	No exit	No access

M4	Eastbound	Westbound
1	Exit to A4 eastbound only	Access from A4 westbound only
2	Access to A4 eastbound only	Access to A4 westbound only
21	No exit	No access
23	No access	No exit
25	No exit	No access
25a	No exit	No access
29	No exit	No access

M4	Eastbound	Westbound
38		No access
39	No exit or access	No exit
41	No access	No exit
41a	No exit	No access
42	Exit to A483 only	Access from A483 only
42	Access from A483 only	No access

M5	Northbound	Southbound
10	No exit	No access
11a	No access from A417 eastbound	No exit to A417 westbound

M6	Northbound	Southbound
3a	No access Exit to M42 northbound only	No exit Access from M6 eastbound only
4a	No exit Access from M42 southbound only	No access Exit to M42 only
5	No access	No exit
10a	No access Exit to M54 only	No exit Access from M54 only
11a	No exit / access No access to M6 Toll	No access / exit
20	No exit to M56 eastbound	No access from M56 westbound
24	No exit	No access
25	No access	No exit
30	No exit Access from M61 northbound only	No access Exit to M61 southbound
31a	No access	No exit

M6 Toll	Northbound	Southbound
T1		No exit
T2	No exit / access	No access
T5	No exit	No access
T7	No access	No exit
T8	No access	No exit

M8	Eastbound	Westbound
8	No exit to M73 northbound	No access from M73 southbound
9	No access	No exit
13	No exit southbound	No access
14	No access	No exit
16	No exit	No access
17	No exit	No access
18		No exit
19	No exit to A814 eastbound	No access from A814 westbound
20	No exit	No access
21	No access	No exit
22	No exit Access from M77 only	No access Exit to M77 only
23	No exit	No access
25	Exit to A739 northbound only Access from A739 southbound only	Exit to A739 northbound only Access from A739 southbound only
25a	No exit	No access
28	No exit	No access
28a	No exit	No access

M9	Eastbound	Westbound
1a	No exit	No access
2	No access	No exit
3	No exit	No access
6	No access	No exit
8	No exit	No access

M11	Northbound	Southbound
4	No exit	No access
5	No access	No exit
9	No access	No exit
13	No access	No exit
14	No exit to A428 westbound	No exit Access from A14 westbound only

Continued on page XV

Stromness
Pentland Firth
John o' Groats
Scrabster
Thurso
Durness
Melvich
Tongue
Eriboll
Dalhalvaig
Mybster
Wick
Laxford Bridge
Kylestrome
Kinloch
Altnaharra
Kinbrace
Latheron
Lochinver
Inchnadamph
Loch Shin
Helmsdale
Ledmore
Lairg
Rosehall
Brora
Inveran
Ullapool
Dornoch
Kincardine
Tain
Aultbea
Ardessie
Braemore
Fionn L.
Gairloch
L. Maree
Invergordon
Cromarty
Moray Firth
Lossiemouth
Elgin
Achnasheen
Garve
Dingwall
Nairn
Forres
Shieldaig
Muir of Ord
Rothes
Inverness
Ferness
Dufftown
Lochcarron
L. Monar
L. Mullardoch
Drumnadrochit
Kyle of Lochalsh
Tomatin
Grantown-on-Spey
Loch Ness
Broadford
Shiel Bridge
Invermoriston
Aviemore
Strathdon
Armadale
Fort Augustus
Loch Quoich
L. Garry
L. Lochy
Newtonmore
Mallaig
L. Arkaig
Braemar
Spean Bridge
Dalwhinnie
Lochailort
Spittal of Glenshee
Fort William
Acharacle
Loch Shiel
L. Treig
L. Ericht
Strontian
Onich
Blair Atholl
L. Rannoch
L. Tummel
Pitlochry
Kirriemuir
Glencoe
Tobermory
Aberfeldy
Blairgowrie
Lochaline
Bridge of Orchy
L. Tay
Lawers
Coupar Angus
Salen
Mull
Connel
Killin
Amulree
Oban
Tyndrum
Fionnphort
Firth of Lorn
Dalmally
Crianlarich
St. Fillans
Perth
Loch Awe
L. Earn
Crieff
Newburgh
Strathyre
Auchtermuchty
Kilmelford
L. Katrine
Greenloaning
Inveraray
Tarbet
Furnace
Strachur
Dunblane
Aberfoyle
Loch Lomond
Glenrothes
Kilmartin
Stirling
Alloa
Kirkcaldy
Garelochhead
Ardlussa
Lochgilphead
Jura
Dunfermline
Cowdenbeath
Burntisland
Helensburgh
Kilsyth
Falkirk
Gourock
Greenock
Edinburgh
Port Askaig
Feolin Ferry
Colintraive
Dunoon
Port Glasgow
Clydebank
Cumbernauld
Tarbert
Airdrie
Livingston
Bonnyrigg
Islay
Bridgend
Rothesay
Glasgow
Paisley
Largs
Penicuik
Hamilton
East Kilbride
Leadburn
Portnahaven
Carnwath
Port Ellen
Tayinloan
Lochranza
Stewarton
Arran
Ardrossan
Irvine
Lanark
Peebles
Kilmarnock
Biggar
Brodick
Troon
Prestwick
Blackwaterfoot
Mauchline
Kilchenzie
Ayr
Campbeltown
Cumnock
Firth of Clyde
Larne
Sanquhar
Turnberry
Maybole
Dalmellington
Moffat
Ballintoy
Port Nis
Barabhas
Stornoway
Port Nan Giuran
Lewis
Outer Hebrides
North Minch
Tairbeart (Tarbert)
Roghadal
Little Minch
Kilmaluag
Uig
North Uist
Loch nam Madadh (Lochmaddy)
Clachan na Luib
Carbost
Dunvegan
Skye
Portree
Tobha Mor
South Uist
Sligachan
Loch Baghasdail (Lochboisdale)
Inner Hebrides
Bagh a Chaisteil (Castlebay)

Restricted motorway junctions

Continuation from page XIII

M20	Eastbound	Westbound
2	No access	No exit
3	No exit Access from M26 eastbound only	No access Exit to M26 westbound only
11a	No access	No exit

M23	Northbound	Southbound
7	No exit to A23 southbound	No access from A23 northbound
10a	No exit	No access

M25	Clockwise	Anticlockwise
5	No exit to M26 eastbound	No access from M26 westbound
19	No access	No exit
21	No exit to M1 southbound Access from M1 southbound only	No exit to M1 southbound Access from M1 southbound only
31	No exit	No access

M27	Eastbound	Westbound
10	No exit	No access
12	No access	No exit

M40	Eastbound	Westbound
3	No exit	No access
7	No exit	No access
8	No exit	No access
13	No exit	No access
14	No access	No exit
16	No access	No exit

M42	Northbound	Southbound
1	No exit	No access
7	No access Exit to M6 northbound only	No exit Access from M6 northbound only
7a	No access Exit to M6 only	No exit Access from M6 northbound only
8	No exit Access from M6 southbound only	Exit to M6 northbound Access from M6 southbound only

M45	Eastbound	Westbound
M1 junc 17	Access to M1 southbound only	No access from M1 southbound
With A45 (Dunchurch)	No access	No exit

M48	Eastbound	Westbound
M4 junc 21	No exit to M4 westbound	No access from M4 eastbound
M4 junc 23	No access from M4 westbound	No exit to M4 eastbound

M49	Southbound
18a	No exit to M5 northbound

M53	Northbound	Southbound
11	Exit to M56 eastbound only Access from M56 westbound only	Exit to M56 eastbound only Access from M56 westbound only

M56	Eastbound	Westbound
2	No exit	No access
4	No exit	No access
7		No access
8	No exit or access	No exit
9	No access from M6 northbound	No access to M6 southbound
15	No exit to M53	No access from M53 northbound

M57	Northbound	Southbound
3	No exit	No access
5	No exit	No access

M58	Eastbound	Westbound
1	No exit	No access

M60	Clockwise	Anticlockwise
2	No exit	No access
3	No exit to A34 northbound	No exit to A34 northbound
4	No access to M56	No exit to M56
5	No exit to A5103 southbound	No exit to A5103 northbound
14	No exit to A580	No access from A580
16	No exit	No access
20	No access	No exit
22		No access
25	No access	
26		No exit or access
27	No exit	No access

M61	Northbound	Southbound
2	No access from A580 eastbound	No exit to A580 westbound
3	No access from A580 eastbound No access from A666 southbound	No exit to A580 westbound
M6 junc 30	No exit to M6 southbound	No access from M6 northbound

M62	Eastbound	Westbound
23	No access	No exit

M65	Eastbound	Westbound
9	No access	No exit
11	No exit	No access

M66	Northbound	Southbound
1	No access	No exit

M67	Eastbound	Westbound
1a	No access	No exit
2	No exit	No access

M69	Northbound	Southbound
2	No exit	No access

M73	Northbound	Southbound
2	No access from M8 or A89 eastbound No exit to A89	No exit to M8 or A89 westbound No access from A89
3	Exit to A80 northbound only	Access from A80 southbound only

M74	Northbound	Southbound
2	No access	No exit
3	No exit	No access
7	No exit	No access
9	No exit or access	No access
10		No exit
11	No exit	No access
12	No access	No exit

M77	Northbound	Southbound
4	No exit	No access
6	No exit	No access
7	No exit or access	
8	No access	No access
M8 junc 22	Exit to M8 eastbound only	Access from M8 westbound only

M80	Northbound	Southbound
3	No access	No exit
5	No access from M876	No exit to M876

M90	Northbound	Southbound
2a	No access	No exit
7	No exit	No access
8	No access	No exit
10	No access from A912	No exit to A912

M180	Northbound	Southbound
1	No access	No exit

M621	Eastbound	Westbound
2a	No exit	No access
4	No exit or access	
5	No exit	No access
6	No access	No exit

M876	Northbound	Southbound
2	No access	No exit

A1(M)	Northbound	Southbound
2	No access	No exit
3		No access
5	No exit	No access
40	No access	No exit
44	No exit, access from M1 only	Exit to M1 only
57	No access	No exit
65	No access	No exit

A3(M)	Northbound	Southbound
1		No access
4	No access	No exit

A38(M)	Northbound	Southbound
With Victoria Road (Park Circus) Birmingham	No exit	No access

A48(M)	Northbound	Southbound
M4 Junc 29	Exit to M4 eastbound only	Access from M4 westbound only
29a	Access from A48 eastbound only	Exit to A48 westbound only

A57(M)	Eastbound	Westbound
With A5103	No access	No exit
With A34	No access	No exit

A58(M)	Southbound
With Park Lane and Westgate, Leeds	No access

A64(M)	Eastbound	Westbound
With A58 Clay Pit Lane, Leeds	No access	No exit
With Regent Street, Leeds	No access	No access

A74(M)	Northbound	Southbound
18	No access	No exit
22	No access	No exit

A167(M)	Northbound	Southbound
With Camden St, Newcastle	No exit	No exit or access

A194(M)	Northbound	Southbound
A1(M) junc 65 Gateshead Western Bypass	Access from A1(M) northbound only	Exit to A1(M) southbound only

Distance table

How to use this table

Distances are shown in miles and kilometres with estimated journey times in hours and minutes.

For example: the distance between Birmingham and Brighton is 163 miles or 262 kilometres with an estimated journey time of 3 hours, 20 minutes.

Estimated driving times are based on an average speed of 60mph on Motorways and 40mph on other roads. Drivers should allow extra time when driving at peak periods or through areas likely to be congested.

(Each cell: miles / kilometres / hours:minutes)

	Swansea	Stranraer	Southampton	Shrewsbury	Sheffield	Portsmouth	Plymouth	Oxford	Oban	Nottingham	Norwich	Newcastle upon Tyne	Manchester	Liverpool	Lincoln	Leicester	Leeds	Land's End	Kyle of Lochalsh	Kingston upon Hull	John o' Groats	Inverness	Holyhead	Harwich	Great Yarmouth	Gloucester	Glasgow	Fort William	Fishguard	Exeter	Edinburgh	Dundee	Dover	Doncaster	Carlisle	Cardiff	Cambridge	Bristol	Brighton	Braemar	Bournemouth	Blackpool	Birmingham	Berwick-upon-Tweed	Ayr	Aberystwyth	Aberdeen	London
Aberdeen																																																51…/83…/11:2…
Aberystwyth																																															445/716/8:40	21…/34…/4:4…
Ayr																																														317/510/6:10	183/295/4:20	39…/63…/7:2…
Berwick-upon-Tweed																																													134/216/3:00	311/501/6:20	182/293/4:40	35…/56…/7:3…
Birmingham																																												274/441/5:30	289/465/5:30	114/183/2:50	420/676/8:30	117/18…/2:5…
Blackpool																																											123/198/2:40	181/291/3:50	180/290/3:30	153/246/3:20	308/496/6:20	22…/364/4:3…
Bournemouth																																										270/435/5:00	147/237/3:10	412/663/7:50	436/702/8:00	207/333/4:30	564/908/10:20	107/17…/2:40
Braemar																																									524/843/9:30	281/452/5:20	385/620/7:10	148/238/3:20	143/230/3:00	405/652/7:50	59/95/1:30	482/776/10:30
Brighton																																								534/859/9:40	92/148/2:10	286/460/5:20	163/262/3:20	409/658/7:40	446/718/8:00	253/407/5:10	573/922/10:30	52/84/1:50
Bristol																																							147/237/4:10	477/768/8:40	82/132/2:30	204/328/3:50	81/130/2:00	362/583/6:50	370/595/6:40	125/201/3:00	493/793/9:10	122/196/2:50
Cambridge																																						169/272/3:10	116/187/2:20	438/705/7:50	154/248/3:00	208/335/3:50	100/161/2:10	306/493/5:40	357/575/6:20	214/344/4:20	471/758/10:00	54/87/1:30
Cardiff																																					190/306/3:30	45/72/1:20	182/293/3:40	483/778/8:40	117/188/3:00	209/336/4:00	103/166/2:20	368/592/7:00	382/615/7:00	105/169/2:40	505/813/9:20	157/253/3:20
Carlisle																																				289/465/5:20	264/425/4:40	277/446/5:00	370/596/6:40	196/316/3:50	343/552/6:20	87/140/1:50	196/315/3:50	87/140/2:10	93/150/2:00	224/360/4:30	221/356/4:30	301/484/5:40
Doncaster																																			142/229/3:00	209/336/4:00	116/187/2:10	175/282/3:20	236/380/4:30	310/499/5:40	235/378/4:20	94/151/1:50	94/151/2:00	184/296/3:50	235/378/4:20	176/283/3:40	344/554/6:50	171/275/3:30
Dover																																		242/390/4:30	389/626/7:00	238/383/4:30	125/201/2:30	202/325/3:50	82/132/2:20	553/890/9:50	174/280/4:30	312/502/5:40	194/312/3:50	424/683/7:50	478/769/8:30	297/478/5:50	588/947/10:40	71/114/2:00
Dundee																																	523/842/9:10	275/443/5:00	152/245/3:00	441/710/8:00	406/654/7:10	430/692/7:40	517/832/9:10	52/84/1:20	495/797/8:50	239/385/4:30	349/562/6:20	113/182/2:40	117/188/2:30	376/605/7:10	67/108/1:50	448/721/8:40
Edinburgh																																56/90/1:30	462/744/8:10	219/352/4:00	96/154/2:00	385/620/7:00	345/555/6:10	373/600/6:50	456/734/8:20	91/146/2:10	439/707/8:00	183/295/3:30	292/470/5:30	57/92/1:40	73/117/1:50	320/515/6:20	125/201/3:10	390/628/7:20
Exeter																															450/724/8:00	518/834/9:10	248/399/4:40	251/404/4:30	353/568/6:20	121/195/2:30	249/401/4:30	76/122/1:40	184/296/5:00	550/885/9:40	82/132/2:20	282/454/5:10	157/253/3:10	428/689/7:50	446/718/7:50	201/323/4:10	569/916/10:20	181/291/3:40
Fishguard																														230/370/4:30	399/642/7:30	460/740/8:30	331/533/6:20	247/398/4:50	297/478/5:40	112/180/2:40	270/435/5:10	154/248/3:20	291/468/5:40	493/794/9:10	222/357/4:40	209/336/4:10	170/274/3:40	371/597/7:20	373/600/7:00	56/90/1:30	504/811/10:10	260/418/5:20
Fort William																													486/782/9:30	560/901/10:20	144/232/3:30	127/204/3:10	596/959/11:00	357/575/7:00	206/332/4:30	485/781/9:10	479/771/9:00	486/782/9:10	575/926/10:50	125/201/3:10	539/867/10:10	296/476/6:00	392/631/7:40	190/306/4:40	133/214/3:20	430/692/8:40	149/240/3:50	510/821/9:50
Glasgow																												101/163/2:50	376/605/7:10	449/723/8:00	44/71/1:20	83/134/2:00	488/786/8:40	249/401/4:40	96/154/2:10	385/620/7:00	372/599/6:40	373/600/6:50	468/753/8:30	110/177/2:30	439/707/8:00	183/295/3:40	292/470/5:30	101/163/2:40	33/53/1:10	320/515/6:20	145/233/3:30	397/639/7:30
Gloucester																											346/557/6:10	454/731/8:30	153/246/3:10	111/179/2:10	349/562/6:10	410/660/7:10	191/307/3:30	150/241/2:50	247/398/4:20	56/90/1:20	123/198/2:20	35/56/1:00	159/256/3:10	443/713/8:00	99/159/2:40	174/280/3:10	56/90/1:20	318/512/6:00	330/531/5:50	102/164/2:30	468/753/8:30	109/175/2:30
Great Yarmouth																										225/362/4:40	419/674/8:00	527/848/10:20	366/589/7:20	335/539/6:30	386/621/7:30	484/779/9:00	185/298/4:00	167/269/3:40	320/515/6:20	284/457/5:50	82/132/2:10	275/443/5:40	180/290/4:10	477/768/9:10	240/386/5:00	252/406/5:10	180/290/4:10	345/555/7:00	402/647/7:40	294/473/6:20	517/832/10:50	128/206/3:40
Harwich																									82/132/2:10	196/316/4:00	432/695/8:10	543/874/10:30	337/542/6:40	279/449/5:20	413/665/7:40	469/755/8:40	125/201/2:50	194/312/4:00	336/541/6:20	246/396/5:00	67/108/1:50	217/349/4:30	128/206/3:00	504/811/9:20	187/301/4:00	275/443/5:20	167/269/3:40	372/599/7:20	425/684/8:00	281/452/5:50	535/861/11:20	76/122/2:20
Holyhead																								349/562/7:10	334/538/7:00	191/307/4:00	330/531/6:40	438/705/8:50	167/269/4:00	282/454/5:40	333/536/6:40	394/634/7:30	360/580/7:00	181/291/3:50	231/372/4:50	216/348/5:40	270/435/5:20	206/332/4:30	334/538/6:40	426/686/8:20	288/463/5:50	141/227/3:20	148/238/3:30	311/501/6:30	305/491/6:10	111/179/2:50	439/707/8:40	269/433/5:40
Inverness																							474/763/9:40	569/916/11:00	553/890/11:00	504/811/9:30	166/267/4:00	66/106/1:40	542/872/10:30	618/995/11:30	158/254/3:50	132/212/3:20	622/1001/11:30	383/617/7:30	262/422/5:30	549/884/10:20	505/813/9:30	539/867/10:10	617/993/11:30	75/121/2:00	597/961/11:20	348/560/7:00	458/737/9:00	215/346/5:10	199/320/4:30	486/782/9:40	105/169/2:50	550/885/10:40
John o' Groats																						129/208/3:20	603/970/12:40	693/1116/14:00	677/1090/14:00	628/1011/12:30	295/475/7:10	195/314/5:00	671/1080/13:40	744/1197/14:30	285/459/7:00	259/417/6:30	746/1201/14:40	507/816/10:30	391/629/8:40	680/1094/13:30	630/1014/12:30	668/1075/13:20	741/1193/14:40	202/325/5:00	724/1165/14:20	478/769/10:00	574/924/11:50	342/550/8:10	328/528/7:40	601/967/12:40	232/373/5:50	663/1067/13:30
Kingston upon Hull																					518/834/10:50	394/634/7:50	231/372/4:50	196/316/4:10	207/333/5:20	169/272/3:10	254/409/4:50	369/594/7:20	280/451/5:30	309/497/5:40	234/377/4:30	295/475/5:30	256/412/4:50	47/76/1:10	158/254/3:00	244/393/4:40	139/224/3:10	233/375/4:20	245/394/4:40	327/526/6:10	264/425/5:00	127/204/2:30	134/216/2:50	185/298/3:50	251/404/4:40	223/359/4:40	364/586/7:20	184/296/3:50
Kyle of Lochalsh																				445/716/9:00	189/304/4:40	84/135/2:10	514/827/10:40	611/983/12:10	602/969/12:10	528/850/10:20	179/288/4:40	79/127/2:00	567/913/11:20	628/1011/12:00	216/348/5:20	186/299/4:40	671/1080/12:50	432/695/8:40	275/443/6:10	564/908/11:10	555/893/10:50	552/888/10:50	651/1048/12:40	159/256/4:00	618/995/12:10	372/599/7:50	471/758/9:40	263/423/6:20	212/341/5:10	499/803/10:20	189/304/4:50	586/943/11:40
Land's End																			763/1228/15:10	421/678/8:20	868/1397/17:20	741/1193/14:20	405/652/8:30	390/628/8:00	446/718/9:10	235/378/5:00	573/922/10:50	686/1104/13:20	353/568/7:20	123/198/3:20	574/924/10:50	642/1033/12:00	381/613/7:40	374/602/7:20	477/768/9:10	245/394/5:20	374/602/7:20	200/322/4:40	308/496/7:50	665/1070/12:30	205/330/5:20	405/652/8:00	281/452/6:00	552/888/10:40	570/917/10:50	313/504/6:50	692/1114/13:10	297/478/6:30
Leeds																		405/652/8:00	394/634/8:20	55/89/1:30	487/784/10:20	360/579/7:10	176/283/4:00	223/359/4:30	196/315/4:20	174/280/3:20	215/346/4:10	329/530/6:40	237/381/4:40	270/435/5:00	202/325/4:00	258/415/4:50	260/418/4:50	29/47/0:50	119/192/2:30	232/373/4:20	145/233/2:50	194/312/3:50	260/419/5:00	293/472/5:30	255/410/4:50	72/116/1:40	113/182/2:30	156/251/3:20	212/341/4:00	169/272/3:40	327/526/6:50	189/304/3:50
Leicester																	95/153/2:00	320/515/6:30	500/805/9:50	102/164/2:10	588/947/11:50	461/742/8:50	190/306/4:00	147/237/3:10	140/225/3:20	85/137/1:40	314/505/5:40	422/679/8:00	209/336/4:10	196/315/3:40	296/476/5:20	349/562/6:20	185/298/3:30	74/119/1:30	206/332/3:50	154/248/3:00	68/109/1:20	120/193/2:30	166/267/3:20	389/626/7:00	158/254/3:10	140/225/2:40	39/63/1:10	252/406/5:00	299/481/5:20	153/246/3:20	414/666/7:40	97/156/2:20
Lincoln																51/82/1:20	68/109/1:50	371/597/7:30	476/766/9:40	44/71/1:20	554/892/11:30	427/687/8:30	216/348/4:40	155/249/3:30	128/206/3:20	159/256/3:10	291/468/5:30	399/642/7:50	272/438/5:30	247/398/4:40	258/415/5:00	314/505/5:50	202/325/4:00	39/63/1:10	191/307/3:40	208/335/4:10	85/137/2:20	183/295/3:40	197/317/4:00	357/575/6:40	209/336/4:10	128/206/2:40	90/145/2:10	224/360/4:40	274/441/5:10	199/320/4:20	383/616/7:20	131/211/3:10
Liverpool															129/208/2:50	130/209/2:40	75/121/1:50	361/581/7:20	407/655/8:30	130/209/2:40	511/822/10:40	382/615/7:40	102/164/2:40	265/427/5:20	240/386/5:00	140/225/2:40	216/348/4:10	329/530/6:40	160/257/3:30	237/381/4:30	216/348/4:10	286/460/5:20	299/481/5:30	86/138/1:50	120/193/2:30	169/272/3:20	194/312/3:40	161/259/3:10	272/438/5:10	318/512/6:00	234/377/4:30	49/79/1:20	93/150/2:10	219/352/4:30	213/343/4:10	104/167/2:40	341/549/6:40	202/325/4:10
Manchester														35/56/1:10	84/135/2:00	92/148/2:00	40/64/1:10	361/581/7:20	406/654/8:30	95/153/2:10	500/805/10:30	373/600/7:30	124/200/3:00	228/367/4:40	212/341/4:30	126/203/2:30	215/346/4:10	329/530/6:40	197/317/4:00	236/380/4:20	215/346/4:10	285/459/5:20	276/444/5:10	61/98/1:30	119/192/2:30	183/295/3:40	165/266/3:10	161/259/3:10	257/414/4:50	318/512/6:00	227/365/4:20	48/77/1:20	80/129/2:00	196/315/4:00	212/341/4:00	129/208/3:00	340/547/6:30	185/298/3:50
Newcastle upon Tyne													132/212/2:50	168/270/3:20	159/256/3:20	187/301/3:40	92/148/2:10	498/802/9:40	318/512/7:00	132/212/2:50	395/636/8:50	268/431/5:40	272/438/5:40	308/496/6:00	281/452/5:40	266/428/4:50	148/238/3:10	253/407/5:20	329/529/6:20	364/586/6:30	110/177/2:20	166/267/3:20	358/576/6:30	114/183/2:20	57/92/1:50	325/523/6:00	241/388/4:20	299/481/5:30	352/567/6:30	201/323/4:00	347/558/6:30	129/208/2:40	207/333/4:10	64/103/1:50	149/240/3:00	257/414/5:20	235/378/4:50	286/460/5:40
Norwich												264/425/5:20	185/298/4:30	220/354/4:40	105/169/2:50	119/192/3:20	176/283/3:50	421/678/8:40	582/937/11:50	149/240/4:00	654/1053/13:30	529/852/10:30	311/501/6:40	73/117/2:00	20/32/0:40	204/328/4:10	385/620/9:00	504/811/10:00	343/552/7:00	308/496/6:00	366/589/7:00	422/679/8:00	174/280/3:50	147/237/3:20	289/465/5:40	262/422/5:20	62/100/1:50	252/406/5:10	175/282/4:00	457/735/8:40	214/344/4:40	232/373/4:50	166/267/3:50	328/528/6:40	382/615/7:20	276/444/6:00	496/798/9:40	114/183/3:30
Nottingham											130/209/3:40	157/253/3:10	73/118/1:40	98/158/2:10	35/56/1:10	25/40/0:50	70/113/1:40	345/555/7:00	479/771/9:40	90/145/2:00	557/896/11:30	430/692/8:20	185/298/4:00	150/241/3:20	153/246/3:30	110/177/2:10	293/472/5:30	401/646/7:50	220/354/4:30	221/356/4:10	262/422/4:50	328/528/6:00	205/330/3:50	43/69/1:10	194/312/3:40	172/277/3:20	83/134/1:40	145/233/3:00	193/311/3:50	353/568/6:30	183/295/3:40	111/179/2:20	50/80/1:20	221/356/4:30	274/441/5:10	164/264/3:40	393/633/7:30	122/196/2:40
Oban										390/628/7:30	492/792/9:40	233/375/4:50	307/494/6:00	308/496/6:10	387/623/7:30	419/674/7:50	307/494/6:00	665/1070/12:50	128/206/3:10	346/557/6:40	244/393/6:10	117/188/3:00	427/687/8:30	524/843/10:00	515/829/10:00	441/710/8:10	92/148/2:30	49/79/1:20	481/774/9:10	549/884/10:00	123/198/3:00	117/188/2:50	585/942/10:40	346/557/6:40	188/303/4:00	477/768/9:00	468/753/8:40	465/748/8:40	565/910/10:30	141/227/3:30	530/853/9:50	285/459/5:40	384/618/7:30	180/290/4:20	94/151/2:20	412/663/8:10	178/286/4:20	499/803/9:30
Oxford									462/744/8:30	109/175/2:10	145/233/3:50	260/418/4:50	144/232/2:50	172/277/3:20	137/221/2:50	73/117/1:30	168/270/3:10	274/441/5:40	550/885/10:40	192/309/3:40	656/1056/13:00	532/856/10:00	238/383/4:50	145/233/3:10	200/322/4:20	52/84/1:30	356/573/6:30	472/760/9:00	205/330/4:10	156/251/3:00	372/599/6:40	433/697/7:40	141/227/2:50	145/233/2:40	260/418/4:40	108/174/2:20	83/134/1:40	74/119/1:40	108/174/2:20	465/749/8:20	90/145/2:00	187/301/3:30	64/103/1:30	324/521/6:10	353/568/6:20	154/248/3:20	483/777/8:50	57/92/1:40
Plymouth								199/320/4:00	587/945/11:00	267/430/5:10	343/552/7:00	410/660/7:40	283/455/5:30	283/455/5:30	293/472/5:50	242/389/4:40	316/509/6:00	89/143/2:20	674/1085/13:10	355/571/6:40	790/1271/15:40	664/1069/12:30	328/528/6:40	309/497/6:10	365/588/7:20	157/253/3:20	495/797/9:10	595/958/11:20	264/425/5:30	46/74/1:30	496/798/9:00	552/888/10:00	300/483/5:50	297/478/5:40	399/642/7:20	167/269/3:40	293/472/5:30	122/196/2:50	224/361/6:00	587/945/10:40	128/206/3:30	328/528/6:10	203/327/4:20	474/763/9:00	492/792/9:00	237/382/5:10	615/990/11:20	218/351/4:40
Portsmouth							176/283/4:50	77/124/1:40	545/877/10:00	191/307/3:40	207/333/4:20	337/542/6:10	236/380/4:30	254/409/4:50	201/323/4:00	162/261/3:10	257/414/4:50	259/417/5:40	633/1019/12:10	269/433/5:00	737/1186/14:30	613/987/11:30	311/501/6:10	166/267/3:40	221/356/4:40	119/192/3:00	448/721/8:10	555/893/10:20	251/404/5:00	135/217/2:40	453/729/8:10	514/827/9:00	130/209/2:50	234/377/4:20	348/560/6:10	142/229/3:00	144/232/2:50	97/156/2:10	48/77/1:40	547/881/9:50	52/84/1:30	264/425/4:50	141/227/3:00	401/645/7:30	430/692/7:40	222/357/4:40	560/901/10:10	70/113/2:00
Sheffield						230/370/4:20	283/455/5:30	135/217/2:40	339/546/6:30	37/60/1:00	146/235/3:20	125/201/2:40	38/61/1:00	72/116/1:40	46/74/1:20	62/100/1:20	33/53/1:00	361/581/7:10	427/687/8:40	65/105/1:30	520/837/10:50	393/632/7:40	168/270/3:40	187/301/3:50	166/267/3:40	126/203/2:20	248/399/4:40	348/560/6:50	215/346/4:20	237/381/4:20	235/378/4:20	291/468/5:20	245/394/4:30	18/29/0:40	152/245/3:00	194/312/3:40	120/193/2:20	161/259/3:10	226/364/4:20	320/515/6:00	216/348/4:10	86/138/1:50	76/122/1:50	190/306/4:00	245/394/4:30	159/256/3:30	360/579/6:50	159/256/3:20
Shrewsbury					82/132/2:10	207/333/3:50	225/362/4:40	106/171/2:10	364/586/7:00	93/150/2:00	205/330/4:20	201/323/3:50	69/111/1:40	58/93/1:50	133/214/2:50	84/135/1:40	109/175/2:20	303/488/6:10	451/726/9:00	169/272/3:10	567/912/11:30	438/705/8:20	113/182/2:50	240/386/4:40	225/362/4:40	77/124/1:30	272/438/5:00	382/615/7:20	145/233/3:10	179/288/3:20	274/441/5:00	330/531/6:00	251/404/4:30	109/175/2:10	176/283/3:20	111/179/2:20	159/256/3:00	103/166/2:50	226/364/4:20	371/597/6:50	185/298/3:40	98/158/2:00	45/72/1:20	265/426/5:10	269/433/5:00	77/124/2:10	399/642/7:30	160/258/3:20
Southampton				185/298/4:10	199/320/3:40	21/34/0:50	151/243/4:10	64/103/1:30	530/853/9:40	176/283/3:20	206/332/4:20	324/521/5:50	221/356/4:10	239/385/4:30	204/328/4:00	137/220/2:40	232/373/4:20	228/367/5:00	618/995/12:00	256/412/4:40	723/1164/14:10	598/963/11:10	293/472/5:50	164/264/3:30	220/354/4:40	105/169/2:40	433/697/7:40	541/871/10:00	233/375/4:40	105/169/3:00	438/705/7:50	500/805/8:50	143/230/2:50	209/336/3:50	324/521/5:50	121/195/2:30	148/238/2:50	76/122/2:20	61/98/1:50	532/856/9:30	31/50/1:00	251/404/4:40	128/206/2:40	388/624/7:10	417/671/7:30	201/323/4:10	547/880/10:00	77/124/2:00
Stranraer			445/716/8:20	277/446/5:30	263/423/5:20	461/742/8:40	500/805/9:40	379/610/7:10	148/238/3:40	290/467/5:50	403/649/8:10	158/254/3:40	220/354/4:40	221/356/4:40	298/480/6:00	330/531/6:20	220/354/4:40	585/942/11:30	263/423/6:30	259/417/5:20	379/610/9:00	262/422/6:00	338/544/7:00	410/660/8:10	426/686/8:40	343/552/6:30	84/135/2:30	195/314/4:50	392/631/7:50	454/731/8:30	124/200/3:00	167/269/3:40	496/798/9:10	257/414/5:10	101/163/2:40	390/628/7:30	379/610/7:10	378/608/7:20	475/765/9:00	194/312/4:20	444/715/8:30	188/303/4:00	297/478/6:00	170/274/4:10	51/82/1:20	325/523/6:50	228/367/5:10	402/647/7:50
Swansea		417/671/7:50	161/259/3:00	118/190/2:20	217/349/4:00	182/293/3:30	206/332/4:10	141/227/2:40	506/815/9:20	192/309/3:40	301/485/6:00	347/559/6:20	187/301/3:30	195/314/3:40	233/375/4:30	177/285/3:20	248/399/4:40	285/459/6:00	594/956/11:30	264/425/4:50	696/1120/13:40	572/921/10:40	184/296/4:50	267/430/5:10	329/530/6:30	89/143/1:50	409/658/7:20	496/798/9:20	67/108/1:50	161/259/3:00	412/663/7:20	473/761/8:20	274/441/5:00	232/373/4:10	309/497/5:30	41/66/1:10	227/365/4:10	85/137/1:50	222/357/4:20	505/813/9:00	167/269/3:20	216/348/4:00	119/192/2:30	383/616/7:10	379/610/6:50	73/117/2:00	507/816/9:20	194/312/4:00
York	272/438/5:10	222/357/4:40	258/415/5:10	133/214/2:40	52/84/1:20	278/448/5:10	333/536/6:20	181/291/3:20	309/497/6:00	77/124/1:40	181/291/4:20	84/135/2:20	64/103/1:30	99/159/2:10	75/121/1:50	108/174/2:10	24/39/0:50	411/661/8:00	407/655/8:20	37/60/1:10	479/771/10:10	352/566/7:00	204/328/4:20	228/367/4:40	201/323/4:20	189/304/3:30	217/349/4:10	330/531/6:30	261/420/5:10	287/462/5:10	194/312/3:40	250/402/4:40	282/454/5:10	34/55/1:00	121/195/2:30	244/393/4:40	165/266/3:10	222/357/4:10	275/443/5:10	285/459/5:20	269/433/5:00	96/154/2:00	130/209/2:40	148/238/3:10	214/344/4:00	195/314/4:10	319/513/6:10	207/333/4:10

Key to 3-mile map pages

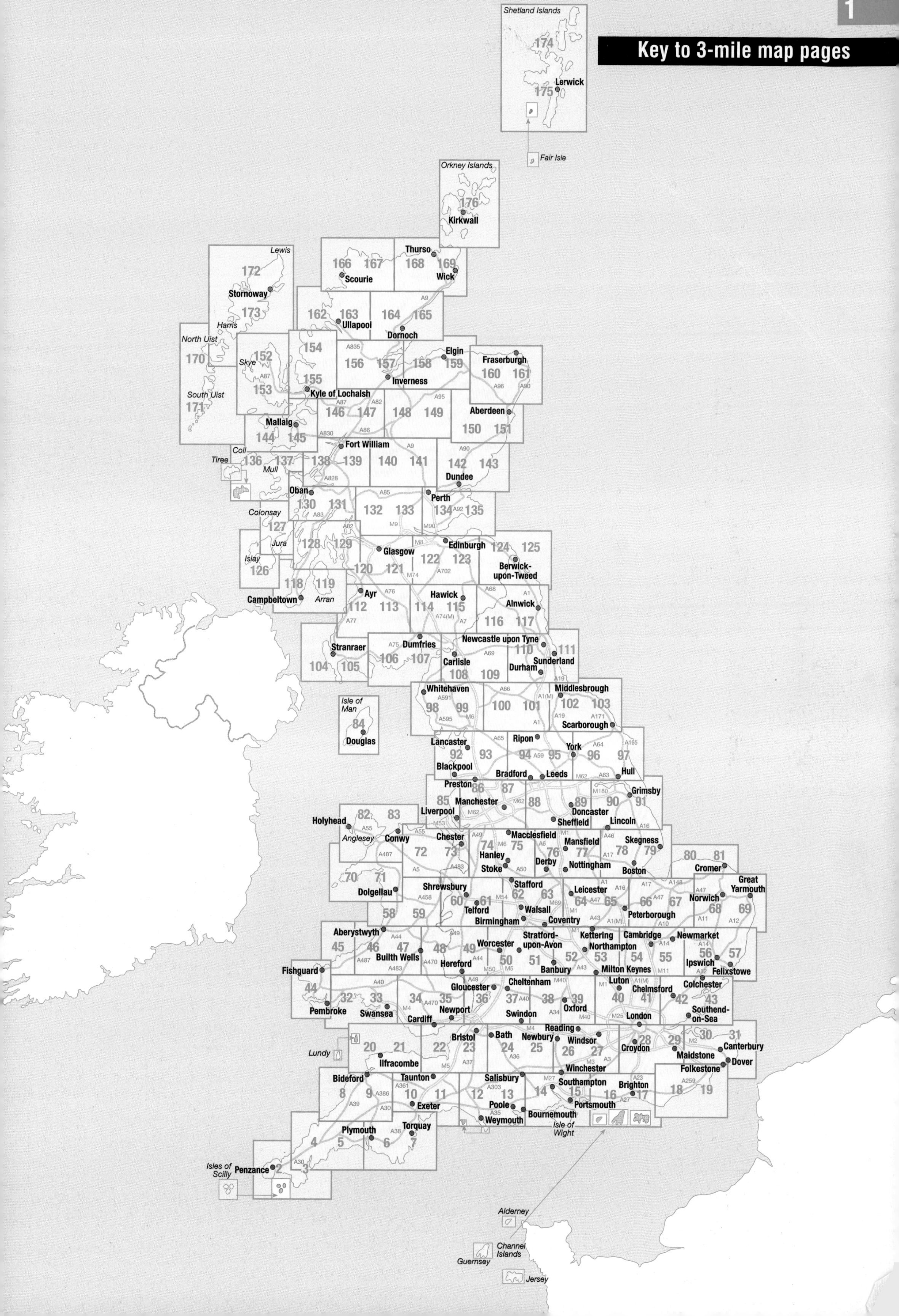

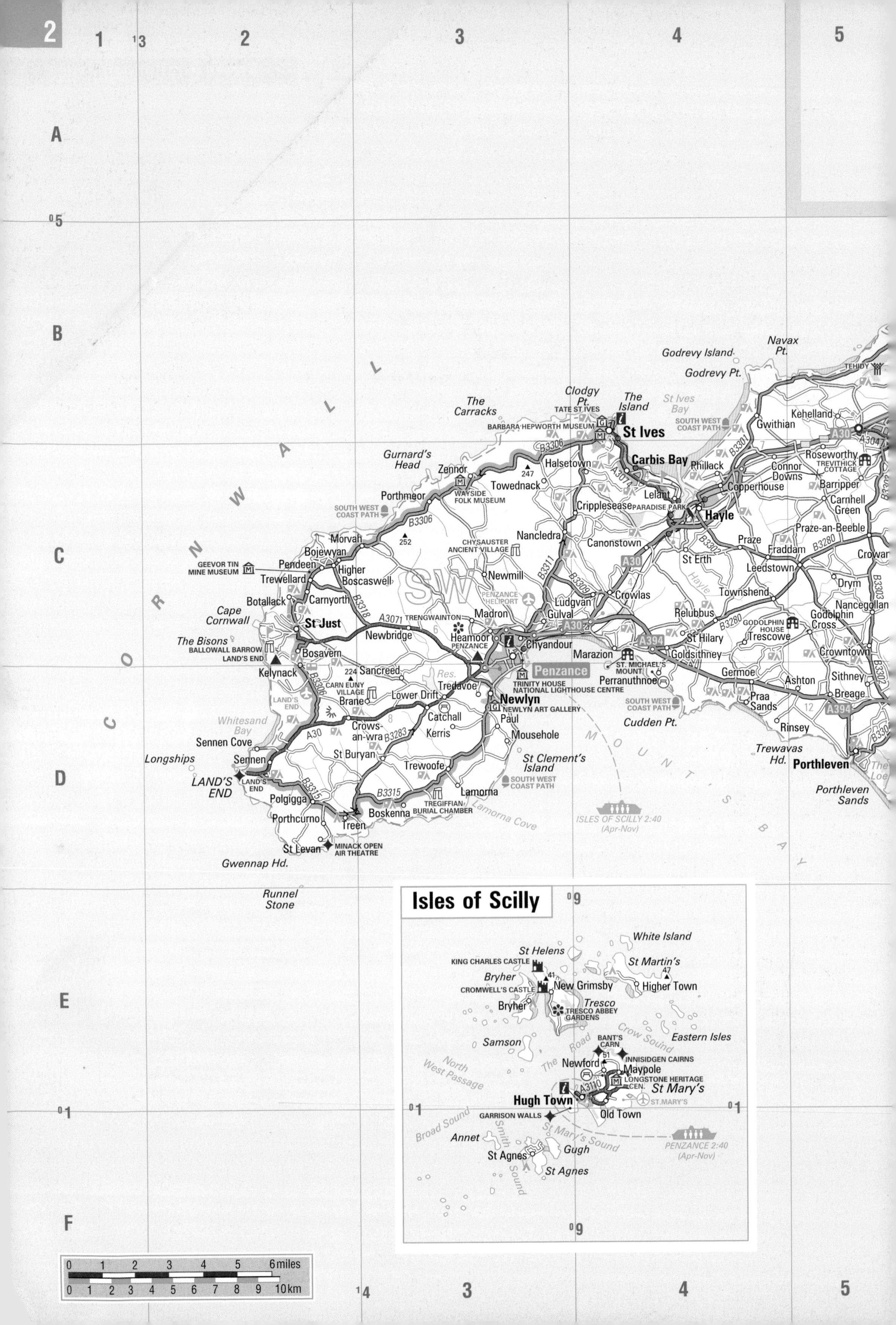

CORNWALL
SW
St Ives
Carbis Bay
Hayle
St Just
Penzance
Newlyn
Porthleven
Marazion
LAND'S END
Sennen
Sennen Cove
Zennor
Towednack
Halsetown
Lelant
Phillack
Gwithian
Kehelland
Roseworthy
Connor Downs
Copperhouse
Barripper
Carnhell Green
Praze-an-Beeble
Crowan
Drym
Nancegollan
Godolphin Cross
Crowntown
Sithney
Breage
Ashton
Germoe
Praa Sands
Rinsey
Trewavas Hd.
Porthleven Sands
Godrevy Island
Godrevy Pt.
Navax Pt.
TEHIDY
The Carracks
Clodgy Pt.
The Island
St Ives Bay
TATE ST IVES
BARBARA HEPWORTH MUSEUM
SOUTH WEST COAST PATH
Gurnard's Head
Porthmeor
WAYSIDE FOLK MUSEUM
Cripplesease
PARADISE PARK
Nancledra
Canonstown
St Erth
Praze
Fraddam
Leedstown
Townshend
Relubbus
St Hilary
Goldsithney
GODOLPHIN HOUSE
Trescowe
Crowlas
Ludgvan
Gulval
Chyandour
Newmill
CHYSAUSTER ANCIENT VILLAGE
PENZANCE HELIPORT
Madron
TRENGWAINTON
Heamoor
PENZANCE
ST. MICHAEL'S MOUNT
Perranuthnoe
TRINITY HOUSE NATIONAL LIGHTHOUSE CENTRE
NEWLYN ART GALLERY
Cudden Pt.
Paul
Mousehole
St Clement's Island
Lamorna
Lamorna Cove
TREGIFFIAN BURIAL CHAMBER
Boskenna
Treen
MINACK OPEN AIR THEATRE
St Levan
Porthcurno
Polgigga
Gwennap Hd.
Runnel Stone
Longships
Whitesand Bay
St Buryan
Trewoofe
Kerris
Catchall
Crows-an-wra
Brane
CARN EUNY VILLAGE
Sancreed
Lower Drift
Tredavoe
Res.
Newbridge
Bosavern
Kelynack
BALLOWALL BARROW
The Bisons
Cape Cornwall
Botallack
Carnyorth
Trewellard
Pendeen
GEEVOR TIN MINE MUSEUM
Bojewyan
Morvah
Higher Boscaswell
MOUNT'S BAY
ISLES OF SCILLY 2:40 (Apr-Nov)
A30
A3071
A3074
A394
A3047
B3306
B3311
B3309
B3302
B3301
B3280
B3318
B3283
B3315
B3303
252
247
224
Isles of Scilly
White Island
St Helens
St Martin's
Higher Town
KING CHARLES CASTLE
Bryher
CROMWELL'S CASTLE
New Grimsby
Tresco
TRESCO ABBEY GARDENS
Eastern Isles
Crow Sound
Samson
BANT'S CARN
INNISIDGEN CAIRNS
The Road
Newford
Maypole
North West Passage
LONGSTONE HERITAGE CEN.
St Mary's
Hugh Town
ST.MARY'S
Old Town
GARRISON WALLS
Broad Sound
Smith Sound
St Mary's Sound
Annet
St Agnes
Gugh
PENZANCE 2:40 (Apr-Nov)
A3110
0 1 2 3 4 5 6 miles
0 1 2 3 4 5 6 7 8 9 10km

Penhale Pt.
Holywell
HOLYWELL BAY FUN PARK
Carines
Kestle Mill
DAIRYLAND FARM WORLD
St Columb Road
Fraddon
Penhale
Indian Queens
St Dennis
Trezaise
Bugle
Hensbarrow
Downs
Whitemoor
Stenalees
Penwithick
Ligger or Perran Bay
Penhale Sands
Cubert
Mount
Rejerrah
St Newlyn East
TRERICE
Gummow's Shop
St Enoder
Retew
Summercourt
Treviscoe
Nanpean
Carthew
Trethurgy
EDEN PROJECT
St Blazey
SOUTH WEST COAST PATH
LAPPA VALLEY STEAM RAILWAY
Rose
PERRAN ROUND
Perranporth
PERRANPORTH
Goonhavern
WORLD IN MINIATURE
Newlyn Downs
Mitchell
Brighton
Trethosa
Foxhole
WHEAL MARTYN CHINA CLAY HER. CENTRE
High Street
Carclaze
Boscoppa
Bolingey
Perranzabuloe
Carland Cross
Trelassick
St Stephen
St Austell
Zelah
Trewoon
Holmbush
St Agnes Hd.
Trevellas
St Mewan
SHIPWRECK HERITAGE CENTRE
Charlestown
St Agnes
Mithian
LEISURE PARK
Callestick
St Allen
Trispen
St Erme
New Mills
Coombe
Grampound Road
Ladock
Sticker
Polgooth
ST AUSTELL BREWERY
Porthpean
Goonbell
CORNISH CYDER FARM
Marazanvose
Hewas Water
TORTOISE GARDEN
Trenarren
Allet
Probus
Grampound
TREWITHEN
Black Hd.
Porthtowan
Mount Hawke
Shortlanesend
PROBUS GDNS.
Creed
THE LOST GARDENS OF HELIGAN
Pentewan
Mevagissey Bay
Three Burrows
Blackwater
Tresillian
Kenwyn
St Ewe
Portreath
Mawla
Truro
CATHEDRAL
Merther
Tresawle
Polmassick
Kestle
WORLD OF MODEL RAILWAY
Illogan
TOLGUS TIN
Scorrier
Chacewater
Threemilestone
ROYAL CORNWALL MUS.
Tregony
Mevagissey
CORNISH MINES & ENGINES
St Day
Baldhu
Kea
St Clement
Portmellon
Chapel Pt.
Roscroggan
Twelve Heads
Redruth
Malpas
Ruan Lanihorne
Trevarrick
Gorran Churchtown
Pool
Tuckingmill
GWENNAP PIT
Carharrack
Bissoe
Playing Place
Old Kea
St Michael Penkevil
Lamorran
St Michael Caerhays
Gorran Haven
Cambrea
Carnkie
Carnon Downs
Portholland
Boswinger
BOSWINGER
CAMBORNE
Gwennap
Lanner
Penpol
Trelissick
Philleigh
Treworga
Penare
SHIRE HORSE FARM
Perranarworthal
Devoran
Feock
Ferry
TRELISSICK
Veryan
Portloe
Veryan Bay
Dodman Pt.
Four Lanes
Troon
Ponsanooth
Treworlas
Carne
Gerrans Bay
Penhalvaen
Stithians
Burnthouse
Mylor Bridge
St Just in Roseland
Trewithian
Nare Hd.
Penmarth
Stithians Res.
Carrick Roads
Gerrans
Portscatho
Burras
Carnkie
Penryn
Flushing
Rame
Longdowns
Mabe Burnthouse
Falmouth
St Mawes
Greeb Pt.
Releath
Porkellis
ART GALLERY
NATIONAL MARITIME
Bohortha
POLDARK MINE
Budock Water
PENDENNIS CASTLE
Pendennis Pt.
Wendron
Seworgan
Treverva
Zone Pt.
Penjerrick
Falmouth Bay
Constantine
Mawnan Smith
Trewennack
Porth Navas
GLENDURGAN
Rosemullion Hd.
Helston
Helford Passage
TREBAH
Mawnan
Helford River
Gweek
NATIONAL SEAL SANCTUARY
FLAMBARDS EXPERIENCE
Helford
St Anthony
Nare Pt.
Mawgan
Manaccan
SW
Garras
St Martins
HALLIGGYE FOGOU
TRELOWARREN
Newtown
Tregidden
Porthallow
Berepper
Gunwalloe
Porthoustock
Cury
Cross Lanes
St Keverne
Manacle Pt.
GOONHILLY SATELLITE EARTH STATION
Traboe
The Manacles
Lowland Pt.
Mullion
Goonhilly Downs
Penhale
THE LIZARD
Trelan
Coverack
COVERACK
Mullion Cove
Mullion Island
Gwenter
Chynhalls Pt.
Kuggar
Predannack Wollas
Black Hd.
St Ruan
Ruan Minor
Vellan Hd.
Grade
Cadgwith
Kynance Cove
Lizard
Llandewednock
Hot Pt.
LIZARD POINT
LIZARD
CORNWALL
A30
A39
A390
A394
A3075
A3076
A3058
A3078
A3083
A3047
B3285
B3284
B3277
B3298
B3289
B3291
B3293
B3294
B3296
B3297
B3280
B3301
B3275
B3279
B3274
B3273
B3287
5
6
7
8
9
A
B
C
D
E
F

C O R N W A L L
Tintagel Hd.
Start Pt.
SOUTH WEST COAST PATH
Port Isaac Bay
Port Isaac
Port Gaverne
Port Quin
Port Quin Bay
Pentire Pt.
New Polzeath
Padstow Bay
Long Cross
Trelights
Pendoggett
Gulland Rock
Polzeath
Trebetherick
St Endellion
Trelill
Gunver Hd.
St Minver
TREVOSE HEAD
Crugmeer
Pityme
Trewethern
St Kew
St Kew Highway
Chapel Amble
Trevone
Prideaux Place
Rock
Treyarnon Bay
Constantine Bay
St Merryn
Padstow
Camel
Treyarnon
Shop
Bodieve
Trevanson
St Mabyn
Wadebridge
Little Petherick
Whitecross
Porthcothan
St Issey
St Breock
Egloshayle
Pencarrow House
Park Hd.
Penrose
St Ervan
Rumford
Tredinnick
Burlawn
Rare Breeds Centre
St Jidgey
Washaway
Crealy Great Adventure Park
St. Breock Downs Monolith
208
St Eval
Trenance
Cornish Birds of Prey Centre
Spirit of the West
Nanstallon
Berryl's Pt.
Ruthernbridge
Trevarrian
St Mawgan
Rosenannon
St Lawrence
Talskiddy
Withiel
Watergate Bay
Tregurrian
St Wenn
Newquay
St Columb Major
Tregonetha
Lanivet
Towan Hd.
Newquay Bay
Porth
St Columb Minor
Castle an Dinas
227
Fistral Bay
Belowda
Victoria
Pentire
Animal World
Colan
Trebudannon
Springfields Fun Park & Pony Centre
Lockengate
Kelsey Hd.
Sea Life Centre
Quintrell Downs
Mountjoy
Ruthvoes
Tregoss
West Pentire
Crantock
Trevarren
Goss Moor
Roche
Bilberry
Lane
Kestle Mill
St Columb Road
Indian Queens
Trezaise
Penhale Pt.
Holywell Bay Fun Park
Dairyland Farm World
Fraddon
Bugle
Holywell
Carines
Penhale
St Dennis
Hensbarrow
Trerice
St Enoder
Whitemoor
Downs
312
Stenalees
Ligger or Perran Bay
Cubert
Gummow's Shop
Retew
Penwithick
Penhale Sands
St Newlyn East
Treviscoe
Nanpean
Mount
Rejerrah
Lappa Valley Steam Railway
Summercourt
Carthew
Trethurgy
Rose
Perran Round
Newlyn Downs
Trethosa
Foxhole
Wheal Martyn China Clay Her. Centre
Eden Project
Perranporth
Mitchell
Brighton
Carclaze
Boscoppa
Goonhavern
World in Miniature
Carland Cross
High Street
St Austell
Bolingey
Trelassick
St Stephen
Holmbush
Perranzabuloe
Zelah
Trewoon
St Agnes Hd.
Trevellas
New Mills
Coombe
St Mewan
Charlestown
St Agnes
Mithian
St Allen
St Erme
Ladock
Grampound Road
Polgooth
St Austell Brewery
Porthpean
Leisure Park
Callestick
Trispen
Sticker
192
Goonbell
Cornish Cyder Farm
Marazanvose
Hewas Water
Tortoise Garden
Trenarren
Allet
Probus
Porthtowan
Mount Hawke
Shortlanesend
Grampound
Trewithen
Black Head
Pentewan
Probus Gdns.
Three Burrows
Tresillian
Creed
The Lost Gardens of Heligan
Mevagissey Bay
Blackwater
St Ewe
Portreath
Mawla
Truro
Kenwyn
Tresawle
Polmassick
Kestle
World of Model Railway
Tolgus Tin
Cathedral
Merther
Mevagissey
Illogan
Scorrier
Chacewater
Threemilestone
Tregony
Portmellon
Cornish Mines & Engines
Royal Cornwall Museum
St Day
Baldhu
Kea
St Clement
Trevarrick
Chapel Pt.
Ruan Lanihorne
Gorran Churchtown
Redruth
Twelve Heads
Malpas
St Michael Caerhays
Gorran Haven
Pool
Bissoe
St Michael Penkevil
Old Kea
Lamorran
Tuckingmill
Cambrea
Playing Place
Portholland
Boswinger
Carnkie
Gwennap Pit
Carharrack
Carnon Downs
Treworga
Penare
Gwennap
Trelissick
Philleigh
114
Camborne
Lanner
Perranarworthal
Penpol
Veryan
Portloe
Veryan Bay
Shire Horse Farm
Four Lanes
Devoran
Feock
Treworlas
Dodman Pt.
Troon
Ponsanooth
Carne
Penhalvaen
Gerrans Bay
252
Stithians
Burnthouse
Trewithian
Nare Hd.
Stithians Res.
Mylor Bridge
St Just in Roseland
Penmarth
Carrick Roads
Gerrans
Portscatho
Burras
Penryn
Flushing
Crowan
Carnkie
Falmouth
St Mawes
Greeb Pt.
Relea
National Maritime Museum
Bohortha
Nancegollan
Pendennis Castle
Wendron
Seworgan
Treverva
Pendennis Pt.
Zone Pt.
0 1 2 3 4 5 6 miles
0 1 2 3 4 5 6 7 8 9 10 km
SW
A39
A30
A390
A392
A3059
A3058
A3075
A3076
A3078
A389
A393
A394
A3047
B3276
B3274
B3275
B3279
B3284
B3285
B3277
B3298
B3289
B3292
B3297
B3280
B3303
B3301
B3287
B3273
B3314
B3267
1 2 3 4 5
A B C D E F

Tintagel
Treknow
Trewarmett
Trebarwith
Delabole
Valley Truckle
Helstone
Camelford
THE ARTHURIAN CENTRE
Davidstow
Trewassa
Tremail
Davidstow Moor
Crowdy Res.
Hallworthy
Treneglos
Tremaine
Tresmeer
Tregeare
Cold Northcott
St Clether
Laneast
Piper's Pool
TRETHORNE LEISURE FARM
Trewen
Tregadillett
North Petherwin
Bridgetown
Werrington
Yeolmbridge
Egloskerry
Langore
St Stephen's
Dutson
Launceston
LAUNCESTON STEAM RAILWAY
CASTLE
Daw's House
South Petherwin
Liftondown
Lifton
Tinhay
Broadwoodwidger
Cross Green
Stowford
DINGLE'S STEAM VILLAGE
Portgate
Thrushelton
Lewdown
Chillaton
Kelly
Lawhitton
Bradstone
Milton Abbot
Dunterton
Polyphant
Altarnun
Lewannick
High Moor
Trewint
BROWN WILLY
Michaelstow
Codda
GARROW TOR
St Breward
Row
St Tudy
MUSEUM OF SMUGGLING
Bolventor
BODMIN MOOR
Bradford
Wenfordbridge
Blisland
Dozmary Pool
COLLIFORD LAKE
Colliford Lake
Temple
KILMAR TOR
Henwood
Congdon's Shop
Trebartha
North Hill
Bathpool
Rilla Mill
Upton Cross
Lezant
Trekenner
Trebullett
Treburley
Coad's Green
Rezare
Sydenham Damerel
Bray Shop
Stoke Climsland
Horsebridge
Luckett
Latchley
Linkinhorne
South Hill
Downgate
Kelly Bray
KIT HILL
Chilsworthy
Gunnislake
Gulworthy
St Ann's Chapel
Drakewalls
Albaston
Golberdon
Haye
Callington
DUPATH WELL HOUSE
Harrowbarrow
MORWELL QUAY
COTEHELE
Calstock
St Dominick
TAMAR VALLEY
Bere Alston
Weir Quay
Helland
Millpool
Maidenwell
THE HURLERS STONE CIRCLE
Minions
Siblyback Lake
CARADON HILL
Darite
Commonmoor
GOLITHA FALLS
TRETHEVY QUOIT
Tremar
Pensilva
Trevigro
Bodmin Forest
Bodmin
BODMIN
BODMIN AND WENFORD RAILWAY
Cardinham
Warleggan
Mount
St Neot
KING DONIERT'S STONE
St Cleer
CARNGLAZE SLATE CAVERNS
Ley
DOBWALLS ADVENTURE PARK
Dobwalls
Merrymeet
Gang
St Ive
Newbridge
Pengover Green
Quethiock
St Mellion
Fowey
LANHYDROCK HOUSE
Trebyan
West Taphouse
East Taphouse
Doublebois
St Pinnock
Liskeard
Menheniot
Blunts
Pillaton
Hatt
Cargreen
Landulph
Botusfleming
SALTASH SERVICES
Tamerton Foliot
Sweethouse
Redmoor
RESTORMEL CASTLE
Braddock
Lostwithiel
Herodsfoot
St Keyne
MUSIC MACHINES
Tideford Cross
Landrake
Tideford
Trematon
Saltash
Lanlivery
Couch's Mill
Trewidland
Trerulefoot
Widegates
Hessenford
St Erney
St Stephens
MARY NEWMAN'S COTTAGE
St Budeaux
Luxulyan
Milltown
Duloe
Bocaddon
Lerryn
Lanreath
Sandplace
Morval
Polbathic
St Germans
ANTONY HOUSE
Penpillick
Muchlarnick
Pelynt
St Martin
Seaton
Sheviock
Crafthole
Antony
Torpoint
Devonport
St Blazey
GOLANT
Golant
St Veep
Penpoll
Tywardreath
Par
Lanteglos Highway
Trenewan
Looe
East Looe
CORNISH MUSEUM
West Looe
Looe Bay
Downderry
Portwrinkle
St John
Cremyll
SOUTH WEST COAST PATH
Whitsand Bay
Freathy
Millbrook
MOUNT EDGCUMBE
SHIPWRECK & HERITAGE CENTRE
Polkerris
Menabilly
ST. CATHERINE'S CASTLE
Fowey
Bodinnick
Polruan
Lansallos
Portballow
Polperro
Talland Bay
St George's or Looe I.
Kingsand
Cawsand
Rame
ST. AUSTELL BAY
Gribbin Hd.
Pencarrow Hd.
Rame Hd.
Penlee Pt.
ROSCOFF 6:00
SANTANDER 18:00
(Mar-Nov)
Cornwall
SX
TOLL
A30
A39
A38
A390
A395
A388
A387
A374
A3082
B3266
B3262
B3263
B3314
B3267
B3254
B3257
B3362
B3268
B3269
B3359
B3252
B3251
B3253
B3247
B3249
B3271
A
B
C
D
E
F
5
6
7
8
9

Broadwoodwidger
Cross Green
Bridestowe
Bridestowe and Sourton Common
BLACK-A-TOR COPSE
621 HIGH WILLHAYS
Gidleigh
Murchington
Sandypark
Easton
Thrushelton
Stowford
DINGLE'S STEAM VILLAGE
Lewdown
Lewtrenchard
Portgate
Shortacombe
566 OKEMENT HILL
585
604 HANGINGSTONE HILL
Teigncombe
Chagford
Frenchbeer
Dutson
LAUNCESTON STEAM RAILWAY
Liftondown
Lifton
Tinhay
Lydford
LYDFORD
DARTMOOR
Lettaford
THE MINIATURE PONY CENTRE
Coryton
LYDFORD GORGE
Black Down
Lawhitton
North Brentor
Willsworthy
604 CUT HILL
537 SITTAFORD TOR
Kelly
Chillaton
GRIMSPOUND
Bradstone
DARTMOOR
529 HAMELDOWN TOR
Milton Abbot
Mary Tavy
Horndon
546 ROUGH TOR
Postbridge
Dunterton
Cudliptown
HOUND TOR
Trekenner
Rezare
NATIONAL
FOREST
Bellever
BELLEVER (Dartmoor)
Bonehill
Peter Tavy
WISTMAN'S WOOD
Widecombe in the Moor
Sydenham Damerel
Lamerton
Wilminstone
539 GT. MIS TOR
PREHISTORIC SETTLEMENT
Merrivale
Two Bridges
Stoke Climsland
Horsebridge
Rundlestone
431
Ponsworthy
Luckett
Latchley
Tavistock
HIGH MOORLAND VISITOR CENTRE
Princetown
W. Dart
Dartmeet
Downgate
Whitchurch
Sampford Spiney
Hexworthy
Buckland in the Moor
Chilsworthy
Gulworthy
Gunnislake
TOLL
Grenofen
PARK
Poundsgate
Kelly Bray
333 KIT HILL
St Ann's Chapel
Higher Walreddon
Whiteworks
RIVER DART ADVENTURES
Haye
KIT HILL
Drakewalls
Albaston
Callington
Harrowbarrow
MORWELLHAM QUAY
Horrabridge
Walkhampton
Holne
DUPATH WELL HOUSE
COTEHELE
Calstock
Buckland Monachorum
GARDEN HOUSE
PAPERWEIGHT CENTRE
Dousland
Burrator Res.
515 RYDER'S HILL
BUCKFAST ABBEY
Buckfast
St Dominick
TAMAR
Crapstone
Yelverton
Sheepstor
Dev
Newbridge
Meavy
Buckfastleigh
Bere Alston
BUCKLAND ABBEY
UPPER PLYM VALLEY
VALLEY
Milton Combe
St Mellion
Weir Quay
Clearbrook
SX
Dean
Lopwell
Plym
493
Pillaton
Dean Prior
Cargreen
Bere Ferrers
Shaugh Prior
475 SHELL TOP
Ugborough Moor
Hatt
Landulph
Bickleigh
464
Didworthy
Botusfleming
Tamerton Foliot
Roborough
Wotter
Lee Moor
DENDLES WOOD
311
Ratte
Landrake
SALTASH SERVICES
PLYMOUTH CITY
CROWNHILL FORT
Plym Forest
South Brent
Tideford
Trematon
TOLL
Crownhill
Drakeland Corner
Lutton
Cornwood
371
Saltash
St Erney
Harford
UGBOROUGH BEACON
Cheston
St Stephens
St Budeaux
Plymouth
DARTMOOR WILDLIFE PARK AND FALCONRY CENTRE
229
Lincombe
MARY NEWMAN'S COTTAGE
Eggbuckland
Sparkwell
Bittaford
Avonwick
St Germans
PLYM VALLEY RAILWAY
Diptford
ANTONY HOUSE
MERCHANT'S HOUSE
Plympton
Lee Mill
Ivybridge
North Huish
St. Germans R.
Ferry
Sheviock
Torpoint
Plymouth
Ugborough
Crafthole
Antony
Devonport
SALTRAM
Curtisknowle
Portwrinkle
Cremyll
ROYAL CITADEL
Elburton
Westlake
St John
Plymstock
Ermington
Brownston
SOUTH WEST COAST PATH
MOUNT EDGCUMBE
Drake's I.
Brixton
118
Yealmpton
Modbury
Freathy
Millbrook
Hooe
Whitsand Bay
MOUNT EDGCUMBE
The Sound
Staddiscombe
Kingsand
Holbeton
Cawsand
Bovisand Bay
Down Thomas
Luson
Rame
Knighton
Loddiswell
Woodleigh
Penlee Pt.
Heybrook Bay
Wembury
Newton Ferrers
Battisborough Cross
Aveton Gifford
St Ann's Chapel
Rame Hd.
Wembury Bay
Noss Mayo
Mothecombe
Kingston
Great Mew Stone
Worswell
SOUTH WEST COAST PATH
SORLEY TUNNEL ADVENTURE WORLDS
Bigbury
Ringmore
Stoke Pt.
Churchstow
E
Bigbury on Sea
Burgh I.
West Alvington
BIGBURY BAY
Bantham
Buckland
Kingsbridge
5
ROSCOFF 6:00
SANTANDER 18:00
(Mar-Nov)
Thurlestone
South Milton
Woolston
Galmpton
Hope
Bolt Tail
Bolberry
Salcombe
Soar
SALCOMBE
Portlemouth
OVERECK MUSEUM & GARDEN
F
Bolt Hd.
SOUTH
0 1 2 3 4 5 6 miles
0 1 2 3 4 5 6 7 8 9 10 km
A30
A386
A388
A390
A38
A374
A379
A381
A3121
B3212
B3357
B3362
B3257
B3271
B3249
B3247
B3413
B3373
B3432
B3417
B3213
B3186
B3392
B3196
B3197
B3206
B3387
9
5
1
2
3
4
5
A
B
C
D

Dunsford
Steps Bridge (Dartmoor)
Shillingford St George
Alphington
Exeter
Adventure Park
Woodbury Salterton
Clyst St George
Newton Poppleford
Sidmouth
Moretonhampstead
Doccombe
Bridford
Bridfordmills
Doddiscombsleigh
Exminster
Kennford
Kenn
Topsham
Ebford
Exton
Woodbury
Colaton Raleigh
Bicton Park
Yettington
Black Hill
Otterton
Ladram Bay
Christow
Higher Ashton
Lower Ashton
Powderham
Powderham Castle
Kenton
Lympstone
A la Ronde
Withycombe Raleigh
Knowle
East Budleigh
Otterton Mill
South West Coast Path
Budleigh Salterton
Danger Pt.
Lustleigh
Manaton
Water
Trusham
Devon & Exeter
Starcross
Littleham
Fairlynch Arts Centre and Museum
Hennock
Cockwood
Exmouth
World of Country Life
Dawlish Warren
Exmouth Model Railway
Straight Pt.
East Dartmoor Woods & Heaths
Bovey Tracey
Chudleigh
Ashcombe
Chudleigh Knighton
Craft Centre
Dawlish Warren
Brimley
Haytor Vale
Ilsington
Heathfield
Ideford
Luton
Little Haldon
Dawlish
Liverton
Stover
Coldeast
Trago Mills
Preston
Holcombe
Sigford
Teigngrace
Bishopsteignton
Teignmouth
Kingsteignton
Bickington
Highweek
Newton Abbot
Shaldon
Shaldon Wildlife Trust
Newton Abbot
Bradley
Combeinteignhead
South West Coast Path
Ashburton
West Ogwell
Wolborough
Netherton
Stokeinteignhead
Plant World
East Ogwell
Prickly Ball Hedgehog Hospital
Babbacombe Bay
Woodland
Denbury
Abbotskerswell
Coffinswell
Kingskerswell
Maidencombe
Forder Grn.
Torbryan
Ipplepen
North Whilborough
Barton
Watcombe
Landscove
Butterfly Farm & Otter Sanctuary
Broadhempston
Model Village
Babbacombe
SX
SY
Shiphay
Compton
Compton Castle
Torquay
Staverton
Cockington
Torre
Torre Abbey
Kent's Cavern Prehistoric Caves
Dartington
Littlehempston
Wellswood
Hope's Nose
Dartington Hall Gardens
Marldon
Cockington
Living Coasts
Berry Pomeroy Castle
Oldway Mansion
Hollicombe
Shinner's Bridge
South Devon Railway
Blagdon
Torbay
Cott
Totnes
Berry Pomeroy
Kirkham
Paignton
Castle
Paignton & Dartmouth Steam Railway
Tigley
Belsford
Motor Museum
Collaton St Mary
Torbay
Zoological & Botanical Gardens
Tor Bay
Harberton
Goodrington
Ashprington
Stoke Gabriel
Brixham
Berry Head
Harbertonford
Aquarium
Churston Ferrers
Berry Head
Galmpton
Tuckenhay
Cornworthy
Crabadon
St Mary's Bay
Washbourne
Dittisham
River Dart
Sharkham Pt.
Halwell
Allaleigh
Capton
Hillhead
Moreleigh
Woodland Leisure Park
Dartmouth
Newcomen Engine House
Woodford
Blackawton
Kingswear
Scabbacombe Hd.
Millcombe
Bayards Cove Fort
Warfleet
Coleton Fishacre
Bowden
Dartmouth Castle
Mew Stone
East Allington
Stoke Fleming
Blackpool
Strete
Goveton
South West Coast Path
Harleston
Slapton
Sherford
Frittiscombe
Slapton Ley
Frogmore
Stokenham
Chillington
Slapton Sands
Charleton
Torcross
Kernborough
Beeson
South Pool
Beesands
Kellaton
Hallsands
South Allington
Start Point
Start Bay
East Prawle
Lannacombe Bay
Prawle Pt.
Devon
A
B
C
D
E
F
5
6
7
8
9

1
2
3
4
5
A
B
C
D
E
F
LUNDY 1:30
BIDEFORD
NORTH
HARTLAND POINT
Windbury Pt.
Titchberry
CLOVELLY VILLAGE
Clovelly
Hartland Quay
Stoke
Hartland
B3248
Higher Clovelly
SOUTH WEST COAST PATH
Philham
Milford
Buck's Cross
Eddistone
THE MILKY WAY AND NORTH DEVON BIRD OF PREY CENTRE
ELMSCOTT
Elmscott
Tosberry
Woolfardisworthy
South Hole
Hartland Forest
Alminstone Cross
Knaps Longpeak
Welcombe
235
Meddon
Ashmansworthy
Woolley
Gooseham
156
Eastcott
Youlstone
Morwenstow
KILLARNEY SPRINGS FAMILY LEISURE PARK
Dinworthy
Higher Sharpnose Pt.
Shop
A39
Bradworthy
Woodford
BROCKLANDS ADVENTURE PARK
Lower Sharpnose Pt.
Bradworthy Cross
14
Alfardisworthy
Coombe
Kilkhampton
Sutcombe
Stibb
Soldon Cross
Strat
DUNSDON
BUDE
Poughill
Hersham
Flexbury
Grimscott
Bude Haven
1643
Stratton
THORNE MANOR
Chilsworthy
Bude
SS
BAY
Launcells
A3072
9
Pancrasweek
Holsworthy
Upton
B3254
Tamar
Derril
Derriton
Marhamchurch
Bridgerule
Widemouth Bay
Pyworthy
162
Chasty
Widemouth Sand
Budd's Titson
Leworthy
Coppathorne
Millook
Dizzard Pt.
Poundstock
Whitstone
SOUTH WEST COAST PATH
Treskinnick Cross
Tregole
North Tamerton
St Genny's
Week St Mary
Trewint
PENHALLAM
Tetcott
Cambeak
Crackington Haven
Rosecare
Lana
Jacobstow
SX
Wainhouse Corner
Luffincott
CORNWALL
Tresparrett Posts
South Wheatley
West Curry
Fire Beacon Pt.
260
B3263
Beeny
A39
Maxworthy
BOSCASTLE HARBOUR
Tresparrett
Marshgate
Bennacott
Northcott
Boyton
Canworthy Water
Boscastle
Brazacott
Otterham
256
Trevalga
Lesnewth
Warbstow
Langdon
Trelash
TAMAR OTTER SANCTUARY
CASTLE
Tremaine
Bridgetown
Tintagel Hd.
OLD POST OFFICE
TINTAGEL
Bossiney
North Petherwin
B3262
Ottery
Tintagel
B3266
Hallworthy
Treneglos
Werrington
308
Davidstow
Yeolmbridge
Treknow
Trewarmett
Tresmeer
B3263
Trewassa
Tremail
13
Egloskerry
Langore
Start Pt.
THE ARTHURIAN CENTRE
Tregeare
St Stephen's
Dutson
Trebarwith
Davidstow Moor
Cold Northcott
B3314
A395
Piper's Pool
Treligga
Launceston
SOUTH WEST COAST PATH
Delabole
Camelford
St Clether
Laneast
Tregadillett
A30
CASTLE
Crowdy Res.
Trewen
Port Isaac Bay
Valley Truckle
TRETHORNE LEISURE FARM
Daw's House
B3254
A388
B3314
B3267
Polyphant
Helstone
Port Quin Bay
Port Isaac
Inny
South Petherwin
Port Quin
Port Gaverne
St Teath
400 ROUGH TOR
High Moor
Altarnun
Lewannick
B3267
LONG CROSS
Trelights
Pendoggett
420 BROWN WILLY
Trewint
B3257
Lezant
369
A30
Polzeath
Michaelstow
Codda
Congdon's Shop
Trekenner
331 GARROW TOR
BODMIN
Trebullett
St Breward
MUSEUM OF SMUGGLING
Trebartha
Cad's Green
Treburley
Pityme
Row
Bolventor
North Hill
B3254
B3257
Chapel
St Kew
MOOR
0 1 2 3 4 5 6 miles
0 1 2 3 4 5 6 7 8 9 10 km

LUNDY 2:15
Braunton Burrows
Chivenor
Barnstaple
Goodleigh
Brayford
High Bray
North Heasley
South Radworthy
Pilton
MUSEUM OF NORTH DEVON
Gunn
West Buckland
Charles
Heasley Mill
Fremington
Bickington
Westacott
Yelland
Bickleton
Newport
Landkey
East Buckland
NORTH DEVON MARITIME MUSEUM
Instow
Bishops Tawton
Swimbridge Newland
NORTH DEVON FARM PARK
Swimbridge
NORTHAM BURROWS
Appledore
Westward Ho!
Northam
Tawstock
North Molton
BAY
DEVON
Westleigh
Filleigh
Orchard Hill
Horwood
Newton Tracey
Eastleigh
THE BIG SHEEP
Bideford
Herner
Cobbaton
QUINCE HONEY FARM
Abbotsham
BURTON GALL. & MUS.
East-the-Water
Ensis
East Stowford
Hiscott
Chapelton
COBBATON COMBAT COLL.
Chittlehampton
South Molton
Bish Mill
Handy Cross
Woodtown
Alverdiscott
Fishleigh Barton
Fairy Cross
ATLANTIC VILLAGE
Landcross
Buck's Mills
Horns Cross
Ford
Woodtown
Umberleigh
Clapworthy
Bishops Nympton
Littleham
Yarnscombe
Atherington
Warkleigh
Alswear
Goldsworthy
Langridge Ford
Satterleigh
George Nympton
Weare Giffard
Chittlehamholt
Marian
Parkham
Buckland Brewer
Monkleigh
High Bullen
Sherwood Green
High Bickington
Parkham Ash
DARTINGTON CRYSTAL
Romansleigh
Frithelstock
St Giles in the Wood
King's Nympton
Frithelstock Stone
Great Torrington
Taddiport
Kingscott
Roborough
Tythecott
Cadbury Barton
R.H.S. GARDEN ROSEMOOR
Week
West Putford
East Putford
Little Torrington
Burrington
Elstone
THE PIXIE KILN & GALLERY
Langtree
Beaford
Bulkworthy
Stibb Cross
Riddlecombe
Chulmleigh
Cheldon
West Worlington
Peters Marland
Ashreigney
Abbots Bickington
Newton St Petrock
Woollaton
Winswell
Merton
Huish
Dolton
Chawleigh
Venn Green
Milton Damerel
Ashley
Hollocombe
Filleigh
Torridge
Buckland Filleigh
Dowland
Petrockstow
Wembworthy
Easting
Holsworthy Beacon
Shebbear
Thornbury
Meeth
Iddesleigh
Winkleigh
Coldridge
Brushford
Lapford
Nymet Rowland
Woodacott
Bradford
Sheepwash
Broadwood Kelly
Black Torrington
Cookbury
Holemoor
Monkokehampton
West Leigh
East Leigh
Bondleigh
Highampton
Hatherleigh
Brandis Corner
Zeal Monachorum
Down St Mary
Whimble
Hollacombe
Graddon Moor
Honeychurch
Chilla
WINSFORD WALLED GARDEN
Exbourne
Jacobstowe
North Tawton
Bow
Halwill Junction
Sampford Courtenay
Nymet Tracey
Colebrooke
Halwill
Beaworthy
Northlew
Inwardleigh
Itton
Clawton
Oak Cross
Hillerton
DARTMOOR RAILWAY
Quoditch
Patchacott
Ashbury
Folly Gate
Taw Green
Spreyton
BROADBURY
Ashwater
Okehampton
Eworthy
Sticklepath
South Tawton
Henford
Germansweek
FINCH FOUNDRY
South Zeal
Boasley Cross
Thorndon Cross
Chapmans Well
Virginstow
Belstone
Whiddon Down
Cheriton Bishop
OKEHAMPTON (Dartmoor)
CASTLE
Okehampton Camp
Roadford Res.
SOURTON CROSS SERVICES
East Panson
Grinacombe Moor
Meldon
Bratton Clovelly
Okehampton Common
COSDON HILL
Throwleigh
Drewsteignton
St Giles on the Hth
CASTLE DROGO
Gridley Corner
YES TOR
Sourton
Bridestowe
Wonson
Sandypark
Broadwoodwidger
BLACK-A-TOR COPSE
HIGH WILLHAYS
Teign
Easton
Gidleigh
Murchington
Bridestowe and Sourton Common
SX
Cross Green
Thrushelton
Chagford
Stowford
DINGLE'S STEAM VILLAGE
Lewdown
OKEMENT HILL
Teigncombe
Shortacombe
DARTMOOR
Liftondown
Lewtrenchard
Frenchbeer
Portgate
HANGINGSTONE HILL
Lifton
Tinhay
Lydford
LYDFORD CASTLE
Lettaford
THE MINIATURE PONY CENTRE
North Bovey
Coryton
LYDFORD GORGE
NATIONAL
CUT HILL
SITTAFORD TOR
Lawhitton
North Brentor
Black Down
Willsworthy
Manaton
Kelly
Chillaton
GRIMSPOUND
Bradstone
HAMELDOWN TOR
PARK
Milton Abbot
Mary Tavy
Horndon
ROUGH TOR
Postbridge
Dunterton
Cudliptown
HOUND TOR
Rezare
Bellever
Bonehill
Haytor Vale
Lamerton
Peter Tavy
FOREST
Widecombe in the Moor
Sydenham Damerel
Wilminstone
GT. MIS TOR
WISTMAN'S WOOD
BELLEVER (Dartmoor)
Merrivale
PREHISTORIC SETTLEMENT
A39
A386
A388
A3072
A3079
A3124
A377
A361
A30
A382
B3227
B3232
B3217
B3226
B3096
B3042
B3220
B3215
B3206
B3212
B3362
B3387
B3233

Brayford
High Bray
Radworthy
North Heasley
Heasley Mill
South Radworthy
Winsford
Exton
Liscombe
Bridgetown
Brompton Regis
Withiel Florey
Clatworthy Res.
West Buckland
Charles
East Buckland
Molland Common
Twitchen
Hawkridge
Wimbleball Lake
North Molton
Anstey Common
West Anstey
Molland
Dulverton
Upton
Huish Champflower
Filleigh
Haddon Hill
Heydon Hill
Quince Honey Farm
East Anstey
Battleton
Skilgate
Chipstable
East Stowford
Chittlehampton
South Molton
Bish Mill
Newtown
Yeo Mill
Nightcott
Brushford
Bury
Morebath
Petton
Oldways End
Exebridge
Clapworthy
Bishops Nympton
Ash Mill
Knowstone
Roachill
Bampton
Shillingford
Clayhanger
Satterleigh
George Nympton
Alswear
Mariansleigh
Rose Ash
Oakfordbridge
Oakford
Romansleigh
Meshaw
Huntsham
King's Nympton
Creacombe
Stoodleigh Beacon
Cove
Stoodleigh
Hockworthy
Rackenford
Cadbury Barton
Week
Queen Dart
Elstone
Lutworthy
Little Dart
Loxbeare
Washfield
East Mere
Chevithorne
Whitnage
Templeton Bridge
Exe Valley
Knightshayes Court
Uplowman
Chulmleigh
Witheridge
Bolham
Chettiscombe
Cheldon
West Worlington
East Worlington
Drayford
Nomansland
Templeton
Calverleigh
Tiverton Castle
Halberton
Sampford Peverell
Cowleymoor
Grand Western Canal
Withleigh
Chawleigh
Thelbridge Barton
Washford Pyne
Cruwys Morchard
Cotteylands
Tiverton
Ashley
Pennymoor
Ash Thomas
Black Dog
Way Village
Filleigh
Dalch
Puddington
Well Town
Willand
Wembworthy
Eastington
Diggerland
Poughill
Cullompton Services
Morchard Bishop
Woolfardisworthy
Cadeleigh
Butterleigh
Brushford
Coldridge
Nymet Rowland
Lapford
Upham
Devonshire's Centre
Bickleigh Mill
Cullompton
Kennerleigh
Stockleigh English
Bickleigh Castle
Bickleigh
Devon Railway Centre
Oldborough
West Leigh
Cheriton Fitzpaine
Ash Bullayne
East Village
Cadbury
Colebrook
East Leigh
Fursdon House
Bradninch
Mutterton
Westcott
Zeal Monachorum
Down St Mary
Newbuildings
Stockleigh Pomeroy
Copplestone
Sandford
Upton Hellions
Silverton
Thorverton
Up Exe
Hele
Langford
Clyst Hydon
North Tawton
Bow
Knowle
Ellerhayes
The Collegiate Church of the Holy Cross
Shobrooke
Efford
Shute
Nether Exe
Nymet Tracey
Coleford
Clyst St Lawrence
Colebrooke
Crediton
Killerton House
Itton
Budlake
Westwood
Sweetham
Brampford Speke
Rewe
Hillerton
Yeoford
Uton
Hookway
Newton St Cyres
Stoke Canon
Broadclyst
Venny Tedburn
Upton Pyne
Spreyton
Poltimore
Whimple
Cowley
Dog Village
Jack in the Green
Hittisleigh
Tedburn St Mary
Pinhoe
Rockbeare
South Tawton
Clyst Honiton
South Zeal
Exwick
Whipton
Exeter International
Whiddon Down
Whitestone
Cheriton Bishop
Cathedral
Marsh Green
Crockernwell
Exeter
Heavitree
Sowton
Exeter Services
Aylesbeare
Bowhill
Drewsteignton
Longdown
Wheatley
St Thomas
Clyst St Mary
Farringdon
Throwleigh
Castle Drogo
Countess Wear
Crealy Adventure Park
Wonson
Sandypark
Ide
Alphington
Exeter
Woodbury Salterton
Teign
Easton
Dunsford
Clyst St George
Gidleigh
Murchington
Shillingford St George
Topsham
Steps Bridge (Dartmoor)
Ebford
Woodbury
Chagford
Doccombe
Exminster
Teigncombe
Bridfordmills
Kenn
Kennford
Exton
Moretonhampstead
Bridford
Doddiscombsleigh
Frenchbeer
Christow
Higher Ashton
Kenn
Powderham
Black Hill
Lympstone
A La Ronde
Lettaford
The Miniature Pony Centre
North Bovey
Lower Ashton
Powderham Castle
Withycombe Raleigh
Kenton
Devon & Exeter
Trusham
Starcross
Littleham
Grimspound
Manaton
Lustleigh
Hennock
Cockwood
Exmouth
Hameldown Tor
Water
Bovey
Ashcombe
Dawlish Warren
Exmouth Model Railway
Posthridge
East Dartmoor Heaths
Bovey Tracey
Chudleigh
Chudleigh Knighton
Straight Pt.
Craft Centre
Dawlish Warren
Brimley
Heathfield
Ideford
Luton
Little Haldon
Dawlish
Ilsington
Liverton
Bell
SS
SX
M5
A361
A396
A3072
A377
A30
A382
A38
A380
A379
A376
B3227
B3222
B3190
B3137
B3226
B3042
B3096
B3220
B3212
B3206
B3193
B3344
B3192
B3181
B3179
B3178
B3052
B3180
B3224
B3387
0 1 2 3 4 5 6 miles
0 1 2 3 4 5 6 7 8 9 10 km

Wiveliscombe
VALE OF TAUNTON DEANE
Taunton
Wellington
BLACKDOWN HILLS
B L A C K D O W N H I L L S
Culm Valley
Culmstock
Hemyock
Churchstanton
Churchinford
Bishopswood
Smeatharpe
Upottery
Luppitt
Broadhembury
Dunkeswell
Sheldon
Kentisbeare
Blackborough
Payhembury
Awliscombe
Honiton
Feniton
Fenny Bridges
Ottery St Mary
Gittisham
Sidbury
Sidford
Sidmouth
Budleigh Salterton
Danger Pt.
Ladram Bay
Otterton
East Budleigh
Newton Poppleford
Colaton Raleigh
Branscombe
Beer
Beer Hd.
Seaton
Seaton Bay
Axmouth
Colyford
Colyton
Southleigh
Farway
Broad Down
Northleigh
Offwell
Wilmington
Shute
Kilmington
Axminster
Musbury
Uplyme
Lyme Regis
Charmouth
Chideock
Seatown
Eype
Bridport
Symondsbury
Morcombelake
Whitchurch Canonicorum
Ryall
Marshwood
Bettiscombe
Pilsdon
Broad Oak
Broadwindsor
Drimpton
Burstock
Birdsmoor Gate
Marshalsea
Hawkchurch
Holditch
Thorncombe
Forde Abbey and Gardens
Tytherleigh
Chardstock
South Chard
Tatworth
Forton
Winsham
Whatley
Chard
Wambrook
Wadeford
Chaffcombe
Cricket St Thomas
Hewish
Crewkerne
Misterton
Clapton
Seaborough
Wayford
Cudworth
Chillington
Cricket Malherbie
Dowlish Wake
Kingstone
Dinnington
Hinton St George
Merriott
Ilminster
Donyatt
Crock Street
Combe St Nicholas
Buckland St Mary
Horton
Broadway
Ashill
Ilton
Puckington
Stocklinch
Ashwell
Dillington House
Seavington St Michael
Seavington St Mary
Lopen
South Petherton
Barrington
Barrington Court
West Lambrook
East Lambrook
Kingsbury Episcopi
Martock
Hambridge
Westport
Isle Brewers
Isle Abbotts
Fivehead
Curry Mallet
Hatch Beauchamp
Beercrocombe
Hatch Green
Bickenhall
Staple Fitzpaine
Staple Hill
Curland
Windmill Hill
Blagdon Hill
Pitminster
Corfe
Orchard Portman
Thurlbear
Stoke St Mary
West Hatch
Henlade
Ruishton
Thornfalcon
Creech St Michael
Creech Heathfield
North Curry
Knapp
Meare Green
West Sedge Moor
Curry Rivel
Drayton
Langport
Huish Episcopi
Muchelney
Aller
High Ham
Low Ham
Othery
Pathe
Burrowbridge
Stathe
Athelney
Stoke St Gregory
Lyng
West Lyng
Durston
North Newton
Hedging
Thurloxton
North Petherton
Huntworth
Northmoor Green or Moorland
Middlezoy
King's Sedge Moor
Goathurst
Broomfield
Cothelstone
Cushuish
Kingston St Mary
Fulford
Pickney
West Monkton
Monkton Heathfield
Cheddon Fitzpaine
Staplegrove
Bathpool
Nailsbourne
Bishops Lydeard
Ash Priors
Combe Florey
East Combe
West Bagborough
Lydeard St Lawrence
Willett
Tolland
Brompton Ralph
Clatworthy
Langley Marsh
Maundown
Fitzhead
Halse
Heathfield
Preston Bowyer
Milverton
Hillcommon
Norton Fitzwarren
Oake
Hillfarance
Bishop's Hull
Bradford on Tone
East Nynehead
Nynehead
Runnington
Langford Budville
Bathealton
Waterrow
Kittisford
Appley
Thorne St Margaret
Holywell Lake
Rockwell Green
Sampford Arundel
Holcombe Rogus
Westleigh
Burlescombe
Appledore
Uffculme
Craddock
Ashill
Smithincott
Wrangway
Ford Street
Angersleigh
West Buckland
Trull
Staplehay
Nicholashayne
Clayhidon
Rosemary Lane
Stapley
Bolham Water
Abbey
Marsh
Whitestaunton
Howley
Yarcombe
Newcott
Rawridge
Beacon
Stockland
Millhayes
Heathstock
Membury
Furley
Churchill
Alston
Smallridge
Weycroft
Dalwood
Ham
Cotleigh
Monkton
Wick
Combe Raleigh
Buckerell
Colestocks
Tale
Plymtree
Norman's Green
Dulford
Kerswell
Talaton
Fairmile
Alfington
Church Green
Whitford
Combpyne
Rousdon
Harcombe
Salcombe Regis
Weston
Vicarage
Sid
Cotmaton
Bowd
Harpford
Venn Ottery
Tipton St John
Wiggaton
West Hill
Hawkerland
Yettington
Knowle
Wootton Fitzpaine
L Y M E B A Y
Charlton Bay
ST
SY
E A S T D E V O N

King's Sedge Moor
Middlezoy
Moorland
Othery
Pathe
Henley
High Ham
Burrow-bridge
Stathe
Athelney
Aller
Low Ham
Stoke St Gregory
West Sedge Moor
Langport
Curry Rivel
Huish Episcopi
Muchelney
Drayton
Fivehead
Isle Brewers
Isle Abbotts
Hambridge
Westport
West Lambrook
East Lambrook
Puckington
Ilton
Barrington
South Petherton
Stocklinch
Shepton Beauchamp
Ashwell
Ilminster
Donyatt
Dowlish Wake
Kingstone
Cricket Malherbie
Cudworth
Chaffcombe
Chillington
Hinton St George
Dinnington
Seavington St Michael
Seavington St Mary
Lopen
Over Stratton
Merriott
Crewkerne
Cricket St Thomas
Hewish
Misterton
Whatley
Winsham
Wayford
Clapton
Seaborough
Drimpton
Thorncombe
Holditch
Burstock
Broadwindsor
Birdsmoor Gate
Hawkchurch
Marshalsea
Bettiscombe
Marshwood
Pilsdon
Wootton Fitzpaine
Whitchurch Canonicorum
Ryall
Morcombelake
Charmouth
Chideock
Symondsbury
Bridport
Lyme Regis
Seatown
Eype
West Bay
Somerton
Dundon
Compton Dundon
Littleton
Pitney
Long Sutton
Kingsdon
Long Load
Stapleton
Kingsbury Episcopi
Martock
Ash
Hurst
Bower Hinton
Tintinhull
Chilthorne Domer
Stoke sub Hamdon
Montacute
Norton sub Hamdon
Odcombe
Chiselborough
West Chinnock
East Chinnock
Haselbury Plucknett
North Perrott
South Perrott
Mosterton
Chedington
Corscombe
Beaminster
Stoke Abbott
Netherbury
Melplash
Broad Oak
Salwayash
Dottery
Bradpole
Loders
Uploders
Walditch
Bothenhampton
Shipton Gorge
Burton Bradstock
Swyre
Puncknowle
West Bexington
Abbotsbury
Rodden
Langton Herring
Chickerell
Charlestown
Wyke Regis
Weymouth
Butleigh
Baltonsborough
Barton St David
Kingweston
Keinton Mandeville
Charlton Adam
Charlton Mackerell
Cary Fitzpaine
Podimore
Ilchester
Northover
Yeovilton
Limington
Ashington
Yeovil Marsh
Mudford
Yeovil
Preston Plucknett
Brympton
West Coker
North Coker
East Coker
Hardington Mandeville
Pendomer
Closworth
Hardington Marsh
Halstock
West Chelborough
Melbury Osmond
Melbury Sampford
Evershot
Rampisham
Wraxall
Hooke
Mapperton
Toller Porcorum
North Poorton
Powerstock
Nettlecombe
West Milton
Eggardon Down
Askerswell
Chilcombe
Litton Cheney
Long Bredy
Littlebredy
Portesham
Southwood
West Lydford
East Lydford
Lydford-on-Fosse
Babcary
Hornblotton Green
Sutton
Alford
Lovington
Galhampton
North Barrow
South Barrow
Sparkford
West Camel
Queen Camel
Bridgehampton
Chilton Cantelo
Marston Magna
Rimpton
Adber
Sandford Orcas
Trent
Nether Compton
Over Compton
Bradford Abbas
Stoford
Thornford
Ryme Intrinseca
Beer Hackett
Yetminster
Leigh
Chetnole
Melbury Bubb
Batcombe
Holywell
Frome St Quintin
Cattistock
Chilfrome
Maiden Newton
Toller Fratrum
Wynford Eagle
West Compton
Compton Valence
Kingston Russell
Winterbourne Abbas
Winterbourne Steepleton
Frampton
Muckleford
Ansford
Castle Cary
Cole
Pitcombe
Redlynch
Shepton Montague
Bratton Seymour
Yarlington
North Cadbury
Holton
Maperton
South Cadbury
Compton Pauncefoot
Blackford
Sutton Montis
Corton Denham
Charlton Horethorne
Stowell
Milborne Wick
Poyntington
Oborne
Sherborne
Goathill
North Wootton
Haydon
Alweston
Folke
Longburton
Lillington
Holnest
Hermitage
Hilfield
Minterne Magna
Up Cerne
Up Sydling
Sydling St Nicholas
Cerne Abbas
Nether Cerne
Godmanstone
Forston
Grimstone
Stratton
Bradford Peverell
Charminster
Dorchester
Martinstown
Winterborne Monkton
Upwey
Broadwey
Nottington
Radipole
Westham
Melcombe Regis
Rodwell
Hardway
Stoney Stoke
Charlton Musgrove
Wincanton
Bayford
Stoke Trister
Lattiford
North Cheriton
South Cheriton
Horsington
Abbas Combe
Temple Combe
Yenston
Henstridge
Henstridge Ash
Henstridge Marsh
Milborne Port
Stalbridge
Purse Caundle
Stalbridge Weston
Stourton Caundle
Bishop's Caundle
Lydlinch
Holwell
Woodbridge
King's Stag
Crouch Hill
Glanvilles Wootton
Pulham
Hazelbury Bryan
Middlemarsh
Westfields
Duntish
Mappowder
Lyon's Gate
Buckland Newton
Alton Pancras
Plush
Piddletrenthide
White Lackington
Piddlehinton
Charlton Down
Stinsford
Kingston Maurward
West Stafford
Whitcombe
Winterborne Herringston
West Knighton
Broadmayne
Bincombe
Poxwell
Littlemoor
Preston
Upton
Overcombe
Osmington
Osmington Mills
BLACKMOOR VALE
DORSET
CHESIL BEACH
Portland Harbour
West Bay
Fortuneswell
Grove
ISLE OF PORTLAND
Easton
Weston
Southwell
Bill of Portland
GUERNSEY 2:00
JERSEY 3:15
ST. MALO 5:00
ST
SY
0 1 2 3 4 5 6 miles
0 1 2 3 4 5 6 7 8 9 10 km

Stourhead
White Sheet Hill
Stourton
Mere
Zeals
Penselwood
Bourton
Queen Oak
West Knoyle
The Green
Bush Farm Bison Centre
East Knoyle
Huntingford
Milton on Stour
Cucklington
Gillingham
Elm Hill
Ham Common
Wyke
Motcombe
Buckhorn Weston
Knap Corner
West Stour
East Stour
Shaftesbury
Ivy Cross
Fifehead Magdalen
Stour Provost
Stour Row
Todber
Guy's Marsh
Cann
Cann Common
Melbury Abbas
Melbury Down
Pillwell
Marnhull
Margaret Marsh
Bedchester
Compton Abbas
Ashmore
East Orchard
West Orchard
Hinton St Mary
Manston
Fontmell Magna
Sutton Waldron
Sturminster Newton
Mill
Hammoon
Iwerne Courtney or Shroton
Iwerne Minster
Fiddleford
Fiddleford Manor
Child Okeford
Hambledon Hill
Newton
Broad Oak
Fifehead Neville
Shillingstone
Okeford Fitzpaine
Kingston
Stourpaine
Pimperne
Durweston
Ibberton
Turnworth
Woolland
Bryanston
Blandford Forum
Blandford St Mary
Stoke Wake
Higher Ansty
Winterborne Houghton
Winterborne Stickland
Winterborne Clenston
Hilton
Milton Abbey
Milton Abbas
Whatcombe
Melcombe Bingham
Charlton Marshall
Thorncombe
Spetisbury
Charlton Down
Winterborne Whitechurch
Cheselbourne
Dewlish
Winterborne Kingston
Winterborne Zelston
Milborne St Andrew
Anderson
Almer
Sturminster Marshall
Puddletown
Tolpuddle
Martyrs Museum
Bere Regis
Athelhampton
Burleston
Affpuddle
Turners Puddle
Briants Puddle
Tincleton
Lane End
Woodsford
Cloud's Hill
Moreton
Bovington Camp
Tank Museum
Monkey World
Crossways
Mill House Cider Museum
Warmwell
Owermoigne
East Burton
Wool
East Stoke
East Knighton
Winfrith Newburgh
Coombe Keynes
Holworth
Chaldon Herring or East Chaldon
Chaldon Down
South West Coast Path
West Lulworth
Lulworth Castle
East Lulworth
Lulworth Cove
Durdle Door
Lulworth Cove
Worbarrow Bay
Ringstead Bay
Bay
Berwick St Leonard
Fonthill Bishop
Hindon
Fonthill Gifford
Chilmark
Ridge
Tisbury
Newtown
Hatch
Sedgehill
Semley
Old Wardour Castle
Swallowcliffe
Ansty
Donhead St Andrew
Donhead St Mary
Milkwell
White Sheet Hill
Berwick St John
Ludwell
Charlton
Win Green
Tollard Royal
Woodcutts
Larmer Tree Victorian Pleasure Garden
Farnham
Dean
Stubhampton
Chettle
Chettle House
Tarrant Gunville
Tarrant Hinton
Tarrant Launceston
Tarrant Monkton
Royal Signals Museum
Tarrant Rawston
Tarrant Rushton
Tarrant Keyneston
Tarrant Crawford
Shapwick
Kingston Lacy
Long Crichel
Moor Crichel
Manswood
Witchampton
Gussage St Michael
Gussage All Saints
Cashmoor
Vale of Wardour
Farmer Giles Farmstead
Teffont Magna
Teffont Evias
Dinton
Chicksgrove
Baverstock
Sutton Mandeville
Fovant
Compton Chamberlayne
Cranborne Chase and West Wiltshire Downs
Prescombe Down
Fifield Bavant
West End
Ebbesbourne Wake
Alvediston
Broad Chalke
Bishopstone
Stoke Farthing
Croucheston
Mount Sorrel
Bowerchalke
Woodminton
Martin Drove End
Woodyates
Deanland
Sixpenny Handley
Pentridge
Pentridge Hill
Martin
Martin Down
Tidpit
Monkton Up Wimborne
Cranborne
Manor Gardens
Wimborne St Giles
Knowlton Church
Knowlton
Edmondsham
Cripplestyle
Edmondsham Ho.
Heavy Horse Centre
Verwood
Woodlands
Horton
Chalbury
Chalbury Common
Mannington
Hinton Martell
Gaunt's Common
Stanbridge
Holt
Holt Heath
Honeybrook Victorian Farm
Broom Hill
Clapgate
Colehill
Canford Bottom
Hillbutts
Pamphill
Walford Mill
Wimborne Minster
Hampreston
Stapehill
Knoll Gdns.
Ferndown
Longham
West Parley
Oakley
Canford Magna
Merley
Bearwood
Bear Cross
Kinson
Parley Cross
Ensbury
Corfe Mullen
East End
Hill View
Broadstone
Canford Heath
Waterloo
Newtown
Poole
Upton
Hamworthy
R.N.L.I. Mus.
Scaplen's Court Museum
Parkstone
Lilliput
Branksome
Branksome Park
Westbourne
Compton Acres
Canford Cliffs
Poole Harbour
Brownsea I.
Brownsea Island
Sandbanks
Ferry
Toll
Poole Bay
Studland Beach and Nature Reserve
Studland
Studland Bay
Studland and Godlingston Heath
Newton Heath
The Foreland
Morden
East Morden
Bloxworth
Slepe
Lytchett Matravers
Lytchett Minster
Farmer Palmer's Farm Park
Wareham Forest
Morden Bog
Holton Heath
Trigon Hill
Sandford
Northport
Wareham
Purbeck Toy Mus.
Arne
Stokeford
Stoborough
Ridge
West Holme
Stoborough Green
Stoborough Heath
Hartland Moor
Middlebere Heath
Wytch Heath
Grange Heath
The Blue Pool
Norden Heath
East Creech
Isle of Purbeck
Purbeck Hills
Corfe Castle
Church Knowle
Model Village & Gardens
Nine Barrow Down
Steeple
Tyneham
Kingston
Kimmeridge
Kimmeridge Bay
Harman's Cross
Langton Matravers
Langton Matravers Mus.
Acton
Worth Matravers
Durlston
Tilly Whim Caves
Ulwell
New Swanage
Swanage Bay
Swanage
Swanage Railway
Peveril Pt.
Durlston Head
Bournemouth
Boscombe
Pokesdown
Southbourne
Moordown
Winton
Talbot Village
Holdenhurst
Jumpers Green
The Red House Museum
Art Gall. and Mus.
Wick
Hurn
Bournemouth International
Alice in Wonderland Maze
Trickett's Cross
The Matchams Experience
St Leonards
Avon Heath
St Ives
St Leonards Services
West Moors
Ashley Heath
Three Legged Cross
Moors Valley
Ashley
Ringwood
Ringwood Forest
Blashford
Ibsley
Bickton
Fordingbridge
Alderholt
Alderholt Mill
Charing Cross
Sandleheath
Ashford
Damerham
Rockbourne
Rockbourne Down
Outwick
Roman Villa
Burgate
Upper Street
Whitsbury
Wick Down
Grovely Wood
Newton
Ditchampton
Wilton
Wilton House
Burcombe
Barford St Martin
Netherhampton
Quidhampton
Stratford sub Castle
Old Sarum
New Sarum
Salisbury
Bemerton
West Harnham
East Harnham
Coombe Bissett
Stratford Tony
Homington
Odstock
Nunton
Ebble
Nadder
Stour
Allen
Piddle or Trent
Frome
Avon
Dorset
SU
SZ
Cherbourg 4:15
Guernsey 2:30
Jersey 3:45
St. Malo 5:25
Cherbourg 2:15
(Apr-Oct)
(May-Sept)
A303
A350
A30
A354
A357
A31
A35
A338
A348
A341
A3049
A3040
A351
A352
B3081
B3092
B3091
B3095
B3089
B3082
B3078
B3072
B3073
B3074
B3075
B3068
B3069
B3070
B3071
B3351
B3390
B3059
B3347
B3369
24
14

Salisbury
Wilton
Laverstock
Milford
Britford
Alderbury
West Grimstead
Whiteparish
Downton
Fordingbridge
Cranborne
Verwood
Ringwood
Ringwood Forest
Ferndown
Bournemouth
Boscombe
CHRISTCHURCH
Mudeford
Highcliffe
New Milton
Barton on Sea
Milford on Sea
LYMINGTON
Brockenhurst
Lyndhurst
NEW FOREST MUSEUM
Totton
Southampton
SOUTHAMPTON
Romsey
Chandler's Ford
Hythe
Dibden Purlieu
Beaulieu
Blackfield
Yarmouth
Totland
Freshwater
Hampshire
NEW FOREST NATIONAL PARK
SU
SZ
POOLE BAY
Christchurch Bay
Hengistbury Head
Studland Bay
The Foreland
The Needles
Sandbanks
Swanage Bay
CHERBOURG 4:15
GUERNSEY 2:30
JERSEY 3:45
(Apr-Oct)
ST. MALO 5:25
CHERBOURG 2:15
(May-Sept)
0 1 2 3 4 5 6 miles
0 1 2 3 4 5 6 7 8 9 10 km

Kings Worthy
New Alresford
Winchester
Petersfield
Liphook
Liss
Eastleigh
Bishopstoke
Fair Oak
Bishop's Waltham
Twyford
West End
Hedge End
Botley
Wickham
Shirrell Heath
Droxford
Meonstoke
Corhampton
Exton
West Meon
Warnford
East Meon
Clanfield
Horndean
Waterlooville
Purbrook
HAVANT
Emsworth
Southbourne
Chichester
Bosham
Fareham
Portchester
Portsmouth
PORTSMOUTH
Cosham
Southsea
GOSPORT
Lee-on-the-Solent
Hill Head
Titchfield
Warsash
Fawley
Calshot
South Hayling
HAYLING ISLAND
East Wittering
West Wittering
Selsey
SELSEY BILL
CHICHESTER HARBOUR
Cowes
East Cowes
RYDE
Isle of Wight
NEWPORT
Bembridge
Sandown
Shanklin
Ventnor
Niton
Blackgang
SOLENT
SPITHEAD
Sandown Bay
Stokes Bay
HAMPSHIRE
EAST
SU
SZ
FOREST OF BERE
M27
A3(M)
M275
A27
A32
A3
A272
CAEN 6:00
CHERBOURG 4:45
LE HAVRE 7:30
ST. MALO 8:45
BILBAO 35:00
GUERNSEY 6:30
JERSEY 10:00
RADICATEL 9:00

West Sussex
SU
SZ
Haslemere
Liphook
Petersfield
Midhurst
Petworth
Billingshurst
Pulborough
Storrington
Arundel
Chichester
Bosham
Bognor Regis
Littlehampton
LITTLEHAMPTON
Rustington
Angmering
Ferring
Goring-by-Sea
West Worthing
Selsey
SELSEY BILL
East Wittering
West Wittering
Middleton-on-Sea
Grayswood
Shottermill
Hammer
Camelsdale
Linchmere
Kingsley Green
Fernhurst
Henley
Lickfold
Lodsworth
Easebourne
Halfway Bridge
Upperton
Tillington
Selham
Byworth
Fittleworth
Stopham
Coates
Coldwaltham
Watersfield
Bury
Amberley
Houghton
North Stoke
South Stoke
Burpham
Offham
Crossbush
Hammerpot
Patching
Clapham
Findon
High Salvington
Salvington
Durrington
Washington
Sullington
Rowhook
Rudgwick
Alfold
Alfold Bars
Tisman's Common
Bucks Green
Park Street
Slinfold
Broadbridge Heath
Strood Green
The Haven
Itchingfield
Five Oaks
Barns Green
Brooks Green
Coneyhurst
Shipley
Whitehall
Broomer's Corner
Goose Green
Spear Hill
Thakeham
Ashington
Wiston
Rock
Marehill
West Chiltington
Nutbourne
Hardham
Wiggonholt
Greatham
Cootham
Rackham
Parbrook
Adversane
Broadford Bridge
North Heath
Gay Street
Codmore Hill
Newpound Common
Roundstreet Common
Wisborough Green
Kirdford
Strood Green
Plaistow
Ifold
Loxwood
Mackerel's Common
Balls Cross
Northchapel
Fisherstreet
Ramsnest Common
Lurgashall
Bedham
Standford
Whitehill
Bramshott
Conford
Greatham
Empshott
Longmoor Camp
Liss Forest
Langley
West Liss
East Liss
Liss
Rake
Milland
Hill Brow
Steep Marsh
Borden
Sheet
Rogate
Chithurst
Iping
Woolbeding
Stedham
Trotton
Minsted
Dumpford
Nyewood
East Harting
Nursted
Buriton
South Harting
Elsted
Didling
Treyford
Bepton
Cocking
Heyshott
Graffham
West Lavington
South Ambersham
Duncton
East Lavington
Barlavington
Sutton
Bignor
West Burton
Upwaltham
North Marden
Compton
Up Marden
West Marden
East Marden
Chilgrove
Singleton
Charlton
East Dean
West Dean
Finchdean
Forestside
Rowlands Castle
Stoughton
Walderton
Woodend
West Stoke
Mid Lavant
East Lavant
Westbourne
Funtington
Woodmancote
East Ashling
West Ashling
Summersdale
Strettington
Halnaker
Westerton
Boxgrove
Hermitage
Hambrook
Nutbourne
Southbourne
Broadbridge
Fishbourne
Chidham
Thorney I.
West Thorney
Apuldram
Donnington
Hunston
North Mundham
South Mundham
Runcton
Merston
Colworth
Westhampnett
Tangmere
Aldingbourne
Oving
Woodgate
Nyton
Norton
Westergate
Eastergate
Fontwell
Slindon
Walberton
Tortington
Barnham
Yapton
Ford
Climping
Bilsham
Wick
Lyminster
Poling
Hangleton
East Preston
Kingston Gorse
Shripney
Flansham
North Bersted
South Bersted
Felpham
Rose Green
Aldwick
Pagham
Nyetimber
Sidlesham
Street End
Birdham
Shipton Green
West Itchenor
Acre Street
Somerley
Highleigh
Earnley
Bracklesham
Norton
Church Norton
Madehurst
Eartham
Arundel Park
CHICHESTER HARBOUR
Chichester Harbour
HOLLYCOMBE STEAM COLLECTION
BLACK DOWN
EBERNOE COMMON
PETWORTH HO.
THE BEAR MUS.
ASHFORD HANGERS
LINCH DOWN
SOUTH DOWNS WAY
ROMAN VILLA
KINGLEY VALE
WEST DEAN GARDENS
WEALD AND DOWNLAND OPEN AIR MUSEUM
GOODWOOD
GOODWOOD HOUSE
ST. ROCHE'S HILL
BOW HILL
STANSTED PARK
STANE STREET
AMBERLEY MUS.
PARHAM
KITHURST HILL
HARROW HILL
COOLHAM AIRFIELD D-DAY MEMORIAL
THE WILDFOWL AND WETLANDS CENTRE
ARUNDEL
MUSEUM AND HERITAGE CENTRE
DENMANS
FONTWELL PARK
TANGMERE AVIATION MUS.
PALLANT HOUSE
FISHBOURNE PALACE
BOSHAM WALK
SUSSEX FALCONRY CENTRE
EARNLEY BUTTERFLIES AND GARDENS
SOUTHCOAST WORLD
HARBOUR PARK
Rother
Arun
A3
A272
A283
A285
A286
A29
A24
A27
A280
A259
A284
A2032
A264
A281
B2131
B2070
B3006
B2146
B2141
B2147
B2148
B2178
B2145
B2179
B2198
B2201
B2166
B2233
B2132
B2187
B2139
B2138
B2133
B3004
27
15
Guernsey
3½ miles to 1 inch
GUERNSEY
POOLE 2:30 (Apr-Oct)
WEYMOUTH 2:00
PORTSMOUTH 6:30
SARK 0:45
ST. HELIER 2:00
ST. HELIER 0:50
ST. MALO 2:40
DIELETTE 1:15 (May-Sept)
L'Ancresse Bay
Le Plomb
La Fontenelle
Grand Havre
St Sampson
L'Islet
Cobo Bay
Vazon Bay
Le Villocq
Belle Greve Bay
Lihou I.
Mont Saint
MUSEUM & ART GALL.
BEAU SEJOUR CENTRE
St Peter Port
VICTOR HUGO'S HOUSE
CASTLE CORNET
Rocquaine Bay
THE LITTLE CHAPEL
Carmel
Fort George
Pleinmont Pt.
Mouilpied
Le Planel
La Planque
St Martin's Pt.
Pointe de la Moye
Icart Pt.
Moulin Huet Bay
Herm
SHELL BEACH
Jethou
Alderney
3½ miles to 1 inch
DIELETTE 1:00 (May-Sept)
Brehou
Quesnard Pt.
Braye
Clonque Bay
Longis Bay
St Anne
ALDERNEY
Telegraph Bay
0 1 2 3 4 5 6 miles
0 1 2 3 4 5 6 7 8 9 10 km

Horsham
Roffey
Buchan Park
Pease Pottage
Pease Pottage Services
Colgate
St Leonard's Forest
Tilgate Forest Row
The High Beeches
Balcombe Lane
Balcombe
Selsfield Common
West Hoathly
Priest House
Wakehurst Place
Sharpthorne
Highbrook
Coleman's Hatch
Wych Cross
Chelwood Gate
Ashdown Forest
Upper Hartfield
Friar's Gate
Lye Green
Boarshead
Crowborough
Poundfield
Jarvis Brook
Rotherfield
Mannings Heath
Ashfold Crossways
Handcross
Nymans Garden
Staplefield
Ardingly
Horsted Keynes
Chelwood Common
Danehill
Nutley
Duddleswell
Monk's Gate
Slaugham
Southwater Street
Nuthurst
Southwater
Lower Beeding
Leonardslee Gardens
Warninglid
Slough Green
Brook Street
Borde Hill Garden
Whitemans Green
Heaven Farm
Cackle Street
Fairwarp
High Hurstwood
Butcher's Cross
Copsale
Crabtree
Cuckfield
Lindfield
Haywards Heath
Sheffield Green
Splayne's Green
Sheffield Park
Maresfield
Pound Green
Hadlow Down
Maplehurst
Bolney
Ansty
Scayne's Hill
Fletching
The Bluebell Railway
Buxted
Ringles Cross
Blackboys
Cross in Hand
Cowfold
West Grinstead
Kent Street
Wivelsfield
Wivelsfield Green
North Common
Newick
Grisling Common
Uckfield
Framfield
Blackboys
Wineham
Hickstead
Twineham
Jumping Course
Burgess Hill
Sayers Common
Ditchling Common
Chailey
South Street
Spithurst
Isfield
Lavender Line Steam Railway
Ridgewood
E. Sussex National
Little Horsted
Waldron
Foxhunt Green
Dial Post
Partridge Green
West End
Blackstone
Albourne
Washbrooks Farm Centre
Hurstpierpoint
Hurst Wickham
Plumpton Green
Plumpton
TQ
Chiltington
Barcombe Cross
Barcombe
Rose Hill
Halland
East Hoathly
Ashurst
Henfield
Woodmancote
Hassocks
Keymer
Ditchling
Ditchling Museum
Streat
East Chiltington
Westmeston
Cooksbridge
Hamsey
Broyle Side
Ringmer
Laughton
Shortgate
Whitesmith
Chiddingly
Chiddingly Parish Church
Golden Cross
Lower Dicker
Small Dole
Poynings
Fulking
Clayton
Pyecombe
Ditchling Beacon
Offham
Mt. Harry
Lewes
South Malling
Glyndebourne
Mark Cross
Ripe
Chalvington
Upper Dicker
Michelham Priory
Steyning
Bramber
Upper Beeding
Truleigh Hill
Edburton
Saddlescombe
Devil's Dyke
St. Mary's House
Botolphs
Wallands Park
Cliffe Hill
Anne of Cleves Ho.
Lewes Downs (Mount Caburn)
Glynde
Glynde Place
Coombes
South Downs
Brighton and Hove
Patcham
Stanmer
Coldean
Falmer
Kingston near Lewes
Mile Oak
Westdene
Withdean
Preston Manor
Moulsecoomb
Bevendean
Castle Hill
Iford
Rodmell
Monks Ho.
Beddingham
West Firle
Firle Pl.
Charleston Farmhouse
Alciston
Selmeston
Arlington
North Lancing
Portslade
West Blatchington
Preston
Brighton
Woodingdean
Southease
South Downs Way
Firle Beacon
Berwick
Drusillas Park
Wilmington
Sompting
Lancing
Shoreham
Kingston by Sea
Southwick
Shoreham-by-Sea
Portslade-by-Sea
Hove
Royal Pavilion
Kemp Town
Ovingdean
Telscombe
Tarring Neville
South Heighton
Clergy House
Alfriston
The Long Man of Wilmington
Lullington Heath
Broadwater
South Lancing
East Worthing
Worthing
Marlipins Museum
Brighton Sea Life
Volk's Electric Railway
Merchants Quay
Rottingdean
Saltdean
Telscombe Cliffs
Peacehaven
Piddinghoe
Newhaven
Denton
Paradise Park
Norton
Bishopstone
Litlington
Charleston Manor
Newhaven Fort
East Blatchington
Westdean
Seaford
Seven Sisters
Friston
East Dean
Birling Gap
Dieppe 4:00
TV
Jersey
3½ miles to 1 inch
Plémont Pt.
Grosnez Pt.
Sorel Pt.
Ronez Pt.
St John's Bay
Belle Hougue Pt.
North Coast Visitor Centre
St John's
Bouley Bay
Tour de Rozel
Rozel
St Mary's
Jersey Flower Centre
Trinity
La Coupe Pt.
Jersey Zoo & Wildlife Park
Carteret 0:45
Portbail 0:45 (Summer only)
JERSEY
St Ouens
Les Mielles Visitor Centre
Res.
St Ouen's Bay
Carrefour Selous
St Peter's
St Martin's
St Catherine's Bay
La Hougie Bie
Mont Orgueil Castle
Gorey
Five Oaks
Red Houses
Corbière Pt.
St Aubin
St Helier
Jersey Museum
Grouville
Royal Bay of Grouville
St Brelade
St Brelades Bay
St Aubin's Bay
St Clements
Sark 0:45 (Summer only)
Elizabeth Castle
Fort Regent Leisure Centre
La Rocque Pt.
Noirmont Pt.
Le Nez Pt.
St Clements Bay
St. Peter Port 0:50
Weymouth 3:15
Poole 3:45 (Apr-Oct)
St. Peter Port 2:00
Portsmouth 10:00
St. Malo 1:10
Granville 1:00 (Apr-Oct)
Dielette 1:30 (May-Sept)
Carteret 0:55 (Apr-Oct)
St. Malo 1:10

HEVER CASTLE AND GARDENS
Penshurst
Markbeech
Haysden
Bidborough
Southborough
High Brooms
Paddock Wood
Claygate
Marden
Headcorn
Staplehurst
Marden Beech
Marden Thorn
Sinkhurst Green
Castle Hill
Matfield
Brenchley
Pembury
Chiddingstone Hoath
Speldhurst
Cowden
Blackham
Fordcombe
Rusthall
Langton Green
Ashurst
ROYAL TUNBRIDGE WELLS
Hawkenbury
Lamberhurst Quarter
BAYHAM ABBEY
Lamberhurst
Bells Yew Green
Petteridge
Horsmonden
SPRIVERS GARDEN
Hazel Street
Goudhurst
Winchet Hill
Knox Bridge
Frittenden
Lashenden
Collier's Green
Cranbrook Common
Three Chimneys
SISSINGHURST
Sissinghurst
Iden Green
Wilsley Pound
CRANBROOK & DIST. MUS.
Cranbrook
East End
FINCHCOCKS
SCOTNEY CASTLE
Kilndown
Hartley
Groombridge
SPA VALLEY RAILWAY
Hartfield
Withyham
Eridge Green
Frant
Hook Green
Cousley Wood
Wood's Green
Bewl Bridge Reservoir
Three Leg Cross
Durgates
Wadhurst
BEDGEBURY PINETUM
Bedgebury Forest
Benenden
Gill's Green
Iden Green
Rolvenden
Upper Hartfield
Lye Green
Friar's Gate
Boarshead
Mark Cross
Bestbeech Hill
Flimwell
High Street
Hawkhurst
Dingleden
Coleman's Hatch
Crowborough
Poundfield
ASHDOWN FOREST LLAMA PARK
ASHDOWN FOREST
Town Row
Riseden
Tidebrook
Shover's Green
Wallcrouch
Union Street
Ticehurst
Horns Corner
The Moor
Four Throws
Sandhurst
Linkhill
Jarvis Brook
Rotherfield
PASHLEY MANOR GARDENS
Stonegate
Swiftsden
Hurst Green
Sandhurst Cross
Newenden
Nutley
Duddleswell
Coggins Mill
Mayfield
Witherenden Hill
Etchingham
Bodiam
GREAT DIXTER
Fairwarp
Hurstwood
Butcher's Cross
Hadlow Down
Five Ashes
Rother
Burwash Common
Burwash
Northbridge Street
Salehurst
ROTHER VALLEY RLY.
Robertsbridge
Northiam
Ewhurst Green
BRICKWALL HOUSE
Millcorner
Clayhill
Maresfield
Pound Green
BATEMAN'S
Burwash Weald
Oxley's Green
Staple Cross
Horns Cross
Buxted
Ringles Cross
BLACKBOYS
Cross in Hand
Broad Oak
Cade Street
Punnett's Town
Brightling
John's Cross
Cripp's Corner
Grisling Common
Uckfield
Framfield
Blackboys
Heathfield
Old Heathfield
Three Cups Corner
Darwell Hole
Mountfield
Vinehall Street
Broad Oak
Broadland Row
Ridgewood
E.SUSSEX NATIONAL
Waldron
Little London
Maynard's Green
Rushlake Green
Dallington
Netherfield
Whatlington
Sedlescombe
Sedlescombe Street
Brede
Isfield
Little Horsted
Foxhunt Green
Vine's Cross
Warbleton
Canadia
Horam
Burlow
Penhurst
Battle
Guestling Thorn
Halland
East Hoathly
Foul Mile
Ponts Green
1066 ABBEY
Telham
Kent Street
Three Oaks
Westfield
Rose Hill
Shortgate
Chiddingly
Gun Hill
CHIDDINGLY PARISH CHURCH
Cowbeech
Bodle Street Green
Catsfield
Broyle Side
Laughton
Whitesmith
Golden Cross
Henley's Down
Crowhurst
Baldslow
HASTINGS
Ringmer
Herstmonceux
Windmill Hill
Ninfield
Hollington
St Helen's
Ore
Glyndebourne
Mark Cross
Lower Dicker
Lower Horsebridge
Hellingly
HERSTMONCEUX CASTLE
Magham Down
Boreham Street
Lunsford's Cross
Ripe
Upper Horsebridge
INTERNATIONAL STUDY CENTRE QUEENS UNIV. CANADA
Hooe Common
Silverhill
LEWES DOWNS (MOUNT CABURN)
Glynde
GLYNDE PLACE
Chalvington
Upper Dicker
Hailsham
Wartling
Hooe
Sidley
St Leonards
Little Common
MICHELHAM PRIORY
Pevensey Levels
West Marina
Bulverhythe
Hastings
FIRLE PL.
West Firle
Selmeston
Arlington
Cooden
BEXHILL
CHARLESTON FARMHOUSE
Alciston
FIRLE BEACON
THE OLD MINT HO.
Hankham
PEVENSEY SERVICES
Norman's Bay
Berwick
DRUSILLAS PARK
Polegate
Pevensey
Westham
Pevensey Bay
Tarring Neville
Wilmington
Folkington
Stone Cross
Friday Street
South Heighton
Alfriston
THE LONG MAN OF WILMINGTON
Hampden Park
Langney
Denton
Norton
PARADISE PARK
ALFRISTON
LULLINGTON HEATH
Willingdon
Jevington
SOUTH DOWNS WAY
St Anthony's Hill
Bishopstone
Litlington
CHARLESTON MANOR
Westdean
Newhaven
East Blatchington
WILLINGDON HILL
Roselands
TOWNER ART GALLERY AND MUS.
Eastbourne
HOW WE LIVED THEN' MUS.
Seaford
SEVEN SISTERS
Friston
East Dean
SEVEN SISTERS SHEEP CENTRE
Holywell
DIEPPE 4:00
SOUTH DOWNS WAY
Birling Gap
BEACHY HEAD
East Sussex
WEALD
HIGH WEALD
TQ
TV
0 1 2 3 4 5 6 miles
0 1 2 3 4 5 6 7 8 9 10 km

Pluckley Thorne
Kennington
Brook
Hastingleigh
Elham
Swingfield Minnis
Smarden
Maltman's Hill
Great Chart
Ashford
Hinxhill
Willesborough Lees
Brabourne
Lymbridge Green
Rhodes Minnis
Ottinge
Densole
Drellingore
Haffenden Quarter
Wissenden
McARTHUR GLEN ASHFORD
Willesborough
Sevington
Stowting
Brabourne Lees
KENT BATTLE OF BRITAIN MUSEUM
Lyminge
Paddlesworth
Hawkinge
West Hougham
Standen
Bethersden
Stubbs Cross
Kingsnorth
Mersham
Smeeth
Postling
Etchinghill
CHANNEL TUNNEL
Capel le Ferne
Biddenden
Tanden
Shadoxhurst
Cheeseman's Green
Sellindge
Sellindge Lees
Beachborough
Stanford
Newington
High Halden
Bromley Green
Aldington Frith
Clap Hill
Aldington
E. Stour
FOLKESTONE
Newingreen
BROCKHILL
ELHAM VALLEY MUSEUM
Cheriton
Folkestone
St Michael's
Henhurst
Shirkoak
Bonnington
Court-at-Street
Pedlinge
Saltwood
RUSSIAN SUB.
ROTUNDA
KENT AND EAST SUSSEX STEAM RAILWAY
Parkgate
Woodchurch
SOUTH OF ENGLAND RARE BREEDS CEN.
Orlestone
HAM STREET WOODS
PORT LYMPNE WILD ANIMAL PARK AND GARDENS
Lympne
Sandgate
CLIFF LIFT
Tenterden
Leigh Green
Brook Street
Kenardington
Ruckinge
Bilsington
Royal Military Canal
West Hythe
Hythe
Palmarsh
Warehorne
Hamstreet
Burmarsh
Newchurch
Small Hythe
Reading Street
Appledore Heath
HORNE'S PLACE CHAPEL
Snave
ROMNEY, HYTHE AND DYMCHURCH LIGHT RAILWAY
Rolvenden Layne
SMALLHYTHE PLACE
ISLE OF OXNEY
Appledore
ROMNEY MARSH
Dymchurch
MARTELLO TOWER
Peening Quarter
Snargate
St Mary in the Marsh
Stone
Wittersham
Brenzett
Ivychurch
AERONAUTICAL MUSEUM
St Mary's Bay
Ham Green
The Stocks
ROTHER LEVELS
FARM WORLD
Brookland
Old Romney
Littlestone on Sea
Four Oaks
New Romney
Romney Sands
Iden
Houghton Green
Walland Marsh
Peasmarsh
Rye Foreign
Playden
Greatstone on Sea
East Guldeford
Lydd
LYDD
Tillingham
Rye
Lydd on Sea
Denge Marsh
RYE HERITAGE CENTRE
Udimore
Camber
Rye Harbour
DUNGENESS
Denge Beach
Brede
Winchelsea
CAMBER CASTLE
DUNGENESS POWER STATION & INFORMATION CENTRE
DUNGENESS
THE OLD LIGHTHOUSE
Rye Bay
Winchelsea Beach
Icklesham
Pett
Guestling Green
Cliff End
Fairlight
Fairlight Cove
HASTINGS CAVES
ENGLISH CHANNEL
TR
A28
A262
A2070
A20
M20
A261
B2067
B2080
B2082
B2081
A259
A268
B2089
B2075
B2068
30
31
A
B
C
D
E
F
G
5
6
7
8
9
60
62
10
09

North West Point
North East Point
LUNDY
LUNDY MARINE NATURE RESERVE
142
ILFRACOMBE 2:15
BIDEFORD 2:15
CLOVELLY 1:30
South West Point
Surf Point
SS
NORTH DEVON
LUNDY 2:15
OLD CORN MILL
Rillage Pt.
Combe Martin Bay
Trentishoe
Ilfracombe
ILFRACOMBE MUSEUM
Hele
WATERMOUTH CASTLE
Girt Down
349
Heale
Bull Pt.
Rockham Bay
Lee
206
Berrynarbor
Combe Martin
Whitestone
Slade
Mortehoe
Sterridge
WILDLIFE & DINOSAUR PARK
Morte Point
ONCE UPON A TIME
269
A3123
A399
Woolacombe
Trimstone
Kentisbury
MORTE BAY
B3343
Cheglinch
Berry Down Cross
B3229
210
Dean
Berry Down
Patchole
Kentisbury Ford
Woolacombe Sand
Bittadon
SOUTH WEST COAST PATH
West Down
East Down
Pickwell
North Buckland
Churchill
Baggy Pt.
Putsborough
B3230
A361
Arlington
ARLINGTON COURT
Georgeham
Nethercott
Milltown
Croyde Bay
Darracott
Halsinger
Muddiford
Loxhore
Croyde
Knowle
A39
B3231
158
Lobb
Marwood
Guineaford
Shirwell
Brattor Fleming
Saunton
Pippacott
198
Kingsheanton
Shirwell Cross
Yeo
Braunton
MARWOOD HILL GARDENS
Prixford
ELLIOT GALLERY
Heanton Punchardon
Stoke Rivers
Saunton Sands
Wrafton
TOLL
Ashford
Burridge
Braunton Burrows
A361
Barnstaple
Goodleigh
Chivenor
LUNDY 2:15
Taw
Pilton
MUSEUM OF NORTH DEVON
Gunn
Fremington
B3233
P&R
Westacott
Yelland
Bickington
Newport
Bickleton
A39
Landkey
LUNDY 1:30
BIDEFORD BAY
NORTH DEVON MARITIME MUSEUM
NORTHAM BURROWS
Instow
Bishops Tawton
Swimbridge Newland
NORTH DEVON FARM PARK
Appledore
Swimbridge
9
Westward Ho!
Westleigh
Northam
A386
Torridge
0 1 2 3 4 5 6 miles
0 1 2 3 4 5 6 7 8 9 10km
Horwood
THE BIG SHEEP
Orchard Hill
Eastleigh
Newton Tracey
A377
Herner
Cobbaton
East Stowford
Titchberry
Abbotsham
BURTON GALL & MUS
Bideford
Hiscott
Ensis
Chapelton
COBBATON COMBAT COLL.
East-the-Water

Kenfig
Mawdlam
Kenfig
Burrows
KENFIG POOL AND DUNES
Kenfig Hill
North Cornelly
Pyle
(Y Pîl)
Cefn Cross
Cefn Cribbwr
Tondu
Aberkenfig
Sarn
Bryncethin
McARTHUR GLEN BRIDGEND
SARN PARK SERVICES
Pen-y-fai
Pendre
Coity
COITY CASTLE
Bridgend
(Pen-y-bont ar Ogwr)
NEW CASTLE
Pencoed
Brynna
Llanharan
Dolau
Bryncae
Llanilid
Llanharry
Brynsadler
Pont-yclun
Miskin
Talygarn
LLANERCH VINEYARD
MODEL CENTRE
South Cornelly
ROYAL PORTHCAWL
Nottage
Newton
Hutchwns
Clevis
Porthcawl
Tythegston
Laleston
Oldcastle
Coychurch
Merthyr Mawr
OGMORE CASTLE
MERTHYR MAWR WARREN
Ogmore
Ogmore-by-Sea
St Brides Major
Southerndown
Tusker Rock
St Mary Hill
Treoes
Corntown
Ewenny
Craig Penllyn
Llangan
Llansannor
Penllyn
Ystradowen
Maendy
Aberthin
Colwinston
Pentre Meyrick
Penuchadre
Llysworney
Llandow
Cowbridge
(Y Bont-Faen)
Llanblethian
Llandough
St Hilary
Welsh St Donats
Wick
Broughton
Llanmihangel
St Mary Church
OLD BEAUPRE CASTLE
Sigingstone
Monknash
Marcross
Llanmaes
Eglwys-Brewis
Flemington
Llanbethery
St Donat's
Llantwit Major
(Llanilltud Fawr)
Boverton
St Athan
CARDIFF INTERNATIONAL (MAES AWYR CAERDYDD CYMRU)
East Aberthaw
Rhoose
(Y Rhws)
Nash Pt.
Trwyn yr As
Breaksea Pt.
Trwyn Breaksea
Vale of Glamorgan
(Bro Morgannwg)
MÔR HAFREN
BRISTOL CHANNEL
SS
Foreland Pt.
Highveer Pt.
Lynmouth Bay
Woody Bay
CLIFF RAILWAY
Lynmouth
Countisbury
Lynton
LYNTON
Martinhoe
WATERSMEET HOUSE
Brendon
Malmsmead
CULBONE HILL
Oare
Porlock Weir
Porlock Bay
Bossington
Porlock
Hurlstone Pt.
SOUTH WEST COAST PATH
SELWORTHY BEACON
Allerford
Selworthy
Woodcombe
Minehead
WEST SOMERSET RAILWAY
SOMERWEST WORLD
Alcombe
Periton
Blue Anchor Bay
LYNTON AND BARNSTAPLE RLY.
Barbrook
East Ilkerton
Cheriton
Martinhoe Cross
Furzehill
Shallowford
Parracombe
West Lyn
EXMOOR
Brendon Common
HAWKCOMBE WOODS
Holnicote Estate
West Luccombe
Luccombe
Wootton Courtenay
Marsh Street
Dunster
MINEHEAD
DOLL MUS.
MILL & YARN MARKET
DUNSTER CASTLE (NT)
Blue Anchor
Old Cleeve
Carhampton
Blackmoor Gate
EXMOOR FOREST
Challacombe Common
Pinkworthy Pond
Exe Plain
THE DUNKERY & HORNER WOOD
DUNKERY BEACON
Cowbridge
Timberscombe
BRENDON
Withycombe
Bilbrook
CLEEVE ABBEY
Washford
EXMOOR ZOO
Challacombe
Exe
NATIONAL
CROYDON HILL
Rodhuish
Shoulsbarrow Common
Simonsbath
Edgcott
Luckwell Bridge
Cutcombe
FOREST
Roadwater
Knightacott
Leworthy
Bray
Exford
EXFORD
Wheddon Cross
Luxborough
LYPE HILL
Kingsbridge
Monksilver
Lydcott
Barle
HORSEN HILL
Withypool
Withypool Common
WINSFORD HILL
BRENDON HILLS
Treborough
Brayford
High Bray
North Radworthy
North Heasley
Winsford
Exton
PARK
Withiel Florey
Clatworthy Res.
Charles
West Buckland
Heasley Mill
South Radworthy
Liscombe
Bridgetown
Brompton Regis
East Buckland
Molland Common
Dane's Brook
Twitchen
Hawkridge
Wimbleball Lake
Huish Champflower
North Molton
Anstey Common
HADDON HILL
Upton
Filleigh
Mole
Molland
West Anstey
Dulverton
Bury
HEYDON HILL
QUINCE HONEY FARM
South Molton
Yeo
East Anstey
Battleton
Skilgate
Chipstable
Yeo Mill
Nightcott
Waterrow
Llanca
Walters
Pend
Llantrith
M4
A4229
A4106
A48
A473
A4222
B4524
B4265
B4268
B4270
B4283
B4265
A39
B3358
B3223
B3224
B3225
B3191
B3190
A396
A399
A361
B3227
B3222
B3190
TOLL
34
35
36
37
22
10

Pencoed
Llantrisant
Talbot Green
Llanharan
Pontyclun
Cross Inn
Creigiau
Pentyrch
Taff's Well
Tongwynlais
Rhiwbina
Llanishen
Lisvane
Llanedeyrn
Castleton
Coedkernew
Marshfield
St Brides Wentlooge
Peterstone Wentlooge
Blacktown
St Mellons
Llanrumney
Rumney
Newton
Whitchurch
Cardiff
(Caerdydd)
Radyr
Birchgrove
Heath
Cathays
Roath
Llandaff
Canton
Ely
St Fagans
Michaelston-super-Ely
Caerau
Butetown
Grangetown
CARDIFF
(CAERDYDD)
MILLENNIUM STADIUM
CARDIFF BAY VISITOR CENTRE
TECHNIQUEST
CARDIFF BAY BARRAGE
Llandough
Cogan
PENARTH
TURNER HOUSE GALLERY
Dinas Powys
Lower Penarth
Lavernock Pt.
Trwyn Larnog
Sully
Sully Island
Ynys Sili
COSMESTON
MEDIEVAL VILLAGE
Cadoxton
Merthyr-Dyfan
Colcot
BARRY
(Y BARRI)
Barry Island
BARRY ISLAND PLEASURE PARK
VALE OF GLAMORGAN RLY.
Porthkerry
Rhoose
(Y Rhws)
CARDIFF INTERNATIONAL (MAES AWYR CAERDYDD CYMRU)
East Aberthaw
Gileston
Breaksea Pt.
Trwyn Breaksea
St Athan
Boverton
Llantwit Major
(Llanilltud Fawr)
Llanmaes
Eglwys-Brewis
Llanbethêry
Penmark
Llancarfan
Flemingston
Moulton
WELSH HAWKING CENTRE
Walterston
Sigingstone
St Mary Church
OLD BEAUPRE CASTLE
Llanmihangel
Llandough
St Hilary
Llantrithyd
Bonvilston
St Nicholas
Wallston
St Lythans
DYFFRYN GARDENS
Wenvoe
Michaelston-le-Pit
Leckwith
St Andrews Major
Llanblethian
Cowbridge
(Y Bont-Faen)
Llandow
Llysworney
Pentre Meyrick
Penllyn
Aberthin
Maendy
Welsh St Donats
Pendoylan
Peterston super-Ely
St Brides super Ely
St George's
Ystradowen
Llansannor
Llangan
Craig Penllyn
St Mary Hill
Vale of Glamorgan
(Bro Morgannwg)
Llanharry
Brynsadler
Talygarn
Groes-faen
Capel Llanilltern
ABER HAFREN
MOUTH OF THE SEVERN
Flat Holm
Steep Holm
MÔR HAFREN
BRISTOL CHANNEL
BRIDGWATER BAY
Sand Pt.
Sand Bay
Kewstoke
Milton
Weston-super-Mare
Weston Bay
Brean Down
Uphill
Brean
BERROW FLATS
ANIMAL FARM COUNTRY PARK
Lympsham
Eastertown
Gore Sands
Berrow
Brent Knoll
Burnham-on-Sea
Edithmead
Highbridge
Watchfield
STERT FLATS
Stolford
Steart
Huntspill
Stretcholt
Pawlett
Dunball
Puriton
Woolavington
Combwich
Otterhampton
Stockland Bristol
Stogursey
Shurton
Burton
Lilstock
Kilton
Stringston
Kilve
East Quantoxhead
West Quantoxhead
Watchet
Minehead
WEST SOMERSET RAILWAY
SOMERWEST WORLD
Alcombe
Woodcombe
Blue Anchor Bay
Marsh Street
Dunster
Wootton Courtenay
Carhampton
Blue Anchor
Old Cleeve
Washford
Williton
Staple
Holford
QUANTOCK HILLS
Nether Stowey
Fiddington
Rodway
Cannington
Over Stowey
Spaxton
Charlynch
Wembdon
Bridgwater
Chilton Trinity
Durleigh
Four Forks
Enmore
Goathurst
North Petherton
Huntworth
Lower Aisholt
Courtway
TEMPLE OF HARMONY
FYNE COURT
Broomfield
Cothelstone
Cushuish
West Bagborough
Flaxpool
Crowcombe
Stogumber
Bicknoller
Sampford Brett
Vellow
Monksilver
Yard
Rodhuish
Roadwater
Luxborough
Kingsbridge
Treborough
BRENDON HILLS
Elworthy
Lower Vexford
Willett
Lydeard St Lawrence
Tolland
Combe Florey
East Combe
Ash Priors
Bishops Lydeard
Fulford
Kingston St Mary
Pickney
Nailsbourne
West Monkton
Monkton Heathfield
Cheddon Fitzpaine
Thurloxton
North Newton
Northmoor Green or Moorland
Hedging
Lyng
West Lyng
Durston
Creech Heathfield
North End
Bathpool
Staplegrove
Norton
Heathfield
Hillcommon
Preston Bowyer
Milverton
VALE OF TAUNTON DEANE
Wiveliscombe
Fitzhead
Halse
Langley Marsh
Clatworthy
Clatworthy Res.
Brompton Ralph
Withiel Florey
Brompton Regis
Wimbleball Lake
Upton
Champflower
Bury
Waterrow
Withycombe
Cowbridge
Timberscombe
BRENDON FOREST
Bilbrook
CLEEVE ABBEY
Cutcombe
LYPE HILL
Somerset
QUANTOCK FOREST
0 1 2 3 4 5 6 miles
0 1 2 3 4 5 6 7 8 9 10 km

North Somerset
Bristol
Bath and N.E. Somerset
Mendip Hills
Polden Hills
Redwick
Whitson
Goldcliff
Almondsbury
Iron Acton
Engine Common
Yate
Old Sodbury
Chipping Sodbury
Over
Easter Compton
Frampton Cotterell
Nibley
Watley's End
Patchway
Hallen
Catbrain
Stoke Gifford
Winterbourne
Coalpit Heath
Winterbourne Down
Westerleigh
Wapley
Dodington
Avonmouth
Henbury
FILTON
Horfield
Hambrook
Codrington
Frenchay
Blackhorse
Battery Pt.
Portishead
Shirehampton
Westbury on Trym
Downend
Hinton
Pucklechurch
Dyrham Park
West Hill
MANGOTSFIELD
Redcliff Bay
Sheepway
Gordano Services
Ham Green
Pill
Bristol Zoo
Stapleton
Fishponds
Siston
Abson
Dyrham
Redland
Soundwell
Easton-in-Gordano
Weston-in-Gordano
Clapton-in-Gordano
Portbury
Abbots Leigh
Eastville
Kingswood
Noah's Ark Zoo Farm
Clifton
Bridge Yate
Doynton
Walton-in-Gordano
Leigh Woods
Warmley
Hanham
Wick
Clifton Suspension Bridge
BRISTOL
Clevedon Court
Stone-edge Batch
Empire & Commonwealth Mus
Warmley Tower
Cold Ashton
Clevedon
Wraxall
Tyntesfield House
Cath.
SS Great Britain
Avon Valley Railway
Tickenham
Knowle
Oldland
Grenville's Mon.
Failand
Brislington
Upton Cheyney
Nailsea
Long Ashton
Bedminster
Arnolfini Gallery
Willsbridge
West End
East End
Farleigh
Bitton
North Stoke
Langridge
Kenn
Flax Bourton
Avon Valley
Woolley
Bishopsworth
KEYNSHAM
Swainswick
Backwell
Barrow Gurney
Chelvey
Kingston Seymour
West Town
Dundry Hill
Dundry
Whitchurch
Kelston
Charlcombe
Brockley
Saltford
Weston
Claverham
Wick St Lawrence
North End
Yatton
Lulsgate Bottom
Upper Town
Queen Charlton
Chewton Keynsham
Bath
Cleeve
Bristol International
North Wick
Norton Malreward
Corston
No.1 Royal Crescent
Bourton
Felton
Winford
Norton Hawkfield
Burnett
Newton St Loe
Twerton
Hewish
Stone Circles
Pensford
Compton Dando
Roman Baths
Puxton
Congresbury
The Oval
Wrington
Chew Magna
Prior Park
Worle
Redhill
Stanton Drew
Stanton Prior
Englishcombe
Odd Down
Ridgehill
Chew Stoke
Chelwood
Hunstrete
West Wick
Brinsea
Lye Cross
Butcombe
Marksbury
Inglesbatch
Lower Langford
Stanton Wick
Priston Mill
Priston
Southstoke
Blagdon Pumping Station
Nempnett Thrubwell
Farmborough
Combe Hay
Churchill
Blagdon Lake
Chew Valley Lake
Dunkerton
Twinhoe
Banwell
Sandford
Burrington
Bishop Sutton
Clutton
Timsbury
Bleadon Hill
Blagdon
Ubley
Temple Cloud
Carlingcott
Wellow
Star
Sutton Wick
High Littleton
Charterhouse
Christon
Winscombe
Shipham
Compton Martin
South Widcombe
Hinton Blewett
Hallatrow
Camerton
Peasedown St John
Norwood
Sidcot
West Harptree
Paulton
Long Barrow
Shoscombe
Compton Bishop
Loxton
East Harptree
Radstock Museum
Clandown
Radstock
King John's Hunting Lodge
Cross
Farrington Gurney
Lower Weare
Axbridge
Cheddar Res.
Cheddar Showcaves and Gorge
Litton
Midsomer Norton
Writhlington
Faulkland
Biddisham
Cheddar
Chewton Mendip
Ston Easton
Hemington
Weare
Kilmersdon
Rooks Bridge
Badgworth
Chilcompton
Hardington
Charlton
Clewer
Stone Allerton
Rodney Stoke
Emborough
Buckland Dinham
Chapel Allerton
Draycott
Priddy
Stratton on the Fosse
Rodney Stoke
Green Ore
Binegar
Great Elm
Cocklake
Gurney Slade
Highbury
Mells
West Stoughton
Westbury-sub-Mendip
Holcombe
Ashwick
Vobster
Little Green
Mark Causeway
Mark
Blackford
Wedmore
Wookey Hole Caves & Papermill
West Horrington
Ebbor Gorge
Nettlebridge
Coleford
Whatley
Easton
Wookey Hole
Oakhill
Leigh upon Mendip
Westham
Latcham
East Horrington
Chantry
Nunney Castle
Theale
Wells
Stoke St Michael
Heath House
Wookey
Nunney
Henton
The Bishop's Palace
Downside
Downhead
Mudgley
Burcott Mill
Dinder
Croscombe
Heale
Westhay Moor
Dulcote
Dean
Tytherington
Burtle
Coxley
Shepton Mallet
East Cranmore
Trudoxhill
Leighton
Polsham
Doulting
West Cranmore
Meare Fish House
Worminster
West Compton
Westhay
Godney
Southway
East Somerset Railway
Wanstrow
Meare
The Peat Moors Visitor Centre
North Wootton
East Compton
Cannard's Grave
Chesterblade
Witham Friary
Ham Wall
Whitelake
Pilton
Prestleigh
Upton Noble
Cossington
Chilton Polden
Edington
Shapwick Heath
Makers of Myth
Glastonbury
Stoney Stratton
Westcombe
Catcott
Stawell
Shapwick
Northover
Glastonbury Tor
West Pennard
Pylle
Evercreech
Batcombe
Edgarley
Moorlinch
Clarks Village
Ashcott
Abbey
East Pennard
Milton Clevedon
Sutton Mallet
Vineyard
Greinton
West Bradley
Ditcheat
Lamyatt
North Brewham
Pedwell
Walton
Shoe Mus
Street
Parbrook
Wraxall
South Brewham
Westonzoyland
Overleigh
Butleigh Wootton
Ham Street
Alhampton
Bruton
Hardway
King Alfred's Tower
King's Sedge Moor
Baltonsborough
Hornblotton Green
Sutton
Cole
Redlynch
Stoney Stoke
Butleigh
Southwood
Ansford
Pitcombe
Middlezoy
Compton Dundon
Henley
Dundon
Barton St David
West Lydford
East Lydford
Alford
Castle Cary
Penselwood
Othery
Pathe
High Ham
Stembridge Tower Mill
Kingweston
Lovington
Shepton Montague
Hadspen Garden
Charlton Musgrove
Leigh Common
Littleton
Keinton Mandeville
Lydford-on-Fosse
Wincanton
Burrowbridge
Aller
Low Ham
Charlton Adam
Babcary
North Barrow
Bratton Seymour
Bayford
Stathe
Pitney
Somerton
Yarlington
Athelney
Haynes Motor Mus
South Barrow
Stoke Trister
Charlton Mackerell
North Cadbury
Stoke St Gregory
Langport
Lytes Cary Manor
Cary Fitzpaine
Sparkford
Holton
Cucklington
West Sedge Moor
Curry Rivel
Langport & R. Parrett
Huish Episcopi
Long Sutton
Kingsdon
South Cadbury
Compton Pauncefoot
Blackford
Maperton
Lattiford
North Cheriton
Parrett
Brue
Yeo
Axe
Avon
Huntspill

Yate
Chipping Sodbury
Little Sodbury
Old Sodbury
Little Badminton
Badminton
Luckington
Alderton
Hullavington
Corston
Brinkworth
Callow Hill
Rodbourne
Startley
Great Somerford
Dauntsey
Grittenham
Lower Stanton St Quintin
Lower Seagry
Tockenham Wick
Stanton St Quintin
Upper Seagry
Acton Turville
Littleton Drew
Grittleton
Leigh Delamere
Dodington
Wapley
Tormarton
Burton
Sutton Benger
Christian Malford
Bradenstoke
Lyneham
Tockenham
Church End
Westerleigh
Codrington
Winterbourne
Coalpit Heath
Hambrook
Frenchay
Blackhorse
Downend
MANGOTSFIELD
Kingswood
Hanham
Warmley
Warmley Tower
Oldland
Willsbridge
Bitton
KEYNSHAM
Saltford
Kelston
Weston
Bath
Corston
Chewton Keynsham
Burnett
Compton Dando
Newton St Loe
Twerton
The Oval
Odd Down
Englishcombe
Inglesbatch
Priston
Marksbury
Stanton Prior
Hunstrete
Farmborough
Timsbury
High Littleton
Hallatrow
Paulton
Camerton
Peasedown St John
Radstock
Midsomer Norton
Writhlington
Kilmersdon
Hinton
Pucklechurch
Dyrham
Abson
Siston
Bridge Yate
Doynton
Wick
Cold Ashton
Marshfield
Upton Cheyney
North Stoke
Langridge
Woolley
Swainswick
Charlcombe
West Littleton
West Kington
Nettleton
Castle Combe
North Wraxall
Ford
Slaughterford
Thickwood
Colerne
St Catherine
Northend
Batheaston
Bathford
Bathampton
Claverton
Combe Down
Monkton Combe
Limpley Stoke
Winsley
Turleigh
Freshford
Westwood
Farleigh Hungerford
Hinton Charterhouse
Wellow
Shoscombe
Norton St Philip
Tellisford
Rode
Woolverton
Laverton
Beckington
Lullington
Oldford
Frome
Berkley
Southwick
North Bradley
Hawkeridge
Rudge
Westbury Leigh
Westbury
Dilton Marsh
Upton Scudamore
Warminster
Corsley
Corsley Heath
Chapmanslade
Yatton Keynell
Kington St Michael
Kington Langley
Langley Burrell
Hardenhuish
Chippenham
Biddestone
Corsham
Easton
Notton
Lacock
Gastard
Neston
Hawthorn
Box
Atworth
Whitley
Shaw
Beanacre
Melksham
Bowerhill
Sells Green
Seend
Seend Cleeve
Semington
Hilperton
Trowbridge
Trowle Common
Staverton
Holt
Bradford-on-Avon
Bradford Leigh
Great Chalfield Manor
Broughton Gifford
Broughton Common
Norrington Common
South Wraxall
Monkton Farleigh
Calne
Derry Hill
Bowood House
Mile Elm
Quemerford
Sandy Lane
Blackland
Calstone Wellington
Bowden Hill
Chittoe
Heddington
Bromham
Sandridge
Rowde
Roundway
Devizes
Etchilhampton
Poulshot
Potterne
Potterne Wick
Worton
Marston
Bulkington
Keevil
Great Hinton
Ashton Common
Steeple Ashton
West Ashton
Yarnbrook
Heywood
Coulston
Great Cheverell
Erlestoke
Little Cheverell
Edington
Bratton
Littleton Pannell
Eastcott
Easterton
Market Lavington
West Lavington
Gore Cross
Urchfont
Stert
Tilshead
Littleton Down
Summer Down
West Lavington Down
Foxham
Preston
Goatacre
East Tytherton
West Tytherton
Spirthill
West End
Bremhill
Studley
Hilmarton
Highway
Compton Bassett
Cherhill
St Edith's
Stockley
Bishops Cannings
Coate
Wilts
SALISBURY PLAIN
Bishopstrow
Boreham
Norton Bavant
Heytesbury
Chitterne
Knook
Upton Lovell
Codford St Peter
Codford St Mary
Sutton Veny
Tytherington
Corton
Boyton
Sherrington
Stockton
Wylye
Deptford
Steeple Langford
Hanging Langford
Little Langford
Grovely
Bugley
Crockerton
Shear Cross
Longbridge Deverill
Horningsham
Longleat
Brixton Deverill
Monkton Deverill
Kingston Deverill
Maiden Bradley
Kilmington
Norton Ferris
Stourhead
Stourton
White Sheet Hill
Mere
Zeals
Queen Oak
Bourton
Huntingford
Penselwood
Stoney Stoke
Charlton Musgrove
Bayford
Wincanton
Milton on Stour
Gillingham
Ham Common
Wyke
Sedgehill
West Knoyle
The Green
Barrow Street
East Knoyle
Fonthill Gifford
Fonthill Bishop
Berwick St Leonard
Chicklade
Pertwood
Keysley Down
Great Ridge
CRANBORNE CHASE
Hindon
Chilmark
Ridge
Teffont Magna
Teffont Evias
Chicksgrove
Tisbury
Dinton
Baverstock
VALE OF WARDOUR
Compton Chamberlayne
Fovant
Sutton Mandeville
Hatch
Newtown
Swallowcliffe
Ansty
Semley
Fifield
Broad Chalke
Donhead
Tythering ton
West Woodlands
Trudoxhill
Leighton
Nunney
The Butts
Chantry
Whatley
Great Elm
Mells
Little Green
Vobster
Coleford
Highbury
Holcombe
Nettlebridge
Stratton on the Fosse
Charlton
Buckland Dinham
Hardington
Hemington
Faulkland
Kilmersdon
Leigh upon Mendip
Downhead
Stoke St Michael
Oakhill
Heale
Dean
East Cranmore
West Cranmore
Doulting
Wanstrow
Chesterblade
Prestleigh
Witham Friary
Bruton Forest
Gare Hill
Upton Noble
Westcombe
Batcombe
Stoney Stratton
Evercreech
Milton Clevedon
Lamyatt
North Brewham
South Brewham
Bruton
Cole
Hardway
Redlynch
Pitcombe
Ansford
Castle Cary
Shepton Montague
Bratton Seymour
Galhampton
Yarlington
North Cadbury
Lattiford
North Cheriton
Compton
Blackford
Dunkerton
Combe Hay
Twinhoe
Southstoke
Carlingcott
Clandown
Farleigh
Wingfield
Alcombe
Luckington
0 1 2 3 4 5 6 miles
0 1 2 3 4 5 6 7 8 9 10 km

Hook
Rodbourne
Walcot
Swindon
The Marsh
Wootton Bassett
Hinton Parva
Idstone
Bishopstone
Ashbury
Kingston Warren
Letcombe Bassett
THE RIDGEWAY
Wanborough
Liddington
Coate
COATE WATER
North Wroughton
Wroughton
GREAT WESTERN (MAIZE) MAZE
Elcombe
Badbury
ASHDOWN PARK
LAMBOURN DOWNS
Upper Lambourn
South Fawley
Fawley
Farnborough
Lilley
Brightwalton
Lambourn
Broadtown Lane
Broad Town
Chiseldon
Baydon
Clyffe Pypard
Uffcott
BARBURY CASTLE
Upper Upham
Eastbury
East Garston
Chaddleworth
Leckhampstead Thicket
Broad Hinton
Woodsend
Aldbourne
MEMBURY SERVICES
Woodlands St Mary
Leckhampstead
Great Shefford
Winterborne Bassett
MARLBOROUGH DOWNS
HACKPEN HILL
Southend
Ogbourne St George
Preston
Shefford Woodlands
Weston
Welford
Berwick Bassett
Ogbourne St Andrew
Whittonditch
Winterbourne
Westbrook
Boxford
SNELSMORE COMMON
WINDMILL HILL
Winterborne Monkton
THE RIDGEWAY
Rockley
FYFIELD DOWN
Ogbourne Maizey
Ramsbury
Hungerford Newtown
Wickham
Yatesbury
AVEBURY MANOR
Avebury
STONE CIRCLE
W. KENNETT AVENUE
Mildenhall
Axford
Kennet
Chilton Foliat
Hungerford
Bagnor
Stockcross
Donnington
Halfway
Avington
Speen
Marlborough
Fyfield
SILBURY HILL
Beckhampton
West Kennett
LONG BARROW
East Kennett
THE SANCTUARY
West Overton
Manton
Lockeridge
Savernake Forest
Froxfield
CHISBURY CHAPEL
Chisbury
Kintbury
Laylands Green
Enborne
Newbury
Clench Common
Cadley
Little Bedwyn
TAN HILL
MILK HILL
PEWSEY DOWNS
Huish
Wootton Rivers
Durley
Great Bedwyn
Bagshot
Inkpen
Upper Green
Hamstead Marshall
Ball Hill
Allington
Stanton St Bernard
West Stowell
Oare
Crofton
Shalbourne
Ham
West Woodhay
North End
Woolton Hill
Broad Laying
All Cannings
Alton Priors
Stibb Green
CROFTON BEAM ENGINES
WILTON WINDMILL
Eastcourt
New Mill
Burbage
Wilton
WALBURY HILL
Honey Street
Wilcot
Pewsey
Easton Royal
Rivar
Buttermere
Combe
East Woodhay
East End
Highclere
Woodborough
Bottlesford
Milton Lilbourne
West Grafton
East Grafton
Marten
Oxenwood
Beechingstoke
Southcott
Wexcombe
Patney
Manningford Bruce
SU
Tidcombe
Linkenholt
Faccombe
HIGHCLERE CASTLE
Chirton
HENGE
Hilcott
Marden
North Newnton
Manningford Bohune
Fosbury
Vernham Street
Netherton
Ashmansworth
Wilsford
Charlton
Pewsey Down
Aughton
Brunton
HAYDOWN HILL
Vernham Dean
Crux Easton
Rushall
Upavon
Collingbourne Kingston
Upton
Lower Everleigh
Sunton
Everleigh
Cadley
Collingbourne Ducis
Upper Chute
Chute Standen
Ibthorpe
Woodcott
Dunley
West Chisenbury
East Chisenbury
Lower Chute
Hurstbourne Tarrant
Binley
Compton
Collingbourne Forest
Tangley
Black Heath
Compton Down
Enford
Fifield
Haxton Down
Doles Wood
Stoke
Wildhern
Coombe
Ludgershall
St Mary Bourne
Enford Down
West Down
Fittleton
Hatherden
Little London
Netheravon
Tidworth
North Tidworth
Clanville
Enham Alamein
Smannell
Orcheston Down
DOVECOTE
Appleshaw
Penton Mewsey
Picket Piece
Whitchurch
Figheldean
South Tidworth
Kimpton
Fyfield
Weyhill
Charlton
FINKLEY DOWN FARM PARK
Hurstbourne Priors
Ablington
Knighton Down
Shipton Bellinger
Thruxton
THRUXTON
THE HAWK CONSERVANCY TRUST
WEYHILL SERVICES
Andover Down
Orcheston
Milston
Andover
Durrington
Middleton
Longparish
Elston
Shrewton
Larkhill
Bulford Camp
BEACON HILL
Amport
Quarley
Monxton
Abbotts Ann
Anna Valley
Upper Clatford
Harewood Forest
Forton
WOODHENGE
Bulford
Countess
STONEHENGE
Amesbury
CHOLDERTON RARE BREEDS
CHOLDERTON (STONEHENGE)
Cholderton
Grateley
Goodworth Clatford
Wherwell
Bullington
West Amesbury
Avon
Newton Stacey
Barton Stacey
Winterbourne Stoke
Palestine
Wilsford
Newton Tony
Chilbolton
SUTTON SCOTNEY SERVICES
Berwick St James
Lake
Great Durnford
Allington
Boscombe
Fullerton
MUSEUM OF ARMY FLYING
Upper Woodford
Bourne
Over Wallop
Middle Wallop
Stapleford
Idmiston
Porton
Longstock
Leckford
Little Wishford
Middle Woodford
Nether Wallop
Gomeldon
Lopcombe Corner
Great Wishford
Stoford
South Newton
Winterbourne Dauntsey
Winterbourne Gunner
Stockbridge
Crawley
Worthy Down
Wood
Lower Woodford
Winterbourne Earls
Firsdown
East Winterslow
Little Somborne
Chilhampton
WILTON
OLD SARUM
Middle Winterslow
The Common
WHITESHOOT HILL
Broughton
Up Somborne
Littleton
Barford St Martin
Ditchampton
Stratford sub Castle
New Sarum
ALL SAINTS CHURCH
Houghton
FLOWERDOWN BARROWS
Wilton
Quidhampton
SALISBURY
Laverstock
West Winterslow
Pitton
Ashley
Sparsholt
Burcombe
WILTON HOUSE
Bemerton
Salisbury
King's Somborne
Horsebridge
Netherhampton
CATH.
Milford
Farley
West Tytherley
FARLEY MOUNT
Weeke
West Harnham
East Harnham
MOMPESSON HOUSE
East Tytherley
Brook
Stanmore
SALISBURY RACECOURSE
Britford
East Grimstead
ABBEY GARDEN
Coombe Bissett
Alderbury
West Dean
Lockerley
Butt's Green
Mottisfont
Michelmersh
Standon
Olivers Battery
Stratford Tony
Odstock
Whaddon
West Grimstead
East Dean
Bodenham
Ebble
N O R T H
W E S S E X
D O W N S
V A L E O F P E W S E Y
s h i r e
B U R Y
M4
A4
A36
A303
A338
A346
A345
A342
A343
A34
A30
A360
A354
B4005
B4000
B4192
B4001
B3087
B3086
B3083
B3084
B3048
B3420
B3400
B3049
A3026
A3057
A3093
26
37
38
14

West Berkshire
Berkshire
Hampshire
Hungerford
Newbury
Thatcham
Reading
Tilehurst
Caversham
Whitley
Goring
Sonning Common
Tadley
Basingstoke
Hook
Overton
Whitchurch
Andover
Alton
Winchester
New Alresford
Kings Worthy
Lambourn
Great Shefford
Shefford Woodlands
Weston
Welford
Hungerford Newtown
Wickham
Winterbourne
Westbrook
Boxford
Snelsmore Common
Chieveley
Chieveley Services
Curridge
Longlane
Hermitage
Oare
Little Hungerford
Frilsham
Yattendon
Stanford Dingley
Bradfield
Englefield
Theale
North Street
Tutts Clump
Southend
Bucklebury
Clay Hill
Cold Ash
Upper Bucklebury
Chapel Row
Beenham
Midgham
Woolhampton
Aldermaston Wharf
Padworth
Aldermaston
Brimpton
Crookham
Wasing
Greenham
Wash Common
Enborne
Hamstead Marshall
Kintbury
Avington
Halfway
Stockcross
Bagnor
Donnington
Donnington Castle
Speen
Shaw
Newbury
Inkpen
Upper Green
West Woodhay
Ball Hill
North End
Woolton Hill
Broad Laying
East Woodhay
East End
Highclere
Highclere Castle
Burghclere
Sandham Memorial Chapel
Tothill Services
Ecchinswell
Whitway
Kingsclere
Sydmonton
Old Burghclere
Newtown
Headley
Plastow Green
Ashford Hill
Heath End
Baughurst
Pamber Green
Pamber Heath
Wolverton Common
West Heath
Wolverton
Ramsdell
Charter Alley
Monk Sherborne
Hannington
Ibworth
North Oakley
Upper Wootton
Wootton St Lawrence
Winklebury
Oakridge
Popley
Chineham
Daneshill
Old Basing
South View
South Ham
Worting
Buckskin
Kempshott
Brighton Hill
Oakley
East Oakley
Deane
Newfound
Ashe
Quidhampton
Cole Henley
Laverstoke
Steventon
North Waltham
Dummer
Cliddesden
Farleigh Wallop
Ellisfield
Nutley
Axford
Preston Candover
Moundsmere
Winslade
Herriard
Tunworth
Upton Grey
Weston Patrick
South Warnborough
Southrope
Lasham
Shalden
Bentworth
Holybourne
Golden Pot
Bradley
Lower Wield
Holt End
Beech
Upper Wield
Wivelrod
Hattingley
Medstead
Mid-Hants Railway
South Town
Four Marks
Lower Farringdon
Upper Farringdon
Chawton
Jane Austen's Ho.
Wilsom
Curtis Museum
West Worldham
Selborne
Newton Valence
Gilbert White's House
East Tisted
Colemore
Hawkley
Ropley
Ropley Dean
Kitwood
Monkwood
Bighton
Soldridge
North Street
Gundleton
Bishop's Sutton
Cheriton
Tichborne
West Tisted
Bramdean
Hinton Ampner
Brockwood
Privett
High Cross
Stoner Hill
Beauworth
New Cheriton
Longwood Warren
Chilcomb
St. Catherine's Hill
Intech Science Technology Centre
Winnall
Weeke
Headbourne Worthy
Easton
Avington
Ovington
Itchen Abbas
Itchen Stoke
Martyr Worthy
Northington
Northington Grange
Brown Candover
East Stratton
Micheldever
Micheldever Wood
Micheldever Forest
Woodmancott
Popham
West Stratton
Stoke Charity
Winchester Services
Sutton Scotney
Sutton Scotney Services
Wonston
South Wonston
Worthy Down
Crawley
Littleton
Flowerdown Barrows
Sparsholt
Farley Mount
Ashley
King's Somborne
Up Somborne
Little Somborne
All Saints Church
Stockbridge
Longstock
Leckford
Fullerton
Chilbolton
Wherwell
Newton Stacey
Barton Stacey
Bullington
Forton
Longparish
Middleton
Harewood Forest
Andover Down
Finkley Down Farm Park
Hurstbourne Priors
Picket Piece
Charlton
Enham Alamein
Smannell
Little London
St Mary Bourne
Upper Clatford
Anna Valley
Goodworth Clatford
Hurstbourne Tarrant
Ibthorpe
Upton
Stoke
Doles Wood
Binley
Woodcott
Dunley
Litchfield
Crux Easton
Ashmansworth
Faccombe
Netherton
Linkenholt
Combe
Walbury Hill
Buttermere
Laylands Green
Tufton
Foliat
Woodlands St Mary
East Garston
Chaddleworth
Leckhampstead
Leckhampstead Thicket
Brightwalton
Lilley
Farnborough
Fawley
South Fawley
West Ilsley
East Ilsley
Catmore
Stanmore
Beedon
Peasemore
World's End
Downend
Compton
Hampstead Norreys
The Living Rainforest
Aldworth
Ashampstead
Quicks Green
Upper Basildon
Pangbourne
Streatley
Streatley on Thames
Lower Basildon
Basildon Park
St. Bartholomew's
Beale Park
Moulsford
South Stoke
Checkendon
Woodcote
Cray's Pond
Goring Heath
Whitchurch Hill
Whitchurch
Purley
Tidmarsh
Sulham
Calcot Row
Mapledurham
Tokers Green
Kidmore End
Binfield Heath
Dunsden Green
Emmer Green
Cane End
Rotherfield Peppard
Rotherfield Greys
Satwell
Shepherd's Green
Highmoor Cross
Greys Court
Stoke Row
Wellplace Zoo
Well
The Ridgeway
Ufton Nervet
Sheffield Bottom
Reading Services
Sulhamstead
Burghfield
Burghfield Hill
Burghfield Common
Grazeley
Wokefield Park
Mortimer
Stratfield Mortimer
Mortimer West End
Silchester
Roman Town
Stratfield Saye
Stratfield Saye House
West End Green
Fair Oak Green
Little London
Stratfield Turgis
Turgis Green
Bramley
Pamber End
Sherfield on Loddon
The Vyne
Sherborne St John
Milestones
Church End
Rotherwick
Hartley Wespall
Newnham
Hatch
Up Nately
Mapledurwell
North Warnborough
Greywell
Odiham
Beech Hill
Riseley
Swallowfield
Farley Hill
Spencers Wood
Three Mile Cross
Shinfield
Arborfield
Wellington
Bramshill
Heckfield
Hazeley
Hound Green
Mattingley
Lyde Green
West Green
Kennet
Pang
M4
M3
A34
A4
A339
A303
A30
A33
A343
A338
B4009
B4494
B4640
B3051
B3400
B3420
B3048
B3046
B3047
A272
A31
A32
A3057
B3049
A340
B3349
TOLL
Portway
SU
38
39
25
15
0 1 2 3 4 5 6 miles
0 1 2 3 4 5 6 7 8 9 10 km

Henley-on-Thames
Windsor and Maidenhead
Maidenhead
Slough
SLOUGH
Uxbridge
Hillingdon
Hayes
Southall
Yiewsley
West Drayton
Iver
Burnham
Cookham Rise
Marlow
Remenham
Aston
Medmenham
Hurley
Pinkneys Grn.
Burchett's Green
Warren Row
Knowl Hill
Littlewick Green
Wargrave
White Waltham
Waltham St Lawrence
Twyford
Woodley
Cox Grn.
Bray
Dorney
Eton
Eton Wick
WINDSOR
Old Windsor
Datchet
Langley
Colnbrook
Harmondsworth
Sipson
Harlington
Cranford
Heston
Brentford
Isleworth
HOUNSLOW
HEATHROW AIRPORT
Stanwell
Feltham
Ashford
Staines
EGHAM
Englefield Green
Windsor Great Park
Winkfield
Ascot
Sunninghill
Sunningdale
Virginia Water
Thorpe
Laleham
Littleton
Sunbury-on-Thames
Teddington
Hampton
Walton-on-Thames
Esher
CHERTSEY
Addlestone
WEYBRIDGE
Byfleet
Cobham
Woodham
Chobham
Ottershaw
Lyne
Binfield
WOKINGHAM
Bracknell
Bracknell Forest
Crowthorne
Sandhurst
CAMBERLEY
Yateley
Bagshot
Lightwater
Windlesham
Bisley
Knaphill
Horsell
WOKING
Pyrford
Ripley
Frimley
Hawley
FARNBOROUGH
Fleet
Church Crookham
ALDERSHOT
Ash
Farnham
Guildford
Shalford
Worplesdon
Pirbright
Ockham
East Horsley
West Horsley
Fetcham
Great Bookham
Effingham
Gomshall
Shere
Albury
Chilworth
Bramley
Godalming
Milford
Elstead
Farncombe
Hindhead
Grayshott
Haslemere
Liphook
Bordon
Chiddingfold
Dunsfold
Cranleigh
Ewhurst
Ockley
Rudgwick
Warnham
Broadbridge Heath
Slinfold
Alfold
Loxwood
Northchapel
Fernhurst
Liss Forest
West Liss
Steep Marsh
Surrey Hills
North Downs Way
Hogs Back
M4
M25
M3
A3
A31
A30
A322
A329(M)
39
40
28
16
27

Uxbridge
Hillingdon
Northolt
Sudbury
Alperton
Willesden
Camden
Islington
East Ham
Barking
Perivale
Harlesden
Kilburn
Bethnal Green
Stratford
Cowley
Yeading
Greenford
Regents Park
Finsbury
Shoreditch
West Ham
Beckton
Yiewsley
Hayes
Southall
EALING
Acton
Paddington
Holborn
City
Poplar
West Drayton
Hanwell
Kensington
Hyde Park
Westminster
Southwark
Bermondsey
Blackwall Tunnel
North Woolwich
Woolwich
Harlington
Heston
Chiswick
Hammersmith
Chelsea
LAMBETH
Greenwich
Sipson
Cranford
Brentford
Kew
Kew Br.
Fulham
Battersea
Deptford
Charlton
Longford
Isleworth
Putney
Peckham
Kidbrooke
HEATHROW AIRPORT
HOUNSLOW
Mortlake
Clapham
Camberwell
New Cross
Lewisham
Richmond
Brixton
Dulwich
West Bedfont
East Bedfont
Roehampton
Wandsworth
Hither Green
Eltham
Stanwell
Richmond Park
Wimbledon Common
Balham
Catford
Feltham
Twickenham
Kingston Vale
Streatham
Mottingham
Grove Park
Staines
Ashford
Hanworth
Ham
Teddington
Upper Tooting
West Norwood
Sydenham
Chislehurst
Hampton
Bushy Park
Wimbledon
Merton
Penge
Laleham
Littleton
Sunbury-on-Thames
Kingston upon Thames
Raynes Park
South Norwood
Beckenham
BROMLEY
Morden
Mitcham
Thornton Heath
Elmers End
Bickley
Petts Wood
West Molesey
East Molesey
Thames Ditton
New Malden
Surbiton
Selhurst
Eden Park
West Wickham
Bromley Common
CHERTSEY
Walton-on-Thames
Long Ditton
Tolworth
Worcester Park
St. Helier
Addiscombe
Hayes
Shirley
Hackbridge
Croydon
WEYBRIDGE
Esher
Hersham
Hook
Carshalton
Keston
Chessington
Cheam
Sutton
Wallington
Beddington
Addington
Farnborough
Claygate
South Croydon
New Haw
Ewell
New Addington
Byfleet
Whiteley Village
Belmont
Purley
Selsdon
Leaves Green
Downe
West Byfleet
Oxshott
Cobham
EPSOM
Woodmansterne
Sanderstead
Hamsey Green
Farleigh
Wisley
Stoke D'Abernon
Wood Field
Kenley
Biggin Hill
Cudham
Pyrford
Downside
Great Burgh
BANSTEAD
Coulsdon
Burgh Heath
Whyteleafe
Warlingham
Ripley
Martyr's Green
Leatherhead Common
Ashtead
Chipstead
Old Coulsdon
South Street
Ockham
Fetcham
Leatherhead
Tadworth
Hooley
Tatsfield
Woldingham
Little Bookham
Kingswood
Chaldon
CATERHAM
Titsey
Effingham
Walton on the Hill
Lower Kingswood
East Horsley
West Horsley
Great Bookham
Headley
Westerham
Mickleham
Merstham
Brewer Street
Godstone
Limpsfield
Limpsfield Chart
Oxted
Westhumble
Ranmore Common
Dorking
Buckland
Redhill
Nutfield
Church Town
Tandridge
Crockham Hill
East Clandon
Newland's Corner
Pixham
Betchworth
Bletchingley
Brockham
Reigate
Earlswood
South Nutfield
Albury
Gomshall
Abinger Hammer
Westcott
Strood Green
Doversgreen
Ridge Green
Crowhurst Lane End
Marlpit Hill
Shere
Wotton
North Holmwood
Sidlow
Salfords
South Godstone
Crowhurst
Crouch House Green
Brook
Sutton
Abinger Common
Leigh
Blindley Heath
Edenbridge
Farley Green
Holmbury St. Mary
Peaslake
South Holmwood
Nalderswood
Outwood
Horne
Marsh Green
Holmbury St Mary
Coldharbour
Parkgate
Norwood Hill
Meath Green
Lingfield
Hurt Wood
Leith Hill
Beare Green
Hookwood
Weatherhill
Horley
Smallfield
Dormansland
Newdigate
Charlwood
GATWICK AIRPORT
Burstow
Newchapel
Felcourt
Rowly
Ewhurst
Forest Green
Capel
Clark's Green
Copthorne
Lullenden
Hammerwood
Cranleigh
Ewhurst Green
Ockley
Felbridge
Blackwell
Walliswood
County Oak
East Grinstead
Ifield
Three Bridges
Crawley Down
Oakwoodhill
Kingsfold
Rusper
Lambs Green
Pound Hill
Worth
Sunnyside
Ashurstwood
Ellen's Green
Crawley
Turners Hill
Saint Hill
Forest Row
Rowhook
Faygate
Broadfield
Tilgate
Alfold
Rudgwick
Warnham
Pease Pottage
Selsfield Common
West Hoathly
Tisman's Common
Bucks Green
Strood Green
Broadbridge Heath
Roffey
Colgate
Balcombe Lane
Sharpthorne
Park Street
Slinfold
St Leonard's Forest
Tilgate Forest Row
Wych Cross
The Haven
Horsham
Balcombe
Highbrook
Chelwood Gate
Handcross
Roundstreet
Ashfold Crossways
Staplefield
Ardingly
Horsted Keynes
Chelwood Common
Monk's Gate
Slaugham
Danehill
Nutley
Lower Beeding
Brook Street
Slough Green
Whitemans
Southwater
Warninglid
0 1 2 3 4 5 6 miles
0 1 2 3 4 5 6 7 8 9 10 km

Dagenham
Hornchurch
Corbets Tey
North Ockendon
Horndon on the Hill
Fobbing
Corringham
CANVEY ISLAND
Leigh Beck
South Hornchurch
Rainham
Thurrock
South Ockendon
Baker Street
Orsett
Stanford-le-Hope
Coryton
Creekmouth
Thamesmead
Wennington
Aveley
North Stifford
Mucking
Thames Haven
THAMES ESTUARY
Belvedere
Erith
Abbey Wood
Purfleet
South Stifford
Little Thurrock
Grays
Chadwell St Mary
Linford
West Tilbury
East Tilbury
West Thurrock
Dartford Crossing
Tilbury
Halstow Marshes
St Mary's Marshes
Allhallows
Allhallows-on-Sea
Lower Stoke
Isle of Grain
Welling
Bexleyheath
Slade Green
Crayford
DARTFORD
Stone
Greenhithe
Swanscombe
NORTHFLEET
GRAVESEND
Chalk
Milton Chantry
Cliffe
Cooling
High Halstow
St Mary Hoo
Stoke
North Street
Bexley
Sidcup
Coldblow
Wilmington
Bean
Betsham
Perry Street
Southfleet
Secret Cold War Bunker
Shorne
Higham
Church Street
Lower Higham
Cliffe Woods
Medway
Hoo St. Werburgh
Chattenden
Upnor Castle
Foots Cray
North Cray
Hextable
Hawley
Darenth
Sutton at Hone
Swanley Village
Swanley
St. Paul's Cray
St Mary Cray
Crockenhill
Orpington
South Darenth
Horton Kirby
Istead Rise
Longfield
New Barn
Singlewell
Thong
Shorne Wood
Cobham
Sole Street
Temple Manor
Wainscott
Strood
Upnor
Frindsbury
Historic Dockyard
Brompton
Grange
Riverside
Ham Green
ROCHESTER
Dickens Centre
Gillingham
Upchurch
CHATHAM
Luton
Farningham
Eynsford
Lullingstone Roman Villa
Lullingstone
Hartley
Meopham Station
Hook Green
Camer Park
Luddesdown
Cuxton
North Halling
Fawkham Green
Meopham
Wayfield
Medway (Rochester)
Capstone Farm
Rainham
Breach
Moor Street
Wigmore
Newington
Hartlip
Chelsfield
Well Hill
Green Street Green
Maplescombe
Brands Hatch
New Ash Green
Ash
Upper Halling
Halling
Wouldham
Rochester Airport
Hempstead
Walderslade
West Kingsdown
Culverstone Green
Blue Bell Hill
Burham
Medway Services
Bredhurst
Stockbury
Pratt's Bottom
Badger's Mount
Shoreham
Halstead
NORTH DOWNS
Stansted
Fairseat
Vigo Village
Trosley
Snodland
Birling
Trottiscliffe
Ryarsh
Kit's Coty House
Eccles
South Green
Knockholt
Knockholt Pound
Otford
Kemsing
Heaverham
Wrotham
Addington
New Hythe
The Friars
Aylesford
Tyland Barn
Boxley
Bicknor
Hucking
Chevening
Borough Green
Wrotham Heath
West Malling
Leybourne
Ditton
British Legion Village
Sandling
Mus. of Kent Life
Detling
Thurnham
Broad Street
Dunton Green
Seal
Chipstead
Riverhead
Platt
Ightham
Great Comp
Offham
St Leonards Tower
Manor Park
East Malling
Maidstone
Roseacre
Maidstone Services
Hollingbourne
Eyhorne Street
Sundridge
Brasted
Sevenoaks
Stone Street
Crouch
Claygate Cross
Kent Street
East Barming
Tovil
Bearsted
Quebec Ho.
Brasted Chart
The Chart
Knole
Cross Keys
Ivy Hatch
Ightham Mote
Plaxtol
Mereworth
Old Soar Manor
Teston
Wateringbury
East Farleigh
Shepway
Otham
Stoneacre
Leeds
Leeds Castle
Broomfield
Emmetts
Whitley Row
Chartwell
Ide Hill
Toy's Hill
Underriver
Dunk's Green
West Peckham
Nettlestead
West Farleigh
Loose
Boughton Monchelsea
Langley
Langley Heath
Kingswood
Sevenoaks Weald
Oakhurst
Coldharbour
Shipbourne
Nettlestead Green
Coxheath
Warmlake
Kent
Broadview Gardens
Pittswood
Hadlow
Hale Street
Yalding
Hunton
Yalding Organic Gdn.
Linton
Chart Corner
Chart Sutton
Sutton Valence
Ulcombe
Pootings
Four Elms
Hildenborough
Hilden Park
Higham Wood
East Peckham
Benover
Laddingford
Chainhurst
Rabbit's Cross
How Green
Chiddingstone Causeway
Golden Green
Barnes Street
Beltring
Whitbread Hop Farm
Bough Beech
Chiddingstone Castle
Leigh
Tonbridge Castle
Brook Street
TONBRIDGE
Whetsted
Five Oak Green
Queen Street
Collier Street
Cross-at-Hand
Milebush
Southernden
Hever
Hever Castle and Gardens
Chiddingstone
Penshurst Place
Haysden
Tudeley
Paddock Wood
Claygate
Marden
Hawkenbury
Headcorn
Penshurst
Bidborough
Markbeech
Castle Hill
Staplehurst
Sinkhurst Green
Marden Beech
Marden Thorn
Farm Mus.
Iden Croft Herbs
Chiddingstone Hoath
Southborough
Speldhurst
High Brooms
Matfield
Brenchley
Knox Bridge
Frittenden
Cowden
Pembury
Winchet Hill
Curtisden Green
Blackham
Fordcombe
Mus. & Art Gall.
Petteridge
Horsmonden
Sprivers Garden
ROYAL TUNBRIDGE WELLS
Hazel Street
Cranbrook Common
Three Chimneys
Ashurst
Langton Green
Hawkenbury
Lamberhurst Quarter
Goudhurst
Sissinghurst
Spa Valley Railway
Groombridge
Bells Yew Green
Bayham Abbey
Lamberhurst
Iden Green
Wilsley Pound
Cranbrook & Dist. Mus.
Finchcocks
Scotney Castle
Cranbrook
East End
Hartfield
Withyham
Eridge Green
Frant
Hook Green
Kilndown
Hartley
Kent Int'l Parkgate
Upper Hartfield
Lye Green
Cousley Wood
Wood's Green
Bedgebury Pinetum
Bedgebury Forest
Benenden
Coleman's Hatch
Friar's Gate
Boarshead
Bewl Bridge Reservoir
Durgates
Three Leg Cross
Gill's Green
Iden Green
Dingleden
Rolvenden
Mark Cross
Wadhurst
Flimwell
High Street
Hawkhurst
Crowborough
Poundfield
Riseden
Bestbeech Hill
Union Street
Four Throws
ASHDOWN FOREST
Town Row
Shover's Green
Wallcrouch
Ticehurst
Horns Corner
The Moor
Rolvenden Layne
Rotherfield
Tidebrook
Pashley Manor Gardens
Jarvis Brook
Swiftsden
Sandhurst
Linkhill
Stonegate
Duddleswell
Coggins Mill
Hurst Green
Sandhurst Cross
Newenden
Cackle Street
Fairwarp
High Hurstwood
Mayfield
Witherenden Hill
Etchingham
Bodiam
Great Dixter
Butcher's Cross
Rother
M25
M20
M26
M2
A2
A13
A20
A21
A25
A26
A227
A228
A229
A264
A268
WEALD

CANVEY ISLAND
Coryton
Thames Haven
Leigh Beck
Shoeburyness
Cambridge Town
THAMES ESTUARY
42
43
(From Dartford)
VLISINGEN 9:30
ZEEBRUGGE 9:00
Halstow Marshes
St Mary's Marshes
Allhallows-on-Sea
Allhallows
St Mary Hoo
Lower Stoke
Isle of Grain
Grain
Cliffe
Cooling
High Halstow
Stoke
North Street
Cliffe Woods
Medway
Hoo St.Werburgh
Chattenden
UPNOR CASTLE
29
Upnor
Frindsbury
HISTORIC DOCKYARD
Brompton
Grange
RIVERSIDE
ROCHESTER
DICKENS CENTRE
Gillingham
CHATHAM
Luton
Wayfield (Rochester)
MEDWAY CAPSTONE FARM
Hempstead
Walderslade
Rainham
Upchurch
Ham Green
Lower Halstow
Iwade
Breach
Moor Street
Wigmore
Newington
Hartlip
Bobbing
MEDWAY SERVICES
Bredhurst
Stockbury
Sheerness
West Minster
Halfway Houses
Minster
ABBEY
Queenborough
Rushenden
Chetney Marshes
Eastchurch
Warden Pt.
Warden
Leysdown-on-Sea
ISLE OF SHEPPEY
ELMLEY
Isle of Harty
THE SWALE
Shell Ness
The Swale
Kemsley
SITTINGBOURNE & KEMSLEY L.T.RLY.
Milton Regis
SITTINGBOURNE
SAILING BARGE MUS.
Borden
Oad Street
Bapchild
Conyer
Barrow Green
Teynham
Uplees
Rodmersham
Tunstall
Highsted
Lynsted
OSPRINGE MAISON DIEU
Ospringe
Faversham
Oare
FLEUR DE LIS HERITAGE CENTRE
CHART GUNPOWDER MILLS
Graveney
Goodnestone
Preston
WHITSTABLE
Tankerton
Swalecliffe
Seasalter
MUSEUM & GALLERY
Chestfield
South Street
Yorkletts
Dargate
Hernhill
FARMING WORLD
MOUNT EPHRAIM
BLEAN WOODS
Blean
Honey Hill
Boughton Street
Dunkirk
Rough Common
Hales Place
Harbledown
CANTERBURY TALES
Thanington
Chartham Hatch
Chartham
South Green
Bredgar
Swanton Street
Milstead
TYLAND BARN
Boxley
Bicknor
Hucking
Thurnham
Detling
Broad Street
MUS. OF KENT LIFE
Sandling
Maidstone
MAIDSTONE SERVICES
Roseacre
Bearsted
Hollingbourne
Eyhorne Street
Wormshill
Frinsted
DODDINGTON PLACE
Newnham
Doddington
Wichling
Eastling
Sheldwich
BELMONT
North Street
Throwley
Badlesmere
Selling
Oversland
South Street
Old Wives Lees
Shottenden
Chilham
Shalmsford Street
Street End
Garlinge Green
Petham
Leaveland
Stalisfield Green
West Street
NORTH DOWNS WAY
Warren Street
Harrietsham
Lenham
Sandway
Lenham Heath
Charing
Challock
Molash
Godmersham
Sole Street
Crundale
Waltham
Bilting
Boughton Aluph
Westwell
Westwell Leacon
Charing Heath
Tovil
Shepway
Otham
STONEACRE
Leeds
LEEDS CASTLE
Broomfield
Kingswood
Langley
Langley Heath
Boughton Monchelsea
Loose
Linton
Warmlake
Chart Corner
Chart Sutton
Sutton Valence
Ulcombe
Grafty Green
Boughton Malherbe
Egerton
Egerton Forstal
Little Chart
Ram Lane
Hothfield
Goat Lees
Boughton Lees
Wye
WYE CROWN
Hassell Street
Bodsham
Elmsted
Hastingleigh
Brook
Kennington
Hinxhill
Rabbit's Cross
Cross-at-Hand
Milebush
Marden
Southernden
Pluckley
Pluckley Thorne
Hawkenbury
Headcorn
Staplehurst
Sinkhurst Green
Smarden Bell
Smarden
Maltman's Hill
Great Chart
Ashford
Willesborough
Willesborough Lees
Sevington
Brabourne
Lymbridge Green
Stowting
Brabourne Lees
Marden Beech
Marden Thorn
FARM MUS.
IDEN CROFT HERBS
Knox Bridge
Frittenden
Lashenden
Standen
Haffenden Quarter
Wissenden
Bethersden
Stubbs Cross
Kingsnorth
Mersham
Smeeth
Postling
Winchet Hill
Curtisden Green
Collier's Green
Cranbrook Common
SISSINGHURST
Three Chimneys
Biddenden
Tanden
Shadoxhurst
Cheeseman's Green
Sellindge
Sellindge Lees
Stanford
Wilsley Pound
Sissinghurst
CRANBROOK & DIST. MUS.
Cranbrook
East End
High Halden
Henghurst
Bromley Green
Aldington Frith
Clap Hill
Aldington
Bonnington
Court-at-Street
Newingreen
FOLKESTONE
Lympne
Pedlinge
Hartley
St Michael's
Shirkoak
Orlestone
SOUTH OF ENGLAND RARE BREEDS CEN.
HAM STREET WOODS
PORT LYMPNE WILD ANIMAL PARK AND GARDENS
KENT AND EAST SUSSEX STEAM RAILWAY
Parkgate
Woodchurch
Tenterden
Leigh Green
Brook Street
Kenardington
Warehorne
Ruckinge
Hamstreet
Bilsington
Royal Military Canal
West Hythe
Palmarsh
Benenden
Gill's Green
Iden Green
Dingleden
Rolvenden
Rolvenden Layne
High Street
Hawkhurst
Four Throws
The Moor
Sandhurst
Small Hythe
SMALLHYTHE PLACE
ISLE OF OXNEY
Reading Street
Appledore Heath
Appledore
HORNE'S PLACE CHAPEL
Snave
Newchurch
Burmarsh
ROMNEY, HYTHE AND DYMCHURCH LIGHT RAILWAY
ROMNEY MARSH
St Mary in the Marsh
Dymchurch
MARTELLO TOWER
St Mary's Bay
Peening Quarter
Stone
Snargate
Brenzett
AERONAUTICAL MUSEUM
Ivychurch
Wittersham
The Stocks
Ham Green
Bodiam
GREAT DIXTER
Brookland
Kent
NORTH DOWNS
0 1 2 3 4 5 6 miles
0 1 2 3 4 5 6 7 8 9 10 km

5
6
7
32
THE SHELL GROTTO
Foreness Pt.
Margate
Cliftonville
Kingsgate
NORTH FORELAND
LIGHTHOUSE
Westgate on Sea
MARGATE
DREAMLAND
Northdown
St Peter's
BROADSTAIRS
BLEAK HOUSE
DICKENS HOUSE MUSEUM
Dumpton
RAMSGATE BOULEVARD
Ramsgate
MARITIME MUSEUM
MOTOR MUSEUM
OOSTENDE 4:00
RECULVER TOWERS AND ROMAN FORT
Minnis Bay
Reculver
HERNE BAY
Hillborough
Birchington
QUEX PARK
Isle of Thanet
SPITFIRE AND HURRICANE MEM
Northwood
Newington
Beltinge
Acol
St Nicholas at Wade
Herne
Broomfield
Boyden Gate
Sarre
WINDMILL
KENT INTERNATIONAL
Manston
Monkton
Minster
Way
Cliffsend
Pegwell
PEGWELL BAY
SANDWICH & PEGWELL BAY
Pegwell Bay
ST. AUGUSTINE'S CROSS
WILDWOOD
Calcott
Hoath
Chislet
Upstreet
Stour
West Stourmouth
Hersden
East Stourmouth
Broadoak
Grove
STODMARSH
Preston
Westmarsh
Ware
RICHBOROUGH CASTLE
Westbere
Sturry
Stodmarsh
Elmstone
Hoaden
AMPHITHEATRE
Great Stonar
Fordwich
Canterbury
Wickhambreux
WINGHAM BIRD PARK
Ickham
Guilton
Ash
Sandwich
Sandwich Bay
ST. AUGUSTINE'S ABBEY
Littlebourne
Wingham
Marshborough
TOLL
ROYAL ST. GEORGE'S
CANTERBURY
HOWLETTS WILD ANIMAL PARK
Bekesbourne
Bramling
Staple
Woodnesborough
Stone Cross
TR
Worth
Nackington
Patrixbourne
Goodnestone
GOODNESTONE PARK
Gore
Eastry
Ham
Finglesham
Bridge
Adisham
Knowlton
Lower Hardres
Chillenden
Betteshanger
Sholden
MARITIME AND LOCAL HISTORY MUSEUM
DEAL
THE DOWNS
DEAL CASTLE
Bishopsbourne
Aylesham
Easole Street
Northbourne
NORTH DOWNS WAY
Kingston
Nonington
Snowdown
Tilmanstone
Elvington
Great Mongeham
Walmer
WALMER CASTLE AND GARDENS
Upper Hardres Court
Barham
Womenswold
Derringstone
Barfreston
EAST KENT RLY.
Ripple
Bossingham
East Studdal
Sutton
Woolage Green
Eythorne
Ringwould
Kingsdown
West Langdon
Coxhill
Shepherdswell
Martin
Denton
East Langdon
LYDDEN
Coldred
Martin Mill
Wingmore
Wootton
Lyminge Forest
Selsted
Lydden
Whitfield
Guston
St Margaret's at Cliffe
LYDDEN TEMPLE EWELL
ST. JOHN'S COMMANDERY
Temple Ewell
West Cliffe
THE BAY MUSEUM
St Margaret's Bay
Elham
Swingfield St
Ewell Minnis
THE PINES GARDEN
Rhodes Minnis
BUTTERFLY CENTRE
CRABBLE CORN MILL
SOUTH FORELAND
Swingfield Minnis
Buckland
Alkham
DOVER
ROMAN PAINTED HOUSE
WHITE CLIFFS (N.T.)
CALAIS 1:10
DUNKERQUE 1:50
Ottinge
Drellingore
Maxton
CASTLE & HELLFIRE CORNER
KENT BATTLE OF BRITAIN MUSEUM
Densole
Lyminge
Paddlesworth
Hawkinge
West Hougham
Farthingloe
DOVER
Etchinghill
Aycliff
DE BRADELEI WHARF
BOULOGNE 0:50
CHANNEL TUNNEL
Capel le Ferne
Newington
East Wear Bay
ELHAM VALLEY MUSEUM
Cheriton
Folkestone
RUSSIAN SUBMARINE
Saltwood
ROTUNDA
Sandgate
CLIFF LIFT
Hythe
19
CHANNEL TUNNEL
C
D
E
F
G
5
6
7
8
9

Crymych
Cwmorgan
Tanglwst
Tegryn
PRESELI
Hermon
Pentre-galar
Llanfyrnach
Hen-feddau fawr
Bryn-Iwan
Cwmduad
Mynachlog-ddu
Rosebush
Dinas
Glandwr
Henry's Moat
Maenclochog
Hebron
Blaen-waun
Blaen-y-coed
Cynwyl Elfed
Woodstock
Llangolman
Glandy Cross
Pant-y-Caws
Llanglydwen
CHOCOLATE FARM
Cwmbach
Llanwinio
Pen-y-bont
New Moat
Cefn-y-pant
Talog
Efailwen
LLYS-Y-FRAN RESERVOIR
Llys-y-frân
Llanycefn
Maesgwynne
Cwmfelin Mynach
Ty-hen
Abernant
Bwlchnewydd
Newchurch
Walton East
Login
Cross-hands
Llanboidy
Gellywen
Pen-ffordd
SN
Dyffryn
Llandissilio
Hiraeth
Clarbeston
Clarbeston Road
Bletherston
Henllan Amgoed
Meidrim
Merthyr
Tre-vaughan
Carmarthen
(Caerfyrddin)
Llanfallteg
Llangynin
Sarnau
Clunderwen
Gelli
Cwmfelin Boeth
Wiston
LLAWHADEN CASTLE
Bethesda
GROVELANDS
Bancyfelin
CORS GOCH, LLANLLWCH
Llanllwch
Llawhaden
Robeston Wathen
Llanddewi Velfrey
Whitland
Pwll-trap
Llangynog
Llangain
Narberth
(Arberth)
WILSON MUSEUM
Trevaughan
Backe
Afon Taf
St Clears
(Sanclêr)
The Rhos
Blackpool
Lampeter Velfrey
Llwyn-y-brain
Llanddowror
PICTON CASTLE GARDENS
HERONS BROOK
Crinow
Morfa Bach
Afon Tywi
Minwear
OAKWOOD
Cross Hands
Cold Blow
Princes Gate
Tavernspite
Halfpenny Furze
Llanybri
Landshipping
Templeton
Red Roses
Llandawke
DYLAN THOMAS BOATHOUSE
Llansteffan
Landshipping Quay
Martletwy
Ludchurch
Llanteg
Laugharne
CASTLE
Ferryside
Longstone
Llansadurnen
Brook
Broadway
Black Tar
Yerbeston
FOLLY FARM
Reynalton
Marros
MUSEUM OF SPEED
Broadlay
Thomas Chapel
Loveston
Stepaside
COLBY WOODLAND GARDEN
Pendine
East Marsh
LAWRENNY
Lawrenny
Cresswell Quay
Begelly
Jeffreyston
Kilgetty
Amroth
Llansaint
Pendine Sands
Traeth Pentywyn
Cresselly
West Williamston
Broadmoor
Hill
PEMBROKESHIRE COAST
ARFORDIR PENFRO
Carew Newton
UPTON CASTLE GROUNDS
East Williamston
Saundersfoot
Cosheston
CAREW CASTLE
Redberth
Carew
Milton
Broadfield
Pembrey Forest
Sageston
New Hedges
Pembroke
(Penfro)
Carew Cheriton
LAMPHEY BISHOP'S PALACE
MANOR HOUSE WILDLIFE PARK
TUDOR MERCHANT'S HOUSE
CARMARTHEN
Lamphey
St Florence
Gumfreston
Tenby
(Dinbych-y-Pysgod)
Hodgeston
Jameston
Penally
BAY
Freshwater East
Lydstep
Giltar Pt.
Caldey Sound
BAE CAERFYRDDIN
MANORBIER CASTLE
Manorbier
Cheriton or Stackpole Elidor
Trewent Pt.
Trwyn Trewent
Old Castle Hd.
Caldey Island
Ynys Bŷr
Chapel Pt.
Trwyn Capel
Stackpole Hd.
Pen Stackpole
SS
Burry Holms
Rhossili Bay
Bae Rhossili
Worms Head
Penrhyn-Gŵyr
A40
A478
A477
A4075
A4115
B4313
B4314
B4316
B4318
B4586
A4139
B4584
B4328
A4066
B4299
B4298
B4312
B4333
A484
44
45
46
0 1 2 3 4 5 6 miles
0 1 2 3 4 5 6 7 8 9 10 km

Carmarthenshire
(Sir Gaerfyrddin)
Swansea
(Abertawe)
Brechfa Forest
Dolgran
Gwernogle
Abergorlech
Edwinsford
Talley
Llandovery
Cwmdwr
Nant-y-ffin
Pen-y-garn
Cwm-byr
Waunclunda
Llansadwrn
Llanwrda
Myrtle Hill
Alltwalis
Brechfa
Cwmdu
Halfway
Felindre
Cilgwyn
Myddfai
Llanpumsaint
Llanllawddog
Horeb
Llanfynydd
Soar
Ashfield
Llangadog
Usk Reservoir
Pontarsais
Hermon
Rhydargaeau
Plâs
Pant-glas
Capel Isaac
Salem
Manordeilo
Cwmifor
Pant-teg
Pant gwyn
Bethlehem
Dyffryn Ceidrych
Talsarn
Felingwm uchaf
Felingwm isaf
Pen-y-banc
Rhosmaen
Twynllanan
Llanddeusant
Peniel
Llanfihangel-uwch-Gwili
Pentrefelin
Broad Oak
Pont-ar-llechau
Capel Gwyn
Court Henry
Pontbren Araeth
Capel Gwynfe
Pont Aber
White Mill
Pont-ar-gothi
Llangathen
Cilsan
Vale of Tywi
Dyffryn Tywi
Llandeilo
Neuadd
Abergwili
Nantgaredig
Llanegwad
Felindre
Dryslwyn
Ffairfach
Carmarthen
Tanerdy
Llangunnor
Capel Dewi
Llanarthne
Golden Grove
Trapp
Carreg Cennen Farm Centre and Castle
Black Mountain
Y Mynydd Du
Foel Fraith
Pensarn
Johnstown
Nantycaws
National Botanic Garden of Wales
Penrhiw-goch
Temple Bar
Milo
Llandyfan
Llanddarog
Maesybont
Carmel
Cwmisfael
Porthyrhyd
Pentre-Gwenlais
Llandybie
Dre-fach
Croesyceiliog
Idole
Bancycapel
Gwendraeth Fach
Llangendeirne
Foel-gastell
Cefneithin
Gorslas
Caer-bryn
Twynmynydd
Brynamman
Rhosaman
Crwbin
Drefach
Cwm-y-glo
Pen-y-groes
Tir-y-dail
Glanaman
Garnant
Pontamman
Cwmllynfell
Ystradowen
Abercraf
Pontantwn
Bancffosfelen
Cwm-mawr
Cross Hands
Morfa
Saron
Ammanford
Gwaun-Leision
Tairgwaith
Cwmgiedd
Llandyfaelog
Pontyberem
Tumble
Capel Hendre
Penybanc
Betws (Rhydaman)
Gwaun-Cae-Gurwen
Upper Cwm-twrch
Lower Cwm-twrch
Meinciau
Pentre
Cwmgwili
Tycroes
Pantyffynnon
Cwmgors
Gurnos
Ystradgynlais
Four Roads
Pont-Henri
Greynor
Garnswllt
Ystalyfera
Mynyddygarreg
Pontyates
Llannon
Llwyn-teg
Mynydd y Gwair
Kidwelly (Cydweli)
Cynheidre
Sylen
Pont Abraham Services
Godre'r-graig
Carway
Five Roads
Horeb
Lliedi Resrs.
Llanedy
Sardis
Pentrebach
Graig Fawr
SN
Climaen gwyn
Ynys-meudwy
Swansea Valley
Cwm Abertawe
Mynydd March-Hywel
Crynant
Trimsaran
Ffrorest
Rhyd-y-fro
Pontardawe
Cilybebyll
Pinged
Waun-y-clyn
Hendy
Pontarddulais
Rhyd-y-gwin
Craig-cefn-parc
Trebanos
Gellinudd
Rhôs
Cwmbach
Cwm-Dulais
Alltwen
Achddu
Felinfoel
Allt
Llangennech
Felindre
Rhyd-y-pandy
Faerdre
Pembrey
Pwll
Furnace
Dafen
Waungron
Pontlliw
Clydach
Ynystawe
Glais
Burry Port
(Porth Tywyn)
Sandy
Bryn
Grovesend
Swansea West Services
Pantlasau
Cilfrew
Aberdulais
Millennium Coastal Park
Llanelli
Llwynhendy
Bynea
Yspitty
Penllergaer
Heol-las
Birchgrove
Bryn-coch
Rhydding
Tonna
Neath Abbey
Cadoxton-Juxta-Neath
Machynys
Morfa
Wildfowl and Wetlands Trust
Loughor
Gorseinon
Llangyfelach
Morriston
Skewen
Neath Museum
Neath
(Castell-Nedd)
Whiteford Pt.
Trwyn Whiteford
Llanrhidian Sands
Traeth Llanrhidian
Pen-clawdd
Gowerton
Waunarlwydd
Cadle
Llansamlet
Swansea Vale Rly.
Pentre-dwr
Cwm
Cimla
Crofty
Blue Anchor
Fforest-fâch
Landore
Bon-y-maen
Llandarcy
Briton Ferry
The Gnoll
Pontrhydyfen
Wernffrwd
Llanmorlais
Three Crosses
Dunvant
Cwmdu
Pentre-chwyth
Foxhole
Swansea (Abertawe)
Crymlyn Bog and Pant-y-Sais
Cheriton
Llanmadoc
Landimore
Weobley Castle
Glynn Vivian
Plantasia
Port Tennant
Baglan
Pwll-y-glaw
Brynbryddan
Burry Green
Llanrhidian
Llethrid
Killay
Sketty
Brynmill
National Waterfront Museum
Swansea Museum
Mynydd Dinas
Cwmafan
Llangennith
Upper Killay
Clyne Valley
Burry
Reynoldston
Ilston
Mayals
Black Pill
Aberavon
Port Talbot
Goybre
The Beacon
Llanddewi
Knelston
Gower Heritage Centre
Lunnon
Kittle
Bishopston
West Cross
Swansea Bay
Taibach
Rhossili
Scurlage
Penrice
Nicholaston
Penmaen
Parkmill
Pennard
Manselfield
Oldway
Newton
Lovespoon Gallery
Oystermouth Castle
The Mumbles
(Y Mwmbwls)
Bae Abertawe
Margam
Groes
Middleton
Pilton Green
Southgate
Oxwich
Oxwich Bay
Bae Oxwich
Mumbles Hd.
Trwyn yr Mwmbwls
Gower Coast
Horton
Overton
Port-Eynon
Port Eynon
Port Eynon Bay
Bae Port Eynon
Port Eynon Pt.
Trwyn Port Eynon
Pwlldu Hd.
Pen Pwlldu
Cork 10:00
SS
Kenfig
Mawdlam
Kenfig Pool and Dunes
Kenfig Burrows
Royal Porthcawl
Hutchwns
Porthcawl
A40
A48
A476
A483
A484
A474
A4069
A4067
A4138
A4240
A4118
A4107
A4109
A4068
A485
B4300
B4310
B4302
B4306
B4309
B4317
B4308
B4297
B4556
B4295
B4296
B4620
B4271
B4247
B4291
B4603
B4290
M4
A B C D E F G
5 6 7 8

Llandovery
Llandeilo'r Fan
Llanfihangel Nant Bran
Pont-faen
Pwllgloyw
Garthbrengy
Felinfach
Sarnau
Talachddu
Llandefaelog Fach
Llanddew
Halfway
Pentre-bach
Myrtle Hill
Llanwrda
Cilgwyn
Myddfai
Llywel
Pentre'r-felin
Trallong
Aberyscir
Brecon
(Aberhonddu)
Llanywern
Llanfaes
Llechfaen
Usk Reservoir
Trecastle
Sennybridge
(Pont Senni)
Penpont
Llanspyddid
Llangadog
Cwmwysg
Pont ar Hydfer
Defynnog
Brecknock Museum
South Wales Borderers
Cathedral
Brecon Gaer Roman Fort
Llanhamlach
Glas Fynydd Forest
Mynydd Illtyd
Mountain Centre
Tai'r-Bull
Libanus
Llanfrynach
Pencelli
Talsarn
Twynllanan
Llanddeusant
Crai
Felin-Crai
Heol Senni
Dyffryn Ceidrych
Pont-ar-llechau
Capel Gwynfe
Trichrug
Pont Aber
Neuadd
Llwyn-y-celyn
Craig Cerrig Gleisiad a Fan Frynych
Glyn Tarell
Fan Brycheiniog
Cray Res.
Pen y Fan
Danywenallt
Brecon Beacons
Talybont Res.
Neuadd Reservoirs
Fan Fawr
Beacons Res.
Ystradfellte Res.
Fan Gihirych
Foel Fraith
Black Mountain
Mynydd Du
Fforest Fawr
Abercynafon
Dan-yr-Ogof Showcaves
Glyntawe
Dan-yr-Ogof
Craig-y-nos
Ogof Ffynnon Ddu
Penwyllt
Cantref Res.
Nant-ddu
Brynamman
Rhosaman
Pen-y-cae
Helen
Garwnant
Garwnant Visitor Centre
Pontsticill Reservoir
Cwmllynfell
Ystradowen
Ystradfellte
Llwyn-on Res.
Gwaun-Leision
Tairgwaith
Gwaun-Cae-Gurwen
Abercraf
Caehopkin
Sarn
Upper Cwm-twrch
Cwmgiedd
Lower Cwm-twrch
Coelbren
Penrhos
Brecon Mountain Railway
Pontsticill
Vaynor
Cwmgors
Gurnos
Ystradgynlais
Onllwyn
Dyffryn Cellwen
Ystalyfera
Seven Sisters
Pontneddfechan
Penderyn
Cefn-coed-y-cymmer
Dowlais
Castle Mus & Art Gall.
Godre'r-graig
Nant-y-cafn
Glyn-Neath
(Glynedd)
Pontbren Llwyd
Rheola Forest
Morfa Glas
Swansea Valley
Cwm Abertawe
Gellideg
Pen-yr-Heolgerrig
Rhigos
Hirwaun
Climaen gwyn
Ynysmeudwy
Mynydd March-Hywel
Cwm-hwnt
Tre-Gibbon
Merthyr Tydfil
(Merthyr Tudful)
Ynysfach Engine House Heritage Centre
Rhyd-y-fro
Pontardawe
Glantawe Riverside
Cilybebyll
Crynant
Vale of Neath
Cwm Nedd
Blaengwrach
Cwmgwrach
Penywaun
Trecynon
Llwydcoed
Pentrebach
Gellinudd
Cefn Coed Colliery Mus.
Resolven Mtn.
Cwmdare
Aberdare
(Aberdâr)
Dare Valley
Abercanaid
Trebanos
Rhôs
Alltwen
Resolven
Aber-nant
Troedyrhiw
Cwmbach
Clydach
Neath
Melincourt
Rhondda
Aberaman
Bedlinog
Aberfan
Cwmfelin
Cilfrew
Aberdulais
Falls
Clyne
Blaenrhondda
Tynewydd
Cwmaman
Mountain Ash
(Aberpennar)
Merthyr Vale
Glais
Bryn-coch
Port Talbot
Cynon
Heol-las
Rhydding
Birchgrove
Neath Abbey
Tonna
Glyncorrwg
Treherbert
Maerdy
Penrhiwceiber
Skewen
Cadoxton-Juxta-Neath
Neath Museum
(Castell-Nedd)
Blaen-gwynfi
Treorchy
(Treorci)
Ferndale
St Gwynno Forest
Treharris
Pentre-dwr
Cimla
Aber-gwynfi
Pentre
Cwm-parc
Rhondda
Taff
Ynysboeth
Abercynon
Llansamlet
Llandarcy
Duffryn
Cymer
Croeserw
Ton-Pentre
Ystrad
Tylorstown
Briton Ferry
The Gnoll
South Wales Miners Museum
Caerau
Werfa
Gelli
Pont-y-gwaith
Wattstown
Crymlyn Bog and Pant-y-Sais
Pontrhydyfen
Afan Argoed
Foel y Dyffryn
Spelter
Nant-y-moel
Craig y Geifri
Llwynypia
Ynysybwl
Baglan
Pwll-y-glaw
Brynbryddan
Dyffryn
Blaengarw
Clydach Vale
Clyndach Vale
Trealaw
Ynyshir
Mynydd Dinas
Bryn
Nantyffyllon
Wyndham
Price Town
Tonypandy
Porth
Rhondda Heritage Park
Glyncoch
Cilfynydd
Cwmafan
Maesteg
Pontycymer
Penygraig
Trehafod
Pontypridd
Glyntaff
Aberavon
Garth
Ogmore Vale
Evanstown
Trebanog
Cwmfelin
Llangynwyd
Pont Rhyd-y-cyff
Ogmore Forest
Gilfach Goch
Bryn Golau
Tonyrefail
Treforest
Port Talbot
Goybre
Taibach
Mynydd Margam
Bridgend
Lewistown
Hendreforgan
Pen-y-coedcae
Rhydyfelin
Hawthorn
Swansea Bay
Bae Abertawe
Margam
Groes
Moel Ton-Mawr
Bettws
Pant-yr-awel
Glynogwr
Castellau
Upper Church Village
Llantwit Fardre
Margam Abbey and Stones Museum
(Pen-y-bont ar Ogwr)
Llangeinor
Blackmill
Mynydd Maendy
Coedely
Beddau
Coytrahen
Bryngarw
Brynmenyn
Tondu
Aberkenfig
Bryncethin
Heol-y-Cyw
Model Centre
Llantrisant
Kenfig Hill
Gefn Cross
Sarn
McArthur Glen Bridgend
Brynna
Talbot Green
Llanharan
Kenfig
Mawdlam
Pyle
(Y Pîl)
Cefn Cribbwr
Pen-y-fai
Pendre
Coity
Coity Castle
Pencoed
Bryncae
Dolau
Pont-y-clun
Cross Inn
Creigiau
Kenfig Pool and Dunes
North Cornelly
Llanilid
Llanharry
Brynsadler
Miskin
Groes-faen
Llanilltern
Kenfig Burrows
South Cornelly
New Castle
Talygarn
Llanerch Vineyard
Royal Porthcawl
Laleston
Oldcastle
Coychurch
St Mary Hill
Craig Penllyn
St Brides super Ely
Peterston super Ely
Newton
Tythegston
Treoes
Llansannor
Ystradowen
Clevis
Merthyr Mawr
Ogmore Castle
Corntown
Llangan
Pendoylan
Merthyr Mawr Warren
Ogmore
Ewenny
Penllyn
Maendy
Welsh St Donats
Porthcawl
0 1 2 3 4 5 6 miles
0 1 2 3 4 5 6 7 8 9 10 km

BLACK MOUNTAINS
Y MYNYDDOEDD DUON
Monmouthshire
(Sir Fynwy)
Torfaen
(Tor-faen)
Caerphilly
(Caerffili)
Newport
(Casnewydd)
Cardiff
(Caerdydd)
Abergavenny
(Y Fenni)
Monmouth
(Trefynwy)
Talgarth
Llanelieu
Michaelchurch Escley
Middle Maes-coed
St Margaret's
Newton
Bacton
Thruxton
Cockyard
Winnal
Dewshall Court
Kivernoll
Didley
St Devereux
Much Dewchurch
Wormelow Tump
Kilpeck
Wormbridge
Abbey Dore
Howton
Ewyas Harold
Pontrilas
Orcop Hill
Llanwarne
Bagwy Llydiart
Orcop
Garway Hill
Kentchurch
Grosmont
White Rocks
Hoaldalbert
Garway
Broad Oak
Skenfrith
Norton
Cross Ash
Llanrothal
Welsh Newton
St Maughans
Crossway
Newcastle
Llangattock Lingoed
Bont
Upper Green
Wayne Green
Llanfaenor
Llangattock-Vibon-Avel
Maypole
Buckholt
Onen
Llanvetherine
Llantilio Crossenny
Llanvihangel-Ystern-Llewern
Wernyrheolydd
Penrhôs
Pen-yr-heol
Wonastow
Dingestow
Mitchel Troy
Tregare
Raglan
Pen-y-clawdd
Cwmcarvan
Mitcheltroy Common
Llangovan
Kingcoed
Twyn-y-Sheriff
Bettws Newydd
Gwehelog
Llandenny
Llansoy
Parkhouse
Trelleck Grange
Llanishen
Gwernesney
Usk
(Brynbuga)
Llangwm
New Inn
Devauden
Wolvesnewton
Kilgwrrwg Common
Newchurch
Chepstow Pk. Wood
Itton Common
Llanbadoc
Llanllowel
Llantrisant
Llangybi
Earlswood
Gaerllwyd
Pen-y-cae-mawr
Shirenewton
Llanvair Discoed
Llanvaches
Penhow
Caerwent
Crick
Highmoor Hill
Caldicot
Rogiet
Llanfihangel Rogiet
Undy
Magor
St Bride's Netherwent
Llanmartin
Langstone
Llanbeder
Cat's Ash
Parc-Seymour
Llanwern
Wilcrick
Bishton
Llandevenny
Redwick
Summerleaze
Whitson
Goldcliff
Nash
Pye Corner
Liswerry
Maindee
Christchurch
Caerleon
(Caerllion)
Ponthir
Llanhennock
Newbridge-on-Usk
Tredunnock
Llandegveth
Coed-y-paen
Croesyceiliog
Cwmbran
(Cwmbrân)
Llanfrechfa
Llantarnam
Oakfield
Pontnewydd
Upper Cwmbran
Lowlands
Griffithstown
Pontypool
(Pont-y-pwl)
New Inn
Glascoed
Little Mill
Monkswood
Llancayo
Kemeys Commander
Goetre
Nant-y-derry
Penperlleni
Abersychan
Trevethin
Garndiffaith
Talywain
Cwmavon
Varteg
Pen-groes-oped
Rhyd-y-meirch
Llanover
Llanvihangel Gobion
Bryngwyn
Llanarth
Llangattock nigh Usk
Coed Morgan
Llanddewi Rhydderch
Llanvapley
Bryn-y-gwenin
Llantilio Pertholey
Mardy
Llanfoist
Llanellen
Govilon
Gilwern
Llanelli
Clydach
Blaenavon
Forge Side
Garn-yr-erw
Blorenge
Llanelly Hill
Brynmawr
Nantyglo
Blaina
Coalbrookvale
Beaufort
Blackrock
Garnlydan
Rassau
Trefil
Dukestown
Sirhowy
Ebbw Vale
(Glyn Ebwy)
Tredegar
Briery Hill
Georgetown
Waunlwyd
Cwm
Abertillery
(Abertyleri)
Cwmtillery
East Bank
Rhymney
(Rhymni)
Pontlottyn
Abertysswg
New Tredegar
(Tredegar Newydd)
Fochriw
Tirphil
Deri
Man-moel
Hollybush
Aberbeeg
St Illtyd
Brynithel
Llanhilleth
(Llanhiledd)
Swffryd
Cwm Ffrwd-oer
Markham
Trinant
Argoed
Bargoed
Gilfach
Pengam
Blackwood
(Coed Duon)
Oakdale
Crumlin
(Crymlyn)
Newbridge
Pontllanfraith
Lanfach
Abercarn
Cwmcarn
Gelligaer
Trelewis
Nelson
Hengoed
Ystrad-mynach
Maesycwmmer
Wyllie
Ynysddu
Cwm-felin-fach
Pontywaun
Crosskeys
Risca
(Rhisga)
Henllys
Castell-y-bwch
Croes-y-mwyalch
Malpas
Bettws
Rogerstone
Lower Machen
Machen
Bedwas
Caerphilly
(Caerffili)
Trecenydd
Penyrheol
Abertridwr
Llanbradach
Nantgarw
Thornhill
Rudry
Rhiwderin
Bassaleg
Pentre-poeth
Duffryn
Michaelston-y-Fedw
Castleton
Coedkernew
Marshfield
St Brides Wentlooge
Peterstone Wentlooge
Blacktown
St Mellons
Llanrumney
Rumney
Newton
Lisvane
Llanedeyrn
Cyncoed
Llanishen
Rhiwbina
Whitchurch
Tongwynlais
Taff's Well
Pentyrch
Radyr
Birchgrove
Heath
Roath
Cathays
Llandaff
Canton
Ely
St Fagans
Michaelston-super-Ely
Crickhowell
Llangattock
Llangenny
Glangrwyney
Cwrt-y-gollen
Llwyn-du
Blaenawey
Llanbedr
Llanfihangel-Crucorney
Stanton
Pandy
Tre-wyn
Cwmyoy
Oldcastle
Walterstone
Llangua
Monmouth Cap
Rowlstone
Clodock
Longtown
Llanthony
Llanveynoe
Capel-y-ffin
Pengenffordd
Trefecca
Tredustan
Llanfilo
Llandefaelog-tre'r-graig
Llanfihangel Tal-y-llyn
Talyllyn
Llangors
Llangorse Lake
Llangasty Talyllyn
Cathedine
Scethrog
Llansantffraed
Bwlch
Cwmrhos
Cwmdu
Tretower
Gaer
Coed-yr-ynys
Llangynidr
Ffawyddog
Mynydd Llangynidr
Mynydd Llangattock
Mynydd Troed
Talybont-on-Usk
Aber-Village
Portishead
Battery Pt.
Redcliff Bay
West Hill
Sheepway
Avonmouth
Second Severn Crossing
Toll

Monmouthshire
(Sir Fynwy)
South
Gloucestershire
Monmouth
(Trefynwy)
Ross-on-Wye
Chepstow
(Cas-gwent)
Lydney
Cinderford
Newent
Coleford
Thornbury
Yate
Chipping Sodbury
Dursley
Wotton-under-Edge
Patchway
FILTON
MANGOTSFIELD
Caldicot
FOREST OF DEAN
River Severn
The Noose
Frampton on Severn
SO
ST
Thruxton
Winnal
Cockyard
Callow
Dewshall Court
Aconbury
Fownhope
Bolstone
Sollers Hope
Donnington
Brown's End
HELLEN'S MANSION
Much Marcle
Bromsberrow Hth.
Broom's Green
Ryton
Redmarley D'Abitot
Playley Green
Pendock
Didley
Kivernoll
King's Thorn
Little Dewchurch
Brockhampton
Falcon
Little Birch
Much Birch
Carey
Ballingham
COURT GARDENS
Crossway
Lyne Down
Dymock
St Devereux
Wormbridge
ABBEY DORE COURT
Kilpeck
KILPECK CHURCH
Howton
Much Dewchurch
Wormelow Tump
Fawley Chapel
Penalt
How Caple
Yatton
Fishpool
ST MARY'S CHURCH
Kempley
Poolhill
Staunton
Corse
Hoarwithy
Llandinabo
Red Rail
King's Caple
Foy
Hole-in-the-Wall
Orcop Hill
Pontrilas
Bagwy Llydiart
Llanwarne
Harewood End
Sellack
Upper Grove Common
Brampton Abbotts
Phocle Green
Crow Hill
Upton Bishop
Gorsley
Brand Green
Upleadon
Monmouth Cap
Orcop
Garway Hill
Pencoyd
Michaelchurch
ROSS SPUR SERVICES
Rudhall
Linton
Kilcot
Hartpury
Kentchurch
GROSMONT CASTLE
Grosmont
White Rocks
St Weonards
St Owens Cross
Tretire
Peterstow
Bridstow
Bromsash
Aston Ingham
BIRDS OF PREY
Malswick
Hoaldalbert
Tudorville
CANDLEMAKERS
Weston under Penyard
Aston Crews
Clifford's Mesne
Kent's Green
Highleadon
Garway
Broad Oak
Three Ashes
Glewstone
Hom Green
Coughton
Pontshill
Lea
Tibberton
Taynton
Rudford
Lassington
Highnam Green
SKENFRITH CASTLE
Norton
Skenfrith
Llangarron
Llancloudy
Pencraig
Walford
Goodrich
Hope Mansell
Glasshouse Hill
Cross Ash
Llanrothal
Welsh Newton
Llangrove
Marstow
Kerne Bridge
Mitcheldean
Longhope
Huntley
Bulley
Highnam
Crossway
St Maughans
WYE VALLEY BUTTERFLY ZOO
Whitchurch
JUBILEE MAZE
WELSH BICKNOR
Welsh Bicknor
Ruardean
Ruardean Woodside
Drybrook
Birdwood
Churcham
Oakle Street
Minsterworth
Wayne Green
Newcastle
Llanfaenor
Maypole
WHITCHURCH SERVICES
Ganarew
Greater Doward
Lower Lydbrook
Upper Lydbrook
Nailbridge
Blaisdon
Northwood Green
Elmore Back
Elmore
Llangattock-Vibon-Avel
Onen
Buckholt
Symonds Yat
English Bicknor
Flaxley
Westbury-on-Severn
Farleys End
GWRT
Llanvihangel-Ystern-Llewern
Rockfield
LADY PARK WOOD
FIDDLER'S ELBOW
Dixton
Christchurch
Edge End
Brierley
Bilson Green
Littledean
Elton
WESTBURY COURT
LITTLEDEAN HALL
Longney
Hardwicke
Boxbush
Wernyrheolydd
Penrhôs
Over
Wyesham
NELSON MUS.
Berry Hill
Five Acres
Staunton
Mile End
COLLIERY MUSEUM
Ruspidge
Newnham
Rodley
Pen-yr-heol
Wonastow
Monnow
Penallt
Coleford
Broadwell
Upper Soudley
DEAN HERITAGE CENTRE
WORKING FARM
Arlingham
Dingestow
Mitchel Troy
Redbrook
G.W.R. MUSEUM
Coalway
Fretherne
Saul
Upper Framilode
Tregare
Mitcheltroy Common
MONMOUTH SERVICES
RAGLAN
Newland
IRON MINES
Milkwall
Moreton Valence
Pen-y-clawdd
Pen-twyn
OFFA'S DYKE PATH
CAVES
Ellwood
Parkend
Awre
Whitminster
Raglan
Cwmcarvan
Caer Llan
Clearwell
Newmills
Yorkley
Nupend
Stowe Green
Trow Green
Whitecroft
Viney Hill
Blakeney
Twyn-y-Sheriff
Kingcoed
Llangovan
Trellech
Whitebrook
Pillowell
The Eaves
WWT SLIMBRIDGE WETLAND CENTRE
Eastington
OFFA'S DYKE
St Briavels
Bream
DEAN FOREST RAILWAY & MUSEUM
Purton
SLIMBRIDGE
Cambridge
Llandenny
Llandogo
ST. BRIAVELS CASTLE
Coldharbour
Newerne
Slimbridge
Moorend
Frocester
Llanishen
Parkhouse
Llansoy
Catbrook
Hewelsfield
Sharpness
Halmore
Gossington
Coaley
Trelleck Grange
Gwernesney
Aylburton
Newtown
Wanswell
Breadstone
Lower Cam
OLD STA.
Tintern Parva
Brockweir
TINTERN ABBEY
Netherend
Alvington
The Quarry
Nympsfield
Llangwm
New Inn
WYE VALLEY CENTRE
ULEY TUMULUS
Cam
Chapel Hill
Woolaston
Brookend
Berkeley
Stinchcombe
Wolvesnewton
Devauden
VEDDW HO.
BERKELEY CASTLE
JENNER MUSEUM
Ham
Tidenham Chase
Kilgwrrwg Common
Chepstow Pk. Wood
Wibdon
Stroat
Uley
Newchurch
Itton Common
Boughspring
Bevington
Woodmancote
Gaerllwyd
St Arvans
Tidenham
Shepperdine
Woodford
Stone
Nibley Green
North Nibley
Pen-y-cae-mawr
Earlswood
Woodcroft
Tutshill
MICHAELWOOD SERVICES
Mynydd-bach
STUART CRYSTAL VISITOR CENTRE
OLDBURY POWER STA. & VISITOR CENTRE
COOMBE VALLEY WOODS
Shirenewton
Mounton
Sedbury
Rockhampton
Falfield
Tortworth
Charfield
Parc-Seymour
Llanvaches
Dinham
Pwll-Meyric
Oldbury-on-Severn
Whitfield
Kingswood
Beachley
RUNSTON CHAPEL
SEVERN ROAD BRIDGE PONT HAFREN
Littleton-on-Severn
Morton
Milbury Heath
Cromhall
Churchend
ABBEY GATEHOUSE
Alderley
Tresham
Llanbeder
Penhow
PENHOW WOODLANDS
Crick
Mathern
SEVERN VIEW SERVICES
Cromhall Common
Llanmartin
Caerwent
Highmoor Hill
St Bride's Netherwent
CALDICOT CASTLE
Hillesley
TOLL
Aust
Elberton
Alveston
MAGOR SERVICES
CALDICOT CASTLE MUSEUM
Portskewett
Wilcrick
Rogiet
Sudbrook
Ingst
OLDOWN COUNTRY PARK
Rudgeway
Tytherington
Wickwar
Hawkesbury Upton
Llanfihangel-Rogiet
Magor
Undy
Redwick
Northwick
Olveston
Itchington
Hawkesbury
Llandevenny
SECOND SEVERN CROSSING
SEVERN BRIDGES VISITOR CENTRE
Severn Beach
Tockington
Rangeworthy
HORTON COURT
Caldicot Level
Summerleaze
Pilning
Awkley
Latteridge
Iron Acton
Engine Common
Horton
Little Sodbury
Almondsbury
Whitson
Over
Easter Compton
Frampton Cotterell
Nibley
Watley's End
Coalpit Heath
Old Sodbury
Hallen
Catbrain
FILTON
Stoke Gifford
Winterbourne
Winterbourne Down
Westerleigh
Wapley
Dodington
Tormarton
Henbury
Horfield
Hambrook
Frenchay
Blackhorse
Downend
Codrington
Shirehampton
Westbury on Trym
Stapleton
Fishponds
Pucklechurch
Hinton
DYRHAM PARK
West Littleton
Redcliff Bay
Sheepway
BRISTOL
P&R
0 1 2 3 4 5 6 miles
0 1 2 3 4 5 6 7 8 9 10 km

Tewkesbury
Bishop's Cleeve
Cheltenham
Charlton Kings
Gloucester
Hucclecote
Churchdown
Stroud
Stonehouse
Nailsworth
Chalford
Cirencester
Tetbury
Malmesbury
South Cerney
Cricklade
Fairford
Lechlade-on-Thames
Highworth
Swindon
Stratton St Margaret
Wootton Bassett
Purton
Stow-on-the-Wold
Bourton-on-the-Water
Northleach
Winchcombe
Stanway
Snowshill
C O T S W O L D S
C O T S W O L D S
c e s t e r
SP
SU
Oakley Wood
The Common
Source of the Thames
M5
M4
A40
A417
A419
A429
A436
A46
A435
A433
A38
B4077
B4425
B4040
B4042
50
51
38
38
24
25

Moreton-in-Marsh
Batsford
Bourton on the Hill
Sezincote
Great Wolford
Barton on the Heath
Little Compton
Long Compton
Whichford
Hook Norton
Great Rollright
Swerford
Wigginton
South Newington
Barford St John
Barford St Michael
Hempton
Deddington
Clifton
Cutsdean
Ford
Temple Guiting
Condicote
Longborough
Donnington
Evenlode
Chastleton
Salford
Over Norton
Chipping Norton
Worton
Great Tew
Little Tew
Over Worton
Duns Tew
North Aston
Somerton
Middle Aston
Heythrop
Sandford St Martin
Westcott Barton
Middle Barton
Steeple Aston
Kineton
Upper Swell
Lower Swell
Stow-on-the-Wold
Broadwell
Adlestrop
Cornwell
Oddington
Daylesford
Maugersbury
Church Enstone
Lidstone
Enstone
Gagingwell
Steeple Barton
Cleveley
Kiddington
Naunton
Upper Slaughter
Lower Slaughter
Kingham
Churchill
Bledington
Sarsden
Icomb
Wyck Rissington
Chadlington
Spelsbury
Taston
Over Kiddington
Glympton
Tackley
Notgrove
Bourton-on-the-Water
Westcote
Bruern Abbey
Lyneham
Charlbury
Wootton
Cold Aston
Little Rissington
Upper Rissington
Idbury
Fifield
Chilson
Ascott-under-Wychwood
Clapton-on-the-Hill
Milton under Wychwood
Shipton-under-Wychwood
Stonesfield
Fawler
Woodstock
Bunkers Hill
Shipton on Cherwell
Turkdean
Great Rissington
Finstock
Combe
Farmington
Leafield
Ramsden
Blenheim Palace
Kidlington
Northleach
Sherborne
Great Barrington
Taynton
Fordwells
Whiteoak Green
East End
North Leigh
Long Hanborough
Bladon
Begbroke
Eastington
Windrush
Little Barrington
Fulbrook
Burford
Swinbrook
Asthall
Asthall Leigh
Minster Lovell
Hailey
New Yatt
Freeland
Church Hanborough
Yarnton
Fossebridge
Coln St Dennis
Lodge Park
Crawley
Barnard Gate
Cassington
Signet
Charterville Allotments
Witney
Cogges
South Leigh
Eynsham
Wolvercote
Coln Rogers
Winson
Aldsworth
Westwell
Holwell
Shilton
Curbridge
High Cogges
Swinford
Wytham
Ablington
Bradwell Grove
Cotswold Wild Life Park
Brize Norton
Ducklington
Farmoor
Botley
Arlington
Bibury
Carterton
Lew
Hardwick
Sutton
Stanton Harcourt
North Hinksey
Coln St Aldwyn's
Eastleach Turville
Eastleach Martin
Hatherop
Filkins
Alvescot
Black Bourton
Yelford
West End
Cumnor
Quenington
Fyfield
Broughton Poggs
Kencot
Broadwell
Brighthampton
Standlake
Eaton
Chawley
Southrop
Aston
Cote
Bampton
Northmoor
Bessels Leigh
Wootton
Boars Hill
Little Faringdon
Langford
Clanfield
Weald
Shifford
Appleton
Poulton
Milton End
Fairford
Horcott
Grafton
Chimney
Duxford
Lamborough Hill
Foxcombe Hill
Sunningwell
Meysey Hampton
Lechlade-on-Thames
Radcot
Carswell Marsh
Hinton Waldrist
Longworth
Netherton
Fyfield
Tubney
Cothill
Whelford
Inglesham
Kelmscott
Eaton Hastings
Buckland
Kingston Bagpuize
Southmoor
Shippon
Marston Meysey
Dunfield
Littleworth
Pusey
Frilford
Garford
Marcham
Caldecott
Down Ampney
Kempsford
Buscot
Upper Inglesham
Latton
Castle Eaton
Hannington Wick
Faringdon
Badbury Hill
Great Coxwell
Charney Bassett
Hatford
Shellingford
Little Coxwell
Stanford in the Vale
Lyford
East Hanney
West Hanney
Drayton
Cricklade
Hannington
Coleshill
Highworth
Fernham
Baulking
Goosey
Denchworth
Steventon
Milton
Broad Blunsdon
Stanton Fitzwarren
Severnhampton
Watchfield
Longcot
Shrivenham
Uffington
Grove
Milton Hill
Rowstock
Harwell
Blunsdon St Andrew
South Marston
West Challow
East Challow
West Hendred
East Hendred
Ardington
Haydon Wick
Penhill
Upper Stratton
Purton
Stratton St Margaret
Gorse Hill
Pinehurst
Woolstone
Kingston Lisle
Sparsholt
Childrey
Wantage
Lockinge
Lydiard Millicent
Rodbourne Cheney
Walcot
Bourton
Compton Beauchamp
Uffington Castle
Letcombe Regis
West Ginge
East Ginge
Swindon
Ashbury
Whitehorse Hill
Wayland's Smithy
Letcombe Bassett
The Ridgeway
Hinton Parva
Idstone
Bishopstone
Kingston Warren
West Ilsley
Coate
Wanborough
Ashdown Park
Lambourn Downs
Farnborough
East Ilsley
North Wroughton
Wroughton
Liddington
Upper Lambourn
Fawley
Catmore
Badbury
Chiseldon
South Fawley
Lilley
Stanmore
Broadtown Lane
Lambourn
Brightwalton
Beedon
Broad Town
Baydon
Leckhampstead Thicket
Peasemore
Eastbury
East Garston
Chaddleworth
World's End
Woodsend
Aldbourne
Vale of White Horse
Oxfordshire
Swindon
SP
SU
0 1 2 3 4 5 6 miles
0 1 2 3 4 5 6 7 8 9 10 km
51
52
37
25
26

Buckingham
Bletchley
Croughton
Aynho
Souldern
Cottisford
Mixbury
Water Stratford
Radclive
Finmere
Tingewick
Gawcott
Thornborough
Nash
Whaddon
Tattenhoe
Far Bletchley
Fenny Stratford
Bletchley Park
Little Brickhill
Barton Hartshorn
Newton Purcell
Preston Bissett
Padbury
Singleborough
Great Horwood
Little Horwood
Whaddon Chase
Newton Longville
Adstock
Fritwell
Baynard's Green
Hardwick
Hethe
Fringford
Chetwode
Addington
Drayton Parslow
Stoke Hammond
Fewcott
Stoke Lyne
Hillesden
Mursley
Cherwell Valley Services
Ardley
Winslow
Steeple Claydon
Swanbourne
North End
Soulbury
Stratton Audley
Twyford
Stewkley
South End
Bucknell
Middle Claydon
East Claydon
Claydon House
Poundon
Granborough
Hoggeston
Linslade
Caversfield
Charndon
Calvert
Botolph Claydon
Dunton
Burcott
Caulcott
Woodfield
Highfield
Middleton Stoney
Bicester
Launton
Marsh Gibbon
North Marston
Creslow
Wing
Ascott House
Buckingham
Edgcott
Cublington
Chesterton
Grendon Underwood
Quainton Windmill
Oving
Whitchurch
Aston Abbotts
Bicester Village
Quainton
Pitchcott
Kirtlington
Ambrosden
Blackthorn
Buckinghamshire Railway Centre
Hardwick
Mentmore
Weston-on-the-Green
Wendlebury
Lower Arncott
Kingswood
Wingrave
Bletchingdon
Merton
Ludgershall
Westcott
Waddesdon
Weedon
Rowsham
Upper Arncott
Piddington
Wotton Underwood
Charlton on Otmoor
Waddesdon Manor
Akeman Street
Long Marston
Hampton Poyle
Murcott
Bierton
Aylesbury
Puttenham
Oddington
Boarstall
Brill Windmill
Brill
Dorton
Ashendon
Upper Winchendon
Upper Pollicott
Islip
Noke
Horton-cum-Studley
Wilstone
Lower Winchendon
Stone
Southcourt
Buckland
Little London
Weston Turville
Woodeaton
Oakley
Chilton
Cuddington
Dinton
Aston Clinton
Beckley
Oxford Services
Stoke Mandeville
Easington
Chearsley
Westlington
Bishopstone
Halton
Elsfield
Summertown
Stanton St John
Townsend
Ford
Marston
Worminghall
Long Crendon
Haddenham
Kimble Wick
North Lee
Terrick
Nash Lee
Wendover
Forest Hill
Aston Sandford
Butler's Cross
Barton
Headington
Holton
Ickford
Shabbington
Little Kimble
University
Owlswick
Meadle
Ellesborough
St Leonard's
Botanic Garden
Oxford
Wheatley
Waterperry
Waterperry Gardens
Waterstock
Kingsey
Great Kimble
Thame
Shotover
Horspath
Rycote Chapel
Towersey
Ilmer
Longwick
Askett
Dunsmore
The Lee
Cowley
Tiddington
Monks Risborough
Oxford Services
Moreton
Iffley
Cuddesdon
Great Milton
Pitch Green
Manor
Little Hampden
Ballinger Common
Littlemore
Denton
Emmington
Henton
Bledlow
Princes Risborough
Sandford on Thames
Garsington
Great Haseley
Tetsworth
Sydenham
Saunderton
Great Hampden
Abbey
Little Milton
Chinnor
Loosley Row
Prestwood
Great Missenden
Toot Baldon
Little Haseley
Oakley
Chinnor & Princes Risborough Railway
Marsh Baldon
Postcombe
Crowell
Lacey Green
Speen
Little Kingshill
Radley
Nuneham Courtenay
St Katherine's
Chislehampton
Stoke Talmage
Adwell
Kingston Blount
Aston Rowant
Upper North Dean
Great Kingshill
Stadhampton
South Weston
Radnage
Bledlow Ridge
Walters Ash
Widmer End
Easington
Lewknor
Bradenham
Cryers Hill
Abingdon
Drayton St Leonard
Chalgrove
The City
Naphill
Clifton Hampden
Newington
Brightwell Baldwin
Pyrton
Shirburn
Stokenchurch
Hughenden Valley
Hughenden Manor
Berinsfield
Burcot
Culham
Dorchester
Berrick Salome
Cuxham
Beacon's Bottom
West Wycombe
West Wycombe Caves
Downley
Hazlemere
Pendon Mus.
Long Wittenham
Dorchester Abbey
Watlington
Christmas Common
West Wycombe Park
Tylers Green
Sutton Courtenay
Appleford
Warborough
Roke
Ibstone
High Wycombe
Little Wittenham
Shillingford
Britwell Salome
The Ridgeway
Northend
Cadmore End
Bolter End
Loudwater
Didcot
Didcot Railway Centre
Benson
Ewelme
Greenfield
Lane End
Booker
Brightwell cum Sotwell
Preston Crowmarsh
Turville Heath
Turville
Fingest
Wycombe Marsh
Cookley Green
Pishill
Skirmett
Wycombe Air Park
Flackwell Heath
Wallingford
Crowmarsh Gifford
Russell's Water
Frieth
Marlow Bottom
Little Marlow
Wooburn Green
East Hagbourne
North Moreton
Cholsey and Wallingford Railway
Park Corner
Stonor
South Moreton
Rockwell End
Lower Woodend
Well End
West Hagbourne
Aston Upthorpe
Nuffield
Hambleden
Bovingdon Green
Bourne End
Cores End
Upton
Cholsey
North Stoke
Nettlebed
Fawley
Marlow
Aston Tirrold
Middle Assendon
Greenlands
Cookham Dean
Cookham
Blewbury
Ipsden
Bix
Lower Assendon
Mill End
Medmenham
Bisham
Maharajahs Well
Wellplace Zoo
Highmoor Cross
Aston
Moulsford
South Stoke
Checkendon
Stoke Row
Greys Court
Remenham
Remenham Hill
The Thames Path
Hurley
Windsor
Cookham Rise
Satwell
Shepherd's Green
Park Corner
Burchett's Green
Pinkneys Grn.
Furze Platt
Woodcote
Rotherfield Greys
Henley-on-Thames
Maidenhead
Streatley
Goring
River & Rowing Museum
Warren Row
Rotherfield Peppard
Compton
Cray's Pond
Harpsden
Knowl Hill
Bray
Cox Grn.
Bray Wick
Streatley on Thames
St. Bartholomew's
Goring Heath
Sonning Common
Lower Shiplake
Littlewick Green
Woodlands Park
Holyport
Aldworth
Lower Basildon
Beale Park
Whitchurch Hill
Cane End
Kidmore End
Shiplake
Wargrave
White Waltham
Basildon Park
Binfield Hth.
Hare Hatch
Waltham St Lawrence
Stud Grn.
Ashampstead
Whitchurch
Tokers Green
Dunsden Green
Sonning Eye
Hampstead Norreys
The Living Rainforest
Quicks
Upper
Pangbourne
Mapledurham
Emmer
Twyford
Ruscombe
Touchen End
Maidenhead
SP
SU
Buckingham
Oxford
Chiltern Hills
Thame
Thames
Cherwell
Ray

Bletchley
Fenny Stratford
Far Bletchley
Tattenhoe
Woburn
Little Brickhill
Great Brickhill
Crawley
WILD ANIMAL KINGDOM
Eversholt
Church End
WOBURN ABBEY
Steppingley
Greenfield
Pulloxhill
Westoning
Higham Gobion
Shillington
Apsley End
Pirton
Icklefo
Tingrith
Harlington
Barton-le-Clay
Sharpenhoe
Pegsdon
HITCHIN
Little Horwood
Newton Longville
Drayton Parslow
Mursley
Stoke Hammond
Milton Bryan
Potsgrove
Battlesden
Toddington
TODDINGTON SERVICES
SUNDON HILLS
Streatley
BARTON HILLS
Charlton
Upper Sundon
Lower Sundon
Lilley
Great Offley
Gosmore
Ippollit
Swanbourne
North End
Soulbury
Heath and Reach
STOCKGROVE PARK
KINGS WOOD
Hockliffe
Tebworth
Wingfield
Chalton
GALLEY HILL
Stewkley
South End
Leighton Buzzard
Linslade
Eggington
Tilsworth
Stanbridge
Houghton Regis
Sundon Park
Limbury
Luton
Stopsley
Preston
Hoggeston
Dunton
Burcott
LEIGHTON BUZZARD RAILWAY
Leagrave
Biscot
WARDOWN PARK MUS
Cockernhoe
Green
King's Walden
SP
Creslow
Wing
ASCOTT HOUSE
Cublington
Ledburn
Billington
MEAD OPEN FM.
Lower End
Totternhoe
PRIORY CHURCH OF ST PETER
Dunstable
Breachwood Green
St Paul's Walden
Whitchurch
Slapton
Eaton Green
Church End
Eaton Bray
Farley Hill
Luton
LONDON LUTON
Whitwell
Aston Abbotts
Hardwick
Mentmore
Wingrave
Edlesborough
DUNSTABLE DOWNS
Kensworth
Caddington
WOODSIDE FARM AND WILDFOWL PARK
STOCKWOOD PARK MUS.
Slip End
Peter's Green
Kimpton
Weedon
Rowsham
Hulcott
Horton
Ivinghoe Aston
Whipsnade
WHIPSNADE WILD ANIMAL PARK
Kensworth Common
East Hyde
Blackmore End
Ayot St Lawrence
Cheddington
Long Marston
Ivinghoe
Pitstone Green
Dagnall
Studham
Markyate
Kinsbourne Green
Batford
SHAW'S CORNER
Bierton
Aylesbury
Puttenham
Marsworth
Pitstone
Ringshall
Jockey End
Flamstead
HARPENDEN
Marshall's Heath
Wilstone
Tring Wharf
ASHRIDGE PARK
Little Gaddesden
Trowley Bottom
Hatching Green
Wheathampstead
Southcourt
Buckland
Drayton Beauchamp
New Mill
Aldbury
Redbourn
Weston Turville
Aston Clinton
Tring
Great Gaddesden
TOLL
Stoke Mandeville
Halton
Wigginton
Nettleden
Water End
Childwick Green
Sandridge
Bishopstone
THE RIDGEWAY PATH
Hastoe
Northchurch
Potten End
Piccotts End
Jersey Farm
Kimble Wick
North Lee
Terrick
Nash Lee
Wendover
BERKHAMSTED CASTLE
Gadebridge
OLD GORHAMBURY HOUSE
Townsend
St Albans
Marshalswic
Butler's Cross
Berkhamsted
ROMAN THEATRE OF VERULAMIUM
Fleetville
Little Kimble
Ellesborough
St Leonard's
Cholesbury
Buckland Common
Bourne End
Boxmoor
Hemel Hempstead
ABBEY
St Stephens
The Camp
Meadle
Great Kimble
Ashley Green
Sopwell
Askett
Dunsmore
Bellingdon
Felden
Chiswell Green
GDNS. OF THE ROSE
London Colney
Monks Risborough
The Lee
Lee Clump
Chartridge
Whelpley Hill
Bedmond
MANOR HOUSE
Princes Risborough
Little Hampden
Ballinger Common
Lye Green
Bovingdon
Primrosehill
Kings Langley
Colney Street
MOSQUITO AIRCRAFT MUS.
Shenleybu
Great Hampden
South Heath
Botley
Leyhill
Bovingdon Green
Abbots Langley
Bricket Wood
Chesham
Chipperfield
Loosley Row
Great Missenden
Prestwood
Hyde Heath
Flaunden
Radlett
Lacey Green
Speen
Little Kingshill
Chesham Bois
Latimer
Sarratt
Green Street
Walters Ash
Great Kingshill
Aldenham
Bledlow Ridge
Upper North Dean
Holmer Green
Little Missenden
Chenies
CHENIES MANOR HO
Letchmore Heath
BRADENHAM
Bradenham
Cryers Hill
Widmer End
Amersham
Watford
BOREHAMWOOD
Naphill
Little Chalfont
Chorleywood
Croxley Green
Hughenden Valley
HUGHENDEN MANOR
Penn Street
ALDENHAM
West Wycombe
WEST WYCOMBE CAVES
Downley
Hazlemere
Coleshill
CHILTERN OPEN AIR MUS.
RICKMANSWORTH
Oxhey
Bushey
Elstree
Winchmore Hill
Tylers Green
Chalfont St Giles
South Oxhey
Bushey Heath
WEST WYCOMBE PARK
High Wycombe
Penn
RICKMANSWORTH AQUADROME
Knotty Green
MILTON'S COTTAGE
Seer Green
Maple Cross
Eastbury
Stanmore
Wycombe Marsh
Forty Green
BEKONSCOT MODEL VILLAGE
Jordans
JORDANS
Chalfont Common
Batchworth Heath
Edgware
Harrow Weald
Booker
Lane End
Loudwater
Beaconsfield
Chalfont St Peter
Northwood
Hatch End
WYCOMBE AIR PARK
Flackwell Heath
Harefield
BAYHURST WOOD
RUISLIP WOODS
Pinner
Wealdstone
Frieth
Little Marlow
Wooburn Green
Marlow Bottom
ODDS FARM PARK
Gerrards Cross
DENHAM
Denham Green
Ruislip Common
HARROW
Greenhill
Lower Woodend
Bovingdon Green
Well End
Wooburn
Hedsor
Hedgerley
Tatling End
Ruislip
Eastcote
Rayners Lane
HARROW SCH.
Harrow on the Hill
FRYENT
Hambleden
Marlow
Bourne End
Cores End
BURNHAM BEECHES
Fulmer
Denham
Ickenham
Wembley
Mill End
STANLEY SPENCER GALLERY
Cookham Dean
Cookham
Bisham
Medmenham
CLIVEDEN
Farnham Common
Stoke Poges
NORTHOLT
Uxbridge
Sudbury
Alperton
Aston
Remenham
THE THAMES PATH
Hurley
Windsor
Park Corner
Cookham Rise
Burnham
Wexham Street
BLACK PARK
Iver Heath
Hillingdon
Northolt
Perivale
Pinkneys Grn.
Furze Platt
Farnham Royal
Stoke Green
LANGLEY PARK
Cowley
Yeading
LONDON MOTORCYCLE MUS
Greenford
Burchett's Green
Maidenhead
Taplow
Slough
SLOUGH
George Green
Iver
Yiewsley
Hayes
Southall
EALING
Warren Row
and
Cox Grn.
Bray
Dorney
Richings Park
West Drayton
Hanwell
Knowl Hill
Littlewick Green
Eton Wick
Langley
THORNEY
HESTON SERVICES
OSTERLEY PARK HO.
Wargrave
Upton
Harmondsworth
Sipson
Harlington
Cranford
Heston
Brentford
Kew
Eton
Datchet
WINDSOR
WINDSOR CASTLE
Colnbrook
Poyle
Longford
LONDON HEATHROW
SYON HO.
KEW GDNS.
Isleworth
Twyford
St Lawrence
Touchen End
Oakley
0 1 2 3 4 5 6 miles
0 1 2 3 4 5 6 7 8 9 10 km

Norton
Baldock
Wallington
Roe Green
Sandon
Mill End
Buckland
Chipping
Langley
Lower Green
Upper Green
Arkesden
Newport
Howlett End
Debden
LETCHWORTH
Willian
Clothall
Rushden
Wyddial
Anstey
Meesden
Clavering
Wicken Bonhunt
Rickling
Priors Hall Barn
Widdington
Mole Hall Wildlife Park
Debden Cross
Walsworth
Weston
Throcking
Hare Street
Brent Pelham
Starlings Green
Berden
Hamperden End
Cutlers Green
Great Wymondley
Little Wymondley
Hall's Green
Cromer Windmill
Cromer
Cottered
Buntingford
Great Hormead
Stocking Pelham
Graveley
Ardeley
Aspenden
Furneaux Pelham
East End
Ugley
Ugley Green
St. Mary's Church
Henham
Glendale Forge
Elsenham
Broxted
Duton Hill
Walkern
Westmill
Hay Street
Manuden
House on the Hill Toy Mus.
Farnham Green
Stevenage
Wood End
Patmore Heath
Braughing
Clapgate
Molehill Green
Brick End
Benington Lordship Garden
Benington
Aston End
Shephall
Nasty
Great Munden
Albury
Albury End
Farnham
Stansted Mountfitchet
Windmill
Stansted Airport
London Stansted
Langley
Hautwick
Levens Green
Puckeridge
Little Hadham
Birchanger
Little Easton
Bambers Green
Aston
Knebworth
Knebworth House
Broadwater
Bragbury End
Dane End
Whempstead
Standon
Wellpond Green
Hadham Ford
Bury Green
BISHOP'S STORTFORD
Birchanger Green Services
Takeley
Takeley Street
Smith's Green
Hope End Green
Dunmow Services
Collier's End
Latchford
Old Knebworth
Datchworth
Watton at Stone
Sacombe
Much Hadham
Thorley Street
Thorley
Hatfield Forest
Gt. Hallingbury
Codicote
Datchworth Green
Barwick
High Cross
Hadham Cross
Perry Green
Spellbrook
Lit. Hallingbury
Great Canfield
Woolmer Green
Oaklands
Bull's Green
Wadesmill
Tonwell
Welwyn
Welwyn Roman Baths
Burnham Green
Stapleford
Thundridge
Baker's End
Allens Green
Hatfield Heath
Hatfield Broad Oak
High Roding
Ayot St Peter
Harmer Green
Bramfield
Chapmore End
Wareside
Widford
Sawbridgeworth
Aythorpe Roding
Digswell Park
Tewin
Waterford
Ware
Hunsdon
High Wych
Leaden Roding
WELWYN GARDEN CITY
Panshanger
Hertford
Great Amwell
Stanstead Abbotts
Eastwick
Gilston
Gibberd Garden
Sheering
White Roding
Margaret Roding
Woodhall
Hall Grove
Hertingfordbury
St Margarets
Matching Tye
Matching
Abbess Roding
Lemsford
Hatfield Hyde
Cole Green
Letty Green
Hertford Heath
Hailey
Rye House Gatehouse
Roydon
Harlow
Netteswell
Churchgate Street
Matching Green
Beauchamp Roding
Hatfield
The Ryde
Hatfield House
Essendon
Bayford
HODDESDON
Rye Park
Gt. Parndon
Tye Green
Potter Street
Foster Street
High Laver
Little Laver
Magdalen Laver
Lea
Little Berkhamsted
Brickendon
Paradise Wildlife Park
Roydon Hamlet
Ada Cole Memorial Stables
Latton Bush
Hastingwood
Fyfield
Willingale
South Hatfield
Wildhill
Woodside
Epping Green
Wormley West End
Broxbourne Woods
Broxbourne
Lower Nazeing
Nazeing
Broadley Common
Moreton
Bell Bar
Welham Green
Newgate Street
Wormley
Thornwood Common
Bovinger
Bobbingworth
Norton Mandeville
Water End
Brookmans Park
Great Wood
Hammond Street
Flamstead End
Goff's Oak
Turnford
River Lee
Hayes Hill Farm
Bumble's Green
Epping Green
Epping Upland
North Weald Bassett
Greensted Church
Shelley
South Mimms
Northaw
Cuffley
CHESHUNT
Lee Valley
Coopersale Common
Epping
Epping Ongar Rly.
Toot Hill
Greensted
Chipping Ongar
High Ongar
Nine Ashes
South Mimms Services
POTTERS BAR
Waltham Cross
WALTHAM ABBEY
Upshire
Gatehouse & Bridge
Ivy Chimneys
Fiddlers Hamlet
Stanford Rivers
Theydon Bois
Little End
Secret Nuclear Bunker
Kelvedon Hatch
Stondon Massey
Doddinghurst
Capel Manor
Botany Bay
Enfield Chase
Forty Hill
Forty Hall Mus. & Gdns.
Enfield Wash
Epping Forest
High Beach
Debden
Stapleford Tawney
Navestock Heath
Navestock Side
Monken Hadley
Trent
ENFIELD
Sewardstone
Sewardstonebury
Loughton
Abridge
Stapleford
Pilgrims Hatch
BARNET
Arkley
Cockfosters
East Barnet
Winchmore Hill
Ponders End
Stapleford Abbotts
London Gateway Services
Totteridge
Southgate
Chingford
Buckhurst Hill
Chigwell
Lambourne End
Hainault Forest
Havering
South Weald
BRENTWOOD
Friern Barnet
Edmonton
Grange Hill
Chigwell Row
Havering-atte-Bower
Noak Hill
Mill Hill
Finchley
Wood Green
Hainault
Woodford Bridge
Harold Hill
Great Warley
Tottenham
Woodford
Collier Row
Hornsey
Vestry House Mus.
Barkingside
Gidea Park
Harold Wood
Hendon
Walthamstow
Romford
Golders Green
Highgate
Hampstead Hth.
Hampstead
Keats Ho.
Stoke Newington
Leytonstone
Wanstead
Newbury Park
Seven Kings
Cranham
Cricklewood
Leyton
Ilford
Manor Park
Becontree
Rush Green
Hornchurch
Elm Park
Upminster
Willesden
Harlesden
Kilburn
Camden
Islington
Hackney
Forest Gate
East Ham
Barking
Dagenham
Hacton
Hornchurch
Corbets Tey
North Ockendon
Lord's
Regents Park
St Pancras
Finsbury
Bethnal Green
Stratford
Shoreditch
South Hornchurch
Paddington
Madame Tussaud's
Oxford St.
Holborn
City
Poplar
West Ham
Beckton
Creekmouth
Rainham
Belhus Woods
South Ockendon
Acton
Hyde Park
Kensington
Holland Ho.
Nat. History Science Mus.
Tate Modern
Tower
Rotherhithe
Blackwall Tunnel
London City
North Woolwich
Woolwich Ferry
Thamesmead
Wennington
Aveley
North Stifford
Chiswick
Westminster
Earls Court
Tate
Southwark
Bermondsey
War Mus.
Belvedere
Thurrock Services
Hammersmith
Chelsea
LAMBETH
The Oval
Cutty Sark
Greenwich
Maritime Mus.
Woolwich
Plumstead
Abbey Wood
Erith
Purfleet
South Stifford
Grays
Fulham
Battersea
Peckham
Deptford
Charlton
Dartford Crossing
West Thurrock
Putney
Camberwell
New Cross
Kidbrooke
Welling
Slade Green
Bexleyheath
Swanscombe Skull Site
Thames
Stort
Rib
Quin
TL
TQ
Greater London
The Rodings
A1(M)
M1
M11
M25
A10
A120
A414
A12
A13
A2
54
55
42
28
29

Newport
Howlett End
Debden
Wicken Bonhunt
Rickling
Quendon
Widdington
PRIORS HALL BARN
MOLE HALL WILDLIFE PARK
Debden Cross
Little Sampford
Howe Street
Finchingfield
Morris Green
Sible Hedingham
Little Maplestead
Pebmarsh
Thaxted
Little Bardfield
Wethersfield
Blackmore End
Halstead
Gosfield
Colne Engaine
Wakes Colne
Hamperden End
Cutlers Green
Great Bardfield
Shalford
Church End
Beazley End
Earls Colne
Chappel
Ugley
Henham
ST. MARY'S CHURCH
GLENDALE FORGE
Monk Street
Lindsell
Shalford Green
Jasper's Green
High Garrett
Greenstead Green
Ugley Green
HOUSE ON THE HILL TOY MUS.
Elsenham
Broxted
Duton Hill
Great Easton
Bardfield Saling
Bocking Churchstreet
Great Tey
Stansted Mountfitchet
Molehill Green
Brick End
Bran End
Great Saling
Panfield
Stisted
ST. JAMES THE LESS CHURCH
STANSTED AIRPORT
Butcher's Pasture
Stebbing
Stebbing Green
Bocking
BRAINTREE
Pattiswick Green
Broad Green
BISHOP'S STORTFORD
LONDON STANSTED
Little Easton
Churchend
FLITCH WAY
Rayne
Bradwell
FREEPORT BRAINTREE
Coggeshall
PAYCOCKES
Bambers Green
Great Dunmow
MALTINGS
Little Dunmow
Bannister Green
Great Notley
Tye Green
GRANGE BARN
Coggeshall Hamlet
Takeley
Takeley Street
BIRCHANGER GREEN SERVICES
Smith's Green
DUNMOW SERVICES
Barnston
Felsted
COUNTRY PARK & DISCOVERY CENTRE
Black Notley
Cressing
Feering
HATFIELD FOREST
Hope End Green
Willows Grn.
Young's End
Silver End
Gore Pit
Kelvedon
Gt. Hallingbury
Bacon End
CRESSING TEMPLE
LOCAL HISTORY MUSEUM
Messing
Bishop's Green
Hounslow Green
North End
Hartford End
White Notley
Inworth
Lit. Hallingbury
Great Canfield
High Roding
Little Leighs
Great Leighs
Faulkbourne
Rivenhall End
Tiptree
Hatfield Broad Oak
Ford End
Fairstead
Fuller Street
Terling
Flack's Green
Chipping Hill
Great Braxted
Witham
High Easter
Howe Street
Pleshey
Aythorpe Roding
Hatfield Heath
THE RODINGS
Sheering
Leaden Roding
White Roding
Great Waltham
Little Waltham
Good Easter
Chignall Smealy
Wickham Bishops
Great Totham
Little Totham
Matching
Matching Tye
Margaret Roding
Abbess Roding
Mashbury
Hatfield Peverel
E
s
s
e
Matching Green
Chignall St James
Broomfield
Nounsley
Beauchamp Roding
Boyton Cross
Parsonage Green
Boreham
Langford
Broad Street Green
Great Totham
High Laver
Little Laver
Foster Street
Magdalen Laver
Shellow Bowells
Roxwell
Springfield
Chelmer Village
Chelmer and Blackwater Navigation
Little Baddow
Woodham Walter
Heybridge
COMBINED MILITARY SERVICES MUSEUM
Heybridge Basin
Fyfield
Moreton
Willingale
Great Oxney Green
Writtle
Chelmsford
MOULSHAM MILL
Maldon
HYTHE QUAY
Northey
Bovinger
Bobbingworth
Norton Mandeville
Cooksmill Green
Widford
Great Baddow
Sandon
Danbury
Runsell Green
Woodham Mortimer
Shelley
North Weald Bassett
Norton Heath
Loves Green
Galleyend
Galleywood
Howe Green
Cock Clarks
Rudley Green
Mundon
GREENSTED CHURCH
EPPING ONGAR RLY.
Toot Hill
Greensted
High Ongar
Chipping Ongar
Nine Ashes
Blackmore
Margaretting
Bicknacre
Purleigh
Stanford Rivers
Mill Green
East Hanningfield
Cold Norton
Latchingdon
Stondon Massey
Fryerning
West Hanningfield
Little End
SECRET NUCLEAR BUNKER
Kelvedon Hatch
Stapleford Tawney
Doddinghurst
Ingatestone
Heybridge
Stock
Reservoir
HYDE HALL
TROPICAL WINGS AND BIRD GARDENS
Woodham Ferrers
Stow Maries
Swallows Cross
Coalhill
Rettendon
South Woodham Ferrers
North Fambridge
Navestock Heath
Navestock Side
Mountnessing
NORSEY WOOD
South Hanningfield
Downham
MARSH FARM
STAPLEFORD
Stapleford Abbotts
Pilgrims Hatch
Ramsden Heath
Rettendon Place
Crouch
South Fambridge
WEALD
South Weald
Hutton
Shenfield
BRENTWOOD
ST. MARY AND ST. HELEN'S CATH.
Billericay
Runwell
Ramsden Bellhouse
Wickford
Shotgate
Battlesbridge
Hullbridge
Canewdon
Havering-atte-Bower
Little Burstead
South Green
ST. MARY MAGDALENE
Rawreth
Ashingdon
Harold Hill
Ingrave
Herongate
Dunton Wayletts
Great Burstead
Crays Hill
BARLEYLANDS CRAFT VILLAGE & FARM CENTRE
Nevendon
Hockley
Hawkwell
Great Stambridge
OLD HOUSE
Collier Row
Great Warley
THORNDON
Little Warley
North Benfleet
Bowers Gifford
RAYLEIGH
Stroud Green
Rochford
Gidea Park
Harold Wood
Romford
Cranham
West Horndon
Laindon
Basildon
Pitsea
Vange
Thundersley
Daws Heath
Hadleigh
Eastwood
Prittlewell
Hornchurch
Upminster
Langdon Hills
LANGDON HILLS
Hope's Grn.
South Benfleet
WAT TYLER
HADLEIGH CASTLE
Leigh on Sea
Southend-on-Sea
CEN. MUS. & PLANETARIUM
Rush Green
Elm Park
Bulphan
Horndon on the Hill
Fobbing
Corringham
Winter Gardens
Westcliff-on-Sea
Dagenham
Hacton
HORNCHURCH
Corbets Tey
North Ockendon
South Hornchurch
BELHUS WOODS
Thurrock
Stanford-le-Hope
Coryton
CANVEY ISLAND
Leigh Beck
ADVENTURE ISLAND
Southend-on-Sea
South Ockendon
Baker Street
Orsett
Rainham
Wennington
Aveley
North Stifford
Mucking
Thames Haven
THAMES ESTUARY
Thames
Belvedere
THURROCK SERVICES
Linford
Chadwell St Mary
West Tilbury
East Tilbury
Halstow Marshes
St Mary's Marshes
St Mary Hoo
Allhallows-on-Sea
Allhallows
Lower Stoke
Isle of Grain
Grain
Cliffe
Cooling
HALSTOW
High Halstow
Slade Green
SWANSCOMBE SKULL SITE
Tilbury
0 1 2 3 4 5 6 miles
0 1 2 3 4 5 6 7 8 9 10km

Bures
Nayland
Stratford St Mary
Boxted
Little Horkesley
Boxted Heath
Boxted Cross
Langham
Wormingford
Great Horkes.
Dedham
Dedham Heath
Bridge Cottage
Sir Alfred Munnings Art Museum
Lawford
Brantham
Cattawade
Upper Street
Holbrook Bay
Harkstead
Shop Corner
Shotley Gate
Stour
HARWICH
Nature Reserve
Mistley Towers
Mistley
Manningtree
Bradfield
Wrabness
Parkeston
Harwich Redoubt
Dovercourt
Upper Dovercourt
Esbjerg 20:00
Hoek van Holland 6:00
Hoek van Holland 3:40
Gothenburg 38:30
Rotterdam 8:00
East Anglian Railway Museum
Fordham
Horkesley Heath
West Bergholt
Colne
Eight Ash Green
Aldham
Mile End
Parson's Heath
Highwoods
St. Botolph's Priory
Colchester
Ardleigh
Little Bromley
Bradfield Heath
Horsleycross Street
Horsley Cross
Little Oakley
Great Oakley
Wix
Stone's Green
Tendring Green
Great Bromley
Fox Street
Crockleford Heath
Elmstead Market
Little Bentley
Beaumont
Horsey Island
The Naze
Hamford Water
Lexden
Beacon End
Stanway
Earth Works
Abbey Field
Old Heath
Wivenhoe Cross
Hare Green
Balls Green
Tendring
Thorpe Green
Thorpe-le-Soken
Kirby-le-Soken
Copford Green
Shrub End
Maypole Green
Bourne Mill
Blackheath
Wivenhoe
Beth Chatto Gdns
Frating Green
Great Bentley
Weeley
Weeley Heath
Walton-on-the-Naze
Colchester Zoo
Heckfordbridge
Layer de la Haye
Easthorpe
Rowhedge
Alresford
Aingers Green
Kirby Cross
Frinton-on-Sea
Birch
Birch Green
Malting Green
Fingringhoe
Thorrington
Row Heath
Little Clacton
Clacton Village
Great Holland
Abberton
Abberton Reservoir
Langenhoe
River Colne
Brightlingsea
St Osyth Heath
Holland Haven
Layer Marney
Layer Breton
Layer Marney Tower
Peldon
St. Osyth's Priory
St Osyth
Great Clacton
Holland-on-Sea
Mersea Island
East Mersea
Cudmore Grove
Point Clear
Clacton-on-Sea
Paternoster Heath
Great Wigborough
Copt Hall Marshes
Blue Row
Salcott
Jaywick
Tolleshunt D'Arcy
West Mersea
Mersea Island Museum
Colne Pt.
The Nass
Virley Channel
Tollesbury
Goldhanger
Sales Pt.
St. Peters on the Wall
Bradwell Waterside
Bradwell on Sea
Blackwater
Osea I.
Ramsey Island
St Lawrence
Steeple
Tillingham
TM
Asheldham
Dengie
Mayland
Southminster
Althorne
Ray Sand
Stoneyhills
Mangapps Railway Mus.
Montsale
Deal Hall
Ostend
Burnham-on-Crouch
Creaksea
Foulness Sand
Foulness Pt.
TR
Crouch
Paglesham Churchend
Courtsend
Pagelsham Eastend
Ballards Gore
Churchend
Potton Island
FOULNESS ISLAND
MAPLIN SANDS
Barling
Havengore Island
Little Wakering
Great Wakering
Bournes Green
North Shoebury
Shoeburyness
Cambridge Town
Thorpe Bay
(From Dartford)
Vlissingen 9:30
Zeebrugge 9:00

ROSSLARE 3:30
ROSSLARE 1:50 (Apr-Sept)
Strumble Head
Pen Caer
Dinas Head
PEMBROKESHIRE COAST
ARFORDIR PENFRO
Tresinwen
PWLL DERI
213
Llanwnda
Goodwick (Wdig)
191
Fishguard Bay
Bae Abergwaun
Brynhenllan
Dinas Cross
Lower Town
A487
Trefasser
Penbwchdy
Dyffryn
Fishguard (Abergwaun)
45
Manorowen
St Nicholas
PEMBROKESHIRE COAST PATH
LLWYBR ARFORDIR PENFRO
TREGWYNT WOOLLEN MILL
A40
Llanychaer
Scleddau
Pontfaen
Ynysduellyn
Abercastle
Granston
B4313
Penclegyr
Porthgain
Trefin
TREFIN
Mathry
CHEESE CENTRE
Newbridge
Trecwn
16
CORSYDD LLANGLOFFAN
Abereiddy
Llanrhian
Penparc
Castlemorris
B4331
14
Croes-goch
B4330
Little Newcastle
Puncheston
ST. DAVID'S HEAD
PENMAEN DEWI
Tretio
Treffynnon
164
Treddiog
Letterston
Castlebythe
Tufton
181
Treleddyd-fawr
Carnhedryn
Treglemais
Llanreithan
Welsh Hook
St Dogwells
B4329
Whitesand Bay
Porth-mawr
ST. DAVID'S
Rhodiad
Caerfarchell
Llandeloy
Pont-yr-hafod
Wolf's Castle
Ambleston
Woodstock
BISHOP'S PALACE
B4583
A487
Whitchurch
Middle Mill
Trefgarn Owen
Hayscastle
Rinaston
Wallis
Rhosson
CATHEDRAL
St David's (Tyddewi)
Nine Wells
Solva
PENYCWM
Hayscastle Cross
Brimaston
Cleddau
LLYS-Y-FRAN RESERVOIR
Ramsey Island
Ynys Dewi
RAMSEY ISLAND
Ramsey Sound
Mountain Water
178
DUDWELL MT.
Triffleton
Treffgarne
Spittal
Penycwm
Leweston
SCOLTON MANOR & COUNTRY PARK
Walton East
Newgale
Pembrokeshire
A487
Roch Gate
Roch
Wolfsdale
W. Cleddau
B4329
Camrose
A40
Rudbaxton
Clarbeston Road
15
Keeston
(Sir Benfro)
Nolton Haven
Simpson Cross
Tangiers
Leechpool
SM
PEMBROKE MOTOR MUSEUM
Pelcomb Cross
B4330
Crundale
ST. BRIDES BAY
BAE SAIN FFRAID
Nolton
Lambston
Slade
Haverfordwest (Hwlffordd)
Wiston
Druidston
Pelcomb Bridge
A487
PEMBROKESHIRE COAST PATH
LLWYBR ARFORDIR PENFRO
Portfield Gate
CASTLE MUSEUM AND ART GALLERY
The Rhos
BROAD HAVEN
Haroldston West
B4341
Dreenhill
Uzmaston
B4327
Broad Haven
Merlin's Bridge
Millin Cross
PICTON CASTLE GARDENS
Broadway
Pope Hill
Little Haven
Walton West
Boulston
Minwear
Talbenny
12
North Johnston
Freystrop
Landshipping
Tower Point
Trwyn Tŵr
82
Walwyn's Castle
8
Hook
Martletwy
St Bride's
Tiers Cross
Landshipping Quay
NATIONAL NATURE RESERVE
79
Wooltack Point
Trwyn Wooltack
Johnston
Skomer Island
Ynys Skomer
SKOMER ISLAND
Hasguard
Robeston Cross
Llangwm
Black Tar
Marloes
B4327
A4076
Rosemarket
MARLOES SANDS
Broad Sound
Thornton
Steynton
10
Hill Mountain
Port Lion
LAWRENNY
Gateholm Island
Ynys Gateholm
St Ishmael's
Sandy Haven
Herbrandston
A477
Houghton
Milford Haven (Aberdaugleddau)
Honeyborough
Lawrenny
West Williamston
Dale
B4325
Burton
Hakin
Waterston
Neyland
MILFORD HAVEN
ABERDAUGLEDDYF
Llanstadwell
UPTON CASTLE GROUNDS
Skokholm Island
Ynys Skokholm
71
Pembroke Dock (Doc Penfro)
TOLL
Cosheston
CAREW CASTLE
Milton
32
Angle
Angle Bay
Bae Angle
Pwllcrochan
Pennar
B4322
St Ann's Hd.
Pentir St. Ann
Pembroke (Penfro)
Rhoscrowther
Monkton
ROSSLARE 3:45
Sheep Island
Ynys y Defaid
LAMPHEY BISHOP'S PALACE
B4320
Hundleton
B4320
Freshwater West
Lamphey
B4584
71
Maiden Wells
HERBERTS MOOR FARM PARK
Hodgeston
B4319
St Twynnells
Castlemartin
B4319
Freshwater East
Warren
St Petrox
Cheriton or Stackpole Elidor
Trewent Pt.
Trwyn Trewent
Linney Hd.
Pentir Linney
Merrion
Stackpole
ELEGUG STACKS
STACKPOLE
Bosherston
The Wash
Stackpole Hd.
Pen Stackpole
PEMBROKESHIRE COAST PATH
LLWYBR ARFORDIR PENFRO
St Govan's Hd.
Pen St Gofan
SR
0 1 2 3 4 5 6 miles
0 1 2 3 4 5 6 7 8 9 10 km

CARDIGAN BAY
BAE CEREDIGION
SN
PEMBROKESHIRE COAST
ARFORDIR PENFRO
PEMBROKESHIRE COAST PATH
LLWYBR ARFORDIR PENFRO
MYNYDD PRESELI
Cwmtudu
Cwmtydu
Ynys-Lochtyn
Llangrannog
Blaencelyn
Pontgarreg
Penbryn
Tresaith
Aberporth
Penmorfa
Brynhoffnant
Sarnau
Parcllyn
Felinwynt
Cardigan I.
Ynys
Aberteifi
Cemaes Head
Pen Cemaes
Gwbert
Ferwig
Blaenannerch
Tremain
Tan-y-groes
Blaenporth
Glynarthen
Rhydlewis
POPPIT SANDS
Cippyn
Penparc
Cardigan
(Aberteifi)
CASTLE
St Dogmaels
ABBEY
Bridgend
Pantgwyn
Bettws
Ifan
Hawen
Beulah
Moylgrove
Llangoedmor
Ponthirwaun
Bryngwyn
Brongest
Capel
Tygwydd
Monington
Llechryd
Llandygwydd
COEDMOR
CILGERRAN CASTLE
Croft
Pen-y-bryn
Cilgerran
Bridell
Carreg-wen
Cwm-cou
Llandyfriog
Aber-banc
Glanrhyd
Llantood
Dinas Head
Newport
Bay
Bae
Trefdraeth
Berry
Hill
Nevern
Pont-gareg
CORACLE CENTRE
& FLOUR MILL
Abercych
Cenarth
Newcastle
Emlyn
(Castell Newydd
Emlyn)
Pentrecagal
Fishguard
Bay
Bae
Abergwaun
Brynhenllan
TREFDRAETH
Parrog
Felindre
Farchog
PENGELLI
FOREST
Rhos-hill
Newchapel
CLYNFYW
Aber-
Arad
NATIONAL
WOOLLEN
MUS
Dinas
Cross
Lower
Town
Newport
(Trefdraeth)
CASTELL
HENLLYS
FORT
Eglwyswrw
Boncath
Cilwendeg
Penrherber
CHEESE
FARM
Felindre
Cwmhiraeth
Fishguard
(Abergwaun)
CARNINGLI
TY CANOL
DYFED SHIRES &
LEISURE FARM
BROMEIGAN
GARDENS
Llanfair-
Nant-Gwyn
Blaenffos
Cilgwyn
Crosswell
Afon Nevern
Bwlchygroes
Cwmcych
Capel Iwan
Llanychaer
Brynberian
Pontyglasier
Eglwyswen
Penygroes
Star
Clydey
MOELFRE
Cwmorgan
Tanglwst
Pontfaen
Trecwn
Crymych
Tegryn
FOEL-
CWMCERWYN
Pentre-galar
Hermon
Llanfyrnach
Hen-feddau
fawr
Bryn-Iwan
Hermon
Little
Newcastle
Puncheston
Castlebythe
New Inn
Rosebush
Mynachlog-ddu
Dinas
Trelech
Glandwr
Afon Taf
Maenclochog
Llangolman
Glandy
Cross
Hebron
Blaen-
waun
Pen-y-bont
Blaen-y-coed
Ambleston
Woodstock
New Moat
Pant-y-
Caws
Llanglydwen
CHOCOLATE
FARM
Cwmbach
Llanwinio
A487
A484
A478
B4548
B4546
B4582
B4570
B4332
B4333
B4334
B4321
B4571
B4329
B4313
B4299
46
44
32
0 1 2 3 4 5 6 miles
0 1 2 3 4 5 6 7 8 9 10 km

Aberystwyth
Arts Centre
National Library
Cliff Railway
Clarach
Plas
Gogerddan
Bow Street
Penrhyncoch
Comins Coch
Capel Dewi
Llanbadarn Fawr
Trefechan
Castle
Penparcau
Southgate
Glanrafon
Rhydyfelin
Moriah
Capel Seion
Llanfarian
Gors
Chancery
New Cross
Blaenplwyf
Llanilar
Pentre-llyn
Rhos-y-garth
Llanddeiniol
Llangwyryfon
Llanrhystud
Lledrod
Trefenter
Rhyd-Rosser
Llyn Eiddwen
Mynydd Bach
Bronnant
Llansantffraed
Rhydfudr
Llanon
Bontnewydd
Nebo
Ceredigion (Sir Ceredigion)
Blaenpennal
Aberarth
Cross Inn
Bethania
Aberaeron
Pennant
Penuwch
Tyncelyn
Monachty
Crynfryn
Ffos-y-ffin
Llanerchaeron
Cilcennin
Llangeitho
New Quay (Ceinewydd)
Cei-bach
Newbridge
Bwlch-Llan
Llwyncelyn
Oakford
Ciliau Aeron
Afon Aeron
Maen-y-groes
Gilfachrheda
Capel Betws Lleucu
Cwmtudu Cwmtydu
Cross Inn
Llanarth
Trefilan
Llundain-fach
Commins Capel Betws
Nanternis
Ystrad Aeron
Tal-sarn
Gartheli
Caerwedros
Dihewyd
Abermeurig
Llwyn-y-groes
Ynys-Lochtyn
Mydroilyn
Felinfach
Felindre
Olmarch
Blaencelyn
Llwyndafydd
Temple Bar
Llangranog
Synod Inn
Pontgarreg
Caledrhydiau
Llangybi
Ffynnon-oer
Plwmp
SN
Penbryn
Tresaith
Penmorfa
Pentregat
Cribyn
Silian
Llanfair Clydogau
Betws Bledrws
Aberporth
Brynhoffnant
Gorsgoch
Sarnau
Talgarreg
Tan-y-groes
Capel Cynon
Rhos Llawr Cwrt
Bwlch-y-fadfa
Maestir
Olwen
Cellan
Glynarthen
Castell-Howell
Aber
Cwrt-newydd
Lampeter (Llanbedr Pont Steffan)
Pentrefelin
Blaenporth
Rhydlewis
Ffostrasol
Llanwnnen
Cwmann
Pantgwyn
Bettws Ifan
Hawen
Maesymeillion
Pont-siân
Cwmsychpant
Pentre-bach
Beulah
Penrhiw-pâl
Alltyblaca
Ram
Ponthirwaun
Bryngwyn
Coed-y-bryn
Llanwenog
Dre-fach
Brongest
Troedyraur
Tregroes
Rhydowen
Pencarreg
Parc-y-rhôs
Llanycrwys
Llandygwydd
Capel Tygwydd
Maesllyn
Croes-lan
Llanybydder
Ffaldybrenin
Prengwyn
Brynteg
Mynydd Pencarreg
Capel Dewi
Rhuddlan
Glan-Duar
Ty Mawr
Harford
Horeb
Rock Mill Woollen Mill
Cwm-cou
Llandyfriog
Aber-banc
Penrhiw-llan
Maesycrugiau
Esgairdawe
Cenarth
Teifi Valley Railway
Llandysul
Newcastle Emlyn (Castell Newydd Emlyn)
Pentrecagal
Henllan
Llanfihangel-ar-arth
Aber-Giâr
Aber-Arad
National Woollen Mus.
Llangeler
Llanllwni
Penrherber
Drefach
Rhydcymerau
Cheese Farm
Felindre
Pentre-cwrt
Saron
Bancyffordd
Cwmhiraeth
Drefelin
Llidiad Nenog
Cwmcych
Capel Iwan
Cwmpengraig
New Inn
Llansawel
Pencader
Moelfre
Gwyddgrug
Rhôs
Carmarthenshire (Sir Gaerfyrddin)
Cwmorgan
Dolgran
Gwernogle
Edwinsford
Tanglwst
Forest
Mynydd Rhos-wen
Abergorlech
Afon Cothi
Cynros
Cwm-byr
Brechfa
Bryn-Iwan
Alltwalis
Nant-y-ffin
Pen-y-garn
Hen-feddau fawr
Cwmduad
Hermon
Trelech
Dinas
Llanllawddog
Brechfa
Llanpumsaint
Soar
Horeb
Llanfynydd
Capel Isaac
Pontarsais
Pant-glas
Rhydargaeau
Plâs
Salem
Blaen-waun
Llanwinio
Afon Duad
A487
A486
A485
A482
A475
A484
B4577
B4337
B4576
B4342
B4339
B4338
B4334
B4321
B4333
B4571
B4459
B4476
B4336
B4310
B4299
B4301
B4578
0 1 2 3 4 5 6 miles
0 1 2 3 4 5 6 7 8 9 10 km
45
58
32
33

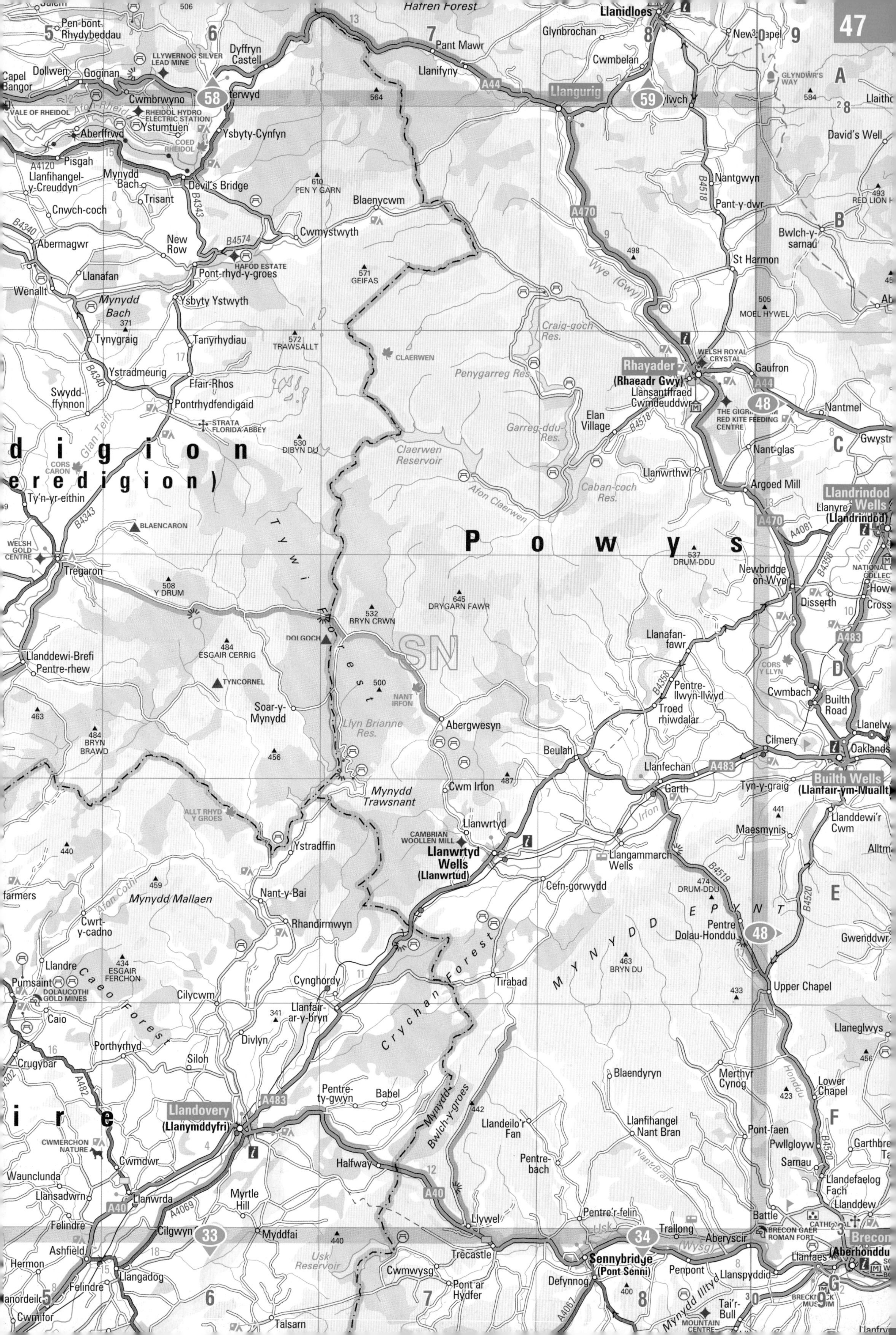
Hafren Forest
Llanidloes
Glynbrochan
New Chapel
Pen-bont Rhydybeddau
Dyffryn Castell
Pant Mawr
Llanifyny
Cwmbelan
LLYWERNOG SILVER LEAD MINE
Capel Bangor
Dollwen
Goginan
Cwmbrwyno
Llangurig
GLYNDWR'S WAY
VALE OF RHEIDOL
RHEIDOL HYDRO ELECTRIC STATION
Ystumtuen
Aberffrwd
COED RHEIDOL
Ysbyty-Cynfyn
Llaithd
David's Well
Pisgah
Llanfihangel-y-Creuddyn
Mynydd Bach
Trisant
Devil's Bridge
PEN Y GARN
Blaenycwm
Nantgwyn
Pant-y-dwr
RED LION H
Cnwch-coch
Abermagwr
New Row
Cwmystwyth
HAFOD ESTATE
Pont-rhyd-y-groes
GEIFAS
Wye (Gwy)
St Harmon
Bwlch-y-sarnau
Llanafan
Wenallt
Mynydd Bach
Ysbyty Ystwyth
MOEL HYWEL
Tynygraig
Tanyrhydiau
TRAWSALLT
CLAERWEN
Craig-goch Res.
Rhayader (Rhaeadr Gwy)
WELSH ROYAL CRYSTAL
Gaufron
Ystradmeurig
Ffair-Rhos
Penygarreg Res.
Llansantffraed Cwmdeuddwr
Swydd-ffynnon
Pontrhydfendigaid
STRATA FLORIDA ABBEY
Elan Village
Garreg-ddu Res.
THE GIGRIN FARM RED KITE FEEDING CENTRE
Nantmel
Nant-glas
Gwystre
Ceredigion
DIBYN DU
Claerwen Reservoir
CORS CARON
Llanwrthwl
Argoed Mill
Caban-coch Res.
Afon Claerwen
Llandrindod Wells (Llandrindod)
Llanyre
Ty'n-yr-eithin
BLAENCARON
Tywi Forest
Powys
DRUM-DDU
WELSH GOLD CENTRE
Tregaron
Newbridge on Wye
Y DRUM
DRYGARN FAWR
BRYN CRWN
Disserth
Cross
Howe
Ithon
DOLGOCH
ESGAIR CERRIG
SN
Llanafan-fawr
Llanddewi-Brefi
Pentre-rhew
TYNCORNEL
NANT IRFON
Pentre-llwyn-llŵyd
CORS Y LLYN
Cwmbach
Builth Road
Soar-y-Mynydd
Llyn Brianne Res.
Abergwesyn
Troed rhiwdalar
Llanelwedd
BRYN BRAWD
Beulah
Cilmery
Oaklands
Llanfechan
Builth Wells (Llanfair-ym-Muallt)
Mynydd Trawsnant
Cwm Irfon
Garth
Tyn-y-graig
ALLT RHYD Y GROES
Llanwrtyd
Irfon
Llanddewi'r Cwm
CAMBRIAN WOOLLEN MILL
Llanwrtyd Wells (Llanwrtud)
Maesmynis
Ystradffin
Llangammarch Wells
Alltmawr
Cefn-gorwydd
DRUM-DDU
farmers
Mynydd Mallaen
Afon Cothi
Nant-y-Bai
Mynydd Epynt
Cwrt-y-cadno
Rhandirmwyn
Pentre Dolau-Honddu
Gwenddwr
Llandre
ESGAIR FERCHON
Caeo Forest
Crychan Forest
BRYN DU
Pumsaint
DOLAUCOTHI GOLD MINES
Cynghordy
Tirabad
Upper Chapel
Cilycwm
Llanfair-ar-y-bryn
Caio
Llaneglwys
Porthyrhyd
Divlyn
Crugybar
Siloh
Blaendyryn
Merthyr Cynog
Honddu
Lower Chapel
Pentre-ty-gwyn
Babel
Mynydd Bwlch-y-groes
Llandovery (Llanymddyfri)
Llandeilo'r Fan
Llanfihangel Nant Bran
Pont-faen
CWMERCHON NATURE
Cwmdwr
Halfway
Pentre-bach
Pwllgloyw
Garthbrengy
Sarnau
Wauncluda
Nant Bran
Llansadwrn
Llanwrda
Myrtle Hill
Llandefaelog Fach
Llanddew
Felindre
Llywel
Pentre'r-felin
Trallong
Battle
Cilgwyn
Myddfai
Usk
Aberyscir
BRECON GAER ROMAN FORT
CATHEDRAL
Brecon (Aberhonddu)
Ashfield
Trecastle
Sennybridge (Pont Senni)
Hermon
Llangadog
Usk Reservoir
Cwmwysg
Pont ar Hydfer
Penpont
Llanspyddid
Llanfaes
Felindre
Defynnog
BRECKNOCK MUSEUM
Cwmifor
Talsarn
Mynydd Illtud
Tai'r-Bull
MOUNTAIN CENTRE
Llanfrynach
A44
A470
A4120
B4343
B4574
B4340
B4518
A483
B4358
B4519
B4520
A4081
A40
A4069
A4067
A482
58
59
48
33
34

A
B
C
D
E
F
1
2
3
4
5
New Chapel
Glyndwr's Way
584
59
thddu
Tylwch
Nantgwyn
Pant-y-dwr
B4518
St Harmon
498
505
Moel Hywel
Rhayader
Rhaeadr Gwy
Llansantffraed Cwmdeuddwr
Welsh Royal Crystal
Gaufron
47
A44
The Gigrin Farm Red Kite Feeding Centre
B4518
Nant-glas
Llanwrthwl
Argoed Mill
A470
537
Drum-ddu
Newbridge on Wye
Llanafan-fawr
Pentre-llwyn-llwyd
Troed rhiwdalar
B4358
Cilmery
Llanfechan
Garth
A483
Irfon
Llangammarch Wells
B4519
474
Drum-ddu
Pentre
Dolau-Honddu
47
463
433
Upper Chapel
B4520
Blaendyryn
Merthyr Cynog
Lower Chapel
423
Honddu
Llanfihangel Nant Bran
Pont-faen
Pwllgloyw
B4520
Sarnau
Llandefaelog Fach
Llanddew
Battle
Aberyscir
Brecon Gaer Roman Fort
Cathedral
Brecon
Aberhonddu
34
Usk
Wysg
400
Bull
Mountain Centre
David's Well
493
Red Lion Hill
Bwlch-y-sarnau
450
Abbey-cwm-hir
Nantmel
Gwystre
Llanyre
A4081
Llandrindod Wells
Llandrindod
Radnorshire Museum
Ridgebourne
National Cycle Collection
Ithon
Howey
Disserth
Crossway
A483
Cors y Llyn
Cwmbach
Builth Road
Llanelwedd
Oaklands
Builth Wells
Llanfair-ym-Muallt
Llanfaredd
451
Tyn-y-graig
441
Llanddewi'r Cwm
Maesmynis
B4567
Aberedw
Alltmawr
A470
Llandeilo Graban
Gwenddwr
Erwood
Crickadarn
Llaneglwys
456
Garthbrengy
Talachddu
Llandefalle
Felinfach
Llanfilo
Tredomen
Llandefaelog-tre'r-graig
Trefecca
Tredustan
Llanywern
Brecon
Llanfihangel Tal-y-llyn
Llechfaen
Tal-y-llyn
Llannamlach
B4560
Llangors
Llangorse Lake
Llangasty Talyllyn
Llanfrynach
A483
528
Cilfaesty Hill
22
Llanbadarn Fynydd
Rhyd-moel-ddu
B4356
Llanbister
393
A483
Llandewi Ystradenny
Fron
Crossgates
Penybont
Dolau
A488
Llanfihangel Rhydithon
411
436
Llandegley
A481
Frank's Bridge
Llansantffraed-in-Elvel
Hundred House
Cregrina
Glascwm
542
Gwaunceste Hill
Rhulen
509
Red Hill
Bryngwyn
Llanbadarn-y-Garreg
Rhosgoch
Rhos Goch
389
Llanbedr
Painscastle
B4594
414
The Begwns
Llanstephan
Rhydnest
Boughrood
B4350
Cwmbach
Glasbury
Pipton
Llyswen
A4079
Three Cocks
Tregoyd
A479
Velindre
Bronllys
Bronllys
A4078
Talgarth
Howell House
Trefeinon Open Farm
Llynfi
A470
609
Mynydd Troed
Pengenffordd
Llanelieu
A479
Anchor
Hall of the Forest
448
Black Mt
Felindre
B4355
Bettws-y-crwyn
Quabbs
Newcastle
Beguildy
Black Mountain
Glyndwr's Way
Dutlas
547
Beacon Hill
Crug
Llangunllo
Bleddfa
Monaughty
1402
Pilleth
B4356
Radnor Forest
Cascob
Maes-Treylow
Beggar's Bush
Kinnerton
New Radnor
B4372
A44
Yardro
Old Radnor
Llanfihangel-nant-Melan
SO
Dolyhir
Gladestry
B4594
Hergest Ridge
Colva
Hengoed
Michaelchurch on Arrow
Newchurch
Dol-y-cannau
Rhydspence
Brilley
Bronydd
Clyro
Hay-on-Wye
Y Gelli Gandryll
B4351
A438
Llowes
B4350
Llanigon
Cusop
677
Hay Bluff
Craswall
703
690
The Tumpa
Capel-y-ffin
Black Mountains
Y Mynyddoedd Duon
35
Afon Honddu
Whitcott Keysett
Bicton
Castle
Clun
Clun Mill
Clunton
B4368
Clun
Llwyn
60
Churchbank
14
Redlake
432
Upper Treverward
Hobarris
A488
Llanfair Waterdine
Purlogue
Offa's Dyke Path
New Invention
Chapel Lawn
B4355
Skyborry Green
Knucklas
Stowe
Knighton
Tref-y-Clawdd
A4113
Milebrook
B4355
Rhos-y-meirch
B4357
B4355
Whitton
Norton
Dolley Green
Discoed
Presteigne
Llanandras
Judges Lodging
Stapleton
Lugg
Combe
Rodd
316
Evenjobb
B4362
B4357
Nash
Knill
Stansbatch
Titley
Walton
Stanner Rocks
391
Offa's Dyke Path
Flintsham
B4355
Burlingjobb
Hergest Croft Gdns.
Kington
Kington
Headbrook
Upper Hergest
Lower Hergest
Oaklands Small Breeds Farm
Kingswood
Lyonshall
Holme Marsh
A4111
Huntington
Hopley's Green
Wootton
Almeley
Lower Welson
Upcott
Kinnersley
Hurstway Common
Millhalf
Eardisley
H
Ailey
Toll
Whitney
Willersley
Winforton
Wye
Letton
Clifford
Priory Wood
Merbach
B4352
Bredwardine
Gardens Gallery
Hardwicke
B4348
The Bage
Brobury
Arthur's Stone
Dorstone
Snodhill
Peterchurch
Hinton
Llanrosser
Urishay Common
Upper Maes-coed
Michaelchurch Escley
Middle Maes-coed
Newton
Lower Maes-coed
Llanveynoe
Longtown
Llanthony
Priory
Clodock
Offa's Dyke Path
Llwybr Clawdd Offa
531
0 1 2 3 4 5 6 miles
0 1 2 3 4 5 6 7 8 9 10 km
P
o
w
y
s

Craven Arms
Ludlow
Leominster
Tenbury Wells
Bromyard
Hereford
Ledbury
Cleobury Mortimer
Kington
Stokesay Castle
The Wernlas Collection
Burford House & Meadow Gallery
Croft Castle
Water Mill and Battle Centre
Berrington Hall
Burton Court
Dunkertons Cider
Hampton Court
Queenswood
Working Dairy Farm
Lower Brockhampton
Heritage Centre
Kenchester Water Gardens
The Weir
Cider Museum
Rotherwas
Hellen's Mansion
Court Gardens
St Mary's Church
Kilpeck Church
Abbey Dore Court
Ross Spur Services
Wyre Forest
Golden Valley
Teme
Arrow
Lugg
Wye
Frome
Lodon
Leadon
Rea
SO
H e r e f o r d s h i r e
Aston on Clun
Sibdon Carwood
Newington
Halford
Dinchope
Seifton
Culmington
Great Sutton
Peaton
St Margaret
Stoke St Milborough
Aston Botterell
Loughton
Wheathill
Chorley
Stottesdon
Kinlet
Hayton's Bent
Cleedownton
Hopton Cangeford
Farlow
Silvington
Clunbury
Purslow
Twitchen
Brandhill
Onibury
Clungunford
Abcott
Shelderton
Wootton
Stanton Lacy
Bromfield
Middleton
Bitterley
Cleeton St Mary
Catherton
Buttonoak
Marlow
Henley
Foxwood
Doddington
Neen Savage
Hopton Wafers
Todding
Kinton
Leintwardine
Downton on the Rock
Snitton
Farden
Cleehill
Hints
Knowbury
Hope Bagot
Knowle
Coreley
Lem Hill
Far Forest
Fingerpost
Pound Bank
Callow Hill
Bliss Gate
Buckton
Ludford
Caynham
Whitton
Milson
Bayton
Walford
Burrington
Aston
Overton
Nash
Neen Sollars
Mamble
Clows Top
Rock
Adforton
Elton
Ashford Carbonell
Ashford Bowdler
Greete
Frith Common
Letton
Leinthall Starkes
Richards Castle
Boraston
Wigmore
Woofferton
Little Hereford
Lindridge
Eardiston
Pensax
Ongar Street
Lower Lye
Leinthall Earls
Brimfield
Gosford
Burford
Newnham Bridge
Lower Rochford
Comberton
Orleton
Yatton
Upper Rochford
Hanley William
Stockton on Teme
Stanford on Teme
Stanford Bridge
Abberley
Limebrook
Aymestrey
Bircher
St Michaels
Callows Grave
Hanley Child
Broad Heath
Great Witley
Middleton on the Hill
Mortimer's Cross
Yarpole
Lucton
Ashton
Eye
The Hundred
Leysters Pole
Kyre Magna
Stoke Bliss
Sapey Common
Upper Sapey
Shelsley Walsh
Shelsley Beauchamp
Clifton upon Teme
Byton
Combe Moor
Ledicot
Luston
Lugg Green
Kingsland
Eyton
Kimbolton
Whyle
Bank Street
Grafton
Sweet Green
High Lane
Harpley
Martley
Shobdon
Cobnash
The Broad
Stockton
Staunton on Arrow
Shirl Heath
Cholstrey
Pudleston
Hatfield
Collington
Thornbury
Edvin Loach
Tedstone Wafre
Tedstone Delamere
Pembridge
Eardisland
Lawton
Monkland
Barons Cross
Steen's Bridge
Edwyn Ralph
Horsham
Berrow
Bearwood
Luntley
Ivington Green
Ivington
Humber
Docklow
Grendon Green
Bredenbury
Bromyard Downs
Whitbourne
Knightwick
Broadwas
Brierley
Stoke Prior
Risbury
Marston Stannett
Sollers Dilwyn
Dilwyn
Haven
Broxwood
Aulden
Upper Hill
Marlbrook
Newton
Hope under Dinmore
Bowley
Hegdon Hill
Pencombe
Linley Green
Alfrick
Alfrick Pound
Birley
Knapton Green
Woonton
Weobley
Weobley Marsh
Bush Bank
Bodenham
Stanford Bishop
Munderfield Row
Little Cowarne
Suckley
Lyonshall
Ledgemoor
King's Pyon
Westhope
Bodenham Moor
Ullingswick
Munderfield Stocks
Acton Beauchamp
Acton Green
Longley Green
Maund Bryan
Urdimarsh
The Vauld
Felton
Moreton Jeffries
Stoke Lacy
Storridge
Canon Pyon
Wormsley
Wellington
Walker's Green
Evesbatch
Bishops Frome
Fromes Hill
Stony Cross
Stifford's Bridge
Cradley
Yarsop
Tillington Common
Marden
Preston Wynne
Burley Gate
Much Cowarne
Ridgeway Cross
Westfield
Moorhampton
Yazor
Mansel Lacy
Tillington
Moreton on Lugg
Sutton St Nicholas
Ocle Pychard
Lower Egleton
Castle Frome
Mathon
West Malvern
Staunton on Wye
Mansell Gamage
Brinsop
Burghill
Pipe and Lyde
Newtown
Norbridge
Ham Green
Credenhill
Westhide
Withington
Stretton Grandison
Stanley Hill
Monnington on Wye
Bishopstone
Kenchester
Stretton Sugwas
Shelwick
Canon Frome
Bosbury
Colwall Stone
Byford
Preston on Wye
Bridge Sollers
Holmer
Shucknall
Yarkhill
Coddington
Canon Bridge
Swainshill
King's Acre
Lugwardine
Hagley
Weston Beggard
Tarrington
Staplow
Colwall Green
Moccas
Ploughfield
Lulham
Breinton Common
Upper Breinton
Bartestree
Munsley
Wellington Heath
Tyberton
Breinton
Tupsley
Dormington
Alder's End
Trumpet
Madley
Eaton Bishop
Ruckhall Common
Priors Frome
Pixley
Bradlow
Shenmore
Cublington
Lower Bullingham
Hampton Bishop
Checkley
Woolhope Cockshoot
Aylton
Vowchurch
Clehonger
Grafton
Dinedor
Mordiford
Putley
Little Marcle
Eastnor
Turnastone
Brampton
Kingstone
Portway
Allensmore
Holme Lacy
Twyford Common
Woolhope
Rushall
Preston
Donnington
Thruxton
Callow
Fownhope
Winnal
Dewshall Court
Cockyard
Aconbury
Sollers Hope
Bromsberrow Hth.
Kerry's Gate
Didley
Kivernoll
Bolstone
King's Thorn
Brockhampton
Much Marcle
Bacton
St Devereux
Little Dewchurch
Falcon
Broom's Green
Ryton
Wormbridge
Little Birch
Much Birch
Carey
Ballingham
Crossway
Lyne Down
Dymock
Redmarley D'Abitot
Kilpeck
Much Dewchurch
Fawley Chapel
How Caple
Kempley
Poolhill
Abbey Dore
Howton
Wormelow Tump
Penalt
Yatton
Hoarwithy
Llandinabo
Red Rail
King's Caple
Foy
Hole-in-the-Wall
Ewyas Harold
Orcop Hill
Llanwarne
Sellack
Brand Green
Pontrilas
Harewood End
Upton Bishop
Rowlstone
Pagwy Llydiart
Upper Grove Common
Brampton Abbotts
Phocle Green
Monmouth Cap
Pencoyd
Orcop
Llangua
Kentchurch
Garway
Michaelchurch
Gorsley
Newent
Hollybush
Brown's End
Leigh

Worcestershire
Potter's Cross
Alveley
Highley
Thorley
Stottesdon
Oreton
Kinlet
Catherton
Neen Savage
Hopton Wafers
Cleobury Mortimer
Milson
Neen Sollars
Bayton
Mamble
Clows Top
Rock
Frith Common
Lindridge
Newnham Bridge
Eardiston
Pensax
Stockton on Teme
Hanley William
Hanley Child
Stanford on Teme
Stanford Bridge
Broad Heath
Sapey Common
Stoke Bliss
Upper Sapey
Shelsley Walsh
Sweet Green
High Lane
Harpley
Edvin Loach
Tedstone Wafre
Tedstone Delamere
Edwyn Ralph
Bromyard
Bromyard Downs
Lower Brockhampton
Whitbourne
Knightwick
Lulsley
Linley Green
Stanford Bishop
Munderfield Row
Acton Beauchamp
Suckley
Alfrick
Alfrick Pound
Evesbatch
Bishops Frome
Frome
Castle Frome
Canon Frome
Stanley Hill
Norbridge
Coddington
Staplow
Munsley
Trumpet
Pixley
Aylton
Putley
Little Marcle
Preston
Donnington
Rushall
Much Marcle
Hellens Mansion
Lyne Down
Dymock
Kempley
Fishpool
Bromsberrow Hth.
Broom's Green
Ryton
Redmarley D'Abitot
Ledbury
Eastnor
Hollybush
Wellington Heath
Bradlow
Colwall Green
Colwall Stone
Malvern Hills
West Malvern
Great Malvern
Malvern Link
Malvern Wells
Little Malvern
Upper Wyche
Lower Wyche
Guarlford
Welland
Mathon
Cradley
Ridgeway Cross
Westfield
Storridge
Longley Green
Acton Green
Stony Cross
Stifford's Bridge
Newland
Madresfield
Leigh Sinton
Bransford
Leigh
Brockamin
Broadwas
Rushwick
Broad Green
Berrow Green
Horsham
Martley
Wichenford
Clifton upon Teme
Shelsley Beauchamp
Great Witley
Little Witley
Abberley
Abberley Hill
Astley
Dunley
Noutard's Green
Shrawley
Sytchampton
Holt Heath
Holt Fleet
Sinton Green
Grimley
Shoulton
Hallow
Lower Broadheath
Upper Broadheath
Moseley
Claines
Fernhill Heath
Hawford
Worcester
St John's
Cherry Orchard
Red Hill
Warndon
Astwood
Bredicot
Spetchley
Whittington
Norton
Littleworth
Powick
Pole Elm
Callow End
Stanbrook
Kempsey
Bowling Green
Kerswell Grn.
Clifton
Severn Stoke
Kinnersley
Hanley Castle
Hanley Swan
Rhydd
Earl's Croome
Holly Grn.
Upton upon Severn
Naunton
Ripple
Queenhill
Newbridge Green
Castlemorton
Birts Street
Rye Street
Longdon
Camer's Green
Sledge Green
Brown's End
Pendock
Playley Green
Eldersfield
Corse Lawn
Chaceley
Forthampton
Long Green
Bushley
Tewkesbury
Walton Cardiff
Puckrup
Twyning Green
Twyning
Shuthonger
Newtown
Deerhurst
Tredington
Apperley
Tirley
Staunton
Corse
Hasfield
Ashleworth
Coombe Hill
Leigh
Hardwicke
Elmstone Hardwicke
Stoke Orchard
Bishop's Cleeve
Woodmancote
Cleeve Hill
Southam
Gotherington
Winchcombe
Langley Hill
Gretton
Greet
Alstone
Dixton
Oxenton
Teddington
Toddington
Alderton
Great Washbourne
Dumbleton
Beckford
Kinsham
Bredon
Kemerton
Overbury
Conderton
Bredon's Norton
Bredon Hill
Kersoe
Ashton under Hill
Hinton on the Green
Sedgeberrow
Aston Cross
Ashchurch
Fiddington
Northway
Upper Strensham
Lower Strensham
Eckington
Birlingham
Great Comberton
Little Comberton
Elmley Castle
Netherton
Bricklehampton
Defford
Besford
Dunstall Common
High Green
Pirton
Wadborough
Stoulton
Hatfield
Drake's Broughton
Pinvin
Pershore
Wyre Piddle
Lower Moor
Fladbury
Cropthorne
Charlton
Evesham
Bengeworth
Hampton
Throckmorton
Peopleton
Bishampton
Naunton Beauchamp
Egdon
White Ladies Aston
Churchill
Upton Snodsbury
North Piddle
Flyford Flavell
Abberton
Broughton Hackett
Kington
Grafton Flyford
Crowle
Huddington
Tibberton
Sale Green
Oddingley
Himbleton
Hindlip
Martin Hussingtree
Shernal Green
Stock Green
Stock Wood
Dormston
Inkberrow
Abbots Morton
Rous Lench
Ab Lench
Church Lench
Atch Lench
Harvington
Norton
Lenchwick
Bradley Green
Feckenham
Astwood Bank
Hanbury
Ham Green
Hunt End
Crabbs Cross
Headless Cross
Webheath
Redditch
Bentley
Woodgate
Woolmere Green
Hadzor
Witton
Droitwich Spa
Salwarpe
Hampton Lovett
Doverdale
Oldfield
Ombersley
Uphampton
Dunhampton
Crossway Green
Lincomb
Hartlebury
Waresley
Astley Cross
Areley Kings
Stourport on Severn
Upper Mitton
Wilden
Elmley Lovett
Cutnall Green
Elmbridge
Upton Warren
Wychbold
Stoke Prior
Aston Fields
Bromsgrove
Charford
Finstall
Tardebigge
Tutnall
Sidemoor
Rushock
Chaddesley Corbett
Dodford
Bournheath
Catshill
Lickey End
Blackwell
Alvechurch
Fairfield
Wildmoor
Bluntington
Mustow Green
Shenstone
Stone
Drayton
Belbroughton
Bell End
Lickey
Marlbrook
Barnt Green
Cofton Hackett
Rubery
Longbridge
Northfield
Frankley
Romsley
Clent
Holy Cross
Broom
Blakedown
Hagley
West Hagley
Churchill
Kidderminster
Franche
Wolverley
Blakebrook
Trimpley
Cookley
Caunsall
Blakeshall
Whittington
Kinver
Kingsford
Stourbridge
Pedmore
Halesowen
Hasbury
Lye
Woodgate
Bartley Green
Harborne
Selly Oak
Bournville
Romsley
Shatterford
Upper Arley
Pound Green
Low Habberley
Buttonoak
Wyre Forest
Far Forest
Lem Hill
Fingerpost
Pound Bank
Callow Hill
Ribbesford
Bewdley
Wribbenhall
Bliss Gate
Severn Valley Railway
West Midland
Kingsford
Bodenham Arboretum & Earth Centre
Strensham Services
Tudor House
Guildhall
Royal Worcester Porcelain
Elgar's Birthplace
Worcester Woods
Croome Park
Three Counties Showground
Odda's Chapel
Avoncroft Historic Buildings
Hanbury Hall
Witley Court
Leigh Court Tithe Barn
Eastnor
Gorsley
Newent
0 1 2 3 4 5 6 miles
0 1 2 3 4 5 6 7 8 9 10 km

Warwick
Coventry
Solihull
Royal Leamington Spa
Warwick
Stratford-upon-Avon
Banbury
Kenilworth
Shirley
Olton
Dorridge
Henley-in-Arden
Studley
Alcester
Southam
Cubbington
Shipston-on-Stour
Moreton-in-Marsh
Chipping Norton
Stow-on-the-Wold
Broadway
Balsall Hth
Sparkhill
Moseley
Springfield
Acock's Green
Sheldon
Birmingham International
NEC
Elmdon
Bickenhill
Elmdon Heath
Hall Green
Sarehole Mill
King's Heath
Railway Mus.
Nat. Motor Cycle Mus.
Butler's End
Meriden
Hampton in Arden
Eastcote
Four Oaks
Berkswell
Hawkes End
Keresley
Longford
Coundon
Allesley
Eastern Green
Little Heath
Foleshill
Walsgrave on Sowe
Transport Mus.
Spon End
Whoberley
Tile Hill
Earlsdon
Stivichall
Pinley
Binley
Binley Woods
Willenhall
Coombe Abbey
Brinklow
Shilton
Ansty
Stretton under Fosse
Easenhall
King's Newnham
Church Lawford
Bretford
Brandon
Wolston
Tollbar End
Baginton
Midland Air Mus.
Lunt Roman Fort
Ryton-on-Dunsmore
Ryton Organic Gardens
Ryton Pools
Bubbenhall
Stoneleigh
National Agricultural Centre
Stareton
Ashow
Princethorpe
Stretton-on-Dunsmore
Bourton on Dunsmore
Frankton
Draycote
Draycote Water
Marton
Birdingbury
Wappenbury
Eathorpe
Weston under Wetherley
Hunningham
Lillington
Old Milverton
Milverton
Leamington Hastings
Jephson Gardens
Offchurch
Long Itchington
Stockton
Grand Union Canal
Bascote
Radford Semele
Whitnash
Ufton
Napton on the Hill
Chapel Green
Harbury
Chesterton Windmill
Chesterton
Ladbroke
Warwick Services
Marston Doles
Cross Green
Bishop's Itchington
Priors Hardwick
Oxford Canal
Knightcote
Gaydon
Lighthorne Heritage Motor Centre
Lighthorne
Moreton Morrell
Ashorne
Ashorne Hall Nickelodeon
Newbold Pacey
Wellesbourne
Wellesbourne Watermill
Compton Verney
Chadshunt
Northend
Burton Dasset Hills
Fenny Compton
Temple Herdewycke
Burton Dassett
Kineton
Little Kineton
Combrook
Butlers Marston
Radway
Edge Hill
Ratley
Warmington
Avon Dassett
Farnborough
Farnborough Hall
Mollington
Claydon
Cropredy
Shotteswell
Hornton
Horley
Hanwell
Upton House
Middle Tysoe
Lower Tysoe
Upper Tysoe
Oxhill
Whatcote
Pillerton Priors
Pillerton Hersey
Ettington
Alkerton
Shenington
Wroxton
Drayton
Neithrop
Grimsbury
Balscott
Epwell
Shutford
Winderton
Upper Brailes
Lower Brailes
Sibford Gower
Sibford Ferris
Swalcliffe
Swalcliffe Barn
Broughton Castle
Broughton
North Newington
Tadmarton
Easington
Bodicote
Bloxham
Milcombe
West Adderbury
Milton
Barford St John
Barford St Michael
South Newington
Wigginton
Hook Norton
Hook Norton Brewery Visitors Centre
Swerford
Great Rollright
Rollright Stones
Hempton
Nether Worton
Over Worton
Great Tew
Little Tew
Duns Tew
Ledwell
Sandford St Martin
Middle Barton
Westcott Barton
Heythrop
Church Enstone
Over Norton
Salford
Cornwell
Chastleton
Chastleton House
Little Compton
Long Compton
Barton on the Heath
Whichford
Ascott
Cherington
Stourton
Sutton under Brailes
Burmington
Willington
Barcheston
Tidmington
Todenham
Little Wolford
Great Wolford
Lower Lemington
Batsford
Arboretum
Bourton on the Hill
Sezincote
Wellington Aviation Art
Aston Magna
Draycott
Blockley
Paxford
Stretton-on-Fosse
Charingworth
Ebrington
Chipping Campden
Broad Campden
Hidcote Boyce
Hidcote Manor Garden
Kiftsgate Court Garden
Cotswold Country Cycles
Mickleton
Meon Hill
Upper Quinton
Lower Quinton
Admington
Newbold on Stour
Armscote
Blackwell
Ilmington
Darlingscott
Halford
Idlicote
Tredington
Honington Hall
Honington
Alderminster
Wimpstone
Preston on Stour
Atherstone on Stour
Ailstone
Clifford Chambers
Shire Horse Centre
Loxley
Walton
Charlecote
Charlecote Park
Hampton Lucy
Wasperton
Alveston
Tiddington
Shakespeare's Birthplace
Anne Hathaway's Cottage
Shottery
Binton
Temple Grafton
Ardens Grafton
Billesley
Haselor
Walcote
Wilmcote
Mary Arden's House
Bishopton
Ingon
Snitterfield
Aston Cantlow
Great Alne
Little Alne
Bearley
Langley
Edstone
Wolverton
Norton Lindsey
Heath End
Sherbourne
Barford
Bishop's Tachbrook
Longbridge
Warwick Castle
St. Mary's
Hampton on the Hill
Budbrooke
Hatton
Hatton Country World
Haseley
Shrewley Common
Rowington
Leek Wootton
Beausale
Kenilworth Castle
Honiley
Wroxall
Baddesley Clinton
Kingswood
Lapworth
Chadwick End
Crackley
Burton Green
Meer End
Catchems Corner
Balsall Common
Fen End
Temple Balsall
Balsall
Barston
Knowle
Copt Heath
Bentley Heath
Hockley Heath
Packwood House
Umberslade Farm
Tanworth-in-Arden
Kemps Green
Lowsonford
Preston Bagot
Claverdon
Wootton Wawen
Shelfield
Oldberrow
Ullenhall
Mapplebourgh Green
Morton Bagot
Gorcott Hill
Holt End
Branson's Cross
Wood End
Portway
Earlswood
Manor Farm Craft Centre
Wythall
Drakes Cross
Whitlock's End
Monkspath
Hollywood
Coughton Court
Coughton
King's Coughton
Cookhill
Overley Green
Arrow
Ragley Hall
Weethley Gate
Exhall
Wixford
Dunnington
Broom
Salford Priors
Bidford-on-Avon
Barton
Marlcliff
Cleeve Prior
Harvington
North Littleton
Middle Littleton
South Littleton
Dorsington
Long Marston
Pebworth
Broad Marston
Honeybourne
Domestic Fowl Trust
Bretforton
Fleece Inn
Aldington
Badsey
Wickhamford
Aston Subedge
Weston-Sub-Edge
Saintbury
Willersey
Welford-on-Avon
Luddington
Stratford
Vale of Evesham
Buckland
Laverton
Broadway Tower
Snowshill Manor
Snowshill Lavender
Snowshill
Stanton
Gloucestershire Warwickshire Steam Railway
Stanway
Stanway House
Didbrook
Hailes Abbey
Cutsdean
Ford
Farmcote
Temple Guiting
Kineton
Cotswold Farm Park
Upper Swell
Lower Swell
Condicote
Longborough
Donnington
Broadwell
Adlestrop
Evenlode
Daylesford
Oddington
M42
M40
M6
A45
A46
A452
A429
A3400
A422
A423
A425
A435
A44
A424
A361
62
63
52
37
38

Barnacle
Shilton
Withybrook
Cross in Hand
A4303
Misterton
Walcote
A4304
North Kilworth
Husbands Bosworth
Sibbertoft
Great Oxendon
Little Heath
Foleshill
Ansty
Oxford Canal
Monks Kirby
Swift
Cotesbach
A5
B4027
Walsgrave on Sowe
M6
Pailton
South Kilworth
Sulby Reservoir
Clipston
Great Heath
Wyken
A4600
Stretton under Fosse
Churchover
Gibbet Hill
Stanford Res.
Welford
1645
Naseby Field
Kelmarsh
A508
Coventry
COOMBE ABBEY
Brinklow
Easenhall
Harborough Magna
Shawell
Swinford
STANFORD HALL
Stanford on Avon
A5199
Naseby Res.
A427
A46
Binley Woods
Pinley
Binley
B4029
B4112
Newbold on Avon
A426
Newton
Catthorpe
A14
Naseby
Haselbech
Maidwell
Willenhall
A428
Bretford
King's Newnham
Church Lawford
Long Lawford
Avon
Lilbourne
Clay Coton
210
Cold Ashby
Thornby
Brandon
Wolston
B4455
Clifton upon Dunsmore
Yelvertoft
Tollbar End
MIDLAND AIR MUS.
New Bilton
Northamptonshire
LUNT ROMAN FORT
Baginton
COVENTRY
Ryton-on-Dunsmore
RYTON ORGANIC GARDENS
Bilton
Rugby
Hillmorton
M1
Winwick
Cottesbrooke
Bubbenhall
A423
A45
A4071
B4038
Crick
A428
Guilsborough
Res.
Creaton
NATIONAL AGRICULTURAL CENTRE
RYTON POOLS
Stretton-on-Dunsmore
B4429
Dunchurch
M45
Kilsby
West Haddon
Coton
COTON MANOR
Hollowell
Princethorpe
Bourton on Dunsmore
Thurlaston
Ravensthorpe
Res.
Teeton
Brixworth
Weston under Wetherley
B4453
Frankton
Draycote
Draycote Water
DRAYCOTE WATER
Barby
Spratton
Wappenbury
Marton
A45
Ashby St Ledgers
Watford
Cubbington
B4453
Eathorpe
Birdingbury
Kites Hardwick
Woolscott
A361
WATFORD GAP SERVICES
B5385
East Haddon
Hunningham
Leam
Holdenby
Leamington Hastings
Willoughby
Long Buckby
N'THAMPTON & LAMPORT RAILWAY
B4455
A426
Grandborough
Braunston
Welton
A5
Chapel Brampton
Offchurch
Broadwell
Sawbridge
DAVENTRY
Daventry Reservoir
Great Brington
A428
Church Brampton
ALTHORP
Grand Union Canal
Long Itchington
Bascote
Stockton
Nethercote
Norton
Whilton
Little Brington
Harlestone
Flecknoe
Lower Shuckburgh
Brockhall
Nobottle
Queen's Park
A425
Ufton
Southam
A425
Napton on the Hill
Staverton
Daventry
New Duston
B4452
Itchen
Dodford
Harpole
Dallington
Chapel Green
Upper Catesby
A45
Flore
141
Duston
Harbury
CHESTERTON WINDMILL
Chesterton
Ladbroke
Badby
Newnham
Upper Weedon
Nene
Weedon Bec
Upper Heyford
A4500
Upton
Kislingbury
A5123
WARWICK SERVICES
Marston Doles
Hellidon
Church Stowe
Nether Heyford
M1
Cross Green
Bishop's Itchington
Priors Marston
Everdon
OLD DAIRY FARM CRAFT CENTRE
Upper Stowe
Bugbrooke
NORTHAMPTON SERVICES
HUNSBURY HILL
B4451
M40
Priors Hardwick
Charwelton
222
SP
Rothersthorpe
Oxford Canal
Preston Capes
Farthingstone
Gayton
Milton Malsor
Lighthorne
HERITAGE MOTOR CENTRE
Knightcote
Gaydon
A423
Wormleighton
Upper Boddington
Byfield
Litchborough
Grimscote
Pattishall
Eastcote
Bliswort
Boddington Reservoir
Hinton
Woodford Halse
Maidford
Cold Higham
Astcote
A43
Northend
BURTON DASSETT HILLS
Temple Herdewycke
Fenny Compton
Lower Boddington
Tiffield
Grand Union Canal
Kineton
203
Burton Dassett
GRANARY MUSEUM OF BYGONES
CANONS ASHBY HOUSE
Adstone
Caldecote
Claydon
Aston le Walls
Eydon
Canons Ashby
Blakesley
Duncote
Little Kineton
B4100
Avon Dassett
Farnborough
FARNBOROUGH HALL
Moreton Pinkney
Woodend
Greens Norton
Shutlanger
Stoke Bruerne
1642
Radway
Cherwell
Towcester
Chipping Warden
CATANGER LLAMA TREKKING
Woodend Green
TOWCESTER
Warmington
Mollington
Bradden
Edge Hill
Ratley
1469
Culworth
182
Weston
Slapton
Alderton
Cropredy
1644
Wardington
Abthorpe
Shotteswell
A361
Upper Wardington
Weedon Lois
Pury End
UPTON HOUSE
Great Bourton
Williamscott
Sulgrave
SULGRAVE MANOR
Wappenham
Paulerspury
Hornton
Thorpe Mandeville
Tysoe
Middle Tysoe
Horley
B4100
Silverstone
Whittlebury
A5
Chacombe
Helmdon
Alkerton
A422
Hanwell
Middleton Cheney
Marston St Lawrence
B4525
SILVERSTONE
Whittlewood Forest
227
Shenington
Wroxton
Drayton
Greatworth
Syresham
A43
Thenford
Crowfield
SILVERSTONE
Balscott
Neithrop
Grimsbury
Overthorpe
Halse
Radstone
Lillingstone Dayrell
Lillingstone Lovell
Epwell
Banbury
Warkworth
A422
Biddlesden
Shutford
North Newington
Farthinghoe
Whitfield
Wicken
SWALCLIFFE BARN
BROUGHTON CASTLE
Easington
STOWE HOUSE AND GARDENS
Sibford Gower
Tadmarton
Broughton
Upper Astrop
Turweston
Dadford
Akeley
Leckhampstead
Bodicote
Sor Brook
Swalcliffe
B4035
Newbottle
Brackley
Shalstone
Res.
Sibford Ferris
A4260
West Adderbury
M40
Astrop
Hinton-in-the-Hedges
A422
Buffler's Holt
Chackmore
Maids Moreton
Bloxham
A361
King's Sutton
Charlton
Great Ouse
Westbury
East Adderbury
Milcombe
Evenley
Water Stratford
Radclive
Buckingham
Thornborough
Milton
B4100
Barford St John
B4031
Croughton
A43
Mixbury
Finmere
A421
NORTON HISTORY VISITORS CENTRE
Hook Norton
Wigginton
South Newington
Barford St Michael
Aynho
Tingewick
Gawcott
Clifton
Swerford
Hempton
B4031
Deddington
Souldern
Cottisford
Barton Hartshorn
Newton Purcell
Padbury
Adstock
Nether Worton
North Aston
B4100
Baynard's Green
Hardwick
Preston Bissett
Great Tew
A361
Over Worton
Duns Tew
Fritwell
Hethe
Chetwode
A413
Addington
Fringford
Hillesden
Somerton
Fewcott
Stoke Lyne
CHERWELL VALLEY SERVICES
Middle Aston
Ardley
A4421
Steeple Claydon
Upper Heyford
B430
Stratton Audley
Twyford
East Claydon
Church
Westcott Barton
Steeple
Bucknell
B4100
Middle Claydon
0 1 2 3 4 5 6 miles
0 1 2 3 4 5 6 7 8 9 10 km
38
39
51
63
64

Desborough
Rushton Triangular Lodge
Rushton
Newton
Geddington
Eleanor Cross
Fermyn Woods
Sudborough
Wadenhoe
Achurch
Aldwincle
Barnwell
All Saints
Wigsthorpe
Luddington in the Brook
Thurning
Great Gidding
Little Gidding
Steeple Gidding
Hamerton Wildlife Centre
Hamerton
Coppingford
Arthingworth
Harrington
Rothwell
Weekley
Boughton House
Warkton
Grafton Underwood
Lowick
Thorpe Waterville
Clopton
Winwick
Titchmarsh
Orton
Loddington
Thorpe Malsor
Kettering
Barton Seagrave
Cranford St Andrew
Cranford St John
Slipton
Twywell
Islip
Thrapston
Woodford
Denford
Old Weston
Buckworth
Draughton
Great Cransley
Mawsley
Broughton
Wicksteed Park
Bythorn
Keyston
Brington
Molesworth
Barham
Leighton Bromswold
Woolley
Lamport
Lamport Hall
Old
Pytchley
Isham
Burton Latimer
Great Addington
Little Addington
Ringstead
Catworth
Spaldwick
Easton
Stow Longa
Scaldwell
Walgrave
Orlingbury
Little Harrowden
Finedon
Raunds
Hannington
Great Harrowden
Irthlingborough
Stanwick
Hargrave
Covington
Tilbrook
Holcot
Hardwick
Chelveston
Caldecott
Higham Ferrers
Chichele College
Shelton
Lower Dean
Upper Dean
Kimbolton
Grafham Water
Pitsford Reservoir
Brixworth
Pitsford
Sywell
Wellingborough
Mears Ashby
Heritage Centre
Little Irchester
Irchester
Knuston
Rushden
Newton Bromswold
Yeldon
Swineshead
West Perry
East Perry
Moulton
Overstone
Sywell Reservoir
Wilby
Little Wymington
Wymington
Melchbourne
Pertenhall
Dillington
Staughton Green
Staughton Highway
Boughton
Boothville
Ecton
New Barton
Great Doddington
Narrow Gauge Railway Mus.
Farndish
Knotting
Riseley
Brook End
Great Staughton
Kingsthorpe
Kingsley Park
Weston Favell
Great Billing
Little Billing
Earls Barton
Wollaston
Podington
Knotting Green
Keysoe
Little Staughton
Hail Weston
Billing Aquadrome
Strixton
Souldrop
Santa Pod
Hinwick
Keysoe Row
Duloe
Northampton
Little Houghton
Cogenhoe
Whiston
Grendon
Bolnhurst
Staploe
Bushmead Priory
Brafield-on-the-Green
Castle Ashby
Castle Ashby Gardens
Easton Maudit
Bozeat
Sharnbrook
Great Houghton
Denton
Yardley Hastings
Odell
Radwell
Bletsoe
Thurleigh
Roothams Green
Colmworth
Hardingstone
Harrold
Felmersham
Harrold-Odell
Milton Ernest
Wootton
Collingtree
Yardley Chase
Chellington
Duck's Cross
Chawston
Hackleton
Quinton
Carlton
Pavenham
Wilden
Colesden
Piddington
Horton
Lavendon
Glenn Miller Museum
Bodyflight
Ravensden
Roxton
Courteenhall
Warrington
West End
Stevington
Oakley
Clapham
Renhold
Green End
Salcey Forest
Cold Brayfield
Stevington Windmill
Salph End
Great Barford
Roade
Eakley Lanes
Weston Underwood
Olney
Turvey
Bromham
Bedford
Blunham
Hartwell
Clifton Reynes
Newton Blossomville
Bromham Mill
Ravenstone
Emberton
Goldington
Willington
Ashton
Stoke Goldington
Box End
Biddenham
Cecil Higgins Art Gallery and Mus.
Priory
Moggerhanger
Long Street
Milton Keynes
Filgrave
Stagsden
Great Denham
Queen's Park
Fenlake
Cople
Moggerhanger Park
Hatch
Tyringham
Kempston
Cardington
Thorncote Green
Grafton Regis
Hanslope
Hardmead
Astwood
Elstow Moot Hall
Harrowden
Shortstown
Elstow
Tathall End
Gayhurst
Sherington
Keeley Green
Northill
Great Ouse
Chicheley
North Crawley
Ickwell Green
Castlethorpe
Lathbury
Bourne End
Wootton
Kempston Hardwick
Cotton End
Littleworth
Yardley Gobion
Newport Pagnell
Upper Shelton
English School of Falconry
Shuttleworth Collection
The Swiss Garden
Old Warden
Potterspury
Newport Pagnell Services
Haversham
Broad Green
Lower Shelton
Stewartby Lake
Stewartby
Wilstead
Cosgrove
Great Linford
Cranfield
Haynes
Southill
Old Stratford
New Bradwell
Willen
Moulsoe
Marston Moretaine
Houghton Conquest
Stony Stratford
Wolverton
Milton Keynes
How End
Haynes Church End
Passenham
Bradwell
Broughton
St. Lawrence's
Salford
Marston Vale Millennium
Houghton House
Ampthill
Clophill
Beadlow
Shefford
Calverton
Bradwell Village
Woolstone
Milton Keynes Village
Lidlington
Millbrook
Maulden
Clifton
Hoo Hedge Maze
Upper Weald
National Hockey
Woughton on the Green
Brogborough
Campton
Loughton
Beachampton
Simpson
Walton
Wavendon
Aspley Guise
De Gray Mausoleum
Upper Gravenhurst
Meppershall
Shenley Church End
Thornton
Woburn Sands
Bow Brickhill
Ridgmont
Denel End
Flitton
Shenley Brook End
Aspley Heath
Husborne Crawley
Flitwick
Silsoe
Wrest Park House
Upper Stondon
Whaddon
Brickhill
Steppingley
Greenfield
Wild Animal Kingdom
Bletchley
Bletchley Park
Fenny Stratford
Woburn
Nash
Pulloxhill
Shillington
Tattenhoe
Far Bletchley
Eversholt
Higham Gobion
Holwell
Church End
Woburn Abbey
Westoning
Apsley End
Singleborough
Little Brickhill
Tingrith
Great Horwood
Little Horwood
Newton Longville
Great Brickhill
Harlington
Barton-le-Clay
Pirton
Milton Bryan
Hexton
Sharpenhoe
Pegsdon
Drayton Parslow
Stoke Hammond
Kings Wood
Stockgrove Park
Potsgrove
Battlesden
Toddington Services
Sundon Hills
Streatley
Barton Hills
Winslow
Mursley
Heath and Reach
Toddington
Upper Sundon
Swanbourne
Soulbury
Hockliffe
Tebworth
Lower Sundon
Lilley
Great Offley
Stewkley
Leighton Buzzard
Galley Hill
Wingfield
Chalton
Sundon
South End
Eggington
Northampton
SP
TL
A6003
A43
A6116
A605
A6
B576
B660
B662
A4300
A14
A510
A509
B574
B571
A45
A4500
B663
B645
A4508
A428
B526
B5388
B565
A508
A509
A422
A421
A603
A600
A5
A4146
A507
A4012
A5130
B530
A5120
B4034
B4033
B4032
B579
B655
A505
M1
H3
H5
H7
H8
H9
V4
V5
V6
V7
V8
V10
64
65
54
39
40
Whaddon Chase
Ouzel
Great Ouse
Til
Ise

Cambridge
Luddington in the Brook
Sawtry
Church End
UPWOOD MEADOWS
Bury
Tick Fen
Ferry Hill
Langwood Fen
Wigsthorpe
Thurning
Great Gidding
Little Gidding
Upwood
Chapel Head
Horseley Fen
Steeple Gidding
HAMERTON WILDLIFE CENTRE
Wood Walton
Great Raveley
Wistow
Pidley Fen
Clopton
Winwick
MONKS WOOD
Little Raveley
Warboys
Fenton
Hamerton
Chatteris Fen
Sutton
Upton
Wennington
Pidley
Somersham
Old Weston
Alconbury Weston
Abbots Ripton
Broughton
King's Ripton
Old Hurst
Hill Row Doles
Bythorn
Brington
Buckworth
Little Stukeley
Colne
Molesworth
Alconbury
Great Stukeley
Woodhurst
Bluntisham
Leighton Bromswold
Barham
Earith
Woolley
Sapley
Aldreth
Catworth
Huntingdon
Hartford
Wyton
Spaldwick
Easton
HUNTINGDON
CROMWELL MUS.
Houghton
HOUGHTON MILL
St Ives
Needingworth
Ellington
HINCHINGBROOKE
Hemingford Abbots
Holywell
Covington
Stow Longa
Brampton
Godmanchester
Hemingford Grey
Over
Willingham
Great Ouse
Tilbrook
Grafham
WOOD GREEN ANIMAL SHELTER
Galley Hill
Fenstanton
Fen Drayton
Swavesey
Rampton
Lower Dean
Grafham Water
Buckden
Upper Dean
Kimbolton
West Perry
East Perry
Offord Cluny
Hilton
Boxworth End
Cottenham
Offord Darcy
Longstanton
Stonely
Swineshead
Dillington
Conington
CAMBRIDGE SERVICES
Staughton Green
Diddington
Papworth St Agnes
Westwick
Pertenhall
Staughton Highway
Boxworth
Oakington
Great Staughton
Southoe
Great Paxton
Graveley
Papworth Everard
Elsworth
Lolworth
Histon
Brook End
Little Staughton
Little Paxton
Bar Hill
Dry Drayton
Impington
Keysoe
Hail Weston
Toseland
Knapwell
Yelling
Girton
Duloe
Madingley
Keysoe Row
St Neots
Eynesbury
Croxton
Staploe
Bolnhurst
BUSHMEAD PRIORY
Eltisley
Cambourne
Highfields
Hardwick
Coton
Newnham
Rootham's Green
Eaton Socon
Caxton
Thurleigh
Colmworth
Little Barford
Bourn
Caldecote
Wyboston
Great Gransden
Toft
Comberton
Chawston
Abbotsley
Barton
Grantchester
Duck's Cross
Colesden
Little Gransden
Kingston
Wilden
Waresley
Longstowe
Roxton
Great Eversden
RUPERT BROOKE MUSEUM
Ravensden
BODYFLIGHT
Green End
Tempsford
Little Eversden
Renhold
Haslingfield
Gamlingay
Harlton
Salph End
Great Barford
Hatley St George
WIMPOLE HALL AND HOME FARM
Hauxton
Bedford
Blunham
Everton
Harston
Goldington
Arrington
WIMPOLE PARK
Barrington
Willington
Girtford
East Hatley
Orwell
Sandy
Potton
CECIL HIGGINS ART GALLERY AND MUS.
PRIORY
New Wimpole
Newton
Moggerhanger
Cockayne Hatley
Croydon
WILLERS MILL WILD ANIMAL SANCTUARY
Fenlake
Cople
Hatch
Beeston
MOGGERHANGER PARK
Wrestlingworth
Tadlow
Shepreth
Foxton
Kempston
Cardington
Thorncote Green
Wendy
ELSTOW MOOT HALL
Harrowden
Sutton
Thriplow
Elstow
Shortstown
Upper Caldecote
Cam or Rhee
Meldreth
Northill
Eyeworth
Whaddon
Ickwell Green
Chiswick End
Fowlmere
Cotton End
Biggleswade
Abington Piggotts
Melbourn
Littleworth
SHUTTLEWORTH COLLECTION
ENGLISH SCHOOL OF FALCONRY
THE SWISS GARDEN
Dunton
Guilden Morden
Kneesworth
Wilstead
Old Warden
Bassingbourn
Haynes
Southill
Broom
Litlington
Steeple Morden
ROYSTON & DISTRICT MUS.
Houghton Conquest
Stanford
Langford
Edworth
Hinxworth
Royston
Heydon
Haynes Church End
HOUGHTON HOUSE
Shefford
Ashwell
Great Chishill
Ampthill
Beadlow
Clifton
Astwick
Caldecote
Barley
Chrishall
Maulden
Clophill
HOD HILL MAZE
Henlow
Campton
Church End
Newnham
Therfield
Little Chishill
DE GRAY MAUSOLEUM
Upper Gravenhurst
Meppershall
Stotfold
BALDOCK SERVICES
Slip End
Kelshall
Flitton
Arlesey
Bygrave
Reed
Barkway
Langley Upper Green
Flitwick
Silsoe
WREST PARK HOUSE
Upper Stondon
Lower Stondon
Radwell
Nuthampstead
Greenfield
Norton
Sandon
Langley Lower Green
Pulloxhill
Shillington
Baldock
Buckland
Higham Gobion
Holwell
Wallington
Roe Green
Mill End
Anstey
Westoning
Apsley End
LETCHWORTH
Chipping
Meesden
Pirton
Clothall
Wyddial
Barton-le-Clay
Ickleford
William
Rushden
Brent Pelham
Hexton
Weston
Hare Street
Sharpenhoe
Pegsdon
HITCHIN
Throcking
SUNDON HILLS
Walsworth
CROMER WINDMILL
Great Hormead
Streatley
BARTON HILLS
Great Wymondley
Hall's Green
Cottered
Buntingford
Little Wymondley
Graveley
Cromer
Aspenden
Furneaux Pelham
Ardeley
Westmill
Hay Street
Ippollitts
Walkern
Patmore Heath
Sundon
GALLEY HILL
Wood End
Quin
Ivel
Hiz
TL
A1
A1(M)
A14
A141
A142
A1123
A1096
A1198
A1303
A1307
A428
A421
A603
A600
A6
A505
A507
A602
A10
A1072
M11
B1043
B1090
B1040
B1050
B1086
B1381
B660
B662
B661
B645
B1046
B1049
B1042
B658
A6001
B656
B197
B1037
B1039
B1038
B1368
P&R
0 1 2 3 4 5 6 miles
0 1 2 3 4 5 6 7 8 9 10 km
53
40
41
65
66

Downham
Chettisham
Prickwillow
Shippea Hill Sta.
Lakenheath
Wangford Warren
Thetford Warren
Welney Hill
West Fen
Coveney
Queen Adelaide
Witcham
Oliver Cromwell's House
Ely
Kenny Hill
Lakenheath Warren
Elveden
Thetford Heath
East of England Tank Museum
Wentworth
Witchford
Middle Fen
Great Fen
Mildenhall Fen
Eriswell
Stuntney
Little Thetford
Broad Hill
Beck Row
Holywell Row
Haddenham
Isleham Fen
Thistley Green
West Row
Wilburton
Stretham
Barway
Soham Cotes
Priory Church
Isleham
Mildenhall
The King's Forest
Soham
Worlington
Barton Mills
Icklingham
Soham Mere
Freckenham
Cavenham Heath
Down Field Windmill
Tuddenham
West Stow
Ingham
Wicken
Fordham
Chittering
Wicken Corn Mill
Upware
Wicken Fen
New River
Chippenham
Red Lodge
Herringswell
Lackford
Culford
Cavenham
Flempton
River Bank
Chippenham Fen
Hengrave
Hengrave Hall
Cottenham
Farmland Mus. & Denny Abbey
Adventures Fen
Landwade
Kennett
Fornham All Saints
Burwell
Snailwell
Reach
Kentford
Risby
Waterbeach
Exning
Higham
Landbeach
Moulton
Packhouse Bridge
Little Saxham
Westley
Commercial End
Swaffham Prior
Newmarket Heath
Newmarket
Gazeley
Barrow
Milton
Lode Mill
Lode
Great Saxham
Cathedral and Abbey Ruins
Bury St Edmunds
Horningsea
Anglesey Abbey
Swaffham Bulbeck
Newmarket
National Stud
National Horseracing Museum
Dalham
Denham
Horringer
Ickworth House
Kings Hedges
Stow cum Quy
Cheveley
Ashley
Bottisham
Dunstall Green
Hargrave
Fen Ditton
Mus. of Technology
Chevington
Saxon Street
Ousden
Hawstead
Cambridge
Romsey Town
Little Wilbraham
Teversham
Woodditton
Whepstead
Fitzwilliam Mus.
Great Wilbraham
Stetchworth
Ditton Green
Upend
Lidgate
Depden Green
Chedburgh
Dullingham
Kirtling
Depden
Six Mile Bottom
Cherry Hinton
Fulbourn
Westley Waterless
Burrough Green
Kirtling Green
Thorns
Rede
Trumpington
Wickhambrook
Clopton Green
Brockley Green
Brinkley
Cowlinge
Weston Colville
Great Bradley
Wickham Street
Wandlebury
Great Shelford
Stapleford
Carlton
Weston Green
Denston
Hawkedon
Stradishall
Stansfield
Hartest
TL
Little Bradley
Little Shelford
Granta
West Wratting
Little Thurlow
Boxted
Shimpling
Babraham
Balsham
Great Thurlow
Fourwentways Services
Little Abington
Stanstead
Sawston
Great Abington
Hildersham
West Wickham
Barnardiston
Hundon
Whittlesford
Duxford Chapel
Pampisford
Streetly End
Great Wratting
Poslingford
Glemsford
Horseheath
Withersfield
Little Wratting
High Street
Linton
Linton Zoo
Kedington
Chilton Street
Cavendish
Sue Ryder Foundation Mus.
Duxford
Haverhill
Clare
Pentlow
Long Melford
Duxford Airfield (Imperial War Museum) American Air Mus.
Hinxton
Bartlow
Boyton End
Clare Castle
Ickleton
Hadstock
Shudy Camps
Stoke by Clare
Clare Ancient House
Foxearth
Stump Cross
Great Chesterford
Castle Camps
Sturmer
Wixoe
Baythorn End
Belchamp St Paul
Borley
Little Chesterford
Ashdon
Helions Bumpstead
Birdbrook
Ashen
Ovington
Belchamp Otten
Ballingdon
Little Walden
Church End
Steeple Bumpstead
Ridgewell
Tilbury Juxta Clare
Belchamp Walter
Bulmer
Strethall
Littlebury
Saffron Walden
Little Yeldham
Elmdon
Stambourne
Bulmer Tye
Gestingthorpe
Henny
Sewards End
Stambourne Green
Great Yeldham
Littlebury Green
Audley End
Radwinter
Toppesfield
Audley End
Great Henny
Bridge Green
Wendens Ambo
Hempstead
Colne Valley Railway
Hedingham Castle
Wimbish
Cornish Hall End
Wickham St Paul
Twinstead Green
Duddenhoe End
Great Sampford
Gainsford End
Castle Hedingham
Highstreet Green
Great Maplestead
Tye Green
Alphamstone
Arkesden
Wimbish Green
Little Sampford
Howe Street
Morris Green
Sible Hedingham
Little Maplestead
Newport
Howlett End
Debden
Finchingfield
Pebmarsh
Clavering
Wicken Bonhunt
Priors Hall Barn
Widdington
Debden Cross
Rickling
Mole Hall Wildlife Park
Wethersfield
Halstead
Starlings Green
Quendon
Thaxted
Little Bardfield
Hamperden End
Cutlers Green
Great Bardfield
Blackmore End
Berden
Stort
St. Mary's Church
Gosfield
Colne
Henham
Glendale Forge
Monk Street
Shalford
Beazley End
Earls Colne
Stocking Pelham
Ugley
Church End
Ugley Green
Lindsell
Shalford Green
Greenstead Green
Manuden
House on the Hill Toy Mus.
Broxted
Duton Hill
Bardfield Saling
Jasper's Green
Stocking Churchstreet
High Garrett
Farnham Green
Elsenham
Molehill Green
Brick End
Great Easton
Pods Brook

Brandon Park
Lodge
Thetford Warren
Thetford
Ancient House Mus.
Brettenham
Shadwell
North Lopham
Heath
Mill Green
Shelfanger
Fersfield
Burston
Wangford Warren
Lakenheath Warren
Rushford
Gasthorpe
Garboldisham
South Lopham
Bressingham
Roydon
Walcot Green
Diss
67
68
Thetford Heath
Elveden
East of England Tank Museum
Barnham
Euston
Knettishall
Knettishall Heath
Coney Weston
Hopton
Market Weston
Blo' Norton
Thelnetham Windmill
Thelnetham
Redgrave
Bressingham Steam Museum and Gardens
Magpie Green
Palgrave
Stuston
Wortham
Hinderclay
Thrandeston
Brome
Fakenham Magna
Sapiston
Honington
Barningham
Hepworth
Botesdale
Rickinghall
Burgate
Mellis
Langton Green
Yaxley
Eye
The King's Forest
Icklingham
Cavenham Heath
Tuddenham
West Stow
West Stow
Ingham
Ampton
Bardwell
Ixworth Thorpe
Troston
Great Livermere
Stanton
Upthorpe
Walsham le Willows
Wattisfield
Cranmer Green
Allwood Green
Gislingham
Thornham Parva
Thornham Magna
Braiseworth
Lackford
Culford
Flempton
Cavenham
Ixworth
Langham
Four Ashes
Crownland
Badwell Ash
Long Thurlow
Westhorpe
Wickham Street
Finningham
Wickham Skeith
Stoke Ash
Thorndon
Hengrave
Hengrave Hall
Timworth Green
Conyers Green
Stowlangtoft
Hunston
Great Ashfield
Wyverstone
Wyverstone Street
Bacton
Cotton
Thwaite
Brockford Street
Wetheringsett
Fornham All Saints
Fornham St Martin
Risby
55
Great Barton
Pakenham
Stanton Street
Norton
Earl's Green
Ford's Green
Higham
Little Saxham
Westley
Thurston
Bacton Green
Canham's Green
Mendlesham
Blacksmith's Green
Bury St Edmunds
Cathedral and Abbey Ruins
Tostock
Elmswell
Haughley Green
Ward Green
Mendlesham Green
Wetherup Street
Barrow
Great Saxham
Blackthorpe
Beyton
Wetherden
Haughley Park
Gipping
Denham
Horringer
Ickworth House
Rougham
Rushbrooke
Hessett
Woolpit
Drinkstone
Woolpit Bygones Museum
Haughley
Saxham Street
Middlewood Green
Mickfield
Sicklesmere
Rougham Green
Bradfield St George
Drinkstone Green
Harleston
Thorney Green
Stowupland
Little Stonham
Hargrave
Chevington
Little Welnetham
Rattlesden
Buxhall Fen Street
Forward Green
Stonham Aspal
Hawstead
Whepstead
Great Welnetham
Bradfield St Clare
Gedding
Poystreet Green
Museum of East Anglian Life
Stowmarket
Earl Stonham
Creeting Bottoms
Depden Green
Bradfield Combust
Bradfield Woods
Felsham
Buxhall
Great Finborough
Combs Ford
Chedburgh
Depden
Cross Green
Hightown Green
Gipping
Creeting St Mary
Crowfield
Thorns
Rede
Hoggard's Green
Great Green
High Street Green
Combs
Moats Tye
Beacon Hill Services
Wickhambrook
Clopton Green
Brockley Green
Lawshall
Cockfield
Thorpe Green
Little Finborough
Battisford
Needham Market
Coddenham
Wickham Street
Denston
Hawkedon
Brettenham
Battisford Tye
Charles Tye
Ringshall
Barking
Stradishall
Stansfield
Hartest
Shimpling Street
Thorpe Morieux
Cross Green
Wattisham Airfield Museum
Barking Tye
Baylham
Barham
Shimpling
Alpheton
Boxted
Preston
Hitcham
Wattisham
Ringshall Stocks
Willisham Tye
Great Blakenham
Claydon
Stanstead
Kettlebaston
Great Bricett
Nedging Tye
Little Blakenham
Hundon
Poslingford
Glemsford
Kentwell Hall
Bridge Street
Lavenham
Guildhall
Bildeston
Offton
Akenham
Monks Eleigh
Chelsworth
Naughton
Somersham
High Street
Brent Eleigh
Chilton Street
Cavendish
Sue Ryder Foundation Mus.
Clare
Pentlow
Long Melford
Melford Hall
Little Waldingfield
Milden
Semer
Ash Street
Elmsett
Whatfield
Flowton
Whitton
Bramford
Westbourne
Clare Castle
Clare Ancient House
Foxearth
Acton
Lindsey
Chapel
Aldham
Sproughton
Great Waldingfield
Wolves Wood RSPB Reserve
Burstall
Ipswich
Borley
Kersey
Hintlesham
Chantry
Ashen
Ovington
Belchamp Otten
Belchamp St Paul
Sudbury
Edwardstone
Mill Green
Hadleigh
Chattisham
Copdock
Ridgewell
Tilbury Juxta Clare
Belchamp Walter
Ballingdon
Bulmer
Great Cornard
Groton
Newton
Boxford
Layham
Coles Green
Mace Green
Belstead
Little Yeldham
Gainsborough's Ho.
Stone Street
Calais Street
Middleton
Little Cornard
Bulmer Tye
Gestingthorpe
Henny Street
Assington
Whitestreet Green
Raydon
Great Wenham
Capel St Mary
Great Yeldham
Audley End
Great Henny
Twinstead
Polstead
Shelley
Holton St Mary
Tattingstone
Colne Valley Railway
Hedingham Castle
Castle Hedingham
Wickham St Paul
Twinstead Green
Lamarsh
Harrow Street
Stoke-by-Nayland
Honey Tye
Bentley
The Heath
Alton Water Res.
Higham
East Bergholt
Sible Hedingham
Great Maplestead
Little Maplestead
Alphamstone
Bures Green
Thorington Street
Stratford St Mary
East Bergholt Place
Brantham
Bures
Dedham Vale
Nayland
Dedham
Bridge Cottage
Cattawade
Pebmarsh
Little Horkesley
Boxted
Boxted Cross
Sir Alfred Munnings Art Museum
Mistley Towers
Mistley
Mount Bures
Boxted Heath
Langham
Dedham Heath
Lawford
Manningtree
Halstead
Colne Engaine
Wormingford
Great Horkesley
Bradfield
Blackmore End
Gosfield
Wakes Colne
East Anglian Railway Museum
Horkesley Heath
Ardleigh
Bradfield Heath
Beazley End
Chappel
Fordham
West Bergholt
Mile End
Little Bromley
Horsley Cross
Horsleycross Street
Bocking Churchstreet
Fordstreet
Eight Ash Green
Highwoods
Colchester
St. Botolph's
Fox Street
Crockleford Heath
Great Bromley
Little Bentley
Tendring Green
Great Tey
Aldham
Stour
Colne
Gipping
Brett
Lark
Little Ouse
Dove
42
43
A11
A1066
A134
A1088
B1106
B1111
B1113
A143
A14
A1101
B1112
A1088
A140
A1120
B1078
A1141
B1115
B1066
B1065
A1092
B1064
A131
B1058
A1017
A1124
B1508
A1071
B1070
B1068
B1087
A12
B1029
A137
A120
B1035
B1077
B1117
A1214
A1232
0 1 2 3 4 5 6 miles
0 1 2 3 4 5 6 7 8 9 10 km
A
B
C
D
E
F
1
2
3
4
5
S
u
f
f
o
TL

Starston
Garlic Street
Harleston
Redenhall
Wortwell
Mendham
St Cross South Elmham
St Margaret South Elmham
SOUTH ELMHAM HALL
St Michael South Elmham
All Saints South Elmham
Ilketshall St Lawrence
Redisham
Stone Street
Cox Common
Brampton
Mill Common
Sotterley
Shadingfield
West End
Stoven
Wrentham
Clay Common
Benacre
BENACRE
Covehithe
Frostenden
South Cove
Cove Bottom
Rushall
Dickleburgh
Needham
100TH BOMB GROUP MEMORIAL MUS.
Thelveton
Withersdale Street
St James South Elmham
Rumburgh
Spexhall
Metfield
Thorpe Abbotts
Brockdish
BILLINGFORD WINDMILL
Oakley
Hoxne
Syleham
WINGFIELD OLD COLLEGE
Wingfield
Fressingfield
Wissett
Linstead Parva
Chediston
Westhall
Broadway
Halesworth
Holton
Blyford
Wangford
Reydon Smear
Reydon
HEN REEDBED NATURE RESERVE
SOUTHWOLD MUSEUM
Southwold
Brome Street
Cross Street
Heckfield Green
Denham
Stradbroke
Chippenhall Green
Battlesea Green
Pixey Green
Little Whittingham Green
Silverley's Green
Cratfield
Swan Green
Cookley
Huntingfield
Walpole
Wenhaston
Blackheath
Blythburgh
Thorington
Walberswick
Bramfield
Blyth
Cranley
Denham Street
Horham
Wilby
Wootton Green
Russel's Green
Ashfield Green
Banyard's Green
Laxfield
Heveningham
Sibton Green
Ubbeston Green
SUFFOLK COAST
Dunwich
Forest
DUNWICH UNDERWATER EXPLORATION EXHIBITION
Redlingfield
Athelington
Foals Green
Brundish Street
Crown Corner
High Street
Darsham
Occold
Fingal Street
Stanway Green
Brundish
Owl's Green
Peasenhall
Sibton
Hemp Green
Yoxford
Westleton
WESTLETON HEATH
Middleton Moor
MINSMERE RSPB NATURE RESERVE
Southolt
Bedingfield
Worlingworth
Tannington
Badingham
Alde
Rotten End
Middleton
Bedfield
Maypole Green
Dennington
Bruisyard
North Green
Theberton
Eastbridge
Kenton
Saxtead
Brabling Green
Cransford
Curlew Green
Kelsale
Monk Soham
SAXTEAD GREEN POST MILL
Rendham
Carlton
LEISTON ABBEY
Saxtead Green
Framlingham
Sweffling
Saxmundham
Leiston
Sizewell
Debenham
Ashfield
Earl Soham
Knodishall
Great Glemham
Cole's Green
Benhall Street
Sternfield
Aldringham
Winston
Deben
Lampardbrook
Coldfair Green
Winston Green
Peats Corner
Brandeston
Stratford St Andrew
Benhall Green
Parham
Friston
Thorpeness
Pettaugh
Framsden
Cretingham
Kettleburgh
Hacheston
Farnham
Gromford
Easton
EASTON FARM PARK
Marlesford
HELMINGHAM HALL GARDENS
Helmingham
Monewden
Letheringham
Little Glemham
SNAPE MALTINGS RIVERSIDE CENTRE
Snape
NORTH WARREN RSPB NATURE RESERVE
AKENFIELD
BLAXHALL
Blaxhall
Aldeburgh
Charsfield
Lower Hacheston
Iken
Wickham Market
Campsey Ash
High Street
Aldeburgh Bay
Otley
Clopton Corner
Dallinghoo
Debach
Pettistree
Ashbocking
Tunstall
Tunstall Forest
Rendlesham
Swilland
Bredfield
Ufford
Sudbourne
Clopton
Chillesford
Witnesham
Grundisburgh
Burgh
Eyke
Henley
Hasketon
Bromeswell
Butley
Melton
ORFORD CASTLE
Orford
Tuddenham St Martin
Culpho
Boot Street
Great Bealings
Woodbridge
Rendlesham Forest
Orford Ness
Butley High Corner
ORFORDNESS-HAVERGATE
SUTTON HOO ARCHAEOLOGICAL SITE
Westerfield
Playford
Maidensgrave
Capel St Andrew
Rushmere St Andrew
Little Bealings
Boyton
Martlesham
CHRISTCHURCH MANSIONS
Waldringfield Heath
Sutton
Stores Corner
Ipswich
Martlesham Heath
Kesgrave
Waldringfield
Duck Corner
Shottisham
Hollesley Bay
Rose Hill
MARTLESHAM HEATH CONTROL TOWER
Hollesley
Stoke
Maidenhall
Brightwell
Newbourne
Warren Heath
Gainsborough
Bucklesham
Hemley
Shingle Street
Alderton
Bawdsey
Wherstead
ORWELL
Nacton
Kirton
Freston
Woolverstone
Levington
Falkenham
Pinmill
Orwell
Thorpe Common
Trimley St Martin
Chelmondiston
Trimley Lower Street
Felixstowe Ferry
Holbrook
Trimley St Mary
Old Felixstowe
Lower Holbrook
Shotley
Walton
TRIMLEY MARSHES NATURE RESERVE
Stutton
Erwarton
Harkstead
Shotley Gate
Shop Corner
FELIXSTOWE
Holbrook Bay
Stour
HARWICH
CHARLES MANNING'S AMUSEMENT PARK
HARWICH REDOUBT
Parkeston
Wrabness
Ramsey
Upper Dovercourt
Dovercourt
Little Oakley
Wix
Great Oakley
Stones Green
ESBJERG 20:00
HOEK VAN HOLLAND 6:00
HOEK VAN HOLLAND 3:40
OOSTENDE (From Ipswich) 9:00
GOTHENBURG 38:30
ROTTERDAM 8:00
TM
A
B
C
D
E
F
G
5
6
7
8
9

1
2
3
4
5
A
B
C
D
E
F
TREMADOG BAY
BAE TREMADOG
Gwynedd
SNOWDONIA NATIONAL PARK
PARC CENEDLAETHOL ERYRI
SH
SN
71
46
47
Eisingrug
Glyn-cywarch
623 MOEL YSGYFARNOGOD
750 MOEL LLYFRANT
Morfa Harlech
Harlech
A496
B4573
A470
Bronaber
Mynydd Bach
Mynydd Bryn-llech
Buarthmeini
Afon Eden
Llanfair
LLANFAIR SLATE CAVERNS
Llandanwg
Pen-sarn
Pen-y-bont
Pentre Gwynfryn
720 RHINOG FAWR
RHINOG
COED Y BRENIN VISITOR CENTRE
SARN HELEN
Bed-y-coedwr
RHAEADR MAWDDACH
Pont Aber-Geirw
Cwm-hesgen
MAES ARTRO HERITAGE MUS.
Llanbedr
LLANBEDR
Morfa Dyffryn
MORFA DYFFRYN
Coed y Brenin Forest
754 Y LLETHR
Capel Hermon
734 RHOBELL FAWR
Pont Fronwydd
Afon Wnion
Coed Ystumgwern
Llanenddwyn
Dyffryn Ardudwy
DIFFWYS 750
Ganllwyd
COED GANLLWYD
ALLT Y BENGLOG
A494
Llanfachreth
Llanddwywe
Cors-y-Gedol
Blaen-y-cwm
Rhydymain
Tal-y-bont
Llanelltyd
CYMMER ABBEY
Bont Newydd
B4416
Brithdir
Plas-canol
Pen-y-bryn
PENMAENPWEL CENTRE
Bontddu
Caerdeon
TOLL
Llanaber
Penmaenpool
A470
Cutiau
Abergwynant
Dolgellau
Y Gribin
A496
Afon Mawddach
KINGS
Rhyd-wen
Afon Cerist
A470
Barmouth (Abermaw)
RNLI LIFEBOAT MUSEUM
A493
670 WAUN-OER
BARMOUTH BAY
The Bar
Arthog
Ynysgyfflog
FAIRBOURNE & BARMOUTH STEAM RAILWAY
893 CADAIR IDRIS
Mynydd Ceiswyn
Mynydd Dolgoed
MEIRIO
BAE BERMO
Fairbourne
Friog
CADER IDRIS
Dyfi Forest
Minffordd
Llwyngwril
Tal-y-llyn
A487
Corris Uchaf
Aberllefenni
Aberangell
A470
Afon Dysynni
Llanfihangel-y-pennant
KING ARTHUR'S LABYRINTH & CRAFT CENTRE
Corris
CORRIS RAILWAY AND MUSEUM
Cwm-Llinau
A493
Llangelynin
Abergynolwyn
Dol-fôr
B4405
Esgairgeiliog
Rhoslefain
Llanegryn
Cemmaes
Llanfendigaid
Peniarth
Plas Llwyngwern
CENTRE FOR ALTERNATIVE TECHNOLOGY
Pantperthog
309
B4404
Tonfanau
633 TARRENHENDRE
Llanwrin
Cemmaes Road
Bryncrug
Pandy
DYFI VALLEY
Pen-y-bont
Abercegir
Commins Coch
Rhyd-yr-onen
TALYLLYN RAILWAY
SENEDD-DY-OWAIN GLYNDWR
A489
Darowen
Tywyn
Machynlleth
Penegoes
FELIN CREWI WATER MILL
Tal-y-wern
Cwrt
Pennal
A493
DOVEY
DYFFRYN
Forge
CELTICA
Caethle
Derwenlas
Melinbyrhedyn
Glaspwll
Pant-glâs
468 MOELFF
279
Aberhosan
Aberdovey
A493
Glandyfi
Dovey
Dyfi
YNYS HIR RESERVE
Eglwys Fach
DYFI FURNACE
Aberdovey Bar
Bae Aberdyfi
DYFI
A487
Glaslyn
Fochno
Ynyslas
B4353
582
Llancynfelyn
Tre'r-ddôl
521 MOEL-Y-LLYN
BORTH
Tre-Taliesin
Borth
Source of R. Severn Blaen Hafren
Upper Borth
Tal-y-bont
Dôl-y-Bont
Nant-y-Moch Reservoir
PLYNLIMON PUMLUMON FAWR
741
752
Source of R. Wye Blaen Gwy
Llandre
Pen-y-garn
Bont-goch
B4572
ARTS CENTRE
Bow Street
Salem
506
NATIONAL LIBRARY
Clarach
Penrhyn-coch
CLIFF RAILWAY
148
Plas Gogerddan
Pen-bont-Rhydybeddau
A4159
Aberystwyth
Comins Coch
Capel Dewi
LLYWERNOG SILVER LEAD MINE
Dyffryn Castell
P&R
Llanbadarn Fawr
Capel Bangor
Dollwen
Goginan
Trefechan
A44
CASTLE
Glanrafon
Ponterwyd
564
Penparcau
Southgate
VALE OF RHEIDOL
Afon Rheidol
Cwmbrwyno
Rhydyfelin
Moriah
RHEIDOL HYDRO ELECTRIC STAT.
Ystumtuen
Capel Seion
Aberffrwd
COED RHEIDOL
Ysbyty-Cynfyn
A487
Llanfarian
Gors
A4120
Pisgah
Mynydd Bach
New Cross
Llanfihangel-y-Creuddyn
Devil's Bridge
610 PEN Y GARN
A485
Blaenplwyf
Trisant
Blaenycwm
0 1 2 3 4 5 6 miles
0 1 2 3 4 5 6 7 8 9 10 km

Parc
Rhos-y-gwaliau
Pennant
Tregeiriog
Llechrydau
Aber-Hirnant
Blaen-y-Cwm
Llanarmon Dyffryn Ceiriog
Llangower
Pont Cwm Pydew
Tyn-y-fedwen
Tyn-y-ffridd
Rhiwlas
Cefn Canol
MOEL SYCH
BALA LAKE RLY.
Llanuwchllyn
Aberhirnant Forest
PISTYLL RHAEADR
Llangadwaladr
Rhydycroesau
Pont-Rhyd-sarn
Tan-y-pistyll
Tai-bach
Llansilin
OFFA'S DYKE PATH
LLWYBR CLAWDD OFFA
Tyn-y-coed
Talardd
FOEL Y GEIFR
Moelfre
Ty-nant
Pencraig
Cefn Coch
Trefonen
Cwm Cynllwyd
Pennant Melangell
Llangynog
Llanrhaeadr-ym-Mochnant
Treflach
Alltforgan
Y BERWYN
Penybontfawr
Llangedwyn
Pen-y-bont
Nant
ARAN AWDDWY
Lake Vyrnwy
Penygarnedd
Afon Tanat
Porth-y-waen
Hirnant
Rhos-y-brithdir
Llanyblodwel
Ty-uchaf
Bwlchyddar
Abernaint
Llansantffraid-ym-Mechain
Llanymynech
Aber-Rhiwlech
Pont y Pennant
Blaen-y-cwm
Llanfechain
Cywarch
Llanwddyn
Abertridwr
Llanfyllin
Hen Gerrig
Llanymawddwy
Tycrwyn
Waen Fach
Bryn Sion
Deuddwr
Aber Cowarch
Ddôl-Cownwy
Llanfihangel-yn-Ngwynfa
Bwlch-y-cibau
Dyfnant Forest
TIR RHIWIOG
Sarnau
Arddleen
Dinas-Mawddwy
Moel y Llyn
Mynydd y Gadfa
Pont-Llogel
Main
Trefnanney
Minllyn
Afon Vyrnwy (Afon Efyrnwy)
Geuffordd
Cwm-Cewydd
Wern
Meifod
Pentrebeirdd
Mallwyd
Wern
Dolanog
Pontrobert
Maesgwyn-Isaf
Glascoed
Pool Quay
Foel
Llangadfan
Groes-lwyd
Guilsfield
Ffridd Goch
GLYNDWR'S WAY
Mynydd y Cemaes
Llanerfyl
Pen Coed
Heniarth
Cloddiau
Welshpool (Y Trallwng)
Four Crosses
Cyfronydd
Butti
Clegyrnant
Dolwen
WELSHPOOL & LLANFAIR LIGHT RAILWAY
POWYSLAND
Neinthirion
Sychtyn
Melin-y-grug
Melin-y-ddôl
Llanfair Caereinion
POWIS CASTLE
Castle Caereinion
Pentre-Celyn
Leighton
Mynydd Waun Fawr
Pandy
Cwmderwen
Bryn-penarth
Waun
Llwynderw
Fron
Powys
Llanbrynmair
Tafolwern
Pant-y-ffridd
Kingswood
Dolfach
Llanllugan
Manafon
Llan
Llanwyddelan
Berriew
Stockton
Rhyd
Forden
Bont-Dolgadfan
Talerddig
Adfa
New Mills
Severn (Hafren)
Brooks
Garthmyl
Tregynon
Pennant
Carno
Fron
Montgomery (Trefaldwyn)
Bettws Cedewain
Green Lane
Llandyssil
Bwlch-y-ffridd
Abermule
Dylife
Clatter
Llanwnog
Llanmerewig
Pentreheyling
Llanllwchaiarn
Staylittle
Caersws
Hodley
Llawryglyn
Gleiniant
Milford
Sarn
Trefeglwys
Newtown (Y Drenewydd)
Glanmule
Kerry
City
Llyn Clywedog
Little London
Mochdre
FAN HILL
Llandinam
Van
Oakley Park
Dolfor
Clun Forest
Pentre
Hafren Forest
Tan Hinon
Old Hall
Glan-y-nant
Anchor
Llanidloes
CILFAESTY HILL
Hall of the Forest
Glynbrochan
Newchapel
BLACK MT.
Newcastle
Pant Mawr
Cwmbelan
Felindre
Bettws-y-crwyn
Quabbs
Llangurig
Tylwch
Llaithddu
Beguildy
David's Well
Black Mountain
Llanbadarn Fynydd
Dutlas
Nantgwyn
RED LION HILL
Rhyd-moel-ddu
BEACON
Llanfair Waterdine
Pant-y-dwr
SJ
SO

Llechrydau
Selattyn
Hengoed
Gobowen
Perthy
Welsh Frankton
Tetchill
Balmer Heath
Lyneal
Colemere
Northwood
Whixall
Waterloo
Quina Brook
Rhiwlas
Llangadwaladr
Cefn Canol
Pant-glas
Llawnt
Old Oswestry Hill Fort
Hindford
Whittington Castle
Whittington
Lower Frankton
Hordley
Lee
Wolverley
Newtown
Edstaston
Oswestry
Babbinswood
Kenwick
English Frankton
Horton
Lowe
Wem
Offa's Dyke Path
Llansilin
Tyn-y-coed
Moelfre
Middleton
Wootton
Lower Hordley
Cockshutt
Loppington
Aston
Rednal
Stanwardine in the Wood
Tilley
Noneley
Lee Brockhurst
Trefonen
Morda
Ball
Queen's Head
Haughton
Bagley
Petton
Grimpo
Burlton
Treflach
Maesbury
Maesbury Marsh
West Felton
Westoncommon
Weston Lullingfields
Preston Brockhurst
Nantmawr
Wykey
Llangedwyn
Pen-y-bont
Morton
Woolston
Eardiston
Marton
Alderton
Clive
Afon Tanat
Porth-y-waen
Llynclys
Stanwardine in the Fields
Myddle
Rhos-y-brithdir
Llanyblodwel
Crickheath
Osbaston
Shotatton
Yorton
Grinshill
Pant
Knockin
Brownhill
Baschurch
Bwlchyddar
Maesbrook
Dovaston
Ruyton-XI-Towns
Harmer Hill
Llanfechain
Llansantffraid-ym-Mechain
Llanymynech
Kinnerley
Prescott
Merrington
Llanfyllin
Kynaston
Hopton
Little Ness
Walford
Walford Heath
Preston Gubbals
Hadnall
Llandysilio
Kinton
Nesscliffe
Yeaton
Bomere Heath
Astley
Crosslanes
Wilcott
Great Ness
Grafton
Leaton
Waen Fach
Four Crosses
Melverley Green
Pentre
Felton Butler
Albrighton
Bwlch-y-cibau
Deuddwr
Forton Heath
Fitz
Llandrinio
Melverley
Ensdon
Forton
Mytton
Battlefield
Main
Sarnau
Arddleen
Shrawardine
Montford Bridge
Haughmond Abbey
Afon Vyrnwy
Trefnanney
Criggion
Coedway
Bicton
Harlescott
Geufforddd
Crewgreen
Alberbury
Montford
Ditherington
Meifod
Wern
Pentrebeirdd
Ford
Shelton
Coton Hill
Uffington
Maesgwyn-Isaf
Middletown
Wollaston
Shrewsbury
Pool Quay
Trewern
Cardeston
Shoot Hill
Copthorne
Groes-lwyd
Guilsfield
Halfway House
Rowton
Wattlesborough Heath
Hortonlane
Porthill
Preston
Glyndŵr's Way
Nox
Cruckton
Meole Brace
Emstrey
Yockleton
Westbury
Cruckmeole
Cloddiau
Welshpool (Y Trallwng)
Buttington
Nelly Andrews Green
Vennington
Stoney Stretton
Edge
Hanwood
Atcham
Cyfronydd
Powysland
Farley
Hinton
Lea
Annscroft
Bayston Hill
Welshpool & Llanfair Light Railway
Hope
Aston Rogers
Westley
Asterley
Plealey
Great Lyth
Cross Houses
Powis Castle
Rowley
Longden
Berrington
Lyth Hill
Castle Caereinion
Leighton
Minsterley
Pontesbury
Condover
Cantlop
Worthen
Oaks
Stapleton
Binweston
Brockton
Wrentnall
Pitchford
Fron
Trelystan
Leigh
Ploxgreen
Great Ryton
Golding
Llwynderw
Habberley
Church Pulverbatch
Dorrington
Acton Pigott
Pant-y-ffridd
Betton
Marton
Snailbeach
Castle Pulverbatch
Kingswood
Berriew
Stockton
Meadowtown
Bentlawnt
Hope
Frodesley
Acton Burnell
Forden
Crowsnest
Longnor
Langley Chapel and Gatehouse
Rorrington
Gravels
Wotherton
Black Marsh
Stiperstones
Garthmyl
Middleton
Mitchell's Fold Stone Circle
Pennerley
Picklescott
Woolstaston
Leebotwood
Ruckley
Church Preen
Chirbury
Shelve
Fron
Priest Weston
The Marsh
The Bog
Montgomery (Trefaldwyn)
Ratlinghope
Green Lane
Corndon Hill
Bridges
Enchmarsh
Plaish
Llandyssil
Coldyeld
Bridges Long Mynd
All Stretton
Cardington
Gretton
Abermule
Church Stoke
Roundton Hill
Hyssington
Llwybr Clawdd Offa
The Long Mynd
Church Stretton
Longville in the Dale
Pentreheyling
Linley
Norbury
Wentnor
Wall Bank
East Wall
Llanmerewig
Snead
Hope Bowdler
Wall under Heywood
Rushbury
Wilderhope Manor
Hodley
Pentre
Owlbury
More
Little Stretton
Sarn
Glanmule
Lydham
Asterton
Minton
Ticklerton
Acton Scott
Hatton
City
Kerry
Myndtown
Marshbrook
Broadstone
Bishop's Castle
House on Crutches
Lea
Eaton
Whittingslow
Working Farm
Eaton
Choulton
Mainstone
Colebatch
Eyton
Plowden
Harton
Middlehope
Wenlock Edge
Ape Dale
Munslow
Aston Munslow
Lydbury North
Woolston
Upper Affcot
Alcaston
Horderley
Wistanstow
Clun Forest
Cefn Einion
Brockton
Edgton
Strefford
Westhope
Diddlebury
Corfton
Boulden
Anchor
Bryn
Acton
Lower Down
Walcot
Cheny Longville
Lower Dinchope
Peaton
Hall of the Forest
Black Mt
Whitcott Keysett
Hopesay
Kempton
Sibdon Carwood
Newington
Halford
Great Sutton
Newcastle
Bicton
Seifton
Craven Arms
Aston on Clun
Little Brampton
Stokesay
Culmington
Clun Mill
Felindre
Bettws-y-crwyn
Quabbs
Clunton
Broome
Stokesay Castle
Norton
Hayton's Bent
Hopton Cangeford
Vernolds Common
Llwyn
Clun
Purslow
Clunbury
Beguildy
Churchbank
Twitchen
Brandhill
The Wernlas Collection
Onibury
Upper
Hobarris
Abcott
Clungunford
Stanton Lacy
Hopton Castle
Hoptonheath
Wootton
Shelderton
Bromfield
Ludlow
Middleton
Henley
New Invention
Chapel Lawn
Bedstone
Marlow
Beacon
0 1 2 3 4 5 6 miles
0 1 2 3 4 5 6 7 8 9 10 km

Telford and Wrekin
Shropshire
Market Drayton
Stone
Stafford
Eccleshall
Newport
Telford
Wellington
Hadley
Oakengates
Donnington
Dawley
Madeley
Shifnal
Much Wenlock
Bridgnorth
Albrighton
Codsall
Brewood
Penkridge
Tettenhall
Wolverhampton
Willenhall
Bilston
Sedgley
Tipton
Wombourne
Dudley
Kingswinford
Brierley Hill
Wordsley
Stourbridge
HALESOWEN
Kinver
Kidderminster
Gnosall
Shawbury
Sandford
Prees
Lowe
Heath
Darliston
Fauls
Bletchley
Longford
Ternhill
Hales
Fairoak
Chatcull
Wetwood
Croxtonbank
Croxton
Slindon
Millmeece
Yarnfield
Walton
Little Stoke
Aston-By-Stone
Burston
Sandon
Norton Bridge
Sugnall
Pershall
Chebsey
Izaak Walton Cottage Museum
Yarlet
Whitgreave
Marston
Salt
Prees Green
Lostford
Sutton
The Four Alls
Woodseaves
Chipnall
Cheswardine
Bishop's Offley
Wollerton
Wollerton Old Hall
Hawkstone Park
Stoke Heath
Marchamley
Hodnet
Hodnet Hall
Weston
Wixhill
Wistanswick
Goldstone Hall
Soudley
Millgreen
Lockleywood
Hinstock
Adbaston
Knighton
Wootton
Great Bridgeford
Ellenhall
High Offley
Stoke on Tern
Moston
Hopton
High Hatton
Ollerton
Child's Ercall
Ellerton
Shebdon
Woodseaves
Seighford
Holmcroft
Stanton upon Hine Heath
Radmoor
Sambrook
Weston Jones
Norbury
Lawnhead
Knightley Dale
Ranton
Coton Clanford
Doxey
Moreton Corbet
Howle
Eaton upon Tern
Pickstock
Derrington
Forebridge
Ellerdine Heath
Edgebolton
Great Bolas
Puleston
Sutton
Long Compton
Whitecross
Moss Pit
Muckleton
Cold Hatton
Meese
Tibberton
Forton
Aqualate Mere
Haughton
Cherrington
Edgmond Marsh
Coton
Gnosall Heath
Allimore Green
Coppenhall
Acton Trussell
Great Wytheford
Rowton
Waters Upton
Edgmond
Walton
Crudgington
Adeney
Outwoods
Apeton
Bradley
Dunston
Bednall
High Ercall
Longford
Church Aston
Chetwynd Aston
Moreton
Church Eaton
Levedale
Kynnersley
Roden
Haughton
Longdon on Tern
Sleapford
Eyton upon the Weald Moors
Preston upon the Weald Moors
Brockton
Lilleshall
Lilleshall Abbey
High Onn
Orslow
Mitton
Longridge
Rodington
Hoo Farm Animal Kingdom
Muxton
Great Chatwell
Whiston
Congreve
Bratton
Heath Hill
Brineton
Marston
Upton Magna
Withington
Admaston
Lilyhurst
Sheriffhales
Weston Heath
Blymhill
Motteý Meadows
Lapley
Wheaton Aston
Stretton
Gailey
Walcot
Wrockwardine
Trench
Granville
Shropshire Union Canal
Charlton
Arleston
Ketley
Ketley Bank
Crackleybank
Weston under Lizard
Weston Park
Belvide Res.
Kiddemore Green
Hatherton
Horsebrook
Norton
Aston
Priorslee
Telford Services
Bishop's Wood
Uppington
Wroxeter
Wroxeter Roman City
Rushton
The Rock
Lawley
Tong Norton
Boscobel House & The Royal Oak
Standeford
Donnington
Eaton Constantine
The Wrekin
Horsehay
Telford Wonderland
Haughton
The Wyke
Tong
White Ladies Priory
Shareshill
Coven
Longwood
Little Wenlock
Horsehay Steam Trust
Stirchley
RAF Museum
Featherstone
Hilton Park Services
Dryton
Leighton
Little Dawley
Rosehill Ho.
Halesfield
Kemberton
Codsall Wood
Buildwas
Coalbrookdale
Ironbridge Gorge
Mus. of Iron
Buildwas Abbey
Cressage
Sheinton
Ironbridge
Blists Hill
Coalport
Brockton
David Austin Roses
Oaken
Moseley Old Hall
Essington
Benthall Hall
Benthall
Tollhouse Mus.
Jackfield Tile Mus.
Grindle
Ryton
Boningale
Fordhouses
Bushbury
Oxley
Homer
Wyke
Broseley
Sutton Maddock
Beckbury
Wood Hayes
Harley
Kenley
Norton
Burnhill Green
Wergs
Bantock House
Wolverhampton
Stretton Westwood
Hughley
Presthope
Callaughton
Willey
Stockton
Stableford
Badger
Ackleton
Pattingham
Wightwick Manor
Perton
Rudge
Chesterton
Trescott
Lower Penn
Bradmore
Blakenhall
Moseley
Ettingshall
Penn
Bourton
Acton Round
Nordley
Astley Abbotts
Worfield
Shipley
Easthope
Haughton
Cross Lane Head
Cliff Railway
Hilton
Hopstone
Seisdon
Trysull
Aston Eyre
Morville
Tasley
Roughton
Claverley
Brockton
Weston
Monkhopton
Morville Heath
Upton Cressett Hall
Stanmore
Heathton
Blakeley
Bagger.
Upper Gornal
Gornalwood
Shipton
Lower Netchwood
Upton Cressett
Farmcote
Halfpenny Green
Himley
Wolverhampton Business Airport
Oldbury
Watermill
Danesford
Swindon
Dudley Zoo & Castle
Stanton Long
Chetton
Quatford
Highgate Common
Bobbington
Wall Heath
Middleton Priors
Eardington
Holdgate
Dudmaston Hall
Quatt
Six Ashes
Netherton
Ditton Priors
Glazeley
Four Ashes
Bromley
Tuckhill
Chelmarsh
Broadfield House Glass Mus.
Enville
Tugford
Neenton
Abdon
Brown Clee Hill
Cleobury North
Middleton Scriven
Sutton
Hampton Loade
Upper Heath
Hampton
Red House Glass Cone
Amblecote
Quarry Bank
Cradley Heath
Stourton
Wollescote
Sidbury
Clee St Margaret
Burwarton
Billingsley
Woodhill
Severn Valley
Birdsgreen
Potter's Cross
Lye
Aston Botterell
Alveley
Chorley
Rays Farm Country Matters
Highley
Romsley
Whittington
Hasbury
Stoke St Milborough
Loughton
Stottesdon
Kingsford
Pedmore
Wheathill
Blakeshall
Caunsall
Cleedownton
Farlow
Oreton
Kinlet
Shatterford
Bodenham Arboretum & Earth Centre
Upper Arley
Cookley
West Hagley
Hagley
Clent
Silvington
Trimpley
Wolverley
Churchill
Broom
Holy Cross
Bell End
Cleeton St Mary
Catherton
Pound Green
Low Habberley
Franche
Blakedown
Bitterley
Foxwood
Buttonoak
Doddington
Cleobury Mortimer
Neen Savage
Hopton Wafers
Wyre Forest
Severn Valley Railway
Blakebrook
Belbroughton
Farden
Wribbenhall
Drayton
Wildmoor
Severn
Worfe
Roden
Tern
Sow
Stour
Rea Brook
Borle Brook
Dale
A53
A41
A529
A442
A518
A519
A5013
A34
A51
A5
A5223
A458
A4169
A454
A449
A4117
A4201
A450
A451
A456
A491
A463
A459
A457
A464
A41
A518
B5026
B5062
B5063
B5061
B4394
B4380
B4375
B4376
B4371
B4378
B4368
B4364
B4363
B4373
B4379
B4176
B4555
B4199
B4188
B4190
B5405
B5066
B5027
M6
M54
74
62
49
50
SJ
P&R
Stafford Services
Ancient High Ho.

Stafford
West Midlands
Stone
Uttoxeter
Eccleshall
Stafford
Rugeley
Lichfield
Cannock
Newport
Shifnal
Albrighton
Codsall
Penkridge
Brewood
Gnosall
Abbots Bromley
Hednesford
Heath Hayes
Burntwood
Brownhills
Aldridge
Walsall
Wednesfield
Willenhall
Wolverhampton
Tettenhall
Bilston
Darlaston
Wednesbury
Sedgley
Coseley
Tipton
Wombourne
Dudley
Oldbury
Rowley Regis
Smethwick
West Bromwich
Handsworth
Birmingham
Sutton Coldfield
Streetly
Kingstanding
Erdington
Great Barr
Kingswinford
Brierley Hill
Wordsley
Stourbridge
Halesowen
Kinver
Harborne
Edgbaston
Solihull
Shirley
Longbridge
Cheslyn Hay
Chatcull
Wetwood
Croxton
Croxtonbank
Fairoak
Slindon
Millmeece
Yarnfield
Walton
Little Stoke
Dayhills
Garshall Green
Milwich
Coton
Coton Hill
Dods Leigh
Field
Bramshall
Blount's Green
Doveridge
Norton Bridge
Aston-By-Stone
Burston
Sandon
Fradswell
Gratwich
Marchington
Bishop's Offley
Pershall
Chebsey
Yarlet
Whitgreave
Marston
Gayton
Grindley
Kingstone
Gorsty Hill
Marchington Woodlands
Adbaston
Knighton
Wootton
Ellenhall
Great Bridgeford
Salt
Weston
Stowe-by-Chartley
Drointon
High Offley
Shebdon
Woodseaves
Hopton
Hixon
Newton
Newborough
Weston Jones
Lawnhead
Knightley Dale
Seighford
Coton Clanford
Ranton
Holmcroft
Ingestre
Norbury
Derrington
Doxey
Forebridge
Tixall
Great Haywood
Admaston
Hoar Cross
Sutton
Puleston
Long Compton
Whitecross
Weeping Cross
Milford
Little Haywood
Colwich
Forton
Aqualate Mere
Haughton
Moss Pit
Walton on the Hill
Trent Vale
Colton
Woodlane
Hadley End
Hamstall Ridware
Coton
Gnosall Heath
Allimore Green
Coppenhall
Brocton
Blithbury
Yoxall
Outwoods
Apeton
Bradley
Dunston
Acton Trussell
Cannock Chase
Etchinghill
Hill Ridware
Morrey
Chetwynd Aston
Moreton
Church Eaton
Bednall
Levedale
Slitting Mill
Orslow
High Onn
Mitton
Longridge
Brereton
Armitage
Handsacre
King's Bromley
Great Chatwell
Pye Green
Upper Longdon
Longdon
Rileyhill
Heath Hill
Brineton
Marston
Whiston
Congreve
Huntington
Hazelslade
Longdon Green
Lilyhurst
Weston Heath
Blymhill
Lapley
Cannock Wood
Elmhurst
Motley Meadows
Wheaton Aston
Stretton
Littleworth
Gentleshaw
Farewell
Oldfallow
Wimblebury
Chorley
Streethay
Weston under Lizard
Belvide Res.
Kiddemore Green
Gailey
Hatherton
Bishop's Wood
Horsebrook
Norton Canes
Norton East
Chasetown
Leamonsley
Hammerwich
Tong Norton
Boscobel House & The Royal Oak
Standeford
Bridgtown
Churchbridge
Muckley Corner
Wall
Tong
White Ladies Priory
Coven
Shareshill
Great Wyrley
Little Wyrley
RAF Museum
Featherstone
Hilton Park Services
Springhill
Codsall Wood
Clayhanger
Shenstone
Moseley Old Hall
Oaken
Fordhouses
Essington
Pelsall
Walsall Wood
Stonnall
David Austin Roses
Ryton
Boningale
Oxley
Bushbury
New Invention
Bloxwich
Shelfield
Leighswood
Little Hay
Beckbury
Wood Hayes
Harden
Rushall
Watford Gap
Burnhill Green
Wergs
Short Heath
Little Aston
Hill
Badger
Pattingham
Wightwick Manor
Bantock House
Heath Town
Arboretum
Hardwick
Roughley
Stableford
Ackleton
Perton
Moseley
Palfrey
Four Oaks
Mere Grn.
Rudge
Chesterton
Trescott
Bradmore
Blakenhall
Lower Penn
Ettingshall
Worfield
Shipley
Penn
Moxley
Wylde Green
Hilton
Seisdon
Bradley
Hopstone
Trysull
Hill Top
Grove Vale
New Oscott
Walmley
Roughton
Claverley
Toll End
Hamstead
Stanmore
Heathton
Baggeridge
Sandwell Valley
Upper Witton
Farmcote
Blakeley
Upper Gornal
Gt. Bridge
Churchfield
Gravelly Hill
Tyburn
Halfpenny Green
Swindon
Gornalwood
Himley
Dudley Zoo & Castle
Dudley Port
Perry Barr
Quatford
Wolverhampton Business Airport
Tividale
Aston
Highgate Common
Bobbington
Wall Heath
Sandwell
Winson Grn.
Aston Hall
Castle Bromwich
Quatt
Six Ashes
Netherton
Tuckhill
Four Ashes
Enville
Broadfield House Glass Mus.
Old Hill
Ward End
Hampton Loade
Blackheath
Bearwood
Chad Valley
Stourton
Amblecote
Red House Glass Cone
Quarry Bank
Cradley Heath
Cradley
Quinton
Botanical Gardens
Blakesley Hall
Yardley
Severn Valley
Birdsgreen
Wollescote
Alveley
Potter's Cross
Woodgate Valley
Lye
Balsall Hth
Sparkhill
Acock's Green
Romsley
Hasbury
Bartley Green
Selly Oak
Moseley
Springfield
Olton
Kingsford
Whittington
Blakeshall
Pedmore
Woodgate
Selly Manor Mus.
King's Heath
Sarehole Mill
Hall Green
Bodenham Arboretum & Earth Centre
Caunsall
Hagley
Clent Hills
Illey
Bartley Res.
Bournville
Cadbury World
Shatterford
Upper Arley
Cookley
West Hagley
Frankley Services
Romsley
Frankley
Trimpley
Wolverley
Churchill
Clent
Northfield
Broom
Holy Cross
King's Norton
Blakedown
Bell End
Waseley Hills
Hollywood
Drakes Cross
Whitlock's End
Monkspath
Wyre Forest
Wribbenhall
Bewdley
Belbroughton
Drayton
Wildmoor
Hopwood
Izaak Walton Cottage Museum
Amerton Working Farm
Shugborough Estate
Ancient High House
Samuel Johnson Birthplace Mus.
Chase Water Rly
Wall (Letocetum)
Brownhills Common
Norton Canes Services
Blithfield Res.
The Piano Workshop
Shropshire Union Canal
Rykneld Street
Stafford Services
Sutton Park
Railway Mus.
Wrens Nest
Stone
Trent
Sow
Stour
Worfe
Kingsford
Nat. Sea Life Birmingham
Westmidlands
Staffordshire
SJ
SO
6 miles
10 km
0 1 2 3 4 5 6 miles
0 1 2 3 4 5 6 7 8 9 10 km
75
61
50
51
M6
M54
M5
M6 Toll
A5
A34
A38
A41
A51
A449
A454
A458
A460
A461
A513
A518
A519
B5013
B5014
B5026
B5027
B5066
B5234
B5405
Toll

Mickleover
Littleover
Normanton
Burnaston
Dalbury
Sutton on the Hill
Church Broughton
Oaks Green
Sudbury
Foston
Etwall
Scropton
Hatton
Tutbury
Marston on Dove
Egginton
Rolleston-on-Dove
Stretton
Draycott in the Clay
Hanbury
Hanbury Woodend
Anslow Gate
Anslow
Horninglow
NEEDWOOD
FOREST
Needwood
Rangemore
Newchurch
Shobnall
Winshill
Burton upon Trent
Tatenhill
Branston
Stapenhill
Dunstall
Woodhouses
Barton-under-Needwood
Walton-on-Trent
Rosliston
Caldwell
Castle Gresley
Linton
Alrewas
Orgreave
Fradley
Coton in the Elms
Croxall
Edingale
Lullington
Netherseal
Elford
Harlaston
Haunton
Clifton Campville
Whittington
Hademore
Wigginton
Thorpe Constantine
Seckington
Newton Regis
Shuttington
Hopwas
Leyfields
Tamworth
Alvecote
Amington
Glascote
Bonehill
Fazeley
Hints
Drayton Bassett
Wilnecote
Dosthill
Polesworth
St Helena
Birchmoor
Dordon
Warton
Austrey
No Man's Heath
Chilcote
Findern
Stenson
Twyford
Willington
Repton
Barrow upon Trent
Milton
Ingleby
Newton Solney
Bretby
Foremark Res.
Upper Midway
Lower Midway
Newhall
Swadlincote
Church Gresley
Hartshorne
Woodville
Smisby
Mount Pleasant
Blackfordby
Norris Hill
Moira
Overseal
Donisthorpe
Oakthorpe
Ashby-de-la-Zouch
Measham
Packington
Chellaston
Allenton
Alvaston
Elvaston
Thulston
Borrowash
Breaston
Draycott
Long Eaton
Sawley
Thrumpton
Shardlow
Cavendish Bridge
Aston-on-Trent
Weston-on-Trent
Swarkestone
Stanton by Bridge
King's Newton
Melbourne
Ticknall
Calke
Breedon on the Hill
Hemington
Lockington
Castle Donington
Isley Walton
Wilson
Diseworth
Tonge
Long Whatton
Kegworth
Ratcliffe on Soar
Kingston on Soar
West Leake
East Leake
New Kingston
Gotham
Sutton Bonington
Normanton on Soar
Hathern
Stanford on Soar
Belton
Worthington
Osgathorpe
Newbold
Shepshed
Thorpe Acre
Loughborough
Lount
Coleorton
Thringstone
Swannington
Whitwick
COALVILLE
Charnwood Forest
Greenhill
Ravenstone
Bardon
Hugglescote
Normanton le Heath
Shelthorpe
Woodthorpe
Quorndon
Woodhouse
Woodhouse Eaves
Swithland
Copt Oak
Markfield
Ellistown
Stanton under Bardon
Field Head
Newtown Linford
Anstey
Groby
Ratby
Glenfield
Kirby Muxloe
Leicester Forest East
Ibstock
Battram
Heather
Swepstone
Snarestone
Newton Burgoland
Appleby Magna
Appleby Parva
Norton-Juxta-Twycross
Shackerstone
Odstone
Nailstone
Bagworth
Thornton
Botcheston
Congerstone
Barton in the Beans
Barlestone
Twycross
Bilstone
Carlton
Market Bosworth
Newbold Verdon
Desford
Newtown Unthank
Orton-on-the-Hill
Wellsborough
Cadeby
Sheepy Magna
Sheepy Parva
Sibson
Peckleton
Kirkby Mallory
Shenton
Sutton Cheney
Upton
Stapleton
Ratcliffe Culey
Grendon
Grendon Common
Baddesley Ensor
Atherstone
Witherley
Mancetter
Fenny Drayton
Higham on the Hill
Dadlington
Stoke Golding
Barwell
Earl Shilton
Elmesthorpe
Thurlaston
Enderby
Narborough
Huncote
Littlethorpe
Croft
Stoney Stanton
Cosby
Sutton in the Elms
Middleton
Wood End
Kingsbury
Bodymoor Heath
Baxterley
Bentley
Hurley
Oldbury
Hartshill
Ridge Lane
Wishaw
Over Green
Curdworth
Marston
Lea Marston
Nether Whitacre
Whiteacre Heath
Church End
Galley Common
Chapel End
Camp Hill
Weddington
Hinckley
Sketchley
Burbage
Sapcote
Aston Flamville
Sharnford
Broughton Astley
Primethorpe
Dunton Bassett
Leire
Frolesworth
Minworth
Water Orton
Furnace End
Over Whitacre
Ansley
Stockingford
Nuneaton
Attleborough
Burton Hastings
Chilvers Coton
Whitestone
Smockington
Claybrooke Magna
Claybrooke Parva
Ashby Parva
Shustoke
Coleshill
Old Arley
New Arley
Astley
Griff
Collycroft
Bramcote
Copston Magna
Wibtoft
Ullesthorpe
Kitt's Green
Tile Cross
Marston Green
Maxstoke
Fillongley
Bedworth Heath
Bedworth
Bulkington
Wolvey
Corley Ash
Corley
Corley Moor
Chapel Green
Ash Green
Neal's Green
Hawkesbury
Barnacle
Shilton
Withybrook
Willey
Bitteswell
Lutterworth
Cross in Hand
Monks Kirby
Cotesbach
Elmdon
Bickenhill
Elmdon Heath
Butler's End
Hawkes End
Keresley
Longford
Little Heath
Foleshill
Ansty
Pailton
Churchover
Gibbet Hill
Meriden
Coundon
Allesley
Walsgrave on Sowe
Great Heath
Wyken
Stretton under Fosse
Hampton in Arden
Eastern Green
Spon End
Four Oaks
Eastcote
Berkswell
Whoberley
Coventry
Brinklow
Harborough Magna
Newbold on Avon
Newton
Catthorpe
Copt Heath
Barston
Tile Hill
Earlsdon
Binley
Binley Woods
Bretford
King's Newnham
Church Lawford
Long Lawford
Knowle
Balsall Common
Stivichall
Willenhall
Brandon
Clifton upon Dunsmore
Bentley Heath
Balsall
Catchems Corner
Tollbar End
Wolston
SK
SP
NATIONAL FOREST
76
51
52
64
M1
M42
M6
M69
M6Toll
A38
A50
A42
A444
A5
A47
A46
A45

LONG EATON
Clifton
Ruddington
Tollerton
Normanton-on-the-Wolds
Plumtree
Keyworth
Owthorpe
Colston Bassett
Kinoulton
Langar
Barkestone-le-Vale
Plungar
Woolsthorpe
Belvoir
Harston
Stathern
Knipton
Branston
Barton in Fabis
Thrumpton
Sawley
Castle Donington
Kegworth
Lockington
Ratcliffe on Soar
Kingston on Soar
New Kingston
West Leake
East Leake
Costock
Wysall
Bunny
Bradmore
Stanton-on-the-Wolds
Widmerpool
Willoughby-on-the-Wolds
Upper Broughton
Nether Broughton
Hickling
Hose
Long Clawson
Eastwell
Eaton
Goadby Marwood
Waltham on the Wolds
Wycomb
Chadwell
Stonesby
Holwell
Scalford
Old Dalby
Wartnaby
Ab Kettleby
Sutton Bonington
Rempstone
Long Whatton
Diseworth
Normanton on Soar
Hathern
Stanford on Soar
Hoton
Wymeswold
Grimston
Saxelbye
Burton on the Wolds
Cotes
Belton
Shepshed
Thorpe Acre
Loughborough
Walton on the Wolds
Six Hills
Ragdale
Shoby
Melton Mowbray
Thorpe Arnold
Freeby
Garthorpe
Coston
Saxby
Wyfordby
Brentingby
Asfordby
Asfordby Hill
Frisby on the Wreake
Hoby
Seagrave
Barrow upon Soar
Shelthorpe
Woodthorpe
Nanpantan
Quorndon
Sileby
Thrussington
Rotherby
Kirby Bellars
Burton Lazars
Stapleford
Whitwick
Charnwood Forest
Woodhouse
Woodhouse Eaves
Mountsorrel
Cossington
Ratcliffe on the Wreake
Rearsby
East Goscote
Great Dalby
Little Dalby
Whissendine
Greenhill
Bardon
Copt Oak
Swithland
Rothley
Queniborough
Gaddesby
Ashby Folville
Thorpe Satchville
Pickwell
Cold Overton
Leicestershire
Markfield
Cropston
Thurcaston
Syston
Barsby
Twyford
Burrough on the Hill
Somerby
Langham
Stanton under Bardon
Field Head
Newtown Linford
Birstall
Thurmaston
Barkby
South Croxton
Marefield
Owston
Knossington
Barleythorpe
Anstey
Beeby
Lowesby
Thornton
Groby
Hungarton
Cold Newton
Leicester
Ratby
Glenfield
Keyham
Scraptoft
Braunston-in-Rutland
Botcheston
Tilton on the Hill
Halstead
Newtown Unthank
Kirby Muxloe
Bushby
Thurnby
Leicester Forest East
Braunstone Town
Desford
Evington
Stoughton
Houghton on the Hill
Billesdon
Skeffington
Loddington
Ridlington
City
Stoneygate
Knighton
Oadby
Gaulby
Belton in Rutland
Peckleton
Kirkby Mallory
Aylestone
Tugby
East Norton
Allexton
Wardley
King's Norton
Rolleston
Little Stretton
Enderby
Thurlaston
Stapleton
Glen Parva
Wigston
Illston on the Hill
Noseley
Goadby
Earl Shilton
Narborough
Blaby
South Wigston
Great Glen
Carlton Curlieu
Newton Harcourt
Burton Overy
Barwell
Huncote
Whetstone
Horninghold
Stockerston
Elmesthorpe
Littlethorpe
Hallaton
Croft
Countesthorpe
Shangton
Stonton Wyville
Glooston
Blaston
Stoney Stanton
Cosby
Kilby
Kibworth Harcourt
Cranoe
Sutton in the Elms
Tur Langton
Slawston
Great Easton
Sapcote
Primethorpe
Peatling Magna
Fleckney
Kibworth Beauchamp
Church Langton
Medbourne
Burbage
Aston Flamville
Broughton Astley
Arnesby
Saddington
Smeeton Westerby
Welham
East Langton
Thorpe Langton
Drayton
Bringhurst
Sharnford
Willoughby Waterleys
Weston by Welland
Frolesworth
Leire
Dunton Bassett
Ashby Magna
Shearsby
Bruntingthorpe
Foxton
Gumley
Sutton Bassett
Ashley
Cottingham
Middleton
Claybrooke Magna
Peatling Parva
Mowsley
Great Bowden
East Carlton
Claybrooke Parva
Ashby Parva
Laughton
Market Harborough
Copston Magna
Wibtoft
Gilmorton
Lubenham
Dingley
Stoke Albany
Wilbarston
Ullesthorpe
Walton
Brampton Ash
Kimcote
Theddingworth
Little Bowden
Bitteswell
Lutterworth
Marston Trussell
East Farndon
Pipewell
Willey
Misterton
Husbands Bosworth
Braybrooke
Withybrook
Cross in Hand
Walcote
North Kilworth
Great Oxendon
Desborough
Monks Kirby
Cotesbach
Sibbertoft
Rushton
South Kilworth
Sulby Reservoir
Clipston
Arthingworth
Rothwell
Pailton
Churchover
Gibbet Hill
Welford
Harrington
Stretton under Fosse
Shawell
Swinford
Stanford on Avon
Naseby Field
Kelmarsh
Orton
Easenhall
Harborough Magna
Naseby
Loddington
Thorpe Malsor
King's Newnham
Coton
Haselbech
Cold Ashby
Maidwell
Draughton
Great Cransley
Mawsley
Clifton upon Dunsmore
Yelvertoft
Thornby
SK
SP
0 1 2 3 4 5 6 miles
0 1 2 3 4 5 6 7 8 9 10km

Ropsley
Sapperton
Folkingham
Billingborough
Donington South Ing
Denton
Harlaxton
HARLAXTON MANOR
Old Somerby
Humby
Pickworth
Hanby
Birthorpe
Pointon
Westhorpe
Gosberton
Little Ponton
Boothby Pagnell
Laughton
Stroxton
Great Ponton
Lenton
Aslackby
Millthorpe
Dowsby
Gosberton Clough
Risegate
Hungerton
Ingoldsby
Graby
Surfleet
Wyville
Keisby
Bassingthorpe
Bitchfield
Hawthorpe
Kirkby Underwood
Rippingale
Stoke Rochford
Easton
Irnham
Crossgate
Northgate
Pinchbeck
Saltby
Skillington
Bulby
Dunsby
Pinchbeck Bars
WOOLSTHORPE MANOR
Burton-le-Coggles
Corby Glen
Stainfield
Haconby
Woolsthorpe
Colsterworth
Elsthorpe
Hanthorpe
Morton
Pinchbeck West
Sproxton
Twyford
Birkholme
TF
Spalding
Buckminster
Grimsthorpe
Dyke
Swinstead
GRANTHAM SOUTH SERVICES
Stainby
Swayfield
Cawthorpe
GRIMSTHORPE CASTLE
Edenham
Pode Hole
Sewstern
Gunby
North Witham
Little London
Clay Lake
Scottlethorpe
Bourne
Twenty
Creeton
Wymondham
South Witham
CRIBBS MEADOW
Castle Bytham
Little Bytham
Lound
Tongue End
Edmondthorpe
Thistleton
Witham on the Hill
Northorpe
Thurlby
Market Overton
Clipsham
Toft
THURLBY
Leigh
Barrow
Stretton
Careby
Manthorpe
Deeping Fen
Deeping St Nicholas
Obthorpe
Thetford
RUTLAND RAILWAY MUS.
Greetham
Pickworth
Carlby
Wilsthorpe
Baston
Hop Pole
Ashwell
Cottesmore
Essendine
Braceborough
Langtoft
Rutland
Exton
Greatford
TOLETHORPE HALL RUTLAND OPEN AIR THEATRE
Ryhall
Barholm
Towngate
Market Deeping
Burley
BARNSDALE PLANTS
Little Casterton
Belmesthorpe
Frognall
Crowland
Oakham
Tickencote
Great Casterton
Deeping Gate
Deeping St James
Whitwell
Empingham
Tallington
West Deeping
Upper Hambleton
Northfields
Uffington
Maxey
Northborough
Egleton
RUTLAND WATER
Stamford
Newborough
Tinwell
Etton
Peakirk
RUTLAND WATER
BURGHLEY
Normanton
Bainton
Glinton
Edith Weston
Ketton
Easton on the Hill
Pilsgate
Barnack
Helpston
Bedford Level (North)
Manton
Lyndon
North Luffenham
Ufford
BARNACK HILLS AND HOLES
Eye Green
Chater
Pilton
Werrington
Gunthorpe
Southorpe
Preston
Wing
Collyweston
Peterborough
Wittering
Eye
South Luffenham
Marholm
Walton
CASTOR HANGLANDS
Thornhaugh
SACREWELL FARM & COUNTRY CENTRE
Upton
Dogsthorpe
Newark
Stone
Glaston
Morcott
Duddington
Barrowden
Tixover
BEDFORD PURLIEUS
Wansford
LONGTHORPE TOWER
PETERBOROUGH
Bisbrooke
Wakerley
Stibbington
Ailsworth
Peterborough
Sutton
Castor
FERRY MEADOWS
Longthorpe
Fengate
FLAG FEN BRONZE AGE EXCAVATIONS
NENE VALLEY RAILWAY
Seaton
Lyddington
Harringworth
King's Cliffe
Yarwell
Water Newton
Old Fletton
Orton Longueville
Stanground
Whittlesey
BEDE HOUSE
Sibson
Laxton
SIBSON
Alwalton
Orton Waterville
King's Delph
Thorpe by Water
Blatherwycke
Nassington
Apethorpe
Chesterton
CROWN LAKES
Farcet
Woodnewton
Gretton
Bulwick
PETERBOROUGH SERVICES
Caldecott
Fotheringhay
ELTON HALL
Elton
Haddon
KIRBY HALL
CASTLE SITE
Farcet Fen
Rockingham
Deene
Deenethorpe
Southwick
Morborne
Yaxley
DEENE PARK
ROCKINGHAM CASTLE
ROCKINGHAM MOTOR SPEEDWAY
Eaglethorpe
Warmington
Tansor
Whittlesey Mere
Little Weldon
Glapthorn
Cotterstock
Folksworth
Norman Cross
Corby
Great Weldon
Upper Benefield
Lower Benefield
Oundle
Ashton
Stilton
Caldecote
TL
HOLME FEN
Rockingham Forest
Stanion
Polebrook
Lutton
Denton
Holme
Little Oakley
BARNWELL
Harper's Brook
Stoke Doyle
Great Oakley
LYVEDEN NEW BIELD
Barnwell St Andrew
Glatton
Conington
Ramsey Heights
Brigstock
HILL FARM HERBS
FERMYN WOODS
Hemington
Pilton
WOODWALTON FEN
Wadenhoe
Barnwell All Saints
Luddington in the Brook
Sawtry
Newton
Geddington
ELEANOR CROSS
Church End
Achurch
Great Gidding
UPWOOD MEADOWS
Sudborough
Wigsthorpe
Thurning
Aldwincle
Little Gidding
Steeple Gidding
Wood Walton
Weekley
BOUGHTON HOUSE
Grafton Underwood
Lowick
Thorpe Waterville
Clopton
Winwick
HAMERTON WILDLIFE CENTRE
Coppingford
Great Raveley
Warkton
MONKS WOOD
Islip
Titchmarsh
Hamerton
Kettering
Twywell
Thrapston
Upton
Wennington
Barton Seagrave
Cranford St Andrew
Cranford St John
Woodford
Old Weston
Alconbury Weston
Abbots Ripton
WICKSTEED PARK
Denford
Bythorn
Brington
Buckworth
Little Stukeley

Donington South Ing
End
Bicker Haven
Quadring
Fosdyke
Gosberton
Westhorpe
Holbeach St Matthew
Holbeach St Marks
Lynn Channel
Gosberton Clough
Daws
79
Risegate
Surfleet Seas End
Surfleet
HOLBEACH MARSH
Gedney Marsh
Gedney Drove End
Moulton Seas End
Saracen's Head
Holbeach Hurn
Holbeach Bank
Holbeach Clough
Crossgate
Northgate
Pinchbeck
Pinchbeck Bars
Halesgate
Gedney Dyke
THE WASH
Lutton
Guy's Head
BAYTREE OWL CENTRE
Weston
Moulton
Whaplode
MOULTON MILL
Holbeach
Fleet Hargate
Chapelgate
Little London
Terrington
Pinchbeck West
Fleet
Gedney
BUTTERFLY AND FALCONRY PARK
Long Sutton
Spalding
SPRINGFIELDS SHOW GARDENS
Low Fulney
Austendike
Gedney Broadgate
Pode Hole
Little London
Clay Lake
AYSCOUGHFEE HALL
Weston Hills
Sutton Bridge
Orange Row
Twenty
Sutton Crosses
Whaplode St Catherine
MUS. OF ENTERTAINMENT
Walpole Cross Keys
Tydd St Mary
Cowbit
Moulton Chapel
Tongue End
Holbeach St Johns
Sutton St James
Tydd Gote
Walpole St Andrew
Hay Green
Four Gotes
Walpole Marsh
Walpole St Peter
65
Deeping St Nicholas
Moulton Eaugate
Tydd St Giles
Deeping Fen
Newton
Ingleborough
St John's Highway
Brotherhouse Bar
Hop Pole
Tydd St Giles Fen
West Walton
St John's
Whaplode Drove
Fitton End
Walpole Highway
Terrington
Sutton St Edmund
West Walton Highway
Shepeau Stow
Holbeach Drove
Marshland
Gedney Hill
Gorefield
St John's Fen End
FENLAND AVIATION MUS.
Leverington
Market Deeping
Frognall
CROWLAND ABBEY
Dowsdale
Walsoken
Deeping St James
Crowland
Throckenholt
Church End
PECKOVER HOUSE
North Fen
Wisbech
Marshland St James
New Walsoken
Parson Drove
WISBECH & FENLAND MUS.
Northborough
Nene Terrace
Morris Fen
Wisbech St Mary
Emneth
Peakirk
Newborough
Murrow
Emneth Hungate
Glinton
Tholomas Drove
Rogue's Alley
Elm
Holly End
Bedford Level (North)
Thorney Toll
Outwell
Eye Green
Thorney
Guyhirn Gull
Waldersey
Friday Bridge
Werrington
Gunthorpe
Guyhirn
Ring's End
Coldham
Laddus Fens
Eye
Upwell
Walton
Dogsthorpe
Newark
Stone Bridge Corner
Chainbridge
Three Holes
Nene (Old Course)
LONGTHORPE TOWER
PETERBOROUGH CATH.
Peterborough
Euximoor Fen
FERRY MEADOWS
Longthorpe
Fengate
FLAG FEN BRONZE AGE EXCAVATIONS
North Side
Eldernell
West Fen
Westry
Euximoor Drove
Upwell
RAILWORLD
Old Fletton
Coates
FEN CAUSEWAY
Norwoodside
South District
Orton Longueville
Stanground
Eastrea
March
Whittlesey
Inham's End
Turves
Binnimoor Fen
Christchurch
Orton Waterville
King's Delph
TL
Town End
Lakesend
PETERBOROUGH SERVICES
CROWN LAKES
Farcet
Twenty Foot River
Tipsend
Upwell Fen
Ranson Moor
BEDFORD LEVEL (MIDDLE)
Flood's Ferry
Welney
Yaxley
Farcet Fen
Wimblington
Whittlesey Mere
Pondersbridge
White Fen
Nene
Doddington
Gold Hill
Norman Cross
Cambridge
Benwick
Sixteen Foot Drain
Middle Moor
Ramsey Mereside
Stilton
HOLME FEN
Wimblington Fen
Manea
Holme
Ramsey St Mary's
Forty Foot Drain
Vermuden's Drain
Fodder Fen
Denton
Ramsey Forty Foot
Horseway
Purls Bridge
Conington
New Bedford River
Ramsey Hollow
Glatton
Ramsey Heights
Chatteris
Welches Dam
Pymoor
Ramsey
RURAL MUSEUM
WOODWALTON FEN
Langwood Fen
Little Downham
Sawtry
Bury
Tick Fen
Ferry Hill
Church End
UPWOOD MEADOWS
Horseley Fen
ELY
Chettisham
Wardy Hill
West Fen
Little Gidding
Upwood
Chapel Head
Coveney
Wood Walton
Great Raveley
Wistow
Pidley Fen
Mepal
OLIVER CROMWELL'S HOUSE
Ely
CATHEDRAL
Witcham
Coppingford
MONKS WOOD
Little Raveley
Warboys
Fenton
Chatteris Fen
55
54
Wennington
Sutton
Wentworth
Witchford
Pidley
Somersham
Hill Row Doles
North Hill
Little Thetford
Little Stukeley
Ripton
Old Hurst
Colne
Haddenham
Alconbury
Woodhurst
0 1 2 3 4 5 6 miles
0 1 2 3 4 5 6 7 8 9 10 km
A17
A16
A151
A15
A47
A1139
A605
A141
A142
A1101
A1122
A10
A1(M)
A1073
B1397
B1357
B1359
B1356
B1180
B1168
B1165
B1166
B1390
B1525
B1443
B1040
B1167
B1169
B1187
B1101
B1098
B1099
B1093
B1096
B660
B1091
B1043
B1090
B1050
B1381
B1411
A1421
A1123

5
6
7
8
9
Snettisham
SNETTISHAM NATURE RESERVE
Shepherd's Port
SNETTISHAM PARK
Ingoldisthorpe
Fring
Great Bircham
Bircham Newton
BIRCHAM MILL
Bircham Tofts
PEDDARS WAY
Barmer
Syderstone
Blenheim Park
Bagthorpe
Wicken Green Village
Sculthorpe
West Barsham
East Barsham
Snoring
Shernborne
Dersingham
DERSINGHAM BOG
Anmer
HOUGHTON HALL
Tattersett
Coxford
Dunton
Shereford
Hempton
Tatterford
Fakenham
FAKENHAM
Little Ryburgh
Great Ryburgh
Sandringham
SANDRINGHAM
Wolferton
West Newton
New Houghton
West Rudham
East Rudham
Toftrees
Flitcham
Harpley
Helhoughton
Colkirk
Hillington
PEDDARS WAY & NORFOLK COAST PATH
Little Massingham
West Raynham
East Raynham
Oxwick
Hamrow
Castle Rising
CASTLE RISING
North Wootton
Ongar Hill
Marsh
South Wootton
Congham
CONGHAM HALL HERB GARDEN
Roydon
Great Massingham
South Raynham
Weasenham St Peter
Whissonsett
Horningtoft
King's Lynn
MARITIME EXHIBITION
ROYDON COMMON
Grimston
Pott Row
Massingham Heath
Weasenham All Saints
EXTREME ADVENTURE
Wellingham
Tittleshall
Stanfield
Brisley
Clenchwarton
GUILDHALL
Gaywood
West Lynn
KING'S LYNN
Fairstead
Gayton
Rougham
Terrington St Clement
Hardwick
Leziate
Ashwicken
Gayton Thorpe
Mileham
Tilney All Saints
Fair Green
Tower End
West Lexham
Litcham
Bittering
NORFOLK RURAL LIFE MUSEUM
West Winch
Middleton
East Walton
TF
East Lexham
Saddle Bow
North Runcton
East Winch
West Bilney
Pentney
West Acre
Castle Acre
CASTLE ACRE PRIORY
Newton
Beeston
Longham
Wiggenhall St Germans
Blackborough End
Setchey
South Acre
Great Dunham
Drury Square
Sparrow Green
Crane's Corner
Wiggenhall St Mary the Virgin
Tottenhill Row
Narborough
Little Dunham
Great Fransham
Wendling
Norfolk
Wiggenhall St Mary Magdalen
Watlington
Wormegay
Great Palgrave
Sporle
Little Dunham
Daffy Green
Tottenhill
Runcton Holme
Shouldham
Marham
Swaffham
Necton
West End
Bradenham
Marshland Fen
South Runcton
Shouldham Thorpe
Beachamwell Warren
PEDDARS WAY & NORFOLK COAST PATH
North Pickenham
Holme Hale
Stowbridge
Stow Bardolph
Fincham
Barton Bendish
Crowshill
West Head
Wimbotsham
Beachamwell
Shingham
Downham Market
Broomhill
Stradsett
Crimplesham
ICENI VILLAGE AND MUSEUMS
Cockley Cley
South Pickenham
Ashill
Saham Hills
Barroway Drove
Bexwell
Eastmoor
GOODERSTONE WATER GARDENS
Saham Toney
Ovington
Nordelph
Denver
Boughton
Wereham
Oxborough
Gooderstone
OXBURGH HALL
Great Cressingham
Caudlesprings
West Dereham
Hilborough
Watton
Griston
Bedford River
Fordham
Wretton
Stoke Ferry
Whitington
Foulden
Bodney
Little Cressingham
Merton
Northacre
Hilgay
Wissey
Northwold
The Arms
Caston
Ten Mile Bank
Brookville
Stow
Thompson
Hilgay Fen
Southery
Cranwich
Ickburgh
LYNFORD ARBORETUM AND LAKES
Methwold Hythe
Methwold
Methwold Fens
Mundford
Southery Fens
Queen's Ground
TL
THETFORD
West Tofts
PEDDARS WAY
Great Hockham
Brandon Creek
Feltwell
B R E C K L A N D
Wretham
Brandon Bank
Feltwell Fens
Hockwold cum Wilton
Weeting
GRIMES GRAVES
FOREST
PEDDARS WAY & NORFOLK COAST PATH
Burnt Fen
Hockwold Fens
WEETING HEATH
Little Ouse
Brandon
Santon Downham
Croxton
Littleport
Bridgham
BEDFORD LEVEL (SOUTH)
BRANDON PARK
THETFORD WARREN LODGE
PARK
Shippea Hill Sta.
Lakenheath
Thetford Warren
Thetford
Brettenham
Shadwell
Prickwillow
Great Ouse
Wangford Warren
ANCIENT HOUSE MUS.
Queen Adelaide
Kenny Hill
Lakenheath Warren
Rushford
Knettishall
KNETTISHALL HEATH
Middle Fen
Mildenhall Fen
Elveden
EAST OF ENGLAND TANK MUSEUM
Barnham
Euston
Stuntney
Great Fen
Eriswell
Broad Hill
Holywell Row
Beck Row
Isleham Fen
Thistley
West Row
Fakenham Magna
Barningham
A
B
C
D
E
F
G
80
68
55
56
A148
A149
A1078
A10
A47
A134
A1122
A1065
A1075
A11
A1066
A1101
A142
A1088
B1440
B1439
B1153
B1155
B1454
B1355
B1146
B1145
B1108
B1112
B1160
B1106
B1107
B1382
B1104

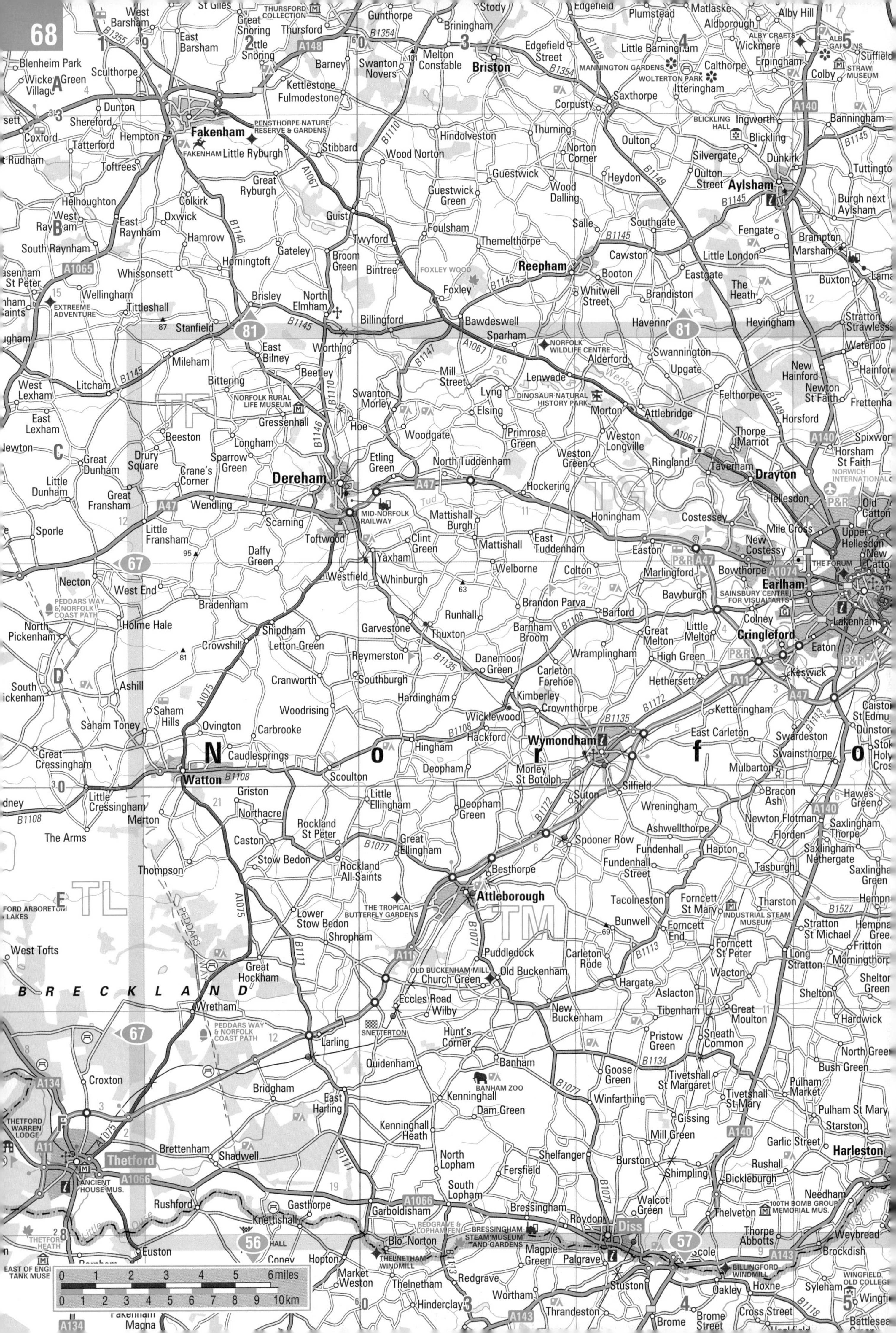
West Barsham
Great Snoring
Little Snoring
East Barsham
Thursford
Thursford Collection
Gunthorpe
Stody
Briningham
Edgefield
Plumstead
Matlaske
Alby Hill
Aldborough
Alby Crafts
Blenheim Park
Wicken Green Village
Sculthorpe
Kettlestone
Fulmodestone
Barney
Swanton Novers
Melton Constable
Briston
Edgefield Street
Little Barningham
Mannington Gardens
Wolterton Park
Calthorpe
Itteringham
Wickmere
Erpingham
Suffield
Colby
Straw Museum
Dunton
Shereford
Coxford
Tatterford
Hempton
Fakenham
Little Ryburgh
Pensthorpe Nature Reserve & Gardens
Rudham
Toftrees
Stibbard
Wood Norton
Hindolveston
Thurning
Corpusty
Saxthorpe
Blickling Hall
Ingworth
Blickling
Banningham
Oulton
Norton Corner
Guestwick
Heydon
Silvergate
Dunkirk
Oulton Street
Aylsham
Tuttington
Burgh next Aylsham
Helhoughton
West Raynham
East Raynham
South Raynham
Colkirk
Oxwick
Great Ryburgh
Hamrow
Guist
Guestwick Green
Wood Dalling
Salle
Southgate
Fengate
Brampton
Marsham
Twyford
Foulsham
Themelthorpe
Reepham
Cawston
Little London
Gateley
Horningtoft
Broom Green
Bintree
Foxley Wood
Booton
Eastgate
The Heath
Buxton
Whissonsett
Foxley
Whitwell Street
Brandiston
Wellingham
Extreme Adventure
Tittleshall
Brisley
North Elmham
Billingford
Bawdeswell
Haveringland
Hevingham
Stratton Strawless
Stanfield
Sparham
Norfolk Wildlife Centre
Swannington
Waterloo
Mileham
East Bilney
Worthing
Alderford
Upgate
New Hainford
Hainford
West Lexham
Litcham
Bittering
Beetley
Mill Street
Lenwade
Lyng
Newton St Faith
Frettenham
East Lexham
Norfolk Rural Life Museum
Gressenhall
Swanton Morley
Dinosaur Natural History Park
Morton
Attlebridge
Felthorpe
Horsford
Hoe
Elsing
Woodgate
Primrose Green
Weston Longville
Thorpe Marriot
Spixworth
Beeston
Longham
Great Dunham
Drury Square
Sparrow Green
Crane's Corner
Dereham
Etling Green
North Tuddenham
Weston Green
Ringland
Taverham
Drayton
Horsham St Faith
Norwich International
Little Dunham
Great Fransham
Wendling
Hockering
Hellesdon
Old Catton
Mid-Norfolk Railway
Mattishall Burgh
Honingham
Costessey
Sporle
Little Fransham
Scarning
Toftwood
Clint Green
Mattishall
East Tuddenham
Easton
Mile Cross
Upper Hellesdon
New Costessey
Daffy Green
Yaxham
Welborne
Colton
Marlingford
Bowthorpe
The Forum
New Catton
Necton
West End
Westfield
Whinburgh
Earlham
Sainsbury Centre for Visual Arts
Peddars Way & Norfolk Coast Path
Bradenham
Brandon Parva
Bawburgh
Runhall
Barford
Colney
Lakenham
North Pickenham
Holme Hale
Shipdham
Garvestone
Thuxton
Barnham Broom
Little Melton
Great Melton
Cringleford
Eaton
Crowshill
Letton Green
Reymerston
Wramplingham
High Green
Keswick
South Pickenham
Ashill
Cranworth
Southburgh
Danemoor Green
Carleton Forehoe
Hethersett
Hardingham
Kimberley
Crownthorpe
Ketteringham
Caistor St Edmund
Saham Hills
Woodrising
Saham Toney
Ovington
Carbrooke
Wicklewood
Hackford
Wymondham
East Carleton
Swardeston
Dunston
Stoke Holy Cross
Great Cressingham
Caudlesprings
Hingham
Deopham
Morley St Botolph
Swainsthorpe
Mulbarton
Watton
Scoulton
Silfield
Griston
Little Ellingham
Suton
Bracon Ash
Hawes' Green
Little Cressingham
Northacre
Deopham Green
Wreningham
Newton Flotman
Saxlingham Thorpe
Merton
The Arms
Caston
Rockland St Peter
Great Ellingham
Ashwellthorpe
Flordon
Spooner Row
Fundenhall
Hapton
Saxlingham Nethergate
Stow Bedon
Rockland All Saints
Besthorpe
Fundenhall Street
Tasburgh
Saxlingham Green
Thompson
Attleborough
Tacolneston
Forncett St Mary
Tharston
Industrial Steam Museum
Hempnall
The Tropical Butterfly Gardens
Lower Stow Bedon
Bunwell
Forncett End
Stratton St Michael
Hempnall Green
Fritton
Shropham
Puddledock
Carleton Rode
Forncett St Peter
Long Stratton
Morningthorpe
West Tofts
Great Hockham
Old Buckenham Mill
Old Buckenham
Church Green
Hargate
Wacton
Shelton Green
Aslacton
Shelton
Breckland
Wretham
Eccles Road
Wilby
New Buckenham
Tibenham
Great Moulton
Hardwick
Peddars Way & Norfolk Coast Path
Larling
Snetterton
Hunt's Corner
Pristow Green
Sneath Common
North Green
Quidenham
Banham
Goose Green
Bush Green
Croxton
Banham Zoo
Tivetshall St Margaret
Tivetshall St Mary
Pulham Market
Bridgham
East Harling
Kenninghall
Winfarthing
Pulham St Mary
Dam Green
Gissing
Starston
Thetford Warren Lodge
Kenninghall Heath
Mill Green
Garlic Street
Harleston
Brettenham
Thetford
Shadwell
North Lopham
Shelfanger
Burston
Rushall
Ancient House Mus.
Fersfield
Shimpling
Dickleburgh
Needham
South Lopham
100th Bomb Group Memorial Mus.
Rushford
Gasthorpe
Garboldisham
Bressingham
Walcot Green
Knettishall
Redgrave & Lopham Fen
Bressingham Steam Museum and Gardens
Roydon
Diss
Thelveton
Thorpe Abbotts
Weybread
Thetford Heath
Euston
Blo' Norton
Magpie Green
Palgrave
Scole
Brockdish
East of England Tank Muse
Coney
Hopton
Thelnetham Windmill
Billingford Windmill
Market Weston
Thelnetham
Redgrave
Stuston
Oakley
Hoxne
Syleham
Wingfield Old College
Wortham
Thrandeston
Cross Street
Hinderclay
Brome
Brome Street
Battlesea
Fakenham Magna
N o r f o
TF
TG
TL
TM
0 1 2 3 4 5 6 miles
0 1 2 3 4 5 6 7 8 9 10 km

North Walsham
Bradfield
Antingham
Swafield
Knapton
Bacton
Keswick
Walcott
Broomholm
Edingthorpe
Edingthorpe Green
Witton Bridge
Ridlington
Spa Common
Crostwight
Happisburgh
Whimpwell Green
Ecclesa on Sea
Happisburgh Common
EAST RUSTON GARDEN
Lessingham
Hempstead
Honing
East Ruston
Ingham Corner
Sea Palling
WAXHAM BARN
Waxham
Ingham
Westwick
Bengate
Worstead
Sloley
Dilham
Smallburgh
Stalham
Stalham Green
MUSEUM OF THE BROADS
Hickling
Sutton
Hickling Green
Scottow
Pennygate
Barton Turf
Hickling Heath
Horsey
Little Hautbois
Tunstead
Sco Ruston
ANT BROADS AND MARSHES
Wood Street
Catfield
Hickling Broad
HORSEY WINDMILL
WINTERTON DUNES
WROXHAM BARNS
Neatishead
Barton Broad
HICKLING BROAD
MARTHAM BROAD
Coltishall
Ashmanhaugh
RA. BOAT TRIP
Irstead
Sharp Street
Potter Heigham
West Somerton
East Somerton
Winterton-on-Sea
Threehammer Common
Hoveton
Belaugh
Wroxham
Lower Street
Ludham
Thurne
Bastwick
Martham
Hemsby
Newport
REDWINGS HORSE SANCTUARY
Upper Street
Horning
Upper Street
Wroxham Broad
BURE MARSHES
Repps
Rollesby
Scratby
California
Crostwick
Woodbastwick
Ranworth
TG
Ormesby St Michael
Rackheath
Salhouse
FAIRHAVEN GARDEN TRUST
Clippesby
Filby Broad
Ormesby St Margaret
Panxworth
South Walsham
Billockby
Burgh St Margaret
Filby
CAISTER ROMAN TOWN
Caister-on-Sea
New Rackheath
Little Plumstead
Upton
THE CANDLEMAKER WORKSHOP
Thrigby
THRIGBY HALL WILDLIFE GARDENS
Mautby
West Caister
Sprowston
Thorpe End
Hemblington
Runham
Blofield Heath
North Burlingham
Acle
Stokesby
West End
NORTH DENES
YARMOUTH
NORWICH
Great Plumstead
Bure
Thorpe St Andrew
Blofield
Damgate
Brundall
Lingwood
Beighton
GREAT YARMOUTH
Tunstall
THE Halvergate Marshes
Runham
Great Yarmouth
Postwick
Strumpshaw
Moulton St Mary
South Burlingham
Breydon Water
SEA LIFE GREAT YARMOUTH
Surlingham
Halvergate
Cobholm Island
ELIZABETHAN HOUSE, MARITIME NELSON/TOLHOUSE MUSEUMS
EXHIBITION GALLERIES
Kirby Bedon
Buckenham
Hassingham
BROADS
Burgh Castle
Southtown
AMAZONIA-WORLD OF REPTILES
PLEASURE BEACH
Bramerton
MID YARE
Southwood
Freethorpe
Wickhampton
BERNEY ARMS AND MILL
Rockland St Mary
Framingham Pigot
Cantley
Limpenhoe
Bradwell
Gorleston-on-Sea
Claxton
Framingham Earl
Hellington
PETTITTS ANIMAL ADVENTURE PARK
Belton
Ashby St Mary
Reedham
Yelverton
Bergh Apton
Langley Street
Hardley Street
Ferry
ST OLAVES PRIORY
Fritton
Hopton on Sea
Howe
Thurton
Chedgrave
Lower Thurlton
Shotesham
Brooke
Sisland
Chet
Thurlton
The Dell
Lound
Stubb's Green
Seething
Loddon
Thorpe
SOMERLEYTON HALL
Blundeston
Mundham
Hales
Herringfleet
Corton
Kirstead Green
Stubbs Green
Raveningham
Haddiscoe
Somerleyton
NEW PLEASUREWOOD HILLS LEISURE PARK
HALES HALL BARN & GARDENS
RAVENINGHAM GARDENS
Maypole Green
TM
Thwaite St Mary
Toft Monks
LOWESTOFT AND EAST SUFFOLK MARITIME MUSEUM
Oulton
Road Green
Woodton
Kirby Cane
Stockton
Wheatacre
Normanstone
Hedenham
Burgh St Peter
HERITAGE/VISITOR CENTRE
Topcroft
Cobbler's Green
Ellingham
Kirby Row
Aldeby
Oulton Broad
Topcroft Street
LOWESTOFT MUSEUM
Lowestoft
Ditchingham
Broome
Geldeston
Gillingham
CARLTON MARSHES NATURE RESERVE
Kirkley
Waveney
Shipmeadow
Beccles
Barnby
Bungay
Mettingham
Worlingham
Carlton Colville
Pakefield
Great Green
Earsham
Barsham
North Cove
Denton
OTTER TRUST
Mutford
Gisleham
Ringsfield
NORFOLK AND SUFFOLK AVIATION MUSEUM
Flixton
Ilketshall St Andrew
Ringsfield Corner
Hulver Street
Rushmere
Kessingland
Ilketshall St Margaret
Ellough
Henstead
SUFFOLK WILDLIFE PARK
Kessingland Beach
Homersfield
St Cross South Elmham
St Michael South Elmham
Ilketshall St Lawrence
Redisham
Sotterley
Benacre
Wortwell
Redenhall
Mendham
St Margaret South Elmham
All Saints South Elmham
Stone Street
Shadingfield
West End
SOUTH ELMHAM HALL
Cox Common
Wrentham
BENACRE
Brampton
Stoven
Clay Common
Withersdale Street
Mill Common
Frostenden
Covehithe
St James South Elmham
Rumburgh
Spexhall
South Cove
Metfield
Westhall
Uggeshall
Cove Bottom
57
Broadway
Wangford
Linstead Parva
Chediston
Reydon Smear
Fressingfield
Holton
Reydon
Little Whittingham Green
Halesworth
Blyford
HEN REEDBED NATURE RESERVE
SOUTHWOLD MUSEUM
Southwold
Chippenhall Green
Silverley's Green
A47
A12
A143
A146
A149
A1062
A1064
A1151
A144
A145
A1117
A1095
B1159
B1152
B1140
B1354
B1150
B1332
B1136
B1074
B1062
B1127
B1437
B1123
B1124
B1126
B1375
81
5
6
7
8
9
A
B
C
D
E
F
G

Malltraeth Bay
Bae Malltraeth
Newborough Forest
MODEL VILLAGE
SEION MARITIME MUSEUM
CASTLE REGIMENTAL MUSEUM
Llanddwyn I.
Ynys Llanddwyn
The Bar
Abermenai Pt.
Trwyn Abermenai
CAERNARFON AIR MUSEUM
Morfa Dinlle
Dinas Dinlle
Llandwrog
GLYNLLIFON
C A E R N A R F O N
B A Y
B A E
C A E R N A R F O N
Pontllyfni
Aberdesach
WELSH LIFE
Clynnog-fawr
82
Capel Uchaf
Gyrn-goch
A499
Bryn-yr-eryr
509 BWLCH MAWR
522 GYRN DDU
Trefor
SH
Llanaelhaearn
564 YR EIFL
Pen-sarn
Llithfaen
B4417
Carreg Ddu
Porth Dinllaen
Pistyll
Llwyndyrys
Pencaenewydd
Llangybi
Morfa Nefyn
Nefyn
LLEYN HISTORIAL MARITIME MUSEUM
Edern
Fron
Tan-y-graig
B4354
Rhos-fawr
Llanarmon
Y Ffôr
PENARTH FAWR MEDIEVAL HOUSE
Chwilog
Porth Ysgadan
Glanrhyd
Rhos-y-llan
CORS GEIRCH
Boduan
A497
Llannor
BODVEL HALL ADVENTURE PARK
Abererch
Tudweiliog
Dinas
Efailnewydd
Rhyd-y-clafdy
Denio
Pwllheli
Carreg yr Imbill
South Beach
Porth Golmon
Garnfadryn
B4415
Bryn-mawr
Llaniestyn
Penrhos
Pen-y-graig
Llangwnnadl
P E N R H Y N   L L Y N
Rhedyn
Sarn Meyllteyrn
Penrhyn Mawr
Pen-y-groeslon
Llanbedrog
Ty-hen
Bryncroes
Botwnnog
Nanhoron
B4413
Mynytho
Trwyn Llanbedrog
Methlem
Rhydlios
Llandegwning
St Tudwal's Road
Angorfa St Tudwal
Capel Carmel
Rhoshirwaun
304 MYNYDD RHIW
PLAS-YN-RHIW
Llawr Dref
Llangian
A499
Abersoch
191
Rhiw
Porth Neigwl or Hell's Mouth
Llanengan
Uwchmynydd
Aberdaron
Llanfaelrhys
Sarn Bach
St Tudwal's Island East
Ynys St Tudwal Dwyrain
Bwlchtocyn
Marchroes
St Tudwal's Island West
Ynys St Tudwal Gorllewin
Bodermid
Bardsey Sound
Swnt Enlli
Pen-y-cil
Cilan Uchaf
Trwyn Cilan
167
YNYS ENLLI
Bardsey Island
Ynys Enlli
L L E Y N
L L E Ŷ N
0 1 2 3 4 5 6 miles
0 1 2 3 4 5 6 7 8 9 10 km

Caernarfon
Waterloo Port
Llanrug
Penisarwaun
Bryn Bras Castle
Deiniolen
Ty'n-y-maes
Pont-rug
Segontium Fort
Clwt-y-bont
Cwm-y-glo
Brynrefail
Caeathro
Power of Wales
Llyn Padarn
Dinorwic
Llanberis Lake Railway
Padarn
Welsh Highland Railway
Inigo Jones Tudor Slateworks
Ceunant
Llanberis
Slate Mus.
Llanfaglan
Croesywaun
Groeslon
Waunfawr
Saron
Bontnewydd
Dolbadarn
Llyn Peris
Rhostryfan
Rhosgadfan
Penyffridd
Betws-Garmon
Groeslon
Fron
Carmel
Cilgwyn
Llyn Cwellyn
Snowdon Ranger
Snowdon Mountain Railway
Nantlle
Talysarn
Tan-yr-allt
Llanllyfni
Nebo
Rhyd-Ddu
Ffridd-Uchaf
Nasareth
Pant-glas
Upper Clynnog
Dafarn Faig
Bryncir
Garndolbenmaen
Dolbenmaen
Llanfihangel-y-pennant
Tyddyn-mawr
Moel-Ddu
Golan
Brynkir Woollen Mill
Rhoslan
Penmorfa
Prenteg
Pentrefelin
Tremadog
Llanystumdwy
Lloyd George Memorial Museum
Criccieth
The Ropeworks
Morfa Bychan
Borth-y-Gest
Porthmadog
Maritime Museum
Welsh Highland Rly.
Pottery
Beddgelert
Beddgelert Forest
Moel Hebog
Pass of Aberglaslyn
Sygun Copper Mine
Nantmor
Croesor
Hafod Garregog
Garreg
Tan-lan
Rhyd
Llanfrothen
Ffestiniog
Tan-y-bwlch
Penrhyndeudraeth
Minffordd
Portmeirion
Portmeirion Village
Cilfor
Traeth Bach
Talsarnau
Glan-y-wern
Eisingrug
Llanfihangel-y-traethau
Tremadog Bay
Bae Tremadog
Morfa Harlech
Glyn-cywarch
Harlech
Llanfair
Llanfair Slate Caverns
Llandanwg
Pen-sarn
Pen-y-bont
Pentre Gwynfryn
Llanbedr
Maes Artro Heritage Mus.
Morfa Dyffryn
Coed Ystumgwern
Llanenddwyn
Dyffryn Ardudwy
Cors-y-Gedol
Llanddwywe
Tal-y-bont
Plas-canol
Llanaber
Caerdeon
Bontddu
Cutiau
Barmouth (Abermaw)
RNLI Lifeboat Museum
Barmouth Bay
The Bar
Bae Bermo
Fairbourne & Barmouth Steam Railway
Fairbourne
Friog
Arthog
Ynysgyfflog
Afon Mawddach
Llwyngwril
Llangelynin
Llanfihangel-y-pennant
Abergynolwyn
Tal-y-llyn
Afon Dysynni
Corris Uchaf
Corris
King Arthur's Labyrinth & Craft Centre
Corris Railway and Museum
Esgairgeiliog
Aberllefenni
Aberangell
Dinas-Mawddwy
Meirion Mill
Cwm-Cewydd
Cwm-Llinau
Dol-fôr
Dyfi Forest
Mynydd Ceiswyn
Mynydd Dolgoed
Waun-Oer
Afon Cerist
Y Gribin
Cywarch
Brithdir
Bont Newydd
Dolgellau
Rhyd-wen
Penmaenpool
Penmaenpwl Centre
Abergwynant
Kings
Cadair Idris
Cader Idris
Minffordd
Pen-y-bryn
Llanelltyd
Cymmer Abbey
Nannau
Blaen-y-cwm
Llanfachreth
Rhydymain
Ganllwyd
Coed Ganllwyd
Coed y Brenin Forest
Coed y Brenin Visitor Centre
Capel Hermon
Rhobell Fawr
Allt-y-Bengloq
Pont Fronwydd
Aran Fawddwy
Pont-Rhyd-sarn
Cwm-hesgen
Pont Aber-Geirw
Bed-y-coedwr
Rhaeadr Mawddach
Sarn Helen
Dolhendre
Mynydd Bach
Bronaber
Mynydd Bryn-llech
Buarthmeini
Moel Llyfrant
Arenig Fawr
Llyn Arenig fawr
Llidiart
Trawsfynydd
Pont Dolydd Prysor
Cwm Prysor
Graig Wen
Llyn Trawsfynydd
Trawsfynydd Nuclear Power Station
Coed y Rhygen
Caerwych
Moel Ysgyfarnogod
Rhinog Fawr
Rhinog
Y Llethr
Diffwys
Gwynedd
Maentwrog
Gellilydan
Ceunant Cynfal
Ceunant Llennyrch
Coed Camlyn
Bont Newydd
Llan Ffestiniog
Rhyd-y-sarn
Coedydd Maentwrog
Moelwyn Mawr
Ffestiniog Power Station
Coed Cymerau
Tanygrisiau
Rhiwbryfdir
Blaenau Ffestiniog
Llechwedd Slate Caverns
Moel Penamnen
Bethania
Congl-y-wal
Pont yr Afon-Gam
Migneint
Arenig Fach
Llyn Celyn
Cwm Penmachno
Carrog
Llyn Conwy
Ysbyty Ifan
Padog
Penmachno
Gwydyr Forest
Pentre-bont
Dolwyddelan
Garnedd
Ty Mawr Wybrnant
Penmachno Woollen Mill
Conwy Falls
Rhaeadr Conwy
Glan-Conwy
Fairy Glen
Capel Garmon
Burial Chamber
Nebo
Betws-y-Coed
Conwy Valley Railway Museum
Pont-y-pant
Mynydd Cribau
Moel Siabod
Pont Cyfyng
Capel Curig
Swallow Falls
Rhaeadr Swallow
Gwydyr Forest Park
Cwm Glas Crafnant
Llyn Crafnant
Cornel
Gwydyr Uchaf
Gwydyr Uchaf Chapel
Tai
Llanrwst
Melin-y-coed
Pentre-tafarn-y-fedw
Llanddoged
Trefriw
Woollen Mill
Tan-lan
Llyn Cowlyd
Carnedd Llywelyn
Carnedd Dafydd
Llyn Ogwen
Pont Rhyd-goch
Pont Pen-y-benglog
Idwal Cottage
Cwm Idwal
Glyder Fawr
Nant Peris
Pass of Llanberis
Pen-y-Pass
Pen-y-Gwryd Hotel
Llyn Llydaw
Snowdon Yr Wyddfa
Yr Wyddfa
Llyn Gwynant
Bryn Gwynant
Bethania
Nantgwynant
Llyn Dinas
Marchlyn Mawr Res.
SH

Llandudno
Great Orme Copper Mines
Tramway
Alice in Wonderland
Penrhynside
Penrhyn Bay
Craig-y-don
Rhos-on-Sea
Llandrillo-yn-Rhos
COLWYN BAY
(BAE COLWYN)
Conwy Sands
Traeth Conwy
Llanrhos
Deganwy
Butterfly Jungle
Tywyn
Llandudno Junction
(Cyffordd Llandudno)
Welsh Mountain Zoo
Mochdre
Old Colwyn
Dinosaur World
Conwy
Gyffin
Aberconwy House/Plas Mawr
Dolwyd
Glan-Conwy
Bryn-y-maen
Llanelian-yn-Rhos
Llysfaen
Llanddulas
Abergele
Rhyd-y-foel
Abergele Roads
Angorfa Abergele
Henryd
Felin Isaf Water Mill
Pentrefelin
Dolwen
Betws-yn-Rhos
Dawn
Rowen
Tal-y-cafn
Bodnant
Graig
Tŷ'n-y-groes
Pontwgan
Hafod-lom
Moelfre Uchaf
Eglwysbach
Vale of Conwy
Dyffryn Conwy
Tal-y-Bont
Pentre'r Felin
Gell
Cefn-coch
Pentre-Isaf
Llangernyw
Dolgarrog
Coed Dolgarrog
Bryn-glas
Hendre-ddu
Woollen Mill
Trefriw
Tan-lan
Llanddoged
Pandy Tudur
Tŷ'n-felin-isaf
Pentre-tafarn-y-fedw
Llanrwst
Tai
Gwydyr Uchaf
Melin-y-coed
Gwytherin
Cornel
Gwydyr Forest
Gwydir Uchaf Chapel
Swallow Falls
Rhaeadr Swallow
Ty-draw
Conwy
Betws-y-Coed
Conwy Valley Railway Museum
Nebo
Moel Seisiog
Capel Garmon
Burial Chamber
Fairy Glen
Mynydd Cribau
Conwy Falls
Rhaeadr Conwy
Ty Mawr Wybrnant
Penmachno Woollen Mill
Gwydyr Forest
Penmachno
Glan-Conwy
Hafod-Dinbych
Padog
Pentrefoelas
Rhydlydan
Snowdonia National Park
Ysbyty Ifan
Cwm Penmachno
Carrog
Llyn Conwy
Migneint
Pont yr Afon-Gam
Carnedd y Filiast
Arenig Fach
Llyn Celyn
Llyn Arenig fawr
Arenig Fawr
Moel Llyfrant
Parc Cenedlaethol Eryri
Cwm Prysor
Mynydd Bryn-llech
Mynydd Bach
Gwynedd
Buarthmeini
Dolhendre
Bala Lake Rly
Llanuwchllyn
Cwm-hesgen
Pont-Rhyd-y-fen
Bed-y-coedwr
Rhaeadr Mawddach
Talardd
Ty-nant
Foel y Geifr
Sealife Centre
RHYL (Y RHYL)
Ocean Beach Amusement Park
Kinmel Bay
Towyn
Pensarn
Y-Ffrith
Prestatyn
Gronant
Gwaenysgor
Meliden
Offa's Dyke Path
Llwybr Clawdd Offa
Rhuddlan
Dyserth
Trelawnyd
Cwm
Llanasa
Picton
Axton
Whitford
Ffynnongroyw
Gwespyr
Talacre
Pant-y-Wacco
Rhuallt
Bodelwyddan
St George
St Asaph (Llanelwy)
St Asaph Cathedral
Glascoed
Groesffordd Marli
Moelfre Isaf
Waen
Tremeirchion
Pen-y-cefn
Caerwys
Goleugoed
Vale of Clwyd
Dyffryn Clwyd
Llanfair Talhaiarn
Llannefydd
Plas-yn-Cefn
Trefnant
Bont-newydd
Graig
Bodfari
Afon-wen
Bryn-nantllech
Cefn Berain
Bryn Rhyd-yr-Arian
Henllan
Green
Llansannan
Denbigh (Dinbych)
Castle & Town Walls
Fron
Llangwyfan
Waen
Llandyrnog
Tan-y-fron
Groes
Clwt-grugoer
Bylchau
Waen
Nantglyn
Peniel
Llanrhaeadr
Prion
Pentre Llanrhaeadr
Llangynhafal
Llanynys
Gellifor
Saron
Rhewl
Hirwaen
Bryn Trillyn
Gorsedd Bran
Meifod
Llanbedr-Dyffryn-Clwyd
Craft Centre
Ruthin (Rhuthun)
Llyn Aled
Llyn Alwen
Mynydd Hiraethog
Cyffylliog
Llanfwrog
Bontuchel
Tai-Ucha
Denbighshire
Nant Uchaf
Efenechtyd
Pwll-glas
Llanfair-Dyffryn-Clwyd
Nilig
Brenig Res.
Hafod Elwy Moor
Alwen Reservoir
Llyn Brenig Visitor Centre
Pennant
Clocaenog
Mwdwl-eithin
Clocaenog Forest
(Sir Ddinbych)
Clawdd-newydd
Pentre-celyn
Pentre-llyn cymmer
Derwen
Glasfryn
Cefn-brith
Llanfihangel Glyn Myfyr
Llanelidan
Rhyd-y-meudwy
Melin-y-Wig
Bryn Saith Marchog
Cerrigydrudion
Garn Prys
Afon Ceirw
Ty Mawr Cwm
Bettws Gwerfil Goch
Gwyddelwern
Bryneglwys
Pen-y-gop
Ty-nant
Dinmael
Morfydd
Llangwm
Maerdy
Llangollen Steam Railway
Carrog
Tai-mawr
Glan-yr-afon
Druid
Corwen
Llidiart-y-parc
Glyndyfrdwy
Glassblobbery
Wenallt
Foel Goch
Cynwyd Forest
Cynwyd
Glan-yr-afon
Ciltalgarth
Bethel
Moel Fferna
Sarnau
Frongoch
Cefn-ddwysarn
Lidiardau
Rhyd-uchaf
Rhiwlas
Llandderfel
Llandrillo
Bala (Y Bala)
Llanfor
Llanycil
Pale
Cefn Coch
Rhos-y-gwaliau
Llyn Tegid or Bala Lake
Parc
Pennant
Pentre
Aber-Hirnant
Berwyn
Llangower
Blaen-y-Cwm
Tyn-y-fedwen
Tyn-y-ffridd
Aberhirnant Forest
Pont Cwm Pydew
Moel Sych
Pistyll Rhaeadr
Tyn-y-pistyll
Pencraig
Llangynog
Pennant Melangell
Cefn Coch
Llanrhaeadr-ym-Mochnant
0 1 2 3 4 5 6 miles
0 1 2 3 4 5 6 7 8 9 10 km

Flintshire
(Sir Y Fflint)
Wrexham
(Wrecsam)
Halton
Chester
Ellesmere Port
Queensferry
Mold
Wrexham
Llangollen
Oswestry
Whitchurch
Runcorn
Garston
Speke
Liverpool Airport
Heswall
Neston
Willaston
Holywell
(Treffynnon)
Flint (Y Fflint)
Connah's Quay
Shotton
Buckley
(Bwcle)
Hawarden
(Penarlâg)
Saltney
Handbridge
Frodsham
Helsby
Kelsall
Tarvin
Hope
(Yr Hôb)
Caergwrle
Llay
Gresford
Holt
Farndon
Malpas
Rhostyllen
Rhosllanerchrugog
Ruabon
(Rhiwabon)
Cefn-mawr
Overton
(Owrtyn)
Chirk
(Y Waun)
Ellesmere
Wem
Mostyn
Greenfield
Bagillt
Northop
Ewloe
Broughton
Rossett
Marford
Acton
Bangor-is-y-coed
Hanmer
Prees
Whittington
Gobowen
Selattyn
Rhydycroesau
Llansilin
Pontfadog
Froncysyllte
Acrefair
Penycae
Minera
Coedpoeth
Brymbo
Ffrith
Llandegla
Llanferres
Cilcain
Gwernaffield
Nercwys
Leeswood
Treuddyn
Pontblyddyn
Penyffordd
Dodleston
Pulford
Aldford
Tattenhall
Beeston
Bunbury
Peckforton
Bickerton
Tilston
Shocklach
Threapwood
Worthenbury
Penley
Dudleston
St Martin's
Weston Rhyn
Welsh Frankton
Tetchill
Cockshutt
Loppington
Lyneal
Welshampton
Bettisfield
Whixall
Tilstock
Edstaston
Ince
Elton
Stanlow
Thornton-le-Moors
Mickle Trafford
Upton
Hoole
Christleton
Waverton
Rowton
Eccleston
Saighton
Huxley
Tarporley
Delamere Forest Park
Manley
Mouldsworth
Alvanley
Kingsley
Willington Corner
Duddon
Clotton
Tiverton
Barton
Broxton
Clutton
Coddington
Churton
Trevalyn
Lavister
Saughall
Mollington
Backford
Capenhurst
Puddington
Burton
Ness
Parkgate
Hinderton
Ledsham
Great Sutton
Little Sutton
Hooton
Eastham
Bromborough
Port Sunlight
Thurstaston
Irby
Pensby
Barnston
Brimstage
Thornton Hough
Raby
Gayton
Dawpool Bank
Gayton Sands
Holywell Bank
River Dee
Afon Dyfrdwy
Llangollen Canal
Shropshire Union Canal
Offa's Dyke Path
Eglwyseg Mountain
Ruabon Mountain
Esclusham Mountain
Cyrn y Brain
Halkyn Mountain
Wrexham Industrial Estate
Chester Zoo
Boat Museum
Blue Planet Aquarium
Cheshire Oaks
Chester Services
Ness Gardens
Erddig
Chirk Castle
Whittington Castle
Old Oswestry Hill Fort
Valle Crucis Abbey
Eliseg's Pillar
Plas Newydd
Llangollen Exhibition Centre
Beeston Castle
Cholmondeley Castle Gdns
Cheshire Workshops
Fenn's, Whixall and Bettisfield Mosses
Wem Moss
Bersham Heritage Centre
Chwarel Wynne Mine & Museum
Speke Hall
Liverpool John Lennon
M53
M56
A55
A5
A41
A483
A51
A534
A495
A539
A525
A5117
A540
A550
A5104
A541
A528
A49
A494
A542
A5026
A548
A549
A5118
A56
A557
A561
M6
85
86
74
60
SJ

Halton
Runcorn
Halton
Hale
Weston
Ince Banks
Frodsham
Helsby
Elton
Daresbury
Norton Priory Mus & Gardens
Preston on the Hill
Dutton
Sutton Weaver
Aston
Newtown
Overton
Fivecrosses
Appleton Thorn
Stretton
Lower Stretton
Higher Whitley
Lower Whitley
Dones Green
Swarton Heath
High Legh
Hoo Green
Mere
Rostherne Mere
Rosthorne
Ashley
Thorns Green
Bucklow Hill
New Mills
Morley Green
Tatton House
Tatton Park
Arley Hall
Arley
Bate Heath
Holehouses
Over Tabley
Knutsford
Over Knutsford
Mobberley
Davenport Green
Wilmslow
Knolls Green
Alderley Edge
Ollerton
Nether Alderley
Marthall
Chelford
Monks Heath
Capesthorne Hall
Siddington
Withington Green
Lower Withington
Gleadsmoss
Great Budworth
Gib Hill
Comberbach
Pickmere
Higher Wincham
Marston
Plumley
Smithy Green
Lower Peover
Over Peover
Peover Heath
Peover Hall
Swan Green
Jodrell Bank Visitor Centre
Blackden Heath
Goostrey
Twemlow Green
Cranage
Holmes Chapel
Swettenham
Newsbank
Sandlow Green
Anderton Boat Lift
Marbury
Anderton
Barnton
Wincham
Northwich
Lostock Gralam
Lostock Green
Broken Cross
Rudheath
Salt Mus
Lach Dennis
Hartford
Weaverham
Little Leigh
Acton Bridge
Crowton
Kingsley
Commonside
Newton
Alvanley
Hapsford
Birch Hill
Delamere Forest Park
Delamere
Norley
Hatchmere
Farmer for a Day
Cuddington
Sandiway
Manley
Mouldsworth
Dunham-on-the-Hill
Bridge Trafford
Picton
Little Barrow
Great Barrow
Guilden Sutton
Ashton
Kelsall
Kelsall Hill
Oscroft
Stamford Bridge
Littleton
Christleton
Cotton Heath
Waverton
Oakmere
Davenham
Moulton
Whitegate
Foxwist Green
Bostock Green
Byley
Puddinglake
Wharton Green
Wharton
Sproston Green
Salterswall
Winsford
Little Budworth
Over
Church Hill
School Green
Middlewich
Willington Corner
Utkinton
Cotebrook
Shire Horse Centre
Oulton Park
Rushton
Eaton
Duddon
Clotton
Burton
Milner's Heath
Hargrave
Tarporley
Rhuddall Heath
Birch Heath
Brassey Green
Four Lane Ends
Tilstone Fearnall
Huxley
Hatton Heath
Shropshire Union Canal
Bruera
Gatesheath
Newton
Tiverton
Beeston Castle
Beeston
Tattenhall
Milton Green
Handley
Chowley
Burwardsley
Higher Burwardsley
Peckforton
Cheshire Workshops
Harthill
Bunbury
Bunbury Heath
Water Mill
Spurstow
Alpraham
Calveley
Wardle
Aston juxta Mondrum
Barbridge
Haughton Moss
Radmore Green
Wettenhall
Church Minshull
Cholmondeston
Occlestone Green
Moston Green
Warmingham
Bradfield Green
Coppenhall Moss
Barrows Green
Maw Green
Wheelock
Wheelock Heath
Elworth
Sandbach Crosses
Sandbach
Sandbach Services
Winterley
Hassall
Hassall Green
Haslington
Crewe
Worleston
Woolstanwood
Wistaston Green
Wistaston
Wells Green
Willaston
Gresty Green
Weston
Shavington
Bradwall Green
Arclid
West Heath
Astbury
Brownlow
Brookhouse Green
Fourlanes End
Little Moreton Hall
Thurlwood
Rode Heath
Scholar Green
Church Lawton
Alsager
Kidsgrove
Radway Green
Talke
Freeport Talke Outlet Mall
Red Street
Audley
Chesterton
Alsagers Bank
Halmer End
Knutton
Silverdale
Madeley Heath
Keele
Newcastle-under-Lyme
Keele Services
Barthomley
Englesea-brook
Hough
Gorstyhill
Balterley
Betley
Wrinehill
Madeley
Onneley
Madeley Park
Whitmore
Hanchurch
Clutton
Barnhill
Broxton
Barton
Tilston
Castletown
Horton Green
Edge Green
Duckington
Fuller's Moor
Bickerton
Gallantry Bank
Bulkeley
Cholmondeley Castle Gdns
Burland
Faddiley
Acton
St Mary's
Nantwich
Stapeley Water Gardens
Butt Green
Stapeley
Wybunbury
Walgherton
Hatherton
Hunsterson
Blakenhall
Checkley
Chorley
Larden Green
Ravensmoor
Burford
Shocklach
Chorlton Lane
Malpas
Ebnal
Hampton Heath
Bickley Moss
No Man's Heath
Cuddington Heath
Threapwood
Bell o' th' Hill
Higher Wych
Wirswall
Marbury
Norbury
Wrenbury
Sound
Sound Heath
Broomhall
Aston
Newhall
Marley Green
Hankelow
Audlem
Buerton
Kinsey Heath
Lightwood Green
Coxbank
Burleydam
Wilkesley
Woore
Ireland's Cross
Pipe Gate
Aston
Knighton
Willoughbridge
The Dorothy Clive Garden
Baldwin's Gate
Adderley
Bearstone
Grindley Brook
Brooklands
Chemistry
Whitchurch
Eglwys Cross
Redbrook
Waymills
Broughall
Ash Magna
The Chequer
Hanmer
Arowry
Bronington
Alkington
Fenn's, Whixall and Bettisfield Mosses
Tilstock
Hollinwood
Welsh End
Llangollen Canal
Bettisfield
Wem Moss
Whixall
Lyneal
Northwood
Colemere
Wolverley
English Frankton
Cockshutt
Loppington
Wem
Lowe
Horton
Newtown
Edstaston
Quina Brook
Waterloo
Prees
Prees Heath
Prees Higher Heath
Prees Lower Heath
Prees Green
Sandford
Darliston
Fauls
Bletchley
Ightfield
Calverhall
New Street Lane
Moreton Say
Longford
Market Drayton
Ternhill
Lostford
Wollerton
Wollerton Old Hall
Hawkstone Park
Marchamley
Hodnet
Hodnet Hall
Stoke Heath
Wistanswick
Stoke on Tern
Hopton
Norton in Hales
Betton
Loggerheads
Almington
Hales
The Four Alls
Sutton
Rosehill
Woodseaves
Chipnall
Cheswardine
Goldstone Hall
Soudley
Millgreen
Lockleywood
Hinstock
Ellerton
Mucklestone
Ashley Heath
Ashley
Hookgate
Blackbrook
Maer
Chapel Chorlton
Stableford
Podmore
Standon
Chatcull
Wetwood
Fairoak
Croxtonbank
Croxton
Millmeece
Slindon
Sugnall
Bishop's Offley
Pershall
Eccleshall
Adbaston
Knighton
High Offley
Shebdon
Woodseaves
Wootton
Ellenhall
Cranberry
Sturbridge
Petton
Burlton
Preston
Child's Ercall
Weaver
Dane
SJ
M6
M56
A49
A51
A41
A54
A556
A530
A533
A534
A500
A5020
A525
A529
A53
A495
A50
A537
A538
A559
B5356
B5082
B5081
B5309
B5392
B5077
B5367
B5069
B5395
B5476
B5065
B5063
B5415
B5026
B5085
B5152
B5393
B5132
A5022
A531
A5182
A535
73
86
87
61
0 1 2 3 4 5 6 miles
0 1 2 3 4 5 6 7 8 9 10 km

Macclesfield
Buxton
Leek
Congleton
Stoke-on-Trent
Ashbourne
Uttoxeter
Stone
Bakewell
PEAK DISTRICT NATIONAL PARK
SK
Chapel-en-le-Frith
Whaley Bridge
Bollington
Prestbury
Hurdsfield
Poynton
Burbage
Tideswell
Castleton
Hathersage
Ashford in the Water
Youlgreave
Hartington
Cheadle
Cheddleton
Biddulph
Tunstall
Burslem
Hanley
Fenton
Longton
Tutbury
Alton
Axe Edge
Brand Side
Dove Dale
Weaver Hills
Stoke-on-Trent
A6
A53
A52
A50
A515
A523
A54
A537
A520
A34
A623
A619
A6020
A518
A51
A522
A521
B5053
B5054
B5055
B5417
B5032
B5033
87
88
76
62
5
6
7
8
9
r
e
a
f
o
r
d
B
C
D
E
F
G

Castleton
Bamford
Thornhill
Aston
Ringinglow
Ecclesall
Millhouses
Whirlow
Abbeydale
Norton
Woodseats
Gleadless
Beighton
Swallownest
Todwick
Kiveton Park
South Anston
Hackenthorpe
Rother Valley
Wales
Thorpe Salvin
Hathersage
Brough
Bradwell
Upper Padley
Dore
Beauchief
Bradway
Jordanthorpe
Highlane
Mosborough
Holbrook
Norwood
Harthill
Netherthorpe
Woodall Services
Coplow Dale
Abney
Longshaw
New Totley
Coal Aston
Eckington
Spinkhill
Great Hucklow
Little Hucklow
Bretton
Nether Padley
Owler Bar
Dronfield Woodhouse
Dronfield
Marsh Lane
Renishaw Hall Gardens
Renishaw
Middle Handley
Barlborough
Grindlow
Grindleford
Holmesfield
Apperknowle
Unstone
West Handley
Lane Head
Foolow
Eyam
Eyam Hall
Froggatt
Unstone Green
Revolution House
Mastin Moor
Whitwell
Clowne
Tideswell
Litton
Derbyshire Dales
Burnt Heath
Stoney Middleton
Common Side
Moorhall
Barlow
New Whittington
Staveley
Creswell
Wardlow
Calver
Curbar
Wilday Green
Old Whittington
Woodthorpe
Poolsbrook
Stanfree
Elmton
Cressbrook
Little Longstone
Rowland
Baslow
Overgreen
Cutthorpe
Newbold
Brimington
Shuttlewood
Ravenstor
Old Brampton
Tapton
Duckmanton
Ashford in the Water
Great Longstone
Hassop
Chatsworth
Eastmoor
Chesterfield
Long Duckmanton
Whaley
Taddington
Pilsley
Wadshelf
Brampton
Hady
Calow
Arkwright Town
Bolsover
Sheldon
Edensor
Hob Hursts House
Holymoorside
St Mary and All Saints
Walton
Sutton Hall
Scarcliffe
Langwith Junction
Bakewell
Slatepit Dale
Birdholme
Hasland
Scarsdale
Temple Normanton
Palterton
Flagg
Haddon Hall
Peak Village
Beeley
Swathwick
Wingerworth
Grassmoor
Heath
Glapwell
Shirebrook
Monyash
Over Haddon
Rowsley
Tupton
Old Tupton
Holmewood
Doe Lea
New Houghton
Youlgreave
Caudwell's Mill
Stanton in Peak
Alport
Uppertown
Northwood
North Wingfield
Stainsby
Pleasley
Mansfield Woodhouse
Arbor Low Henge
Nine Ladies Stone Circle
Bradford
Brockhurst
Kelstedge
Alton
Clay Cross
Parkhouse Green
Hardstoft
Hardwick Hall
Radmanthwaite
Parsley Hay
Churchtown
Two Dales
Ashover
Fallgate
Pilsley
Teversal
Middleton
Upper Hackney
Darley Bridge
Peak Rail
Birchover
Milltown
Stretton
Tibshelf
Tibshelf Services
Skegby
Mansfield
The Pennine Bridleway
Elton
Wensley
Tansley Knoll
Woolley
Morton
Stanton Hill
Newhaven
Winster
Matlock
Tansley
Brackenfield
Higham
Stonebroom
Heathcote
Biggin
Pikehall
Brightgate
The Heights of Abraham
Bonsall
Starkholmes
Newton
Huthwaite
Sutton in Ashfield
Grangemill
Gulliver's Kingdom
Matlock Bath
Lea
Wessington
Shirland
West-houses
Blackwell
Hilcote
Biggin Dale
Aldwark
Ible
Arkwright's Cromford Mill
Masson Mills
Wheatcroft
South Normanton
Kirkby in Ashfield
Cox Moor
Cromford
Holloway
The National Tramway Mus.
Fourlane Ends
Alfreton
McArthur Glen Mansfield
Alsop en le Dale
Alstonefield
Longcliffe
Middleton
National Stone Cen.
Leawood Pumphouse
South Wingfield
Middleton Top Engine House
Bolehill
Milldale
Ballidon
Wirksworth
Wirksworth Moor
Whatstandwell
Oakerthorpe
Pinxton
Nuncargate
Newstead Abbey
Parwich
Brassington
Wingfield Manor
Crich
Alfreton Services
Somercotes
Selston
Annesley
Bradbourne
Carsington
Miller's Green
Alderwasley
Fritchley
Swanwick
Leabrooks
Annesley Woodhouse
Newstead
Tissington
Ecclesbourne Valley Rly.
Shining Cliff
Bullbridge
Pentrich
Riddings
Jacksdale
Carsington Res.
Ambergate
Ridgeway Cottage Industrial Centre
Ironville
Bagthorpe
Felley Priory
Papplewick
Linby
Dove Dale
Ilam
Thorpe
Fenny Bentley
Hognaston
Beighton Hill
Toadmoor
Heage
Midland Railway Centre
New Brinsley
Underwood
Kniveton
Kirk Ireton
Belper Lane End
Nether Heage
Ripley
Codnor
Hucknall
Shottle
Derwent Valley Visitor Cen.
Broadholme
Marehay
Brinsley
Atlow
Biggin
Idridgehay
Mount Pleasant
Far Laund
Cross Hill
Loscoe
Mapleton
Hulland Ward
Hillcliffiane
Blackbrook
Openwoodgate
Aldercar
Moorgreen
Westville
Ashbourne
Shottlegate
De Bradelei Mill
Denby
Heanor
D H Lawrence Birthplace Mus.
Eastwood
Hulland
Cowers Lane
Belper
Kilburn
Horsley Woodhouse
Marlpool
Watnall
Bulwell
Mayfield
Bradley
Cross o' th' hands
Turnditch
Hazelwood
Milford
Shipley
Nuthall
Church Mayfield
Clifton
Windley
Holbrook
Smalley
American Adventure
Kimberley
Osmaston
Horsley
Awsworth
Swingate
Weston Underwood
Coxbench
Cotmanhay
Mapperley
Erewash Museum
Snelston
Wyaston
Duffield
Cossall
Mugginton
Little Eaton
Stanley Common
Ilkeston
Bilborough
Strelley
Castle Mus. & Gall.
Darley Moor
Brailsford
Kedleston
Flaxholme
West Hallam
Trowell Services
Shirley
Ednaston
Quarndon
Morley
Breadsall
Stanley
Kirk Hallam
Trowell
Yeaveley
Rodsley
Hollington
Kedleston Hall
Allestree
Wollaton
Wollaton Hall
Bentley Fields Open Farm
Cubley Common
Great Cubley
Alkmonton
Hollington Grove
Kirk Langley
Dale Abbey
Chaddesden
Marston Montgomery
Thurvaston
Longlane
Mackworth
Stanton-by-Dale
Bramcote
Beeston
Lees
Langley Common
Sandiacre
Risley
Stapleford
Longford
Longfordlane
Radbourne
Derby
Spondon
Ockbrook
Chilwell
Attenborough
Boylestone
City Mus. & Art Gall.
Oaks Green
Trusley
Mickleover
Littleover
Normanton
Osmaston
Elvaston Castle
Castle & Mus.
Borrowash
Elvaston
Breaston
Draycott
Toton
Long Eaton
Barton in Fabis
Dalbury
Sutton on the Hill
Burnaston
Alvaston
Thulston
Thrumpton
Church Broughton
Foston
Etwall
Allenton
Sawley
Sudbury
Scropton
Hilton
Findern
Chellaston
Shardlow
Cavendish Bridge
Gotham
Sudbury Hall
Hatton
Tutbury
Stenson
Aston-on-Trent
Shardlow Services
Ratcliffe on Soar
Swarkestone
Lockington
New Kingston
Willington
Twyford
Barrow upon Trent
Weston-on-Trent
Hemington
Castle Donington
Kingston on Soar
West Leake
Repton
Ingleby
Stanton by Bridge
King's Newton
Donington Park
Nottingham East Midlands
Grand Prix Racing Cars
Kegworth
Hanbury Woodend
Anslow
Milton
Melbourne
Derbyshire
Nottinghamshire
Derby City
SK
0 1 2 3 4 5 6 miles
0 1 2 3 4 5 6 7 8 9 10 km

Lindrick
Woodsetts
Wigthorpe
Gateford
Shireoaks
Kilton
Manton
Worksop
Scofton
Ranby
Babworth
West Retford
Ordsall
RETFORD
Bassetlaw Museum
Sutton
Hayton
Clarborough
Welham
North Leverton with Habblesthorpe
North Leverton Windmill
Sturton le Steeple
Littleborough
South Leverton
Coates
Treswell
Cottam
Sundown Adventureland
Rampton
Grove
Eaton
Headon
Woodbeck
Stokeham
Gamston
Upton
Church Laneham
Laneham
Askham
Elkesley
West Drayton
Markham Moor
Markham Moor Services
Darlton
East Drayton
Dunham
Ragnall
Laughterton
Newton on Trent
Bothamsall
Haughton
Milton
Bevercotes
West Markham
East Markham
Walks of Life
Tuxford
Fledborough
Walesby
High Marnham
Normanton on Trent
Low Marnham
Kirton
Egmanton
Weston
Grassthorpe
Boughton
New Ollerton
Ollerton
Wellow
Laxton
Moorhouse
Beth Shalom Holocaust Centre
Sutton on Trent
Ompton
Kneesall
Ossington
Carlton on Trent
Norwell Woodhouse
Norwell
The Vina Cooke Museum of Dolls
Cromwell
Kersall
Eakring
Maplebeck
Caunton
Knapthorpe
Winkburn
Bathley
Holme
North Muskham
Langford
Little Carlton
South Muskham
Kelham
Winthorpe
Newark Air Museum
Hockerton
Kirklington
Farnsfield
Edingley
Normanton
The Workhouse
Upton
Halam
Southwell
Southwell Minster
Easthorpe
Averham
Staythorpe
Rolleston
Farndon
Newark-on-Trent
Balderton
Hawton
Coddington
Beckingham
Barnby in the Willows
Halloughton
Park Hill
Morton
Fiskerton
Thurgarton
Bleasby
East Stoke
Thorpe
Elston
Epperstone
Gonalston
Hoveringham
Syerston
Flintham
Cotham
Lowdham
Caythorpe
Kneeton
Sibthorpe
Shelton
Staunton in the Vale
Gunthorpe
East Bridgford
Screveton
Hawksworth
Flawborough
Thoroton
Kilvington
Alverton
Car Colston
Scarrington
Orston
Bingham
Aslockton
Whatton
Normanton
Allington
Bottesford
Elton
Easthorpe
Sedgebrook
Muston
Muston Meadows
Redmile
Stenwith
Barrowby
Granby
Sutton
Cropwell Butler
Tithby
Barnstone
Langar
Naturescape Wild Flower Farm
Vale of Belvoir
Barkestone-le-Vale
Plungar
Belvoir
Woolsthorpe
Denton
Harston
Knipton
Harlaxton
Harlaxton Manor
Stathern
Harby
Hose
Eaton
Branston
Croxton Kerrial
Eastwell
Hungerton
Wyville
Stroxton
Great Ponton
Little Ponton
Grantham
Grantham Mus
Earlsfield
Great Gonerby
Manthorpe
Belton
Belton House
Syston
Barkston
Honington
Grantham North Services
Boundary Mills
Foston
Marston
Hougham
Westborough
Long Bennington
Gelston
Hough-on-the-Hill
Brandon
Caythorpe
Frieston
Stubton
Fenton
Claypole
Dry Doddington
Stragglethorpe
Brant Broughton
Leadenham
Fulbeck
Manor Stables Craft Workshops
Norton Disney
Stapleford
Carlton le Moorland
Bassingham
Brough
Collingham
South Scarle
Besthorpe
Girton
Thurlby
Swinderby
Morton
Eagle Barnsdale
Eagle
North Scarle
Eagle Moor
Whisby
Thorpe on the Hill
Aubourn
Haddington
South Hykeham
North Hykeham
Spalford
Wigsley
South Clifton
North Clifton
Harby
Doddington
Doddington Hall
Birchwood
Boultham
Bracebridge
Lincolnshire Road Transport Museum
Thorney
Skellingthorpe
Broadholme
Saxilby
Kettlethorpe
Fenton
Torksey
Brampton
Sturton by Stow
Marton
Gate Burton
Knaith
Willingham by Stow
Normanby by Stow
Stow
Cammeringham
Thorpe in the Fallows
Aisthorpe
Bransby
Ingleby
Broxholme
North Carlton
South Carlton
Burton
Museum of Lincolnshire Life
Odder
Scampton
Brattleby
Cuckney
Norton
Carburton
Clumber Park
Hardwick
Great Lake
Perlethorpe
Hamlyn Lodge Cottage Industry
Budby
Meden Vale
Market Warsop
Sherwood Forest
Sherwood Forest Visitors Centre
Edwinstowe
Lidgett
Sherwood Forest Farm Park
Old Clipstone
Rufford
Clipstone
Forest Town
Sherwood Pines Forest Park
Bilsthorpe
Bilsthorpe Moor
Rainworth
Wonderland Pleasure Park
White Post Farm Centre
White Post
Blidworth
Haywood Oaks
Ravenshead
Longdale Rural Craft Centre
Papplewick Pumping Station
Burntstump
Oxton
Calverton
Bestwood
Woodborough
Arnold
Tumble Town
Lambley
Burton Joyce
Bulcote
Gedling
Porchester
Mapperley Park
The Tales of Robin Hood
Green's Mill & Science Cen
Carlton
Colwick
Shelford
Newton
Stoke Bardolph
Radcliffe on Trent
Saxondale
Harlequin
Nottingham
Holme Pierrepont
Trent Bridge Cricket Grd
West Bridgford
Bassingfield
Edwalton
Nottingham
Cotgrave
Cropwell Bishop
Tollerton
Owthorpe
Normanton-on-the-Wolds
Colston Bassett
Framework Knitters Mus.
Plumtree
Ruddington
Keyworth
Kinoulton
Bradmore
Stanton-on-the-Wolds
Bunny
Hickling
Widmerpool
Wysall
East Leake
Costock
Manor Farm
Willoughby-on-the-Wolds
Upper Broughton
Long Clawson
Goadby Marwood
Waltham
Saltby
Skillington
Stoke Rochford
Easton
Woolsthorpe Manor
Nottingham
SK
Trent
Witham
Maun
Poulter
Till
Brant

Lincoln
Saxilby
Nettleham
Washingborough
Bardney
Wragby
North Hykeham
South Hykeham
Waddington
Metheringham
Woodhall Spa
Bassingham
Navenby
Leadenham
Ruskington
Leasingham
Sleaford
Billinghay
Heckington
Helpringham
Swineshead
Caythorpe
Claypole
Barkston
Great Gonerby
Grantham
Sedgebrook
Folkingham
Horbling
Billingborough
Donington
Rippingale
Great Ponton
Gosberton
Pinchbeck
Coningsby
Boultham
Bracebridge
Skellingthorpe
Birchwood
Doddington
Whisby
Eagle
Thorpe on the Hill
Morton
Swinderby
Thurlby
Norton Disney
Stapleford
Brant Broughton
Welbourn
Wellingore
Coleby
Boothby Graffoe
Harmston
Aubourn
Haddington
Canwick
Branston
Heighington
Potterhanworth
Nocton
Dunston
Blankney
Scopwick
Kirkby Green
Rowston
Digby
Dorrington
Martin
Timberland
Walcott
Thorpe Tilney
Tattershall
Cranwell
Fulbeck
Ancaster
Wilsford
Quarrington
Silk Willoughby
North Rauceby
South Rauceby
Osbournby
Aswarby
Threekingham
Pointon
Dowsby
Lenton
Ingoldsby
Bitchfield
Irnham
Bulby
Dunsby
Little Ponton
Harlaxton
Denton
Woolsthorpe
Barrowby
Allington
Foston
Marston
Hougham
Westborough
Long Bennington
Dry Doddington
Stubton
Brandon
Hough-on-the-Hill
Gelston
Carlton Scroop
Sudbrook
Normanton
Honington
Belton
Manthorpe
Londonthorpe
Welby
Syston
Scampton
Welton
Dunholme
Sudbrooke
Reepham
Cherry Willingham
Fiskerton
Langworth
Snelland
Scothern
Riseholme
Burton
Broadholme
Torksey
Stow
Sturton by Stow
Fenton
Kettlethorpe
Newton on Trent
Thorney
Harby
Wigsley
Spalford
Collingham
Brough
Coddington
Beckingham
Barnby in the Willows
Stragglethorpe
Carlton le Moorland
Bracebridge Heath
Bracebridge Low Fields
Bloxholm
Ashby de la Launde
Anwick
North Kyme
South Kyme
South Kyme Fen
Holland Fen
HOLLAND FEN
Amber Hill
East Heckington
Great Hale
Little Hale
Burton Pedwardine
Scredington
Swaton
Bicker
Northorpe
Bridge End
Stow
Birthorpe
Pickworth
Walcot
Newton
Haceby
Braceby
Sapperton
Ropsley
Humby
Hanby
Boothby Pagnell
Old Somerby
Stroxton
Hungerton
Keisby
Kirkby Underwood
Hawthorpe
Graby
Millthorpe
Gosberton Clough
Risegate
Westhorpe
Quadring
Church End
Donington South Ing
Evedon
Ewerby
Ewerby Thorpe
Howell
Asgarby
Kirkby la Thorpe
Holdingham
Culverthorpe
Kelby
Swarby
Heydour
Oasby
Aisby
Aunsby
Dembleby
Spanby
Northbeck
Laughton
Aslackby
Bardney Limewoods
Southrey
Stixwould
Kirkstead
Martin Dales
Tattershall Bridge
Tattershall Thorpe
Dogdyke
Chapel Hill
Scrub Hill
Haven Bank
Thimbleby
Langton
Horsington
Bucknall
Edlington
Wispington
Gautby
Minting
Baumber
Hatton
Panton
Sotby
Great Sturton
Langton by Wragby
Kingthorpe
Apley
Stainfield
Bullington
Rand
Fulnetby
Stainton by Langworth
Friesthorpe
Wickenby
Holton cum Beckering
Lissington
East Torrington
West Torrington
South Willingham
Benniworth
East Barkwith
West Barkwith
Market Stainton
Ranby
Hemingby
Young Wood
Low Barlings
Greetwell
Potterhanworth Booths
Branston Booths
Wasps Nest
Sots Hole
Reeds Beck
Roughton Moor
Kirkby on Bain
Hawthorn Hill
Snarford
Welton Hill
Hackthorn
Cold Hanworth
Cammeringham
Ingham
Thorpe in the Fallows
Aisthorpe
Brattleby
Bransby
Broxholme
North Carlton
South Carlton
Ingleby
Brampton
Odder
Eagle Moor
North Scarle
South Scarle
Skillington
Croxton Kerrial
Saltby
A15
A17
A46
A52
A57
A153
A158
A607
A1
B1188
B1190
B1191
B1202
B6403
65
77
90
91
SK
TF
0 1 2 3 4 5 6 miles
0 1 2 3 4 5 6 7 8 9 10 km

Raithby
Vithcall
Little Cawthorpe
South Reston
Gayton le Marsh
Strubby
Trusthorpe
Tathwell
North Reston
Withern
Thorpe
Sutton on Sea
Haugham
Muckton
Tothill
Maltby le Marsh
Stenigot
CADWELL PARK
Authorpe
Sandilands
Cawkwell
Maidenwell
Burwell
Woodthorpe
Beesby
WOODY'S TOP
Hannah
Goulceby
Scamblesby
Farforth
Ruckland
Belleau
CLAYTHORPE WATER MILL AND WILDFOWL GARDENS
Saleby
Markby
White Pit
Aby
Swaby
Oxcombe
Ketsby
South Thoresby
ALFORD WINDMILL
Asserby
ALFORD MANOR HOUSE
Bilsby
Huttoft
Belchford
South Ormsby
Rigsby
Alford
Haugh
Calceby
Anderby
ON YOUR MARQUES
Tetford
Farlesthorpe
Mumby
Authorpe Row
Brinkhill
Driby
Fulletby
Well
Cumberworth
Salmonby
Somersby
Ulceby
Helsey
Chapel St Leonards
Bonthorpe
Hogsthorpe
West Ashby
Sutterby
Bag Enderby
Claxby
Ashby Puerorum
Harrington
Willoughby
High Toynton
Langton
Sloothby
Greetham
Aswardby
HARDY'S ANIMAL FARM
Horncastle
Skendleby
Hagworthingham
Sausthorpe
Ingoldmells
Scrafield
SNIPE DALES
Partney
Addlethorpe
FANTASY ISLAND CHILDREN'S PLAYDROME & THE MILLENNIUM ROLLERCOASTER
Mareham on the Hill
Hameringham
Lusby
Welton le Marsh
Mavis Enderby
Raithby
Scremby
FUNCOAST WORLD
Orby
Candlesby
Orby Marsh
Scrivelsby
Asgarby
Spilsby
Ashby by Partney
GUNBY HALL
Winthorpe
Old Bolingbroke
Hundleby
Burgh le Marsh
Seathorne
Hareby
NORTHCOTE HEAVY HORSE CENTRE
Bratoft
Great Steeping
Wood Enderby
Moorby
BOLINGBROKE
Halton Holegate
NATURELAND SEAL SANCTUARY
Miningsby
West Keal
Toynton All Saints
Irby in the Marsh
BURGH LE MARSH WINDMILL
CHURCH FARM MUS.
Skegness
OSLINC OSTRICH FARM
East Keal
Toynton St Peter
Firsby
THE LIFEBOAT STATION
East Kirkby
Toynton Fen Side
Little Steeping
Mareham le Fen
Revesby
LINCOLNSHIRE AVIATION HERITAGE CENTRE
Keal Cotes
Thorpe Culvert
Thorpe St Peter
Croft
Seacroft
Croft Marsh
Revesby Bridge
Thorpe Fendykes
Wainfleet All Saints
Stickford
GIBRALTAR POINT
New Bolingbroke
Wainfleet Bank
MAGDALEN MUSEUM
Fen Side
GIBRALTAR POINT
New Leake
Wainfleet Tofts
Wainfleet St Mary
Tumby Woodside
Midville
Eastville
Stickney
Friskney Eaudike
Medlam
Wainfleet Sand
Sandy Bank
East Fen
Friskney
Carrington
Bunker's Hill
Lade Bank
Wrangle Bank
Friskney Tofts
West Fen
Northlands
Leake Commonside
SIBSEY TRADER MILL
Sibsey
Wrangle Lowgate
Friskney Flats
Frithville
Old Leake
Gipsey Bridge
Wrangle
Fishtoft Drove
Hurn's End
Langrick
Anton's Gowt
Hill Dyke
Boston Long Hedges
Leverton Outgate
Frith Bank
Leverton Highgate
Leverton
Cowbridge
Leverton Lucasgate
BOSTON DEEPS
Borthertoft
Benington
Boston West
Haltoft End
LYNN DEEPS
Boston
GUILDHALL
Butterwick
Freiston
TF
Chain Bridge
Skirbeck
Skirbeck Quarter
Kirton Holme
Wyberton
Fishtoft
THE WASH
Frampton West End
Scrane End
Hunstanton
SEA LIFE SANCTUARY
Kirton End
Frampton
Kirton
Asperton
Sandholme
Skeldyke
Heacham
Wigtoft
Seadyke
Sutterton
Bucklegate
Algarkirk
Fosdyke
Lynn Channel
Holbeach St Matthew
SNETTISHAM NATURE RESERVE
Holbeach St Marks
Dawsmere
Surfleet Seas End
HOLBEACH MARSH
Gedney Marsh
Gedney Drove End
DERSINGHAM B
Moulton Seas End
Saracen's Head
Holbeach Hurn
THE WASH
Wolferton
Holbeach Bank
Halesgate
Holbeach Clough
Gedney Dyke
Lutton
Guy's
BAYTREE
A153
A157
A1104
B1373
A1111
A52
B1449
A1104
A16
A1028
B1196
A158
B1195
B1183
A155
A16
B1183
B1184
B1192
A52
A1121
B1391
A17
B1357
B1359
91
80
66
66
5 6 7 8 9
A B C D E F G

NATURELAND SEAL SANCTUARY
THE LIFEBOAT STATION
Skegness
Seacroft
Croft Marsh
GIBRALTAR POINT
Wainfleet Sand
TF
NORFOLK COAST
BRANCASTER ROADS
LYNN DEEPS
79
67
Holkham Bay
SCOLT HEAD ISLAND
Brancaster Bay
HOLME DUNES
BIRD OBSERVATORY RESERVE
Holme next the Sea
Titchwell
Brancaster Staithe
Burnham Deepdale
Brancaster
Burnham Norton
Burnham Market
Burnham Overy Staithe
Burnham Overy Town
Burnham Thorpe
PEDDARS WAY & NORFOLK COAST PATH
WELLS-NEXT-THE-SEA
Wells-next-the-Sea
Holkham
HOLKHAM HALL
WELLS AND WALSINGHAM RAILWAY
Warham
Wighton
Copy's Green
Great Walsingham
Little Walsingham
SHIREHALL MUS.
Houghton St Giles
North Barsham
West Barsham
East Barsham
Great Snoring
Old Hunstanton
Thornham
Hunstanton
SEA LIFE SANCTUARY
Ringstead
HUNSTANTON
New Holkham
CREAKE ABBEY
North Creake
South Creake
SOUTH CREAKE MAIZE MAZE
Waterden
Summerfield
Docking
Heacham
NORFOLK LAVENDER
Sedgeford
Stanhoe
Fring
Bircham Newton
Snettisham
SNETTISHAM PARK
Ingoldisthorpe
SNETTISHAM NATURE RESERVE
Shepherd's Port
Great Bircham
BIRCHAM MILL
Bircham Tofts
Barmer
Syderstone
Blenheim Park
Wicken Green Village
Bagthorpe
Sculthorpe
Shernborne
Dersingham
DERSINGHAM BOG
Anmer
HOUGHTON HALL
Tattersett
Dunton
Shereford
Hempton
Coxford
Tatterford
Fakenham
FAKENHAM
West Rudham
East Rudham
Toftrees
SANDRINGHAM
Sandringham
Wolferton
West Newton
New Houghton
Flitcham
Harpley
Helhoughton
Colkirk
West Raynham
East Raynham
Oxwick
Hamrow
Castle Rising
CASTLE RISING
North Wootton
Hillington
Little Massingham
South Raynham
Horningtoft
Terrington Marsh
Ongar Hill
South Wootton
Congham
CONGHAM HALL HERB GARDEN
Roydon
Great Massingham
Weasenham St Peter
Whissonsett
ROYDON COMMON
Grimston
Wellingham
Weasenham All Saints
EXTREEME ADVENTURE
Tittleshall
King's Lynn
MARITIME EXHIBITION
GUILDHALL
Gaywood
Pott Row
Massingham Heath
Stanfield
Clenchwarton
Terrington St Clement
West Lynn
KING'S LYNN
Fairstead
Gayton
Rougham
Mileham
Hardwick
Leziate
Ashwicken
Gayton Thorpe
Tilney All Saints
Tilney High End
Fair Green
Tower End
West Lexham
Litcham
Bittering
Saddle Bow
West Winch
Middleton
East Walton
East Lexham
Terrington St John
Tilney St Lawrence
North Runcton
East Winch
West Bilney
Pentney
Castle Acre
CASTLE ACRE PRIORY
West Acre
Newton
South Acre
Beeston
Great Dunham
Drury Square
Crane's Corner
Wiggenhall St Germans
Setchey
Blackborough End
Little Dunham
Great Fransham
Wiggenhall St Mary the Virgin
Tottenhill Row
Narborough
Wendling
Wiggenhall St Mary Magdalen
Watlington
Wormegay
Great Palgrave
Sporle
Little Fransham
Tottenhill
Runcton Holme
Marham
Shouldham
Necton
West End
Swaffham
Bradenham
Beachamwell Warren
Holme Hale
North Pickenham
Crowshill
Barton Bendish
Fincham
Bardolph
West Head
0 1 2 3 4 5 6 miles
0 1 2 3 4 5 6 7 8 9 10 km

TG
Blakeney Point
HOLKHAM
BLAKENEY
GUILDHALL
CLEY MILL
Cley next the Sea
PEDDARS WAY AND NORFOLK COAST PATH
Morston
Salthouse
MUCKLEBURGH COLLECTION
NORTH NORFOLK RAILWAY
Sheringham
PRIORY MAZE & GARDENS
NORFOLK SHIRE HORSE CENTRE
CROMER MUSEUM
Cromer
Stiffkey
Blakeney
Wiveton
Newgate
Kelling
Weybourne
SHERINGHAM PARK
Upper Sheringham
Beeston Regis
West Runton
East Runton
Overstrand
Cockthorpe
Langham
Glandford
High Kelling
Bodham
East Beckham
Aylmerton
Felbrigg
Northrepps
Sidestrand
Westgate
Binham
Saxlingham
Letheringsett
Holt
PICTURECRAFT GALLERY
West Beckham
Gresham
FELBRIGG HALL
Crossdale Street
Trimingham
WAYSIDE CROSS
Field Dalling
LETHERINGSETT WATERMILL
BACONSTHORPE CASTLE
Frogshall
Lower Green
Bale
Sharrington
Hempstead
Baconsthorpe
Sustead
Roughton
Southrepps
Gimingham
Mundesley
Hindringham
Brinton
Thornage
Hunworth
Bessingham
Hanworth
Thorpe Market
Lower Street
STOW MILL
Paston
THURSFORD COLLECTION
Stody
Edgefield
Plumstead
Matlaske
Thurgarton
Alby Hill
Trunch
Knapton
Bacton
Gunthorpe
Briningham
Aldborough
ALBY CRAFTS
ALBY GARDENS
Antingham
Bradfield
Broomholm
Keswick
Thursford
Edgefield Street
Little Barningham
Wickmere
Suffield
Edingthorpe
Barney
Swanton Novers
Melton Constable
Briston
MANNINGTON GARDENS
WOLTERTON PARK
Calthorpe
Erpingham
Colby
STRAW MUSEUM
Swafield
Edingthorpe Green
Witton Bridge
Ridlington
Kettlestone
Fulmodestone
Saxthorpe
Itteringham
North Walsham
Spa Common
Crostwight
Corpusty
BLICKLING HALL
Ingworth
Banningham
Stibbard
Hindolveston
Thurning
Oulton
Blickling
Felmingham
Wood Norton
Norton Corner
Silvergate
Dunkirk
Tuttington
Honing
Guestwick
Heydon
Oulton Street
Aylsham
Westwick
Bengate
Worstead
East Ruston
Guestwick Green
Wood Dalling
Burgh next Aylsham
Skeyton
Guist
Salle
Southgate
Swanton Abbot
Sloley
Dilham
Smallburgh
Twyford
Foulsham
Themelthorpe
Fengate
Marsham
Brampton
BURE VALLEY RAILWAY
Gateley
Broom Green
Bintree
FOXLEY WOOD
Reepham
Cawston
Little London
Lamas
Scottow
Pennygate
Booton
Eastgate
Buxton
Little Hautbois
Tunstead
North Elmham
Foxley
Whitwell Street
Brandiston
The Heath
Sco Ruston
WROXHAM BARNS
Neatishead
ANT BROADS AND MARSHES
Billingford
Bawdeswell
Haveringland
Hevingham
Stratton Strawless
Coltishall
Ashmanhaugh
Worthing
Sparham
NORFOLK WILDLIFE CENTRE
Swannington
Waterloo
Threehammer Common
Beetley
Mill Street
Alderford
Upgate
New Hainford
Hainford
Belaugh
Hoveton
Lenwade
Lyng
DINOSAUR NATURAL HISTORY PARK
Frettenham
Wroxham
Lower Street
Swanton Morley
Elsing
Morton
Attlebridge
Felthorpe
REDWINGS HORSE SANCTUARY
Upper Street
Horning
Hoe
Horsford
Newton St Faith
Wroxham Broad
BURE MARSHES
Woodgate
Primrose Green
Weston Longville
Thorpe Marriott
Crostwick
Woodbastwick
Etling Green
North Tuddenham
Weston Green
Ringland
Taverham
Horsham St Faith
Spixworth
Rackheath
Salhouse
Dereham
Hockering
Drayton
NORWICH INTERNATIONAL
Panxworth
Hellesdon
Old Catton
New Rackheath
MID-NORFOLK RAILWAY
Mattishall Burgh
Honingham
Costessey
Sprowston
Little Plumstead
Scarning
Toftwood
Clint Green
Mattishall
East Tuddenham
Mile Cross
Upper Hellesdon
Thorpe End
Blofield Heath
Yaxham
Easton
New Costessey
THE FORUM
New Catton
Thorpe St Andrew
Great Plumstead
Westfield
Whinburgh
Welborne
Colton
Marlingford
Bowthorpe
Earlham
CATHEDRAL
SAINSBURY CENTRE FOR VISUAL ARTS
NORWICH
Blofield
Brundall
Brandon Parva
Bawburgh
Runhall
Barford
Colney
Lakenham
Postwick
Garvestone
Thuxton
Barnham Broom
Great Melton
Little Melton
Cringleford
Trowse Newton
Kirby Bedon
Surlingham
Letton Green
Reymerston
Danemoor
Wramplingham
High Green
Eaton
NORFOLK
COAST
A149
A148
A1082
A140
A1067
A47
A1074
A1151
B1156
B1110
B1354
B1149
B1145
B1436
B1150
B1135
B1108
B1140
68
69

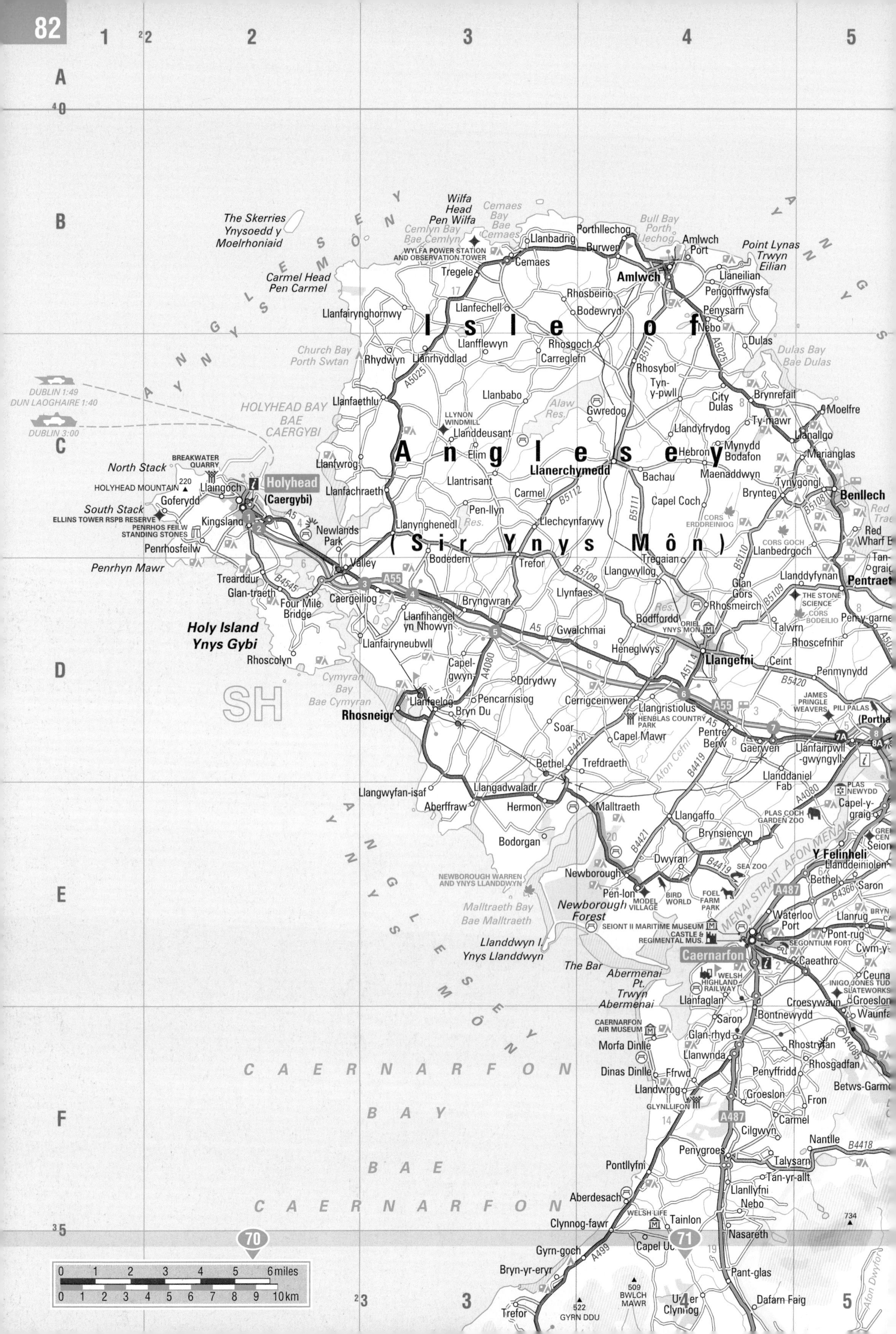

1
2
3
4
5
A
B
C
D
E
F
Isle of Anglesey
(Sir Ynys Môn)
ANGLESEY
YNYS MÔN
CAERNARFON BAY
BAE CAERNARFON
SH
The Skerries
Ynysoedd y Moelrhoniaid
Carmel Head
Pen Carmel
Wilfa Head
Pen Wilfa
Cemlyn Bay
Bae Cemlyn
Cemaes Bay
Bae Cemaes
WYLFA POWER STATION AND OBSERVATION TOWER
Llanbadrig
Porthllechog
Bull Bay
Porth Llechog
Amlwch Port
Point Lynas
Trwyn Eilian
Cemaes
Burwen
Amlwch
Tregele
Llaneilian
Pengorffwysfa
Llanfechell
Rhosbeirio
Bodewryd
Penysarn
Llanfairynghornwy
Nebo
Dulas
Llanfflewyn
Rhosgoch
Carreglefn
Church Bay
Porth Swtan
Rhydwyn
Llanrhyddlad
Dulas Bay
Bae Dulas
Rhosybol
Tyn-y-pwll
DUBLIN 1:49
DUN LAOGHAIRE 1:40
DUBLIN 3:00
Llanbabo
Alaw Res.
Gwredog
City Dulas
Brynrefail
Moelfre
HOLYHEAD BAY
BAE CAERGYBI
Llanfaethlu
LLYNON WINDMILL
Llanddeusant
Llandyfrydog
Ty-mawr
Llanallgo
Hebron
Mynydd Bodafon
Marianglas
Elim
Llanerchymedd
Llanfwrog
Bachau
Maenaddwyn
Tynygongl
North Stack
BREAKWATER QUARRY
Llantrisant
HOLYHEAD MOUNTAIN
220
Llaingoch
Holyhead
(Caergybi)
Llanfachraeth
Carmel
Capel Coch
Brynteg
Benllech
Goferydd
South Stack
ELLINS TOWER RSPB RESERVE
Kingsland
PENRHOS FEILW STANDING STONES
Penrhosfeilw
Newlands Park
Pen-llyn
Llanynghenedl
Res.
Llechcynfarwy
CORS ERDDREINIOG
Red Wharf B
CORS GOCH
Llanbedrgoch
Penrhyn Mawr
Valley
Bodedern
Trefor
Tregaian
Llangwyllog
Llanddyfnan
Pentraet
Treardddur
Glan-traeth
Four Mile Bridge
Caergeiliog
Llynfaes
Glan Gors
THE STONE SCIENCE
Bryngwran
Rhosmeirch
CORS BODEILIO
Pen-y-garne
Holy Island
Ynys Gybi
Llanfihangel yn Nhowyn
Bodffordd
ORIEL YNYS MÔN
Talwrn
Gwalchmai
Llanfairyneubwll
Heneglwys
Rhoscefnhir
Rhoscolyn
Llangefni
Ceint
Capel-gwyn
Penmynydd
Cymyran Bay
Bae Cymyran
Ddrydwy
Rhosneigr
Llanfaelog
Pencarnisiog
Bryn Du
Cerrigceinwen
Llangristiolus
HENBLAS COUNTRY PARK
JAMES PRINGLE WEAVERS
PILI PALAS
(Portha
Soar
Capel Mawr
Pentre Berw
Gaerwen
Llanfairpwll-gwyngyll
Bethel
Trefdraeth
Afon Cefni
Llanddaniel Fab
PLAS NEWYDD
Llangwyfan-isaf
Llangadwaladr
Capel-y-graig
Aberffraw
Hermon
Malltraeth
Llangaffo
PLAS COCH GARDEN ZOO
Bodorgan
Brynsiencyn
Y Felinheli
MENAI STRAIT AFON MENAI
Dwyran
SEA ZOO
Llanddeiniolen
NEWBOROUGH WARREN AND YNYS LLANDDWYN
Newborough
Bethel
Saron
Pen-lon
MODEL VILLAGE
BIRD WORLD
FOEL FARM PARK
Malltraeth Bay
Bae Malltraeth
Newborough Forest
Waterloo Port
Llanrug
SEIONT II MARITIME MUSEUM
CASTLE & REGIMENTAL MUS.
SEGONTIUM FORT
Pont-rug
Llanddwyn I.
Ynys Llanddwyn
Caernarfon
Cwm-y-
Caeathro
The Bar
Abermenai Pt.
Trwyn Abermenai
WELSH HIGHLAND RAILWAY
Ceuna
INIGO JONES TUD SLATEWORKS
Llanfaglan
Groeslon
Croesywaun
Waunfa
Saron
Bontnewydd
CAERNARFON AIR MUSEUM
Glan-rhyd
Morfa Dinlle
Llanwnda
Rhostryfan
Dinas Dinlle
Ffrwd
Rhosgadfan
Penyffridd
Betws-Garm
Llandwrog
GLYNLLIFON
Groeslon
Fron
Carmel
Cilgwyn
Nantlle
Penygroes
Talysarn
Pontllyfni
Tan-yr-allt
Llanllyfni
Aberdesach
Nebo
WELSH LIFE
Tainlon
734
Clynnog-fawr
Nasareth
70
71
Capel Uc
Gyrn-goch
Bryn-yr-eryr
Pant-glas
509 BWLCH MAWR
522 GYRN DDU
Uwchmynydd Clynnog
Dafarn Faig
Afon Dwyfor
Trefor
A5025
A5
A55
A4080
B5111
B5112
B5109
B5110
B5108
B4545
A5114
B5420
B4422
B4419
B4421
A4080
A487
B4366
A4085
B4418
A499
0 1 2 3 4 5 6 miles
0 1 2 3 4 5 6 7 8 9 10 km

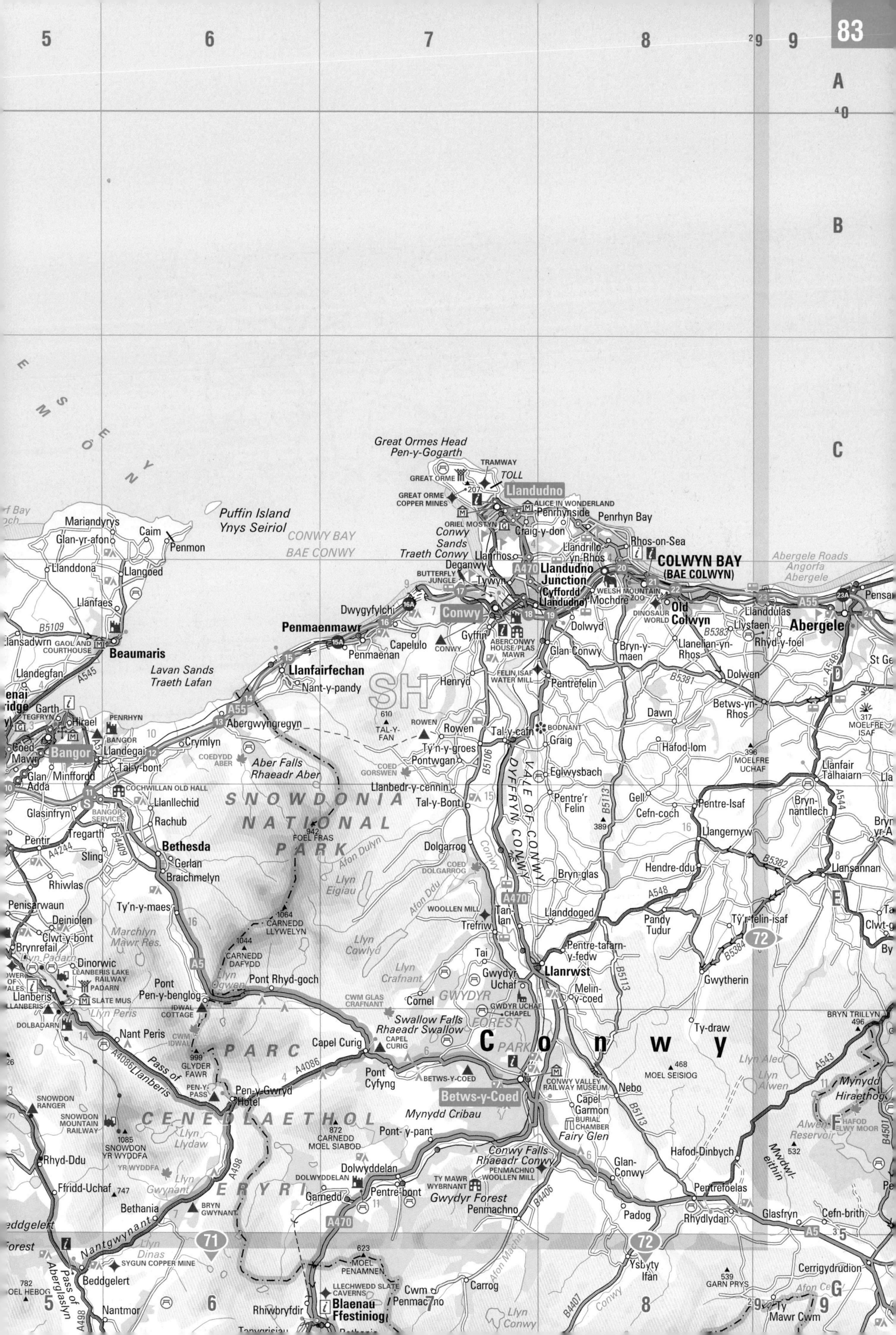

5
6
7
8
9
A
B
C
D
E
F
G
MENAI YNYS MÔN
Great Ormes Head
Pen-y-Gogarth
TRAMWAY
GREAT ORME
TOLL
Llandudno
GREAT ORME COPPER MINES
ALICE IN WONDERLAND
Penrhynside
Penrhyn Bay
ORIEL MOSTYN
Craig-y-don
Conwy Sands
Traeth Conwy
Puffin Island
Ynys Seiriol
CONWY BAY
BAE CONWY
Mariandyrys
Glan-yr-afon
Caim
Penmon
Llanddona
Llangoed
Llanfaes
Beaumaris
GAOL AND COURTHOUSE
Llandegfan
Lavan Sands
Traeth Lafan
Llanrhos
Deganwy
Tywyn
BUTTERFLY JUNGLE
Llandrillo-yn-Rhos
Rhos-on-Sea
COLWYN BAY
(BAE COLWYN)
Llandudno Junction
(Cyffordd Llandudno)
WELSH MOUNTAIN ZOO
Mochdre
DINOSAUR WORLD
Old Colwyn
Abergele Roads
Angorfa Abergele
Llanddulas
Abergele
Pensarn
Llysfaen
Rhyd-y-foel
Llanelian-yn-Rhos
Dolwen
St George
Dwygyfylchi
Conwy
Penmaenmawr
Penmaenan
Capelulo
Gyffin
ABERCONWY HOUSE/PLAS MAWR
Llanfairfechan
Nant-y-pandy
Henryd
FELIN ISAF WATER MILL
Pentrefelin
Glan-Conwy
Dolwyd
Bryn-y-maen
Dawn
Betws-yn-Rhos
MOELFRE ISAF
Garth
Hirael
PENRHYN
Bangor
Llandegai
Tal-y-bont
Abergwyngregyn
Crymlyn
COEDYDD ABER
Aber Falls
Rhaeadr Aber
TAL-Y-FAN
ROWEN
Rowen
Tŷ'n-y-groes
Pontwgan
COED GORSWEN
Tal-y-cafn
BODNANT
Graig
Eglwysbach
Hafod-lom
MOELFRE UCHAF
Llanfair Talhaiarn
Glan Adda
Minffordd
COCHWILLAN OLD HALL
Llanllechid
BANGOR SERVICES
Rachub
Glasinfryn
Tregarth
Pentir
Sling
Bethesda
Gerlan
Braichmelyn
Rhiwlas
SNOWDONIA NATIONAL PARK
FOEL FRAS
Llanbedr-y-cennin
Tal-y-Bont
DYFFRYN CONWY
VALE OF CONWY
Pentre'r Felin
Gell
Cefn-coch
Pentre-Isaf
Bryn-nantllech
Llangernyw
Dolgarrog
COED DOLGARROG
Afon Dulyn
Llyn Eigiau
Afon Ddu
Bryn-glas
Hendre-ddu
Llansannan
Penisarwaun
Deiniolen
Clwt-y-bont
Brynrefail
Ty'n-y-maes
Marchlyn Mawr Res.
CARNEDD LLYWELYN
CARNEDD DAFYDD
WOOLLEN MILL
Trefriw
Tan-lan
Llanddoged
Pandy Tudur
Tŷ'r-felin-isaf
Llyn Padarn
Dinorwic
LLANBERIS LAKE RAILWAY
PADARN
SLATE MUS
Llanberis
DOLBADARN
Llyn Peris
Llyn Cowlyd
Llyn Crafnant
Tai
Gwydyr Uchaf
Pentre-tafarn-y-fedw
Llanrwst
Gwytherin
Pont Pen-y-benglog
Pont Rhyd-goch
Llyn Ogwen
IDWAL COTTAGE
CWM GLAS CRAFNANT
Cornel
GWYDYR FOREST PARK
GWYDYR UCHAF CHAPEL
Melin-y-coed
Ty-draw
BRYN TRILLYN
Nant Peris
CWM IDWAL
Swallow Falls
Rhaeadr Swallow
Capel Curig
CAPEL CURIG
Conwy
MOEL SEISIOG
Llyn Aled
Llyn Alwen
Mynydd Hiraethog
Pass of Llanberis
GLYDER FAWR
PEN-Y-PASS
Pen-y-Gwryd Hotel
PARC CENEDLAETHOL ERYRI
Pont Cyfyng
BETWS-Y-COED
CONWY VALLEY RAILWAY MUSEUM
Betws-y-Coed
Nebo
Capel Garmon
BURIAL CHAMBER
Fairy Glen
SNOWDON RANGER
SNOWDON MOUNTAIN RAILWAY
SNOWDON YR WYDDFA
Llyn Llydaw
CARNEDD MOEL SIABOD
Mynydd Cribau
Pont-y-pant
Alwen Reservoir
HAFOD ELWY MOOR
Mwdwl-eithin
Rhyd-Ddu
Ffridd-Uchaf
Llyn Gwynant
Dolwyddelan
DOLWYDDELAN
Conwy Falls
Rhaeadr Conwy
PENMACHNO WOOLLEN MILL
TY MAWR WYBRNANT
Gwydyr Forest
Glan-Conwy
Hafod-Dinbych
Bethania
BRYN GWYNANT
Garnedd
Pentre-bont
Penmachno
Padog
Pentrefoelas
Rhydlydan
Glasfryn
Cefn-brith
Beddgelert
Forest
Nantgwynant
Llyn Dinas
SYGUN COPPER MINE
MOEL PENAMNEN
Afon Machno
Ysbyty Ifan
GARN PRYS
Cerrigydrudion
Afon Ce
Pass of Aberglaslyn
MOEL HEBOG
LLECHWEDD SLATE CAVERNS
Cwm Penmachno
Carrog
Blaenau Ffestiniog
Rhiwbryfdir
Nantmor
Llyn Conwy
Ty Mawr Cwm
Tanygrisiau
A55
A470
A5
A4086
A498
A4244
A545
A548
A543
A544
A5025
B5109
B5106
B5113
B5381
B5382
B5383
B5384
B4406
B4407
B4409
B4501
71
72

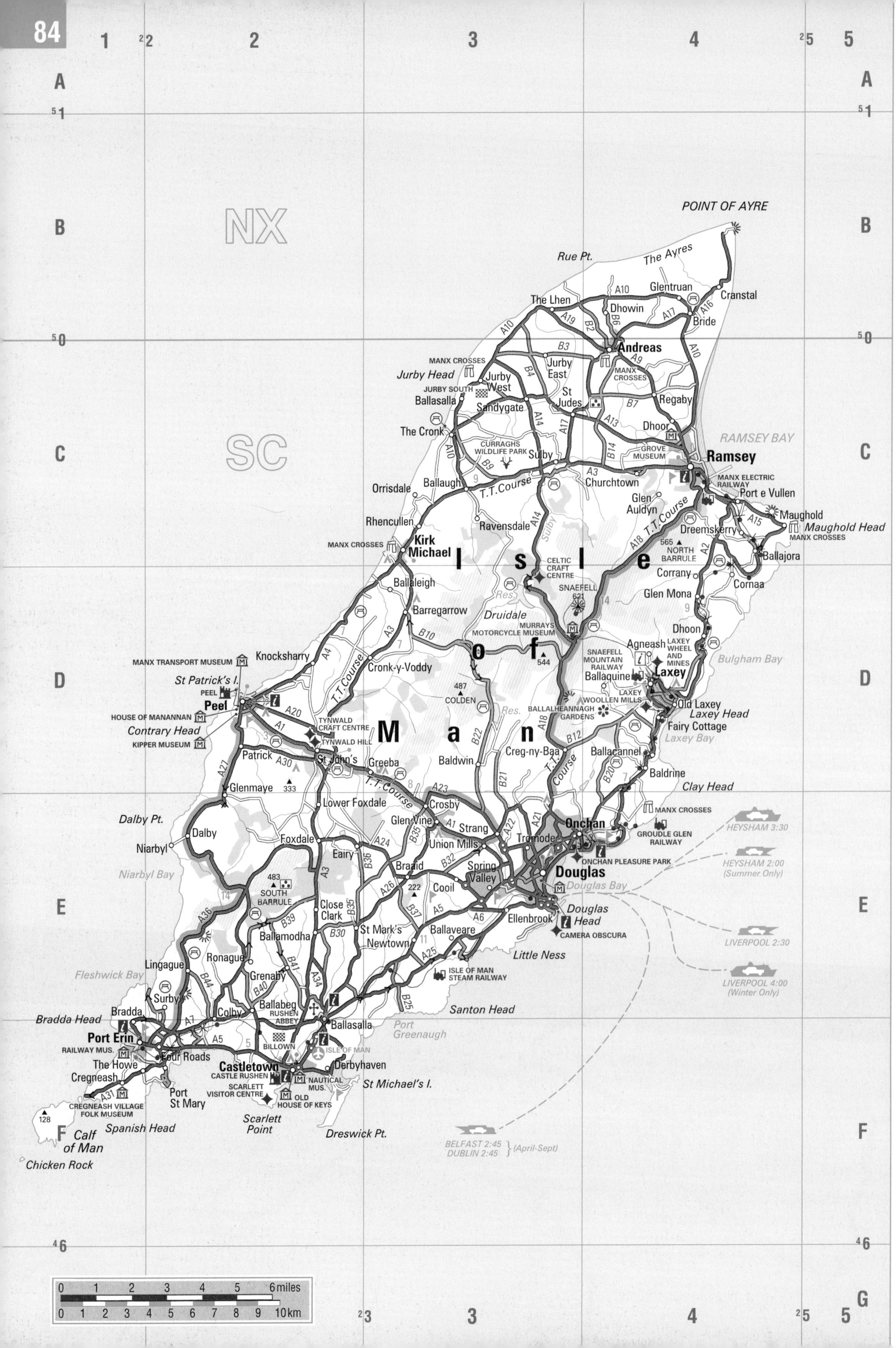

NX
SC
POINT OF AYRE
The Ayres
Rue Pt.
Glentruan
Cranstal
The Lhen
Dhowin
Bride
Andreas
MANX CROSSES
Jurby Head
Jurby West
Jurby East
JURBY SOUTH
Ballasalla
Sandygate
St Judes
Regaby
Dhoor
The Cronk
CURRAGHS WILDLIFE PARK
GROVE MUSEUM
Sulby
RAMSEY BAY
Ramsey
Churchtown
MANX ELECTRIC RAILWAY
Port e Vullen
Orrisdale
Ballaugh
T.T.Course
Glen Auldyn
Maughold
Maughold Head
Rhencullen
Ravensdale
Dreemskerry
Kirk Michael
Isle of Man
NORTH BARRULE
Ballajora
CELTIC CRAFT CENTRE
Corrany
Cornaa
Ballaleigh
SNAEFELL 621
Glen Mona
Barregarrow
Druidale
Dhoon
MURRAYS MOTORCYCLE MUSEUM
Agneash
LAXEY WHEEL AND MINES
Bulgham Bay
MANX TRANSPORT MUSEUM
Knocksharry
SNAEFELL MOUNTAIN RAILWAY
St Patrick's I.
Cronk-y-Voddy
Ballaquine
Laxey
PEEL
Peel
487 COLDEN
LAXEY WOOLLEN MILLS
Old Laxey
HOUSE OF MANANNAN
BALLALHEANNAGH GARDENS
Laxey Head
Contrary Head
TYNWALD CRAFT CENTRE
TYNWALD HILL
Fairy Cottage
KIPPER MUSEUM
Laxey Bay
Patrick
St John's
Greeba
Baldwin
Creg-ny-Baa
Ballacannel
Baldrine
Glenmaye
333
Clay Head
Lower Foxdale
Crosby
MANX CROSSES
Dalby Pt.
Glen Vine
Strang
Onchan
HEYSHAM 3:30
Dalby
Tromode
GROUDLE GLEN RAILWAY
Niarbyl
Foxdale
Union Mills
ONCHAN PLEASURE PARK
HEYSHAM 2:00 (Summer Only)
Eairy
Braaid
Spring Valley
Douglas
Niarbyl Bay
483 SOUTH BARRULE
222
Cooil
Douglas Bay
Close Clark
Ellenbrook
Douglas Head
CAMERA OBSCURA
Ballamodha
St Mark's
Newtown
Ballaveare
LIVERPOOL 2:30
Ronague
Little Ness
Lingague
Grenaby
ISLE OF MAN STEAM RAILWAY
LIVERPOOL 4:00 (Winter Only)
Fleshwick Bay
Surby
Santon Head
Bradda Head
Bradda
Colby
Ballabeg
RUSHEN ABBEY
Ballasalla
Port Erin
Port Greenaugh
RAILWAY MUS.
BILLOWN
ISLE OF MAN
The Howe
Four Roads
Castletown
Derbyhaven
CASTLE RUSHEN
NAUTICAL MUS.
Cregneash
SCARLETT VISITOR CENTRE
St Michael's I.
Port St Mary
OLD HOUSE OF KEYS
CREGNEASH VILLAGE FOLK MUSEUM
128
Scarlett Point
Dreswick Pt.
Spanish Head
Calf of Man
Chicken Rock
BELFAST 2:45
DUBLIN 2:45
(April-Sept)
0 1 2 3 4 5 6 miles
0 1 2 3 4 5 6 7 8 9 10 km

WAXWORKS
CYBERDOME CRYSTAL MAZE
South Shore
BLACKPOOL PLEASURE BEACH
Hawes Side
Mereside
Common Edge
Little Plumpton
Great Plumpton
Westby
Wesham
Kirkham
Dowbridge
Squires Gate
BLACKPOOL
Moss Side
Wrea Green
Newton
Scales
TOY AND TEDDY BEAR MUSEUM
ROYAL LYTHAM & ST. ANNES
Ansdell
LYTHAM HALL
St Annes
Lytham St Anne's
Lytham
Fairhaven
Salters Bank
Warton
Freckleton
A584
Ribble
Banks Sands
Great Bank
RIBBLE MARSHES
Hesketh Bank
Becconsall
Hundred End
Banks
Tarleton
Horse Bank
Crossens
Marshside
Southport
PLEASURELAND
NEW MODEL VILLAGE
Churchtown
Mere Brow
Holmeswood
B5246
Blowick
Birkdale
Brown Edge
MARTIN MERE WILDFOWL AND WETLAND CENTRE
Rufford
Snape Green
Bescar
New Lane
Hillside
ROYAL BIRKDALE
Scarisbrick
Shirdley Hill
Ainsdale-on-Sea
Ainsdale
Pinfold
Burscough
Burscough Bridge
Woodvale
Halsall
Formby Hills
AINSDALE SAND DUNES
Barton
Haskayne
ORMSKIRK
Freshfield
Formby
Downholland Cross
Westhead
Formby Pt.
Little Altcar
Great Altcar
B5195
Aughton Park
Blaguegate
CABIN HILL
Stanley Gate
Hightown
Ince Blundell
Lydiate
Aughton
Royal Oak
Bickerstaffe
Maghull
Barrow Nook
Lunt
Little Crosby
Melling Mount
Sefton
Thornton
Netherton
Melling
Great Crosby
Kirkby
I R I S H S E A
SD
LIVERPOOL BAY
SJ
BELFAST 8:00
DOUGLAS 4:00 (Winter only)
DUBLIN 7:45
DOUGLAS 2:30
Crosby Channel
LITHERLAND
Aintree
AINTREE
Southdene
Waterloo
Seaforth
Orrell
Fazakerley
Knowsley
Bootle
New Brighton
Walton
Norris Green
CROXTETH
Merseyside
Kirkdale
Anfield
West Derby
Mockbeggar Wharf
Liscard
Egremont
Longview
Wallasey
HISTORIC WARSHIPS
Everton
LIVERPOOL
Knotty Ash
Huyton
Leasowe
Seacombe
MARITIME MUS.
Roby
Meols
Moreton
Poulton
Bidston
HOYLAKE
Edge Hill
Childwall
West Hoyle Bank
Upton
Claughton
TATE
Wavertree
Netherley
Hilbre I.
Greasby
Birkenhead
ALBERT DOCK
Toxteth
Mossley Hill
Gateacre
Grange
Woodchurch
Rock Ferry
Dingle
MENDIPS
West Kirby
Frankby
Tranmere
SUDLEY
Allerton
Woolton
Welsh Channel
ARROWE
Prenton
New Ferry
Aigburth
HALEWOOD
Point of Ayr
Yr Parlwr Du
River Dee
Afon Dyfrdwy
PORT SUNLIGHT HERITAGE CENTRE
LADY LEVER ART GALLERY
Grassendale
Hunt's Cross
Talacre
Caldy
Irby
Thingwall
BEBINGTON
Storeton
Port Sunlight
Thurstaston
Gwespyr
Pensby
Barnston
Garston
Gronant
WIRRAL
Brimstage
SPEKE HALL
Speke
Prestatyn
Ffynnongroyw
Picton
Bromborough
Gwaenysgor
Llanasa
Heswall
EASTHAM
Eastham Ferry
LIVERPOOL JOHN LENNON
Liverpool Airport
OFFA'S DYKE PATH
LLWYBR CLAWDD OFFA
Mostyn
Mostyn Quay
Dawpool Bank
Thornton Hough
Axton
Trelogan
Gayton
Eastham
Trelawnyd
Raby
Mersey
Parkgate
Hinderton
Willaston
Hooton
Ellesmere Port
Ince Banks
GREENFIELD VALLEY HERITAGE PARK
Holywell Bank
Gayton Sands
Neston
Childer Thornton
RIVACRE
BOAT MUSEUM
Walwen
Little Sutton
Overpool
Whitby
Ince
Elton
Little Neston
Ness
Gorsedd
Holywell
0 1 2 3 4 5 6 miles
0 1 2 3 4 5 6 7 8 9 10 km

Lancashire
Merseyside
Warrington
Halton
Blackburn with Darwen
Preston
Fulwood
Ribbleton
Kirkham
Wrea Green
Freckleton
Warton
Lytham
Ansdell
Banks Sands
Ribble
Ribble Marshes
Hesketh Bank
Becconsall
Hundred End
Banks
Crossens
Marshside
Churchtown
Tarleton
Bretherton
Much Hoole
Walmer Bridge
Longton
Hutton
Penwortham
Higher Penwortham
Walton-le-Dale
Bamber Bridge
Lostock Hall
Farington
Leyland
Broadfield
Euxton
Chorley
Croston
Sollom
Mere Brow
Holmeswood
Rufford
Rufford Old Hall
Martin Mere Wildfowl and Wetland Centre
Tarlscough
Eccleston
Mawdesley
Heskin Green
Bispham Green
Wrightington Bar
Parbold
Newburgh
Burscough
Burscough Bridge
Pinfold
Scarisbrick
Shirdley Hill
Halsall
Barton
Haskayne
Ormskirk
Westhead
Aughton Park
Skelmersdale
Digmoor
Orrell
Up Holland
Appley Bridge
Shevington
Standish
Coppull
Adlington
Horwich
Blackrod
Aspull
Westhoughton
Wigan
Pemberton
Ince in Makerfield
Hindley
Atherton
Tyldesley
Leigh
Bolton
Darwen
Blackburn
Turton Moor
Anglezarke Moor
White Coppice
Rivington
Belmont
Edgworth
Egerton
Maghull
Lydiate
Lunt
Sefton
Netherton
Crosby
Litherland
Aintree
Kirkby
Melling
Fazakerley
Knowsley
Knowsley Safari Park
Rainford
Billinge
St Helens
Eccleston
Haydock
Ashton-in-Makerfield
Golborne
Lowton
Newton-le-Willows
Culcheth
Glazebury
Chat Moss
Irlam
Cadishead
Partington
Prescot
Huyton
Roby
Liverpool
Everton
Toxteth
Dingle
Childwall
Woolton
Halewood
Speke
Garston
Liverpool John Lennon Airport
Hale
Widnes
Runcorn
Weston
Frodsham
Warrington
Penketh
Great Sankey
Lymm
Latchford
Stockton Heath
Appleton Thorn
Daresbury
Preston Brook
Sutton Weaver
Aston
Dutton
Lower Stretton
Arley
Great Budworth
Comberbach
Northwich
Manchester Ship Canal
Dunham Massey
Rostherne
Mere
Over Tabley
Bromborough
Eastham
Port Sunlight
New Ferry
0 1 2 3 4 5 6 miles
0 1 2 3 4 5 6 7 8 9 10 km

Padiham
Burnley
Altham
Habergham
Hapton
Rose Grove
Worsthorne
Hurstwood
Rose Hill
Lane Ends
Mereclough
Huncoat
Walk Mill
Heptonstall Moor
ACCRINGTON
Clow Bridge
Holme Chapel
Dunnockshaw
Love Clough
Forest of Rossendale
THIEVELEY PIKE
Oswaldtwistle
Baxenden
Rising Bridge
Goodshaw
Acre
Crawshawbooth
Water
Weir
Portsmouth
Cornholme
Lydgate
Whitewell Bottom
Haslingden
Lane Side
RAWTENSTALL
Greave
Bacup
Edgeside
Britannia
Bent Gate
Helmshore
Waterfoot
Nun Hills
Shawforth
Cowpe
Clough Foot
Todmorden
Shade
Walsden
Mankinholes
Walshaw Dean Res.
Widdop Res.
Wadsworth Moor
Colden
Pecket Well
Blackshaw Head
Heptonstall
Hebden Bridge
Chiserley
Wainstalls
Mytholm
Charlestown
Midgley
Mytholmroyd
Eastwood
Cragg Vale
Sowerby
Triangle
Lumb
Mill Bank
Sowerby Bridge
Ripponden
Soyland Moor
Rishworth
Rishworth Moor
Booth Wood
Denholme
Allerton
Denholme Clough
Thornton
Lidget Green
Clayton
Queensbury
Illingworth
Causeway Foot
Mountain
Mount Tabor
Ovenden
Wheatley
Luddenden
Luddenden Foot
Pellon
Halifax
Savile Park
Southowram
BRIGHOUSE
Shelf
Stone Chair
Northowram
Buttershaw
Ambler Thorn
Elland
Rastrick
Greetland
Barkisland
Stainland
Holywell Green
Sowood
Outlane
Birchencliffe
Fartown
Scapegoat Hill
Oakes
Leymoor
Golcar
Huddersfield
Lockwood
Wilberlee
Slaithwaite
Linthwaite
Netherton
Edenfield
Turn
Whitworth
Facit
Calderbrook
Stubbins
Ramsbottom
Wardle
Broadley
Healey
Littleborough
Smallbridge
Syke
Hollingworth Lake
Rakewood
Woodhey
Summerseat
Norden
Cutgate
Rochdale
Bamford
Walmersley
Limefield
Firgrove
Milnrow
Moss Moor
Bury
Walshaw
Ainsworth
HEYWOOD
Marland
Lower Place
Castleton
Haugh
Newhey
Denshaw
Marsden
Lingards Wood
Meltham
Honley
Brockholes
Netherthong
Wooldale
HOLMFIRTH
Upperthong
Burnlee
Flush House
Hepworth
Holmbridge
Holme
Redvales
Broadfield
Hopwood
Slattocks
Summit
Shaw
Bleak Hey Nook
Black Lane
Hollins
Top of Hebers
ROYTON
Heyside
Birch
Delph
Diggle
Radcliffe
Whitefield
Middleton
Long Sight
Moorside
Dobcross
Wessenden Moor
Saddleworth Moor
Kearsley
Stand
Rhodes
Chadderton Fold
Chadderton
Lees
Grasscroft
Uppermill
Greenfield
Tunstead
Oldham
PRESTWICH
Clifton
Blackley
Hathershaw
Mossley
Dove Stone Res.
Chew Res.
Swinton
Pendlebury
Crumpsall
Moston
Hollinwood
Failsworth
Broughton Park
Harpurhey
Waterloo
Ashton-under-Lyne
Hazelhurst
Charlestown
Newton Heath
SALFORD
MANCHESTER
STALYBRIDGE
Crowden
LONGDENDALE
Eccles
Droylsden
Dukinfield
Tintwistle
Hadfield
Padfield
Ardwick
Audenshaw
Trafford Park
Hulme
Old Trafford
Gorton
Newton
Mottram in Longdendale
Hollingworth
URMSTON
Stretford
Rusholme
Denton
Hyde
Godley
Broadbottom
Gamesley
Old Glossop
BLEAKLOW HILL
Levenshulme
Fallowfield
Reddish
Chorlton cum Hardy
Withington
Haughton Grn.
Gee Cross
Simmondley
GLOSSOP
Shelf Moor
HOPE FOREST
Ashton upon Mersey
SALE
West Didsbury
Heaton Moor
Woodley
Chisworth
Charlesworth
Charlestown
FEATHERBED TOP
Brooklands
Northenden
Didsbury
Bredbury
Romiley
Compstall
Chunal
Timperley
Cheadle
Cheadle Heath
Heaviley
Stepping Hill
Stockport
Marple
Marple Bridge
Little Hayfield
Wythenshawe
GATLEY
Hawk Green
Mellor
Altrincham
Hale
Halebarns
Cheadle Hulme
HAZEL GROVE
Strines
Thornsett
Birch Vale
Hayfield
KINDER SCOUT
Nether Booth
Woodhouse Park
Heald Green
Bramhall
Windlehurst
High Lane
Disley
Low Leighton
New Mills
Edale
Manchester Airport
Kitt's Moss
Newtown
Chinley Head
Barber Booth
MAM TOR
Ashley
Thorns Green
Styal
Handforth
Woodford
Poynton
Midway
LYME PARK
Furness Vale
Chinley
Chapel Milton
Malcoff
CASTLETON
New Mills
Morley Green
Hope Green
Wood Lanes
Bridgemont
Buxworth
Whaley Bridge
Whitehough
Slackhall
Perryfoot
Sparrowpit
Chapel-en-le-Frith
WILMSLOW
Dean Row
Davenport Green
Mobberley
Knolls Green
Whiteley Green
Pott Shrigley
Kettleshume
Horwich End
Taxal
Lower Crossings
Peak Forest
Knutsford
Over Knutsford
Alderley Edge
Hough
Mottram St Andrew
Prestbury
Bollington
Fernilee
Combs
Dove Holes
Peak Dale
Ollerton
Marthall
Nether Alderley
Bollington Cross
Rainow
Upper
Wheston
Tideswell
Little Hucklow
Coplow Dale
M60
M62
M66
M67
M56
M602
M65
A627(M)
A6144(M)
A56
A58
A646
A6033
A640
A62
A635
A628
A57
A6
A34
A560
A538
A523
A623
A5103
A6010
A663
A627
A6018
93
94
88
74
75

Bradford
LEEDS
PUDSEY
GARFORTH
Queensbury
Illingworth
Halifax
Sowerby Bridge
BRIGHOUSE
Elland
Cleckheaton
Liversedge
Heckmondwike
BATLEY
MORLEY
Birstall
Dewsbury
OSSETT
Rothwell
Middleton
Wakefield
Normanton
CASTLEFORD
Featherstone
Pontefract
Mirfield
Horbury
Huddersfield
Slaithwaite
Marsden
Meltham
HOLMFIRTH
Skelmanthorpe
Denby Dale
Clayton West
Darton
Royston
Barnsley
Hemsworth
Cudworth
Dodworth
Penistone
Worsbrough
Wombwell
Hoyland
Stocksbridge
Chapeltown
Sheffield
Wath upon Dearne
Swinton
Rawmarsh
Dronfield
ECKINGTON
Hathersage
Castleton
Chapel-en-le-Frith
GLOSSOP
Tideswell
Beighton
Handsworth
Kippax
Swillington
Crigglestone
Emley
Kirkburton
Honley
Netherthong
Holmbridge
Hepworth
Crowden
Langsett
Midhopestones
Deepcar
Grenoside
Ecclesfield
Oughtibridge
Bradfield
Hope
Edale
Hayfield
Chinley
Bamford
West Yorkshire
South Yorkshire
PEAK DISTRICT NATIONAL PARK
HIGH PEAK
HOPE FOREST
Midhope Moors
Howden Moors
Broomhead Moor
Bradfield Moors
Wharncliffe Wood
Wessenden Moor
1 2 3 4 5 6 miles
0 1 2 3 4 5 6 7 8 9 10km
94
95
87
75
76

Sherburn in Elmet
Little Fenton
Barlby
Selby Abbey
Osgodby
Menthorpe
The Real Aeroplane Museum
Breighton
Spaldington
Newthorpe
Steeton Hall Gateway
Selby
Lund
South Duffield
Foulness
Thorpe Willoughby
Cliffe
Wressle
North Howden
South Milford
Hambleton
Toll
East Common
Hemingbrough
Portington
Hive
Lumby
Monk Fryston
Brayton
Brind
Sedsham
Newsholme
Cavil
Sandholme
Eastrington
Scalby
Howden Minster
Gilberdyke
Hillam
Gateforth
Burn
Barlow
Long Drax
Barmby on the Marsh
Howden
Staddlethorpe
Fairburn
Selby Canal
Yorkshire Garden World
West Haddlesey
Asselby
Knedlington
Balkholme
Burton Salmon
Birkin
Chapel Haddlesey
Drax
Boothferry
Kilpin Pike
Kilpin
New Fryston
Brotherton
Temple Hirst
Camblesforth
Newland
Ouse
Laxton
Beal
Kellington
Aire
Hirst Courtney
Airmyn
Hook
Skelton
Sutton
Saltmarshe
Yokefleet
Blacktoft
Ferrybridge
Kellingley
Carlton
Goole
Ousefleet
Knottingley
Eggborough
Hensall
Sobriety Waterways Adventure Centre
Reedness
Whitgift
Black Toft RSPB
Snaith
East Cowick
Rawcliffe
Rawcliffe Bridge
Swinefleet
Little Reedness
Gowdall
Ferrybridge Services
High Eggborough
West Cowick
Old Goole
Chequerfield
Cridling Stubbs
Whitley
Great Heck
Dutch River
Adlingfleet
Southfield Reservoir
Pollington
Darrington
Womersley
Balne
Aire and Calder Navigation
Goole Fields
Fockerby
Garthorpe
East Hardwick
Went
Burton Stather
Wentbridge
Little Smeaton
Walden Stubbs
Goole Moors
Luddington
Ackworth
Sykehouse
Pincheon Green
Kirk Smeaton
Fenwick
Moorends
Humberhead Peatlands
Thorpe Audlin
Thorne Waste or Moors
Amcotts
Badsworth
Barnsdale Bar Services
Norton
Fosterhouses
Campsall
Moss
Fishlake
Wrangbrook
Upton
Instoneville
Askern
Far Bank
Thorne
Crowle
North Elmshall
Sutton
Doncaster North Services
Canal Side
Stainforth & Keadby Canal
Windsor
Burghwallis
Haywood
Braithwaite
Wike Well End
Skelbrooke
Moorthorpe
Owston
Thorpe in Balne
Kirk Bramwith
Stainforth
Ealand
Keadby
Gunness
South Elmsall
Carcroft
Hampole
Skellow
Hatfield
Hatfield Chase
Burringham
Adwick le Street
Barnby Dun
Althorpe
Hooton Pagnell
Dunscroft
Clayton
Almholme
Kirk Sandall
Hatfield Woodhouse
Sandtoft
Woodhouse
Derrythorpe
Brodsworth
Toll Bar
Woodlands
Dunsville
West End
Sandtoft Transport Centre
Grey Green
Highfields
Westgate
Belton
Beltoft
Thurnscoe
Brodsworth Hall
Arksey
Edenthorpe
Bentley
Church Town
East Butterwick
Thurnscoe East
Hickleton
Marr
Scawsby
Museum & Art Gallery
Armthorpe
Hatfield Moors
West Butterwick
Cusworth
Wheatley
Isle of Axholme
Epworth
Old Rectory
Goldthorpe
Melton Wood
Newton
Intake
Nutwell
Doncaster
Wroot
Barnburgh
Cusworth Hall Museum
Epworth Turbary
Bolton upon Dearne
Harlington
Sprotbrough
Hyde Park
Cantley
Low Burnham
Susworth
Scotter
Bessacarr
Branton
Kelfield
Adwick upon Dearne
High Melton
Balby
Lakeside Village
Auckley
Owston Ferry
Mexborough
Cadeby
Aeroventure
Lidget
Blaxton
Upperthorpe
Warmsworth
Haxey
East Lound
Denaby Main
Old Denaby
New Edlington
Loversall
Rossington
Finningley
Westwoodside
East Ferry
Laughton Forest
Conisbrough
Conisbrough/Ivanhoe
Robin Hood Airport Doncaster Sheffield
Craiselound
Wildsworth
Old Edlington
New Rossington
Laughton
Hooton Roberts
Wadworth
Idle
Thrybergh
Clifton
Ravenfield
Misson
Misterton
West Stockwith
Blyton
Micklebring
Austerfield
East Stockwith
Dalton
Braithwell
Stainton
Spital Hill
Newington
Bawtry
Walkerith
Bramley
Hellaby
Maltby
Tickhill
Harworth
Walkeringham
Morton
Gainsborough
Gringley on the Hill
Gainsborough Old Hall
Wickersley
Hooton Levitt
Bircotes
Scaftworth
Everton
Styrrup
Scrooby
Carr
Stone
Cuckoo Hill
Wiseton
Beckingham
Thurcroft
Roche Abbey
Serlby
Mattersey Thorpe
Mattersey
Firbeck
Oldcotes
Blyth Services
Ranskill
Clayworth
Saundby
Brampton en le Morthen
Laughton en le Morthen
Ulley
Langold
Blyth
Torworth
Bole
Lea
Knaith Park
Letwell
Aughton
Laughton Common
Dinnington
North Wheatley
Aston
Gildingwells
Lound
Wetlands Waterfowl Reserve
South Wheatley
Knaith
Carlton in Lindrick
Barnby Moor
Sutton
Hayton
Sturton le Steeple
North Anston
Swallownest
Todwick
Woodsetts
Kiveton Park
South Anston
Clarborough
Gate Burton
Rother Valley
Wigthorpe
North Leverton with Habblesthorpe
Wales
Bassetlaw Museum
Welham
Littleborough
Norwood
Thorpe Salvin
Gateford
West Retford
North Leverton Windmill
Marton
Killamarsh
Harthill
Netherthorpe
Shireoaks
Scofton
Ranby
Babworth
Retford
Coates
Woodall Services
Rhodesia
Kilton
Ordsall
Grove
South Leverton
Cottam
Brampton
Spinkhill
Darfoulds
Worksop
Treswell
Sundown Adventureland
Rampton
Torksey
Manton
Eaton
Barlborough
Woodbeck
Stokeham
Church Laneham
Whitwell
Hodthorpe
Headon
Upton
Fenton
Clumber Park
Gamston
Laneham
Clowne
Mastin Moor

North
Lincolnshire
Kingston-upon-Hull
KINGSTON UPON HULL
HUMBER
Humber Bridge
Scunthorpe
Goole
Gainsborough
Hotham
High Hunsley
Skidby
Cottingham
Bransholme
Sutton on Hull
Bursea
North Cave
Everthorpe
South Cave
Rowley
Little Weighton
SKIDBY WINDMILL
Inglemire
Sutton Ings
Stoneferry
Summergangs
WILBERFORCE HOUSE
Marfleet
STREETLIFE
Newland
Sculcoates
Epplewordth
Riplingham
West End
YORKSHIRE WOLDS WAY
Kirk Ella
Willerby
East Ella
West Ella
Anlaby
Northfield
Hessle
FERENS ART GALLERY
HUMBER BRIDGE
Swanland
Welton
Brantingham
Ellerker
Elloughton
Brough
North Ferriby
Portington
Hive
Cavil
Eastrington
Sandholme
Scalby
Newport
Gilberdyke
Staddlethorpe
Howden
North Howden
Kilpin
Kilpin Pike
Balkholme
Broomfleet
Market Weighton Canal
Foulness
Laxton
Skelton
Hook
Saltmarshe
Yokefleet
Blacktoft
Faxfleet
Whitton
Redcliff Channel
Read's Island
WATERS EDGE
Barton Waterside
ST PETER'S CHURCH
FAR INGS
Barton-upon-Humber
New Holland
Goxhill Haven
Barrow Haven
Goxhill
Ousefleet
BLACKTOFT SANDS RSPB
Reedness
Swinefleet
Whitgift
Little Reedness
JULIAN'S BOWER
Alkborough
Winteringham
West Halton
Walcot
Adlingfleet
Old Goole
Goole Fields
Goole Moors
Fockerby
Garthorpe
Coleby
Winterton
South Ferriby
BAYSGARTH HO. MUS.
Barrow upon Humber
South End
East Halton
THORNTON ABBEY
Kingsforth
Horkstow
Burton Stather
Burton upon Stather
Thealby
NORMANBY HALL
Normanby
Roxby
Saxby All Saints
Burnham
Thornton Curtis
North Killingholme
Wootton
Luddington
Eastoft
New River Ancholme
Flixborough
Flixborough Stather
Amcotts
Appleby
Bonby
Ulceby
Ulceby Skitter
Habrough
Dragonby
Worlaby
Crowle
Windsor
Ealand
Keadby
Gunness
Crosby
Frodingham
Santon
ELSHAM HALL
Elsham
Croxton
Kirmington
Brocklesby
Melton Ross
New Barnetby
HUMBERSIDE INTERNATIONAL
Barnetby le Wold
Althorpe
Burringham
Brumby
Wressle
Woodhouse
SANDTOFT TRANSPORT CENTRE
Derrythorpe
Grey Green
Westgate
Ashby
Broughton
Wrawby
Brigg
Great Limber
Yaddlethorpe
Bottesford
Bigby
Church Town
Belton
Beltoft
East Butterwick
West Butterwick
Mill Place
Scawby
Somerby
Searby
Owmby
Grasby
Clixby
ISLE OF AXHOLME
Epworth
OLD RECTORY
Messingham
Sturton
Howsham
Epworth Turbary
Low Burnham
Manton
Cadney
North Kelsey Moor
Cabourne
Susworth
Scotterthorpe
GAINSTHORPE DESERTED MEDIEVAL VILLAGE
Hibaldstow
Caistor
Kelfield
Owston Ferry
Scotter
North Kelsey
Nettleton
Upperthorpe
Haxey
Westwoodside
East Lound
Laughton Forest
Scotton
Kirton in Lindsey
Redbourne
Moortown
South Kelsey
Craiselound
East Ferry
Wildsworth
Laughton
Northorpe
Holton le Moor
Waddingham
Brandy Wharf
Thornton le Moor
Grayingham
Blyton
Misterton
West Stockwith
East Stockwith
Blyborough
Snitterby
North Owersby
Claxby
Normanby le Wold
Pilham
Aisby
Willoughton
South Owersby
Usselby
Kingerby
Osgodby
Atterby
Walkeringham
Morton
Gringley on the Hill
GAINSBOROUGH OLD HALL
Corringham
Hemswell
Bishop Norton
Kirkby
Bishopbridge
Walesby
Spital in the Street
Glentham
West Rasen
Middle Rasen
Market Rasen
Beckingham
Springthorpe
Harpswell
Hemswell Cliff
Caenby Corner
Caenby
Normanby-by-Spital
Toft next Newton
MARKET RASEN
Saundby
Heapham
Glentworth
Newton by Toft
Bole
Lea
Upton
Ownby-by-Spital
North Wheatley
Knaith Park
Kexby
Saxby
Linwood
Legsby
Fillingham
Buslingthorpe
South Wheatley
Sturton le Steeple
Knaith
Willingham by Stow
Spridlington
Faldingworth
Bleasby
Harborough
Gate Burton
Normanby by Stow
Ingham
Cold Hanworth
Friesthorpe
East Torrington
North Leverton with Habblesthorpe
Littleborough
Lissington
West Torrington
NORTH LEVERTON WINDMILL
Marton
Stow
Cammeringham
Hackthorn
Snarford
Wickenby
Thorpe in the Fallows
Holton cum Beckering
Coates
Welton Hill
REDHURST B&B
South Leverton
Sturton by Stow
Brattleby
DAMBUSTERS INN & HERITAGE CENTRE
Aisthorpe
Welton
Snelland
Scampton
Fulnetby
Treswell
Cottam
Dunholme
Rand
RAND FARM PARK
Wragby
Bransby
Broxholme
Stainton by Langworth
Ingleby
North Carlton
Scothern
Bullington
Upton
Saxilby
South Carlton
Sudbrooke
Langworth
Laneham
SE
SK
0 1 2 3 4 5 6 miles
0 1 2 3 4 5 6 7 8 9 10km

Thirtleby
Sproatley
Humbleton
Fitling
Hilston
Ganstead
Bilton
Lelley
Elstronwick
Owstwick
Tunstall
Preston
Burton Pidsea
North End
Roos
West End
Salt End
Waxholme
Owthorne
Hedon
Haven Side
Rimswell
Withernsea
Burstwick
Halsham
East End
Paull
Thorngumbald
Camerton
FORT PAULL
Ryehill
Keyingham
Ottringham
Hollym
Little Humber
Winestead
Holmpton
Thorney Crofts
Patrington
Out Newton
Cherry Cob Sands
TA
Welwick
Weeton
Sunk Island
Skeffling
Easington
Kilnsea
SPURN
SPURN HEAD
ROTTERDAM 12:30
ZEEBRUGGE 12:45
ROTTERDAM
ZEEBRUGGE
HOEK VAN HOLLAND 13:00
OOSTENDE 15:00
MOUTH OF THE HUMBER
BREVIK 33:00
CUXHAVEN 22:00
ESBJERG 22:00
GOTHENBURG 26:00
KRISTIANSAND 30:00
ROTTERDAM 11:45
ZEEBRUGGE 14:00
South Killingholme
Immingham
MUSEUM
Stallingborough
Pyewipe
Grimsby
Healing
West Marsh
Keelby
Great Coates
CLEETHORPES
NATIONAL FISHING HERITAGE CENTRE
Old Clee
Riby Cross Roads
Aylesby
CLEETHORPES COAST LIGHT RAILWAY
Riby
Laceby
Nunsthorpe
PLEASURE ISLAND THEME PARK
Bradley
Scartho
CLEETHORPES
Humberston
North East Lincolnshire
Irby upon Humber
Waltham
New Waltham
Barnoldby le Beck
WALTHAM WINDMILL
Holton le Clay
Swallow
Tetney Lock
Beelsby
Brigsley
Ashby cum Fenby
North Cotes
Cuxwold
Hatcliffe
Tetney
Waithe
East Ravendale
Grainsby
Marshchapel
Donna Nook
Rothwell
Croxby
North Thoresby
Eskham
Wragholme
Thoresway
Thorganby
Grainthorpe
Wold Newton
Fulstow
North Somercotes
Swinhope
DONNA NOOK
LINCOLNSHIRE WOLDS RLY
Skidbrooke North End
Brookenby
Ludborough
Covenham St Bartholomew
Conisholme
Stainton le Vale
Binbrook
TF
Covenham St Mary
South Somercotes
Saltfleet
Utterby
North Ormsby
Yarburgh
Skidbrooke
Kirmond le Mire
ALVINGHAM POTTERY AND CRAFTS
Alvingham
Fotherby
Saltfleetby St Clements
Little Grimsby
SALTFLEETBY THEDDLETHORPE
North Elkington
North Cockerington
Tealby
Great Tows
Kelstern
RUSHMOOR
Saltfleetby All Saints
Theddlethorpe St Helen
North Willingham
Ludford
South Elkington
South Cockerington
Saltfleetby St Peter
Keddington
Grimoldby
Welton le Wold
Louth
Theddlethorpe All Saints
Burgh on Bain
Stewton
Manby
SEAL SANCTUARY & NATURE CENTRE
Sixhills
ST JAMES
Grimblethorpe
Little Carlton
Meers Bridge
Gayton le Wold
Hallington
Great Carlton
Mablethorpe
Hainton
Biscathorpe
Legbourne
South Willingham
Raithby
South Reston
Gayton le Marsh
Trusthorpe
Donington on Bain
Little Cawthorpe
North Reston
Withcall
Strubby
Thorpe
Sutton on Sea
Tathwell
Benniworth
Withern
Maltby le Marsh
Haugham
Muckton
Tothill
Beesby
Sandilands
East Barkwith
CADWELL PARK
Stenigot
Authorpe
Market Stainton
West Barkwith
Cawkwell
Woodthorpe
Maidenwell
Burwell
Hannah
Sotby
Saleby
WOODY'S TOP
CLAYTHORPE WATER MILL AND WILDFOWL GARDENS
Markby
Panton
Goulceby
Belleau
Ranby
Scamblesby
Ruckland
Farforth
Aby
White Pit
Swaby
Asserby
Oxcombe
ALFORD WINDMILL
Hatton
Ketsby
South Thoresby
Bilsby
Huttoft
ALFORD MANOR HOUSE
Great Sturton
Belchford
South Ormsby
Rigsby
Alford
LINCOLNSHIRE WOLDS
A1033
B1362
B1242
B1239
B1240
B1238
A1033
B1445
A160
A180
A180
B1213
A46
A1098
B1219
A16
A18
A1173
A46
B1203
A1031
B1201
A16
A1031
B1203
A631
B1200
A157
A153
A157
A16
A1104
A157
B1373
B1225
A1111
A52
B1449
97
78
79

Green
The Hill
Whicham
Millom
MILLOM FOLK MUSEUM
Haverigg
DUDDON ESTUARY
DUDDON SANDS
Kirkby-in-Furness
Beck Side
Soutergate
Askam in Furness
Ireleth
Lindal in Furness
Gawthwaite
Bridge
Penny Bridge
Broughton Beck
Greenodd
Arrad Foot
Mansriggs
Backbarrow
ARTCRYSTAL
Haverthwaite
Ayside
Witherslack
High Newton
Low Newton
Mill Side
Town End
Field Broughton
Meathop
Lindale
ROUDSEA WOOD AND MOSSES
LAUREL & HARDY MUS.
Ulverston
Pennington
Swarthmoor
CONISHEAD PRIORY & BUDDHIST TEMPLE
CARTMEL PRIORY
Cartmel
Holker
Allithwaite
Grange-over-Sands
Cark
Flookburgh
Kents Bank
Ravenstown
LAKELAND RIDING CENTRE
Cartmel Sands
Humphrey Head Pt.
SANDSCALE HAWS
SOUTH LAKES WILD ANIMAL PARK
Dalton-in-Furness
DALTON CASTLE
Great Urswick
Little Urswick
Stainton with Adgarley
Bardsea
Scales
Baycliff
NORTH WALNEY
WALNEY ISLAND
Hawcoat
BOW BRIDGE
Ormsgill
Newton
FURNESS ABBEY
Newbarns
Dendron
GLEASTON WATERMILL
Gleaston
Aldingham
Barrow-in-Furness
Yarlside
CUSTOM HO.
Newbiggin
Leece
North Scale
THE DOCK MUSEUM
Vickerstown
Barrow Island
Roosebeck
Biggar
Rampside
Roa Island
Foulney Island
Piel Island
South End
Isle of Walney
South End Point
South Channel
MORECAMBE
BAY
Crooklands
Leasgill
Heversham
Milnthorpe
Farleton
Storth
HERON CORN MILL
Beetham
Holme
ARNSIDE
Arnside
LAKELAND WILDLIFE OASIS
GAIT BARROWS
Clawthorpe
Yealand Redmayne
Burton-in-Kendal
BURTON-IN-KENDAL (Northbound Only)
ARNSIDE AND SILVERDALE
Silverdale
Yealand Conyers
LEIGHTON HALL
Priest Hutton
Warton Sands
Warton
Borwick
Capernwray
OLD RECTORY
Millhead
Carnforth
Over Kellet
Nether Kellet
Bolton le Sands
Aughton
Hest Bank
Bolton Town End
Slyne
Halton
Caton Green
Caton
Morecambe
Bare
Torrisholme
Skerton
Sandylands
MARITIME MUS.
White Lund
Heysham
Lancaster
ASHTON MEMORIAL
PRIORY CHURCH
CITY
Aldcliffe
Heaton
LEISURE PARK
Scotforth
Middleton
Overton
Quernmore
DOUGLAS 3:30
DOUGLAS 2:00 (Summer Only)
BELFAST 9:00
DUBLIN 9:00
LARNE 8:00
Glasson
Conder Green
Sunderland Pt.
Shoulder of Lune
Lune
Galgate
Smith Green
Thurnham
Ortner
Dolphinholme
LANCASTER (FORTON) SERVICES
Cockerham Sands
Cockerham
Braides
Forton
Street
Hollins Lane
Knott End-on-Sea
Dam Side
Pilling Lane
Pilling
Stake Pool
Winmarleigh
Scorton
Fleetwood
Rossall Point
Preesall
FREEPORT, FLEETWOOD
Cabus
Oakenclough
Eagland Hill
Garstang
GARSTANG DISCOVERY CENTRE
Calder Vale
SD
Stalmine
Staynall
Wyre
Nateby
Bowgreave
MARSH MILL-IN-WYRE
WYRE ESTUARY
Cleveleys
Trunnah
Hambleton
Churchtown
Catterall
Out Rawcliffe
Moss Edge
Ratten Row
Claughton
Anchorsholme
Thornton
Norbreck
Little Eccleston
TOLL
St Michael's on Wyre
Inglewhite
Bispham
Skippool
Carleton
Little Singleton
Great Eccleston
Bilsborrow
Blackpool
Warbreck
Poulton-le-Fylde
Singleton
Elswick
Myerscough
Crossmoor
North Shore
Thistleton
Inskip
Cuddy Hill
Queenstown
Normoss
Esprick
Roseacre
Barton
Blackpool
Layton
Staining
BLACKPOOL TOWER
SEA LIFE CENTRE
LOUIS TUSSAUD'S WAXWORKS
ZOO PARK
Great Marton
L a n c a
Corner Row
Catforth
Wharles
CATFORTH GARDENS
Woodplumpton
Broughton
Weeton
CYBERDOME CRYSTAL MAZE
Hawes Side
Mereside
Great Plumpton
South Shore
BLACKPOOL PLEASURE BEACH
Common Edge
Little Plumpton
Wesham
Treales
Lower Bartle
Higher Bartle
Cottam
Sharoe Green
Fulwood
Kirkham
Westby
Dowbridge
Lea Town
Ingol
Cadley
Squires Gate
BLACKPOOL
Moss Side
Wrea Green
Newton
Scales
Clifton
Higher Ballam
TOY AND TEDDY BEAR MUSEUM
ROYAL LYTHAM ST. ANNES
LYTHAM HALL
Preston
Freckleton
St Annes
Lytham St Anne's
Ansdell
Lytham
Warton
Bottom of Hutton
Higher Penwortham
Middleforth Green
Fairhaven
Salters Bank
Ribble
Hutton
Longton
Lostock
Lancaster Canal
98
99
85
86
0 1 2 3 4 5 6 miles
0 1 2 3 4 5 6 7 8 9 10 km

YORKSHIRE DALES NATIONAL PARK
FOREST OF BOWLAND
Deepdale
Old Town
Barbon
Mansergh
Lupton
Kearstwick
Casterton
Kirkby Lonsdale
Hutton Roof
Whittington
Cowan Bridge
Nether Burrow
Newton
Leck
Ireby
Masongill
Westhouse
Ingleton
Tunstall
Cantsfield
Arkholme
Melling
Wrayton
Burton in Lonsdale
Low Bentham
BENTHAM POTTERY
Tatham
Wennington
Hornby
High Bentham
Wray
Farleton
Claughton
Caton Moor
Salter
Goodber Common
Lowgill
Tatham Fells
Burn Moor
Crossgill
Haylot Fell
Mallowdale Fell
WARD'S STONE
WHITE HILL
Lee Fell
Tarnbrook Fell
Croasdale Fell
Tarnbrook
Lee
Abbeystead
Trough of Bowland
WHINS BROW
Marshaw
Hawthornthwaite Fell
FELL TOP
Sykes
Hareden
Sykes Fell
Dunsop Bridge
Bleasdale Moors
FAIR SNAPE FELL
Whitewell
Bleasdale
Cow Ark
LEAGRAM GARDENS
BEACON FELL
Chipping
Hodder
Bashall Eaves
Walker Fold
Whitechapel
Hesketh Lane
Longridge Fell
Knowle Green
New Row
Longridge
Goosnargh
ST SAVIOUR'S CHURCH
Little Town
Ribchester
MUS. OF CHILDHOOD
ROMAN MUSEUM
Grimsargh
Balderstone
Salesbury
Ribbleton
SAMLESBURY HALL
Samlesbury
Osbaldeston
Mellor Brook
Mellor
Samlesbury Bottoms
COUNTY AND REGIMENTAL MUS.
Walton-le-Dale
Higher Walton
Coup Green
HOGHTON TOWER
Bamber Bridge
Gregson Lane
Hoghton
Pleasington
Riley Green
Feniscowles
Blackburn
Pleckgate
Wilpshire
Brownhill
Rishton
Great Harwood
Clayton-le-Moors
Church
Accrington
Oswaldtwistle
Dunnockshaw
Love Clough
Baxenden
Rising Bridge
Shadsworth
Guide
Lower Darwen
West End
Scaitcliffe
Milnshaw
Huncoat
Altham
Read
Simonstone
Padiham
Hapton
Habergham
Rose Grove
Rose Hill
Burnley
Brunshaw
Worsthorne
Hurstwood
Mereclough
Lane Ends
TOWNELEY HALL ART GALL. & MUS.
Clow Bridge
Holme Chapel
Forest of Rossendale
GOODSHAW CHAPEL
Goodshaw
Water
THIEVELEY PIKE
Portsmouth
Cornholme
Lydgate
Charles
Blackshaw Head
Heptonstall Moor
Widdop Res.
Walshaw Dean Res.
BOULSWORTH HILL
THE FOREST OF TRAWDEN
Trawden
HOLLIN HALL SEWING CENTRE
WYCOLLER
Wycoller
Winewall
Laneshaw Bridge
Colne
BRITISH IN INDIA MUS.
Nelson
Little Marsden
Brierfield
Haggate
Harle Syke
Burnley Lane
Higham
Fence
THE FOREST OF PENDLE
TRAPP FORGE
GAWTHORPE HALL
Sabden
Wiswell
Whalley
WHALLEY ABBEY
Billington
Langho
Old Langho
Copster Green
Hurst Green
Great Mitton
Barrow
Pendleton
Worston
Clitheroe
CLITHEROE CASTLE MUSEUM
Low Moor
Waddington
Chatburn
Downham
PENDLE HILL
Barley
Roughlee
PENDLE HERITAGE CENTRE
Newchurch
Barrowford
Blacko
Colne Edge
Foulridge
Kelbrook
Salterforth
Barnoldswick
Coates
Earby
Thornton in Craven
Elslack
West Marton
East Marton
Broughton
PENNINE WAY
Gargrave
Bank Newton
Coniston Cold
Eshton
Flasby
Bell Busk
Hetton
Winterburn
Calton
Airton
Otterburn
Hellifield
Long Preston
HORSES HEALTH FARM
Rathmell
Wigglesworth
Tosside
Grunsagill
Knotts
Halton West
Nappa
Newsholme
Paythorne
Horton
Bracewell
Gisburn
Lane End
Rimington
Newby
Twiston
Sawley
ABBEY
Grindleton
West Bradford
Holden
Bolton-by-Bowland
Forest Becks
Lane Ends
Easington Fell
Newton
Slaidburn
Stocks Reservoir
Gisburn Forest
Catlow Fell
SD
Mearbeck
Wham
Settle
Giggleswick
GIGGLESWICK SCHOOL CHAPEL
Langcliffe
Stackhouse
WATERSHED MILL VISITOR CENTRE
Stainforth
Little Stainforth
THE SETTLE LOOP
MALHAM TARN
Malham Tarn
MALHAM COVE
KIRKBY FELL
Malham
Hanlith
Kirkby Malham
Bordley
NEW HOUSE FARM, MALHAM
Eldroth
YORKSHIRE DALES FALCONRY AND CONSERVATION CENTRE
Lawkland
Keasden
Mewith Head
Wenning
Austwick
Feizor
Clapham
Newby
Wharfe
Helwith Bridge
INGLEBOROUGH SHOW CAVE
GAPING GILL
Ingleborough Common
WHITE SCAR CAVES
SIMON FELL
INGLEBOROUGH
Chapel-le-Dale
Scales Moor
LECK FELL
CRAG HILL
Whernside
Blea Moor
Gayle Moor
Ribblehead
Cam Fell
Cam Beck
High Birkwith
Horton Moor
New Houses
Horton in Ribblesdale
PEN-Y-GHENT
FOUNTAINS FELL
Darnbrook Fell
Oughtershaw
LANGSTROTHDALE CHASE
Yockenthwaite
Hubberholme
Foxup
Halton Gill
Cragdale Moor
MIDDLE TONGUE
Cray
Buckden
Litton
Littondale
Skirfare
Wharfe
SCOSKA WOOD
Arncliffe
Kettlewell
Hawkswick
KILNSEY PARK
Ribble
RIBBLESDALE
Lune
DOCKER PARK FARM
A65
A683
A687
A682
A59
A56
A666
A671
A680
A678
A679
A6068
A646
B6479
B6480
B6478
B6255
B6254
B6243
B6245
B6246
B6230
B6231
B6160
B6251
B6252
B6383
M65
M6

YORKSHIRE
DALES
NATIONAL
PARK
NIDDERDALE
North
SD
SE
Cragdale Moor
Oughtershaw
MIDDLE TONGUE
Kidstones
Walden Head
Carlton Moor
Walden
Gammersgill
West Scrafton
Horsehouse
Coverdale
Braidley
Woodale
Hindlethwaite Moor
Colsterdale Moor
Colsterdale
Ellingstring
High Ellington
Low Ellington
Low Burton
Masham
UREDALE GLASS
THEAKSTON BREWERY VISITOR CENTRE
Healey
Fearby
Swinton
Leighton
Warthermarske
Leighton Res.
Ilton
Roundhill Res.
Grewelthorpe
Kirkby Malzeard
Yockenthwaite
Hubberholme
Cray
BUCKDEN PIKE
Buckden
GREAT HAW
Masham Moor
LITTLE WHERNSIDE
Scar House Res.
Angram Res.
Foxup
Halton Gill
Starbotton
Litton
Littondale
SCOSKA WOOD
KETTLEWELL
GREAT WHERNSIDE
Kettlewell
Riggs Moor
Middlesmoor
Stean
Lofthouse
HAMBLETON HILL
Carlesmoor
Swetton
Laverton
Greygarth
Dallowgill Moor
Dallow
Low Grantley
Grantley
Darnbrook Fell
FOUNTAINS FELL
PENNINE WAY
Arncliffe
Hawkswick
Conistone Moor
Stean Moor
Ramsgill
Bouthwaite
Gouthwaite Res.
Heathfield Moor
Wath
Pateley Moor
Eavestone
Risplith
Sawley
Malham Tarn
MALHAM TARN
THE SETTLE LOOP
Kilnsey
KILNSEY PARK
Conistone
Hebden Moor
Grimwith Res.
NIDDERDALE MUSEUM
Pateley Bridge
Bewerley
Glasshouses
Wilsill
BRIMHAM ROCKS
MALHAM COVE
KIRKBY FELL
MALHAM
Malham
Bordley
NEW HOUSE FARM, MALHAM
Threshfield
Grassington
UPPER WHARFEDALE MUSEUM
Linton
Hebden
Greenhow Hill
STUMP CROSS CAVERNS
Low Laithe
New York
Dacre Banks
Summer Bridge
Hanlith
Kirkby Malham
Threapland
Thorpe
Burnsall
PARCEVALL HALL GARDENS
Skyreholme
Pockstones Moor
Dacre
Airton
Calton
Winterburn
Hetton
Cracoe
Rylstone
Upper Barden Res.
Appletreewick
Drebley
Barden Fell
Padside
Darley Head
Darley
Birstwith
Thruscross Res.
Thornthwaite
Otterburn
Hellifield
Bell Busk
Flasby
Eshton
Barden Scale
West End
Kettlesing Bottom
Lower Barden Res.
BOLTON ABBEY ESTATE
Bolton Abbey
Hill End
Blubberhouses
Kettlesing Head
Coniston Cold
Gargrave
Eastby
Embsay
EMBSAY STEAM RAILWAY
Halton East
Pace Gate
Fewston
Fewston Res.
Swinsty Res.
BUFFERS
Hazlewood
Timble
Bland Hill
Jack Hill
Halton West
Bank Newton
Nappa
Thorlby
Broughton
East Marton
Newsholme
Horton
West Marton
Skipton
Draughton
Bolton Bridge
Beamsley
Langbar
Addingham
Carleton
Elslack
Middleton
Denton
Lindley Wood Res.
Lindley Green
Bracewell
Thornton in Craven
Low Bradley
Cringles
Askwith
Clifton
Farnley
Lane End
Coates
Barnoldswick
Earby
EARBY
Cononley
Farnhill
Kildwick
Silsden
ILKLEY
Weston
Newall
Otley
ROMBALDS MOOR
Ilkley Moor
Burley in Wharfedale
Salterforth
Kelbrook
Lothersdale
Glusburn
Eastburn
Steeton
Lane Ends
Cowling
Sutton-in-Craven
New Road Side
Menston
CHEVIN FOREST
East Carlton
Pool
Guiseley
Yeadon
CLIFFE CASTLE
Riddlesden
EAST RIDDLESDEN HALL
East Morton
Micklethwaite
Hawksworth
Foulridge
Blacko
Roughlee
Colne Edge
Keighley
Braithwaite
Laycock
Knowle Park
Thwaites
Crossflatts
Eldwick
BRACKEN HALL COUNTRYSIDE CENTRE
Baildon
Esholt
Rawdon
Barrowford
COLNE
Laneshaw Bridge
Winewall
Wycoller
WYCOLLER
KEIGHLEY MOOR
Goose Eye
Exley Head
Oakworth
Thwaites Brow
VINTAGE RAILWAY CARRIAGE MUS.
Ingrow
BINGLEY
1853 GALLERY
Saltaire
Apperley Bridge
Horsforth
Trawden
HOLLIN HALL SEWING CENTRE
BRITISH IN INDIA MUS.
NELSON
Little Marsden
THE FOREST OF TRAWDEN
Dockroyd
BRONTE PARSONAGE MUS.
Lees
HAWORTH
Haworth
Harden
Cullingworth
Cottingley
Wilsden
SHIPLEY
Idle
Calverley
Rodley
Brierfield
Stanbury
PENISTONE HILL
Marsh
Haworth Moor
KEIGHLEY AND WORTH VALLEY RAILWAY
Oxenhope
Lingbob
Moorhead
Frizinghall
Eccleshill
CARTWRIGHT HALL ART GALLERY
Heaton
Manningham
BRADFORD IND. MUS.
Undercliffe
Thornbury
Farsley
Bramley
Stanningley
Haggate
Harle Syke
Burnley Lane
BOULSWORTH HILL
PENNINE WAY
Walshaw Dean Res.
Wadsworth Moor
Denholme
Denholme Well Heads
Allerton
Bradford
CATH.
COLOUR MUS.
Laisterdyke
Swinnow Moor
PUDSEY
Burnley
Brunshaw
Worsthorne
WEAVERS TRIANGLE
Walk Mill
Hurstwood
Mereclough
Widdop Res.
Warley Moor Res.
Denholme Clough
Thornton
Lidget Green
Clayton
Great Horton
Little Horton
Bowling
West Bowling
Holme Wood
New Farnley
TOWNELEY HALL ART GALL. & MUS.
Heptonstall Moor
Dean Head Res.
Causeway Foot
Mountain
NAT. MUS. OF PHOTOGRAPHY
BOLLING HALL
Tong
Holme Chapel
Colden
Pecket Well
Queensbury
Illingworth
Ambler Thorn
Butterfield
Wibsey
Bierley
Drighlington
Gildersome
AUTOMOBILIA
Chiserley
Wainstalls
Shelf
Low Moor
Birkenshaw
Adwalton
Hebden Bridge
Mount Tabor
Booth
Ovenden
Stone Chair
Oakenshaw
BANKFIELD MUSEUM
Northowram
SHIBDEN HALL
Wyke
OAKWELL HALL
RED HOUSE
Birstall
Portsmouth
Lydgate
WALKLEY CLOGS
Mytholmroyd
Midgley
Wheatley
Luddenden
Halifax
Scholes
Gomersal
BAGSHAW MUS.
Water
0 1 2 3 4 5 6 miles
0 1 2 3 4 5 6 7 8 9 10 km

Yorkshire
City of York
SE
Snape
Carthorpe
Pickhill
Holme
Sinderby
Sandhutton
Ainderby Quernhow
Kirklington
Nosterfield
Thornborough
Sutton Howgrave
Middleton Quernham
Baldersby
Skipton-on-Swale
Catton
Topcliffe
Asenby
Baldersby St James
Melmerby
Wath
North Stainley
Lightwater Valley
Sutton Grange
Norton Conyers
Nunwick
Rainton
Hutton Conyers
Azerley
Galphay
Ure Bank
Sharow
Ripon
Ripon Cathedral
Copt Hewick
Bridge Hewick
Marton-le-Moor
Winksley
Bishopton
Studley Roger
Littlethorpe
Studley Royal Water Gdns
Fountains Abbey
Skelton-on-Ure
Newby Hall
Park Hill
Langthorpe
Boroughbridge
Aldborough
Aldborough Roman Town
Roecliffe
Bishop Monkton
Markington
Minskip
Wormald Green
Burton Leonard
Copgrove
Bishop Thornton
South Stainley
Staveley
Bedlam
Brearton
Farnham
Ferrensby
Ripley
Ripley Castle
Nidd
Scotton
Scriven
Killinghall
Knaresborough
Knaresborough Castle & Mus.
Mother Shipton's Cave
New Park
Starbeck
Forest Lane Head
Woodlands
Mercer Art Gallery
Harrogate
RHS Garden Harlow Carr
Harlow Hill
Oatlands
Pannal
Rossett Green
Follifoot
Spofforth Castle
Spofforth
Spacey Houses
North Rigton
Kirby Overblow
Sicklinghall
Huby
Weeton
Netherby
Dunkeswick
Castley
Arthington
Harewood
Harewood House
Weardley
East Keswick
Bramhope
Bardsey
East Rigton
Eccup
Wike
Scarcroft
Scarcroft Hill
Thorner
Shadwell
Alwoodley
Moor Allerton
Adel
Holt Park
Roundhay
Chapel Allerton
Meanwood
Headingley
Potternewton
Harehills
Seacroft
Woodhouse
Kirkstall
Burley
Sheepscar
Whitkirk
Manston
Armley
Leeds
Halton
Colton
Wortley
Holbeck
Hunslet
Beeston
Thwaite Mills Industrial Mus.
Temple Newsam
Swillington
Churwell
Middleton Railway
Rothwell
Rothwell Haigh
Robin Hood
Morley
Middleton
Carlton
Tingley
East Ardsley
Oulton
Methley
Mickletown
Allerton Bywater
Great Preston
Kippax
Ledston
Ledston Luck
Ledsham
Garforth
Micklefield
Mickle field Garden Village
New Micklefield
Barwick-in-Elmet
Scholes
Potterton
Aberford
Lotherton Hall
Bramham Park
Bramham
Boston Spa
Clifford
Thorp Arch
Walton
Wetherby
Linton
Collingham
Kirk Deighton
North Deighton
Little Ribston
Goldsborough
Walshford
Hunsingore
Cowthorpe
Bickerton
Allerton Mauleverer
Flaxby
Coneythorpe
Arkendale
Whixley
Hopperton
Cattal
Kirk Hammerton
Green Hammerton
Little Ouseburn
Great Ouseburn
Thorpe Underwood
Marton
Grafton
Upper Dunsforth
Lower Dunsforth
Myton-on-Swale
Helperby
Brafferton
Kirby Hill
Norton-le-Clay
Dishforth
Cundall
Crakehill
Fawdington
Sessay
Dalton
Hutton Sessay
Birdforth
Little Sessay
Thormanby
Raskelf
Easingwold
Tholthorpe
Flawith
Alne
Aldwark
Tollerton
Youlton
Linton-on-Ouse
Newton on Ouse
Beningbrough Hall
Beningbrough
Nun Monkton
Moor Monkton
Overton
Nether Poppleton
Upper Poppleton
Hessay
Marston Moor
Tockwith
Long Marston
Bilton in Ainsty
Hutton Wandesley
Rufforth
Knapton
Acomb
Angram
Askham Bryan
Askham Richard
Bilbrough
Healaugh
Wighill
Catterton
Copmanthorpe
York West Services
Tadcaster
Newton Kyme
Stutton
Kirkby Wharfe
Bolton Percy
Ulleskelf
Towton
Saxton
Barkston
Church Fenton
Biggin
Little Fenton
Sherburn in Elmet
Steeton Hall Gateway
South Milford
Lumby
Monk Fryston
Hambleton
Newthorpe
Fairburn
Burton Salmon
Brotherton
Hillam
Birkin
Beal
Castleford
Thirsk
Old Thirsk
World of James Herriot
Sowerby
South Kilvington
Carlton Miniott
Bagby
Balk
Great Thirkleby
Little Thirkleby
Monk Park Farm
Kilburn
Mouseman Visitors Centre
High Kilburn
Oldstead
Carlton Husthwaite
Husthwaite
Coxwold
Byland Abbey
Wass
Ampleforth
Oulston
Yearsley
Brandsby
Crayke
Stillington
Huby
Sutton-on-the-Forest
Sutton Park
Cross Lanes
Shipton
Wigginton
Skelton
Haxby
Strensall
Towthorpe
Earswick
Huntington
New Earswick
West Huntington
Rawcliffe
Clifton
York
York Minster
Jorvik Centre
Holgate
National Railway Museum
Castle Mus.
Heworth
Osbaldwick
Heslington
Nunthorpe
Woodthorpe
Fulford
Bishopthorpe
McArthur Glen York
Crockey Hill
Naburn
Acaster Malbis
Colton
Appleton Roebuck
Acaster Selby
Holme Green
Deighton
Escrick
Stillingfleet
Ryther
Kelfield
Cawood
Riccall
Skipwith
Wistow
Barlby
Selby
Selby Abbey
Osgodby
Thorpe Willoughby
Brayton
East Common
Hemingbrough
Barlow
Gateforth
Burn
West Haddlesey
Chapel Haddlesey
Yorkshire Garden World
Temple
Camblesforth
Helmsley
Rye Dale
Duncombe Park
Sprxton
Nunnington
Oswaldkirk
Gilling East
Cawton
Hovingham
Coulton
Scackleton
Stearsby
Dalby
Skewsby
Whenby
Farlington
Sheriff Hutton
West Lilling
Thirlby
Felixkirk
Sutton Bank Visitor Centre
Cold Kirby
Scawton
Sutton-under-Whitestonecliffe
Bob Hunter - Home of the Wren
Harome
A1
A1(M)
A19
A59
A61
A64
A168
A170
A658
A661
A6120
A63
A659
A162
B1223
B1224
B6265
M1
M62
M621

Helmsley
Rye Dale
DUNCOMBE PARK
Nawton
Wombleton
Great Edstone
Marton
Pickering
PICKERING CASTLE
Ellerburn
Thornton-le-Dale
Wilton
Allerston
Ebberston
Snainton
Harome
Sproxton
Normanby
Muscoates
Little Barugh
FLAMINGO LAND
NUNNINGTON HALL
Nunnington
West Ness
Salton
Kirby Misperton
Great Barugh
Wass
Ampleforth
BYLAND ABBEY
Oswaldkirk
Stonegrave
East Ness
Brawby
High Marishes
Low Marishes
Yedingham
Coxwold
Gilling East
South Holme
Butterwick
Little Habton
Great Habton
Ryton
West Heslerton
East Heslerton
Cawton
Hovingham
HOWARDIAN HILLS
Yearsley
Wath
Fryton
Slingsby
Barton-le-Street
Wykeham
Scampston
SCAMPSTON HALL
West Knapton
East Knapton
Rillington
WOLDS WAY LAVENDER
Coulton
Appleton-le-Street
Amotherby
EDEN CAMP MUSEUM
Thorpe Bassett
Wintringham
Brandsby
Scackleton
Swinton
Broughton
Malton
Old Malton
Norton-on-Derwent
Scagglethorpe
Place Newton
Stearsby
Dalby
Terrington
Skewsby
YORKSHIRE LAVENDER
Ganthorpe
Coneysthorpe
CASTLE HOWARD
Settrington
Crayke
Whenby
Whitewall Corner
East Lutton
West Lutton
Stillington
Farlington
Bulmer
Welburn
High Hutton
North Grimston
Low Hutton
Kirby Grindalythe
Duggleby
Sheriff Hutton
West Lilling
Thornton-le-Clay
Whitwell-on-the-Hill
Firby
Kirkham
Langton
Kennythorpe
Birdsall
Wharram le Street
Huby
Sutton-on-the-Forest
SUTTON PARK
Foston
Crambe
KIRKHAM PRIORY
Westow
Burythorpe
WHARRAM PERCY MEDIEVAL VILLAGE
Sledmere
Leavening
Barton-le-Willows
Howsham
Flaxton
Harton
Leppington
Acklam
Thixendale
Strensall
Bossall
Claxton
Scrayingham
Fimber
Towthorpe
Sand Hutton
Kirby Underdale
Shipton
Wigginton
Haxby
City of York
Earswick
Upper Helmsley
Buttercrambe
Bugthorpe
Skirpenbeck
Painsthorpe
Fridaythorpe
Skelton
Moor End
Stockton on the Forest
Gate Helmsley
Stamford Bridge
YORKSHIRE WOLDS WAY
Huntington
West Huntington
New Earswick
Warthill
Youlthorpe
Bishop Wilton
Huggate
Holtby
Full Sutton
Gowthorpe
Rawcliffe
Clifton
Low Catton
High Catton
Great Givendale
Fangfoss
Upper Poppleton
YORK MINSTER
Murton
Dunnington
YORKSHIRE MUSEUM OF FARMING
Bolton
Meltonby
Millington
North Dalton
Knapton
York
Heworth
Osbaldwick
JORVIK CENTRE
Holgate
Acomb
NATIONAL RAILWAY MUSEUM
CASTLE MUS.
Grimston
Kexby
Wilberfoss
Yapham
Warter
Kilnwick Percy
Middleton-on-the-Wolds
Nunthorpe
Heslington
Woodthorpe
Fulford
Barmby Moor
Pocklington
Newton upon Derwent
Bishopthorpe
McARTHUR GLEN YORK
Crockey Hill
YORKSHIRE AIR MUSEUM
Elvington
Nunburnholme
BURNBY HALL GARDENS & MUSEUM TRUST
Burnby
Copmanthorpe
Sutton upon Derwent
Allerthorpe
Acaster Malbis
Naburn
Wheldrake
Thornton
Hayton
Londesborough
Colton
Deighton
Storwood
Melbourne
Pocklington Canal
Thorpe le Street
Goodmanham
Appleton Roebuck
Escrick
LOWER DERWENT VALLEY
Bielby
Shiptonthorpe
Market Weighton
Acaster Selby
Everingham
Seaton Ross
Holme Green
East Cottingwith
Thorganby
Harswell
Stillingfleet
Sancton
Ryther
Kelfield
Ellerton
Laytham
Water End
Holme-on-Spalding-Moor
Cawood
Skipwith
North Duffield
Aughton
Harlthorpe
Moor End
Sand Hole
Foggathorpe
North Newbald
North Cliffe
South Newbald
Riccall
Bubwith
Highfield
Rascal Moor
Wistow
Gunby
THE REAL AEROPLANE MUSEUM
Willitoft
Gribthorpe
South Cliffe
Hotham
Barlby
SELBY ABBEY
Osgodby
Menthorpe
Breighton
Spaldington
Bursea
Foulness
North Cave
Everthorpe
Lund
South Duffield
Selby
Cliffe
Thorpe Willoughby
Wressle
Brind
North Howden
Portington
Hive
South Cave
West End
Brayton
East Common
Hemingbrough
Newsholme
HOWDEN MINSTER
Cavil
Sandholme
Eastrington
Newport
Brantingham
Barmby on the Marsh
Howden
Gilberdyke
Staddlethorpe
Ellerker
Asselby
Knedlington
Kilpin Pike
Kilpin
Balkholme
Elloughton
Brough
Drax
Boothferry
Broomfleet
Haddlesey
Temple
Camblesforth
Laxton
Selby Canal
Market Weighton Canal
0 1 2 3 4 5 6 miles
0 1 2 3 4 5 6 7 8 9 10 km

Yons Nab
CLEVELAND WAY
Seamer
Irton
Eastfield
Cayton
Lebberston
Gristhorpe
Filey Brigg
Filey
Filey Bay
Wykeham
Flixton
Folkton
Muston
Willerby
Staxton
Ganton
YORKSHIRE WOLDS WAY
Primrose Valley
Hunmanby Moor
Hunmanby
Reighton Sands
Reighton Gap
Potter Brompton
Fordon
Reighton
Speeton
Wold Newton
Foxholes
Burton Fleming
Buckton
Bempton
Butterwick
Grindale
FLAMBOROUGH HEAD
Flamborough
Weaverthorpe
Thwing
Octon
Octon Cross Roads
SEWERBY HALL AND GARDENS
Sewerby
BONDVILLE MODEL VILLAGE
Boynton
PRIORY
Rudston
BAYLE MUSEUM
Bridlington
Langtoft
Bessingby
West Hill
OLD PENNY MEMORIES
Carnaby
Hilderthorpe
Haisthorpe
Cottam
BURTON AGNES HALL
Thornholme
Kilham
BRIDLINGTON BAY
PARK ROSE POTTERY AND LEISURE PARK
BURTON AGNES MANOR HOUSE
Burton Agnes
Ruston Parva
Harpham
Fraisthorpe
Garton-on-the-Wolds
Lowthorpe
Gransmoor
Nafferton
Barmston
Great Kelk
Lissett
Elmswell
Little Driffield
Driffield
Gembling
Ulrome
Kelleythorpe
Foston on the Wolds
TA
Wansford
SKIPSEA CASTLE
Kirkburn
Skerne
CRUCKLEY ANIMAL FARM
Skipsea
Southburn
Church End
Beeford
Skipsea Brough
Hutton
Brigham
North Frodingham
Bainton
Hutton Cranswick
Rotsea
Dunnington
Hempholme
Watton
Bewholme
Atwick
Kilnwick
North Cliff
Lund
Beswick
Watton Beck
Burshill
Hornsea
FREEPORT HORNSEA
HORNSEA MUSEUM
Lockington
Baswick Steer
Brandesburton
Seaton
Thorpe
Hornsea Bridge
Hornsea Mere
Scorborough
Aike
Leven
Leven Canal
Sigglesthorne
Rolston
Catwick
Goxhill
Arram
Mappleton
Etton
Leconfield
Eske
Little Hatfield
Cherry Burton
Routh
Long Riston
Rise
Great Hatfield
Great Cowden
Tickton
Arnold
Withernwick
Molescroft
Beverley
New Ellerby
Bishop Burton
Weel
Meaux
Skirlaugh
Marton
West Newton
Aldbrough
BEVERLEY FRIARY
MINSTER
Woodmansey
East Newton
Walkington
BURTON CONSTABLE HALL
Old Ellerby
Flinton
Wawne
Thearne
Bentley
Swine
Coniston
Garton
Dunswell
Grimston
Thirtleby
Sproatley
Humbleton
Fitling
Hilston
Skidby
Bransholme
Sutton on Hull
Ganstead
Little Weighton
Cottingham
Kingston-upon-Hull
SKIDBY WINDMILL
Rowley
Inglemire
Bilton
Lelley
Owstwick
Tunstall
Epplewor th
Sutton Ings
Elstronwick
Riplingham
Stoneferry
North End
Newland
Summergangs
Preston
Burton Pidsea
Roos
Willerby
Kirk Ella
Sculcoates
WILBERFORCE HOUSE
West End
Waxholme
Salt End
Owthorne
West Ella
Anlaby
Marfleet
STREETLIFE
Hedon
Rimswell
Swanland
Haven Side
Burstwick
Halsham
Withernsea
Welton
Northfield
Hessle
KINGSTON UPON HULL
FERENS ART GALLERY
Camerton
East End
Paull
Thorngumbald
North Ferriby
Keyingham
A
B
C
D
E
F
G
7
8
9
Wolds
East Riding of Yorkshire

Flimby
Broughton Moor
Standingstone
Dovenby
Bridekirk
Blindcrake
Bewaldeth
Orthwaite
Siddick
Camerton
Great Broughton
Little Broughton
Papcastle
Wordsworth Ho.
Cockermouth
Castlegate Ho.
Embleton
Bassenthwaite
Seaton
Great Clifton
Brigham
Derwent
Skiddaw Forest
North Side
Workington
Stainburn
Helena Thompson Mus.
Bridgefoot
Greysouthen
Little Clifton
Cockermouth
Wythop Mill
Bassenthwaite Lake
Mirehouse
931 Skiddaw
Westfield
Eaglesfield
Sandybeck Meadow
Thornthwaite Forest
Mossbay
Deanscales
Lorton Vale
Harrington
High Harrington
Winscales
Dean
Low Lorton
High Lorton
Thornthwaite
Thornthwaite Galleries
Whinlatter Pass
Cumberland Pencil Museum
Millbeck
Applethwaite
Cars of the Stars Motor Mus.
Mosser
Branthwaite
Pardshaw
Ullock
Mockerkin
Thackthwaite
Distington
Heritage/Visitor Centre
Braithwaite
Keswick
790 Grisedale Pike
Whinlatter Forest Park
Portinscale
Lowca
Pica
Keekle
247
Loweswater
Lamplugh
Brackenthwaite Fell
851
Stair
Derwent Water
Parton
Moresby
Asby
Bransty
Moresby Parks
Arlecdon
573
Loweswater Fell
Little Town
Derwentwater
The Rum Story
Rowrah
High Leys
512
Rannerdale
Grange
Derwent Fells
Whitehaven
Haig Colliery Mining Museum
Frizington
Kirkland
Croasdale
Crummock Water
Buttermere
608 High Seat
Hensingham
Cleator Moor
Ehen
616 Great Borne
Buttermere Fell
Borrowdale
Thirlmere
Watendlath
Saltom Bay
Mirehouse
Ennerdale Bridge
Ennerdale Forest
Ennerdale
High Stile
608
753
Rosthwaite
St Bees Head
Sandwith
Moor Row
Wath Brow
Ennerdale Water
Borrowdale
Seatoller
Honister Hause
Stonethwaite
Rottington
Cleator
Ennerdale Fell
Liza
892 Pillar
Black Sail
Seathwaite
726 Ullscarf
St Bees
Egremont
Wilton
NY
Lake
899 Great Gable
High White Stones
762
Coulderton
Thornhill
Middletown
Haile
Seatallan 692
Wasdale Head
Nethertown
Beckermet
322
Copeland Forest
National
977 Scafell Pike
902 Bow Fell
Langdale Pikes
NX
Braystones
Calder Bridge
Calder
Bleng
Wast Water
Burnmoor Tarn
Cumbrian
High Sellafield
Sellafield Visitors Centre
Calder Hall
Wellington
Wastwater
Nether Wasdale
The Screes
609
Gosforth
Hardknott Fort
Hard Knott Pass
Wrynose Pass
Brathay
Seascale
Santon Bridge
Boot
Eskdale
Eskdale Green
Beckfoot
Cockley Beck
Furness Fells
Holmrook
Irt
649 Harter Fell
Seathwaite Tarn
Coniston Coppermines
Coniston Holly How
Drigg
Mite
231
Esk
Birker Fell
801 The Old Man of Coniston
Saltcoats
Ravenglass and Eskdale Railway & Mus.
Ravenglass
Bath House
Third Millennium Muncaster Owl Trust World HQ
Devoke Water
Woodend
Hall Dunnerdale
Seathwaite
Broad Oak
Ulpha Fell
529 Caw
Newbiggin
Lane End
572 Whitfell
Ulpha
Hoses
Torver
Corney Fell
Stub Place
Corney
Broughton Mills
High Nibthwaite
Water Yeat
Blawith
Hycemoor
Selker Bay
Bootle
Duddon Bridge
Lower Hawthwaite
SC
SD
Broughton in Furness
Lowick Bridge
Black Combe
600
Hallthwaites
Duddon Mosses
Grizebeck
Lowick Green
Whitbeck
The Green
Foxfield
Gawthwaite
The Hill
333
Kirkby-in-Furness
Beck Side
Broughton Beck
Silecroft
Whicham
Millom
Millom Folk Museum
Soutergate
Mansriggs
Kirksanton
Haverigg
Duddon Estuary
Duddon Sands
Laurel & Hardy Mus.
Ulverston
Askam in Furness
Ireleth
Pennington
Lindal in Furness
Swarthmoor
A596
A595
A66
A5086
B5292
B5289
A591
B5291
B5294
B5295
B5345
B5344
A593
A5084
A5092
B5281
A5093
107
92
0 1 2 3 4 5 6 miles
0 1 2 3 4 5 6 7 8 9 10 km

Penrith
Carleton
Eamont Bridge
Clifton
Appleby-in-Westmorland
Ambleside
Windermere
Bowness-on-Windermere
Staveley
Kendal
Sedbergh
Kirkby Lonsdale
Milnthorpe
Grange-over-Sands
Arnside
Coniston
Hawkshead
Grasmere
Rydal
Glenridding
Patterdale
Shap
Tebay
Orton
Keswick
Threlkeld
Scales
Mungrisdale
Greystoke
Penruddock
Pooley Bridge
Askham
Lowther
Hackthorpe
Bampton
Haweswater Reservoir
Ullswater
Kirkstone Pass
Troutbeck
Troutbeck Bridge
Kentmere
Sadgill
Long Sleddale
Shap Fells
Ralfland Forest
Borrowdale
Grayrigg
Lambrigg Fell
Oxenholme
Natland
Sedgwick
Levens
Heversham
Beetham
Holme
Burton-in-Kendal
Carnforth
Cartmel
Lindale
Newby Bridge
Haverthwaite
Grizedale
Satterthwaite
Rusland
Langdale Fell
Howgill Fell
Ravenstonedale Common
Great Asby
Crosby Ravensworth
Brough Sowerby
Temple Sowerby
Kirkby Thore
Morland
Great Strickland
Little Strickland
Dufton
Brampton
Crackenthorpe
Milburn
Culgaith
Langwathby
Edenhall
Kirkland
Ousby
Skirwith
Blencarn
Catterlen
Johnby
Hutton Roof
Mosedale
Berrier
Motherby
Troutbeck
Matterdale End
Dockray
Dowthwaitehead
Stanah
Fisher Place
Wythburn
Helvellyn
Howtown
Sandwick
Martindale Common
Bampton Common
High Street
Harter Fell
Lowbridge House
Forest Hall
Garnett Bridge
Watchgate
Burneside
Crook
Winster
Crosthwaite
Underbarrow
Brigsteer
Cartmel Fell
Bowland Bridge
Witherslack
Meathop
Storth
Yealand Redmayne
Whittington
Casterton
Barbon
Mansergh
Middleton
Killington
Dent
Gawthrop
Cautley
Millthrop
Lakeside
Finsthwaite
Backbarrow
Cark
Holker
Allithwaite
Kents Bank
Cartmel Sands
Flookburgh
LAKE DISTRICT NATIONAL PARK
NY
SD
M6
A6
A66
A591
A592
A685
A683
A684
A65
A590
A5074
B5284
B6260
B6261

Ousby
Skirwith
Kirkland
893
CROSS FELL
Tees
MILBURN
FOREST
Trout Beck
MOOR HOUSE-
UPPER TEESDALE
Blencarn
Crowdundle Beck
Harwood
Harwood Beck
639
VIEWING
HILL
Langdon
Common
696
CHAPELFELL
TOP
Westernhope
Moor
675
Newbiggin
Common
Bollihope
Common
Middleton
Common
Langdon Beck
LANGDON BECK
B6277
B6412
A
109
110
Culgaith
772
ACORN
BANK
Newbiggin
Milburn
Cow Green
Reservoir
Dufton Fell
767
Widdybank
Fell
CAULDRON
SNOUT
Forest
Ettersgill
Tees
HIGH FORCE
BOWLEES VISITOR CENTRE
Newbiggin
565
Temple
Sowerby
Knock
PENNINE WAY
Maize Beck
Cronkley Fell
TEESDALE
B6277
Holwick
Middleton-in-
Teesdale
B6282
Lowmoor Row
Kirkby Thore
DUFTON
Dufton
BURN MOSS
Cliburn
B
Long Marton
Brampton
Murton Fell
673
NORTH
Mickle Fell
776
LUNE FOREST
Lune Moor
Bowbank
Thringarth
Mickleton
EGGLESTON
HALL
Eggleston
Morland
Bolton
Crackenthorpe
Murton
B6276
Grassholme
Reservoir
Romaldkirk
B6277
King's
Meaburn
Newby
Lyvennet
Colby
APPLEBY
CASTLE
Appleby-in-
Westmorland
Hilton
Warcop Fell
15
Lune
Grassholme
Hunderthwaite
Selset Reservoir
Hury
DOW CRAG
549
Hunderthwaite Moor
Hury
Reservoir
PENNINES
Eden
B6542
B6276
Burrells
Balder
Balderhead
Reservoir
Clove Lodge
BALDERSDALE
Cotherstone Moor
Reagill
Hoff
A66
Great
Ormside
Stainmore
Common
99
B6260
Sandford
Maulds
Meaburn
Warcop
8
Hillbeck
North
Stainmore
Deep Dale
Deepdale Beck
C
Crosby
Ravensworth
Drybeck
BROUGH
CASTLE
A66
13
Bowes
PENNINE
WAY
Oddendale
Great Asby
Bleatarn
B6259
Great
Musgrave
Brough
South
Stainmore
Little
Musgrave
Brough
Sowerby
A66
Gilmonby
Kaber
Barras
Moudy Mea
Soulby
A685
Crosby
Ravensworth
Fell
GREAT ASBY SCAR
Winton
Heggerscales
Bowes Moor
STAINMORE
FOREST
Sleightholme
Crosby
Garrett
Hartley
Belah
Scargill
412
B6261
Little
Asby
KIRKBY
STEPHEN
Kirkby
Stephen
Winton Fell
NY
Sleightholme Moor
M6
Orton
B6260
B6261
Raisbeck
Smardale
Waitby
510
CLEASBY HILL
SERVICES
D
SMARDALE GILL
Nateby
662
Lune
Gaisgill
Kelleth
Newbiggin-
on-Lune
Ash
Fell
B6270
Arkengarthdale
Moor
38
A685
10
Tebay
Bowderdale
Coldbeck
385
A683
Stonesdale Moor
Whaw
Weasdale
Ravenstonedale
B6259
Ravenseat
ROGAN'S SEAT
671
Birkdale
Common
West Stonesdale
583
GREAT PINSEAT
Outhgill
709
B6270
KELD
Keld
Melbecks Moor
A685
Langdale Fell
Ravenstonedale
Common
Angram
494
587
11
Angram Common
Kearton
Gunnerside
Feetham
Howgill
Fell
708
Mallerstang
Common
Thwaite
Satron
Muker
B6270
Low Row
716
GREAT SHUNNER FELL
Lowgill
676
THE CALF
13
A683
Crackpot
Beck Foot
Brant Fell
B6259
BUTTERTUBS
PASS
Abbotside
Common
YORKSHIRE
PENNINE WAY
Abbotside
Common
E
B6257
Cautley
SD
Cotterdale
M6
Askrigg Common
37
99
Baugh Fell
North Yo
Sedbergh
FARFIELD MILL
ARTS & HERITAGE
CENTRE
Garsdale Head
A684
High Shaw
Askrigg
A684
676
Mossdale
Moor
Hardrow
Sedbusk
LOW MILL
OUTDOOR CENTRE
Newbiggin
KILLINGTON SERVICES
(Southbound Only)
Millthrop
Garsdale
Appersett
DALES COUNTRYSIDE
MUSEUM
Bainbridge
Woodhall
WENSLEYDALE POTTERY
Hawes
Worton
Cubeck
Killington
Dee
11
Garsdale
Widdale Fell
HAWES
Gayle
Burtersett
WENSLEYDALE
Thornton
Rust
556
RISE HILL
Countersett
A683
Gawthrop
Dent
Dentdale
Cowgill
672
WENSLEYDALE
CREAMERY
Semer Water
Wether Fell
Carpley Green
BISHOPDALE
VALLEY
614
Middleton
Stone
House
DENTDALE
Wold Fell
B6255
Dodd
Fell
Marsett
Stalling Busk
Newbiggin
F
609
CALF TOP
Deepdale
10
668
Bishopdale Beck
B6160
Old Town
682
CRAG HILL
PENNINE WAY
Cragdale Moor
Barbon
Whernside
Gayle Moor
NATIONAL
Mansergh
736
Blea
Moor
Oughtershaw
Kidstones
Cam Fell
643
MIDDLE TONGUE
26
Walden Head
Kirkby Lonsdale
Casterton
93
LANGSTROTHDALE
CHASE
94
627
Ribblehead
Yockenthwaite
702
BUCKDEN
PIKE
Cray
Hubberholme
0 1 2 3 4 5 6 miles
0 1 2 3 4 5 6 7 8 9 10 km
Dale
INGLEBOROUGH
B6479
Cam Beck
Gligh Birkwith
Foxup
Halton Gill
Buckden
610
Cowan
Bridge
Ireby
PARK

Fir Tree
Howden-le-Wear
Hunwick
Newfield
Byers Green
Spennymoor
Ferryhill
Cornforth
Trimdon
Middlestone Moor
Ferryhill Station
Fishburn
Pikeston Fell
Bedburn
Redford
Hamsterley
Witton-le-Wear
High Grange
Binchester Blocks
Kirk Merrington
Mainsforth
Bishop Middleham
Hamsterley Forest
Witton Park
Toronto
Westerton
Middlestone
Chilton Lane
Butterwick
Escomb
Coundon
Leasingthorne
Chilton
Low Etherley
High Etherley
Bishop Auckland
Rushyford
Sedgefield
Forest
Eldon
Bradbury
Morley
Toft Hill
Coundon Grange
Old Eldon
Woodland
St Helen Auckland
Shildon
Middridge
NEWTON AYCLIFFE
Mordon
Woodland Fell
Howle
Butterknowle
West Auckland
Wynyard Village
Copley
High Lands
Evenwood
Thorpe Larches
Bildershaw
Royal Oak
Redworth
Foxton
Cockfield
Evenwood Gate
Aycliffe
Stillington
Burnt Houses
Bolam
Heighington
Elstob
Thorpe
Wackerfield
Whitton
RABY CASTLE
Hilton
Houghton-le-Side
Great Stainton
Redmarshall
Carlton
Kinninvie
Ingleton
Brafferton
Bishopton
Walworth Gate
Staindrop
Killerby
Coatham Mundeville
Little Stainton
Cotherstone
Langton
Denton
Skerne
Headlam
Summerhouse
Walworth
Beaumont Hill
Barmpton
Stainton
Cleatlam
Little Newsham
BARNARD CASTLE
THE BOWES MUSEUM
Gainford
Harrowgate Hill
Great Burdon
Sadberge
Elton
Barnard Castle
Winston
High Coniscliffe
Darlington
Haughton Le Skerne
Longnewton
Startforth
Westwick
Whorlton
Piercebridge
Low Coniscliffe
Urlay Nook
Boldron
EGGLESTONE ABBEY
ROKEBY PARK
Ovington
ROMAN BRIDGE
Manfield
DURHAM TEES VALLEY
Egglescliffe
Caldwell
Middleton St George
Greta Bridge
Eppleby
Cleasby
Aislaby
Hutton Magna
Forcett
Carlton
Stapleton
Blackwell
Middleton One Row
Brignall
STANWICK IRON AGE FORTIFICATIONS
Lane Head
Stanwick-St-John
Aldbrough St John
Low Dinsdale
Scargill
West Layton
Neasham
Low Worsall
Barningham
Newsham
East Layton
Newton Morrell
Croft-on-Tees
Hurworth Place
The Stang Forest
Barton
Eryholme
Dalton
Melsonby
Girsby
Ravensworth
BARTON PARK SERVICES
Dalton-on-Tees
Picton
Gayles
CROFT
Sockburn
Kirby Hill
Hartforth
Whashton
Middleton Tyas
Hornby
Appleton Wiske
SCOTCH CORNER SERVICES
NZ
Gilling West
Scotch Corner
Great Smeaton
West Rounton
Moulton
North Cowton
Welbury
Langthwaite
Arkle Town
Washfold
Atley Hill
East Cowton
Birkby
Hurst
Skeeby
Uckerby
Richmond
Deighton
EASBY ABBEY
Skelton
Easby
Scorton
RICHMOND CASTLE
Marske
Hudswell
Whitwell
Streetlam
Lovesome Hill
East Harlsey
SWALEDALE FOLK MUSEUM
Colburn
Brompton-on-Swale
CATTERICK
Bolton-on-Swale
Reeth
Fremington
Catterick Bridge
Danby Wiske
Grinton
Marrick
Downholme
Hipswell
Walkerville
Catterick
SWALE DALE
GRINTON LODGE
Catterick Garrison
Brompton
Winton
Stainton
Hipswell Moor
Scotton
Tunstall
Great Langton
Kirby Sigston
SE
East Appleton
Kirkby Fleetham
Yafforth
Stainton Moor
Redmire Moor
Great Fencote
Bullamoor
Barden
Hornby
Hackforth
Thrintoft
Northallerton
East Hauxwell
Ainderby Steeple
Romanby
Yorkshire
Bellerby
Garriston
Hunton
Arrathorne
Little Fencote
Castle Bolton
BOLTON CASTLE
Constable Burton
Scruton
Langthorne
SWINESIDE CERAMICS
Preston-under-Scar
Redmire
Patrick Brompton
Little Crakehall
CRAKEHALL WATER MILL
Morton-on-Swale
Warlaby
Leyburn
Great Crakehall
Leeming
North Otterington
Thornton-le-Beans
Carperby
Wensley
YORKSHIRE MUSEUM OF CARRIAGES
Swinithwaite
Harmby
WENSLEYDALE RLY.
Finghall
Newton-le-Willows
Leeming Bar
Sowber Gate
Thornton-le-Moor
WHITE ROSE CANDLES
Spennithorne
Leeming
AYSGARTH FALLS
West Witton
Middleham
Bedale
Aiskew
Gatenby
Cowling
Londonderry
Newby Wiske
South Otterington
PENHILL
Agglethorpe
Burrill
MIDDLEHAM CASTLE
Thornton Steward
JERVAULX ABBEY
Exelby
Firby
Maunby
Thornton-le-Street
West Burton
Coverham
East Witton
Thirn
Thornton Watlass
Theakston
Melmerby
Carlton
THORP PERROW ARBORETUM
Burneston
Kirby Wiske
Newsham
SION HILL HALL & BIRDS OF PREY CENTRE
Caldbergh
Ellingstring
Snape
Carthorpe
Pickhill
Carlton Moor
West Scrafton
High Ellington
Low Ellington
AERIAL EXTREME
Holme
Walden
Gammersgill
Sinderby
Sandhutton
Horsehouse
Colsterdale
UREDALE GLASS
Low Burton
Well
Kirklington
Ainderby Quernhow
Coverdale
Fearby
Healey
Masham
Nosterfield
Colsterdale Moor
Braidley
Hindlethwaite Moor
THEAKSTON BREWERY VISITOR CENTRE
Binsoe
Howe
Carlton Miniott
Skipton-on-Swale
GREAT HAW
Leighton
Swinton
Thornborough
Sutton Howgrave
Warthermarske
Baldersby
Masham Moor
West Tanfield
MARMION TOWER
Middleton Quernham
Catton
LITTLE WHERNSIDE
Scar House Res.
Leighton Res.
Ilton
Roundhill Res.
Mickley
North Stainley
Wath
NORTON CONYERS
Melmerby
Baldersby St James
Topcliffe
Grewelthorpe
LIGHTWATER

Hartlepool
Trimdon
High Throston
Elwick
West Park
Saint Hilda's Parish Church
Hartlepool's Maritime Experience
Hartlepool Bay
Landing
Fishburn
Ferryhill Station
Mainsforth
Bishop Middleham
Chilton
Dalton Piercy
Rift House
Seaton Carew
Butterwick
Hardwick Hall
Sedgefield
Bradbury
Mordon
Tees Bay
Rotterdam 16:00
Zeebrugge 16:30
Greatham
Energy Information Centre
Graythorp
Wynyard Village
Wynyard Woodland
Thorpe Larches
Newton Bewley
Cowpen Bewley
Wolviston
Teesmouth
Foxton
Stillington
Thorpe Thewles
Billingham Art Gallery
BILLINGHAM
Haverton Hill
Port Clarence
Elstob
Whitton
Redmarshall
Carlton
Stockton-on-Tees
Norton
Roseworth
Billingham Beck
Great Stainton
Brafferton
Bishopton
Coatham Mundeville
Little Stainton
Fairfield
Skerne
Beaumont Hill
Barmpton
Great Burdon
Sadberge
Hartburn
Green Dragon Mus
Stockton-on-Tees
Salt Scar
REDCAR
Coatham
Dormanstown
Kirkleatham Old Hall Museum
Kirkleatham
Marske-by-the-Sea
Miniature Railway
Saltburn Smugglers Heritage Centre
Saltburn-by-the-Sea
Yearby
New Marske
Grangetown
South Bank
North Ormesby
Toll
Middlesbrough
Lazenby
Wilton
Upleatham
Dunsdale
Tocketts Water Mill
Skelton
North Skelton
Eston
Normanby
Dorman Museum
Middlesbrough
Thornaby on Tees
Acklam
Natures World
Park End
Ormesby
Redcar and Cleveland
Guisborough
Guisborough Priory
Boosbeck
Lingdale
Margrove Park
Stanghow
Elton
Longnewton
Preston Hall Museum
Ormesby Hall
Marton
Coulby Newham
Captain Cook Birthplace
Hutton Gate
Charltons
Darlington
Haughton Le Skerne
Urlay Nook
Eaglescliffe
Ingleby Barwick
Stainton
Thornton
Hemlington
Nunthorpe
Hutton Village
Gisborough Moor
Res.
Moorsholm
Durham Tees Valley
Middleton St George
Egglescliffe
Maltby
Newton under Roseberry
Aislaby
High Leven
Middleton One Row
Yarm
Low Dinsdale
Newby
Tanton
Great Ayton
Commondale Moor
Commondale
Hilton
Seamer
Little Ayton
New Row
Neasham
Low Worsall
Kirklevington
Hurworth Place
Eryholme
Dalton-on-Tees
Sockburn
Girsby
Middleton-on-Leven
Stokesley
Easby
Kildale
Kildale Moor
Tame Bridge
Picton
Crathorne
Rudby
Battersby
Castleton
Hutton Rudby
Leven
Great Broughton
Kirkby
Ingleby Greenhow
Westerdale
Hornby
Appleton Wiske
Great Smeaton
Enterpen
Great Busby
Cleveland Way
West Rounton
Potto
Carlton in Cleveland
Wiske
East Cowton
Birkby
Welbury
East Rounton
Faceby
Whorlton
Swainby
Urra
Westerdale Moor
Deighton
Ingleby Arncliffe
Seave Green
Farndale Moor
Streetlam
East Harlsey
Lovesome Hill
Whorlton Moor
Chop Gate
Cockayne Ridge
Cockayne
Wake Lady Green
Danby Wiske
Mount Grace Priory
Osmotherley
Cleveland Hills
Brompton
Winton
Ellerbeck
Kirby Sigston
Snilesworth Moor
Bilsdale West Moor
Bilsdale East Moor
Church Houses
Blakey Ridge
Rudland Rigg
Bransdale
North York Moors National Park
Thimbleby
Yafforth
Fangdale Beck
Low Mill
Great Fencote
Thrintoft
Northallerton
Bullamoor
Over Silton
East Moors
Ainderby Steeple
Romanby
Scruton
Morton-on-Swale
Nether Silton
Arden Great Moor
Warlaby
Leeming
Leeming Bar
Swale
North Otterington
Thornton-le-Beans
Kepwick
Helmsley Moor
Skiplam Moor
Gillamoor
Leake
Sowber Gate
Thornton-le-Moor
Borrowby
Cowesby
Hawnby
Rievaulx Moor
Fadmoor
Gatenby
Londonderry
Newby Wiske
South Otterington
Knayton
Kirby Knowle
Yorks
Upsall
Hambleton Hills
Maunby
Thornton-le-Street
Boltby
Old Byland
Carlton
Kirkbymoorside
Burneston
Kirby Wiske
Newsham
North Kilvington
Rievaulx
Pockley
Beadlam
Sion Hill Hall & Birds of Prey Centre
Felixkirk
Thirlby
Rievaulx Abbey
Cleveland Way
Helmsley
Welburn
Carthorpe
Pickhill
South Kilvington
Sutton Bank Visitor Centre
Cold Kirby
Nawton
Wombleton
Aerial Extreme
Holme
World of James Herriot
Thirsk
Bob Hunter - Home of the Wren
Scawton
Rye Dale
Duncombe Park
Sinderby
Sandhutton
Old Thirsk
Sutton-under-Whitestonecliffe
Harome
Kirklington
Ainderby Quernhow
Monk Park Farm
Sproxton
Riccal
Carlton Miniott
Sowerby
Bagby
Balk
Oldstead
Muscoates
Howe
Skipton-on-Swale
Great Thirkleby
Kilburn
High Kilburn
Wass
Nunnington
Nunnington Hall
West Ness
Sutton
Howgrave
Little Thirkleby
Mouseman Visitors Centre
Byland Abbey
Ampleforth
Oswaldkirk
East Ness
Carlton Husthwaite
Coxwold
Stonegrave
South Holme
Norton Conyers
Melmerby
Baldersby St James
Topcliffe
Dalton
Hutton Sessay
Gilling East
Cawton
Hovingham
0 1 2 3 4 5 6 miles
0 1 2 3 4 5 6 7 8 9 10 km
A179
A177
B1278
A19
A178
B1276
A689
A1(M)
A167
A1185
A66
A1046
B1275
A1032
A1085
B1269
A1042
A174
A1053
A171
A173
A135
A1043
A172
A67
B6280
B1380
B1365
B1292
A1044
B1265
B1264
B1263
B1257
A684
A167
B6271
A168
B6285
A170
A61
A1
B1363
111
101
95
96
60
Tees
Ure
Seph
Rye
Dove

5
6
7
8
A
B
C
D
E
F
G
NZ
OV
SE
TA
Skinningrove
Carlin How
Boulby
Loftus
Staithes
A174
Easington
Port Mulgrave
Runswick Bay
Hinderwell
Runswick Bay
Liverton
Roxby
Newton Mulgrave
Kettleness
Goldsborough
B1366
Ellerby
Scaling
A174
Lythe
B1266
Sandsend
THE DRACULA EXPERIENCE
Mickleby
East Barnby
Sandsend Wyke
SUTCLIFFE GALLERY
Scaling Dam Res.
West Barnby
East Row
Whitby
Saltwick Bay
Dunsley
Ugthorpe
WHITBY ABBEY
Low Moor
Lealholm Moor
Newholm
WHITBY
THE MOORS CENTRE
299
Stonegate
A171
Ruswarp
CAPTAIN COOK MEMORIAL MUSEUM
B1410
Houlsyke
Aislaby
Stainsacre
High Hawsker
Lealholm
Sleights
Briggswath
Sneaton
Ugglebarnby
Ness Pt.
CLEVELAND WAY
Low Garth
Street
Glaisdale
Egton
Grosmont
B1416
Sneatonthorpe
Raw
Robin Hood's Bay
Egton Bridge
GROSMONT GALLERY
Littlebeck
Fylingthorpe
BOGGLE HOLE
Esk Valley
Robin Hood's Bay
A169
A171
Glaisdale
Glaisdale Moor
Egton High Moor
Beck Hole
Old Peak
Goathland
Ravenscar
Flask Inn
Rosedale Moor
Fylingdales Moor
WHEELDALE MOOR ROMAN ROAD
299
Staintondale
STAINTONDALE SHIRE HORSE FARM
YORK MOORS
Harwood Dale Forest
CLEVELAND WAY
Wheeldale Moor
Goathland Moor
Harwood Dale
Rosedale Abbey
Cloughton Newlands
PICKERING MOOR
Cloughton Wyke
Pickering Forest
Saltergate
Langdale Forest
Cloughton
ROSEDALE
Cropton Forest
Broxa Forest
A171
Burniston
Hartoft End
Stape
NAL PARK
Cromer Pt.
Spaunton Moor
Forest
MOORLAND EXPERIENCE
TOLL
A165
Silpho
SCARBOROUGH
Scalby Ness Rocks
SEA LIFE AND MARINE SANCTUARY
Lastingham
Newton Dale
Levisham
Broxa
Suffield
Scalby
KINDERLAND
Langdale End
Hackness
North Bay
Newton-on-Rawcliffe
LOCKTON
Lockton
Staindale Forest
248
Wrench Green
Everley
Barrowcliff
Newby
WATERSPLASH WORLD
Spaunton
Appleton-le-Moors
Cropton
NORTH RIDING FOREST PARK
Trouts Dale
Wykeham Forest
SCARBOROUGH CASTLE
ROTUNDA MUSEUM
Scarborough
NORTH YORKSHIRE MOORS RAILWAY
Low Dalby
Dalby Forest
P&R
South Bay
Falsgrave
Keldholme
Sinnington
Wrelton
Aislaby
ST PETER AND ST PAUL CHURCH
FORGE VALLEY WOODLANDS
East Ayton
Cayton Bay
Kirkby Mills
Middleton
West Ayton
THE HONEY FARM
Osgodby
Sawdon
Hutton Buscel
Irton
Eastfield
Yons Nab
CLEVELAND WAY
Great Edstone
PICKERING CASTLE
Ellerburn
WORDSWORTH GALLERY
A170
Pickering
Ruston
Seamer
A165
Marton
A170
Thornton-le-Dale
Wilton
Ebberston
Snainton
Wykeham
B1261
Cayton
Allerston
B1415
Brompton
A64
Lebberston
Gristhorpe
Normanby
Costa Beck
Little Barugh
FLAMINGO LAND
Flixton
Folkton
Salton
96
97
Muston
Great Barugh
Kirby Misperton
Yedingham
THE CARRS
Staxton
A1039
Brawby
High Marishes
East Heslerton
YORKSHIRE WOLDS WAY
Butterwick
Derwent
Sherburn
Ganton
Little Habton
Great Habton
Low Marishes
West Knapton
East Knapton
Potter Brompton
Hunmanby
Ryton
Scampston
A64
West

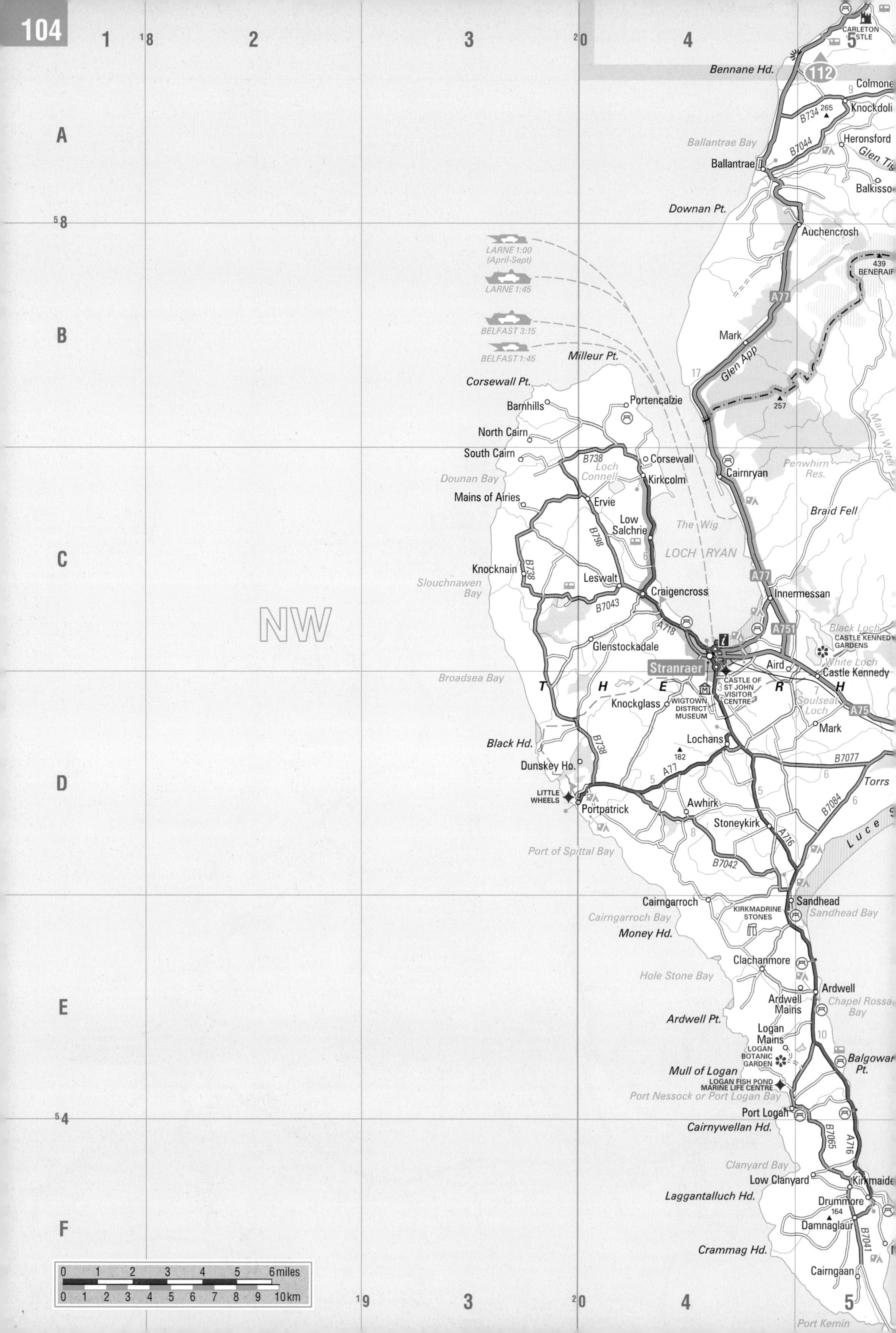

CARLETON CASTLE
Bennane Hd.
112
Colmone
B734
265
Knockdoli
Ballantrae Bay
B7044
Heronsford
Glen Tig
Ballantrae
Balkisso
Downan Pt.
Auchencrosh
439
BENERAIF
A77
LARNE 1:00 (April-Sept)
LARNE 1:45
BELFAST 3:15
BELFAST 1:45
Milleur Pt.
Mark
Glen App
17
257
Corsewall Pt.
Portencalzie
Barnhills
North Cairn
Main Water
South Cairn
B738
Loch Connell
Corsewall
Cairnryan
Penwhirn Res.
Dounan Bay
Kirkcolm
Mains of Airies
Ervie
Braid Fell
Low Salchrie
B798
The Wig
LOCH RYAN
Knocknain
B738
Leswalt
A77
Slouchnawen Bay
Craigencross
Innermessan
NW
B7043
A718
A751
Black Loch
CASTLE KENNEDY GARDENS
Glenstockadale
Stranraer
Aird
White Loch
Castle Kennedy
Broadsea Bay
T
H
E
CASTLE OF ST JOHN VISITOR CENTRE
R
H
Soulseat Loch
A75
Knockglass
WIGTOWN DISTRICT MUSEUM
Mark
Lochans
Black Hd.
182
B738
B7077
Dunskey Ho.
A77
Torrs
LITTLE WHEELS
Portpatrick
Awhirk
B7084
Stoneykirk
A716
Luce
Port of Spittal Bay
B7042
Cairngarroch
Sandhead
KIRKMADRINE STONES
Sandhead Bay
Cairngarroch Bay
Money Hd.
Clachanmore
Hole Stone Bay
Ardwell
Ardwell Mains
Chapel Rossa Bay
Ardwell Pt.
Logan Mains
LOGAN BOTANIC GARDEN
Balgowar Pt.
Mull of Logan
LOGAN FISH POND MARINE LIFE CENTRE
Port Nessock or Port Logan Bay
Port Logan
Cairnywellan Hd.
B7065
A716
Clanyard Bay
Low Clanyard
Kirkmaide
Laggantalluch Hd.
Drummore
164
Damnaglaur
B7041
Crammag Hd.
Cairngaan
Port Kemin
0 1 2 3 4 5 6 miles
0 1 2 3 4 5 6 7 8 9 10 km

Dumfries and Galloway
GALLOWAY FOREST PARK
Pinmore Mains
Poundland
Pinwherry
Bellamore
PINDONNAN
Ballochmorrie
Black Clauchrie
Water of Tig
Barrhill
Laggan
Eldrick
A714
B734
Arecleoch Forest
B7027
Drumlamford Loch
Dornal
Loch Dornal
Chirmorrie
Loch Ochiltree
Loch Maberry
Craig Airie Fell
Loch Derry
Polbae
Miltonise
LAGGANGAIRN STANDING STONES
Knowe
Cross Water of Luce
Artfield Fell
Loch Moan
Water of Minnoch
Palgowan
Glentrool
Forest
Glen Trool Lodge
BRUCE'S STONE
Loch Trool
Glentrool Village
GLEN TROOL VISITOR CENTRE
MULLWHARCHAR
MERRICK
Loch Enoch
Loch Neldricken
Loch Valley
SILVER FLOWE
RHINNS OF KELLS
CORSERINE
Loch Harrow
Forrest Lodge
Loch Dungeon
Drumb
Clatteringshaws Forest
Clatteringshaws Loch
Loch Dee
LAMACHAN HILL
Clachaneasy
Kirroughtree Forest
Loch Middle
WILD GOAT PARK
Loch Grannoch
FELL OF
Penninghame Forest
B7027
A714
Penkiln Burn
A712
Palnure Burn
Carseriggan
Challoch
Minnigaff
MINNIGAFF
Creebridge
Newton Stewart
NX
CAIRNSMORE OF FLEET
Black Loch
Loch Heron
Loch Ronald
New Luce
SOUTHERN UPLAND WAY
Drumphail
Benfield
Shennanton
A75
B735
B733
Kirkcowan
Palnure
Clints of Dromore
Tarf Water
Baltersan
Cree
Causeway End
Whitecairn
Carscreugh
Craighlaw Mains
GLENLUCE ABBEY
CASTLE OF PARK
Glenluce
Dernaglar Loch
Knock Moss
High Mindork
Spittal
Carsegowan
Torhousemuir
GEM ROCK MUSEUM
Creetown
Glen
Wigtown Sands
TORHOUSE STONE CIRCLE
Bladnoch
B7052
B733
B7005
Wigtown
Whitefield Loch
A747
Fell Loch
THE MACHARS
Bladnoch
SCOTLAND'S BOOK TOWN
VISITOR CENTRE
A714
Carsluith
CARSLUITH CASTLE
CAIRNHARROW
CAIRNHOLY CAIRNS
Milton
Stairhaven
Castle Loch
Culmazie
Auchenmalg
Mochrum Loch
Braehead
Kirkinner
Baldoon Sands
Ravenshall Pt.
Fleet Bay
Ringdoo Pt.
Auchenmalg Bay
Culshabbin
B7085
Alticry
B7005
Loch Head
Barrachan
Whauphill
A746
B7004
CHAPEL FINIAN
Elrig
MOTE OF DRUCHTAG
Sorbie
B7052
Garlieston
Eggerness Pt.
Mochrum
Airyhassen
Milton Pt.
Drumtroddan
Drummoddie
GALLOWAY HOUSE GARDENS
DRUMTRODDAN STONES
B7063
Port William
B7085
Monreith Mains
B7021
Moor of Ravenstone
Cults
LUCE BAY
CRUGGLETON CHURCH AND CASTLE
BARSALLOCH FORT
Barsalloch Pt.
Monreith
MONREITH ANIMAL WORLD, SHORE CENTRE AND MUSEUM
Bishopton
PRIORY AND MUSEUM
Whithorn
Port Allen
Monreith Bay
WHITHORN TRUST DISCOVERY CENTRE
A747
Portyerrock Bay
Glasserton
Cairn Hd.
FELL OF CARLETON
B7004
ST NINIAN'S CHAPEL
ST NINIAN'S CAVE
Isle of Whithorn
Port Castle Bay
Cutcloy
BURROW HEAD
Cailliness Pt.
MULL OF GALLOWAY
112
106

Dumfries and Galloway
NX
Loch Dungeon
Millquarter
Earlstoun Loch
St John's Town of Dalry
Bogue
Corriedoo Forest
Sundaywell
Loch Urr
Drumbuie
Garroch
Glenlee
Silver Flowe
Loch Valley
Clatteringshaws Forest
Clatteringshaws Loch
Loch Dee
New Galloway
Balmaclellan
Blackcraig
Knocklearn
Gibbshill
Glenkiln
Glen
Blowplain Open Farm
Ironmacannie
Craig
Corsock
Clatteringshaws Forest Wildlife Centre
Raiders Road Forest Drive
Merkland
Brooklands
Crocketford
Ninemile Bar
Auchenreoch Loch
Bennan Forest
Cairn Edward Hill
Drumrash
Loch Ken
Wild Goat Park
Loch Grannoch
Fell of Fleet
Mossdale
Parton
Kirkpatrick Durham
Springholm
Stroan Loch
Loch Skerrow
Woodhall Loch
Old Bridge of Urr
Crossmichael
Cainsmore of Fleet
Cairnsmore of Fleet
Palnure Burn
Fleet Forest
Lochenbreck Loch
Craig
Clarebrand
Haugh of Urr
Townhead of Greenlaw
Mote of Urr
Clints of Dromore
Laurieston
Laurieston Forest
Palnure
Big Water of Fleet
Loch Glentoo
Threave Castle
Castle Douglas
Old Buittle Tower
Barhill
Dalbeattie
Loch Whinyeon
Loch Mannoch
Kelton Mains Open Farm
Threave Gardens
Loch Bargatton
Carlingwark Loch
Glengap Forest
Bengray
Glengap
Bridge of Dee
Rhonehouse or Kelton Hill
Gelston
Cree
Gem Rock Museum
Creetown
Glen
Fleet
Wigtown Sands
Anworth
Mill on the Fleet
Gatehouse of Fleet
Ringford
Valleyfield
Airieland
Palnackie
Barnbarroch
Orchardton Tower
Wigtown
Scotland's Book Town
Carsluith
Carsluith Castle
Cairnharrow
Cardoness Castle
Valley
Girthon
Twynholm
Galloway Hydro Visitor Centre
Tongland
Broughton House and Garden
Bengairn
Kippford or Scaur
Mote of Mark
Rough Island
East Stewartry Coast
Cairnholy Cairns
Baldoon Sands
Ravenshall Pt.
Fleet Bay
Sandgreen
Barharrow
Maclellan's Castle
Whinnieliggate
Ringdoo Pt.
Stewartry Museum
Kirkcudbright
Auchencairn
Knockbrex
Islands of Fleet
Kirkandrews
Borgue
St Mary's Isle
Mutehill
Kirkcarswell
Dundrennan
Rascarrel
Balcary Pt.
Rascarrel Bay
Orroland
Wigtown Bay
Sorbie
Garlieston
Eggerness Pt.
Borness
Kirkcudbright Bay
Townhead
Dundrennan Abbey
Netherlaw
Port Mary
Galloway House Gardens
Ross
Balmae
Borness Pt.
Abbey Hd.
Cults
Cruggleton Church and Castle
Little Ross
Whithorn
Port Allen
Portyerrock Bay
Cairn Hd.
St Ninian's Chapel
Isle of Whithorn
Cutcloy
A702
A712
A762
A713
A75
A711
A745
A755
B7075
B794
B795
B796
B727
B736
B7004
B7052
B7063
A746
113
105
0 1 2 3 4 5 6 miles
0 1 2 3 4 5 6 7 8 9 10 km

Dunscore
ELLISLAND FARM
Duncow
Applegarthtown
A74(M)
B723
5
6
Gallaberry
Amisfield
7 Lochmaben
Marjoriebanks
8
Water of Milk
9
240
B729
A76
Kirkton
A701
Tinwald
Lockerbie
B7068
319
Bankshill
A
LOCHMABEN CASTLE
Castle Loch
A709
Newtonairds
Holywood
114
Locharbriggs
114
B7068
Heck
Heathhall
DUMFRIES AND GALLOWAY AVIATION MUS.
Irongray
LINCLUDEN COLLEGE
Newbridge
The Grove
A709
Torthorwald
Hightae
287
Burnswark
BURNSWARK FORT
Birkshaw Forest
Castlemilk
Waterbeck
Lincluden
OLD BRIDGE HOUSE MUS.
Terregles Banks
Greystone
RAMMERSCALES HOUSE
249
Kettleholm
B725
B722
Kirtle Water
KIRKCONNEL CHURCH
Maxwelltown
Dumfries
Collin
Middleshaw
Middlebie
BIRRENS FORT
Springkell
A75
B7020
B7076
Eaglesfield
Cargenbridge
BURNS HOUSE
ROBERT BURNS CENTRE
Greenlea
Annan
Ecclefechan
THOMAS CARLYLE'S BIRTHPLACE
B
Brae
Lochfoot
Lochrutton Loch
A711
DUMFRIES MUSEUM & CAMERA OBSCURA
Racks
Lochar Water
Cleughbrae
Dalton
B725
B723
Hoddomcross
Kingholm Quay
Mouswald
Kirtlebridge
A74(M)
Islesteps
B725
B724
Carrutherstown
B725
Hoddom Mains
Mabie Forest
Mabie
A710
Kelton
Lochar Moss
B722
Creca
Lochaber Loch
Loch Arthur
KIRKCONNELL FLOW
Brydekirk
B7020
B723
Beeswing
DRUMCOLTRAN TOWER
Glencaple
Bankend
B725
A75
Charlesfield
108
Clarencefield
B6357
Kirkgunzeon
Kirkconnell
River Nith
RUTHWELL CROSS
SHAMBELLIE HOUSE COSTUME MUSEUM
B725
Ruthwell
DUNCAN SAVINGS BANK MUSEUM
B721
Annan
A75
New Abbey
Shearington
Blackshaw
Cummertrees
B724
Dornock
New Abbey Pow
SWEETHEART ABBEY
B725
CAERLAVEROCK CASTLE
Eastpark
Powfoot
Welldale
Shawhill
Eastriggs
NEW ABBEY CORN MILL
NITH
Bowhouse
CAERLAVEROCK
C
383 LONG FELL
Overton
WILDFOWL AND WETLAND CENTRE
Blackshaw Bank
Loch Kindar
ESTUARY
Bowness-on-Solway
Port Carlisle
Drumburn
569 CRIFFELL
SOLWAY COAST
Glasson
Bowness Common
Carsethorn
B793
Cardurnock
Drumburgh
Kirkbean
ARBIGLAND GARDENS
Anthorn
DRUMBURGH MOSS
Drumstinchall
Prestonmill
Whitrigg
Caulkerbush
A710
JOHN PAUL JONES BIRTHPLACE MUSEUM
Kirkbride
Finglandrigg
Mainsriddle
MERSEHEAD RSPB NATURE RESERVE
Skinburness
Newton Arlosh
Sandyhills
D
Colvend
Southerness
Wedholme Flow
Rockcliffe
Portling
Southerness Pt.
Silloth
Calvo
Seaville
Wampool
Mersehead Sands
Greenrow
Causewayhead
B5307
Castlehill Pt.
Kingside Hill
SOUTH SOLWAY MOSSES
B5302
Blitterlees
Abbey Town
Waver
Oulton
B5300
Highlaws
Kelsick
Lessonhall
Beckfoot
Dundraw
Waverbridge
Pelutho
B5302
Wigton
Newtown
Blencogo
NX
Holme St Cuthbert
Bromfield
Waverton
Mawbray
Langrigg
Waterside
Dubmill Pt.
B5301
E
A595
Edderside
New Cowper
Westnewton
Bolton Low Houses
NY
Allonby
Watchhill
108
Aspatria
A596
B5299
Allonby Bay
Hayton
Ellen
Mealsgate
Prospect
Blennerhasset
Boltongate
B5300
Oughterside
Sandale
Torpenhow
Allerby
Threapland
Crosscanonby
Crosby Villa
Parsonby
Plumbland
Whitrigg
Crosby
Bullgill
Gilcrux
Bothel
Ireby
B5301
A591
MARYPORT MARITIME MUSEUM
Uldale
High Ireby
Maryport
Dearham
447 BINSEY
Over Water
A594
Tallentire
A595
Sunderland
Blindcrake
Bewaldeth
F
Flimby
Dovenby
Bridekirk
Orthwaite
Broughton Moor
Standingstone
Derwent
A596
Great Broughton
Little Broughton
B5291
Bassenthwaite
Siddick
Papcastle
Camerton
WORDSWORTH HO.
Cockermouth
Embleton
Seaton
Derwent
Brigham
CASTLEGATE HO.
BASSENTHWAITE LAKE
Great Clifton
A66
COCKERMOUTH
98
WYTHOP MILL
Wythop Mill
North Side
Bridgefoot
Greysouthen
98
Bassenthwaite Lake
MIREHOUSE
931 SKIDDAW
Workington
Stainburn
HELENA THOMPSON MUS.
Little Clifton
A5086
B5292
Thornthwaite Forest
Westfield
A595
Eaglesfield
SANDYBECK MEADOW
Mossbay
Deanscales
Marron
A596
5
6
7
8
9
G
Winscales
Low Lorton
Thornthwaite
A66

Langholm
MALCOLM MONUMENT
Tinnisburn Forest
Kershopefoot
Kershope Forest
Lockerbie
Paddockhole
Bankshill
Kirtleton
Caulside
Baileyhead
Burnswark
BURNSWARK FORT
Castlemilk
Waterbeck
GILNOCKIE TOWER
Claygate
Rowanburn
Catlowdy
Crossings
Evertown
Canonbie
Middlebie
KIRKCONNEL CHURCHYARD
Springkell
BIRRENS FORT
Milltown
Woodhouselees
Riddings
Roughsike
Roadhead
Ecclefechan
THOMAS CARLYLE'S BIRTHPLACE
Eaglesfield
Haggbeck
Moat
Hoddomcross
Chapelknowe
SCOTS DYKE
Hoddom Mains
Kirtlebridge
MERKLAND CROSS
Netherby
Easton
Stapleton
Kirkpatrick-Fleming
Brydekirk
Creca
Newton
GRETNA GREEN SERVICES
OLD BLACKSMITHS SHOP CENTRE
Charlesfield
Hollee
Springfield
Longtown
Boltonfellend
Kirkcambeck
Gretna Green
Kirklinton
Hethersgill
Annan
Rigg
Gretna
GRETNA GATEWAY
Powfoot
Welldale
Shawhill
Dornock
Eastriggs
Browhouses
Sandysike
Westlinton
Smithfield
Walton
VALLUM
Scaleby Hill
Scaleby
Newtown
NY
Bowness-on-Solway
Port Carlisle
Todhills
TODHILLS SERVICES
Blackford
Laversdale
Irthington
Brampton
COURSE OF HADRIAN'S WALL
Rockcliffe
Glasson
Bowness Common
Harker
CARLISLE
Cardurnock
Drumburgh
HADRIAN'S WALL PATH
Burgh-by-Sands
Beaumont
Cargo
Kingstown
Houghton
Low Crosby
Newby East
Anthorn
Easton
Boustead Hill
Linstock
DRUMBURGH MOSS
Grinsdale
Edentown
Hayton
Whitrigg
Kirkandrews upon Eden
Warwick on Eden
Kirkbride
Fingland
FINGLANDRIGG WOODS
Thurstonfield
Stanwix
Carlisle
Moorhouse
Newton Arlosh
Kirkbampton
Oughterby
TULLIE HOUSE MUS. & GALL.
CATH
Warwick Bridge
How
Castle Carrock
Heads Nook
Faugh
Little Bampton
Little Orton
Botcherby
Scotby
Morton
Harraby
Wetheral
Great Corby
WETHERAL PRIORY GATEHOUSE
Calvo
Seaville
Wedholme Flow
Aikton
Great Orton
Newby West
Upperby
Wiggonby
Cummersdale
Carleton
Cumwhinton
Cumwhitton
SOUTH SOLWAY MOSSES
Baldwinholme
Brisco
Kingside Hill
Durdar
Oulton
Abbey Town
Kelsick
Lessonhall
Thursby
Dalston
Cotehill
Hornsby
Dundraw
Waverbridge
Buckabank
Wreay
Blencogo
Wigton
West Curthwaite
East Curthwaite
Holmwrangle
Bromfield
Waverton
Gaitsgill
Aiketgate
Langrigg
Waterside
Brackenthwaite
Low Hesket
Armathwaite
Red Dial
Raughton Head
Stockdalewath
SOUTHWAITE SERVICES
Rosley
Westnewton
Westward
Southwaite
High Hesket
Bolton Low Houses
Welton
HIGH HEAD SCULPTURE VALLEY
Old Town
Watchhill
Fletchertown
Ivegill
Low Braithwaite
Aspatria
Brocklebank
Sebergham
Mealsgate
Blennerhasset
Boltongate
Cumbria
Inglewood Forest
Thomas Close
Calthwaite
Sandale
Torpenhow
Caldbeck
Sowerby Row
Lazonby Fell
Townhead
Threapland
Hesket Newmarket
Plumbland
Whitrigg
Ireby
Hutton End
Bothel
Fell Side
Branthwaite
Uldale
Millhouse
High Ireby
New Rent
HUTTON-IN-THE-FOREST
Plumpton
Brockleymoor
Low Row
Lamonby
Unthank
Skelton
BINSEY
Over Water
Ellonby
Unthank End
Plumpton Head
Blindcrake
Sunderland
HIGH PIKE
High Row
Bewaldeth
Orthwaite
Hutton Roof
Little Blencow
Catterlen
Johnby
KNOTT
Mosedale
Laithes
Great Blencow
Newton Reigny
Bassenthwaite
Derwent
Caldew
Fair Hill
Embleton
SKIDDAW FOREST
GREAT CALVA
Greystoke
Penrith
BASSENTHWAITE LAKE
Mungrisdale
Carleton
Wythop Mill
Berrier
Newbiggin
Motherby
BLENCATHRA
SADDLEBACK OR BLENCATHRA
Penruddock
Eamont Bridge
Stainton
RHEGED
Sockbridge
Scales
TARN MOSS
Troutbeck
DALEMAIN
Clifton
Hutton
Dacre
Tirril
Thornthwaite
Applethwaite
Threlkeld
0 1 2 3 4 5 6 miles
0 1 2 3 4 5 6 7 8 9 10 km

NORTHUMBERLAND
NATIONAL PARK
NY
Wark Forest
Bellingham
Bower
Hesleyside
Ridsdale
Redesmouth
Hopehouse
Sighty Crag
Whitelyne Common
Kielder Mires
Paddaburn Moor
The Flatt
Churnsike Lodge
White Preston
Blacka Burn
Birtley
Colt Crag Reservoir
Warks Burn
Wark
Whygate
Stonehaugh
Bewcastle
Park End
Great Swinburne
Gunnerton
Butterburn
Black Fell
Spadeadam Forest
Pennine Way
Simonburn
Barrasford
Haughton Common
Haughton Castle
Chollerton
Humshaugh
Chollerford
Spadeadam Farm
Wiley Sike
Irthing
Course of Hadrian's Wall
Hadrian's Wall Path
Greenlee Lough
Broomlee Lough
Old Repeater Station
Walwick
Low Brunton
Brunton Turret
Chesters Roman Fort
Thirlwall Common
Whiteside
Housesteads Roman Fort
Visitor Centre
Vallum
Wall
Hill Head
West Hall
Gilsland Spa
Birdoswald Roman Fort
Roman Army Museum
Hadrian's Wall
Fourstones
Newbrough
Birdoswald
Gilsland
Greenhead
Once Brewed
Chesterholm Museum
Warden
Acomb
Upper Denton
Bardon Mill
Chesterwood
Henshaw
Tyne Green
Lanercost
Haltwhistle
Melkridge
Redburn
Haydon Bridge
Low Gate
Moothall
Abbey
Hexham
Border History Mus.
Low Row
Plenmeller
South Tyne
Denton Fell
Plenmellar Common
Langley
Milton
Rowfoot
Farlam
Hallbankgate
Tindale
Midgeholme
Halton Lea Gate
Tindale Tarn
Tindale Fells
Forest Head
Maiden Way
Lambley
Stonehouse
Whitfield
Catton
Bearsbridge
Dye House
Dalton
Whitley Chapel
Slaley Forest
Gelt
Cold Fell
Glendue Fell
Eals
West Allen
Allendale Town
King's Forest of Geltsdale
Knarsdale
Whitfield Moor
Broadwell House
Hexhamshire Common
Devil's Water
Slaggyford
Ninebanks
Sinderhope
Allendale Common
Blanchland Moor
Geltsdale Middle
Ninebanks
East Allen
Blanchland
Newbiggin
Ayle
Spartylea
Hunstanworth
Nookton Fell
Croglin
South Tynedale Railway
Blagill
Gossipgate Gallery
Carrshield
Scale Houses
Watch Hill
Raise
Alston
Nenthall
Dirt Pot
Allenheads
Bolt's Law
Bayles
Middle Fell
Coalcleugh
Gilderdale Forest
Renwick
Haresceugh
Leadgate
Nenthead
Nenthead Mines Heritage Centre
Killhope Leadmining Centre
Rookhope
Rookhope Nurseries
High Bankhill
Garrigill
Lanehead
Middlehope Moor
Unthank
Cowshill
Wearhead
Weardale
Gamblesby
Burnhope Reservoir
Eastgate
Glassonby
Maiden Way
Altston Moor
Ireshopeburn
Westgate
Melmerby
Melmerby Fell
St John's Chapel
Daddry Shield
Little Salkeld
Black Burn
Burnhope Seat
Ireshope Moor
Hunsonby
Round Hill
Pennines
Winskill
Ousby
Cross Fell
Tees
Harwood
Westernhope Moor
Briggle Beck
Skirwith
Kirkland
Milburn Forest
Trout Beck
Viewing Hill
Harwood Beck
Langdon Common
Chapelfell Top
Edenhall
Eden
Moor House-Upper Teesdale
Newbiggin Common
Blencarn
Crowdundle Beck
Langdon Beck
Widdybank Fell
Forest
Ettersgill
Culgaith
Milburn
Cow Green Reservoir
High Force
Bowlees Visitor Centre
Acorn Bank
Newbiggin
Dufton Fell
Cauldron Snout
Temple Sowerby
Cronkley Fell
Knock
Maize Beck
Holwick
Middleton-in-Teesdale
Lowmoor Row
Cliburn Moss
Brougham Castle
A69
A689
A686
A68
A6079
B6318
B6319
B6320
B6305
B6304
B6295
B6303
B6294
B6277
B6306
B6412
A66
116
110
99
100

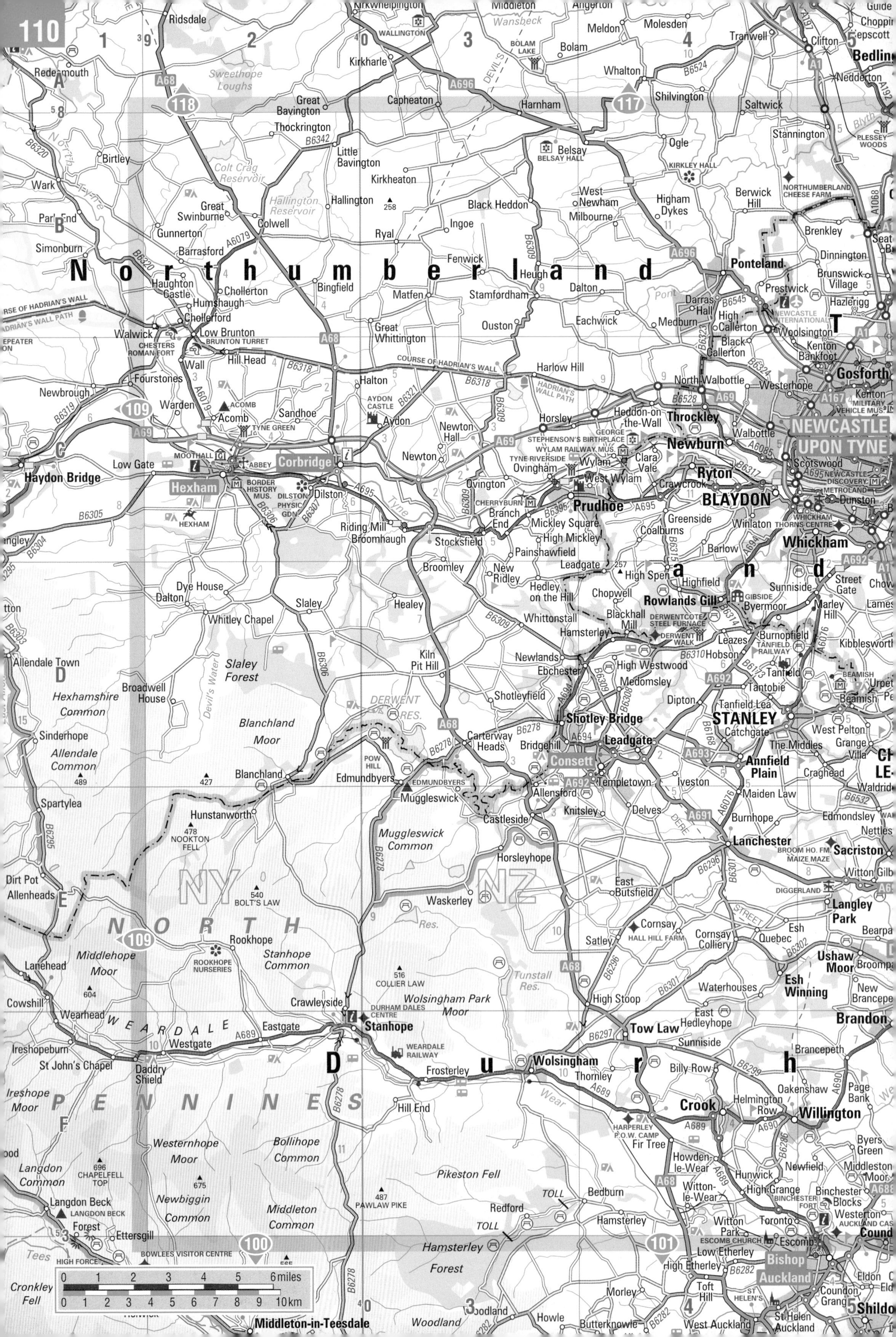
Northumberland
Durham
NORTH PENNINES
NEWCASTLE UPON TYNE
Ridsdale
Redesmouth
Kirkwhelpington
WALLINGTON
Kirkharle
Middleton
Wansbeck
Angerton
Meldon
Molesden
BOLAM LAKE
Bolam
Tranwell
Clifton
Bedlington
Nedderton
Whalton
Shilvington
Saltwick
Sweethope Loughs
Great Bavington
Capheaton
Harnham
Thockrington
Little Bavington
Belsay
BELSAY HALL
Ogle
Stannington
KIRKLEY HALL
Birtley
Colt Crag Reservoir
Kirkheaton
Wark
Hallington Reservoir
Hallington
West Newham
Milbourne
Higham Dykes
Berwick Hill
NORTHUMBERLAND CHEESE FARM
Black Heddon
Great Swinburne
Colwell
Ingoe
Park End
Gunnerton
Ryal
Brenkley
Simonburn
Barrasford
Fenwick
Ponteland
Dinnington
Brunswick Village
Heugh
Haughton Castle
Chollerton
Bingfield
Dalton
Prestwick
Hazlerigg
Humshaugh
Matfen
Stamfordham
Darras Hall
High Callerton
Woolsington
COURSE OF HADRIAN'S WALL
HADRIAN'S WALL PATH
Chollerford
Eachwick
Medburn
NEWCASTLE INTERNATIONAL
Black Callerton
Kenton Bankfoot
Walwick
Low Brunton
BRUNTON TURRET
Great Whittington
Ouston
CHESTERS ROMAN FORT
Wall
Hill Head
Harlow Hill
Gosforth
Fourstones
Halton
North Walbottle
Westerhope
Kenton
Newbrough
AYDON CASTLE
Aydon
Warden
ACOMB
Acomb
Sandhoe
Throckley
Heddon-on-the-Wall
Horsley
Walbottle
TYNE GREEN
Newton Hall
GEORGE STEPHENSON'S BIRTHPLACE
WYLAM RAILWAY MUS.
Newburn
MOOTHALL
ABBEY
Corbridge
Newton
TYNE RIVERSIDE
Ovingham
Wylam
Clara Vale
Ryton
Scotswood
Haydon Bridge
Low Gate
Hexham
BORDER HISTORY MUS.
DILSTON PHYSIC GDN
Dilston
Tyne
Ovington
West Wylam
Crawcrook
BLAYDON
NEWCASTLE DISCOVERY
METROLAND
Dunston
CHERRYBURN
Prudhoe
Branch End
Mickley Square
Greenside
Winlaton
THORNS CENTRE
Whickham
HEXHAM
Riding Mill
Broomhaugh
Stocksfield
High Mickley
Coalburns
Painshawfield
Barlow
Broomley
New Ridley
Leadgate
High Spen
Highfield
Street Gate
Dye House
Dalton
Hedley on the Hill
Chopwell
Rowlands Gill
GIBSIDE
Byermoor
Sunniside
Marley Hill
Slaley
Healey
Whitley Chapel
Whittonstall
Blackhall Mill
DERWENTCOTE STEEL FURNACE
Hamsterley
DERWENT WALK
Leazes
Burnopfield
TANFIELD RAILWAY
Kibblesworth
Allendale Town
Slaley Forest
Kiln Pit Hill
Newlands
Ebchester
High Westwood
Hobson
Tanfield
BEAMISH
Beamish
Medomsley
Tantobie
Hexhamshire Common
Broadwell House
DERWENT RES.
Shotleyfield
Dipton
Tanfield Lea
Blanchland Moor
Shotley Bridge
STANLEY
West Pelton
Sinderhope
Carterway Heads
Bridgehill
Leadgate
Catchgate
The Middles
Grange Villa
Allendale Common
POW HILL
Consett
Annfield Plain
Craghead
Blanchland
Edmundbyers
EDMUNDBYERS
Templetown
Iveston
Waldridge
Muggleswick
Allensford
Maiden Law
Spartylea
Hunstanworth
Castleside
Knitsley
Delves
Burnhope
Edmondsley
NOOKTON FELL
Muggleswick Common
Lanchester
BROOM HO. FM. MAIZE MAZE
Sacriston
Horsleyhope
Witton Gilbert
Dirt Pot
Allenheads
East Butsfield
DIGGERLAND
NY
NZ
BOLT'S LAW
Waskerley
Langley Park
Cornsay
HALL HILL FARM
Esh
Cornsay Colliery
Quebec
Rookhope
Satley
Middlehope Moor
ROOKHOPE NURSERIES
Stanhope Common
Ushaw Moor
Lanehead
Tunstall Res.
COLLIER LAW
Esh Winning
Waterhouses
New Brancepeth
Cowshill
Crawleyside
Wolsingham Park Moor
High Stoop
DURHAM DALES CENTRE
Stanhope
East Hedleyhope
Brandon
Wearhead
WEARDALE
Eastgate
Tow Law
Ireshopeburn
Westgate
WEARDALE RAILWAY
Sunniside
Brancepeth
St John's Chapel
Daddry Shield
Frosterley
Wolsingham
Thornley
Billy Row
Oakenshaw
Page Bank
Ireshope Moor
PENNINES
Hill End
Wear
Crook
Helmington Row
Willington
HARPERLEY P.O.W. CAMP
Fir Tree
Howden-le-Wear
Byers Green
Westernhope Moor
Bollihope Common
Newfield
Middlestone Moor
Langdon Common
CHAPELFELL TOP
Pikeston Fell
Hunwick
High Grange
Binchester Blocks
BINCHESTER FORT
Newbiggin Common
PAWLAW PIKE
Bedburn
Witton-le-Wear
Langdon Beck
LANGDON BECK
Middleton Common
Redford
TOLL
Hamsterley
Witton Park
Toronto
Westerton
AUCKLAND CASTLE
Forest
Ettersgill
ESCOMB CHURCH
Escomb
Coundon
Tees
HIGH FORCE
BOWLEES VISITOR CENTRE
Hamsterley Forest
Low Etherley
High Etherley
Bishop Auckland
Eldon
Cronkley Fell
Toft Hill
ST HELEN'S
Coundon Grange
Morley
Shildon
Middleton-in-Teesdale
Woodland
Howle
Butterknowle
West Auckland
St Helen Auckland
0 1 2 3 4 5 6 miles
0 1 2 3 4 5 6 7 8 9 10 km

6
7
8
9
A
B
C
D
E
F
G
117
BLYTH
West Sleekburn
Cambois
East Sleekburn
Cowpen
Bebside
Newsham
New Delaval
New Hartley
Seaton
Seaton Sluice
SEATON DELAVAL HALL
Hartley
ST MARY'S LIGHTHOUSE
St Mary's or Bait I.
Seaton Delaval
East Cramlington
Seghill
Holywell
Annitsford
Burradon
Backworth
Earsdon
WHITLEY BAY
Monkseaton
Shiremoor
Cullercoats
SEA LIFE CENTRE
Marden
TYNEMOUTH CASTLE & PRIORY
STAVANGER 20:45
HAUGESUND 23:00
BERGEN 27:00
KRISTIANSAND 18:00
GOTHENBURG 26:00
AMSTERDAM 15:00
Camperdown
Longbenton
STEPHENSON RAILWAY MUSEUM
Tynemouth
North Shields
THE RISING SUN
Willington
ARBEIA ROMAN FORT AND MUSEUM
South Shields
SOUTH SHIELDS MUSEUM
Jesmond
WALLSEND
Heaton
NEWCASTLE-U-TYNE
Byker
Tyne Tunnel
TOLL
ROYAL QUAYS
SEGEDUNUM FORT
Jarrow
BEDE'S WORLD
ST PAUL'S MONASTERY
Westoe
THE LEAS AND MARSDEN ROCK
Marsden Bay
Harton
Marsden
CASTLE KEEP
Walker
Gateshead
Hebburn
A1300
SOUTER LIGHTHOUSE
INTERNATIONAL STADIUM
Hedworth
Whiteleas
Cleadon
Whitburn Colliery
Pelaw
Boldon Colliery
Whitburn
Felling
Boldon
A1018
Carr Hill
FULWELL WINDMILL
Fulwell
Downhill
Hylton Castle
Southwick
Roker
Wrekenton
N.E. AIRCRAFT MUS.
BOWES RLY.
Monkwearmouth
NATIONAL GLASS CENTRE
Springwell
Usworth
Castletown
STATION MUS.
SAINT PETER'S CHURCH
SUNDERLAND MINSTER
Blackfell
OLD HALL
South Hylton
Pallion
WASHINGTON
High Barnes
Sunderland
WASHINGTON SERVICES
Pennywell
Hendon
Lambton
THE WILDFOWL & WETLANDS TRUST
PENSHAW MON.
NZ
New Silksworth
Fatfield
Barley Mow
Rickleton
Penshaw
East Herrington
Shiney Row
Tunstall
Ryhope
RYHOPE ENGINES MUS.
New Herrington
Doxford Park
Bournmoor
Burdon
Newbottle
THE ANKERS HOUSE
Fence Houses
Seaton
Northlea
SEAHAM
HOUGHTON-LE-SPRING
Great Lumley
Colliery Row
West Lea
Dalton-le-Dale
East Rainton
Hetton-le-Hole
Plawsworth
West Rainton
Cold Hesledon
FINCHALE PRIORY
Murton
Leamside
Low Moorsley
Easington Lane
Hawthorn
Pity Me
South Hetton
Beacon Pt.
Framwellgate Moor
Pittington
Easington Colliery
DURHAM LIGHT INFANTRY MUS.
Carrville
DALTON PARK
Littletown
Easington
Haswell
Sherburn
DURHAM CITY
DURHAM CATH.
Sherburn Hill
Haswell Plough
Shotton Colliery
Horden
DURHAM UNIV. ORIENTAL MUS.
Ludworth
Shadforth
Shincliffe
PETERLEE
Old Cassop
Thornley
Shotton
CASTLE EDEN DENE
Blackhall Colliery
Wheatley Hill
CASTLE EDEN WALKWAY
Blackhall Rocks
Old Cassop
Old Quarrington
CASSOP VALE
Castle Eden
High Hesleden
Bowburn
Hesleden
DURHAM COAST
DURHAM SERVICES
Quarrington Hill
Wingate
Deaf Hill
Station Town
Hett
Hart Station
Kelloe
Trimdon Colliery
Trimdon Grange
Hutton Henry
Sheraton
Hart
JACKSONS LANDING
Coxhoe
Cornforth
Trimdon
High Throston
SAINT HILDA'S PARISH CHURCH
Ferryhill
THRISLINGTON
Ferryhill Station
HARTLEPOOL'S MARITIME EXPERIENCE
Hartlepool Bay
Elwick
West Park
Hartlepool
Kirk Merrington
Fishburn
Hartlepool
Mainsforth
Seaton Carew
Middlestone
Bishop Middleham
Dalton Piercy
Rift House
Leasingthorne
Chilton Lane
Butterwick
Chilton
101
102
ROTTERDAM 16:00
ZEEBRUGGE 16:30
Rushyford
Sedgefield
Tees Bay
Greatham
ENERGY INFORMATION CENTRE
Bradbury
SEDGEFIELD
Graythorp
NEWTON AYCLIFFE
Mordon
Wynyard Village
Newton Bewley
Thorpe
Salt Scar

Troon
Lady Isle
North Bay
South Bay
ROYAL TROON
LARNE 1:49
(March-Sept)
LARNE 4:30
Barassie
Muirhead
Loans
Dundonald
DUNDONALD CASTLE
Symington
Bogend
Craigie
Crossroads
Sornhill
Hansel Village
Millburn
Auchmillan
Mossgiel
Monkton
Tarbolton
BACHELOR'S CLUB
BURNS HOUSE MUSEUM
Mauchline
GLASGOW PRESTWICK INTERNATIONAL
Prestwick
St Quivox
Mossblown
Failford
AYR GORGE WOODLANDS
Haugh
Woodfield
Newton on Ayr
Wallacetown
Annbank
Stair
Crosshill
Whitletts
Ayr
Trabboch
Ochiltree
Seafield
Belston
Masonhill
Coylton
Coalhall
BURNS COTTAGE
Belmont
MACLAURIN GALLERY & ROZELLE HOUSE
Hillhead
Drongan
Heads of Ayr
HEADS OF AYR FARM PARK
Doonfoot
Alloway
Laigh Glengall
BURNS NATIONAL HERITAGE PARK
TAM O'SHANTER EXPERIENCE
Joppa
Barbieston
Martnaham Loch
Fisherton
Dunure
Sinclairston
Hayhill
Littlemill
Hollybush
Rankinston
Culroy
Minishant
Dalrymple
ELECTRIC BRAE
Water of Coyle
Culzean Bay
Polnessan
KILMEIN HILL
NS
CULZEAN CASTLE
CULZEAN
Whitefaulds
Maybole
COLLEGIATE CHURCH
Patna
Burnfoot
Maidenhead Bay
Kirkmichael
Aitkenhead
Waterside
DOON VALLEY HERITAGE MUSEUM
BENBEOCH
Maidens
Loch Spallander Reservoir
SCOTTISH INDUSTRIAL RAILWAY CENTRE
Burnton
TURNBERRY
Kirkoswald
CROSSRAGUEL ABBEY
Crosshill
Turnberry Bay
SOUTER JOHNNIE'S COTTAGE
Turnberry
Brest Rocks
BLAIRQUHAN
Dalmellington
CATHCARTSON VISITOR CENTRE
Bogton Loch
Ruglen
Straiton
Bellsbank
Townhead
South
Wallacetown
Water of Girvan
Dipple
Burnhead
Dailly
BIG HILL OF GLENMOUNT
BARGANY GARDENS
Old Dailly
Ayrshire
Girvan
Penkill
Houston
Linfern Loch
Tairlaw Forest
Loch Finlas
Glendoune
Penwhapple Res.
LOCH DOON
Loch Bradan
Woodland Bay
MULL OF MILJOAN
Dalwyne
LOCH DOON CASTLE
Craigmalloch
Lamlo
South Balloch
ARDWELL GARDENS
Tormitchell
Pinminnoch
CARRICK
Kennedy's Pass
Auchensoul
Barr
Changue Forest
CARRICK FOREST
GREY HILL
Loch Riecawr
Pinmore
Stinchar
Loch Macaterick
Currarie
Merkland
CRAIGENREOCH
MEAUL
Lendalfoot
Straid
Pinmore Mains
CARLETON CASTLE
NX
CORSERINE
Poundland
Pinwherry
PINDONNAN
Colmonell
Bellamore
GALLOWAY
MULLWHARCHAR
Knockdolian
Cree
Loch Moan
Water of Minnoch
MERRICK
Loch Enoch
RHINNS OF KELLS
Heronsford
Ballochmorrie
Black Clauchrie
Glen Tig
Water of Tig
Duisk
Palgowan
Loch Neldricken
SILVER FLOWE
Barrhill
Laggan
FOREST
Loch Valley
Balkissock
Eldrick
Glentrool
Forest
Glen Trool Lodge
BRUCE'S STONE
Trool
Arecleoch Forest
Chencrosh
Glentrool Village
GLEN TROOL VISITOR CENTRE
Glen
Loch Trool
PARK
Loch Dee
Drumlamford Loch
Dornal
Loch Dornal
Bargrennan
LAMACHAN HILL
0 1 2 3 4 5 6 miles
0 1 2 3 4 5 6 7 8 9 10 km

East Ayrshire
Dumfries and Galloway
LOWTHER HILLS
THE GLENKENS
Glengavel Reservoir
522 NUTBERRY HILL
434 WEDDER HILL
466 MIDDLEFIELD LAW
465 HARESHAW HILL
Braehead
Happendon
CAIRN LODGE (HAPPENDON) SERVICES
Uddington
Douglas West
Glenbuck
Netherwood
Glespin
Roberton Law
392 AUCHENSAUGH HILL
Middle Muir
SORN CASTLE
Catrine
Sorn
Smallburn
Muirkirk
Kames
Airds Moss
593 CAIRN TABLE
Glentaggart
Crawfordjohn
Cronberry
Back Rogerton
Auchinleck
Lugar
497 WARDLAW HILL
Glenmuir
Glenmuirshaw
Holmhead
Logan
KEIR HARDIE STATUE
Cumnock
Netherthird
BAIRD INSTITUTE MUS.
Craigens
Dalblair
Glenmuir Water
Duneaton Water
DRAKE LAW 483
478 MOUNT STUART
Fingland
494 RAKE LAW
553 WELLGRAIN DOD
DOON VALLEY RARE BREEDS CENTRE
509 KIRKLAND HILL
Kirkland
Pathhead
Mansfield
Connel Park
Bankglen
New Cumnock
Nith
Kirkconnel
Kelloholm
Crawick Water
Leadhills
LEADHILLS & WANLOCKHEAD RLY.
MUSEUM OF LEAD MINING
WANLOCKHEAD BEAM ENGINE
Wanlockhead
485 CONRIG HILL
732 GREEN LOWTHER
725 LOWTHER HILL
Mennock Pass
Burnside
Dalleagles
THE KNIPE 575
Crawick
Sanquhar
TOLBOOTH MUSEUM
SANQUHAR POST OFFICE
Mennock
Kello Water
SOUTHERN UPLAND WAY
Afton Water
569 ENOCH HILL
700 BLACKCRAIG HILL
Afton Reservoir
Euchan Water
449 CAIRN HILL
Potrail Water
Durisdeermill
DURISDEER PARISH CH.
Durisdeer
BALLENCLEUCH
Enterkinfoot
478
Scar Water
554 CAIRNKINNA HILL
Enoch
Carsphairn Forest
Holestane
MORTON CASTLE
DRUMLANRIG CASTLE
Carronbridge
797 CAIRNSMORE OF CARSPHAIRN
Corlae
580 BENBRACK
500
Auchenbrack
Auchenbainzie
Gatelawbridge
Benbuie
Shinnel Water
Burnhead
Thornhill
Brochloch
Penpont
Dalwhat Water
Water of Ken
372
Tynron
Keir Mill
Carsphairn
CAIRN AVEL
Bardennoch
SOUTHERN UPLAND WAY
Closeburn
Dundeugh Forest
Knowehead
Craigdarroch
Moniaive
JAMES PATERSON MUSEUM
Kirkland
357
Park
Kendoon Loch
MAXWELTON HOUSE
Glencrosh
Black Water
Straith
Wallaceton
Dalmacallan Forest
Glenmidge
Auldgirth
Dundeugh
KENDOON
Kendoon
Glenhoul
385 WETHER HILL
Castlefairn
Forrest Lodge
Carsfad Loch
Holmhead
Lochurr
432 BOGRIE HILL
Loch Dungeon
Lochinvar
417
Dunscore
Sundaywell
Loch Urr
Millquarter
Milton
Cairn Water
Earlstoun Loch
Drumbuie
St John's Town of Dalry
Bogue
Corriedoo Forest
373
240
Garroch
Blackcraig
Newtonairds
Drumpark
Holywood
Glenlee
Knocklearn
Glenkiln Res.
Irongray
381
New Galloway
Balmaclellan
Gibbshill
BLOWPLAIN OPEN FARM
Glenkiln
Terregles Banks
CLATTERINGSHAWS FOREST WILDLIFE CENTRE
Ironmacannie
317
398
Glen
Corsock
Shawhead
A70
A76
A702
A713
A712
A762
B729
B743
B705
B741
B740
B797
B7000
B7078
B7040
M74
NS
NX
121
114
106

Happendon
Uddington
Douglas
ST BRIDES
West
Roberton Law
M74
Roberton
Wiston
Newton
DUNGAVEL HILL
Lamington
Coulter
A702
Clyde
Culter Water
CULTER FELL
748
Cowgill Upper Reservoir
Culter Waterhead Reservoir
Holms Water
BLAKEHOPE HEAD
543
Drumelzier
PYKESTONE HILL
737
Langhaugh
Manor Water
Stanhope
637
817
DOLLAR LAW
Crookhaugh
510
Hearthstane
GLENWHAPPEN RIG
688
Tweedsmuir
Tweed
A701
392
AUCHENSAUGH HILL
Middle Muir
B7078
Glentaggart
Crawfordjohn
B740
ABINGTON SERVICES
Abington
569
TEWSGILL HILL
Camps Water
Camps Reservoir
DRAKE LAW
483
Kirkton
Crawford
550
Glenbreck
840
BROAD LAW
Meggethead
Megget Reservoir
Talla Reservoir
Talla Linnfoots
Fruid Reservoir
LOCHCRAIG HEAD
800
690
553
CRAIGMAID
546
CLYDE LAW
WELLGRAIN DOD
553
494
RAKE LAW
B797
B7040
Elvanfoot
LOWTHER HILLS
Elvan Water
Leadhills
LEADHILLS & WANLOCKHEAD RLY.
MUSEUM OF LEAD MINING
WANLOCKHEAD
WANLOCKHEAD BEAM ENGINE
Wanlockhead
485
CONRIG HILL
732
GREEN LOWTHER
725
LOWTHER HILL
Mennock Pass
SOUTHERN UPLAND WAY
B797
Mennock
A702
March
Watermeetings
Source of River Tweed
Loch Skeen
GREY MARE'S TAIL WATERFALLS
882
WHITE COOMB
808
HART FELL
DEVIL'S BEEF TUB
753
SADDLE YOKE
Blackhope Burn
Birkhill
677
Nether Howecleuch
Ericstane
Granton
Howslack
Roundstonefoot
Capplegill
A708
B719
A74(M)
Daer Reservoir
Potrail Water
SOUTHERN UPLAND WAY
NS NT
449
CAIRN HILL
A76
Moffat
MUSEUM
Moffat Water
TWEEDHOPE SHEEPDOGS
Coatsgate
678
CAPEL FELL
692
ETTRICK PEN
688
LOCH FELL
Dumcrieff
Durisdeermill
DURISDEER PARISH CHURCH
Durisdeer
691
BALLENCLEUCH LAW
407
Easter Earshaig
Garpol Water
Beattock
Kinnelhead
Enterkinfoot
Enoch
668
GANA HILL
NITHSDALE
ANNANDALE
Holestane
443
MORTON CASTLE
512
QUEENSBERRY
DRUMLANRIG CASTLE
A701
Wamphray Water
484
Laverhay
Eskdale
Carronbridge
Locherben
Auchenbainzie
Gatelawbridge
399
Lochwood
Scar Water
Burnhead
Penpont
Thornhill
Loch Ettrick
NX NY
Kinnel Water
Newton
Waterhead
Sandyford
B7020
B7076
Keir Mill
St Ann's
Closeburn
353
Forest of Ae
A702
357
Park
Blackacre
Johnstonebridge
ANNANDALE WATER SERVICES
Chapelhill
Dinwoodie Mains
Boreland
MAXWELTON HOUSE
Courance
B729
Straith
Wallaceton
Ae Village
Dumfries and
Dryfe Water
Water of Ae
Nethermill
Sibbaldbie
Dalmacallan Forest
Glenmidge
Parkgate
Auldgirth
Nith
Templand
Corrie Common
Dalswinton
Shieldhill
Dunscore
ELLISLAND FARM
Auchencairn
Millhousebridge
Sundaywell
Milton
Cairn Water
Duncow
Applegarthtown
A74(M)
B723
Water of Milk
Gallaberry
Amisfield
Lochmaben
Marjoriebanks
240
Kirkton
Tinwald
Lockerbie
LOCHMABEN CASTLE
Castle Loch
A709
Bankshill
Newtonairds
Holywood
Locharbriggs
Heck
B7068
Drumpark
Heathhall
DUMFRIES AND GALLOWAY AVIATION MUS.
Irongray
Glenkiln
LINCLUDEN COLLEGE
The Grove
Torthorwald
Hightae
287
Burnswark
BURNSWARK FORT
OLD BRIDGE HOUSE MUS.
Birkshaw Forest
Castlemilk
398
Glen
Greystone
RAMMERSCALES HOUSE
Kettleholm
Shawhead
Maxwelltown
Collin
249
Middleshaw
Middlebie
A75
0 1 2 3 4 5 6 miles
0 1 2 3 4 5 6 7 8 9 10 km
113
122
107

Traquair
Caddonfoot
Abbotsford House
Boleside
Darnick
Melrose
Newstead
A6091
Priorwood Gdns.
Trimontium Exhibition
Dryburgh Abbey
Mertoun Gdn
Eildon Hills
Newtown St. Boswells
St. Boswells
B6404
B6398
B6359
Glensax
Law
Kirkhouse
Glen Ho
576
Minch Moor
Yair Hill Forest
373
B7060
B709
743 Dun Rig
Blake Muir
123
Broadmeadows
Ovenscloss
Lindean
323
Whitlaw Mosses
Selkirk Glass
Selkirk
A707
A708
A699
Maxton
Douglas Burn
504
Yarrow Water
Yarrow
501 Fasteheugh Hill
Bowhill
Bowhill House & Country Park
B7039
Philiphaugh
Halliwell's House Museum
Sir Walter Scott's Courtroom
B6453
Midlem
Longnewton
B6359
Muir
Southern Upland Way
543
Dryhope Tower
Mountbenger
Sundhope
Yarrow Feus
Scottish
B7009
Clerklands
Lilliesleaf
Belses
B6400
Bloomfield
Ancrum
A68
Dryhope
Ettrickbridge
Kirkhope
Aikwood Tower James Hogg Exhibition
A7
Greenhouse
Chesters
Cappercleuch
Ettrick Forest
Black Knowe Head
550
St. Mary's Loch
Caver's Hill
369
Woll
Ashkirk
Akermoor Loch
B6359
276
Minto
Lanton
A698
Mary Queen of Scots House
Jedburgh Abbey
589 The Wiss
Gilmanscleuch
Ettrick Water
Hassendean
B6405
Newton
Loch of the Lowes
Crosslee
Newburgh
Todrig
Shaws Under Loch
Horsleyhill
Teviot
Borders
Hellmoor Loch
Ale Water
Clarilaw
Appletreehall
Denholm
B6358
Bedrule
338
Hunda
A708
Ramsey Knowe
Tushielaw
471
333 Smasha Hill
Ashybank
116
B6357
590
Wardlaw
Redfordgreen
Borthwickshiels
Burnfoot
424
Rubers Law
Ettrickhill
Ettrick
Ramseycleuch
B711
Buccleuch
Robertson
Wilton
Museum and Scott Gallery
Hawick
A698
Cauldmill
Kirkton
Hallrule
James Hogg Monument
498
Borthwickbrae
Burnfoot
Drumlanrig's Tower
A6088
Bonchester Bridge
Deanburnhaugh
Branxholm Park
Branxholme
301
Glenkerry
390 Redcleuch Edge
Newmill
Hobkirk
Chesters
Cleuch Head
Craik Forest
Borthwick Water
B6399
Southdean
Nether Dalgliesh
B709
Craik
Broadhaugh
393
488
Howpasley
Northhouse
Dodburn
Slitrig Water
B6357
Cragbank Wood
Riddell Monument
417 Pike Hill
Allan Water
NT
The Pike 462
Wauchope Forest
Teviothead
Priesthaugh
Langburnshiels
Davington
477
Castleweary
532
514 Fanna Hill
Singdean
Kagyu Samye Ling Tibetan Centre
Caldcleuch Head 608
599
602 Peel Fell
White Esk
Eskdalemuir Forest
Wisp Hill
599 Tudhope Hill
21
Jamestown
Gorrenberry
Hermitage Castle
Deadwater
Saughtree
529
446
Hermitage
Meggat Water
NY
Castle O'er Forest
B709
492
14
Ewes Water
499 Pike Fell
568 Roan Fell
Newlands
Larriston
Kielder
Castle O'er
Steele Road
Larriston Fells
Eskdale
Georgefield
Ewes
Dinlabyre
329
Bentpath
Old Castleton
Galloway
Tarras Water
446 Black Edge
Liddesdale
Janet Armstrong House
Newcastleton Forest
Newcastleton or Copshaw Holm
450 Calkin Rig
Craigcleuch Castle Collection
Potholm
Glendhu Hill
Langholm
Malcolm Monument
Kershope Burn
Black Lyne
Paddockhole
B7068
Tinnisburn Forest
Kershopefoot
319
Kershope Forest
Bewcastle Fells
Kirtleton
Caulside
White Lyne
518 Sighty Crag
108
B6318
Gilnockie Tower
Claygate
Baileyhead
Whitelyne Common
B722
Kirtle Water
Liddel Water
The Flatt
Blackpool Gate
Rowanburn
B6357
B6318
Crossings
Kirkconnel Churchyard
127
Evertown
B720
Canonbie
B6357
Catlowdy
424 White Preston

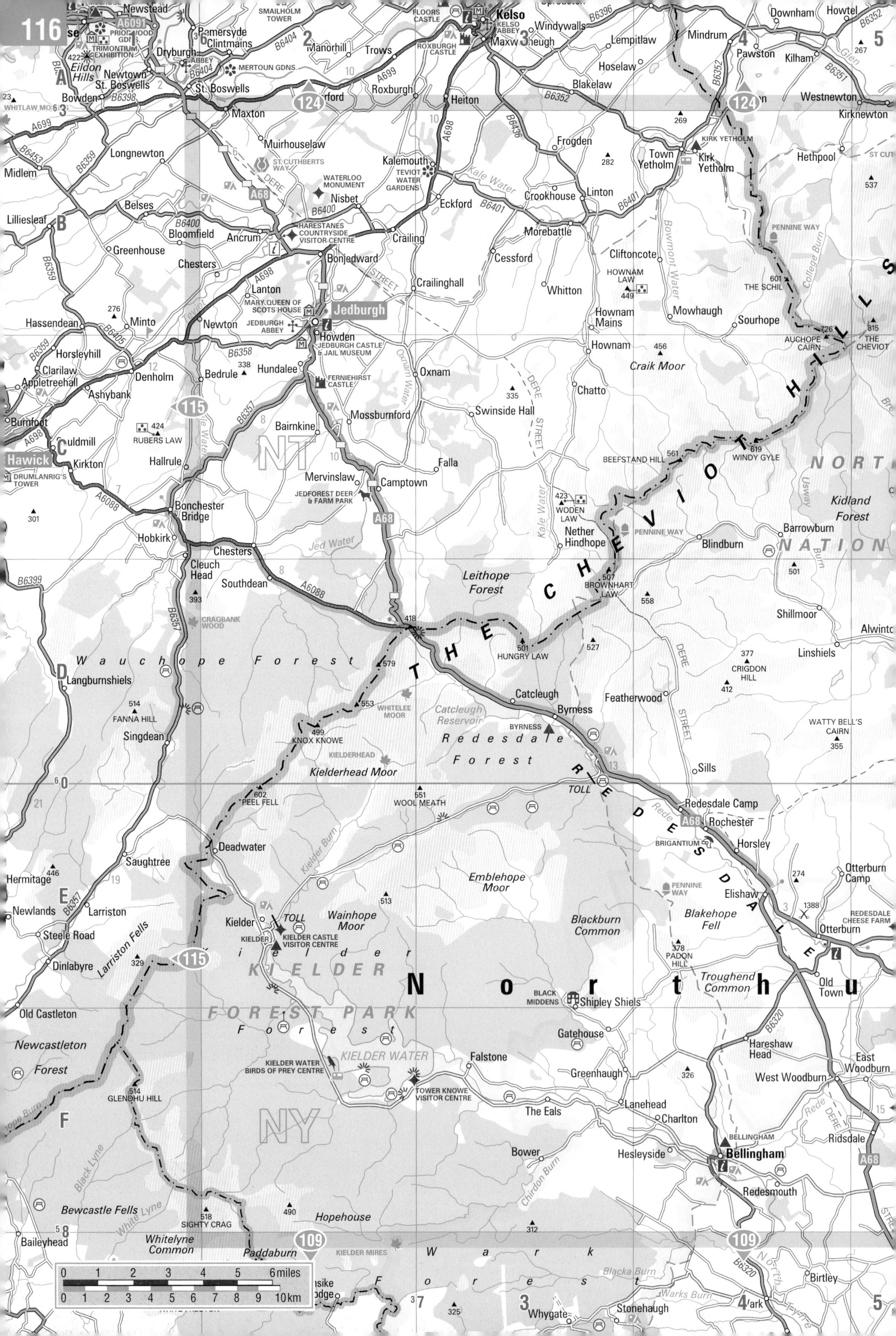

Newstead
SMAILHOLM TOWER
FLOORS CASTLE
Kelso
KELSO ABBEY
Windywalls
B6396
Downham
Howtel
B6352
A6091
PRIORWOOD GDNS
Pemersyde
Clintmains
B6404
Manorhill
Trows
ROXBURGH CASTLE
Maxwheugh
Lempitlaw
Mindrum
Pawston
Kilham
TRIMONTIUM EXHIBITION
Dryburgh
ABBEY
Eildon Hills
Newtown St. Boswells
MERTOUN GDNS.
A699
Hoselaw
Glen
B6351
Bowden
B6398
St. Boswells
Roxburgh
Blakelaw
124
WHITLAW MOSS
Maxton
Heiton
B6352
269
Westnewton
Kirknewton
A699
Longnewton
Muirhouselaw
A698
B6436
Frogden
KIRK YETHOLM
Town Yetholm
Kirk Yetholm
Hethpool
ST CUTHBERT'S WAY
Midlem
B6453
B6359
ST. CUTHBERTS WAY
Kalemouth
TEVIOT WATER GARDENS
Kale Water
282
537
WATERLOO MONUMENT
DERE
A68
Nisbet
B6400
Eckford
B6401
Crookhouse
Linton
B6401
Belses
Lilliesleaf
B6400
Bloomfield
Ancrum
HARESTANES COUNTRYSIDE VISITOR CENTRE
Crailing
Morebattle
Bowmont Water
PENNINE WAY
Greenhouse
Cessford
Cliftoncote
College Burn
Chesters
Bonjedward
STREET
HOWNAM LAW
449
THE SCHIL
601
Lanton
A698
Crailinghall
Whitton
MARY QUEEN OF SCOTS HOUSE
Jedburgh
Mowhaugh
276
Teviot
JEDBURGH ABBEY
Hownam Mains
Sourhope
Hassendean
Minto
Newton
Howden
AUCHOPE CAIRN
726
815
THE CHEVIOT
B6359
B6405
JEDBURGH CASTLE & JAIL MUSEUM
Hownam
456
Horsleyhill
B6358
Craik Moor
Clarilaw
338
Bedrule
Hundalee
Oxnam Water
Oxnam
Appletreehall
Denholm
FERNIEHIRST CASTLE
Chatto
Ashybank
335
DERE STREET
115
B6357
Mossburnford
Swinside Hall
Burnfoot
424
RUBERS LAW
Bairnkine
A698
Cauldmill
NT
Hawick
Kirkton
Hallrule
BEEFSTAND HILL
561
619
WINDY GYLE
NORTH
Falla
DRUMLANRIG'S TOWER
Mervinslaw
Camptown
Usway
Kidland Forest
A6088
JEDFOREST DEER & FARM PARK
423
WODEN LAW
301
Bonchester Bridge
A68
Kale Water
Nether Hindhope
PENNINE WAY
Barrowburn
Blindburn
Hobkirk
Jed Water
NATION
Chesters
Burn
Cleuch Head
501
B6399
Southdean
A6088
Leithope Forest
507
BROWNHART LAW
558
393
Shillmoor
B6357
CRAGBANK WOOD
418
Alwinton
THE CHEVIOT HILLS
501
HUNGRY LAW
527
377
CRIGDON HILL
Linshiels
Wauchope Forest
579
DERE
Langburnshiels
412
553
WHITELEE MOOR
Catcleugh
Catcleugh Reservoir
Byrness
Featherwood
514
FANNA HILL
BYRNESS
WATTY BELL'S CAIRN
Singdean
499
KNOX KNOWE
Redesdale Forest
STREET
355
KIELDERHEAD
Kielderhead Moor
13
Sills
TOLL
REDESDALE
602
PEEL FELL
551
WOOL MEATH
Redesdale Camp
Rochester
Rede
A68
21
BRIGANTIUM
Horsley
Deadwater
Kielder Burn
Saughtree
446
Hermitage
19
Emblehope Moor
PENNINE WAY
274
Otterburn Camp
Elishaw
B6357
513
1388
REDESDALE CHEESE FARM
Newlands
Larriston
TOLL
Wainhope Moor
Blackburn Common
Blakehope Fell
Otterburn
Kielder
KIELDER
KIELDER CASTLE VISITOR CENTRE
Steele Road
Larriston Fells
378
PADON HILL
Kielder
329
115
Dinlabyre
KIELDER
Troughend Common
Old Town
Northumberland
BLACK MIDDENS
Shipley Shiels
Old Castleton
FOREST PARK
Forest
B6320
Gatehouse
Hareshaw Head
Newcastleton Forest
KIELDER WATER BIRDS OF PREY CENTRE
KIELDER WATER
Falstone
East Woodburn
Greenhaugh
326
West Woodburn
514
GLENDHU HILL
TOWER KNOWE VISITOR CENTRE
Lanehead
The Eals
Charlton
Rede
DERE
NY
BELLINGHAM
Ridsdale
Black Lyne
Bower
Chirdon Burn
Hesleyside
Bellingham
A68
Redesmouth
Bewcastle Fells
White Lyne
518
SIGHTY CRAG
490
Hopehouse
312
Baileyhead
Whitelyne Common
Paddaburn
109
KIELDER MIRES
Wark Forest
109
North Tyne
B6320
Blacka Burn
Birtley
Warks Burn
Whygate
Stonehaugh
Wark
325
0 1 2 3 4 5 6 miles
0 1 2 3 4 5 6 7 8 9 10 km

NORTHUMBERLAND COAST
Belford
Seahouses
Beadnell
Wooler
Alnwick
Alnmouth
Amble
Rothbury
Morpeth
Ashington
Newbiggin-by-the-Sea
Bedlington
BLYTH
Cramlington
Seaton Delaval
Longhoughton
Craster
Embleton
Warkworth
Longframlington
Lynemouth
Pegswood
Harwood Forest
Thrunton Wood
ROTHBURY FOREST
Coquet I.
Alnmouth Bay
Druridge Bay
Beadnell Bay
Embleton Bay
Howick Haven
Boulmer Haven
DUNSTANBURGH CASTLE
CRAGSIDE HOUSE
CHILLINGHAM CASTLE
WALLINGTON
BELSAY HALL
A1
A697
A68
A696
A1068
A189
B6341
B6342
B6343
B6346
B6347
B6348
B1340
NT
NU
NY
NZ

1
2
3
4
5
A
B
C
D
E
F
NR
Carraig Mhór
Ardtalla
Claggain Bay
Kintour
Ardmore Pt.
KILDALTON CHURCH AND CROSSES
Eilean Craobhach
Eilean a'Chuirn
Eilean Bhride
126
Eilean Garbh
West Tarbert Bay
East Tarbert Bay
Tarbert
Gigha Island
100
Druimyeon More
Ardminish
Ardminish Bay
ACHAMORE GARDENS
0:20
Gigalum Island
Cara Island
SOUND OF GIGHA
Ardpatrick Ho.
Ardpatrick Pt.
Eilean Tràighe
Port Achoillan
Ronachan Pt.
A83
Clachan
Loch Ciaran
Gartnagrenach
269 CRUACH NAM FIADH
128
Balochroy
Crossaig Glen
Loch Garasdale
248 CRUACH MHIC GOUGAN
Rhunahaorine
Cour
Cour Bay
241 BEINN BHREAC
13
Tayinloan
322 CNOC NAN CRAOBH
Carradale Water
Grogport
Killean
Beacharr
CRUACH MHIC-AN T-SAOIR 364
354 CRUACH NAN GABHAR
Brackley
Clachaig Water
Muasdale
KINTYRE
Amod
426 BEINN BHREAC
Carradale
Port Righ
Glenacardoch Pt.
Belloch
Glenbarr
Barr Water
CLAN MACALISTER CENTRE
Bridgend
Torrisdale-Square
Carradale Pt.
454 BEINN AN TUIRC
Carradale Bay
Saddell Glen
Cleongart
19
Bellochantuy Bay
Bellochantuy
Saddell
SADDELL ABBEY
341 A'CHRUACH
Saddell Bay
Killocraw
Lussa Loch
14
397 SGREADAN HILL
Ugadale
Tangy Loch
Skeroblingarry
B842
Black Bay
KILBRANNAN
Westport
Glenlussa Water
Kilchenzie
Peninver
Ardnacross Bay
Kilmichael
West Darlochan
Low Smerby
Machrihanish Bay
CAMPBELTOWN
CAMPBELTOWN HERITAGE CENTRE
Machrihanish
Trodigal
Campbeltown
Campbeltown Loch
Island Davaar
DAVAAR ISLAND CAVE PAINTING
Drumlemble
B843
Stewarton
Kilkerran
Knocknaha
Kildalloig
Earadale Pt.
352 BEINN GHUILEAN
Achinhoan Hd.
10
385 THE SLATE
Woodbank
446 CNOC MOY
NORTH CHANNEL
Feochaig
Rubh'a'Mharaiche
277 CNOC ODHAR
Glen Breackerie
Conie Glen
Johnston's Pt.
Keprigan
North Carrine
Strone Glen
Macharioch
Polliwilline Bay
428
Southend
Carskiey
Cove Pt.
Brunerican Bay
Port Mean
MULL OF KINTYRE
Rubha Chlachan
Sheep I.
123
Sanda Island
0 1 2 3 4 5 6 miles
0 1 2 3 4 5 6 7 8 9 10 km

Inchmarnock
Scalpsie
Ardscalpsie Pt.
Scalpsie Bay
Stravanan Bay
Kingarth
Kilchattan Bay
ST BLANE'S CHAPEL
SOUND OF BUTE
Glenreasdell Mains
Skipness
SKIPNESS CASTLE
Skipness Pt.
Skipness Bay
Claonaig Bay
B8001
0:30
Great Cumbrae Island
CHRISTIAN HERITAGE MUSEUM
MUSEUM OF THE CUMBRAES
Millport
Downcraig Ferry
Fairlie Roads
Largs
OLD KIRK
HOUSE AND GARDEN
Muirhead Reservoir
KELBURN COUNTRY CENTRE
Fairlie
KAIM HILL
Knockendon Reservoir
The Tan
Little Cumbrae Island
HUNTERSTON POWER STATION VISITOR CENTRE
Thirdpart
Portencross
Farland Hd.
West Kilbride
Seamill
BLACKSHAW FARM PARK
Chapelhill
Dykes
Horse Isle
Ardrossan
NORTH AYRSHIRE MUSEUM
Saltcoats
Garroch Hd.
Cock of Arran
Loch Ranza
LOCHRANZA CASTLE
Lochranza
LOCHRANZA
ISLE OF ARRAN DISTILLERY
Catacol Bay
Catacol
Millstone Pt.
North Ayrshire
NORTH SANNOX FARM PARK
Sannox
Sannox Bay
Glen Sannox
MEALL NAN DAMH
Thundergay
Pirnmill
NORTH
Loch Tanna
CIR MHÓR
Corrie
Whitefarland
BEINN BHARRAIN
BEINN TARSUINN
GOAT FELL
Imachar
ISLE OF ARRAN
Glen Iorsa
Glen Rosa
BRODICK
BRODICK CASTLE
ARRAN AROMATICS VISITOR CENTRE
Brodick Bay
ISLE OF ARRAN HERITAGE MUSEUM
Brodick
Strathwhillan
Dougarie
Machrie Water
Auchagallon
Glenloig
A'CHRUACH
Glen Cloy
Machrie Bay
Clauchlands Pt.
Tormore
MACHRIE MOOR STANDING STONES
BALMICHAEL VISITOR CENTRE
Balmichael
KING'S CAVE
Blairbeg
Margnaheglish
Lamlash
Lamlash Bay
Cordon
Holy Island
Drumadoon Pt.
Torbeg
Shiskine
Blackwaterfoot
Drumadoon Bay
Kilpatrick
KILPATRICK DUN
Kingscross Pt.
Kingscross
TIGHVEIN
Auchencairn
Knockenkelly
Sliddery Water
Whiting Bay
North Kiscadale
South Kiscadale
GLENASHDALE FALLS
WHITING BAY
Largymore
Glenree
Brown Hd.
CARN BAN
Corriecravie
Kilmory Water
Largybeg
Sliddery
Dippen
Dippin Head
Lagg
Levencorroch
Kilmory
SOUTH BANK FARM PARK
TORRYLINN CAIRN
Bennan
Kildonan
Bennan Hd.
Sound of Pladda
Pladda
FIRTH OF CLYDE
0:55
120
128
129
112
NR
NS
Dunure
Culzean Bay
CULZEAN CASTLE
CULZEAN
Maidenhead Bay
Maidens
TURNBERRY
Turnberry Bay
Turnberry
Brest Rocks
Kirkoswald
SOUTER JOHNNIE'S COTTAGE
Townhead
Wallacetown
Dipple
Burnhead
A841
B880
A78
A738
A719
A77
B741
B881
B896
B899
A844
A
B
C
D
E
F
5
6
7
8
9

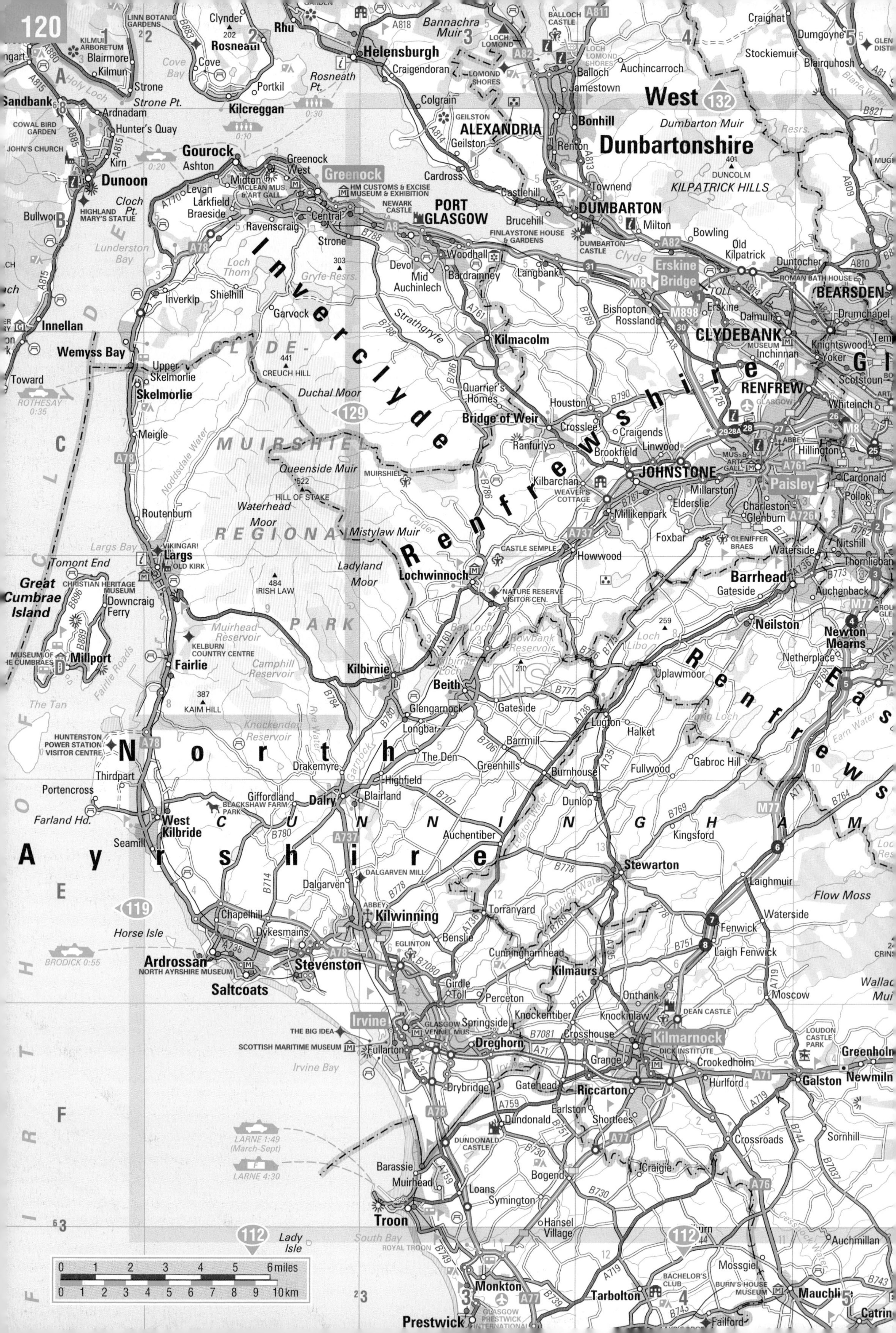
Helensburgh
Rhu
Rosneath
Clynder
Kilcreggan
Cove
Craigendoran
Bannachra Muir
Balloch
Jamestown
Alexandria
Bonhill
Renton
West Dunbartonshire
Dumbarton Muir
KILPATRICK HILLS
DUNBARTON
Dunoon
Sandbank
Kirn
Gourock
Greenock
PORT GLASGOW
Cardross
Bowling
Old Kilpatrick
Erskine Bridge
CLYDEBANK
BEARSDEN
RENFREW
Inverclyde
Renfrewshire
East Renfrewshire
Kilmacolm
Bridge of Weir
Houston
JOHNSTONE
Paisley
Barrhead
Neilston
Newton Mearns
Lochwinnoch
Howwood
Inverkip
Wemyss Bay
Skelmorlie
Innellan
Toward
Largs
Great Cumbrae Island
Millport
Fairlie
CLYDE-MUIRSHIEL REGIONAL PARK
Kilbirnie
Beith
Dalry
West Kilbride
Seamill
Portencross
North Ayrshire
CUNNINGHAME
Stewarton
Kilwinning
Stevenston
Ardrossan
Saltcoats
Irvine
Dreghorn
Kilmarnock
Kilmaurs
Riccarton
Galston
Newmilns
Fenwick
Dundonald
Troon
Symington
Monkton
Prestwick
Tarbolton
Mauchline
Irvine Bay
Horse Isle
Lady Isle
0 1 2 3 4 5 6 miles
0 1 2 3 4 5 6 7 8 9 10 km

Campsie Fells
Kilsyth Hills
Carron Valley Forest
Carron Valley Res.
Denny
Dunipace
Stenhousemuir
Larbert
Grangemouth
Falkirk
Bonnybridge
Falkirk Millennium Wheel
Laurieston
Polmont
Brightons
Falkirk
East Dunbartonshire
Lennoxtown
Kilsyth
Milngavie
Kirkintilloch
Cumbernauld
Bishopbriggs
Lenzie
Muirhead
Glasgow
Coatbridge
Airdrie
North Lanarkshire
Caldercruix
Armadale
Westrigg
Blackridge
Harthill
Whitburn
Fauldhouse
Rutherglen
Cambuslang
Uddingston
Bellshill
Bothwell
Motherwell
Hamilton
Wishaw
Shotts
East Kilbride
Carluke
Larkhall
Eaglesham
Strathaven
Stonehouse
Lanark
New Lanark
Lesmahagow
Kirkmuirhill
Blackwood
Coalburn
Douglas
Douglas West
Glespin
Glenbuck
Muirkirk
Darvel
Kype Muir
Rough Moss
Broken Cross Muir
Tinto Hills
Roberton Law
Middle Muir
South Lanarkshire
Clyde
Clydesdale
Kingshill Plantation
M8
M73
M74
M80
M876
M9
A71
A70
A73

Falkirk
West Lothian
Edinburgh
Mid
GRANGEMOUTH
FALKIRK
Bo'ness
Linlithgow
Rosyth
Inverkeithing
Dalgety Bay
Queensferry
Forth Road Bridge
Kirkliston
Winchburgh
Broxburn
Uphall
Bathgate
Armadale
LIVINGSTON
Blackburn
Whitburn
Harthill
Fauldhouse
Shotts
West Calder
Mid Calder
East Calder
Currie
Balerno
Penicuik
Carlops
West Linton
PENTLAND HILLS REGIONAL PARK
Carluke
Lanark
New Lanark
Carnwath
Carstairs
Forth
Wilsontown
Biggar
Symington
TINTO HILLS
Broughton
Drumelzier
Stobo
UPPER TWEEDDALE
Romannobridge
Blyth Bridge
Dolphinton
Dunsyre
Douglas
Abington
Lamington
Coulter
Skirling
Elsrickle
Ratho
Cramond
Corstorphine
Barnton
0 1 2 3 4 5 6 miles
0 1 2 3 4 5 6 7 8 9 10 km

Inchkeith
F I R T H O F F O R T H
Gullane Bay
Muirfield
& Gardens
Dirleton
Auldhame
Scoughall
Gullane
West Fenton
Fenton Barns
Kingston
Whitekirk
Aberlady Bay
Aberlady
Tyne Mouth
Myreton Motor Museum
Drem
Craigielaw
Zeebrugge 17:30
The Chesters Fort
Museum of Flight
East Fortune
Tyninghame
Belhaven
John Muir
West Barns
Gosford Bay
Gosford House
Spittal
Ballencrieff
Athelstaneford
Preston
East Linton
Black Rocks
HMY Britannia
Newhaven
Leith
Cockenzie and Port Seton
Seton Collegiate Church
Longniddry
Hopetoun Mon.
Jane Welsh Carlyle Museum
Preston Mill & Phantassie Doocot
Hailes Castle
Traprain
Biel Water
Pitcox
EDINBURGH
Prestonpans
Industrial Heritage Museum
Musselburgh
Huntington
Elvington
Palace of Holyroodhouse
Portobello
Joppa
Duddingston
Royal Mus. of Scotland
Gladsmuir
St. Mary's Collegiate Ch.
Haddington
Luggate Burn
Stenton
Halls
Newhailes
Inveresk Lodge Gdns.
Inveresk
Wallyford
Tranent
Penston
Macmerry
Lennoxlove
Papple
Craigmillar
Craigmillar Castle
Newcraighall
Edinburgh Services
Elphinstone
New Winton
New Town
East
Samuelston
Garvald
Whitecraig
Dunbar Common
Danderhall
Millerhill
Crossgatehall
Ormiston
Bolton
Liberton
Gilmerton
Dalkeith Park
Cousland
Carfrae
Pencaitland
Lothian
Kaimes
Dalkeith
Glenkinchie Distillery
East Saltoun
West Saltoun
Gifford
Danskine
Straiton
Butterfly Farm
Eskbank
Peastonbank
Loanhead
Newbattle
Easthouses
Gilchriston
Quarryford
Bilston
Mayfield
Peaston
Long Newton
Longyester
Polton
Bonnyrigg and Lasswade
Mining Museum
Vogrie
Pathhead
Spartleton Edge
Roslin
Newtongrange
Newlandrig
Whiteadder Reservoir
Rosslyn Chapel
Rosewell
Humbie
Stobshiel
Arniston Engine
Crichton
Fala Dam
Blegbie
Auchendinny
Edinburgh Crystal Visitor Centre
Arniston House
Crichton Castle
Lammer Law
Meikle Says Law
Hopes Reservoir
Carrington
Gorebridge
Fala
North Middleton
Tynehead
Lammermuir Hills
Lothian
Temple
Middleton
Fala Moor
Hunt Law
Dye Water
Gilston
Falahill
Rosebery Reservoir
Hillhouse
Soonhope Burn
Watch Water Reservoir
Kirktonhill
Hog's Law
Torfichen Hill
Addinston
Oxton
Moorfoot Hills
Carcant
Heriot
NT
Gladhouse Reservoir
Gala Water
Leader Water
Wedderlie
Collie Law
Westruther
Blyth
Thornydykes
Fountainhall
Dewar
Blackhope Scar
Torquhan
Thirlestane Castle
Lauder
Lauderdale
Whiteburn
Thirlestane
Houndslow
Scottish Borders
Killochyett
Lugate Water
Boon
Eden Water
Whitehope Law
Stow
Nether Blainslie
Legerwood
Green Knowe Tower
Glentress Forest
Leithen Water
Windlestraw Law
Gordon
West Morriston
Bow
Southern Upland Way
Fans
Peebles
Black Law
Colquhar
Great Law
Tweeddale Mus. & Gall.
Glentress
Caitha Bowland
Langshaw
Kings Muir
Kailzie Gardens
Kirkburn
Robert Smail's Printing Works
Blackhaugh
Buckholm
Earlston
Mellerstain House
Cardrona
St Ronan's Well Interpretative Centre
Tweed
Galashiels
Smailholm
Cardrona Forest
Walkerburn
Peter Anderson Woollen Mill
Innerleithen
Clovenfords
Old Gala House
Eildon and Leaderfoot
Redpath
Brotherstone
Traquair House
Elibank and Traquair Forest
Gattonside
Abbey
Melrose
Newstead
Smailholm Tower
Traquair
Caddonfoot
Abbotsford House
Darnick
Priorwood Gdns.
Glen Ho
Kirkhouse
Minch Moor
Yair Hill Forest
Boleside
Trimontium Exhibition
Bemersyde
Clintmains
Dryburgh Abbey
Eildon Hills
Mertoun Gdns.
Newtown St. Boswells
St. Boswells
Lindean
Broadmeadows
Ovenscloss
Blake Muir
Whitlaw Mosses
Bowden
Rutherford
Selkirk Glass
Maxton
Yarrow
Yarrow Water
Selkirk
Muirhouselaw
Douglas Burn
Bowhill
Fastheugh Hill
Bowhill House & Country Park
Philiphaugh
Halliwell's House Museum
Sir Walter Scott's Courtroom
Midlem
Longnewton
St. Cuthberts Way
Southern Upland Way
Dryhope
Yarrow
Belses

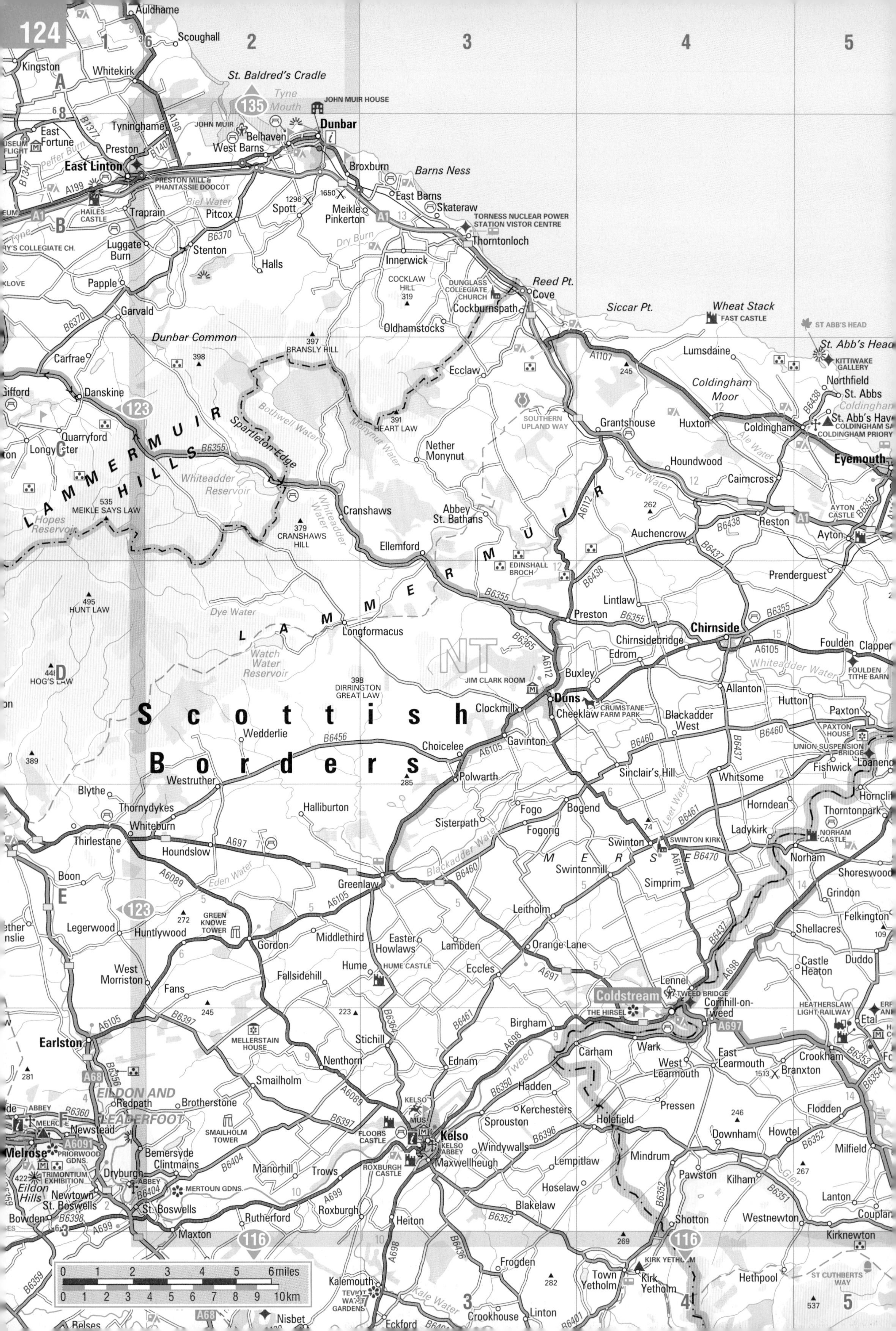
Auldhame
Scoughall
Kingston
Whitekirk
St. Baldred's Cradle
Tyne Mouth
135
JOHN MUIR HOUSE
Dunbar
JOHN MUIR
Belhaven
West Barns
Tyninghame
East Fortune
Preston
East Linton
PRESTON MILL & PHANTASSIE DOOCOT
Broxburn
Barns Ness
East Barns
Skateraw
Spott
Meikle Pinkerton
TORNESS NUCLEAR POWER STATION VISTOR CENTRE
Thorntonloch
HAILES CASTLE
Traprain
Pitcox
Biel Water
Stenton
Luggate Burn
Halls
Dry Burn
Innerwick
COCKLAW HILL 319
DUNGLASS COLLEGIATE CHURCH
Reed Pt.
Cove
Cockburnspath
Papple
Garvald
Oldhamstocks
Siccar Pt.
Wheat Stack
FAST CASTLE
ST ABB'S HEAD
St. Abb's Head
KITTIWAKE GALLERY
Dunbar Common
397 BRANSLY HILL
398
Carfrae
Ecclaw
Lumsdaine
Coldingham Moor
Northfield
St. Abbs
Danskine
123
Bothwell Water
Monynut Water
391 HEART LAW
SOUTHERN UPLAND WAY
Grantshouse
Huxton
Coldingham
COLDINGHAM PRIORY
Quarryford
LAMMERMUIR HILLS
Spartleton Edge
Whiteadder Reservoir
Nether Monynut
Houndwood
Eye Water
Cairncross
Eyemouth
535 MEIKLE SAYS LAW
Hopes Reservoir
Cranshaws
379 CRANSHAWS HILL
Whiteadder Water
Abbey St. Bathans
Auchencrow
Reston
AYTON CASTLE
Ayton
Ellemford
EDINSHALL BROCH
Prenderguest
495 HUNT LAW
LAMMERMUIR
Lintlaw
Preston
Chirnside
Dye Water
Longformacus
Watch Water Reservoir
NT
Chirnsidebridge
Edrom
Foulden
FOULDEN TITHE BARN
Whiteadder Water
448 HOG'S LAW
398 DIRRINGTON GREAT LAW
JIM CLARK ROOM
Buxley
Duns
Allanton
Hutton
Paxton
PAXTON HOUSE
Scottish Borders
Clockmill
Cheeklaw
CRUMSTANE FARM PARK
Blackadder West
UNION SUSPENSION BRIDGE
Fishwick
Wedderlie
Choicelee
Gavinton
389
Westruther
Polwarth
285
Sinclair's Hill
Whitsome
Blythe
Thornydykes
Halliburton
Fogo
Bogend
Horndean
Thorntonpark
Whiteburn
Sisterpath
Fogorig
Leet Water
Ladykirk
NORHAM CASTLE
Thirlestane
Houndslow
Swinton
SWINTON KIRK
Norham
MERSE
Swintonmill
Boon
Eden Water
Blackadder Water
Greenlaw
Simprim
Shoreswood
Grindon
272
GREEN KNOWE TOWER
Legerwood
Huntlywood
Gordon
Middlethird
Easter Howlaws
Lambden
Leitholm
Felkington
Shellacres
Orange Lane
West Morriston
Hume
HUME CASTLE
Fallsidehill
Eccles
Castle Heaton
Duddo
Fans
245
223
Lennel
TWEED BRIDGE
Coldstream
THE HIRSEL
Cornhill-on-Tweed
HEATHERSLAW LIGHT RAILWAY
Etal
Earlston
MELLERSTAIN HOUSE
Stichill
Birgham
Carham
Wark
Nenthorn
Ednam
Tweed
West Learmouth
East Learmouth
Crookham
Branxton
281
Smailholm
Hadden
EILDON AND LEADERFOOT
Redpath
Brotherstone
KELSO
Kerchesters
Pressen
Flodden
Newstead
Melrose
SMAILHOLM TOWER
FLOORS CASTLE
Kelso
Sprouston
Holefield
246
Downham
Howtel
Milfield
PRIORWOOD GDNS.
Bemersyde
Clintmains
KELSO ABBEY
Maxwellheugh
Windywalls
Lempitlaw
Mindrum
TRIMONTIUM EXHIBITION
Eildon Hills
Dryburgh
ABBEY
Manorhill
Trows
ROXBURGH CASTLE
Pawston
Kilham
267
Newtown St. Boswells
MERTOUN GDNS.
Hoselaw
Glen
Lanton
St. Boswells
Roxburgh
Blakelaw
Bowden
Rutherford
Heiton
Shotton
Westnewton
Coupland
Maxton
116
269
Kirknewton
Frogden
282
KIRK YETHOLM
Town Yetholm
Kirk Yetholm
Hethpool
ST CUTHBERTS WAY
Kalemouth
TEVIOT WATER GARDENS
Kale Water
537
Crookhouse
Linton
Eckford
Nisbet
Belses
0 1 2 3 4 5 6 miles
0 1 2 3 4 5 6 7 8 9 10 km

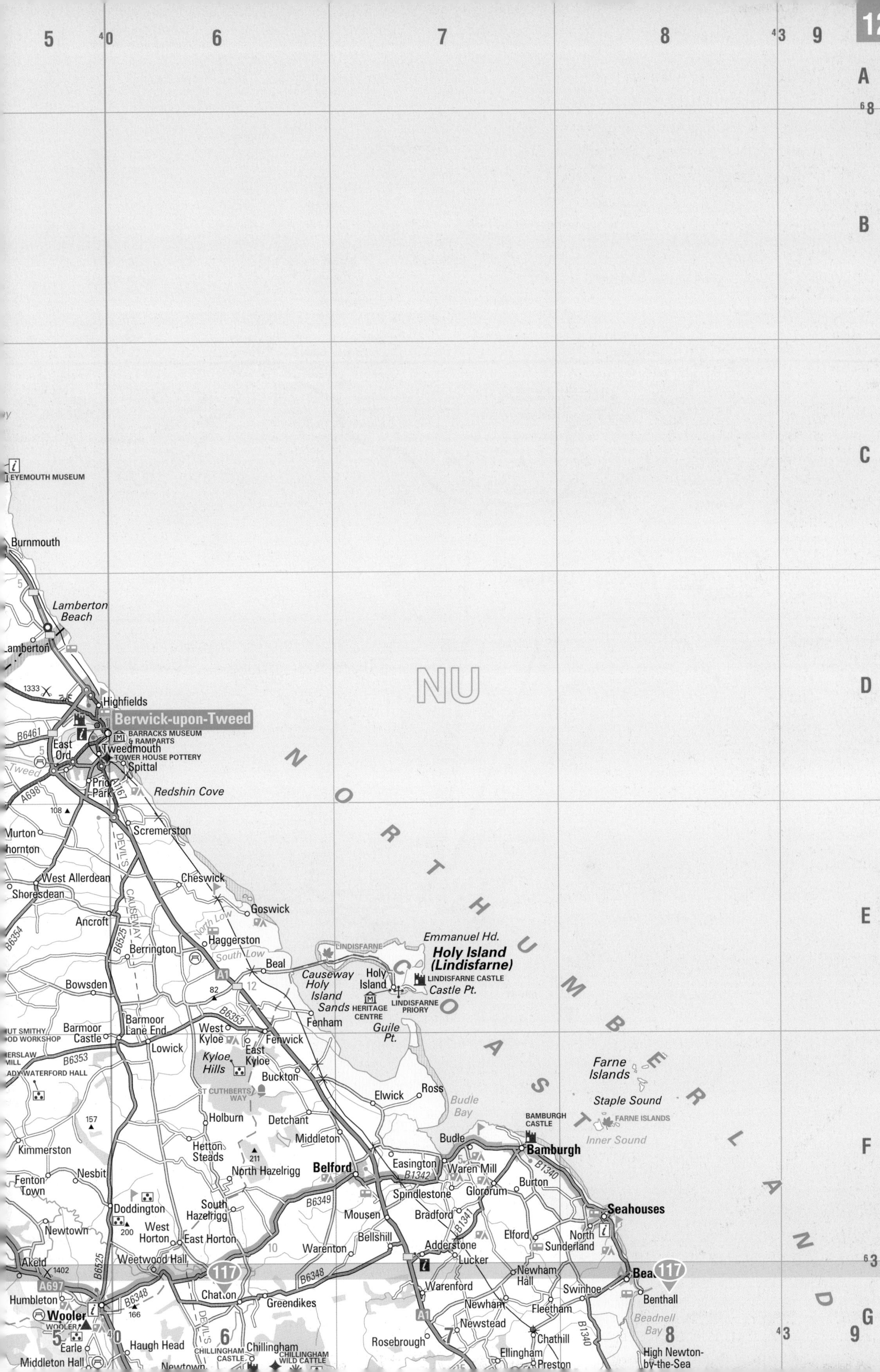

NU
NORTHUMBERLAND COAST
Eyemouth Museum
Burnmouth
Lamberton Beach
Lamberton
Highfields
Berwick-upon-Tweed
Barracks Museum & Ramparts
East Ord
Tweedmouth
Tower House Pottery
Spittal
Tweed
Prior Park
Redshin Cove
Murton
Thornton
Scremerston
Devil's Causeway
West Allerdean
Cheswick
Shoresdean
Goswick
Ancroft
North Low
Haggerston
Berrington
South Low
Beal
Emmanuel Hd.
Lindisfarne
Holy Island (Lindisfarne)
Causeway
Holy Island Sands
Holy Island
Lindisfarne Castle
Castle Pt.
Heritage Centre
Lindisfarne Priory
Bowsden
Fenham
Guile Pt.
Barmoor Lane End
Barmoor Castle
Lowick
West Kyloe
East Kyloe
Fenwick
Kyloe Hills
Buckton
St Cuthbert's Way
Elwick
Ross
Budle Bay
Farne Islands
Staple Sound
Farne Islands
Bamburgh Castle
Inner Sound
Holburn
Detchant
Middleton
Budle
Bamburgh
Kimmerston
Hetton Steads
North Hazelrigg
Belford
Easington
Waren Mill
Fenton Town
Nesbit
Spindlestone
Glororum
Burton
Doddington
South Hazelrigg
Mousen
Bradford
Seahouses
Newtown
West Horton
East Horton
Bellshill
Warenton
Adderstone
Elford
North Sunderland
Lucker
Akeld
Weetwood Hall
Newham Hall
Beadnell
Humbleton
Wooler
Chatton
Greendikes
Warenford
Swinhoe
Benthall
Newham
Fleetham
Beadnell Bay
Newstead
Earle
Haugh Head
Chillingham
Chillingham Castle
Chillingham Wild Cattle
Rosebrough
Chathill
Middleton Hall
Newtown
Ellingham
Preston
High Newton-by-the-Sea
A1
A697
A698
A1167
B6461
B6354
B6525
B6353
B6349
B1342
B1341
B1340
B6348
117

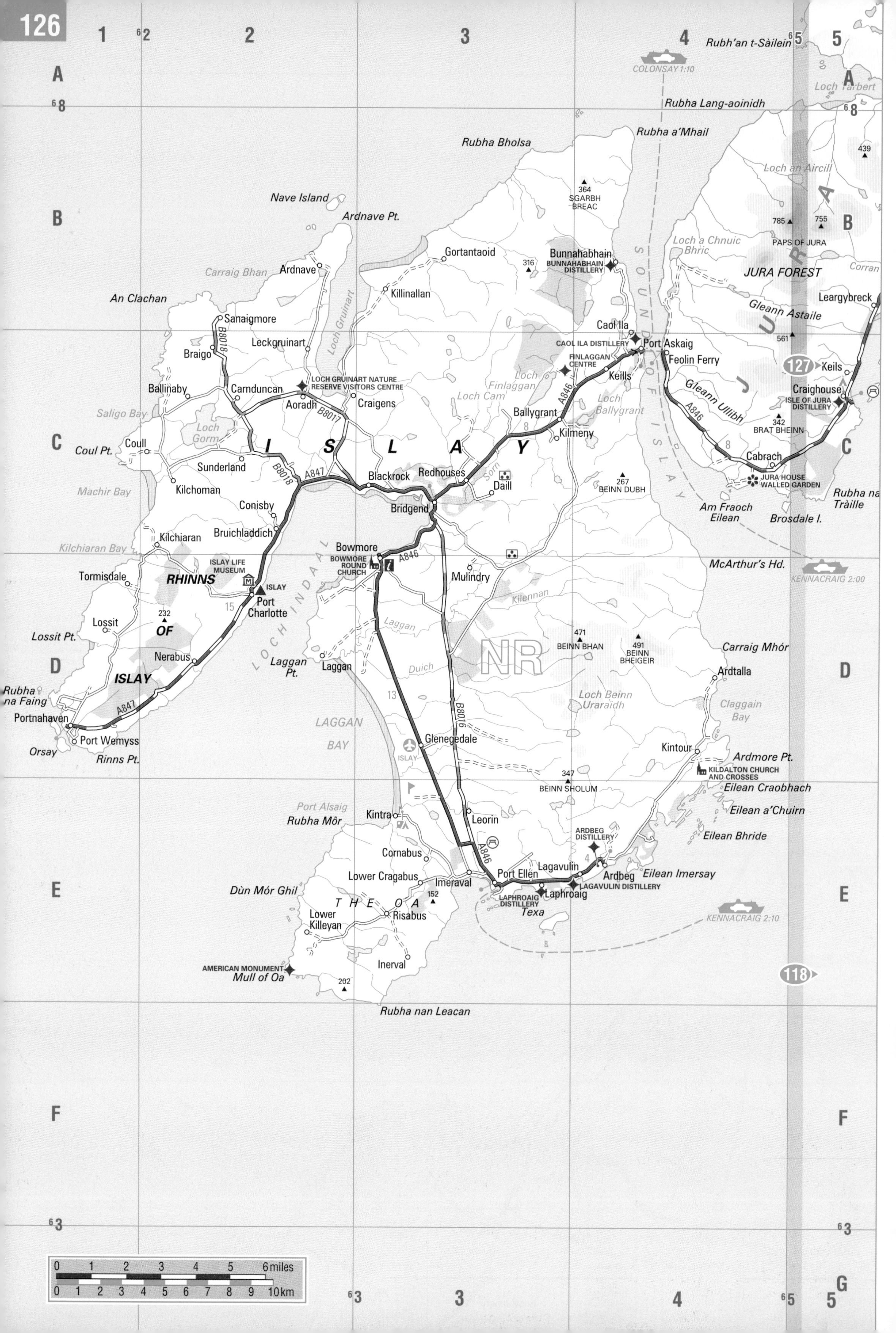

Rubh'an t-Sàilein
COLONSAY 1:10
Loch Tarbert
Rubha Lang-aoinidh
Rubha a'Mhail
Rubha Bholsa
439
Loch an Aircill
364
SGARBH BREAC
Nave Island
Ardnave Pt.
785
755
PAPS OF JURA
Loch a Chnuic Bhric
Corran
JURA FOREST
Gortantaoid
Bunnahabhain
BUNNAHABHAIN DISTILLERY
316
Carraig Bhan
Ardnave
Killinallan
An Clachan
Leargybreck
Gleann Astaile
SOUND OF ISLAY
Sanaigmore
Caol Ila
561
CAOL ILA DISTILLERY
Port Askaig
B8018
Leckgruinart
Loch Gruinart
Braigo
Feolin Ferry
FINLAGGAN CENTRE
127
Keils
Loch Finlaggan
Keills
LOCH GRUINART NATURE RESERVE VISITORS CENTRE
Ballinaby
Carnduncan
Craighouse
Gleann Ullibh
ISLE OF JURA DISTILLERY
Loch Cam
Aoradh
Craigens
Loch Ballygrant
B8017
JURA
Saligo Bay
Ballygrant
A846
342
BRAT BHEINN
Loch Gorm
Coull
ISLAY
Kilmeny
Coul Pt.
Cabrach
Sunderland
B8018
A847
Blackrock
Redhouses
267
BEINN DUBH
JURA HOUSE WALLED GARDEN
Kilchoman
Sorn
Daill
Rubha na Tràille
Machir Bay
Conisby
Bridgend
Am Fraoch Eilean
Brosdale I.
Bruichladdich
Kilchiaran
Bowmore
Kilchiaran Bay
BOWMORE ROUND CHURCH
A846
McArthur's Hd.
ISLAY LIFE MUSEUM
Tormisdale
RHINNS
ISLAY
Mulindry
KENNACRAIG 2:00
Port Charlotte
Kilennan
232
Lossit
OF
LOCH INDAAL
Laggan
Lossit Pt.
471
BEINN BHAN
491
BEINN BHEIGEIR
Carraig Mhór
Nerabus
Laggan Pt.
Laggan
Duich
NR
Rubha na Faing
ISLAY
Ardtalla
A847
Loch Beinn Uraraidh
Claggain Bay
Portnahaven
LAGGAN BAY
B8016
Port Wemyss
Glenegedale
Orsay
Rinns Pt.
ISLAY
Kintour
Ardmore Pt.
KILDALTON CHURCH AND CROSSES
347
BEINN SHOLUM
Eilean Craobhach
Port Alsaig
Eilean a'Chuirn
Rubha Mòr
Kintra
Leorin
ARDBEG DISTILLERY
Eilean Bhride
Cornabus
A846
Lagavulin
Lower Cragabus
Imeraval
Port Ellen
Ardbeg
Eilean Imersay
Dùn Mór Ghil
152
THE OA
Laphroaig
LAGAVULIN DISTILLERY
LAPHROAIG DISTILLERY
Lower Killeyan
Risabus
Texa
KENNACRAIG 2:10
Inerval
AMERICAN MONUMENT
Mull of Oa
118
202
Rubha nan Leacan
0 1 2 3 4 5 6 miles
0 1 2 3 4 5 6 7 8 9 10 km

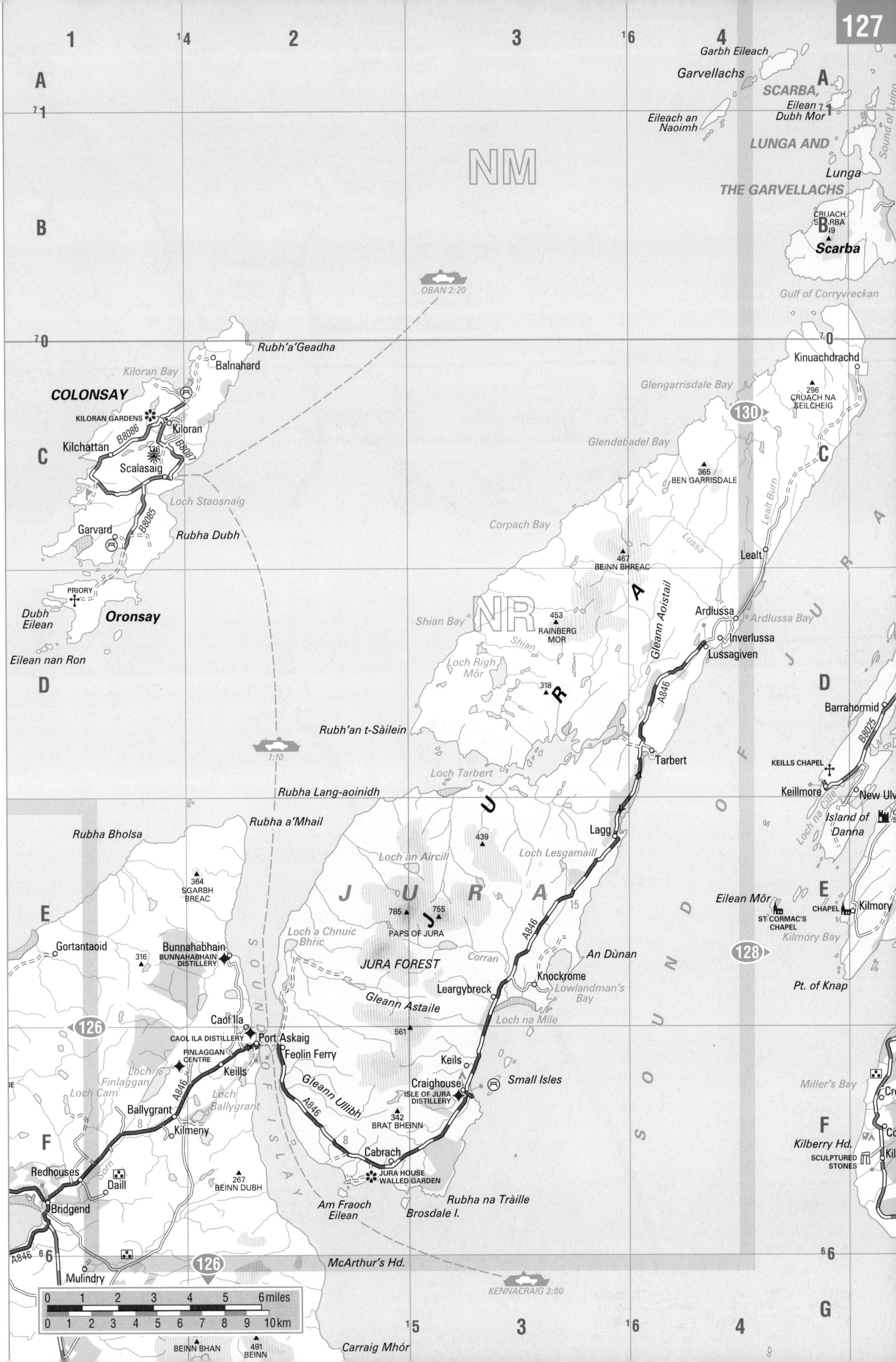
NM
NR
COLONSAY
Oronsay
Kiloran Bay
Balnahard
Rubh'a'Geadha
KILORAN GARDENS
Kiloran
Kilchattan
Scalasaig
Loch Staosnaig
Garvard
Rubha Dubh
PRIORY
Dubh Eilean
Eilean nan Ron
OBAN 2:20
1:10
KENNACRAIG 2:00
Garbh Eileach
Garvellachs
Eileach an Naoimh
SCARBA, LUNGA AND THE GARVELLACHS
Eilean Dubh Mor
Lunga
Scarba
Sound of Luing
Gulf of Corryvreckan
Kinuachdrachd
296 CRUACH NA SEILCHEIG
Glengarrisdale Bay
Glendebadel Bay
365 BEN GARRISDALE
Corpach Bay
467 BEINN BHREAC
Lealt
Leaft Burn
Lussa
Gleann Aoistail
Ardlussa
Ardlussa Bay
Inverlussa
Lussagiven
Shian Bay
453 RAINBERG MOR
Shian
Loch Righ Mòr
318
Rubh'an t-Sàilein
Tarbert
Loch Tarbert
Rubha Lang-aoinidh
Rubha a'Mhail
Rubha Bholsa
Lagg
439
Loch an Aircill
Loch Lesgamaill
JURA
785
755
PAPS OF JURA
JURA FOREST
Loch a Chnuic Bhric
Corran
An Dùnan
Knockrome
Lowlandman's Bay
Leargybreck
Loch na Mile
Gleann Astaile
561
Keils
Small Isles
Craighouse
ISLE OF JURA DISTILLERY
Gleann Ullibh
342 BRAT BHEINN
Cabrach
JURA HOUSE WALLED GARDEN
Rubha na Tràille
Am Fraoch Eilean
Brosdale I.
McArthur's Hd.
Carraig Mhór
SOUND OF JURA
SOUND OF ISLAY
364 SGARBH BREAC
Gortantaoid
316
Bunnahabhain
BUNNAHABHAIN DISTILLERY
Caol Ila
CAOL ILA DISTILLERY
Port Askaig
Feolin Ferry
FINLAGGAN CENTRE
Keills
Loch Finlaggan
Loch Cam
Loch Ballygrant
Ballygrant
Kilmeny
Redhouses
Daill
Sorn
Bridgend
267 BEINN DUBH
Mulindry
BEINN BHAN
491 BEINN
A846
B8086
B8087
B8085
B8025
Barrahormid
KEILLS CHAPEL
Keillmore
New Ulva
Loch na Cille
Island of Danna
Eilean Môr
ST CORMAC'S CHAPEL
CHAPEL
Kilmory
Kilmory Bay
Pt. of Knap
Miller's Bay
Kilberry Hd.
SCULPTURED STONES
130
128
126
0 1 2 3 4 5 6 miles
0 1 2 3 4 5 6 7 8 9 10 km

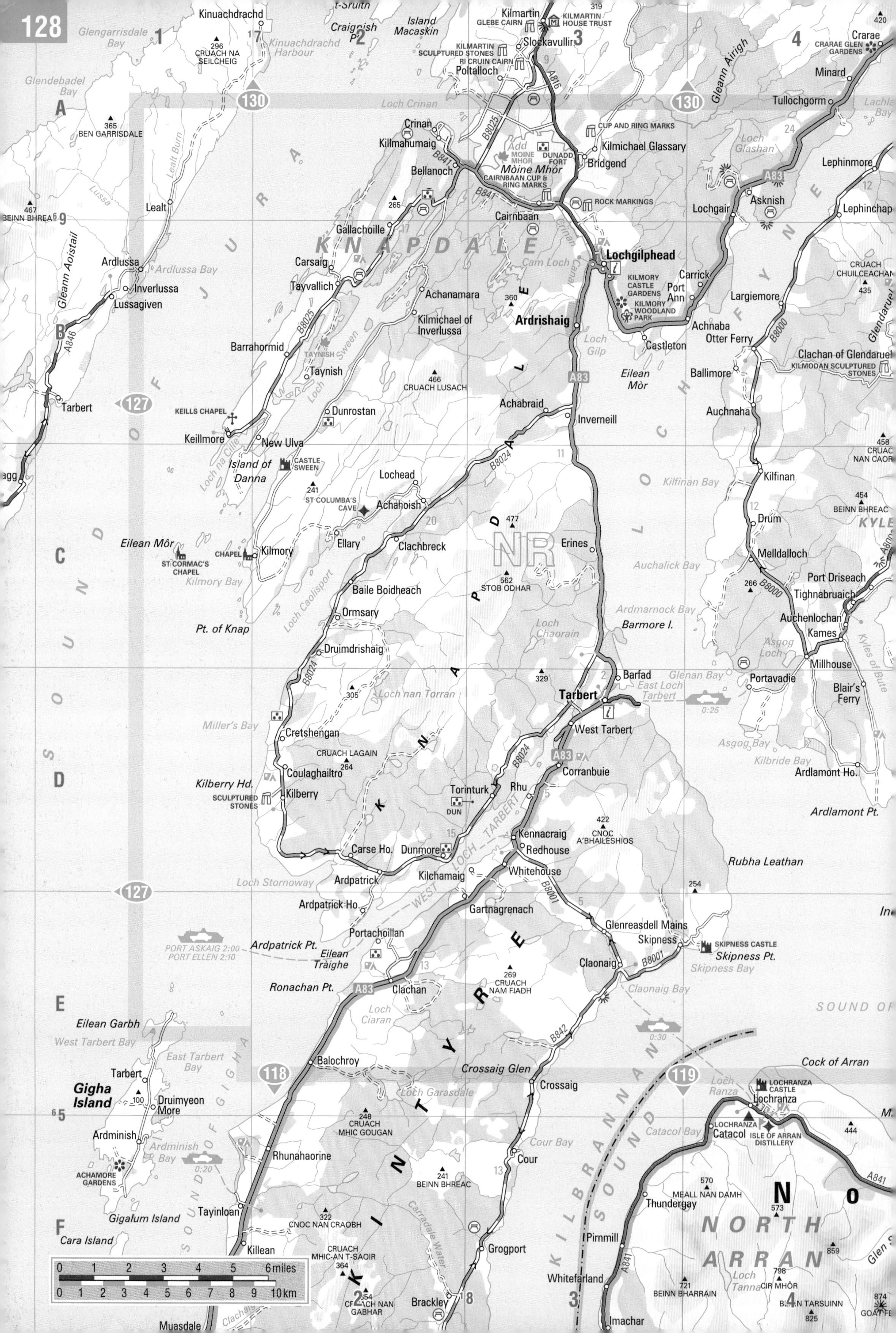
Kinuachdrachd
Glengarrisdale Bay
296 CRUACH NA SEILCHEIG
Kinuachdrachd Harbour
Craignish Pt.
Island Macaskin
Kilmartin
GLEBE CAIRN
KILMARTIN HOUSE TRUST
KILMARTIN SCULPTURED STONES
RI CRUIN CAIRN
Slockavullin
Poltalloch
Crarae
CRARAE GLEN GARDENS
Minard
Glendebadel Bay
130
Loch Crinan
Gleann Airigh
Tullochgorm
Lachlan Bay
365 BEN GARRISDALE
Crinan
Killmahumaig
B8025
B841
A816
CUP AND RING MARKS
Kilmichael Glassary
Bridgend
MOINE MHOR
DUNADD FORT
Mòine Mhór
CAIRNBAAN CUP & RING MARKS
Loch Glashan
Bellanoch
Lephinmore
A83
Lealt Burn
Lussa
467 BEINN BHREAC
Lealt
265
Cairnbaan
ROCK MARKINGS
Lochgair
Asknish
Lephinchapel
Gallachoille
KNAPDALE
JURA
Gleann Aoistail
Ardlussa
Ardlussa Bay
Inverlussa
Lussagiven
Carsaig
Tayvallich
Cam Loch
Crinan Canal
Lochgilphead
KILMORY CASTLE GARDENS
KILMORY WOODLAND PARK
Carrick
Port Ann
CRUACH CHUILCEACHAN 435
Largiemore
Achanamara
360
Kilmichael of Inverlussa
Ardrishaig
Achnaba
Otter Ferry
B8000
Glendaruel
A846
Barrahormid
TAYNISH
Loch Sween
Taynish
Loch Gilp
Castleton
Clachan of Glendaruel
KILMODAN SCULPTURED STONES
466 CRUACH LUSACH
Eilean Mòr
Ballimore
Tarbert
127
KEILLS CHAPEL
Dunrostan
Achabraid
Inverneill
Auchnaha
Keillmore
New Ulva
Loch na Cille
Island of Danna
CASTLE SWEEN
LOCH FYNE
458 CRUACH NAN CAORACH
Lochead
Kilfinan Bay
Kilfinan
241
ST COLUMBA'S CAVE
Achahoish
B8024
454 BEINN BHREAC
20
Drum
KYLES
SOUND OF JURA
Eilean Mòr
ST CORMAC'S CHAPEL
CHAPEL
Kilmory
Ellary
Clachbreck
477
NR
Erines
Melldalloch
Kilmory Bay
Loch Caolisport
Auchalick Bay
Port Driseach
Baile Boidheach
562 STOB ODHAR
266
Tighnabruaich
Ormsary
Ardmarnock Bay
Barmore I.
Auchenlochan
Pt. of Knap
Loch Chaorain
Kames
Asgog Loch
Druimdrishaig
Millhouse
Kyles of Bute
329
Barfad
Glenan Bay
Portavadie
305
Loch nan Torran
Tarbert
East Loch Tarbert
0:25
Blair's Ferry
Miller's Bay
Cretshengan
West Tarbert
Asgog Bay
CRUACH LAGAIN 264
Kilbride Bay
Coulaghailtro
Corranbuie
Ardlamont Ho.
Kilberry Hd.
Torinturk
Rhu
SCULPTURED STONES
Kilberry
DUN
Ardlamont Pt.
KNAPDALE
WEST LOCH TARBERT
422 CNOC A'BHAILESHIOS
Kennacraig
Redhouse
Carse Ho.
Dunmore
Rubha Leathan
Ardpatrick
Kilchamaig
Whitehouse
Loch Stornoway
B8001
254
Ardpatrick Ho.
Gartnagrenach
PORT ASKAIG 2:00
PORT ELLEN 2:10
Ardpatrick Pt.
Portachoillan
Glenreasdell Mains
Skipness
SKIPNESS CASTLE
Skipness Pt.
Eilean Traighe
269 CRUACH NAM FIADH
Claonaig
Skipness Bay
Ronachan Pt.
Clachan
Claonaig Bay
SOUND OF BUTE
Loch Ciaran
KINTYRE
Eilean Garbh
West Tarbert Bay
East Tarbert Bay
B842
0:30
Balochroy
Crossaig Glen
Cock of Arran
118
119
Crossaig
Tarbert
Gigha Island
100
Druimyeon More
SOUND OF GIGHA
Loch Garasdale
248 CRUACH MHIC GOUGAN
Loch Ranza
LOCHRANZA CASTLE
Lochranza
KILBRANNAN SOUND
Ardminish
Ardminish Bay
Catacol Bay
Catacol
ISLE OF ARRAN DISTILLERY
444
Cour Bay
ACHAMORE GARDENS
0:20
Rhunahaorine
Cour
241 BEINN BHREAC
570 MEALL NAN DAMH
A841
Thundergay
573
Tayinloan
Gigalum Island
322 CNOC NAN CRAOBH
Carradale Water
NORTH ARRAN
Cara Island
Grogport
Pirnmill
859
Killean
CRUACH MHIC-AN T-SAOIR 364
Loch Tanna
798 CIR MHÒR
721 BEINN BHARRAIN
Whitefarland
354 CRUACH NAN GABHAR
Brackley
BEINN TARSUINN 825
874 GOATFELL
Glen Sannox
Muasdale
Imachar
0 1 2 3 4 5 6 miles
0 1 2 3 4 5 6 7 8 9 10 km

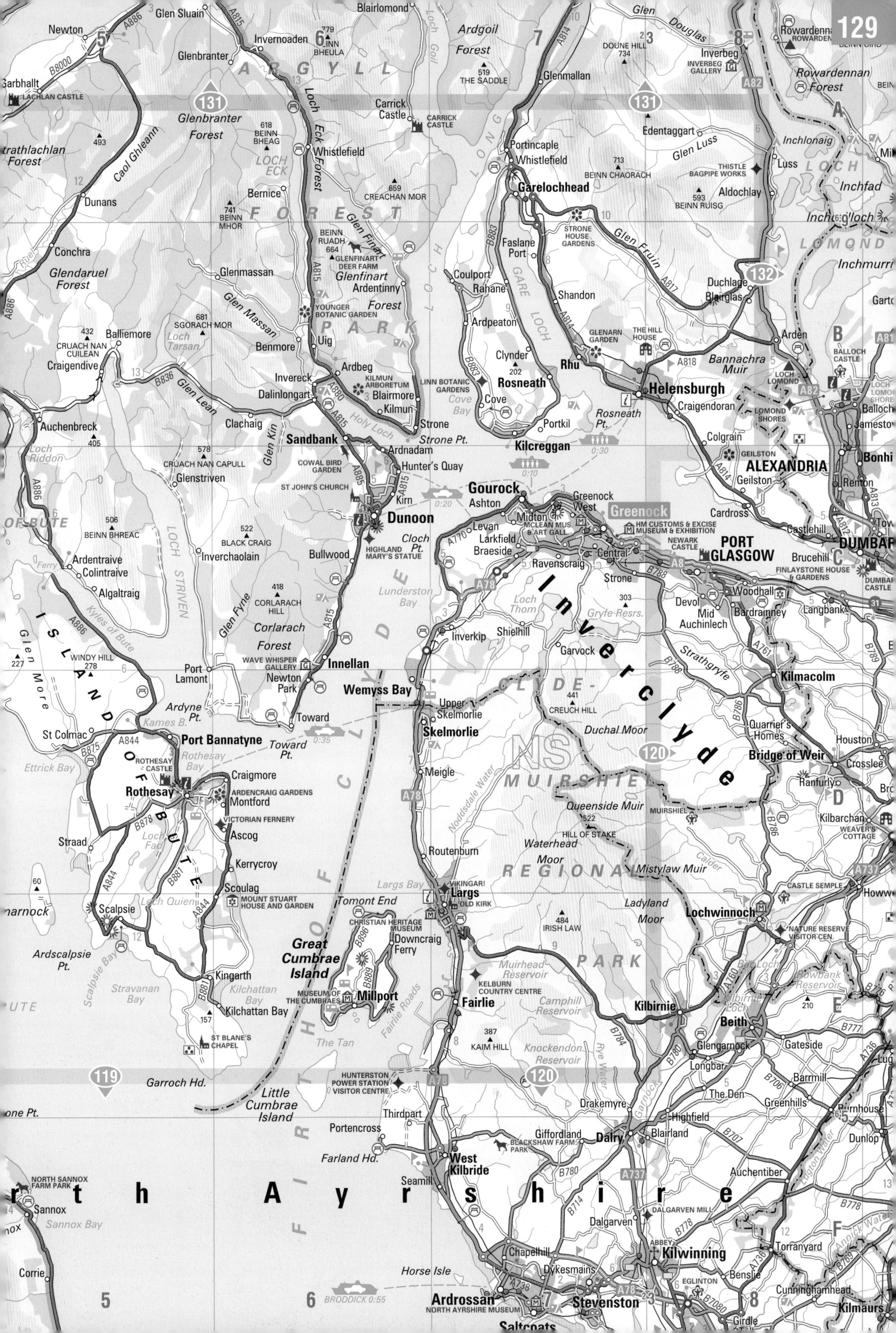
A R G Y L L
F O R E S T
P A R K
Ardgoil Forest
Glen Sluain
Blairlomond
Glen Douglas
Newton
Invernoaden
779 BEINN BHEULA
Loch Goil
Glenbranter
519 THE SADDLE
Glenmallan
DOUNE HILL 734
Inverbeg
INVERBEG GALLERY
Rowardennan
ROWARDENNAN
Rowardennan Forest
Garbhallt
LACHLAN CASTLE
131
Glenbranter Forest
618 BEINN BHEAG
LOCH ECK
Loch Eck
Eck Forest
Carrick Castle
CARRICK CASTLE
Edentaggart
Glen Luss
Inchlonaig
Luss
493
Strathlachlan Forest
Caol Ghleann
Whistlefield
Portincaple
Whistlefield
LONG
713 BEINN CHAORACH
THISTLE BAGPIPE WORKS
LOCH
Inchfad
Dunans
Bernice
659 CREACHAN MOR
Garelochhead
593 BEINN RUISG
Aldochlay
741 BEINN MHOR
Glen Finart
STRONE HOUSE GARDENS
Glen Fruin
Inchcailloch
LOMOND
Inchmurrin
Conchra
BEINN RUADH 664
GLENFINART DEER FARM
Faslane Port
Glenfinart Forest
Glendaruel Forest
Glenmassan
Ardentinny
Coulport
Rahane
GARE LOCH
Shandon
Duchlage
Blairglas
132
Glen Massan
YOUNGER BOTANIC GARDEN
681 SGORACH MOR
Ardpeaton
Loch Tarsan
432 CRUACH NAN CUILEAN
Balliemore
Craigendive
Benmore
Uig
Clynder
202
GLENARN GARDEN
THE HILL HOUSE
Arden
BALLOCH CASTLE
Bannachra Muir
LOCH LOMOND
Ardbeg
KILMUN ARBORETUM
LINN BOTANIC GARDENS
Rosneath
Rhu
Helensburgh
Craigendoran
LOMOND SHORES
Balloch
Jamestown
Glen Lean
Invereck
Dalinlongart
Blairmore
Cove Bay
Cove
Kilmun
Strone
Portkil
Rosneath Pt.
Auchenbreck
405
Loch Riddon
Clachaig
Glen Kin
Holy Loch
Strone Pt.
Kilcreggan
Colgrain
GEILSTON
ALEXANDRIA
Bonhill
578 CRUACH NAN CAPULL
Glenstriven
Sandbank
Ardnadam
COWAL BIRD GARDEN
Hunter's Quay
ST JOHN'S CHURCH
Kirn
Gourock
Ashton
Greenock West
Greenock
Geilston
Renton
OF BUTE
506 BEINN BHREAC
LOCH STRIVEN
522 BLACK CRAIG
Dunoon
HIGHLAND MARY'S STATUE
Cloch Pt.
Levan
Larkfield
Braeside
Midton
MCLEAN MUS. & ART GALL.
HM CUSTOMS & EXCISE MUSEUM & EXHIBITION
NEWARK CASTLE
PORT GLASGOW
Cardross
Castlehill
DUMBARTON
Inverchaolain
Bullwood
Ravenscraig
Central
Brucehill
Ardentraive
Colintraive
Algaltraig
418 CORLARACH HILL
Lunderston Bay
Strone
FINLAYSTONE HOUSE & GARDENS
DUMBARTON CASTLE
Woodhall
303
Devol
Mid Auchinlech
Bardrainney
Langbank
Loch Thom
Gryfe Resrs.
I N V E R C L Y D E
Kyles of Bute
Glen Fyne
Corlarach Forest
Inverkip
Shielhill
Garvock
Strathgryfe
ISLAND OF BUTE
Glen More
227
WINDY HILL 278
WAVE WHISPER GALLERY
Innellan
Port Lamont
Newton Park
Wemyss Bay
CLYDE
Kilmacolm
Ardyne Pt.
Upper Skelmorlie
441 CREUCH HILL
Toward
Skelmorlie
Duchal Moor
Quarrier's Homes
Houston
Kames B.
St Colmac
Port Bannatyne
Toward Pt.
NS
120
Bridge of Weir
Crosslee
Ettrick Bay
ROTHESAY CASTLE
Rothesay Bay
M U I R S H I E L
Ranfurly
Craigmore
Meigle
Noddsdale Water
Rothesay
ARDENCRAIG GARDENS
Montford
Queenside Muir
MUIRSHIEL
Kilbarchan
WEAVER'S COTTAGE
VICTORIAN FERNERY
522 HILL OF STAKE
Straad
Loch Fad
Ascog
Waterhead Moor
Routenburn
R E G I O N A L
Mistylaw Muir
Calder
Kerrycroy
60
Largs Bay
VIKINGAR!
Largs
OLD KIRK
CASTLE SEMPLE
Howwood
Scoulag
MOUNT STUART HOUSE AND GARDEN
Tomont End
Ladyland Moor
Lochwinnoch
Kilmarnock
Scalpsie
Loch Quien
CHRISTIAN HERITAGE MUSEUM
484 IRISH LAW
NATURE RESERVE VISITOR CEN.
Ardscalpsie Pt.
Great Cumbrae Island
Downcraig Ferry
P A R K
Barr Loch
Bowbank Reservoir
Scalpsie Bay
Kingarth
Muirhead Reservoir
KELBURN COUNTRY CENTRE
Stravanan Bay
Kilchattan Bay
MUSEUM OF THE CUMBRAES
Millport
Fairlie Roads
Fairlie
Camphill Reservoir
Kilbirnie
Kilbirnie Loch
210
BUTE
Kilchattan Bay
157
Beith
ST BLANE'S CHAPEL
The Tan
387 KAIM HILL
Knockendon Reservoir
Rye Water
Glengarnock
Gateside
Longbar
119
Garroch Hd.
HUNTERSTON POWER STATION VISITOR CENTRE
Barrmill
The Den
Little Cumbrae Island
FIRTH OF CLYDE
Drakemyre
Greenhills
Burnhouse
Bone Pt.
Thirdpart
Highfield
Portencross
Giffordland
Dalry
Blairland
Dunlop
BLACKSHAW FARM PARK
Lugton Water
Farland Hd.
West Kilbride
NORTH SANNOX FARM PARK
Seamill
Auchentiber
North Ayrshire
Sannox
DALGARVEN MILL
Sannox Bay
Dalgarven
ABBEY
Torranyard
Chapelhill
Kilwinning
Annick Water
Corrie
Horse Isle
Dykesmains
Bensley
EGLINTON
Cunninghamhead
BRODDICK 0:55
Ardrossan
NORTH AYRSHIRE MUSEUM
Stevenston
Kilmaurs
Girdle
Saltcoats
A815
A886
B8000
A880
B836
A885
A814
B833
A817
A818
A82
A770
A78
A8
B788
A761
B789
B786
A737
A760
B777
B776
A736
B706
B707
B780
B714
B778
A738
B7080
B769
B875
A844
B878
B881
B896
B899
B784
A813
A812

SOUND OF MULL
ISLAND OF MULL
FIRTH OF LORN
LYNN OF LORN
LORN
BENDERLOCH
NM
NR
Killundine
Claggan
Larachbeg
KINLOCHALINE CASTLE
ARDTORNISH GARDENS
Achranich
Loch Aline
Loch Tearnait
Rannoch
437 BEINN A' CHAISIL
Loch nan Clach
Glensanda
Shuna I.
Portnacroish
Appin
Port Appin
Port Ramsay
Clachan
Eriska
North Shian
South Shian
SCOTTISH SEA LIFE SANCTUARY
Lismore
Achnacroish
Fiunary
Savary
Lochaline
GLAIS BHEINN 479
AN SLEAGHACH 513
Eignaig
ARDTORNISH CASTLE
Ardtornish Pt.
Aros Mains
Rubha Mor
Salen
Pennygown
Fishnish Bay
Killbeg
Corrynachenchy
Inninmore Bay
Garbh Shlios
Camas Gorm
Garmony
Scallastle Bay
Rubha an Ridire
Bernera I.
Achinduin
Kilcheran
Baravullin
Ferlochan
Kiel Crofts
Benderloch
Ledaig
Achnaba
Eilean Dubh
Ardmucknish Bay
Knock
412
Loch Bà
591 BEINN GHRAIG
Scallastle
Java
Craignure Bay
Craignure
MULL AND WEST HIGHLAND NARROW GAUGE RAILWAY
766 DUN DA GHAOITHE
TOROSAY CASTLE & GARDEN
Duart Bay
Duart Pt.
DUART CASTLE
Eilean Musdile
Eilean Mor
DUNSTAFFNAGE CASTLE
North Connel
Connel
Black Croft
FALLS OF LORA
Glen Cannel
761 BEINN TALAIDH
Lochdon
CASTLEBAY 5:10
COLL 2:40
TIREE 3:40
LOCHBOISDALE 5:15
Dunbeg
Ganavan
Dunollie
OBAN/ OBAN LODGE
MCCAIG'S TOWER
OBAN VISITOR CENTRE
OBAN DISTILLERY
OBAN RARE BREEDS FARM PARK
Altnacraig
Oban
Black Lochs
704 CORRA-BHEINN
Glen More
Lussa
Loch Don
Grass Pt.
Strathcoil
Coladoir
Kerrera
Balliemore
Glenamachrie
Loch Airdeglais
248
Loch Spelve
BEN BUIE 717
698 CREACH BEINN
Loch Fuaron
Kinlochspelve
Croggan
Rubha nan Sailthean
Bach I.
Ardmore
Gallanach
Sound of Kerrera
Loch Nell
Lochbuie
Barachandroman
Loch Uisg
503 BEINN NA CROISE
Rubha Seanach
Kilbride
Kilmore
Barran
Am Buth
Loch Feochan
Glen Feochan
GLENFEOCHAN HOUSE GARDENS
Leidle
Loch Buie
Carsaig
405 DRUIM FADA
Laggan Deer Forest
LORD LOVAT'S CAVE
Carsaig Bay
Rubha Dubh
Kilninver
Barochreal
368 A' CHRUACH
Musdale
Glen Euchar
Bragleenmore
CLACHAN BRIDGE
Loch Scamadale
515 BEINN CHAPULL
Insh I.
Sound of Insh
Frank Lockwood's Island
Clachan-Seil
Clachan
Seil
AN CALA GARDENS
438 CARN DEARG
Easdale
EASDALE ISLAND FOLK MUSEUM
Balvicar
Braes of Lorn
Blaran
267 CRUACH RAREY
Seil Sound
Loch Tralaig
Lochavich
Drissa
Dubh-fheith
Cuan
Kilmun
Ferry
Torsa
Kilchoan
Ardanstur
Melfort
Cullipool
94
Kilmelford
Loch Avich
Garbh Eileach
Garvellachs
Loch Melfort
Glenmore
Luing
Sound of Luing
SCARBA, LUNGA AND THE GARVELLACHS
Eilean Dubh Mor
Eileach an Naoimh
Achafolla
ARDUAINE GARDEN
Arduaine
Kames
365
Lagalochan
491 CARN DUCHARA
Inverliever Forest
Kilmaha
Garraron
Barbreck
Liever
COLONSAY 2:20
Toberonochy
Shuna Sound
Shuna
Craobh Haven
Barravullin
Lunga
Shuna Pt.
350 CRUACH AN EACHLAICH
Arichamish
Kintraw
Rubha Aird Luing
Torran
CRUACH SCARBA 449
Scarba
Ardfern
Ford
Finchairn
FINCHAIRN CASTLE
Ederline
227 CREAG MHOR
Gulf of Corryvreckan
Eilean Righ
CARNASSARIE CASTLE
Loch Craignish
CRUACH FHION
Aird
Loch Gaineamh
Rèisa an t-Sruith
319
Kinuachdrachd
Kilmartin
GLEBE CAIRN
KILMARTIN HOUSE TRUST
Island Macaskin
Craignish Pt.
Glengarrisdale Bay
296 CRUACH NA SEILCHEIG
Kinuachdrachd Harbour
KILMARTIN SCULPTURED STONES
RI CRUIN CAIRN
Slockavullin
Poltalloch
Gleann Airigh
Glendebadel Bay
Loch Crinan
231 DUN DUBH
365 BEN GARRISDALE
Crinan
CUP AND RING MARKS
Kilmahumaig
Add
MOINE MHOR
DUNADD FORT
Kilmichael Glassary
Loch Glashan
Bellanoch
Mòine Mhòr
Bridgend
CAIRNBAAN CUP & RING MARKS
265
Lussa
Lealt
ROCK MARKINGS
Lochgair
Asknish
A848
A849
A884
B8035
B849
A828
B8045
A816
B844
B8003
B8002
B8025
B841
A83
B840
137
138
127
128
0 1 2 3 4 5 6 miles
0 1 2 3 4 5 6 7 8 9 10 km

Elleric
Glen Creran
Invercreran
Glasdrum
Glasdrum Wood
Creagan
South Creagan
Druimavuic
Barcaldine
Barcaldine Forest
Glen Ure
Beinn Sgulaird
Gualachulain
Inverchamnan
Glenceitlein
Stob Dubh
Beinn Fhionnlaidh
Beinn Trilleachan
Ben Starav
Stob Coir'an Albannaich
Stob Ghabhar
Clach Leathad
Black Mount
West Highland Way
Loch Tulla
Achallader
Forest Lodge
Inveroran Hotel
Loch Dochard
Allt Dochard
Allt Coire a' Chaolain
Creach Bheinn
Beinn nan Aighenan
Bridge of Orchy
Beinn Dorain
Beinn Odhar
Gleann Salach
Beinn Mheadhonach
Ardchattan Priory
Ardchattan Priory Gardens
Achnacloich
Achnacloich Garden
Bonawe
Loch Etive
Glen Kinglass
Glen Liver
Glen Noe
Beinn Eunaich
Beinn Mhic Mhonaidh
Glen Strae
Glen Orchy
Arichastlich
Beinn Udlaidh
Glen Lochy
Clifton
Tyndrum
Arrivain
Bonawe Iron Furnace
Inverawe Fisheries and Smokeries Exhibition
Brochroy
Taynuilt
Ichrachan
Bridge of Awe
Ben Cruachan
Pass of Brander
Cruachan Reservoir
Falls of Cruachan
Barguillean Gardens
Glen Nant
Kilchurn Castle
Lochawe
Stronmilchan
Strath of Orchy
Achnafalnich
Inverlochy
Dalmally
McIntyre Monument
Cruachan Dam Visitor Centre
Loch Tromlee
Loch Nant
Ardanaiseig Gardens
Ardanaiseig
Innis Chonain
Inishail Chapel
Inishail
Teatle Water
Eas a' Ghaill
Ben Lui
Beinn Dubhchraig
Inverherive
Sior Loch
Kilchrenan
Annat
North Port
Cladich
Allt Fearna
NN
Meall nan Tighearn
Allt Fionn Ghlinne
Dubh Eas
Glen Falloch
Falls of Falloch
Portsonachan
South Port
Argyll
Lochan Shira
Loch Stron Mor
Troisgeach
Inverarnan
Ben Glas Burn
Inverinan
Ballimeanoch
Allt Beochlich
Tullich
Glen Aray
Beinn Ghlas
Glen Shira
Beinn Bhuidhe
Brannie Burn
Allt na Lairige
Glen Fyne
Glenfyne Lodge
Maol Breac
Ardlui
Dalavich
Blarghour
Cruach Mhor
Kilblaan Burn
Clachan
Dubh Loch
Ardchonnell Castle
Portinnisherrich
Drishaig
Cairndow
Loch Sloy
Ben Vorlich
and
Inveraray Castle
Bell Tower
Ardkinglas Woodland Garden
Glen Kinglas
Inveruglas
Rob Roy's Cave
Combined Operations Museum Inveraray
Inveraray Jail
Inveraray
Maritime Museum
Newtown
Ardno
St Catherine's
Eredine
Durran
An Suidhe
Douglas Water
Beinn an Lochain
Hell's Glen
Rest and Be Thankful
Beinn Ime
Inversnaid Hotel
West Highland Way
Argyll Wildlife Park
Dalchenna
Eredine Forest
Cruach nan Capull
Monevechadan
Glen Croe
Forest
Succoth
Tarbet
Arrochar
Craig Rostan
Beinn Dearg
Loch Leacann
Auchindrain
Auchindrain Open Air Museum
Ben Donich
Ardgartan
Stuckgowan
Ardmay
Bute
Creggans
Clachan Strachur
Strachur Bay
Drimsynie
European Sheep and Wool Centre
Lochgoilhead
Beinn Lochain
Corrow
Cnoc Coinnich
Ardgartan
Loch Long
Ptarr
Furnace
Glen Sluain
Blairlomond
Loch Goil
Ardgoil Forest
Glen Douglas
Crarae
Crarae Glen Gardens
Newton
Invernoaden
Beinn Bheula
Doune Hill
Inverbeg
Inverbeg Gallery
Minard
Glenbranter
Glenbranter Forest
Argyll Forest Park
The Saddle
Glenmallan
Tullochgorm
Garbhallt
Lachlan Castle
Lachlan Bay
Loch Eck
Carrick Castle
Beinn Eich
Edentaggart
Glen Luss
Strathlachlan Forest
Beinn Bheag
Whistlefield
NS
Portincaple
Whistlefield
Lephinmore
Caol Ghleann
Beinn Chaorach
Thistle Bagpipe Works
Aldochlay
Lephinchapel
Dunans
Bernice
Creachan Mor
Garelochhead
Beinn Ruisg
A85
A82
A819
A83
A815
A886
A814
A817
B845
B840
B8074
B8077
B828
B839
B8000
138
139
132
129

Glen Lochy
Arrivain
Clifton
Tyndrum
139
Cononish
Strath Fillan
BEINN UDLAIDH
BEINN ODHAR
BEN CHALLUM
BEINN CHEATHAICH
Auchlyne West Burn
Auchlyne
Ardchyle
GLEN DOCHART
Ledcharrie
Lochdochart House
Loch Iubhair
Loch Dochart
Inverherive
Benmore
Portnellan
Crianlarich
CRIANLARICH
BEN MORE
STOB BINNEIN
BEN LUI
BEINN DUBHCHRAIG
Allt Fionn Ghlinne
WEST HIGHLAND WAY
Glen Falloch
Falls of Falloch
MEALL NAN TIGHEARN
Dubh Eas
Boreland
MOIRLANICH LONGHOUSE
Finlarig
Killin
BREADALBANE FOLKLORE CENTRE
Achmore
FALLS OF DOCHART
Dochart
140
Glen Ogle
Beich Burn
Dalveich
Lochearnhead
EDINAMPLE FALLS
Edinample
Ardvorlich
LOCH LOMOND
AND THE
TROSSACHS
NATIONAL
PARK
Braes of Balquhidder
Balquhidder
ROB ROY'S GRAVE
Auchtubh
Monachylemore
Craigruie
Loch Doine
Loch Voil
Inverlochlarig
Ballimore
Calair Burn
Strathyre
Strathyre Forest
BEN VORLICH
TROISGEACH
Inverarnan
Ben Glas Burn
BEINN A'CHROIN
131
Ardlui
MAOL BREAC
STOB A'CHOIN
NN
BEINN BHREAC
BENVANE
BEINN EACH
Ardchullarie More
Loch Lubnaig
Stirling
Loch Sloy
Strath Gartney
Glen Finglas Res.
Anie
Pass of Leny
Leny Ho.
Inveruglas
ROB ROY'S CAVE
Stronachlachar
LOCH KATRINE
BEN LEDI
FALLS OF LENY
Kilmahog
Bochastle
Callander
BEINN IME
Inversnaid Hotel
Loch Arklet
Loch Ard Forest
The Trossachs
TROSSACHS PIER COMPLEX
SS SIR WALTER SCOTT
Trossachs Hotel
Brig o'Turk
Coilantogle
Frenich
BEN VENUE
Loch Achray
Duncraggan
Lendrick Lodge
THE TROSSACHS
Loch Venachar
Succoth
Tarbet
Arrochar
Glen Croe
Ardgartan Forest
Ardgartan
Craig Rostan
Loch Chon
Achray Forest
Loch Drunkie
Menteith Hills
Torrie
Loch Rusky
Stuckgowan
Ardmay
BEN LOMOND
Kinlochard
Altskeith
FOREST PARK VISITOR CENTRE
SCOTTISH WOOL CENTRE
TROSSACHS DISCOVERY CENTRE
Milton
Aberfoyle
Kirkton
Port of Menteith
DUNAVER FARMLIFE CENTRE
Ptarmigan Lodge
QUEEN ELIZABETH
Loch Ard
INCHMAHOME PRIORY
Malling
Ruskie
Goodie Water
Lake of Menteith
Glen Douglas
Rowardennan
BEINN UIRD
Duchray Water
Cobleland
Loch Ard Forest
FOREST PARK
Inverbeg
INVERBEG GALLERY
DOUNE HILL
Glenmallan
Rowardennan Forest
Gartmore
Dykehead
FLANDERS MOSS
Flanders Moss
Kelty Water
Dalmary
Flanders Moss
BEINN EICH
Edentaggart
NS
Arnprior
Cauldhame
Portincaple
Whistlefield
129
Glen Luss
Inchlonaig
Milarrochy
Buchlyvie
THISTLE BAGPIPE WORKS
Luss
Moor Park
Buchlyvie Muir
Kippen
Muir
Garelochhead
BEINN CHAORACH
Aldochlay
Inchfad
Balmaha
Milton of Buchanan
Garadhban Forest
BEINN RUISG
STRONE HOUSE GARDENS
Inchcailloch
ROWAN GALLERY
Balfron Station
Balfron
Harvieston
Faslane Port
Glen Fruin
LOMOND
LOCH LOMOND
Inchmurrin
Drymen
Fintry Hills
CULCREUCH CASTLE
Endrick Water
Shandon
GARE LOCH
Duchlage
Blairglas
Gartness
Boquhan
Spittal
Killearn
Ballikinrain
Fintry
Gartocharn
Croftamie
GLENARN GARDEN
THE HILL HOUSE
Arden
BALLOCH CASTLE
EARL'S SEAT
Rhu
Bannachra Muir
Craighat
CAMPSIE FELLS
Helensburgh
LOCH LOMOND
GLENGOYNE DISTILLERY
Rosneath
Dumgoyne
Blairquhosh
Kilcreggan
Rosneath Pt.
Craigendoran
LOMOND SHORES
LOCH LOMOND SHORES
Balloch
Auchincarroch
Stockiemuir
Strathblane Hills
Blane Water
Portkil
ALEXANDRIA
Jamestown
West
Dunbartonshire
Bonhill
120
Dumbarton Muir
Blanefield
Netherton
Strathblane
Clachan of Campsie
121
East
Lennoxtown
Balgrochan
Dunbartonshire
0 1 2 3 4 5 6 miles
0 1 2 3 4 5 6 7 8 9 10 km
Gourock
Greenock West
Greenock
MCLEAN MUS. & ART GALL.
HM CUSTOMS & EXCISE MUSEUM & EXHIBITION
Cardross
Castlehill
Renton
Townend
DUMBARTON
DUNCOLM
KILPATRICK HILLS
MUGDOCK
Mugdock
Resrs.

Perth and Kinross
Clackmannanshire
Falkirk
NN
NS
140
141
134
121
122
Almond
CREAG UCHDAG
BEN CHONZIE
MEALL NAN CAORAICH
Little Glenshee
Newton
Logiealmond Lodge
Logiealmond
Chapelhill
Harrietfield
GLEN ALMOND
Sma' Glen
MEALL TARSUINN
Shaggie Burn
Loch Lednock Reservoir
Invergeldie Burn
Loch Turret Reservoir
Glen Lednock
Invergeldie
Funtullich
Glen Turret
Buchanty
Methven
Almondbank
Lochty
Keillour
Braegrum
Tibbermore
St Fillans
LOCH EARN
RIVER EARN
Ardtrostan
Dunira
MELVILLE MONUMENT
Comrie
Lawers
FALLS OF TURRET
Ochtertyre
Quoig
Monzie
Monzie Castle
Hosh
Gilmerton
Fowlis Wester
STANDING STONES
Keillour Forest
Pow Water
GLENTURRET DISTILLERY
Crieff
Tullybannocher
EARTHQUAKE HOUSE
Ross
Dalginross
Lochlane
Madderty
Findo Gask
Clathy
St David's
Dupplin Castle
Forteviot
AUCHINGARRICH WILDLIFE & HIGHLAND CATTLE CENTRE
CRIEFF VISITORS' CENTRE
STUART CRYSTAL VISITOR CENTRE
The Balloch
Forest of Glenartney
Torlum Wood
DRUMMOND CASTLE GARDENS
INNERPEFFRAY LIBRARY
Kirkton
Culloch
Water of Ruchill
Glen Artney
Dalchruin
Tigh-na-Blair
OLD CHURCH & TOWER
Muthill
Kinkell Bridge
STRATHEARN
Earn
Allt Strath a' Ghlinne
Auchnashelloch
Ochtermuthill
Machany Water
Aberuthven
BEN CLACH
Dunning
Tullibardine
TULLIBARDINE CHAPEL
Auchterarder
Langside
Glenlichorn
Knaik
Garrick
Muirton
Milton
AUCHTERARDER HERITAGE
UAMH BHEAG
BLACKHALL ROMAN CAMPS
Gleneagles Hotel
GLENEAGLES
ARDOCH ROMAN CAMP
QUEEN ELIZABETH FOREST PARK AND TROSSACHS
BRACKLINN FALLS
Bullie Burn
Braco
STRATHALLAN
Blackford
Gleneagles House
Common of Dunning
Middle Rigg
Muckle Burn
Annet Burn
Greenloaning
Braes of Ogilvie
Glen Eagles
STEEL'S KNOWE
INNERDOUNY HILL
Allan Water
Ardoch Burn
Braes of Doune
Kinbuck
Glendevon Resvrs.
GLENDEVON
Glendevon
Glen Devon
South Queich
Drumvaich
Burn of Cambus
Ashfield
Balhaldie
Sheriff Muir
Burnfoot
Castle Hill Reservoir
Carnbo
Doune
Deanston
CATHEDRAL
Dunblane
Pisgah
LEIGHTON LIBRARY
BLAIRDENON HILL
BEN CLEUCH
Pool o' Muckhart
Yetts o' Muckhart
Thornhill
Blair Drummond
Easter Row
BLAIR DRUMMOND SAFARI PARK
Sunnylaw
KING'S SEAT HILL
CASTLE CAMPBELL
Rumbling Bridge
RUMBLING BRIDGE GORGE
Crook of Devon
Drum
Blairdrummond Moss
Bridge of Allan
Blairlogie
MILL TRAIL VISITOR CENTRE
Menstrie
Tillicoultry
Dollar
Powmill
Alva
Fishcross
STERLING MILLS
Devonside
Blairingone
Drip Moss
Causewayhead
NATIONAL WALLACE MONUMENT
Tullibody
Coalsnaughton
GARTMORN DAM
Hill End
Kippen
Glentirranmuir
Gargunnock
STIRLING CASTLE
OLD TOWN JAIL
Raploch
Cambuskenneth
ABBEY
Cambus
Branshill
Sauchie
Forest Mill
Keilarsbrae
Balgonar
KNOCK HILL
SMITH ART GALL & MUSEUM
Stirling
CARLEATHERAN
Touch Hills
Cambusbarron
Torbrex
ALLOA
ALLOA TOWER
Saline
Gargunnock Hills
St Ninians
Fallin
Throsk
Clackmannan
South Alloa
Kennet
Kilbagie
Cowstrandburn
BANNOCKBURN HERITAGE CENTRE
Bannockburn
Earlsburn Reservoirs
Cowie
THE PINEAPPLE
Dunmore
Blairhall
Comrie
Oakley
Carnock
Gowkhall
Devilla Forest
Craigend
STIRLING SERVICES
Kincardine
CULROSS ABBEY
High Valleyfield
Loch Walton
Loch Coulter
Plean
PLEAN
Airth
CULROSS PALACE
Low Torry
Torryburn
Cairneyhill
Easter Cringate
Letham
Kincardine Bridge
Culross
Torry Bay
CHARLESTOWN WORKSHOPS
Charlestown
Muirmill
Carron
Torwood
Antonshill
Carron Valley Forest
Carron Valley Res.
Carron Bridge
Dunipace
DENNY
Stenhousemuir
Skinflats
Fankerton
Stoneywood
Larbert
Carron
MUSEUM
GRANGEMOUTH
Grangepans
TOMTAIN
Bainsford
BO'NESS AND KINNEIL RAILWAY
Carriden
Head of Muir
P&R
FALKIRK MILLENNIUM WHEEL
Bo'ness
Muirhouses
Kilsyth Hills
Bonnybridge
Dennyloanhead
FALKIRK
Laurieston
BIRKHILL CLAY MINE
Blackness
COLZIUM HOUSE
Banton
Longcroft
ROUGH CASTLE
Grougfoot
Kilsyth
Banknock
High Bonnybridge
Glen Village
Redding
CALLENDAR HOUSE
Polmont
Brightons
Whitecross
Linlithgow
Linlithgow Bridge
Philpstoun
Queenzieburn
Greenhill
Reddingmuirhead
Castlecary
Dullatur
Cumbernauld Village
Croy
Shieldhill
California
Maddiston
Loan
PALACE
Bridgend
A85
A822
A9
A823
A824
A91
A84
A820
A811
A907
A905
A876
A977
A985
A994
A883
A872
A803
A904
A905
A706
A993
A801
A88
M9
M80
M876
B8063
B8062
B934
B9141
B9112
B827
B8033
B8032
B826
B824
B8031
B822
B8075
B9140
B9096
B908
B910
B913
B914
B818
B9124
B816
B805
B8023
B802
B803
B9080
B903
B977

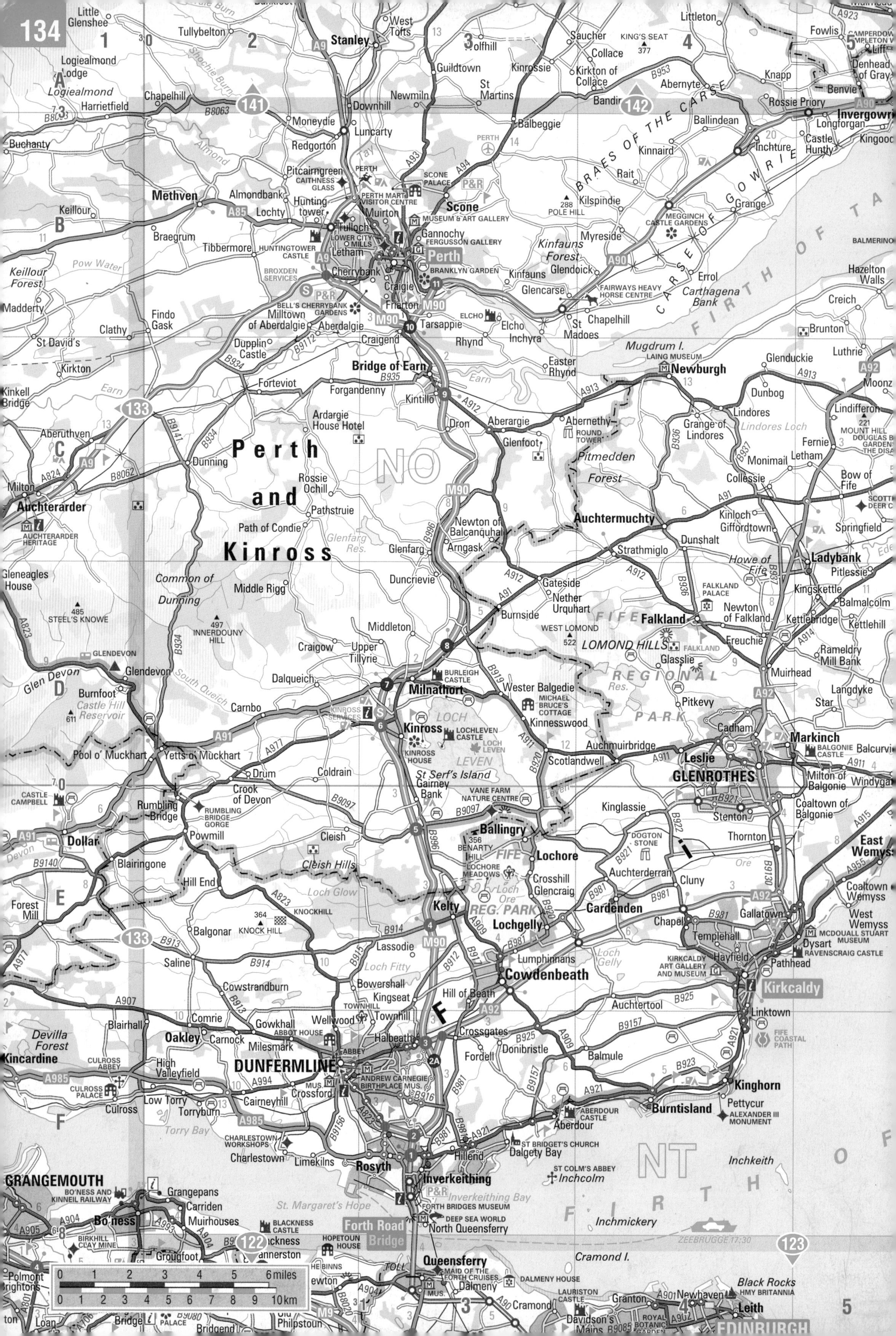

Little Glenshee
Tullybelton
Stanley
West Tofts
Wolfhill
Saucher
KING'S SEAT 377
Littleton
Fowlis
Logiealmond Lodge
Logiealmond
Guildtown
Kinrossie
Collace
Kirkton of Collace
Abernyte
Knapp
Benvie
Chapelhill
Harrietfield
B8063
141
Downhill
Newmiln
St Martins
Bandir
142
Rossie Priory
Invergowrie
Longforgan
Buchanty
Moneydie
Luncarty
Balbeggie
BRAES OF THE CARSE
Ballindean
Castle Huntly
Inchture
Redgorton
PERTH
Kinnaird
Almond
Pitcairngreen
CAITHNESS GLASS
SCONE PALACE
P&R
Rait
Methven
Almondbank
Huntingtower
PERTH MART VISITOR CENTRE
Scone
Kilspindie
Grange
Keillour
Lochty
Muirton
MUSEUM & ART GALLERY
288 POLE HILL
MEGGINCH CASTLE GARDENS
A85
Tulloch
Gannochy
FERGUSSON GALLERY
Myreside
CARSE OF GOWRIE
Braegrum
Tibbermore
HUNTINGTOWER CASTLE
LOWER CITY MILLS
Letham
Perth
Kinfauns Forest
BALMERINO
Pow Water
Keillour Forest
BROXDEN SERVICES
Cherrybank
BRANKLYN GARDEN
Kinfauns
Glendoick
A90
Errol
Hazelton Walls
Craigie
Glencarse
FAIRWAYS HEAVY HORSE CENTRE
Carthagena Bank
FIRTH OF TAY
Madderty
Findo Gask
BELL'S CHERRYBANK GARDENS
Friarton
M90
Creich
Clathy
Milltown of Aberdalgie
Aberdalgie
ELCHO
Tarsappie
Elcho
St Madoes
Chapelhill
Brunton
St David's
Dupplin Castle
Craigend
Rhynd
Inchyra
Mugdrum I.
Luthrie
Kirkton
B934
B9112
Bridge of Earn
Easter Rhynd
LAING MUSEUM
Newburgh
Glenduckie
Kinkell Bridge
Earn
Forteviot
B935
Forgandenny
Kintillo
A913
Dunbog
Moonzie
133
Aberuthven
Ardargie House Hotel
Dron
Aberargie
Abernethy
ROUND TOWER
Grange of Lindores
Lindores
Lindores Loch
Lindifferon
221 MOUNT HILL
B9141
Glenfoot
B936
Fernie
Perth and Kinross
NO
Pitmedden Forest
Monimail
Letham
A9
Dunning
B8062
Rossie Ochill
Collessie
Bow of Fife
A824
Milton
Auchterarder
Pathstruie
Auchtermuchty
A91
Kinloch
Giffordtown
AUCHTERARDER HERITAGE
Path of Condie
Newton of Balcanquhal
Springfield
Glenfarg Res.
Glenfarg
Arngask
Strathmiglo
Dunshalt
Howe of Fife
Ladybank
Pitlessie
Gleneagles House
Common of Dunning
Middle Rigg
Duncrievie
A912
Gateside
Nether Urquhart
FALKLAND PALACE
Kingskettle
Balmalcolm
485 STEEL'S KNOWE
497 INNERDOUNY HILL
Burnside
FIFE
Falkland
Newton of Falkland
Kettlebridge
Kettlehill
A823
Middleton
WEST LOMOND 522
LOMOND HILLS
FALKLAND
Freuchie
Rameldry Mill Bank
GLENDEVON
Craigow
Upper Tillyrie
Glasslie
Muirhead
Glen Devon
Glendevon
South Queich
Dalqueich
BURLEIGH CASTLE
Milnathort
B919
REGIONAL PARK
Langdyke
Burnfoot
Castle Hill Reservoir
611
Carnbo
Wester Balgedie
MICHAEL BRUCE'S COTTAGE
Pitkevy
Star
KINROSS SERVICES
Kinross
LOCHLEVEN CASTLE
LOCH LEVEN
Kinnesswood
Cadham
Markinch
Pool o' Muckhart
Yetts o' Muckhart
A977
KINROSS HOUSE
Auchmuirbridge
A911
Leslie
BALGONIE CASTLE
Balcurvie
Drum
Coldrain
St Serf's Island
Scotlandwell
GLENROTHES
Milton of Balgonie
Windygates
CASTLE CAMPBELL
Crook of Devon
Gairney Bank
VANE FARM NATURE CENTRE
Kinglassie
Coaltown of Balgonie
Rumbling Bridge
RUMBLING BRIDGE GORGE
B9097
Ballingry
B921
Stenton
A915
Dollar
Powmill
Cleish
356 BENARTY HILL
DOGTON STONE
Thornton
East Wemyss
Devon
B9140
Blairingone
Cleish Hills
LOCHORE MEADOWS
Lochore
Auchterderran
Cluny
Hill End
Loch Glow
Crosshill
Glencraig
B981
Coaltown of Wemyss
Forest Mill
A823
Kelty
LOCHORE REG. PARK
Cardenden
Gallatown
West Wemyss
364 KNOCK HILL
KNOCKHILL
B914
Lochgelly
Chapel
Templehall
Dysart
MCDOUALL STUART MUSEUM
133
B913
Balgonar
B915
Lassodie
Lumphinnans
Loch Gelly
Hayfield
RAVENSCRAIG CASTLE
A971
Saline
Loch Fitty
B912
B917
Cowdenbeath
KIRKCALDY ART GALLERY AND MUSEUM
Pathhead
Kirkcaldy
Cowstrandburn
Bowershall
Hill of Beath
A907
TOWNHILL
Kingseat
Townhill
A92
Auchtertool
B925
Linktown
Blairhall
Comrie
Gowkhall
Wellwood
ABBOT HOUSE
F
Crossgates
B9157
FIFE COASTAL PATH
Devilla Forest
Oakley
Carnock
Halbeath
Fordell
Donibristle
A909
Balmule
Milesmark
ABBEY
Kincardine
CULROSS ABBEY
High Valleyfield
DUNFERMLINE
ANDREW CARNEGIE BIRTHPLACE MUS.
Kinghorn
A985
A994
MUS.
Crossford
B916
Pettycur
CULROSS PALACE
Low Torry
Cairneyhill
ABERDOUR CASTLE
Burntisland
ALEXANDER III MONUMENT
Culross
Torryburn
Aberdour
Torry Bay
CHARLESTOWN WORKSHOPS
B9156
B981
A921
ST BRIDGET'S CHURCH
NT
Charlestown
Limekilns
Rosyth
Hillend
Dalgety Bay
Inchkeith
ST COLM'S ABBEY
Inchcolm
FIRTH OF
GRANGEMOUTH
BO'NESS AND KINNEIL RAILWAY
Grangepans
Inverkeithing
Inverkeithing Bay
Carriden
St. Margaret's Hope
FORTH BRIDGES MUSEUM
A904
Bo'ness
A993
Muirhouses
BLACKNESS CASTLE
Forth Road Bridge
DEEP SEA WORLD
North Queensferry
Inchmickery
A905
BIRKHILL CLAY MINE
122
Blackness
HOPETOUN HOUSE
ZEEBRUGGE 17:30
123
Grougfoot
Philpstoun
Queensferry
Cramond I.
Polmont
Brightons
THE BINNS
MAID OF THE FORTH CRUISES
DALMENY HOUSE
Black Rocks
HMY BRITANNIA
Dalmeny
LAURISTON CASTLE
Granton
A901
Newhaven
Leith
A90
Cramond
A902
B8020
PALACE
Bridgend
Davidson's Mains
ROYAL BOTANIC GARDEN
EDINBURGH
M9
0 1 2 3 4 5 6 miles
0 1 2 3 4 5 6 7 8 9 10 km

Dundee
Downfield
Fintry
Douglas & Angus
Baldovie
Craigie
West Ferry
Broughty Ferry
Lochee
VERDANT WORKS
MUS. AND ART GALL.
MILLS OBSERVATORY
CLAYPOTTS CASTLE
Stannergate
FRIGATE UNICORN
BROUGHTY CASTLE MUSEUM
Tay Bridge
TOLL
DUNDEE
DISCOVERY POINT
UNIVERSITY BOTANIC GARDENS
Newport-on-Tay
Tayport
Scotscraig
TENTSMUIR POINT
Woodhaven
Tay Rail Bridge
Wormit
Tentsmuir Forest
MORTON LOCHS
Kirkton
Bottomcraig
Balmerino
Gauldry
Pickletillem
Rhynd
Carrick
Kilmany
Lucklawhill
Leuchars
LEUCHARS NORMAN CHURCH
EARLSHALL CASTLE AND GARDENS
Rathillet
Logie
Balmullo
Eden Mouth
Guardbridge
EDEN ESTIVANT CENTRE
ST ANDREWS BAY
Dairsie or Osnaburgh
Kincaple
ST ANDREWS
ST ANDREWS AQUARIUM
BRITISH GOLF MUS.
St Andrews
CATH. & ST RULE'S TOWER
Kilmaron Castle
Newpark
Strathkinness
Cupar
Kemback
Blebocraigs
B939
Balone
CRAIGTOUN
ST ANDREWS BOTANIC GARDEN
Brownhills
Buddo Ness
Boarhills
Babbet Ness
Denhead
Prior Muir
217
Pitscottie
HILL OF TARVIT MANSIONHOUSE
Bridgend
Ceres
Cameron Res.
Cameron Burn
Stravithie
Dunino
Kingsbarns
Cambo Ness
CAMBO GARDENS
Carr Brigs
Tullybothy Craigs
Craighead
Balcomie
Fife Ness
SCOTSTARVIT TOWER
Craigrothie
FIFE FOLK MUSEUM
Baldinnie
Peat Inn
Radernie
Kingsmuir
Lochty
CRAIL TOLBOOTH
SCOTLAND'S SECRET BUNKER
Crail
CRAIL MUSEUM AND HERITAGE CENTRE
West Ness
Woodside
New Gilston
Lathones
Largoward
Montrave
Carnbee
Pitcorthie
Pitkierie
Wester Newburn
KELLIE CASTLE AND GARDEN
Kilrenny
FIFE COASTAL PATH
PRAYTIS FARM PARK
SCOTLAND'S LARDER
Kirkton of Largo
Arncroach
Anstruther Easter
SCOTTISH FISHERIES MUSEUM
NO
Bonnybank
Lundin Links
Drumeldrie
Colinsburgh
Kennoway
Scoonie
ROBINSON CRUSOE STATUE
Lower Largo
Balchrystie
Abercrombie
Kilconquhar
Pittenweem
Anstruther Wester
ST FILLAN'S CAVE
ST MONAN'S WINDMILL
St Monans
ST MONAN'S CHURCH
SILVERBURN ESTATE
LETHAM GLEN
Leven
Largo Bay
Ardross
Ruddons Pt.
Innerleven
Methil
Earlsferry
Elie
Sauchar Pt.
Chapel Ness
ISLE OF MAY
Isle of May
MUSEUM
Buckhaven
FIFE COASTAL PATH
Souterrain Ardestie
Barry
Mains of Ardestie
Carnoustie
CARNOUSTIE
Barry Links
Monifieth
Barnhill
Buddon Ness
142
143
F O R T H
Fidra
Craigleith
Bass Rock
Eyebroughy
North Berwick
SCOTTISH SEABIRD CENTRE
MUSEUM
TANTALLON CASTLE
NT
DIRLETON CASTLE & GARDENS
MUIRFIELD
Dirleton
Auldhame
Gullane Bay
187
Gullane
Scoughall
West Fenton
Kingston
Whitekirk
Fenton Barns
St. Baldred's Cradle
Aberlady Bay
Aberlady
MYRETON MOTOR MUSEUM
Tyne Mouth
JOHN MUIR HOUSE
123
Craigielaw
Drem
Tyninghame
124
JOHN MUIR
Dunbar
THE CHESTERS FORT
MUSEUM OF FLIGHT
East Fortune
Preston
Belhaven
West Barns
Gosford Bay
GOSFORD HOUSE
Ballencrieff
Athelstaneford
Peffer Burn
East Linton
Broxburn
Barns Ness
Spittal
PRESTON MILL & PHANTASSIE DOOCOT
5 Cockenzie and Port Seton
SETON COLLEGIATE CHURCH
HOPETOUN MON.
181
JANE WELSH
Biel Water
Longniddry
1296
1650
Spott
Meikle
East Barns
Skateraw
A
B
C
D
E
F
G

1
2
3
4
A
B
C
D
E
F
G
144
Ardna
ARDNAMURCHAN
Cairns of Coll
Eilean Mor
Rubha Mor
Sorisdale
Bousd
B8072
Cliad Bay
Arnabost
Gallanach
Grishipoll
B8071
73
COLL
OBAN 2:40
Ballyhaugh
104
Loch Cliad
Hogh Bay
Arinagour
B8070
Totronald
Feall Bay
Arileod
Acha
Loch Eatharna
Eilean Ornsay
Breachacha Castle
Friesland
Calgary Pt.
Gunna
Crossapol Bay
Soa
Loch Breachacha
Quinis
Rubha an Aird
Caliach Pt.
Sunipol
M o r n i s
Calgary
Calgary Bay
Ensay
Treshnish Pt.
Haunn
B8073
Rubh a'Chaoil
Kilninia
Burg
TIREE
Vaul Bay
Salum
Caolas
Rubha Dubh
Balephetrish Bay
Vaul
B8069
Ruaig
B8068
Gott Bay
Soa
0:55
Kenovay
Scarinish
TIREE
B8065
NM
Heanish
Crossapol
Rubha Traigh an Duin
Hynish Bay
Balemartine
Mannal
Treshnish Isles
Fladda
LOCH
Eilean Dioghlum
Lunga
Gometra
Bearn
U
Bac Mor
Little Colonsay
Staffa
STAFFA
FINGAL'S CAVE
Argyll
Erisgeir
0 1 2 3 4 5 6 miles
0 1 2 3 4 5 6 7 8 9 10 km
(April-Oct) 0:45
NL
Hough Skerries
Balevullin
R. Chraiginis
Kilkenneth
Moss
Middleton
Heylipol
Port Mor
Barrapol
Loch a'Phuill
B8067
Rinn Thorbhais
Balephuil
141
Balephuil Bay
Port Snoig
Hynish
COLL 0:55
MACLEAN'S CROSS
Eilean Annraidh
Rubha nan Cearc
IONA ABBEY AND CATHEDRAL
IONA HERITAGE CENTRE
Iona
Baile Mor
Kintra
ST COLUMBA EXHIBITION & WELCOME CENTRE
Aridhglas
Loch na Lathach
Stac an Aoineidh
Sound of Iona
Fionnphort
A849
Eorabus
Fidden
Tiraghoil
Bunessan
Loch Assapol
Erraid
ROSS OF
Soa I.
Ardalanish
Uisken
Ardchiavaig
125
Eilean a'Chalmain
Rubh Ardalanish

5
6
7
8
A
B
C
D
E
F
G
Rubha Aird Druimnich
Eilean Shona
Farquhar's Pt.
Invermoidart
Kinlochmoidart
MOIDART
Gaskan
Gorstar
Castle Tioram
Loch Moidart
Ardmolich
Brunery
Ockle Pt.
Sanna Point
144
Fascadale
Kilmory
Ockle
Ardtoe
Newton of Ardtoe
Shielfoot
145
A861
Sanna
Sanna Bay
Branault
Kentra
Kentra Bay
B8044
Blain
Dalnabreck
Dalelia
Polloch
Portuairk
Achnaha
357 Beinn Bhreac
Moss
Claish Moss
Achosnich
401
ARDNAMURCHAN
Acharacle
Ardshealach
Loch Mudle
SUNART
B8007
845 Beinn Resipol
Salen
Resipole
Ariundle
Scotstown
Anaheilt
Ardnastang
Ormsaigmore
Ormsaigbeg
Kilchoan
Mingary Castle
Ardnamurchan Natural History Visitor Centre
490 Meall nan Each
528 Ben Hiant
Glenbeg
512 Ben Laga
Loch Sunart
Glencripesdale
Kilchoan Bay
Maclean's Nose
Ardslignish
Eilean Mor
Glenborrodale
Laga
Camuschoirk
Ardmore Bay
Ardmore Pt.
Oronsay
Carna
Glencripesdale
Liddesdale
Bloody Bay
Auliston Pt.
169
516 Meall an Damhain
138
Glengorm Castle
Mull and Iona Folklore Museum
Highland
582 Beinn nam Beathrach
Tobermory
Calve I.
Loch Teacuis
571 Beinn Iadain
Lochuisge
Quinish
Mishnish
'S Airde-Beinn
Tobermory Distillery
292
B8073
Drimnin
Bonnavoulin
MORVERN
Gleann Dubh
A884
B8043
Loch Uisge
Mull Little Theatre
Upper Druimfin
451 Beinn Bhuidhe
Beach
Penmore Mill
Dervaig
Achnadrish
Loch Arienas
The Old Byre Heritage Centre
Speinne Mor 444
550 Stithean na Raplaich
Acharn
739 Beinn Mheadhoin
Rhemore
Gleann Geal
AROS
Ardnacross
Killundine
Lettermore
Loch Frisa
NM
Claggan
Larachbeg
Kinlochaline Castle
Ardtornish Gardens
Achranich
Loch Teàrnait
SOUND OF MULL
B849
Achnacraig
Fiunary
Savary
437 Beinn a' Chaisil
Loch Aline
Loch nan Clach
Achleck
Cranmich
Aros Mains
Lochaline
Fanmore 390
Rubha Mor
Glais Bheinn 479
An Sleaghach 513
Eignaig
Ballygown
Salen
A848
Fishnish Bay
Ardtornish Castle
Ardtornish Pt.
Eas Fors Waterfall
424 Beinn na Drise
Pennygown
Lagganulva
Killiechronan
B8035
Killbeg
Corrynachenchy
A849
Inninmore Bay
Garbh Shlios
Camas Gorm
Laggan Bay
Oskamull
Kellan
B8073
Gruline
412
Garmony
Scallastle Bay
Rubha an Ridire
Bernera I.
Achinduin
Ulva
Ulva House
Killiemor
Knock
ISLAND OF MULL
Loch Bà
Java
Craignure Bay
Scallastle
Kilchera
Lismore
Loch na Keal
Sound of Ulva
Eorsa
591 Beinn a' Ghràig
Craignure
Mull and West Highland Narrow Gauge Railway
Inch Kenneth Chapel
Inch Kenneth
Isle of Mull
Derryguaig
Glen Cannel
766 Dun da Ghaoithe
Duart Bay
Duart Pt.
Torosay Castle & Gardens
Duart Castle
Eilean Musdile
Balnahard
761 Beinn Talaidh
Argyll and Bute
Mackinnon's Cave
966 Ben More
130
Lochdon
Oban 0:45
561
704 Corra-Bheinn
Glen More
Lussa
Loch Don
Grass Pt.
519 Beinn na Sreine
Glen Seilisdeir
Strathcoil
ARDMEANACH
Killiemore House
B8035
Coladoir
A849
Loch Airdeglais
248
Aird of Kinloch
Kilfinichen Bay
Ben Buie 717
698 Creach Beinn
Loch Spelve
Kerrera
Balliemore
The Burg
Loch Fuaron
Croggan
Rubha nan Sailthean
Bach I.
Ardmore
Loch Scridain
Pennycross
Kinlochspelve
Rubha Seanach
Torrans
Lochbuie
Barachandroman
503 Beinn na Croise
Loch Uisg
FIRTH OF LORN
Leidle
BROLASS
Loch Buie
Lee
Carsaig
405 Druim Fada
Laggan Deer Forest
376 Cruachan Min
376
Carsaig Bay
Rubha Dubh
Lord Lovat's Cave
Kilninver
B844
Clachan Bridge
Insh I.
Sound of Insh
Mull
Scoor
Carsaig Arches
Frank Lockwood's Island
Clachan-Seil
Seil
Clachan
An Cala Gardens
Malcolm's Pt.
Easdale
Easdale Island Folk Museum
Rubha nam Braithrean
Balvicar
267 Cruach

UAMH CAIRN
Loch Beoraid
Polnish
Lochailort
A830
Ranochan
796 SGURR AN UTHA
Glen Finnan
Glen Dubh Lighe
Gleann Suileag
Druim Fada
Loch Eilt
Inverailort
A861
STATION MUSEUM
GLENFINNAN MONUMENT
Wauchan
Ardnish
Laggan
Loch Ailort
145
Glenfinnan
146
Alisary
Callop
Kinlocheil
Fassfern
869 DRUIM FIACHLACH
Drumsallie
LOCH EIL
TREASURES OF THE EARTH
Roshven
882 ROIS-BHEINN
882 BEINN ODHAR BHEAG
South Garvan
Duisky
Blaich
Corpach
Achaphubuil
Camusnagaul
Trislaig
MOIDART
666 BEINN GAIRE
755 MEALL NAN CREAG LEAC
Glen Garvan
Kinlochmoidart
Ardmolich
Loch Moidart
Brunery
Gaskan
Scamodale
LOCH SHIEL
SGOR AN TARMACHAIN 756
Gorstanvorran
Glen Hurich
Cona Glen
770 STOB COIRE A'CHEARCAILL
Stronchreggan
Ach'an Todhair
Drumarbin
A82
A861
Dalnabreck
Dalelia
Polloch
786 BEINN MHEADHOIN
Conaglen House
Blarmachfoldach
Glenhurich
Loch Doilet
888 SGURR DHOMHNUILL
Scaddle
Aryhoulan
Coruanan Lodge
CLAISH MOSS
Kinlochan
Glen Scaddle
Inverscaddle Bay
Ardshealach
SUNART
Ardgour
SGURR NA H-EANCHAINNE 730
616 BEINN NA GUCAIG
Resipole
845 BEINN RESIPOL
ARIUNDLE CENTRE
ARIUNDLE OAKWOOD
Ariundle
Glen Gour
701
Glenrigh Forest
Scotstown
Strontian
Clovullin
Corran
Inchree
Corran Narrows
LOCH SUNART
Anaheilt
Sallachan
Keppanach
Onich
GLENCRIPESDALE
Ardnastang
Strontian
885 GARBH BHEINN
Sallachan Pt.
North Ballachulish
Camuschoirk
Glen Tarbert
LOCH LINNHE
Liddesdale
Inversanda Bay
Inversanda
HIGHLAND MYSTERYWORLD
South Ballachulish
Glencoe
516 MEALL AN DAMHAIN
NM
583 CREACH BHEINN
B8043
Kentallen
A828
Ballachulish
582 BEINN NAM BEATHRACH
765 FUAR BHEINN
Kilmalieu
Glenduror Forest
947
571 BEINN IADAIN
Lochuisge
Duror
Rubha Mor
Cuil Bay
Beinn a'Bheithir
Glen an Fhiodh
Loch Uisge
Eilean Balnagowan
Keil
Glen Duror
Gleann Dubh
Beach
Kingairloch
Camasnacroise
Salachan Glen
Loch Arienas
Loch a'Choire
879 FRAOCHAIDH
Acharn
739 BEINN MHEADHOIN
KINGAIRLOCH
Gleann Geal
Shuna I.
Appin House
655
Glen Creran
Elleric
Claggan
137
Glen Stockdale
Fasnacloich
Glen Ure
ARDTORNISH GARDENS
Achranich
Loch Tearnait
Rannoch
437 BEINN A' CHAISIL
Glensanda
Portnacroish
KINLOCHLAICH HOUSE GARDENS
An Iola
Invercreran
BEINN CHURALAIN 546
GLASDRUM WOOD
Glasdrum
937 BEINN SGULAIRD
Loch Aline
Loch nan Clach
Appin
Strath of Appin
Port Ramsay
Port Appin
Creagan
Druimavuic
GLAIS BHEINN 479
LYNN OF LORN
ARDTORNISH CASTLE
AN SLEAGHACH 513
Eignaig
Clachan
Eriska
North Shian
South Creagan
839 BEINN TRILLEACHAN
Loch Creran
South Shian
Lismore
B8045
SCOTTISH SEA LIFE SANCTUARY
Barcaldine
810 CREACH BHEINN
Abhainn Dalach
Allt Easach
Inninmore Bay
Garbh Shlios
Camas Gorm
Achnacroish
Barcaldine Forest
LORN
Baravullin
BENDERLOCH
Ferlochan
Scallastle Bay
Rubha an Ridire
Bernera I.
130
Achinduin
131
Kilcheran
Eilean Dubh
Kiel Crofts
Benderloch
Gleann Salach
B845
LOCH ETIVE
Java
Craignure Bay
Scallastle
Craignure
MULL AND WEST HIGHLAND NARROW GAUGE RAILWAY
Ledaig
Achnaba
715 BEINN MHEADHONACH
Ardmucknish Bay
0:50
ARDCHATTAN PRIORY GARDENS
ARDCHATTAN PRIORY
Duart Bay
Duart Pt.
DUART CASTLE
TOROSAY CASTLE & GARDEN
Eilean Musdile
0:45
Eilean Mor
DUNSTAFFNAGE CASTLE
North Connel
Connel
Black Crofts
FALLS OF LORA
Achnacloich
ACHNACLOICH GARDEN
Glen Liver
Bonawe
Glen Noe
Lochdon
CASTLEBAY 5:10
COLL 2:40
TIREE 3:40
LOCHBOISDALE 5:15
Dunbeg
Ganavan
A85
BONAWE IRON FURNACE
Brochroy
INVERAWE FISHERIES AND SMOKERIES EXHIBITION
A849
Loch Don
Grass Pt.
Dunollie
OBAN/OBAN LODGE
Black Lochs
Fearnoch Forest
BEN CRUACHAN 1126
OBAN VISITOR CENTRE
McCAIG'S TOWER
OBAN DISTILLERY
Taynuilt
Ichrachan
Bridge of Awe
Pass of Brander
Cruachan Res.
Altnacraig
OBAN RARE BREEDS FARM PARK
BARGUILLEAN GARDENS
Kerrera
COLONSAY 2:20
Oban
Glen Nant
GLEN NANT
Awe
Falls of Cruachan
Loch Spelve
Glenamachrie
383
Glen Lonan
0 1 2 3 4 5 6 miles
0 1 2 3 4 5 6 7 8 9 10 km
Gallanach
Loch Nell
CRUACHAN DAM VISITOR CENTRE
Barran
Loch Tromlee
Loch Nant

Gairlochy
Stronaba
Glen Loy
Kilmonivaig
COMMANDO MEMORIAL
Bohuntine
Bohenie
Moy Forest
1049 BEINN A' CHAORUINN
Moy
Moy Lodge
Glen Loy Forest
Brackletter
Highbridge
Spean Bridge
Inverroy
Roybridge
Achluachrach
Murlaggan
Roughburn
Strone
Muirshearlich
146
Killiechonate
A86
Spean
MONESSIE FALLS
Braes o'Lochaber
147
B8004
TOR CASTLE
A82
GLEN SPEAN
GEAL
Leanachan Forest
724 BEINN CHLIANAIG
Fersit
Allt Loraich
Allt Cam
Banavie
NEPTUNE'S STAIRCASE LOCKS
Torlundy
NEVIS RANGE SKI CENTRE
1087 BEINN A'CHLACHAIR
Lochyside
The Cour
Allt Làire
BEN NEVIS DISTILLERY VISITOR CENTRE
Claggan
Loch Ghuilbinn
Fort William
Achintee
WEST HIGHLAND MUSEUM
1177 STOB CHOIRE CLAURIGH
1106
Lairig Leacach
1115 STOB COIRE EASAIN
LOCH TREIG
1046 CHNO DEARG
1114 AONACH BEAG
GLEN NEVIS VISITOR CENTRE
GLEN NEVIS
Glen Nevis House
Water of Nevis
Allt na Lairige
Ossian
1344 BEN NEVIS
1234 AONACH BEAG
1094
1148 BEN ALDER
Uisge Labhair
937 BEINN NA LAP
Corrour Shooting Lodge
Creaguaineach Lodge
Prince Charlie's Cave
Amhainn Rath
LOCH OSSIAN
Loch Ossian
Corrour Forest
Achriabhach
Nevis
952 SGOR GAIBHRE
583
1099 SGURR A' MHAIM
1130 BINNEIN MOR
630
Loch Eilde Beag
140
MAMORE FOREST
Allt na Caim
Rannoch Forest
WEST HIGHLAND WAY
789
Loch Eilde Mor
Ciaran Water
906 LEUM UILLEIM
796 MAM NA GUALAINN
Kinlochmore
Kinlochleven
THE ALUMINIUM STORY
B863
BLACKWATER RESERVOIR
Black Water
Ericht
Leven
867
GLENCOE AND NORTH LORN FOLK MUSEUM
AONACH 967
953
GLENCOE
NN
Rannoch Station
B846
Glen Coe
Altnafeadh
857 BEINN A' CHRULAISTE
Black Corries Lodge
739 STOB NA CRUAICHE
Loch Eigheach
Gaur
Bridge of Gaur
BEN NEVIS AND GLEN COE
1150 BIDEAN NAM BIAN
925
Coupall
Kingshouse Hotel
Loch Gaineamhach
Loch Laidon
Royal Forest
Etive
GLENCOE SKI CENTRE
A82
RANNOCH MOOR
Allt Camghouran
994 SGOR NA H-ULAIDH
Dalness
MUSEUM OF SCOTTISH SKIING AND MOUNTAINEERING
1188
547
Glen Etive
Alltchaorunn
Loch Bà
883 STOB DUBH
1099 CLACH LEATHAD
Allt Coire a'Chaolain
Loch na h-Achlaise
Bà
931 MEALL BUIDHE
Invercharnan
Glenceitlein
BLACK MOUNT
Water of Tulla
Loch an Daimh
879
Eas Daimh
Gualachulain
Allt Dochard
1090 STOB GHABHAR
WEST HIGHLAND WAY
Loch Tulla
907 MEALL BUIDHE
1081 BEINN A' CHREACHAIN
960 STUCHD AN LOCHAIN
1044 STOB COIR'AN ALBANNAICH
Achallader
Black Mount
Forest Lodge
1078 BEN STARAV
Loch Dochard
Pubil
Cashlie
Inveroran Hotel
Loch Lyon
Stronuich Reservoir
957 BEINN NAN AIGHENAN
Allt Hallater
1004 BIENN AN DOTHAIDH
953 BEINN MHANACH
Bridge of Orchy
Allt Chonoghlais
BEINN HEASGARNICH 1076
639
1076 BEINN DÒRAIN
Orchy
701
Kenknock
Glen Lochay
Kinglass
1047 CREAG MHOR
A82
Breadalbane
796 BEINN MHIC-MHONAIDH
GLEN ORCHY
Arichastlich
Glen Strae
Strae
901 BEINN ODHAR
989 BEINN EUNAICH
840 BEINN UDLAIDH
937 BEINN CHEATHAICH
B8074
1025 BEN CHALLUM
Auchlyne West Burn
Allt Mhoille
Glen Lochy
A85
Lochy
Clifton
Tyndrum
Allt Riobain
Arrivain
131
132
Auchlyne
B8077
Stronmilchan
Achnafalnich
880
Cononish
KILCHURN CASTLE
Strath of Orchy
Inverlochy
Strath Fillan
Lochdochart House
GLEN DOCHART
A85
Dalmally
BEN LUI
A82
Inverherive
Loch Dochart
Loch Iubhair
MCINTYRE MONUMENT
1130
Crianlarich
Benmore

139
Moy Lodge
674
BEINN EILDE
911
Lochan na h-Earba
Ardverikie Forest
147
1049
GEAL CHARN
Pattack
Loch Ericht Forest
A9
941
CARN NA CAIM
Gaick
Forest
Loch Bhrodainn
Allt Gharbh Ghaig
148
Loch an Duin
774
CREAGAN MOR
Loch Pattack
Ben Alder Lodge
Cama Choire
Sronphadruig Lodge
Dail-na-Mine Forest
816
SRON A'CHLEIR
1087
BEINN A'CHLACHAIR
Allt Cam
917
936
A'BHUIDHEANACH BHEAG
Allt a'Chaoil-reidhe
Ben Alder Forest
LOCH ERICHT
B
Loch Ghuilbinn
934
BEINN UDLAMAIN
803
THE SOW OF ATHOLL
Dalnacardoch Forest
Edendon Water
Allt Glas Choire
Allt a' Mhuilinn
FOREST
1114
AONACH BEAG
Loch a' Bhealaich Bheithe
Dalnaspidal Lodge
ATHOLL
Allt a' Chireachain
Ossian
Corrievarkie Lodge
Allt na Glaise
Dalnaspidal Forest
Loch Garry
775
MEALL NA LEITREACH
Dalnacardoch Lodge
1148
BEN ALDER
Uisge Labhair
GLEN GARRY
Garry
Corrour Shooting Lodge
Loch Ossian
Prince Charlie's Cave
855
Talla Bheith Forest
Loch Con
Corrour Forest
952
SGOR GAIBHRE
GRAMPIAN
Loch Errochty
C
Rannoch Forest
Allt Ghlas
841
BEINN MHOLACH
NN
612
Dalchalloch
Trinafour
B847
Errochty Water
GLEN ERROCHTY
515
SRON BHEAG
Aulich Burn
891
BEINN A'CHUALLAICH
Tummel Forest
477
Erich
Killichonan Burn
Craiganor Lodge
Kinloch Rannoch
Tummel Bridge
B8019
Rannoch Station
B846
Bridge of Ericht
Killichonan
LOCH RANNOCH
Dunalastair
Dunalastair Water
Tummel
Foss
Loch Eigheach
Gaur
Bridge of Gaur
Finnart
Carie
Inverhadden
Camghouran
Black Wood of Rannoch
Loch Kinardochy
D
Rannoch Forest
Dall Burn
Allt na Bogair
Innerhadden Burn
TAY FOREST
1083
SCHIEHALLION
Allt Mor
Allt Camghouran
LOCH RANNOCH AND GLEN LYON
GLENGOULANDIE DEER PARK
Keltney Burn
1042
CARN MAIRG
745
MEALL A'MHUIC
931
MEALL BUIDHE
1029
CARN GORM
Keltneyburn
Appin of Dull
Camusvrachan
Invervar
ST FILLAN'S CHURCH & FORTINGALL YEW
Loch an Daimh
GLEN LYON GALLERY
Innerwick
Lyon
Fortingall
Taymouth Castle
Eas Daimh
Bridge of Balgie
Allt Conait
Gallin
Kenmore
E
907
MEALL BUIDHE
960
STUCHD AN LOCHAIN
Allt Bail a' Mhuilinn
Allt Gleann Da-Eig
Fearnan
SCOTTISH CRANNOG CENTRE
Remony
Acharn
Falls of Acharn
780
1118
Lawers Burn
LOCH TAY
Glen Lyon
Pubil
Cashlie
Loch Lyon
Stronuich Reservoir
1214
BEN LAWERS
BEN LAWERS
Loch na Lairige
716
BEINN BHREAC
MEALL NAN TARMACHAN
1043
Lawers
Ardtalnaig
BEINN HEASGARNICH
1076
BEN LAWERS VISITOR CENTRE (N.T.S.)
Carie
A827
Gleann a' Chilleine
Kenknock
Glen Lochay
888
1047
CREAG MHOR
Breadalbane
Lochay
Milton Morenish
Morenish
Ardeonaig
F
FALLS OF LOCHAY AND FISH LIFT
Boreland
MOIRLANICH LONGHOUSE
Finlarig
Finglen Burn
Killin
BREADALBANE FOLKLORE CENTRE
Achmore
637
937
BEINN CHEATHAICH
FALLS OF DOCHART
879
CREAG UCHDAG
1025
BEN CHALLUM
Allt Riobain
Auchlyne West Burn
Dochart
A827
Loch Lednock Reservoir
Invergeldie Burn
931
BEN CHONZIE
132
Auchlyne
A85
133
Ardchyle
Beich Burn
Glen Ogle
Glen Lednock
Invergeldie
Innertullich
672
SRON MHOR
Ledcharrie
Benmore
1 2 3 4 5 6 miles
1 2 3 4 5 6 7 8 9 10 km

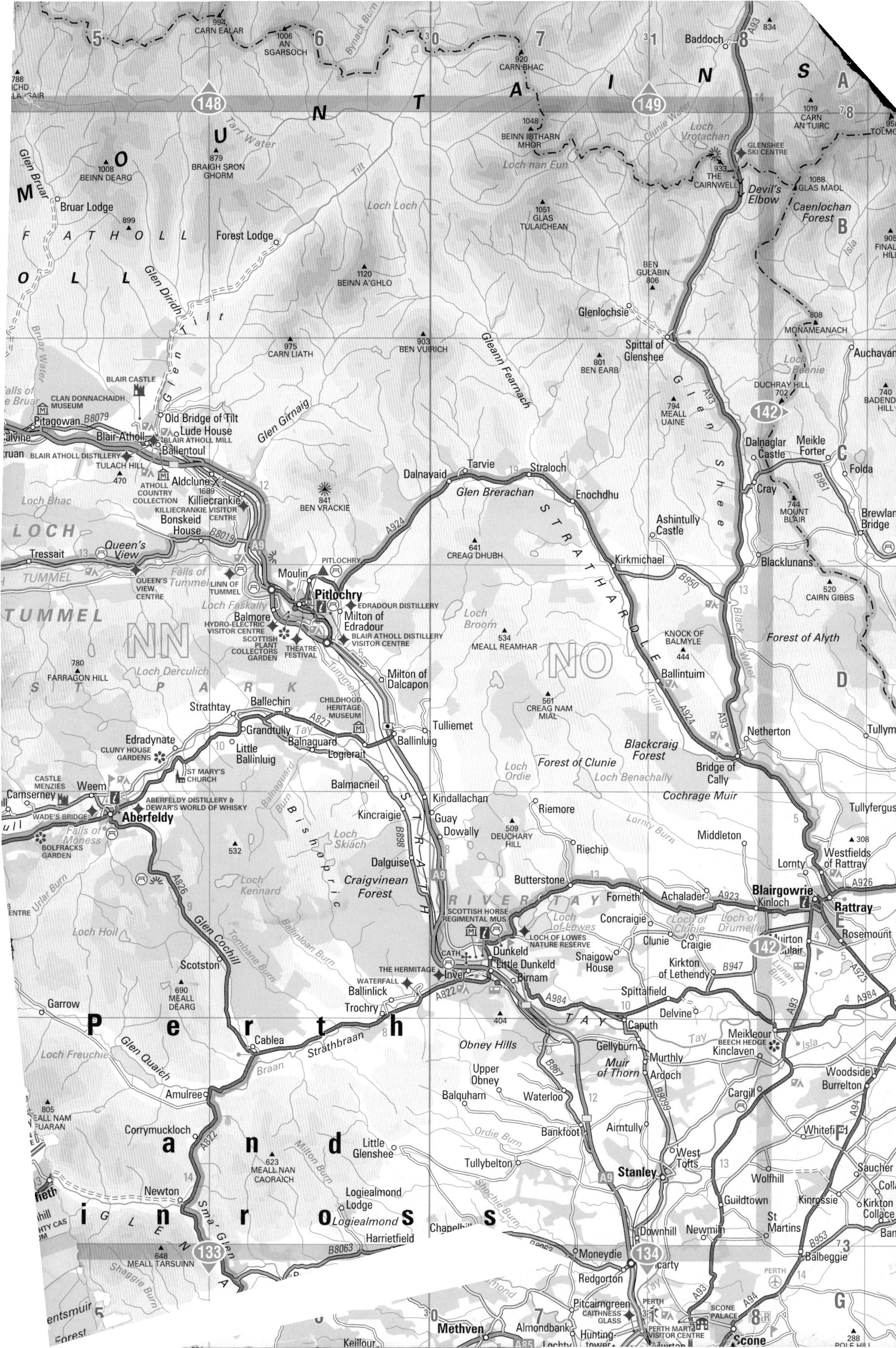
CARN EALAR
AN SGARSOCH
Bynack Burn
CARN BHAC
Baddoch
A93
GLENSHEE SKI CENTRE
THE CAIRNWELL
Devil's Elbow
Caenlochan Forest
GLAS MAOL
CARN AN TUIRC
TOLMOUNT
BEINN IUTHARN MHOR
Loch nan Eun
Loch Vrotachan
Clunie Water
Tarf Water
BRAIGH SRON GHORM
BEINN DEARG
Glen Bruar
Bruar Lodge
Forest Lodge
Loch Loch
GLAS TULAICHEAN
BEINN A'GHLO
BEN GULABIN
FINALTY HILL
Isla
Glen Diridh
Tilt
Glen Tilt
Glenlochsie
Spittal of Glenshee
MONAMEANACH
Auchavan
Loch Beanie
DUCHRAY HILL
BADENDUN HILL
CARN LIATH
BEN VUIRICH
Gleann Fearnach
BEN EARB
MEALL UAINE
Glen Shee
Bruar Water
Falls of Bruar
BLAIR CASTLE
CLAN DONNACHAIDH MUSEUM
Pitagowan
B8079
Old Bridge of Tilt
Lude House
BLAIR ATHOLL MILL
Blair Atholl
Ballentoul
BLAIR ATHOLL DISTILLERY
TULACH HILL
ATHOLL COUNTRY COLLECTION
Aldclune
Killiecrankie
KILLIECRANKIE VISITOR CENTRE
Glen Girnaig
BEN VRACKIE
Dalnavaid
Tarvie
Straloch
Glen Brerachan
Enochdhu
Dalnaglar Castle
Meikle Forter
Folda
Cray
B951
MOUNT BLAIR
Brewlands Bridge
Loch Bhac
LOCH
Bonskeid House
B8019
A9
Tressait
Queen's View
TUMMEL
QUEEN'S VIEW CENTRE
Falls of Tummel
LINN OF TUMMEL
Moulin
PITLOCHRY
Pitlochry
A924
CREAG DHUBH
Ashintully Castle
Kirkmichael
B950
Blacklunans
CAIRN GIBBS
Loch Faskally
EDRADOUR DISTILLERY
Milton of Edradour
BLAIR ATHOLL DISTILLERY VISITOR CENTRE
Balmore
HYDRO-ELECTRIC VISITOR CENTRE
SCOTTISH PLANT COLLECTORS GARDEN
THEATRE FESTIVAL
Loch Broom
MEALL REAMHAR
STRATHARDLE
KNOCK OF BALMYLE
Black Water
Forest of Alyth
NN
NO
FARRAGON HILL
Loch Derculich
TUMMEL
Milton of Dalcapon
Ballintuim
Ardle
CREAG NAM MIAL
Strathtay
Ballechin
CHILDHOOD HERITAGE MUSEUM
Grandtully
A827
Tay
Tulliemet
Ballinluig
Edradynate
CLUNY HOUSE GARDENS
Little Ballinluig
Balnaguard
Logierait
Blackcraig Forest
Netherton
Tullymurdoch
CASTLE MENZIES
Weem
Camserney
ST MARY'S CHURCH
Balmacneil
Loch Ordie
Forest of Clunie
Loch Benachally
Bridge of Cally
ABERFELDY DISTILLERY & DEWAR'S WORLD OF WHISKY
WADE'S BRIDGE
Aberfeldy
Falls of Moness
BOLFRACKS GARDEN
Balnaguard Burn
Bishopric
Kincraigie
Kindallachan
Guay
Dowally
Riemore
DEUCHARY HILL
Cochrage Muir
Tullyfergus
Loch Skiach
B898
Riechip
Lornty Burn
Middleton
Westfields of Rattray
Lornty
Urlar Burn
A826
Loch Kennard
Dalguise
Craigvinean Forest
Butterstone
Forneth
Achalader
A923
Blairgowrie
Kinloch
Rattray
A926
Loch Hoil
Glen Cochill
Tombane Burn
Ballinloan Burn
RIVER TAY
SCOTTISH HORSE REGIMENTAL MUS.
Loch of Lowes
LOCH OF LOWES NATURE RESERVE
Concraigie
Loch of Clunie
Loch of Drumellie
Rosemount
Clunie
Craigie
Muirton of Ballochblair
CATH
Dunkeld
Little Dunkeld
Snaigow House
Kirkton of Lethendy
B947
Lunan Burn
Scotston
THE HERMITAGE
Inver
Birnam
WATERFALL
Ballinlick
MEALL DEARG
A822
A984
Spittalfield
Garrow
Trochry
TAY
Caputh
Delvine
Perth
Cablea
Strathbraan
Obney Hills
Gellyburn
Meikleour
BEECH HEDGE
Kinclaven
Isla
Loch Freuchie
Glen Quaich
Braan
Upper Obney
B867
Muir of Thorn
Murthly
Ardoch
Woodside
Burrelton
Amulree
Balquharn
Waterloo
B9099
Cargill
A94
MEALL NAM FUARAN
Corrymuckloch
and
Ordie Burn
Bankfoot
Airntully
Whitefield
Milton Burn
Little Glenshee
MEALL NAN CAORAICH
Tullybelton
West Tofts
Saucher
Collace
Stanley
Wolfhill
Newton
Sma' Glen
Shochie Burn
Logiealmond Lodge
Guildtown
Kinrossie
Kirkton of Collace
GLEN
Logiealmond
St Martins
Ross
Chapelhill
Downhill
Newmill
Harrietfield
B953
Balbeggie
B8063
MEALL TARSUINN
Moneydie
Redgorton
PERTH
Shaggie Burn
Luncarty
Pitcairngreen
CAITHNESS GLASS
SCONE PALACE
Methven
Almondbank
PERTH MART VISITOR CENTRE
Scone
Huntingtower
A85
Keillour
Lochty
Forest
Bandirran
POLE HILL
Fossoway
Scone Palace
Ballechin
ATHOLL
FOREST OF ATHOLL
MOUNTAINS
148
149
142
133
134

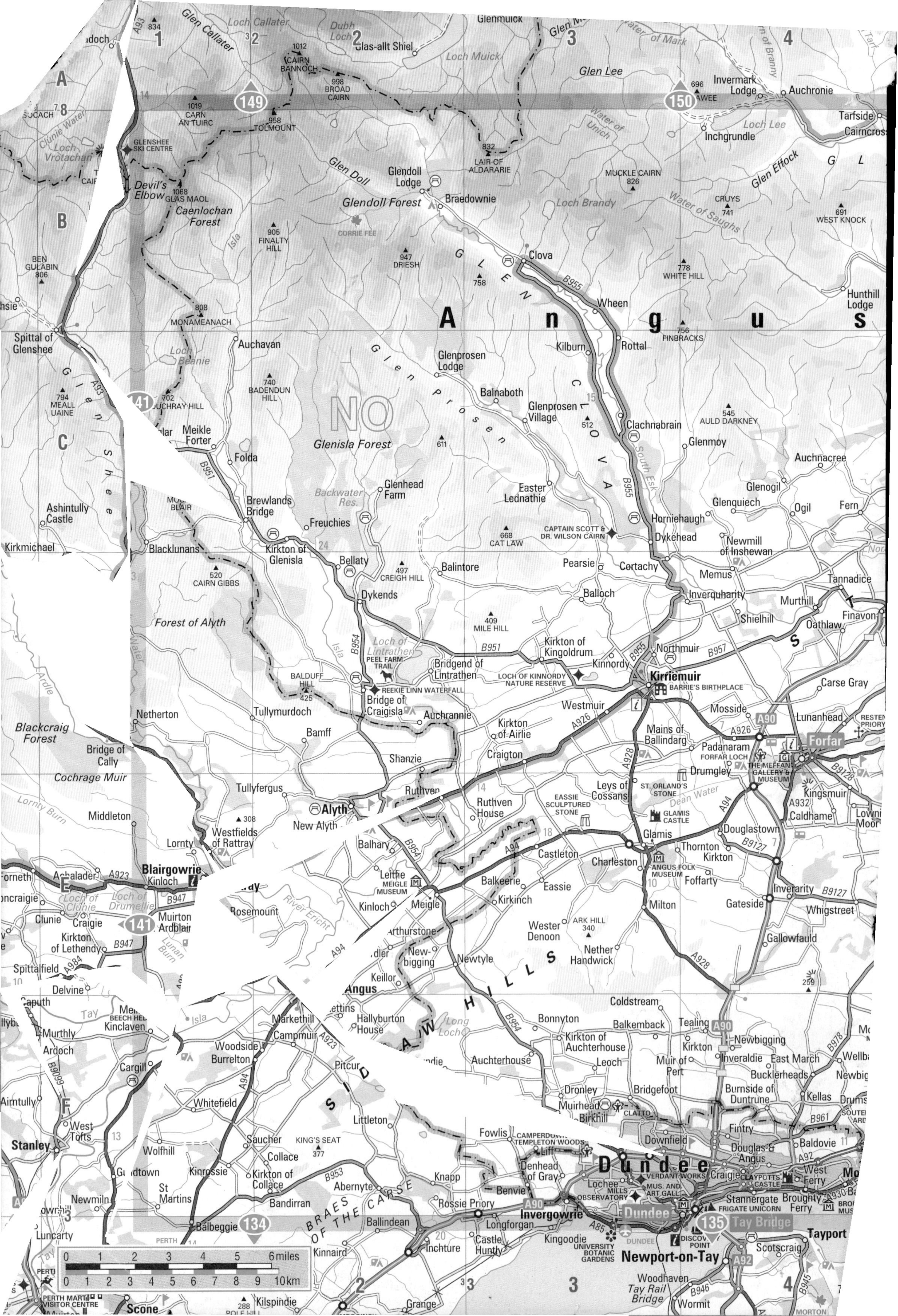

Glen Callater
Loch Callater
Dubh Loch
Glas-allt Shiel
Glenmuick
Loch Muick
Water of Mark
Glen Lee
Invermark Lodge
Auchronie
Tarfside
Cairncross
Loch Lee
Inchgrundle
CAIRN BANNOCH
BROAD CAIRN
CARN AN TUIRC
TOLMOUNT
GLENSHEE SKI CENTRE
Loch Vrotachan
Cluanie Water
Devil's Elbow
GLAS MAOL
Caenlochan Forest
LAIR OF ALDARARIE
Water of Unich
MUCKLE CAIRN
Glen Effock
Glen Doll
Glendoll Lodge
Glendoll Forest
Braedownie
CORRIE FEE
Loch Brandy
Water of Saughs
CRUYS
WEST KNOCK
FINALTY HILL
DRIESH
Clova
GLEN CLOVA
B955
Wheen
WHITE HILL
Hunthill Lodge
BEN GULABIN
Spittal of Glenshee
MONAMEANACH
Auchavan
Loch Beanie
Glen Shee
Angus
FINBRACKS
Kilburn
Rottal
Glenprosen Lodge
Glen Prosen
Balnaboth
Glenprosen Village
Clachnabrain
AULD DARKNEY
Glenmoy
MEALL UAINE
BADENDUN HILL
DUCHRAY HILL
Meikle Forter
Folda
NO
Glenisla Forest
Auchnacree
Glenogil
Backwater Res.
Glenhead Farm
Easter Lednathie
South Esk
Glenquiech
Ogil
Fern
Ashintully Castle
Brewlands Bridge
Freuchies
CAPTAIN SCOTT & DR. WILSON CAIRN
Horniehaugh
Dykehead
Newmill of Inshewan
Kirkmichael
Blacklunans
Kirkton of Glenisla
CAT LAW
Pearsie
Cortachy
Bellaty
CREIGH HILL
Balintore
Memus
Tannadice
CAIRN GIBBS
Dykends
Balloch
Inverquharity
Murthill
Forest of Alyth
MILE HILL
Shielhill
Finavon
Oathlaw
Loch of Lintrathen
PEEL FARM TRAIL
Kirkton of Kingoldrum
Northmuir
B957
Bridgend of Lintrathen
Kinnordy
Kirriemuir
BARRIE'S BIRTHPLACE
BALDUFF HILL
REEKIE LINN WATERFALL
LOCH OF KINNORDY NATURE RESERVE
Carse Gray
Bridge of Craigisla
Westmuir
Mosside
Lunanhead
Netherton
Tullymurdoch
Auchrannie
Kirkton of Airlie
A926
Mains of Ballindarg
Padanaram
FORFAR LOCH
Forfar
Ardle
Blackcraig Forest
Bamff
Craigton
A928
Drumgley
THE MEFFAN GALLERY & MUSEUM
Bridge of Cally
Shanzie
B9128
Cochrage Muir
Tullyfergus
Ruthven
Leys of Cossans
ST. ORLAND'S STONE
Dean Water
Kingsmuir
Lornty Burn
Middleton
Alyth
Ruthven House
EASSIE SCULPTURED STONE
GLAMIS CASTLE
A932
Caldhame
New Alyth
Westfields of Rattray
Balhary
Glamis
Douglastown
Lornty
Castleton
Thornton
Kirkton
Blairgowrie
Kinloch
Achalader
A923
Leitfie
MEIGLE MUSEUM
Balkeerie
Charleston
ANGUS FOLK MUSEUM
Foffarty
Loch of Clunie
Loch of Drumellie
B947
Rosemount
River Ericht
Eassie
Kinloch
Meigle
Kirkinch
Milton
Inverarity
B9127
Clunie
Craigie
Muirton
Ardblair
Gateside
Whigstreet
Arthurstone
Wester Denoon
ARK HILL
Kirkton of Lethendy
Lunan Burn
Nether Handwick
Gallowfauld
New-bigging
Newtyle
SIDLAW HILLS
Spittalfield
A984
Keillor
Delvine
Caputh
Tay
Meikleour
BEECH HEDGE
Kinclaven
Isla
Coldstream
Bettins
Markethill
Hallyburton House
Long Loch
Bonnyton
Balkemback
Tealing
A90
Murthly
Ardoch
Woodside
Burrelton
Campmuir
Kirkton of Auchterhouse
Newbigging
B978
Leoch
Auchterhouse
Inveraldie
East March
Muir of Pert
Bucklerheads
Wellbank
Cargill
Pitcur
B9099
Aimtully
Bridgefoot
Burnside of Duntrune
Kellas
Whitefield
Dronley
Muirhead
Birkhill
CLATTO
Littleton
West Tofts
Stanley
Fowlis
CAMPERDOWN
TEMPLETON WOODS
Liff
Downfield
Fintry
Baldovie
Wolfhill
Saucher
KING'S SEAT
Collace
Douglas & Angus
A92
Guildtown
Kinrossie
Kirkton of Collace
B953
Abernyte
Knapp
Denhead of Gray
Dundee
VERDANT WORKS
Craigie
CLAYPOTTS CASTLE
West Ferry
Lochee
MILLS OBSERVATORY
MUS. AND ART GALL.
St Martins
Newmiln
Bandirran
Benvie
Rossie Priory
Stannergate
FRIGATE UNICORN
Broughty Ferry
BRAES OF THE CARSE
A90
Invergowrie
Balbeggie
Luncarty
Ballindean
Longforgan
Dundee
Tay Bridge
Tayport
A85
PERTH
Kingoodie
UNIVERSITY BOTANIC GARDENS
DISCOVERY POINT
Inchture
Castle Huntly
Scotscraig
Kinnaird
Newport-on-Tay
A92
0 1 2 3 4 5 6 miles
0 1 2 3 4 5 6 7 8 9 10 km
PERTH MART VISITOR CENTRE
Kilspindie
Woodhaven
Tay Rail Bridge
B946
B945
Wormit
Scone
Grange
MORTON

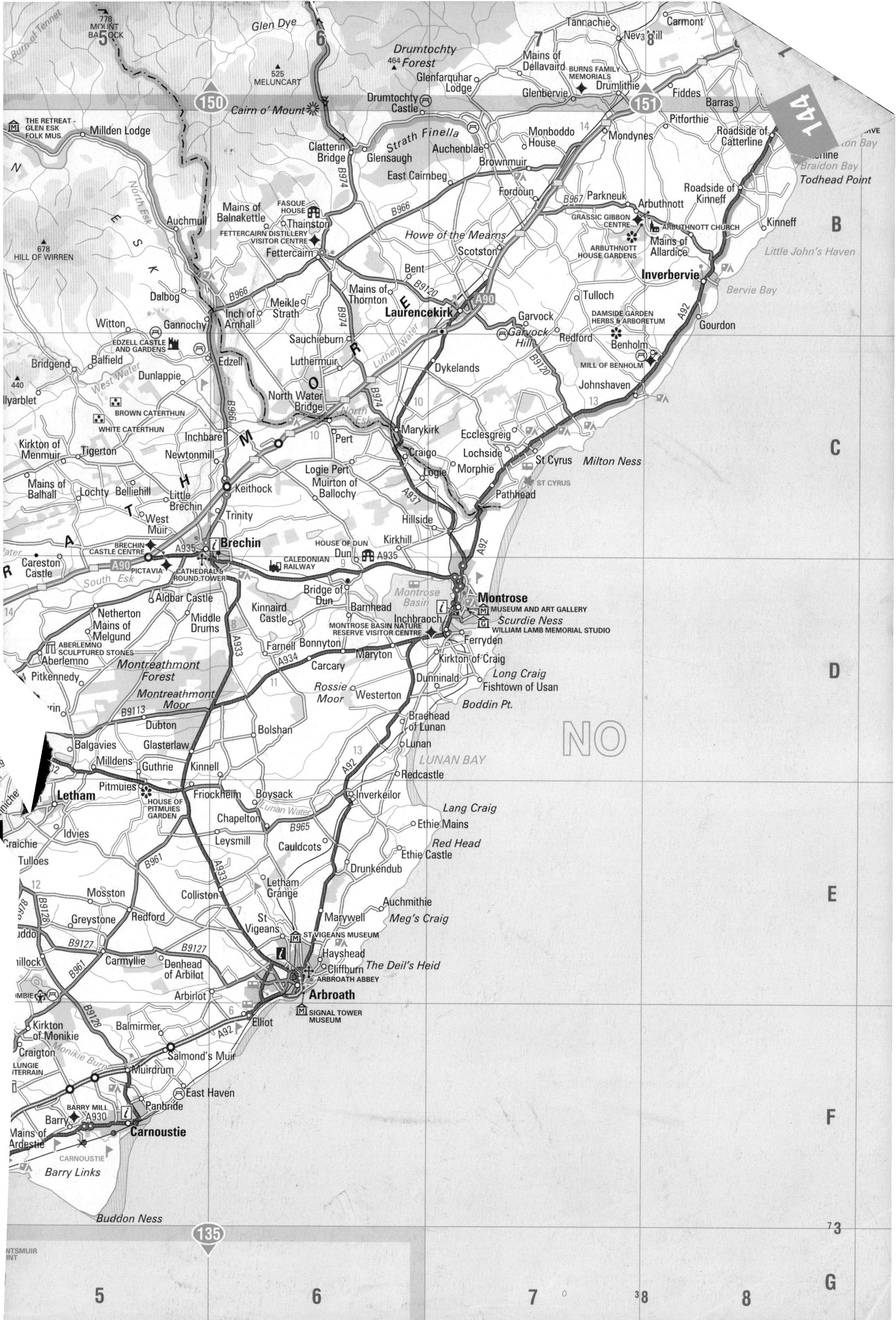

Glen Dye
778 MOUNT BATTOCK
Burn of Tennet
Drumtochty Forest
464
525 MELUNCART
Tannachie
Carmont
Nevay Hill
Mains of Dellavaird
BURNS FAMILY MEMORIALS
Drumlithie
Glenfarquhar Lodge
Glenbervie
Fiddes
Barras
Drumtochty Castle
150
151
144
Cairn o' Mount
THE RETREAT - GLEN ESK FOLK MUS.
Millden Lodge
Clatterin Bridge
Glensaugh
Strath Finella
Auchenblae
Monboddo House
Mondynes
Pitforthie
Roadside of Catterline
Braidon Bay
Todhead Point
East Cairnbeg
Brownmuir
Fordoun
Parkneuk
Arbuthnott
Roadside of Kinneff
Kinneff
North Esk
Auchmull
Mains of Balnakettle
FASQUE HOUSE
Thainston
FETTERCAIRN DISTILLERY VISITOR CENTRE
Fettercairn
B966
B974
B967
Howe of the Mearns
Scotston
GRASSIC GIBBON CENTRE
ARBUTHNOTT CHURCH
ARBUTHNOTT HOUSE GARDENS
Mains of Allardice
Little John's Haven
678 HILL OF WIRREN
Bent
B9120
Inverbervie
Bervie Bay
Dalbog
Mains of Thornton
Meikle Strath
Inch of Arnhall
Laurencekirk
A90
Tulloch
DAMSIDE GARDEN HERBS & ARBORETUM
Gourdon
A92
Witton
Gannochy
EDZELL CASTLE AND GARDENS
Edzell
Saucbieburn
Luthermuir
Luther Water
Garvock
Garvock Hill
Redford
Benholm
MILL OF BENHOLM
Bridgend
Balfield
West Water
Dunlappie
440
Dykelands
Johnshaven
Ballyarblet
BROWN CATERTHUN
WHITE CATERTHUN
North Water Bridge
Marykirk
Ecclesgreig
Kirkton of Menmuir
Tigerton
Inchbare
Newtonmill
Pert
Craigo
Lochside
Morphie
St Cyrus
Milton Ness
ST CYRUS
Logie
Logie Pert
Muirton of Ballochy
Mains of Balhall
Lochty
Belliehill
Little Brechin
Keithock
Pathhead
Trinity
West Muir
A937
Hillside
BRECHIN CASTLE CENTRE
A935
Brechin
HOUSE OF DUN
Kirkhill
Dun
CALEDONIAN RAILWAY
Careston Castle
PICTAVIA
CATHEDRAL & ROUND TOWER
South Esk
Montrose Basin
Montrose
MUSEUM AND ART GALLERY
Scurdie Ness
WILLIAM LAMB MEMORIAL STUDIO
Aldbar Castle
Bridge of Dun
Netherton
Mains of Melgund
Middle Drums
Kinnaird Castle
Barnhead
Inchbraoch
MONTROSE BASIN NATURE RESERVE VISITOR CENTRE
Ferryden
ABERLEMNO SCULPTURED STONES
Aberlemno
A933
Farnell
Bonnyton
Maryton
Kirkton of Craig
Montreathmont Forest
A934
Carcary
Long Craig
Fishtown of Usan
Pitkennedy
Dunninald
Rossie Moor
Westerton
Boddin Pt.
Montreathmont Moor
B9113
Dubton
Braehead of Lunan
NO
Balgavies
Glasterlaw
Bolshan
Lunan
Milldens
Guthrie
Kinnell
LUNAN BAY
Redcastle
Pitmuies
Letham
HOUSE OF PITMUIES GARDEN
Friockheim
Boysack
Inverkeilor
Lunan Water
Lang Craig
Chapelton
Ethie Mains
B965
Idvies
Leysmill
Cauldcots
Red Head
Ethie Castle
Tulloes
B961
Drunkendub
Mosston
Colliston
Letham Grange
Auchmithie
Greystone
Redford
B9128
Marywell
Meg's Craig
St Vigeans
ST VIGEANS MUSEUM
B9127
Hayshead
Carmyllie
Denhead of Arbilot
Cliffburn
The Deil's Heid
ARBROATH ABBEY
Arbroath
Arbirlot
SIGNAL TOWER MUSEUM
Elliot
Kirkton of Monikie
Balmirmer
A92
Craigton
Monikie Burn
Salmond's Muir
Muirdrum
East Haven
Panbride
BARRY MILL
A930
Barry
Mains of Ardestie
Carnoustie
CARNOUSTIE
Barry Links
Buddon Ness
135
B
C
D
E
F
G
5
6
7
8

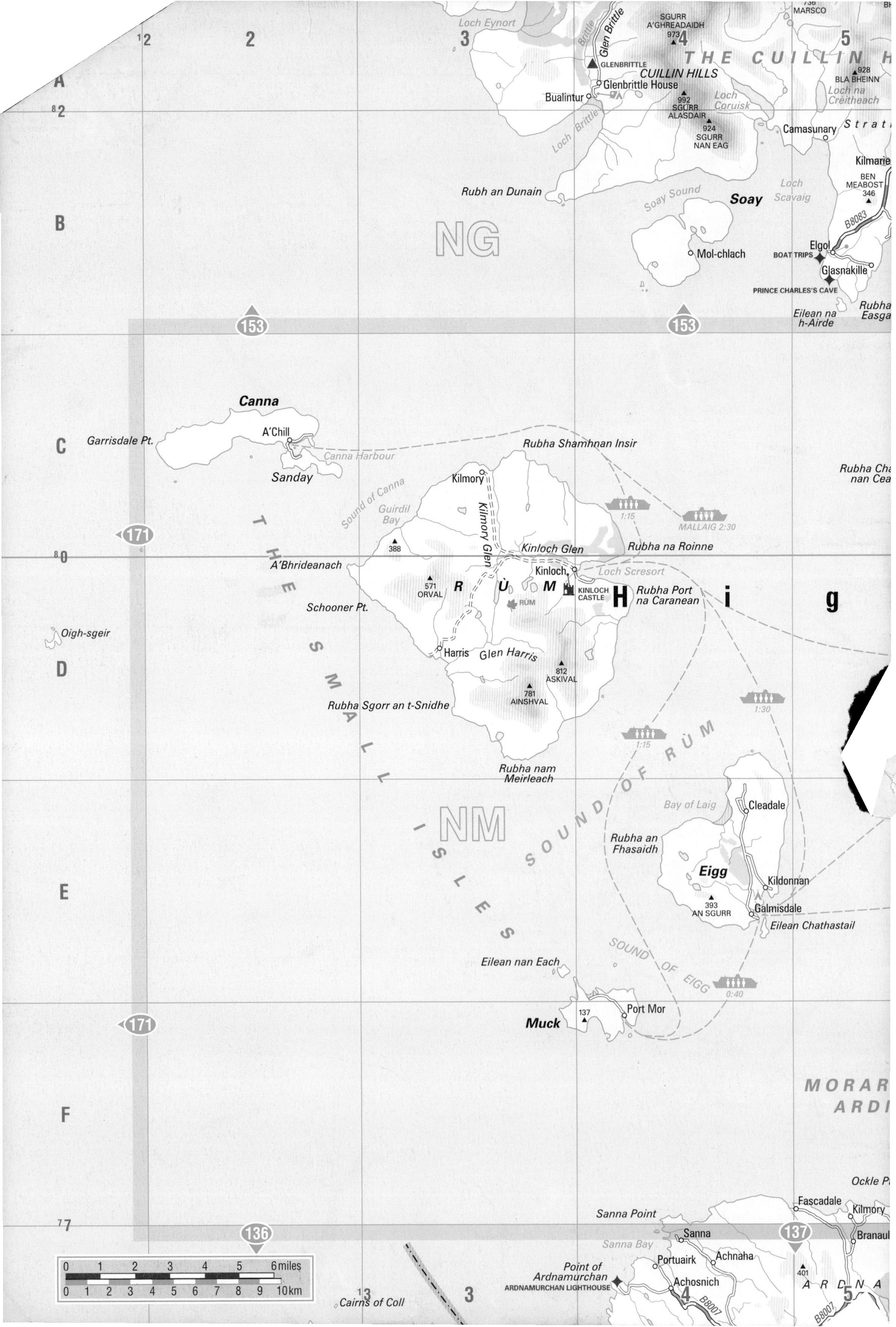
Loch Eynort
Glen Brittle
Brittle
SGURR A'GHREADAIDH
973
MARSCO
THE CUILLIN H
GLENBRITTLE
CUILLIN HILLS
928
BLA BHEINN
Glenbrittle House
Bualintur
992
SGURR ALASDAIR
Loch Coruisk
Loch na Creitheach
924
SGURR NAN EAG
Loch Brittle
Camasunary
Strat
Kilmarie
BEN MEABOST
346
Rubh an Dunain
Soay Sound
Soay
Loch Scavaig
B8083
NG
Mol-chlach
Elgol
BOAT TRIPS
Glasnakille
PRINCE CHARLES'S CAVE
Eilean na h-Airde
Rubha Easga
153
153
Canna
A'Chill
Garrisdale Pt.
Canna Harbour
Sanday
Rubha Shamhnan Insir
Rubha Cha nan Cea
Kilmory
Sound of Canna
Guirdil Bay
Kilmory Glen
1:15
MALLAIG 2:30
171
388
Kinloch Glen
Rubha na Roinne
A'Bhrideanach
Kinloch
Loch Scresort
571
ORVAL
R Ù M
KINLOCH CASTLE
Rubha Port na Caranean
H i g
Schooner Pt.
RÙM
Oigh-sgeir
THE SMALL ISLES
Harris
Glen Harris
812
ASKIVAL
781
AINSHVAL
Rubha Sgorr an t-Snidhe
1:30
1:15
SOUND OF RÙM
Rubha nam Meirleach
Bay of Laig
Cleadale
NM
Rubha an Fhasaidh
Eigg
Kildonnan
393
AN SGURR
Galmisdale
Eilean Chathastail
SOUND OF EIGG
Eilean nan Each
0:40
137
Port Mor
Muck
171
MORAR
ARDI
Ockle P
Fascadale
Kilmory
Sanna Point
Sanna
Sanna Bay
136
137
Branaul
Portuairk
Achnaha
401
Point of Ardnamurchan
ARDNAMURCHAN LIGHTHOUSE
Achosnich
ARDNA
B8007
B8007
Cairns of Coll
0 1 2 3 4 5 6 miles
0 1 2 3 4 5 6 7 8 9 10 km

RED HILLS
Corry
Broadford
Waterloo
Lower Breakish
Upper Breakish
Harrapool
SKYE ENVIRONMENTAL CENTRE
WORLD OF WOOD
Skulamus
Torrin
Kilbride
Strath Suardal
Heast
Kinloch
Drumfearn
Loch Eishort
Rubha Suisnish
Ord
DUNSGIATH CASTLE
Tokavaig
Tarskavaig
Tarskavaig Pt.
Achnacloich
Camuscross
Isleornsay
Ornsay
Duisdalemore
Teangue
KNOCK CASTLE
Knock Bay
Ferindonald
Kilbeg
Kilmore
Armadale Castle
ARMADALE GARDENS
CLAN DONALD CENTRE
ARMADALE
Armadale Bay
Glen Meadhonach
Calligarry
Ardvasar
Aird of Sleat
Ard Thurinish
SLEAT
SOUND OF SLEAT
Rubha Raonuill
Mallaig
MALLAIG HERITAGE CENTRE
MALLAIG MARINE WORLD
Glasnacardoch
Beoraidbeg
Morar
Bunacaimb
Portnaluchaig
Eilean Ighe
Back of Keppoch
Kinloid
Arisaig
Luinga Bheag
Luinga Mhor
Loch nan Ceall
Druimindarroch
SOUND OF ARISAIG
Loch nan Uamh
Polnish
LOCH NAN UAMH CAIRN
Ardnish
Laggan
Eilean nan Gobhar
Loch Ailort
Samalaman I.
Glenuig Bay
Smirisary
Glenuig
Roshven
Alisary
MOIDART AND ARDNAMURCHAN
Eilean Shona
Invermoidart
Kinlochmoidart
Farquhar's Pt.
CASTLE TIORAM
Ardmolich
Brunery
Ardtoe
Newton of Ardtoe
Shielfoot
Ockle
Kentra
Kentra Bay
Blain
Moss
Dalnabreck
Dalelia
CLAISH MOSS
Acharacle
Ardshealach
BEINN BHREAC
SGURR NA COINNICH
KYLERHEA OTTER HAVEN
Kylerhea
Glen Arroch
BEN ASLAK
Bernera
Galltair
Glenelg
BERNERA BARRACKS
Glenelg Bay
Eilanreach
GLENELG BROCHS
Balvraid
Glen More
Upper Sandaig
Sandaig Is.
BEINN A'CHAPAILL
BEINN SGRITHEALL
BEINN NAN CAORACH
Arnisdale
Glen Arnisdale
Corran
LOCH HOURN
Rubha Ard Slisneach
Inverguseran
Airor
Sandaig
Sandaig Bay
Scottas
Inverie
Inverie Bay
KNOYDART
BEINN NA CAILLICH
LADHAR BHEINN
Gleann na Guiserein
Gleann an Dubh-Lochain
LUINNE BHEINN
MEALL BUIDHE
BEINN BHUIDHE
LOCH NEVIS
Camusrory
Stoul
Kylesknoydart
Kylesmorar
Bracara
Bracorina
Brinacory
Tarbet
Swordland
North Morar
Kinlochmorar
LOCH MORAR
Scamadale
Lettermorar
South Morar
Meoble
SIDHEAN MOR
MEITH BHEINN
Oban
AN STAC
Kinlochbeoraid
Loch Beoraid
SGURR AN UTHA
Lochailort
Inveraillort
Loch Eilt
Ranochan
STATION MUSEUM
Glenfinnan
GLENFINNAN MONUMENT
DRUIM FIACLACH
ROIS-BHEINN
BEINN ODHAR BHEAG
BEINN GAIRE
MOIDART
Gaskan
Scamodale
SGOR AN TARMACHAIN
Gorstanvorran
LOCH SHIEL
MEALL NAN CREAG LEAC
Glen Hurich
Polloch
Glenhurich
Loch Doilet
Kinlochan
BEINN MHEADHOIN
SGURR DHOMHNUILL
SUNART
Keppoch
Letterfearn
Inverinate
Ruarach
Loch Duich
BEINN A'CHUIRN
Ratagan
Aultachruinn
Invershiel
Shiel Bridge
Glenshiel Forest
THE SADDLE
Kinlochhourn Forest
DRUIM FADA
BUIDHE BHEINN
Barrisdale Bay
Glen Barrisdale
Abhainn Chosaidh
SGURR NA CICHE
Glen Dessarry
Glen Pean
CARN MOR
SGURR NAN COIREACHAN
SGURR THUILM
Glen Finnan
Glen Dubh Lighe
Drumsallie
Glen Garvan
Cona Glen
Glen Scaddle
Highland
NG
NM
155
146
138
137
A87
A851
A830
A861
B8083
B8008
B8044

Killilan Forest
899 AONACH BUIDHE
1086 AN RIABHACHAN
1150 SGURR NA LAPAICH
1069
Glencannich
Mullardoch House
East Benula Forest
Gleann Udalain
Sallachy
Allt-nan-sùgh
SGUMAN COINNTICH 879
155
156
Loch Mullardoch
Glen Cannich
Loch Long
Camas-luinie
Carnach
Allt na Doire Gairbhe
Auchertyre
Bundalloch
Glen Elchaig
Loch nan Eun
Loch na Leitreach
Elchaig
Gleann Sithidh
West Benula Forest
Gleann A'Choilich
1005
1053 TOLL CREAGACH
1111 TOM A CHOINICH
1183 CARN EIGE
Gleann nam Fiadh
A87
Nostie
Ardelve
Dornie
EILEAN DONAN CASTLE
634
FALLS OF GLOMACH
Glas Eilean
Totaig
Keppoch
Letterfearn
SGURR NAN CEATHREAMHNAN 1151
GLEN AFFRIC
Affric Lodge
Glen Affric
SGURR AN AIRGID 841
Inverinate
Dorusduain
Loch a'Bhealaich
Loch Affric
539
Loch Duich
Ruarach
Morvich
Carn-gorm
Ault a'chruinn
Glenaffric
Guisach
603 BEINN A'CHUIRN
Ratagan
RATAGAN
Inverhiel
Shiel Bridge
BEINN FADA OR BEN ATTOW 1032
GLEN AFFRIC
Forest
Glen Gniomhaidh
GLEN AFFRIC
Allt Garbh
Allt Riabhach
KINTAIL
Kintail Forest
GLENELG BROCHS
Balvraid
145
Glen More
779
888 AONACH SHASUINN
706 CARN A CHAOCHAIN
1067 FIVE SISTERS
979 CISTE DHUBH
NG
NH
C
Shiel
1027
1719
Glenshiel Forest
1120 A'CHRALAIG
1109 SGURR NAN CONBHAIREAN
Ceannacroc Forest
Doe
BEINN NAN CAORACH 774
974 BEINN SGRITHEALL
1010 THE SADDLE
31
Cluanie Inn
Ceannacroc Lodge
GLEN SHIEL
918
SGURR AN LOCHAIN 1004
Cluanie Lodge
Lundie
Arnisdale
Glen Arnisdale
Kinlochhourn Forest
Cluanie Forest
LOCH CLUANIE
A887
Bun Loyne
Corran
LOCH HOURN
879 BUIDHE BHEINN
906 SGURR THIONAIL
Glen Quoich
1021 AONACH AIR CHRITH
Bunloinn Forest
713 DRUIM FADA
Kinloch Hourn
Beinneun Forest
Barrisdale Bay
1027 SGURR A'MHAORAICH
Highland
Loyne
LOCH LOYNE
1035 GLEOURAICH
D
KNOYDART
894
Glen Barrisdale
Glenquoich Forest
540
A87
Abhainn Chosaidh
LOCH QUOICH
Kingie
Aultnaslat
Inchlaggan
Ardochy House
LUINNE BHEINN 939
Garry
Tomdoun
Glen Garry
Greenfield
919 GAIRICH
Glen Kingie
Kingie
946 MEALL BUIDHE
1003 SGURR MOR
Allt Choire a' Bhalachain
556 GLAS BHEINN
901 BEN TEE
Carnach
1040 SGURR NA CICHE
Camusrory
E
656 MEALL BLAIR
Glengarry Forest
Loch Blàir
858
880 SGURR MHURLAGAIN
804 GEAL CHARN
935 SRON A'CHOIRE GHAIRBH
859
Glen Dessarry
Dessarry
Murlaggan
Strathan
LOCH ARKAIG
Kinlochmorar
829 CARN MOR
Glen Pean
Pean
Ardechvie
Oban
Achnasaul
Clunes Forest
Altrua
718 AN STAC
Gleann Camgharaidh
727
Locheil Forest
Inver Mallie
B8005
Clunes
965 SGURR NAN COIREACHAN
963 SGURR THUILM
987 GAOR BHEINN
Glen Mallie
Mallie
Achnacarry
Bunarkaig
A82
NM
NN
796 BEINN BHAN
CLAN CAMERON MUSEUM
Gairlochy
Stronaba
Kinlochbeoraid
F
Glen Finnan
Glen Dubh Lighe
Gleann Suileag
Glen Loy
Loy
GREAT GLEN WAY
Kilmonivaig
COMMANDO MEMORIAL
796 SGURR AN UTHA
Druim Fada
Brackletter
Spean Bridge
STATION MUSEUM
GLENFINNAN MONUMENT
Wauchan
Glen Loy Forest
Strone
Highbridge
Muirshearlich
Lochy
Killiechonate
Glenfinnan
138
139
Kinlocheil
Fassfern
A830
TOR CASTLE
B8004
A82
LOCH EIL
TREASURES OF THE EARTH
Corpach
Banavie
Leanachan Forest
NEPTUNE'S STAIRCASE LOCKS
Torlundy
NEVIS RANGE SKI CENTRE
882 BEINN AR BHEA
South Garvan
Duisky
A861
Blaich
Caol
Lochyside
INVERLOCHY CASTLE
Achaphubuil
0 1 2 3 4 5 6 miles
0 1 2 3 4 5 6 7 8 9 10 km

Muchrachd
Balmore
Glass
428
MEALL NAN
CAORACH
Balchraggan
Dores
Cannich
A831
457
CARN NAM BAD
465
MEALL NA
H-EILRIG
A833
A82
Cannich
CANNICH
Glen
Balbeg
Urquhart
LOCH NESS
MONSTER
EXHIBITIONS
Loch
Duntelchaig
Fasnakyle Forest
CAIRN
Corrimony
156
Buntait
Braefield
12
Balnain
Milton
Drumnadrochit
157
Achnabat
446
STAC NA
CATHAIG
DOG FALLS
Shenval
Loch
Meiklie
Enrick
DRUM FARM
Urquhart
Bay
464
Affric
Fasnakyle Ho
Lewiston
Strone
Tullich
Nairn
Glenurquhart Forest
URQUHART CASTLE
B852
B862
Tomich
Divach
Upper
Lenie
Lower Lenie
Torness
Loch Ruthven
East
Croachy
Abhainn Deabhag
Enrick
578
COBB MEMORIAL
Balcladaich
Balmacaan Forest
Coiltie
Bunloit
13
1:20
(May-Dec)
Aberarder
House
B857
Beinn
Meadhoin
Farigaig
Balbeg
PLODDA
FALLS
Loch nam
Breac
Dearga
Inverfarigaig
25
MEALL A'
CHRATHAICH
679
Loch ma
Stac
Easter
Boleskine
FARIGAIG
FOREST
CENTRE
Aultnagoire
Errogie
Loch nan
Eun
Loch a'
Chràthaich
Creagnaneun Forest
A82
Foyers
Farigaig Forest
Dunmaglass
Lodge
771
Forest
Lyne of
Gorthleck
Loch na
Beinne Bàine
Allt Bhlàraidh
Levishie Forest
LOCH NESS
Alltsigh
B852
B862
Wester Aberchalder
Achnaconeran
Lochgarthside
Allt Uisg an t-Sidhein
680
Levishie
Loch Mhor
Dundreggan
Forest
Bailebeag
802
CARN ODHAR
Aberchalder Burn
148
Allt na Muic
A887
Moriston
FALLS OF
MORISTON
Invermoriston
Portclair Forest
Whitebridge
Dundreggan Lodge
15
Dundreggan
Loch
Knockie
588
River E
C
607
BURACH
Portclair
Knockie
Lodge
811
CARN NA
SAOBHAIDHE
Coignafearn Forest
Dalchreichart
6
Inverwick Forest
Feehlin
Tomchrasky
GREAT
GLEN WAY
Glenbrein
Lodge
Garrogie Lodge
MONADHLIATH
555
B862
Eskin
Allt Phocaichain
Inchnacardoch
Hotel
A82
Loch
Tarff
809
CARN NA LARAICHE
MAOILE
CLANSMAN
CENTRE
Fort Augustus
Glendoe
Lodge
Loch Killin
Glen Brein
Killin Lodge
MOUNTAINS
Inchnacardoch
Forest
Glendoebeg
Glen Markie
826
CARN COIRE NA
CREICHE
Auchteraw
828
BURRACH
MOR
NH
Allt Doe
Allt Breinag
Killin
Abhainn Crò Chlach
FORT AUGUSTUS
ABBEY AND
VISITOR CENTRE
Allt Lundie
Oich
Caledonian Canal
Allt Cam Ban
779
CARN EASGANN
BANA
l
a
n
d
D
Bridge
of Oich
Newtown
CARN
A'CHUILINN
816
Glendoe
Forest
Allt Odhar
Munerigie
Tarff
Glen
942
CARN BAN
Invergarry
Loch Oich
Calder Burn
Tarff
MEALL NA
H-AISRE
862
Mandally
A82
80
Culachy Forest
Allt Choire Lain Oig
Fèith Talagain
Glen Markie
925
GEAL
CHARN
Allt Madagain
WELLS OF THE
SEVEN HEADS
LOCH
LOCHY
LAGGAN LOCKS
896
GAIRBEINN
Corrieyairack
Forest
884
CARN LEAC
832
MARG NA
CRAIGE
Laggan
815
CARN DEARG
Melgarve
Kilfinnan
Spey
Garvamore
Balgowan
E
A86
Drummin
Crathie
Laggan
Cluny
Castle
Loch Crunachdan
148
Gaskmore
Catlodge
Glenshero
Lodge
Strath Mashie
15
NN
Turret
Strathmashie
House
636
Brae Roy
Lodge
622
Letterfinlay
CARN LIATH
1006
Aberarder
Lodge
Cromra
571
Glen Gloy
Roy
Loch
Caoldair
PARALLEL ROADS
Burn of Agie
Aberarder Forest
Kinloch
Laggan
A86
A889
Upper
Glenfintaig
834
CARN DEARG
LAGGAN
9
684
Roy
Aberarder
Mashie
GLEN ROY
1128
CREAG
MEAGAIDH
CREAG
MEAGAIDH
Glen
915
674
BEINN EILDE
Allt Glas Dhoire
Dalwhinnie
LOCH
F
1049
BEINN A'
CHAORUINN
Moy Forest
DALWHINNIE DISTILLERY
911
Lochan na h-Earba
Ardverikie Forest
Pattack
Bohuntine
28
Moy
Moy
Lodge
Bohenie
Loch Ericht Forest
A9
Inverroy
Roybridge
Achluachrach
Murlaggan
Roughburn
A86
1049
GEAL CHARN
774
CREAGAN
MOR
Spean
MONESSIE
FALLS
Braes o'Lochaber
139
Loch Pattack
140
Ben
Alder
Lodge
ERICHT
78
GLEN
SPEAN
Allt Loraich
724
BEINN CHLIANAIG
Fersit
Allt Cam
1087
BEINN A'CHLACHAIR
Allt a'Chaoil-reidhe
Ben Alder Forest
917
G
936
5
6
7
8
26
9
Allt Laire
LOCH
A
B
Ballindaloch

Dores
Loch Ashie
Dunlichity Lodge
STRATHNAIRN
Tombreck
Farr
Farr House
Moy
Strathdearn Forest
A9
Ruthven
465
ALL NA EILRIG
Loch Duntelchaig
616
CARN NA H-EASGAINN
Upper Inverbrough
Balvraid
635
CARN AN T-SEAN-LIATHANAICH
Tomlachlan Burn
157
158
Achnabat
446
STAC NA CATHAIG
464
B852
B862
Tullich
Nairn
Brinmore
TOMATIN DISTILLERY
Tomatin
627
CARN A' CHOIRE MHOIR
659
CARN GLAS-CHOIRE
B9007
Findhorn Bridge
Torness
Loch Ruthven
East Croachy
601
BEINN BHREAC
Aberarder House
B851
Farigaig
Glen Kyllachy
STRATHDEARN
Kyllachy House
Clune
CLAN GRANT & CHURCH
Dulnain Burn
A938
Slochd
Corrievorrie
714
CARN NA SAOBHAIDH
Duthil
Aultnagoire
Errogie
B862
Dalmigavie Lodge
Ellan
Carrbridge
Lochanhully
LANDMARK HERITAGE & ADVENTURE PARK
Dunmaglass Lodge
771
Glen Mazeran
Sluggan
Lyne of Gorthleck
Highland
B9153
Drumuillie
Wester Aberchalder
Allt Uisg an t-Sidhein
807
BEINN BHREAC MHOR
750
Dalnahaitnach
Chapelton
Boat of Garten
Loch Mhor
Dalmigavie
Dulnain
Kinveachy
Findhorn
802
CARN ODHAR
Eil
Allt Lorgy
Avielochan
Aberchalder Burn
147
NH
STRATHSPEY RAILWAY
Auchgourish
677
CARN SLEAMHUINN
River E.
Coignafearn Lodge
CARN COIRE NA H-EASGAINN
790
745
CNOC FRAING
Granish
Pityoulish
B970
811
CARN NA SAOBHAIDHE
Coignafearn Forest
AVIEMORE
Dalfaber
CRAIGELLACHIE
Aviemore
THE AVIEMORE SKI CENTRE
MONADHLIATH MOUNTAINS
824
GEAL CHARN MOR
CAIRNGORM WHISKY CENTRE
Coylumbridge
Eskin
CALPA MOR
814
Inverdruie
Druie
809
CARN NA LARAICHE MAOILE
Loch Alvie
Polchar
ROTHIEMURCHUS VISITOR CENTRE
Glen Markie
826
CARN COIRE NA CREICHE
Elrick Burn
Abhainn Cro Chlach
812
CARN SGULAIN
A9
Alvie
LOCH AN EILEIN VISITOR CENTRE
B970
B9152
Rothiemurchus
828
BURRACH MOR
878
CARN AN FHREICEADAIN
541
AN SUIDHE
Loch an Eilein
Allt Cam Ban
Kincraig
Insh Forest
Inshriach Forest
Raitts Burn
Invereshie House
Feshiebridge
742
CARN EILR
Allt Mor
HIGHLAND WILDLIFE PARK
Loch Insh
930
A'CHAILLEACH
942
CARN BAN
HIGHLAND FOLK MUSEUM
Balavil
Farr
Spey
Insh
Lynchat
B970
SGORAN DUBH MOR
1111
CLAN MCPHERSON MUS.
Pitmain
Kingussie
INSH MARSHES
Inveruglass
Newtonmore
WALTZING WATERS
Drumguish
Tolvah
THE
925
GEAL CHARN
Glen Markie
Calder
Allt Madagain
Glen Banchor
HIGHLAND FOLK MUSEUM AULTLARIE
Ruthven
RUTHVEN BARRACKS
B9150
Achlean
Loch Einich
Feith Talagain
832
MARG NA CRAIGE
Glentromie Lodge
Allt Chomhraig
1052
CARN BAN MOR
Glen Tromie
CH
Feshie
Glen Feshie
Balgowan
A86
Glentruim House
A9
Allt Mor
Crathie
Laggan
Cluny Castle
Truim
Glenfeshie Lodge
Eidart
Drumgask
Catlodge
Glenshero Lodge
Strath Mashie
147
Strathmashie House
Etteridge
592
GARBH-MHEALL MOR
1019
MULLACH CLACH A'BHLAIR
Glenfeshie Forest
622
Crubenmore Lodge
768
MEALLACH MHOR
857
CARN DEARG MOR
Cromra
A86
571
Loch Caoldair
A889
Allt Bhran
Mashie
BADENOCH
951
Loch Cuaich
Allt Cuaich
NN
Loch an t-Seilich
912
Feshie
674
BEINN EILDE
Dalwhinnie
DALWHINNIE DISTILLERY
Gaick Lodge
994
CARN EALAR
1006
AN SGARSOCH
911
Gaick Forest
Loch Bhrodainn
Allt Gharbh Ghaig
Pattack
Loch Ericht Forest
LOCH ERICHT
A9
941
CARN NA CAIM
788
UCHD A'CHLARSAIR
GRAMPIAN
774
CREAGAN MOR
Loch an Duin
Tarf Water
Ben Alder Lodge
140
141
Cama Choire
Sronphadruig Lodge
879
BRAIGH SRON GHORM
0 1 2 3 4 5 6 miles
0 1 2 3 4 5 6 7 8 9 10 km
Allt Glas Choire
Dail-na-Mine Forest
Glen Bruar
1008
BEINN DEARG
816
SRON A'CHLEIRICH
BHEAG
Bruar Lodge

484
CARN-RUIGH CHARRACH
5
6
7
8
Upper Derraid
Auchnagallin
Lettoch
Dalchirach
B9008
A939
Glaschoil
Dellefure
Mains of Dalvey
Camerory
158
B9102
14
A95
Drumin
GLENLIVET DISTILLERY
Glenlivet
Glenbeg
471
BEINN MHOR
Grantown-on-Spey
Cromdale
Auchroisk
1690
Haughs of Cromdale
HILLS OF CROMDALE
710
Ballcorach
B9136
Strath Avon
Tomnavoulin
Glen Fiddich
Glenfiddich Forest
Blackwater
MAUSOLEUM
Craggan
Anagach
Congash
Dulnain Bridge
Speybridge
REVACK ESTATE
569
CARN DAIMH
Skye of Curr
Spey
Lynemore
722
CREGGAN A'CHAISE
HEATHER HERITAGE CENTRE
Glenlivet Forest
742
150
B9009
732
CARN AN SUIDHE
B970
Burn of Lochy
Bridge of Brown
Livet
A95
Nethy Bridge
Dirdhu
Fodderletter
Cullachie
B970
Birchfield
Dell Lodge
A939
East Croftmore
Lettoch
GLENLIVET ESTATE
TOMINTOUL MUSEUM
Tomintoul
TOMINTOUL
588
ABERNETHY FOREST NATURE RESERVE
568
BADDOCH
Chapeltown
Loch Garten
804
CARN MOR
Lodge
658
Abernethy Forest
Delnabo
Dorback Lodge
588
CARN MEADHONACH
Conglass Water
150
Aundorach
Forest Lodge
LADDER
ABERNETHY FOREST
Dorback Burn
Braes of Abernethy
Blairnamarrow
CAIRNGORMS
688
Water of Ailnack
11
718
THE SOCACH
Glen More Forest Park
NJ
LECHT SKI CENTRE
A939
Bellabeg
MEALL A'BHUACHAILLE
810
821
GEAL CHARN
Glen Ernan
Ernan Water
The Queen's Forest
792
CARN EALASAID
Invererrnan Ho.
A944
Candacraig Ho.
CAIRNGORM LODGE
CAIRNGORM REINDEER CENTRE
Water of Caiplich
Avon
711
673
Glenmore Lodge
Nethy
Burn of Loin
Allt Tuileach
Don
GLENMORE VISITOR CENTRE
742
742
BIG GARVOUN
Delnadamph
Cock Bridge
Colnabaichin
Corgarff
Tornahaish
Loch Morlich
CORGARFF CASTLE
NATIONAL
GLEN AVON
1090
BYNACK MORE
CAIRNGORM CHAIRLIFT, FUNICULAR RLY & SKI CENTRE
749
CAIRNGORM
715
THE BRUACH
Forest of Glenavon
A939
D
1245
CAIRN GORM
1245
Loch Builg
823
BROWN COW HILL
744
Lairig Ghru
Loch Avon
1107
10
Glen Fenzie
MOUNTAINS
1082
BEINN A' CHAORRUINN
1171
BEN AVON
Gairnshiel Lodge
12
Gairn
Loch Etchachan
Lary
BEN MACDUI
1309
S
CAIRNGORM MOUNTAINS
1089
CARN EAS
900
CULARDOCH
B976
743
GEALLAIG HILL
Glen Gairn
A939
Bridge of Gairn
Coilacriech
Culsh
1155
DERRY CAIRNGORM
931
BEINN BHREAC
Bush Crathie
CRATHIE CHURCH
Dee
Littlemill
MCEWAN GALLERY
PARK
MOUNTAINS
Glen Dee
Derry Burn
A93
Crathie
E
CARN NA DROCHAIDE
818
BALMORAL CASTLE AND GARDENS
B976
Inver
Invergelder
150
Easter Balmoral
ROYAL LOCHNAGAR DISTILLERY VISITOR CENTRE
Birkhall
BRAEMAR
BRAEMAR CASTLE
Lui Water
Glen Lui
Invercauld House
Girnock Burn
Mill of Sterin
BRAEMAR HIGHLAND HERITAGE CENTRE
Allanaquoich
Braemar
Glen Gelder
601
157
BHROTAIN
Mar Lodge
KINDROCHIT CASTLE
BRAEMAR
Aucholzie
Forest of Mar
Claybokie
INVEREY
Tomintoul
Ballochbuie Forest
LINN OF MUICK WATERFALL
LINN OF DEE
Muir
Inverey
DEESIDE AND
Dee
Auchallater
Muick
Glen Muick
BALMORAL FOREST
Geldie Burn
LOCHNAGAR
818
CARN LIATH
Glen Ey
Ey Burn
NO
Callater Burn
850
CONACHCRAIG
1150
LOCHNAGAR
Dubh Loch
Glas-allt Shiel
674
Allt Connie
998
BROAD CAIRN
Bynack Burn
Glen Callater
Loch Callater
Glen Doll
Baddoch
A93
834
Dubh Loch
Glendoll Forest
920
CARN BHAC
1012
CAIRN BANNOCH
998
BROAD CAIRN
14
939
AN SOCACH
1019
CARN AN TUIRC
1048
BEINN IUTHARN MHOR
141
Clunie Water
958
TOLMOUNT
142
Loch Vrotachan
GLENSHEE SKI CENTRE
Glen Doll
Braedownie
Loch nan Eun
Tilt
933
THE CAIRNWELL
1068
GLAS MAOL
Devil's Elbow
Glendoll Forest
Loch Loch
1051

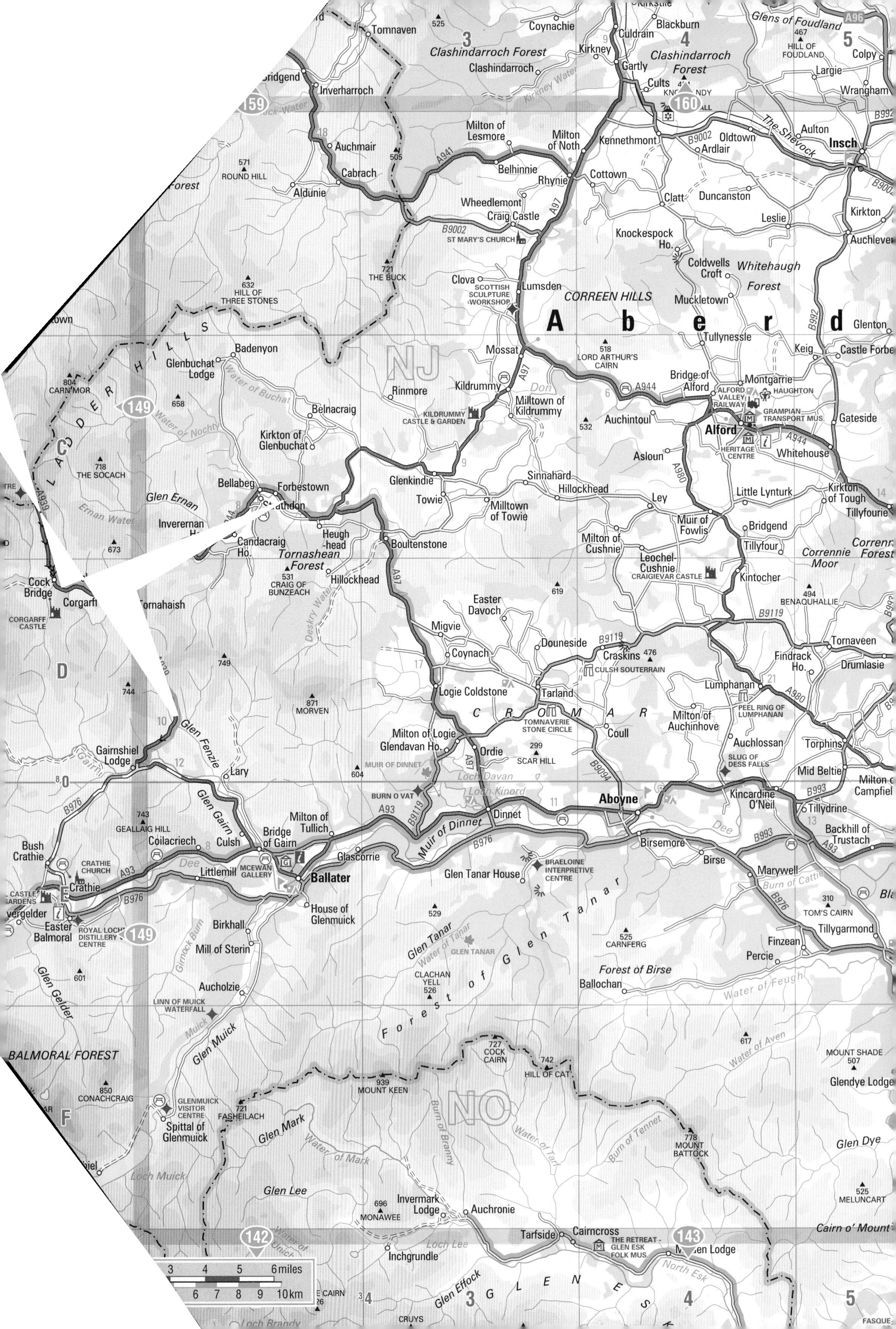

Tomnaven
525
Coynachie
Culdrain
Blackburn
Glens of Foudland
A96
3
4
5
Clashindarroch Forest
Kirkney
Gartly
Clashindarroch Forest
467
HILL OF FOUDLAND
Colpy
Bridgend
Clashindarroch
Largie
Inverharroch
Cults
Wrangham
159
160
Milton of Lesmore
Milton of Noth
Kennethmont
B9002
Oldtown
Aulton
The Shevock
Insch
Auchmair
505
Ardlair
571
ROUND HILL
A941
Belhinnie
Cabrach
Rhynie
Cottown
Forest
Aldunie
Clatt
Duncanston
Wheedlemont
Kirkton
Craig Castle
A97
Leslie
B9002
ST MARY'S CHURCH
Knockespock Ho.
Auchleven
721
THE BUCK
Coldwells Croft
Whitehaugh Forest
Clova
SCOTTISH SCULPTURE WORKSHOP
Lumsden
632
HILL OF THREE STONES
CORREEN HILLS
Muckletown
B992
A b e r d
Glenton
Tullynessle
Badenyon
518
LORD ARTHUR'S CAIRN
Mossat
Keig
Castle Forbe
Glenbuchat Lodge
NJ
804
CARN MOR
658
149
Rinmore
Kildrummy
Bridge of Alford
Montgarrie
A944
ALFORD VALLEY RAILWAY
HAUGHTON
Belnacraig
KILDRUMMY CASTLE & GARDEN
Milltown of Kildrummy
GRAMPIAN TRANSPORT MUS.
Gateside
Water of Buchat
Water of Nochty
Auchintoul
532
Alford
Kirkton of Glenbuchat
718
THE SOCACH
HERITAGE CENTRE
Whitehouse
A944
Asloun
A980
Bellabeg
Forbestown
Glenkindie
Sinnahard
Hillockhead
Little Lynturk
Kirkton of Tough
Glen Ernan
Strathdon
Towie
Milltown of Towie
Ley
Tillyfourie
Ernan Water
Inverernan
Muir of Fowlis
Bridgend
A939
Candacraig Ho.
Heugh-head
Boultenstone
Milton of Cushnie
Tillyfour
673
Tornashean Forest
Correnie Forest
Correnie Moor
Cock Bridge
531
CRAIG OF BUNZEACH
Hillockhead
Leochel-Cushnie
CRAIGIEVAR CASTLE
Kintocher
Corgarff
Tornahaish
619
494
BENAQUHALLIE
CORGARFF CASTLE
Deskry Water
Easter Davoch
B9119
Migvie
Douneside
B9119
Tornaveen
749
Coynach
Craskins
476
CULSH SOUTERRAIN
Findrack Ho.
Drumlasie
D
744
17
Logie Coldstone
Tarland
Lumphanan
21
A980
871
MORVEN
C R O M A R
TOMNAVERIE STONE CIRCLE
Milton of Auchinhove
PEEL RING OF LUMPHANAN
Glen Fenzie
Milton of Logie
Glendavan Ho.
Coull
Auchlossan
Torphins
Gairnshiel Lodge
Ordie
299
SCAR HILL
604
MUIR OF DINNET
SLUG OF DESS FALLS
Mid Beltie
Milton of Campfield
Lary
Loch Davan
B9094
B976
Glen Gairn
BURN O VAT
Loch Kinord
Aboyne
Kincardine O'Neil
B993
Tillydrine
743
GEALLAIG HILL
Milton of Tullich
A93
B9119
Dinnet
Backhill of Trustach
Bush
Crathie
Coilacriech
Culsh
Bridge of Gairn
Muir of Dinnet
B976
Birsemore
Birse
B993
A93
CRATHIE CHURCH
Littlemill
MCEWAN GALLERY
Glascorrie
BRAELOINE INTERPRETIVE CENTRE
Marywell
Dee
Burn of Cattie
Ballater
Glen Tanar House
Crathie
CASTLE GARDENS
B976
House of Glenmuick
529
310
TOM'S CAIRN
Invergelder
Easter Balmoral
ROYAL LOCHNAGAR DISTILLERY CENTRE
149
Birkhall
Glen Tanar
Water of Tanar
GLEN TANAR
525
CARNFERG
Tillygarmond
Finzean
Mill of Sterin
Girnock Burn
Percie
Glen Gelder
601
CLACHAN YELL
526
Forest of Birse
Aucholzie
Ballochan
Water of Feugh
LINN OF MUICK WATERFALL
Forest of Glen Tanar
Muick
Glen Muick
727
COCK CAIRN
617
Water of Aven
MOUNT SHADE
507
BALMORAL FOREST
742
HILL OF CAT
939
MOUNT KEEN
Glendye Lodge
850
CONACHCRAIG
GLENMUICK VISITOR CENTRE
721
FASHEILACH
NO
Burn of Branny
Water of Tarf
Burn of Tennet
778
MOUNT BATTOCK
Glen Dye
F
Spittal of Glenmuick
Glen Mark
Water of Mark
Loch Muick
Glen Lee
525
MELUNCART
696
MONAWEE
Invermark Lodge
Auchronie
Cairn o' Mount
142
Water of Unich
Tarfside
Cairncross
THE RETREAT - GLEN ESK FOLK MUS.
143
Loch Lee
Inchgrundle
North Esk
3 4 5 6 miles
6 7 8 9 10km
Glen Effock
3
G L E N E S K
4
5
CRUYS
FASQUE

Kirkton of Culsalmond
B922
Rothmaise
5
Folla Rule
St Katherine's
6
Cross of Jackston
Chapel
Earlsford
HADDO HOUSE AND GARDENS
B9005
Ythanbank
Hilton
8
Mains of Birness
40
Neth Leask
9
Wedderlairs
Balgove
Newseat
A920
Cairnhill
Tocher
Meikle Wartle
Jackstown
Tulloch
Raxton
MEDIEVAL TOMB
Inverebrie
Broomfield
A90
Artrochie
Auchmacoy
West Kinharrachie
A948
P&R
Bonnyton
160
Kirkton of Rayne
Craigdam
Tarves
Ythsie
Esslemont
Ellon
161
SLAINS CASTLE
Newton Ho.
Old Rayne
LOANHEAD STONE CIRCLE
Mounie Castle
Meldrum Ho.
Auquhorthies
F O R M A R T I N E
TOLQUHON CASTLE
Kirkton of Logie Buchan
VISITOR CENTRE
Kirktown of Slains
Collieston
Pitmachie
Durno
Daviot
Fingask
A920
PITMEDDEN GARDENS
Pitmedden
Waterside
Ardoyne
CHAEOLINK PREHISTORY PARK
Westhall
Whiteford
Pitcaple
Barra Castle
Oldmeldrum
Cairnbrogie
B9000
Tipperty
Meikle Tarty
FORVIE
St Catherine's Dub
Hackley Hd. or Forvie Ness
Sands of Forvie
Oyne
Kirkton of Oyne
A96
Harlaw Ho.
1411
193
NJ
Mill of Kingoodie
Udny Green
Tarty Burn
B9000
Chapel of Garioch
Pittodrie
Kirkton of Bourtie
Hattoncrook
Pettymuick
Culterculen
Foveran
Newburgh
BENNACHIE 528
BATTLE OF HARLAW MEMORIAL
Balhalgardy
BRANDSBUTT STONE
Hillbrae
Whiterashes
Affleck
Udny Station
Foveran Burn
Minnes
Rashiereive
A975
Drums
Newburgh Bar
Burgh Muir
INVERURIE MUSEUM
Inverurie
186
Tillygreig
Tillycorthie
518
237
G A R I O C H
Nether Crimond
Tillykerrie
Straloch
Ardo Ho.
A b e r d e e n s h i r e
Upper Woodend
Bograxie
Manar Ho.
Port Elphinstone
B993
Middlemuir
Delfrigs
Burnhervie
Aquhythie
Kinmuck
KINKELL CHURCH
Middleton
Balbithan Ho.
Newmachar
B979
Craigie
Causeyend
Whitecairns
Belhelvie
Don
Blairdaff
Dalmadilly
Clovenstone
Balbithan
Wester Fintray
Cairnpark
Kinmundy
B977
BALMEDIE
Balmedie
Grantlodge
Pitfichie
MONYMUSK ARTS CENTRE
Kemnay
B994
Cottown
Kintore
Hatton of Fintray
OLD CHURCH
B977
Cothall
A947
Drumligair
Potterton
A90
C
Pitmunie
Monymusk
Craigearn
Leylodge
B977
Overton
Parkhill Ho.
Corby Loch
Blackdog
Todlachie
B993
Lauchintilly
CASTLE FRASER
13
Blackburn
Dyce
ABERDEEN
Mundurno
B999
Haughs of Clinterty
A96
A b e r d e e n C i t y
Stoneywood
Denmore
KIRKWALL 6:00
LERWICK 14:00
Ordhead
Sauchen
Achath
Lyne of Skene
East Auchronie
Bankhead
Bridge of Don
A944
B9126
Bucksburn
Hayton
BRIG O' BALGOWNIE
CRUICKSHANK BOTANIC GARDEN
Milton of Corsindae
Old Kinnernie
Corsindae
Dunecht
Skene Ho.
266
Woodside
ST MACHAR'S CATHEDRAL
Old Aberdeen
Bankhead
Kirkton of Skene
Kittybrewster
KING'S COLLEGE VISITOR CENTRE
Midmar
STONE CIRCLE
274
Loch of Skene
Northfield
Mastrick
A90
Aberdeen
Comers
Tillybirloch
Marionburgh
Echt
Westhill
Kingswells
A944
SATROSPHERE
MARISCHAL MUSEUM
B9119
B9119
Garlogie
Cairnie
Elrick
B9119
P&R
GORDON HIGHLANDERS MUSEUM
ABERDEEN
Ferryhill
Torry
Girdle Ness
Midmar Forest
South Kirkton
B979
Blacktop
Mannofield
DUTHIE PARK WINTER GARDENS
D
Nigg Bay
Landerberry
Redhill
Leuchar Burn
Easter Ord
Cults
Ruthrieston
Kincorth
Greg Ness
433 HILL OF FARE
B9125
West Cullery
Benthoul
Contlaw
Bieldside
Garthdee
Burn of Corrichie
Hardgate
Craigton
Milton of Murtle
Milltimber
A93
Banchory-Devenick
Nigg
Cove Bay
B977
DRUM CASTLE
Peterculter
B9077
Charlestown
A956
Hirn
A980
Myrebird
Mains of Drum
Kirkton of Maryculter
Auchlunies
A90
Hare Ness
80
Brathens
Drumoak
The Neuk
Marywell
Hillside
Findon Ness
Bridge of Canny
East Mains
Upper Lochton
CRATHES CASTLE AND GARDENS
A93
Dee
B9077
Findon
BANCHORY MUSEUM
Woodside of Arbeadie
Crathes
Muirskie
Auchlee
Portlethen
Arbeadie
Deebank
Banchory
ROYAL DEESIDE RLY.
Kirkton of Durris
Woodlands
Denside
Upper Burnhaugh
Downies
Cammachmore Bay
E
Auchattie
Bridge of Feugh
A957
Crossroads
Cammachmore
Belts of Collonach
Borrowfield
Newtonhill
B974
Durris Forest
Netherley
Cookney
Strachan
CAIRN-MON-EARN 378
Muchalls
Lochton
NO
B979
RAEDYKES ROMAN CAMP
Bridge of Muchalls
Union Cottage
Garrol Hill
376 MONGOUR
Water of Dye
Burn of Sheeoch
Mergie
Rickarton
Garron Pt.
534 KERLOCH
Cowie Water
A957
Cowie
Bridge of Dye
Kirktown of Fetteresso
Fetteresso Forest
Tewel
TOLBOOTH MUSEUM
Stonehaven
F
Tannachie
Carmont
Castle Haven
DUNNOTTAR CASTLE
New Mill
A90
Drumtochty Forest
464
A92
Thornyhive Bay
Mains of Dellavaird
BURNS FAMILY MEMORIALS
Glenfarquhar Lodge
Glenbervie
Drumlithie
Fiddes
Mill of Uras
Drumtochty Castle
Barras
Crawton
143
Pitforthie
FOWLSHEUGH NATURE RESERVE
78
Strath Finella
Monboddo House
Mondynes
Roadside of Catterline
Crawton Bay
Auchenblae
Catterline
Glensaugh
Brownmuir
Braidon Bay
G
5
East Cairnbeg
6
Todhead Point
8
40
9
B974
Fordoun
Roadside of Kinneff
7
B966
B967
Parkneuk
Arbuthnott

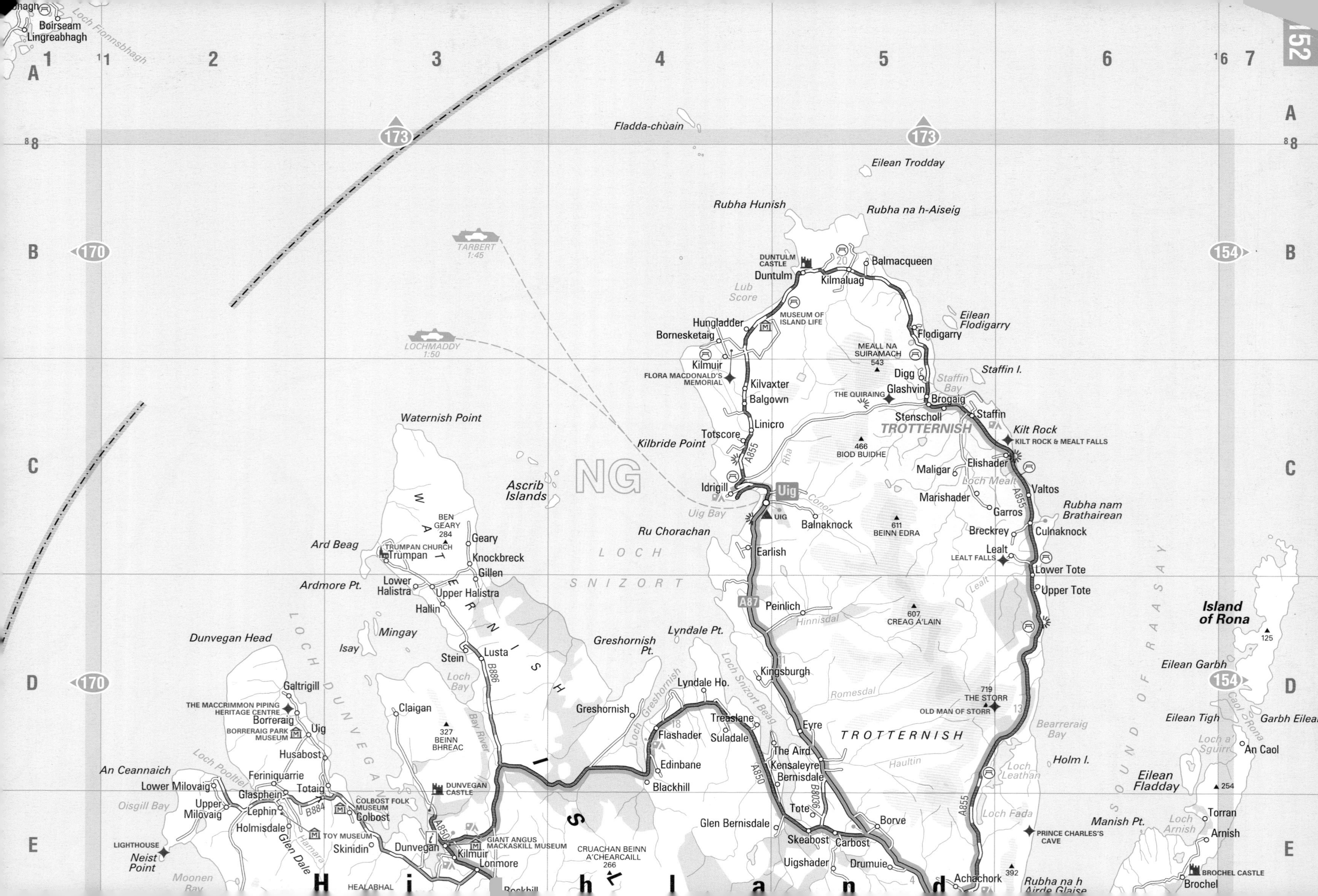
Fladda-chùain
Eilean Trodday
Rubha Hunish
Rubha na h-Aiseig
TARBERT 1:45
LOCHMADDY 1:50
Duntulm Castle
Duntulm
Kilmaluag
Balmacqueen
Lub Score
Museum of Island Life
Hungladder
Bornesketaig
Kilmuir
Flora MacDonald's Memorial
Kilvaxter
Balgown
Linicro
Totscore
Kilbride Point
Idrigill
Uig
Uig Bay
Eilean Flodigarry
Flodigarry
Meall na Suiramach 543
Digg
Staffin Bay
Staffin I.
The Quiraing
Glashvin
Brogaig
Stenscholl
Staffin
Trotternish
Kilt Rock
Kilt Rock & Mealt Falls
Biod Buidhe 466
Maligar
Elishader
Loch Mealt
Valtos
Marishader
Garros
Rubha nam Brathairean
Balnaknock
Beinn Edra 611
Breckrey
Culnaknock
Lealt
Lealt Falls
Lower Tote
Upper Tote
Waternish Point
Ascrib Islands
NG
Ru Chorachan
Ard Beag
Ben Geary 284
Trumpan Church
Trumpan
Geary
Knockbreck
Gillen
Ardmore Pt.
Lower Halistra
Upper Halistra
Hallin
Loch Snizort
Earlish
Peinlich
Hinnisdal
Creag A'Lain 607
Island of Rona
Dunvegan Head
Mingay
Isay
Waternish
Stein
Lusta
B886
Loch Bay
Greshornish Pt.
Lyndale Pt.
Kingsburgh
Eilean Garbh
Galtrigill
The MacCrimmon Piping Heritage Centre
Borreraig
Borreraig Park Museum
Uig
Loch Dunvegan
Claigan
Beinn Bhreac 327
Bay River
Greshornish
Loch Greshornish
Lyndale Ho.
Loch Snizort Beag
Romesdal
The Storr 719
Old Man of Storr
Eilean Tigh
Garbh Eilean
Caol Rona
Loch a' Sguirr
An Caol
Husabost
An Ceannaich
Loch Pooltiel
Feriniquarrie
Lower Milovaig
Glasphein
Totaig
Oisgill Bay
Upper Milovaig
Lephin
B884
Colbost Folk Museum
Colbost
Holmisdale
Toy Museum
Glen Dale
Hamara
Skinidin
Dunvegan Castle
A850
Dunvegan
Giant Angus MacAskill Museum
Kilmuir
Lonmore
Lighthouse
Neist Point
Moonen Bay
Healabhal
Rockhill
Cruachan Beinn A'Chearcaill 266
Treaslane
Flashader
Suladale
Edinbane
Blackhill
Eyre
The Aird
Kensaleyre
Bernisdale
B8036
Tote
Glen Bernisdale
Skeabost
Carbost
Borve
Uigshader
Drumuie
Haultin
Bearreraig Bay
Holm I.
Loch Leathan
Loch Fada
Sound of Raasay
Eilean Fladday
Manish Pt.
Prince Charles's Cave
Loch Arnish
Torran
Arnish
Brochel Castle
Brochel
Achachork
Rubha na h Airde Glaise
Highland
A87
A855
Boirseam
Lingreabhagh
Loch Fionnsbhagh

ISLAND OF RAASAY
Portree
Torvaig
AN TUIREANN ARTS CENTRE
Shulishadermor
THE AROS EXPERIENCE
Glengrasco
Heatherfield
Penifiler
BEN TIANAVAIG
Glenmore
Mugeary
Camastianavaig
Conordan
Lower Ollach
Upper Ollach
Gedintailor
BATTLE OF THE BRAES MONUMENT
The Braes
Peinchorran
BEN LEE
Raasay Ho.
Clachan
RAASAY OUTDOOR CENTRE
Inverarish
East Suisnish
Eyre
Eyre Point
North Fearns
Oskaig
Balachuirn
Balmeanach
Glame
DUN CAAN
Rubha na'Leac
Holoman Bay
Tianavaig Bay
Narrows of Raasay
Caol Mór
Loch Sligachan
Sconser
GLAMAIG
Moll
Scalpay
Scalpay Ho.
Caolas Scalpay
Loch Ainort
Luib
Dunan
OLD SKYE CROFTER'S HOUSE
GLAS BHEINN MHOR
RED HILLS
BROADFORD
Corry
Harrapool
WORLD OF WOOD
Suardal
Strath
Torrin
Kilbride
Loch Slapin
Sligachan Hotel
Glen Sligachan
MARSCO
THE CUILLIN HILLS
SKYE
MINGINISH
DOF
AND
SGURR NAN GILLEAN
SGURR A'GHREADAIDH
CUILLIN HILLS
SGURR ALASDAIR
SGURR NAN EAG
BLA BHEINN
Loch na Creitheach
Loch Coruisk
Camasunary
Strathaird
Kirkibost
Kilmarie
BEN MEABOST
Elgol
BOAT TRIPS
Glasnakille
PRINCE CHARLES'S CAVE
Eilean na h-Airde
Rubha na h-Easgainne
Loch Scavaig
Soay
Soay Sound
Mol-chlach
Rubha Suisnish
Loch Eishort
Ord
DUNSGIATH CASTLE
Tokavaig
Tarskavaig
Tarskavaig Pt.
Achnacloich
Glen Meadhonach
Rubha Charn nan Cearc
SLEAT
Glen Brittle
GLENBRITTLE
Glenbrittle House
Bualintur
Loch Brittle
Glen Brittle Forest
Grula
Eynort
Loch Eynort
BEINN BHREAC
Talisker
Talisker Bay
Gleann Oraid
Carbost
TALISKER DISTILLERY
Merkadale
Drynoch
Crossal
ROINEVAL
Fernilea
ARNAVAL
Fiskavaig
Portnalong
Loch Harport
Oronsay
Rubha nan Clach
Coillore
Bracadale
Struan
Ullinish
Tarner I.
Loch Bracadale
Wiay
Harlosh I.
Idrigill Point
MACLEOD'S MAIDENS
Ose
Loch Caroy
Vatten
Harlosh
Balmore
Roag
Orbost
Loch Varkasaig
Macleod's Tables
HEALABHAL BHEAG
Ramasaig
Hoe Rape
Hoe Point
Geodha Mor
Loch Connan
Tungadal
Loch Duagrich
Snizort
Glen Varragill
Varragill
A87
A863
B885
B883
B8009
B8083
NG
Canna
A'Chill
Sanday
Canna Harbour
MALLAIG 2:30
RUM 1:15
Garrisdale Pt.
Kilmory
Rubha Shamhnan Insir
Rubh an Dunain
0 1 2 3 4 5 6 miles
0 1 2 3 4 5 6 7 8 9 10 km

Ullapool
Carnach
Rireavach
Stattic Pt.
Little Loch Broom
Rubha Mor
Mellon Udrigle
Gruinard I.
Gruinard Bay
Badluarach
Mungasdale
Gruinard House
Dundonnell
Durnamuck
Badcaul
Badrallach
Allt na h-Airbhe
Blarnalearoch
Rhiroy
Ardindrean
Camusnagaul
Ardessie
767
SAIL MHOR
Dundonnell Hotel
Eilean Darach
Strath Beag
Dundonnell House
AN TEALLACH
1062
Strathnasheallag Forest
Loch na Sealga
Strath na Sealga
Dundonnell Forest
A832
Fisherfield Forest
680
BEINN A'CHAISGEIN BEAG
908
BEINN DEARG MHOR
914
BEINN A' CHLAIDHEIMH
807
NH
1019
MULLACH COIRE MHIC FHEARCHAIR
Letterewe Forest
Lochan Fada
748
GROBAN
999
A'CHAILLEACH
Loch a'Bhraoin
Abhainn a'Chadh'Bhuidhe
BEINN NAN RAM
711
933
FIONN BHEINN
635
BEINN GHOBHLACH
302
Eilean Furadh Mór
Srón a' Gheodha Dhuibh
Camas Mór
Rubha Reidh
Loch an Draing
Cove
Achgarve
155
Laide
Mellon Charles
Ormiscaig
Sand
First Coast
Second Coast
Little Gruinard
Tighnafiline
Aultbea
Isle of Ewe
Drumchork
Loch a'Bhaid-luachraich
Loch Fada
Little Gruinard
296
AN CUAIDH
Loch Sguod
Melvaig
Aultgrishan
Inverasdale
Midtown
Brae
Loch Ewe
Rubha 'Ard na Bà
Naast
B8057
Tournaig
Aird Dubh
Fionn Loch
Seana Chamas
Peterburn
B8021
INVEREWE GARDEN
Londubh
Loch Bad a'Chreamh
Port Erradale
North Erradale
Poolewe
Loch Kernsary
Rubha Bàn
Big Sand
Ewe
Longa Island
Caolas Beag
CARN DEARG
Strath
Loch Tollaidh
GAIRLOCH HERITAGE MUSEUM
Smithstown
Gairloch
MEALL AN DOIREAN
420
Dubh Loch
791
BEINN AIRIGH CHARR
LOCH GAIRLOCH
Charlestown
NG
BEINN LAIR
860
Port Henderson
Aird
B8056
Badachro
Kerrysdale
Loch Maree
Eilean Subhainn
LOCH MAREE ISLANDS
Letterewe
Opinan
Shieldaig
Kerry
Loch Bad an Sgalaig
VICTORIA FALLS
Talladale
Loch Clàir
South Erradale
Abhainn a' Gharbh Choire
Loch Garbhaig
Redpoint
Erradale
Abhainn Braigh-horrisdale
Dubh Loch
19
A832
980
SLIOCH
Loch Gaineamhach
WESTER ROSS
Flowerdale Forest
875
BAOSBHEINN
Loch na h-Oidhche
Glen Grudie
692
Kinlochewe Forest
156
152
173
Shieldaig Forest
624
BEINN BHREAC
Loch a'Bhealaich
878
Taagan
Heights of Kinlochewe
Leckie
Craig
Kinlochewe Forest
Anancaun
Abhainn Bruachaig
BEINN EIGHE NATIONAL NATURE RESERVE
Incheril
Kinlochewe
Rubha na Fearn
Fearnmore
Loch Torridon
985
BEINN ALLIGIN
1010
BEINN EIGHE
Lower Diabaig
Glen Docherty
Fearnbeg
WESTER ROSS
Torridon Forest
Arinacrinachd
Alligin Shuas
A896
Badavanich
Achnasheen
1054
LIATHACH
Rechullin
A'Ghairbhe
Loch a'Chroisg
Island of Rona
125
Cuaig
Kenmore
Loch a' Chracaich
Inveralligin
Glen Torridon
Loch Clair
Abhainn Dubh
Ledgowan Forest
Ardheslaig
Torridon Ho.
Fasag
17
TORRIDON
Torridon
Upper Loch Torridon
Loch Shieldaig
782
Loch Coulin
550
Eilean Garbh
RAASAY
162
163
A
B
C
D
E
1
2
3
4
5
6
7

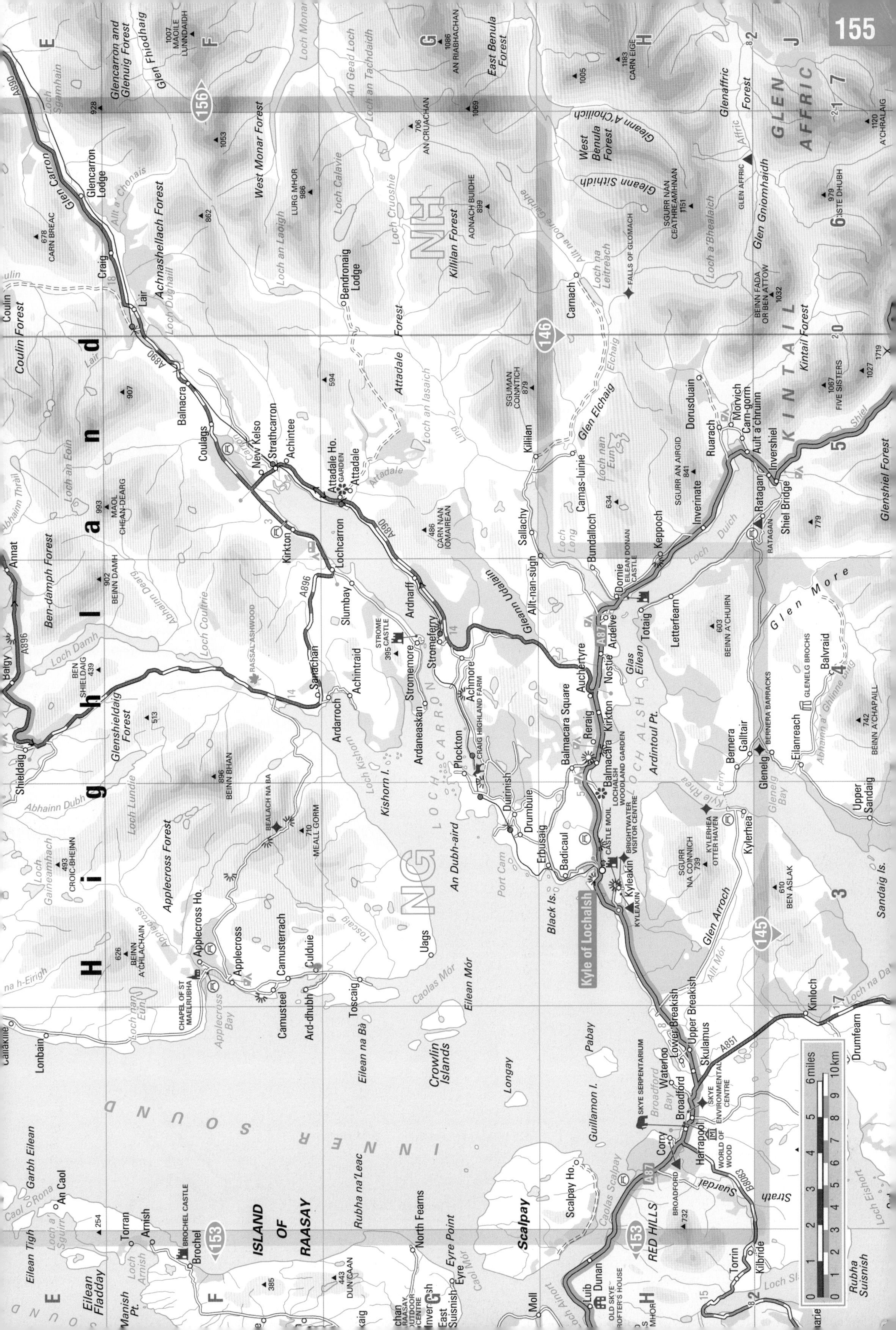
Highland
Kyle of Lochalsh
ISLAND OF RAASAY
Scalpay
INNER SOUND
LOCH CARRON
LOCH ALSH
GLEN AFFRIC
KINTAIL
NG
NH
Applecross
Applecross Forest
Applecross Ho.
Applecross Bay
Camusterrach
Camusteel
Culduie
Ard-dhubh
Toscaig
Shieldaig
Glenshieldaig Forest
Ben-damph Forest
Annat
Coulin Forest
Achnashellach Forest
Glen Carron
Glencarron Lodge
Glencarron and Glenuig Forest
Glen Fhiodhaig
West Monar Forest
Craig
Lair
Balnacra
Coulags
New Kelso
Strathcarron
Achintee
Attadale Ho.
Attadale
Attadale Forest
Lochcarron
Kirkton
Slumbay
Sanachan
Ardarroch
Achintraid
Kishorn I.
Strome Castle
Stromemore
Stromeferry
Ardaneaskan
Ardnarff
Achmore
Craig Highland Farm
Plockton
Duirinish
Drumbuie
Erbusaig
Badicaul
Kyleakin
Balmacara
Balmacara Square
Reraig
Auchertyre
Nostie
Ardelve
Dornie
Eilean Donan Castle
Bundalloch
Totaig
Letterfearn
Allt-nan-sùgh
Sallachy
Killilan
Killilan Forest
Camas-luinie
Glen Elchaig
Carnach
Falls of Glomach
Bendronaig Lodge
Keppoch
Inverinate
Ruarach
Dorusduain
Morvich
Carn-gorm
Ault a'chruinn
Invershiel
Shiel Bridge
Ratagan
Glenshiel Forest
Kintail Forest
Five Sisters
West Benula Forest
East Benula Forest
Glenaffric Forest
Glen Gniomhaidh
Glen More
Glenelg
Glenelg Bay
Bernera
Bernera Barracks
Galltair
Eilanreach
Balvraid
Glenelg Brochs
Upper Sandaig
Sandaig Is.
Kylerhea
Kylerhea Otter Haven
Glen Arroch
Kinloch
Drumfearn
Broadford
Broadford Bay
Harrapool
Waterloo
Skulamus
Lower Breakish
Upper Breakish
Skye Serpentarium
Skye Environmental Centre
World of Wood
Corry
Strath Suardal
Red Hills
Torrin
Kilbride
Luib
Dunan
Old Skye Crofter's House
Scalpay Ho.
Caolas Scalpay
Guillamon I.
Pabay
Longay
Crowlin Islands
Eilean Mòr
Eilean na Bà
Rubha na' Leac
North Fearns
Eyre Point
East Suisnish
Brochel
Brochel Castle
Arnish
Torran
An Caol
Eilean Fladday
Eilean Tigh
Manish Pt.
Black Is.
An Dubh-aird
Lonbain
Uags
A890
A896
A87
A851
B8083
0 1 2 3 4 5 6 miles
0 1 2 3 4 5 6 7 8 9 10 km

1
2
3
4
5
A
B
C
D
E
F
Inverbroom
Lael Forest
Deanich Lodge
Dieb
Gleann Beag
Crom Loch
BEINN THARSUINN
Glen Diebidale
Strath More
Dundonnell Forest
163
Auchindrean
Braemore
889
1084 BEINN DEARG
Tollomuick Forest
628
787 BEINN A'CHAISTEIL
Strath na Sealga
Fain
Dundonnell
A832
CORRIESHALLOCH GORGE
MEALL LEACACHAIN 618
954
Loch Vaich
Abhainn Cuileig
772 MEALL A' GHRIANAIN
Inchbae Forest
914 BEINN A' CHLAIDHEIMH
Braemore Forest
Abhainn Droma
Dirrie More
Lochdrum
Loch Droma
Strathvaich Forest
742
Strathvaich Lodge
Strathrannoch
807
Loch a'Bhraoin
934
Loch Glascarnoch
Strath Vaich
Strath Rannoch
1019 MULLACH COIRE MHIC FHEARCHAIR
A835
1110 SGURR MOR
BEINN LIATH MHOR A 'GHIUBHAIS LI 766
Aultguish Inn
748 GROBAN
999 A'CHAILLEACH
Lochan Fada
Highland
Abhainn a'Chadh'Bhuidhe
949 MEALL GORM
Kinlochluichart Forest
Garbat Forest
Fannich Forest
MEALL MHIC IOMHAIR 607
Garbat
154
BEINN NAN RAMH 711
Fannich Lodge
479
Kinlochewe Forest
LOCH FANNICH
Aultdearg
Corriemoillie Forest
Grudie
Black Water
Heights of Kinlochewe
Leckie
Strath Chrombuill
LITTLE WYVIS 764
Lochrosque Forest
558 AN CABAR
Corriemoillie
Strathgarve Forest
Abhainn Bruachaig
Lochluichart
Incheril
933 FIONN BHEINN
Achanalt
Grudie
Gorstan
Loch Luichart
Garve
Glen Docherty
A832
Strath Bran
Loch Achanalt
Loch Garve
Badavanich
Achnasheen
580 SGURR MARCASAIDH
Loch Bhad Ghaineamhaich
Glenmarksie
Tarvie
Craigdarroch
Loch a'Chroisg
NH
Abhainn Dubh
Ledgowan Forest
Little Scatwell
Loch Achilty
Loch Meig
879 SGURR A'MHUILINN
Milton
Porin
Dalnacroich
Torrachilty Wood
550 CARN-BEAG
Loch Gowan
Meig
STRATHCONON
Loch Achonachie
Gleann Meinich
A890
538 CARN MHARTUIN
STRATHCONON
591
678 CARN BREAC
Glen Carron
Loch Sgamhain
Scardroy
457
Loch Beannacharain
Carnoch
673 CARN NA COINNICH
Cabaan Forest
Glencarron Lodge
928
Inverchoran
Orrin
FOREST
Orrin Reservoir
Allt a' Chonais
Glencarron and Glenuig Forest
849 BAC AN EICH
Corriehallie Forest
Glen Fhiodhaig
Gleann Goibhre
Achnashellach Forest
Orrin
Glen Orrin
Loch na Caoidhe
862
1007 MAOILE LUNNDAIDH
814
766
BEINN A'BHA'ACH ARD 862
1053
155
Erchless Forest
West Monar Forest
East Monar Forest
1083 SGURR A'CHOIRE GHLAIS
Neaty Burn
Loch Laoigh
Erchless Castle
Aigas Forest
LURG MHOR 986
Culligran Falls
Inchmore
Craigdhu
Loch Monar
Monar Lodge
GLEN
Struy
Mid Main
Loch Calavie
Glen Strathfarrar
Farrar
An Gead Loch
Uisge Misgeach
Loch Beannacharan
Loch an Tachdaidh
Glenstrathfarrar Forest
STRATHFARRAR
Mauld
Struy Forest
Loch a'Mhuillidh
Loch Cruoshie
818 SGOR NA DIOLLAID
Carnoch
A831
706 AN CRUACHAN
STRATHGLASS
F
1150 SGURR NA LAPAICH
676 CAIRN GORM
1086 AN RIABHACHAN
Glencannich Forest
Muchrachd
Glassburn
Killilan Forest
Glass
Balmore
457 CARN NAM BAD
AONACH BUIDHE 899
1069
Liatrie
Cannich
East Benula Forest
Mullardoch House
Cannich
CANNICH
Fasnakyle Forest
Glen
CAIRN
Buntait
Braefield
Loch Doire Gairbhe
Loch Mullardoch
Corrimony
Glen Cannich
Balnain
146
147
Shenval
A831
Loch Meikle
DOG FALLS
Affric
Fasnakyle Ho
0 1 2 3 4 5 6 miles
0 1 2 3 4 5 6 7 8 9 10 km
1053 TOLL CREAGACH
Glenurquhart
Tomich
Enrick
578
TOM A' CHOINICH
1183
Deabhag
Balcladaich
Balmacaan Forest

Forest
838 CARN CHUINNEAG
Loch a'Chairn
West
Easter Fearn Burn
546
Balleigh
Meikle Gluich
A836
Tarlogie
Morangie
GLENMORANGIE DISTILLERY
ALDIE WATERMILL
TAIN THROUGH TIME VISITOR CENTRE
Tain
ST DUTHUS'S CHAPEL
TAIN TOLBOOTH
Balnagall
Lochslin
Aultnamain Inn
B9176
321
Quarryhill
Morangie Forest
602
164
Glasa
Loch a'Chaorainn
692 BEINN THARSUINN
Aldie
Hilton
Loch Eye
Rhynie
Fearn Station
Fearn
Hill of Fearn
B9165
FEARN ABBEY
B9166
Loans of Tullich
Kildermorie Forest
Kildermorie Lodge
Braeantra
Strath Rusdale
Black Water
Strath Rory
CNOC CORR GUINIE
397
East Lamington
Lamington
Newfield
Logie Hill
Torran
Scotsburn
Kildary
Arabella
Loch Morie
Inchlumpie
Ardross
Ardross Forest
Easter Ardross
Stittenham
Dalnavie
Tullich Muir
Milton
Tarbat Ho.
B9175
Ankerville
Chapelhill
Wyvis Lodge
738
Boath
Ardross Castle
Wester Lealty
Alness
Stonyfield
Kilmuir
Nigg Bay
Pitcalnie
QUEEN'S CAIRN 645
Loch Glass
NH
Culzie Lodge
Achandunie
Nonikiln
Rhicullen
Barbaraville
Nigg
203
King's Cave
I a n d
523
Mossfield
Tomich
B817
Sands of Nigg
Mount Canisp
Balintraid
Alness
Achnagarron
Rosskeen
Saltburn
Balnabruaich
Balnapaling
Castlecraig
BEN WYVIS 1046
Glen Glass
Eileanach Lodge
FYRISH MONUMENT
Novar House
Dalmore
DALMORE DISTILLERY
Invergordon
Ferry
Nigg Ferry
Allt nan Caorach
Assynt Ho.
Redburn
Culcairn
Evanton
Alness Bay
CROMARTY FIRTH
Balblair
Newhall Point
Cromarty
CROMARTY COURT HOUSE
HUGH MILLER'S COTTAGE
Sutors of Cromarty
Cromarty Bay
Udale Bay
Swordale
Drummond
Resolis
Newhall House
B9163
Shore Mill
Newton
158
Foulis Castle
Cullicudden
Jemimaville
A832
Strath Sgitheach
Clach Liath Forest
Ardullie
STOREHOUSE OF FOULIS
Muirton
482 CIOCH MHOR
Shoreton
Millbuie Forest
Glenurquhart
Upper Eathie
Woodlands
BLACK ISLE
Heights of Brae
Mountgerald
Findon Mains
B9169
Culbo
B9160
A862
A9
Tulloch Castle
Bottacks
Fodderty
Balmungie
Raddery
Whiteness Head
Auchterneed
A834
Dingwall
HIGHLAND MUS. OF CHILDHOOD
Knockfarrel
MACDONALD MONUMENT
Culbokie
256 MOUNT EAGLE
Killen
GROAM HOUSE MUSEUM AND PICTISH CENTRE
Rosemarkie
Rosemarkie Bay
Strathpeffer
Loch Ussie
Urquhart
Alcaig
FORTROSE CATHEDRAL
FORT GEORGE
Fort George
Kirkton
Baddock
Tradespark
Jamestown
Maryburgh
Corntown
Duncanston
Belmaduthy
Rosehaugh Mains
Fortrose
QUEEN'S OWN HIGHLANDERS MUS.
B9006
B9092
Contin
CORR ACHILTY FARM FISH LIFT
Conon Bridge
Conon House
Easter Kinkell
Knockbain
Suddie
Roskill House
A832
Avoch
HERITAGE EXHIBITION
Chanonry Pt.
Ardersier
Moss-side
Leanaig
Avoch Bay
MORAY FIRTH
Marybank
Conon
A835
Gollanfield
Muirton Mains
Urray
A832
Muir of Fairburn
Muckernich
Munlochy
Munlochy Bay
Milton of Gollanfield
Muir of the Clans
Gedde
Lochside
B9039
INVERNESS
B9091
Ross
GLEN ORD DISTILLERY
Balvaird
Kilcoy
Tore
Allangrange Mains
Drumderfit
BLACK ISLE WILDLIFE AND COUNTRY PARK
Fisherton
Clephanton
B9090
Cawdor
Fettes
Bogallan
CASTLE STUART
Tornagrain
Muir of Ord
Ardnagrask
Arpafeelie
Redcastle
A832
Milton
B9161
Kilmuir
Alturlie Pt.
Castle Stuart
Croy
KILRAVOCK CASTLE
CAWDOR CASTLE AND GARDENS
Loch nan Euin
Corry of Ardnagrask
Windhill
Tomich House
Clashandorran
DOLPHINS & SEALS OF THE MORAY FIRTH
Charlestown
North Kessock
Longman Pt.
A96
Newton
Cantraywood
Easter Galcantray
Loch nam Bonnach
BEAULY FIRTH
Balloch
Culloden
Culloden Forest
Nairn
Kirkton of Barevan
Mains
Ruilick
BEAULY PRIORY
MADE IN SCOTLAND
Beauly
Kirkhill
South Kessock
Bunchrew
Smithton
Newlands
Cantraydoune
Cantraybruich
Assich Forest
Allt Dearg
A862
Lentran
CRAIG PHADRIG FORT
BALNAIN HOUSE
INVERNESS MUS. AND ART GALLERY
CULLODEN BATTLEFIELD
1746
CLAVA CAIRNS
B9164
Drumchardine
Leachkin
Culcabock
BUGHT FLORAL HALL VISITOR CENTRE
CASTLE GARRISON ENCOUNTER
Westhill
B9006
Kilmorack
Breakachy
AIGAS DAM FISH LADDER
Balchraggan
HIGHLAND WINERIES
Easter Moniack
Newtonhill
INVERNESS
376
Crask of Aigas
Beaufort Castle
Cabrich
THE AIRD
Dunain Ho.
Caledonian Canal
Castletown
Riereach Burn
Culburnie
Kiltarlity
B851
BEINN BHUIDHE MHOR 548
414 AN LEACAINN
Dochgarroch
Leys Castle
House of Daviot
Camault Muir
Ness
Daviot
Craggie
Eskadale
Dochfour Ho.
DOCHFOUR GARDENS
Strath Dores
Essich
615 CARN NAN TRI-TIGHEARNAN
A833
Lochend
B862
B861
DRUMMOSSIE MUIR
Scatraig
BEINN BHREAC 511
Boblainy Forest
Lairgmore
B9154
Moy Burn
Loch Bruicheach
501
A82
Drumashie Moor
MEALL MOR 492
MEALL A'BHREACRAIBH 551
Glen Convinth
GREAT GLEN WAY
Moy Hall
Balnafoich
B851
Loch Moy
Abriachan
ABRIACHAN GARDEN NURSERY
Dores
Tombreck
A9
Moy
Strathdearn Forest
428 MEALL NAN CAORACH
Balchraggan
Loch Ashie
Dunlichity Lodge
Ruthven
STRATHNAIRN
Farr
LOCH NESS
465 MEALL NA H-EILRIG
LOCH NESS MONSTER EXHIBITIONS
616 CARN NA H-EASGAINN
Balbeg
Urquhart
Farr House
Loch Duntelchaig
Upper Inverbrough
Balvraid
Milton
Achnabat
446 STAC NA CATHAIG
Drumnadrochit
Enrick
464
Urquhart Bay
147
148
TOMATIN DISTILLERY
Tomatin
Lewiston
DRUM FARM
Strone
B852
B862
Tullich
Nairn
Brinmore
627 CARN A'CHOIRE BHOIR
Forest
Divach
Upper Lenie
Lower Lenie
URQUHART CASTLE
Findhorn Bridge
Torness
Loch Ruthven
East Croachy
601 BEINN BHREAC
COBB MEMORIAL
Aberarder House
B851
Glen Kyllachy
Kyllachy
A B C D E F G
5 6 7 8 9

GLENMORANGIE DISTILLERY
TAIN THROUGH TIME VISITOR CENTRE
TAIN-TOLBOOTH
Tain
Aldie
Hilton
Loch Eye
TARBAT DISCOVERY CENTRE
Portmahomack
Bindal
Rockfield
Inver
Arboll
Tarrel
Balnagall
Lochslin
165
Rhynie
Geanies House
Fearn Station
East Lamington
Newfield
Logie Hill
Hill of Fearn
Fearn
FEARN ABBEY
Loans of Tullich
Hilton of Cadboll
Balintore
SHANDWICK STONE
Shandwick
Arabella
Kildary
Milton
Tarbat Ho.
Kilmuir
Ankerville
Chapelhill
Nigg Bay
Barbaraville
Pitcalnie
Port an Righ
Nigg
Sands of Nigg
203
King's Cave
Mount Canisp
Balnabruaich
Balnapaling
Castlecraig
Nigg Ferry
Ferry
Cromarty
CROMARTY COURT HOUSE
HUGH MILLER'S COTTAGE
157
Sutors of Cromarty
Cromarty Bay
Newton
Shore Mill
Upper Eathie
MORAY FIRTH
NH
Balmungie
Whiteness Head
The Bar
Culbin Forest
Kincorth Ho.
Findhorn
Findhorn Bay
BURGHEAD BAY
BURGHEAD MUSEUM
Burghead
Hopeman
Cummingston
Roseisle
Roseisle Forest
Lower Hempriggs
Coltfield
Miltonhill
Alves
KINLOSS ABBEY
Kinloss
Grange Hall
Kintessack
Springfield
SUENO'S STONE
Moy Ho.
Forres
NELSON TOWER
FALCONER MUSEUM
Mains of Burgie
Monaughty Forest
PLUSCARDEN ABBEY
Barnhill
Dyke
BRODIE CASTLE
NAIRN FISHERTOWN MUSEUM
NAIRN LITERARY INSTITUTE MUSEUM
Nairn
GROAM HOUSE MUSEUM AND PICTISH CENTRE
Rosemarkie Bay
FORT GEORGE
Fort George
QUEEN'S OWN HIGHLANDERS MUS.
Kirkton
Baddock
Chanonry Pt.
Ardersier
Tradespark
BOATH DOVECOTE
Auldearn
Earlsmill
1645
Blervie Castle
DALLAS DHU DISTILLERY
Califer
Rafford
Moss-side
Blackhills
Whitemire
Conicavel
Easter Milton
Altyre Ho.
Moor of Granary
Black Burn
Dallas Forest
319
Briach
Gollanfield
Milton of Gollanfield
Muir of the Clans
Geddes House
Laiken Forest
Wester Milton
Altyre Woods
Branchill
Dallas
INVERNESS
Lochside
Rosefield
Regoul
Darnaway Forest
Newtyle Forest
Clephanton
Cawdor
Piperhill
Logie
Drumine Forest
Craigroy
Tornagrain
Croy
KILRAVOCK CASTLE
CAWDOR CASTLE AND GARDENS
Culcharry
Littlemill
Mid Urchany
371
MILL BUIE
Newton
Easter Galcantray
Cantraywood
Culloden Forest
Achavraat
Muckle Burn
Relugas
Loch Dallas
Kirkton of Barevan
Mains of Clunas
Redburn
Glenernie
Beachans
Newlands
Cantraydoune
Cantraybruich
Allt Dearg
Assich Forest
Newlands of Fleenas Wood
ARDCLACH TOWER
Mount
NJ
CULLODEN BATTLEFIELD
CLAVA CAIRNS
1746
Balmore
Ferness
Lossie
Castletown
Riereach Burn
Glenferness House
Dorback Burn
Divie
CARN KITTY
521
BEINN BHUIDHE MHOR
548
CARN SGUMAIN
417
Dulsie
455
545
LARIG HILL
516
Findhorn
406
Aitnoch
HILL OF AITNOCH
Dava
Allt a Ghealaidh
BEINN BHREAC
511
615
CARN NAN TRI-TIGHEARNAN
Daless
Rhilean Burn
Leonach Burn
Burn of Tulchan
Moy Burn
MEALL A'BHREACRAIBH
551
Lochindorb
LOCHINDORB CASTLE
Moy Hall
Loch Moy
Moy
Strathdearn Forest
Highland
Tomlachlan Burn
Lochindorb Lodge
484
CARN-RUIGH CHARRACH
549
CARN NA LOINE
Upper Derraid
Auchnagallin
Advie
Lettoch
Ruthven
616
CARN NA CASGAINN
Upper Inverbrough
Balvraid
635
CARN AN T-SEAN-LIATHANAICH
Glaschoil
Camerory
Cottartown
Dellefure
Mains of Dalvey
TOMATIN DISTILLERY
Tomatin
148
149
659
CARN GLAS-CHOIRE
710
Glenbeg
Cromdale
Auchroisk
Haughs of Cromdale
1690
Achnahannet
471
BEINN MHOR
Grantown-on-Spey
Anagach
Craggan
Congash
Speybridge
Dulnain
Kyllachy
BEINN
HILLS OF CROMDALE
STRATHSPEY
A9
A96
A939
A940
A832
A95
B9163
B9165
B9166
B9175
B9006
B9039
B9090
B9091
B9092
B9101
B9007
B9010
B9011
B9089
B9102
B851
B9154
0 1 2 3 4 5 6 miles
0 1 2 3 4 5 6 7 8 9 10km

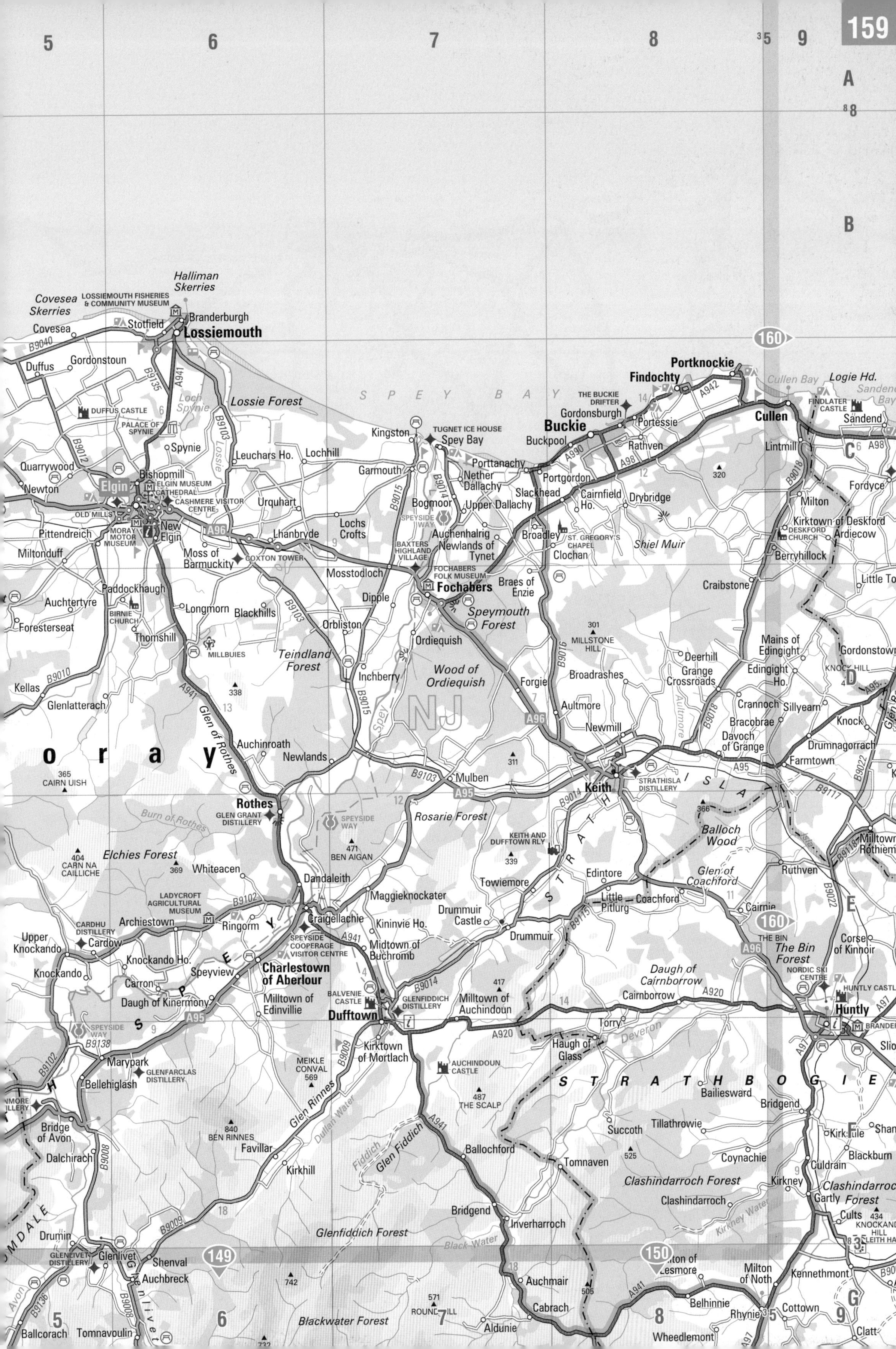
5
6
7
8
9
A
B
C
D
E
F
G
Halliman Skerries
Covesea Skerries
LOSSIEMOUTH FISHERIES & COMMUNITY MUSEUM
Covesea
Stotfield
Branderburgh
Lossiemouth
160
Portknockie
Findochty
Cullen Bay
Logie Hd.
Sandend Bay
Duffus
Gordonstoun
DUFFUS CASTLE
PALACE OF SPYNIE
Loch Spynie
Lossie Forest
S P E Y B A Y
THE BUCKIE DRIFTER
Gordonsburgh
Portessie
Cullen
FINDLATER CASTLE
Sandend
Spynie
Leuchars Ho.
Lochhill
Kingston
TUGNET ICE HOUSE
Spey Bay
Buckie
Buckpool
Rathven
Lintmill
Quarrywood
Bishopmill
Garmouth
Porttanachy
Portgordon
Fordyce
Newton
Elgin
ELGIN MUSEUM
CATHEDRAL
CASHMERE VISITOR CENTRE
Urquhart
Nether Dallachy
Upper Dallachy
Slackhead
Cairnfield Ho.
Drybridge
Milton
OLD MILLS
MORAY MOTOR MUSEUM
New Elgin
Bogmoor
SPEYSIDE WAY
Pittendreich
Lhanbryde
Lochs Crofts
Auchenhalrig
Newlands of Tynet
Broadley
ST. GREGORY'S CHAPEL
Clochan
Shiel Muir
Kirktown of Deskford
DESKFORD CHURCH
Ardiecow
Miltonduff
Moss of Barmuckity
COXTON TOWER
BAXTERS HIGHLAND VILLAGE
FOCHABERS FOLK MUSEUM
Berryhillock
Mosstodloch
Fochabers
Braes of Enzie
Craibstone
Little Toux
Paddockhaugh
Auchtertyre
BIRNIE CHURCH
Longmorn
Blackhills
Dipple
Speymouth Forest
Orbliston
Foresterseat
Thornshill
MILLBUIES
Ordiequish
301 MILLSTONE HILL
Mains of Edingight
Gordonstown
Teindland Forest
Wood of Ordiequish
Deerhill
Edingight Ho.
KNOCK HILL
Kellas
Inchberry
Broadrashes
Grange Crossroads
Glenlatterach
338
Forgie
NJ
Aultmore
Crannoch
Sillyearn
Glen of Rothes
Bracobrae
Knock
Glen Barry
Newmill
Davoch of Grange
Drumnagorrach
o r a y
Auchinroath
Newlands
Farmtown
311
365 CAIRN UISH
Mulben
Keith
STRATHISLA DISTILLERY
I S L A
Rothes
GLEN GRANT DISTILLERY
SPEYSIDE WAY
Rosarie Forest
366
Burn of Rothes
KEITH AND DUFFTOWN RLY
Balloch Wood
Milltown of Rothiemay
404 CARN NA CAILLICHE
Elchies Forest
471 BEN AIGAN
339
369
Whiteacen
Dandaleith
Edintore
Glen of Coachford
Ruthven
Towiemore
LADYCROFT AGRICULTURAL MUSEUM
Maggieknockater
Little Pitlurg
Coachford
Cairnie
Archiestown
Ringorm
Craigellachie
Drummuir Castle
CARDHU DISTILLERY
Kininvie Ho.
Drummuir
THE BIN
Corse of Kinnoir
Upper Knockando
Cardow
SPEYSIDE COOPERAGE VISITOR CENTRE
Midtown of Buchromb
The Bin Forest
Knockando Ho.
Daugh of Cairnborrow
NORDIC SKI CENTRE
Knockando
Speyview
Charlestown of Aberlour
HUNTLY CASTLE
Carron
417
Cairnborrow
Daugh of Kinermony
Milltown of Edinvillie
BALVENIE CASTLE
GLENFIDDICH DISTILLERY
Milltown of Auchindoun
Huntly
Dufftown
Torry
Deveron
SPEYSIDE WAY
Haugh of Glass
BRANDER M
Sliach
Kirktown of Mortlach
Marypark
GLENFARCLAS DISTILLERY
MEIKLE CONVAL 569
AUCHINDOUN CASTLE
Bellehiglash
487 THE SCALP
S T R A T H B O G I E
Glen Rinnes
Bailiesward
Bridgend
Bridge of Avon
840 BEN RINNES
Succoth
Tillathrowie
Kirk Tule
Shanqu
Favillar
Dullan Water
Glen Fiddich
Fiddich
Ballochford
525
Blackburn
Dalchirach
Kirkhill
Tomnaven
Coynachie
Culdrain
Clashindarroch Forest
Kirkney
Clashindarroch Forest
Clashindarroch
Gartly
Bridgend
Inverharroch
Cults
434 KNOCKANDY HILL
LEITH HALL
Drumin
Glenfiddich Forest
Black Water
Kirkney Water
GLENLIVET DISTILLERY
Glenlivet
Shenval
149
150
Milton of Lesmore
Milton of Noth
Kennethmont
Auchbreck
742
Auchmair
505
Belhinnie
Rhynie
Cottown
571 ROUND HILL
Cabrach
Ballcorach
Tomnavoulin
Blackwater Forest
Aldunie
Wheedlemont
Clatt
732
Avon
Livet

1
2
3
4
5
A
B
C
D
E
F
Findochty
Portknockie
Cullen Bay
Logie Hd.
Sandend Bay
Redhythe Pt.
Boyne Bay
Knock Hd.
Boyndie Bay
Head of Garness
Gamrie Bay
Troup Hd.
Portessie
Rathven
Cullen
FINDLATER CASTLE
Sandend
Portsoy
Seatown
Whitehills
Macduff
MACDUFF MARINE AQUARIUM
Crovie
Gardenstown
Pennan
Lintmill
Drybridge
Shiel Muir
Fordyce
JOINER'S WORKSHOP
Easter Whyntie
Boyndie
Auds
Inverboyndie
Banff
BANFF MUSEUM
Easter Silverford
Dubford
Milton
Kirktown of Deskford
DESKFORD CHURCH
Ardiecow
Berryhillock
COLLEONARD SCULPTURE GARDEN & GALLERY
DUFF HOUSE
Doune Park
West Greenskares
Longmanhill
Wester Culbeuchly
Montcoffer Ho.
Cushnie
Craibstone
Newmills of Boyne
Little Toux
Oldtown of Ord
Kirktown of Alvah
Keilhill
Minnonie
Netherbrae
Mid Cloch Forbie
Cornhill
Fattahead
Greenlaw
King Edward
Gorrachie
Mains of Edingight
Gordonstown
Weachyburn
The Pole of Itlaw
Milltown of Craigston
HILL OF FISHRIE
Deerhill
Crange Crossroads
Edingight Ho.
KNOCK HILL
Blacklaw Finnygaud
Plaidy
Craigston Castle
Glen Barry
Crannoch
Sillyearn
Knowes of Elrick
Hill of Mountblairy
Muirden
Fintry
New Byth
Bracobrae
Davoch of Grange
Knock
Drumnagorrach
Cranna
Aberchirder
Forglen Ho.
Garmond
Whitestone
Farmtown
Old Crombie
Bogton
Muiryfold
Balthangie
STRATHISLA DISTILLERY
Knauchland
Marnoch
Clunie
Carnousie
Turriff
DELGATIE CASTLE
Cuminestown
Middle Cairncake
Kirkton
Balloch Wood
Deveron
Little Colp
Delgaty Forest
Milltown of Rothiemay
Mains of Mayen
Hillbrae
Inverkeithny
Mill of Muiresk
Auchininna
Hatton Castle
Howe of Teuchar
Ruthven
Glen of Coachford
Coachford
Yonder Bognie
Bogniebrae
FOURMAN HILL
Darra
Birkenhills
Rush-head
Cairnie
Aberdeen
Fortrie
Brownhill
Crofts of Inverthernie
THE BIN
The Bin Forest
Corse of Kinnoir
GLENDRONACH DISTILLERY
Drumblair
NJ
Dykeside
Cairnbanno Ho.
South Millbrex
Steinmanhill
Daugh of Cairnborrow
Cairnborrow
NORDIC SKI CENTRE
HUNTLY CASTLE
Lessendrum
Denmoss
Gourdas
Inverythan
Nether Lenshie
Kirkton of Auchterless
Tifty
Lethenty
Cottown
Monkshill
Huntly
BRANDER MUSEUM
Drumblade
Corse
Aucharnie
Balgaveny
Brideswell
Slioch
Logie Newton
Backhill
FYVIE CASTLE
Fyvie
Woodhead
Ardo
Crofts of Haddo
Denend
Ythanwells
Gordonstown
Badenscoth
Rothiebrisbane
STRATHBOGIE
Bailiesward
Thomastown
Redhill
Bridgend
Hillhead
Fisherford
Rothienorman
Petty
Collynie
Tillathrowie
Kirkstile
Shanquhar
Bainshole
Cromblet
Barthol Chapel
Coynachie
Blackburn
Culdrain
Glens of Foudland
HILL OF FOUDLAND
Kirkton of Culsalmond
Rothmaise
Newseat
Folla Rule
St Katherine's
Earlsford
Clashindarroch Forest
Kirkney
Clashindarroch
Gartly
Colpy
Cairnhill
Tocher
Cross of Jackston
Balgove
Largie
Meikle Wartle
Jackstown
Tulloch
Cults
KNOCKANDY HILL
Kirkney Water
Wrangham
Bonnyton
Craigdam
Milton of Lesmore
Milton of Noth
Kennethmont
Oldtown
Ardlair
Aulton
The Shevock
Insch
Newton Ho.
Kirkton of Rayne
Old Rayne
LOANHEAD STONE CIRCLE
Mounie Castle
FORMARTINE
Meldrum Ho.
Auquhorthies
Belhinnie
Rhynie
Cottown
Pitmachie
Ardoyne
Durno
Daviot
Fingask
Oldmeldrum
Wheedlemont
Craig Castle
Clatt
Duncanston
ARCHAEOLINK PREHISTORY PARK
Westhall
Whiteford
Pitcaple
Barra Castle
Mill of Kingoodie
ST MARY'S CHURCH
Leslie
Kirkton
Oyne
Kirkton of Oyne
Harlaw Ho.
Kirkton of Bourtie
Hattoncrook
Knockespock Ho.
Auchleven
Pittodrie
Chapel of Garioch
Balhalgardy
Coldwells Croft
Whitehaugh Forest
BENNACHIE
BATTLE OF HARLAW MEMORIAL
BRANDSBUTT STONE
Hillbrae
Nether Crimond
Clova
SCOTTISH SCULPTURE WORKSHOP
Lumsden
CORREEN HILLS
Muckletown
GARIOCH
Burgh Muir
INVERURIE MUSEUM
Inverurie
Tillykerrie
Glenton
Manar Ho.
Tullynessle
Upper Woodend
Bograxie
Port Elphinstone
Kinmuck
Middleton
Mossat
LORD ARTHUR'S
Keig
Castle Forbes
Burnhervie
Aquhythie
KINKELL CHURCH
Balbithan Ho.
Kildrummy
Montgarrie
HAUGHTON
Rorandle
Pitfichie
Blairdaff
Dalmadilly
Clovenstone
Balbithan
Wester Fintray
Cairnpark
Auchintoul
Alford
GRAMPIAN TRANSPORT MUS.
Gateside
Pitfichie Forest
Grantlodge
MONYMUSK ARTS CENTRE
Kemnay
Hatton of Fintray
0 1 2 3 4 5 6 miles
0 1 2 3 4 5 6 7 8 9 10 km

5
6
7
8
9
A
B
C
D
E
F
G
NJ
NK
Fraserburgh
FRASERBURGH HERITAGE MUSEUM
SANDHAVEN MEAL MILL
Kinnaird Head
KINNAIRD CASTLE LIGHTHOUSE & SCOTLAND'S LIGHTHOUSE MUSEUM
Rosehearty
Pittulie
Broadsea
PITSLIGO CASTLE
Sandhaven
Quarry Hd.
Peathill
Percyhorner
Pitblae
Fraserburgh Bay
Cairnbulg Pt.
Inverallochy
MAGGIE'S HOOSIE
Coburty
Towie
Upper Boyndlie
Mid Ardlaw
New Aberdour
Tyrie
Memsie
Cairnbulg Castle
St Combs
Inzie Head
Gowanhill
MEMSIE BURIAL CAIRN
Whitewell
Ladysford
Strathellie
Rathen
Cairness
Loch of Strathbeg
Nether Glasslaw
Craigmaud
Hillhead of Auchentumb
Newburgh
Crimonmogate
LOCH OF STRATHBEG NATURE RESERVE VISITOR CENTRE
Lonmay
Old Rattray
Rattray Head
Crimond
New Pitsligo
Knowhead
230
MORMOND HILL
Nether Park
Blackhill
Strichen
New Leeds
Longhill
Balearn
Bonnykelly
Adziel
North Ugie Water
Leys
St Fergus Moss
Little Skillymarno
Ironside
Denhead
Backfolds
Kirktown
St Fergus
Scotstown Hd.
Oldwhat
Fetterangus
Hythie
Rora Moss
North Kirkton
Mains of Fedderate
Forest of Deer
Toux
Rora
Lunderton
Kirkton Hd.
Culsh
DEER ABBEY
Dunshillock
Woodside
Maud
Mintlaw
Newseat
Inverugie
INVERUGIE CASTLE
UGIE SALMON FISH HOUSE
Buchanhaven
New Deer
MAUD RAILWAY MUSEUM
Backhill of Clackriach
Old Deer
ABERDEENSHIRE FARMING MUSEUM
Longside
Torterston
Peterhead
Flushing
South Ugie
Stuartfield
Inverquhomery
ARBUTHNOT MUSEUM & ART GALLERY
Keith Inch
Drymuir
Bulwark
Millbreck
Hillhead of Cocklaw
PETERHEAD MARITIME
Peterhead Bay
Mains of Crichie
Crichie
Nether Kinmundy
Invernettie
Sandford Bay
Nethermuir
Knaven
Kinnadie
Clola
Little Dens
Skelmuir
Blackhill
Millbank
Boddam
Buchan Ness
Stirling
Crofts of Meikle Ardo
Barrack
Mains of Annochie
Kinknockie
Auchnagatt
Backhill of Fortree
Smallburn
Sandfordhill
Cairnorrie
Brownhill
Mains of Inkhorn
Moss of Cruden
Coldwells
Longhaven
Backhill
Stoneygate
Skelmonae
Teuchan
Quilquox
Milton Coldwells
North Haven
Auchiries
BULLERS OF BUCHAN
Methlick
Hatton
Ythan
Muirtack
Drumwhindle
Arthrath
Eastertown of Auchleuchries
Twa Havens
Cruden Bay
Port Erroll
HADDO
HADDO HOUSE AND GARDENS
Toll of Birness
Bogbrae
Chapel Hill
Bay of Cruden
Ythanbank
Hilton
Mains of Birness
Wedderlairs
Inverebrie
Nether Leask
Whinnyfold
Broomfield
Raxton
MEDIEVAL TOMB
West Kinharrachie
Artrochie
Auchmacoy
Tarves
Ythsie
Esslemont
Ellon
SLAINS CASTLE
Kirkton of Logie Buchan
Kirktown of Slains
VISITOR CENTRE
FORMARTINE
TOLQUHON CASTLE
PITMEDDEN GARDENS
Pitmedden
Waterside
Collieston
St Catherine's Dub
Meikle Tarty
FORVIE
Sands of Forvie
Tipperty
Fairnbrogie
Udny Green
Hackley Hd. or Forvie Ness
Tarty Burn
Pettymuick
Cultercullen
Newburgh
Foveran
Foveran Burn
Affleck
Udny Station
Newburgh Bar
Whiterashes
Minnes
Tillygreig
Tillycorthie
Rashiereive
Drums
186
Ardo Ho.
Straloch
Delfrigs
Middlemuir
Newmachar
Craigie
Causeyend
Whitecairns
Kinmundy
Belhelvie
BALMEDIE
Drumligair
Balmedie
Cothall
A90
A98
A950
A981
A952
A948
A975
A920
A947
A982
B9031
B9033
B9107
B9032
B9093
B9029
B9030
B9106
B9170
B9005
B999
B9000
B979
B977
151
P&R

1
2
3
4
A
B
C
D
E
F
NB
NC
NG
NH
166
154
154
Eilean Chrona
Culkein
Clashnessie Bay
Cluas Deas
Achnacarnin
Clashmore
Clashnessie
Balchladich
Rienachait
Stoer
Rubh'a' Mhill Dheirg
Bay of Stoer
Clachtoll
Loch Cròcach
R. Leumair
Achmelvich Bay
B869
Rhicar
Achmelvich
ACHMELVICH BEACH
ASSYNT VISITOR CENTRE
Rubha Rodha
Baddidarach
Lochinver
Soyea I.
Loch Inver
Kirkaig Pt.
A'Chleit
Badnaban
Inverkirkaig
Loch Kirkaig
Rubha na Breige
Rubha Coigeach
Eilean Mór
ENARD BAY
Rubh'a' Choin
Camas Eilean Ghlais
Rubha Mor
Inverpolly Lodge
Reiff
Brae of Achnahaird
Altandhu
SUMMER ISLES SMOKEHOUSE
Eilean Mullagrach
Loch Vatachan
Loch Osgaig
Aird of Coigach
Isle Ristol
Polbain
Glas-leac Mór
Loch Bad a'Ghaill
Achiltibuie
HYDROPONICUM GARDENS
Tanera Beg
Badentarbat Bay
Polglass
ACHENINVER
Summer Isles
Tanera Mór
Horse Sound
Horse I.
Glas-leac Beag
Culnacraig
BEINN COIG
Achduart
Eilean Dubh
Priest I.
Bottle I.
Carn nan Sgeir
Camas
Isle Martin
Greenstone Point
Cailleach Hd.
STORNOWAY 2:40
Annat Bay
Rubha Beag
Opinan
Scoraig
Carnach
Stattic Pt.
LITTLE LOCH BROOM
Rubha Mor
Rireavach
Mellon Udrigle
635
BEINN GHOBHLACH
Gruinard I.
Badluarach
Eilean Furadh Mór
Sròn a' Gheodha Dhuibh
Achgarve
Mungasdale
Durnamuck
Rubha Reidh
Camas Mór
155
Gruinard Bay
Gruinard House
A832
Badcaul
Badrallach
Laide
Mellon Charles
Loch an Draing
Sand
First Coast
Ormiscaig
Cove
Second Coast
Inchina
Tighnafiline
Isle of Ewe
Aultbea
Little Gruinard
302
Camusnagaul
Ardessie
296
AN CUAIDH
767
SAIL MHOR
Drumchork
Loch Sguod
Loch a'Bhaid-luachraich
Dundonnell Hotel
Dundonnell
Melvaig
Inverasdale
LOCH EWE
Little Gruinard
Loch Fada
WESTER ROSS
Strathnasheallag Forest
Aultgrishan
Midtown
Seana Chamas
Brae
B8057
Rubha 'Ard na Bà
AN TEALLACH
1062
Tournaig
Peterburn
Naast
Aird Dubh
Loch na Sealga
INVEREWE GARDEN
680
BEINN A'CHAISGEIN BEAG
Port Erradale
Loch Bad a'Chreamh
B8021
Londubh
FIONN LOCH
Fisherfield Forest
Strath na Sealga
North Erradale
Poolewe
Loch Kernsary
908
BEINN DEARG MHOR
Rubha Bàn
Big Sand
Ewe
Loch Tollaidh
Dubh Loch
914
BEINN A' CHLAIDHEIMH
0 1 2 3 4 5 6 miles
0 1 2 3 4 5 6 7 8 9 10 km
MEALL AN DOIREAN
420

Culkein Drumbeg
Drumbeg
Nedd
B869
Gleann Leireag
Kylestrome
Kylesku
Unapool
Newton
Loch Glencoul
Loch Glendhu
Glendhu Forest
547
Gleann Dubh
530 BEINN AIRD DA LOCH
Glen Coul
Kinloch
A838
566
873 BEN HEE
Loch a'Ghorm-choire
Loch Merkland
Merkland Lodge
792 BEINN LEOID
Loch an Eircill
Loch Dubh a'Chuail
Loch a'Ghriama
Loch Fiag
404
312 CNOC AN ALASKIE
Fiag Plantation
Glen Fiag
Loch an Leothaid
808 QUINAG
Loch Beannach
Lochassynt Lodge
LOCH ASSYNT
A894
EAS COUL AULIN WATERFALL
776
BEINN UIDHE 740
Corrykinloch
Little Assynt
Inver
A837
Brackloch
Skiag Bridge
ARDVRECK CASTLE
Gorm Loch Mor
Fionn Loch Mor
Overscaig Hotel
LOCH SHIN
Glencanisp Lodge
Loch Feith an Leòthaid
540
Inchnadamph
Inchnadamph Forest
512 MAOVALLY
Fiag Bridge
ASSYNT-
Glencanisp Forest
SUILVEN 731
846 CANISP
Stronchrubie
INCHNADAMPH
998 BEN MORE ASSYNT
391
Allt Car
Strath an Lòin
Falls
Fionn Loch
Loch na Gainimh
718 BREABAG
MEALL AN AONAICH 715
Duchally
COIGACH
Loanan
Loch Awe
NC
Benmore Forest
Glen Cassley
Loch Veyatie
Cam Loch
Ledbeg
Loch Sionascaig
Ledmore
BEINN SGEIREACH 476
Allt a'Bhunn
Inverpolly Forest
849 CUL MOR
HIGHLAND & RARE BREEDS FARM
Elphin
Altnacealgach Hotel
Loch Ailsh
Benmore Lodge
Drumrunie Forest
Loch an Doire Dhuibh
613
Knockan
Loch Urigill
KNOCKAN CRAG
Glen Oykel
364 AN STUC
BEINN AN EOIN 554
Loch Urgainn
769 CUL BEAG
A835
CROMALT HILLS
Crom Allt
517
Glencassley Castle
Loch na Fuaralaich
Drumrunie
COIGACH
Loch Craggie
Loch na Claise Moire
Oykel
Glenrossal
402 CNOC A'CHOIRE
Oykel Forest
Langwell Lodge
Runie
Kanaird
Strathcanaird
Rappach
Strath nan Lon
578 MEALL AN FHUARAIN
18
Lubcroy
Oykel Bridge
Strath Oykel
Invercassley
Rosehall
Strath Kanaird
Brae
Doune
Oape
Altass
415
Allt-Beinn Donuill
Rappach Water
340
Einig
Glen Einig
Ardmair
Highland
Rhidorroch Forest
493 BEINN ULBHAIDH
Morefield
Ullapool
Loch Achall
Rhidorroch Ho.
ULLAPOOL MUSEUM
548
Loch an Daimh
Strath Mulzie
Corriemulzie Lodge
412 CREAG LOISGTE
Strath Cuileannach
507 MEALL DHEIRGIDH
Braelangwell Lodge
ULLAPOOL
Ullapool
LOCHBROOM MUSEUM
Glen Achall
Rhidorroch
East Rhidorroch Lodge
Corriemulzie
Carron
Western Gruinards
Rubha Cadail
Allt na h-Airbhe
A835
558 BEINN EILIDEACH
LECKMELM SHRUBBERY AND ARBORETUM
Leckmelm
Glasha Burn
701 CARN A' CHOIN DEIRG
CROICH CHURCH
Croich
The Craigs
Amatnatua
Amat Forest
279
Blarnalearoch
Rhiroy
642 MEALL DUBH
677 MEALL NAM BRADHAN
Loch a'Choire Mhoir
822
Freevater Forest
Alladale Lodge
Alladale
Ardcharnich
Ardindrean
LOCH BROOM
Douchary
927 SEANA BHRAIGH
Glencalvie Lodge
Eilean Darach
Letters
845 CARN BAN
Gleann Mór
Glencalvie Forest
Inverlael Forest
EASTER ROSS
CARN SALACHAIG
Little Loch Broom
Beag
Dundonnell House
Inverlael
LAEL FOREST GARDEN
Lael Forest
NH
735
Deanich Lodge
Diebidale Forest
Inverbroom
Lael
928
Gleann Beag
Crom Loch
714 BEINN THARSUINN
Glen Diebidale
838 CARN CHUINNEAG
Strath More
Broom
628
Dundonnell Forest
Auchindrean
889
1084 BEINN DEARG
Tollomuick Forest
Fain
Braemore
CORRIESHALLOCH GORGE
954
787 BEINN A'CHAISTEIL
Abhainn na Glasa
Loch a'Chaorainn
Dundonnell
A832
Abhainn Cuileig
MEALL LEACACHAIN 618
Loch Vaich
Kildermorie Forest
Kildermorie Lodge
772 MEALL A' GHRIANAIN
Inchbae Forest
Abhainn Droma
Braemore Forest
166
167
164
156

Highland
EASTER ROSS
NC
NH
873 BEN HEE
Loch a'Ghorm-choire
Mudale
Clebrig
A836
Strath Vagastie
Kilbreck Burn
Loch Truderscaig
272
Loch an Alltan Fhearna
Loch Badanloch
Badanloch Lodge
328
721 BEN KLIBRECK
Loch Choire Forest
Loch Choire Lodge
167
168
473
961 MEALL NAN CON
Loch Choire
A838
Merkland Lodge
404
Loch Fiag
312 CNOC AN ALASKIE
542
704 BEN ARMINE
Gorm-loch Beag
Borrobol Forest
Glen Fiag
Fiag Plantation
Crask Inn
Loch a'Bhealaich
581 MEALL A'BHATA
Overscaig Hotel
Loch Gaineamhach
713 CREAG MHOR
Gorm-loch Mór
365
486
BEN ARMINE FOREST
Fiag Bridge
Strath Tirry
LOCH SHIN
Ben Armine Lodge
Glas-loch Mor
Strath na Seilge
Strath Skinsdale
Skinsdale
391
Allt Car
Strath an Loin
163
461 MEALLAN LIATH MOR
Tirry
Rhian
Shinness
Dalnessie
Black Water
Glen Cassley
Allt a'Bhunn
Achnairn
BEINN SGEIREACH 476
Loch Beannach
Brora
Dalchork
Dalchork Wood
Colaboll
Achnaluachrach
299
West Langwell
Strath Brora
Allt na Luibe
BEINN AN EOIN 554
Saval
Sallachy
Lairg Lodge
Loch Craggie
Dalreavoch
Glencassley Castle
Lairg Muir
Rhilochan
323
Loch na Fuaralaich
Lairg
A839
East Langwell
Farlary
FERRYCROFT COUNTRYSIDE CENTRE
Grudie Burn
Claonel
Muie
Strath Fleet
Glenrossal
Gruids
Torroble
402 CNOC A'CHOIRE
Cassley
Loch Cracail Mor
Ardachu
Rogart
Oykel Forest
Pittentrail
Invercassley
Rosehall
B864
336
HECTOR MACDONALD MONUMENT
Rogart Station
466 BEINN LUNN
Oykel Bridge
Strath Oykel
Achany
Shin Forest
Achany Glen
Shin
A837
Brae
Oape
Doune
Altass
Achinduich
Morvich
Fleet
Linsidemore
FALLS OF SHIN VISITOR CENTRE
Loch Laro
Loch Buidhe
Torboll Farm
Achnahanat
Little Torboll
Inveran
Invershin
Cambusmore Lodge
493 BEINN ULBHAIDH
349 BEINN DOMHNAILL
Craigton
Loch Fleet
Cambusavie Farm
Kyle of Sutherland
CARBISDALE CASTLE
297
Skelbo
507 MEALL DHEIRGIDH
1650
Culrain
Balblair
Achvaich
Badninish
Strath Cuileannach
Airdens
Evelix
Braelangwell Lodge
Clashcoig
Rearquhar
Poles
701 CARN A' CHOIN DEIRG
Carron
Strathcarron
Migdale
Proncy
B9168
Wester Gruinards
Soyal
Gablon
Pitgrudy
CROICH CHURCH
Croich
Bonar Bridge
Lower Gledfield
Loch Migdale
Evelix
HISTORYLINKS EXHIBITION
The Craigs
Amatnatua
Amat Forest
Dounie
Ardgay
Spinningdale
Ospisdale
Clashmore
Camore
A949
279
Alladale Lodge
Kincardine
DORNOCH
Whiteface
Skibo Castle
DORNOCH CATHEDRAL
Dornoch
Lonemore
Alladale
Glencalvie Lodge
Upper Ardchronie
Fearn Lodge
Dornoch Sands
Glencalvie Forest
645 CARN SALACHAIDH
Meikle Ferry
Ardmore
Cambuscurrie Bay
Easter Fearn
FIRTH
Wester Fearn Burn
Ferry Point
Edderton
Diebidale
Forest
Loch a'Chairn
B9176
Balleigh
GLENMORANGIE DISTILLERY
ALDIE WATERMILL
Crom Loch
Tarlogie
838 CARN CHUINNEAG
Meikle Gluich
Morangie
TAIN THROUGH TIME VISITOR CENTRE
Tain
714 BEINN THARSUINN
Glen Diebidale
Easter Fearn Burn
546
Aultnamain Inn
Quarryhill
321
602
Morangie Forest
Aldie
Hilton
157
Abhainn na Glasa
692 BEINN THARSUINN
0 1 2 3 4 5 6 miles
0 1 2 3 4 5 6 7 8 9 10 km
Braeantra
Strath Rusdale
East Lamington
Lamington
Newfield
Inchbae Forest
Black Water
Strath Rory
Logie Hill
Torran
CNOC CORR GUINIE

Loch Arichlinie
Knockfin Heights
Strath Beg
Achentoul
Kinbrace
B871
A897
Helmsdale
318 CNOC LOCH MHADADH
Dunbeath Water
Smerral
Latheronwheel Ho.
Latheronwheel
168
169
Kinbrace Burn
438 CNOC COIRE NA PEARNA
Berriedale Water
Braemore
283
Balnabruich
LAIDHAY CROFT MUSEUM
DUNBEATH HERITAGE CENTRE
Dunbeath
Dunbeath Bay
Knockally
DUNBEATH CASTLE
705 MORVEN
517 CNOC AN EIREANNAICH
Abhainn na Frithe
Suisgill Burn
Wag
626 SCARABEN
Ramscraigs
Altanduin
Borrobol Lodge
Langwell Forest
Borgue
Newport
Ceann Leathad nam Bò
Aultibea
STRATH OF KILDONAN
387 CREAG NAM FIADH
Kildonan Burn
555 CREAG SCALABSDALE
Langwell Water
Langwell Ho.
Berriedale
BADBEA CLEARANCE VILLAGE
Kildonan Lodge
BAILE AN ÒR GOLDRUSH SITE
BEINN DUBHAIN 414
422
Tuarie Burn
A9
Ousdale
Craggie
Craggie Burn
Torrish
Kilphedir
Ord Point
345
ELDRABLE HILL 417
Marrel
HELMSDALE
Navidale
TIMESPAN HERITAGE CENTRE
West Helmsdale
NC
628 BEINN DHORAIN
Glen Loth
592
Gartymore
Helmsdale
ND
Glen Sletdale
Portgower
Balnacoil
Lothmore
538 COL-BHEINN
Lothbeg
Gordonbush
Lothbeg Pt.
Loch Brora
HORN 521
Loch Horn
Achrimsdale
East Clyne
West Clyne
Clynelish
Dalchalm
CLYNELISH DISTILLERY
377 CAGAR FEOSAIG
Brora
Doll
Backies
DUNROBIN CASTLE MUSEUM & GARDENS
Golspie
Culmaily
LOCH FLEET
Littleferry
Fourpenny
Embo
Embo Street
WITCHES STONE
OLD POST OFFICE VISITOR CENTRE
NH
NJ
Tarbat Ness
TARBAT NESS LIGHTHOUSE
Wilkhaven
Whiteness Sands
TARBAT DISCOVERY CENTRE
Bindal
Portmahomack
Rockfield
Inver
Balnagall
Arboll
Tarrel
Lochslin
Loch Eye
158
B9165
Geanies House
Rhynie
Fearn Station
Hill of Fearn
Fearn
FEARN ABBEY
Loans of Tullich
Hilton of Cadboll
A
B
C
D
E
F
G
5
6
7
8
30
31
93
90
88

CAPE WRATH
Kearvaig
371 SGRIBHIS-BHEINN
Geodha Ruadh na Fola
Bay of Keisgaig
Inshore
Loch Keisgaig
Geodha Ruadh
457 FASHVEN
Am Balg
423 BEINN DEARG
Loch Airigh na Beinne
Sandwood Loch
Rubh'an Fhir Léithe
485 CREAG RIABHACH
Strath Shinary
Loch na Gainimh
332 GHLAS BHEINN
Sheigra
Balchrick
Droman
Oldshore Beg
Oldshoremore
Eilean Roin Mor
A838
521 FARRMHEALL
NC
Kinlochbervie
Loch Clash
Gualin Ho.
B801
Badcall
Achriesgill
Bagh Loch an Roin
Loch Inchard
Strath Dionard
L. na Claise Carnaich
Achlyness
Loch Dughaill
Ceathramh Garbh
Rhiconich
Ardmore Pt.
Rubha Ruadh
Ardmore
GANU MOR 908
Foinaven
Fanagmore
Tarbet
NORTH-WEST SUTHERLAND
Loch Laxford
Loch a'Garbh-bhaid Mór
Handa Island
Foindle
Sound of Handa
A894
Loch nam Brac
Laxford Bridge
Loch an Easain Uaine
Scourie Bay
787 ARKLE
Laxford
Scourie More
Scourie
Gorm Loch
Rubh'Aird an t-Sionnaich
A838
Lochstack Lodge
Upper Badcall
Lower Badcall
719 BEN STACK
Loch Stack
Strath Stack
Badcall Bay
BEINN AUSKAIRD 386
18
Eil. a'Bhreitheimh
LOCH A'MHUILINN
Loch Crocach
Achfary
332
REAY FOREST
A894
Lochmore Lodge
Rubha a'Mhucard
Loch More
Meall Mór
Calbha Mór
Loch na Creige Duibhe
Duartmore Forest
Eddrachillis Bay
Calbha Beag
Loch an Leathaid Bhuain
Aultanrynie
Point of Stoer
Oldany Island
Loch a'Chairn Bhain
R. nan Còsan
Cirean Geardail
Kylestrome
Kinloch
161
Eilean Chrona
Loch Nedd
547
Culkein Drumbeg
Glendhu
Forest
Kylesku
Culkein
Clashnessie Bay
Oldany
B869
Loch Glendhu
Glean Dubh
Cluas Deas
Unapool
Drumbeg
Nedd
Loch Glencoul
530 BEINN AIRD DA LOCH
Achnacarnin
8
Loch Poll
Newton
Clashmore
Gleann Leireag
Glen Coul
Clashnessie
Balchladich
Rienachait
162
13
163
792 BEINN LEOID
Loch an Leothaid
808 QUINAG
Stoer
Loch an Eircill
0 1 2 3 4 5 6 miles
0 1 2 3 4 5 6 7 8 9 10 km
Loch Cròcach
Loch Beannach
EAS COUL AULIN WATERFALL
Lochassynt Lodge
A894
A837
776
BEINN UIDHE
R. Leumair
B869
1 2 3 4 5
A B C D E F

5
6
7
8
9
A
B
C
D
E
F
G
Faraid Head
Balnakeil Bay
BALNAKEIL CHURCH
Balnakeil
DURNESS VISITOR CENTRE
SMOO CAVE
Durness
DURNESS
BALNAKEIL CRAFT VILLAGE
Sangomore
Leirinmore
Keoldale
Sangobeg
Rispond
Kyle of Durness
Sarsgrum
422
MEALL MEADHONACH
Eilean Hoan
Whiten Head
Geodh'a' Bhrideoin
Eilean Clùimhrig
LOCH ERIBOLL
Portnancon
Heilam
Hope
Lochside
230
Eilean Choraidh
Eriboll
A838
Polla
Strath Beag
772
BEINN SPIONNAIDH
521
AN LEAN-CHARN
Loch Hope
Rubha Thormaid
408
BEN HUTIG
Strathan
Midfield
Port Vasgo
West Strathan
Talmine
Skinnet
Midtown
A'Mhoine
A838
Achuvoldrach
NC
Druim nan Cliar
KYLE OF TONGUE
CASTLE VARRICH
TONGUE
Kirkiboll
Tongue
Rabbit Is.
Tongue Bay
Skullomie
Coldbackie
310
A836
Ribigill
Kinloch Lodge
Loch na Seilg
Eilean nan Ron
Caol Raineach
Neave I. or Coombe I.
Skerray
Achtoty
Airdtorrisdale
Torrisdale
Torrisdale Bay
Borgie
Borgie Forest
Loch Craggie
168
Kirtomy Pt.
Farr Pt.
Kirtomy
Farr
STRATHNAVER MUSEUM
Swordly
A836
Bettyhill
Achina
Invernaver
Clachan Burn
Leckfurin
ACHANLOCHY CLEARANCE VILLAGE
Skelpick
B871
Skelpick Burn
Achagary
STRATHNAVER
Carnachy
Rhifail
293
BEINN RIFA-GIL
Skail
Langdale
Naver
Syre
Dalvina Lo.
ROSAL CLEARANCE TRAIL
B873
168
B871
Rimsdale Burn
Loch Dionard
Loch Crocach
927
BEN HOPE
Loch a' Ghobha-Dhuibh
764
BEN LOYAL
Loch an Dherue
527
BEINN STUMANADH
Loch Loyal
Loch Loyal Lodge
557
CNOC NAN CULLEAN
FEINNE-BHEINN MOR
465
Strath More
Alltnacaillich
DUN DORNAIGIL BROCH
Loch Haluim
Loch Syre
Glen Golly
416
Loch Coulside
Inchkinloch
Gobernuisgach Lodge
Loch Meadie
Loch Eileanach
294
POLE HILL
Highland
759
A836
Allt a' Chraois
Meadie Burn
Loch Coire na Saidhe Duibhe
Mudale
Altnaharra
B873
Loch Naver
Mallart
Naver Forest
Clebrig
Loch Rimsdale
Loch nan Cl
873
BEN HEE
Loch a'Ghorm-choire
Loch Truderscaig
272
Loch an Alltan Fhearna
328
838
34
Loch Merkland
473
Strath Vagastie
Kilbreck Burn
721
BEN KLIBRECK
Loch Choire Lodge
Merkland Lodge
163
Loch Fiag
404
961
MEALL NAN CON
Loch Choire Forest
164
Loch Choire
A836
Loch a'Ghriama
312
CNOC AN
642
581
704
BEN ARMINE
Gorm-loch Beag
orrykinloch
Dubh huail
ckiemore
CKIE

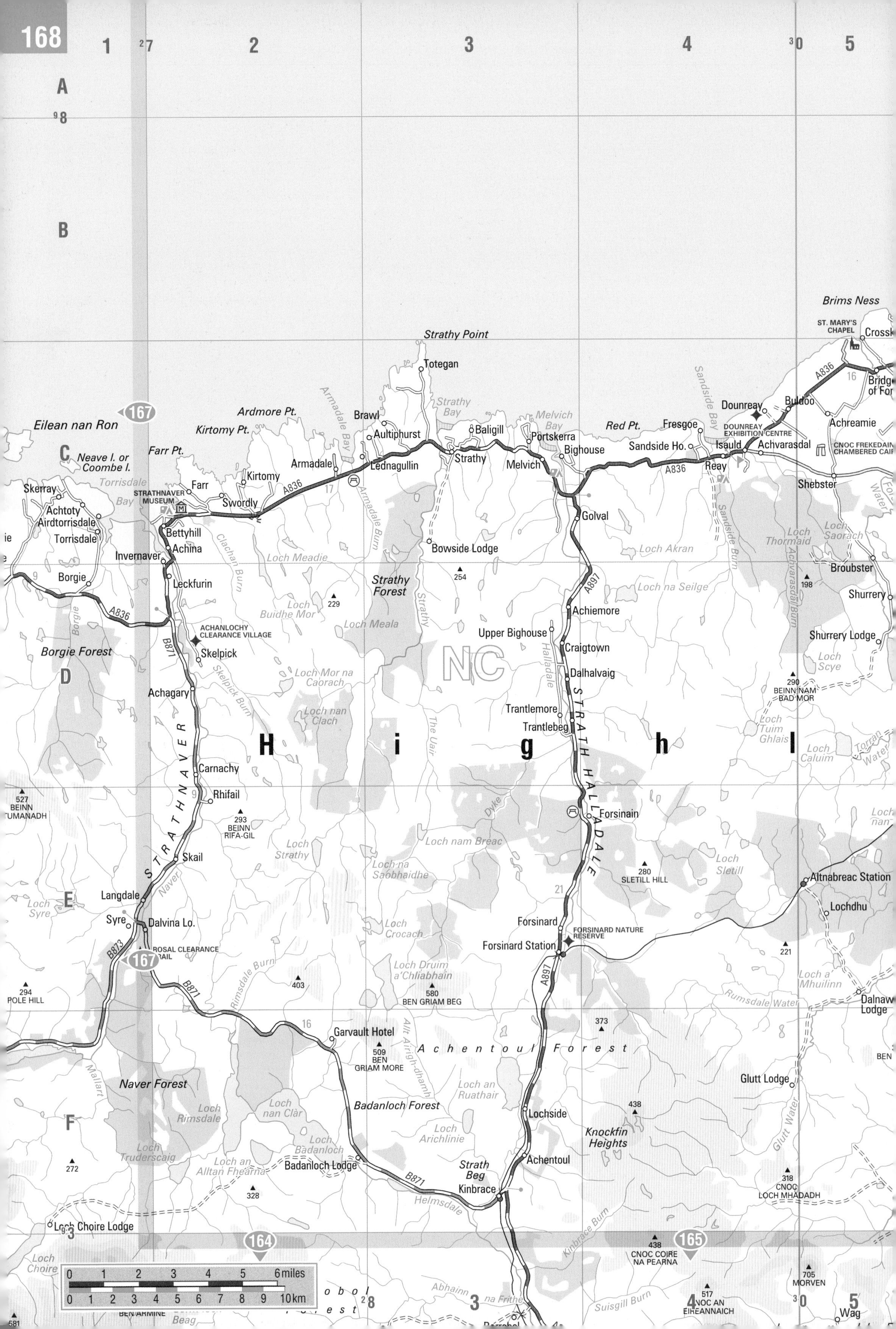

1
2
3
4
5
A
B
C
D
E
F
Strathy Point
Totegan
Brims Ness
ST. MARY'S CHAPEL
Crossk
A836
Bridg of For
Buldoo
Dounreay
DOUNREAY EXHIBITION CENTRE
Achreamie
Sandside Bay
Eilean nan Ron
167
Ardmore Pt.
Kirtomy Pt.
Armadale Bay
Strathy Bay
Melvich Bay
Red Pt.
Fresgoe
Brawl
Aultiphurst
Baligill
Portskerra
Bighouse
Sandside Ho.
Isauld
Achvarasdal
CNOC FREKEDAIN CHAMBERED CAIR
Neave I. or Coombe I.
Farr Pt.
Armadale
Lednagullin
Strathy
Melvich
A836
Reay
Torrisdale Bay
Kirtomy
Skerray
Farr
STRATHNAVER MUSEUM
Swordly
Shebster
Achtoty
Airdtorrisdale
Torrisdale
Bettyhill
Achina
Invernaver
Borgie
Leckfurin
Clachan Burn
Armadale Burn
Golval
Bowside Lodge
Loch Meadie
Loch Akran
Loch Thormaid
Loch Saorach
Broubster
Strathy Forest
254
A897
Loch na Seilge
198
Shurrery
Borgie
A836
Loch Buidhe Mor
229
Loch Meala
Strathy
Achiemore
Achvarasdal Burn
Sandside Burn
ACHANLOCHY CLEARANCE VILLAGE
Upper Bighouse
Shurrery Lodge
Borgie Forest
B871
Skelpick
NC
Craigtown
Halladale
Loch Scye
Dalhalvaig
Loch Mor na Caorach
Skelpick Burn
290
BEINN NAM BAD MOR
Achagary
Loch nan Clach
Trantlemore
Trantlebeg
STRATH HALLADALE
The Uair
Loch Tuim Ghlais
H
i
g
h
l
STRATHNAVER
Loch Caluim
Torran Water
Carnachy
Rhifail
527
BEINN TUMANADH
293
BEINN RIFA-GIL
Dyke
Forsinain
Loch nan
Loch Strathy
Loch nam Breac
Skail
Loch na Saobhaidhe
280
SLETILL HILL
Loch Sletill
Altnabreac Station
Naver
Loch Syre
Langdale
21
Lochdhu
Syre
Dalvina Lo.
Loch Crocach
Forsinard
FORSINARD NATURE RESERVE
Forsinard Station
ROSAL CLEARANCE TRAIL
B873
167
221
Rimsdale Burn
Loch Druim a'Chliabhain
A897
580
BEN GRIAM BEG
403
Loch a' Mhuilinn
294
POLE HILL
B871
Rumsdale Water
Dalnaw Lodge
16
373
Garvault Hotel
509
BEN GRIAM MORE
Allt Airigh-dhamh
Achentoul Forest
BEN
Mallart
Naver Forest
Loch an Ruathair
Glutt Lodge
Loch nan Clàr
Badanloch Forest
438
Loch Rimsdale
Lochside
Knockfin Heights
Glutt Water
Loch Arichlinie
Loch Badanloch
Loch Truderscaig
Achentoul
Strath Beg
Loch an Alltan Fhearna
Badanloch Lodge
B871
272
318
CNOC LOCH MHADADH
Kinbrace
328
Helmsdale
Kinbrace Burn
Loch Choire Lodge
164
165
438
CNOC NA PEARNA
Loch Choire
0 1 2 3 4 5 6 miles
0 1 2 3 4 5 6 7 8 9 10 km
705
MORVEN
517
NOC AN EIREANNAICH
Abhainn na Frithe
Suisgill Burn
Wag
581
BEN ARMINE
Beag

5
6
7
8
9
A
B
C
D
E
F
G
Swona
ST MARGARETS HOPE 1:00
176
Langaton Point
Nethertown
Red Head
Island of Stroma
Mell Head
Uppertown
BURWICK 0:45 (May-Sept)
DUNNET HEAD
Briga Hd.
Scarfskerry Pt.
Men of Mey
St John's Pt.
Boars of Duncansby
Scarfskerry
Gills Bay
East Mey
Brough
Ham
CASTLE OF MEY
Huna
DUNCANSBY HEAD
Hunspow
Rattar
Kirkstyle
STROMNESS 1:30
The Thirl
St John's Loch
Mey
Gills
A836
JOHN O'GROATS
John o' Groats
Spear Hd.
Holborn Hd.
MARY-ANN'S COTTAGE
Corsback
Barrock
Canisbay
Stacks of Duncansby
NATURAL HISTORY DISPLAY
Dunnet
Thurso Bay
Clardon Hd.
DUNNET BAY
Inkstack
Scrabster
THURSO CASTLE
THURSO FOLK MUSEUM
FLAGSTONE INTERPRETATIVE TRAIL
Castlehill
Loch Heilen
Brabster
Skirza
Skirza Head
Clardon
Murkle
Greenland
Lochend
Gill Burn
Tofts
Thurso
Thurso East
A836
Castletown
Freswick
Freswick Bay
Millbank
Haimer
CASTLETOWN
Tain
Slickly
Newlands of Geise
Olrig Ho.
Ness Head
BUCHOLLY CASTLE
Reaster
Geise
Hilliclay
Alterwall
NORTHLANDS VIKING CENTRE
Westfield
Weydale
Durran
Bowermadden
Lyth
LYTH ARTS CENTRE
Sortat
Auckengill
Nybster
Achingills
Barrock Ho.
Brough Head
Lieurary
Buckies
Stemster
Howe
Sordale
Bowertower
Keiss
KEISS CASTLE
Knockdee
Stemster Ho.
Braal Castle
Halcro
Mireland
Loch Calder
Hastigrow
Calder Mains
Roadside
Gillock
Kirk
Loch of Wester
Clayock
Loch Scarmclate
SINCLAIR'S
Halkirk
North Watten
Myrelandhorn
BAY
Banniskirk Ho.
Killimster
Loch Olginey
Scotscalder Station
Harpsdale
Mains of Watten
Loch Watten
Dorrery
Olgrinmore
CASTLE SINCLAIR
CASTLE GIRNIGOE
Noss Head
Reiss
Watten
Winless
Spittal
Backlass
Wick
Ackergill
Sealky Head
Loch of Toftingall
Bilbster
Staxigoe
Mybster
WICK HERITAGE CENTRE
Papigoe
Westerdale
Acharole
Strath
A882
Wick
Broadhaven
Burn of Acharole
Strath Burn
Stirkoke Ho.
Milton
Wick Bay
Loch Meadie
Achairn Burn
Newton
Old Wick
South Hd.
Badlipster
CASTLE OF OLD WICK
Whiterow
Gote O'Tram
Loch Eileanach
Strathmore Lodge
Little River
Tannach
Hempriggs House
Loch Gaineimh
Camster Burn
Loch Hempriggs
Helman Hd.
Lochmore Cottage
HILL OF OLICLETT
Thrumster
ND
Rangag
Gansclet
Loch More
GREY CAIRNS OF CAMSTER
Sarclet
Loch Ruard
Loch of Yarrows
Achavanich
Sarclet Hd.
Loch Thulachan
STEMSTER HILL
Camster
Ulbster
Loch Sand
Loch Rangag
CAIRN OF GET
Whaligoe
Roster
Crofts of Benachielt
HILL O' MANY STANES
Bruan
Loch Breac
Rumster Forest
Upper Lybster
Mid Clyth
Braehungie
Reisgill Burn
Loch Dubh
LYBSTER ART GALLERY
West Clyth
CNOCAN CONACHREAG
Forse Ho.
Swiney
Lybster
Houstry
WAG OF FORSE
Burn of Houstry
Smerral
Latheron
Forse
Dunbeath Water
CLAN GUNN HERITAGE CENTRE
Latheronwheel Ho.
Latheronwheel
Braemore
LAIDHAY CROFT MUSEUM
Balnabruich
165
DUNBEATH HERITAGE CENTRE
Dunbeath
Knockally
Dunbeath Bay
DUNBEATH CASTLE
Ramscraigs
SCARABEN

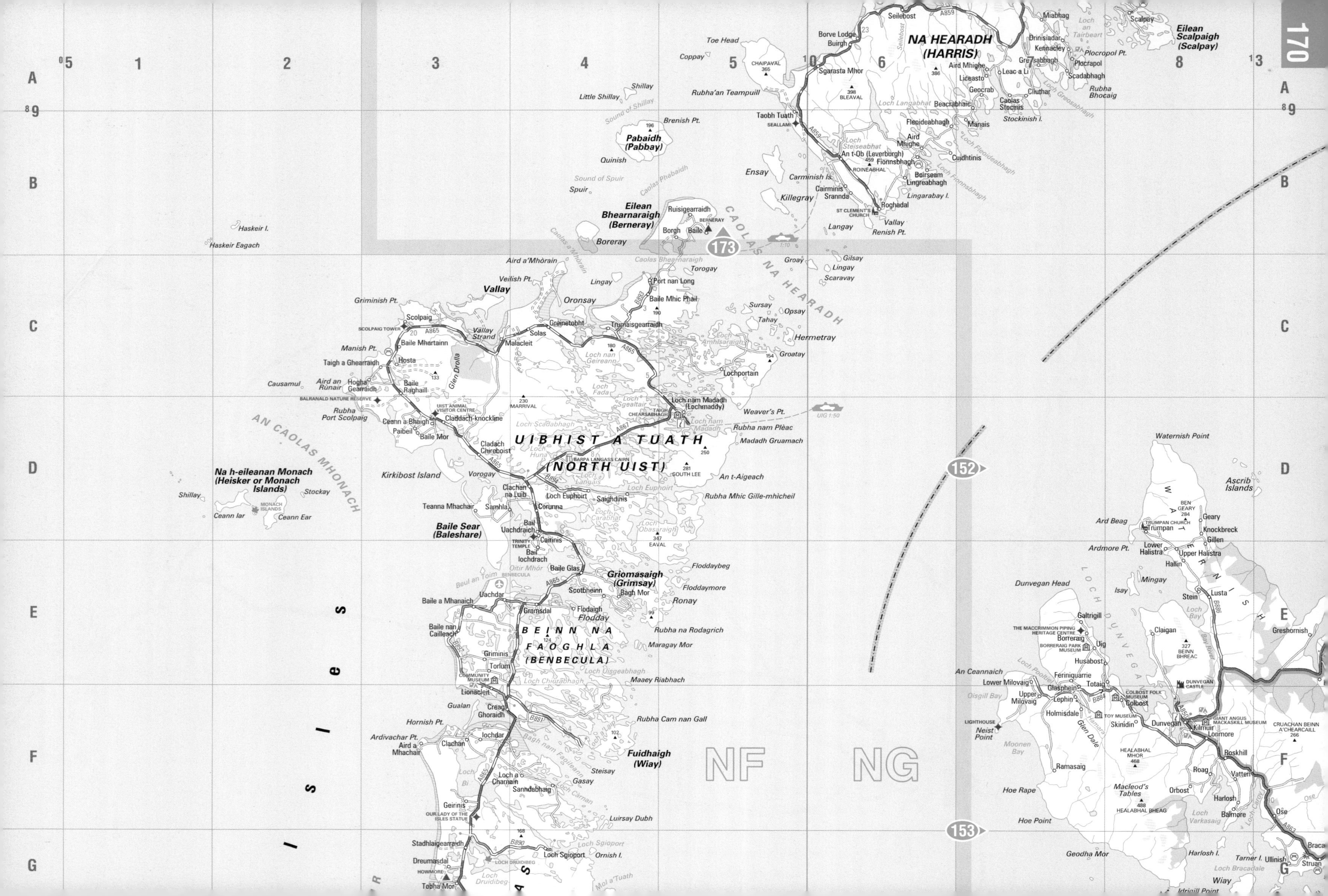
NA HEARADH (HARRIS)
Eilean Scalpaigh (Scalpay)
Pabaidh (Pabbay)
Eilean Bhearnaraigh (Berneray)
CAOLAS NA HEARADH
UIBHIST A TUATH (NORTH UIST)
BEINN NA FAOGHLA (BENBECULA)
Griomasaigh (Grimsay)
Fuidhaigh (Wiay)
Baile Sear (Baleshare)
Na h-eileanan Monach (Heisker or Monach Islands)
AN CAOLAS MHONACH
Loch nam Madadh (Lochmaddy)
Vallay
Oronsay
Kirkibost Island
Haskeir I.
Haskeir Eagach
Shillay
Ceann Iar
Ceann Ear
Stockay
Ensay
Killegray
Boreray
Lingay
Toe Head
Coppay
An t-Ob (Leverburgh)
Taobh Tuath
Tairbeart
Waternish Point
Ascrib Islands
Dunvegan Head
LOCH DUNVEGAN
Dunvegan
Neist Point
Macleod's Tables
Hoe Point
Hoe Rape
Glen Dale
NF
NG
152
153
173
Isles

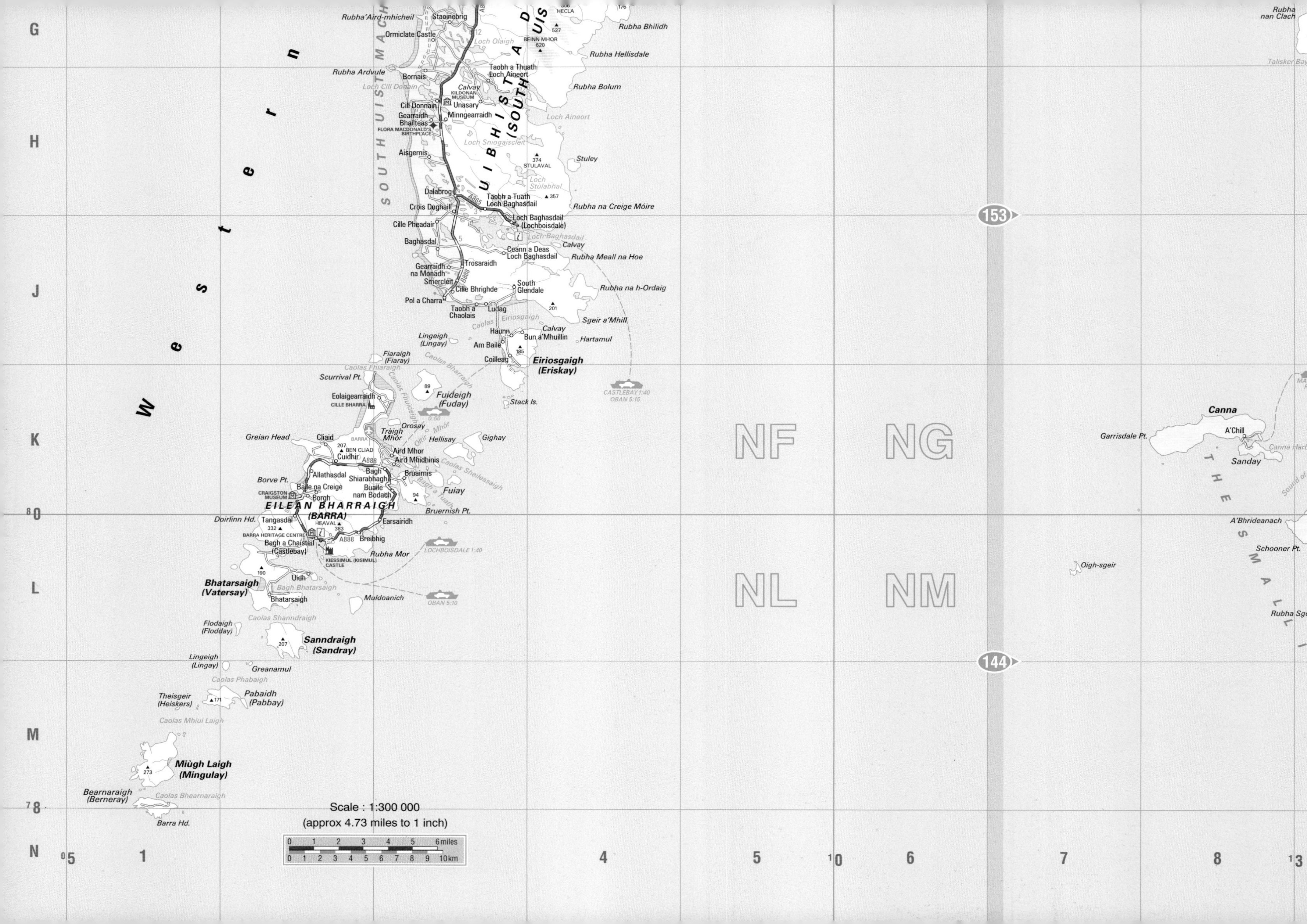
Western
UIBHIST A DEAS (SOUTH UIST)
SOUTH UIST MACHAIR
Rubha'Aird-mhicheil
Staoinebrig
Ormiclate Castle
Loch Olaigh
BEINN MHOR 620
HECLA
Rubha Bhilidh
Rubha Hellisdale
Rubha Ardvule
Bornais
Loch Cill Donain
Taobh a Thuath Loch Aineort
Calvay
KILDONAN MUSEUM
Unasary
Cill Donnain
Gearraidh Bhailteas
FLORA MACDONALD'S BIRTHPLACE
Minngearraidh
Rubha Bolum
Loch Aineort
Loch Sniogaiscleit
Aisgernis
374 STULAVAL
Loch Stùlabhal
Stuley
Dalabrog
Taobh a Tuath Loch Baghasdail
357
Crois Dughaill
Rubha na Creige Móire
Cille Pheadair
Loch Baghasdail (Lochboisdale)
Loch Baghasdail
Calvay
Baghasdal
Ceann a Deas Loch Baghasdail
Rubha Meall na Hoe
Trosaraidh
Gearraidh na Monadh
Smercleit
Cille Bhrighde
South Glendale
Rubha na h-Ordaig
Pol a Charra
Taobh a Chaolais
Ludag
201
Caolas Eiriosgaigh
Sgeir a'Mhill
Lingeigh (Lingay)
Haunn
Calvay
Bun a'Mhuillin
Hartamul
Am Baile
185
Coilleag
Eiriosgaigh (Eriskay)
Fiaraigh (Fiaray)
Caolas Fhiaraigh
Caolas Bharraigh
Scurrival Pt.
Caolas Fhuideigh
89
Fuideigh (Fuday)
CASTLEBAY 1:40 OBAN 5:15
Eolaigearraidh
CILLE BHARRA
0:50
Stack Is.
Orosay
Tràigh Mhòr
Oitir Mhòr
Greian Head
Cliaid
BARRA
Hellisay
Gighay
207 BEN CLIAD
Cuidhir
A888
Aird Mhor
Aird Mhidhinis
Caolas Sheileasaigh
Allathasdal
Bagh Shiarabhagh
Bruairnis
Borve Pt.
CRAIGSTON MUSEUM
Baile na Creige
Buaile nam Bodach
94
Fuiay
Bagh a Tuath
Borgh
EILEAN BHARRAIGH (BARRA)
Bruernish Pt.
Doirlinn Hd.
Tangasdal
HEAVAL 383
Earsairidh
332
BARRA HERITAGE CENTRE
Bagh a Chaisteil (Castlebay)
A888
Breibhig
KIESSIMUL (KISIMUL) CASTLE
Rubha Mor
LOCHBOISDALE 1:40
190
Uidh
Bhatarsaigh (Vatersay)
Bagh Bhatarsaigh
Bhatarsaigh
Muldoanich
OBAN 5:10
Caolas Shanndraigh
Flodaigh (Flodday)
Sanndraigh (Sandray)
207
Lingeigh (Lingay)
Greanamul
Caolas Phabaigh
Theisgeir (Heiskers)
171
Pabaidh (Pabbay)
Caolas Mhiui Laigh
273
Miùgh Laigh (Mingulay)
Bearnaraigh (Berneray)
Caolas Bhearnaraigh
Barra Hd.
Scale : 1:300 000
(approx 4.73 miles to 1 inch)
0 1 2 3 4 5 6 miles
0 1 2 3 4 5 6 7 8 9 10km
NF
NG
NL
NM
153
144
Rubha nan Clach
Fiskavaig
Gleann Oraid
Talisker
Talisker Bay
BEINN B
MALLAIG 2:30 RUM 1:15
Canna
A'Chill
Garrisdale Pt.
Canna Harbour
Sanday
Sound of Canna
Guirdil Bay
THE SMALL ISLES
A'Bhrideanach
571 ORVAL
Schooner Pt.
Oigh-sgeir
Harr
Rubha Sgorr an t-Snidhe
G
H
J
K
L
M
N
1
4
5
6
7
8
80
78
05
10
13

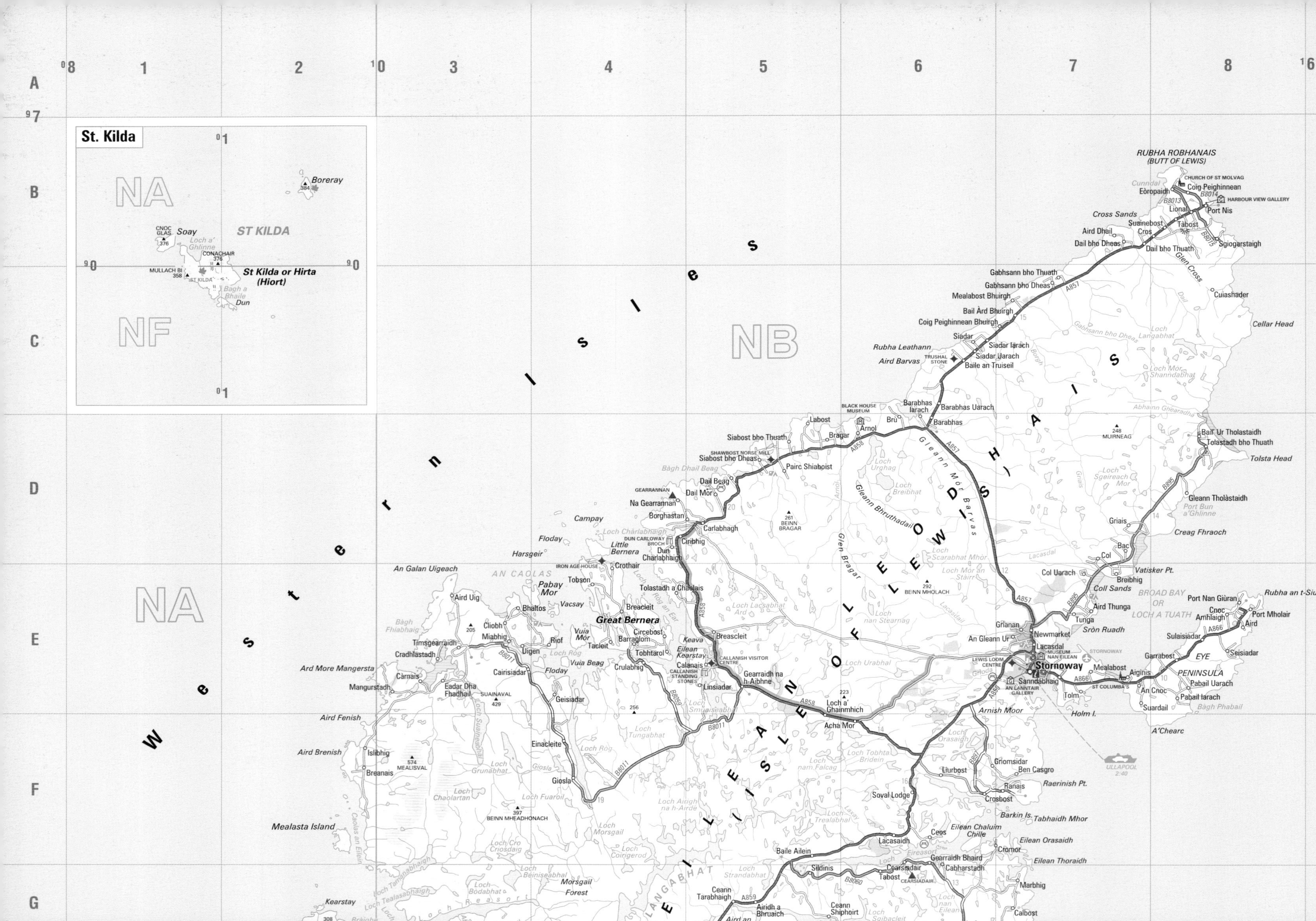
St. Kilda
St Kilda or Hirta (Hiort)
ST KILDA
Boreray
Soay
Dun
CONACHAIR
MULLACH BI
NA
NF
NB
NA
Western Isles
ISLE OF LEWIS
EILEAN LEÒDHAIS
RUBHA ROBHANAIS (BUTT OF LEWIS)
CHURCH OF ST MOLVAG
HARBOUR VIEW GALLERY
Coig Peighinnean
Port Nis
Eòropaidh
Lional
Tabost
Sgiogarstaigh
Suainebost
Cross
Cuiashader
Cellar Head
Glen Cross
Cross Sands
Dail bho Thuath
Dail bho Dheas
Aird Dhail
Gabhsann bho Thuath
Gabhsann bho Dheas
Mealabost Bhuirgh
Bail Àrd Bhuirgh
Siadar Iarach
Siadar Uarach
Baile an Truiseil
Siadar
Coig Peighinnean Bhuirgh
Rubha Leathann
Aird Barvas
TRUSHAL STONE
Barabhas Uarach
Barabhas
Barabhas Iarach
Brù
Arnol
BLACK HOUSE MUSEUM
Bragar
Labost
Siabost bho Thuath
Siabost bho Dheas
SHAWBOST NORSE MILL
Pairc Shiabost
Bàgh Dhail Beag
Dail Beag
Dail Mòr
Carlabhagh
GEARRANNAN
Na Gearrannan
Borghastan
Dun Charlabhaigh
DUN CARLOWAY BROCH
Cirbhig
Little Bernera
Great Bernera
IRON AGE HOUSE
Crothair
Campay
Floday
Harsgeir
Pabay Mòr
Vacsay
Vuia Mòr
Vuia Beag
Tobson
Bhaltos
Cliobh
Miabhig
Uigean
Riof
Aird Uig
An Galan Uigeach
AN CAOLAS
Timsgearraidh
Cradhlastadh
Càrnais
Mangurstadh
Ard More Mangersta
Aird Fenish
Aird Brenish
Mealasta Island
Kearstay
Breanais
Islibhig
Eadar Dha Fhadhail
Cairisiadar
SUAINAVAL
MEALISVAL
BEINN MHEADHONACH
Einacleite
Giosla
Geisiadar
Breascleit
Calanais
CALLANISH VISITOR CENTRE
CALLANISH STANDING STONES
Linsiadar
Keava
Eilean Kearstay
Tobhtarol
Crulabhig
Circebost
Barraglom
Tacleit
Breacleit
Tolastadh a Chaolais
Gearraidh na h-Aibhne
Acha Mòr
Loch a' Ghainmhich
Glen Bragar
Gleann Mòr Barvas
Gleann Bhruthadail
BEINN MHOLACH
MUIRNEAG
BEINN BRAGAR
Tolastadh bho Thuath
Bail' Ur Tholastaidh
Tolsta Head
Gleann Tholàstaidh
Port Bun a' Ghlinne
Creag Fhraoch
Griais
Bac
Col
Col Uarach
Vatisker Pt.
Breibhig
Coll Sands
BROAD BAY OR LOCH A TUATH
Aird Thunga
Tunga
Sròn Ruadh
Newmarket
Lacasdal
Stornoway
MUSEUM NAN EILEAN
AN LANNTAIR GALLERY
LEWIS LOOM CENTRE
Grianan
An Gleann Ur
Sanndabhaig
Mealabost
Aiginis
ST COLUMBA'S
Holm I.
Tolm
Suardail
An Cnoc
Pabail Iarach
Pabail Uarach
Seisiadar
EYE PENINSULA
Garrabost
Sulaisiadar
Port Nan Giùran
Cnoc Amhlaigh
Aird
Port Mholair
Rubha an t-Siumpain
Bàgh Phabail
A'Chearc
ULLAPOOL 2:40
Arnish Moor
Griomsidar
Ben Casgro
Raerinish Pt.
Ranais
Crosbost
Liurbost
Soval Lodge
Barkin Is.
Tabhaidh Mhor
Eilean Orasaidh
Eilean Thoraidh
Marbhig
Calbost
Eilean Chaluim Chille
Cromor
Ceos
Gearraidh Bhaird
Cabharstadh
Lacasaidh
Tabost
Cearsiadar
Ceann Shiphoirt
Baile Ailein
Sildinis
Airidh a Bhruaich
Ceann Tarabhaigh
Aird an Troim
Morsgail Forest
LANGABHAT
A857
A858
A859
A866
B895
B897
B8011
B8013
B8014
B8015
B8059
B8060

SOUTH LEWIS
HARRIS AND
CEANN A TUATH NA HEARADH
Forest of Harris
LOCH A SIAR
NORTH UIST
NA HEARADH
(HARRIS)
Eilean Scalpaigh
(Scalpay)
Tarasaigh
(Taransay)
Pabaidh
(Pabbay)
Eilean Bhearnaraigh
(Berneray)
CAOLAS NA HEARADH
UIBHIST A TUATH
(NORTH UIST)
Griomasaigh
(Grimsay)
Baile Sear
(Baleshare)
PARK OR PAIRC
Na h-Eileanan Mòra
(Shiant Islands)
CAOLAS NAN EILEAN
Eilean Iubhard
TROTTERNISH
WATERNISH
LOCH SNIZORT
LOCH DUNVEGAN
SOUND OF RAASAY
Eilean Garbh
NF
NG
170
152
Huisinis
Tairbeart
(Tarbert)
An t-Ob (Leverburgh)
Loch nam Madadh
(Lochmaddy)
Uig
Staffin
Kilt Rock
Duntulm
Aline Lodge
Scale : 1:300 000
(approx 4.73 miles to 1 inch)
0 1 2 3 4 5 6 miles
0 1 2 3 4 5 6 7 8 9 10 km

Shetland
HO
HP
HT
HU
UNST
YELL
FETLAR
MAINLAND
Muckle Flugga
Herma Ness
The Noup
Holm of Skaw
The Garths
Lamba Ness
Grunka Hellier
Orknagable
Norwick
North Stane
Valsgarth
Haroldswick
UNST BOAT HAVEN
The Nev
North Holms
South Holms
Burrafirth
Quoys
Baliasta
Buness
Baltasound
Balta
Valla Field
Spoo Ness
Caldback
Westing
Huney
Underhoull
Lund
Brough Taing
The Vere
Gloup Holm
Gloup Ness
Ness of Houlland
Gloup
Greenbank
Cullivoe
Stonganess
Geo of Markamouth
Belmont
Uyeasound
Clivocast
Muness
MUNESS CASTLE
Mu Ness
Ramnageo
Ness of Ramnageo
Haaf Gruney
Gutcher
South Garth
Uyea
The Hall
Wedder Holm
Linga
Winna Ness
Sellafirth
North Sandwick
Colvister
Cunnister
Sound Gruney
Urie Lingey
Daaey
Stack of Birrier
Nev of Stuis
Ramna Stacks
Gruney
Pt. of Fethaland
Isle of Fethaland
Lanyar Taing
Garmus Taing
Basta
Burra Ness
Hamars Ness
Brough Lodge
Strandburgh Ness
Head of Hosta
Grimister
Camb
Windhouse
Mid Yell
Hascosay
Tresta
Houbie
Aith
Funzie
Funzie Bay
FETLAR INTERPRETATIVE CENTRE
Lamb Hoga
Head of Lambhoga
The Snap
Rams Ness
COLGRAVE SOUND
Birrier
Aywick
Uyea
Fugla Ness
Isbister
Ness of Burravoe
Holm of West Sandwick
Harkland
North Roe
Hevdadale Hd.
South-haa
West Sandwick
Muckle Holm
Gruna Stack
The Faither
Otterswick
Hill of Arisdale
Swarister
Ness of Gossabrough
Gossabrough
Horse of Burravoe
Muckle Ossa
Ockran Hd.
Housetter
Little Holm
Hd. of Brough
West Yell
Neap of Skea
North Collafirth
RONAS HILL
The Brough
Ness of Sound
Brother Isle
Setter
Head of Stanshi
Hamnavoe
Scarff
Heylor
Voe
Ollaberry
Lamba
Uynarey
Ulsta
Hamnavoe
Houlland
Burravoe
Brough
VISITOR CENTRE
OLD HAA
Heoga Ness
Copister
ESHA NESS
TANGWICK HAA MUSEUM
Ure
Braehoulland
Burnside
Urafirth
Eastwick
Little Roe
Mio Ness
Gluss Isle
North Gluss
Bigga
Isle of Stenness
Stenness
Tangwick
Hillswick
Bardister
Calback Ness
Brough
Samphrey
Skerry of Eshaness
Dore Holm
Ness of Hillswick
Baa Taing
Burraland
Sullom Voe Oil Terminal
Mossbank
Lunna Holm
Lunna Ness
Fish Holm
Linga
Muckle Skerry
Housay
Bruray
Out Skerries
Grunay
Mio Ness
Isle of Nibon
Nibon
Sullom
Fugla Ness
Scatsta
Graven
Laxobigging
Hamnavoe
Mangaster
Haggrister
Trondavoe
Fora Ness
Lang Hd.
Egilsay
Islesburgh
Mavis Grind
Voxter
Lunna
The Guens
Filla
Brae
Busta
Burravoe
Button Hills
Collafirth
Swining
Lunning
Challister Ness
Skaw
Skaw Taing
WHALSAY
ST. MAGNUS BAY
SHETLAND

SHETLAND
Lerwick
Scalloway
Bressay
Isle of Noss
Whalsay
Vementry
Papa Little
Papa Stour
Foula
Fair Isle
West Burra
Trondra
Mousa
Vaila
Sumburgh
SUMBURGH HEAD
FITFUL HEAD
Mid Kame
Cliff Hills
Ward of Scousburgh
HT
HU
HZ
Fair Isle
FAIR ISLE LODGE & BIRD OBSERVATORY
GEORGE WATERSTON MUSEUM
Stoneybreck
SUMBURGH 2:40
TORSHAVN 12:00
BERGEN 12:30
SEYDISFJORDUR 30:00
(May-Sept)
ABERDEEN 14:00
KIRKWALL 6:00
WALLS 2:30
FOULA 2:30
FAIR ISLE 2:40
SHETLAND TEXTILE WORKING MUS.
TINGWALL AGRICULTURAL MUS.
SHETLAND MUSEUM
UP HELLY AA EXHIBITION
FORT CHARLOTTE
CROFT TRAIL
MOUSA BROCH
SHETLAND CROFT HOUSE MUSEUM
JARLSHOF PREHISTORIC SITE
STANEYDALE TEMPLE
CAVE OF THE BARD
A970
A971
B9071
B9074
B9075
B9073
B9122
Scale : 1:300 000
(approx 4.73 miles to 1 inch)
0 1 2 3 4 5 6 miles
0 1 2 3 4 5 6 7 8 9 10 km

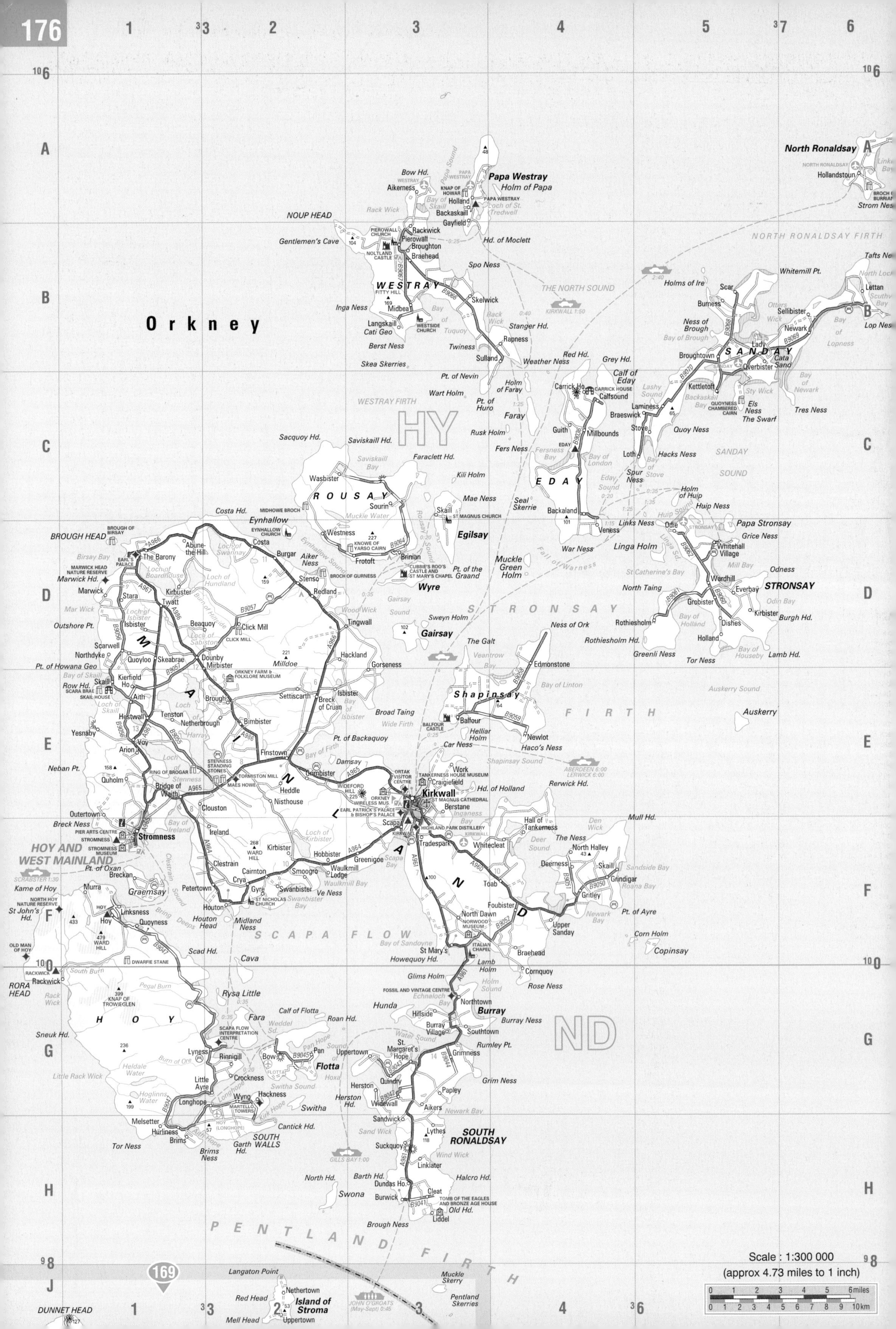

Orkney
North Ronaldsay
Hollandstoun
Strom Ness
NORTH RONALDSAY FIRTH
Tafts Ness
Lettan
Lop Ness
Papa Westray
Holm of Papa
Bow Hd.
Aikerness
Holland
Backaskaill
Gayfield
NOUP HEAD
Rack Wick
Gentlemen's Cave
Pierowall
Rackwick
Broughton
Braehead
Hd. of Moclett
Spo Ness
WESTRAY
Inga Ness
Midbea
Skelwick
Langskaill
Cati Geo
Berst Ness
Twiness
Rapness
Skea Skerries
Sulland
Stanger Hd.
Weather Ness
THE NORTH SOUND
Red Hd.
Grey Hd.
Calf of Eday
Carrick Ho.
Calfsound
Holms of Ire
Scar
Burness
Whitemill Pt.
Sellibister
Newark
Ness of Brough
Bay of Brough
Broughtown
SANDAY
Overbister
Kettletoft
Cata Sand
Bay of Lopness
Bay of Newark
Tres Ness
Laminess
Braeswick
Stove
Quoy Ness
Els Ness
The Swarf
Loth
Hacks Ness
SANDAY SOUND
Pt. of Nevin
Wart Holm
Holm of Faray
Pt. of Huro
Faray
WESTRAY FIRTH
HY
Sacquoy Hd.
Saviskaill Hd.
Faraclett Hd.
Rusk Holm
Fers Ness
Guith
Millbounds
EDAY
Spur Ness
Kili Holm
Mae Ness
Wasbister
ROUSAY
Sourin
Westness
Skaill
Egilsay
Seal Skerrie
Backaland
Veness
Holm of Huip
Huip Ness
Papa Stronsay
Grice Ness
Links Ness
Odie
Linga Holm
Whitehall Village
War Ness
Costa Hd.
Eynhallow
BROUGH HEAD
The Barony
Abune-the-Hill
Costa
Burgar
Aiker Ness
Brinian
Frotoft
Muckle Green Holm
Fall of Warness
St Catherine's Bay
Mill Bay
Odness
Marwick Hd.
Marwick
Stenso
Redland
Pt. of the Graand
Wyre
North Taing
Wardhill
Everbay
STRONSAY
Stara
Kirbuster
Twatt
Mar Wick
Outshore Pt.
Isbister
Beaquoy
Click Mill
Tingwall
Gairsay Sound
Gairsay
Sweyn Holm
STRONSAY
Ness of Ork
Rothiesholm
Grobister
Dishes
Kirbister
Burgh Hd.
Bay of Holland
Holland
Rothiesholm Hd.
Scarwell
Northdyke
Quoyloo
Skeabrae
Dounby
Mirbister
Milldoe
Hackland
Gorseness
The Galt
Edmonstone
Greenli Ness
Tor Ness
Lamb Hd.
Pt. of Howana Geo
Row Hd.
Skaill
Kierfield Ho
Aith
Brough
Settiscarth
Breck of Cruan
Isbister
Shapinsay
Bay of Linton
Auskerry Sound
Auskerry
Hestwall
Tenston
Netherbrough
Bimbister
Broad Taing
Balfour
Helliar Holm
Newlott
Haco's Ness
FIRTH
Yesnaby
Voy
Arion
Finstown
Pt. of Backaquoy
Car Ness
Neban Pt.
Quholm
Bridge of Waith
Damsay
Grimbister
Heddle
Nisthouse
Work
Craigiefield
Kirkwall
Hd. of Holland
Berstane
Rerwick Hd.
Shapinsay Sound
Outertown
Breck Ness
Clouston
Ireland
Stromness
Scapa
Kirbister
Hobbister
Tradespark
Whitecleat
Hall of Tankerness
Mull Hd.
Deer Sound
The Ness
North Halley
Deerness
Skaill
Grindigar
HOY AND WEST MAINLAND
Pt. of Oxan
Breckan
Clestrain
Cairnton
Crya
Smoogro
Greenigoe
Waulkmill Lodge
Toab
Gritley
Pt. of Ayre
Kame of Hoy
Murra
Graemsay
Petertown
Gyre
Swanbister
Ve Ness
Foubister
St John's Hd.
Linksness
Hoy
Quoyness
Houton
Houton Head
Midland Ness
North Dawn
Upper Sanday
Corn Holm
Copinsay
SCAPA FLOW
Bay of Sandoyne
Braehead
Scad Hd.
Cava
Howequoy Hd.
St Mary's
Lamb Holm
Cornquoy
Rose Ness
RORA HEAD
Rackwick
Glims Holm
Rysa Little
Hunda
Northtown
Burray
Burray Ness
Fara
Calf of Flotta
Roan Hd.
Hillside
Burray Village
Southtown
ND
Sneuk Hd.
HOY
Lyness
Rinnigill
Bow
Pan
Flotta
Uppertown
St. Margaret's Hope
Grimness
Rumley Pt.
Little Rack Wick
Crockness
Little Ayre
Hoxa
Quindry
Herston
Papley
Grim Ness
Longhope
Wyng
Hackness
Herston Hd.
Widewall
Aikers
Switha
Melsetter
Hurliness
Brims
Cantick Hd.
Sandwick
Lythes
SOUTH RONALDSAY
Tor Ness
Brims Ness
Garth Hd.
SOUTH WALLS
Suckquoy
Linklater
North Hd.
Swona
Barth Hd.
Dundas Ho.
Halcro Hd.
Burwick
Cleat
Old Hd.
Liddel
Brough Ness
PENTLAND FIRTH
Scale : 1:300 000
(approx 4.73 miles to 1 inch)
Langaton Point
Red Head
Nethertown
Island of Stroma
Mell Head
Uppertown
Muckle Skerry
Pentland Skerries
DUNNET HEAD
169

Aberdeen

0 Miles ¼

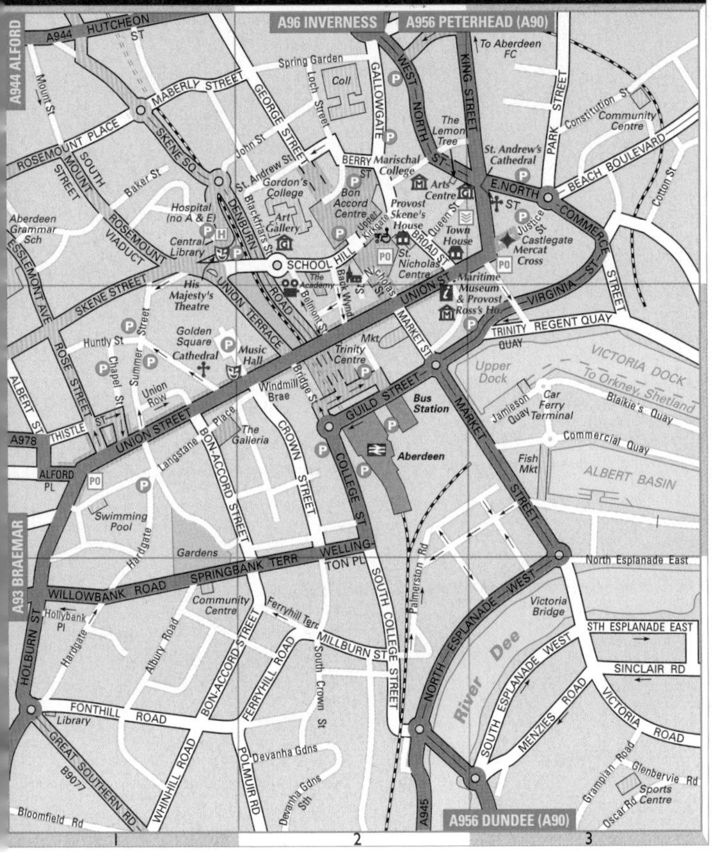

Aberystwyth

0 Miles ¼

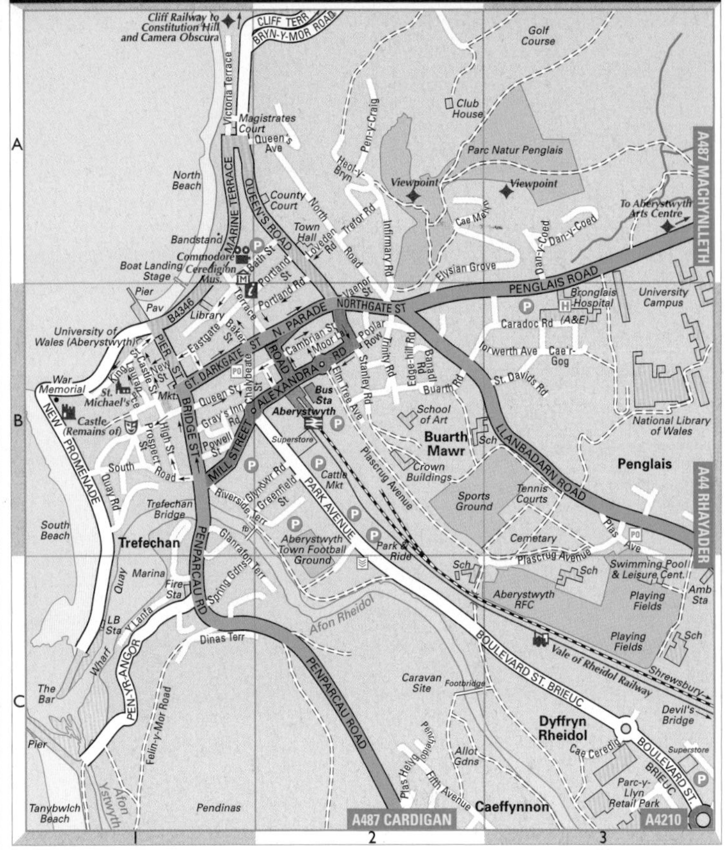

Aberdeen

ɔerdeen ⇌ B2
ɔerdeen Grammar
School A1
ɔademy, The B2
bert Basin B3
bert St B1
bury Rd C1
ford Pl B1
t Gallery 🏛 A2
ts Centre 🏛 A2
ack Wynd A2
aker St A1
each Blvd A3
elmont St B2
erry St A2
ackfriars St A2
aikie's Quay B3
oomfield Rd C1
on-Accord Centre . . . A2
on-Accord St B1
idge St B2
us Station B2
ar Ferry Terminal B3
astlegate A3
athedral ✝ B1
entral Library A1
hapel St B1
ollege St B2
ommerce St A3
ommercial Quay B3
ommunity
Centre A3/C1
onstitution St A3
Cotton St A3
Crown St B2
Denburn Rd A2
Devanha Gdns C2
Devanha Gdns South . C2
East North St A3
Esslemont Ave A1
Ferryhill Rd C2
Ferryhill Terr C2
Fish Market B3
Fonthill Rd C1
Galleria, The B1
Gallowgate A2
George St A2
Glenbervie Rd C3
Golden Sq B1
Gordon's College A2
Grampian Rd C3
Great Southern Rd . . . C1
Guild St B2
Hardgate B1
His Majesty's
Theatre 🎭 A1
Holburn St C1
Hollybank Pl C1
Hospital H A1
Huntly St B1
Hutcheon St A1
Information Ctr ℹ B2
Jamieson Quay B3
John St A2
Justice St A3
King St A2
Langstane Pl B1
Lemon Tree, The A2
Library C1
Loch St A2
Maberly St A1
Marischal College 🏛 . . A2
Maritime Museum &
Provost Ross's
House 🏛 B2
Market St B3
Menzies Rd C3
Mercat Cross ✦ A3
Millburn St C2
Miller St A3
Market B2
Market St B2
Mount St A1
Music Hall 🎭 B1
North Esp East C3
North Esp West C2
Oscar Rd C3
Palmerston Rd C2
Park St A3
Police Station ▣ A2
Polmuir Rd C2
Post Office PO . A2/A3/B1
Provost Skene's
House 🏛 A2
Queen St A2
Regent Quay B3
Rose St B1
Rosemount Pl A1
Rosemount Viaduct . . . A1
St Andrew St A2
St Andrew's
Cathedral ✝ A3
St Nicholas Centre . . . A2
St Nicholas St A2
School Hill A2
Sinclair Rd C3
Skene Sq A1
Skene St B1
South College St C2
South Crown St C2
South Esp East C3
South Esp West C3
South Mount St A1
Sports Centre C3
Spring Garden A2
Springbank Terr C1
Summer St B1
Swimming Pool B1
Thistle St B1
Town House 🏛 A2
Trinity Centre B2
Trinity Quay B3
Union Row B1
Union St B1
Union Terr B2
Upper Dock B3
Upper Kirkgate A2
Victoria Bridge C3
Victoria Dock B3
Victoria Rd C3
Virginia St A3
Wellington Pl B2
West North St A2
Whinhill Rd C1
Willowbank Rd C1
Windmill Brae B2

Aberystwyth

Aberystwyth RFC C3
Aberystwyth
Station ⇌ B2
Aberystwyth Town
Football Ground B2
Alexandra Rd B2
Ambulance Station . . . C3
Baker St B1
Banadl Rd B2
Bandstand A1
Bath St A2
Boat Landing Stage . . A1
Boulevard St. Brieuc . . C3
Bridge St B1
Bronglais Hospital H . . B3
Bryn-y-Mor Rd A2
Buarth Rd B2
Bus Station B2
Cae Ceredig C3
Cae Melyn A2
Cae'r-Gog B3
Cambrian St B2
Caradoc Rd B3
Caravan Site C2
Castle (Remains of) 🏰 . B1
Castle St B1
Cattle Market B2
Cemetary B3
Ceredigion
Museum 🏛 A1
Chalybeate St B1
Cliff Terr A2
Club House A2
Commodore 🎦 A1
County Court A2
Crown Buildings B2
Dan-y-Coed A3
Dinas Terr C1
Eastgate B1
Edge-hill Rd B2
Elm Tree Ave B2
Elysian Gr A2
Felin-y-Mor Rd C1
Fifth Ave C2
Fire Station C1
Glanrafon Terr B1
Glyndwr Rd B2
Golf Course A3
Gray's Inn Rd B1
Great Darkgate St B1
Greenfield St B2
Heol-y-Bryn A2
High St B1
Infirmary Rd A2
Information Ctr ℹ B1
Iorwerth Ave B3
King St B1
Lauraplace B1
Library B1
Lifeboat Station C1
Llanbadarn Rd B3
Loveden Rd A2
Magistrates Court A1
Marina C1
Marine Terr A1
Market B1
Mill St B1
Moor La B2
National Library
of Wales B3
New Promenade B1
New St B1
North Beach A1
North Parade B2
North Rd A2
Northgate St B2
Parc Natur Penglais . . A3
Parc-y-Llyn
Retail Park C3
Park & Ride B2
Park Ave B2
Pavillion B1
Pendinas C1
Penglais Rd B3
Penparcau Rd C1/C2
Penrheidol C2
Pen-y-Craig A2
Pen-yr-angor C1
Pier St B1
Plas Ave B3
Plas Helyg C2
Plascrug Ave B2/C3
Police Station ▣ C2
Poplar Row B2
Portland Rd B2
Portland St A2
Post Office PO B1/B3
Powell St B1
Prospect St B1
Quay Rd B1
Queen St B1
Queen's Ave A2
Queen's Rd A2
Riverside Terr B1
St. Davids Rd B3
St. Michael's ⛪ B1
School of Art B2
South Beach B1
South Rd B1
Sports Ground B2
Spring Gdns C1
Stanley Rd B2
Swimming Pool &
Leisure Centre C3
Tanybwlch Beach C1
Tennis Courts B3
Terrace Rd B1
The Bar C1
Town Hall A2
Trefechan Bridge B1
Trefor Rd A2
Trinity Rd B2
University Campus . . . B3
University of Wales
(Aberystwyth) B1
Vaenor St B2
Vale of Rheidol
Railway 🚂 C3
Victoria Terr A1
Viewpoint ✦ A2
Viewpoint ✦ A3
War Memorial B1
Y Lanfa C1

Barrow-in-Furness

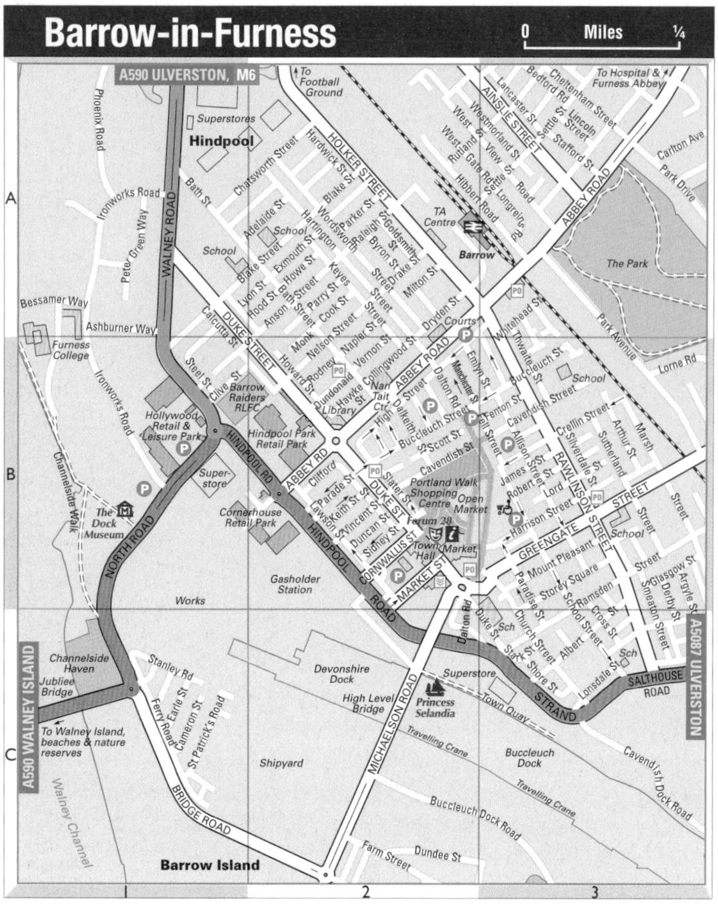

Bath

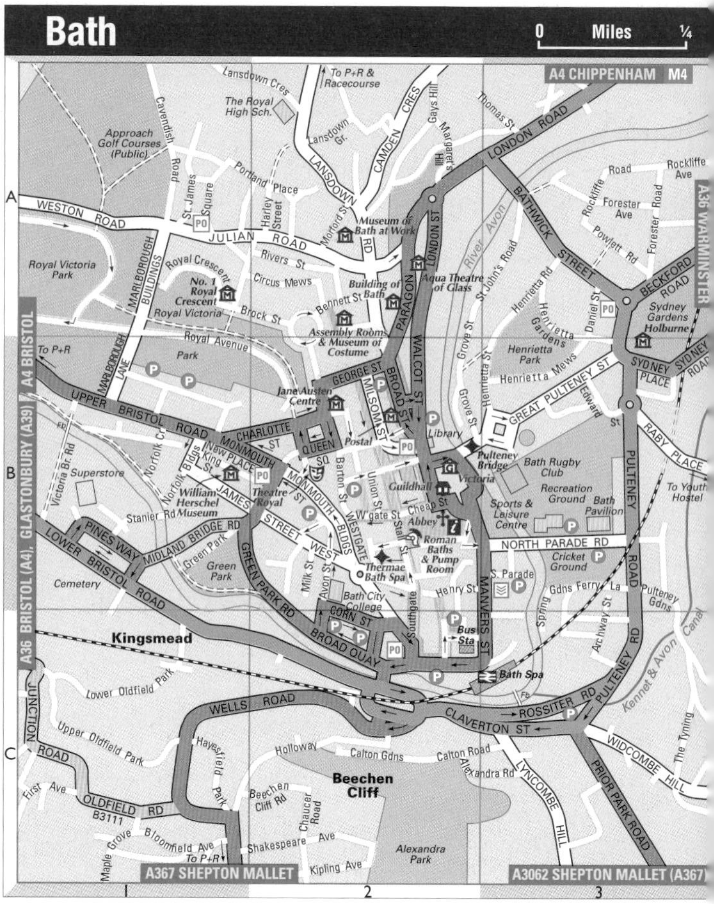

Barrow-in-Furness

Abbey Rd A3/B2
Adelaide St A2
Ainslie St A3
Albert St C3
Allison St B3
Anson St A2
Argyle St B3
Arthur St B3
Ashburner Way A1
Barrow Raiders RLFC . B1
Barrow Station ⇌ . . . A2
Bath St A1/B2
Bedford Rd A3
Bessamer Way A1
Blake St. A1/A2
Bridge Rd C1
Buccleuch Dock C3
Buccleuch
Dock Rd C2/C3
Buccleuch St. B2
Byron St A2
Calcutta St A1
Cameron St C1
Carlton Ave A3
Cavendish Dock Rd . . C3
Cavendish St. B2/B3
Channelside Walk B1
Channelside Haven . . . C1
Chatsworth St A2
Cheltenham St. A3
Church St C3
Clifford St B2
Clive St B1
Collingwood St B2
Cook St. A2
Cornerhouse
Retail Park. B2
Cornwallis St. B2
Courts A2
Crellin St B3
Cross St. C3
Dalkeith St. B2
Dalton Rd B2/C2
Derby St B3
Devonshire Dock. C2
Dock Museum,
The 🏛 B1
Drake St A2
Dryden St A2
Duke St A1/B2/C3
Duncan St B2
Dundee St C2
Dundonald St B2
Earle St C1
Emlyn St B2
Exmouth St A2
Farm St C2
Fell St B3
Fenton St. B3
Ferry Rd. C1
Forum 28 🎭. B2
Furness College B1
Glasgow St B3
Goldsmith St A2
Greengate St B3
Hardwick St. A2
Harrison St B3
Hartington St. A2
Hawke St. B2
Hibbert Rd. A2
High Level Bridge C2
High St B2
Hindpool Park
Retail Park. B2
Hindpool Rd B2
Holker St A2
Hollywood Retail &
Leisure Park B1
Hood St. A2
Howard St B2
Howe St. A2
Information Ctr ℹ B2
Ironworks Rd. A1/B1
James St B3
Jubliee Bridge C1
Keith St B2
Keyes St A2
Lancaster St A3
Lawson St. B2
Library B2
Lincoln St A3
Longreins Rd. A3
Lonsdale St C3
Lord St. B3
Lorne Rd B3
Lyon St A2
Manchester St. B2
Market B2
Market St. B2
Marsh St B3
Michaelson Rd C2
Milton St A2
Monk St. B2
Mount Pleasant B3
Nan Tait Centre B2
Napier St B2
Nelson St. B2
North Rd B1
Open Market B2
Parade St B2
Paradise St B3
Park Ave A3
Park Dr A3
Parker St A2
Parry St A2
Peter Green Way A1
Phoenix Rd A1
Police Station 🏛 B2
Portland Walk
Shopping Centre. . . . B2
Post Office PO . A3/B2/B3
Princess Selandia ⛵. . C2
Raleigh St A2
Ramsden St. B3
Rawlinson St B3
Robert St. B3
Rodney St B2
Rutland St A2
St Patrick's Rd. C1
Salthouse Rd. C3
School St B2
Scott St. B2
Settle St. A3
Shore St C3
Sidney St. B2
Silverdale St B3
Slater St. B2
Smeaton St B3
Stafford St. A3
Stanley Rd. C1
Stark St C3
Steel St B1
Storey Sq. B3
Strand C3
Sutherland St B3
TA Centre. A2
The Park A3
Thwaite St. B3
Town Hall. B2
Town Quay C3
Vernon St. B2
Vincent St B2
Walney Rd. A1
West Gate Rd A3
West View Rd A3
Westmorland St. A3
Whitehead St. A3
Wordsworth St. A2

Bath

Alexandra Park C2
Alexandra Rd. C2
Approach Golf
Courses (Public) A1
Aqua Theatre
of Glass 🏛 A2
Archway St C3
Assembly Rooms
& Museum of
Costume 🏛. A2
Avon St B2
Barton St. B2
Bath Abbey ✝ B2
Bath City College B2
Bath Pavilion B3
Bath Rugby Club. B3
Bath Spa Station ⇌. . . C3
Bathwick St. A3
Beechen Cliff Rd C2
Bennett St A2
Bloomfield Ave C1
Broad Quay C2
Broad St B2
Brock St A1
Building of Bath
Museum 🏛 A2
Bus Station C2
Calton Gdns C2
Calton Rd C2
Camden Cr A2
Cavendish Rd A1
Cemetery. B1
Charlotte St. B2
Chaucer Rd C2
Cheap St. B2
Circus Mews A2
Claverton St C2
Corn St C2
Cricket Ground B3
Daniel St A3
Edward St A3
Ferry La B3
First Ave C1
Forester Ave A3
Forester Rd A3
Gays Hill A2
George St B3
Great Pulteney St B3
Green Park B1
Green Park Rd. B2
Grove St. B2
Guildhall 🏛 B2
Harley St A2
Hayesfield Park C1
Henrietta Gdns A3
Henrietta Mews B3
Henrietta Park B3
Henrietta Rd A3
Henrietta St B3
Henry St B2
Holburne Museum 🏛 . B3
Holloway C2
Information Ctr ℹ B2
James St West . . . B1/B2
Jane Austen
Centre 🏛. B2
Julian Rd A1
Junction Rd C1
Kipling Ave C2
Lansdown Cr. A1
Lansdown Gr. A2
Lansdown Rd A2
Library B2
London Rd. A3
London St A2
Lower Bristol Rd B1
Lower Oldfield Park. . . C1
Lyncombe Hill C3
Manvers St B3
Maple Gr C1
Margaret's Hill A2
Marlborough
Buildings A1
Marlborough La. B1
Midland Bridge Rd . . . B1
Milk St B2
Milson St B2
Monmouth St B2
Morford St A2
Museum of Bath
at Work 🏛. A2
New King St B1
No. 1 Royal
Crescent 🏛. A1
Norfolk Bldgs A1
Norfolk Cr B1
North Parade Rd B3
Oldfield Rd C1
Paragon. A2
Pines Way A1
Police Station 🏛 B3
Portland Pl. A2
Post Office PO . . . .
. . . . A1/A3/B2/C2
Postal Museum 🏛. . . . B2
Powlett Rd. A3
Prior Park Rd. C3
Pulteney Bridge ✦ . . . B2
Pulteney Gdns. B3
Pulteney Rd. B3
Queen Sq B2
Raby Pl B3
Recreation Ground . . . B3
Rivers St A2
Rockliffe Ave A3
Rockliffe Rd. . . . . A
Roman Baths &
Pump Room 🏛 . . . . . B
Rossiter Rd C
Royal Ave . . . . A
Royal Cr. . . . . A
Royal High
School, The. . . . . A
Royal Victoria Park . . . A
St James Sq . . . . A
St John's Rd . . . . A
Shakespeare Ave C
Southgate C
South Pde . . . . B
Sports & Leisure
Centre . . . . B
Spring Gdns C
Stall St. . . . . B
Stanier Rd . . . . A
Sydney Gdns. . . . . A
Sydney Pl . . . . B
Theatre Royal 🎭 . . . . . B
Thermae Bath Spa ✦ . B
The Tyning C
Thomas St. . . . . A
Union St . . . . B
Upper Bristol Rd . . . . . B
Upper Oldfield Park. . . C
Victoria Art Gallery 🏛 . B
Victoria Bridge Rd . . . . B
Walcot St. . . . . B
Wells Rd C
Westgate St. . . . . B
Weston Rd. . . . . A
Widcombe Hill. C
William Herschel
Museum 🏛 . . . . B

Birmingham

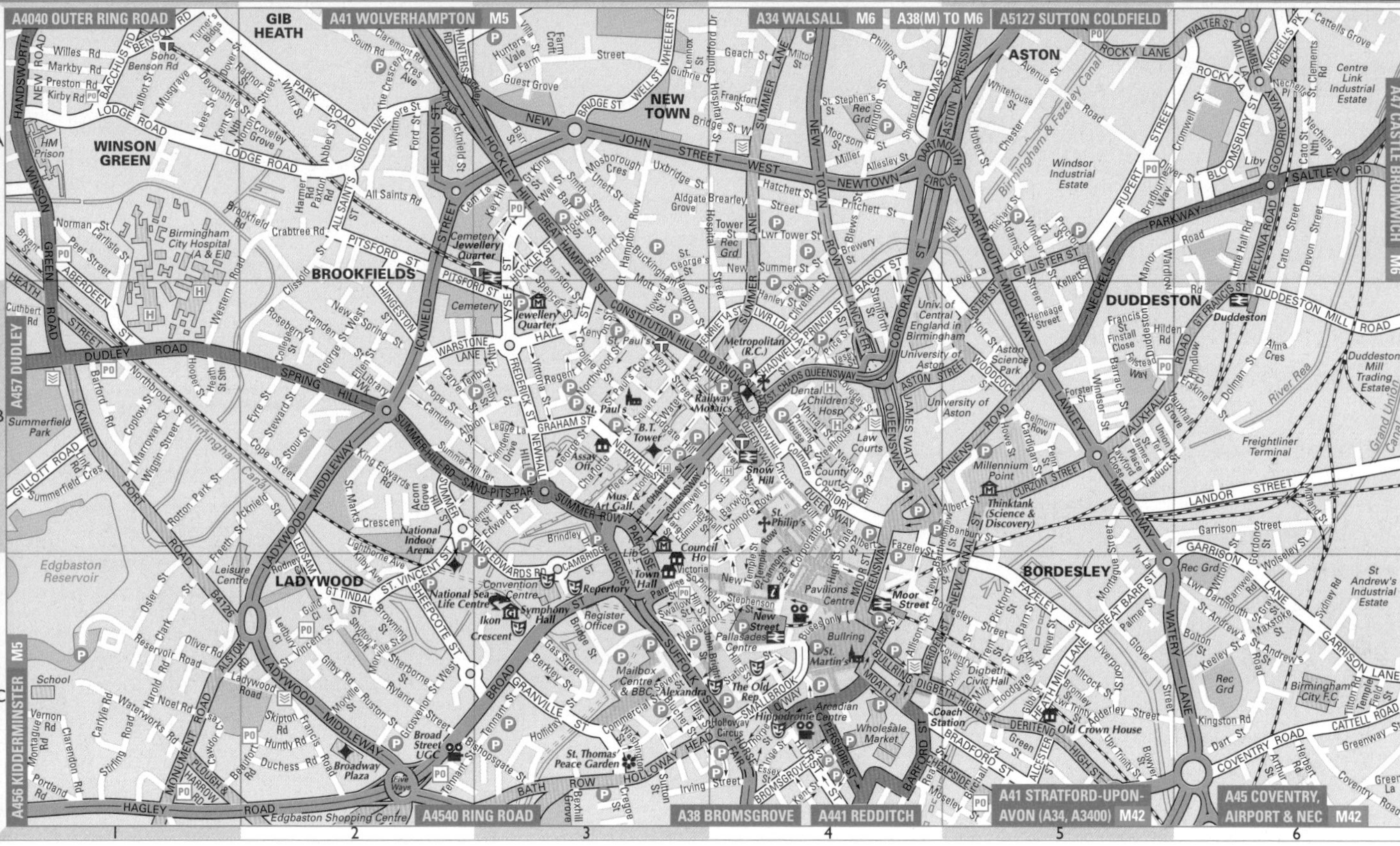

Birmingham

bbey St . . . A2
berdeen St . . . A1
corn Gr . . . B2
dams St. . . . A5
dderley St . . . C5
bert St . . . B4/B5
bion St . . . B2
cester St. . . . C5
dgate Gr. . . . A3
exandra Theatre . . C3
l Saint's St . . . A2
l Saints Rd . . . A2
lcock St . . . C5
lesley St . . . A4
lison St . . . C4
ma Cr . . . B6
ston Rd. . . . C1
rcadian Centre . . . C4
rthur St . . . C6
ssay Office . . . B3
ston Expressway. . . A5
ston Science Park. . . B5
ston St. . . . B4
venue Rd. . . . A5
T Tower ✦ . . . B3
acchus Rd. . . . A1
agot St . . . B4
anbury St . . . B5
arford Rd. . . . B1
arford St . . . C4
arn St . . . C5
arnwell Rd. . . . C6
arr St. . . . A3
arrack St . . . B5
artholomew St. . . . C4
arwick St. . . . B4
ath Row. . . . C3
eaufort Rd. . . . C1
elmont Row. . . . B5
enson Rd. . . . A1
erkley St . . . C3
exhill Gr. . . . C3
rchall St . . . C5
rmingham City F.C.
(St Andrew's). . . . C6
rmingham City
Hospital (A&E) . . . A1
shopsgate St . . . C3
ews St . . . A4
oomsbury St. . . . A6
ucher St . . . C3
ordesley St . . . C4
owyer St . . . C5
radburne Way . . . A5
radford St . . . C5
ranston St. . . . A3
rearley St. . . . A4
rewery St. . . . A4
ridge St . . . A3
ridge St . . . C3
ridge St West . . . A4
rindley Dr. . . . B3
road St . . . C3
road St UGC . . . C2
roadway Plaza ✦ . . . C2
Bromley St. . . . C5
Bromsgrove St . . . C4
Brookfield Rd . . . A2
Browning St. . . . C2
Bryant St . . . A1
Buckingham St . . . A3
Bullring . . . C4
Bull St . . . B4
Cambridge St . . . C3
Camden Dr . . . B3
Camden St . . . B2
Cannon St . . . C4
Cardigan St . . . B5
Carlisle St . . . A1
Carlyle Rd . . . C1
Caroline St. . . . B3
Carver St . . . B2
Cato St . . . A6
Cato St North . . . A6
Cattell Rd . . . C6
Cattells Gr . . . A6
Cawdor Cr. . . . C1
Cecil St . . . B4
Cemetery. . . . A2/B2
Cemetery La . . . A2
Centre Link
Industrial Estate . . . A6
Charlotte St. . . . B3
Cheapside . . . C4
Chester St . . . A5
Children's Hospital . B4
Church St . . . B4
Claremont Rd . . . A2
Clarendon Rd . . . C1
Clark St . . . C1
Clement St . . . B3
Clissold St . . . B2
Cliveland St . . . B4
Coach Station . . . C5
College St . . . B2
Colmore Circus . . . B4
Colmore Row . . . B4
Commercial St. . . . C3
Constitution Hill. . . . B3
Convention Centre . . . C3
Cope St . . . B2
Coplow St . . . B1
Corporation St. . . . B4
Council House . . . B3
County Court. . . . B4
Coveley Gr. . . . A2
Coventry Rd . . . C6
Coventry St . . . C5
Cox St . . . B3
Crabtree Rd. . . . A2
Cregoe St . . . C3
Crescent Ave. . . . A2
Crescent Theatre . . . C3
Cromwell St. . . . A6
Cromwell St. . . . B3
Curzon St . . . B5
Cuthbert Rd. . . . B1
Dale End . . . B4
Dart St. . . . C6
Dartmouth Circus . . . A4
Dartmouth Middleway. A5
Dental Hospital . . . B4
Deritend. . . . C5
Devon St . . . A6
Devonshire St . . . A1
Digbeth Civic Hall . . . C5
Digbeth High St. . . . C4
Dolman St . . . B6
Dover St . . . A1
Duchess Rd. . . . C2
Duddeston ⇌. . . . B6
Duddeston Manor Rd . B5
Duddeston Mill Rd . . . B6
Duddeston Mill
Trading Estate . . . B6
Dudley Rd . . . B1
Edgbaston Shopping
Centre . . . C2
Edmund St . . . B3
Edward St . . . B3
Elkington St. . . . A4
Ellen St . . . B2
Ellis St . . . C3
Erskine St . . . B6
Essex St . . . C4
Eyre St. . . . B2
Farm Croft. . . . A3
Farm St . . . A3
Fazeley St . . . B4
Felstead Way. . . . B5
Finstall Cl. . . . B5
Five Ways . . . C2
Fleet St . . . B3
Floodgate St . . . C5
Ford St. . . . A2
Fore St. . . . C4
Forster St. . . . B5
Francis Rd . . . C2
Francis St . . . B5
Frankfort St . . . A4
Frederick St. . . . B3
Freeth St . . . C1
Freightliner Terminal . . B6
Garrison La . . . C6
Garrison St . . . B6
Gas St . . . C3
Geach St . . . A4
George St . . . B3
George St West. . . . B2
Gibb St . . . C5
Gillott Rd . . . B1
Gilby Rd. . . . C2
Glover St . . . C5
Goode Ave . . . A2
Goodrick Way . . . A6
Gordon St . . . B6
Graham St. . . . B3
Granville St . . . C3
Gray St . . . C6
Great Barr St. . . . C5
Great Charles St . . . B3
Great Francis St . . . B6
Great Hampton Row . . A3
Great Hampton St. . . . A3
Great King St. . . . A3
Great Lister St. . . . A5
Great Tindal St . . . C2
Green La . . . C6
Green St . . . C5
Greenway St . . . C6
Grosvenor St West . . . C2
Guest Gr . . . A3
Guild Cl . . . C2
Guildford Dr. . . . A4
Guthrie Cl . . . A3
Hagley Rd . . . C1
Hall St . . . B3
Hampton St. . . . B3
Handsworth New Rd. . A1
Hanley St. . . . B4
Harford St . . . A3
Harmer Rd. . . . A2
Harold Rd . . . C1
Hatchett St . . . A4
Heath Mill La. . . . C5
Heath St . . . B1
Heath St South . . . B1
Heaton St . . . A2
Heneage St . . . B5
Henrietta St. . . . B4
Herbert Rd. . . . C6
High St . . . C4
High St . . . C5
Hilden Rd. . . . B5
Hill St. . . . C3
Hindlow Cl. . . . B6
Hingeston St . . . B2
Hippodrome
Theatre . . . C4
HM Prison . . . A1
Hockley Circus . . . A2
Hockley Hill . . . A3
Hockley St. . . . A3
Holliday St. . . . C3
Holloway Circus . . . C4
Holloway Head . . . C3
Holt St. . . . B5
Hooper St . . . B1
Horse Fair . . . C4
Hospital St. . . . A4
Howard St . . . B3
Howe St. . . . B5
Hubert St. . . . A5
Hunters Rd . . . A2
Hunters Vale . . . A3
Huntly Rd . . . C2
Hurst St. . . . C4
Icknield Port Rd. . . . B1
Icknield Sq. . . . B2
Icknield St . . . A2
Ikon Gallery . . . C3
Information Ctr . . . C4
Inge St. . . . C4
Irving St. . . . C3
Ivy La. . . . C5
James Watt
Queensway . . . B4
Jennens Rd . . . B5
Jewellery Quarter ⇌ . A3
Jewellery Quarter
Museum . . . B3
John Bright St. . . . C4
Keeley St. . . . C6
Kellett Rd. . . . B5
Kent St . . . C4
Kent St North . . . A1
Kenyon St . . . B3
Key Hill . . . A3
Kilby Ave . . . C2
King Edwards Rd . . . B2
King Edwards Rd . . . C3
Kingston Rd. . . . C6
Kirby Rd . . . A1
Ladywood Middleway . C2
Ladywood Rd . . . C1
Lancaster St . . . B4
Landor St. . . . B6
Law Courts . . . B4
Lawford Cl. . . . B5
Lawley Middleway. . . . B5
Ledbury Cl. . . . C2
Ledsam St. . . . B2
Lees St . . . A1
Legge La . . . B3
Lennox St . . . A3
Library . . . A6/C3
Library Walk. . . . B2
Lighthorne Ave . . . B2
Link Rd . . . B1
Lionel St . . . B3
Lister St. . . . B5
Little Ann St. . . . C5
Little Hall Rd . . . A6
Liverpool St. . . . C5
Livery St . . . B3
Lodge Rd. . . . A1
Lord St. . . . A5
Love La . . . A5
Loveday St . . . B4
Lower Dartmouth St . . C6
Lower Loveday St . . . B4
Lower Tower St . . . A4
Lower Trinty St . . . C5
Ludgate Hill . . . B3
Mailbox Centre
& BBC . . . C3
Margaret St . . . B3
Markby Rd. . . . A1
Marroway St . . . B1
Maxstoke St . . . C6
Melvina Rd . . . A6
Meriden St. . . . C4
Metropolitan (R.C.) ✝ . B4
Midland St. . . . B6
Milk St . . . C5
Mill St . . . A5
Millennium Point . . . B5
Miller St . . . A4
Milton St . . . A4
Moat La . . . C4
Montague Rd. . . . C1
Montague St . . . C5
Monument Rd . . . C1
Moor Street ⇌. . . . C4
Moor St Queensway . . C4
Moorsom St. . . . A4
Morville St . . . C2
Mosborough Cr . . . A3
Moseley St . . . C4
Mott St . . . B3
Museum &
Art Gallery . . . B3
Musgrave Rd. . . . A1
National Indoor
Arena ✦ . . . B2
National Sea Life
Centre . . . C3
Navigation St. . . . C3
Nechell's Park Rd . . . A6
Nechells Parkway . . . A5
Nechells Pl . . . A6
New Bartholomew St . C4
New Canal St . . . B5
New John St West. . . . A3
New Spring St. . . . B2
New St. . . . C4
New Street ⇌ . . . C4
New Summer St . . . A4
New Town Row . . . A4
Newhall Hill . . . B3
Newhall St. . . . B3
Newton St . . . B4
Newtown . . . A4
Noel Rd . . . C1
Norman St. . . . A1
Northbrook St . . . B1
Northwood St . . . B3
Norton St. . . . A2
Old Crown House . . C5
Old Rep Theatre,
The . . . C4
Old Snow Hill. . . . B4
Oliver Rd . . . C1
Oliver St. . . . A5
Osler St . . . C1
Oxford St. . . . C5
Pallasades Centre . . . C4
Palmer St. . . . C5
Paradise Circus. . . . C3
Paradise St . . . C3
Park Rd . . . A2
Park St. . . . C4
Pavilions Centre . . . C4
Paxton Rd . . . A2
Peel St. . . . A1
Penn St . . . B5
Pershore St . . . C4
Phillips St . . . A4
Pickford St. . . . C5
Pinfold St. . . . C4
Pitsford St . . . A2
Plough & Harrow Rd . . C1
Police Station . . .
. . . A4/B1/B4/C2/C4
Pope St . . . B2
Portland Rd . . . C1
Post Office . A1/A3/A5/
. . B1/B5/C1/C2/C3/C5
Preston Rd . . . A1
Price St . . . B4
Princip St. . . . B4
Printing House St . . . B4
Priory Queensway. . . . B4
Pritchett St . . . A4
Proctor St . . . A5
Queensway . . . B3
Radnor St . . . A2
Railway Mosaics ✦ . . . B4
Rea St . . . C4
Regent Pl. . . . B3
Register Office. . . . C3
Repertory Theatre . . C3
Reservoir Rd . . . C1
Richard St . . . A5
River St . . . C5
Rocky La . . . A5
Rodney Cl . . . C2
Roseberry St . . . B2
Rotton Park St. . . . B1
Rupert St . . . A5
Ruston St . . . C2
Ryland St. . . . C2
St Andrew's Industrial
Estate . . . C6
St Andrew's Rd . . . C6
St Andrew's St. . . . C6
St Bolton St. . . . C6
St Chads Circus . . . B4
St Chads Queensway . B4
St Clements Rd. . . . A6
St George's St. . . . A3
St James Pl. . . . B5
St Marks Cr. . . . B2
St Martin's . . . C4
St Paul's . . . B3
St Paul's
(Metro station). . . . B3
St Paul's Sq. . . . B3
St Philip's ✝. . . . B4
St Stephen's St . . . A4
St Thomas' Peace
Garden . . . C3
St Vincent St . . . C2
Saltley Rd . . . A6
Sand Pits Pde . . . B3
Severn St. . . . C3
Shadwell St . . . B4
Sheepcote St. . . . C2
Shefford Rd . . . A4
Sherborne St . . . C2
Shylton's Croft. . . . C2
Skipton Rd . . . C2
Smallbrook
Queensway . . . C4
Smith St. . . . A3
Snow Hill ⇌. . . . B4
Snow Hill Queensway . B4
Soho, Benson Rd
(Metro station). . . . A1
South Rd . . . A2
Spencer St . . . B3
Spring Hill . . . B2
Staniforth St . . . B4
Station St. . . . C4
Steelhouse La . . . B4
Stephenson St. . . . C4
Steward St. . . . B2
Stirling Rd . . . C1
Stour St . . . B2
Suffolk St. . . . C3
Summer Hill Rd . . . B2
Summer Hill St . . . B2
Summer Hill Terr . . . B2
Summer La . . . A4
Summer Row. . . . B3
Summerfield Cr . . . B1
Summerfield Park . . . B1
Sutton St . . . C3
Swallow St. . . . C3
Sydney Rd. . . . C6
Symphony Hall . . . C3
Talbot St . . . A1
Temple Row. . . . C4
Temple St . . . C4
Templefield St . . . C6
Tenby St . . . B3
Tenby St North . . . B2
Tennant St . . . C2
The Crescent. . . . A2
Thimble Mill La . . . A6
Thinktank (Science
& Discovery) . . . B5
Thomas St. . . . A4
Thorpe St. . . . C4
Tilton Rd . . . C6
Tower St . . . A4
Town Hall . . . C3
Trent St . . . C5
Turner's Buildings . . . A1
Unett St. . . . A3
Union Terr . . . B5
University of Central
England in
Birmingham. . . . B4
University of
Aston. . . . B4/B5
Upper Trinity St . . . C5
Uxbridge St . . . A3
Vauxhall Gr . . . B5
Vauxhall Rd . . . B5
Vernon Rd . . . C1
Vesey St . . . B4
Viaduct St . . . B5
Victoria Sq. . . . C3
Villa St . . . A3
Vittoria St. . . . B3
Vyse St . . . B3
Walter St . . . A6
Wardlow Rd. . . . A5
Warstone La . . . B2
Washington St. . . . C3
Water St. . . . B3
Waterworks Rd . . . C1
Watery La . . . C5
Well St . . . A3
Western Rd . . . B1
Wharf St . . . A2
Wheeler St. . . . A3
Whitehouse St. . . . A5
Whitmore St . . . A2
Whittall St . . . B4
Wholesale Market . . . C4
Wiggin St. . . . B1
Willes Rd . . . A1
Windsor Industrial
Estate . . . A5
Windsor St. . . . A5
Windsor St. . . . B5
Winson Green Rd . . . A1
Witton St . . . C6
Wolseley St . . . C6
Woodcock St. . . . B5

WEDNESFIELD
Perton
Wightwick Manor
WOLVERHAMPTON
Bantock House Museum
Castlecroft
Staffordshire and Worcestershire Canal
WILLENHALL
Bentley
Birchills Canal Museum
WALSALL
Bescot Stadium
BILSTON
DARLASTON
Penn
WEDNESBURY
COSELEY
SEDGLEY
WOMBOURNE
Baggeridge Country Park
TIPTON
Nature Centre
Upper Gornal
Himley Park
Himley Hall
Himley
Wildlife Centre
Lyndon
WEST BROMWICH
Sandwell Valley Country Park
Black Country Museum
Dudley Zoological Gardens
Gornalwood
DUDLEY
Swindon
Wall Heath
Oakham
Sandwell
The Public Site
Kingswinford
Pensnett
OLDBURY
Ashwood
Broadfield House Glass Museum
Ridgehill Wood
Netherton
SMETHWICK
Langley Green
ROWLEY REGIS
Merry Hill Centre
BRIERLEY HILL
Wordsley
Red House Glass Cone
Old Hill
Blackheath
Warley Woods
Stourbridge Canal
AMBLECOTE
Hurst Green
Stourton
Lye
Cradley
World's End
Gibbet Wood
STOURBRIDGE
HALESOWEN
Woodgate Valley Country Park
Whittington Common
Bunker's Hill Wood
Pedmore
Wychbury Hill
Woodgate
Weoley Castle
Hagley Wood
Uffmoor Wood
Frankley Services
Bartley Resr
Hagley
Hagley Park
Twiland Wood
Shenley Fields
Frankley Resr
West Hagley
Clent
Clent Hills Country Park
Romsley
Egg Hill
Ell Wood
Frankley Hill
Frankley
Blakedown
Holy Cross
Broome
Hurcott Wood
Great Farley Wood
Waseley Hills Country Park
Turves Green
Bissell Wood
Rubery
Longbridge
Lickey Hills
Lickey Hills Country Park
Belbroughton
Upper Bittell Reservoir
0 1 2 3 miles
0 1 2 3 4 5 km

ALDRIDGE
Little Aston
Hardwick
Roughley
Four Oaks
Streetly
Upper Nut Hurst
SUTTON PARK COUNTRY PARK
Doe Bank Wood
Pheasey
Westwood Coppice
Holly Hurst
Visitor Centre
SUTTON COLDFIELD
Reddicap Heath
Trickley Coppice
New Park Wood
Middleton
ASH END HOUSE FARM
CROFT FARM
North Wood
KINGSBURY WATER PARK
Kingstanding
Over Green
Curdworth
Short Heath
Walmley
Perry Park
Erdington
WATER ORTON
Bromford
CASTLE BROMWICH
COLESHILL
Aston
VILLA PARK
ASTON HALL
Perry Barr
Winson Green
BIRMINGHAM
Kingshurst
Tile Cross
Lea Hall
Chelmsley Wood
NATIONAL INDOOR ARENA
Edgbaston Resr
BIRMINGHAM ECO PARK
BLAKESLEY HALL
Bordesley Green
Yardley
Lyndon Green
Marston Green
SHELDON COUNTRY PARK
Sheldon
BIRMINGHAM INTERNATIONAL AIRPORT
Bickenhill Plantations
NATIONAL EXHIBITION CENTRE
BIRMINGHAM BOTANICAL GARDENS
EDGBASTON
Cannon Hill Park
Nature Centre
Moseley
RAILWAY MUSEUM
Acock's Green
NATIONAL MOTOR CYCLE MUSEUM
Selly Park
Selly Oak
Moor Green
SAREHOLE MILL
Elmdon Park
Ulverley Green
CADBURY WORLD
Stirchley
Bournville
Elmdon Heath
Hampton Coppice
Lode Heath
Barber's Coppice
HAMPTON-IN-ARDEN
Catherine de Barnes Heath
Yardley Wood
Shirley
SOLIHULL
Eastcote
King's Norton
Tudor Grange Park
Hillfield
Bill's Wood
Major's Green
Hawkesley
Hollywood
Trueman's Heath
Drakes Cross
Monkspath
KNOWLE
Cheswick Green
Bentley Heath
Wythall
M6
M6 Toll
M42
A38
A34
A45
A41
A452
A453
A4040
A435
A441
Grand Union Canal
Stratford-Upon-Avon Canal
Birmingham & Fazeley Canal
River Tame
River Cole

Blackpool

0 Miles ¼

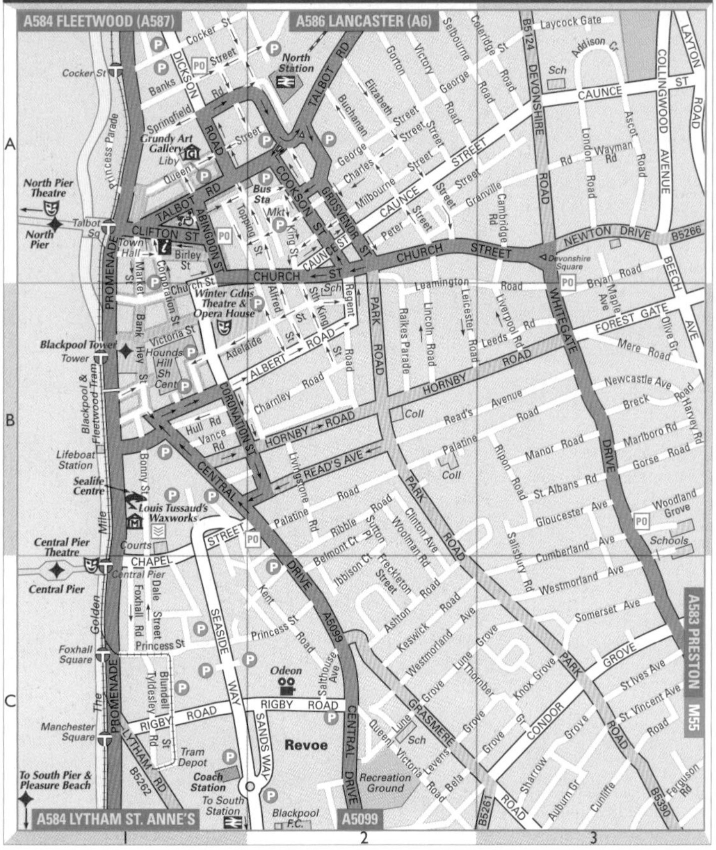

Bournemouth

0 Miles ¼

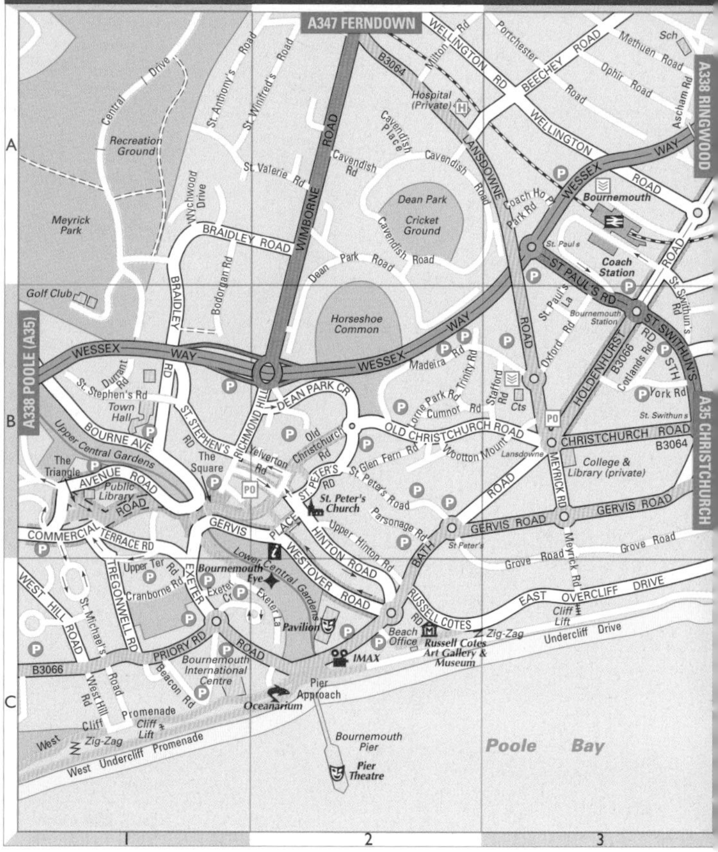

Blackpool

Abingdon St A1
Addison Cr A3
Adelaide St B1
Albert Rd B2
Alfred St B2
Ascot Rd A3
Ashton Rd C2
Auburn Gr C3
Bank Hey St B1
Banks St A1
Beech Ave B3
Bela Gr C2
Belmont Ct B2
Birley St A1
Blackpool & Fleetwood Tram B1
Blackpool F.C. C2
Blackpool Tower ✦ B1
Blundell St C1
Bonny St B1
Breck Rd B3
Bryan Rd A3
Buchanan St A2
Bus Station A2
Cambridge Rd A3
Caunce St A2
Central Dr B1
Central Pier ✦ C1
Central Pier (Tram stop) C1
Central Pier Theatre C1
Chapel St C1
Charles St A2
Charnley Rd B2
Church St A1
Clifton St A1
Clinton Ave B2
Coach Station C1
Cocker St A1
Cocker St (Tram stop) A1
Coleridge Rd A3
Collingwood Ave A3
Condor Gr C3
Cookson St A2
Coronation St B1
Corporation St A1
Courts B1
Cumberland Ave B3
Cunliffe Rd C3
Dale St C1
Devonshire Rd A3
Devonshire Sq A3
Dickson Rd A1
Elizabeth St A2
Ferguson Rd C3
Forest Gate B3
Foxhall Rd C1
Foxhall Sq (Tram stop) C1
Freckleton St C2
George St A2
Gloucester Ave B3
Golden Mile, The C1
Gorse Rd B3
Gorton St A2
Granville Rd A2
Grasmere Rd C2
Grosvenor St A2
Grundy Art Gallery A1
Harvey Rd B3
Hornby Rd B2
Hounds Hill Shopping Centre B1
Hull Rd B1
Ibbison Ct C2
Information Ctr A1
Kent Rd C2
Keswick Rd C2
King St A2
Knox Gr C3
Laycock Gate A3
Layton Rd A3
Leamington Rd B2
Leeds Rd B3
Leicester Rd B2
Levens Gr C2
Library A1
Lifeboat Station B1
Lincoln Rd B2
Liverpool Rd B3
Livingstone Rd B2
London Rd A3
Louis Tussaud's Waxworks B1
Lune Gr C2
Lytham Rd C1
Manchester Sq (Tram stop) C1
Manor Rd B3
Maple Ave B3
Market A2
Market St A1
Marlboro Rd B3
Mere Rd B3
Milbourne St A2
Newcastle Ave B3
Newton Dr A3
North Pier ✦ A1
North Pier Theatre A1
North Station A2
Odeon C2
Olive Gr B3
Palatine Rd B2
Park Rd B2
Peter St A2
Police Station B1
Post Office A1/B2/B3
Princess Pde A1
Princess St C1/C2
Promenade A1/C1
Queen St A1
Queen Victoria Rd C2
Raikes Pde B2
Read's Ave B2
Regent Rd B2
Ribble Rd B2
Rigby Rd C1
Ripon Rd B3
St Albans Rd B3
St Ives Ave C3
St Vincent Ave C3
Salisbury Rd B3
Salthouse Ave C2
Sands Way C2
Sealife Centre B1
Seaside Way C1
Selbourne Rd A2/A3
Sharrow Gr C3
Somerset Ave C3
Springfield Rd A1
South King St B2
Sutton Pl B2
Talbot Rd A1
Talbot Sq (Tram stop) A1
Thornber Gr C2
Topping St A1
Tower (Tram stop) B1
Town Hall A1
Tram Depot C1
Tyldesley Rd C1
Vance Rd B1
Victoria St B1
Victory Rd A2
Wayman Rd A3
Westmorland Ave C2
Whitegate Dr B3
Winter Gardens Theatre & Opera House B1
Woodland Gr B3
Woolman Rd B2

Bournemouth

Ascham Rd A3
Avenue Rd B1
Bath Rd C2
Beacon Rd C1
Beach Office C2
Beechey Rd A3
Bodorgan Rd B1
Bourne Ave B1
Bournemouth Eye ✦ C2
Bournemouth International Ctr C1
Bournemouth Pier C2
Bournemouth Station A3
Bournemouth Station (r'about) B3
Braidley Rd A1
Cavendish Place A2
Cavendish Rd A2
Central Drive A1
Christchurch Rd B3
Cliff Lift C1/C3
Coach House La A3
Coach Station A3
College & Library B3
Commercial Rd B1
Cotlands Rd B3
Courts B3
Cranborne Rd C1
Cricket Ground A2
Cumnor Rd B2
Dean Park A2
Dean Park Cr B2
Dean Park Rd A2
Durrant Rd B1
East Overcliff Dr C3
Exeter Cr C1
Exeter La C2
Exeter Rd C1
Gervis Place B1
Gervis Rd B3
Glen Fern Rd B2
Golf Club A1
Grove Rd B3
Hinton Rd C2
Holdenhurst Rd B3
Horseshoe Common B2
Hospital (Private) A2
IMAX C2
Information Ctr B2
Lansdowne (r'about) B3
Lansdowne Rd A2
Lorne Park Rd B2
Lower Central Gdns B2
Madeira Rd B2
Methuen Rd A3
Meyrick Park A1
Meyrick Rd B3
Milton Rd A2
Oceanarium C2
Old Christchurch Rd B2
Ophir Rd A3
Oxford Rd B3
Park Rd A3
Parsonage Rd B2
Pavilion C2
Pier Approach C2
Pier Theatre C2
Police Station A3/B3
Portchester Rd A3
Post Office B1/B3
Priory Rd C1
Recreation Ground A1
Richmond Hill Rd B1
Russell Cotes Art Gallery & Museum C2
Russell Cotes Rd C2
St Anthony's Rd A1
St Michael's Rd C1
St Paul's (r'about) B3
St Paul's La B3
St Paul's Rd A3
St Peter's B2
St Peter's (r'about) B2
St Peter's Rd B2
St Stephen's Rd B1
St Swithun's (r'about) B3
St Swithun's Rd A3
St Swithun's Rd South B
St Valerie Rd A
St Winifred's Rd A
Stafford Rd B
Terrace Rd B
The Square B
The Triangle B
Town Hall B
Tregonwell Rd C
Trinity Rd B
Undercliff Drive C
Upper Central Gdns B
Upper Hinton Rd B
Upper Terr Rd C
Wellington Rd A
Wessex Way B
West Cliff Promenade C
West Hill Rd C
West Undercliff Promenade C
Westover Rd B
Wimborne Rd A
Wootton Mount B
Wychwood Dr A
Yelverton Rd B
York Rd B
Zig-Zag Walks C1/C

Bradford

0 Miles ¼

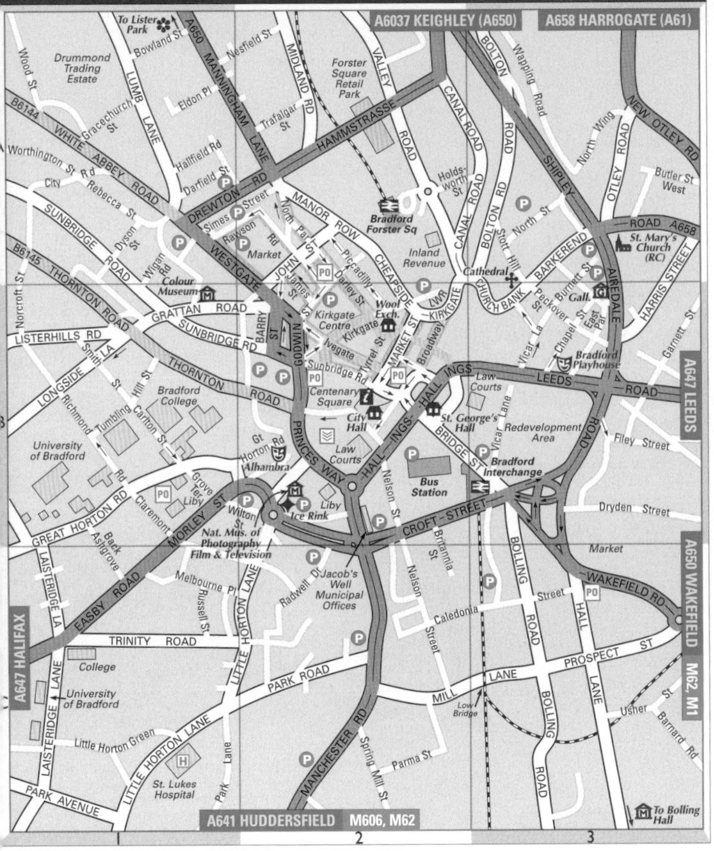

Brighton

0 Miles ¼

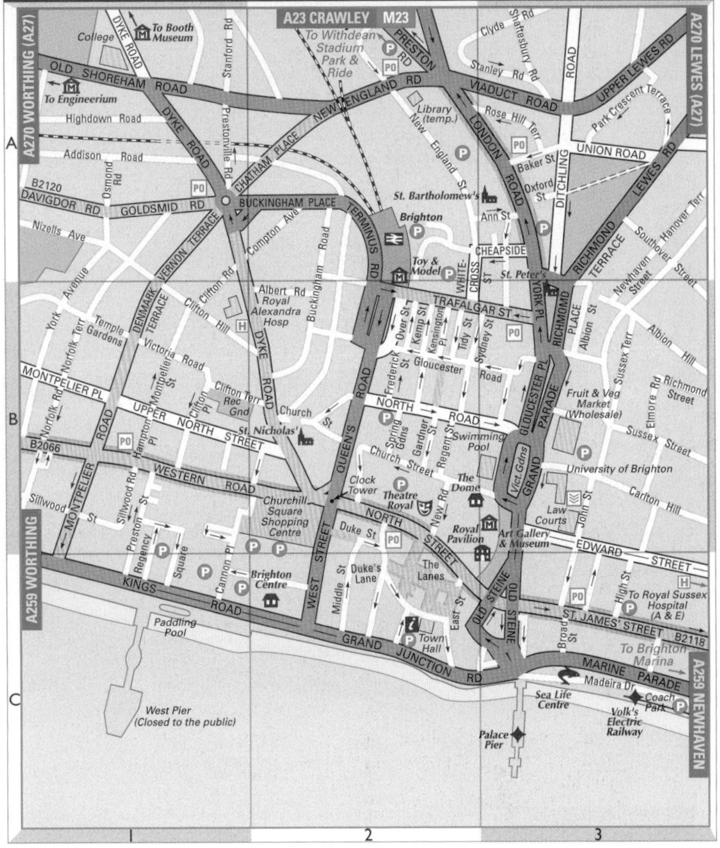

Bradford

Alhambra ♉ B2
Back Ashgrove B1
Barkerend Rd A3
Barnard Rd C3
Barry St B2
Bolling Rd C3
Bolton Rd A3
Bowland St A1
Bradford College B1
Bradford Forster Sq ⇌ A2
Bradford Interchange ⇌ B3
Bradford Playhouse ♉ B3
Bridge St B2
Britannia St B2
Broadway B2
Burnett St B3
Bus Station B2
Butler St West A3
Caledonia St C2
Canal Rd A2
Carlton St B1
Cathedral ✝ A3
Centenary Sq B2
Chapel St B3
Cheapside A2
Church Bank B3
City Hall 🏛 B2
City Rd A1
Claremont B1
Colour Museum 🏛 . . . B1
Croft St B2
Darfield St A1
Darley St A2
Drewton Rd A1
Drummond Trading Estate A1
Dryden St B3
Dyson St A1
Easby Rd C1
East Parade B3
Eldon Pl A1
Filey St B3
Forster Square Retail Park A2
Gallery 🏛 B3
Garnett St B3
Godwin St B2
Gracechurch St A1
Grattan Rd B1
Great Horton Rd B1
Grove Terr B1
Hall Ings B2
Hall La C3
Hallfield Rd A1
Hammstrasse A2
Harris St B3
Holdsworth St A2
Ice Rink ✦ B2
Information Ctr ℹ B2
Ivegate B2
James St A2
John St A2
Kirkgate B2
Kirkgate Centre B2
Laisteridge La C1
Law Courts B3
Leeds Rd B3
Library B1/B2
Listerhills Rd B1
Little Horton La C1
Little Horton Gn C1
Longside La B1
Lower Kirkgate B2
Lumb La A1
Manchester Rd C2
Manningham La A1
Manor Row A2
Market A2/C3
Market St B2
Melbourne Place C1
Midland Rd A2
Mill La C2
Morley St B1
Nat. Museum of Photography, Film & Television 🏛 B2
Nelson St B2
Nesfield St A2
New Otley Rd A3
Norcroft St B1
North Parade A2
North St A3
North Wing A3
Otley Rd A3
Park Ave C1
Park La C1
Park Rd C2
Parma St C2
Peckover St B3
Piccadilly A2
Police Station 🅂 B2
Post Office 🅿 A2/B1/B2/C3
Princes Way B2
Prospect St C3
Radwell Drive C2
Rawson Rd A1
Rebecca St A1
Richmond Rd B1
Russell St C1
St George's Hall 🏛 . . . B2
St Lukes Hospital H . . C1
St Mary's ⛪ A3
Shipley Airedale Rd A3/B3
Simes St A1
Smith St B1
Spring Mill St C2
Stott Hill A3
Sunbridge Rd A1
Thornton Rd A1
Trafalgar St A2
Trinity Rd C1
Tumbling Hill St B1
Tyrrel St B2
University of Bradford B1/C1
Usher St C3
Valley Rd A2
Vicar La B3
Wakefield Rd C3
Wapping Rd A3
Westgate A1
White Abbey Rd A1
Wigan Rd A1
Wilton St B1
Wood St A1
Wool Exchange 🏛 . . . B2
Worthington St A1

Brighton

Addison Rd A1
Albert Rd B2
Albion Hill B3
Albion St B3
Ann St A3
Art Gallery & Museum 🏛 B3
Baker St A3
Brighton ⇌ A2
Brighton Centre 🏛 . . . C2
Broad St C3
Buckingham Pl A2
Buckingham Rd B2
Cannon Pl C1
Carlton Hill B3
Chatham Pl A1
Cheapside A3
Church St B2
Churchill Square Shopping Centre B2
Clifton Hill B1
Clifton Pl B1
Clifton Rd B1
Clifton Terr B1
Clock Tower B2
Clyde Rd A3
Coach Park C3
Compton Ave A2
Davigdor Rd A1
Denmark Terr B1
Ditchling Rd A3
Dome, The 🏛 B2
Duke St B2
Duke's La C2
Dyke Rd A1
East St C2
Edward St B3
Elmore Rd B3
Frederick St B2
Fruit & Veg Market (wholesale) B3
Gardner St B2
Gloucester Pl B3
Gloucester Rd B2
Goldsmid Rd A1
Grand Junction Rd . . . C2
Grand Pde B3
Hampton Pl B1
Hanover Terr A3
High St C3
Highdown Rd A1
Information Ctr ℹ C2
John St B3
Kemp St B2
Kensington Pl B2
Kings Rd C1
Law Courts B3
Lewes Rd A3
Library (temp) A2
London Rd A3
Madeira Dr C3
Marine Pde C3
Middle St C2
Montpelier Pl B1
Montpelier Rd B1
Montpelier St B1
New England Rd A2
New England St A2
New Rd B2
Newhaven St A3
Nizells Ave A1
Norfolk Rd B1
Norfolk Terr B1
North Rd B2
North St B2
Old Shoreham Rd A1
Old Steine C3
Osmond Rd A1
Over St B2
Oxford St A3
Paddling Pool C1
Palace Pier ✦ C3
Park Crescent Terr A3
Police Station 🅂 B3
Post Office 🅿 . . . . A1/A2/ A3/B1/B2/B3/C3
Preston Rd A2
Preston St B1
Prestonville Rd A1
Queen's Rd B2
Regency Sq C1
Regent St B2
Richmond Pl B3
Richmond St B3
Richmond Terr A3
Rose Hill Terr A3
Royal Alexandra Hospital H B2
Royal Pavilion 🏛 B2
St Bartholomew's ⛪ . . A2
St James' St C3
St Nicholas' ⛪ B2
St Peter's ⛪ A3
Sea Life Centre 🐟 . . . C3
Shaftesbury Rd A3
Sillwood Rd B1
Sillwood St B1
Southover St A3
Spring Gdns B2
Stanford Rd A1
Stanley Rd A3
Sussex St B3
Sussex Terr B3
Swimming Pool B3
Sydney St B3
Temple Gdns B1
Terminus Rd A2
The Lanes C2
Theatre Royal ♉ B2
Tidy St B2
Town Hall C2
Toy & Model Museum 🏛 A1
Trafalgar St B2
Union Rd A3
University of Brighton . B3
Upper Lewes Rd A3
Upper North St B1
Vernon Terr A1
Viaduct Rd A3
Victoria Gdns B3
Victoria Rd B1
Volk's Electric Railway ✦ C3
West Pier (Closed to the Public) C1
West St C2
Western Rd B1
Whitecross St B2
York Ave B1
York Pl B3

Bristol

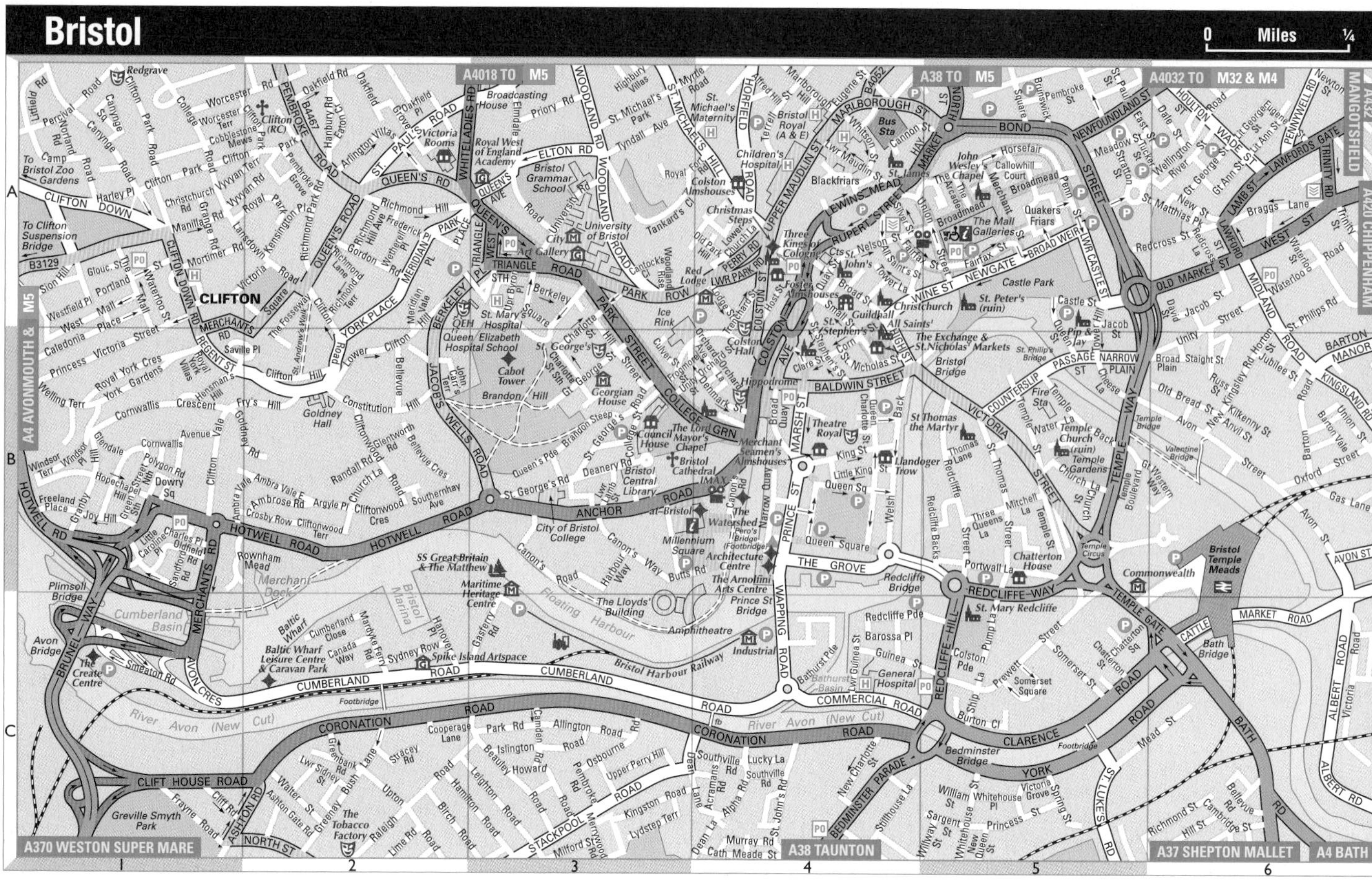
Bristol
0 Miles ¼
A4018 TO M5
A38 TO M5
A4032 TO M32 & M4
A432 MANGOTSFIELD
A420 CHIPPENHAM
A4 AVONMOUTH & M5
A370 WESTON SUPER MARE
A38 TAUNTON
A37 SHEPTON MALLET
A4 BATH
CLIFTON
HOTWELL ROAD
CUMBERLAND ROAD
CORONATION ROAD
River Avon (New Cut)
Floating Harbour
TEMPLE WAY
BOND ST
BALDWIN STREET
REDCLIFFE WAY
CLARENCE ROAD
COMMERCIAL ROAD
Bristol Temple Meads
Cabot Tower
Castle Park
Castle St
Victoria Rooms
Theatre Royal
Millennium Square
Bristol Cathedral
SS Great Britain & The Matthew
Plimsoll Bridge
Avon Bridge
Create Centre
Greville Smyth Park
Cumberland Basin
Bathurst Basin
Merchant Dock
Bristol Marina
A
B
C
1
2
3
4
5
6

Bristol

Acramans Rd C4
Albert Rd C6
Alfred Hill A4
All Saint's St A4
All Saints' B4
Allington Rd C3
Alpha Rd C4
Ambra Vale B1
Ambra Vale East B2
Ambrose Rd B2
Amphitheatre C3
Anchor Rd B3
Anvil St B6
Architecture Centre ✦ B4
Argyle Pl B2
Arlington Villas A2
Arnolfini Arts Centre, The ✦ B4
Art Gallery A3
Ashton Gate Rd C2
Ashton Rd C1
at-Bristol ✦ B3
Avon Bridge C1
Avon Cr C1
Avon St B6
Baldwin St B4
Baltic Wharf C2
Baltic Wharf Leisure Centre & Caravan Park ✦ C2
Barossa Pl C4
Barton Manor B6
Barton Rd B6
Barton Vale B6
Bath Rd C6
Bathurst Basin C4
Bathurst Parade C4
Beauley Rd C3
Bedminster Bridge C5
Bedminster Parade C4
Bellevue Cr B2
Bellevue B2
Bellevue Rd C6
Berkeley Pl A2
Berkeley Sq A3
Birch Rd C2
Blackfriars A4
Bond St A5
Braggs La A6
Brandon Hill B3
Brandon Steep B3
Bristol Bridge B5
Bristol Cathedral (CE) B3
Bristol Grammar School A3
Bristol Harbour Railway C3
Bristol Marina C2
Bristol Royal (A & E) A4
Bristol Temple Meads Station B6
Broad Plain B6
Broad Quay B4
Broad St A4
Broad Weir A5
Broadcasting House A3
Broadmead A5
Brunel Way C1
Brunswick Sq A5
Burton Cl C5
Bus Station A4
Butts Rd B3
Cabot Tower ✦ B3
Caledonia Pl B1
Callowhill Ct A5
Cambridge St C6
Camden Rd C3
Camp Rd A1
Canada Way C2
Cannon St A4
Canon's Rd B3/B4
Canon's Way B3
Cantock's Cl A3
Canynge Rd A1
Canynge Sq A1
Castle Park A5
Castle St A5
Catherine Meade St C4
Cattle Market Rd C6
Charles Pl B1
Charlotte St B3
Charlotte St South B3
Chatterton House B5
Chatterton Sq C5
Chatterton St C5
Cheese La B5
Children's Hospital A4
Christchurch A4
Christchurch Rd A1
Christmas Steps ✦ A4
Church La B5
Church St B5
City Museum A3
City of Bristol College B3
Clare St B4
Clarence Rd C5
Cliff Rd C1
Clift House Rd C1
Clifton Cathedral (RC) A2
Clifton Down Rd A1
Clifton Down A1
Clifton Hill B2
Clifton Park A2
Clifton Park Rd A1
Clifton Rd A2
Cliftonwood Cr B2
Cliftonwood Rd B2
Cliftonwood Terr B2
Clifton Vale B1
Cobblestone Mews A1
College Green B3
College Rd A1
College St B3
Colston Almshouses A4
Colston Ave B4
Colston Hall B4
Colston Parade C5
Colston St A4
Commercial Rd C4
Commonwealth Museum B6
Constitution Hill B2
Cooperage La C2
Corn St B4
Cornwallis Ave B1
Cornwallis Cr B1
Coronation Rd C3
Council House B3
Counterslip B5
Courts A4
Create Centre, The ✦ B1
Crosby Row B2
Culver St B3
Cumberland Basin C1
Cumberland Cl C2
Cumberland Rd C2
Dale St A6
David St A6
Dean La C4
Deanery Rd B3
Denmark St B4
Dowry Sq B1
East St A5
Eaton Cr A2
Elmdale Rd A3
Elton Rd A3
Eugene St A5
Exchange, The and St Nicholas' Mkts B4
Fairfax St A4
Fire Station B5
Floating Harbour C3
Foster Almshouses A4
Frayne Rd C1
Frederick Pl A2
Freeland Pl B1
Frogmore St B3
Fry's Hill B2
Gas La B6
Gasferry Rd C3
General Hospital C4
Georgian House B3
Glendale B1
Glentworth Rd B2
Gloucester St A1
Goldney Hall B2
Goldney Rd B1
Gordon Rd A2
Granby Hill B1
Grange Rd A1
Great Ann St A6
Great George St A6
Great George St B3
Great Western Way B6
Green St North B1
Green St South B1
Greenay Bush La C2
Greenbank Rd C2
Greville Smyth Park C1
Guildhall A4
Guinea St C4
Hamilton Rd C3
Hanbury Rd A2
Hanover Pl C2
Harbour Way B3
Harley Pl A1
Haymarket A5
Hensman's Hill B1
High St B4
Highbury Villas A3
Hill St B3
Hill St C6
Hippodrome B4
Hopechapel Hill B1
Horfield Rd A4
Horton St B6
Host St A4
Hotwell Rd B2
Houlton St A6
Howard Rd C3
Ice Rink B3
IMAX Cinema B4
Industrial Museum C4
Information Ctr B4
Islington Rd C3
Jacob St A5/A6
Jacob's Wells Rd B2
John Carr's Terr B2
John Wesley's Chapel A5
Joy Hill B1
Jubilee St B6
Kensington Pl A2
Kilkenny St B6
King St B4
Kingsland Rd B6
Kingston Rd C3
Lamb St A6
Lansdown Rd A2
Lawford St A6
Lawfords Gate A6
Leighton Rd C3
Lewins Mead A4
Lime Rd C2
Little Ann St A6
Little Caroline Pl B1
Little George St A6
Little King St B4
Litfield Rd A1
Llandoger Trow B4
Lloyds' Building, The C3
Lodge St A4
Lord Mayor's Chapel A4
Lower Castle St A5
Lower Church La A4
Lower Clifton Hill B2
Lower Guinea St C4
Lower Lamb St B3
Lower Maudlin St A4
Lower Park Rd A4
Lower Sidney St C2
Lucky La C4
Lydstep Terr C3
Manilla Rd A1
Mardyke Ferry Rd C2
Maritime Heritage Centre B3
Marlborough Hill A4
Marlborough St A4
Marsh St B4
Maternity Hospital A4
Mead St C5
Meadow St A5
Merchant Dock B2
Merchant Seamen's Almshouses B4
Merchant St A5
Merchants Rd A1
Merchants Rd C1
Meridian Pl A2
Meridian Vale A2
Merrywood Rd C3
Midland Rd A6
Milford St C3
Millennium Sq B3
Mitchell La B5
Mortimer Rd A1
Murray Rd C4
Myrtle Rd A3
Narrow Plain B5
Narrow Quay B4
Nelson St A4
New Charlotte St C4
New Kingsley Rd B6
New Queen St C5
New St A6
Newfoundland St A5
Newgate A5
Newton St A6
Norland Rd A1
North St C2
Oakfield Gr A2
Oakfield Pl A2
Oakfield Rd A2
Old Bread St B6
Old Market St A6
Old Park Hill A4
Oldfield Rd B1
Orchard Ave B4
Orchard La B4
Orchard St B4
Osbourne Rd C3
Oxford St B6
Park Pl A2
Park Rd C3
Park Row A3
Park St A3
Passage St B5
Pembroke Gr A2
Pembroke Rd A2
Pembroke Rd C3
Pembroke St A5
Penn St A5
Pennywell Rd A6
Percival Rd A1
Pero's Bridge B4
Perry Rd A4
Pip & Jay A5
Plimsoll Bridge B1
Police Sta A4/A6
Polygon Rd B1
Portland St A1
Portwall La B5
Post Office A1/A3/A4/A5/A6/B1/B4/C4/C5
Prewett St C5
Prince St B4
Prince St Bridge C4
Princess St C5
Princess Victoria St B1
Priory Rd A3
Pump La C5
QEH Theatre A2
Queen Charlotte St B4
Quakers Friars A5
Quay St A4
Queen Elizabeth Hospital School A2
Queen Sq B4
Queen St A5
Queen's Ave A3
Queen's Parade B3
Queen's Rd A2
Raleigh Rd C2
Randall Rd B2
Redcliffe Backs B5
Redcliffe Bridge B4
Redcliffe Hill C5
Redcliffe Parade C4
Redcliffe St B5
Redcliffe Way B5
Redcross La A6
Redcross St A6
Redgrave Theatre A1
Red Lodge A4
Regent St B1
Richmond Hill A2
Richmond Hill Ave A2
Richmond La A2
Richmond Park Rd A2
Richmond St C6
Richmond Terr A2
River St A6
Rownham Mead B2
Royal Fort Rd A3
Royal Park A2
Royal West of England Academy A3
Royal York Cr B1
Royal York Villas B1
Rupert St A4
Russ St B6
St Andrew's Walk B2
St George's B3
St George's Rd B3
St James A4
St John's A4
St John's Rd C4
St Luke's Rd C5
St Mary Redcliffe C5
St Mary's Hospital A3
St Matthias Park A6
St Michael's Hill A3
St Michael's Park A3
St Nicholas St B4
St Paul St A5
St Paul's Rd A2
St Peter's (ruin) A5
St Philip's Bridge B5
St Philips Rd A6
St Stephen's B4
St Stephen's St B4
St Thomas St B5
St Thomas the Martyr B5
Sandford Rd B1
Sargent St C5
Saville Pl B1
Ship La C5
Silver St A4
Sion Hill A1
Small St A4
Smeaton Rd C1
Somerset Sq C5
Somerset St C5
Southernhay Ave B2
Southville Rd C4
Spike Island Artspace C2
Spring St C5
SS Great Britain and The Matthew C3
Stackpool Rd C3
Staight St B6
Stillhouse La C4
Stracey Rd C2
Stratton St A5
Sydney Row C2
Tankard's Cl A3
Temple Back B5
Temple Boulevard B5
Temple Bridge B5
Temple Church B5
Temple Gate C5
Temple St B5
Temple Way B5
Terrell St A4
The Arcade A5
The Fosseway A2
The Mall Galleries Shopping Ctr A5
The Grove B4
The Horsefair A5
The Mall A5
Theatre Royal B4
Thomas La B5
Three Kings of Cologne A4
Three Queens La B5
Tobacco Factory, The C
Tower Hill B
Tower La A
Trenchard St A
Triangle South A
Triangle West A
Trinity Rd A
Trinity St A
Tucker St A
Tyndall Ave A
Union St A
Union St B
Unity St A
Unity St B
University of Bristol A
University Rd A
Upper Maudlin St A
Upper Perry Hill C
Upper Byron Pl A
Upton Rd C
Valentine Bridge B
Victoria Gr C
Victoria Rd C
Victoria Rooms A
Victoria Sq A
Victoria St B
Vyvyan Rd A
Vyvyan Terr A
Wade St A
Walter St C
Wapping Rd C
Water La B
Waterloo Rd A
Waterloo St A
Waterloo St A
Watershed, The ✦ B
Welling Terr B
Wellington Rd A
Welsh Back B
West Mall A
West St A
Westfield Pl A
Wetherell Pl A
Whitehouse Pl C5
Whitehouse St C5
Whiteladies Rd A
Whitson St A
William St C5
Willway St C5
Windsor Pl B
Windsor Terr B
Wine St A
Woodland Rise A
Woodland Rd A
Worcester Rd A
Worcester Terr A
YHA ▲ B
York Gdns B
York Pl A
York Rd C5

BRISTOL
YATE
Goose Green
Nibley
Engine Common
Mayshill
Westerleigh
Pucklechurch
Westerleigh Hill
Abson
Wick
Holbrook Common
Beach
North Stoke
Kelston
Upton Cheyney
Swineford
Saltford
Bitton
Iron Acton
Frampton End
Coalpit Heath
Ram Hill
Henfield
Shortwood
Siston
Webb's Heath
Bridge Yate
North Common
Goose Green
Siston Common
Warmley
Cadbury Heath
Oldland
Longwell Green
KEYNSHAM
Frampton Cotterell
Watley's End
Kendleshire
Winterbourne Down
Mangotsfield
Soundwell
KINGSWOOD
Latteridge
North Corner
Winterbourne
Frogland Cross
Pye Corner
Whiteshill
Bromley Heath
Downend
Hillfields
Frenchay
Fishponds
Speedwell
St. George
Hanham
Hanham Green
Conham
Queen Charlton
Stoke Gifford
Harry Stoke
Bradley Stoke
Great Stoke
Little Stoke
Broomhill
Clay Hill
Crew's Hole
St. Anne's Park
Broom Hill
Brislington
Flowers Hill
Stockwood
Whitchurch
PATCHWAY
Broad Mead
Lockleaze
Stapleton
Eastville
Arno's Vale
Knowle
Hengrove
Almondsbury
FILTON
Horfield
Ashley Down
Montpelier
Windmill Hill
Filwood Park
Hengrove Park
Over
Cribbs Causeway
Catbrain
Bristol (Filton)
Southmead
Henleaze
Golden Hill
Bishopston
Redland
Cotham
Lower Knowle
Novers Park
Hartcliffe
Easter Compton
Brentry
Eastfield
Westbury Park
HARTCLIFFE
Bedminster Down
Headley Park
Withywood
Gilslake
Marsh Common
Compton Greenfield
Henbury
Westbury on Trym
Stoke Bishop
Clifton
Hotwells
Bedminster
Bishopsworth
Highridge
Berwick
Blaise Castle House
Sneyd Park
Leigh Woods
Avon Gorge
Ashton Vale
Bower Ashton
Hallen
Sea Mills
Abbots Leigh
Barrow Common
Severn Beach
Crook's Marsh
Lawrence Weston
Shirehampton
Long Ashton
Barrow Wood
Ham Green
AVONMOUTH
Pill
Easton-in-Gordano
Ashton Hill Plantation
Cambridge Batch
Barrow Gurney
To Bristol International Airport
Failand
Tyntesfield Plantation
Flax Bourton
Avonmouth Docks
River Avon
Portbury
Lower Failand
The Royal Portbury Dock
Tyntesfield
Sheepway
Farleigh
Church Town
Bristol Channel
Prior's Wood
Wraxall
PORTISHEAD
Backwell
Nailsea
Clapton in Gordano
Lime Breach Wood
Stone-edge Batch
Chelvey
M4
M5
M32
M49
3 miles
5 km

Cardiff / Caerdydd

0 Miles ¼

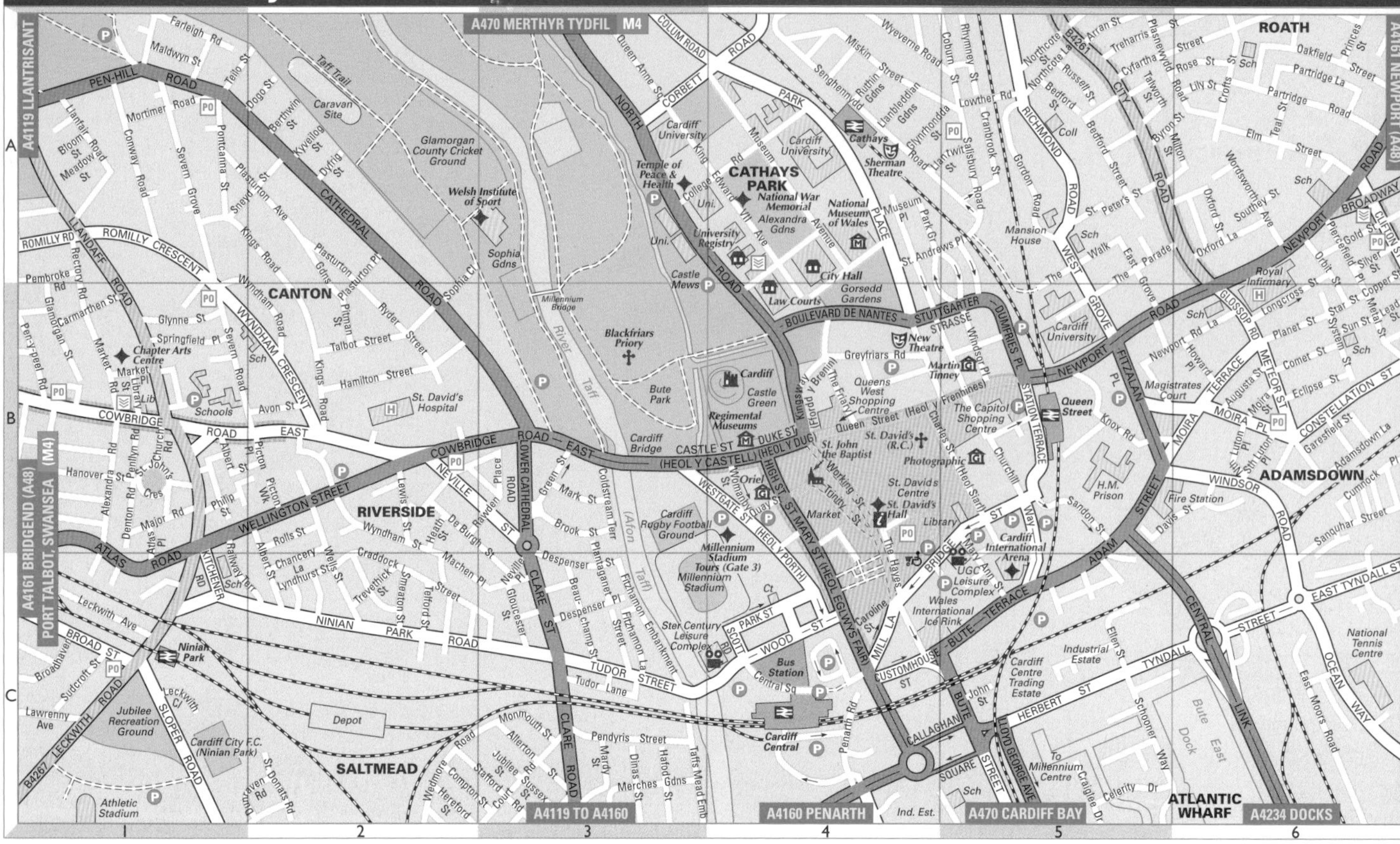

Cardiff/ Caerdydd

Adam St B5
Adamsdown La B6
Albert St B1
Alexandra Gdns A4
Alexandra Rd B1
Allerton St C3
Arran St A5
Athletic Stadium C1
Atlas Place B1
Atlas Rd C1
Augusta St B6
Avon St B2
Beauchamp St C3
Bedford St A5
Berthwin St A2
Blackfriars Priory ✝ B3
Bloom St A1
Boulevard De Nantes B4
Bridge St B5
Broad St C1
Broadhaven C1
Broadway A6
Brook St B3
Bus Station C4
Bute East Dock C6
Bute Park B3
Bute St C4
Bute Terr C5
Byron St A5
Callaghan Sq C4/C5
Capitol Shopping Centre, The B5
Caravan Site A2
Cardiff Bridge B3
Cardiff Castle B4
Cardiff Central Station C4
Cardiff Centre Trading Estate C5
Cardiff City F.C. (Ninian Park) C1
Cardiff International Arena ✦ C5
Cardiff Rugby Football Ground B3
Cardiff University A3/A4/B5
Carmarthen St B1
Caroline St C4
Castle Green B4
Castle Mews A3
Castle St (Heol y Castell) B3
Cathays Station A4
Cathedral Rd A2
Celerity Drive C5
Central Link C6
Central Sq C4
Chancery La C2
Chapter Arts Centre ✦ B1
Charles St (Heol Siarl) B5
Church Rd B1
Churchill Way B5
City Hall A4
City Rd A5
Clare Rd C3
Clare St C3
Clifton St A6
Coburn St A5
Coldstream Terr B3
College of Cardiff A3
College Rd A3
Colum Rd A3
Comet St B6
Compton St C2
Constellation St B6
Conway Rd A1
Copper St B6
Corbett Rd A3
Court C4
Court Rd C3
Cowbridge Rd East B1/B2
Craddock St C2
Craiglee Drive C5
Cranbrook St A5
Crofts St A6
Cumnock Place B6
Customhouse St C4
Cyfartha St A5
Davis St B5
De Burgh St B2
Denton Rd B1
Despenser Place C3
Despenser St C3
Dinas St C3
Dogo St A2
Duke St (Heol y Dug) B4
Dumfries Place B5
Dunraven Rd C1
Dyfrig St A2
East Grove A5
East Moors Rd C6
East Tyndall St C6
Eclipse St B6
Ellen St C5
Elm St A6
Farleigh Rd A1
Fire Station B5
Fitzalan Place B5
Fitzhamon Embankment C3
Fitzhamon La C3
Garesfield St B6
Glamorgan County Cricket Ground A2
Glamorgan St B1
Glossop Rd B6
Gloucester St C3
Glynne St B1
Glynrhondda St A4
Gold St A6
Gordon Rd A5
Gorsedd Gdns B4
Green St B3
Greyfriars Rd B4
H.M. Prison B5
Hafod St C3
Hamilton St B2
Hanover St B1
Heath St B2
Herbert St C5
Hereford St C2
High St B4
Howard Place B6
Industrial Estate C5
Information Ctr B4
John St C5
Jubilee Rec Gnd C1
Jubilee St C3
King Edward VII Ave A3
Kings Rd A1/B2
Kingsway (Ffordd y Brenin) B4
Kitchener Rd C1
Knox Rd B5
Kyveilog St A2
Law Courts B4
Lawrenny Ave C1
Lead St B6
Leckwith Ave C1
Leckwith Close C1
Leckwith Rd C1
Lewis St B2
Library B1/B5
Library St B1
Lily St A6
Llanbleddian Gdns A4
Llandaff Rd A1
Llanfair Rd A1
Llantwit St A4
Lloyd George Ave C5
Longcross St B6
Lower Cathedral Rd B3
Lowther Rd A5
Lyndhurst St C2
Machen Place C2
Magistrates Court B5
Major Rd B1
Maldwyn St A1
Mansion House A5
Mardy St C3
Mark St B3
Market B4
Market Place B1
Market Rd B1
Martin Tinney B5
Mary Ann St C5
Meadow St A1
Merches Gdns C3
Metal St B6
Meteor St B6
Mill La C4
Millennium Bridge B3
Millennium Stadium C3
Millennium Stadium Tours (Gate 3) ✦ B4
Milton St A5
Miskin St A4
Moira Place B6
Moira St B6
Moira Terr B6
Monmouth St C3
Mortimer Rd A1
Museum Ave A4
Museum Place A4
National Museum of Wales A4
National Tennis Centre C6
National War Memorial ✦ A4
Neville Place C3
Neville St B2
New Theatre B4
Newport Rd A6/B5
Newport Rd La B5
Ninian Park C1
Ninian Park Rd C2
North Rd A3
Northcote La A5
Northcote St A5
North Luton Place B6
Oakfield St A6
Ocean Way C6
Orbit St A6
Oriel B4
Oxford La A6
Oxford St A6
Park Grove A4
Park Place A4
Park St C4
Partridge La A6
Partridge Rd A6
Pembroke Rd A1
Pen-Hill Rd A1
Pen-y-Peel Rd B1
Penarth Rd C4
Pendyris St C3
Penllyn Rd B1
Philip St B1
Photographic Library B5
Picton Place B2
Picton Walk B2
Piercefield Place A6
Pitman St B2
Plat St B6
Plantaganet St C3
Plasnewydd Rd A5
Plasturton Ave A1
Plasturton Gdns A2
Plasturton Place A2
Police Station A4/A6/B1
Pontcanna St A1
Post Office A1/A5/A6/B1/B2/B4/B6/C1
Princes St A6
Quay St B4
Queen Anne Sq A3
Queen St (Heol y Frenhines) B4
Queen St Station B5
Queens West Shopping Centre B4
Railway Terr C1
Rawden Place B3
Rectory Rd A1
Regimental Museums B4
Rhymney St A5
Richmond Rd A5
Rolls St B2
Romilly Cr A1
Romilly Rd A1
Rose St A6
Royal Infirmary A6
Russell St A5
Ruthin Gdns A4
Ryder St B2
St Andrews Place A4
St David's ✝ B4
St David's Centre B4
St David's Hall B4
St David's Hospital B2
St Donats Rd C2
St John The Baptist B4
St John's Cr B1
St Mary St (Heol Eglwys Fair) B4
St Peter's St A5
Salisbury Rd A5
Sandon St B5
Sanquhar St B6
Schooner Way C5
Scott Rd C4
Senghennydd Rd A4
Severn Green A1
Severn Rd A1
Sherman Theatre A4
Silver St A6
Sloper Rd C1
Smeaton St C2
Sneyd St A1
Sophia Cl B2
Sophia Gdns A3
South Luton Place B6
Southey St A6
Springfield Place B1
Stafford Rd C3
Ster Century Leisure Complex C3
Star St B6
Station Terr B5
Stuttgarter Strasse B4
Sudcroft St C1
Sun St B6
Sussex St C3
System St B6
Taffs Mead Embankment C
Taff Trail A
Talbot St B
Talworth St A
Teal St A
Teilo St A
Telford St C
Temple of Peace & Health ✦ A
The Friary B
The Hayes B
The Parade A
The Walk A
Treharris St A
Trevethick St C
Trinity St B
Tudor La C
Tudor St C
Tyndall St C
UGC Leisure Complex C
University Registry A
Wales International Ice Rink C
Wedmore Rd C
Wellington St B
Wells St C
Welsh Institute of Sport ✦ A
West Green A
Westgate St (Heol y Porth) B
Windsor Place B
Windsor Rd B
Womanby St B
Wood St C
Wordsworth Ave A
Working St B
Wyeverne Rd A
Wyndham Cr A
Wyndham Rd B
Wyndham St B

NEWPORT
(CASNEWYDD)
CARDIFF
(CAERDYDD)
CAERPHILLY
(CAERFFILI)
MOUTH OF THE SEVERN
ABER HAFREN
Risca
(Rhisga)
Pontymister
Bassaleg
Pye Corner
High Cross
Rogerstone
(Ty-du)
Ridgeway
Allt-yr-yn
Maindee
Beechwood
St Julians
Somerton
Uskmouth
Pillgwenlly
Maes-glas
Duffryn
Tredegar House
Gaer
Stelvio
Glasllwch
St Brides Wentlooge
(Llansanffraid Gwynllŵg)
Coedkernew
(Coedcernyw)
Marshfield
Castleton
Peterstone Wentlooge
(Llanbedr Gwynllŵg)
Wentlooge Level
Michaelston-y-Fedw
Blacktown
St. Mellons
(Llaneirwg)
Trowbridge
Newton
Rumney
(Rhymni)
Pwll-Mawr
Llanrumney
Began
Lower Machen
Machen
Chatham
Draethen
Ochrwyth
Lisvane
(Llys Faen)
Llanedeyrn
Pentwyn
Cyncoed
Roath Park
Roath
Splott
Tremorfa
Cathays
Maindy
Heath
Gabalfa
Llandaff
(Llandaf)
Llandaff North
Whitchurch
Rhiwbina
Birchgrove
Llanishen
Thornhill
Pontcanna
Canton
Riverside
Grangetown
Butetown
Ely
(Tre-lai)
Caerau
Fairwater
St Fagans
(Sain Ffagan)
Michaelston-super-Ely
Culverhouse Cross
Leckwith
Llandough
Michaelston-le-Pit
Wenvoe
Wallston
Twyn-yr-odyn
Downs
Drope
St Georges
St Brides-super-Ely
(Llansanffraid-ar-Elai)
St Nicholas
(Sain Nicolas)
St Lythans
Radyr
Morganstown
Pentyrch
Gwaelod-y-garth
Taff's Well
(Ffynnon-Taf)
Tongwynlais
Nantgarw
Groes-wen
Upper Boat
Rhydyfelin
Hawthorn
Church Village
Abertridwr
Senghenydd
Penyrheol
Trecenydd
Energlyn
Pwllypant
Llanbradach
Bedwas
Trethomas
Lansbury Park
Van
Watford
Rudry
Berllangollen
Llwyncelyn
Graig-y-Rhacca
Waterloo
Rhymney Valley
Taf Vale
Mynydd Meio
Garth Wood
Cefn Mably Woods
Coed Craig Ruperra
Coed Cefn-pwll-du
Parc Cefn Onn
Forest Farm
Park Wood
M4
A48(M)
A48
A470
A469
A4232
A467
A468
25
25A
26
27
28
29
29A
30
32
33
CARDIFF GATE SERVICES
CARDIFF WEST SERVICES
MUSEUM OF WELSH LIFE
NATIONAL MUSEUM OF WALES
CARDIFF CASTLE
MILLENNIUM STADIUM
WALES MILLENNIUM CENTRE
NATIONAL ASSEMBLY
CARDIFF BAY VISITOR CENTRE
TECHNIQUEST
CAERPHILLY CASTLE
CASTELL COCH
LLANDAFF CATHEDRAL
FOURTEEN LOCKS
WELSH NATIONAL VELODROME
Transporter Bridge
River Usk
Ebbw River
River Taff
River Ely
Cardiff Bay Barrage
0 1 2 3 miles
0 1 2 3 4 5 km

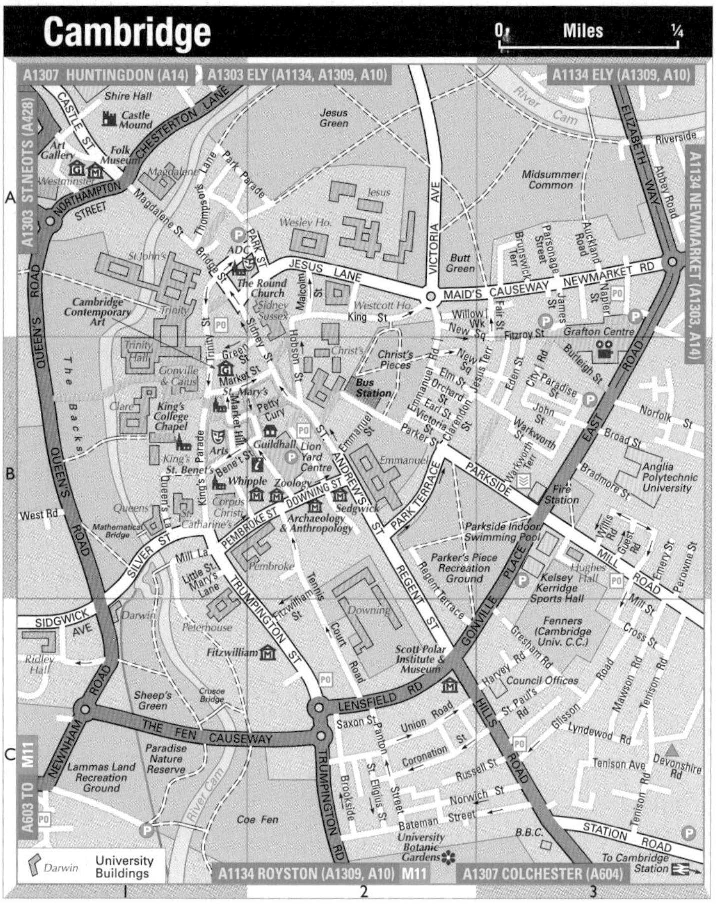

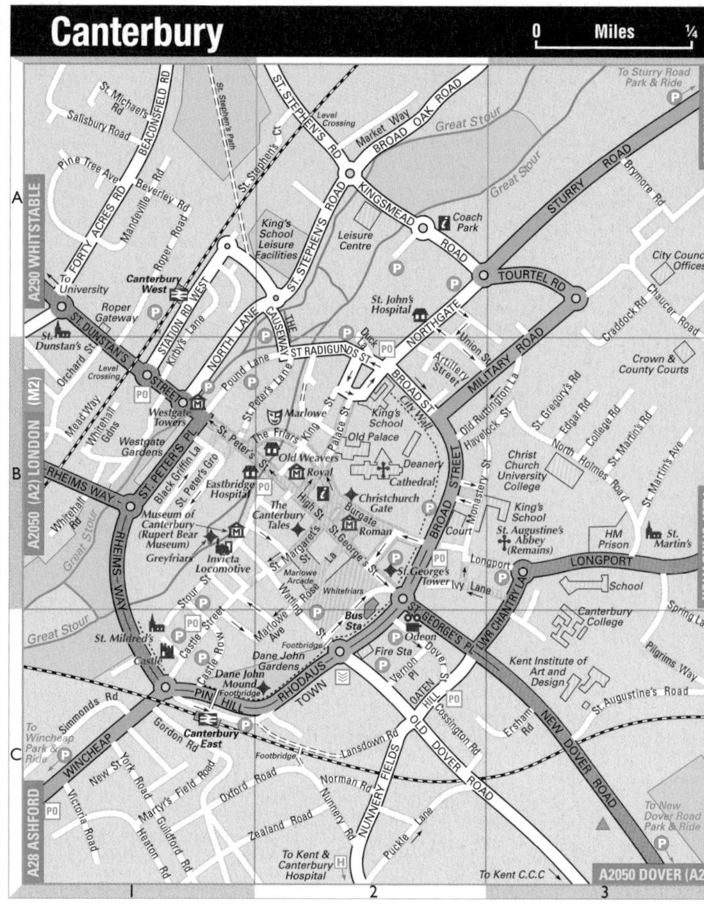

Cambridge

Abbey Rd . . . A3
ADC 🎭 . . . A2
Anglia Polytechnic University . . . B3
Archaeology & Anthropology 🏛 . . . B2
Art Gallery 🏛 . . . A1
Arts Theatre 🎭 . . . B1
Auckland Rd . . . A3
Bateman St . . . C2
B.B.C. . . . C3
Bene't St . . . B1
Bradmore St . . . B3
Bridge St . . . A1
Broad St . . . B3
Brookside . . . C2
Brunswick Terr . . . A3
Burleigh St . . . B3
Bus Station . . . B2
Butt Green . . . A2
Cambridge Contemporary Art Gallery 🏛 . . . B1
Castle Mound ♜ . . . A1
Castle St . . . A1
Chesterton La . . . A1
Christ's (Coll) . . . B2
Christ's Pieces . . . B2
City Rd . . . B3
Clare (Coll) . . . B1
Clarendon St . . . B2
Coe Fen . . . C2
Coronation St . . . C2
Corpus Christi (Coll) . . B1
Council Offices . . . C3
Cross St . . . C3
Crusoe Bridge . . . C1
Darwin (Coll) . . . C1
Devonshire Rd . . . C3
Downing (Coll) . . . B2
Downing St . . . B2
Earl St . . . B2
East Rd . . . B3
Eden St . . . B3
Elizabeth Way . . . A3
Elm St . . . B2
Emery St . . . B3
Emmanuel (Coll) . . . B2
Emmanuel Rd . . . B2
Emmanuel St . . . B2
Fair St . . . A3
Fenners (Cambridge Univ. C. C.) . . . C3
Fire Station . . . B3
Fitzroy St . . . A3
Fitzwilliam Museum 🏛 . . . C1
Fitzwilliam St . . . B2
Folk Museum 🏛 . . . A1
Glisson Rd . . . C3
Gonville & Caius (Coll) . B1
Gonville Place . . . B3
Grafton Centre . . . A3
Gresham Rd . . . C3
Green St . . . B1
Guest Rd . . . B3
Guildhall 🏛 . . . B2
Harvey Rd . . . C3
Hills Rd . . . C3
Hobson St . . . B2
Hughes Hall (Coll) . . . B3
Information Ctr ℹ . . . B2
James St . . . A3
Jesus (Coll) . . . A2
Jesus Green . . . A2
Jesus La . . . A2
Jesus Terr . . . B3
John St . . . B3
Kelsey Kerridge Sports Hall . . . B3
King St . . . A2
King's (Coll) . . . B1
King's College Chapel ⛪ . . . B1
King's Parade . . . B1
Lensfield Rd . . . C2
Lion Yard Centre . . . B2
Little St Mary's La . . . B1
Lyndewod Rd . . . C3
Magdalene (Coll) . . . A1
Magdalene St . . . A1
Maid's Causeway . . . A3
Malcolm St . . . A2
Market Hill . . . B1
Market St . . . B1
Mathematical Bridge . . B1
Mawson Rd . . . C3
Midsummer Common . A3
Mill La . . . B1
Mill Rd . . . B3
Napier St . . . A3
New Square . . . A2
Newmarket Rd . . . A3
Newnham Rd . . . C1
Norfolk St . . . B3
Northampton St . . . A1
Norwich St . . . C2
Orchard St . . . B2
Panton St . . . C2
Paradise Nature Reserve . . . C1
Paradise St . . . B3
Park Parade . . . A1
Park St . . . A2
Park Terr . . . B2
Parker St . . . B2
Parker's Piece . . . B2
Parkside . . . B3
Parkside Swimming Pool . . . B3
Parsonage St . . . A3
Pembroke (Coll) . . . B2
Pembroke St . . . B1
Perowne St . . . B3
Peterhouse (Coll) . . . C1
Petty Cury . . . B2
Police Station 🅿 . . . B3
Post Office 📮 . . . A1/A3/B2/B3/C1/C2/C3
Queens' (Coll) . . . B1
Queen's La . . . B1
Queen's Rd . . . B1
Regent St . . . B2
Regent Terr . . . B2
Ridley Hall (Coll) . . . C1
Riverside . . . A3
Round Church, The ⛪ . A1
Russell St . . . C2
St Andrew's St . . . B2
St Benet's ⛪ . . . B1
St Catharine's (Coll) . . B1
St Eligius St . . . C2
St John's (Coll) . . . A1
St Mary's ⛪ . . . B1
St Paul's Rd . . . C3
Saxon St . . . C2
Scott Polar Institute & Museum 🏛 . . . C2
Sedgwick Museum 🏛 . B2
Sheep's Green . . . C1
Shelly Row . . . A1
Shire Hall . . . A1
Sidgwick Ave . . . C1
Sidney St . . . A1
Sidney Sussex (Coll) . . A2
Silver St . . . B1
Station Rd . . . C3
Tenison Ave . . . C3
Tenison Rd . . . C3
Tennis Court Rd . . . B2
The Backs . . . B1
The Fen Causeway . . . C1
Thompson's La . . . A1
Trinity (Coll) . . . A1
Trinity Hall (Coll) . . . B1
Trinity St . . . B1
Trumpington Rd . . . C2
Trumpington St . . . C2
Union Rd . . . C2
University Botanic Gardens ✿ . . . C2
Victoria Ave . . . A2
Victoria St . . . B2
Warkworth St . . . B3
Warkworth Terr . . . B3
Wesley House (Coll) . . A2
West Rd . . . B1
Westcott House (Coll) . A2
Westminster (Coll) . . . A1
Whipple 🏛 . . . B2
Willis Rd . . . B3
Willow Walk . . . A2
Zoology 🏛 . . . B2

Canterbury

Artillery St . . . B2
Beaconsfield Rd . . . A1
Beverley Rd . . . A1
Black Griffin La . . . B1
Broad Oak Rd . . . A2
Broad St . . . B2
Brymore Rd . . . A3
Burgate . . . B2
Bus Station . . . C2
Canterbury College . . . C3
Canterbury East ⇌ . . C1
Canterbury Tales, The ✦ . . . B2
Canterbury West ⇌ . . A1
Castle ♜ . . . C1
Castle Row . . . C1
Castle St . . . C1
Cathedral ✝ . . . B2
Chaucer Rd . . . A3
Christ Church University College . . . B3
Christchurch Gate ✦ . . B2
City Council Offices . . . A3
City Wall . . . B2
Coach Park . . . A2
College Rd . . . B3
Cossington Rd . . . C2
Court . . . B2
Craddock Rd . . . A3
Crown & County Courts . . . B3
Dane John Gdns . . . C2
Dane John Mound ✦ . C1
Deanery . . . B2
Dover St . . . C2
Duck La . . . B2
Eastbridge Hospital 🏛 B1
Edgar Rd . . . B3
Ersham Rd . . . C3
Fire Station . . . C2
Forty Acres Rd . . . A1
Gordon Rd . . . C1
Greyfriars ✦ . . . B1
Guildford Rd . . . C1
Havelock St . . . B2
Heaton Rd . . . C1
High St . . . B2
HM Prison . . . B3
Information Ctr ℹ . A2/B2
Invicta Locomotive 🚂 . B1
Ivy La . . . B2
Kent Institute of Art and Design . . . C3
King St . . . B2
King's School . . . B3
Kingsmead Rd . . . A2
Kirby's La . . . B1
Lansdown Rd . . . C2
Leisure Centre . . . A2
Longport . . . B3
Lower Chantry La . . . C3
Mandeville Rd . . . A1
Market Way . . . A2
Marlowe Arcade . . . B2
Marlowe Ave . . . C2
Marlowe Theatre 🎭 . . B2
Martyr's Field Rd . . . C1
Mead Way . . . B1
Military Rd . . . B2
Monastery St . . . B2
Museum of Canterbury (Rupert Bear Museum) 🏛 . . . B1
New Dover Rd . . . C3
New St . . . C1
Norman Rd . . . C2
North Holmes Rd . . . B3
North La . . . B1
Northgate . . . A2
Nunnery Fields . . . C2
Nunnery Rd . . . C2
Oaten Hill . . . C2
Odeon Cinema 🎥 . . . C2
Old Dover Rd . . . C2
Old Palace . . . B2
Old Ruttington La . . . B2
Old Weavers 🏛 . . . B2
Orchard St . . . B1
Oxford Rd . . . C1
Palace St . . . B2
Pilgrims Way . . . C3
Pin Hill . . . C1
Pine Tree Ave . . . A1
Police Station 🅿 . . . C2
Post Office 📮 . . . B1/B2/C1/C2
Pound La . . . B1
Puckle La . . . C2
Rheims Way . . . B1
Rhodaus Town . . . C2
Roman Museum 🏛 . . B2
Roper Gateway . . . A1
Roper Rd . . . A1
Rose La . . . B2
Royal Museum 🏛 . . . B2
St Augustine's Abbey (remains) ✝ . . . B3
St Augustine's Rd . . . C3
St Dunstan's ⛪ . . . A1
St Dunstan's St . . . A1
St George's Pl . . . C2
St.George's St . . . B2
St.George's Tower ✦ . B
St Gregory's Rd . . . B
St John's Hospital 🏛 . A
St Margaret's St . . . B
St Martin's ⛪ . . . B
St Martin's Ave . . . B
St Martin's Rd . . . B
St Michael's Rd . . . A
St Mildred's ⛪ . . . C
St Peter's Gr . . . B
St Peter's La . . . B
St Peter's Pl . . . B
St Peter's St . . . B
St Radigunds St . . . B
St Stephen's Ct . . . A
St Stephen's Path . . . A
St Stephen's Rd . . . A
Salisbury Rd . . . A
Simmonds Rd . . . C
Spring La . . . C
Station Rd West . . . B
Stour St . . . B
Sturry Rd . . . A
The Causeway . . . A
The Friars . . . B
Tourtel Rd . . . A
Union St . . . B
Vernon Pl . . . C
Victoria Rd . . . C
Watling St . . . B
Westgate Towers 🏛 . . B
Westgate Gdns . . . B
Whitefriars . . . B
Whitehall Gdns . . . B
Whitehall Rd . . . B
Wincheap . . . C
York Rd . . . C1
Zealand Rd . . . C

Carlisle

0 Miles ¼

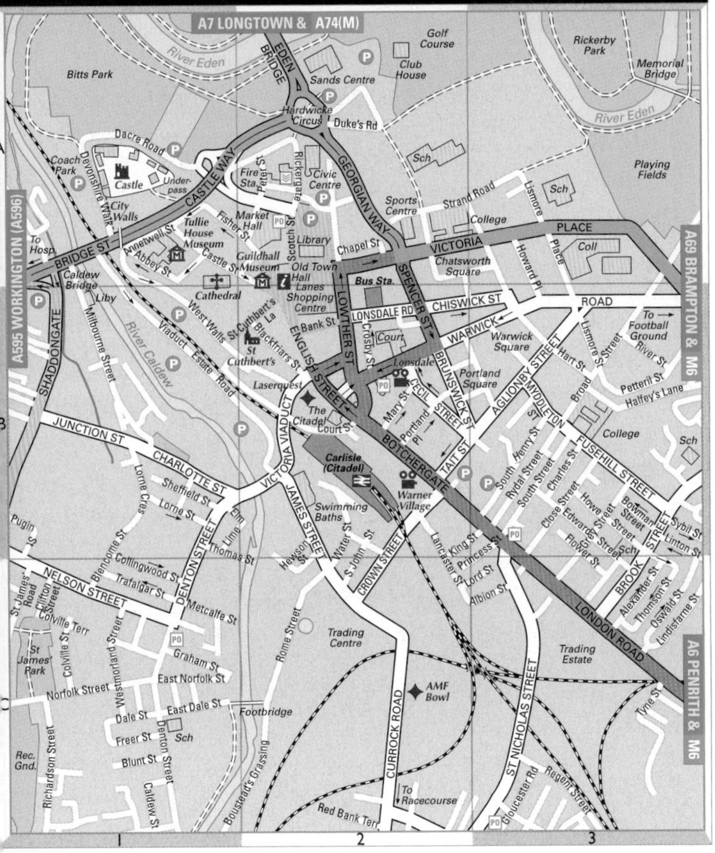

Cheltenham

0 Miles ¼

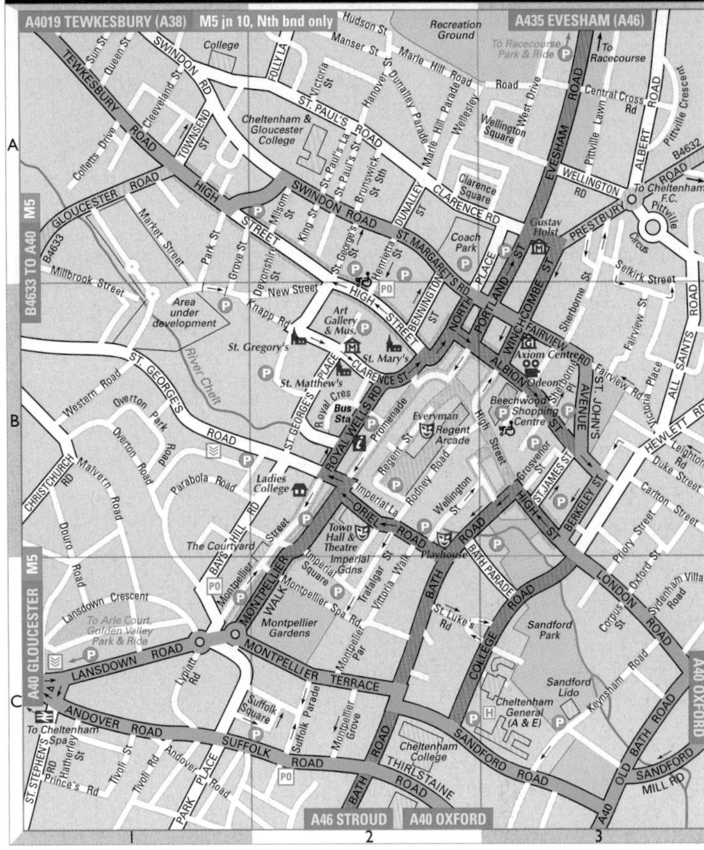

Carlisle

Abbey St A1
Aglionby St B3
Albion St C3
Alexander St C3
AMF Bowl ✦ C2
Annetwell St A1
Bank St B2
Bitts Park. A1
Blackfriars St. B2
Blencome St C1
Blunt St C1
Botchergate. B2
Boustead's Grassing . . C2
Bowman St B3
Broad St B3
Bridge St A1
Brook St C3
Brunswick St B2
Bus Station B2
Caldew Bridge. A1
Caldew St C1
Carlisle (Citadel)
Station B2
Castle A1
Castle St A1
Castle Way A1
Cathedral ✝ A1
Cecil St B2
Chapel St. A2
Charles St B3
Charlotte St B1
Chatsworth Square . . . A2
Chiswick St B2
Citadel, The B2
City Walls. A1
Civic Centre. A2
Clifton St C1
Close St. B3
Collingwood St C1
Colville St C1
Colville Terr C1
Court B2
Court St. B2
Crosby St B2
Crown St C2
Currock Rd C2
Dacre Rd A1
Dale St. C1
Denton St C1
Devonshire Walk A1
Duke's Rd A2
East Dale St. C1
East Norfolk St C1
Eden Bridge. A2
Edward St B3
Elm St B1
English St B2
Fire Station A2
Fisher St A1
Flower St. C3
Freer St C1
Fusehill St B3
Georgian Way A2
Gloucester Rd C3
Golf Course A2
Graham St. C1
Grey St B3
Guildhall Museum 🏛 . . A2
Halfey's La. B3
Hardwicke Circus A2
Hart St. B3
Hewson St. C2
Howard Pl A3
Howe St. B3
Information Ctr ℹ A2
James St B2
Junction St B1
King St. B2
Lancaster St C2
Lanes Shopping
Centre A2/B2
Laserquest ✦ B2
Library A2/B1
Lime St B1
Lindisfarne St C3
Linton St B3
Lismore Pl A3
Lismore St. B3
London Rd. C3
Lonsdale B2
Lonsdale Rd B2
Lord St. C3
Lorne Cres. B1
Lorne St. B1
Lowther St. B2
Market Hall A2
Mary St B2
Memorial Bridge A3
Metcalfe St C1
Milbourne St B1
Myddleton St. B3
Nelson St. C1
Norfolk St C1
Old Town Hall A2
Oswald St C3
Peter St A2
Petteril St. B3
Police Station A2
Portland Pl. B2
Portland Sq B2
Post Office . . . .
. . . . . A2/B2/B3/C1/C3
Princess St C3
Pugin St. B1
Red Bank Terr C2
Regent St C3
Richardson St C1
Rickerby Park A3
Rickergate A2
River St B3
Rome St C2
Rydal St. B3
St Cuthbert's B2
St Cuthbert's La B2
St James' Park C1
St James' Rd. C1
St Nicholas St C3
Sands Centre A2
Scotch St. A2
Shaddongate. B1
Sheffield St B1
South Henry St B3
South John St C2
South St B3
Spencer St B2
Sports Centre A2
Strand Rd A2
Swimming Baths B2
Sybil St B3
Tait St B2
Thomas St. B1
Thomson St. C3
Trafalgar St C1
Tullie House
Museum 🏛 A1
Tyne St. C3
Viaduct Estate Rd B1
Victoria Pl A2/A3
Victoria Viaduct B2
Warner Village B2
Warwick Rd B3
Warwick Sq B3
Water St. B2
West Walls. B1
Westmorland St. C1

Cheltenham

Albert Rd A3
Albion St B3
All Saints Rd B3
Andover Rd C1
Art Gallery & Mus. 🏛 . B2
Axiom Centre 🏛 B3
Bath Pde B2
Bath Rd C2
Bays Hill Rd. B1
Beechwood Shopping
Centre B3
Bennington St B2
Berkeley St B3
Brunswick St South. . . A2
Bus Station B2
Carlton St B3
Cheltenham &
Gloucester College . . A2
Cheltenham College . . C2
Cheltenham F.C. A3
Cheltenham General
(A & E) H C3
Christchurch Rd B1
Clarence Rd. A3
Clarence Sq. A2
Clarence St B2
Cleeveland St A1
Coach Park A2
College Rd. C2
Colletts Dr A1
Corpus St C3
Devonshire St A2
Douro Rd. B1
Duke St B3
Dunalley Pde A2
Dunalley St A2
Everyman B2
Evesham Rd A3
Fairview Rd B3
Fairview St. B3
Folly La A2
Gloucester Rd A1
Grosvenor St B3
Grove St A1
Gustav Holst 🏛. A3
Hanover St A2
Hatherley St. C1
Henrietta St A2
Hewlett Rd. B3
High St B2/B3
Hudson St A2
Imperial Gdns C2
Imperial La. B2
Imperial Sq C2
Information Ctr ℹ B2
Keynsham Rd C3
King St. A2
Knapp Rd B2
Ladies College B2
Lansdown Cr. C1
Lansdown Rd C1
Leighton Rd. B3
London Rd. C3
Lypiatt Rd C1
Malvern Rd B1
Manser St A2
Market St. A1
Marle Hill Pde A2
Marle Hill Rd A2
Millbrook St. A1
Milsom St A2
Montpellier Gdns. C2
Montpellier Gr C2
Montpellier Pde. C2
Montpellier Spa Rd . . . C2
Montpellier St C1
Montpellier Terr C2
Montpellier Walk C2
New St. B2
North Pl B2
Odeon B3
Old Bath Rd. C3
Oriel Rd B2
Overton Park Rd B1
Overton Rd B1
Oxford St. C3
Parabola Rd B1
Park Pl. C1
Park St. A1
Pittville Circus A3
Pittville Cr A3
Pittville Lawn A3
Pittville Pump Room &
Racecourse ✦ A3
Playhouse B2
Police Station . . B1/C1
Portland St B3
Post Office . B2/C1/C2
Prestbury Rd A3
Prince's Rd C1
Priory St. B3
Promenade B2
Queen St A1
Recreation Ground . . . A2
Regent Arcade B2
Regent St B2
Rodney Rd B2
Royal Cr. B2
Royal Wells Rd B2
Sandford Lido C3
Sandford Park C3
Sandford Rd C2
Selkirk St. A3
Sherborne Pl B3
Sherborne St. B3
St George's Pl B2
St George's Rd B1
St George's St. A1
St Gregory's B2
St James St. B3
St John's Ave B3
St Luke's Rd C2
St Margaret's Rd A2
St Mary's B2
St Matthew's B2
St Paul's La A2
St Paul's Rd. A2
St Paul's St A2
St Stephen's Rd C1
Suffolk Pde C2
Suffolk Rd C1
Suffolk Sq C1
Sun St A1
Swindon Rd. B2
Sydenham Villas Rd . . C3
Tewkesbury Rd A1
The Courtyard B1
Thirlstaine Rd C2
Tivoli Rd C1
Tivoli St C1
Town Hall &
Theatre B2
Townsend St A1
Trafalgar St C2
Victoria Pl B3
Victoria St A2
Vittoria Walk C2
Wellesley Rd A2
Wellington Rd A3
Wellington Sq A3
Wellington St. B2
West Drive. A3
Western Rd B1
Winchcombe St. B3

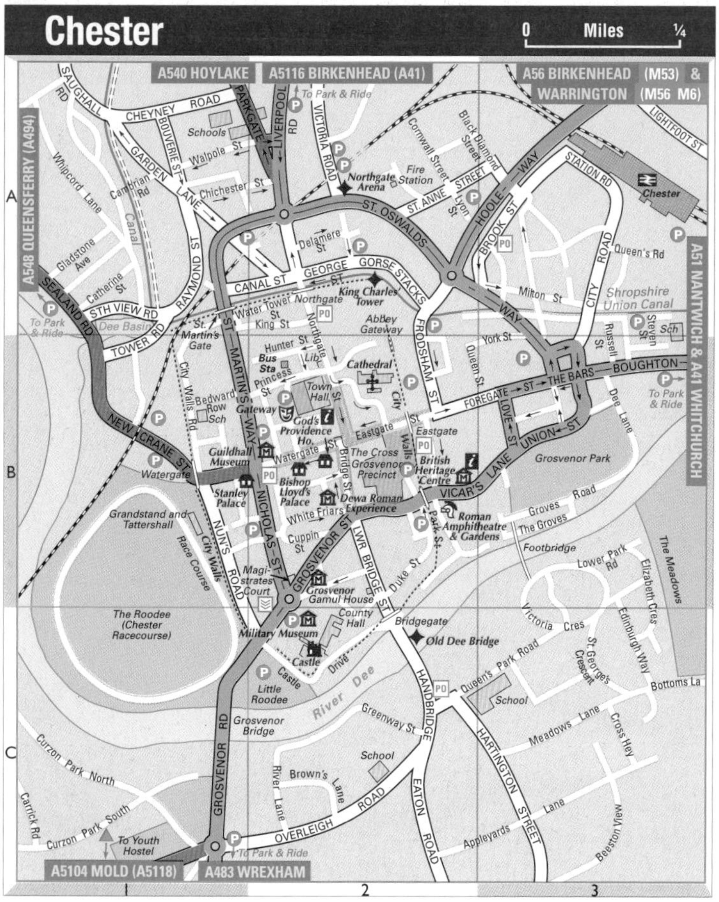
Chester
0 Miles ¼
A540 HOYLAKE
A5116 BIRKENHEAD (A41)
A56 BIRKENHEAD (M53) & WARRINGTON (M56 M6)
A548 QUEENSFERRY (A494)
A51 NANTWICH & A41 WHITCHURCH
A5104 MOLD (A5118)
A483 WREXHAM
Chester
Northgate Arena
Fire Station
King Charles Tower
Cathedral
Town Hall
Abbey Gateway
Gateway
God's Providence Ho.
Guildhall Museum
Bishop Lloyd's Palace
Stanley Palace
Dewa Roman Experience
British Heritage Centre
The Cross
Grosvenor Precinct
Roman Amphitheatre & Gardens
Grosvenor Park
Magistrates Court
Grosvenor Gamul House
County Hall
Military Museum
Castle
Little Roodee
Grosvenor Bridge
Old Dee Bridge
Bridgegate
The Roodee (Chester Racecourse)
Grandstand and Tattershall
Race Course
River Dee
The Meadows
School
Shropshire Union Canal
Dee Basin
To Park & Ride
To Youth Hostel
A
B
C
1
2
3

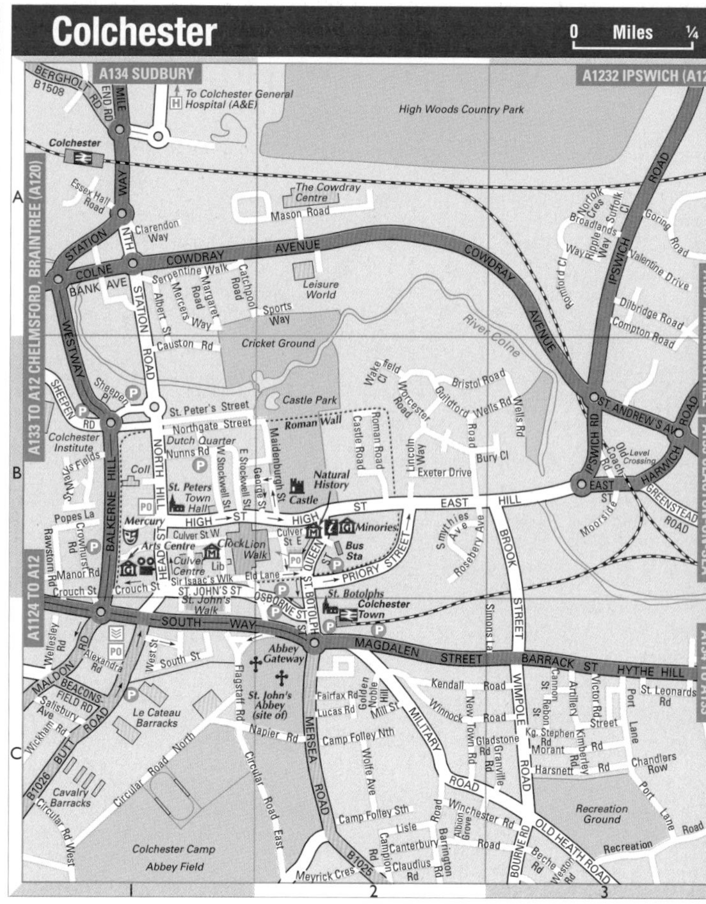
Colchester
0 Miles ¼
A134 SUDBURY
A1232 IPSWICH (A12)
A133 TO A12 CHELMSFORD, BRAINTREE (A120)
A1124 TO A12
A137 MANNINGTREE
A133 CLACTON-ON-SEA
A134 TO A133
To Colchester General Hospital (A&E)
High Woods Country Park
Colchester
The Cowdray Centre
Leisure World
Cricket Ground
Castle Park
Roman Wall
Natural History
Castle
Minories
Bus Sta
St. Peters
Town Hall
Mercury
Arts Centre
Culver Centre
Lion Walk
St. John's Walk
St. Botolphs
Colchester Town
Abbey Gateway
St. John's Abbey (site of)
Le Cateau Barracks
Cavalry Barracks
Colchester Camp
Abbey Field
Recreation Ground
Colchester Institute
River Colne
A
B
C
1
2
3

Chester

Abbey Gateway . . . A2
Appleyards La . . . C3
Bedward Row . . . B1
Beeston View . . . C3
Bishop Lloyd's Palace . . . B2
Black Diamond St . . . A2
Bottoms La . . . C3
Boughton . . . B3
Bouverie St . . . A1
Bridge St . . . B2
Bridgegate . . . C2
British Heritage Centre . . . B2
Brook St . . . A3
Brown's La . . . C2
Bus Station . . . B2
Cambrian Rd . . . A1
Canal St . . . A2
Carrick Rd . . . C1
Castle . . . C2
Castle Dr . . . C2
Cathedral . . . B2
Catherine St . . . A1
Chester . . . A3
Cheyney Rd . . . A1
Chichester St . . . A1
City Rd . . . A3
City Walls . . . B1/B2
City Walls Rd . . . B1
Cornwall St . . . A2
County Hall . . . C2
Cross Hey . . . C3
Cuppin St . . . B2
Curzon Park North . . . C1
Curzon Park South . . . C1
Dee Basin . . . A1
Dee La . . . B3
Delamere St . . . A2
Dewa Roman Experience . . . B2
Duke St . . . B2
Eastgate . . . B2
Eastgate St . . . B2
Eaton Rd . . . C2
Egerton St . . . A3
Elizabeth Cr . . . B3
Fire Station . . . A2
Foregate St . . . B2
Frodsham St . . . B2
Gamul House . . . B2
Garden La . . . A1
Gateway Theatre . . . B2
George St . . . A2
Gladstone Ave . . . A1
God's Providence House . . . B2
Gorse Stacks . . . A2
Greenway St . . . C2
Grosvenor Bridge . . . C1
Grosvenor Museum . . . B2
Grosvenor Park . . . B3
Grosvenor Precinct . . . B2
Grosvenor Rd . . . C1
Grosvenor St . . . B2
Groves Rd . . . B3
Guildhall Museum . . . B1
Handbridge . . . C2
Hartington St . . . C3
Hoole Way . . . A2
Hunter St . . . B2
Information Ctr . . . B2
King Charles' Tower . . . A2
King St . . . A2
Library . . . B2
Lightfoot St . . . A3
Little Roodee . . . C2
Liverpool Rd . . . A2
Love St . . . B3
Lower Bridge St . . . B2
Lower Park Rd . . . B3
Lyon St . . . A2
Magistrates Court . . . B2
Meadows La . . . C3
Military Museum . . . C2
Milton St . . . A3
New Crane St . . . B1
Nicholas St . . . B2
Northgate . . . A2
Northgate Arena . . . A2
Northgate St . . . A2
Nun's Rd . . . B1
Old Dee Bridge . . . C2
Overleigh Rd . . . C2
Park St . . . B2
Police Station . . . B2
Post Office . . . A2/A3/B2/C2
Princess St . . . B2
Queen St . . . B2
Queen's Park Rd . . . C3
Queen's Rd . . . A3
Raymond St . . . A1
River La . . . C2
Roman Amphitheatre & Gardens . . . B2
Roodee, The (Chester Racecourse) . . . B1
Russell St . . . A3
St Anne St . . . A2
St George's Cr . . . C3
St Martin's Gate . . . A1
St Martin's Way . . . B1
St Oswalds Way . . . A2
Saughall Rd . . . A1
Sealand Rd . . . A1
South View Rd . . . A1
Stanley Palace . . . B1
Station Rd . . . A3
Steven St . . . A3
The Bars . . . B3
The Cross . . . B2
The Groves . . . B3
The Meadows . . . B3
Tower Rd . . . B1
Town Hall . . . B2
Union St . . . B3
Vicar's La . . . B2
Victoria Cr . . . C3
Victoria Rd . . . A2
Walpole St . . . A1
Water Tower St . . . A1
Watergate . . . B1
Watergate St . . . B2
Whipcord La . . . A1
White Friars . . . B2
York St . . . B3

Colchester

Abbey Gateway . . . C2
Albert St . . . A1
Albion Grove . . . C2
Alexandra Rd . . . C1
Artillery St . . . C3
Arts Centre . . . B1
Balkerne Hill . . . B1
Barrack St . . . C3
Barrington Rd . . . C2
Beaconsfield Rd . . . C1
Beche Rd . . . C3
Bergholt Rd . . . A1
Bourne Rd . . . C3
Bristol Rd . . . B2
Broadlands Way . . . A3
Brook St . . . B3
Bury Cl . . . B2
Bus Station . . . B2
Butt Rd . . . C1
Camp Folley North . . . C2
Camp Folley South . . . C2
Campion Rd . . . C2
Cannon St . . . C3
Canterbury Rd . . . C2
Castle . . . B2
Castle Rd . . . B2
Catchpool Rd . . . A1
Causton Rd . . . B1
Cavalry Barracks . . . C1
Chandlers Row . . . C3
Circular Rd East . . . C2
Circular Rd North . . . C1
Circular Rd West . . . C1
Clarendon Way . . . A1
Claudius Rd . . . C2
Clock . . . B1
Colchester Institute . . . B1
Colchester . . . A1
Colchester Town . . . C2
Colne Bank Ave . . . A1
Compton Rd . . . A3
Cowdray Ave . . . A1/A3
Cowdray Centre, The . . . A2
Crouch St . . . B1
Crowhurst Rd . . . B1
Culver Centre . . . B1
Culver St East . . . B2
Culver St West . . . B1
Dilbridge Rd . . . A3
East Hill . . . B2
East St . . . B3
East Stockwell St . . . B1
Eld La . . . B1
Essex Hall Rd . . . A1
Exeter Dr . . . B2
Fairfax Rd . . . C2
Flagstaff Rd . . . C1
George St . . . B2
Gladstone Rd . . . C2
Golden Noble Hill . . . C2
Goring Rd . . . A3
Granville Rd . . . C3
Greenstead Rd . . . B3
Guildford Rd . . . B2
Harsnett Rd . . . C3
Harwich Rd . . . B3
Head St . . . B1
High St . . . B1
Hythe Hill . . . C3
Information Ctr . . . B2
Ipswich Rd . . . A3
Kendall Rd . . . C2
Kimberley Rd . . . C3
King Stephen Rd . . . C3
Le Cateau Barracks . . . C1
Leisure World . . . A2
Library . . . B1
Lincoln Way . . . B2
Lion Walk Shopping Centre . . . B1
Lisle Rd . . . C2
Lucas Rd . . . C2
Magdalen St . . . C2
Maidenburgh St . . . B2
Maldon Rd . . . C1
Manor Rd . . . B1
Margaret Rd . . . A1
Mason Rd . . . A2
Mercers Way . . . A1
Mercury . . . B1
Mersea Rd . . . C2
Meyrick Cr . . . C2
Mile End Rd . . . A1
Military Rd . . . C2
Mill St . . . C2
Minories . . . B2
Moorside . . . B3
Morant Rd . . . C3
Napier Rd . . . C2
Natural History . . . B2
New Town Rd . . . C2
Norfolk Cr . . . A3
North Hill . . . B1
North Station Rd . . . A1
Northgate St . . . B1
Nunns Rd . . . B1
Odeon . . . B1
Old Coach Rd . . . B3
Old Heath Rd . . . C3
Osborne St . . . B2
Police Station . . . C1
Popes La . . . B1
Port La . . . C3
Post Office . . . B1/B2/C1
Priory St . . . B2
Queen St . . . B2
Rawstorn Rd . . . B1
Rebon St . . . C3
Recreation Rd . . . C3
Ripple Way . . . A3
Roman Rd . . . B2
Roman Wall . . . B2
Romford Cl . . . A3
Rosebery Ave . . . B2
St Andrew's Ave . . . B3
St Botolph St . . . B2
St Botolphs . . . B2
St John's Abbey (site of) . . . C2
St John's St . . . B1
St John's Walk Shopping Centre . . . B1
St Leonards Rd . . . C3
St Marys Fields . . . B1
St Peters . . . B1
St Peter's St . . . B1
Salisbury Ave . . . C1
Serpentine Walk . . . A1
Sheepen Pl . . . B1
Sheepen Rd . . . B1
Simons La . . . C3
Sir Isaac's Walk . . . B1
Smythies Ave . . . B2
South St . . . C1
Sports Way . . . A2
Station Way . . . A1
Suffolk Cl . . . A3
Town Hall . . . B1
Turner Rd . . . A1
Valentine Dr . . . A3
Victor Rd . . . C3
Wakefield Cl . . . B2
Wellesley Rd . . . C1
Wells Rd . . . B2
West St . . . C1
West Stockwell St . . . B1
Weston Rd . . . C3
Westway . . . A1
Wickham Rd . . . C1
Wimpole Rd . . . C3
Winchester Rd . . . C2
Winnock Rd . . . C2
Wolfe Ave . . . C2
Worcester Rd . . . B2

Coventry

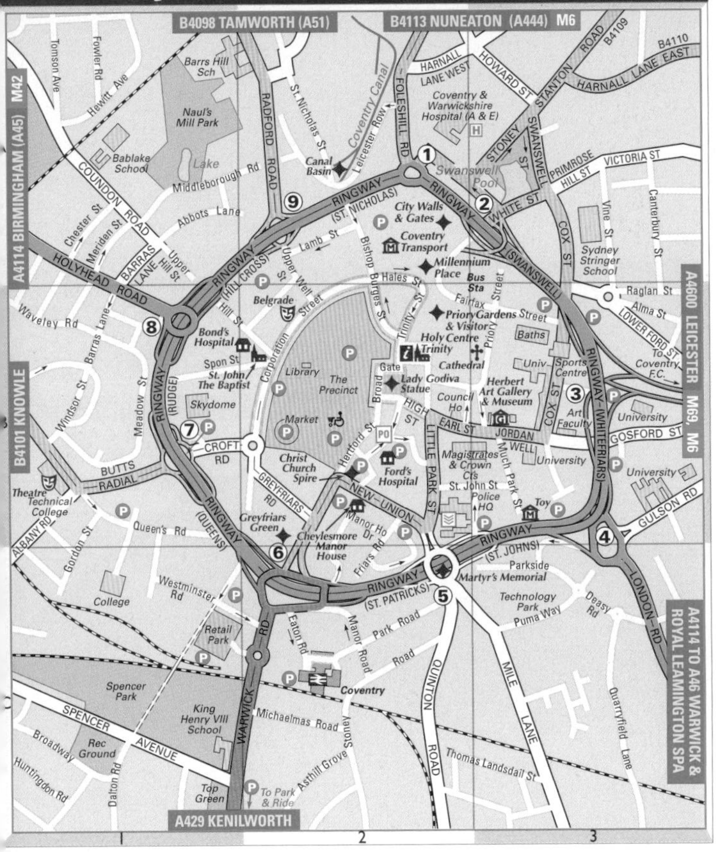

Derby

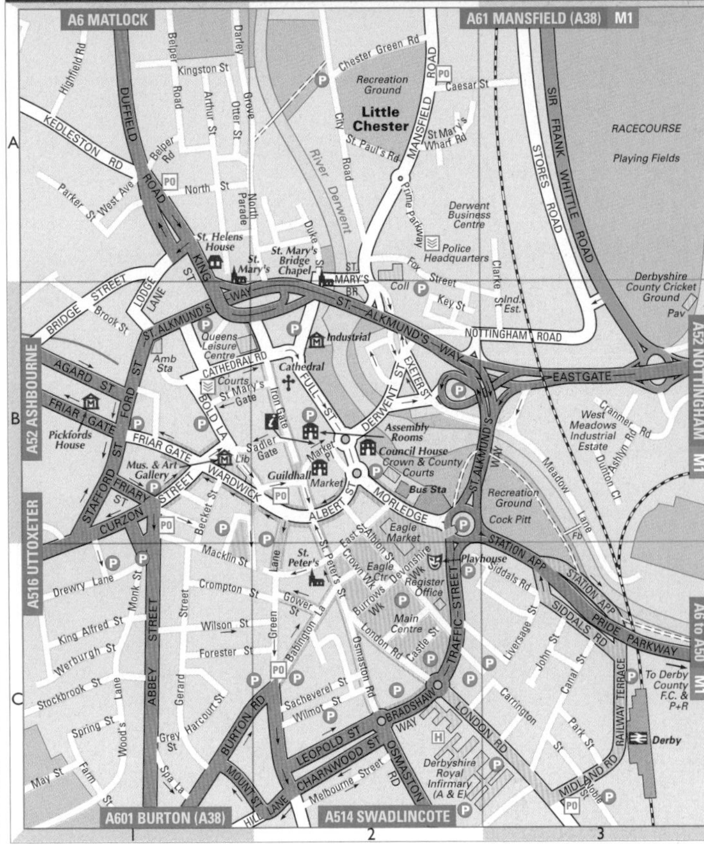

Coventry

Abbots La A1
Albany Rd B1
Alma St B3
Art Faculty. B3
Asthill Grove C2
Bablake School A1
Barras La. A1
Barrs Hill School A1
Belgrade B2
Bishop Burges St A2
Bond's Hospital . . . B1
Broadgate B2
Broadway C1
Bus Station A3
Butts Radial. B1
Canal Basin ✦. A2
Canterbury St A3
Cathedral ✝. B3
Chester St A1
Cheylesmore Manor House B2
Christ Church Spire ✦ B2
City Walls & Gates ✦ . A2
Coach Park A3
Corporation St. B2
Council House. B2
Coundon Rd A1
Coventry & Warwickshire Hospital (A&E) H. . . . A2
Coventry Station . . C2
Coventry Transport Museum A2
Cox St A3
Croft Rd. B1
Deasy Rd. C3
Earl St B2
Eaton Rd C2
Fairfax St. B2
Foleshill Rd A2
Ford's Hospital B2
Fowler Rd A1
Friars Rd C2
Gordon St C1
Gosford St. B3
Greyfriars Green B2
Greyfriars Rd B2
Gulson Rd B3
Hales St. A2
Harnall Lane East A3
Harnall Lane West. . . . A2
Herbert Art Gallery & Museum B3
Hertford St. B2
Hewitt Ave. A1
High St B2
Hill St. B1
Holy Trinity B2
Holyhead Rd A1
Howard St A3
Huntingdon Rd C1
Information Ctr i B2
Jordan Well B3
King Henry VIII School. C1
Lady Godiva Statue ✦. B2
Lamb St. A2
Leicester Row A2
Library B2
Little Park St B2
London Rd. C3
Lower Ford St B3
Magistrates & Crown Courts B2
Manor House Drive . . . B2
Manor Rd C2
Market B2
Martyr's Memorial ✦ . . C2
Meadow St B1
Meriden St. A1
Michaelmas Rd C2
Middleborough Rd . . . A1
Mile La. C3
Millennium Place A2
Much Park St B3
Naul's Mill Park A1
New Union. B2
Park Rd C2
Parkside. C3
Police HQ B3
Post Office PO B2
Primrose Hill St A3
Priory Gardens & Visitor Centre B2
Priory St. B3
Puma Way C3
Quarryfield La C3
Queen's Rd B1
Quinton Rd C2
Radford Rd A2
Raglan St. B3
Retail Park C1
Ringway (Hill Cross) . . A1
Ringway (Queens) B1
Ringway (Rudge) B1
Ringway (St Johns) . . . B3
Ringway (St Nicholas) . A2
Ringway (St Patricks) . C2
Ringway (Swanswell). . A2
Ringway (Whitefriars). . B3
St John St B2
St John The Baptist B2
St Nicholas St A2
Skydome B1
Spencer Ave C1
Spencer Park. C1
Spencer Rd C1
Spon St B1
Sports Centre B3
Stoney Rd C2
Stoney Stanton Rd . . . A3
Swanswell Pool. A3
Swanswell St. A3
Sydney Stringer School A3
Technical College B1
Technology Park C3
The Precinct B2
Theatre B1
Thomas Landsdail St . C2
Tomson Ave. A1
Top Green C1
Toy Museum B3
Trinity St B2
University. B3
Upper Hill St A1
Upper Well St A2
Victoria St A3
Vine St. A3
Warwick Rd C2
Waveley Rd B1
Westminster Rd. C1
White St. A3
Windsor St. B1

Derby

Abbey St C1
Agard St B1
Albert St B2
Albion St B2
Ambulance Station . . . B1
Arthur St A1
Ashlyn Rd B3
Assembly Rooms . . B2
Babington La. C2
Becket St. B1
Belper Rd A1
Bold La B1
Bradshaw Way C2
Bridge St. B1
Brook St B1
Burrows Walk C2
Burton Rd C1
Bus Station B2
Caesar St. A2
Canal St. C3
Carrington St. C3
Castle St C2
Cathedral ✝. B2
Cathedral Rd B1
Charnwood St. C2
Chester Green Rd A2
City Rd A2
Clarke St A3
Cock Pitt B3
Council House B2
Cranmer Rd. B3
Crompton St C1
Crown & County Courts B2
Crown Walk. C2
Curzon St B1
Darley Grove A1
Derby C3
Derbyshire County Cricket Ground B3
Derbyshire Royal Infirmary (A&E) H . . . C2
Derwent Business Centre A2
Derwent St B2
Devonshire Walk C2
Drewry La C1
Duffield Rd. A1
Duke St A2
Dunton Cl B3
Eagle Market C2
Eastgate B3
East St B2
Exeter St B2
Farm St C1
Ford St B1
Forester St. C1
Fox St A2
Friar Gate B1
Friary St. B1
Full St B2
Gerard St. C1
Gower St C2
Green La C2
Grey St C1
Guildhall B2
Harcourt St C1
Highfield Rd. A1
Hill La C2
Industrial B2
Information Ctr i B2
Iron Gate B2
John St C3
Kedleston Rd. A1
Key St B2
King Alfred St C1
King St. A1
Kingston St A1
Leopold St. C2
Library B1
Liversage St C3
Lodge La. B1
London Rd. C2
Macklin St C1
Main Centre. C2
Mansfield Rd A2
Market B2
Market Pl B2
May St. C1
Meadow La B3
Melbourne St. C2
Midland Rd C3
Monk St. C1
Morledge B2
Mount St C1
Museum & Art Gallery B1
Noble St C3
North Parade A1
North St. A1
Nottingham Rd B3
Osmaston Rd C2
Otter St A1
Park St. C3
Parker St A1
Pickfords House . . . B1
Playhouse C2
Police HQ A2
Police Station B1
Post Office PO A1/A2/B1/B2/C2/C3
Pride Parkway C3
Prime Parkway A2
Queens Leisure Centre B1
Racecourse A3
Railway Terr. C3
Register Office. B2
Sacheverel St C2
Sadler Gate B1
St Alkmund's Way . B1/B2
St Helens House ✦. . . A1
St Mary's A1
St Mary's Bridge Chapel A2
St Mary's Gate. B1
St Paul's Rd. A2
St Peter's C2
St Peter's St C2
Siddals Rd. C3
Sir Frank Whittle Rd . . A3
Spa La. C1
Spring St C1
Stafford St. B1
Station Approach C3
Stockbrook St C1
Stores Rd A3
Traffic St C2
Wardwick. B1
Werburgh St C1
West Ave A1
West Meadows Industrial Est B3
Wharf Rd A2
Wilmot St. C2
Wilson St. C1
Wood's La C1

Dorchester

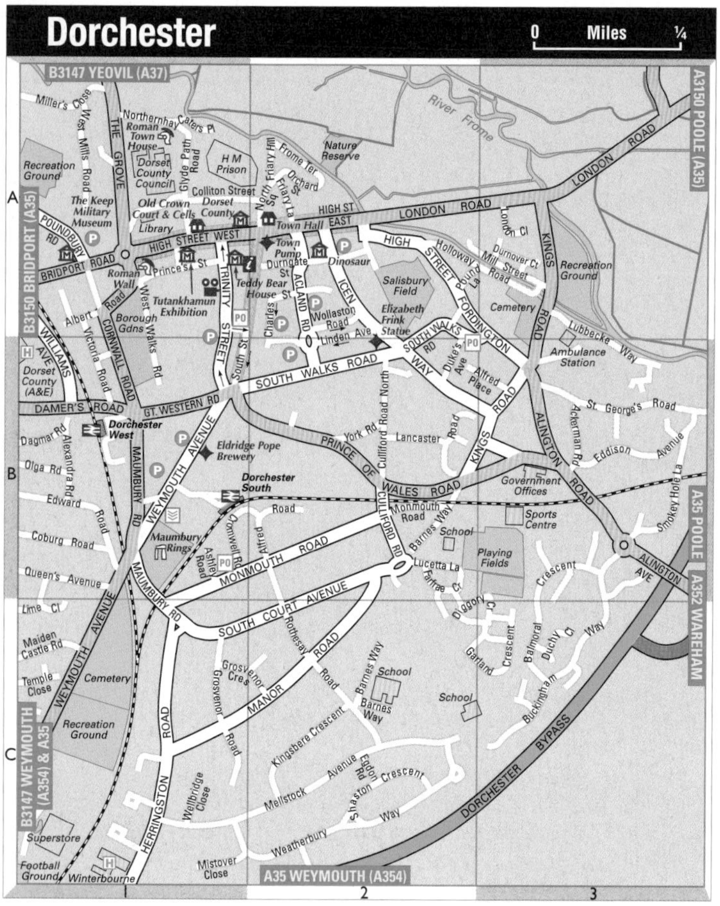

Dundee

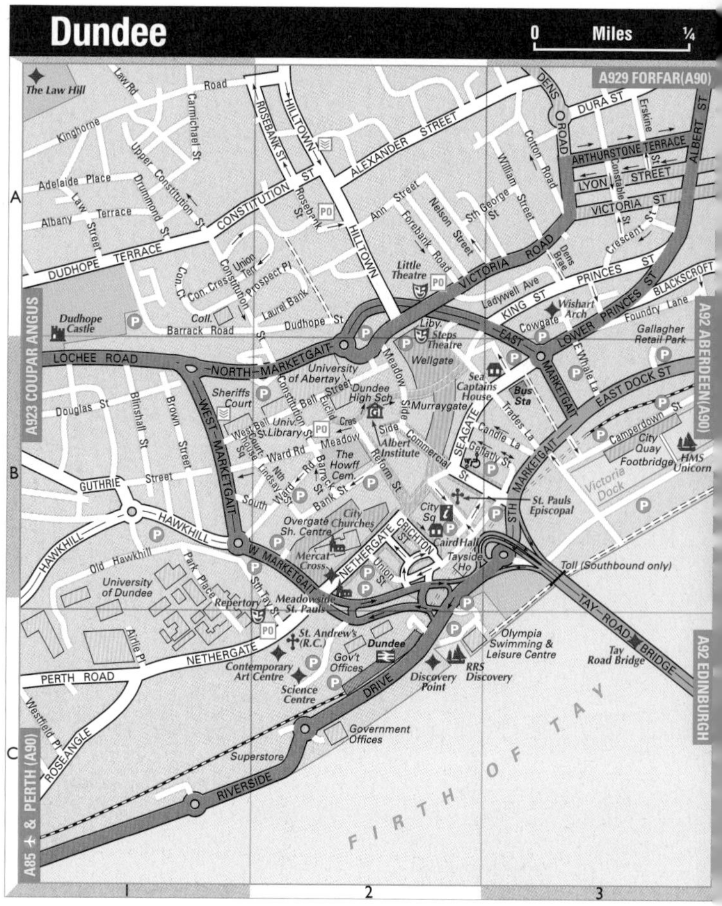

Dorchester

Ackerman Rd. B3
Acland Rd A2
Albert Rd A1
Alexandra Rd. B1
Alfred Place. B3
Alfred Rd B2
Alington Ave B3
Alington Rd B3
Ambulance Station . . . B3
Ashley Rd B1
Balmoral Cres C3
Barnes Way. B2/C2
Borough Gdns. A1
Bridport Rd A1
Buckingham Way C3
Caters Place A1
Charles St A2
Coburg Rd. B1
Colliton St A1
Cornwall Rd. A1
Cromwell Rd B1
Culliford Rd B2
Culliford Rd North B2
Dagmar Rd B1
Damer's Rd B1
Diggory Cres B2
Dinosaur Museum 🏛 . A2
Dorchester Bypass . . . C3
Dorchester South Station ⇌. B1
Dorchester West Station ⇌. B1
Dorset County Council Offices A1
Dorset County (A+E) H B1
Dorset County Museum 🏛 A1
Duchy Close C3
Duke's Ave. B2
Durngate St. A2
Durnover Court A3
Eddison Ave B3
Edward Rd. B1
Egdon Rd C2
Eldridge Pope Brewery ✦ B1
Elizabeth Frink Statue ✦. B2
Farfrae Cres. B2
Friary Hill A2
Friary Lane. A2
Frome Terr A2
Garland Cres C3
Glyde Path Rd. A1
Gt. Western Rd B1
Grosvenor Cres C1
Grosvenor Rd C1
H M Prison A1
Herringston Rd C1
High St East A2
High Street Fordington. A2
High Street West A1
Holloway Rd A2
Icen Way A2
Keep Military Museum, The 🏛 A1
Kings Rd A3/B3
Kingsbere Cres C2
Lancaster Rd. B2
Library A1
Lime Cl B1
Linden Ave. B2
London Cl A3
London Rd. A3
Lubbecke Way. A3
Lucetta La B2
Maiden Castle Rd C1
Manor Rd C2
Maumbury Rd B1
Maumbury Rings ⛫ . . . B1
Mellstock Ave C2
Mill St A3
Miller's Cl. A1
Mistover Cl C1
Monmouth Rd B1
North Sq A2
Northernhay. A1
Old Crown Court & Cells 🏛 A1
Olga Rd B1
Orchard St. A2
Police Station ☒ B1
Post Office PO . A1/B1/B2
Pound Lane. A2
Poundbury Rd A1
Prince of Wales Rd . . . B2
Prince's St. A1
Queen's Ave B1
Roman Town House ⛫ A1
Roman Wall ⛫. A1
Rothesay Rd C2
St George's Rd B3
Salisbury Field. A2
Shaston Cres. C2
Smokey Hole La B3
South Court Ave C1
South St B1
South Walks Rd. B2
Teddy Bear House 🏛 . A1
Temple Cl C1
The Grove A1
Town Hall 🏛 A2
Town Pump ✦. A2
Trinity St A1
Tutankhamun Exhibition 🏛 A1
Victoria Rd. B1
Weatherbury Way C2
Wellbridge Cl. C1
West Mills Rd A1
West Walks Rd A1
Weymouth Ave C1
Williams Ave B1
Winterbourne Hospital H C1
Wollaston Rd. A2
York Rd B2

Dundee

Adelaide Pl A1
Airlie Pl C1
Albany Terr A1
Albert 🏛 B2
Albert St A3
Alexander St A2
Ann St A2
Arthurstone Terr. A3
Bank St B2
Barrack Rd A1
Barrack St B2
Bell St B2
Blackscroft A3
Blinshall St. B1
Brown St B1
Bus Station B3
Caird Hall. B2
Camperdown St B3
Candle La B3
Carmichael St A1
Carnegie St A2
City Churches ⛪ B2
City Quay. B3
City Sq. B2
Commercial St. B2
Constable St A3
Constitution Ct A1
Constitution Cres A1
Constitution St . . . A1/B2
Contemporary Art Centre ✦ C2
Cotton Rd A3
Courthouse Sq B1
Cowgate A3
Crescent St A3
Crichton St B2
Dens Brae A3
Dens Rd. A3
Discovery Point ✦. . . . C2
Douglas St. B1
Drummond St A1
Dudhope Castle 🏰 . . . A1
Dudhope St. A2
Dudhope Terr. A1
Dundee ⇌ C2
Dundee High School . . B2
Dura St A3
East Dock St B3
East Whale La B3
East Marketgait B3
Erskine St A3
Euclid Cr B2
Forebank Rd A2
Foundry La A3
Gallagher Retail Park. . B3
Gellatly St B3
Government Offices . . C2
Guthrie St B1
Hawkhill. B1
Hilltown A2
HMS Unicorn ✦ B3
Howff Cemetery, The. . B2
Information Ctr ℹ B2
King St. A3
Kinghorne Rd A1
Ladywell Ave A3
Laurel Bank A2
Law Hill, The ✦ A1
Law Rd A1
Law St. A1
Library A2
Little Theatre 🎭 A2
Lochee Rd. B1
Lower Princes St. A3
Lyon St A3
Meadow Side B2
Meadowside St. Pauls ⛪. B2
Mercat Cross ✦ B2
Murraygate B2
Nelson St. A2
Nethergate. B2/C1
North Marketgait B2
North Lindsay St B2
Old Hawkhill B1
Olympia Swimming & Leisure Centre C3
Overgate Shopping Centre B2
Park Pl. B1
Perth Rd C1
Police Station ☒ . . A2/B1
Post Office PO . A2/B2/C2
Princes St A3
Prospect Pl A2
Reform St B2
Repertory 🎭 C1
Riverside Dr. C2
Roseangle C1
Rosebank St A2
RRS Discovery ⛵ C2
St Andrew's ⛪. C2
St Pauls Episcopal ⛪ . B3
Science Centre ✦ C2
Sea Captains House 🏛. B3
Sheriffs Court B1
South Ward Rd B2
South George St A2
South Marketgait. B3
South Tay St B2
Steps 🎭. A2
Tay Road Bridge ✦ . . . C3
Tayside House. B2
Trades La. B3
Union St B2
Union Terr A1
University Library B2
University of Abertay. . B2
University of Dundee. . B1
Upper Constitution St . A1
Victoria Rd. A2
Victoria St A3
West Marketgait . . B1/B2
Ward Rd B1
Wellgate. B2
West Bell St. B1
Westfield Pl C1
William St A3
Wishart Arch ✦ A3

Durham

0 Miles ¼

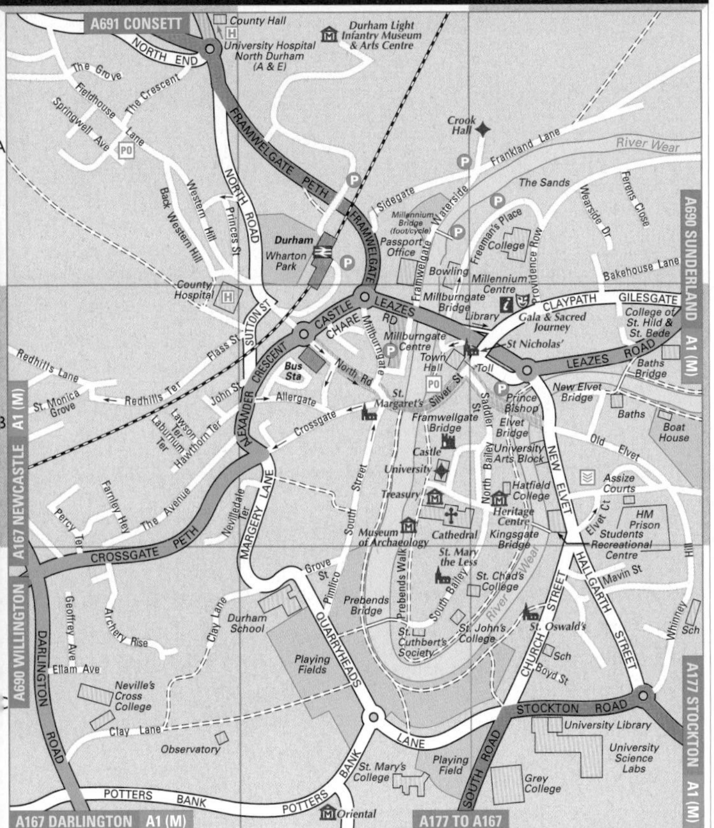

Exeter

0 Miles ¼

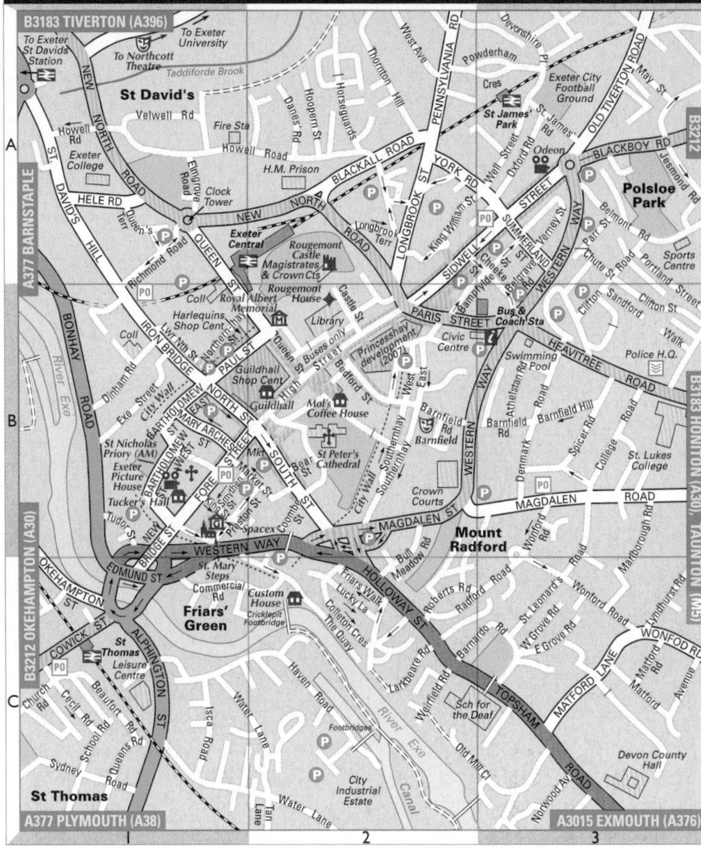

Durham

Alexander Cr B2
Allergate B2
Archery Rise C1
Assize Courts B3
Back Western Hill A1
Bakehouse La A3
Baths Bridge B3
Boat House B3
Boyd St C3
Bus Station B2
Castle B2
Castle Chare B2
Cathedral ✝ B2
Church St C3
Clay La C1
Claypath B3
College of St. Hild & St. Bede B3
County Hall A1
County Hospital H . . . B1
Crook Hall ✦ A3
Crossgate B2
Crossgate Peth C1
Darlington Rd C1
Durham Station . . . A2
Durham Light Infantry Museum & Arts Centre A2
Durham School C2
Ellam Ave. C1
Elvet Bridge B3
Elvet Court. B3
Farnley Hey B1
Ferens Cl. A3
Fieldhouse La A1
Flass St B1
Framwelgate A2
Framwelgate Bridge . . B2
Framwelgate Peth A2
Framwelgate Waterside A2
Frankland La A3
Freeman's Pl A3
Gala & Sacred Journey B3
Geoffrey Ave C1
Gilesgate B3
Grey College C3
Grove St C2
Hallgarth St C3
Hatfield College. B3
Hawthorn Terr B1
Heritage Centre B3
HM Prison B3
Information Ctr B2
John St B1
Kingsgate Bridge. B3
Laburnum Terr. B1
Lawson Terr. B1
Leazes Rd B2/B3
Library B2
Margery La B2
Mavin St C3
Millburngate. B2
Millburngate Bridge. . . B2
Millburngate Centre. . . B2
Millennium Bridge (foot/cycle) A2
Millennium Centre B3
Museum of Archaeology B2
Neville's Cross College C1
Nevilledale Terr B1
New Elvet B3
New Elvet Bridge. B3
North Bailey. B3
North End A1
North Rd A1/B2
Observatory. C1
Old Elvet B3
Oriental Museum . . . C2
Passport Office A2
Percy Terr B1
Pimlico. C2
Police Station B3
Post Office A1/B2
Potters Bank C1/C2
Prebends Bridge C2
Prebends Walk C2
Princes St A1
Providence Row A3
Quarryheads La. C2
Redhills La. B1
Redhills Terr. B1
Saddler St B3
St Chad's College C3
St Cuthbert's Society . C2
St John's College C2
St Margaret's B2
St Mary The Less . . C2
St Mary's College C2
St Monica Grove B1
St Nicholas' B3
St Oswald's C3
Sidegate A2
Silver St B2
South Bailey C2
South Rd C3
South St B2
Springwell Ave. A1
Stockton Rd C3
Students' Rec Centre . B3
Sutton St B2
The Avenue B1
The Crescent. A1
The Grove A1
The Sands A3
Town Hall. B2
Treasury Museum . . B2
University ✦ B2
University Arts Block . B3
University Library C3
University Science Labs C3
Wearside Dr. A3
Western Hill A1
Wharton Park A2
Whinney Hill. C3

Exeter

Alphington St. C1
Athelstan Rd B3
Bampfylde St. B2
Barnardo Rd C3
Barnfield Hill B3
Barnfield Rd B2/B3
Barnfield Theatre . . . B2
Bartholomew St East . B1
Bartholomew St West . B1
Bear St B2
Beaufort Rd. C1
Bedford St. B2
Belgrave Rd. A3
Belmont Rd A3
Blackall Rd A2
Blackboy Rd A3
Bonhay Rd. B1
Bull Meadow Rd C2
Bus & Coach Sta. B3
Castle St B2
Cecil Rd. C1
Cheeke St A3
Church Rd. C1
Chute St A3
City Industrial Estate. . C2
City Wall B1/B2
Civic Centre. B2
Clifton Rd B3
Clifton St B3
Clock Tower. A1
College Rd. B3
Colleton Cr C2
Commercial Rd C1
Coombe St B2
Cowick St C1
Crown Courts B2
Custom House C2
Danes' Rd A2
Denmark Rd B3
Devon County Hall . . . C3
Devonshire Pl A3
Dinham Rd B1
East Grove Rd. C3
Edmund St C1
Elmgrove Rd A1
Exe St B1
Exeter Central Station A1
Exeter City Football Ground A3
Exeter College. A1
Exeter Picture House B1
Fire Station A1
Fore St. B1
Friars Walk. C2
Guildhall B2
Guildhall Shopping Centre B2
Harlequin's Shopping Centre B1
Haven Rd. C2
Heavitree Rd B3
Hele Rd A1
High St B2
HM Prison A2
Holloway St. C2
Hoopern St A2
Horseguards A2
Howell Rd A1
Information Ctr B3
Iron Bridge. B1
Isca Rd C1
Jesmond Rd A3
King William St A2
King St. B1
Larkbeare Rd. C2
Leisure Centre. C1
Library B2
Longbrook St. A2
Longbrook Terr A2
Lucky La C2
Lower North St B1
Lyndhurst Rd. C3
Magdalen Rd. B3
Magdalen St B2
Magistrates & Crown Courts A2
Market B2
Market St. B2
Marlborough Rd C3
Mary Arches St B1
Matford Rd C3
Matford Ave. C3
Matford La. C3
May St. A3
Mol's Coffee House B2
New Bridge St. B1
New North Rd A1/A2
North St. B1
Northernhay St B1
Norwood Ave. C3
Odeon A3
Okehampton St. C1
Old Mill Cl C2
Old Tiverton Rd. A3
Oxford Rd A3
Paris St B2
Parr St. A3
Paul St. B1
Pennsylvania Rd A2
Police H.Q. B3
Portland Street A3
Post Office A3/B1/B3/C1
Powderham Cr A3
Preston St B1
Princesshay development B2
Queen St A1
Queen's Rd C1
Queen's Terr A1
Radford Rd C2
Richmond Rd A1
Roberts Rd C2
Rougemont Castle . A2
Rougemont House ✦ . B2
Royal Albert Memorial Museum B2
St David's Hill A1
St James' Park Station A3
St James' Rd. A3
St Leonard's Rd. C3
St Lukes College. B3
St Mary Steps C1
St Nicholas Priory (AM) ✝ B1
St Peter's Cathedral ✝. B2
St Thomas Station C1
Sandford Walk. B3
School for the Deaf . . C2
School Rd C1
Sidwell St A2
Smythen St B1
South St B2
Southernhay East B2
Southernhay West. . . . B2
Spacex Gallery B1
Spicer Rd B3
Sports Centre A3
Summerland St A3
Swimming Pool B3
Sydney Rd. C1
Tan La C2
The Quay. C2
Thornton Hill A2
Topsham Rd C3
Tucker's Hall B1
Tudor St. B1
Velwell Rd A1
Verney St. A3
Water La C1/C2
Weirfield Rd. C2
Well St. A3
West Ave A2
West Grove Rd C3
Western Way . . A3/B1/B2
Wonford Rd B3/C3
York Rd A2

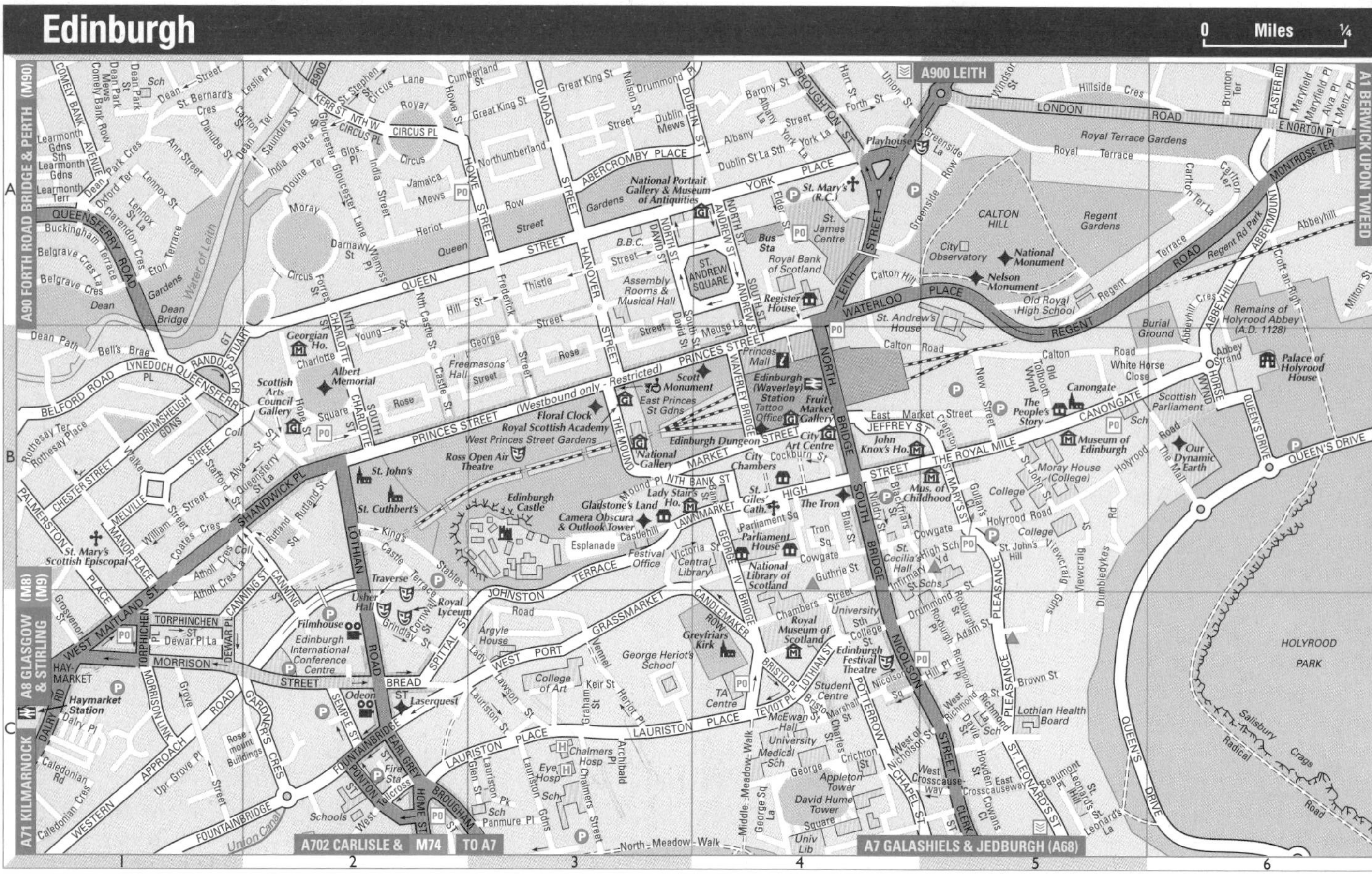
Edinburgh
0 Miles ¼
A90 FORTH ROAD BRIDGE & PERTH (M90)
A900 LEITH
A1 BERWICK UPON TWEED
A8 GLASGOW & STIRLING (M8) (M9)
A71 KILMARNOCK
A702 CARLISLE & M74
TO A7
A7 GALASHIELS & JEDBURGH (A68)
HOLYROOD PARK
CALTON HILL
Royal Terrace Gardens
Regent Gardens
Edinburgh Castle
Palace of Holyrood House
Princes Street
Queen Street
George Street
The Royal Mile
Haymarket Station
Edinburgh (Waverley) Station

Edinburgh

Abbey Strand B6
Abbeyhill B6
Abbeyhill Cr. B6
Abbeymount A6
Abercromby Pl. A3
Adam St C5
Albany La A4
Albany St. A4
Albert Memorial ✦ . . . B2
Alva Pl A6
Alva St. B1
Ann St A1
Appleton Tower C4
Archibald Pl C3
Argyle House C3
Assembly Rooms & Musical Hall. A3
Atholl Cr B1
Atholl Crescent La. . . . C1
BBC. A3
Bank St B4
Barony St. A4
Beaumont Pl C5
Belford Rd B1
Belgrave Cr A1
Belgrave Crescent La . . A1
Bell's Brae B1
Blackfriars St. B4
Blair St. B4
Bread St C2
Bristo Pl. C4
Bristo St C4
Brougham St C2
Broughton St A4
Brown St C5
Brunton Terr. A6
Buckingham Terr A1
Burial Ground A6
Bus Station A4
Caledonian Cr C1
Caledonian Rd. C1
Calton Hill A4
Calton Hill A5
Calton Rd B4
Camera Obscura & Outlook Tower ✦ . . . B3
Candlemaker Row. . . . C4
Canning St. B2
Canongate. B5
Canongate B5
Carlton St A1
Carlton Terr A6
Carlton Terrace La. . . . A6
Castle St B2
Castle Terr B2
Castlehill B3
Central Library. B4
Chalmers Hospital [H] . C3
Chalmers St. C3
Chambers St. C4
Chapel St. C4
Charles St C4
Charlotte Sq B2
Chester St B1
Circus La A2
Circus Pl A2
City Art Centre B4
City Chambers B4
City Observatory A5
Clarendon Cr. A1
Clerk St C5
Coates Cr B1
Cockburn St B4
College of Art C3
Comely Bank Ave A1
Comely Bank Row. . . . A1
Cornwall St C2
Cowans Cl. C5
Cowgate B4
Cranston St. B5
Crichton St C4
Croft-An-Righ A6
Cumberland St A2
Dalry Pl C1
Dalry Rd. C1
Danube St A1
Darnaway St A2
David Hume Tower . . . C4
Davie St C5
Dean Bridge A1
Dean Gdns A1
Dean Park Cr. A1
Dean Park Mews. A1
Dean Park St. A1
Dean Path B1
Dean St A1
Dean Terr A1
Dewar Pl C1
Dewar Place La C1
Doune Terr. A2
Drummond Pl A3
Drummond St C5
Drumsheugh Gdns . . . B1
Dublin Mews A3
Dublin St A4
Dublin Street Lane South A4
Dumbiedykes Rd. B5
Dundas St A3
Earl Grey St C2
East Norton Pl A6
East Crosscauseway . . C5
East Market St. B4
East Princes St Gdns . B3
Easter Rd. A6
Edinburgh (Waverley) ≋ B4
Edinburgh Castle . . . B3
Edinburgh Dungeon ✦ B4
Edinburgh Festival Theatre C4
Edinburgh International Conference Ctr C2
Elder St A4
Esplanade B3
Eton Terr A1
Eye Hospital [H] C3
Festival Office B3
Filmhouse C2
Fire Station C2
Floral Clock ✦. B3
Forres St A2
Forth St A4
Fountainbridge C2
Frederick St. A3
Freemasons' Hall. B3
Fruit Market B4
Gardner's Cr C2
George Heriot's School. C3
George IV Bridge. B4
George Sq. C4
George Sq La C4
George St B2
Georgian House . . . B2
Gladstone's Land . . B3
Glen St C3
Gloucester La A2
Gloucester Pl. A2
Gloucester St A2
Graham St. C3
Grassmarket C3
Great King St. A3
Great Stuart. B1
Greenside La. A5
Greenside Row A5
Greyfriars Kirk C4
Grindlay St. C2
Grosvenor St C1
Grove St C1
Gullan's Cl. B5
Guthrie St B4
Hanover St A3
Hart St A4
Haymarket. C1
Haymarket Station ≋. C1
Heriot Pl. C3
Heriot Row A2
High School Yard B5
High St B4
Hill Pl C5
Hill St. A2
Hillside Cr A5
Holyrood Park C6
Holyrood Rd B5
Home St C2
Hope St. B2
Horse Wynd. B6
Howden St C5
Howe St. A2
India Pl A2
India St A2
Infirmary St B4
Information Ctr [i] B4
Jamaica Mews A2
Jeffrey St. B4
John Knox's House B4
Johnston Terr C3
Keir St C3
Kerr St A2
King's Stables Rd B2
Lady Lawson St C3
Lady Stair's House . B4
Laserquest ✦ C2
Lauriston Gdns C3
Lauriston Park C3
Lauriston Pl C3
Lauriston St. C3
Lawnmarket. B3
Learmonth Gdns A1
Learmonth Terr A1
Leith St A4
Lennox St A1
Lennox St La. A1
Leslie Pl. A2
London Rd. A5
Lothian Health Board . C5
Lothian Rd. B2
Lothian St C4
Lower Menz Pl A6
Lynedoch Pl. B1
Manor Pl B1
Market St. B4
Marshall St C4
Maryfield A6
Maryfield Pl A6
McEwan Hall C4
Medical School C4
Melville St B1
Meuse La. B4
Middle Meadow Walk . C4
Milton St A6
Montrose Terr A6
Moray Circus A2
Moray House (college). B5
Morrison Link C1
Morrison St C1
Mound Pl. B3
Museum of Childhood B5
Museum of Edinburgh B5
National Gallery B3
National Library of Scotland B4
National Monument ✦ A5
National Portrait Gallery & Museum of Antiquities A3
Nelson Monument ✦ . A5
Nelson St. A3
New St. B5
Nicolson Sq. C4
Nicolson St C4
Niddry St B4
North Bridge B4
North Meadow Walk . . C3
North Bank St B3
North Castle St A2
North Charlotte St. . . . A2
North St Andrew St . . . A3
North St David St A3
North West Circus Pl. . A2
Northumberland St . . . A3
Odeon C2
Old Royal High School A5
Old Tolbooth Wynd . . . B5
Our Dynamic Earth ✦ . B6
Oxford Terr A1
Palace of Holyrood House B6
Palmerston Pl B1
Panmure Pl C3
Parliament House . . B4
Parliament Sq B4
People's Story, The B5
Playhouse Theatre . A4
Pleasance C5
Police Station A4
Ponton St C2
Post Office . A2/A4/B2/B4/B5/C1/C2/C4/C5
Potterrow. C4
Princes Mall. B4
Princes St B3
Queen St. A2
Queen Street Gdns . . . A3
Queen's Dr. B6/C6
Queensferry Rd A1
Queensferry St B1
Queensferry Street La . B2
Radical Rd. C6
Randolph Cr B1
Regent Gdns A5
Regent Rd B5
Regent Rd Park. A6
Regent Terr A5
Register House . . . A4
Remains of Holyrood Abbey (AD 1128). . . . A6
Richmond La. C5
Richmond Pl C5
Rose St B2
Rosemount Bldgs C1
Ross Open Air Theatre B3
Rothesay Pl. B1
Rothesay Terr B1
Roxburgh Pl. C5
Roxburgh St C5
Royal Bank of Scotland A4
Royal Circus A2
Royal Lyceum C2
Royal Museum of Scotland C4
Royal Scottish Academy B3
Royal Terr A5
Royal Terrace Gdns. . . A5
Rutland Sq B2
Rutland St B2
St Andrew Sq A3
St Andrew's House . . . A4
St Bernard's Cr A1
St Cecilia's Hall B4
St Cuthbert's B2
St Giles' ✝. B4
St James Centre A4
St John St B5
St John's B2
St John's Hill B5
St Leonard's Hill C5
St Leonard's La C5
St Leonard's St C5
St Mary's ✝ (R.C.) A4
St Mary's Scottish Episcopal ✝ B1
St Mary's St. B5
St Stephen St A2
Salisbury Crags C6
Saunders St. A2
Scott Monument ✦. . . . B4
Scottish Arts Council Gallery B2
Scottish Parliament B6
Semple St C2
Shandwick Pl. B2
South Bridge B4
South Charlotte St. . . . B2
South College St C4
South Learmonth Gdns . . . . A
South St Andrew St . . . A
South St David St . . . . A
Spittal St C
Stafford St. . . . . B
Student Centre C
TA Centre. C
Tattoo Office . . . . B
Teviot Pl. C
The Mall. . . . . B
The Mound . . . . B
The Royal Mile. . . . . . . B
Thistle St . . . . A
Torphichen Pl. C
Torphichen St C
Traverse Theatre . . . B
Tron Sq . . . . B
Tron, The ✦ . . . . B
Union St . . . . A
University. C
University Library C
Upper Grove Pl C
Usher Hall C
Vennel C
Victoria St . . . . B
Viewcraig Gdns . . . . . . B
Viewcraig St . . . . B
Walker St. . . . . B
Waterloo Pl . . . . A
Waverley Bridge . . . . . B
Wemyss Pl. . . . . A
West Crosscauseway . . C
West Maitland St. C
West of Nicolson St. . C
West Port. C
West Princes Street Gardens. . . . . B
West Richmond St C
West Tollcross C
Western Approach Rd. . C
White Horse Cl . . . . . . B
William St . . . . B
Windsor St. . . . . A
York La . . . . A
York Pl . . . . A
Young St . . . . B

FIRTH OF FORTH
EDINBURGH
Leith
Newhaven
Granton
Portobello
Musselburgh
Dalkeith
Lasswade
Bonnyrigg
Loanhead
Queensferry
Kirkliston
Ratho
Currie
Balerno
Kirknewton
Newbridge
Pentland Hills
Inchkeith
Inchcolm
Inchmickery
Cramond Island
Drum Sands
Dalmeny Park
Forth Bridge
Forth Road Bridge
Edinburgh Airport
Union Canal
River Almond
Holyrood Park
Arthur's Seat
THE CITY OF EDINBURGH BY-PASS
Rosyth
North Queensferry
Inverkeithing Bay

Kilpatrick Hills
Birny Hills
Cochno Loch
Black Loch
Loch Humphrey
Creigarestie
Jaw Reservoir
Greenside Reservoir
The Slacks
Fyn Loch
Black Linn Reservoir
Lily Loch
Carneddans Wood
Mugdock Wood
MUGDOCK COUNTRY PARK
Mugdock
Mugdock Loch
Loch Ardinning Nature Reserve
Craigend Muir
Craigmaddie Muir
Blairskaith Muir
Mugdock Reservoir
Craigmaddie Reservoir
MILNGAVIE
LILLIE ART GALLERY
Dougalston Loch
Bardowie Loch
TORRANCE
Balmore
Kilpatrick Braes
DUNTOCHER
OLD KILPATRICK
Faifley
BEARSDEN
Sports Complex
Big Wood
Erskine Bridge
GLENHEAD PARK
ROMAN BATHHOUSE
ANTONINE WALL
Bargarran
Dalmuir
Drumchapel
Kessington
Drumry
ERSKINE
Newshot Island
CLYDEBANK MUSEUM
CLYDEBANK
Inchinnan
Yoker
Knightswood
Dawsholm Park
Possil Loch
Nature Reserve
BISHOPBRIGGS
Milton
Wilderness Plantation
Forth and Clyde Canal
River Kelvin
River Clyde
Passenger Ferry
Blythswood
Jordanhill
Kelvinside
GLASGOW BOTANIC GARDENS
Firhill
FIRHILL PARK
Springburn
SPRINGBURN MUSEUM
Black Cart Water
White Cart Water
Braehead Shopping Centre
CLYDEBUILT
Victoria Park
GLASGOW INTERNATIONAL AIRPORT
RENFREW
Partick
ART GALLERY
MUSEUM & ART GALLERY
TRANSPORT MUSEUM
GLASGOW
Clyde Tunnel
Govan
Town Hall
EXHIBITION CENTRE
SCIENCE CENTRE
Queen Street
City Hall
Central
CATH.
Gallowhill
LINWOOD
PAISLEY
Hillington
Oldhall
Ibrox
Ferguslie Park
MUS. & ART GALL
ABBEY
ELDERSLIE
Bellahouston Park
Glasgow Green
Gallowgate
Pollokshields
Richmond Park
Crookston
HAGG'S CASTLE
POLLOK COUNTRY PARK
BURRELL COLLECTION
POLLOK HOUSE
Crossmyloof
Queen's Park
Govanhill
Foxbar
Stanely Reservoir
Glenburn
Langside
HAMPDEN PARK
RUTHERGLEN
GLENIFFER BRAES COUNTRY PARK
Priesthill
Govt Offices
Nitshill
Hillpark
Cathcart
King's Park
Croftfoot
Glenniffer Reservoir
Brownside Braes
Crossmill
Muirend
HOLMWOOD HOUSE
Nature Trail Linn Park
Castlemilk
Harelaw Reservoir
Fereneze Hills
Orchard Park
Giffnock
CATHKIN BRAES COUNTRY PARK
BARRHEAD
ROUKEN GLEN COUNTRY PARK
Netherlee
Waulkmill Glen Reservoir
Lochliboside Hills
Williamwood
Carmunnock
NEILSTON
Balgray Reservoir
Ryatt Linn Resr
Crookfur
CLARKSTON
Broom
Busby
GREENBANK GARDEN
Kirkton Dam
Glanderston Dam
MUSEUM OF SCOTTISH COUNTRY LIFE
College Milton
Walton Dam
NEWTON MEARNS
Mearns
Thorntonhall
Snypes Dam
Craighall Dam
Knockenae Plantation
Commore Dam
Waterfoot
Hairmyres
Brother Loch
Moyne Moor
Long Loch
EAGLESHAM
Mossneuk
0 1 2 3 miles
0 1 2 3 4 5 km

LENNOXTOWN
Queenzieburn
KILSYTH
Milton of Campsie
Antermony Loch
Dullatur
Cumbernauld Village
Croy
Croy Hill
Bar Hill
Twechar
Carrickstone
Abronhill
Forth and Clyde Canal
Balloch
CUMBERNAULD
Fannyside Muir
KIRKINTILLOCH
AULD KIRK MUSEUM
River Kelvin
BROADWOOD STADIUM
Broadwood Loch
Carbrain
Greenfaulds
PALACERIGG COUNTRY PARK
Gartshore Moss
Westfield
Condorrat
Luggiebank
Luggie Water
Lenzie
Gadloch
Auchinloch
Moodiesburn
Greengairs
Chryston
MUIRHEAD
Robroyston
STEPPS
Marnock
Glenboig
Johnston Loch
Gartcosh
Frankfield Loch
Hogganfield Loch
Glenmavis
Bishop Loch
Woodend Loch
Craigend
Riddrie
PROVAN HALL
DRUMPELLIER COUNTRY PARK
Lochend Loch
Gartsherrie
AIRDRIE
Plains
Easterhouse
SUMMERLEE HERITAGE CENTRE
Blairhill
Dunbeth
Whinhall
WEAVER'S COT. MUS.
Drumgelloch
Carntyne
Springboig
COATBRIDGE
TIME CAPSULE
Whifflet
Gartlea
SHYBERRY EXCELSIOR
Swinton
Bargeddie
Dundyvan
Tollcross Park
Kirkwood
Muirhead
Mont Vernon
Braidfauld
Shawhead
Carnbroe
Chapelhall
Calderbank
Broomhouse
North Calder Water
River Clyde
Tannochside
Westburn
Hattonrig
Eurocentral (Rail Depot)
Holytown
CAMBUSLANG
UDDINGSTON
Mossend
New Stevenston
BELLSHILL
Newarthill
BOTHWELL CASTLE
BOTHWELL SERVICES (SOUTH ONLY)
Flemington
Orbiston
South Calder Water
Grotto
DAVID LIVINGSTONE CENTRE
STRATHCLYDE COUNTRY PARK
Forgewood
Carfin
Cleland
BOTHWELL
Dechmont Hill
Strathclyde Loch
Blantyre
MOTHERWELL
Ravenscraig
HAMILTON PARK RACE COURSE
HAMILTON SERVICES (NORTH ONLY)
Nerston
Whitehill
WATER SPORTS CENTRE
NEW DOUGLAS PARK
CAMERONIANS MUSEUM
Udston
Calderwood
HAMILTON
Airbles
Craigneuk
WISHAW
FIR PARK
DALZELL PARK
Nature Reserve
East Mains
West Mains
Earnock
Muirhouse
VISITOR CENTRE
CHATELHERAULT COUNTRY PARK
Netherton
EAST KILBRIDE
St Leonards
Avon Water
Carbarns Wood
CALDERGLEN COUNTRY PARK
Blantyre Muir
Eddlewood
Hamilton High Parks
Whitehills
M80
M8
M73
M74
A80
A8
A73
A725
A721
A724
A749
A726
A723
A72
27
67
66

Glasgow

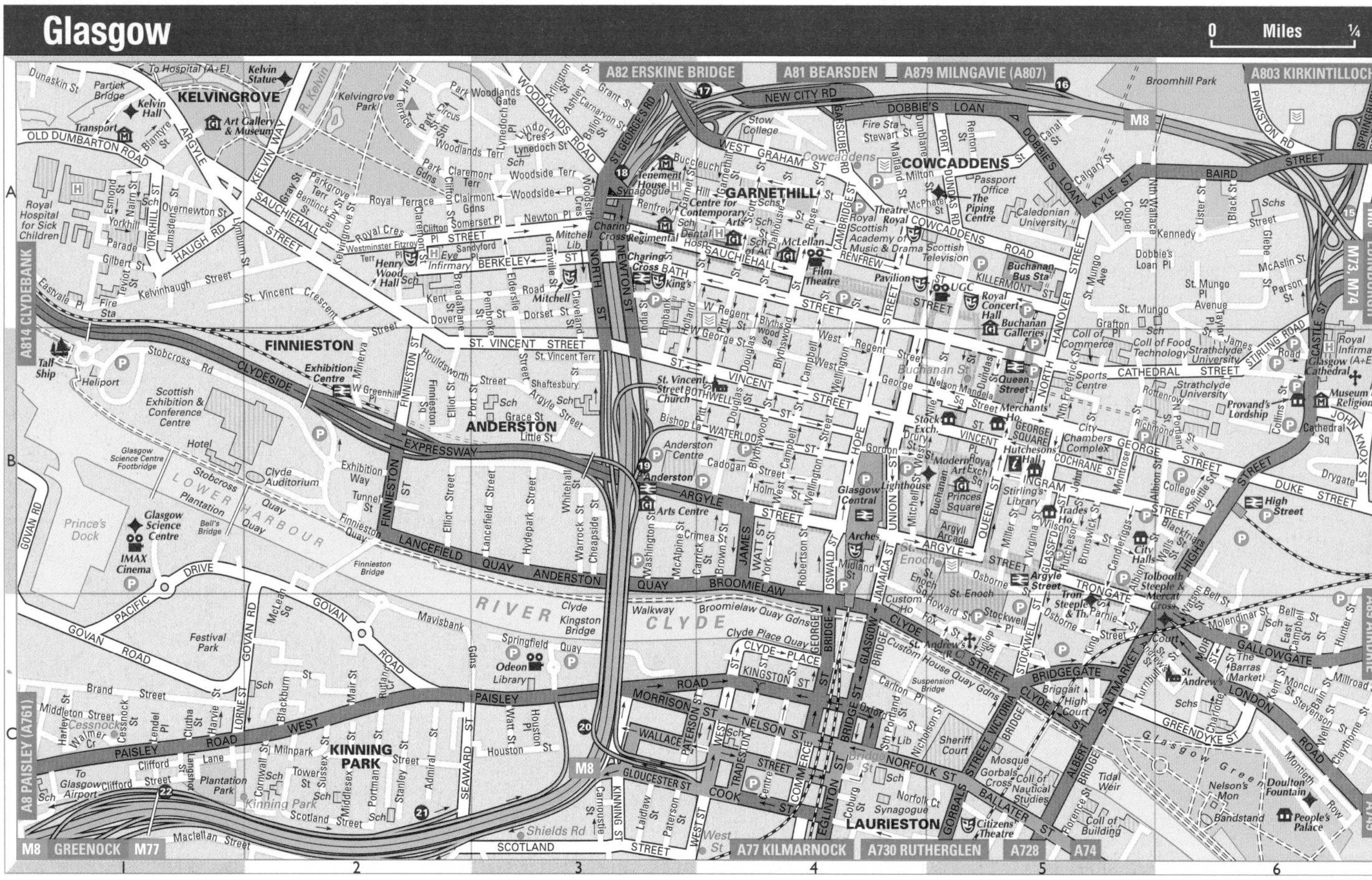

Glasgow

Admiral St . . . C2
Albert Bridge . . . C5
Albion St . . . B5
Anderston Centre . . . B3
Anderston Quay . . . B3
Anderston Station ⇌ . . . B3
Arches 🎭 . . . B4
Argyle St . . . A1/A2/B3/B4/B5
Argyle Street Station ⇌ . . . A3
Argyll Arcade . . . B5
Arlington St . . . A3
Art Gallery & Museum 🏛 . . . A1
Arts Centre 🏛 . . . B3
Ashley St . . . A3
Bain St . . . C6
Baird St . . . A6
Baliol St . . . A3
Ballater St . . . C5
Barras, The (Market) . . C6
Bath St . . . A3
Bell St . . . C6
Bell's Bridge . . . B1
Bentinck St . . . A2
Berkeley St . . . A3
Bishop La . . . B3
Black St . . . A6
Blackburn St . . . C2
Blackfriars St . . . B6
Blantyre St . . . A1
Blythswood Sq . . . A4
Blythswood St . . . B4
Bothwell St . . . B4
Brand St . . . C1
Breadalbane St . . . A2
Bridge St . . . C4
Bridge St (Metro Station) . . . C4
Bridgegate . . . C5
Briggait . . . C5
Broomhill Park . . . A6
Broomielaw . . . B4
Broomielaw Quay Gdns . . . B3
Brown St . . . B4
Brunswick St . . . B5
Buccleuch St . . . A3
Buchanan Bus Station A5
Buchanan Galleries 🏛 A5
Buchanan St . . . B5
Buchanan St (Metro Station) . . . B5
Cadogan St . . . B4
Caledonian University . A5
Calgary St . . . A5
Cambridge St . . . A4
Campbell St . . . B4
Canal St . . . A5
Candleriggs . . . B5
Carlton Pl . . . C4
Carnarvon St . . . A3
Carnoustie St . . . C3
Carrick St . . . B4
Castle St . . . B6
Cathedral Sq . . . B6
Cathedral St . . . B5
Centre for Contemporary Arts 🏛 . . . A4
Centre St . . . C4
Cessnock (Metro Station) . . . C1
Cessnock St . . . C1
Charing Cross Station ⇌ . . . A3
Charlotte St . . . C6
Cheapside St . . . B3
Citizens' Theatre 🎭 . . . C5
City Chambers Complex . . . B5
City Halls 🏛 . . . B5
Clairmont Gdns . . . A2
Claremont St . . . A2
Claremont Terr . . . A2
Claythorne St . . . C6
Cleveland St . . . A3
Clifford La . . . C1
Clifford St . . . C1
Clifton Pl . . . A2
Clifton St . . . A2
Clutha St . . . C1
Clyde Auditorium . . . B2
Clyde Pl . . . C4
Clyde Place Quay . . . C4
Clyde St . . . C5
Clyde Walkway . . . C3
Clydeside Expressway . . . B2
Coburg St . . . C4
Cochrane St . . . B5
College of Building . . . C5
College of Commerce . B5
College of Food Technology . . . B5
College of Nautical Studies . . . C5
College St . . . B6
Collins St . . . B6
Commerce St . . . C4
Cook St . . . C4
Cornwall St . . . C2
Couper St . . . A5
Cowcaddens (Metro Station) . . . A4
Cowcaddens Rd . . . A4
Crimea St . . . B3
Custom House 🏛 . . . C4
Custom House Quay Gdns . . . C4
Dalhousie St . . . A4
Dental Hospital [H] . . . A4
Derby St . . . A2
Dobbie's Loan . . . A4/A5
Dobbie's Loan Pl . . . A5
Dorset St . . . A3
Douglas St . . . B4
Doulton Fountain ✦ . . C6
Dover St . . . A2
Drury St . . . B4
Drygate . . . B6
Duke St . . . B6
Dunaskin St . . . A1
Dunblane St . . . A4
Dundas St . . . B5
Dunlop St . . . C5
East Campbell St . . . C6
Eastvale Pl . . . A1
Eglinton St . . . C4
Elderslie St . . . A3
Elliot St . . . B2
Elmbank St . . . A3
Esmond St . . . A1
Exhibition Centre Station ⇌ . . . B2
Exhibition Way . . . B2
Eye Infirmary [H] . . . A2
Festival Park . . . C1
Film Theatre 🎥 . . . A4
Finnieston Bridge . . . B2
Finnieston Quay . . . B2
Finnieston Sq . . . B2
Finnieston St . . . B2
Fitzroy Pl . . . A2
Florence St . . . C5
Fox St . . . C5
Gallowgate . . . C6
Garnet St . . . A3
Garnethill St . . . A4
Garscube Rd . . . A4
George Sq . . . B5
George St . . . B5
George V Bridge . . . C4
Gilbert St . . . A1
Glasgow Bridge . . . C4
Glasgow Cathedral ✝ . B6
Glasgow Central Station ⇌ . . . B4
Glasgow Green . . . C6
Glasgow Science Centre ✦ . . . B1
Glasgow Science Centre Footbridge . . . B1
Glassford St . . . B5
Glebe St . . . A6
Gloucester St . . . C3
Gorbals Cross . . . C5
Gorbals St . . . C5
Gordon St . . . B4
Govan Rd . . . B1/C1/C2
Grace St . . . B3
Grafton Pl . . . A5
Grant St . . . A3
Granville St . . . A3
Gray St . . . A2
Greendyke St . . . C6
Harley St . . . C1
Harvie St . . . C1
Haugh Rd . . . A1
Heliport . . . B1
Henry Wood Hall 🎭 . . . A2
High St . . . B6
High Street Station ⇌ . . . B6
Hill St . . . A3
Holland St . . . A3
Holm St . . . B4
Hope St . . . A5
Houldsworth St . . . B2
Houston Pl . . . C3
Houston St . . . C3
Howard St . . . C5
Hunter St . . . C6
Hutcheson St . . . B5
Hydepark St . . . B3
Imax Cinema 🎥 . . . B1
India St . . . A3
Information Ctr [i] . . . B5
Ingram St . . . B5
Jamaica St . . . B4
James Watt St . . . B4
John Knox St . . . B6
John St . . . B5
Kelvin Hall ✦ . . . A1
Kelvin Statue ✦ . . . A2
Kelvin Way . . . A2
Kelvingrove Park . . . A2
Kelvingrove St . . . A2
Kelvinhaugh St . . . A1
Kennedy St . . . A6
Kent Rd . . . A2
Killermont St . . . A5
King St . . . B5
King's 🎭 . . . A3
Kingston Bridge . . . C3
Kingston St . . . C4
Kinning Park (Metro Station) . . . C2
Kinning St . . . C3
Kyle St . . . A5
Laidlaw St . . . C3
Lancefield Quay . . . B2
Lancefield St . . . B3
Langshot St . . . C1
Lendel Pl . . . C1
Lighthouse ✦ . . . B4
Lister St . . . A6
Little St . . . B3
London Rd . . . C6
Lorne St . . . C1
Lower Harbour . . . B1
Lumsden St . . . A1
Lymburn St . . . A1
Lyndoch Cr . . . A3
Lynedoch Pl . . . A3
Lynedoch St . . . A3
Maclellan St . . . C1
Mair St . . . C2
Maitland St . . . A4
Mavisbank Gdns . . . C2
Mcalpine St . . . B3
Mcaslin St . . . A6
McLean Sq . . . C2
McLellan Gallery 🏛 . . . A4
McPhater St . . . A4
Merchants' House 🏛 . B5
Middlesex St . . . C2
Middleton St . . . C1
Midland St . . . B4
Miller St . . . B5
Millroad St . . . C6
Milnpark St . . . C2
Milton St . . . A4
Minerva St . . . A2
Mitchell Library . . . A3
Mitchell St West . . . B4
Mitchell Theatre 🎭 . . A3
Modern Art Gallery 🏛 . B5
Moir St . . . C6
Molendinar St . . . C6
Moncur St . . . C6
Montieth Row . . . C6
Montrose St . . . B5
Morrison St . . . C3
Mosque . . . C5
Museum of Religion 🏛 . . . B6
Nairn St . . . A1
Nelson Mandela Sq . . . B5
Nelson St . . . C4
Nelson's Monument . . C6
New City Rd . . . A4
Newton St . . . A3
Newton Pl . . . A3
Nicholson St . . . C4
Nile St . . . A5
Norfolk Court . . . C4
Norfolk St . . . C4
North Frederick St . . . B5
North Hanover St . . . B5
North Portland St . . . B5
North St . . . A3
North Wallace St . . . A5
Odeon 🎥 . . . C3
Old Dumbarton Rd . . . A1
Osborne St . . . B5/C5
Oswald St . . . B4
Overnewton St . . . A1
Oxford St . . . C4
Pacific Dr . . . B1
Paisley Rd . . . C3
Paisley Rd West . . . C1
Park Circus . . . A2
Park Gdns . . . A2
Park St South . . . A2
Park Terr . . . A2
Parkgrove Terr . . . A2
Parnie St . . . C5
Parson St . . . A6
Partick Bridge . . . A1
Passport Office . . . A5
Paterson St . . . C3
Pavilion Theatre 🎭 . . . A4
Pembroke St . . . A3
People's Palace 🏛 . . . C6
Pinkston Rd . . . A6
Piping Centre, The ✦ . A5
Pitt St . . . A4/B4
Plantation Park . . . C1
Plantation Quay . . . B1
Police Station ▤ . . . A4/A6/B5
Port Dundas Rd . . . A5
Port St . . . B2
Portman St . . . C2
Prince's Dock . . . B1
Princes Sq . . . B5
Provand's Lordship 🏛 . . . B6
Queen St . . . B5
Queen Street Station ⇌ . . . B5
Regimental Museum 🏛 . . . A3
Renfrew St . . . A3/A4
Renton St . . . A5
Richmond St . . . B5
Robertson St . . . B4
Rose St . . . A4
Rottenrow . . . B5
Royal Concert Hall 🎭 . A5
Royal Cr . . . A2
Royal Exchange Sq . . . B5
Royal Hospital For Sick Children [H] . . . A1
Royal Infirmary [H] . . . B6
Royal Scottish Academy of Music & Drama . . . A4
Royal Terr . . . A2
Rutland Cr . . . C2
St Kent St . . . C6
St Andrew's (R.C.) ✝ . . C5
St Andrew's ⛪ . . . C6
St Andrew's St . . . C5
St Enoch (Metro Station) . . . B5
St Enoch Shopping Centre . . . B5
St Enoch Sq . . . B4
St George's Rd . . . A3
St James Rd . . . B6
St Mungo Ave . . . A5/A6
St Mungo Pl . . . A6
St Vincent Cr . . . A2
St Vincent Pl . . . B5
St Vincent St . . . B3/B4
St Vincent Street Church ⛪ . . . B4
St Vincent Terr . . . B3
Saltmarket . . . C5
Sandyford Pl . . . A3
Sauchiehall St . . . A2/A4
School of Art . . . A4
Scotland St . . . C2/C3
Scott St . . . A4
Scottish Exhibition & Conference Centre . . B1
Scottish Television . . . A5
Seaward St . . . C2
Shaftesbury St . . . B3
Sheriff Court . . . C5
Shields Rd . . . C3
Shields Rd (Metro Station) . . . C3
Shuttle St . . . B6
Somerset Pl . . . A2
Springburn Rd . . . A6
Springfield Quay . . . C3
Stanley St . . . C2
Stevenson St . . . C6
Stewart St . . . A4
Sth Portland St . . . C4
Stirling Rd . . . B6
Stirling's Library . . . B5
Stobcross Quay . . . B1
Stobcross Rd . . . B1
Stock Exchange 🏛 . . . B5
Stockwell Pl . . . C
Stockwell St . . . B
Stow College . . . A
Strathclyde University . B
Sussex St . . . C
Synagogues . . . A3/C
Tall Ship ⛵ . . . B
Taylor Pl . . . A
Tenement House 🏛 . . A
Teviot St . . . A
Theatre Royal 🎭 . . . A
Tolbooth Steeple & Mercat Cross ✦ . . . C
Tower St . . . C
Trades House 🏛 . . . B
Tradeston St . . . C
Transport Museum 🏛 . A
Tron Steeple & Theatre 🎭 . . . C
Trongate . . . B
Tunnel St . . . B
Turnbull St . . . C
UGC 🎥 . . . A
Union St . . . B
Victoria Bridge . . . C
Virginia St . . . B
West Greenhill Pl . . . B
West Regent St . . . A
Wallace St . . . C
Walls St . . . B
Walmer Cr . . . C
Warrock St . . . B
Washington St . . . B
Waterloo St . . . B
Watson St . . . B
Watt St . . . C
Well St . . . C
Wellington St . . . B
West George St . . . B
West Graham St . . . A
West Regent St . . . B
West St . . . C
West St (Metro Station) . . . C
Westminster Terr . . . A
Whitehall St . . . B
Wilson St . . . B
Woodlands Gate . . . A
Woodlands Rd . . . A
Woodlands Terr . . . A
Woodside Cr . . . A
Woodside Pl . . . A
Woodside Terr . . . A
York St West . . . B
Yorkhill Pde . . . A
Yorkhill St . . . A

Gloucester

0 Miles ¼

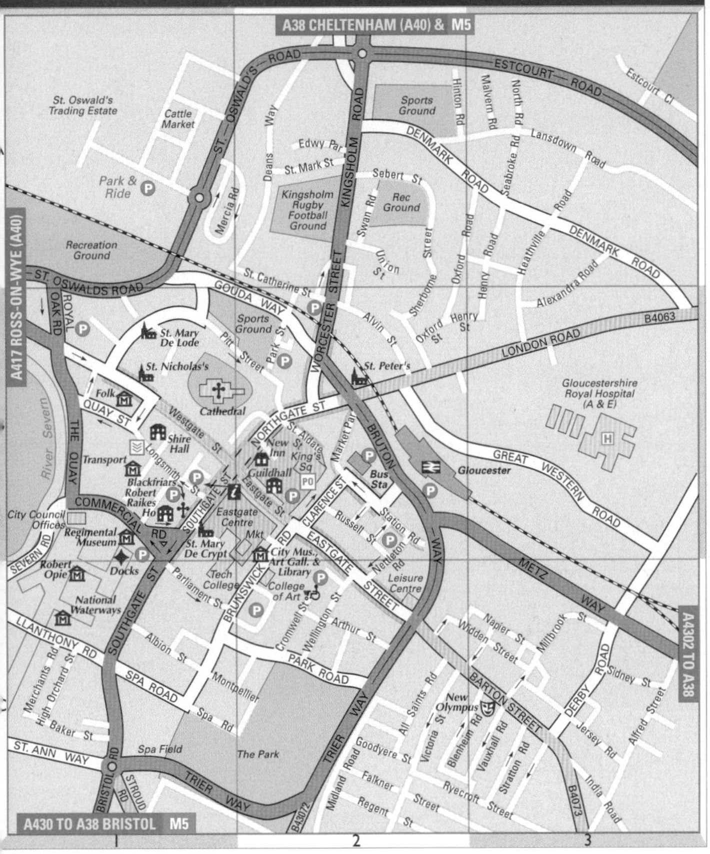

Hull

0 Miles ¼

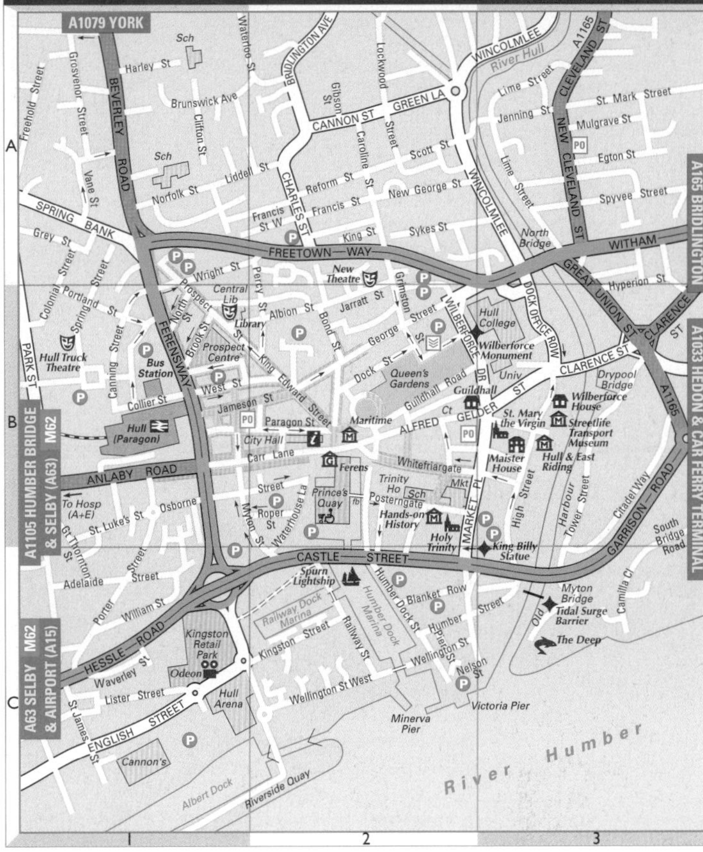

Gloucester

lbion St . . . C1
lexandra Rd . . . B3
lfred St . . . C3
ll Saints Rd . . . C2
lvin St . . . B2
rthur St . . . C2
aker St . . . C1
arton St . . . C2
lackfriars ✝ . . . B1
lenheim Rd . . . C2
ristol Rd . . . C1
runswick Rd . . . C2
ruton Way . . . B2
us Station . . . B2
attle Market . . . A1
ity Council Offices . . . B1
ity Mus., Art Gall. & Library . . . B2
larence St . . . B2
ollege of Art . . . C2
ommercial Rd . . . B1
romwell St . . . C2
eans Way . . . A2
enmark Rd . . . A3
erby Rd . . . C3
ocks ✦ . . . C1
astgate Centre . . . B1
astgate St . . . B2
dwy Pde . . . A2
stcourt Cl . . . A3
stcourt Rd . . . A3
alkner St . . . C2
Folk Museum . . . B1
Gloucester Cathedral ✝ . . . B1
Gloucester Station . . . B2
Gloucestershire Royal Hospital (A & E) . . . B3
Goodyere St . . . C2
Gouda Way . . . A1
Great Western Rd . . . B3
Guildhall . . . B2
Heathville Rd . . . A3
Henry Rd . . . B3
Henry St . . . B2
High Orchard St . . . C1
Hinton Rd . . . A2
India Rd . . . C3
Information Ctr . . . B1
Jersey Rd . . . C3
King's Sq . . . B2
Kingsholm Rd . . . A2
Kingsholm Rugby Football Ground . . . A2
Lansdown Rd . . . A3
Leisure Centre . . . C2
Llanthony Rd . . . C1
London Rd . . . B3
Longsmith St . . . B1
Malvern Rd . . . A3
Market Pde . . . B2
Merchants Rd . . . C1
Mercia Rd . . . A1
Metz Way . . . C3
Midland Rd . . . C2
Millbrook St . . . C3
Market . . . B2
Montpellier . . . C1
Napier St . . . C3
National Waterways . . . C1
Nettleton Rd . . . C2
New Inn . . . B2
New Olympus . . . C3
North Rd . . . A3
Northgate St . . . B2
Oxford Rd . . . A2
Oxford St . . . B2
Park & Ride Gloucester . . . A1
Park Rd . . . C2
Park St . . . B2
Parliament St . . . C1
Pitt St . . . B1
Police Station . . . B1
Post Office . . . B2
Quay St . . . B1
Recreation Gd . . . A1/A2
Regent St . . . C2
Regimental . . . B1
Robert Opie . . . C1
Robert Raikes House . . . B1
Royal Oak Rd . . . B1
Russell St . . . B2
Ryecroft St . . . C2
St Aldate St . . . B2
St Ann Way . . . C1
St Catherine St . . . A2
St Mark St . . . A2
St Mary De Crypt . . . B1
St Mary De Lode . . . B1
St Nicholas's . . . B1
St Oswald's Rd . . . A1
St Oswald's Trading Estate . . . A1
St Peter's . . . B2
Seabroke Rd . . . A3
Sebert St . . . A2
Severn Rd . . . C1
Sherborne St . . . B2
Shire Hall . . . B1
Sidney St . . . C3
Southgate St . . . B1/C1
Spa Field . . . C1
Spa Rd . . . C1
Sports Ground . . . A2/B2
Station Rd . . . B2
Stratton Rd . . . C3
Stroud Rd . . . C1
Swan Rd . . . A2
Technical College . . . C1
The Park . . . C2
The Quay . . . B1
Transport . . . B1
Trier Way . . . C1/C2
Union St . . . A1
Vauxhall Rd . . . C3
Victoria St . . . C2
Wellington St . . . C2
Westgate St . . . B1
Widden St . . . C2
Worcester St . . . B2

Hull

Adelaide St . . . C1
Albion St . . . B2
Alfred Gelder St . . . B2
Anlaby Rd . . . B1
Beverley Rd . . . A1
Blanket Row . . . C2
Bond St . . . B2
Bridlington Ave . . . A2
Brook St . . . B1
Brunswick Ave . . . A1
Bus Station . . . B1
Camilla Cl . . . C3
Canning St . . . B1
Cannon St . . . A2
Cannon's . . . C1
Caroline St . . . A2
Carr La . . . B2
Castle St . . . B2
Central Library . . . B1
Charles St . . . A2
Citadel Way . . . B3
City Hall . . . B2
Clarence St . . . B3
Cleveland St . . . A3
Clifton St . . . A1
Collier St . . . B1
Colonial St . . . B1
Court . . . B2
Deep, The . . . C3
Dock Office Row . . . B3
Dock St . . . B2
Drypool Bridge . . . B3
Egton St . . . A3
English St . . . C1
Ferens Gallery . . . B2
Ferensway . . . B1
Francis St . . . A2
Francis St West . . . A2
Freehold St . . . A1
Freetown Way . . . A2
Garrison Rd . . . B3
George St . . . B2
Gibson St . . . A2
Great Union St . . . A3
Green La . . . A2
Grey St . . . A1
Grimston St . . . B2
Grosvenor St . . . A1
Gt Thornton St . . . B1
Guildhall . . . B2
Guildhall Rd . . . B2
Hands-on History . . . B2
Harley St . . . A1
Hessle Rd . . . C1
High St . . . B3
Holy Trinity . . . B2
Hull & East Riding Museum . . . B3
Hull Arena . . . C1
Hull College . . . B3
Hull (Paragon) Station . . . B1
Hull Truck Theatre . . . B1
Humber Dock Marina . . . C2
Humber Dock St . . . C2
Humber St . . . C2
Hyperion St . . . A3
Information Ctr . . . B2
Jameson St . . . B1
Jarratt St . . . B2
Jenning St . . . A3
King Billy Statue ✦ . . . C2
King Edward St . . . B2
King St . . . A2
Kingston Retail Park . . . C1
Kingston St . . . C2
Library Theatre . . . B1
Liddell St . . . A1
Lime St . . . A3
Lister St . . . C1
Lockwood St . . . A2
Maister House . . . B3
Maritime Museum . . . B2
Market . . . B2
Market Place . . . B2
Minerva Pier . . . C2
Mulgrave St . . . A3
Myton Bridge . . . C3
Myton St . . . B1
Nelson St . . . C2
New Cleveland St . . . A3
New George St . . . A2
New Theatre . . . A2
Norfolk St . . . A1
North Bridge . . . A3
North St . . . B1
Odeon . . . C1
Osborne St . . . B1
Paragon St . . . B2
Park St . . . B1
Percy St . . . A2
Pier St . . . C2
Police Station . . . B2
Post Office . . . A3/B1/B2
Porter St . . . C1
Portland St . . . B1
Posterngate . . . B2
Prince's Quay . . . B2
Prospect Centre . . . B1
Prospect St . . . B1
Queen's Gdns . . . B2
Railway Dock Marina . . . C2
Railway St . . . C2
Reform St . . . A2
Riverside Quay . . . C2
Roper St . . . B2
St James St . . . C1
St Luke's St . . . B1
St Mark St . . . A3
St Mary the Virgin . . . B3
Scott St . . . A2
South Bridge Rd . . . B3
Spring Bank . . . A1
Spring St . . . B1
Spurn Lightship . . . C2
Spyvee St . . . A3
Streetlife Transport Museum . . . B3
Sykes St . . . A2
Tidal Surge Barrier ✦ . . . C3
Tower St . . . B3
Trinity House . . . B2
University . . . B3
Vane St . . . A1
Victoria Pier . . . C2
Waterhouse La . . . B2
Waterloo St . . . A1
Waverley St . . . C1
Wellington St . . . C2
Wellington St West . . . C2
West St . . . B1
Whitefriargate . . . B2
Wilberforce Dr . . . B2
Wilberforce House . . . B3
Wilberforce Monument ✦ . . . B3
William St . . . C1
Wincolmlee . . . A3
Witham . . . A3
Wright St . . . A1

Ipswich

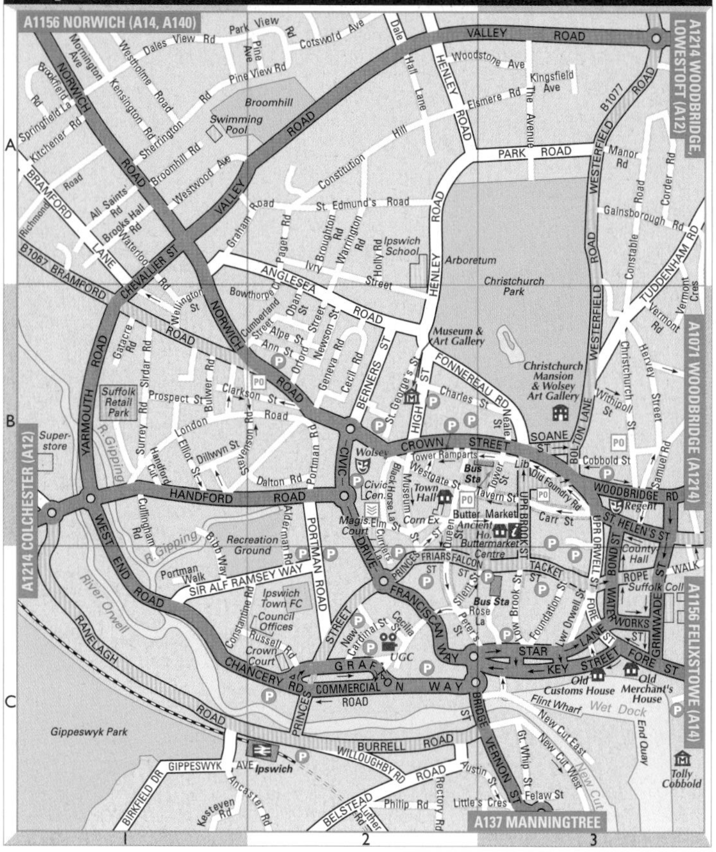

Lancaster

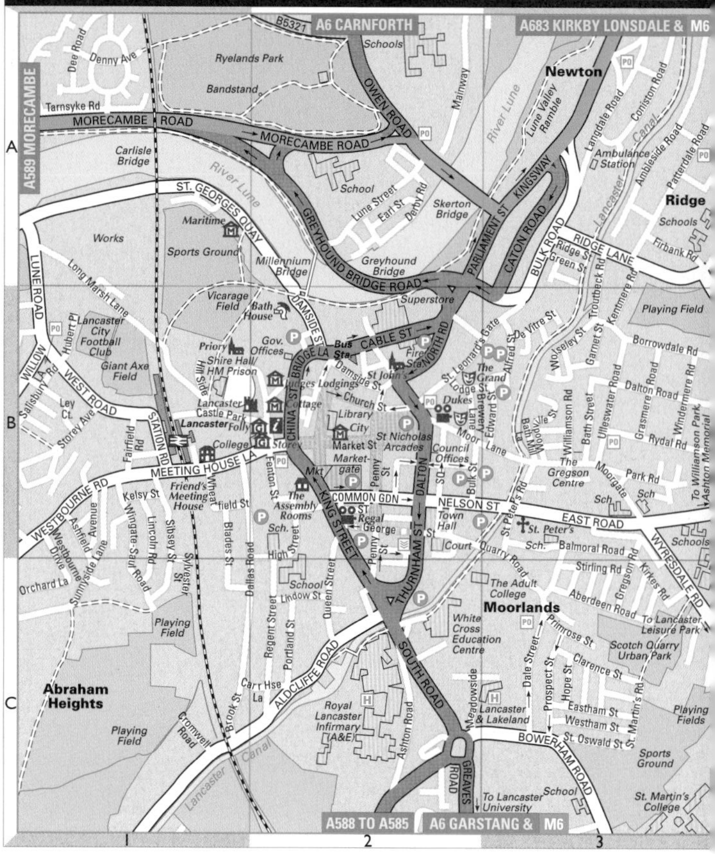

Ipswich

Alderman Rd ... B2
All Saints' Rd ... A1
Alpe St ... B2
Ancaster Rd ... C1
Ancient House ... B3
Anglesea Rd ... B2
Ann St ... B2
Austin St ... C2
Belstead Rd ... C2
Berners St ... B2
Bibb Way ... B1
Birkfield Dr ... C1
Black Horse La ... B2
Bolton La ... B3
Bond St ... C3
Bowthorpe Cl ... B2
Bramford La ... A1
Bramford Rd ... A1
Bridge St ... C2
Brookfield Rd ... A1
Brooks Hall Rd ... A1
Broomhill Rd ... A1
Broughton Rd ... A2
Bulwer Rd ... B1
Burrell Rd ... C2
Bus Station ... B2/C3
Butter Market ... B2
Butter Market Centre ... B3
Carr St ... B3
Cecil Rd ... B2
Cecilia St ... C2
Chancery Rd ... C2
Charles St ... B2
Chevallier St ... A1
Christchurch Mansion & Wolsey Art Gallery ... B3
Christchurch Park ... A3
Christchurch St ... B3
Civic Centre ... B2
Civic Dr ... B2
Clarkson St ... B1
Cobbold St ... B3
Commercial Rd ... C2
Constable Rd ... A3
Constantine Rd ... C1
Constitution Hill ... A2
Corder Rd ... A3
Corn Exchange ... B2
Cotswold Ave ... A2
Council Offices ... C2
County Hall ... B3
Crown Court ... C2
Crown St ... B2
Cullingham Rd ... B1
Cumberland St ... B2
Curriers La ... B2
Dale Hall La ... A2
Dales View Rd ... A1
Dalton Rd ... B2
Dillwyn St ... B1
Elliot St ... B1
Elm St ... B2
Elsmere Rd ... A3
End Quay ... C3
Falcon St ... C2
Felaw St ... C3
Flint Wharf ... C3
Fonnereau Rd ... B2
Fore St ... C3
Foundation St ... C3
Franciscan Way ... C2
Friars St ... C2
Gainsborough Rd ... A3
Gatacre Rd ... B1
Geneva Rd ... B2
Gippeswyk Ave ... C1
Gippeswyk Park ... C1
Grafton Way ... C2
Graham Rd ... A1
Grimwade St ... C3
Great Whip St ... C3
Handford Cut ... B1
Handford Rd ... B1
Henley Rd ... A2
Hervey St ... B3
High St ... B2
Holly Rd ... A2
Information Ctr ... B3
Ipswich School ... A2
Ipswich Station ... C2
Ipswich Town FC (Portman Road) ... C2
Ivry St ... A2
Kensington Rd ... A1
Kesteven Rd ... C1
Key St ... C3
Kingsfield Ave ... A3
Kitchener Rd ... A1
Magistrates Court ... B2
Little's Cr ... C2
London Rd ... B1
Low Brook St ... C3
Lower Orwell St ... C3
Luther Rd ... C2
Manor Rd ... A3
Mornington Ave ... A1
Museum & Art Gallery ... B2
Museum St ... B2
Neale St ... B3
New Cardinal St ... C2
New Cut East ... C3
New Cut West ... C3
Newson St ... B2
Norwich Rd ... A1/B1
Oban St ... B2
Old Customs House ... C3
Old Foundry Rd ... B3
Old Merchant's House ... C3
Orford St ... B2
Paget Rd ... A2
Park Rd ... A3
Park View Rd ... A2
Peter's St ... C2
Philip Rd ... C2
Pine Ave ... A2
Pine View Rd ... A2
Police Station ... B2
Portman Rd ... B2
Portman Walk ... C1
Post Office ... B2/B3
Princes St ... C2
Prospect St ... B1
Queen St ... B2
Ranelagh Rd ... C1
Rectory Rd ... C2
Regent Theatre ... B3
Richmond Rd ... A1
Rope Walk ... C3
Rose La ... C2
Russell Rd ... C1
St Edmund's Rd ... A2
St George's St ... B2
St Helen's St ... B3
Samuel Rd ... B3
Sherrington Rd ... A1
Silent St ... C2
Sir Alf Ramsey Way ... C1
Sirdar Rd ... B1
Soane St ... B3
Springfield La ... A1
Star La ... C3
Stevenson Rd ... B1
Suffolk College ... C3
Suffolk Retail Park ... B1
Superstore ... B1
Surrey Rd ... B1
Swimming Pool ... A1
Tacket St ... C3
Tavern St ... B3
The Avenue ... A3
Tolly Cobbold Museum ... C3
Tower Ramparts ... B2
Tower St ... B3
Town Hall ... B2
Tuddenham Rd ... A3
UGC ... C2
Upper Brook St ... B3
Upper Orwell St ... B3
Valley Rd ... A2
Vermont Cr ... B3
Vermont Rd ... B3
Vernon St ... C3
Warrington Rd ... A2
Waterloo Rd ... A1
Waterworks St ... C3
Wellington St ... B1
West End Rd ... B1
Westerfield Rd ... A3
Westgate St ... B2
Westholme Rd ... A1
Westwood Ave ... A1
Willoughby Rd ... C2
Withipoll St ... B3
Wolsey Theatre ... B2
Woodbridge Rd ... B3
Woodstone Ave ... A3
Yarmouth Rd ... B1

Lancaster

Aberdeen Rd ... C3
Adult College, The ... C3
Aldcliffe Rd ... C2
Alfred St ... B3
Ambleside Rd ... A3
Ambulance Sta ... A3
Ashfield Ave ... B1
Ashton Rd ... C2
Assembly Rooms, The ... B2
Balmoral Rd ... B3
Bath House ... B2
Bath Mill La ... B3
Bath St ... B3
Blades St ... B1
Borrowdale Rd ... B3
Bowerham Rd ... C3
Brewery La ... B2
Bridge La ... B2
Brook St ... C1
Bulk Rd ... A3
Bulk St ... B2
Bus Station ... B2
Cable St ... B2
Carlisle Bridge ... A1
Carr House La ... C2
Castle ... B1
Castle Park ... B1
Caton Rd ... A3
China St ... B2
Church St ... B2
City Museum ... B2
Clarence St ... C3
Common Gdn St ... B2
Coniston Rd ... A3
Cottage Museum ... B2
Council Offices ... B2
Court ... B2
Cromwell Rd ... C1
Dale St ... C3
Dallas Rd ... B1/C1
Dalton Rd ... B3
Dalton Sq ... B2
Damside St ... B2
De Vitre St ... B3
Dee Rd ... A1
Denny Ave ... A1
Derby Rd ... A2
Dukes ... B2
Earl St ... A2
East Rd ... B3
Eastham St ... C3
Edward St ... B3
Fairfield Rd ... B1
Fenton St ... B2
Firbank Rd ... A3
Fire Station ... B2
Folly Gallery ... B2
Friend's Meeting House ... B1
Garnet St ... B3
George St ... B2
Giant Axe Field ... B1
Gov. Offices ... B2
Grand, The ... B2
Grasmere Rd ... B3
Greaves Rd ... C2
Green St ... A3
Gregson Centre, The ... B3
Gregson Rd ... C3
Greyhound Bridge Rd ... A2
Greyhound Bridge ... A2
High St ... B2
Hill Side ... B1
Hope St ... C3
Hubert Pl ... B1
Information Ctr ... B2
Judges Lodgings ... B2
Kelsy St ... B1
Kentmere Rd ... B3
King St ... B2
Kingsway ... A3
Kirkes Rd ... C3
Lancaster & Lakeland ... C3
Lancaster City Football Club ... B1
Lancaster Station ... B1
Langdale Rd ... A3
Ley Ct ... B1
Library ... B2
Lincoln Rd ... B1
Lindow St ... C2
Lodge St ... B2
Long Marsh La ... B1
Lune Rd ... A1
Lune St ... A2
Lune Valley Ramble ... A3
Mainway ... A2
Maritime Museum ... A1
Market St ... B2
Marketgate Shopping Centre ... B2
Meadowside ... C2
Meeting House La ... B1
Millennium Bridge ... A2
Moorgate ... B3
Moor La ... B2
Morecambe Rd ... A1/A2
Nelson St ... B2
North Rd ... B2
Orchard La ... C1
Owen Rd ... A2
Park Rd ... B3
Parliament St ... A3
Patterdale Rd ... A3
Penny St ... B2
Police Station ... B2
Portland St ... C2
Post Office ... A2/A3/B1/B2/B3/C3
Primrose St ... C3
Priory ... B1
Prospect St ... C3
Quarry Rd ... B3
Queen St ... C2
Regal ... B2
Regent St ... C2
Ridge La ... A3
Ridge St ... A3
Royal Lancaster Infirmary (A&E) ... C2
Rydal Rd ... B3
Ryelands Park ... A
St. John's ... B
St. Nicholas Arcades Shopping Centre ... B
St. Peter's Rd ... B
St. Georges Quay ... A
St. Leonard's Gate ... B
St. Martin's College ... C
St. Martin's Rd ... C
St. Oswald St ... C
St. Peter's ... B
Salisbury Rd ... B
Scotch Quarry Urban Park ... C
Shire Hall/HM Prison ... B
Sibsey St ... B
Skerton Bridge ... A
South Rd ... C
Station Rd ... B
Stirling Rd ... C
Storey Ave ... B
Storey Gallery ... B
Sunnyside La ... C
Sylvester St ... C
Tarnsyke Rd ... A
Thurnham St ... C
Town Hall ... B
Troutbeck Rd ... B
Ulleswater Rd ... B
Vicarage Field ... B
West Rd ... B
Westbourne Dr ... C
Westbourne Rd ... B
Westham St ... C
Wheatfield St ... B
White Cross Education Centre ... C
Williamson Rd ... B
Willow La ... B
Windermere Rd ... B
Wingate-Saul Rd ... B
Wolseley St ... B
Woodville St ... B
Wyresdale Rd ... C

Leeds

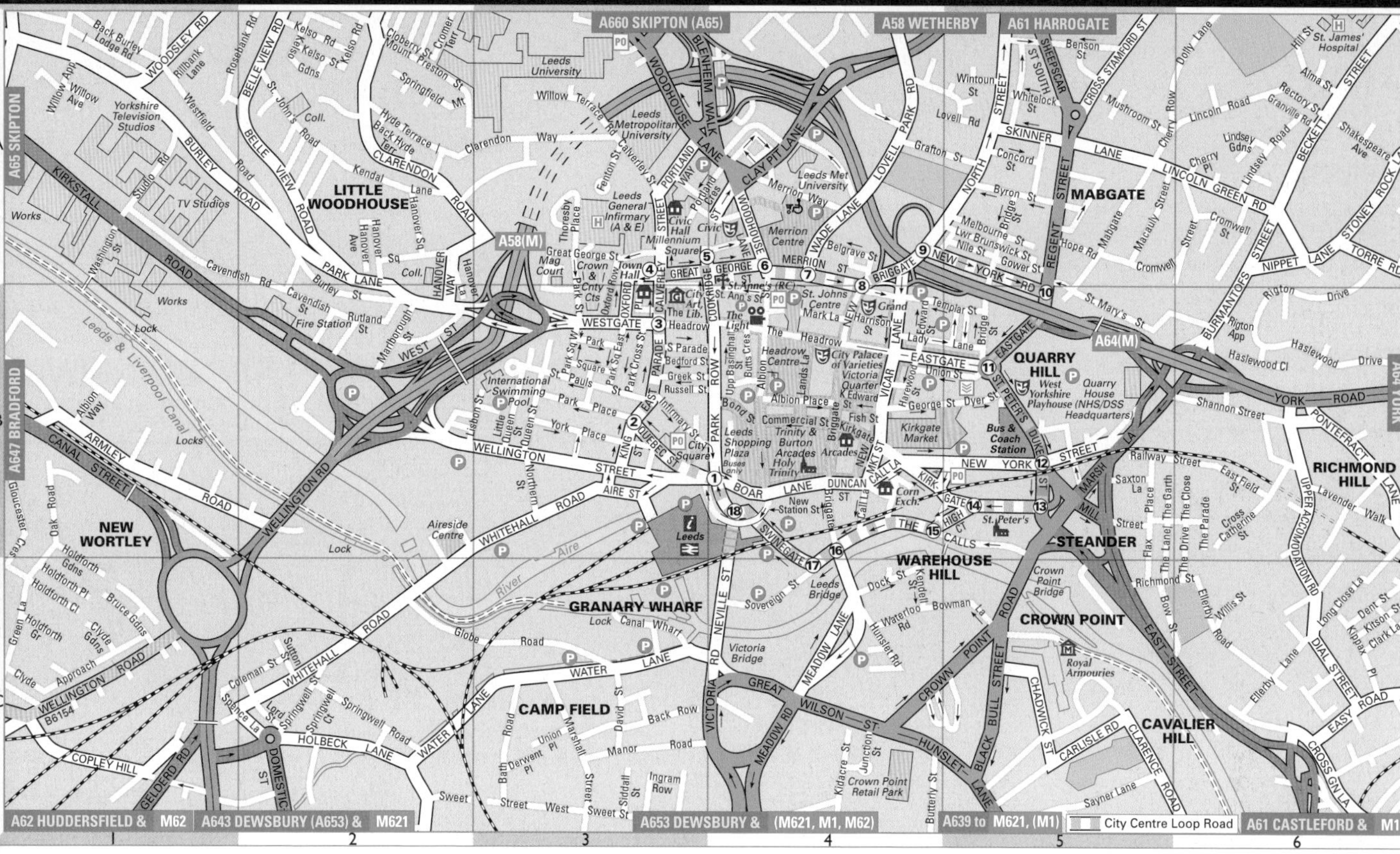

.eeds	Carlisle Rd. C5	Derwent Pl. C3	Haslewood Drive B6	Leeds Metropolitan University A3/A4	New Station St B4	St Ann's St. B4	Town Hall 🏛 A3
·e St B3	Cavendish Rd A1	Dial St C6	Headrow Centre B4	Leeds Shopping Plaza B4	New Wade La A4	St Anne's Cathedral (RC) ✝ A4	Trinity & Burton Arcades B4
·eside Centre B2	Cavendish St. A2	Dock St C4	High Court. B5	Leeds Station ⇌ B3	New York Rd A5	St James' Hospital H . A6	Union Pl. C3
·bion Pl B4	Chadwick St C5	Dolly La A6	Hill St. A6	Leeds University A3	New York St. B5	St Johns Centre B4	Union St B5
·bion St A4	Cherry Pl A6	Domestic St. C2	Holbeck La C2	Light, The 🎥 B4	Nile St A5	St John's Rd A2	Upper Basinghall St . . B4
·bion Way B1	Cherry Row A5	Duke St B5	Holdforth Cl. C1	Lincoln Green Rd A6	Nippet La. A6	St Mary's St. B5	Upper Accomodation Rd B6
·na St A6	City Art Gallery & Library 🏛 B3	Duncan St B4	Holdforth Gdns B1	Lincoln Rd A5	North St. A4	St Pauls St. B3	Vicar La B4
·cades 🏛 B4	City Palace of Varieties 🎭 B4	Dyer St B5	Holdforth Gr C1	Lindsey Gdns A6	Northern St B3	St Peter's ⛪ B5	Victoria Bridge. C4
·mley Rd B1	City Sq. B3	East Field St B6	Holdforth Pl C1	Lindsey Rd A6	Oak Rd B1	Saxton La B5	Victoria Quarter B4
·ck Burley Lodge Rd A1	Civic Theatre 🎭 A4	East Pde B3	Holy Trinity ⛪ B4	Lisbon St. B3	Oxford Pl. B3	Sayner La C5	Victoria Rd. C4
·ck Hyde Terr A2	Civic Hall 🏛 A3	East St. C5	Hope Rd A5	Little Queen St B3	Oxford Row A3	Shakespeare Ave A6	Washington St. A1
·ck Row C3	Clarendon Rd A2	Eastgate B5	Hunslet La. C4	Long Close La. C6	Park Cross St B3	Shannon St B6	Water La C3
·ath Rd C3	Clarendon Way A3	Easy Rd C6	Hunslet Rd. C4	Lord St. C2	Park La A2	Sheepscar St South . . A5	Waterloo Rd C3
·ckett St A6	Clark La. C6	Edward St B4	Hyde Terr. A2	Lovell Park Rd. A4	Park Pl. B3	Siddall St. C3	Wellington Rd B2/C1
·dford St. B3	Clay Pit La. A4	Ellerby La. C6	Infirmary St B3	Lovell Rd A5	Park Row. B4	Skinner La A5	Wellington St. B3
·lgrave St A4	Cloberry St A2	Ellerby Rd C6	Information Ctr ℹ B3	Lower Brunswick St . . A5	Park Sq B3	South Pde B3	West St B1
·lle View Rd A2	Clyde Approach C1	Fenton St. A3	Ingram Row. C3	Mabgate A5	Park Sq East B3	Sovereign St C4	West Yorkshire Playhouse 🎭 B5
·nson St A5	Clyde Gdns C1	Fire Station B2	International Swimming Pool B3	Macauly St A5	Park Sq West. B3	Spence La. C2	Westfield Rd A1
·ack Bull St C5	Coleman St C2	Fish St B4	Junction St C4	Magistrates Court A3	Park St. B3	Springfield Mount A2	Westgate B3
·enheim Walk. A3	Commercial St. B4	Flax Pl B5	King Edward St B4	Manor Rd C3	Police Station 🏛 B5	Springwell Ct. C2	Whitehall Rd B3/C2
·ar La B4	Concord St A5	Gelderd Rd C1	Kelso Gdns A2	Mark La. B4	Pontefract La. B6	Springwell Rd C2	Whitelock St A5
·nd St. B4	Cookridge St A4	George St B4	Kelso Rd A2	Marlborough St B1	Portland Cr A3	Springwell St. C2	Willis St C6
·w St. C5	Copley Hill. C1	Globe Rd. C2	Kelso St. A2	Marsh La B6	Portland Way. A3	Stoney Rock La. A6	Willow Approach A1
·wman La. C4	Corn Exchange 🏛 B4	Gloucester Cr B1	Kendal La A2	Marshall St C3	Post Office 🏤 . . A3/B3/B5	Studio Rd A1	Willow Ave. A1
·idge St. A5/B5	Cromer Terr A2	Gower St A5	Kendell St C4	Meadow La C4	Quarry House (NHS/DSS Headquarters) B5	Sutton St C2	Willow Terrace Rd A3
·iggate. B4	Cromwell St. A5	Grafton St A4	Kidacre St C4	Meadow Rd. C4	Quebec St. B3	Sweet St C3	Wintoun St. A5
·uce Gdns C1	Cross Catherine St . . . B6	Grand Theatre 🎭 B4	King St. B3	Melbourne St. A5	Queen St B3	Sweet St West. C3	Woodhouse La . . . A3/A4
·rley Rd. A1	Cross Green La C6	Granville Rd. A6	Kippax Pl. C6	Merrion Centre A4	Railway St B5	Swinegate B4	Woodsley Rd A1
·rley St B1	Cross Stamford St. . . . A5	Great George St A3	Kirkgate B4	Merrion St A4	Rectory St A6	Templar St B5	York Pl B3
·rmantofs St B6	Crown & County Courts A3	Great Wilson St C4	Kirkgate Market. B4	Merrion Way A4	Regent St A5	The Calls B5	York Rd B6
·s & Coach Station. . B5	Crown Point Bridge. . . C5	Greek St B3	Kirkstall Rd A1	Mill St B5	Richmond St C5	The Close B6	Yorkshire Television Studios A1
·tterly St C4	Crown Point Retail Park. C4	Green La C1	Kitson St C6	Millennium Sq A3	Rigton Approach B6	The Drive B6	
·tts Cr. B4	Crown Point Rd. C4	Hanover Ave A2	Lady La B4	Mount Preston St A2	Rigton Dr. B6	The Garth B5	
·ron St A5	David St. C3	Hanover La A2	Lands La B4	Mushroom St. A5	Rillbank La. A1	The Headrow. B3/B4	
·ll La B4	Dent St C6	Hanover Sq A2	Lavender Walk. B6	Neville St. C4	Rosebank Rd. A1	The Lane B5	
·lverley St. A3/B3		Hanover Way. A2	Leeds Bridge. C4	New Briggate. A4/B4	Royal Armouries 🏛 . . . C5	The Parade B6	
·nal St. B1		Harewood St B4	Leeds General Infirmary (A&E) H A3	New Market St B4	Russell St B3	Thoresby Pl A3	
·nal Wharf. C3		Harrison St B4			Rutland St. B1	Torre Rd. A6	
		Haslewood Cl B6					

Menston
Guiseley
Yeadon
Leeds Bradford International Airport
Riddlesden
East Riddlesden Hall
Keighley
Keighley & Worth Valley Light Rly
Vintage Railway Carriage Museum
Hawksworth Moor
Bingley Moor
East Morton
Micklethwaite
Eldwick
Baildon Moor
Baildon
Bracken Hall Countryside Centre
Bingley
Ferncliffe
Harden
Esholt
Rawdon
Tranmere Park
Kelcliff
Westfield
Larkfield
Thackley
Shipley
Baildon Wood Bottom
1853 Gallery
Cottingley
Nab Wood
Cullingworth
Wilsden
Moorhead
Frizinghall
West Royd
Wrose
Eccleshill
Thorpe
Greengates
Calverley
Farsley
Ravenscliffe
Bradford Industrial Museum
Heaton
Cartwright Hall Art Gallery
Daisy Hill
Bolton
Fagley
Denholme
Allerton
Fairweather Green
Thornton
Bradford
Colour Museum
National Museum of Photography
Barkerend
Thornbury
Stanningley
Pudsey
Tyersal
Fulneck
Clayton
Horton Bank
West Bowling
Bolling Hall
Holme Wood
Queensbury
Buttershaw
Bierley
Tong
Odsal Stadium
Shelf
Illingworth
Wesley Place
East Bierley
Drighlington
Birkenshaw
Woodside
Moor Side
Upper Common
Mixenden
Ovenden
Northowram
Wheatley
Woodlands
Bankfield Museum
Wyke
Hunsworth
Gomersal
Red House
Oakwell Hall Country Park
Birstall
Hipperholme
Scholes
Pellon
Halifax
Piece Hall
Eureka!
Bailiff Bridge
Cleckheaton
Marsh
Bank Top
Hove Edge
Hightown Heights
Hartshead Moor Services
Liversedge
Heckmondwike
Nunroyd
Savile Park
Sowerby Bridge
Siddal
Southowram
Brighouse
Waring Green
Clifton
Norland Town
Exley
Robertown
Hartshead
Lindwell
Greetland
West Vale
Rastrick
Elland
Bradley Wood
Mirfield
Ravensthorpe
Northope
Dewsbury Moor
Fixby
Stainland
Holywell Green
Brackenhall
Cowcliffe

Bog Plantation
Harewood House
Harewood Park
Crag Wood
BRAMHOPE
Beech Bank
Lady Wood
West Woods
Eccup Reservoir
Bramham Park
Scarcroft
Coakridge
York Gate Garden
Alwoodley
Slaid Hill
Whittle Carr
Thorner
Adel
Blackwood
Shadwell
Govt Bldgs
Saw Wood
HORSFORTH
Ireland Wood
Park Villas
Tropical World
Roundhay Park
Lady Wood
Arthursdale
Cragg Hill
West Park
Meanwood
Barwick in Elmet
Hawksworth
Met Univ
Monkswood
Scholes
Barwick Bank
Beckett Park
Headingley
Oakwood
Kirkstall Abbey
Headingley
Brooklands
Swarcliffe
Hyde Park
Parklands
Parlington Hollins
Bramley
Hill Top
Burley
University
Harehills
Manston
Leeds Industrial Museum
Civic Hall
Austhorpe
Town Hall
City Art Gall
Whitekirk
Armley
Garforth
Park Spring
Bank
Osmondthorpe
East End Park
Halton Moor
Colton
Barrowby Park
Swillington Common
Church Garforth
Upper Wortley
LEEDS
Royal Armouries
Farnley
Holbeck
Knowsthorpe
Home Farm
Temple Newsam House
Temple Newsam Country Park
Hunslet
Thwaitemills Industrial Museum
Dawson's Wood
Avenue Wood
Brecks Wood
New Farnley
Elland Road
Cross Flatts Park
River Aire
Aire & Calder Navigation
Beeston
South Leeds Stadium
Newsam Green
Swillington
KIPPAX
Little Preston
Country Park
Middleton Railway
Rothwell Haigh
Woodlesford
Great Preston
Cockpit Round
Churwell
White Rose Centre
Middleton Park
Troy Hill
Town Hall
ROTHWELL
Oulton
Bruntcliffe
MORLEY
Middleton
Robin Hood
Carlton
Mickletown
Almshouses Wood
Topcliffe
Thorpe on the Hill
Oulzewell Green
Moss Carr Wood
Methley
Sports Centre
The Fall
Upper Batley
Upper Green
EAST ARDSLEY
Ardsley Resr
Lee Moor
Lofthouse Gate
Fairies Hill
Lower Soothill
The Mill
Haigh Moor
River Calder
Dum Wood
STANLEY
Brandy Carr
OUTWOOD
Nature Reserve
Altofts
BATLEY
Dogloitch Wood
Brag Lane End
Batley Carr
Hanging Heaton
Chidswell
Kirkhamgate
Newton Hill
NORMANTON
Gawthorpe
Wrenthorpe
DEWSBURY
Ossett Street Side
Woodhouse
Alverthorpe
Chickenley
Kirkthorpe
Canal Museum
WAKEFIELD
OSSETT
Flanshaw
Town Hall
Coll
Cath
Warmfield
Streethouse
Runtlings
Lupset
Thornhill Lees
South Ossett
Sharlston Common
Sharlston
Belle Vue
A58
A61
A64
A63
A62
A65
A639
A642
A650
A653
A654
A655
A660
A6120
A647
M1
M62
M621
0 1 2 3 miles
0 1 2 3 4 5 km

Liverpool

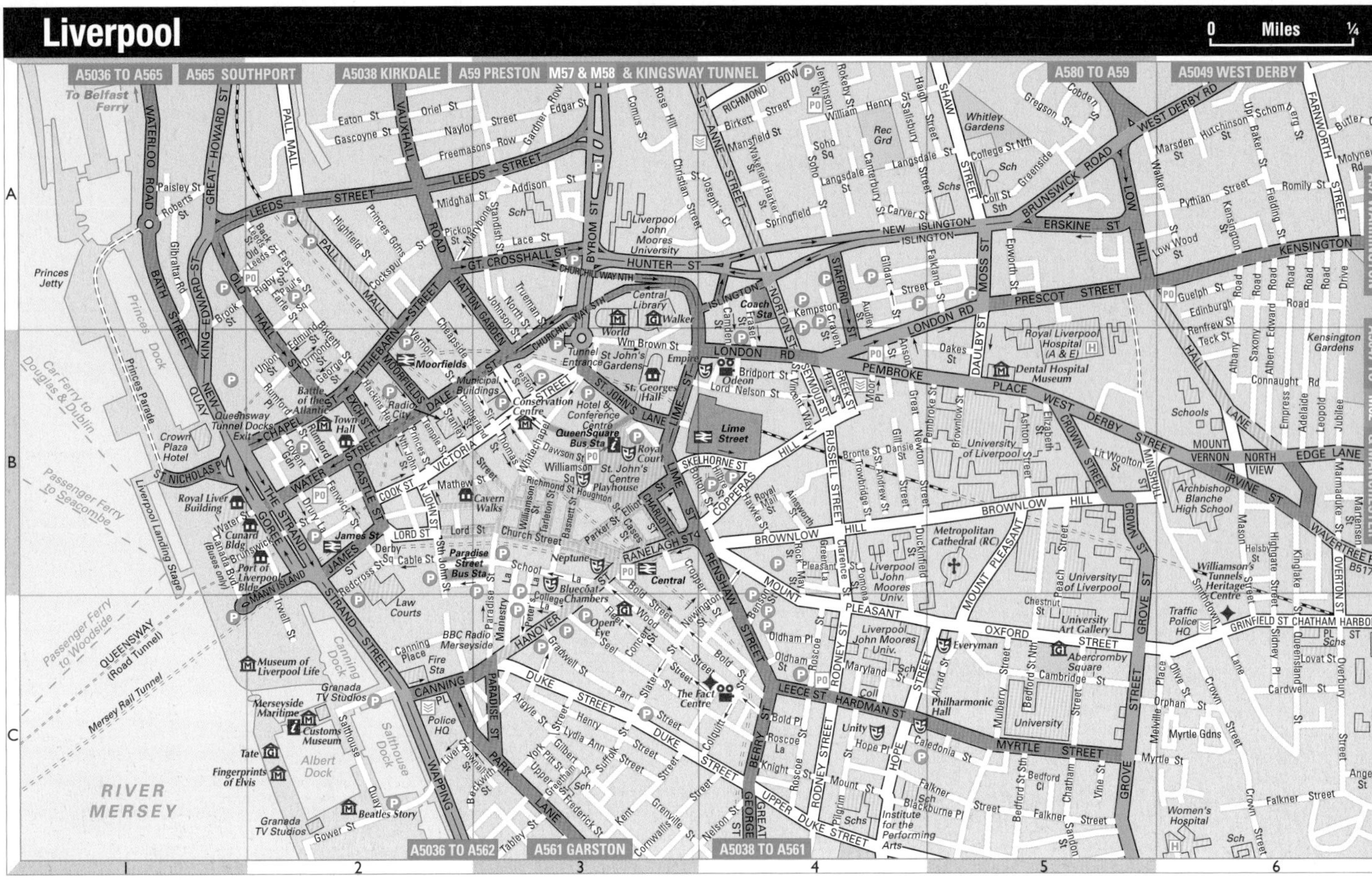

Liverpool

Abercromby Sq C5
Addison St. A3
Adelaide Rd. B6
Ainsworth St B4
Albany Rd B6
Albert Dock C2
Albert Edward Rd B6
Angela St. C6
Anson St B4
Archbishop Blanche High School B6
Argyle St C2
Arrad St. C4
Ashton St. B5
Audley St. A4
Back Leeds St. A2
Basnett St B3
Bath St A1
Battle of the Atlantic 🏛 B2
BBC Radio Merseyside C2
Beatles Story 🏛 C2
Beckwith St. C3
Bedford Close C5
Bedford St North. C5
Bedford St South C5
Benson St C4
Berry St. C4
Birkett St A4
Bixteth St. B2
Blackburne Place C4
Bluecoat Chambers B3
Bold Place. C4
Bold St C4
Bolton St B3
Bridport St. B4
Bronte St. B4
Brook St A1
Brownlow Hill B4/B5
Brownlow St B5
Brunswick Rd A5
Brunswick St. B1
Butler Cr A6
Byrom St. A3
Cable St. B2
Caledonia St C4
Cambridge St C5
Camden St A4
Canada Blvd B1
Canning Dock C2
Canning Place C2
Canterbury St A4
Cardwell St C6
Carver St. A4
Cases St B3
Castle St B2
Cavern Walks B3
Central Library. A3
Central Station . . . B3
Chapel St. B2
Charlotte St. B3
Chatham Place C6
Chatham St. C5
Cheapside B2
Chestnut St C5
Christian St A3
Church St B3
Churchill Way North . . A3
Churchill Way South . . B3
Clarence St B4
Coach Station A4
Cobden St. A5
Cockspur St A2
College La. C3
College St North A5
College St South. A5
Colquitt St C4
Comus St A3
Concert St. C3
Connaught Rd. B6
Conservation Centre 🏛. B3
Cook St B2
Copperas Hill. B3
Cornwallis St. C3
Covent Garden B2
Craven St A4
Cropper St. B3
Crown St B5/C6
Cumberland St B2
Cunard Building B1
Dale St. B2
Dansie St. B4
Daulby St B5
Dawson St. B3
Dental Hospital Museum 🏛 B5
Derby Sq B2
Drury La. B2
Duckinfield St B4
Duke St C3
Earle St A2
East St. A2
Eaton St. A2
Edgar St A3
Edge La. B6
Edinburgh Rd A6
Edmund St B2
Elizabeth St. B5
Elliot St B3
Empire Theatre B4
Empress Rd. B6
Epworth St A5
Erskine St A5
Everyman Theatre . . C5
Exchange St East B2
Fact Centre, The ✦ . C4
Falkland St A5
Falkner St C5/C6
Farnworth St A6
Fenwick St. B2
Fielding St A6
Fingerprints of Elvis 🏛 C2
Fleet St C3
Fraser St A4
Freemasons Row A2
Gardner Row. A3
Gascoyne St A2
George St B2
Gibraltar Row A1
Gilbert St C3
Gildart St A4
Gill St. B4
Goree. B2
Gower St C2
Gradwell St C3
Granada TV Studios . . . C2
Great Crosshall St A3
Great George St C4
Great Howard St A1
Great Newton St B4
Greek St B4
Green La B4
Greenside A5
Greetham St C3
Gregson St A5
Grenville St C3
Grinfield St C6
Grove St C5
Guelph St A6
Hackins Hey B2
Haigh St. A4
Hall La. B6
Hanover St B3
Harbord St. C6
Hardman St C4
Harker St. A4
Hart St. B4
Hatton Garden. A2
Hawke St B4
Helsby St. B6
Henry St C3
HM Customs & Excise National Museum 🏛 . C2
Highfield St A2
Highgate St B6
Hilbre St. B4
Hope Place C4
Hope St C4
Houghton St B3
Hunter St. A3
Hutchinson St A6
Information Ctr . B3/C2
Institute For The Performing Arts. C4
Irvine St B6
Irwell St B2
Islington. A4
James St B2
James St Station . . B2
Jenkinson St A4
Johnson St A3
Jubilee Drive B6
Kempston St A4
Kensington A6
Kensington Gdns. B6
Kensington St A6
Kent St C3
King Edward St A1
Kinglake St B6
Knight St C4
Lace St A3
Langsdale St A4
Law Courts C2
Leece St C4
Leeds St A2
Leopold Rd B6
Lime St B3
Lime St Station . . . B4
Little Woolton St B5
Liver St C2
Liverpool John Moores University . . . A3/B4/C4
Liverpool Landing Stage. B1
London Rd. A4/B4
Lord Nelson St B4
Lord St. B2
Lovat St. C6
Low Hill A5
Low Wood St. A6
Lydia Ann St C3
Manestry La. C3
Mann Island. B2
Mansfield St A4
Marmaduke St. B6
Marsden St A6
Martensen St. B6
Marybone A3
Maryland St C4
Mason St. B6
Mathew St B2
May St. B4
Melville Place C6
Merseyside Maritime Museum 🏛 C2
Metropolitan Cathedral (RC) ✝. B5
Midghall St A2
Molyneux Rd A6
Moor Place B4
Moorfields B2
Moorfields Station . B2
Moss St. A5
Mount Pleasant . . . B4/B5
Mount St C4
Mount Vernon View . . . B6
Mulberry St C5
Municipal Buildings . . . B2
Museum of Liverpool Life 🏛 C2
Myrtle Gdns. C6
Myrtle St C5
Naylor St A2
Nelson St. C4
Neptune Theatre . . . B3
New Islington. A4
New Quay B1
Newington St C3
North John St B2
North St. A3
North View. B6
Norton St. A4
Oakes St B5
Odeon B4
Old Hall St. A1
Old Leeds St A2
Oldham Place C4
Oldham St C4
Olive St C5
Open Eye Gallery 🏛 . . C3
Oriel St A2
Ormond St. B2
Orphan St C6
Overbury St C6
Overton St B6
Oxford St. C5
Paisley St. A1
Pall Mall. A2
Paradise St C3
Paradise St Bus Station B2
Park La C3
Parker St B3
Parr St C3
Peach St B5
Pembroke Place B4
Pembroke St B5
Peter's La C3
Philharmonic Hall . . C5
Pickop St. A2
Pilgrim St. C4
Pitt St. C3
Playhouse Theatre . . B3
Pleasant St B4
Police Headquarters C2
Police Station . . A4/B4
Pomona St B4
Port of Liverpool Building B2
Post Office A2/A4/A6/B2/B3/B4/C4
Pownall St C2
Prescot St A5
Preston St B3
Princes Dock. A1
Princes Gdns. A2
Princes Jetty A1
Princes Pde. B1
Princes St B2
Pythian St A6
Queen Square Bus Station B3
Queensland St. C6
Queensway Tunnel (Docks exit). B1
Queensway Tunnel (Entrance) B3
Radio City B2
Ranelagh St. B3
Redcross St. B2
Renfrew St. B6
Renshaw St. B4
Richmond Row A4
Richmond St B3
Rigby St. A2
Roberts St A1
Rock St B4
Rodney St C4
Rokeby St A4
Romily St. A6
Roney St C4
Roscoe La. C4
Roscoe St C4
Rose Hill A3
Royal Court Theatre B3
Royal Liver Building B1
Royal Liverpool Hospital (A&E) B5
Royal Mail St. B4
Rumford Place. B2
Rumford St B2
Russell St B4
St Andrew St. B4
St Anne St. A4
St Georges Hall B3
St John's Centre B3
St John's Gdns B3
St John's La B3
St Joseph's Cr. A4
St Minishull St. B5
St Nicholas Place B1
St Paul's Sq. A2
St Vincent Way B4
Salisbury St A4
Salthouse Dock C2
Salthouse Quay C2
Sandon St C5
Saxony Rd. B6
Schomberg St A6
School La B2
Seel St. C3
Seymour St B4
Shaw St A5
Sidney Place C6
Sir Thomas St B3
Skelhorne St B4
Slater St. C3
Smithdown La. B5
Soho Sq A4
Soho St A4
Springfield A4
Stafford St A4
Standish St
Stanley St
South John St
Strand St
Suffolk St
Tabley St
Tarleton St
Tate Gallery 🏛
Teck St
Temple St
The Strand
Tithebarn St
Town Hall
Traffic Police Headquarters
Trowbridge St
Trueman St
Union St
Unity Theatre
University Art Gallery 🏛
University
University of Liverpool
Upper Duke St
Upper Frederick St
Upper Baker St
Vauxhall Rd
Vernon St
Victoria St
Vine St
Wakefield St
Walker Art Gallery 🏛
Walker St
Wapping
Water St. B1/
Waterloo Rd
Wavertree Rd
West Derby Rd
West Derby St
Whitechapel
Whitley Gdns
Williamson Sq
Williamson St
Williamson's Tunnels Heritage Centre ✦
William Brown St
Willian Henry St
Women's Hospital
Wood St
World Museum, Liverpool 🏛
York St

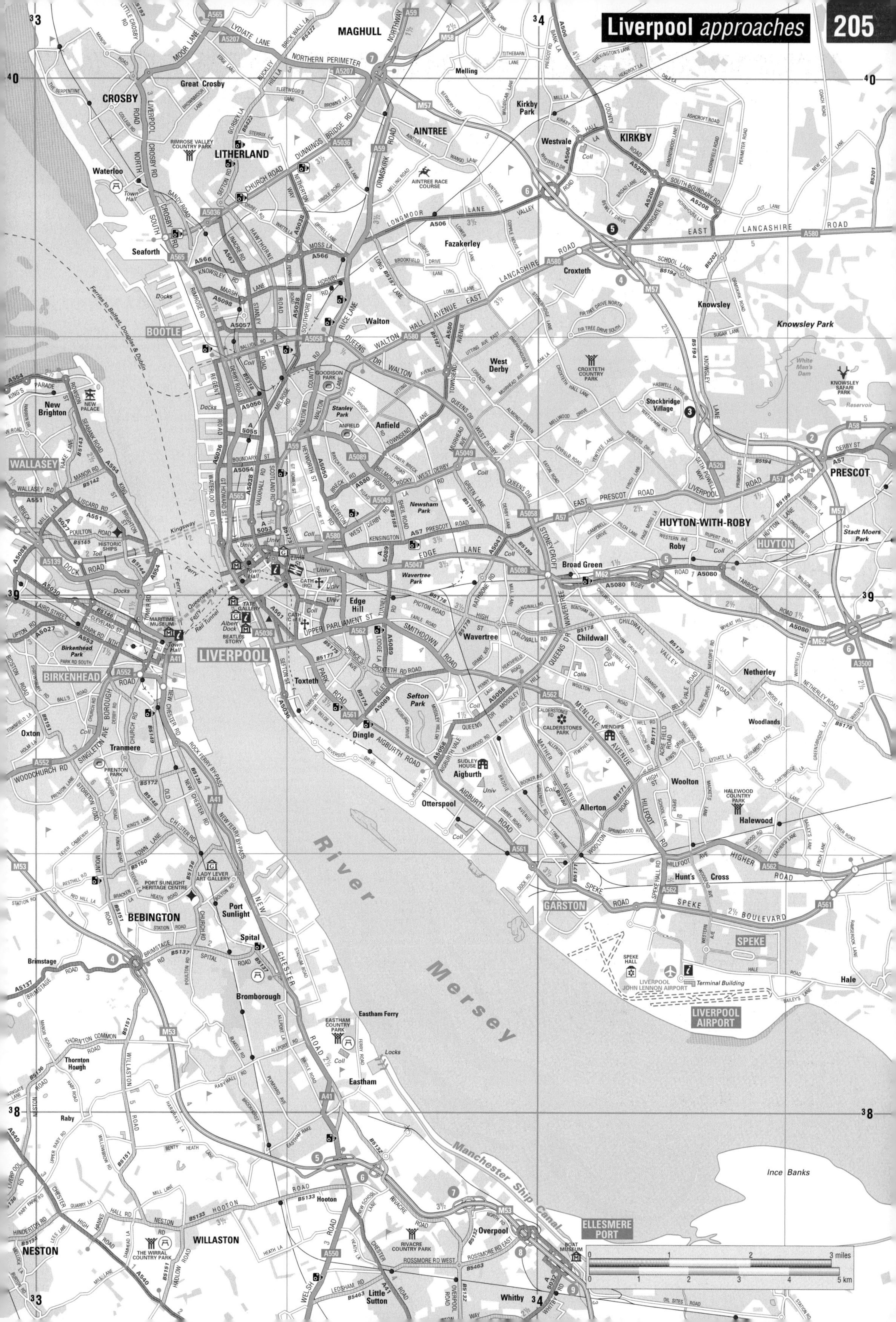
MAGHULL
Melling
Kirkby Park
KIRKBY
Westvale
CROSBY
Great Crosby
LITHERLAND
RIMROSE VALLEY COUNTRY PARK
AINTREE
AINTREE RACE COURSE
Waterloo
Seaforth
Fazakerley
Croxteth
Knowsley
Knowsley Park
KNOWSLEY SAFARI PARK
BOOTLE
Ferries to Belfast, Douglas & Dublin
Walton
West Derby
CROXTETH COUNTRY PARK
Stockbridge Village
New Brighton
NEW PALACE
WALLASEY
Anfield
Stanley Park
GOODISON PARK
PRESCOT
HUYTON-WITH-ROBY
Roby
HUYTON
Stadt Moers Park
HISTORIC SHIPS
Kingsway
Broad Green
Newsham Park
Wavertree Park
Edge Hill
Birkenhead Park
MARITIME MUSEUM
TATE GALLERY
Albert Dock
BEATLES STORY
Queensway
Rail Tunnel
LIVERPOOL
BIRKENHEAD
Wavertree
Childwall
Netherley
Woodlands
Toxteth
Sefton Park
Dingle
Oxton
Tranmere
PRENTON PARK
CALDERSTONES PARK
MENDIPS
SUDLEY HOUSE
Aigburth
Otterspool
Allerton
Woolton
HALEWOOD COUNTRY PARK
Halewood
Hunt's Cross
GARSTON
SPEKE
SPEKE HALL
LIVERPOOL JOHN LENNON AIRPORT
Terminal Building
LIVERPOOL AIRPORT
Hale
River Mersey
LADY LEVER ART GALLERY
PORT SUNLIGHT HERITAGE CENTRE
Port Sunlight
BEBINGTON
Spital
Brimstage
Bromborough
Eastham Ferry
EASTHAM COUNTRY PARK
Locks
Eastham
Thornton Hough
Raby
Manchester Ship Canal
Ince Banks
Hooton
ELLESMERE PORT
BOAT MUSEUM
RIVACRE COUNTRY PARK
Overpool
NESTON
WILLASTON
THE WIRRAL COUNTRY PARK
Little Sutton
Whitby
0 1 2 3 miles
0 1 2 3 4 5 km

Leicester

0 Miles ¼

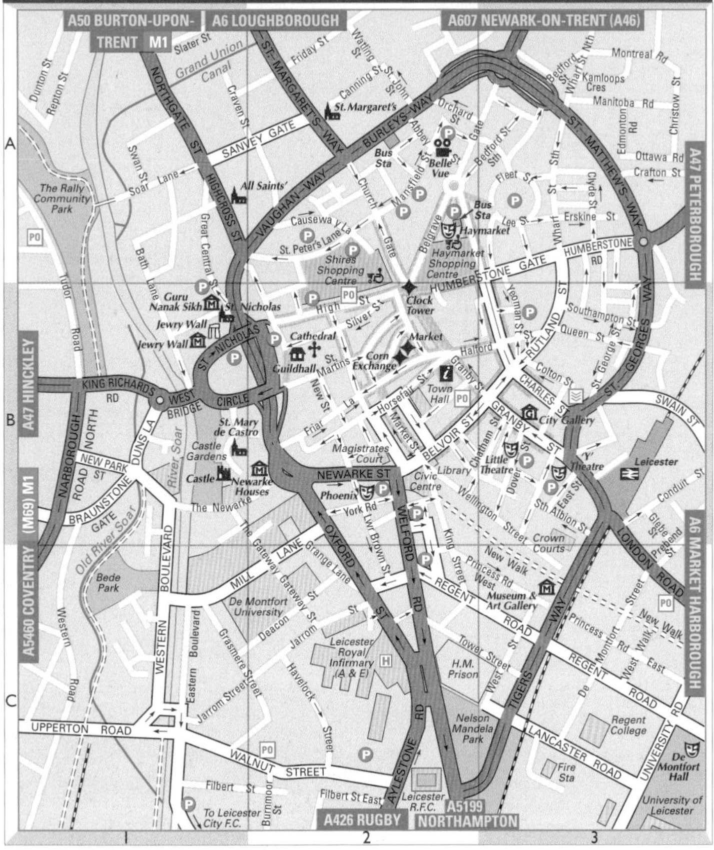

Lincoln

0 Miles ¼

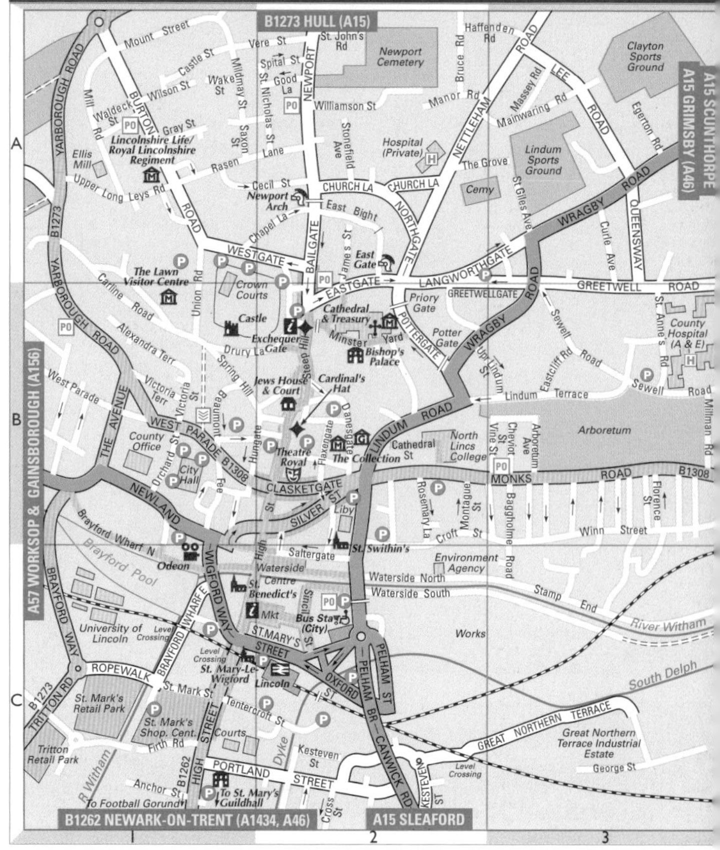

Leicester

Abbey St A2
All Saints' A1
Aylestone Rd C2
Bath La A1
Bede Park C1
Bedford St A3
Bedford St South A3
Belgrave Gate A2
Belle Vue A2
Belvoir St B2
Braunstone Gate B1
Burleys Way A2
Burnmoor St C2
Bus Station A2
Canning St A2
Castle B1
Castle Gardens B1
Cathedral B2
Causeway La A2
Charles St B3
Chatham St B2
Christow St A3
Church Gate A2
City Gallery B3
Civic Centre B2
Clock Tower B2
Clyde St A3
Colton St B3
Conduit St B3
Corn Exchange B2
Crafton St A3
Craven St A1
Crown Courts B3
Deacon St C2
De Montfort Hall C3
De Montfort St C3
De Montfort University C1
Dover St B3
Duns La B1
Dunton St A1
East St B3
Eastern Boulevard C1
Edmonton Rd A3
Erskine St A3
Filbert St C1
Filbert St East C2
Fire Station C3
Fleet St A3
Friar La B2
Friday St A2
Gateway St C2
Glebe St B3
Granby St B3
Grange La C2
Grasmere St C1
Great Central St A1
Guildhall B2
Guru Nanak Sikh Museum B1
Halford St B2
Havelock St C2
Haymarket A2
Haymarket Shopping Centre A2
High St A2
Highcross St A1
H.M. Prison C2
Horsefair St B2
Humberstone Gate B2
Humberstone Rd A3
Information Ctr B2
Jarrom St C2
Jewry Wall B1
Kamloops Cr A3
King Richards Rd B1
King St B2
Lancaster Rd C3
Lee St A3
Leicester Station B3
Leicester R.F.C. C2
Leicester Royal Infirmary (A & E) C2
Library B2
Little Theatre B3
London Rd C3
Lower Brown St B2
Magistrates Court B2
Manitoba Rd A3
Mansfield St A2
Market B2
Market St B2
Mill La C2
Montreal Rd A3
Museum & Art Gallery C3
Narborough Rd North B1
Nelson Mandela Park C2
New St B2
New Walk C3
New Park St B1
Newarke Houses B2
Newarke St B2
Northgate St A1
Orchard St A2
Ottawa Rd A3
Oxford St C2
Phoenix B2
Police Station B3
Post Office A1/B2/C2/C3
Prebend St C3
Princess Rd East C3
Princess Rd West C3
Queen St B3
Regent College C3
Regent Rd C2/C3
Repton St A1
Rutland St B3
St George St B3
St Georges Way B3
St John St A2
St Margaret's A2
St Margaret's Way A2
St Martins B2
St Mary de Castro B1
St Matthew's Way A3
St Nicholas B1
St Nicholas Circle B1
St Peter's La A2
Sanvey Gate A2
Shires Shopping Centre A2
Silver St B2
Slater St A1
Soar La A1
South Albion St B3
Southampton St B3
Swain St B3
Swan St A1
The Gateway C2
The Newarke B1
The Rally Community Park A2
Tigers Way C3
Tower St C3
Town Hall B2
Tudor Rd B1
University of Leicester C3
University Rd C3
Upperton Rd C1
Vaughan Way A2
Walnut St C2
Watling St A2
Welford Rd B2
Wellington St B2
West Bridge B1
West St C3
West Walk C3
Western Boulevard C1
Western Rd C1
Wharf St North A3
Wharf St South A3
'Y' Theatre B3
Yeoman St B3
York Rd B2

Lincoln

Alexandra Terr B1
Anchor St C1
Arboretum B3
Arboretum Ave B3
Baggholme Rd B3
Bailgate A2
Beaumont Fee B1
Bishop's Palace B2
Brayford Way C1
Brayford Wharf East C1
Brayford Wharf North B1
Bruce Rd A2
Burton Rd A1
Bus Station (City) C2
Canwick Rd C2
Cardinal's Hat B2
Carline Rd B1
Castle B1
Castle St A1
Cathedral & Treasury B2
Cathedral St B2
Cecil St A2
Chapel La A2
Cheviot St B3
Church La A2
City Hall B1
Clasketgate B2
Clayton Sports Ground A3
Collection, The B2
County Hospital (A & E) B3
County Office B1
Courts C1
Croft St B2
Cross St C2
Crown Courts B1
Curle Ave A3
Danesgate B2
Drury La B1
East Bight A2
East Gate A2
Eastcliff Rd B3
Eastgate B2
Egerton Rd A3
Ellis Mill A1
Environment Agency C2
Exchequer Gate B2
Firth Rd C1
Flaxengate B2
Florence St B3
George St C3
Good La A2
Gray St A1
Great Northern Terr C3
Great Northern Terrace Industrial Estate C3
Greetwell Rd B3
Greetwellgate B3
Haffenden Rd A2
High St B2/C1
Hospital (Private) A2
Hungate B2
Information Ctr B2
James St A2
Jews House & Court B2
Kesteven St C2
Langworthgate A2
Lee Rd A3
Lawn Visitor Centre, The B1
Library B2
Lincoln Station C2
Lincolnshire Life/Royal Lincolnshire Regiment Museum A1
Lindum Rd B2
Lindum Sports Ground A3
Lindum Terr B3
Mainwaring Rd A3
Manor Rd A2
Massey Rd A3
Mildmay St A1
Mill Rd A1
Millman Rd B3
Minster Yard B2
Market C2
Monks Rd B3
Montague St B2
Mount St A1
Nettleham Rd A2
Newland B1
Newport A2
Newport Arch A2
Newport Cemetery A2
North Lincs College B2
Northgate A2
Odeon C1
Orchard St B1
Oxford St C2
Pelham Bridge C2
Pelham St C2
Police Station B1
Portland St C2
Post Office A1/A2/B1/B3/C2
Potter Gate B2
Priory Gate B2
Queensway A3
Rasen La A1
Ropewalk C1
Rosemary La B2
St Anne's Rd B3
St Benedict's C1
St Giles Ave A3
St John's Rd A2
St Mark St C1
St Mark's Retail Park C1
St Mark's Shopping Centre C1
St Mary-Le-Wigford C1
St Mary's St C
St Nicholas St A
St Swithin's B
Saltergate C
Saxon St A
Sewell Rd B
Silver St B
Sincil St C
Spital St A
Spring Hill B
Stamp End C
Steep Hill B
Stonefield Ave A
Tentercroft St C
The Avenue B
The Grove A
Theatre Royal B
Tritton Retail Park C
Tritton Rd C
Union Rd B
University of Lincoln C
Upper Lindum St B
Upper Long Leys Rd A
Vere St A
Victoria St B
Victoria Terr B
Vine St B
Wake St A
Waldeck St A
Waterside Centre C
Waterside North C
Waterside South C
West Pde B
Westgate A
Wigford Way C
Williamson St A
Wilson St A
Winn St B
Wragby Rd A
Yarborough Rd A

.ondon

obey Orchard St E3
ochurch La D6
oingdon St E4
chilles Way D2
cton St B4
ddington St E4
r St D3
bany St B2
bemarle St D3
bert Embankment F4
'denham St A3
dersgate St C6
dford St D2
dgate C7
dgate High St C7
dwych C4
lsop Pl B1
mwell St B5
ndrew Borde St C3
ngel ⊖ A5
opold St C7
rgyle Sq B4
rgyle St B4
rgyll St C3
rnold Circus B7
rtillery La C7
rtillery Row E3
ssociation of
Photographers
Gallery 🏛 B6
aker St B1
aker Street ⊖ B1
aldwin's Gdns C5
altic St B6
ank ⊖ C6
ank Museum 🏛 C6
ank of England C6
ankside D5
ankside Gallery 🏛 D5
anner St B6
arbican ⊖⇌ C6
arbican Centre
for Arts, The C6
arbican Gallery 🏛 C6
asil St E1
asinghall St C6
astwick St B6
ateman's Row B7
ath St B6
ayley St C3
aylis Rd E5
eak St D3
edford Row C4
edford Sq C3
edford St D4
edford Way B3
eech St C6
elgrave Pl E2
elgrave Sq E2
ell La C7
elvedere Rd E4
erkeley Sq D2
erkeley St D2
ernard St B4
erners Pl C3
erners St C3
erwick St C3
ethnal Green Rd B7
evenden St B6
evis Marks C7
FI London IMAX
Cinema 🎥 D5
idborough St B4
nney St C2
rdcage Walk E3
shopsgate C7
ackfriars ⊖⇌ D5
ackfriars Bridge D5
ackfriars Rd E5
andford St C1
omfield St C6
oomsbury St C3
oomsbury Way C4
olton St D2
ond Street ⊖ C2
orough High St D6/E6
orough Rd E5
oswell St C4
owling Green La B5
ow St C4
ad St D5
essenden Pl E2
ewer St D3
ick St D3
idge St E4
itain at War 🏛 D7
itannia Walk B6
itish Airways
London-Eye ✦ E4
itish Library 🏛 B3
itish Museum 🏛 C4
itton St B5
oad Sanctuary E3
oadway E3
ook Dr F5
ook St D2
unswick Pl B6
unswick Sq B4
ushfield St C7
uton St D2
yanston St C1
ickingham Gate E3

Buckingham
Palace 🏰 E3
Buckingham
Palace Rd E2
Bunhill Row B6
Byward St D7
Cabinet War Rooms
& Churchill
Museum 🏛 E3
Cadogan La E2
Cadogan Pl E1/E2
Cadogan Sq F1
Caledonian Rd A4
Calshot St A4
Calthorpe St B4
Calvert Ave B7
Cambridge Circus C3
Camomile St C7
Cannon St D6
Cannon St ⊖⇌ D6
Carey St C4
Carlisle La E4
Carlisle Pl E3
Carlton House Terr D3
Carmelite St D5
Carnaby St C3
Carter La C5
Carthusian St C6
Cartwright Gdns B4
Castle Baynard St D5
Cavendish Pl C2
Cavendish Sq C2
Caxton Hall E3
Caxton St E3
Central St B6
Chalton St B3
Chancery Lane ⊖ C5
Chapel St E2
Charing Cross ⊖⇌ D4
Charing Cross Rd C3
Charles II St D3
Charles Sq B6
Charles St D2
Charlotte Rd B7
Charlotte St C3
Charterhouse Sq C5
Charterhouse St C5
Chart St B6
Cheapside C6
Chenies St C3
Chesham St E2
Chesterfield Hill D2
Chester Sq F2
Chiltern St C2
Chiswell St C6
City Garden Row A5
City Rd B6
City Thameslink ⇌ C5
City University, The B5
Claremont Sq A5
Clarges St D2
Clerkenwell Cl B5
Clerkenwell Green B5
Clerkenwell Rd B5
Cleveland St C3
Clifford St D3
Clink Prison
Museum 🏛 D6
Clock Museum 🏛 C6
Club Row B7
Cockspur St D3
Coleman St C6
Collier St A4
Columbia Rd B7
Commercial St B7
Compton St B5
Conduit St D2
Constitution Hill E2
Copperfield St E5
Coptic St C4
Cornhill C6
Cornwall Rd D5
Coronet St B7
Courtauld Gallery 🏛 D4
Covent Garden ⊖ D4
Covent Garden ✦ D4
Cowcross St C5
Cowper St B6
Cranbourne St D3
Craven St D4
Crawford St C1
Creechurch La C7
Cremer St A7
Cromer St B4
Cumberland Gate D1
Cumberland Terr A2
Curtain Rd B7
Curzon St D2
Dalí Universe 🏛 E4
D'arblay St C3
Davies St C2
Dean St C3
Deluxe Gallery 🏛 B7
Denmark St C3
Dering St C2
Devonshire St C2
Diana, Princess of Wales
Memorial Walk E3
Dingley Rd B6
Dorset St C1
Doughty St B4
Dover St D2
Downing St E4
Druid St E7

Drummond St B3
Drury La C4
Drysdale St B7
Duchess St C2
Dufferin St B6
Duke of Wellington Pl E2
Duke St C2
Duke St D3
Duke St Hill D6
Duke's Pl C7
Duncannon St D4
Eastcastle St C3
Eastcheap D7
Eastman Dental
Hospital [H] B4
East Rd B6
Eaton Pl E2
Eaton Sq E2
Eccleston Bridge F2
Eccleston St E2
Edgware Rd C1
Eldon St C6
Embankment ⊖ D4
Endell St C4
Endsleigh Pl B3
Euston ⊖⇌ B3
Euston Rd B3
Euston Square ⊖ B3
Eversholt St A3/B3
Exmouth Market B5
Eyestorm 🏛 C3
Fair St E7
Fann St B6
Farringdon ⊖⇌ C5
Farringdon Rd C5
Farringdon St C5
Featherstone St B6
Fenchurch St D7
Fenchurch St ⇌ D7
Fetter La C5
Finsbury Circus C6
Finsbury Pavement C6
Finsbury Sq B6
Fitzalan St F5
Fitzmaurice Pl D2
Fleet St C5
Floral St D4
Florence Nightingale
Museum 🏛 E4
Folgate St C7
Foot Hospital [H] B3
Fore St C6
Foster La C6
Francis St F3
Frazier St E5
Freemason's Hall C4
Friday St C6
Gainsford St E7
Garden Row E5
Gee St B6
George St C1
Gerrard St D3
Giltspur St C5
Glasshouse St D3
Gloucester Pl C1
Golden Hinde ⛵ D6
Golden La B6
Golden Sq D3
Goodge St C3
Goodge Street ⊖ C3
Gordon Sq B3
Goswell Rd B5
Gough St B4
Goulston St C7
Gower St B3
Gracechurch St D6
Grafton Way B3
Graham St A5/A6
Gray's Inn Rd B4
Great College St E4
Great Cumberland Pl C1
Great Eastern St B7
Great Guildford St D6
Great Marlborough St C3
Great Ormond St B4
Great Ormond
Street Childrens
Hospital [H] B4
Great Percy St B4
Great Peter St E3
Great Portland St C2
Great Portland St ⊖ B2
Great Queen St C4
Great Russell St C3
Great Scotland Yd D4
Great Smith St E3
Great Suffolk St E5
Great Titchfield St C3
Great Tower St D7
Great Windmill St D3
Greek St C3
Greencoat Pl F3
Green Park ⊖ D3
Green St D2
Gresham St C6
Greville St B4
Greycoat Hospital
School E3
Greycoat Pl E3
Grosvenor Cr E2
Grosvenor Gdns E2
Grosvenor Pl E2
Grosvenor Sq D2
Grosvenor St D2

Guards Museum &
Chapel 🏛 E3
Guildhall Art
Gallery 🏛 C6
Guilford St B4
Guy's Hospital [H] D6
Haberdasher St B6
Hackney Rd B7
Half Moon St D2
Halkin St E2
Hallam St C2
Hall St B5
Hampstead Rd B3
Hanover Sq C2
Hans Cr E1
Hanway St C3
Hardwick St B5
Harley St C2
Harrison St B4
Hastings St B4
Hatfields D5
Hayles St F5
Haymarket D3
Hayne St C5
Hay's Galleria D7
Hay's Mews D2
Hayward Gallery 🏛 D4
Helmet Row B6
Herbrand St B4
Hercules Rd E4
Hertford St D2
High Holborn C4
Hill St D2
HMS Belfast ⛴ D7
Hobart Pl E2
Holborn C5
Holborn ⊖ C4
Holborn Viaduct C5
Holland St D5
Holmes Museum 🏛 B1
Holywell La B7
Horseferry Rd F3
Horse Guards' Rd D3
Houndsditch C7
Houses of
Parliament 🏛 E4
Howland St C3
Hoxton Sq B7
Hoxton St B7
Hunter St B4
Hunterian Museum 🏛 C4
Hyde Park D1
Hyde Park Corner ⊖ E4
Imperial War
Museum 🏛 E5
Inner Circle B2
Institute of Archaeology
(London Univ) B2
Ironmonger Row B6
James St C2
James St D4
Jermyn St D3
Jockey's Fields C4
John Carpenter St D5
John St B4
Judd St B4
Kennington Rd E5
Killick St A4
King Charles St E4
Kingley St C3
King's Cross ⇌ A4
King's Cross Rd B4
King's Cross
St Pancras ⊖ A4
King's Cross
Thameslink ⇌ B4
Kingsland Rd B7
King's Rd E2
King St D3
King St D6
Kingsway C4
King William St C6
Kinnerton St E2
Knightsbridge E1/E2
Knightsbridge ⊖ E1
Lambeth Bridge F4
Lambeth High St F4
Lambeth North ⊖ E5
Lambeth Palace 🏰 E4
Lambeth Palace Rd E4
Lambeth Rd E4/E5
Lambeth Walk F4
Lamb's Conduit St C4
Lamb St C7
Lancaster Pl D4
Lancaster St E5
Langham Pl C2
Leadenhall St C7
Leake St E4
Leather La C5
Leicester Sq ⊖ D3
Leicester St D3
Leonard St B6
Lever St B6
Lexington St D3
Lidlington Pl A3
Lime St D7
Lincoln's Inn Fields C4
Lindsey St C5
Lisle St D3
Liverpool St C7
Liverpool Street ⊖⇌ C7
Lloyd Baker St B5
Lloyd Sq B5

Lollard St F4
Lombard St C6
London Aquarium 🐟 E4
London Bridge ⊖⇌ D6
London Bridge
Hospital [H] D6
London City Hall D7
London Dungeon 🏛 D6
London Guildhall
University C6
London Rd E5
London Transport
Museum 🏛 D4
London Wall C6
Long Acre D4
Longford St B2
Long La C5
Lower Belgrave St E2
Lower Grosvenor Pl E2
Lower Marsh E5
Lower Thames St D6
Lowndes St E2
Ludgate Circus C5
Ludgate Hill C5
Luxborough St C2
Lyall St E2
Macclesfield Rd B6
Madame Tussaud's ✦ B2
Maddox St D2
Malet St C3
Manchester Sq C2
Manchester St C2
Mandeville Pl C2
Mansion House ⊖ D6
Mansion House 🏛 C6
Maple St C3
Marble Arch D1
Marble Arch ⊖ C1
Marchmont St B4
Margaret St C3
Margery St B5
Mark La D7
Marlborough Rd D3
Marshall St C3
Marsham St E3/F3
Marylebone High St C2
Marylebone La C2
Marylebone Rd B2
Marylebone St C2
Mecklenburgh Sq B4
Middlesex St
(Petticoat La) C7
Middle Temple La C5
Midland Rd A3/B3
Mildmay Mission
Hospital [H] B7
Millbank E4
Minories C7
Monck St E3
Monkton St F5
Monmouth St C4
Montagu Pl C1
Montagu Sq C1
Montagu St C4
Montague Pl C3
Monument ⊖ D6
Monument, The ✦ D6
Monument St D6
Moorfields C6
Moorfields Eye
Hospital [H] B6
Moorgate C6
Moorgate ⊖⇌ C6
Moor La C6
Moreland St B5
Morley St E5
Mortimer St C3
Mount Pleasant B5
Mount St D2
Murray Gr A6
Museum of Garden
History 🏛 E4
Museum of London 🏛 C6
Museum St C4
Myddelton Sq B5
Myddelton St B5
National Film
Theatre 🎥 D4
National Gallery 🏛 D3
National Hospital [H] B4
National Portrait
Gallery 🏛 D3
Neal St C4
Nelson's Column ✦ D4
New Bond St C2/D2
New Bridge St C5
New Cavendish St C2
New Change C6
New Fetter La C5
Newgate St C5
New Inn Yard B7
New North Rd A6
New Oxford St C3
New Scotland Yard E3
New Sq C4
Newton St C4
Nile St B6
Noble St C6
Noel St C3
Northampton Sq B5
North Audley St D2
North Cr C3
Northington St B4
North Row D2

Northumberland Ave D4
Norton Folgate C7
Nottingham Pl C2
Obstetric Hospital [H] B3
Old Bailey C5
Old Broad St C6
Old Compton St C3
Old County Hall E4
Old Gloucester St C4
Old King Edward St C6
Old Nichol St B7
Old Paradise St F4
Old Spitalfields Market C7
Old St B6
Old Street ⊖⇌ B6
Old Town Hall C4
Old Vic 🎭 B2
Open Air Theatre 🎭 B2
Operating Theatre
Museum 🏛 D6
Orange St D3
Orchard St C2
Ossulston St A3
Outer Circle B2
Oxford Circus ⊖ C3
Oxford St C2/C3
Paddington St C2
Palace St E3
Pall Mall D3
Pall Mall East D3
Pancras Rd A4
Panton St D3
Paris Gdns D5
Park Cr B2
Parker St C4
Park La D2
Park Rd B1
Park St D2
Park St D6
Parliament Sq E4
Parliament St E4
Paternoster Sq C5
Paul St B6
Pear Tree St B5
Penton Rise B4
Penton St A5
Pentonville Rd A4/A5
Percival St B5
Petticoat La
(Middlesex St) C7
Petty France E3
Phoenix Pl B4
Phoenix Rd A3
Photo Gallery 🏛 D3
Piccadilly D2/D3
Piccadilly Circus ⊖ D3
Pitfield St B7
Pocock St E5
Pollock's Toy Mus 🏛 C3
Polygon Rd A3
Pont St E1
Portland Pl C2
Portman Mews C2
Portman Sq C2
Portman St C2
Portugal St C4
Poultry C6
Primrose St C7
Princes St C6
Procter St C4
Provost St B6
Quaker St B7
Queen Anne St C2
Queen Elizabeth
Hall 🎭 D4
Queens Gallery 🏛 E3
Queen Sq B4
Queen St D6
Queen St Pl D6
Queen Victoria St D5
Radnor St B6
Rathbone Pl C3
Rawstorne St B5
Redchurch St B7
Redcross Way D6
Red Lion Sq C4
Red Lion St C4
Regency St F3
Regent's Park B2
Regent's Park ⊖ A2
Regent Sq B4
Regent St C3
Richmond Terr E4
Ridgmount St C3
Rivington St B7
Robert St B2
Rochester Row E3/F3
Rodney St A4
Ropemaker St C6
Rosebery Ave B5
Roupell St D5
Royal Academy
of Arts 🏛 D3
Royal Academy of
Dramatic Art B3
Royal Academy
of Music B2
Royal College
of Nursing C2
Royal College of
Surgeons C4
Royal Festival Hall 🎭 D4
Royal National
Theatre 🎭 D5

Royal National Throat,
Nose & Ear
Hospital [H] B4
Russell Sq B3
Russell Sq ⊖ B4
Royal Opera House 🎭 D4
Sackville St D3
Sadlers Wells 🎭 B5
Saffron Hill C5
St Alban's St D3
St Andrew St C5
St Bartholomew's
Hospital [H] C5
St Botolph St C7
St Bride St C5
St George's Rd E5
St Giles High St C3
St James's Palace 🏰 D3
St James's Park ⊖ E3
St James's St D3
St John St B5
St Margaret St E4
St Mark's Hospital [H] B5
Martin's La D4
St Martin's le Grand C6
St Mary Axe C7
St Pancras ⇌ A4
St Paul's ⊖ C6
St Paul's Cathedral ✝ C6
St Paul's Churchyard C5
St Peter's Hospital [H] D4
St Thomas'
Hospital [H] E4
St Thomas St D6
Savile Row D3
Savoy Pl D4
Savoy St D4
School of Hygiene &
Tropical Medicine C3
Sclater St B7
Scrutton St B7
Sekforde St B5
Serpentine Rd D1
Seven Dials C4
Seward St B5
Shad Thames D7
Shaftesbury Ave D3
Shakespeare's Globe
Theatre 🎭 D6
Shepherdess Wk A6/B6
Shepherd Market D2
Sherwood St D3
Shoe La C5
Shoreditch High St B7
Shorts Gardens C4
Sidmouth St B4
Silk St C6
Sir John Soane's
Museum 🏛 C4
Skinner St B5
Sloane St E1
Snow Hill C5
Soho Sq C3
Somerset House 🏛 D4
Southampton Row C4
Southampton St D4
South Audley St D2
South Bank University E5
South Carriage Dr E1
South Molton St C2
South Pl C6
South St D2
Southwark ⊖ D5
Southwark Bridge D6
Southwark Bridge Rd D6
Southwark
Cathedral ✝ D6
Southwark St D6
Speakers' Corner D1
Spencer St B5
Spital Sq C7
Stamford St D5
Stanhope St B3
Stephenson Way B3
Stoney St D6
Strand C5/D4
Stratton St D2
Sumner St D5
Swanfield St B7
Swinton St B4
Tabernacle St B6
Tate Modern 🏛 D6
Tavistock Pl B4
Tavistock Sq B3
Temple ⊖ D5
Temple Ave D5
Temple Pl D4
Terminus Pl E2
Thayer St C2
The Cut E5
The Mall E3
Theobald's Rd C4
Thorney St F4
Threadneedle St C6
Throgmorton St C6
Tonbridge St B4
Tooley St D7
Torrington Pl B3
Tothill St E3
Tottenham Court
Rd B3/C3
Tottenham Court
Rd ⊖ C3
Tottenham St C3

Tower Bridge ✦ D7
Tower Bridge
Approach D7
Tower Bridge Rd D7
Tower Hill ⊖ D7
Tower of London,
The 🏰 D7
Toynbee St C7
Trafalgar Sq D3
Trinity Sq D7
Trocadero Centre D3
Tudor St D5
Turnmill St C5
Ufford St E5
Union St D5
University College
Hospital [H] B3
University of London C3
University of
Westminster C2
University St B3
Upper Belgrave St E2
Upper Berkeley St C1
Upper Brook St D2
Upper Grosvenor St D2
Upper Ground D5
Upper Montague St C1
Upper St Martin's La D4
Upper Thames St D6
Upper Wimpole St C2
Upper Woburn Pl B3
Vauxhall Bridge Rd F3
Vere St C2
Vernon Pl C4
Vestry St B6
Victoria ⊖⇌ E2
Victoria Embankment D4
Victoria St E3
Villiers St D4
Vincent Sq F3
Vinopolis City
of Wine 🏛 D6
Virginia Rd B7
Wakley St B5
Walbrook C6
Walcot Sq F5
Wallace Collection 🏛 C2
Walnut Tree Walk F5
Wardour St C3/D3
Warner St B5
Warren St B3
Warren Street ⊖ B3
Waterloo ⊖⇌ E4
Waterloo Bridge D4
Waterloo East ⇌ D5
Waterloo
International ⇌ E4
Waterloo Rd E5
Watling St C6
Webber St E5
Welbeck St C2
Wellington Arch ✦ E2
Wellington
Museum 🏛 E2
Wells St C3
Wenlock Rd A6
Wenlock St A6
Wentworth St C7
Wernington St A3
Westminster ⊖ E4
Westminster Abbey ✝ E4
Westminster Bridge E4
Westminster
Bridge Rd E5
Westminster
Cathedral (RC) ✝ E3
Westminster City Hall E3
Westminster Hall 🏛 E4
West Smithfield C5
West Sq E5
Weymouth St C2
Wharf Rd A6
Wharton St B4
Whitcomb St D3
Whitecross St B6
Whitefriars St C5
Whitehall D4
Whitehall Pl D4
White Lion Hill D5
Wigmore Hall C2
Wigmore St C2
William IV St D4
Wilmington Sq B5
Wilson St C6
Wilton Cr E2
Wilton Rd F3
Wimpole St C2
Windmill Walk D5
Woburn Pl B4
Woburn Sq B3
Women's Hospital [H] C3
Woodbridge St B5
Wood St C6
Wootton St D5
Wormwood St C7
Worship St B6
Wren St B4
Wynyatt St B5
York Rd E4
York St C1
York Terr B2
York Way A4

REGENT'S PARK
REGENT'S PARK
SOMERS TOWN
BLOOMSBURY
FITZROVIA
SOHO
MAYFAIR
ST. JAMES'S
WESTMINSTER
HYDE PARK
GREEN PARK
ST. JAMES'S PARK
BELGRAVIA
MARYLEBONE ROAD
EUSTON ROAD
OXFORD STREET
PICCADILLY
REGENT STREET
KNIGHTSBRIDGE
VICTORIA STREET
WHITEHALL
STRAND
HORSEFERRY ROAD
LAMBETH BRIDGE
WESTMINSTER BRIDGE
British Museum
Buckingham Palace
Houses of Parliament
Westminster Abbey
Trafalgar Square
Piccadilly Circus
Oxford Circus
Euston
St. Pancras
King's Cross
Charing Cross
Victoria
Marble Arch
Wellington Arch
Queen Victoria Memorial
Westminster Cathedral (R.C.)
Miles
0
½

HOXTON
SHOREDITCH
FINSBURY
CLERKENWELL
HOLBORN
THE CITY
SOUTHWARK
LAMBETH
RIVER THAMES
London Docklands
STEPNEY
POPLAR
CANNING TOWN
WAPPING
ROTHERHITHE
BERMONDSEY
MILLWALL
ISLE OF DOGS
DEPTFORD
GREENWICH
Congestion Charging Zone
Extended Charging Zone
– operational from February 2007
0 Miles 1

KINGS LANGLEY
Bovingdon Green
Tower Hill
Venus Hill
Chipperfield
Hogspit Bottom
Flaunden
Chipperfield Common
Belsize
Commonwood
Hunton Bridge
ABBOTS LANGLEY
Waterdale
BRICKET WOOD
Woodside
Frogmore
Broad Colney
Colney Street
Radlett
Sarratt
WATFORD
Chenies
CHENIES MANOR HOUSE
Whippendell Wood
Aldenham
Letchmore Heath
ELSTREE AERODROME
Hilfield Park Reservoir
ALDENHAM
Watford Junction
Cassiobury Park
Loudwater
Chorleywood West
CHORLEYWOOD
Croxley Green
VICARAGE ROAD
BUSHEY
OXHEY
Holywell
Philipshill Wood
CHILTERN OPEN AIR MUSEUM
RICKMANSWORTH
Newland Park
Bottom Wood
SHIRE HORSE CENTRE
Mill End
RICKMANSWORTH AQUADROME
Stocker's Lake
Carpenders Park
Stanmore Common
Maple Cross
MOOR PARK MANSION
Moor Park
Oxhey Woods
Chalfont Common
NORTHWOOD
BISHOP'S WOOD
STANMORE
Hatch End
Mount Pleasant
Grand Union Canal
Harefield
CHALFONT ST. PETER
Headstone
Belmont
Copse Wood
HARROW MUSEUM
Wealdstone
Civic Centre
HARROW
Mad Bess Wood
South Harefield
BAYHURST WOOD
Ruislip Lido
Park Wood
RUISLIP LIDO
PINNER
DENHAM AERODROME
Denham Green
Eastcote
Higher Denham
RUISLIP
Rayners Lane
Harrow on the Hill
DENHAM
Fulmer
Ickenham
Ruislip Gardens
NORTHOLT AERODROME
New Denham
NORTHOLT
North Hillingdon
UXBRIDGE
BLACK PARK
Blackpark Lake
Iver Heath
Perivale
GREENFORD
LONDON MOTORCYCLE MUSEUM
HILLINGDON
Univ
LANGLEY PARK
Yeading
Cowley
Langley Park
IVER
EALING
HAYES
YIEWSLEY
SOUTHALL
West Ealing
HANWELL
WEST DRAYTON
Norwood Green
Osterley Park
WEM
0 1 2 3 miles
0 1 2 3 4 5 km

North Mymms Park
THE DE HAVILLAND AIRCRAFT HERITAGE CENTRE & MOSQUITO MUSEUM
Shenleybury
South Mimms
Shenley
Ridge
SOUTH MIMMS SERVICES
POTTERS BAR
Swanley Bar
Leggatts Park
Little Heath
Northaw
Goff's Oak
Churchgate
Bury Green
Waltham Cross
Whitewebbs Park
CAPEL MANOR
FORTY HALL
Clay Hill
Forty Hill
Enfield Chase
Hadley Wood
Monken Hadley Common
TRENT
BOREHAMWOOD
Film Studios
Cockfosters
New Barnet
BARNET
Arkley
Oakwood
Grange Park
ENFIELD
Bush Hill Park
Ponders End
EAST BARNET
Oak Hill Park
Scratchwood
LONDON GATEWAY SERVICES
Totteridge
Whetstone
SOUTHGATE
Grovelands Park
Winchmore Hill
Lower Edmonton
Palmers Green
Broomfield Park
Pymmes Park
EDGWARE
Mill Hill
North Finchley
FRIERN BARNET
Bowes Park
EDMONTON
Colney Hatch
WOOD GREEN
BRUCE CASTLE MUSEUM
WHITE HART LANE
Burnt Oak
RAF MUSEUM
FINCHLEY
Coldfall Wood
Alexandra Palace
Alexandra Park
TOTTENHAM
HENDON
CHURCH FARM MUSEUM
Queensbury
Muswell Hill
East Finchley
Highgate Wood
Queen's Wood
HORNSEY
South Tottenham
Kingsbury
Crouch End
Stamford Hill
FRYENT
Barn Hill
Brent Cross Shopping Centre
Brent Cross
Golders Green
HAMPSTEAD HEATH
KENWOOD HOUSE
Highgate
Brent Reservoir (Welsh Harp)
Hampstead Heath
Highgate Ponds
Parliament Hill
Golders Hill Park
Archway
STOKE NEWINGTON
Clapton
Lea Bridge
Wembley Park
WEMBLEY ARENA
WEMBLEY STADIUM
GRANGE MUSEUM
Neasden
Gladstone Park
Cricklewood
FENTON HOUSE
HAMPSTEAD
KEATS HOUSE
Gospel Oak
Tufnell Park
EMIRATES STADIUM
Canonbury
WILLESDEN
FREUD
Swiss Cottage
West Hampstead
Kentish Town
Dalston
HACKNEY
Harlesden
Kilburn
Primrose Hill
JEWISH MUSEUM
CAMDEN TOWN
ISLINGTON
SHOREDITCH
LONDON ZOO
Regents Park
St. John's Wood
LORDS
Maida Vale
Park Royal
BETHNAL GREEN
FINSBURY
MADAME TUSSAUD'S
Wormwood Scrubs Park
MARYLEBONE
BRITISH MUSEUM
Holborn
PADDINGTON
MUSEUM OF BRANDS
TOY & MODEL MUSEUM
ROYAL ACADEMY
NATIONAL GALLERY
LONDON TRANSPORT MUS
GUILDHALL
Stepney
Aldgate
ACTON
Hyde Park
Kensington Gardens
KENSINGTON PALACE
Green Park
BUCKINGHAM PALACE
St James's Park
MILLENNIUM BRIDGE
GLOBE THEATRE
TOWER OF LONDON
Wapping
Holland Park
ROYAL ALBERT HALL
NATURAL HISTORY
Houses of Parliament
WESTMINSTER ABBEY
DESIGN MUSEUM
BRUNEL ENGINE HOUSE MUSEUM
Bedford Park
BERMONDSEY
Gunnersbury Park
HAMMERSMITH
CHELSEA
NATIONAL ARMY MUSEUM
TATE BRITAIN
IMPERIAL WAR MUSEUM
LAMBETH
Elephant & Castle
M25
M1
A1
A406
NORTH CIRCULAR ROAD
A10
A40
52
53

Waltham Abbey
Upshire
Waltham Cross
Whitewebbs Park
Capel Manor
Enfield Chase
Hadley Wood
Clay Hill
Forty Hill
Enfield Lock
Epping Forest
High Beach
Sewardstone
Brimsdown
Enfield
Cockfosters
New Barnet
Oakwood
Grange Park
Bush Hill Park
Ponders End
Sewardstonebury
Loughton
East Barnet
Southgate
Winchmore Hill
Chingford Green
Chingford
Whetstone
Palmers Green
Lower Edmonton
Buckhurst Hill
Woodford Wells
North Finchley
Friern Barnet
Edmonton
Chingford Hatch
Higham's Park
Hale End
Woodford
Woodford Bridge
Finchley
Wood Green
Tottenham
Higham Hill
Woodford Green
Clayhall
Muswell Hill
Walthamstow
Snaresbrook
East Finchley
Hornsey
South Tottenham
Redbridge
Crouch End
Wanstead
Highgate
Hampstead
Archway
Stamford Hill
Finsbury Park
Stoke Newington
Clapton
Leytonstone
Lea Bridge
Leyton
Hampstead Heath
Gospel Oak
Tufnell Park
Manor Park
Kentish Town
Canonbury
Hackney
Stratford
Forest Gate
Swiss Cottage
Camden Town
Dalston
Upton
West Ham
Islington
Shoreditch
Bethnal Green
Bow
Old Ford
Victoria Park
Plaistow
St. John's Wood
Regents Park
Finsbury
Maida Vale
Marylebone
Holborn
Stepney
Poplar
Canning Town
Aldgate
Wapping
Canary Wharf
Hyde Park
Rotherhithe
Isle of Dogs
Silvertown
Bermondsey
Chelsea
Lambeth
Elephant & Castle
Woolwich
Kennington
Deptford
Greenwich
Battersea Park
Peckham
Camberwell
New Cross Gate
Kidbrooke
Battersea

0 1 2 3 miles
0 1 2 3 4 5 km
Stanford Rivers
Mount End
Fiddlers Hamlet
Little End
Theydon Bois
Hobbs Cross
Stapleford Tawney
Doddinghurst
Kelvedon Hatch
Secret Nuclear Bunker
Swallows Cross
Navestock Heath
Navestock Side
Stapleford Aerodrome
Abridge
Debden
Horseman Side
South Weald Common
Coxtie Green
Crow Green
Pilgrims Hatch
Stapleford Abbots
Navestock
Lambourne End
Weald Park
Shenfield
BRENTWOOD
St. Mary & St. Helens Cathedral
Chigwell Row
Hainault Forest
Old Macdonald's
Noak Hill
South Weald
Brook Street
Shenfield Common
CHIGWELL
Havering-atte-Bower
Havering
Warley
Grange Hill
Chase Cross
Harold Hill
Harold Park
Thorndon
Thorndon Park
Hainault
Collier Row
Harold Wood
Great Warley
Fairlop
Fulwell Cross
Marks Gate
Little Warley
Barkingside
Ardleigh Green
Gants Hill
Newbury Park
Seven Kings Park
Chadwell Heath
ROMFORD
Emerson Park
Heath Park
Tithe Barn Agricultural & Folk Museum
Cranham
Seven Kings
Goodmayes
Rush Green
Hornchurch
Upminster
Redbridge Museum
ILFORD
Loxford
Becontree
Elm Park
Corbets Tey
Univ
North Ockenden
Mayesbrook Park
Hacton
Hornchurch
BARKING
DAGENHAM
South Hornchurch
Eastbury Manor House
Creekmouth
Rainham Hall (N.T.)
Rainham
Belhus Woods
South Ockendon
Grangewater
River Thames
Belhus Park
Wennington
Aveley
North Stifford
Thamesmead
North Woolwich
Wennington Marshes
Channel Tunnel Rail Link (u/c)
Thurrock Services
Aveley Marshes
Mar Dyke
Abbey Wood
Lakeside Shopping Centre
Plumstead
Erith
Purfleet
West Thurrock
South Stifford
Bostall Heath
West Heath
Lessness Heath
GRAYS
North End
Crayford Marshes
Dartford Marshes
Dartford Crossing
Dartford Tunnel
West Thurrock Marshes
Northumberland Heath
Shooters Hill
Barnehurst
Slade Green
Welling
Queen Elizabeth II Bridge
M25
M11
A12
A13
A127
River Roding
River Ingrebourne
Weald Brook

Colnbrook
Harmondsworth
HARLINGTON
Sipson
Longford
Cranford Park
Cranford
North Hyde
HESTON
Norwood Green
Osterley Park
BRENTFORD
HOUNSLOW
ISLEWORTH
Hounslow West
Syon Park
Old Deer Park
Poyle
Horton
The Queen Mother Reservoir
London Heathrow
Heathrow Airport
Wraysbury
Wraysbury Reservoir
Stanwell Moor
STANWELL
West Bedfont
Hatton Cross
Hounslow Heath
Whitton
TWICKENHAM
King George VI Reservoir
Staines Reservoirs
STAINES
Runnymede Park
EGHAM
FELTHAM
Hanworth Park
HANWORTH
ASHFORD
TEDDINGTON
Ham
Milton Park
Stroude
Queen Mary Reservoir
Hampton
Bushy Park
Hampton Wick
SUNBURY
Laleham
Virginia Water
Thorpe
Shepperton Green
Upper Halliford
Hampton Court Park
East Molesey
Molesey Reservoirs
Shepperton
Thames Ditton
Lyne
CHERTSEY
Fieldcommon
WALTON ON THAMES
Woburn Park
WEYBRIDGE
Hinchley Wood
ADDLESTONE
HERSHAM
ESHER
Ottershaw
Burwood Park
St George's Hill
West End Common
CLAYGATE
Arbrook Common
Woodham
Anningsley Park
Whiteley Village
Esher Common
Oxshott
Fairmile
Malden Rushett
Prince's Coverts
Horsell Common
West Byfleet
Sheerwater
Byfleet
Silver Mere
Cobham
Stoke Wood
Little Heath
Pain's Hill
Foxwarren Park
Pyrford
Wisley
Cobham Park
Stoke D'Abernon
Maybury
Pyrford Green
Wisley Common
Telegraph Hill
Pachesham Park
WOKING
Bolder Mere
Downside
Elm Corner
Ripley Green
Leatherhead Common
Old Woking
Bridge End
Ripley
LEATHERHEAD
Westfield
Ockham Park
Church End
Ockham
Banks Common
Great Bookham Common
Little Bookham Common
Fetcham
Hungry Hill
Effingham Common
Little Bookham
Givons Grove
Sutton Green
Great Bookham
Fetcham Downs
3 miles
5 km

Gunnersbury Park
HAMMERSMITH
CHELSEA
LAMBETH
DEPTFORD
CHISWICK
Kew
FULHAM
BARNES
Battersea Park
BATTERSEA
Kennington
Peckham
Camberwell Green
CAMBERWELL
North Sheen
Mortlake
CLAPHAM
BRIXTON
East Dulwich
Nunhead
RICHMOND
PUTNEY
WANDSWORTH
Clapham Common
Roehampton
Putney Heath
Wandsworth Common
Brockwell Park
Dulwich Park
Petersham
Richmond Park
Balham
Tulse Hill
West Dulwich
Upper Tooting
Tooting Bec Common
STREATHAM
Wimbledon Park
Wimbledon Common
Kingston Vale
WIMBLEDON
Tooting
Streatham Common
Colliers Wood
Coombe
KINGSTON UPON THAMES
Norbiton
NEW MALDEN
MERTON
Raynes Park
Morden Hall Park
MITCHAM
Norbury
Anerley
MORDEN
Mitcham Common
SOUTH NORWOOD
THORNTON HEATH
Berrylands
Motspur Park
Morden Park
St Helier
CROYDON
ADDISCOMBE
Tolworth
Hackbridge
Beddington Park
Worcester Park
North Cheam
CARSHALTON
BEDDINGTON
Waddon
Coombe Park
Stoneleigh
WALLINGTON
SUTTON
CHESSINGTON
Nonsuch Park
West Ewell
CHEAM
South Croydon
Ewell
Belmont
Carshalton on the Hill
Selsdon
Little Woodcote
Oaks Park
Purley
Sanderstead
Epsom Common
EPSOM
North Looe
Woodmansterne
Kings Wood
Nork
BANSTEAD
Kenley
Hamsey Green
Coulsdon
Great Burgh
Park Downs
Kenley Common
Whyteleafe
Langley Vale
Chipstead
Banstead Wood
Warlingham
Ashtead
Walton Downs
Burgh Heath
Old Coulsdon
Kingswood
Hooley
Tadworth
Chaldon
Tyrell's Wood
Walton on the Hill
CATERHAM
Nower Wood
Headley
Banstead Heath
Lower Kingswood

Barnes
Battersea
Clapham
Brixton
Camberwell
Peckham
New Cross Gate
Blackheath
Lewisham
Putney
Wandsworth
Roehampton
Balham
Streatham
East Dulwich
Nunhead
Brockley
Catford
Wimbledon
Wimbledon Common
Tooting
Upper Tooting
West Dulwich
Forest Hill
Bellingham
Penge
Crystal Palace National Sports Centre
Merton
Morden
Colliers Wood
Mitcham
Norbury
Anerley
Beckenham
Raynes Park
Thornton Heath
Elmers End
Shirley
West Wickham
Croydon
Addiscombe
Carshalton
St Helier
Hackbridge
Beddington
Wallington
Waddon
Sutton
Cheam
Nonsuch Park
North Cheam
Belmont
South Croydon
Spring Park
Addington
Upper Shirley
New Addington
Selsdon
Sanderstead
Purley
Little Woodcote
Oaks Park
Woodmansterne
Banstead
Nork
Great Burgh
Burgh Heath
Coulsdon
Kenley
Whyteleafe
Warlingham
Farleigh
Fickleshole
Chelsham
Hamsey Green
Chipstead
Banstead Wood
Kingswood
Tadworth
Hooley
Old Coulsdon
Chaldon
Caterham
Woldingham
Woldingham Garden Village
Walton on the Hill
Banstead Heath
Lower Kingswood
Merstham
Gravelly Hill
Winders Hill
Mogador
Margery
Buckland Hills
Warwick Wold
Oxted
M25

Woolwich Common
Shooters Hill
Kidbrooke
Eltham Common
Oxleas Wood
Welling
Barnehurst
Slade Green
Dartford Crossing
Dartford Tunnel
Queen Elizabeth II Bridge
Falconwood
Danson Park
Bexleyheath
Crayford
Temple Hill
Stone
ELTHAM
Avery Hill
BEXLEY
Old Bexley
Hall Place
DARTFORD
Stone Lodge Farm Park
Eltham Palace
New Eltham
Coldblow
Mottingham
Maypole
Darenth Wood
Grove Park
Longlands
SIDCUP
North Cray
Joyden's Wood
Hook Green
Wilmington
Lane End
Elmstead Wood
Foots Cray
Darenth
Hawley
Scadbury Park Nature Reserve
St John's Jerusalem (N.T.)
Sundridge Park
Chislehurst Common
CHISLEHURST
Ruxley
Hextable
Clement Street
Sutton-at-Hone
Chislehurst Caves
St Paul's Cray
Hockenden
Swanley Village
South Darenth
BROMLEY
Bickley
Petts Wood
Swanley
Horton Kirby
Jubilee
Farningham Wood
Southborough
St Mary Cray
Kevingtown
Farningham
Bromley Common
Crockenhill
ORPINGTON
Eynsford Castle
Horton Wood
Locksbottom
Bird of Prey Centre
Eynsford
Lullingstone Roman Villa
Keston
Lullingstone Castle
Brands Hatch
Farnborough
Chelsfield
Beechen Wood
Maplescombe
Nash
Maypole
Well Hill
High Castle Wood
High Elms
Pratt's Bottom
West Kingsdown
Cuckoo Wood
Knatts Valley
Leaves Green
Downe
Shoreham
Down House (Charles Darwin Museum)
Hazelwood
Romney Street
Halstead
Biggin Hill Aerodrome
Magpie Bottom
Woodlands
Newyears Wood
Cudham
Knockholt Pound
Berry's Green
Otford
Knockholt
Kemsing
Heaverham
Biggin Hill
Horns Green
Chevening
South Street
Tatsfield
Dunton Green
Seal
Chipstead
Riverhead
Hill Park
Force Green
Seal Chart
Godden Green
Sundridge
Stone Street
Titsey
Brasted
SEVENOAKS
Farley Common
Quebec House (N.T.)
Titsey Wood
Clacket Lane Services
Westerham
Knole (N.T.)
Knole Park
Fawke Common
Lower Bitchet
Bitchet Green
Squerryes Court
Brasted Chart
Mill Bank Wood
Limpsfield
Hosey Hill
French Street
The High Chart
Goathurst Common
Whitley Row
Emmetts (N.T.)
River Darent
River Hill
M25
M26
M20
A20
A21
A2
A25
A225
A224
A233
0 1 2 3 miles
0 1 2 3 4 5 km

Manchester

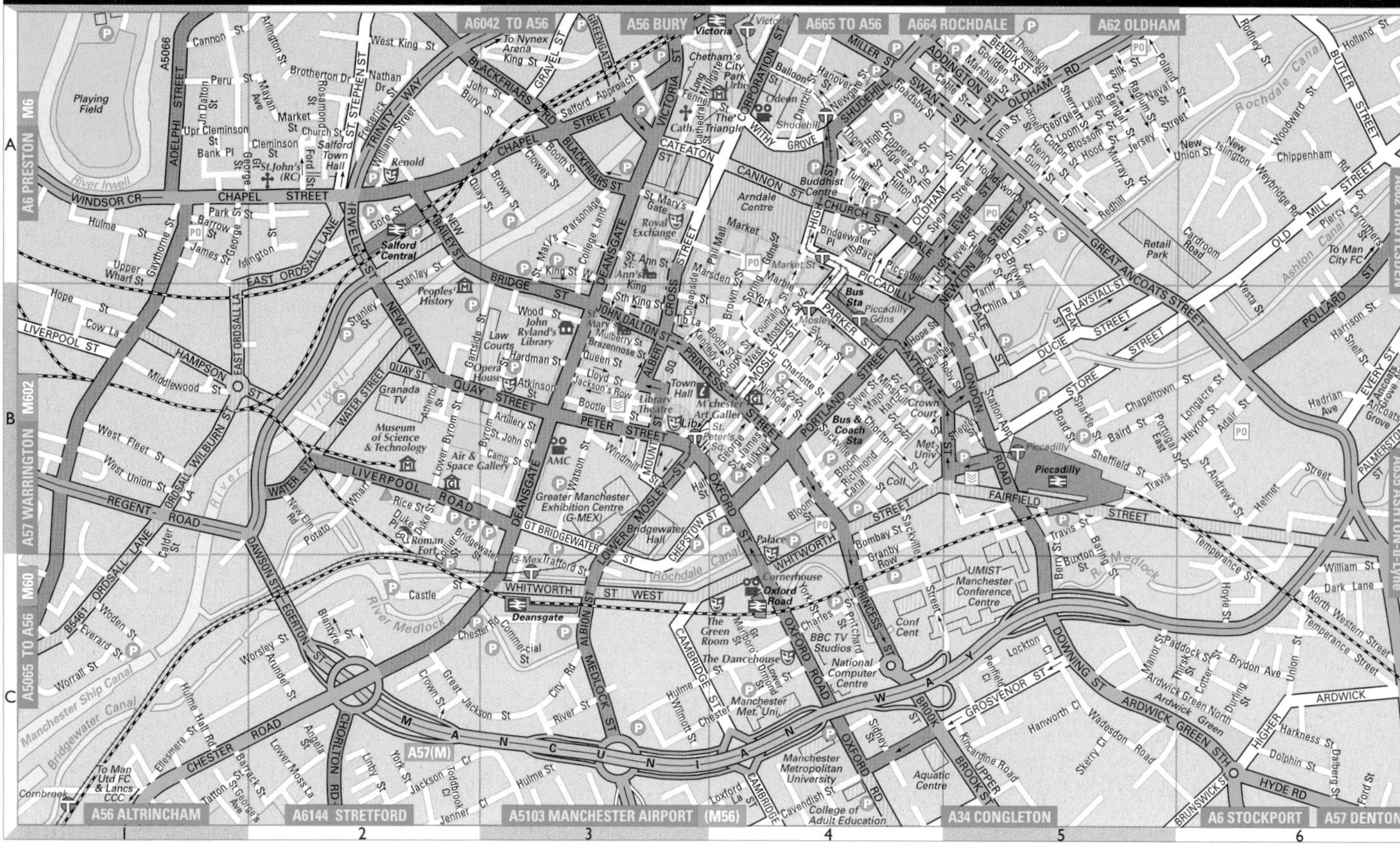

Manchester

Adair St B6
Addington St A5
Adelphi St A1
Air & Space Gallery B2
Albert Sq B3
Albion St C3
AMC Great Northern B3
Ancoats Gr B6
Ancoats Gr North B6
Angela St C2
Aquatic Centre C4
Ardwick Green C5
Ardwick Green North C5
Ardwick Green South C5
Arlington St A2
Arndale Centre A4
Artillery St B3
Arundel St C2
Atherton St B2
Atkinson St B3
Aytoun St B4
Back Piccadilly A4
Baird St B5
Balloon St A4
Bank Pl A1
Baring St B5
Barrack St C1
Barrow St A1
BBC TV Studios C4
Bendix St A5
Bengal St A5
Berry St C5
Blackfriars Rd A3
Blackfriars St A3
Blantyre St C2
Bloom St B4
Blossom St A5
Boad St B5
Bombay St B4
Booth St A3
Booth St B4
Bootle St B3
Brazennose St B3
Brewer St A5
Bridge St A3
Bridgewater Hall B3
Bridgewater Pl A4
Bridgewater St B2
Brook St C4
Brotherton Dr A2
Brown St A3
Brown St B4
Brunswick St C6
Brydon Ave C6
Buddhist Centre A4
Bury St A2
Bus & Coach Station B4
Bus Station B4
Butler St A6
Buxton St C5
Byrom St B3
Cable St A5
Calder St B1
Cambridge St C3/C4
Camp St B3
Canal St B4
Cannon St A1
Cannon St A4
Cardroom Rd A6
Carruthers St A6
Castle St C2
Cateaton St A3
Cathedral A3
Cathedral St A3
Cavendish St C4
Chapel St A1/A3
Chapeltown St B5
Charles St C4
Charlotte St B4
Chatham St B4
Cheapside A3
Chepstow St B3
Chester Rd C1/C2
Chester St C4
Chetham's (Dept Store) A3
China La B5
Chippenham Rd A6
Chorlton Rd C2
Chorlton St B4
Church St A2
Church St A4
City Park A4
City Rd C3
Cleminson St A2
Clowes St A3
College Land A3
College of Adult Education C4
Collier St B2
Commercial St C3
Conference Centre C4
Cooper St B4
Copperas St A4
Cornbrook (Metro Station) C1
Cornell St A5
Cornerhouse C4
Corporation St A4
Cotter St C6
Cotton St A5
Cow La B1
Cross St B3
Crown Court B4
Crown St C2
Dalberg St C6
Dale St A4/B5
Dancehouse, The C4
Dantzic St A4
Dark La C6
Dawson St C2
Dean St A5
Deansgate A3/B3
Deansgate Station C3
Dolphin St C6
Downing St C5
Ducie St B5
Duke Pl B2
Duke St B2
Durling St C6
East Ordsall La A2/B1
Edge St A4
Egerton St C2
Ellesmere St C1
Everard St C1
Every St B6
Fairfield St B5
Faulkner St B4
Fennel St A3
Ford St A2
Ford St C6
Fountain St B4
Frederick St A2
Gartside St B2
Gaythorne St A1
George Leigh St A5
George St A1
George St B4
G-Mex (Metro Station) C3
Goadsby St A4
Gore St A2
Goulden St A5
Granada TV Studios B2
Granby Row B4
Gravel St A3
Great Ancoats St A5
Great Bridgewater St B3
Great George St A1
Great Jackson St C2
Great Marlborough St C4
Greater Manchester Exhibition Centre (G-Mex) B3
Greengate A3
Green Room, The C4
Grosvenor St C5
Gun St A5
Hadrian Ave B6
Hall St B3
Hampson St B1
Hanover St A4
Hanworth Cl C5
Hardman St B3
Harkness St C6
Harrison St B6
Hart St B4
Helmet St B6
Henry St A5
Heyrod St B6
High St A4
Higher Ardwick C6
Hilton St A4/A5
Holland St A6
Hood St A5
Hope St B1
Hope St B4
Houldsworth St A5
Hoyle St C6
Hulme Hall Rd C1
Hulme St A1
Hulme St C3
Hyde Rd C6
Information Ctr B3
Irwell St A2
Islington St A2
Jackson Cr C2
Jackson's Row B3
James St A1
Jenner Cl C2
Jersey St A5
John Dalton St A1
John Dalton St B3
John Ryland's Library B3
John St A2
Kennedy St B3
Kincardine Rd C4
King St A3
King St West A3
Law Courts B3
Laystall St B5
Lever St A5
Library B3
Library Theatre B3
Linby St C2
Little Lever St A4
Liverpool Rd B2
Liverpool St B1
Lloyd St B3
Lockton Cl C5
London Rd B5
Long Millgate A3
Longacre St B6
Loom St A5
Lower Byrom St B2
Lower Mosley St B3
Lower Moss La C2
Lower Ormond St C4
Loxford La C4
Luna St A5
Major St B4
Manchester Art Gallery B4
Manchester Metropolitan University B4/C4
Mancunian Way C3
Manor St C5
Marble St A4
Market St A2
Market St A4
Market St (Metro Station) A4
Marsden St A3
Marshall St A4
Mayan Ave A2
Medlock St C3
Middlewood St B1
Miller St A4
Minshull St B5
Mosley St A4
Mosley St (Metro Station) B4
Mount St B3
Mulberry St B3
Murray St A5
Museum of Science & Technology B2
Nathan Dr A2
National Computer Centre C4
Naval St A5
New Bailey St A2
New Elm Rd B2
New Islington A6
New Quay St B2
New Union St A6
Newgate St A4
Newton St A5
Nicholas St B4
North George St A1
North Western St C6
Oak St A4
Odeon A4
Old Mill St A6
Oldfield Rd A1/C1
Oldham Rd A5
Oldham St A4
Opera House B3
Ordsall La C1
Oxford Rd C4
Oxford Road Station C4
Oxford St B4
Paddock St C6
Palace Theatre B4
Pall Mall A3
Palmerston St B6
Park St A1
Parker St B4
Peak St B5
Penfield Cl C5
Peoples' History Museum B2
Peru St A1
Peter St B3
Piccadilly A4
Piccadilly (Metro Station) B5
Piccadilly Gdns (Metro Station) B4
Piccadilly Station B5
Piercy St A6
Poland St A5
Police Station B3/B5
Pollard St B6
Port St A5
Portland St B4
Portugal St East B5
Post Office A1/A4/A5/B4/B6
Potato Wharf B2
Princess St B3/C4
Pritchard St C4
Quay St A2
Quay St B2
Queen St B3
Radium St A5
Redhill St A5
Regent Rd B1
Renold Theatre A2
Retail Park A5
Rice St B2
Richmond St B4
River St C3
Roby St B5
Rodney St A6
Roman Fort B2
Rosamond St A2
Royal Exchange A3
Sackville St B4
St Andrew's St B6
St Ann St A3
St George's Ave C1
St James St B4
St John St B3
St John's Cathedral (RC) A2
St Mary's B3
St Mary's Gate A3
St Mary's Parsonage A3
St Peter's Sq (Metro Station) B3
St Stephen St A2
Salford Approach A3
Salford Central A2
Sheffield St B5
Shepley St B5
Sherratt St A5
Shudehill A4
Shudehill (Metro Station) A4
Sidney St C4
Silk St A5
Silver St B4
Skerry Cl C5
Snell St B6
South King St B3
Sparkle St B5
Spear St A4
Spring Gdns A4
Stanley St A2/B2
Station Approach B5
Store St B5
Swan St A4
Tariff St B5
Tatton St C1
Temperance St B6/C6
The Triangle A
Thirsk St C
Thomas St A
Thompson St A
Tib La B
Tib St A
Toddbrook Cl C
Town Hall (Manchester) B
Town Hall (Salford) A
Trafford St C
Travis St B
Trinity Way A
Turner St A
UMIST Manchester Conference Centre C
Union St C
Upper Brook St C
Upper Cleminson St A
Upper Wharf St A
Urbis Museum A
Vesta St B
Victoria (Metro Station) A
Victoria Station A
Victoria St A
Wadesdon Rd C
Water St B
Watson St B
Wellington St A
West Fleet St B
West King St A
West Mosley St B
West Union St B
Weybridge Rd A
Whitworth St B
Whitworth St West C
Wilburn St B
William St A
William St C
Wilmott St C
Windmill St B
Windsor Cr A
Withy Gr A
Woden St C
Wood St B
Woodward St A
Worrall St C
Worsley St C
York St B
York St C
York St C

MANCHESTER
SALFORD
TRAFFORD PARK
STOCKPORT
OLDHAM
BURY
MANCHESTER AIRPORT
RADCLIFFE
LITTLE LEVER
KEARSLEY
WALKDEN
SWINTON
PENDLEBURY
ECCLES
URMSTON
STRETFORD
SALE
ALTRINCHAM
HALE
WHITEFIELD
PRESTWICH
MIDDLETON
CHADDERTON
ROYTON
FAILSWORTH
DROYLSDEN
REDDISH
CHEADLE
CHEADLE HULME
BRAMHALL
HAZEL GROVE
GATLEY
WYTHENSHAWE
Redvales
Hollins
Unsworth
Outwood
Prestolee
Ringley
Park Lane
Simister
Birch
Langley
Higher Boarshaw
Heaton Park
Higher Blackley
Crumpsall
Broughton Park
Kersal
Charlestown
Moston
Harpurhey
New Moston
Hollinwood
Newtown
Clifton Green
Linnyshaw
Broadoak Park
Ellesmere Park
Westwood Park
Patricroft
Little Bolton
Seedley
Barton upon Irwell
Miles Platting
Clayton
Openshaw
Ardwick
Gorton
Hulme
Old Trafford
Moss Side
Rusholme
Levenshulme
Whalley Range
Firswood
Davyhulme
Chorlton-cum-Hardy
Withington
Burnage
Heaton Mersey
Heaton Norris
Barlow Moor
West Didsbury
Ashton upon Mersey
Carrington
Woodhouses
Brooklands
Northern Moor
Broadheath
Timperley
Roundthorn
Bowdon
Well Green
Newall Green
Davenport Green
Woodhouse Park
Halebarns
Bowgreen
Ashley
Heald Green
Handforth
Kitt's Moss
Bramhall Park
Norbury Moor
Gale Green
Ardswood
Brinnington
South Reddish
North Reddish
Debdale
Ryder Brow
Greeside
Woodhouses
Busk
Moorclose
Alkrington Garden Village
Healds Green
Rhodes
Sunny Bank
Besses o' th' Barn
0 1 2 3 miles
0 1 2 3 4 5 km

Middlesbrough

0 Miles ¼

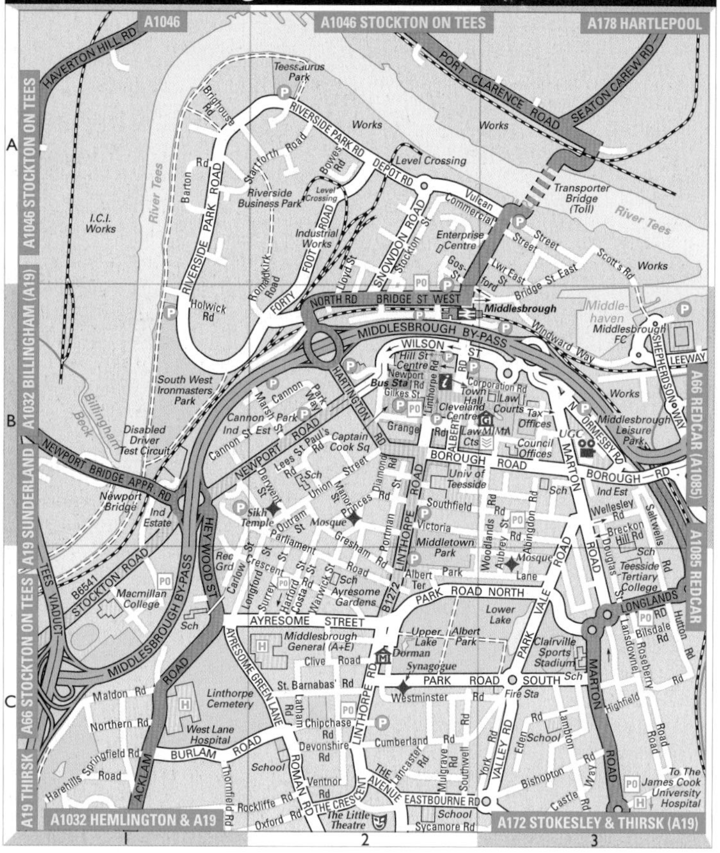

Milton Keynes

0 Miles ¼

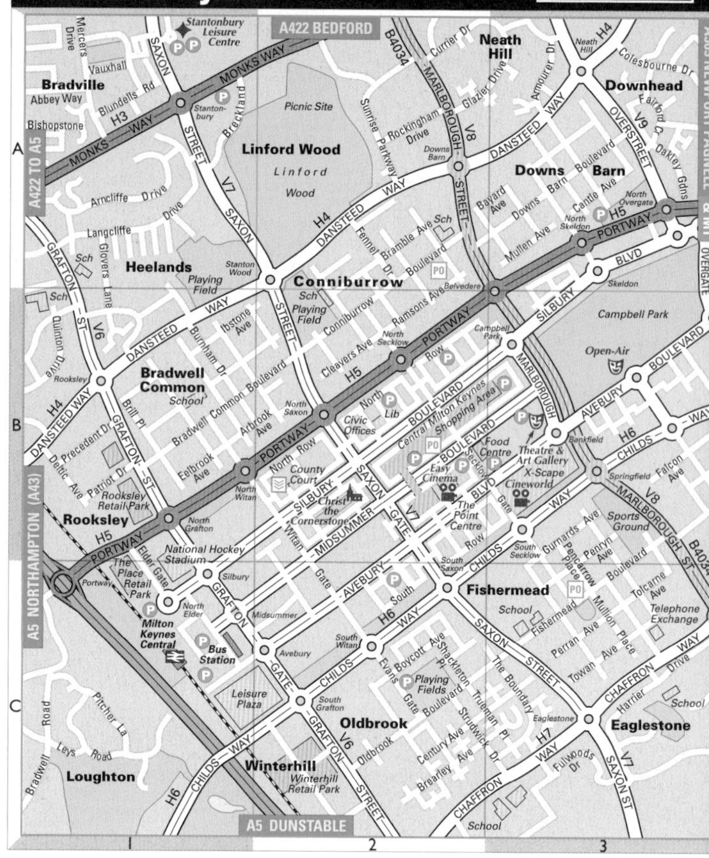

Middlesbrough

Abingdon Rd C3
Acklam Rd C1
Albert Park C2
Albert Rd B2
Albert Terr C2
Aubrey St C3
Ayresome Gdns C2
Ayresome Green La C1
Ayresome St C2
Barton Rd A1
Bilsdale Rd C3
Bishopton Rd C2
Borough Rd B2/B3
Bowes Rd A2
Breckon Hill Rd B3
Bridge St East B3
Bridge St West B2
Brighouse Rd A1
Burlam Rd C1
Bus Station B2
Cannon Park B1
Cannon Park Way B2
Cannon St B1
Captain Cook Sq B2
Carlow St B1
Castle Way C3
Chipchase Rd C2
Clairville Sports Stadium C3
Cleveland Centre B2
Clive Rd C2
Commercial St A2
Corporation Rd B2
Costa St C2
Council Offices B3
Crescent Rd C1
Cumberland Rd C2
Depot Rd A2
Derwent St B1
Devonshire Rd C2
Diamond Rd B2
Disabled Driver Test Circuit B1
Dorman Museum C2
Douglas St B3
Eastbourne Rd C2
Eden Rd C3
Enterprise Centre A2
Forty Foot Rd A2
Gilkes St B2
Gosford St A2
Grange Rd B2
Gresham Rd B2
Harehills Rd C1
Harford St C2
Hartington Rd B2
Haverton Hill Rd A1
Hey Wood St B1
Highfield Rd C3
Hill St Centre B2
Holwick Rd B1
Hutton Rd C3
I.C.I. Works A1
Information Ctr B2
Lambton Rd C3
Lancaster Rd C2
Lansdowne Rd C3
Latham Rd C2
Law Courts B2/B3
Lees Rd B2
Leeway B3
Linthorpe Cemetery C1
Linthorpe Rd B2
Little Theatre, The C2
Longford St C2
Longlands Rd C3
Lower East St A3
Lower Lake C3
Macmillan College C1
Maldon Rd C1
Manor St B2
Marsh St B1
Marton Rd B3
Middlehaven B3
Middlesbrough By-Pass B2/C1
Middlesbrough F.C. B3
Middlesbrough General (A+E) C2
Middlesbrough Leisure Park B3
Middlesbrough ≷ B2
Middletown Park C2
MIMA B3
Mosque ✦ B2
Mosque ✦ C3
Mulgrave Rd C2
North Ormesby Rd B3
Newport Bridge B1
Newport Bridge Approach Rd B1
Newport Rd B2
North Rd B2
Northern Rd C1
Outram St B2
Oxford Rd C2
Park La C2
Park Rd North C2
Park Rd South C2
Park Vale Rd C3
Parliament Rd B1
Police Station B3
Port Clarence Rd A3
Portman St B2
Post Office B2/B3/C1/C2/C3
Princes Rd B2
Riverside Business Park A2
Riverside Park Rd A1
Rockliffe Rd C2
Romaldkirk Rd B1
Roman Rd C2
Roseberry Rd C3
St Paul's Rd B2
St Barnabas' Rd C2
Saltwells Rd B3
Scott's Rd A3
Seaton Carew Rd A3
Shepherdson Way B3
Sikh Temple ✦ B2
Snowdon Rd A2
South West Ironmasters Park B1
Southfield Rd B3
Southwell Rd C2
Springfield Rd C1
Startforth Rd A2
Stockton Rd C1
Stockton St A2
Surrey St C2
Sycamore Rd C2
Synagogue ✦ B2
Tax Offices B3
Tees Viaduct C1
Teessaurus Park A2
Teesside Tertiary College C3
The Avenue C2
The Crescent C2
Thornfield Rd C1
Town Hall B2
Transporter Bridge (Toll) A3
UGC B3
Union St B2
University of Teesside B2
Upper Lake C2
Valley Rd C3
Ventnor Rd C2
Victoria Rd B2
Vulcan St A2
Warwick St C2
Wellesley Rd B3
West Lane Hospital C1
Westminster Rd C2
Wilson St B2
Windward Way B3
Woodlands Rd B2
York Rd C3

Milton Keynes

Abbey Way A1
Arbrook Ave B1
Armourer Dr A3
Arncliffe Dr A1
Avebury (r'about) C2
Avebury Blvd C2
Bankfield (r'about) B3
Bayard Ave A2
Belvedere (r'about) A2
Bishopstone A1
Blundells Rd A1
Boycott Ave C2
Bradwell Common Blvd B1
Bradwell Rd C1
Bramble Ave A2
Brearley Ave C2
Breckland A1
Brill Place B1
Burnham Dr B1
Bus Station C1
Campbell Park (r'about) B3
Cantle Ave A3
Central Milton Keynes Shopping Area B2
Century Ave C2
Chaffron Way C3
Childs Way C1
Christ the Cornerstone B2
Cineworld B2
Civic Offices B2
Cleavers Ave B2
Colesbourne Dr A3
Conniburrow Blvd B2
County Court B2
Currier Dr A2
Dansteed Way A2/A3/B1
Deltic Ave B1
Downs Barn (r'about) A2
Downs Barn Blvd A3
Eaglestone (r'about) C3
Easy Cinema B2
Eelbrook Ave B1
Elder Gate B1
Evans Gate C2
Fairford Cr A3
Falcon Ave B3
Fennel Dr A2
Fishermead Blvd C3
Food Centre B3
Fulwoods Dr C3
Glazier Dr A2
Glovers La A1
Grafton Gate C1
Grafton St A1/C2
Gurnards Ave B3
Harrier Dr C3
Ibstone Ave B1
Langcliffe Dr A1
Leisure Plaza C1
Leys Rd C1
Library B2
Linford Wood A2
Marlborough Gate B3
Marlborough St A2/B3
Mercers Dr A1
Midsummer (r'about) C2
Midsummer Blvd B2
Milton Keynes Central ≷ C1
Monks Way A1
Mullen Ave A3
Mullion Pl C3
National Hockey Stadium B1
Neath Hill (r'about) A3
North Elder (r'about) C1
North Grafton (r'about) B1
North Overgate (r'about) A3
North Row B2
North Saxon (r'about) B2
North Secklow (r'about) B2
North Skeldon (r'about) A3
North Witan (r'about) B1
Oakley Gdns A3
Oldbrook Blvd C2
Open-Air Theatre B3
Overgate A3
Overstreet A3
Patriot Dr B1
Pencarrow Pl B3
Penryn Ave B3
Perran Ave C3
Pitcher La C1
Place Retail Park, The C1
Point Centre, The B2
Police Station B2
Portway (r'about) B2
Post Office A2/B2/C3
Precedent Dr B1
Quinton Dr B1
Ramsons Ave B2
Rockingham Dr A2
Rooksley (r'about) B
Rooksley Retail Park C
Saxon Gate B
Saxon St A1/C
Secklow Gate B
Shackleton Pl C
Silbury (r'about) C
Silbury Blvd B
Skeldon (r'about) A
South Grafton (r'about) C
South Row C
South Saxon (r'about) C
South Secklow (r'about) B
South Witan (r'about) C
Springfield (r'about) B
Stanton Wood (r'about) A
Stantonbury (r'about) A
Stantonbury Leisure Centre ✦ A
Strudwick Dr C
Sunrise Parkway A
Telephone Exchange C
The Boundary C
Theatre & Art Gallery B
Tolcarne Ave C
Towan Ave C
Trueman Pl C
Vauxhall A
Winterhill Retail Park C
Witan Gate B
X-Scape B

Newport / Casnewydd

0 Miles ¼

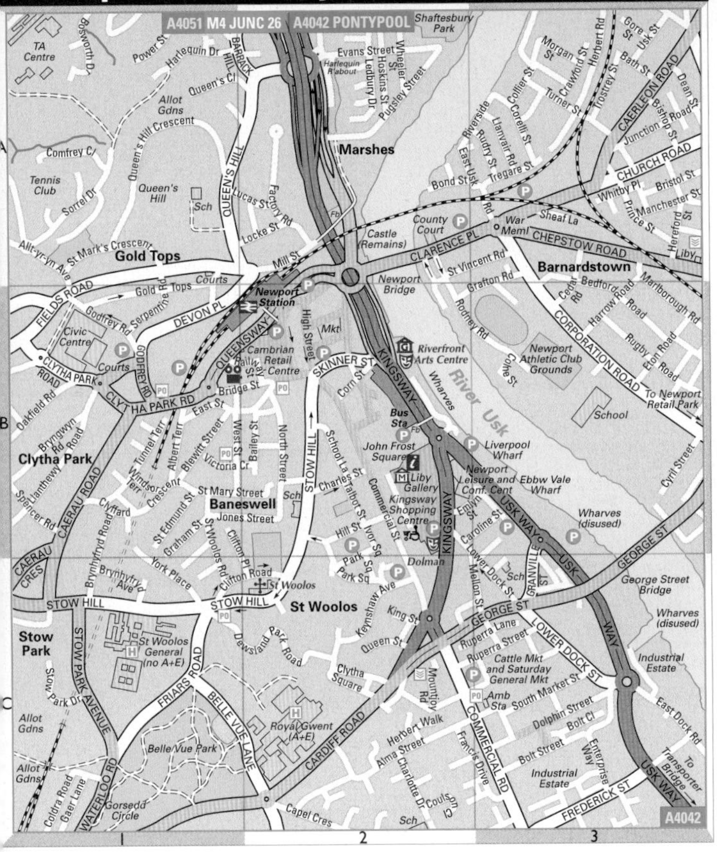

Northampton

0 Miles ¼

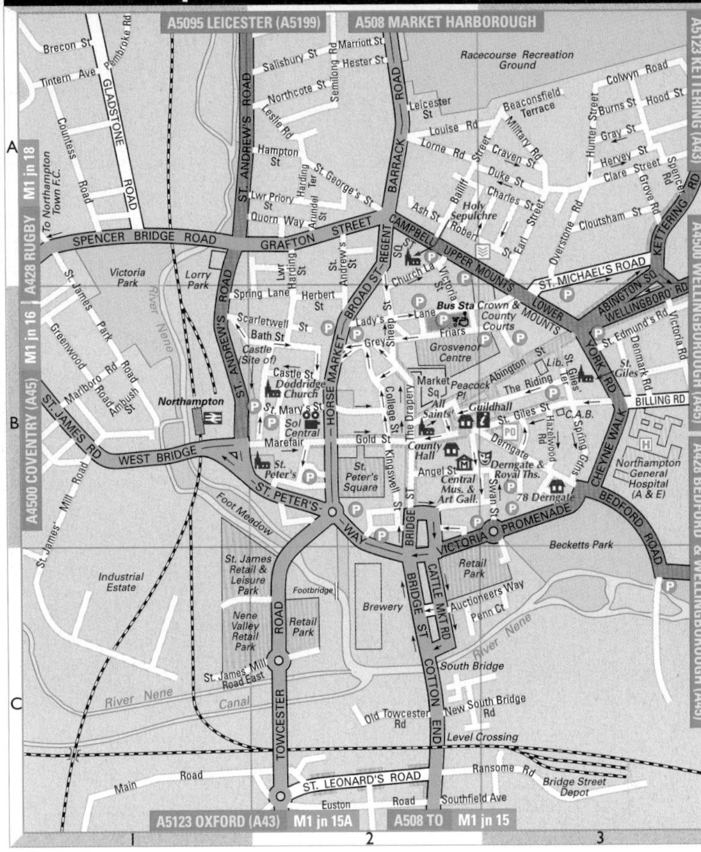

Newport / Casnewydd

Albert Terr B1
Allt-yr-Yn Ave A1
Alma St C2
Ambulance Station C3
Bailey St B2
Barrack Hill A2
Bath St A3
Bedford Rd B3
Belle Vue La C1
Belle Vue Park C1
Bishop St A3
Blewitt St B1
Bolt Cl C3
Bolt St C3
Bond St A2
Bosworth Dr A1
Bridge St B1
Bristol St A3
Bryngwyn Rd B1
Brynhyfryd Ave C1
Brynhyfryd Rd C1
Bus Station B2
Caerau Cres C1
Caerau Rd B1
Caerleon Rd A3
Cambrian Retail Centre B2
Capel Cres C2
Cardiff Rd C2
Caroline St B3
Castle (Remains) A2
Cattle Market and Saturday General Market C3
Cedar Rd B3
Charles St B2
Charlotte Dr C2
Chepstow Rd A3
Church Rd A3
City Cinema B1
Civic Centre B1
Clarence Pl A2
Clifton Pl B1
Clifton Rd C1
Clyffard Cres B1
Clytha Park Rd B1
Clytha Sq C2
Coldra Rd C1
Collier St A3
Colne St B3
Comfrey Cl A1
Commercial Rd C3
Commercial St B2
Corelli St A3
Corn St B2
Corporation Rd B3
Coulson Cl C2
County Court A2
Courts A1
Courts B1
Crawford St A3
Cyril St B3
Dean St A3
Devon Pl B1
Dewsland Park Rd C2
Dolman B2
Dolphin St C3
East Dock Rd C3
East St B1
East Usk Rd A3
Ebbw Vale Wharf B3
Emlyn St B2
Enterprise Way C3
Eton Rd B3
Evans St A2
Factory Rd A2
Fields Rd B1
Francis Dr C2
Frederick St C3
Friars Rd C1
Gaer La C1
George St C3
George Street Bridge C3
Godfrey Rd B1
Gold Tops B1
Gore St A3
Gorsedd Circle C1
Grafton Rd A3
Graham St B1
Granville St C3
Harlequin Dr A1
Harrow Rd B3
Herbert Rd A3
Herbert Walk C2
Hereford St A3
High St B2
Hill St B2
Hoskins St A2
Information Ctr B2
Ivor Sq B2
John Frost Sq B2
Jones St B1
Junction Rd A3
Keynshaw Ave C2
King St C2
Kingsway B2
Kingsway Shopping Centre B2
Ledbury Dr A2
Library A3
Library, Museum & Art Gallery B2
Liverpool Wharf B3
Llanthewy Rd B1
Llanvair Rd A3
Locke St A2
Lower Dock St C3
Lucas St A2
Manchester St A3
Market B2
Marlborough Rd B3
Mellon St C3
Mill St A2
Morgan St A3
Mountjoy Rd C2
Newport Athletic Club Grounds B3
Newport Bridge A2
Newport Leisure and Conference Ctr B2
Newport Station B2
North St B2
Oakfield Rd B1
Park Sq C2
Police Station A3/C2
Post Office B1/B2/C1/C3
Power St A1
Prince St A3
Pugsley St A2
Queen St C2
Queen's Cl A1
Queen's Hill A1
Queen's Hill Cres A1
Queensway B2
Railway St B2
Riverfront Arts Centre B2
Riverside A3
Rodney Rd B2
Royal Gwent (A+E) C2
Rudry St A3
Rugby Rd B3
Ruperra La C3
Ruperra St C3
St. Edmund St B1
St. Mark's Cres A1
St. Mary St B1
St. Vincent Rd A3
St. Woolos C2
St. Woolos General (no A+E) C1
St. Woolos Rd B1
School La B2
Serpentine Rd B1
Shaftesbury Park A2
Sheaf La A3
Skinner St B2
Sorrel Dr A1
South Market St C3
Spencer Rd B1
Stow Hill B2/C1/C2
Stow Park Ave C1
Stow Park Dr C1
TA Centre A1
Talbot St B2
Tennis Club A1
Tregare St A3
Trostrey St A3
Tunnel Terr B1
Turner St A3
Usk St A3
Usk Way B3/C3
Victoria Cr B1
War Memorial A3
Waterloo Rd C1
West St B1
Wharves B2
Wheeler St A2
Whitby Pl A3
Windsor Terr B1
York Pl C1

Northampton

78 Derngate B3
Abington Sq B3
Abington St B3
All Saints' B2
Ambush St B1
Angel St B2
Arundel St A2
Ash St A2
Auctioneers Way C2
Bailiff St A2
Barrack Rd A2
Bath St B2
Beaconsfield Terr A3
Becketts Park C3
Bedford Rd B3
Billing Rd B3
Brecon St A1
Brewery C2
Bridge St C2
Bridge St Depot C3
Broad St B2
Burns St A3
Bus Station B2
Campbell St A2
Castle (Site of) B2
Castle St B2
Cattle Market Rd C2
Central Museum & Art Gallery B2
Charles St A3
Cheyne Walk B3
Church La A2
Clare St A3
Cloutsham St A3
College St B2
Colwyn Rd A3
Cotton End C2
Countess Rd A1
County Hall B2
Craven St A3
Crown & County Courts B3
Denmark Rd B3
Derngate B3
Derngate & Royal Theatres B3
Doddridge Church B2
Duke St A3
Earl St A3
Euston Rd C2
Foot Meadow B2
Gladstone Rd A1
Gold St B2
Grafton St A2
Gray St A3
Greenwood Rd B1
Grey Friars B2
Grosvenor Centre B2
Grove Rd A3
Guildhall B2
Hampton St A2
Harding Terr A2
Hazelwood Rd B3
Herbert St B2
Hervey St A3
Hester St A2
Holy Sepulchre A2
Hood St A3
Horse Market B2
Hunter St A3
Industrial Estate C1
Information Ctr B2
Kettering Rd A3
Kingswell St B2
Lady's La B2
Leicester St A2
Leslie Rd A2
Library B3
Lorne Rd A2
Lorry Park A1
Louise Rd A2
Lower Harding St A2
Lower Mounts B3
Lower Priory St A2
Main Rd C1
Marefair B2
Market Sq B2
Marlboro Rd B1
Marriott St A2
Military Rd A3
Nene Valley Retail Park C1
New South Bridge Rd C2
Northampton General Hospital (A & E) B3
Northampton Station B1
Northcote St A2
Old Towcester Rd C2
Overstone Rd A3
Peacock Pl B2
Pembroke Rd A1
Penn Court C2
Police Station B3
Post Office B3
Quorn Way A2
Ransome Rd C3
Regent Sq A2
Retail Park C2
Robert St A2
St Andrew's Rd B1
St Andrew's St A2
St Edmund's Rd B3
St George's St A2
St Giles B3
St Giles St B3
St Giles' Terr B3
St James' Mill Rd B1
St James' Mill Rd East C1
St James Park Rd B1
St James Retail & Leisure Park C1
St James Rd B1
St Leonard's Rd C2
St Mary's St B2
St Michael's Rd A3
St Peter's B2
St Peter's Square Shopping Precinct B2
St Peter's Way B2
Salisbury St A2
Scarletwell St B2
Semilong Rd A2
Sheep St B2
Sol Central (Leisure Centre) B2
South Bridge C2
Southfield Ave C2
Spencer Bridge Rd A1
Spencer Rd A3
Spring Gdns B3
Spring La B2
Swan St B3
The Drapery B2
The Riding B3
Tintern Ave A1
Towcester Rd C2
Upper Mounts A2
Victoria Park A1
Victoria Promenade B2
Victoria Rd B3
Victoria St A2
Wellingborough Rd B3
West Bridge B1
York Rd B3

Newcastle upon Tyne

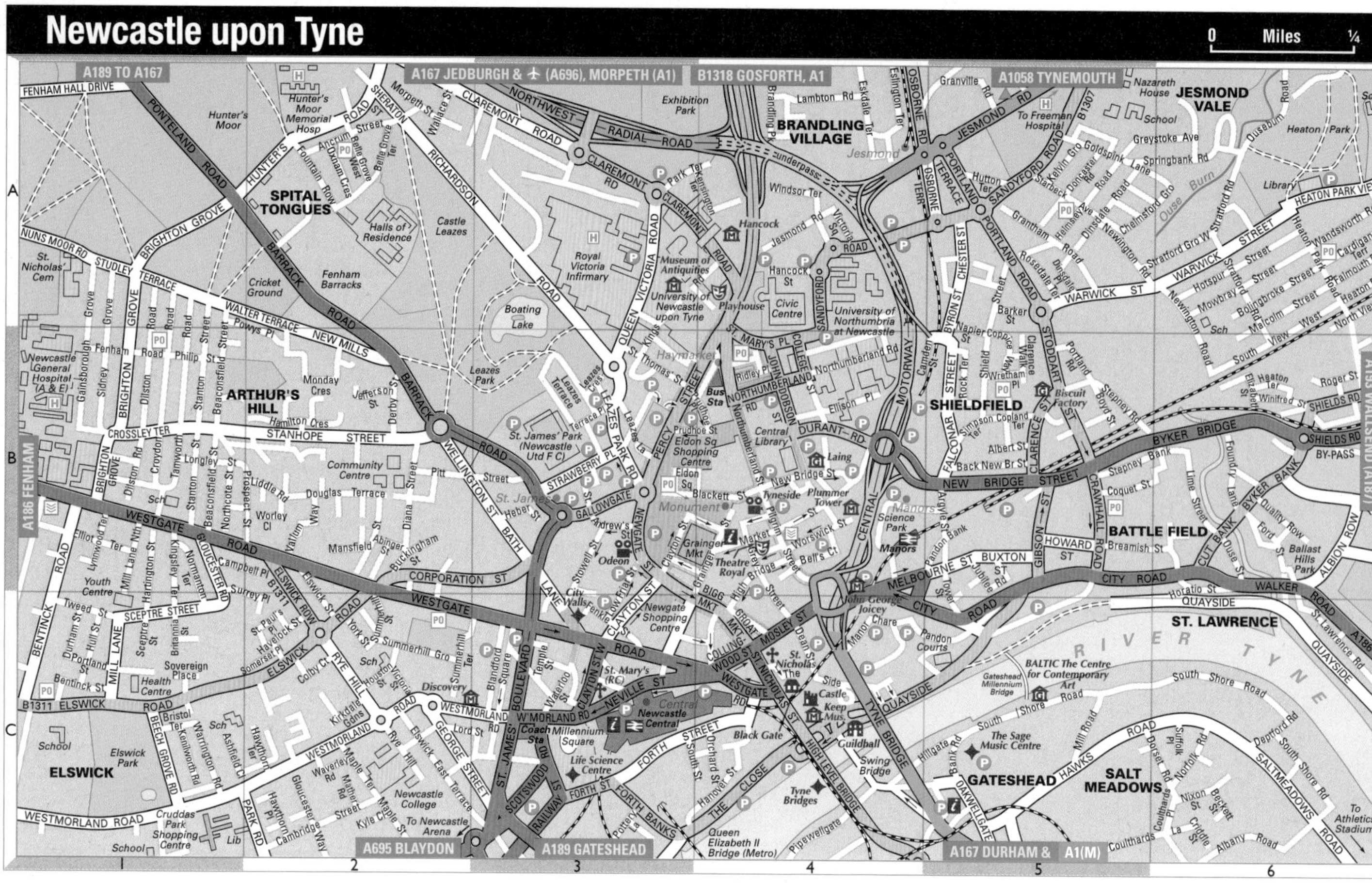

Newcastle upon Tyne

Abinger St B2
Albany Rd C6
Albert St B5
Albion Row B6
Ancrum St A2
Argyle St B5
Arthur's Hill B1
Ashfield Cl C1
Athletics Stadium C6
Back New Bridge St B5
Ballast Hills Park B6
BALTIC The Centre for Contemporary Art 🏛 C5
Bank Rd C5
Barker St A5
Barrack Rd A2/B2
Bath La B3
Beaconsfield St B1
Beckett St C6
Beech Grove Rd C1
Belle Grove Terr A2
Belle Grove West A2
Bell's Court B4
Bentinck Rd C1
Bentinck St C1
Bigg Market C4
Biscuit Factory 🏛 B5
Black Gate 🏛 C4
Blackett St B4
Blandford Sq C3
Boating Lake A3
Bolingbroke St A6
Boyd St B5
Brandling Park A4
Breamish St B5
Brighton Gr A1/B1
Bristol Terr C1
Britannia St C1
Buckingham St B2
Bus Station B4
Buxton St B5
Byker Bank B6
Byker Bridge B6
Byron St A5
Cambridge St C2
Camden St B4
Campbell Pl B1
Cardigan Terr A6
Castle ♜ C4
Castle Leazes A2
Central (metro station) C3
Central Library B4
Central Motorway B4
Chelmsford Gr A5
Chester St A5
City Rd B5/C5
City Walls ✦ C3
Civic Centre A4
Claremont Rd A3
Clarence St B5
Clarence Walk B5
Clayton St B3
Clayton St West C3
Coach Station C3
Colby Court C2
College St B4
Collingwood St C4
Community Centre B2
Copland Terr B5
Coppice Way B5
Coquet St B5
Corporation St B2
Coulthards La C5
Coulthards Pl C6
Courts C5
Crawhall Rd B5
Cricket Ground A2
Criddle St C6
Crossley Terr B1
Croydon Rd B1
Cruddas Park Shopping Centre C1
Cut Bank B6
Dean St C4
Deptford Rd C6
Derby St B2
Diana St B2
Dilston Rd B1
Dinsdale Pl A5
Dinsdale Rd A5
Discovery Museum 🏛 C2
Doncaster Rd A5
Dorset Rd C6
Douglas Terr B2
Durant Rd B4
Durham St C1
Eldon Sq B3
Eldon Sq Shopping Centre B3
Elizabeth St B6
Elliot Terr B1
Ellison Pl B4
Elswick East Terr C2
Elswick Park C1
Elswick Rd C1/C2
Elswick Row B2
Elswick St B2
Eskdale Terr A4
Eslington Terr A4
Exhibition Park A3
Falconar St B5
Falmouth Rd A6
Fenham Barracks A2
Fenham Hall Dr A1
Fenham Rd B1
Fenkle St C3
Ford St B6
Forth Banks C3
Forth St C3
Foundry La B6
Fountain Row A2
Gainsborough Gr B1
Gallowgate B3
Gateshead Millennium Bridge C5
George St C2
Gibson St B5
Gloucester Rd B1
Gloucester Way C2
Goldspink La A5
Grainger Market B4
Grainger St B4
Grantham Rd A5
Granville Rd A5
Grey St B4
Greystoke Ave A5
Groat Market C4
Guildhall 🏛 C4
Halls of Residence A2
Hamilton Cr B2
Hancock Museum 🏛 A4
Hanover St C4
Hartington St B1
Havelock St C2
Hawks Rd C5
Hawthorn Pl C2
Hawthorn Terr C2
Haymarket (metro station) B4
Health Centre C1
Heaton Park A6
Heaton Park Rd A6
Heaton Park View A6
Heaton Rd A6
Heaton Terr B6
Heber St B3
Helmsley Rd A5
High Bridge B4
High Level Bridge C4
Hillgate C5
Horatio St B6
Hotspur St A6
Houston St C2
Howard St B5
Hull St C1
Hunter's Moor A1
Hunter's Moor Memorial Hospital H A2
Hunter's Rd A2
Hutton Terr A5
Information Ctr i B3/B4/C3
Jefferson St B2
Jesmond (metro station) A4
Jesmond Rd A4/A5
John Dobson St B4
John George Joicey Museum 🏛 C4
Jubilee Rd B5
Keep Museum 🏛 C4
Kelvin Gr A5
Kenilworth Rd C1
Kensington Terr A4
Kings Rd B3
Kingsley Terr B1
Kirkdale Gdns C2
Kyle Cl C2
Laing Gallery 🏛 B4
Lambton Rd A4
Leazes Cr B3
Leazes La B3
Leazes Park B3
Leazes Park Rd B3
Leazes Terr B3
Library A6/C1
Liddle Rd B2
Life Science Centre ✦ C3
Lime St B6
Longley St B1
Lord St C2
Low Friar St C3
Lynnwood Terr B1
Malcolm St A6
Manor Chare C4
Manors (metro station) B4
Manors Station ⇌ B4
Mansfield St B2
Maple St C2
Maple Terr C2
Market St B4
Mather Rd C2
Melbourne St B4
Mill La C1
Mill La North B1
Mill Rd C5
Millennium Sq C3
Monday Cr B2
Monument (metro station) B4
Morpeth St A2
Mosley St C4
Mowbray St A6
Museum of Antiquities 🏛 A3
Napier St A5
Nazareth House A5
Neville St C3
New Bridge St B4/B5
New Mills B2
Newcastle Central Station ⇌ C3
Newcastle College C2
Newcastle General Hospital (A&E) H B1
Newgate Shopping Centre C3
Newgate St B3
Newington Rd A5/A6
Nixon St C6
Norfolk Rd C6
Normanton Terr B1
North View A6
Northcote St B1
Northumberland Rd B4
Northumberland St B4
Northwest Radial Rd A3
Nuns Moor Rd A1
Oakwellgate C5
Odeon 🎥 B3
Orchard St C4
Osborne Rd A4
Osborne Terr A5
Ouse Burn A6
Ouse St B6
Ouseburn Rd A6
Oxnam Cr A2
Pandon Bank B4
Pandon C5
Park Rd C2
Park Terr A3
Percy St B3
Philip St B1
Pilgrim St B4
Pipewellgate C4
Pitt St B2
Playhouse Theatre ♥ A4
Plummer Tower 🏛 B4
Police Station B1/B4/C4
Ponteland Rd A1
Portland Rd A5/B5
Portland St C1
Portland Terr A5
Post Office PO A2/A5/A6/B1/B3/B4/B5/C1/C2
Pottery La C3
Powys Pl A1
Prospect St B2
Prudhoe Pl B3
Prudhoe St B3
Quality Row B6
Quayside C4/C6
Queen Elizabeth II Bridge C4
Queen Victoria Rd A3
Railway St C3
Richardson Rd A3
Ridley Pl B4
Rock Terr B5
Roger St B6
Rosedale Terr A5
Royal Victoria Infirmary H A3
Rye Hill C2
Sage Music Centre, The ✦ C5
St Andrew's St B3
St James (metro station) B3
St James' Blvd C3
St James' Park (Newcastle Utd FC) B3
St Lawrence Rd C6
St Mary's (RC) ✝ C3
St Mary's Place B4
St Nicholas ✝ C4
St Nicholas' Cem A1
St Nicholas St C4
St Paul's Pl C2
St Thomas' St B3
Saltmeadows Rd C6
Sandyford Rd A4/A5
Sceptre St C1
Science Park B4
Scotswood Rd C3
Sheraton St A2
Shield St B5
Shieldfield B5
Shields Rd B6
Shields Rd By-Pass B6
Sidney Gr B1
Simpson Terr B5
Somerset Pl C2
South Shore Rd C5
South St C3
South View West B6
Sovereign Pl C1
Springbank Rd A6
Stanhope St B2
Stanton St B1
Starbeck Ave A5
Stepney Bank B5
Stepney Rd B5
Stoddart St B5
Stowell St B3
Stratford Gr West A6
Stratford Rd A6
Strawberry Pl B3
Studley Terr A1
Suffolk Pl C6
Summerhill Gr C2
Summerhill St C2
Summerhill Terr C2
Surrey Pl B1
Swing Bridge C4
Tamworth Rd B1
Temple St C3
Terrace Pl B3
The Close C4
The Side C4
Theatre Royal ♥ B4
Tower St B5
Tweed St C1
Tyne Bridge C4
Tyne Bridges ✦ C4
Tyneside 🎥 B4
University of Newcastle upon Tyne A3
University of Northumbria at Newcastle A4
Vallum Way B2
Victoria Sq A4
Victoria St C2
Walker Rd B6
Wallace St A2
Walter Terr A1
Wandsworth Rd A6
Warrington Rd C1
Warwick St A5/A6
Waterloo St C3
Waverley Rd C2
Wellington St B2
Westgate Rd B1/C2/C4
Westmorland Rd C1/C2/C3
Windsor Terr A4
Winifred St B6
Worley Cl B2
Worswick St B4
Wretham Pl B5
York St C2
Youth Centre C1

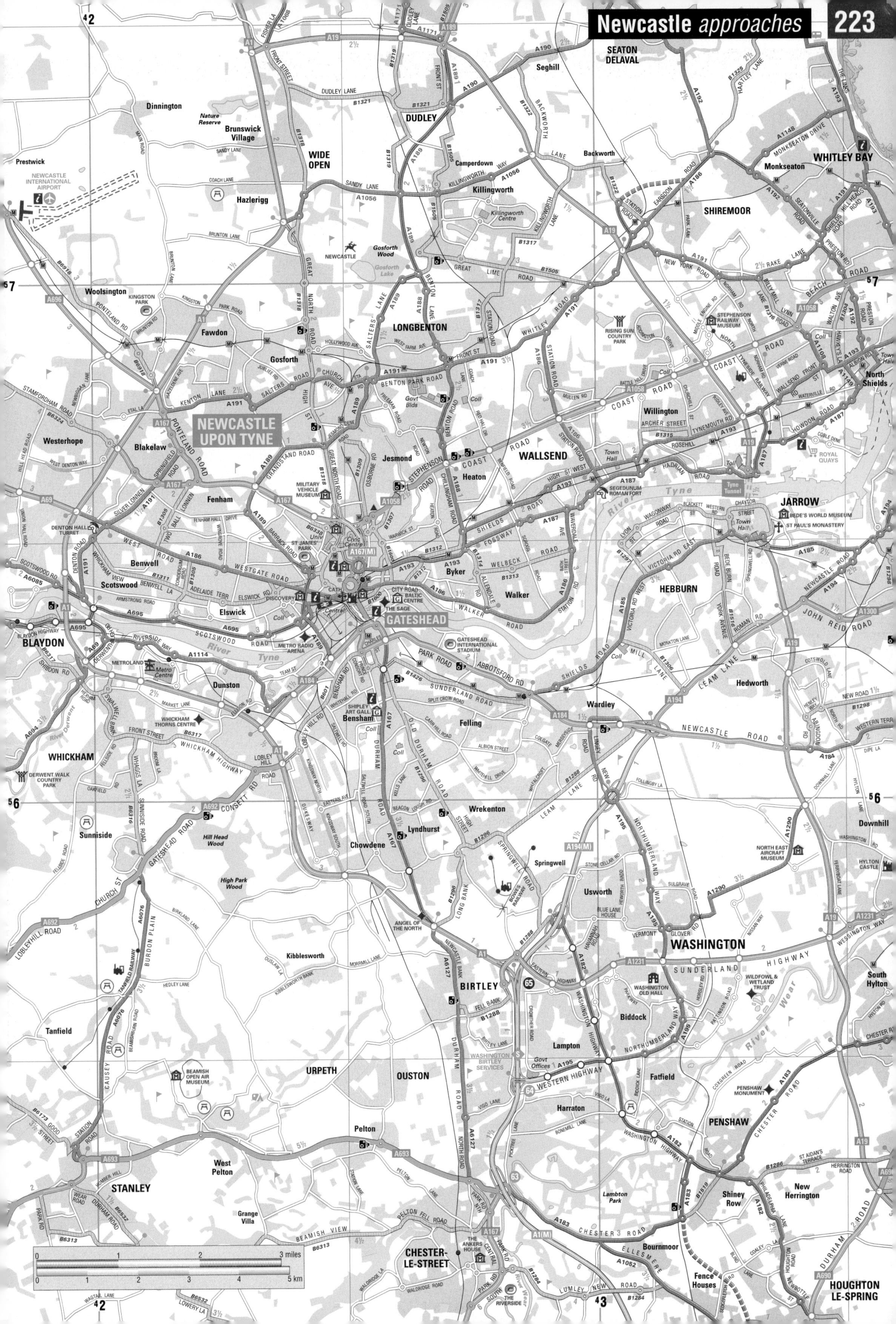
NEWCASTLE UPON TYNE
GATESHEAD
SEATON DELAVAL
Seghill
DUDLEY
WIDE OPEN
Dinnington
Brunswick Village
Prestwick
NEWCASTLE INTERNATIONAL AIRPORT
Hazlerigg
Camperdown
Killingworth
Backworth
WHITLEY BAY
Monkseaton
SHIREMOOR
Woolsington
Fawdon
Gosforth
LONGBENTON
Westerhope
Blakelaw
Jesmond
WALLSEND
Willington
North Shields
Heaton
Fenham
JARROW
Benwell
Scotswood
Byker
Walker
HEBBURN
BLAYDON
Elswick
Dunston
Hedworth
Wardley
Felling
Bensham
WHICKHAM
Sunniside
Wrekenton
Lyndhurst
Chowdene
Springwell
Usworth
Downhill
WASHINGTON
Kibblesworth
BIRTLEY
South Hylton
Tanfield
Lampton
Biddock
URPETH
OUSTON
Fatfield
Harraton
PENSHAW
Pelton
West Pelton
STANLEY
Shiney Row
New Herrington
Grange Villa
Lambton Park
Bournmoor
CHESTER-LE-STREET
Fence Houses
HOUGHTON LE-SPRING
River Tyne
River Wear
0 1 2 3 miles
0 1 2 3 4 5 km

Norwich

0 Miles ¼

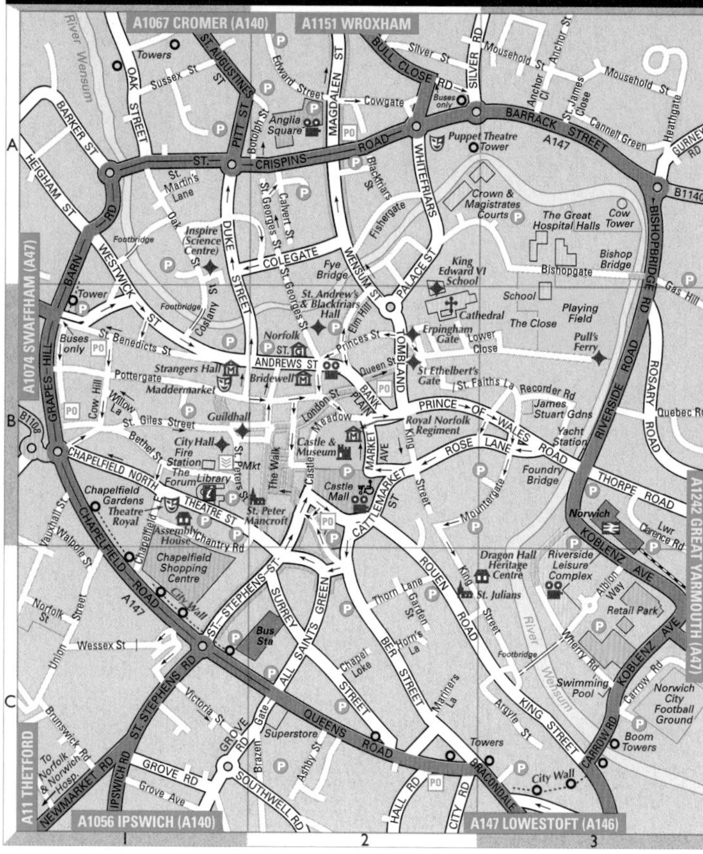

Nottingham

0 Miles ¼

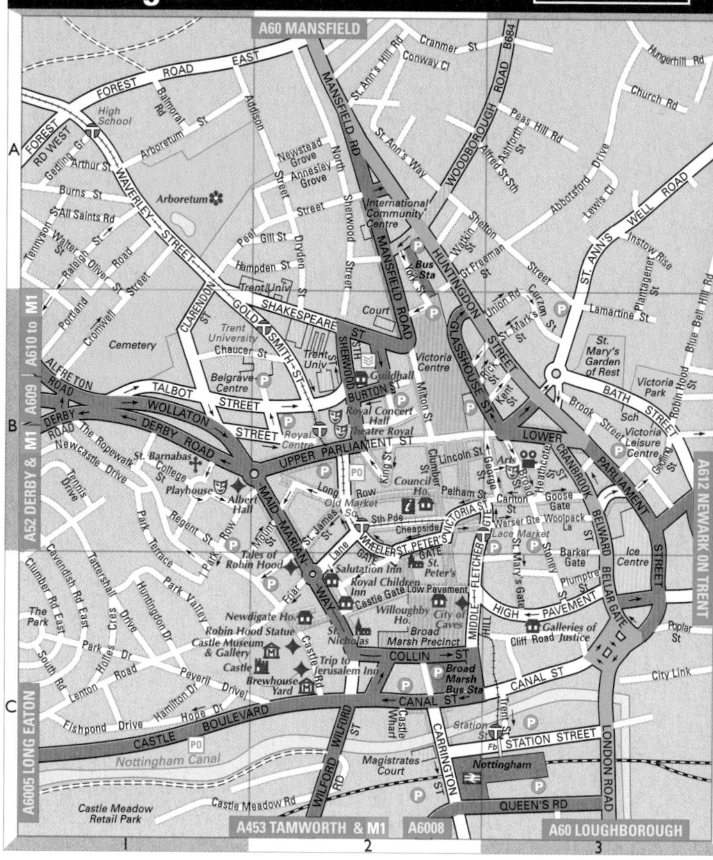

Norwich

Albion Way C3
All Saints Green. C2
Anchor Cl A3
Anchor St A3
Anglia Sq. B2
Argyle St C3
Ashby St C2
Assembly House 🏛 . . B1
Bank Plain B2
Barker St A1
Barn Rd A1
Barrack St A3
Ber St C2
Bethel St B1
Bishop Bridge A3
Bishopbridge Rd A3
Bishopgate A3
Blackfriars St. A2
Botolph St A2
Bracondale C3
Brazen Gate C2
Bridewell 🏛 B2
Brunswick Rd C1
Bull Close Rd A2
Bus Station C2
Calvert St. A2
Cannell Green A3
Carrow Rd C3
Castle Mall. B2
Castle Meadow B2
Castle & Museum ♜ . . B1
Cathedral ✝ B2
Cattlemarket St B2
Chantry Rd B1
Chapel Loke C2
Chapelfield East B1
Chapelfield Gdns. B1
Chapelfield North B1
Chapelfield Rd. B1
Chapelfield Shopping Centre C1
City Hall ✦ B1
City Rd C2
City Wall C1/C3
Colegate A2
Coslany St. B1
Cow Hill. B1
Cow Tower A3
Cowgate A2
Crown & Magistrates Courts B2
Dragon Hall Heritage Centre 🏛 C3
Duke St A1
Edward St A2
Elm Hill B2
Erpingham Gate ✦ . . . B2
Fire Station B1
Fishergate A2
Foundry Bridge B3
Fye Bridge. A2
Garden St C2
Gas Hill B3
Grapes Hill. B1
Great Hospital Halls, The A3
Grove Ave C1
Grove Rd. C1
Guildhall ✦ B1
Gurney Rd. A3
Hall Rd. C2
Heathgate A3
Heigham St A1
Horn's La. C2
Information Ctr ℹ B1
Inspire (Science Centre) ✦ A1
Ipswich Rd C1
James Stewart Gdns. . B3
King Edward VI School ✦ B2
King St. B2
King St. C3
Koblenz Ave C3
Library B1
London St B2
Lower Clarence Rd . . . B3
Lower Cl B3
Maddermarket 🎭. B1
Magdalen St A2
Mariners La C2
Market B2
Market Ave B2
Mountergate B3
Mousehold St A3
Newmarket Rd C1
Norfolk Gallery 🏛 B2
Norfolk St C1
Norwich City FC C3
Norwich Station ⇌. . . B3
Oak St A1
Palace St. A2
Pitt St. A1
Police Station ▤ B1
Post Office PO A2/B1/B2/C2
Pottergate B1
Prince of Wales Rd . . . B2
Princes St B2
Pull's Ferry ✦ B3
Puppet Theatre 🎭 A2
Quebec Rd B3
Queen St B2
Queens Rd C2
Recorder Rd B3
Retail Park. C3
Riverside Leisure Complex C3
Riverside Rd B3
Rosary Rd B3
Rose La. B2
Rouen Rd C2
Royal Norfolk Regiment Museum 🏛 B2
St Andrew's & Blackfriars Hall ✦ . . . B2
St Andrews St B2
St Augustines St A1
St Benedicts St B1
St Crispins Rd A1
St Ethelbert's Gate ✦ . B2
St Faiths La B3
St Georges St A2
St Giles St B1
St James Cl. A3
St Julians ⛪ C2
St Martin's La A1
St Peter Mancroft ⛪ . . B2
St Peters St. B1
St Stephens Rd. C1
St Stephens St C1
Silver Rd A2
Silver St. A2
Southwell Rd. C2
Strangers Hall 🏛 B1
Superstore. C2
Surrey St C2
Sussex St A1
Swimming Pool B3
The Close B3
The Forum. B1
The Walk B2
Theatre Royal 🎭 B1
Theatre St B1
Thorn La C2
Thorpe Rd B3
Tombland. B2
Union St C1
Vauxhall St. B1
Victoria St C1
Walpole St. B1
Wensum St A2
Wessex St C1
Westwick St. A1
Wherry Rd C3
Whitefriars A2
Willow La. B1
Yacht Station. B3

Nottingham

Abbotsford Dr A3
Addison St. A1
Albert Hall ✦ B1
Alfred St South A3
Alfreton Rd B1
All Saints Rd A1
Annesley Gr. A2
Arboretum ✿ A1
Arboretum St. A1
Arthur St A1
Arts Theatre 🎭. B3
Ashforth St A3
Balmoral Rd. A1
Barker Gate. B3
Bath St B3
Belgrave Centre. B1
Bellar Gate. B3
Belward St. B3
Blue Bell Hill Rd B3
Brewhouse Yard 🏛 . . . C2
Broad Marsh Bus Station C2
Broad Marsh Precinct . C2
Broad St B3
Brook St B3
Burns St A1
Burton St. B2
Bus Station A2
Canal St. C2
Carlton St B3
Carrington St. C2
Castle Blvd C1
Castle ♜ C2
Castle Gate C2
Castle Meadow Retail Park. C1
Castle Meadow Rd . . . C2
Castle Museum & Gallery 🏛. C2
Castle Rd. C2
Castle Wharf C2
Cavendish Rd East . . . C1
Cemetery. B1
Chaucer St B1
Cheapside B2
Church Rd. A3
City Link C3
City of Caves ✦ C2
Clarendon St. B1
Cliff Rd. C3
Clumber Rd East. C1
Clumber St B2
College St B1
Collin St. C2
Conway Cl. A2
Council House 🏛 B2
Court B2
Cranbrook St. B3
Cranmer St A2
Cromwell St. B1
Curzon St B3
Derby Rd B1
Dryden St A2
Fishpond Dr. C1
Fletcher Gate. B3
Forest Rd East. A1
Forest Rd West A1
Friar La C2
Galleries of Justice 🏛. C3
Gedling Gr. A1
Gedling St B3
George St B3
Gill St. A2
Glasshouse St. B2
Goldsmith St B2
Goose Gate B3
Great Freeman St A2
Guildhall 🏛 B2
Hamilton Dr C1
Hampden St A1
Heathcote St B3
High Pavement C3
High School (tram stop). A1
Holles Cr C1
Hope Dr. C1
Hungerhill Rd. A3
Huntingdon Dr. C1
Huntingdon St. A2
Ice Centre C3
Information Ctr ℹ B2
Instow Rise A3
International Community Centre A2
Kent St B3
King St. B2
Lace Market (tram stop). B3
Lamartine St B3
Lenton Rd C1
Lewis Cl. A3
Lincoln St B2
London Rd. C3
Long Row B2
Low Pavement C2
Lower Parliament St . . B3
Magistrates Court C2
Maid Marian Way B2
Mansfield Rd A2/B2
Middle Hill C2
Milton St B2
Mount St B2
Newcastle Dr. B1
Newdigate House 🏛. . C2
Newstead Gr A2
North Sherwood St . . . A2
Nottingham Station ⇌. C3
Old Market Square (tram stop). B2
Oliver St. A1
Park Dr C1
Park Row. C1
Park Terr B1
Park Valley. C1
Peas Hill Rd. A3
Peel St. A1
Pelham St B2
Peveril Dr. C1
Plantagenet St. A3
Playhouse Theatre 🎭 . B1
Plumptre St C3
Police Station ▤ B2
Poplar St C3
Portland Rd. B1
Post Office PO B2/C1
Queen's Rd C3
Raleigh St A1
Regent St B1
Rick St. B3
Robin Hood Statue ✦. C2
Robin Hood St. B3
Royal Centre (tram stop). B2
Royal Children Inn 🏛 . C2
Royal Concert Hall 🎭 . B2
St Ann's Hill Rd A2
St Ann's Way. A2
St Ann's Well Rd A3
St Barnabas ✝. B1
St James' St B2
St Mark's St. B3
St Mary's Garden of Rest B3
St Mary's Gate. B3
St Nicholas ⛪ C2
St Peter's ⛪. C2
St Peter's Gate B2
Salutation Inn 🏛. C2
Shakespeare St. B2
Shelton St A2
South Pde B2
South Rd C1
South Sherwood St. . . B2
Station St. C3
Station Street (tram stop). C3
Stoney St. B3
Talbot St B1
Tales of Robin Hood ✦ C2
Tattershall Dr C1
Tennis Dr B1
Tennyson St. A1
The Park C1
The Ropewalk B1
Theatre Royal 🎭 B2
Trent St C3
Trent University . . . A2/B2
Trent University (tram stop). B2
Trip To Jerusalem Inn ✦. C2
Union Rd B3
Upper Parliament St . . B2
Victoria Centre. B2
Victoria Leisure Centre B3
Victoria Park B3
Victoria St B2
Walter St A1
Warser Gate B3
Watkin St. A2
Waverley St A1
Wheeler Gate. B2
Wilford Rd C2
Wilford St. C2
Willoughby House 🏛 . C2
Wollaton St B1
Woodborough Rd A2
Woolpack La B3
York St. A2

Bagthorpe
Underwood
New Brinsley
Brinsley
Felley Priory
William Wood
Willey Spring
Moorgreen Reservoir
High Park Wood
Misk Hill
Watnall Coppice
Eastwood
D. H. LAWRENCE BIRTHPLACE MUSEUM
Moorgreen
Greasley
Beavale
Bogend
Hill Top
Newthorpe
New Eastwood
Giltbrook
Newthorpe Common
Kimberley
Watnall
Nuthall
Awsworth
Swingate
Cotmanhay
Ilkeston
Cossall Marsh
Cossall
EREWASH MUSEUM
Larklands
Gallows Inn
Hallam Fields
Trowell
TROWELL SERVICES
Strelley
Catstone Hill
Trowell Moor
New Stanton
Stanton-by-Dale
Stanton Gate
Stapleford Hill
Bramcore Hills
Stapleford
Sandiacre
Toton
Long Eaton
New Sawley
Sawley
Trentlock
Lindy
Papplewick
Dobpark
Long Hill
Beauvale
Ruffs
Hazelgrove
Hucknall
Westville
Butler's Hill
Broomhill
Cobbler's Hill
Bestwood Park
Bestwood Village
BESTWOOD
The Warren
Gaunt's Hill
Raceground Hill
Rise Park
Top Valley
Bestwood
Redhill
Arnold
TUMBLE TOWN
PLAYWORLD
Bulwell
Highbury Vale
Old Basford
Cinderhill
Broxtowe
Aspley
Whitemoor
Bilborough
New Basford
Carrington
Sherwood
Mapperley
Mapperley Park
Woodthorpe
Porchester
Gelding
Carlton
Thorneywood
St. Ann's
Nottingham
Netherfield
Radford
Wollaton
Wollaton Park
WOLLATON HALL
Nottingham University
New Lenton
TALES OF ROBIN HOOD
CASTLE MUSEUM & GALLERY
GALLERIES OF JUSTICE
GREENS MILL & SCIENCE CENTRE
Sneinton
Meadows
Colwick
HOLME PIERREPONT
NATIONAL WATER SPORTS CENTRE
Holme Pierrepont
THE CITY GROUND
TRENT BRIDGE
Bramcote
Chilwell
Rylands
Beeston
Attenborough
ATTENBOROUGH NATURE RESERVE
Clifton
Wilford
West Bridgford
Gamston
Bassingfield
NOTTINGHAM AIRPORT
Edwalton
Wilford Hill
Sharp Hill
Tollerton
Clipston
Brook Hill
Manor Park
FRAMEWORK KNITTERS' MUSEUM
Ruddington
Ruddington Fields
RUSHCLIFFE
Mill Hill
Barton in Fabis
Clifton Pasture
Barton Moor
Ruddington Moor
Bradmore
Bradmore Moor
Bunny Moor
Plumtree
Plumtree Park
Normanton-on-the-Wolds
Keyworth
Stanton on the Wolds
Thrumpton
THRUMPTON HALL
Red Hill
Gotham Hill
Cottagers Hill
Gotham Moor
Gotham
Winking Hill
Bunny
Bunny Park
Keyworth Wolds
Ratcliffe on Soar
Kingston on Soar
New Kingston
Crownend Wood
West Leake Hills
Crow Wood Hill
Windmill Hill
Old Wood
Bunny Hill
Lockington
Kegworth
Moulter Hill
Fox Hill
The Heavers
Wysall
Calverton
Oxton Bogs
Thorndale Plantation
Epperstone Park
Bonner Hill
Woodborough
Ploughman Wood
Hunger Hill
Lambley
Wicketwood Hill
Burton Joyce
Peas Hill
Hoe Hill
Plumtree Wolds
Normanton Wolds
Stanton Lo
North Lo
0 1 2 3 miles
0 1 2 3 4 5 km

Oxford

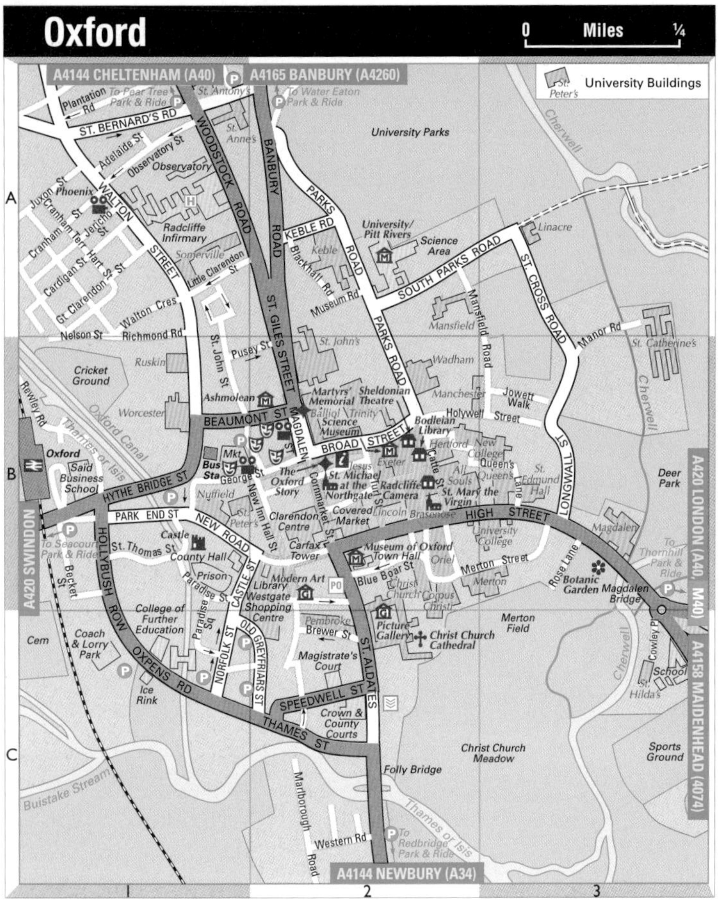

Plymouth

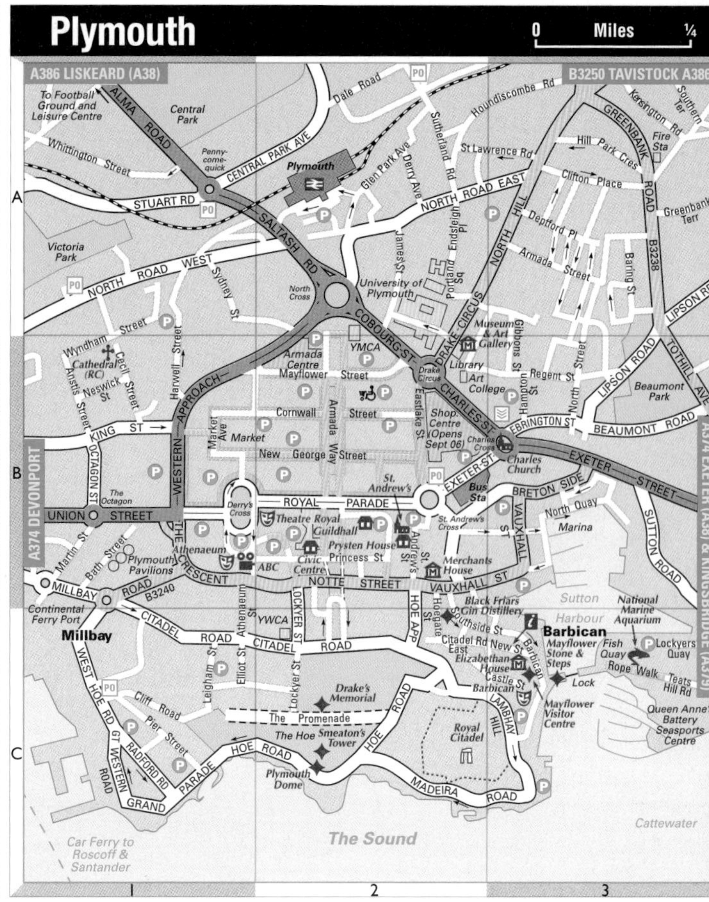

Oxford

Adelaide St A1
All Souls (Coll) B2
Ashmolean
  Museum 🏛 B2
Balliol (Coll) B2
Banbury Rd A2
Beaumont St B1
Becket St. B1
Blackhall Rd A2
Blue Boar St B2
Bodleian Library B2
Botanic Garden B3
Brasenose (Coll) B2
Brewer St. C2
Broad St B2
Burton-Taylor
  Theatre B2
Bus Station B1
Cardigan St A1
Carfax Tower B2
Castle B1
Castle St B1
Catte St. B2
Cemetery. C1
Christ Church (Coll). . . B2
Christ Church
  Cathedral ✝. C2
Christ Church
  Meadow C2
Clarendon Centre B2
Coach & Lorry Park. . . C1
College of Further
  Education C1
Cornmarket St. B2
Corpus Christi (Coll) . . B2
County Hall B1
Covered Market. B2
Cowley Pl C3
Cranham St. A1
Cranham Terr. A1
Cricket Ground B1
Crown & County
  Courts C2
Deer Park B3
Exeter (Coll). B2
Folly Bridge C2
George St B1
Great Clarendon St . . . A1
Hart St. A1
Hertford (Coll) B2
High St B3
HM Prison B1
Hollybush Row B1
Holywell St B2
Hythe Bridge St. B1
Ice Rink C1
Information Ctr ℹ B2
Jericho St A1
Jesus (Coll) B2
Jowett Walk. B3
Juxon St A1
Keble (Coll) A2
Keble Rd A2
Library B2
Linacre (Coll) A3
Lincoln (Coll) B2
Little Clarendon St . . . A1
Longwall St B3
Magdalen (Coll) B3
Magdalen Bridge. B2
Magdalen St B2
Magistrate's Court. . . . C2
Manchester (Coll) B2
Manor Rd B3
Mansfield (Coll) A2
Mansfield Rd A3
Market B1
Marlborough Rd C2
Martyrs' Memorial ✦. . B2
Merton Field B3
Merton (Coll) B3
Merton St B2
Museum of
  Modern Art 🏛 B2
Museum of Oxford 🏛 . B2
Museum Rd. A2
New College (Coll). . . . B3
New Inn Hall St B2
New Rd B1
New Theatre B2
Norfolk St C1
Nuffield (Coll). B1
Observatory. A1
Observatory St A1
Odeon B1/B2
Old Fire Station B1
Old Greyfriars St C2
Oriel (Coll) B2
Oxford Station B1
Oxford Story, The ✦. . B2
Oxpens Rd C1
Paradise Sq. C1
Paradise St B1
Park End St. B1
Parks Rd A2/B2
Pembroke (Coll). C2
Phoenix A1
Picture Gallery 🏛 C2
Plantation Rd. A1
Playhouse B2
Police Station C2
Post Office B2
Pusey St B1
Queen's La B3
Queen's (Coll) B3
Radcliffe Camera . . . B2
Radcliffe Infirmary H. . A1
Rewley Rd B1
Richmond Rd A1
Rose La B3
Ruskin (Coll) B1
Saïd Business School . B1
St Aldates C2
St Anne's (Coll) A1
St Antony's (Coll). A1
St Bernard's Rd. A1
St Catherine's (Coll). . . B3
St Cross Rd. A3
St Edmund Hall (Coll) . B3
St Giles St A2
St Hilda's (Coll) C3
St John St B2
St John's (Coll) B2
St Mary the Virgin . . B2
St Michael at the
  Northgate B2
St Peter's (Coll) B1
St Thomas St B1
Science Area. A2
Science Museum 🏛 . . B2
Sheldonian
  Theatre B2
Somerville (Coll). A1
South Parks Rd A2
Speedwell St C2
Sports Ground. C3
Thames St. C2
Town Hall. B2
Trinity (Coll) B2
Turl St B2
University College
  (Coll) B3
University Museum & Pitt
  Rivers Museum 🏛 . . A2
University Parks A2
Wadham (Coll). B2
Walton Cr A1
Walton St. A1
Western Rd C2
Westgate Shopping
  Centre B2
Woodstock Rd. A1
Worcester (Coll). B1

Plymouth

ABC B2
Alma Rd. A1
Anstis St B1
Armada Centre B2
Armada St A3
Armada Way B2
Art College. B2
Athenaeum St C1
Athenaeum B1
Barbican C3
Barbican C3
Baring St A3
Bath St B1
Beaumont Park B3
Beaumont Rd B3
Black Friars Gin
  Distillery ✦ C2
Breton Side B3
Bus Station B2
Castle St C3
Cathedral (RC) ✝. B1
Cecil St B1
Central Park A1
Central Park Ave A2
Charles Church B3
Charles Cross
  (r'about). B3
Charles St B2
Citadel Rd C2
Citadel Rd East C2
Civic Centre B2
Cliff Rd. C1
Clifton Pl A3
Cobourg St A2
Continental Ferry Port. B1
Cornwall St B2
Dale Rd A2
Deptford Pl A3
Derry Ave. A2
Derry's Cross
  (r'about). B1
Drake Circus B2
Drake's Memorial ✦ . . C2
Eastlake St B2
Ebrington St B3
Elizabethan
  House 🏛. C3
Elliot St C1
Endsleigh Pl. A2
Exeter St B3
Fire Station A3
Fish Quay C3
Gibbons St A3
Glen Park Ave A2
Grand Pde. C1
Great Western Rd C1
Greenbank Rd A3
Greenbank Terr A3
Guildhall B2
Hampton St. B3
Harwell St B1
Hill Park Cr A3
Hoe Approach B2
Hoe Rd C2
Hoegate St C2
Houndiscombe Rd . . . A2
Information Ctr ℹ C3
James St A2
Kensington Rd. A3
King St. B1
Lambhay Hill C3
Leigham St C1
Library B2
Lipson Rd A3/B3
Lockyer St. C2
Lockyers Quay C3
Madeira Rd C2
Marina B3
Market B1
Market Ave B1
Martin St B1
Mayflower St B2
Mayflower Stone
  & Steps ✦. C3
Mayflower Visitor
  Centre ✦ C3
Merchants House 🏛 . . B2
Millbay Rd B1
Museum & Art
  Gallery 🏛 B2
National Marine
  Aquarium C3
Neswick St B1
New George St B2
New St. C3
North Cross (r'about). . A2
North Hill. A3
North Quay B2
North Rd East A2
North Rd West. A1
North St. B3
Notte St. B2
Octagon St B1
Pennycomequick
  (r'about). A1
Pier St C1
Plymouth Dome ✦ . . . C2
Plymouth Pavilions . . . B1
Plymouth Station . . A2
Police Station B3
Portland Sq. A2
Post Office . . . .
  . . . . A1/A2/B2/C1
Princess St B2
Prysten House B2
Queen Anne's Battery
  Seasports Centre . . . C3
Radford Rd C1
Regent St B3
Rope Walk. C3
Royal Citadel C2
Royal Pde B2
St.Andrew's B2
St Andrew's Cross
  (r'about). B2
St Andrew's St. B2
St Lawrence Rd. A2
Saltash Rd. A2
Smeaton's Tower ✦ . . C2
Southern Terr. A3
Southside St C2
Stuart Rd. A1
Sutherland Rd A2
Sutton Rd B3
Sydney St A1
Teats Hill Rd C3
The Crescent. B1
The Hoe. C2
The Octagon (r'about) . B1
The Promenade. C2
Theatre Royal B2
Tothill Ave B3
Union St B1
University of
  Plymouth. A2
Vauxhall St. B2/3
Victoria Park A1
West Hoe Rd C1
Western Approach. . . . B1
Whittington St A1
Wyndham St B1
YMCA B2
YWCA C2

Poole

0 Miles ¼

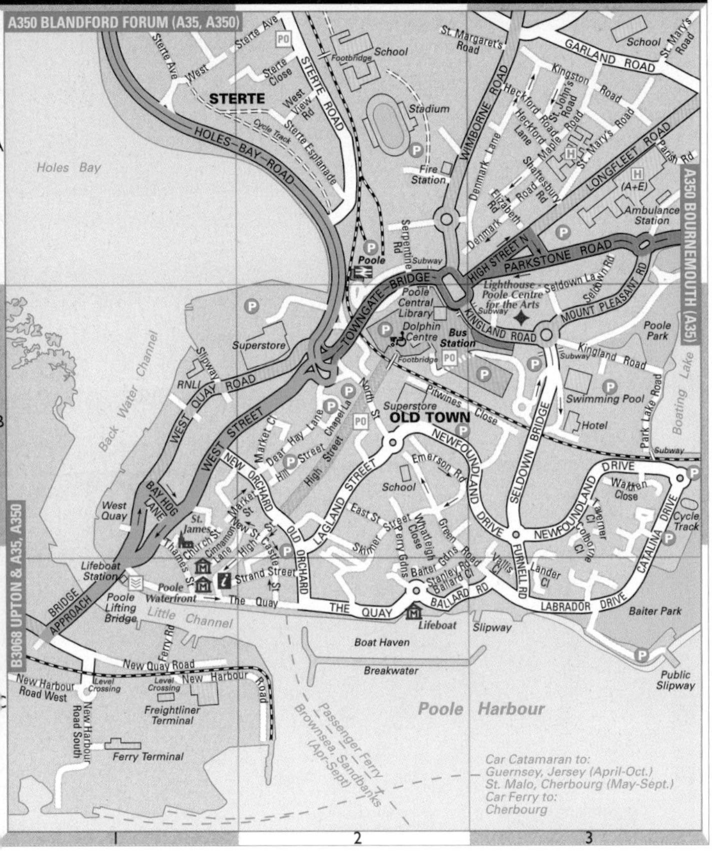

Portsmouth

0 Miles ¼

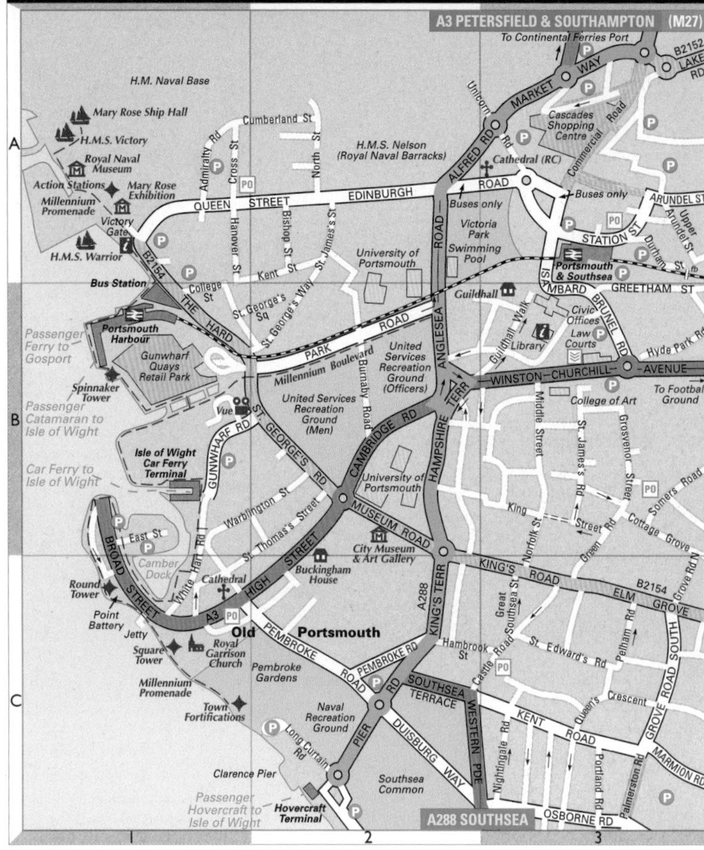

Poole

ımbulance Station . . . A3
aiter Gdns C2
aiter Park C3
allard Cl C2
allard Rd C2
ay Hog La B1
ridge Approach C1
us Station B2
astle St B2
atalina Dr. B3
hapel La B2
hurch St B1
innamon La B1
olborne Cl B3
ear Hay La B2
enmark La A3
enmark Rd A3
ast St. B2
lizabeth Rd A3
merson Rd. B2
erry Rd. C1
erry Terminal C1
ire Station A2
reightliner Terminal . . C1
urnell Rd B3
Garland Rd A3
Green Rd. B2
Heckford La. A3
Heckford Rd A3
High St B2
High St North A3
Hill St. B2
Holes Bay Rd A1
Hospital (A+E) H A3
Information Ctr i C1
Kingland Rd. B3
Kingston Rd. A3
Labrador Dr. C3
Lagland St. B2
Lander Cl. C3
Lifeboat 🏛 C2
Lighthouse - Poole
  Centre for
  the Arts ✦ B3
Longfleet Rd A3
Maple Rd. A3
Market Cl. B2
Market St. B2
Mount Pleasant Rd . . . B3
New Harbour Rd C1
New Harbour Rd
  South. C1
New Harbour Rd West C1
New Orchard B1
New Quay Rd C1
New St. B2
Newfoundland Dr B2
North St. B2
Old Orchard. B2
Parish Rd. A3
Park Lake Rd. B3
Parkstone Rd. A3
Perry Gdns B2
Pitwines Cl B2
Police Station ▤ C1
Poole Lifting Bridge. . . C1
Poole Central Library . B2
Poole Park. B2
Poole Station ⇌. A2
Poole Waterfront
  Museum 🏛 C1
Post Office PO A2/B2
RNLI. B2
St John's Rd A3
St Margaret's Rd A2
St Mary's Rd A3
Seldown Bridge. B3
Seldown La B3
Seldown Rd. B3
Serpentine Rd A2
Shaftesbury Rd A3
Skinner St B2
Slipway B1
Stanley Rd. C2
Sterte Ave A2
Sterte Ave West. A1
Sterte Cl A2
Sterte Esplanade. A2
Sterte Rd A2
Strand St. C2
Swimming Pool B3
Taverner Cl B3
Thames St. B1
The Quay. C2
Towngate Bridge B2
Vallis Cl C3
Waldren Cl. B3
West Quay. B1
West Quay Rd B1
West St B1
West View Rd A2
Whatleigh Cl B2
Wimborne Rd A3

Portsmouth

Action Stations ✦ C1
Admiralty Rd A1
Alfred Rd A2
Anglesea Rd B2
Arundel St B3
Bishop St. A2
Broad St C1
Buckingham
  House 🏛. C2
Burnaby Rd. B2
Bus Station B1
Camber Dock C1
Cambridge Rd. B2
Car Ferry to
  Isle of Wight B1
Cascades Shopping
  Centre A3
Castle Rd. C3
Cathedral ✝. C1
Cathedral (RC) ✝. A3
City Museum & Art
  Gallery 🏛 B2
Civic Offices B3
Clarence Pier. C2
College of Art B3
College St B1
Commercial Rd A3
Cottage Gr. B3
Cross St. A1
Cumberland St A2
Duisburg Way C2
Durham St A3
East St. B1
Edinburgh Rd A2
Elm Gr. C3
Great Southsea St. . . . C3
Green Rd. B3
Greetham St B3
Grosvenor St B3
Grove Rd North. C3
Grove Rd South. C3
Guildhall 🏛. B3
Guildhall Walk B3
Gunwharf Quays
  Retail Park. B1
Gunwharf Rd B1
Hambrook St. C2
Hampshire Terr B2
Hanover St A1
High St C2
HM Naval Base A1
HMS Nelson (Royal
  Naval Barracks). A2
HMS Victory ⛴ A1
HMS Warrior ⛴ A1
Hovercraft Terminal . . . C2
Hyde Park Rd B3
Information Ctr i . A1/B3
Isambard Brunel Rd . . B3
Isle of Wight Car
  Ferry Terminal B1
Kent Rd C3
Kent St A2
King St. B3
King's Rd. C3
King's Terr C2
Lake Rd. A3
Law Courts B3
Library B3
Long Curtain Rd C2
Market Way. A3
Marmion Rd. C3
Mary Rose
  Exhibition 🏛 A1
Mary Rose
  Ship Hall ⛴. A1
Middle St. B3
Millennium Blvd. B2
Millennium
  Promenade A1/C1
Museum Rd. B2
Naval Recreation
  Ground C2
Nightingale Rd. C3
Norfolk St B3
North St. A2
Osborne Rd. C3
Park Rd B2
Passenger Catamaran
  to Isle of Wight B1
Passenger Ferry
  to Gosport. B1
Pelham Rd. C3
Pembroke Gdns C2
Pembroke Rd C2
Pier Rd. C2
Point Battery C1
Police Station ▤ B3
Portsmouth &
  Southsea ⇌. A3
Portsmouth
  Harbour ⇌. B1
Post Office PO . . . .
  . . . . . .A1/A3/B3/C1/C3
Queen St A1
Queen's Cr C3
Round Tower ✦. C1
Royal Garrison
  Church ⛪ C1
Royal Naval
  Museum 🏛 A1
St Edward's Rd C3
St George's Rd B2
St George's Sq B1
St George's Way B2
St James's Rd. B3
St James's St A2
St Thomas's St B2
Somers Rd B3
Southsea Common . . . C2
Southsea Terr C2
Station St. A3
Spinnaker Tower ✦. . . B1
Square Tower ✦ C1
Swimming Pool A2
The Hard B1
Town Fortifications ✦ . C1
Unicorn Rd A2
United Services
  Recreation Ground . . B2
University of
  Portsmouth A2/B2
Upper Arundel St A3
Victoria Park A2
Victory Gate. A1
Vue 🎬 B1
Warblington St. B1
Western Pde C2
White Hart Rd C1
Winston Churchill Ave . B3

Preston

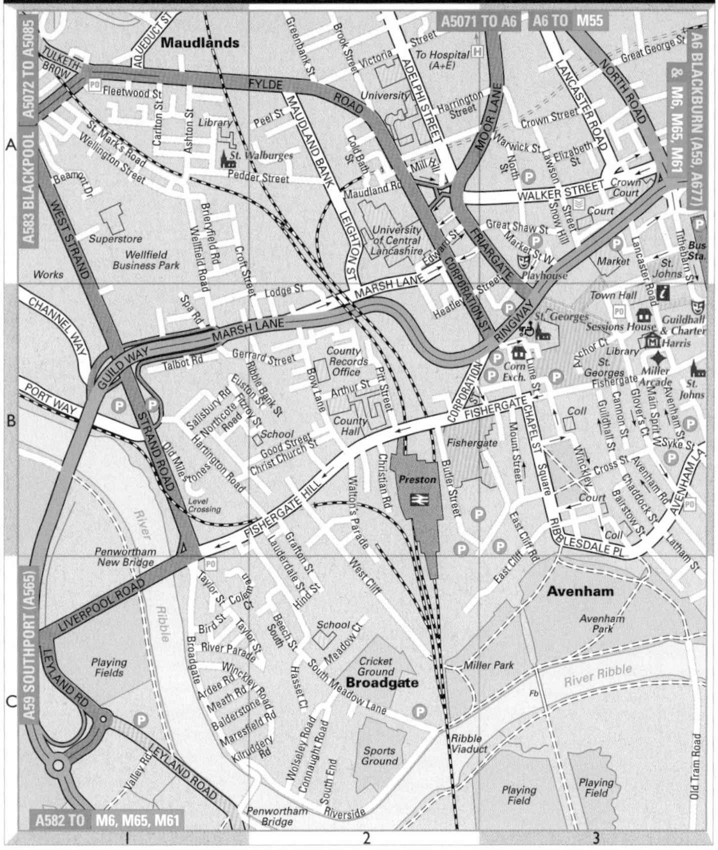

Reading

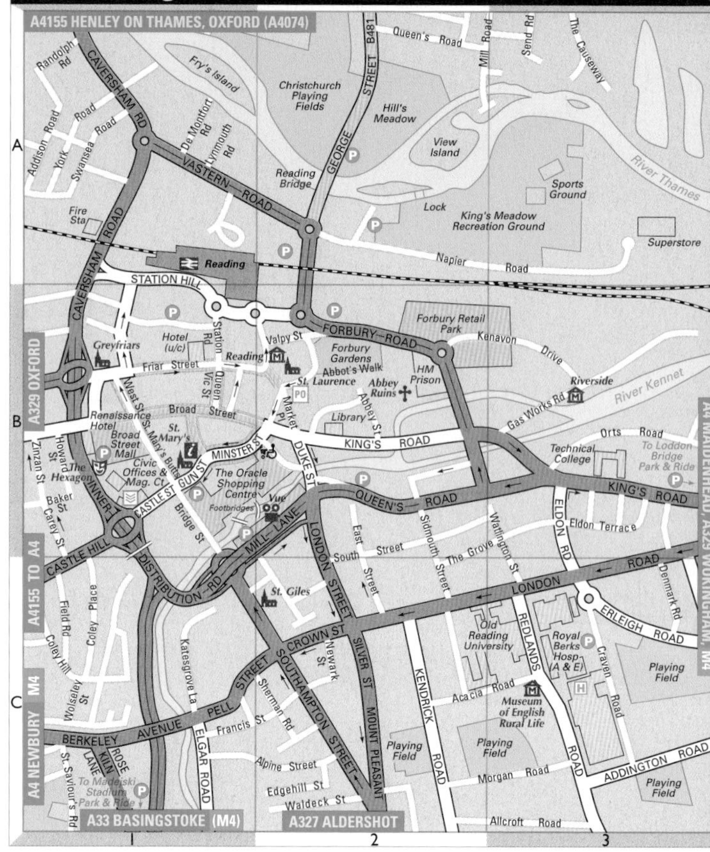

Preston

Adelphi St A2
Anchor Ct B3
Aqueduct St A1
Ardee Rd C1
Arthur St B2
Ashton St. A1
Avenham La B3
Avenham Park C3
Avenham Rd B3
Avenham St. B3
Bairstow St B3
Balderstone Rd C1
Beamont Dr. A1
Beech St South C2
Bird St C1
Bow La B2
Brieryfield Rd. A1
Broadgate C1
Brook St A2
Bus Station A3
Butler St B2
Cannon St. B3
Carlton St A1
Chaddock St. B3
Channel Way B1
Chapel St. B3
Christ Church St B2
Christian Rd. B2
Cold Bath St A2
Coleman Ct C1
Connaught Rd C2
Corn Exchange B3
Corporation St.... A2/B2
County Hall B2
County Records Office B2
Court A3
Court B3
Cricket Ground C2
Croft St A1
Cross St. B3
Crown Court A3
Crown St A3
East Cliff C3
East Cliff Rd B3
Edward St A2
Elizabeth St A3
Euston St. B1
Fishergate B2/B3
Fishergate Hill B2
Fishergate Shopping Centre B2
Fitzroy St. B1
Fleetwood St. A1
Friargate A3
Fylde Rd A1/A2
Gerrard St B2
Glover's Ct. B3
Good St. B2
Grafton St B2
Great George St A3
Great Shaw St. A3
Greenbank St A2
Guild Way B1
Guildhall & Charter B3
Guildhall St B3
Harrington St. A2
Harris Museum B3
Hartington Rd B1
Hasset Cl. C2
Heatley St B2
Hind St C2
Information Ctr B3
Kilruddery Rd C1
Lancaster Rd. A3/B3
Latham St B3
Lauderdale St C2
Lawson St A3
Leighton St A2
Leyland Rd C1
Library A1
Library B3
Liverpool Rd C1
Lodge St B2
Lune St B3
Main Sprit West. B3
Maresfield Rd C1
Market St West A3
Marsh La. B1/B2
Maudland Bank. A2
Maudland Rd. A2
Meadow Ct C2
Meath Rd. C1
Mill Hill. A2
Miller Arcade ✦ B3
Miller Park C3
Moor La. A3
Mount St B3
North Rd A3
North St. A3
Northcote Rd B1
Old Milestones B1
Old Tram Rd C3
Pedder St A1/A2
Peel St. A2
Penwortham Bridge .. C2
Penwortham New Bridge C1
Pitt St. B2
Playhouse A3
Police Station A3
Port Way B1
Post Office .A1/B3//C1
Preston Station B2
Ribble Bank St B2
Ribble Viaduct C2
Ribblesdale Pl B3
Ringway. B3
River Parade C1
Riverside C2
St. Georges B3
St. Georges Shopping Centre B3
St. Johns B3
St. Johns Shopping Centre A3
St. Mark's Rd. A1
St. Walburges A1
Salisbury Rd B1
Sessions House B3
Snow Hill A3
South End C2
South Meadow La. C2
Spa Rd B1
Sports Ground. C2
Strand Rd B1
Syke St B3
Talbot Rd. B1
Taylor St C1
Tithebarn St. A3
Town Hall. B3
Tulketh Brow A1
University of Central Lancashire. A2
Valley Rd C1
Victoria St A2
Walker St. A3
Walton's Parade B2
Warwick St A3
Wellfield Business Park. A1
Wellfield Rd A1
Wellington St. A1
West Cliff. C2
West Strand. A1
Winckley Rd C1
Winckley Square B3
Wolseley Rd. C2

Reading

Abbey Ruins ✝ B2
Abbey St. B2
Abbot's Walk B2
Acacia Rd C2
Addington Rd C3
Addison Rd A1
Allcroft Rd C3
Alpine St C2
Baker St. B1
Berkeley Ave C1
Bridge St B1
Broad St B1
Broad Street Mall B1
Carey St. B1
Castle Hill C1
Castle St B1
Caversham Rd. A1
Christchurch Playing Fields A2
Civic Offices & Magistrate's Court. .. B1
Coley Hill. C1
Coley Pl. C1
Craven Rd C3
Crown St C2
De Montfort Rd A1
Denmark Rd C3
Duke St B2
East St. B2
Edgehill St. C2
Eldon Rd B3
Eldon Terr B3
Elgar Rd. C1
Erleigh Rd C3
Field Rd. C1
Fire Station A1
Forbury Gdns B2
Forbury Retail Park . .. B2
Forbury Rd B2
Francis St C1
Friar St. B1
Gas Works Rd B3
George St A2
Greyfriars B1
Gun St. B1
Hexagon Theatre, The B1
Hill's Meadow A2
HM Prison B2
Howard St. B1
Information Ctr B1
Inner Distribution Rd . . B1
Katesgrove La C1
Kenavon Dr B2
Kendrick Rd. C2
King's Meadow Rec Ground. A2
King's Rd B2
Library B2
London Rd. C3
London St B2
Lynmouth Rd. A1
Market Pl. B2
Mill La B2
Mill Rd A2
Minster St B1
Morgan Rd. C3
Mount Pleasant C2
Museum of English Rural Life C3
Napier Rd A2
Newark St C2
Old Reading University C3
Oracle Shopping Centre, The B1
Orts Rd B3
Pell St C1
Queen Victoria St ... B1
Queen's Rd A2
Queen's Rd B2
Police Station B1
Post Office B2
Randolph Rd A1
Reading Bridge A2
Reading Station ... A1
Redlands Rd C3
Renaissance Hotel ... B1
Riverside Museum . B3
Rose Kiln La C
Royal Berks Hospital (A & E) C
St Giles C
St Laurence ...... B
St Mary's ...... B
St Mary's Butts ...... B
St Saviour's Rd C
Send Rd ...... A
Sherman Rd C
Sidmouth St ...... B
Silver St. C
South St ...... B
Southampton St C
Station Hill. ...... A
Station Rd ...... B
Superstore. ...... A
Swansea Rd ...... A
Technical College .... B
The Causeway. ...... A
The Grove ...... B
Valpy St ...... B
Vastern Rd. ...... A
Vue ...... B
Waldeck St C
Watlington St. ...... B
West St ...... B
Wolseley St C
York Rd ...... A
Zinzan St ...... B

Salisbury

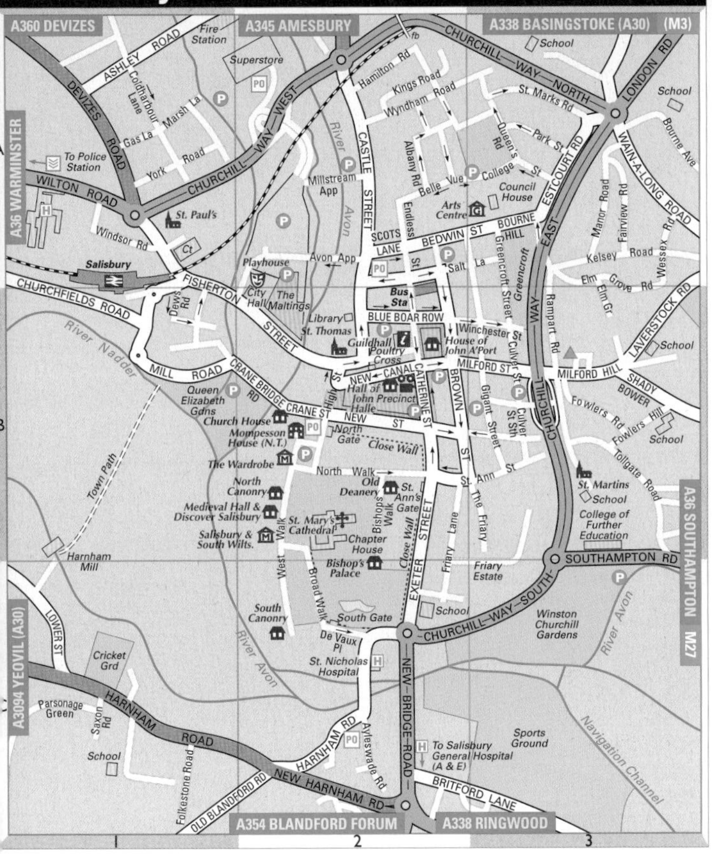

Scarborough

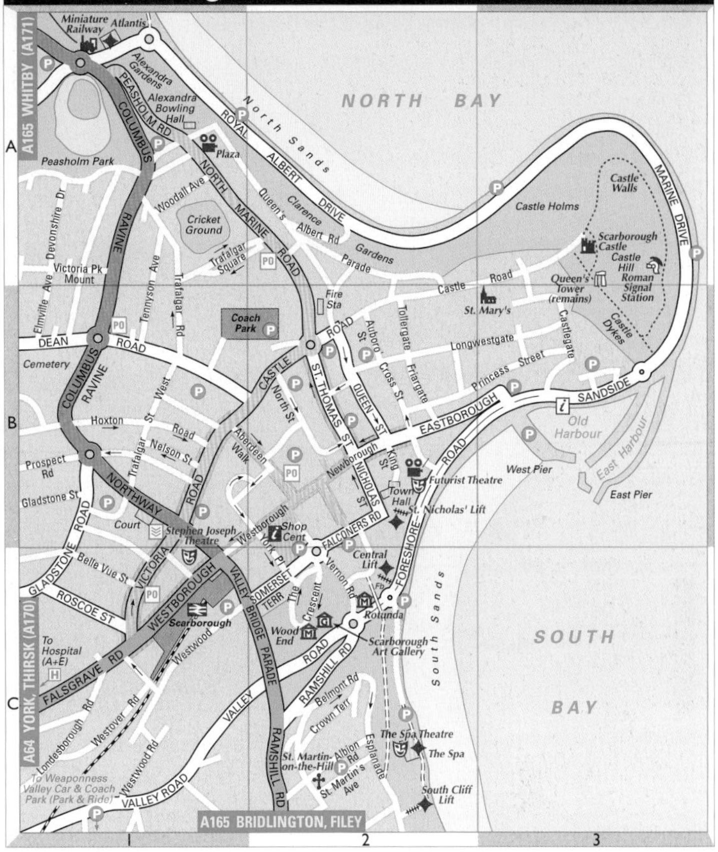

Salisbury

lbany Rd ... A2
rts Centre 🏛 ... A3
shley Rd ... A1
von Approach ... A2
yleswade Rd ... C2
edwin St ... A2
elle Vue ... A2
ishop's Palace ... C2
ishops Walk ... B2
lue Boar Row ... B2
ourne Ave ... A3
ourne Hill ... A3
ritford La ... C2
road Walk ... C2
rown St ... B2
us Station ... B2
astle St ... A2
atherine St ... B2
hapter House ... B2
hurch House ... B2
hurchfields Rd ... B1
hurchill Way East ... B3
hurchill Way North ... A3
hurchill Way South ... C2
hurchill Way West ... A1
ity Hall ... B2
lose Wall ... B2
oldharbour La ... A1
ollege of Further Education ... B3
ollege St ... A3
ouncil House ... A3
ourt ... A1
rane Bridge Rd ... B2
Crane St ... B2
Cricket Ground ... C1
Culver St South ... B3
De Vaux Pl ... C2
Devizes Rd ... A1
Dews Rd ... B1
Elm Grove ... B3
Elm Grove Rd ... A3
Endless St ... A2
Estcourt Rd ... A3
Exeter St ... C2
Fairview Rd ... A3
Fire Station ... A1
Fisherton St ... A1
Folkestone Rd ... C1
Fowlers Hill ... B3
Fowlers Rd ... B3
Friary Estate ... C3
Friary La ... B2
Gas La ... A1
Gigant St ... B3
Greencroft ... B3
Greencroft St ... A3
Guildhall ... B2
Hall of John Halle ... B2
Hamilton Rd ... A2
Harnham Mill ... B1
Harnham Rd ... C1/C2
High St ... B2
Hospital H ... A1
House of John A'Port ... B2
Information Ctr i ... B2
Kelsey Rd ... A3
King's Rd ... A2
Laverstock Rd ... B3
Library ... B2
London Rd ... A3
Lower St ... C1
Maltings, The ... B2
Manor Rd ... A3
Marsh La ... A1
Medieval Hall & Discover Salisbury ... B2
Milford Hill ... B3
Milford St ... B3
Mill Rd ... B1
Millstream Approach ... A2
Mompesson House (N.T.) ... B2
New Bridge Rd ... C2
New Canal ... B2
New Harnham Rd ... C2
New St ... B2
North Canonry ... B2
North Gate ... B2
North Walk ... B2
Old Blandford Rd ... C1
Old Deanery ... B2
Park St ... A3
Parsonage Green ... C1
Playhouse Theatre ... A2
Post Office PO ... A2/B2/C2
Poultry Cross ... B2
Precinct ... B2
Queen Elizabeth Gdns ... B1
Queen's Rd ... A3
Rampart Rd ... B3
St Ann's Gate ... B2
St Ann St ... B2
St Marks Rd ... A3
St Martins ... B3
St Mary's Cathedral ✝ ... B2
St Nicholas Hospital H ... C2
St Paul's ... A1
St Thomas ... B2
Salisbury & South Wiltshire Museum 🏛 ... B2
Salisbury General Hospital (A & E) H ... C2
Salisbury Station ... A1
Salt La ... A3
Saxon Rd ... C1
Scots La ... A2
Shady Bower ... B3
South Canonry ... C2
South Gate ... C2
Southampton Rd ... B2
Sports Ground ... C3
The Friary ... B3
Tollgate Rd ... B3
Town Path ... B1
Wain-a-Long Rd ... A3
Wardrobe, The 🏛 ... B2
Wessex Rd ... A3
West Walk ... C2
Wilton Rd ... A1
Winchester St ... B3
Windsor Rd ... A1
Winston Churchill Gdns ... C3
Wyndham Rd ... A2
YHA ▲ ... B3
York Rd ... A1

Scarborough

Aberdeen Walk ... B2
Albert Rd ... A2
Albion Rd ... C2
Alexandra Bowling Hall ... A1
Alexandra Gardens ... A1
Atlantis ✦ ... A1
Auborough St ... B2
Belle Vue St ... C1
Belmont Rd ... C2
Brunswick Shopping Centre ... B2
Castle Dykes ... B3
Castlegate ... B3
Castle Holms ... A3
Castle Hill ... A3
Castle Rd ... B2
Castle Walls ... A3
Cemetery ... B1
Central Lift ✦ ... C2
Clarence Gardens ... A2
Coach Park ... B1
Columbus Ravine ... A1
Court ... B1
Cricket Ground ... A1
Cross St ... B2
Crown Terr ... C2
Dean Rd ... B1
Devonshire Dr ... A1
East Harbour ... B3
East Pier ... B3
Eastborough ... B2
Elmville Ave ... B1
Esplanade ... C2
Falconers Rd ... B2
Falsgrave Rd ... C1
Fire Station ... B2
Foreshore Rd ... B2
Friargate ... B2
Futurist Theatre ... B2
Gladstone Rd ... B1
Gladstone St ... B1
Hoxton Rd ... B1
Information Ctr i ... B2/B3
King St ... B2
Londesborough Rd ... C1
Longwestgate ... B3
Marine Dr ... A3
Miniature Railway ... A1
Nelson St ... B1
Newborough ... B2
Nicolas St ... B2
North Marine Rd ... A1
North St ... B2
Northway ... B1
Old Harbour ... B3
Peasholm Park ... A1
Peasholm Rd ... A1
Plaza ... A1
Police Station ... B1
Post Office PO ... A2/B1/B2/C1
Princess St ... B3
Prospect Rd ... B1
Queen St ... B2
Queen's Parade ... A2
Queen's Tower (Remains) ... A3
Ramshill Rd ... C2
Roman Signal Station ... A3
Roscoe St ... C1
Rotunda Museum 🏛 ... C2
Royal Albert Dr ... A2
St Martin-on-the-Hill ... C2
St Martin's Ave ... C2
St Mary's ... B3
St Nicholas' Lift ✦ ... B2
St Thomas St ... B2
Sandside ... B3
Scarborough Art Gallery 🏛 ... C2
Scarborough Castle ... A3
Scarborough Station ... C1
Somerset Terr ... C2
South Cliff Lift ✦ ... C2
Spa, The ✦ ... C2
Spa Theatre, The ... C2
Stephen Joseph Theatre ... B1
Tennyson Ave ... B1
The Crescent ... C2
Tollergate ... B2
Town Hall ... B2
Trafalgar Rd ... B1
Trafalgar Square ... A1
Trafalgar St West ... B1
Valley Bridge Parade ... C2
Valley Rd ... C1
Vernon Rd ... C2
Victoria Park Mount ... A1
Victoria Rd ... B1
West Pier ... B3
Westborough ... C1
Westover Rd ... C1
Westwood ... C1
Woodall Ave ... A1
Wood End Museum 🏛 ... C2
York Pl ... B2

Sheffield

0 Miles ¼

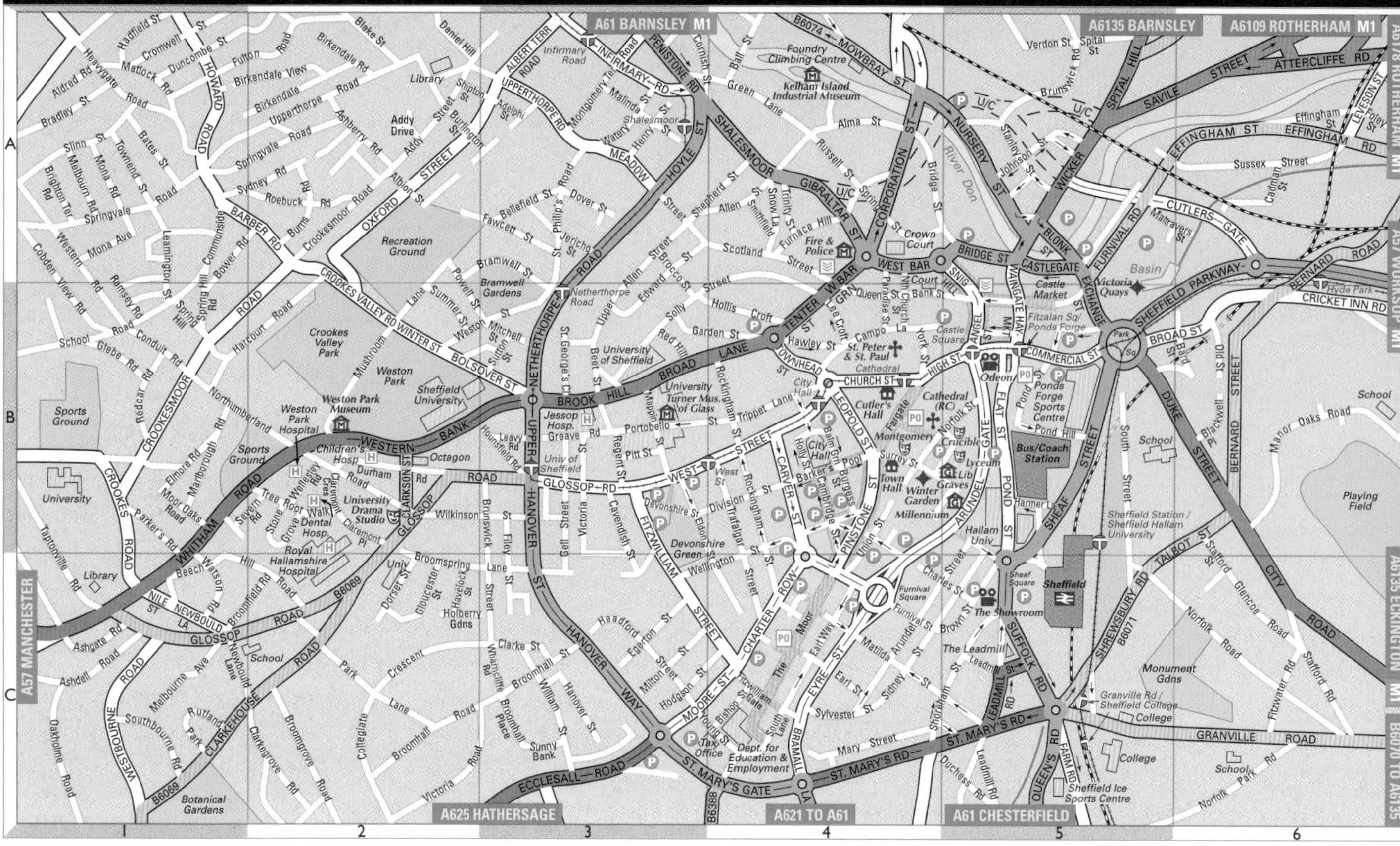

Sheffield

Addy Dr A2
Addy St A2
Adelphi St A3
Albert Terrace Rd A3
Albion St A2
Aldred Rd A1
Allen St A4
Alma St A4
Angel St. B5
Arundel Gate B5
Arundel St C4
Ashberry Rd A2
Ashdell Rd. C1
Ashgate Rd C1
Attercliffe Rd A6
Ball St A4
Balm Green B4
Bank St B4
Barber Rd A2
Bard St B5
Barker's Pool. B4
Bates St. A1
Beech Hill Rd C1
Beet St B3
Bellefield St A3
Bernard Rd A6
Bernard St. B6
Birkendale A2
Birkendale Rd A2
Birkendale View. A1
Bishop St. C4
Blackwell Pl. B6
Blake St. A2
Blonk St. A5
Bolsover St B2
Botanical Gdns C1
Bower Rd A1
Bradley St A1
Bramall La C4
Bramwell Gdns B3
Bramwell St. A3
Bridge St A4/A5
Brighton Terrace Rd . . A1
Broad La B3
Broad St B6
Brocco St A3
Brook Hill. B3
Broomfield Rd C1
Broomgrove Rd. C2
Broomhall Pl C3
Broomhall Rd C2
Broomhall St C3
Broomspring La. C2
Brown St C5
Brunswick Rd A5
Brunswick St. B3
Burgess St. B4
Burlington St A2
Burns Rd A2
Bus/Coach Station . . . B5
Cadman St A6
Cambridge St B4
Campo La B4
Carver St B4
Castle Market B5
Castle Square (tram station). B5
Castlegate A5
Cathedral (RC) ✝. B4
Cathedral (tram station). B4
Cavendish St. B3
Charles St C4
Charter Row C4
Children's Hospital 🄷 B2
Church St B4
City Hall. B4
City Hall (tram station). B4
City Rd C6
Claremont Cr. B2
Claremont Pl B2
Clarke St C3
Clarkegrove Rd C2
Clarkehouse Rd. C1
Clarkson St B2
Cobden View Rd A1
Collegiate Cr C2
Commercial St. B5
Commonside. A1
Conduit Rd B1
Cornish St A3
Corporation St. A4
Court B4
Cricket Inn Rd B6
Cromwell St. A1
Crookes Rd B1
Crookes Valley Park . . B2
Crookes Valley Rd. . . . B2
Crookesmoor Rd. A2
Crown Court A4
Crucible Theatre 🎭 . . . B5
Cutlers Gate A6
Cutler's Hall 🏛 B4
Daniel Hill A2
Dental Hospital 🄷 B2
Dept for Education & Employment C4
Devonshire Green B3
Devonshire St B3
Division St B4
Dorset St C2
Dover St A3
Duchess Rd. C5
Duke St B5
Duncombe St A1
Durham Rd B2
Earl St C4
Earl Way C4
Ecclesall Rd. C3
Edward St B3
Effingham Rd. A6
Effingham St A6
Egerton St C3
Eldon St. B3
Elmore Rd B1
Exchange St B5
Eyre St. C4
Fargate B4
Farm Rd. C5
Fawcett St. A3
Filey St. B3
Fire & Police Museum 🏛 A4
Fitzalan Sq / Ponds Forge (tram station). . B5
Fitzwater Rd C6
Fitzwilliam Gate C4
Fitzwilliam St. B3
Flat St B5
Foley St A6
Foundry Climbing Centre A4
Fulton Rd. A1
Furnace Hill A4
Furnival Rd A5
Furnival Sq C4
Furnival St. C4
Garden St B3
Gell St B3
Gibraltar St A4
Glebe Rd B1
Glencoe Rd C6
Glossop Rd . . . B2/B3/C1
Gloucester St C2
Granville Rd. C6
Granville Rd / Sheffield College (tram station). C5
Graves Gallery 🏛 B5
Greave Rd B3
Green La A4
Hadfield St. A1
Hallam University B5
Hanover St C3
Hanover Way. C3
Harcourt Rd. B1
Harmer La B5
Havelock St. C2
Hawley St B4
Haymarket. B5
Headford St. C3
Heavygate Rd A1
Henry St A3
High St B4
Hodgson St. C3
Holberry Gdns. C2
Hollis Croft. B4
Holly St B4
Hounsfield Rd B3
Howard Rd A1
Hoyle St. A3
Hyde Park (tram station). A6
Infirmary Rd. A3
Infirmary Rd (tram station). A3
Jericho St A3
Jessop Hospital 🄷 . . . B3
Johnson St A5
Kelham Island Industrial Museum 🏛 A4
Leadmill Rd C5
Leadmill St C5
Leadmill, The. C5
Leamington St. A1
Leavy Rd B3
Lee Croft B4
Leopold St. B4
Leveson St A6
Library A2
Library B5
Library C1
Lyceum Theatre 🎭 . . . B5
Malinda St A3
Maltravers St. A5
Manor Oaks Rd. B6
Mappin St B3
Marlborough Rd B1
Mary St C4
Matilda St C4
Matlock Rd A1
Meadow St A3
Melbourn Rd A1
Melbourne Ave C1
Millennium Galleries 🏛 B5
Milton St C3
Mitchell St B3
Mona Ave A1
Mona Rd A1
Montgomery Terrace Rd. A3
Montgomery Theatre 🎭 B4
Monument Gdns C6
Moor Oaks Rd. B1
Moore St C3
Mowbray St. A4
Mushroom La B2
Netherthorpe Rd B3
Netherthorpe Rd (tram station). B3
Newbould La. C1
Nile St C1
Norfolk Park Rd. C6
Norfolk Rd. C6
Norfolk St B4
North Church St B4
Northumberland Rd. . . B1
Nursery St A5
Oakholme Rd C1
Octagon. B2
Odeon 🎥. B5
Old St B6
Oxford St. A2
Paradise St B4
Park La C2
Park Sq B5
Parker's Rd B1
Penistone Rd. A3
Pinstone St B4
Pitt St. B3
Police Station 🄿 . . A4/B5
Pond Hill B5
Pond St. B5
Ponds Forge Sports Centre B5
Portobello St B3
Post Office 🄿 B5/C4
Powell St A2
Queen St B4
Queen's Rd C5
Ramsey Rd B1
Red Hill B3
Redcar Rd B1
Regent St B3
Rockingham St B4
Roebuck Rd A2
Royal Hallamshire Hospital 🄷 C2
Russell St A4
Rutland Park C1
St George's Cl B3
St Mary's Gate. C3
St Mary's Rd C4/C5
St Peter & St Paul Cathedral ✝. B4
St Philip's Rd. A3
Savile St A5
School Rd B1
Scotland St A4
Severn Rd B1
Shalesmoor A4
Shalesmoor (tram station). A3
Sheaf Sq C5
Sheaf St. B5
Sheffield Ice Sports Centre C5
Sheffield Parkway A6
Sheffield Station ⇌ . . C5
Sheffield Station / Sheffield Hallam University (tram station). B5
Sheffield University . . . B2
Shepherd St A3
Shipton St A2
Shoreham St C4
Showroom, The 🎥. . . . C5
Shrewsbury Rd C5
Sidney St. C4
Slinn St A1
Smithfield A4
Snig Hill. A5
Snow La A4
Solly St B3
South La C4
South St B5
Southbourne Rd C1
Spital Hill. A5
Spital St. A5
Spring Hill B1
Spring Hill Rd B1
Spring St A4
Springvale Rd A1
Stafford Rd C6
Stafford St. B6
Stanley St A5
Stone Gr B2
Suffolk Rd C5
Summer St B2
Sunny Bank. C3
Surrey St B4
Sussex St A6
Sutton St. B3
Sydney Rd. A2
Sylvester St. C4
Talbot St B5
Taptonville Rd B1
Tax Office C4
Tenter St B4
The Moor. C4
Town Hall 🏛 . . . . B
Townend St . . . . A
Townhead St . . . . B
Trafalgar St . . . . B
Tree Root Walk . . . . . . B
Trinity St . . . . A
Trippet La . . . . B
Turner Museum of Glass 🏛 . . . . B
Union St . . . . B
University Drama Studio 🎭 . . . . B
University of Sheffield (tram station). . . . . . . B
Upper Allen St. . . . . . . A
Upper Hanover St . . . . B
Upperthorpe Rd . . A2/A
Verdon St. . . . . A
Victoria Quays ✦. . . . . B
Victoria Rd. C
Victoria St . . . . B
Waingate . . . . B
Watery St. . . . . A
Watson Rd. C
Wellesley Rd . . . . B
Wellington St. C
West Bar . . . . A
West Bar Green. . . . . . A
West St . . . . B
West St (tram station) . B
Westbourne Rd C
Western Bank . . . . B
Western Rd . . . . A
Weston Park . . . . B
Weston Park Hospital 🄷 . . . . B
Weston Park Museum 🏛 . . . . B
Weston St . . . . B
Wharncliffe Rd. C
Whitham Rd. . . . . B
Wicker . . . . A
Wilkinson St . . . . B
William St C
Winter Garden ✦. . . . . B
Winter St . . . . B
York St. . . . . B
Young St C

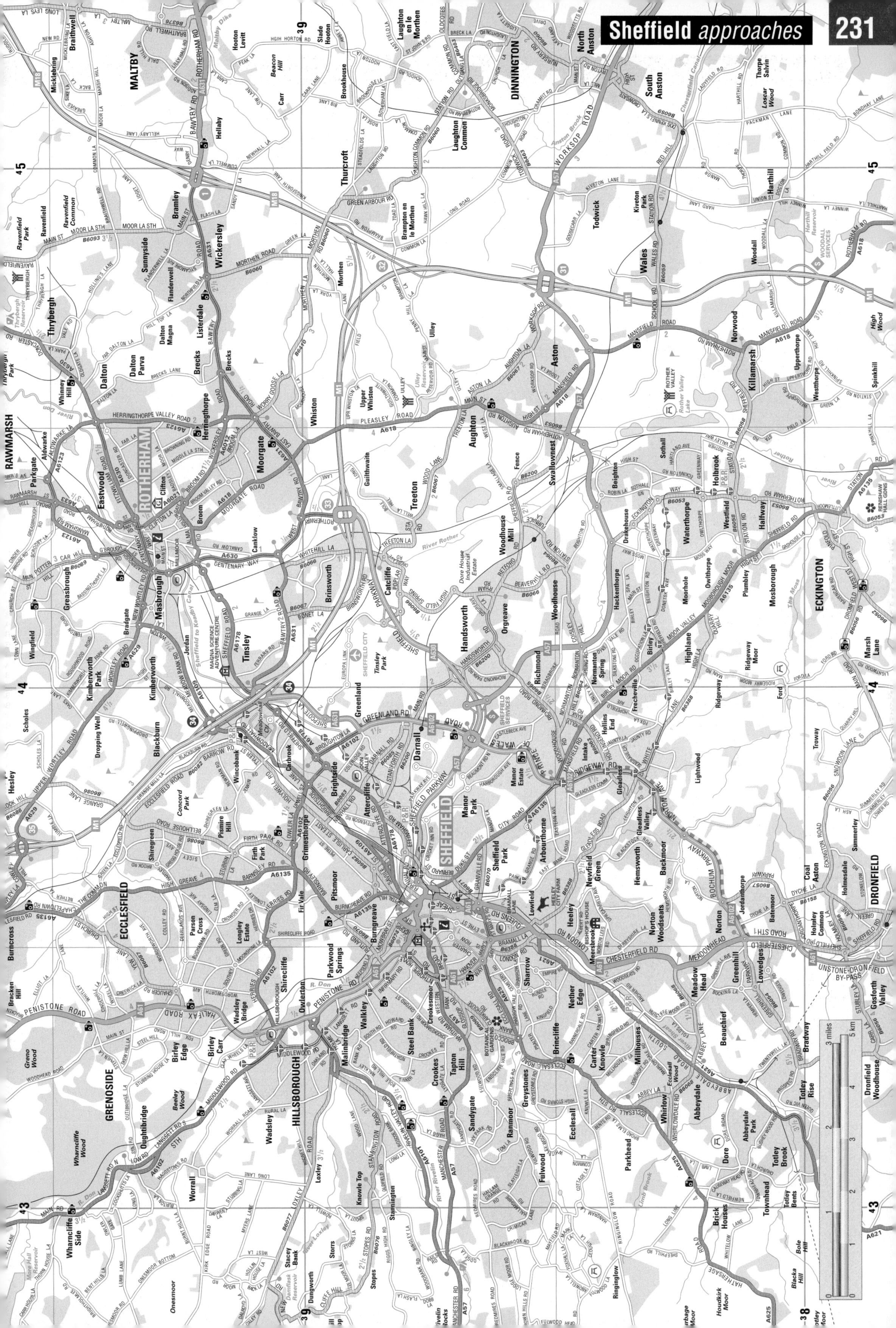
MALTBY
DINNINGTON
North Anston
South Anston
Thurcroft
Wickersley
Bramley
Sunnyside
Thrybergh
Dalton
Listerdale
Brecks
Whiston
Ulley
Aston
Aughton
Treeton
Swallownest
Killamarsh
Norwood
Kiveton Park
Wales
Todwick
Harthill
Woodall
RAWMARSH
Parkgate
ROTHERHAM
Eastwood
Moorgate
Herringthorpe
Canklow
Masbrough
Greasbrough
Kimberworth
Tinsley
Brinsworth
Catcliffe
Handsworth
Woodhouse
Orgreave
Beighton
Hackenthorpe
Mosborough
ECKINGTON
Halfway
Westfield
Waterthorpe
SHEFFIELD
Darnall
Attercliffe
Brightside
Manor Park
Richmond
Intake
Gleadless
Heeley
Norton
Meadow Head
ECCLESFIELD
Shiregreen
Firth Park
Pitsmoor
Burngreave
Parson Cross
Grenoside
HILLSBOROUGH
Walkley
Crookes
Broomhill
Nether Edge
Ecclesall
Greystones
Fulwood
Dore
Totley
Bradway
Beauchief
Millhouses
Abbeydale
Whirlow
Stannington
Loxley
Oughtibridge
Worrall
Wadsley
Stocksbridge
Coal Aston
DRONFIELD
Dronfield Woodhouse
Ringinglow
3 miles
5 km

Shrewsbury

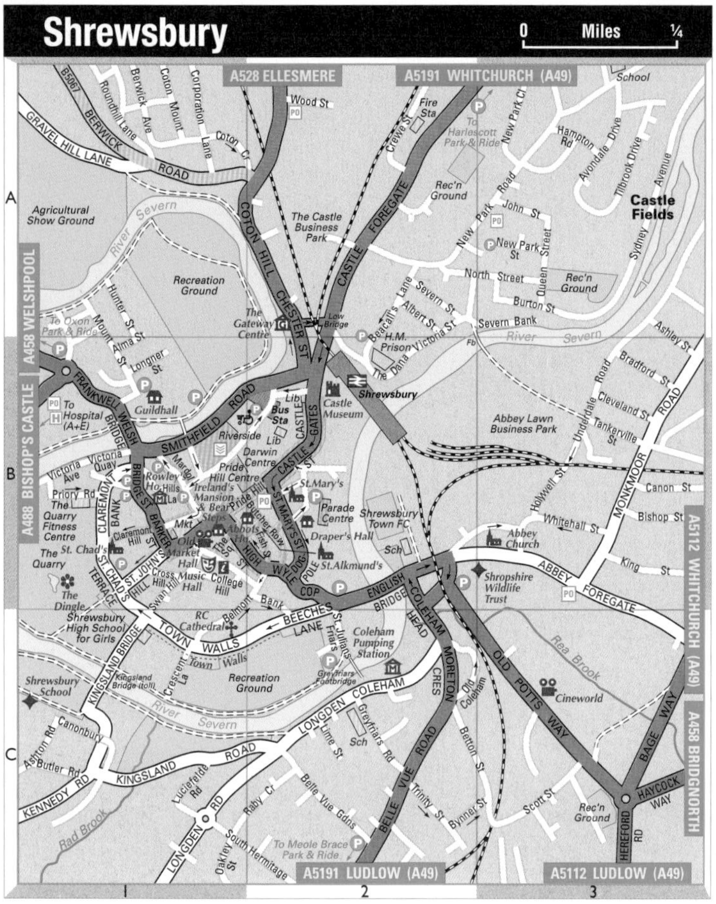

Southampton

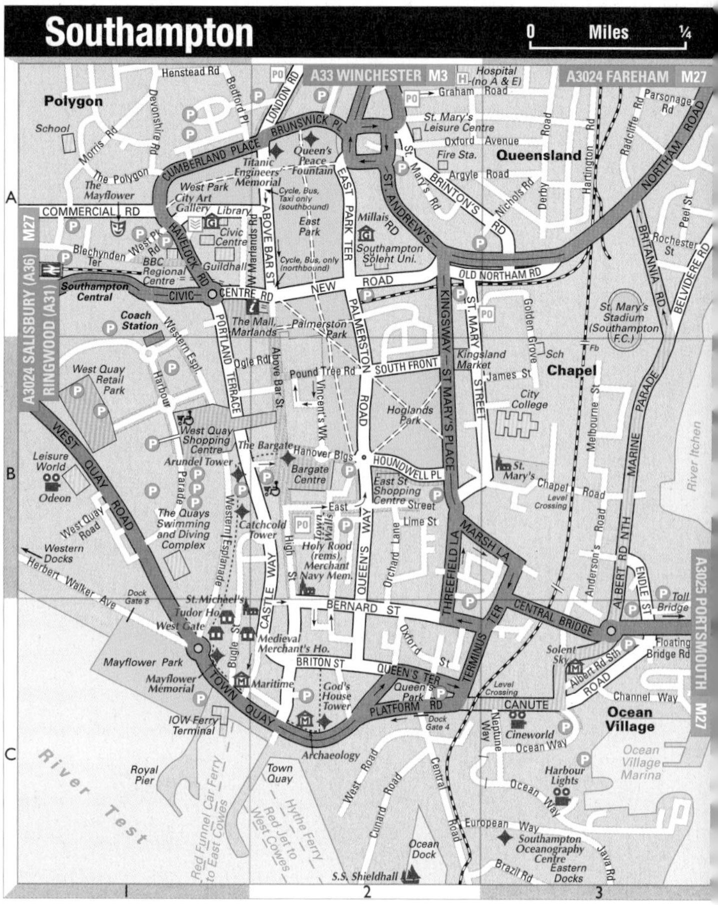

Shrewsbury

Abbey Church ... B3
Abbey Foregate ... B3
Abbey Lawn
  Business Park ... B3
Abbots House ... B2
Agricultural Show
  Ground ... A1
Albert St ... A2
Alma St ... B1
Ashley St ... A3
Ashton Rd ... C1
Avondale Dr. ... A3
Bage Way ... C3
Barker St ... B1
Beacall's La ... A2
Beeches La ... C2
Belle Vue Gdns ... C2
Belle Vue Rd ... C2
Belmont Bank ... C1
Berwick Ave ... A1
Berwick Rd ... A1
Betton St ... C2
Bishop St. ... B3
Bradford St ... B3
Bridge St ... B1
Bus Station ... B2
Butcher Row ... B2
Burton St. ... A3
Butler Rd ... C1
Bynner St. ... C2
Canon St ... B3
Canonbury. ... C1
Castle Foregate ... A2
Castle Gates ... B2
Castle Museum ... B2
Castle St ... B2
Cathedral (RC) ✝ ... C1
Chester St ... A2
Cineworld ... C3
Claremont Bank ... B1
Claremont Hill ... B1
Cleveland St ... B3
Coleham Head ... B2
Coleham Pumping
  Station ... C2
College Hill ... B1
Corporation La ... A1
Coton Cres ... A1
Coton Hill. ... A2
Coton Mount ... A1
Crescent La. ... C1
Crewe St ... A2
Cross Hill. ... B1
Darwin Centre ... B2
Dingle, The ... B1
Dogpole. ... B2
Draper's Hall ... B2
English Bridge ... B2
Fish St ... B2
Frankwell ... B1
Gateway Centre,
  The ... A2
Gravel Hill La ... A1
Greyfriars Rd ... C2
Guildhall ... B1
Hampton Rd ... A3
Haycock Way ... C3
HM Prison ... B2
Hereford Rd. ... C3
High St ... B1
Hills La. ... B1
Holywell St ... B3
Hunter St. ... A1
Information Ctr ... B1
Ireland's Mansion
  & Bear Steps ... B1
John St ... A3
Kennedy Rd. ... C1
King St. ... B3
Kingsland Bridge ... C1
Kingsland Bridge (toll) . C1
Kingsland Rd. ... C1
Library ... B2
Lime St ... C2
Longden Coleham ... C2
Longden Rd. ... C1
Longner St. ... B1
Luciefelde Rd ... C1
Mardol ... B1
Market ... B1
Monkmoor Rd ... B3
Moreton Cr ... C2
Mount St ... A1
Music Hall ... B1
New Park Cl ... A3
New Park Rd ... A2
New Park St ... A3
North St. ... A2
Oakley St. ... C1
Old Coleham ... C2
Old Market Hall ... B1
Old Potts Way ... C3
Parade Centre ... B2
Police Station ... B1
Post Office ... A2/B1/B2/B3
Pride Hill ... B1
Pride Hill Centre ... B1
Priory Rd ... B1
Queen St ... A3
Raby Cr ... C2
Rad Brook ... C1
Rea Brook ... C3
Riverside ... B1
Roundhill La ... A1
Rowley's House ... B1
St.Alkmund's ... B2
St Chad's ... B1
St Chad's Terr ... B1
St John's Hill ... B1
St Julians Friars. ... C2
St.Mary's ... B2
St Mary's St. ... B2
Scott St ... C3
Severn Bank ... A3
Severn St. ... A2
Shrewsbury ⇌ ... B2
Shrewsbury High
  School for Girls ... C1
Shrewsbury School ✦ . C1
Shrewsbury Town FC . B2
Shropshire Wildlife
  Trust ✦ ... B3
Smithfield Rd. ... B1
South Hermitage ... C1
Swan Hill ... B1
Sydney Ave ... A3
Tankerville St ... B3
The Castle Business
  Park. ... A2
The Dana ... B2
The Quarry. ... B1
The Square ... B1
Tilbrook Dr. ... A3
Town Walls ... C1
Trinity St ... C2
Underdale Rd ... B3
Victoria Ave ... B1
Victoria Quay. ... B1
Victoria St ... B2
Welsh Bridge ... B1
Whitehall St. ... B3
Wood St. ... A2
Wyle Cop. ... B2

Southampton

Above Bar St. ... A2
Albert Rd North ... B3
Albert Rd South. ... C3
Anderson's Rd. ... B3
Archaeology
  Museum ... C2
Argyle Rd. ... A2
Arundel Tower ✦ ... B1
Bargate, The ✦ ... B2
Bargate Centre ... B2
BBC Regional Centre . A1
Bedford Pl ... A1
Belvidere Rd ... A3
Bernard St. ... C2
Blechynden Terr ... A1
Brazil Rd ... C3
Brinton's Rd. ... A2
Britannia Rd. ... A3
Briton St ... C2
Brunswick Pl ... A2
Bugle St. ... C1
Canute Rd ... C3
Castle Way ... C2
Catchcold Twr ✦ ... B1
Central Bridge ... C3
Central Rd ... C2
Channel Way ... C3
Chapel Rd ... B3
Cineworld ... C3
City Art Gallery ... A1
City College. ... B3
Civic Centre. ... A1
Civic Centre Rd ... A1
Coach Station ... B1
Commercial Rd ... A1
Cumberland Pl ... A1
Cunard Rd. ... C2
Derby Rd ... A3
Devonshire Rd. ... A1
Dock Gate 4 ... C2
Dock Gate 8 ... B1
East Park. ... A2
East Park Terr ... A2
East St. ... B2
East St Shopping
  Centre ... B2
Endle St. ... B3
European Way ... C2
Fire Station ... A2
Floating Bridge Rd ... C3
God's House
  Tower ✦ ... C2
Golden Gr ... A3
Graham Rd ... A2
Guildhall. ... A1
Hanover Bldgs. ... B2
Harbour Lights ... C3
Harbour Pde ... B1
Hartington Rd ... A3
Havelock Rd ... A1
Henstead Rd ... A1
Herbert Walker Ave ... B1
High St ... B2
Hoglands Park. ... B2
Holy Rood (Rems),
  Merchant Navy
  Memorial ... B2
Hospital ... A2
Houndwell Pl. ... B2
Hythe Ferry ... C2
Information Ctr ... A1
Isle of Wight
  Ferry Terminal ... C1
James St. ... B3
Java Rd ... C3
Kingsland Market ... B2
Kingsway. ... A2
Leisure World ... B1
Library ... A1
Lime St ... B2
London Rd. ... A2
Marine Pde ... B3
Maritime ... C1
Marsh La ... B2
Mayflower
  Memorial ✦ ... C1
Mayflower Park ... C1
Mayflower Theatre,
  The ... A1
Medieval Merchant's
  House ... C1
Melbourne St. ... B3
Millais ... A2
Morris Rd. ... A1
Neptune Way. ... C3
New Rd ... A2
Nichols Rd. ... A3
Northam Rd. ... A3
Ocean Dock ... C2
Ocean Village Marina . C3
Ocean Way ... C3
Odeon ... B1
Ogle Rd ... B1
Old Northam Rd ... A2
Orchard La ... B2
Oxford Ave ... A2
Oxford St. ... C2
Palmerston Park ... A2
Palmerston Rd. ... A2
Parsonage Rd ... A3
Peel St. ... A3
Platform Rd ... C2
Police Station ... A1
Portland Terr ... B1
Post Office . A2/A3/B2
Pound Tree Rd ... B2
Quays Swimming &
  Diving Complex, The. B1
Queen's Park. ... C2
Queen's Peace
  Fountain ✦ ... A2
Queen's Terr ... C2
Queen's Way ... B2
Radcliffe Rd. ... A3
Rochester St ... A3
Royal Pier ... C1
St Andrew's Rd ... A2
St Mary St ... A
St Mary's ... B
St Mary's Leisure
  Centre ... A
St Mary's Pl. ... B
St Mary's Rd ... A
St Mary's Stadium
  (Southampton F.C.) . . A
St Michael's ... C
Solent Sky ... C
South Front ... B
Southampton Central
  Station ⇌ ... A
Southampton Solent
  University ... A
Southhampton
  Oceanography
  Centre ✦ ... C
SS Shieldhall ... C
Terminus Terr. ... C
The Mall, Marlands ... A
The Polygon ... A
Threefield La ... B
Titanic Engineers'
  Memorial ✦ ... A
Town Quay ... C
Town Walls ... B
Tudor House ... C
Vincent's Walk ... B
West Gate ... C
West Marlands Rd. ... A
West Park ... A
West Park Rd ... A
West Quay Rd ... B
West Quay
  Retail Park. ... B
West Quay Shopping
  Centre ... B
West Rd. ... C
Western Esplanade ... B

Stoke-on-Trent (Hanley)

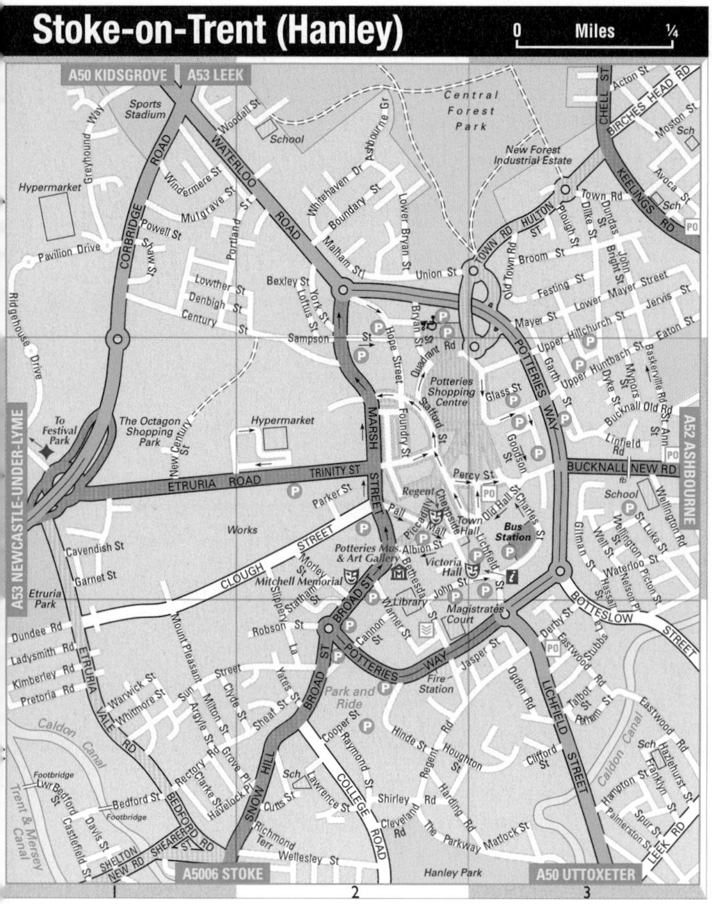

Stratford-upon-Avon

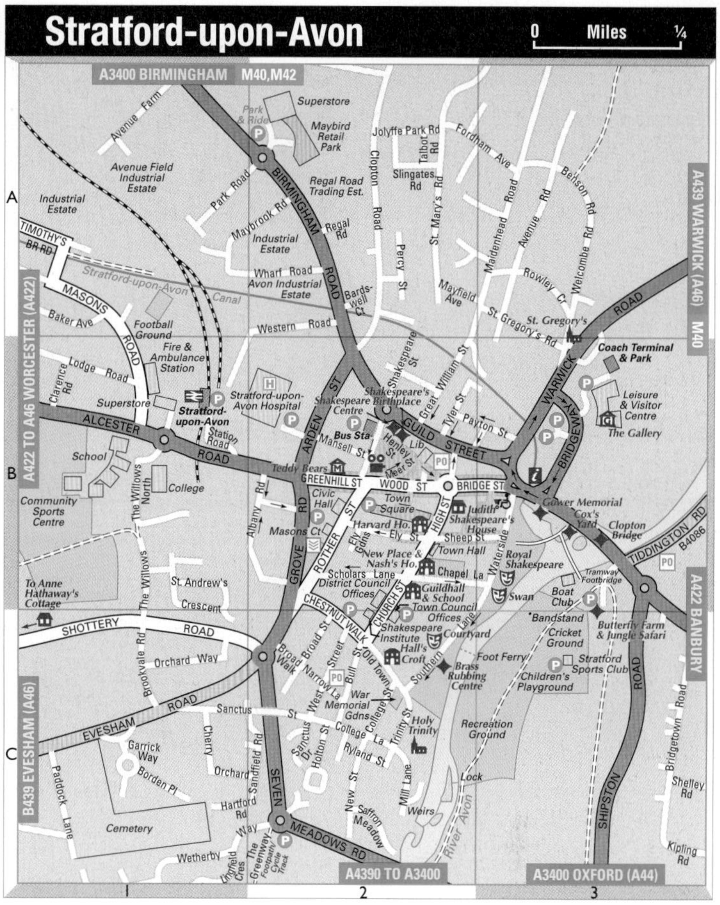

Stoke-on-Trent (Hanley)

cton St A3
bion St B2
rgyle St C1
shbourne Gr A2
voca St A3
askerville Rd B3
edford Rd C1
edford St C1
ethesda St B2
exley St A2
irches Head Rd A3
otteslow St C3
oundary St A2
road St C2
room St A3
ryan St A2
ucknall New Rd B3
ucknall Old Rd B3
us Station B3
annon St C2
astlefield St C1
anley Park C2
avendish St B1
entral Forest Park A2
harles St B3
heapside B2
hell St A3
larke St C1
leveland Rd C2
lifford St C3
lough St B2
lyde St C1
ollege Rd C2
ooper St C2
orbridge Rd A1
utts St C2
avis St C1
enbigh St A1
erby St C3
lke St A3
undas St A3
undee Rd C1
Dyke St B3
Eastwood Rd C3
Eaton St A3
Etruria Park B1
Etruria Rd B1
Etruria Vale Rd C1
Festing St A3
Fire Station C2
Foundry St B2
Franklyn St C3
Garnet St B1
Garth St B3
George St A3
Gilman St B3
Glass St B3
Goodson St B3
Greyhound Way A1
Grove Pl C1
Hampton St C3
Hanley Park C2
Harding Rd C2
Hassall St B3
Havelock Pl C1
Hazlehurst St C3
Hinde St C2
Hope St B2
Houghton St C2
Hulton St A3
Hypermarket A1/B2
Information Ctr B3
Jasper St C2
Jervis St A3
John Bright St A3
John St B2
Keelings Rd A3
Kimberley Rd C1
Ladysmith Rd C1
Lawrence St C2
Leek Rd C3
Library C2
Lichfield St C3
Linfield Rd B3
Loftus St A2
Lower Bedford St C1
Lower Bryan St A2
Lower Mayer St A3
Lowther St A1
Magistrates Court C2
Malham St A2
Marsh St B2
Matlock St C3
Mayer St A3
Milton St C1
Mitchell Memorial Theatre B2
Morley St B2
Moston St A3
Mount Pleasant C1
Mulgrave St A1
Mynors St B3
Nelson Pl B3
New Century St B1
New Forest Industrial Estate A3
Octagon Shopping Park, The B1
Ogden Rd C3
Old Hall St B3
Old Town Rd A3
Pall Mall B2
Palmerston St C3
Park and Ride C2
Parker St B2
Pavilion Dr A1
Pelham St C3
Percy St B2
Piccadilly B2
Picton St B3
Plough St A3
Police Station C2
Portland St A1
Post Office A3/B3/C3
Potteries Museum & Art Gallery B2
Potteries Shopping Centre B2
Potteries Way C2
Powell St A1
Pretoria Rd C1
Quadrant Rd B2
Ranelagh St C2
Raymond St C2
Rectory Rd C1
Regent Rd C2
Regent Theatre B2
Richmond Terr C2
Ridgehouse Dr A1
Robson St C2
St Ann St B3
St Luke St B3
Sampson St B2
Shaw St A1
Sheaf St C2
Shearer St C1
Shelton New Rd C1
Shirley Rd C2
Slippery La B2
Snow Hill C2
Sports Stadium A1
Spur St C3
Stafford St B2
Statham St B2
Stubbs La C3
Sun St C1
Talbot St C3
The Parkway C2
Town Hall B2
Town Rd A3
Trinity St B2
Union St A2
Upper Hillchurch St A3
Upper Huntbach St B3
Victoria Hall Theatre B3
Warner St C2
Warwick St C1
Waterloo Rd A1
Waterloo St B3
Well St B3
Wellesley St C2
Wellington Rd B3
Wellington St B3
Whitehaven Dr A2
Whitmore St C1
Windermere St A1
Woodall St A1
Yates St C2
York St A2

Stratford-upon-Avon

Albany Rd B1
Alcester Rd B1
Ambulance Station B1
Arden St B2
Avenue Farm A1
Avenue Field Industrial Estate A1
Avenue Rd A3
Avon Industrial Estate A2
Baker Ave A1
Bandstand C3
Benson Rd A3
Birmingham Rd A2
Boat Club B3
Borden Pl C1
Brass Rubbing Centre ✦ C2
Bridge St B2
Bridgetown Rd C3
Bridgeway B3
Broad St C2
Broad Walk C2
Brookvale Rd C1
Bull St C2
Butterfly Farm & Jungle Safari ✦ C3
Bus Station B2
Cemetery C1
Chapel La B2
Cherry Orchard C1
Chestnut Walk B2
Children's Playground C3
Church St C2
Civic Hall B2
Clarence Rd B1
Clopton Bridge ✦ B3
Clopton Rd A2
Coach Terminal & Park B3
College B1
College La C2
College St C2
Community Sports Centre B1
Council Offices (District) B2
Council Offices (Town) B2
Courtyard C2
Cox's Yard ✦ B3
Cricket Ground C3
Ely Gdns B2
Ely St B2
Evesham Rd C1
Fire Station B1
Foot Ferry C3
Football Ground A1
Fordham Ave A2
Gallery, The B3
Garrick Way C1
Gower Memorial ✦ B3
Great William St B2
Greenhill St B2
Grove Rd B2
Guild St B2
Guildhall & School B2
Hall's Croft C2
Hartford Rd C1
Harvard House B2
Henley St B2
High St B2
Holton St C2
Holy Trinity C2
Information Ctr B3
Jolyffe Park Rd A2
Judith Shakespeare's House B2
Kipling Rd C3
Leisure & Visitor Centre B3
Library B2
Lodge Rd B1
Maidenhead Rd A3
Mansell St B2
Masons Court B2
Masons Rd A1
Maybird Retail Park A2
Maybrook Rd A1
Mayfield Ave A2
Meer St B2
Mill La C2
Moat House Hotel B3
Narrow La C2
New Place & Nash's House B2
New St C2
Old Town C2
Orchard Way C1
Paddock La C1
Park Rd A1
Payton St B2
Percy St A2
Police Station B2
Post Office B2/B3/C2
Recreation Ground C2
Regal Road A2
Regal Road Trading Estate A2
Rother St B2
Rowley Cr A3
Royal Shakespeare Theatre B3
Ryland St C2
Saffron Meadow C2
St Andrew's Cr B1
St Gregory's A3
St Gregory's Rd A3
St Mary's Rd A2
Sanctus Dr C2
Sanctus St C1
Sandfield Rd C2
Scholars La B2
Seven Meadows Rd C2
Shakespeare Centre ✦ B2
Shakespeare Institute C2
Shakespeare St B2
Shakespeare's Birthplace ✦ B2
Sheep St B2
Shelley Rd C3
Shipston Rd C3
Shottery Rd C1
Slingates Rd A2
Southern La C2
Station Rd B1
Stratford Sports Club B1
Stratford-upon-Avon Hospital B2
Stratford-upon-Avon Station B1
Swan Theatre B3
Talbot Rd A2
Teddy Bears Museum B2
The Greenway C2
The Willows B1
The Willows North B1
Tiddington Rd B3
Timothy's Bridge Rd A1
Town Hall B2
Town Sq B2
Tramway Bridge B3
Trinity St C2
Tyler St B2
War Memorial Gdns B3
Warwick Rd B3
Waterside B3
Welcombe Rd A3
West St C2
Western Rd A2
Wharf Rd A2
Wood St B2

Sunderland

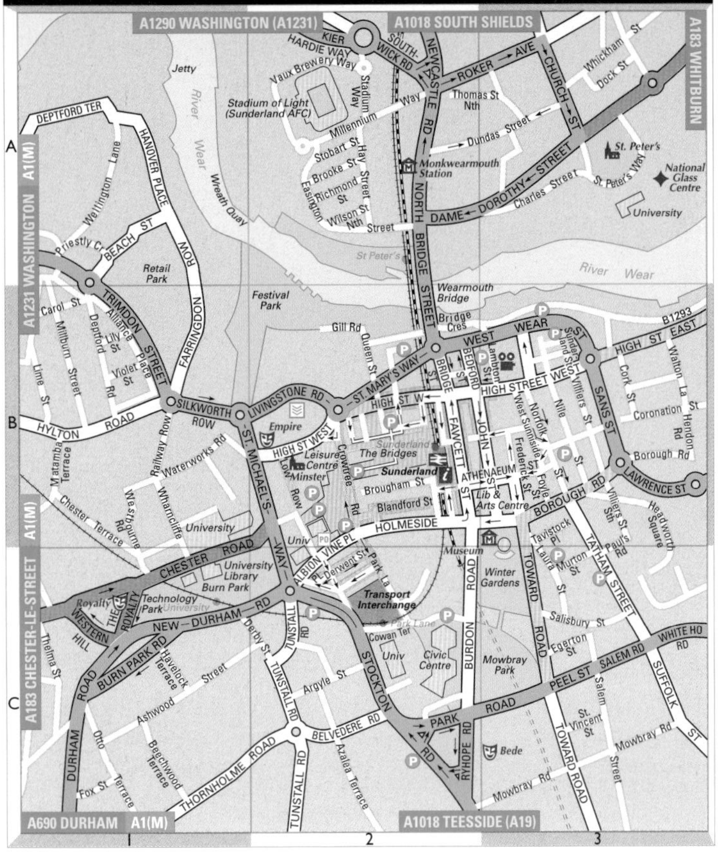

Swansea / Abertawe

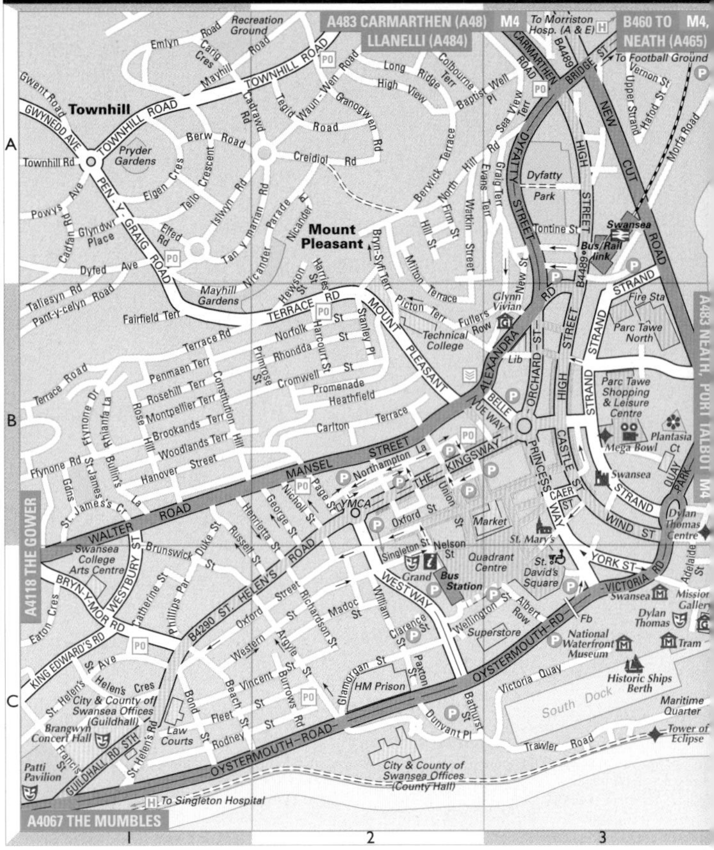

Sunderland

Albion Pl C2
Alliance Pl B1
Argyle St C2
Ashwood St. C1
Athenaeum St B2
Azalea Terr. C2
Beach St A1
Bede Theatre 🎭. C3
Bedford St. B2
Beechwood Terr C1
Belvedere Rd. C2
Blandford St B2
Borough Rd. B3
Bridge Cr. B2
Bridge St. B2
Brooke St A2
Brougham St B2
Burdon Rd. C2
Burn Park C1
Burn Park Rd. C1
Carol St B1
Charles St A3
Chester Rd C1
Chester Terr. B1
Church St A3
Cineworld 🎦 B2
Civic Centre. C2
Cork St B3
Coronation St B3
Cowan Terr C2
Crowtree Rd B2
Dame Dorothy St. A2
Deptford Rd. B1
Deptford Terr A1
Derby St C2
Derwent St C2
Dock St A3
Dundas St A2
Durham Rd C1
Easington St A2
Egerton St C3
Empire Theatre 🎭 B2
Farringdon Row. B1
Fawcett St. B2
Festival Park B2
Fox St C1
Foyle St B3
Frederick St. B3
Gill Rd B2
Hanover Pl. A1
Havelock Terr C1
Hay St A2
Headworth Sq B3
Hendon Rd B3
High St East B3
High St West B2/B3
Holmeside B2
Hylton Rd B1
Information Ctr ℹ B2
John St B3
Kier Hardie Way. A2
Lambton St B3
Laura St. C3
Lawrence St B3
Leisure Centre B2
Library & Arts Centre . . B3
Lily St. B1
Lime St B1
Livingstone Rd B2
Low Row B2
Matamba Terr B1
Millburn St. B1
Millennium Way A2
Minster ⛪ B2
Monkwearmouth Station Museum 🏛 A2
Mowbray Park C3
Mowbray Rd C3
Murton St C3
Museum 🏛 B3
National Glass Centre ✦. A3
New Durham Rd C1
Newcastle Rd A2
Nile St B3
Norfolk St B3
North Bridge St A2
Otto Terr C1
Park La C2
Park Lane (metro station). C2
Park Rd C2
Paul's Rd B3
Peel St. C3
Police Station 🏢 B2
Post Office 📮 B2
Priestly Cr A1
Queen St B2
Railway Row B1
Retail Park A1
Richmond St A2
Roker Ave A2
Royalty Theatre 🎭 C1
Ryhope Rd C2
St Mary's Way B2
St Michael's Way. B2
St Peter's ⛪. A3
St Peter's (metro station). A2
St Peter's Way A3
St Vincent St C3
Salem Rd. C3
Salem St C3
Salisbury St. C3
Sans St B3
Silkworth Row B1
Southwick Rd A2
Stadium of Light (Sunderland AFC) . . . A2
Stadium Way A2
Stobart St A2
Stockton Rd C2
Suffolk St. C3
Sunderland (metro station) B2
Sunderland Station ⇌. B2
Sunderland St B3
Tatham St C3
Tavistock Pl B3
Technology Park C1
The Bridges B2
The Royalty C1
Thelma St C1
Thomas St North. A2
Thornholme Rd C1
Toward Rd. C3
Transport Interchange . C2
Trimdon St Way. B1
Tunstall Rd. C2
University. A3/B1/C2
University (metro station). C1
University. A3/B1/C2
University Library C1
Vaux Brewery Way . . . A2
Villiers St B3
Villiers St South. B3
Vine Pl C2
Violet St. B1
Walton La B3
Waterworks Rd B1
Wearmouth Bridge . . . B2
Wellington La. A1
West Sunniside B3
West Wear St. B3
Westbourne Rd B1
Western Hill C1
Wharncliffe B1
Whickham St. A3
White House Rd C3
Wilson St North. A2
Winter Gdns C3
Wreath Quay A1

Swansea/ Abertawe

Adelaide St C3
Albert Row. C3
Alexandra Rd. B3
Argyle St C1
Baptist Well Pl A2
Beach St C1
Belle Vue Way B3
Berw Rd A1
Berwick Terr A2
Bond St. C1
Brangwyn Concert Hall 🎭 C1
Bridge St A3
Brookands Terr B1
Brunswick St. C1
Bryn-Syfi Terr. A2
Bryn-y-Mor Rd C1
Bullins La. B1
Burrows Rd C1
Bus/Rail link A3
Bus Station C2
Cadfan Rd. A1
Cadrawd Rd A1
Caer St B3
Carig Cr. A1
Carlton Terr B2
Carmarthen Rd A3
Castle St B3
Catherine St C1
City & County of Swansea Offices (County Hall) . C2
City & County of Swansea Offices (Guildhall) . . . C1
Clarence St C2
Colbourne Terr. A2
Constitution Hill. B1
Court B3
Creidiol Rd. A2
Cromwell St. B2
Duke St B1
Dunvant Pl. C2
Dyfatty Park. A3
Dyfatty St. A3
Dyfed Ave A1
Dylan Thomas Ctr ✦. . B3
Dylan Thomas Theatre 🎭 C3
Eaton Cr C1
Eigen Cr. A1
Elfed Rd. A1
Emlyn Rd. A1
Evans Terr A3
Fairfield Terr. B1
Ffynone Dr. B1
Ffynone Rd B1
Fire Station B3
Firm St. A2
Fleet St C1
Francis St C1
Fullers Row B2
George St B2
Glamorgan St C2
Glyndwr Pl. A1
Glynn Vivian 🏛 B3
Graig Terr. A3
Grand Theatre 🎭. C2
Granogwen Rd A2
Guildhall Rd South . . . C1
Gwent Rd A1
Gwynedd Ave A1
Hafod St A3
Hanover St B1
Harcourt St B2
Harries St A2
Heathfield B2
Henrietta St. B1
Hewson St. B2
High St A3/B3
High View A2
Hill St. A2
Historic Ships Berth ⛴. C3
HM Prison C2
Information Ctr ℹ C2
Islwyn Rd. A1
King Edward's Rd C1
Law Courts C1
Library B3
Long Ridge A2
Madoc St C2
Mansel St B2
Maritime Quarter C3
Market B3
Mayhill Gdns B1
Mayhill Rd A1
Mega Bowl ✦ 🎦 B3
Milton Terr A2
Mission Gallery 🏛 C3
Montpellier Terr B1
Morfa Rd A3
Mount Pleasant B2
National Waterfront Museum 🏛 C3
Nelson St. C2
New Cut Rd. A3
New St. A3
Nicander Pde A2
Nicander Pl A2
Nicholl St B2
Norfolk St B2
North Hill Rd A2
Northampton La B2
Orchard St. B3
Oxford St B2
Oystermouth Rd C1
Page St B2
Pant-y-Celyn Rd B1
Parc Tawe North B3
Parc Tawe Shopping & Leisure Centre. B3
Patti Pavilion 🎭 C1
Paxton St. C2
Penmaen Terr B1
Pen-y-Graig Rd A1
Phillips Pde C1
Picton Terr. B2
Plantasia ✿ B3
Police Station 🏢 B2
Post Office 📮 . . . . A1/A2/ A3/B2/C1/C2/C3
Powys Ave. A1
Primrose St B2
Princess Way. B3
Promenade B2
Pryder Gdns A1
Quadrant Centre C2
Quay Park B3
Rhianfa La B1
Rhondda St B2
Richardson St C2
Rodney St C1
Rose Hill B1
Rosehill Terr. B1
Russell St . . . . B
St David's Sq. C
St Helen's Ave C
St Helen's Cr C
St Helen's Rd C
St James Gdns . . . . . . B
St James's Cr . . . . B
St Mary's ⛪ . . . . B
Sea View Terr. . . . . A
Singleton St. C
South Dock C
Stanley Pl . . . . B
Strand . . . . B
Swansea Castle 🏰 . . . B
Swansea College Arts Centre C
Swansea Museum 🏛 . C
Swansea Station ⇌. . A
Taliesyn Rd . . . . B
Tan y Marian Rd . . . . . A
Technical College . . . . B
Tegid Rd . . . . A
Teilo Cr . . . . A
Terrace Rd. B1/B
The Kingsway . . . . B
Tontine St . . . . A
Tower of Eclipse ✦ . . . C
Townhill Rd . . . . A
Tram Museum 🏛. C
Trawler Rd C
Union St . . . . B
Upper Strand. . . . . A
Vernon St. . . . . A
Victoria Quay. C
Victoria Rd. . . . . B
Vincent St C
Walter Rd. . . . . B
Watkin St. . . . . A
Waun-Wen Rd . . . . A
Wellington St. C
Westbury St. C
Western St. C
Westway C
William St C
Wind St . . . . B
Woodlands Terr . . . . . . B
YMCA . . . . B
York St. C

Swindon

0 Miles ¼

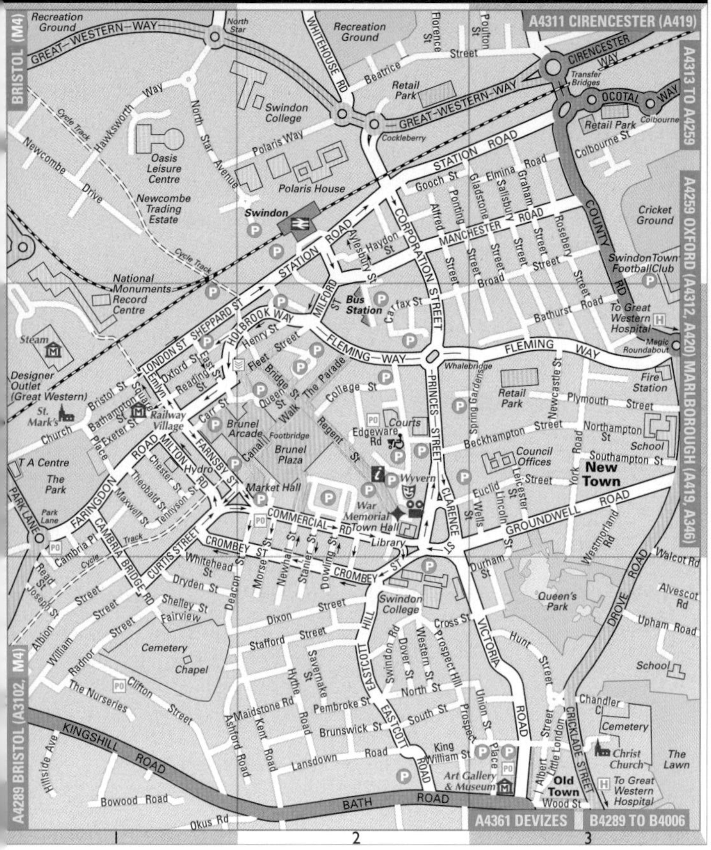

Telford

0 Miles ¼

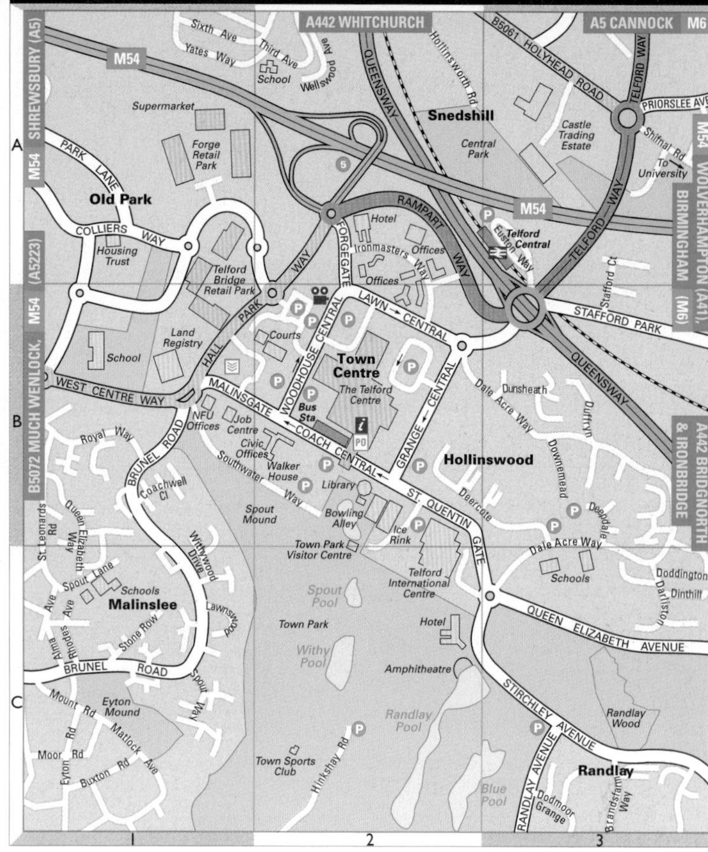

Swindon

bert St C3
bion St C1
fred St A2
vescot Rd C3
t Gallery & Museum 🏛 C3
shford Rd C1
vlesbury St A2
ath Rd C2
athampton St B1
athurst Rd B3
eatrice St A2
eckhampton St B3
owood Rd C1
istol St B1
oad St A3
unel Arcade B2
unel Plaza B2
unswick St C2
us Station B2
ambria Bridge Rd B1
ambria Place B1
anal Walk B2
arfax St B2
arr St B1
emetery C1/C3
handler Cl C3
hapel C1
hester St B1
hrist Church ⛪ C3
hurch Place B1
rencester Way A3
arence St B2
ifton St C1
ockleberry Rdbt A2
olbourne Rdbt A3
olbourne St A3
ollege St B2
ommercial Rd B2
orporation St A2
ouncil Offices B3
ounty Rd A3
ourts B2
icket Ground A3
cklade Street C3
Crombey St B1/C2
Cross St C2
Curtis St B1
Deacon St C1
Designer Outlet (Great Western) B1
Dixon St C2
Dover St C2
Dowling St C2
Drove Rd C3
Dryden St C1
Durham St C3
East St B1
Eastcott Hill C2
Eastcott Rd C2
Edgeware Rd B2
Elmina Rd A3
Emlyn Square B1
Euclid St B3
Exeter St B1
Fairview C1
Faringdon Rd B1
Farnsby St B1
Fire Station B3
Fleet St B2
Fleming Way B2/B3
Florence St A2
Gladstone St A3
Gooch St A2
Graham St A3
Great Western Way A1/A2
Groundwell Rd B3
Hawksworth Way A1
Haydon St A2
Henry St B2
Hillside Ave C1
Holbrook Way B2
Hunt St C3
Hydro B1
Hythe Rd C2
Information Ctr ℹ B2
Joseph St C1
Kent Rd C2
King William St C2
Kingshill Rd C1
Lansdown Rd C2
Leicester St B3
Library B2
Lincoln St B3
Little London C3
London St B1
Magic Rdbt B3
Maidstone Rd C2
Manchester Rd A3
Market Hall B2
Maxwell St B1
Milford St B2
Milton Rd B1
Morse St C2
National Monuments Record Centre B1
Newcastle St B3
Newcombe Drive A1
Newcombe Trading Estate A1
Newhall St C2
North St C2
North Star Rdbt A1
North Star Ave A1
Northampton St B3
Oasis Leisure Centre A1
Ocotal Way A3
Okus Rd C1
Old Town C3
Oxford St B1
Park Lane B1
Park Lane Rdbt B1
Pembroke St C2
Plymouth St B3
Polaris House A2
Polaris Way A2
Police Station B2
Ponting St A2
Post Office B1/B2/C1/C3
Poulton St A3
Princes St B2
Prospect Hill C2
Prospect Place C2
Queen St B2
Queen's Park C3
Radnor St C1
Railway Village 🏛 B1
Read St C1
Reading St B1
Regent St B2
Retail Park A2/A3/B3
Rosebery St A3
St Mark's ⛪ B1
Salisbury St A3
Savernake St C2
Shelley St C1
Sheppard St B1
South St C2
Southampton St B3
Spring Gardens B3
Stafford Street C2
Stanier St C2
Station Road A2
Steam 🏛 B1
Swindon Station ⇌ A2
Swindon College A2/C2
Swindon Rd C2
Swindon Town Football Club A3
T A Centre B1
Tennyson St B1
The Lawn C3
The Nurseries C1
The Parade B2
The Park B1
Theobald St B1
Town Hall B2
Transfer Bridges Rdbt A3
Union St C2
Upham Rd C3
Victoria Rd C3
Walcot Rd B3
War Memorial ✦ B2
Wells St B3
Western St C2
Westmorland Rd B3
Whalebridge Rdbt B2
Whitehead St C1
Whitehouse Rd A2
William St C1
Wood St C3
Wyvern Theatre & Arts Centre B2
York Rd B3

Telford

Alma Ave C1
Amphitheatre C2
Bowling Alley B2
Brandsfarm Way C3
Brunel Rd B1
Bus Station B2
Buxton Rd C1
Castle Trading Estate A3
Central Park A2
Civic Offices B2
Coach Central B2
Coachwell Cl B1
Colliers Way A1
Courts B2
Dale Acre Way B3
Darliston C3
Deepdale B3
Deercote B2
Dinthill C3
Doddington C3
Dodmoor Grange C3
Downemead B3
Duffryn B3
Dunsheath B3
Euston Way A3
Eyton Mound C1
Eyton Rd C1
Forge Retail Park A1
Forgegate A2
Grange Central B2
Hall Park Way B1
Hinkshay Rd C2
Hollinsworth Rd A2
Holyhead Rd A3
Housing Trust A1
Ice Rink B2
Information Ctr ℹ B2
Ironmasters Way A2
Job Centre B1
Land Registry B1
Lawn Central B2
Lawnswood C1
Library B2
Malinsgate B1
Matlock Ave C1
Moor Rd C1
Mount Rd C1
NFU Offices B1
Park Lane A1
Police Station B1
Post Office B2
Priorslee Ave A3
Queen Elizabeth Ave C3
Queen Elizabeth Way B1
Queensway A2/B3
Rampart Way A2
Randlay Ave C3
Randlay Wood C3
Rhodes Ave C1
Royal Way B1
St Leonards Rd B1
St Quentin Gate B2
Shifnal Rd A3
Sixth Ave A1
Southwater Way B1
Spout Lane C1
Spout Mound B1
Spout Way C1
Stafford Court B3
Stafford Park B3
Stirchley Ave C3
Stone Row C1
Telford Bridge Retail Park A1
Telford Central Station ⇌ A3
Telford Centre, The B2
Telford International Centre C2
Telford Way A3
Third Ave A2
Town Park C2
Town Park Visitor Centre B2
Town Sports Club C2
Walker House B2
Wellswood Ave A2
West Centre Way B1
Withywood Drive C1
Woodhouse Central B2
Yates Way A1

Torquay

0 Miles ¼

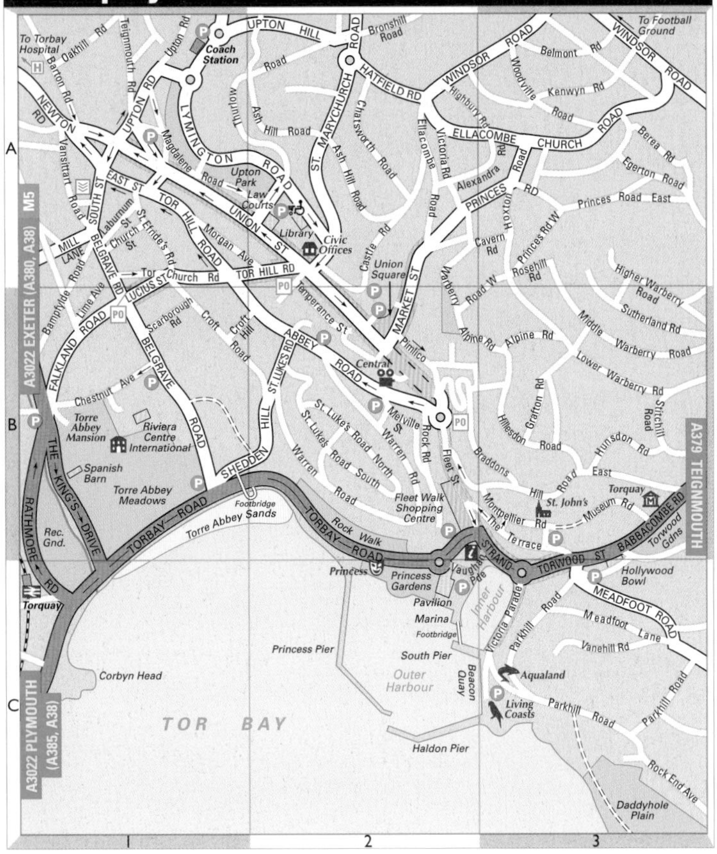

Winchester

0 Miles ¼

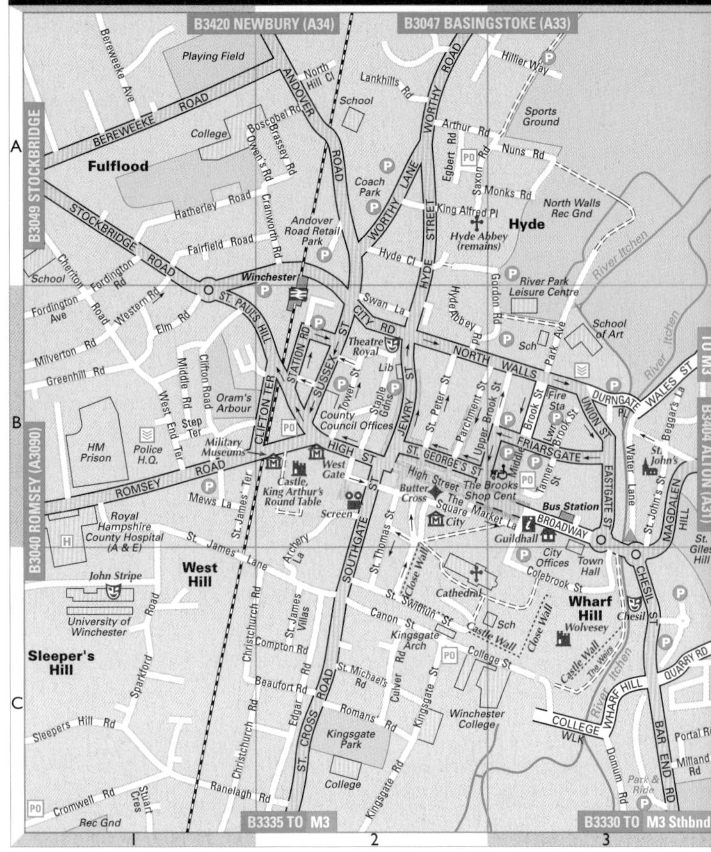

Torquay

Abbey Rd B2
Alexandra Rd. A2
Alpine Rd. B3
Aqualand C3
Ash Hill Rd. A2
Babbacombe Rd B3
Bampfylde Rd B1
Barton Rd A1
Beacon Quay. C2
Belgrave Rd. A1/B1
Belmont Rd A3
Berea Rd A3
Braddons Hill Rd East. B3
Bronshill Rd. A2
Castle Rd. A2
Cavern Rd A3
Central B2
Chatsworth Rd A2
Chestnut Ave. B1
Church St A1
Civic Offices A2
Coach Station A1
Corbyn Head. C1
Croft Hill B1
Croft Rd. B1
Daddyhole Plain C3
East St. A1
Egerton Rd A3
Ellacombe Church Rd . A3
Ellacombe Rd A2
Falkland Rd B1
Fleet St B2
Fleet Walk Shopping Centre B2
Grafton Rd. B3
Haldon Pier C2
Hatfield Rd A2
Highbury Rd A2
Higher Warberry Rd. . . A3
Hillesdon Rd B3
Hollywood Bowl C3
Hoxton Rd. A3
Hunsdon Rd B3
Information Ctr B2
Inner Harbour C3
Kenwyn Rd A3
Laburnum St A1
Law Courts A2
Library A2
Lime Ave B1
Living Coasts C3
Lower Warberry Rd . . . B3
Lucius St B1
Lymington Rd A1
Magdalene Rd A1
Marina C2
Market St. B2
Meadfoot Lane C3
Meadfoot Rd C3
Melville St. B2
Middle Warberry Rd . . B3
Mill Lane A1
Montpellier Rd. B3
Morgan Ave. A1
Museum Rd. B3
Newton Rd A1
Oakhill Rd A1
Outer Harbour C2
Parkhill Rd. C3
Pavilion C2
Pimlico. B2
Police Station A1
Post Office . A2/B1/B2
Princes Rd. A3
Princes Rd East. A3
Princes Rd West A3
Princess Theatre . . . C2
Princess Gdns. C2
Princess Pier C2
Rathmore Rd. B1
Recreation Grd B1
Riviera Centre International B1
Rock End Ave C3
Rock Rd B2
Rock Walk. B2
Rosehill Rd A3
St Efride's Rd A1
St John's B3
St Luke's Rd B2
St Luke's Rd North . . . B2
St Luke's Rd South . . . B2
St Marychurch Rd. . . . A2
Scarborough Rd B1
Shedden Hill B2
South Pier C2
South St A1
Spanish Barn. B1
Stitchill Rd. B3
Strand B3
Sutherland Rd B3
Teignmouth Rd A1
Temperance St B2
The King's Drive B1
The Terrace B3
Thurlow Rd A1
Tor Bay B1
Tor Church Rd. A1
Tor Hill Rd A1
Torbay Rd B2
Torquay Museum . . B3
Torquay Station . . . C1
Torre Abbey Mansion B1
Torre Abbey Meadows B1
Torre Abbey Sands . . . B1
Torwood Gdns. B3
Torwood St C3
Union Square A2
Union St A1
Upton Hill A2
Upton Park A1
Upton Rd. A1
Vanehill Rd. C3
Vansittart Rd A1
Vaughan Parade C2
Victoria Parade C3
Victoria Rd. A2
Warberry Rd West. . . . B2
Warren Rd B2
Windsor Rd A2/A3
Woodville Rd A3

Winchester

Andover Rd A2
Andover Road Retail Park. A2
Archery La. C2
Arthur Rd. A2
Bar End Rd C3
Beaufort Rd C2
Beggar's La. B3
Bereweeke Ave A1
Bereweeke Rd. A1
Boscobel Rd A2
Brassey Rd A2
Broadway B3
Brooks Shopping Centre, The B3
Bus Station B3
Butter Cross B2
Canon St. C2
Castle Wall C2/C3
Castle, King Arthur's Round Table B2
Cathedral C2
Cheriton Rd. A1
Chesil St C3
Chesil Theatre C3
Christchurch Rd C1
City Museum B2
City Offices C3
City Rd B2
Clifton Rd B1
Clifton Terr. B2
Close Wall C2/C3
Coach Park A2
Colebrook St. C3
College St C2
College Walk C3
Compton Rd C2
County Council Offices. B2
Cranworth Rd A2
Cromwell Rd C1
Culver Rd C2
Domum Rd C3
Durngate Pl B3
Eastgate St B3
Edgar Rd. C2
Egbert Rd A2
Elm Rd. B1
Fairfield Rd A1
Fire Station B3
Fordington Ave B1
Fordington Rd A1
Friarsgate B3
Gordon Rd. B3
Greenhill Rd. B1
Guildhall B3
HM Prison B1
Hatherley Rd A1
High St B2
Hillier Way A3
Hyde Abbey (Remains) A2
Hyde Abbey Rd. B2
Hyde Cl A2
Hyde St A2
Information Ctr B3
Jewry St B2
John Stripe Theatre C1
King Alfred Pl. A2
Kingsgate Arch C2
Kingsgate Rd. C2
Kingsgate Park C2
Kingsgate St C2
Lankhills Rd. A2
Library B2
Lower Brook St B3
Magdalen Hill B3
Market La B2
Mews La B1
Middle Brook St B3
Middle Rd B1
Military Museums . . B2
Milland Rd C3
Milverton Rd B1
Monks Rd A3
North Hill Cl. A2
North Walls B2
North Walls Rec Gnd . A3
Nuns Rd A3
Oram's Arbour. B1
Owen's Rd. A2
Parchment St B2
Park & Ride C3
Park Ave B3
Playing Field A1
Police H.Q. B1
Police Station B3
Portal Rd C3
Post Office A2/B2/B3/C1/C2
Quarry Rd C3
Ranelagh Rd C1
River Park Leisure Centre B3
Romans' Rd C2
Romsey Rd B1
Royal Hampshire County Hospital (A & E) . . B1
St Cross Rd. C2
St George's St. B2
St Giles Hill C3
St James' La B1
St James' Terr. B1
St James Villas C2
St John's B3
St John's St. B3
St Michael's Rd C
St Paul's Hill . . . . E
St Peter St. . . . . E
St Swithun St C
St Thomas St C
Saxon Rd. . . . . A
School of Art . . . . E
Screen . . . . E
Sleepers Hill Rd. C
Southgate St . . . . E
Sparkford Rd. C
Staple Gdns . . . . E
Station Rd . . . . E
Step Terr . . . . E
Stockbridge Rd . . . . . A
Stuart Cres C
Sussex St . . . . E
Swan Lane. . . . . E
Tanner St. . . . .
The Square . . . . E
The Weirs. C
Theatre Royal . . . . . E
Tower St . . . . E
Town Hall. C
Union St . . . . E
University of Winchester C
Upper Brook St. . . . . . E
Wales St . . . . E
Water Lane . . . . E
West End Terr . . . . E
West Gate . . . . E
Western Rd . . . . E
Wharf Hill. C
Winchester College. . . C
Winchester . . . . A
Wolvesey Castle . . . C
Worthy Lane . . . . A
Worthy Rd . . . . A

Windsor

0 Miles ¼

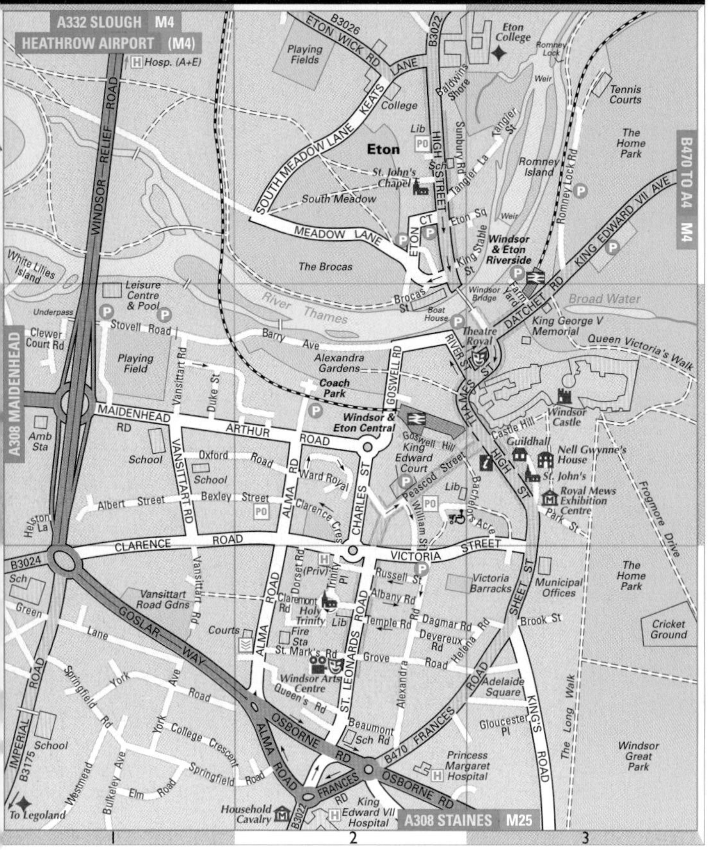

Wolverhampton

0 Miles ¼

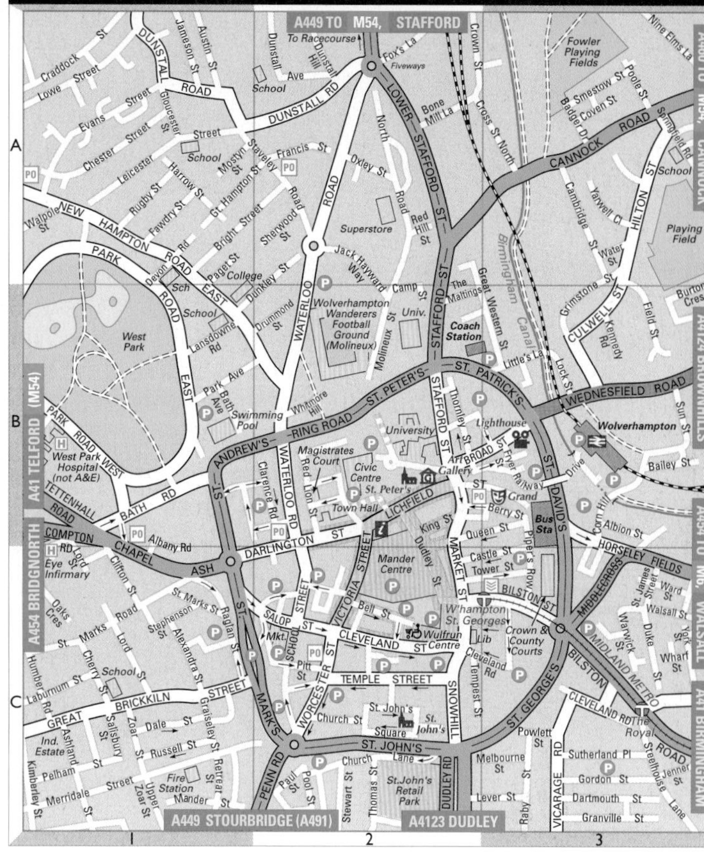

Windsor

delaide Sq C3
lbany Rd C2
lbert St B1
exandra Gdns B2
exandra Rd C2
ma Rd B2
mbulance Station B1
rthur Rd B2
achelors Acre B3
arry Ave B2
eaumont Rd C2
exley St B1
oat House B2
rocas St B2
rook St C3
ulkeley Ave C1
astle Hill B3
harles St B2
laremont Rd C2
larence Cr B2
larence Rd B1
lewer Court Rd B1
oach Park B2
ollege Cr C1
ourts C2
ricket Ground C3
agmar Rd C2
atchet Rd B3
evereux Rd C2
orset Rd C2
uke St B1
Elm Rd C1
Eton College ✦ A3
Eton Ct A2
Eton Sq A2
Eton Wick Rd A2
Fire Station C2
Farm Yard B3
Frances Rd C2
Frogmore Dr B3
Gloucester Pl C3
Goslar Way C1
Goswell Hill B2
Goswell Rd B2
Green La C1
Grove Rd C2
Guildhall B3
Helena Rd C2
Helston La B1
High St A2/B3
Holy Trinity C2
Hospital (Private) C2
Household Cavalry C2
Imperial Rd C1
Information Ctr B3
Keats La A2
King Edward Ct B2
King Edward VII Ave A3
King Edward VII Hospital C2
King George V Memorial B3
King's Rd C3
King Stable St A2
Leisure Centre & Pool B1
Library C2
Maidenhead Rd B1
Meadow La A2
Municipal Offices C3
Nell Gwynne's House B3
Osborne Rd C2
Oxford Rd B1
Park St B3
Peascod St B2
Police Station C2
Post Office A2/B2
Princess Margaret Hospital C2
Queen Victoria's Walk B3
Queen's Rd C2
River St B2
Romney Island A3
Romney Lock A3
Romney Lock Rd A3
Russell St C2
St John's B3
St John's Chapel A2
St Leonards Rd C2
St Mark's Rd C2
Sheet St C3
South Meadow A2
South Meadow La A2
Springfield Rd C1
Stovell Rd B1
Sunbury Rd A2
Tangier La A2
Tangier St A3
Temple Rd C2
Thames St B3
The Brocas A2
The Home Park A3/C3
The Long Walk C3
Theatre Royal B3
Trinity Pl C2
Vansittart Rd B1/C1
Vansittart Rd Gdns C1
Victoria Barracks C2
Victoria St C2
Ward Royal B2
Westmead C1
White Lilies Island A1
William St B2
Windsor Arts Centre C2
Windsor Castle B3
Windsor & Eton Central B2
Windsor & Eton Riverside A3
Windsor Bridge B3
Windsor Great Park C3
Windsor Relief Rd A1
York Ave C1
York Rd C1

Wolverhampton

Albany Rd B1
Albion St B3
Alexandra St C1
Gallery B2
Ashland St C1
Austin St A1
Badger Dr A3
Bailey St B3
Bath Ave B1
Bath Rd B1
Bell St C2
Berry St B3
Bilston Rd C3
Bilston St C3
Birmingham Canal A3
Bone Mill La A2
Bright St A1
Burton Cres B3
Bus Station B3
Cambridge St A3
Camp St B2
Cannock Rd A3
Castle St C2
Chapel Ash C1
Cherry St C1
Chester St A1
Church La C2
Church St C2
Civic Centre B2
Clarence Rd B2
Cleveland Rd C2
Cleveland St C2
Clifton St C1
Coach Station B2
Compton Rd B1
Corn Hill B3
Coven St A3
Craddock St A1
Cross St North A2
Crown & County Courts C3
Crown St A2
Culwell St B3
Dale St C1
Darlington St C1
Dartmouth St C3
Devon Rd A1
Drummond St B2
Dudley Rd C2
Dudley St B2
Duke St C3
Dunkley St B1
Dunstall Ave A2
Dunstall Hill A2
Dunstall Rd A1/A2
Evans St A1
Eye Infirmary C1
Fawdry St A1
Field St B3
Fire Station C1
Fiveways (r'about) A2
Fowler Playing Fields A3
Fox's La A2
Francis St A2
Fryer St B3
Gloucester St A1
Gordon St C3
Graiseley St C1
Grand B3
Granville St C3
Great Western St A2
Great Brickkiln St C1
Grimstone St B3
Gt. Hampton St A1
Harrow St A1
Hilton St A3
Horseley Fields C3
Humber Rd C1
Jack Hayward Way A2
Jameson St A1
Jenner St C3
Kennedy Rd B3
Kimberley St C1
King St B2
Laburnum St C1
Lansdowne Rd B1
Leicester St A1
Lever St C3
Library C3
Lichfield St B2
Lighthouse B3
Little's La B3
Lock St B3
Lord St C1
Lowe St A1
Lower Stafford St A2
Magistrates Court B2
Mander Centre C2
Mander St C1
Market St B2
Market C2
Melbourne St C3
Merridale St C1
Middlecross C3
Molineux St B2
Mostyn St A1
New Hampton Rd East A1
Nine Elms La A3
North Rd A2
Oaks Cres C1
Oxley St A2
Paget St A1
Park Ave B1
Park Rd East A1
Park Road West B1
Paul St C2
Pelham St C1
Penn Rd C2
Piper's Row B3
Pitt St C2
Police Station C3
Pool St C2
Poole St A3
Post Office A1/A2/B2/B2/C2
Powlett St C3
Queen St B2
Raby St C3
Raglan St C1
Railway Dr B3
Red Hill St A2
Red Lion St B2
Retreat St C1
Ring Rd B2
Rugby St A1
Russell St C1
St. Andrew's B1
St. David's B3
St. George's C3
St. James St C3
St. John's C2
St. John's C2
St. John's Retail Park C2
St. John's Square C2
St. Mark's C1
St. Marks Rd C1
St. Marks St C1
St. Patrick's B2
St. Peter's B2
St. Peter's B2
Salisbury St C1
Salop St C2
School St C2
Sherwood St A2
Smestow St A3
Snowhill C2
Springfield Rd A3
Stafford St B2
Staveley Rd A1
Steelhouse La C3
Stephenson St C1
Stewart St C2
Sun St B3
Sutherland Pl C3
Tempest St C2
Temple St C2
Tettenhall Rd B1
The Maltings B2
The Royal (Metro) C3
Thomas St C2
Thornley St B2
Tower St C2
Town Hall B2
University B2
Upper Zoar St C1
Vicarage Rd C3
Victoria St C2
Walpole St A1
Walsall St C3
Ward St C3
Warwick St C3
Water St A3
Waterloo Rd B2
Wednesfield Rd B3
West Park (not A&E) B1
West Park Swimming Pool B1
Wolverhampton St. Georges (Metro) C2
Wharf St C3
Whitmore Hill B2
Wolverhampton B3
Wolverhampton Wanderers Football Gnd. (Molineux) B2
Worcester St C2
Wulfrun Centre C2
Yarwell Cl A3
York St C3
Zoar St C1

Worcester

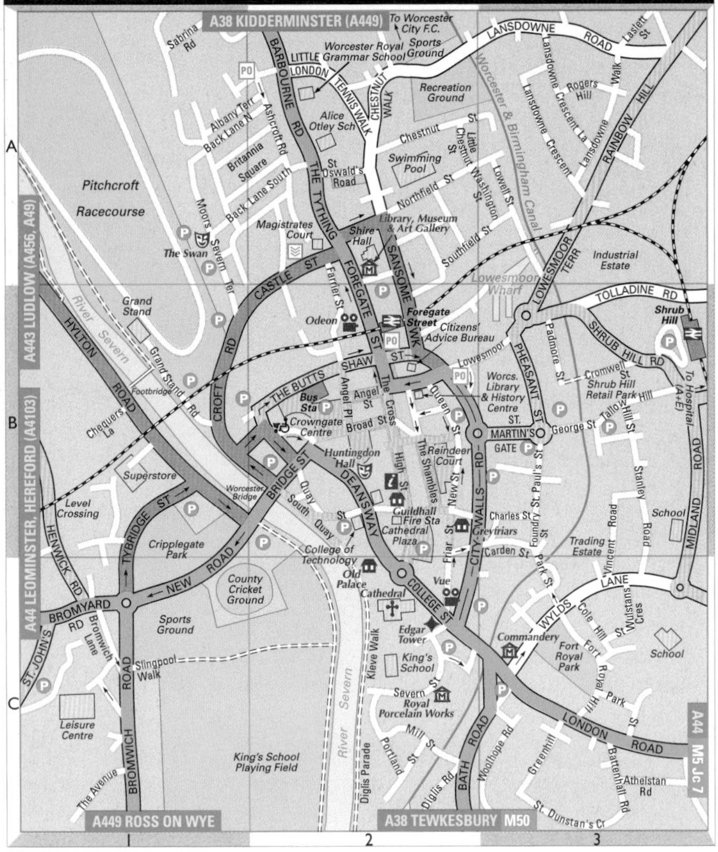

York

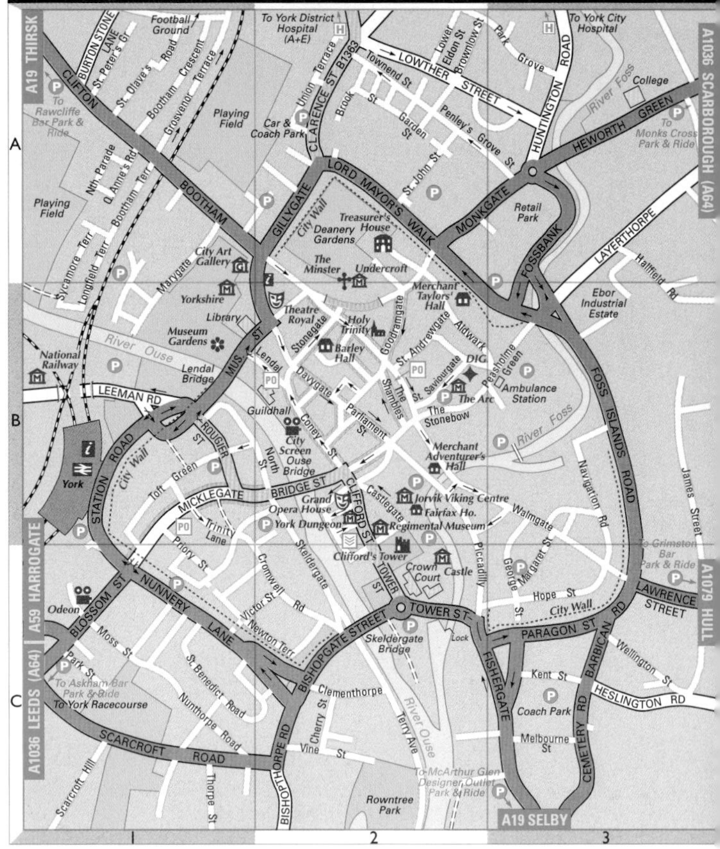

Worcester

Albany Terr A1
Alice Otley School. . . . A2
Angel Pl. B2
Angel St. B2
Ashcroft Rd A2
Athelstan Rd C3
Back Lane North A1
Back Lane South. A1
Barbourne Rd A2
Bath Rd C2
Battenhall Rd. C3
Bridge St B2
Britannia Sq. A1
Broad St B2
Bromwich La C1
Bromwich Rd. C1
Bromyard Rd C1
Bus Station B2
Carden St B3
Castle St A2
Cathedral ✝. C2
Cathedral Plaza. B2
Charles St B3
Chequers La B1
Chestnut St A2
Chestnut Walk. A2
Citizens' Advice Bureau. B2
City Walls Rd. B2
Cole Hill. C3
College of Technology B2
College St C2
Commandery 🏛 C3
County Cricket Ground C1
Cripplegate Park B1
Croft Rd. B1
Cromwell St. B3
Crowngate Centre. . . . B2
Deansway B2
Diglis Pde C2
Diglis Rd C2
Edgar Tower ✦ C2
Farrier St A2
Fire Station B2
Foregate St B2
Fort Royal Hill C3
Fort Royal Park C3
Foundry St. B3
Friar St. C2
George St B3
Grand Stand Rd B1
Greenhill C3
Greyfriars 🏛 B2
Guildhall 🏛 B2
Henwick Rd. B1
High St B2
Hill St. B3
Huntingdon Hall 🎭 . . . B2
Hylton Rd B1
Information Ctr ℹ B2
King's School C2
King's School Playing Field C2
Kleve Walk. C2
Lansdowne Cr. A3
Lansdowne Rd A3
Lansdowne Walk. A3
Laslett St A3
Leisure Centre. A3
Library, Museum & Art Gallery 🏛 A2
Little Chestnut St A2
Little London A2
London Rd. C3
Lowell St A3
Lowesmoor B2
Lowesmoor Terr A3
Lowesmoor Wharf. . . . A3
Magistrates Court A2
Midland Rd B3
Mill St C2
Moors Severn Terr. . . . A1
New Rd C1
New St. B2
Northfield St A2
Odeon 🎥 B2
Old Palace 🏛 B2
Oswald's Rd A2
Padmore St B3
Park St. C3
Pheasant St. B3
Pitchcroft Racecourse. A1
Police Station 🏢 A2
Portland St C2
Post Office PO . A1/A2/B2
Quay St B2
Queen St B2
Rainbow Hill A3
Recreation Ground . . . A2
Reindeer Court B2
Rogers Hill. A3
Royal Porcelain Works 🏛. C2
Sabrina Rd A1
St Dunstan's Cr C3
St John's C1
St Martin's Gate B3
St Paul's St B3
St Wulstans Cr C3
Sansome Walk A2
Severn St. C2
Shaw St. B2
Shire Hall. A2
Shrub Hill ⇌. B3
Shrub Hill Retail Park . B3
Shrub Hill Rd. B3
Slingpool Walk. C1
South Quay B2
Southfield St A2
Sports Ground. . . . A2/C1
Stanley Rd. B3
Swimming Pool A2
Swan, The 🎭. A1
Tallow Hill B3
Tennis Walk A2
The Avenue C1
The Butts. B2
The Cross B2
The Shambles B2
The Tything A2
Tolladine Rd. B3
Tybridge St B1
Vincent Rd. B3
Vue 🎥. C2
Washington St. A3
Woolhope Rd. C3
Worcester Bridge. B2
Worcester Library & History Centre. B3
Worcester Royal Grammar School. . . . A2
Wylds La C3

York

Aldwark B2
Ambulance Station . . . B3
Arc Museum, The 🏛 . . B2
Barbican Rd C3
Barley Hall 🏛 B2
Bishopgate St C2
Bishopthorpe Rd. C2
Blossom St C1
Bootham A1
Bootham Cr. A1
Bootham Terr. A1
Bridge St B2
Brook St A2
Brownlow St A2
Burton Stone La A1
Castle Museum 🏛 . . . C2
Castlegate B2
Cemetery Rd C3
Cherry St C2
City Art Gallery 🏛 A1
City Screen 🎥 B2
City Wall A2/B1/C3
Clarence St A2
Clementhorpe C2
Clifford St B2
Clifford's Tower 🏰 B2
Clifton A1
Coach park A2/C3
Coney St B2
Cromwell Rd C2
Crown Court C2
Davygate B2
Deanery Gdns A2
DIG ✦ B2
Ebor Industrial Estate . B3
Fairfax House 🏛 B2
Fishergate C3
Foss Islands Rd. B3
Fossbank. A3
Garden St A2
George St C3
Gillygate. A2
Goodramgate B2
Grand Opera House 🎭 B2
Grosvenor Terr. A1
Guildhall. B2
Hallfield Rd A3
Heslington Rd C3
Heworth Green A3
Holy Trinity ⛪ B2
Hope St C3
Huntington Rd. A3
Information Ctr ℹ A2
James St B3
Jorvik Viking Centre 🏛 B2
Kent St C3
Lawrence St C3
Layerthorpe A3
Leeman Rd B1
Lendal B2
Lendal Bridge B1
Library B1
Longfield Terr. A1
Lord Mayor's Walk. . . . A2
Lower Eldon St A2
Lowther St. A2
Margaret St C3
Marygate A1
Melbourne St. C3
Merchant Adventurer's Hall 🏛. B2
Merchant Taylors' Hall 🏛. B2
Micklegate B1
Minster, The ✝. A2
Monkgate A2
Moss St C1
Museum Gdns ✲. B1
Museum St B1
National Railway Museum 🏛 B1
Navigation Rd B3
Newton Terr. C2
North Pde A1
North St. B2
Nunnery La C1
Nunthorpe Rd C1
Odeon 🎥 C1
Ouse Bridge B2
Paragon St C3
Park Gr A3
Park St. C1
Parliament St. B2
Peasholme Green B3
Penley's Grove St A2
Piccadilly B2
Police Station 🏢 B2
Post Office PO B1/B2
Priory St. B1
Queen Anne's Rd A1
Regimental Museum 🏛 B2
Rowntree Park. C
St Andrewgate. . . . . . . B
St Benedict Rd C
St John St . . . . A
St Olave's Rd. . . . . A
St Peter's Gr . . . . A
St Saviourgate. . . . . . . B
Scarcroft Hill C
Scarcroft Rd C
Skeldergate C
Skeldergate Bridge . . . C
Station Rd . . . . B
Stonegate . . . . B
Sycamore Terr . . . . A
Terry Ave C
The Shambles . . . . B
The Stonebow . . . . B
Theatre Royal 🎭 . . . . . B
Thorpe St. C
Toft Green . . . . B
Tower St C
Townend St . . . . A
Treasurer's House 🏛. . A
Trinity La . . . . B
Undercroft Museum 🏛 . . . . A
Union Terr . . . . A
Victor St. C
Vine St. C
Walmgate . . . . B
Wellington St C
York Dungeon 🏛 . . . . . B
York Station ⇌. . . . . . . B
Yorkshire Museum 🏛 . B

M25 *and routes into London*

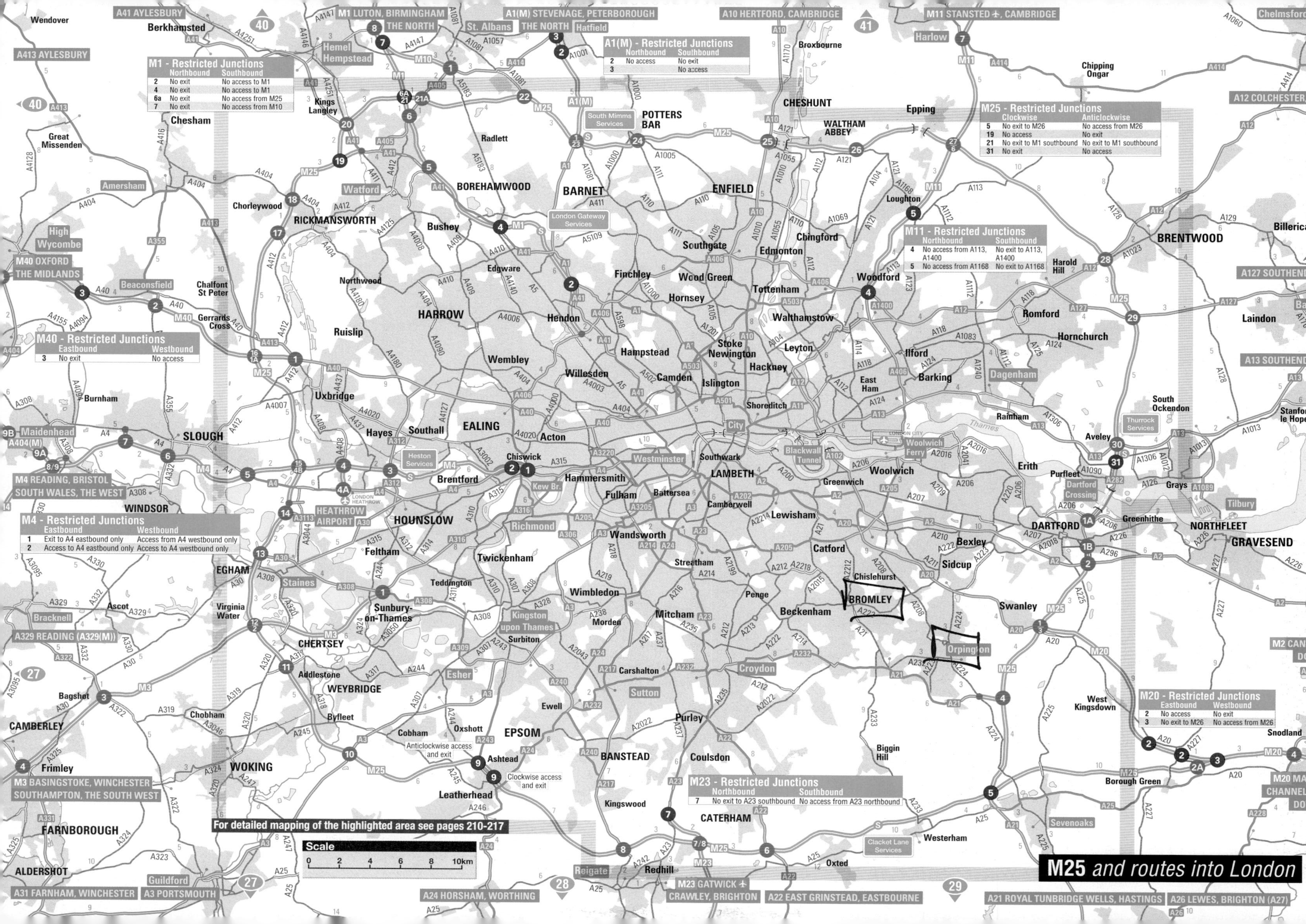

Restricted Junctions

M6	Northbound	Southbound
20	No exit to M56 eastbound	No access from M56 westbound
24	No exit	No access
25	No access from A49	No exit

M53	Northbound	Southbound
11	No exit to M56 westbound	No exit to M56 westbound

M56	Eastbound	Westbound
2	No exit	No access
4	No exit	No access
7		No access
8	No exit or access	No exit
9	No access from M6 northbound	No access to M6 southbound
15	No exit to M53	No access from M53 northbound

M57	Northbound	Southbound
3	No exit	No access
5	No exit	No access

M58	Eastbound	Westbound
1	No exit	No access

M60	Clockwise	Anticlockwise
2	No exit	No access
3	No exit to A34 northbound	No exit to A34 northbound
4	No access to M56	No exit to M56
5	No exit to A5103 southbound	No exit to A5103 northbound
14	No exit to A580	No access from A580
16	No exit	No access
20	No access	No exit
22		No access
25	No access	
26		No exit or access
27	No exit	No access

M61	Northbound	Southbound
2	No access from A580 eastbound	No exit to A580 westbound
3	No access from A580 eastbound No access from A666 southbound	No exit to A580 westbound

M66	Northbound	Southbound
1	No access	No exit

M67	Eastbound	Westbound
1a	No access	No exit
2	No exit	No access

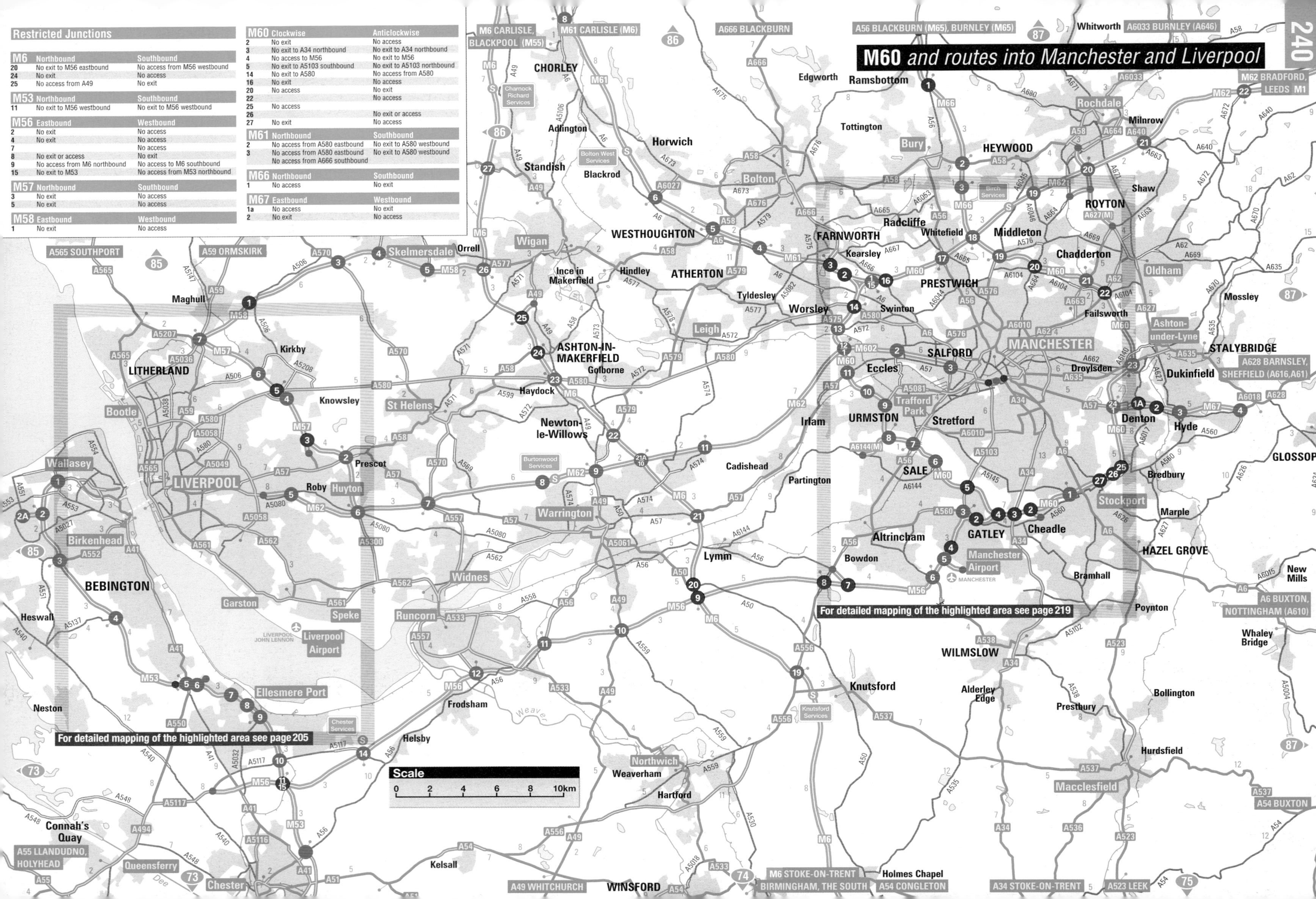

Heathrow Airport (London)

0 Miles ¼

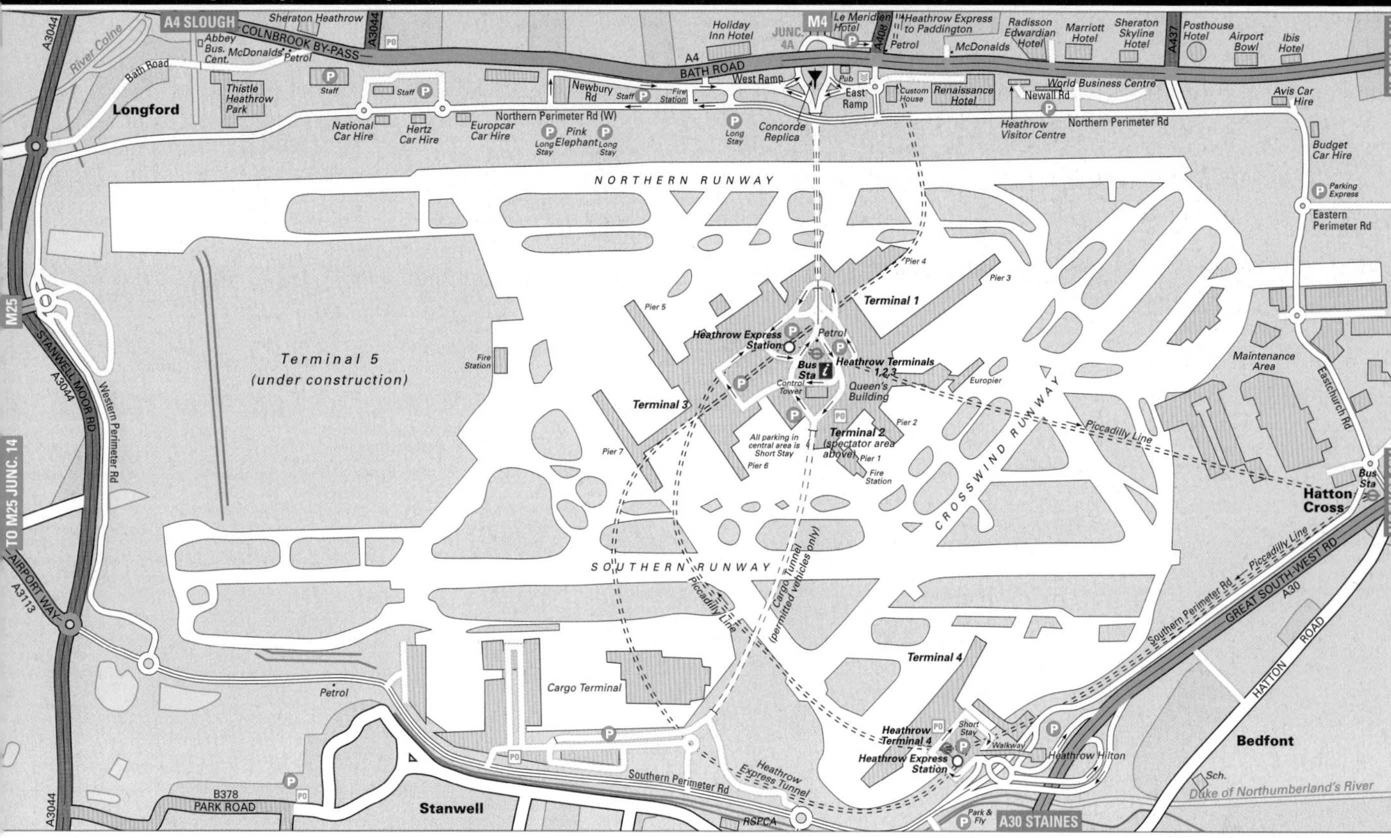

Gatwick Airport (London)

0 Miles ¼

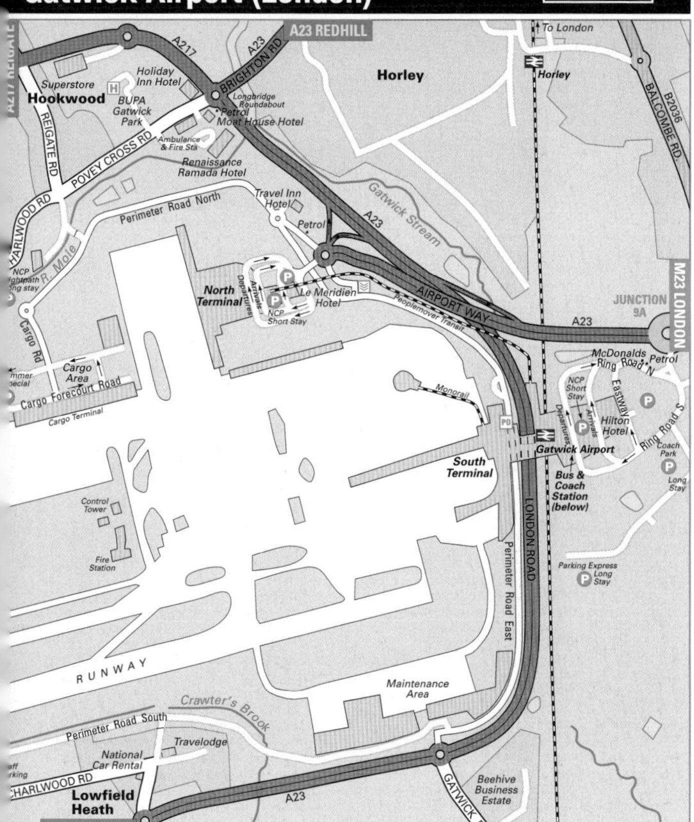

Manchester Airport

0 Miles ¼

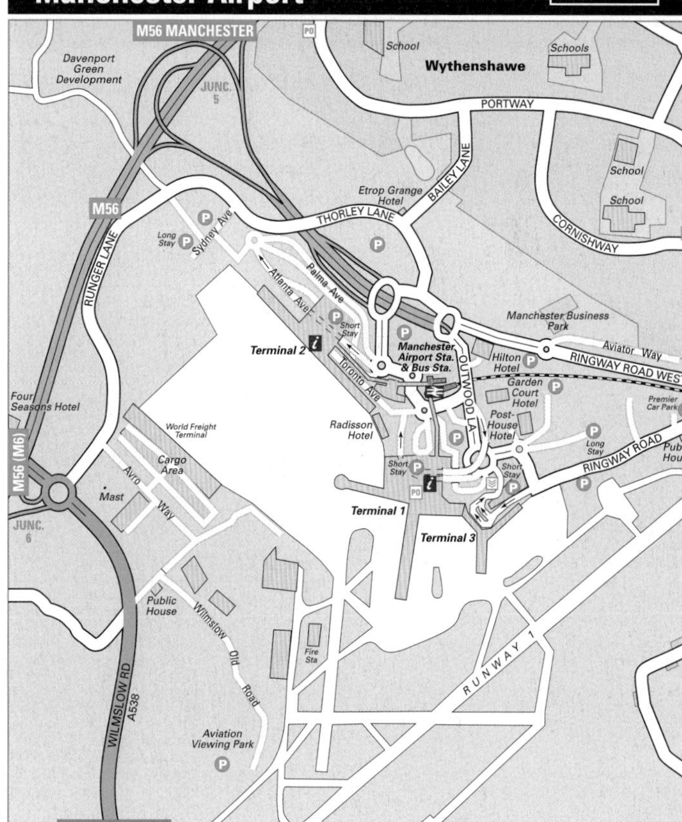

Port of Dover

0 Miles ¼

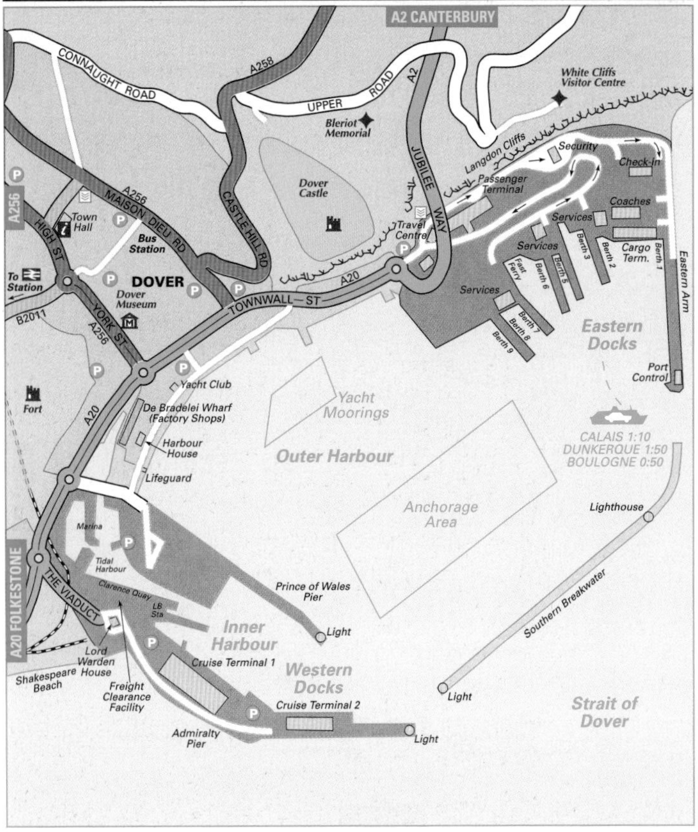

Port of Felixstowe

0 Miles ¼

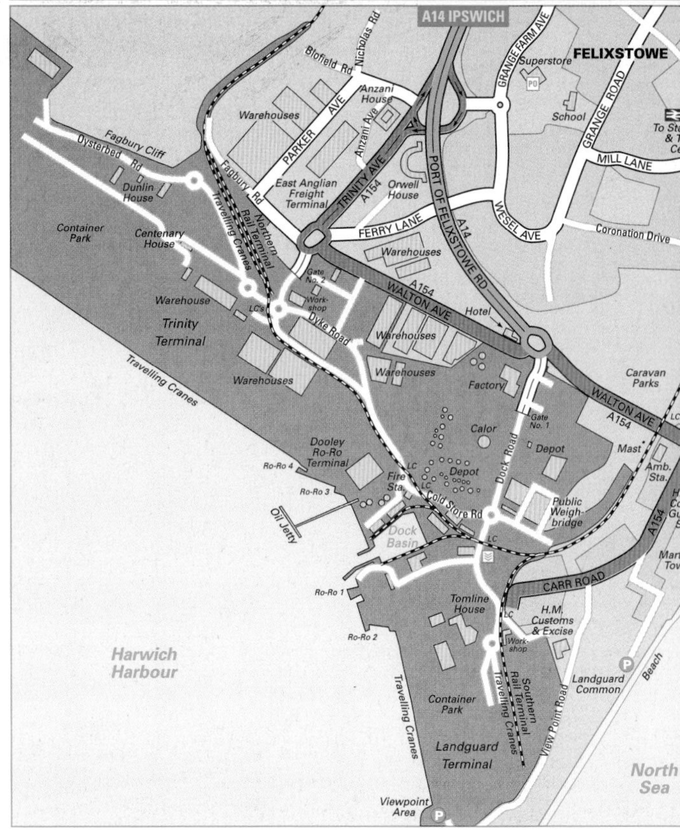

Portsmouth-Continental Ferry Port

0 Miles ¼

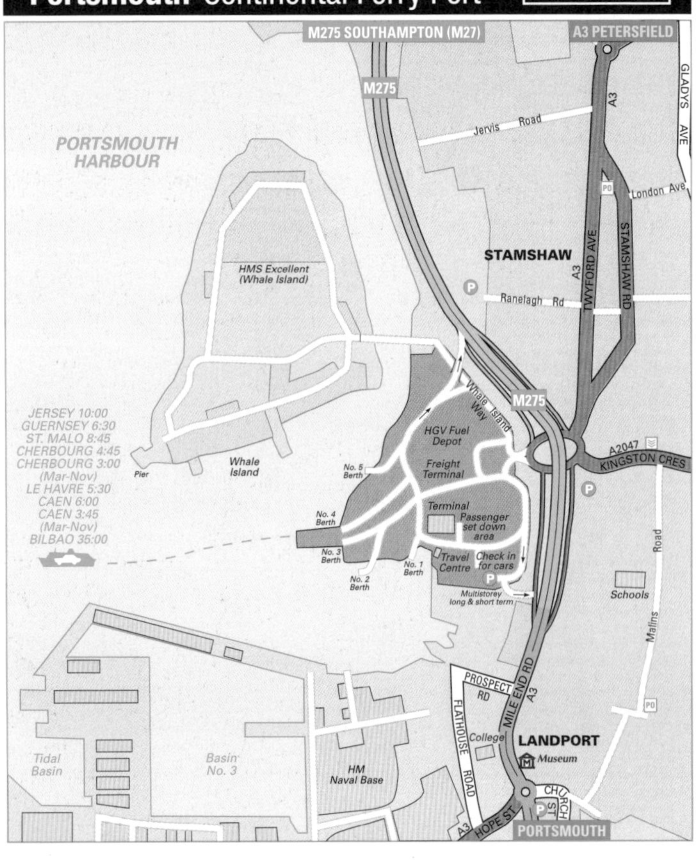

Port of Southampton

0 Miles 1

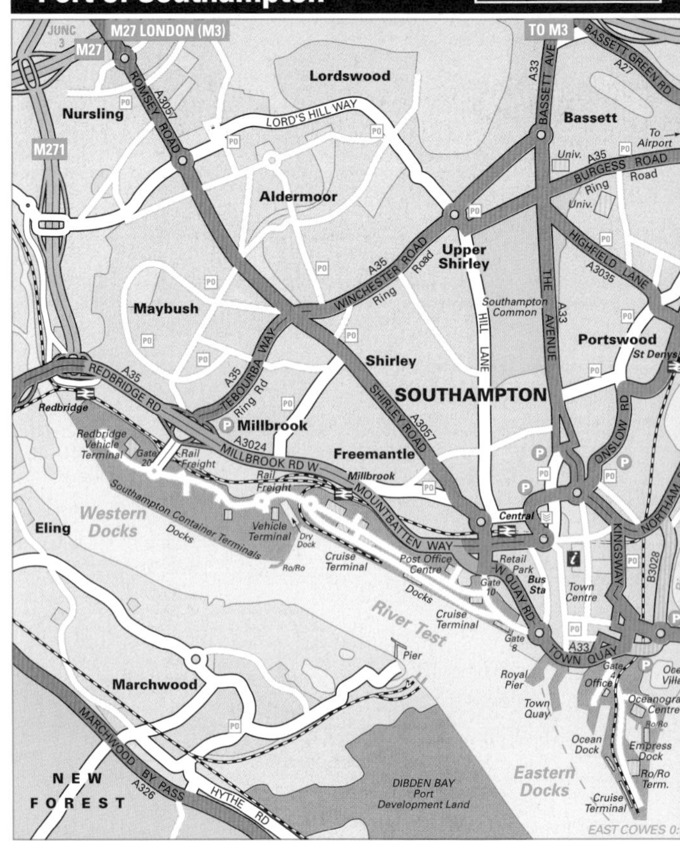

Boulogne

0 Miles ¼

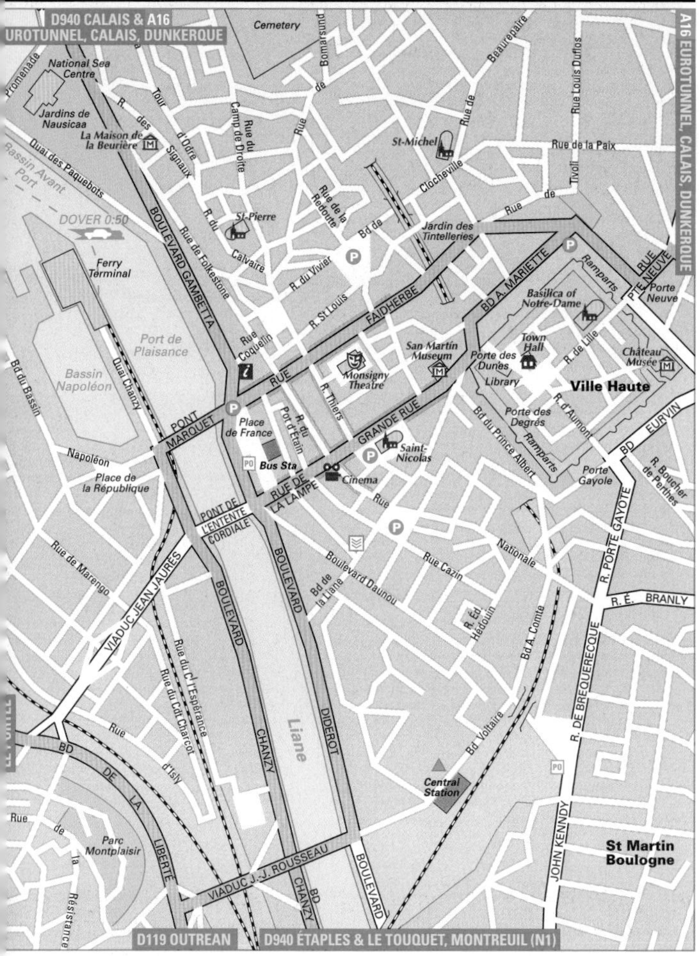

Calais

0 Miles ¼

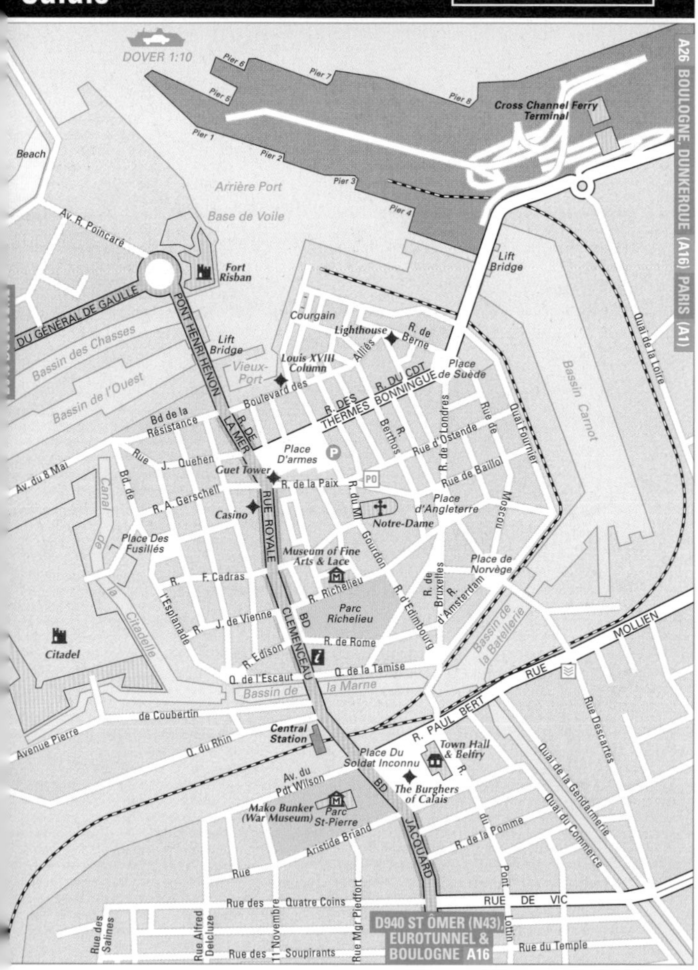

Boulogne and Calais *approaches*

Motorway full / restricted junction
Toll motorway
Principal trunk road single / dual carriageway
Other main road single / dual carriageway
Other important road
Other Road, scenic route
E25 European road number
A49 135 Motorway number, national road number
0 5 10 15 20 25 30miles
0 10 20 30 40km
Poole – St Malo via Guernsey and Jersey
Condor 5hrs:25mins May–Sept
Guernsey 2:30
Jersey 3:45 (Apr-Oct)
Bilbao 35:00
Poole – Cherbourg
Brittany Ferries
4hrs:15mins all year
5hrs:45mins all year
2hrs:15mins May–Sept
Guernsey 6:30
Jersey 10:00
Portsmouth – Cherbourg
Brittany Ferries
4hrs:45mins all year
7hrs:30mins all year
3hrs:00mins Mar-Nov
(Monday-Thursday)
Rosslare 17:30 (Mar-Dec)
Newhaven – Diepp
Transmanche Ferries
4hrs all year
Portsmouth – Le Havre
LD Lines
5hrs:30mins all year
7hrs:30mins all year
Portsmouth – Caen
Brittany Ferries
6hrs:00mins all year
7hrs:00mins all year
3hrs:45mins Mar-Nov
(Friday-Sunday)
Portsmouth – St Malo
Brittany Ferries
8hrs:45mins all year
10hrs:30mins all year
ENGLISH CHANN
Baie de la Seine
Côte de Nacre
Côte Fleurie
Omaha Beach
Gold Beach
Juno Beach
Sword Beach
Utah Beach
Baie du Mont-St. Michel
50°
49°
Basingstoke
Guildford
Reigate
Crawley
Horsham
Petersfield
Eastleigh
Fareham
Havant
Portsmouth
Chichester
Worthing
Hove
Brighton
Lewes
Eastbourne
Newhaven
Poole
Bournemouth
Christchurch
Weymouth
Swanage
Newport
Ryde
Cowes
Sandown
Shanklin
Ventnor
Isle of Wight
Alderney
Cherbourg
Valognes
Jersey
St. Helier
Le Havre
Honfleur
Deauville
Caen
Bayeux
Lisieux
St. Lô
Coutances
Granville
Avranches
St. Malo
Dinard
Vire
Flers
Falaise
Argentan
Fécamp
Étretat

Ramsgate – Oostende
Transeuropa Ferries
4hrs all year
Dover – Dunkirk
Norfolk Line
1:50mins all year
Dover – Calais
P&O Ferries 1:15mins all year
SeaFrance 1:10mins all year
Dover – Boulogne
Speedferries
50 mins
Brittany Ferries
www.brittany-ferries.com
08703 665 333
Condor Ferries
www.condorferries.co.uk
0845 345 2000
LD Lines
www.ldlines.com
0870 428 4335
Norfolk Line
www.norfolkline.com
0870 870 1020
P&O Ferries
www.poferries.com
08705 980 333
SeaFrance
www.seafrance.com
08705 711 711
Speedferries
www.speedferries.com
0870 220 0570
Transeuropa Ferries
www.transeuropaferries.com
01843 595 522
Transmanche Ferries
www.transmancheferries.com
0800 917 1201
Canterbury
Dover
Folkestone
Ashford
Ramsgate
Oostende
Brugge
Gent
Dunkerque
Dunkirk
Calais
Boulogne-sur-Mer
St. Omer
Lille
Roubaix
Tourcoing
Kortrijk
Béthune
Lens
Douai
Valenciennes
Arras
Cambrai
Abbeville
Amiens
St. Quentin
Dieppe
Rouen
Beauvais
Compiègne
Évreux
Pontoise
PARIS
Versailles
Nord
Pas de Calais
Picardie
Île de France

DONEGAL
NORTHERN
TYRONE
FERMANAGH
LEITRIM
SLIGO
ROSCOMMON
CAVAN
MON
LONDO
INISHOWEN PEN.
Malin Hd.
Ballykillin
Ballygorman
Malin Pen.
Glengad Hd.
Trawbreaga B.
Dunaff Hd.
Fanad Hd.
Mulroy B.
Lough Swilly
Tory I.
Horn Hd.
Sheep Haven
Inishbofin
Bloody Foreland
Gola I.
Inishfree B.
Rosses B.
The Rosses
ARAN I.
Crohy Hd.
Gweebarra B.
Dawros Hd.
Loughros More B.
Glen B.
Rossan Pt.
Rathlin O'Birne I.
Carrigan Hd.
Muckros Hd.
Mc Swyne's Bay
Inver Bay
Donegal Harbour
St. John's Pt.
Donegal Bay
Inishmurray I.
Sligo Bay
Derryveagh Mts
GLENVEAGH NAT. PARK
ERRIGAL 752
SLIEVE SNAGHT 615
Blue Stack Mts.
LAVAGH MORE 676
SLIEVE TOOEY 444
SLIEVE LEAGUE 601
SPERRIN
Lough Foyle
Derry/Londonderry
Letterkenny
Buncrana
Moville
Carndonagh
Strabane
Donegal
Ballyshannon
Bundoran
Omagh
Enniskillen
Sligo
Ballymote
Boyle
Carrick-on-Shannon
Lower Lough Erne
Upper L. Erne
Lough Melvin
L. Macnean
L. Gill
L. Arrow
Lough Key
L. Allen
Curlew Mts
TRUSKMORE 644
KNOCKALONGY 544
CUILCAGH 667
SLIEVE ANIERIN 587
CORRY MT. 391
SLIEVE BEAGH 372
CORN HILL 279
CARNBANE EAST 278
MULLAGHMEEN 261
Ballyshannon
Belleek
Manorhamilton
Kinlough
Cliffony
Tobercurry
Charlestown
Swinford
Ballyhaunis
Castlerea
Knock
KNOCK SHRINE
Claremorris
Strokestown
Longford
Mohill
Drumshanbo
Ballinamore
Belturbet
Cavan
Clones
Lisnaskea
Newtownbutler
Irvinestown
Kesh
Pettigo
Castlederg
Newtownstewart
Sion Mills
Ballybofey
Stranorlar
Glenties
Ardara
Killybegs
Dunglow
Falcarragh
Dunfanaghy
Creeslough
Milford
Ramelton
Rathmullan
Kilmacrenan
Churchill
248
CONNAUGHT

5
6
7
8
6°W
5°W
55°N
54°N
A
B
C
D
Campbeltown
Machrihanish
Earadale Pt.
446 CNOC MOY
Southend
Johnston's Pt.
Sanda I.
Mull of Kintyre
Ailsa Craig
Pladda
Rathlin Island
Fair Hd.
Giants Causeway
Benbane Hd.
Inishowen Hd.
Stroove
Magilligan Pt.
The Skerries
Portballintrae
Ballintoy
Ballycastle
Ballyvoy
Portrush
Portstewart
Bushmills
Castlerock
Downhill
Coleraine
Articlave
Ballybogy
Armoy
Moss-side
Carrowreagh
517 KNOCKLAYD
Loughran
Runabay Hd.
Cushendun
Mullarts
Cushendall
Red B.
Garron Pt.
Glenariff
554 TROSTAN
Loughguile
Ballymoney
Macosquin
Limavady
Dungiven
Drumdallagh
Dervock
Ardreagh
Finvoy
Dunloy
Garvagh
Kilrea
Rasharkin
Newtown Crommelin
Clogh
Carnlough
Cullinane
Glenarm
Islandtown
Parkview
Milltown
The Sheddings
Carncastle
MOUNTAINS OF ANTRIM
DERRY
ANTRIM
Swatragh
Teeshan
Broughshane
Ballymena
Portglenone
Inishrush
Maghera
Gulladuff
Ahoghill
Larne
Larne Lough
AGNEWS HILL 476
Moorfields
Glynn
Glenoe
I. Magee
Black Hd.
Ballycarry
Whitehead
Carrickfergus
Ballyclare
Ballynure
Doagh
Kells
Connor
Randalstown
Toome
Moneyglass
Magherafelt
Castledawson
Tobermore
Bellaghy
L. Beg
Antrim
Templepatrick
Mossley
Greenisland
Glengormly
Newtownabbey
Belfast Lough
Bangor
Groomsport
Copeland I.
Donaghadee
Millisle
Holywood
Conlig
Newtownards
Dundonald
BELFAST
ULSTER MUSEUM
Newtownbreda
Comber
BELFAST INTERNATIONAL
Nutts Corner
Crumlin
Dundrod
Legoniel
Glenavy
Lough Neagh
N IRELAND
Cookstown
Coagh
Arboe
The Loup
Ballyronan
Moneymore
Tullaghoge
Stewartstown
Coalisland
Killeen
Dungannon
Donaghmore
Maghery
Derrytrasna
Dunmurry
Ballinderry Upr.
Aghalee
Magheragall
Lisburn
Drumbeg
Carryduff
Lisbane
Greyabbey
Ballywalter
Ballyhalbert
Kircubbin
Glastry
Portavogie
Ardkeen
Cloghy
Ards Peninsula
Strangford Lough
Ballygowan
Saintfield
The Temple
Moira
Lurgan
Craigavon
Portadown
Hillsborough
Annahilt
Derryboy
Crossgar
Killyleagh
Shrigley
Portaferry
Strangford
Ballynahinch
Waringstown
Dromore
Moy
Charlemont
Armagh
Killylea
Caledon
Tynan
Middletown
Richhill
Gilford
Tandragee
Lawrencetown
Banbridge
Mount Ida
Garvaghy
Finnis
Dromara
Annacloy
Downpatrick
Frankville
Tobermoney
Ballyquintin Pt.
Killard Pt.
Ballyhornan
ARMAGH
DOWN
Scarva
Loughbrickland
Katesbridge
Acton
Poyntz Pass
Markethill
Castlewellan
Clough
Ballydugan
Ardglass
Killough
St. John's Pt.
Dundrum
Dundrum Bay
Newcastle
Mountnorris
Keady
Milltown
Darkley
Newtown Hamilton
Whitecross
Bessbrook
Belleek
Camlough
Newry
Beech Hill
Rathfriland
Hilltown
Mayo Bridge
Kilcoo
Tollymore
MOURNE MTS.
852 SLIEVE DONARD
Glasdrumman
Annalong
Burren
Rostrevor
Attical
Moyad
Warrenpoint
Omeath
Killowen
Ballymartin
Kilkeel
Lisnacree
Greencastle
Carlingford
590 SLIEVE FOYE
Greenore
Carlingford Lough
Cranfield Pt.
Ballagan Pt.
Castleblaney
Cullyhanna
Slieve Gullion 577
Crossmaglen
Forkill
Cullaville
Kilcurry
Dundalk
Rampark
Rathcor
Black Rock
Lurgangreen
Dundalk Bay
LOUTH
Louth
Carrickmacross
Tallanstown
Dromiskin
Castlebellingham
Annagassan
Salterstown
Dunany Pt.
Ardee
Dunleer
Togher
Clogher Head
Clogher Hd.
Termonfeckin
Baltray
Collon
Monasterboice
Kells
Drogheda
Kingscourt
North Channel
TROON 1:49 (April-Sept)
CAIRNRYAN 1:45
FLEETWOOD 8:00
STRANRAER 1:45
LIVERPOOL 8:00
DOUGLAS 2:45 (April-Sept)
Corsewall Pt.
Milleur Pt.
Kirkcolm
Cairnryan
Leswalt
L. Ryan
STRANRAER
Innermessan
Lochans
Portpatrick
Stoneykirk
Sandhead
Ardwell
Port Logan
Drummore
Lendalfoot
Bennane Hd.
Ballantrae
Scale : 1:625 000
(approx 10 miles to 1 inch)
0 10 20 miles
0 10 20 30 km

1
2
3
4
A
B
C
D
11°W
10°W
54°N
53°N
Broad Haven
Benwee Hd.
Portacloy
Erris Hd.
Belderg
MAUMAKEOGH
380
Downpatrick Hd.
Ballycastle
Rathlacken
Lenadoon Pt.
Killala Bay
Graghil
Corlogh
Annagh Hd.
Belmullet
Knockalina
Glenamoy
R314
Creeragh
Killala
Inishcrone
An Geata Mór
Bunahowen
Carrowmore L.
Mullet Pen.
Inishkea North
Inishkea South
R313
Srahmore
Bangor
Largan
Owenmore
Beville
Bellacorick
Crossmolina
Ballina
Crockets Town
Ardnaree
Fallmore
Gwessalia
OWEN DUFF NAT. PARK
N59
NEPHIN BEG RANGE
722
627
Blacksod Pt.
Blacksod Bay
Deel
L. Conn
N26
Ridge Pt.
Saddle Hd.
SLIEVEMORE
672
Doogort
Ballycroy
Castlehill
Lahardaun
806
NEPHIN
Achill Hd.
Dooagh
Keel
R319
Chasel
714
L. Feeagh
Pontoon
L. Cullin
Foxford
ACHILL I.
Achill
Beltra
Strade Friary
Dooega Hd.
Mallaranny
Corraun Pen.
Rosturk
Beltra L.
Newport
R311
Bellavary
Bohola
Achill Sd.
Achillbeg I.
Newport B.
Castlebar
Derrycoosh
Manulla
Kiltamagh
CLARE I.
Clew Bay
Westport B.
Westport
N5
Balla
R330
Ballyhean
N84
Louisburgh
R335
Killadangan
765
CROAGH PATRICK
Aghagower
Killavally
Ballintober
Mayo
Ballyglass
Lugatemple
Caher I.
Inishturk
Killadoon
Cregganbaun
M
A
Y
O
C
Carrowkennedy
392
Partry
Cornanagh
L. Carra
Sheeffry Hills
763
PARTRY MTS.
Killary Harbour
Inishbofin
819
MWEELREA
683
Toomakeady
Hollymount
Inishshark
Srahnalong
Lough Mask
Ballinrobe
Tully Cross
Gowlaun
KYLEMORE ABBEY
Leenaun
Kilmaine
Cleggan
Letterfrack
MAUMTURK MTS.
Joyce Country
Neale
Moyard
Streamstown
BENBAUN
730
CONNEMARA NAT. PARK
Clonbur
Cong
Maum
Cornamona
Shrule
Clifden
Clifden B.
Recess
660
Maam Cross
Headford
Ballyconneely
CONNEMARA
Toombeola
Oughterard
Ballyhale
Lough Corrib
Kilgarriff
Slyne Hd.
R341
Roundstone
Callow
Ballyconneely Bay
Derryrush
Screeb
Rosscahill
Glinsk
Kylesa
Kilbrickan
G
A
L
Bertraghboy Bay
Kilkieran
Kilkieran Bay
Moycullen
Carna
Ardmore
Lettermore I.
Lettermore
Costelloe
Ballagh
Menlough
Galway
Carraroe
Rossaveel
Lettermullan
Gorumna I.
Inveran
Caher
Barna
Spiddle
Salthill
Cashla Bay
Galway Bay
North Sound
Black Hd.
Burren
Kilmurvy
Kilronan
Murrough
INISHMORE
Inishmaan
Ballyvaghan
AILLWEE CAVE
ARAN IS.
South Sd.
345
SL. ELVA
N67
Carran
Inisheer
Lisdoonvarna
Doolin
Kilfenora
BURREN NAT. PARK
Kilshanny
Killinaboy
Cliffs of Moher
Hags Hd.
Liscannor
Ennistimon
Corrofin
Liscannor Bay
Lehinch
N85
C
L
A
Spanish Pt.
Milltown Malbay
Inagh
Fountain Cross
250
Mal Bay
SLIEVECALLEN
391
Mutton I.
Quilty
Shanovogh
Kilmaley
Kilmurry
Darragh

Donegal Bay
Sligo Bay
FERMANAGH
LEITRIM
SLIGO
CAVAN
ROSCOMMON
LONGFORD
WESTMEATH
REPUBLIC OF IRELAND
OFFALY
LAOIS
CONNAUGHT
Lower Lough Erne
Upper L. Erne
Lough Ree
Lough Melvin
L. Allen
L. Key
L. Gill
L. Derg
L. Oughter
L. Sheelin
L. Ennell
L. Owel
L. Derravaragh
Slieve Bloom
Slieve Aughty
Curlew Mts
Arra Mts.
Ballyshannon
Bundoran
Single Street
Belleek
Mullaghmore
Roskeeragh Pt.
Inishmurray I.
Tullaghan
Kinlough
Cliffony
Grange
Ballyconnell
Mullaghnaneane
TRUSKMORE 644
Carney
Drumcliff
Rosses Point
Sligo
Strandhill
Easky
Dromore West
Templeboy
Dromard
Beltra
Ballysadare
Collooney
Ballygawley
KNOCKALONGY 544
Coolaney
Manorhamilton
Glenade
Leckanarainey
Kiltyclogher
Rossinver
Garrison
Glen
Scribbagh
Tullycrossmearan
Lissinagroagh
Glenfarn
Belcoo
Letterbreen
Enniskillen
Lisbellaw
Irvinestown
Ballinamallard
Tempo
Fivemiletown
SLIEVE BEAGH 372
Clogher
Augher
Fintona
Tummery
Trillick
Clabby
Killarbran
Cooneen
Brookeborough
Maguiresbridge
Lisnaskea
Newtownbutler
Clones
Monaghan
Scotstown
Emyvale
Smithborough
Rosslea
Donagh
Magheraveely
Killeevan
Newbliss
Lisnaveane
Rockcorry
Cootehill
Drum
Tullyvin
Belturbet
Ballyconnell
Bawnboy
Derrylin
Swanlinbar
CUILCAGH 667
Florence Court
Mullan
Kinawley
Derrynacreeve
Glengavlen
Dowra
Blacklion
Killarga
Lackagh Hills
Killargue
Drumkeeran
CORRY MT. 391
Greevagh
Ballyfarnan
Keadow
Drumshanbo
SLIEVE ANIERIN 587
Ballinamore
Newtown Gore
Killashandra
Butler's Bridge
Cavan
Ballyhaise
Stradone
Lavey
Bailieborough
Ballyjamesduff
Virginia
Mount Nugent
Kilnaleck
Crossdoney
Arvagh
Ballymote
Tobercurry
Bunnanaddan
Ballinafad
Boyle
Cloonloogh
Gorteen
Charlestown
Curry
Aclare
Mullanys Cross
Carracastle
Tawnyinah
Kilkelly
Knock
KNOCK SHRINE
Ballyhaunis
Claremorris
Castlerea
Ballaghaderreen
Frenchpark
Breedoge
Loughglinn
Carrowbehy
Croghan
Elphin
Strokestown
Tulsk
Carrick-on-Shannon
Drumsna
Mohill
Cloone
Dromod
Roosky
Drumlish
CORN HILL 279
Ballinalee
Granard
Longford
Edgeworthstown
Ardagh
Lanesborough
Roscommon
Ballymurray
Knockcroghery
Athleague
Mount Talbot
Ballygar
Newbridge
Mountbellew Bridge
Castleblakeney
Tuam
Dunmore
Milltown
Glenamaddy
Ballinlough
Ballymoe
Williamstown
Castlepollard
Collinstown
Delvin
Crookedwood
Mullingar
Kinnegad
Rochfortbridge
Tyrrellspass
Kilbeggan
Moate
Horseleap
Clara
Tullamore
Daingean
Edenderry
Rhode
Portarlington
Monasterevin
Mountmellick
Portlaoise
Stradbally
Abbeyleix
Durrow
Ballyragget
Castlecomer
Rathdowney
Borris-in-Ossory
Mountrath
Roscrea
Templemore
DEVILSBIT 482
Nenagh
Toomyvara
Borrisokane
Birr
Banagher
Ferbane
Shannonbridge
Clonmacnoise
Athlone
Glassan
Ballymahon
Ballinasloe
Kilconnell
Aughrim
Athenry
Loughrea
Craughwell
Oranmore
Clarinbridge
Kilcolgan
Ardrahan
Gort
Peterswell
Kinvarra
Portumna
Eyrecourt
Terryglass
Woodford
Scarriff
Mountshannon
Tulla
Killaloe
Ballina
Feakle
Whitegate
Dolla
Silvermines
GLENNAGALLIAGH 533
Broadford
Kilkishen
Clarecastle
Quin
Moymore
Spancelhill
Barefield
Crusheen
Ruan
ARDERIN 529
Shinrone
Cloughjordan
Moneygall
Dunkerrin
Kilcormac
Cadamstown
Kinnitty
Clonaslee
Rosenallis
Ballyfin
Killeigh
Geashill
Rathangan
Bracknagh
MULLAGHMEEN 261
CARNBANE EAST 278
Oldcastle
Finnea
Kilcogy
Crossakiel
Clonmellon
Killucan
Raharney
Ballycumber
Cloghan
Grand Canal
Royal Canal
54°N
53°N
251
252
246
247

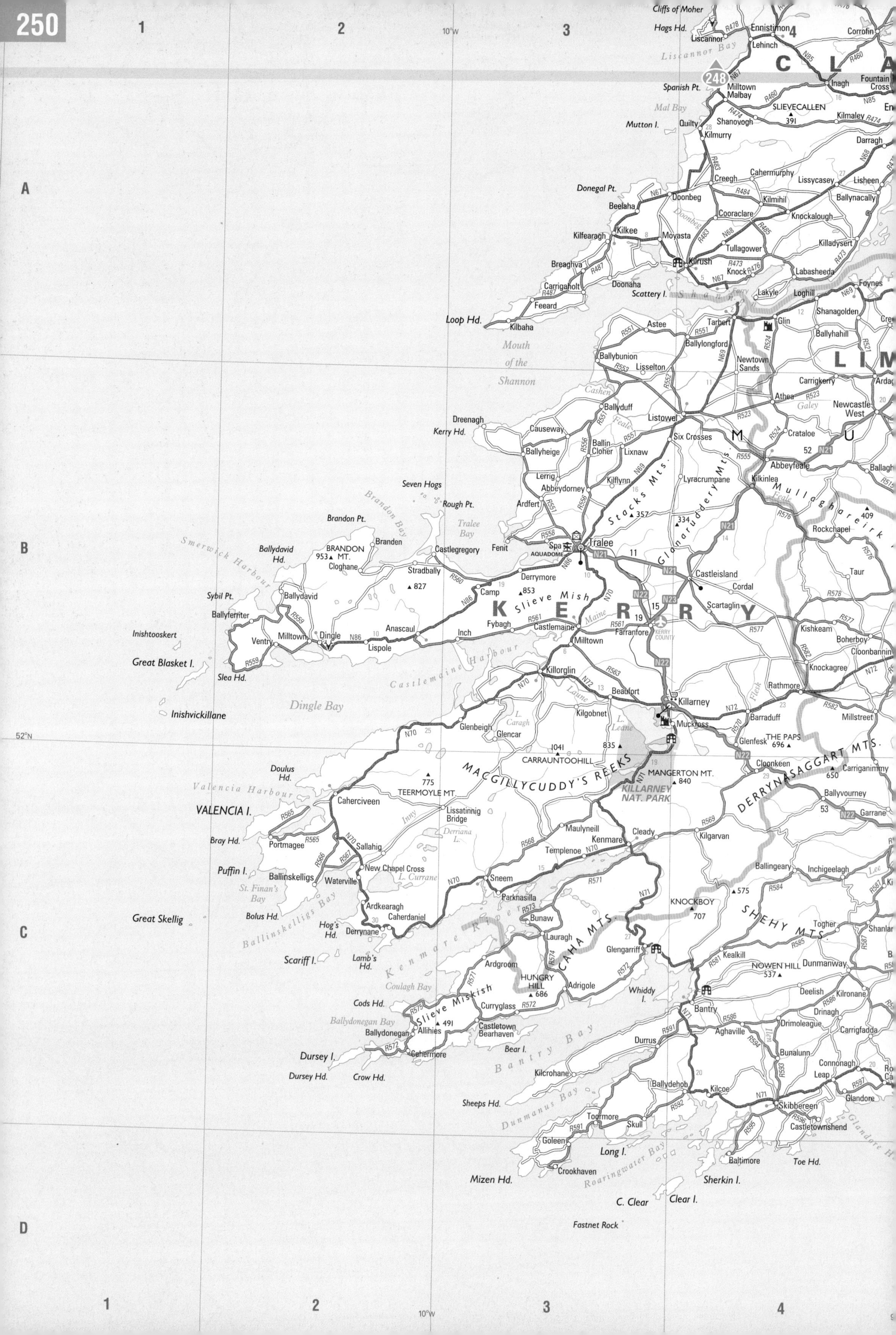
1
2
3
4
A
B
C
D
10°W
52°N
248
CLA
LIM
K E R R Y
M U
Cliffs of Moher
Hags Hd.
Liscannor
Liscannor Bay
Ennistimon
Lehinch
Corrofin
Spanish Pt.
Milltown Malbay
Inagh
Fountain Cross
Mal Bay
SLIEVECALLEN
391
Shanovogh
Kilmaley
Mutton I.
Quilty
Kilmurry
Darragh
Creegh
Cahermurphy
Lissycasey
Lisheen
Donegal Pt.
Doonbeg
Kilmihil
Ballynacally
Beelaha
Cooraclare
Knockalough
Kilkee
Moyasta
Kilfearagh
Tullagower
Killadysert
Breaghva
Kilrush
Knock
Labasheeda
Carrigaholt
Doonaha
Scattery I.
Lakyle
Loghill
Foynes
Feeard
Loop Hd.
Kilbaha
Glin
Shanagolden
Astee
Tarbert
Ballylongford
Ballyhahill
Mouth of the Shannon
Ballybunion
Lisselton
Newtown Sands
Cashen
Carrigkerry
Ardagh
Ballyduff
Athea
Newcastle West
Galey
Dreenagh
Kerry Hd.
Causeway
Listowel
Six Crosses
Ballyheige
Ballin Cloher
Lixnaw
Cratalone
Abbeyfeale
Lerrig
Kilflynn
Lyracrumpane
Kilkinlea
Seven Hogs
Abbeydorney
Stacks Mts.
Glanaruddery Mts.
Mullaghareirk
Brandon Bay
Rough Pt.
Ardfert
Tralee Bay
357
334
409
Brandon Pt.
Rockchapel
Smerwick Harbour
Ballydavid Hd.
BRANDON MT.
953
Branden
Cloghane
Castlegregory
Fenit
Spa
Tralee
AQUADOME
11
Castleisland
Stradbally
827
Derrymore
853
Cordal
Taur
Sybil Pt.
Ballydavid
Camp
Slieve Mish
Scartaglin
Ballyferriter
Anascaul
Fybagh
Castlemaine
Farranfore
KERRY COUNTY
Kishkeam
Inishtooskert
Ventry
Milltown
Dingle
Lispole
Inch
Boherboy
Great Blasket I.
Slea Hd.
Castlemaine Harbour
Killorglin
Knockagree
Cloonbannin
Dingle Bay
Beaufort
Killarney
Rathmore
Inishvickillane
Kilgobnet
L. Caragh
L. Leane
Millstreet
Glenbeigh
Glencar
Muckross
Barraduff
Glenfesk
THE PAPS
696
1041
835
CARRAUNTOOHILL
Doulus Hd.
MACGILLYCUDDY'S REEKS
MANGERTON MT.
840
Cloonkeen
DERRYNASAGGART MTS.
Carriganimmy
650
Valencia Harbour
775
TEERMOYLE MT.
KILLARNEY NAT. PARK
Ballyvourney
53
Garrane
VALENCIA I.
Caherciveen
Lissatinnig Bridge
Derriana L.
Maulyneill
Cleady
Kilgarvan
Bray Hd.
Portmagee
Sallahig
Templenoe
Kenmare
Puffin I.
Ballinskelligs
New Chapel Cross
L. Currane
Sneem
Ballingeary
Inchigeelagh
St. Finan's Bay
Waterville
Parknasilla
575
Ballinskelligs Bay
Ardkearagh
Caherdaniel
KNOCKBOY
707
SHEHY MTS.
Great Skellig
Bolus Hd.
Bunaw
Togher
Hog's Hd.
Derrynane
Kenmare River
CAHA MTS.
Lauragh
Glengarriff
Kealkill
Dunmanway
Scariff I.
Lamb's Hd.
Ardgroom
HUNGRY HILL
686
NOWEN HILL
537
Coulagh Bay
Adrigole
Whiddy I.
Deelish
Kilronane
Cods Hd.
Slieve Miskish
Curryglass
Bantry
Drinagh
Ballydonegan Bay
491
Castletown Bearhaven
Drimoleague
Ballydonegan
Allihies
Aghaville
Carrigfadda
Dursey I.
Cahermore
Bear I.
Durrus
Bunalunn
Bantry Bay
Connonagh
Dursey Hd.
Crow Hd.
Kilcrohane
Leap
Ballydehob
Kilcoe
Glandore
Sheeps Hd.
Dunmanus Bay
Skibbereen
Toormore
Skull
Castletownshend
Goleen
Long I.
Glandore Harbour
Roaringwater Bay
Baltimore
Toe Hd.
Crookhaven
Mizen Hd.
Sherkin I.
C. Clear
Clear I.
Fastnet Rock

TIPPERARY
WATERFORD
CORK
Limerick
CORK
Waterford
Clonmel
Nenagh
Roscrea
Thurles
Kilkenny
Cashel
Tipperary
Mitchelstown
Fermoy
Mallow
Dungarvan
Youghal
Midleton
Cobh
Kinsale
Bandon
Clonakilty
Carrick-on-Suir
Callan
Templemore
Lismore
Cappoquin
Tramore
Charleville
Kilmallock
Macroom
Kanturk
SILVERMINE MTS.
KEEPER HILL
GOLDEN VALE
GALTY MTS.
GALTYMORE
BALLYHOURA MTS.
KNOCKMEALDOWN MTS.
COMERAGH MTS.
MONAVULLAGH MTS.
SLIEVENAMON
Nagles Mts.
KNOCKNASKAGH
Kilworth Mts.
Arra Mts.
DEVILSBIT
Youghal Bay
Cork Harbour
Kinsale Harbour
Courtmacsherry Bay
Clonakilty Bay
Tramore Bay
Dungarvan Harbour
Helvick Hd.
Mine Hd.
Ardmore Hd.
Old Head of Kinsale
Seven Heads
Galley Hd.
SWANSEA 10:00
ROSCOFF 11:00 (Mar-Nov)
249
252
5
6
7
8
C
D
52°N
8°W

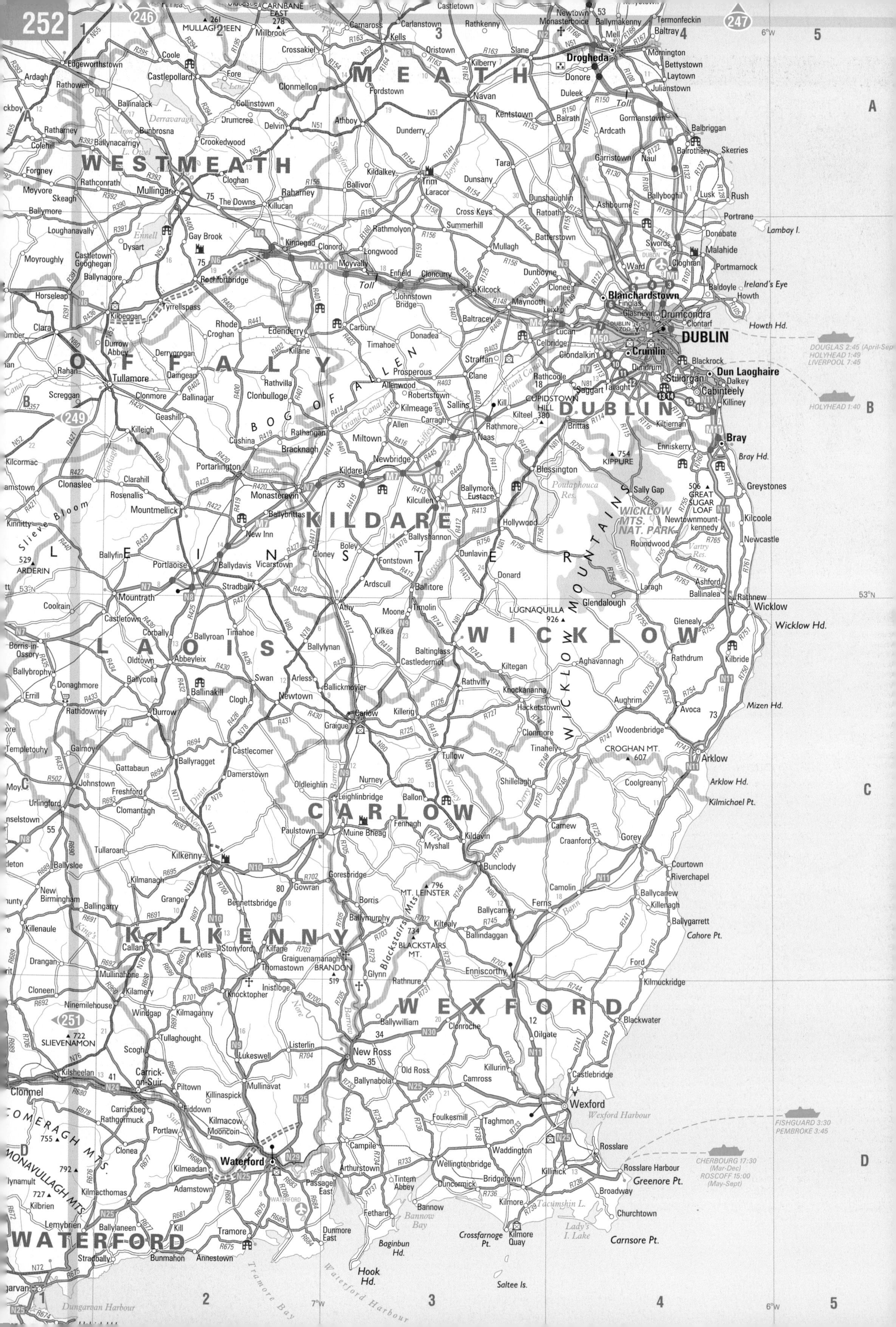
246
247
249
251
MEATH
WESTMEATH
OFFALY
BOG OF ALLEN
KILDARE
DUBLIN
LEINSTER
LAOIS
WICKLOW
WICKLOW MOUNTAINS
CARLOW
KILKENNY
WEXFORD
WATERFORD
Drogheda
Termonfeckin
Baltray
Newtown
Monasterboice
Ballymakenny
Mell
Mornington
Bettystown
Laytown
Julianstown
Donore
Duleek
Slane
Castletown
Carnaross
Carlanstown
Rathkenny
Kells
Oristown
Kilberry
Crossakiel
Navan
Fordstown
Clonmellon
Kentstown
Balrath
Gormanstown
Balbriggan
Balrothery
Skerries
Athboy
Dunderry
Delvin
Collinstown
Drumcree
Crookedwood
Kildalkey
Trim
Laracor
Tara
Dunsany
Ardcath
Garristown
Naul
Lusk
Rush
Ballyboghil
Ashbourne
Dunshaughlin
Ratoath
Batterstown
Portrane
Donabate
Lambay I.
Swords
Malahide
Portmarnock
Cloghran
Baldoyle
Ireland's Eye
Howth
Howth Hd.
Blanchardstown
Finglas
Glasnevin
Drumcondra
Clontarf
DUBLIN
Crumlin
Blackrock
Dun Laoghaire
Dalkey
Stillorgan
Dundrum
Cabinteely
Killiney
Tallaght
Saggart
Clondalkin
Lucan
Leixlip
Celbridge
Maynooth
Kilcock
Dunboyne
Clonee
Ward
Mullagh
Summerhill
Cross Keys
Ballivor
Raharney
Longwood
Rathmolyon
Enfield
Clonard
Kinnegad
Moyvally
Cloncurry
Johnstown Bridge
Carbury
Donadea
Timahoe
Edenderry
Kilane
Baltracey
Straffan
Clane
Prosperous
Allenwood
Robertstown
Kilmeage
Sallins
Kill
Naas
Rathmore
Kilteel
Cupidstown Hill 380
Rathcoole
Brittas
Kiltiernan
Enniskerry
Bray
Bray Hd.
Greystones
Kippure 754
Blessington
Poulaphouca Res.
Sally Gap
Great Sugar Loaf 506
Wicklow Mts. Nat. Park
Newtownmountkennedy
Kilcoole
Newcastle
Roundwood
Ashford
Ballinalea
Laragh
Glendalough
Rathnew
Wicklow
Wicklow Hd.
Lugnaquilla 926
Glenealy
Rathdrum
Kilbride
Aghavannagh
Aughrim
Avoca
Mizen Hd.
Woodenbridge
Croghan Mt. 607
Arklow
Arklow Hd.
Kilmichael Pt.
Coolgreany
Gorey
Courtown
Riverchapel
Ballycanew
Kilenagh
Ballygarrett
Cahore Pt.
Ford
Kilmuckridge
Blackwater
Edgeworthstown
Ardagh
Rathowen
Coole
Castlepollard
Fore
L. Lene
Ballinalack
L. Derravaragh
Rathharney
Ballynacarrigy
Bunbrosna
Coleshill
Forgney
Rathconrath
Mullingar
Cloghan
The Downs
Killucan
Moyvore
Skeagh
Ballymore
Loughanavally
Dysart
Gay Brook
L. Ennell
Moyroughly
Castletown Geoghegan
Ballynagore
Rochfortbridge
Horseleap
Kilbeggan
Tyrrellspass
Clara
Durrow Abbey
Rhode
Croghan
Derrygrogan
Daingean
Rahan
Tullamore
Rathvilla
Clonbullogue
Screggan
Clonmore
Ballinagar
Geashill
Killeigh
Cushina
Rathangan
Bracknagh
Allen
Carragh
Miltown
Newbridge
Kildare
Portarlington
Monasterevin
Kilcullen
Ballymore Eustace
Hollywood
Clonaslee
Clarahill
Rosenallis
Mountmellick
Ballybrittas
New Inn
Ballyshannon
Dunlavin
Donard
Slieve Bloom
Kilcormac
Kinnitty
Arderin 529
Ballyfin
Portlaoise
Ballydavis
Vicarstown
Cloney
Boley
Fontstown
Ardscull
Ballitore
Stradbally
Mountrath
Coolrain
Castletown
Corbally
Athy
Timolin
Moone
Kilkea
Baltinglass
Kiltegan
Borris-in-Ossory
Ballyroan
Timahoe
Ballylynan
Castledermot
Oldtown
Abbeyleix
Ballybrophy
Donaghmore
Ballycolla
Swan
Arless
Ballickmoyler
Rathvilly
Knockananna
Errill
Ballinakill
Clogh
Newtown
Hacketstown
Rathdowney
Durrow
Carlow
Graigue
Killerig
Clonmore
Templetouhy
Galmoy
Castlecomer
Tullow
Tinahely
Shillelagh
Gattabaun
Ballyragget
Johnstown
Freshford
Damerstown
Nurney
Oldleighlin
Leighlinbridge
Ballon
Urlingford
Clomantagh
Fennagh
Muine Bheag
Paulstown
Myshall
Kildavin
Carnew
Craanford
Tullaroan
Kilkenny
Bunclody
Ballysloe
Kilmanagh
Gowran
Goresbridge
Mt. Leinster 796
Camolin
New Birmingham
Grange
Bennettsbridge
Borris
Ballingarry
Ferns
Ballycarney
Killenaule
Ballymurphy
Kiltealy
Ballindaggan
Blackstairs Mt. 734
Callan
Kells
Stonyford
Kilfane
Graiguenamanagh
Brandon 519
Drangan
Thomastown
Glynn
Enniscorthy
Mullinahone
Kilamery
Inistioge
Rathnure
Cloneen
Knocktopher
Ninemilehouse
Windgap
Kilmaganny
Ballywilliam
Clonroche
Oilgate
Slievenamon 722
Tullaghought
Scogh
Listerlin
New Ross
Killurin
Kilsheelan
Carrick-on-Suir
Lukeswell
Old Ross
Camross
Castlebridge
Clonmel
Piltown
Mullinavat
Ballynabola
Wexford
Wexford Harbour
Killinaspick
Fiddown
Kilmacow
Foulkesmill
Taghmon
Carrickbeg
Rathgormuck
Portlaw
Mooncoin
Comeragh Mts.
Monavullagh Mts.
Clonea
Campile
Waddington
Rosslare
Waterford
Kilmeadan
Arthurstown
Wellingtonbridge
Rosslare Harbour
Greenore Pt.
Killinick
Tintern Abbey
Duncormick
Bridgetown
Kilmacthomas
Adamstown
Passage East
Broadway
Kilbrien
Fethard
Bannow
Bannow Bay
Kilmore
Tacumshin L.
Churchtown
Lemybrien
Ballylaneen
Kill
Tramore
Dunmore East
Crossfarnoge Pt.
Kilmore Quay
Lady's I. Lake
Carnsore Pt.
Stradbally
Bunmahon
Annestown
Baginbun Hd.
Hook Hd.
Saltee Is.
Dungarvan Harbour
Tramore Bay
Waterford Harbour
Lough Owel
L. Iron
Royal Canal
Grand Canal
Boyne
Liffey
Barrow
Nore
Slaney
Suir
Avoca
Vartry Res.
DOUGLAS 2:45 (April-Sept)
HOLYHEAD 1:49
LIVERPOOL 7:45
HOLYHEAD 1:40
FISHGUARD 3:30
PEMBROKE 3:45
CHERBOURG 17:30 (Mar-Dec)
ROSCOFF 15:00 (May-Sept)
53°N
6°W
7°W

Belfast

0 Miles ¼

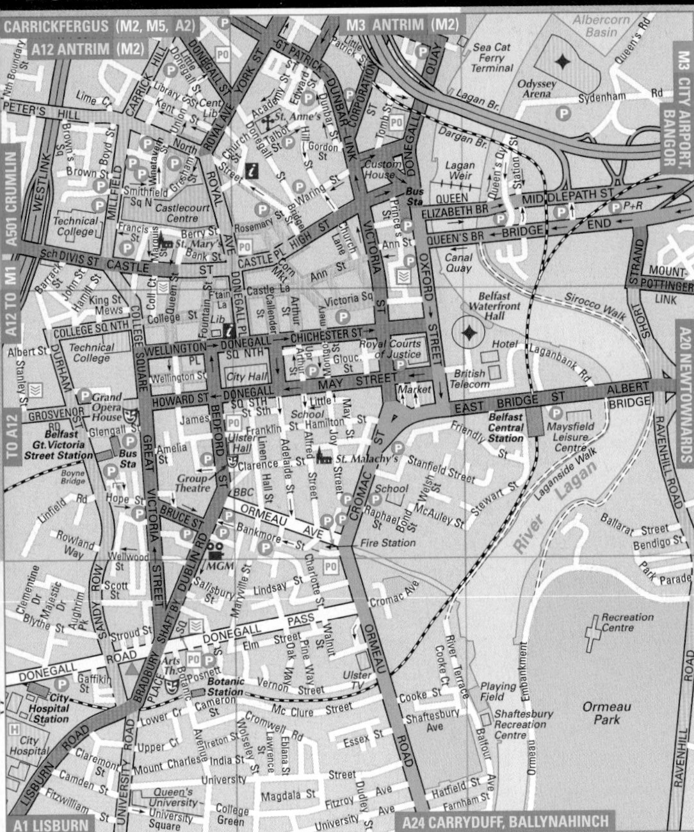

Cork

0 Miles ¼

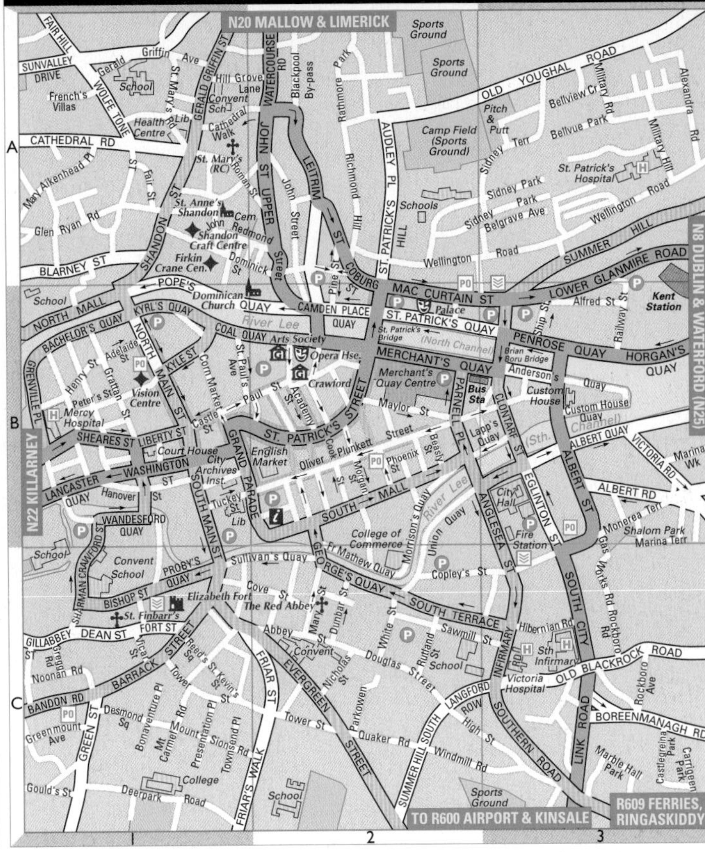

Belfast

Academy St A2
Adelaide St B2
Albert Bridge B3
Albert St B1
Alfred St B2
Amelia St B1
Ann St A2
Arthur St B2
Arts Theatre C1
Aughrim Park C1
Balfour Ave C3
Ballarat St B3
Bank St A1
Bankmore St B2
Barrack St A1
BBC B2
Bedford St B1
Belfast Great Victoria Street Station B1
Belfast Central Station B3
Belfast Waterfront Hall ✦ B3
Bendigo St B3
Berry St A1
Blythe St C1
Bond St B2
Botanic Ave C1
Botanic Station C1
Boyd St A1
Boyne Bridge B1
Bradbury Pl C1
Bridge End A3
Bridge St A2
British Telecom B3
Brown St A1
Brown's Sq A1
Bruce St B1
Bus Station B1
Callender St B2
Camden St C1
Cameron St C1
Canal Quay A2
Carrick Hill A1
Castle La B2
Castle Pl A2
Castle St A1
Castlecourt Centre A1
Central Library A1
Charlotte St C2
Chichester St B2
Church La A2
Church St A2
Cinema (MGM) B1
City Hall B2
City Hospital C1
City Hospital Station C1
Claremont St C1
Clarence St B2
Clementine Dr C1
College Court B1
College Green C1
College Sq North B1
College Sq B1
College St B1
Cooke Court C2
Cooke St C2
Corn Market A2
Corporation St A2
Cromac Ave C2
Cromac St B2
Cromwell Rd C2
Custom House A2
Dargan Bridge A2
Divis St A1
Donegall Pass C1/C2
Donegall Pl A2
Donegall Quay A2
Donegall Rd C1
Donegall Sq North B2
Donegall Sq South B2
Donegall St A1
Dublin Rd B1
Dudley St C2
Dunbar Link A2
Dunbar St A2
Durham St B1
East Bridge St B3
Eblana St C2
Edward St A2
Elm St C2
Essex St C2
Farnham St C2
Fire Station B2
Fitzroy Ave C2
Fitzwilliam St C1
Fountain La B1
Fountain St B1
Francis St A1
Franklin St B1
Friendly St B3
Gaffikin St C1
Glengall St B1
Gloucester St B2
Gordon St A2
Grand Opera House B1
Great Patrick St A2
Great Victoria St B1
Gresham St A1
Grosvenor Rd B1
Group Theatre B1
Hamill St B1
Hamilton St B2
Hatfield St C2
High St A2
Hill St A2
Hope St B1
Howard St B1
India St C1
Information Ctr A2/B1
Ireton St C1
James St South B1
John St A1
Joy St B2
Kent St A1
King St Mews B1
Lagan Bridge A3
Lagan Weir A2
Laganbank Rd B3
Laganside Walk B3
Lawrence St C2
Library B1
Library St A1
Lime Court A1
Lindsay St C2
Linen Hall St B2
Linfield Rd B1
Lisburn Rd C1
Little Donegall St A1
Little May St B2
Little Patrick St A2
Lower Cr C1
McAuley St B2
McClure St C2
Magdala St C2
Majestic Dr C1
Market B2
Marquis St A1
Maryville St C2
May St B2
Maysfield Leisure Centre B3
Middlepath St A3
Millfield A1
Montgomery St B2
Mount Charles C1
Mountpottinger Link A3
North St A1
North Boundary St A1
Oak Way C2
Odyssey Arena ✦ A3
Ormeau Ave B2
Ormeau Embankment C3
Ormeau Park C3
Ormeau Rd C2
Oxford St A2
Park Pde B3
Peter's Hill A1
Pine Way C2
Police Station A1/A2/B1/C1
Posnett St C1
Post Office A2/B2/C1
Prince's St A2
Queen Elizabeth Bridge A2
Queen St A1
Queen's Bridge A2
Queen's Quay A3
Queen's Rd A3
Queen's University C1
Raphael St B2
Ravenhill Rd B3/C3
River Terr C2
Rosemary St A2
Rowland Way B1
Royal Ave A1
Royal Courts of Justice B2
St Anne's Cathedral ✝ A2
St Malachy's B2
St Mary's A1
Salisbury St C1
Sandy Row C1
Scott St C1
Sea Cat Ferry Terminal A3
Shaftesbury Sq C1
Shaftesbury Ave C2
Shaftesbury Recreation Centre C3
Short Strand B3
Sirocco Walk B3
Smithfield Sq North A1
Stanfield St B2
Stanley St B1
Station St A3
Stewart St B3
Stroud St C1
Sydenham Rd A3
Talbot St A2
Technical College A1/B1
Tomb St A2
Ulster Hall B2
Ulster Television C2
Union St A1
University Ave C2
University Rd C1
University Sq C1
University St C1/C2
Upper Cr C1
Upper Arthur St B2
Vernon St C1
Victoria Sq B2
Victoria St A2
Walnut St C2
Waring St A2
Wellington Pl B1
Wellington St B1
Wellwood St B1
Welsh St B2
Westlink A1
Winetavern St A1
Wolseley St C2
York St A2

Cork

Abbey St C2
Academy St B2
Adelaide St B1
Albert St B3
Albert Quay B3
Albert Rd B3
Alexandra Rd A3
Alfred St B3
Anderson's Quay B3
Anglesea St B3
Arts Society B2
Audley Pl A2
Bachelor's Quay B1
Bandon Rd C1
Barrack St C1
Beasly St B2
Belgrave Ave A3
Bellview Cr A3
Bellvue Park A3
Bishop St C1
Blackpool By-Pass A2
Blarney St A1
Bonaventure Pl C1
Boreenmanagh Rd C3
Brian Boru Bridge B3
Bus Station B2
Camden Pl Quay B2
Camp Field (Sports Ground) A2
Carrigeen Park C3
Castle St B1
Castlegreina Park C3
Cathedral Rd A1
Cathedral Walk A1
City Archives Institute B1
City Hall B3
Clontarf St B3
Coal Quay B1
Coburg St A2
College of Commerce C2
Convent C2
Cook St B2
Copley's St C2
Corn Market B1
Court House B1
Cove St C2
Crawford Gallery B2
Custom House B3
Custom House Quay B3
Dean St C1
Deerpark Rd C1
Desmond Sq C1
Dominican Church B1
Dominick St A1
Douglas St C2
Dunbar St C2
Eglinton St B3
Elizabeth Fort C1
English Market B2
Evergreen St C2
Fair Hill A1
Fair St A1
Father Mathew Quay C2
Fire Station B3
Firkin Crane Centre ✦ A1
Fort St C1
French's Villas A1
Friar St C2
Friar's Walk C1
Gas Works Rd C3
George's Quay C2
Gerald Griffin Ave A1
Gerald Griffin St A1
Gillabbey St C1
Glen Ryan Rd A1
Gould's St C1
Grand Pde B1
Grattan St B1
Green St C1
Greenmount Ave C1
Gregg Rd C1
Grenville Pl B1
Hanover St B1
Health Centre A1
Henry St B1
Hibernian Rd C3
High St C2
Hill Grove La A1
Horgan's Quay B3
Infirmary Rd C3
Information Ctr B2
John St A2
John St Upper A2
John Redmond St A1
Kent Station B3
Kyle St B1
Kyrl's Quay B1
Lancaster Quay B1
Langford Row C2
Lapp's Quay B3
Leitrim St A2
Liberty St B1
Library B1
Link Rd C3
Lower Glanmire Rd A3
Mac Curtain St B2
Marble Hall Park C3
Marina Terr B3
Marina Walk B3
Mary Aikenhead Pl A1
Mary St C2
Maylor St B2
Merchant's Quay B2
Merchant's Quay Centre B2
Mercy Hospital B1
Military Hill A3
Military Rd A3
Monerea Terr B3
Morgan St B2
Morrison's Quay B2
Mount Carmel Rd C1
Mount Sion Rd C1
Nicholas St C2
Noonan Rd C1
North Main St B1
North Mall B1
Old Blackrock Rd C3
Old Youghal Rd A3
Oliver Plunkett St B2
Opera House B2
Palace Theatre B2
Parkowen C2
Parnell Pl B2
Paul St B1
Penrose Quay B3
Peter's St B1
Phoenix St B2
Pine St B2
Pitch & Putt A3
Police Station B3/C1/C3
Pope's Quay B1
Post Office B1/B2/B3/C1
Presentation Pl C1
Proby's Quay C1
Quaker Rd C2
Railway St B3
Rathmore Park A2
Red Abbey, The ✝ C2
Reed's Sq C1
Richmond Hill A2
Rockboro Ave C3
Rockboro Rd C3
Roman St A1
Rutland St C2
St Anne's Shandon A1
St Finbarr's ✝ C1
St Kevin's St C1
St Mary's A1
St Mary's Rd A1
St Patrick's Bridge B2
St Patrick's Hill A2
St Patrick's Hospital A3
St Patrick's Quay B2
St Patrick's St B2
St Paul's Ave B1
Sawmill St C2
Shalom Park B3
Shandon St A1
Shandon Craft Centre ✦ A1
Sharman Crawford St C1
Sheares St B1
Ship St B3
Sidney Park A2
Sidney Terr A3
South City C3
South Infirmary C3
South Main St B1
South Mall B2
South Terr C2
Southern Rd C3
Sullivan's Quay C1
Summer Hill A3
Summer Hill South C2
Sunvalley Dr A1
Tower St C1/C2
Townsend Pl C1
Tuckey St B1
Union Quay C2
Vicar St C1
Victoria Hospital C3
Victoria Rd B3
Vision Centre ✦ B1
Wandesford Quay B1
Washington St B1
Watercourse Rd A2
Wellington Rd A2/A3
White St C2
Windmill Rd C2
Wolfe Tone St A1

Derry/Londonderry

0 Miles ¼

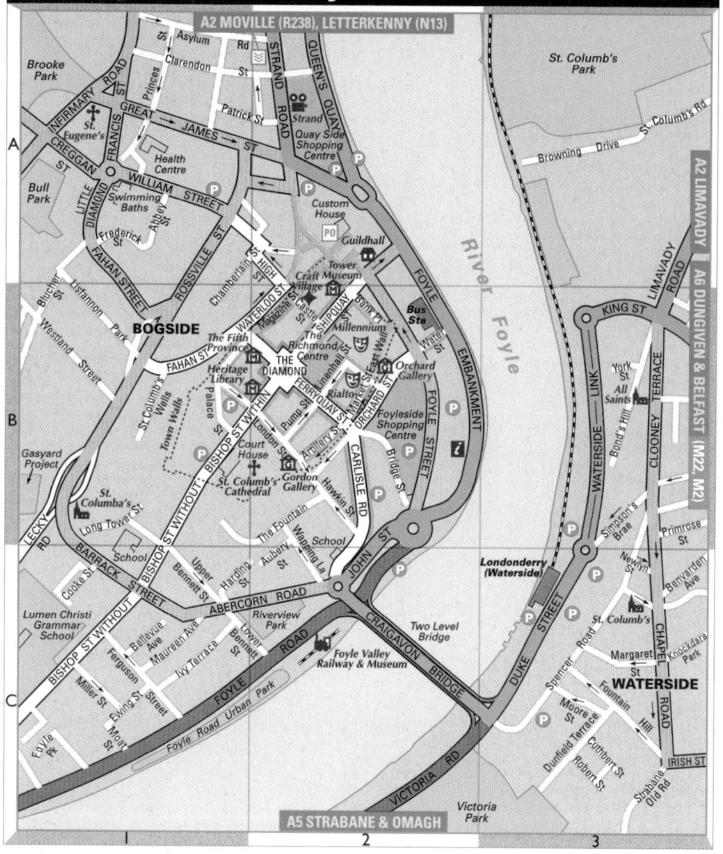

Dublin

0 Miles ¼

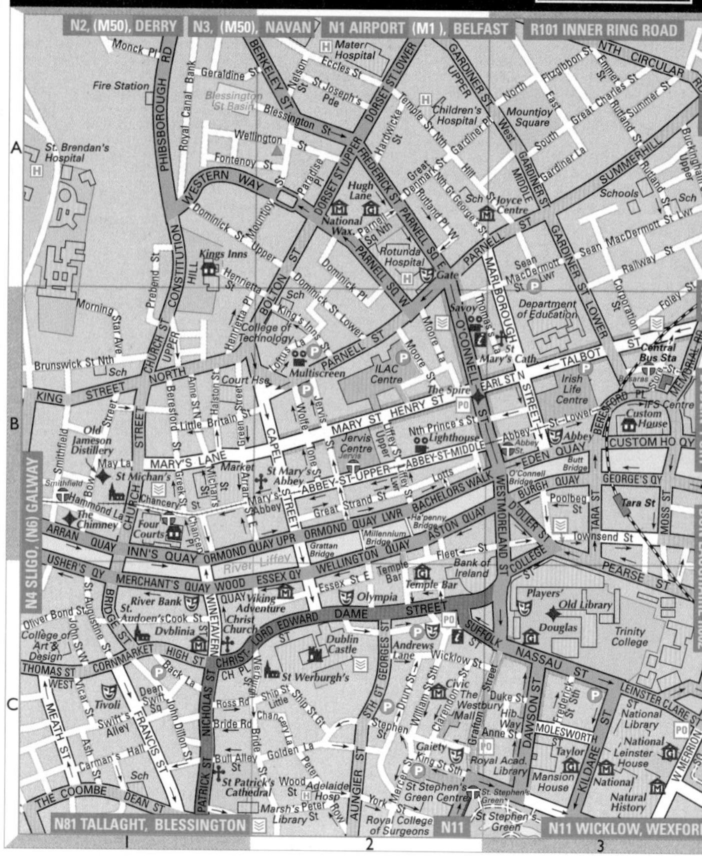

Derry/ Londonderry

- Abbey St . . . A1
- Abercorn Rd . . . C1
- All Saints . . . B3
- Artillery St . . . B2
- Asylum Rd . . . A1
- Aubery St . . . C2
- Bank Pl . . . A2
- Barrack St . . . C1
- Bellevue Ave . . . C1
- Benvarden Ave . . . C3
- Bishop St Within . . . B1
- Bishop St Without . B1/C1
- Blucher St . . . B1
- Bond's Hill . . . B3
- Bridge St . . . B2
- Brooke Park . . . A1
- Browning Dr . . . A3
- Bull Park . . . A1
- Bus Station . . . B2
- Carlisle Rd . . . B2
- Castle St . . . B2
- Chamberlain St . . . A1
- Chapel Rd . . . C3
- Clarendon St . . . A1
- Clooney Terr . . . B3
- Cooke St . . . C1
- Court House . . . B1
- Craft Village ✦ . . . B2
- Craigavon Bridge . . . C1
- Creggan St . . . A1
- Custom House . . . A2
- Cuthbert St . . . C3
- Duke St . . . C2
- Dunfield Terr . . . C3
- East Wall . . . B2
- Ewing St . . . C1
- Fahan St . . . A1
- Ferguson St . . . C1
- Ferryquay St . . . B2
- Fifth Province, The . B1
- Fountain Hill . . . C3
- Foyle Embankment . . . A2
- Foyle Park . . . C1
- Foyle Rd Urban Park . . C1
- Foyle St . . . B2
- Foyle Valley Railway & Museum . . . C2
- Foyleside Shopping Centre . . . B2
- Francis St . . . A1
- Frederick St . . . A1
- Gasyard Project . . . B1
- Gordon Gallery . . . B2
- Great James St . . . A1
- Guildhall . . . A2
- Harding St . . . C1
- Hawkin St . . . B2
- Health Centre . . . A1
- Heritage Library . . . B1
- High St . . . A2
- Infirmary Rd . . . A1
- Information Ctr . . . B2
- Irish St . . . C3
- Ivy Terr . . . C1
- John St . . . C2
- King St . . . B3
- Knockdara Park . . . C3
- Lecky Rd . . . B1
- Limavady Rd . . . A3
- Linenhall St . . . B2
- Lisfannon Park . . . B1
- Little Diamond St . . . A1
- London St . . . B2
- Long Tower St . . . B1
- Lower Bennett St . . . C1
- Lumen Christi Grammar School . . . C1
- Magazine St . . . A2
- Margaret St . . . C3
- Market St . . . B2
- Maureen Ave . . . C1
- Millennium Theatre . B2
- Miller St . . . C1
- Moat St . . . C1
- Moore St . . . C3
- Newlyn St . . . C3
- Orchard Gallery . . . B2
- Orchard St . . . B2
- Palace St . . . B1
- Patrick St . . . A1
- Police Station . . . A2
- Post Office . . . A2
- Primrose St . . . B3
- Princes St . . . A1
- Pump St . . . B2
- Quay Side Shopping Centre . . . A2
- Queen's Quay . . . A2
- Rialto Theatre . . . B2
- Richmond Centre, The . . . B2
- Riverview Park . . . C2
- Robert St . . . C3
- Rossville St . . . A1
- St Columb's . . . C3
- St Columb's Cathedral ✝ . . . B2
- St Columb's Park . . . A3
- St Columb's Rd . . . A3
- St Columb's Wells . . . B1
- St Columba's . . . B1
- St Eugene's Cathedral ✝ . . . A1
- Shipquay . . . B2
- Simpson's Brae . . . B3
- Spencer Rd . . . C3
- Strabane Old Rd . . . C3
- Strand . . . A2
- Strand Rd . . . A2
- Swimming Baths . . . A1
- The Diamond . . . B2
- The Fountain . . . B2
- Tower Museum . . . A2
- Town Walls . . . B1
- Two Level Bridge . . . C2
- Upper Bennett St . . . C1
- Victoria Park . . . C2
- Victoria Rd . . . C2
- Wapping La . . . B2
- Water St . . . B2
- Waterloo St . . . A2
- Londonderry (Waterside) . . . C3
- Waterside Link . . . B3
- William St . . . A1
- York St . . . B3

Dublin

- Abbey St Lower . . . B3
- Abbey St Middle . . . B2
- Abbey St Upper . . . B2
- Abbey Theatre . . . B3
- Adelaide Hospital . . C2
- Andrews Lane Theatre . . . C2
- Anne St . . . C3
- Anne St North . . . B1
- Arran Quay . . . B1
- Arran St East . . . B1
- Ash St . . . C1
- Aston Quay . . . B2
- Aungier St . . . C2
- Bachelors Walk . . . B2
- Back La . . . C1
- Bank of Ireland . . . B2
- Beresford Pl . . . B3
- Beresford St . . . B1
- Berkeley St . . . A2
- Blessington St . . . A2
- Blessington St Basin . . A1
- Bolton St . . . B2/A2
- Bow St . . . B1
- Bride Rd . . . C1
- Bride St . . . C2
- Bridge St . . . C1
- Brunswick St North . . . B1
- Buckingham St Upper . A3
- Bull Alley St . . . C1
- Burgh Quay . . . B3
- Butt Bridge . . . B3
- Capel St . . . B2
- Carman's Hall . . . C1
- Central Bus Station . . . B3
- Chancery La . . . C2
- Chancery Pl . . . B1
- Chancery St . . . B1
- Children's Hospital . A2
- Chimney, The ✦ . . . B1
- Christ Church Cathedral ✝ . . . C1
- Christchurch Pl . . . C1
- Church St Upper . . . B1
- Church St . . . B1
- Civic Museum . . . C2
- Clare St . . . C3
- Clarendon St . . . C2
- College of Art & Design . . . C1
- College of Technology . B1
- College St . . . B3
- Constitution Hill . . . A1/B1
- Cook St . . . C1
- Cornmarket . . . C1
- Corporation St . . . A3
- Court House . . . B1
- Custom House . . . B3
- D'Olier St . . . B3
- Dame St . . . C2
- Dawson St . . . C3
- Dean St . . . C1
- Dean Swift Sq . . . C1
- Department of Education . . . B3
- Dominick Pl . . . A2
- Dominick St Lower . . . B2
- Dominick St Upper . . . A1
- Dorset St Lower . . . A2
- Dorset St Upper . . . A2
- Douglas Art Gallery . C3
- Drury St . . . C2
- Dublin Castle . . . C2
- Duke St . . . C3
- Dvblinia . . . C1
- Earl St North . . . B3
- Eccles St . . . A2
- Eden Quay . . . B3
- Emmet St . . . A3
- Essex Quay . . . C2
- Essex St East . . . C2
- Fitzgibbon St . . . A3
- Fleet St . . . B2
- Foley St . . . B3
- Fontenoy St . . . A1
- Four Courts . . . B1
- Francis St . . . C1
- Frederick St . . . A2
- Frederick St South . . . C3
- Gaiety Theatre . . . C2
- Gardiner La . . . A3
- Gardiner Pl . . . A2
- Gardiner St Lower . A3/B3
- Gardiner St Middle . . . A3
- Gardiner St Upper . . . A2
- Gate Theatre . . . A2
- George's Quay . . . B3
- Geraldine St . . . A1
- Golden La . . . C2
- Grafton St . . . C2
- Grattan Bridge . . . B2
- Great Charles St . . . A3
- Great Denmark St . . . A2
- Great Strand St . . . B2
- Greek St . . . B1
- Green St . . . B1
- Ha'penny Bridge . . . B2
- Halston St . . . B1
- Hammond La . . . B1
- Hardwicke St . . . A2
- Henrietta Pl . . . B1
- Henrietta St . . . A1
- Henry St . . . B2
- Hibernian Way . . . C3
- High St . . . C1
- Hill St . . . A2
- Hugh Lane Gallery . A2
- ILAC Centre . . . B2
- Information Ctr . B2/C2
- Inn's Quay . . . B1
- International Financial Services Centre . . . B3
- Irish Life Centre . . . B3
- Jervis St . . . B2
- John Dillon St . . . C1
- John St West . . . C1
- Joyce Centre . . . A2
- Kildare St . . . C3
- King St South . . . C2
- King St North . . . B1
- King's Inns St . . . B2
- Kings Inns . . . A1
- Leinster House . . . C3
- Leinster St . . . C3
- Liffey St Lower . . . B2
- Liffey St Upper . . . B2
- Lighthouse Cinema . B2
- Little Britain St . . . B1
- Loftus La . . . B2
- Lord Edward St . . . C2
- Lotts . . . B2
- Mansion House . . . C3
- Marlborough St . . . B3
- Marsh's Library . . . C2
- Mary St . . . B2
- Mary's Abbey . . . B2
- Mary's La . . . B1
- Mater Hospital . . . A2
- May La . . . B1
- Meath St . . . C1
- Memorial Rd . . . B3
- Mercer St . . . C2
- Merchant's Quay . . . C1
- Millennium Bridge . . . B2
- Molesworth St . . . C3
- Monck Pl . . . A1
- Moore La . . . B2
- Moore St . . . B2
- Morning Star Ave . . . B1
- Moss St . . . B3
- Mountjoy Sq . . . A3
- Mountjoy St . . . A1
- Multiscreen Cinema . . . B2
- Nassau St . . . C3
- National Gallery . . . C3
- Natural History Museum . . . C3
- National Library . . . C3
- National Museum . . C3
- National Wax Museum . . . A2
- Nelson St . . . A2
- Nicholas St . . . C1
- North Circular Rd . . . A3
- North Great George's St . . . A2
- North Prince's St . . . B2
- O'Connell St . . . B2
- O'Connell Bridge . . . B3
- Old Jameson Distillery ✦ . . . B1
- Old Library ✦ . . . C3
- Oliver Bond St . . . C1
- Olympia Theatre . . . C2
- Ormond Quay Lower . . B2
- Ormond Quay Upper . . . B1/B2
- Paradise Pl . . . A2
- Parnell Sq East . . . A2
- Parnell Sq North . . . A2
- Parnell Sq West . . . A2
- Parnell St . . . A2/B2
- Patrick St . . . C1
- Pearse St . . . C3
- Peter Row . . . C2
- Peter St . . . C2
- Phibsborough Rd . . . A1
- Players' Theatre . . . C3
- Police Station . . . B1/B2/B3/C2
- Poolbeg St . . . B3
- Post Office . . B2/C2/C3
- Prebend St . . . B1
- Railway St . . . A3
- River Bank Theatre . C
- Ross Rd . . . C
- Rotunda Hospital . . A
- Royal Academy Library C
- Royal Canal Bank . . . A
- Royal College of Surgeons . . . C
- Rutland Pl West . . . A
- Rutland St . . . A
- St Audoen's . . . C
- St Augustine St . . . C
- St Brendan's Hospital . . . A
- St Joseph's Pde . . . A
- St Mary's Abbey ✝ . . . B
- St Mary's Cathedral ✝ . B
- St Michan's . . . B1
- St Michan's St . . . B1
- St Patrick's Cathedral ✝ . . . C1
- St Stephen's Green . . . C
- St Stephen's Green Centre . . . C2
- St Werburgh's . . . C2
- Savoy . . . B2
- Sean Macdermott St Lower . . . A3
- Ship St Great . . . C2
- Ship St Little . . . C2
- Smithfield . . . B1
- Spire, The ✦ . . . B2
- Stephen St . . . C2
- South Great Georges St . . . C2
- Store St . . . B3
- Suffolk St . . . C2
- Summer St . . . A3
- Summerhill . . . A3
- Swift's Alley . . . C1
- Talbot St . . . B3
- Tara St . . . B3
- Tara Street Station . . . B3
- Taylor Gallery . . . C3
- Temple Bar . . . C2
- Temple Bar Gallery . C2
- Temple St North . . . A2
- The Coombe . . . C1
- Thomas St West . . . C1
- Thomas's La . . . B2
- Tivoli Theatre . . . C1
- Townsend St . . . B3
- Trinity College . . . C3
- Usher's Quay . . . C1
- Vicar St . . . C1
- Viking Adventure . . . C2
- Wellington Quay . . . B2
- Wellington St . . . A1
- Werburgh St . . . C2
- West Merrion Sq . . . C3
- Westbury Mall, The . . . C2
- Western Way . . . A1/A2
- Westmoreland St . . . B3
- Wicklow St . . . C2
- William St South . . . C2
- Winetavern St . . . C1
- Wolfe Tone St . . . B2
- Wood Quay . . . C1
- Wood St . . . C2
- York St . . . C2

A

Abbey Galway 249 C6
Abbeydorney Kerry 250 B3
Abbeyfeale Limerick 250 B4
Abbeyleix Laois 252 C2
Abington Limerick 251 A6
Achill Mayo 248 B3
Aclare Sligo 249 A5
Acton Armagh 247 C6
Adamstown Waterford 252 D2
Adare Limerick 251 A5
Adcarn Roscommon 249 B6
Adrigole Cork 250 C3
Aghagower Mayo 248 B4
Aghalee Antrim 247 B6
Aghavannagh Wicklow 252 C4
Aghaville Cork 250 C4
Aghern Cork 251 B6
Aghnacliff Longford 249 B7
Aglish Waterford 251 B7
Ahascragh Galway 249 C6
Ahoghill Antrim 247 B6
Allen Kildare 252 B3
Allenwood Kildare 252 B3
Allihies Cork 250 C2
An Geata Mór Mayo 248 A2
Anacotty Limerick 251 A5
Anascaul Kerry 250 B2
Annacarty Tipperary 251 A6
Annacloy Down 247 C7
Annagassan Louth 247 D6
Annahilt Down 247 C7
Annalong Down 247 C7
Annestown Waterford 252 D2
Antrim Antrim 247 B6
Araglin Tipperary 251 B6
Arboe Tyrone 247 B5
Ardagh Limerick 250 B4
Ardagh Longford 249 B7
Ardahy Monaghan 247 C5
Ardara Donegal 246 B2
Ardcath Meath 252 A4
Ardcrony Tipperary 249 D6
Ardee Louth 247 D5
Ardfert Kerry 250 B3
Ardfinnane Tipperary 251 B7
Ardglass Down 247 C7
Ardgroom Cork 250 C3
Ardkearagh Kerry 250 C2
Ardkeen Down 247 C7
Ardmore Galway 248 C3
Ardmore Waterford 251 C7
Ardnacrusha Clare 251 A5
Ardnamona Donegal 246 B2
Ardnaree Mayo 248 A4
Ardnasodan Galway 249 C5
Ardpatrick Limerick 251 B5
Ardrahan Galway 249 C5
Ardreagh Londonderry 247 A5
Ardscull Kildare 252 B3
Ardstraw Tyrone 246 B4
Arklow Wicklow 252 C4
Arless Laois 252 C2
Armagh Armagh 247 C5
Armoy Antrim 247 A6
Arney Fermanagh 246 C3
Arthurstown Wexford 252 D3
Articlave Londonderry 247 A5
Artigarvan Tyrone 246 B4
Arvagh Cavan 249 B7
Ashbourne Meath 252 A4
Ashford Wicklow 252 B4
Ashville Louth 247 D5
Askeaton Limerick 251 A5
Astee Kerry 250 A3
Athboy Meath 252 A3
Athea Limerick 250 B4
Athenry Galway 249 C5
Athlacca Limerick 251 B5
Athleague Roscommon 249 B6
Athlone Westmeath 249 C7
Athy Kildare 252 C3
Attical Down 247 C6
Attymon Galway 249 C5
Aucloggeen Galway 249 C5
Augher Tyrone 246 C4
Aughnacloy Tyrone 247 C5
Aughrim Clare 249 C5
Aughrim Galway 249 C6
Aughrim Wicklow 252 C4
Avoca Wicklow 252 C4

B

Bailieborough Cavan 247 D5
Balbriggan Dublin 252 A4
Baldoyle Dublin 252 B4
Balla Mayo 248 B4
Ballagh Galway 248 C4
Ballagh Limerick 250 B4
Ballagh Tipperary 251 A7
Ballaghaderreen Roscommon 249 B5
Ballickmoyler Laois 252 C2
Ballin Cloher Kerry 250 B3
Ballina Mayo 248 A4
Ballina Tipperary 251 A6
Ballinadee Cork 251 C5
Ballinafad Sligo 246 C2
Ballinagar Offaly 252 B2
Ballinakill Laois 252 C2
Ballinalack Westmeath 252 A2
Ballinalea Wicklow 252 B4
Ballinalee Longford 249 B7
Ballinamallard Fermanagh 246 C3
Ballinameen Roscommon 249 B6
Ballinamore Leitrim 246 C3
Ballinamore Bridge Galway 249 C6
Ballinascarty Cork 251 C5
Ballinasloe Galway 249 C6
Ballincollig Cork 251 C5
Ballincurrig Cork 251 C6
Ballindaggan Wexford 252 C3
Ballinderreen Galway 249 C5
Ballinderry Tipperary 249 C6
Ballinderry Upr. Antrim 247 B6
Ballindine Mayo 249 B5
Ballindooly Galway 248 C4
Ballineen Cork 251 C5
Ballingarry Limerick 251 B5
Ballingarry Tipperary 251 A7
Ballingarry Tipperary 249 C6
Ballingeary Cork 250 C4
Ballinhassig Cork 251 C5
Ballinlea Antrim 247 A6
Ballinlough Roscommon 249 B5
Ballinrobe Mayo 248 B4
Ballinskelligs Kerry 250 C2
Ballinspittle Cork 251 C5
Ballintober Mayo 248 B4
Ballintober Roscommon 249 B6
Ballintoy Antrim 247 A6
Ballintra Donegal 246 B2
Ballintrohan Donegal 246 A4
Ballinunty Tipperary 251 A7
Ballinure Tipperary 251 A7
Ballitore Kildare 252 B3
Ballivor Meath 252 A3
Ballon Carlow 252 C3
Ballure Donegal 246 B2
Ballyagran Limerick 251 B5
Ballybay Monaghan 247 C5
Ballybofey Donegal 246 B3
Ballyboghil Dublin 252 A4
Ballybogy Antrim 247 A5
Ballybritt Offaly 249 C7
Ballybrittas Laois 252 B2
Ballybrophy Laois 249 D7
Ballybunion Kerry 250 A3
Ballycahill Tipperary 251 A7
Ballycanew Wexford 252 C4
Ballycarney Wexford 252 C3
Ballycarry Antrim 247 B7
Ballycastle Mayo 248 A4
Ballycastle Antrim 247 A6
Ballyclare Antrim 247 B7
Ballyclerahan Tipperary 251 B7
Ballyclogh Cork 251 B5
Ballycolla Laois 252 C2
Ballyconneely Galway 248 C2
Ballyconnell Cavan 246 C3
Ballyconnell Sligo 246 C1
Ballycotton Cork 251 C6
Ballycrossaun Galway 249 C6
Ballycroy Mayo 248 A3
Ballycumber Offaly 249 C7
Ballydangan Roscommon 249 C6
Ballydavid Galway 249 C6
Ballydavid Kerry 250 B2
Ballydavis Laois 252 B2
Ballydehob Cork 250 C4
Ballydonegan Cork 250 C2
Ballyduff Kerry 250 B3
Ballyduff Waterford 251 B6
Ballydugan Down 247 C7
Ballyfarnan Roscommon 246 C2
Ballyferriter Kerry 250 B2
Ballyfin Laois 252 B2
Ballyforan Roscommon 249 C6
Ballygar Galway 249 B6
Ballygarrett Wexford 252 C4
Ballygawley Sligo 246 C2
Ballygawley Tyrone 246 C4
Ballyglass Mayo 248 B4
Ballygorman Donegal 246 A4
Ballygowan Down 247 B7
Ballyhaght Limerick 251 B5
Ballyhahill Limerick 250 A4
Ballyhaise Cavan 246 C4
Ballyhalbert Down 247 C8
Ballyhale Galway 248 C4
Ballyhaunis Mayo 249 B5
Ballyhean Mayo 248 B4
Ballyheige Kerry 250 B3
Ballyhooly Cork 251 B6
Ballyhornan Down 247 C7
Ballyjamesduff Cavan 246 D4
Ballykelly Londonderry 246 A4
Ballykillin Donegal 246 A4
Ballylanders Limerick 251 B6
Ballylaneen Waterford 252 D2
Ballyliffin Donegal 246 A4
Ballylongford Kerry 250 A4
Ballylooby Tipperary 251 B7
Ballylynan Laois 252 C2
Ballymacarbry Waterford 251 B7
Ballymacoda Cork 251 C7
Ballymagorry Tyrone 246 B4
Ballymahon Longford 249 B7
Ballymakenny Louth 247 D6
Ballymartin Down 247 C7
Ballymena Antrim 247 B6
Ballymoe Galway 249 B6
Ballymoney Antrim 247 A5
Ballymore Westmeath 249 C7
Ballymore Eustace Kildare 252 B3
Ballymote Sligo 246 C1
Ballymullakill Roscommon 249 C6
Ballymurphy Carlow 252 C3
Ballymurray Roscommon 249 B6
Ballynabola Wexford 252 D3
Ballynacally Clare 250 A4
Ballynacarrigy Westmeath 249 B7
Ballynacorra Cork 251 C6
Ballynagore Westmeath 252 B2
Ballynahinch Down 247 C7
Ballynahown Westmeath 249 C7
Ballynamona Cork 251 B5
Ballynamult Waterford 251 B7
Ballyneety Limerick 251 A5
Ballynure Antrim 247 B7
Ballyporeen Tipperary 251 B6
Ballyragget Kilkenny 252 C2
Ballyroan Laois 252 C2
Ballyroe Cork 251 B6
Ballyronan Londonderry 247 B5
Ballyroney Down 247 C6
Ballysadare Sligo 246 C1
Ballyshannon Donegal 246 C2
Ballyshannon Kildare 252 B3
Ballyshrule Galway 249 C6
Ballysloe Tipperary 251 A7
Ballysteen Limerick 251 A5
Ballyvaghan Clare 248 C4
Ballyvourney Cork 250 B4
Ballyvoy Antrim 247 A6
Ballywalter Down 247 B8
Ballyward Down 247 C6
Ballywilliam Wexford 252 D3
Balrath Meath 252 A4
Balrothery Dublin 252 A4
Baltimore Cork 250 D4
Baltinglass Wicklow 252 C3
Baltracey Kildare 252 B3
Baltray Louth 252 A4
Banagher Offaly 249 C7
Banbridge Down 247 C6
Bandon Cork 251 C5
Bangor Mayo 248 A3
Bangor Down 247 B7
Bannow Wexford 252 D3
Banteer Cork 251 B5
Bantry Cork 250 C4
Baranailt Londonderry 246 B4
Barefield Clare 249 D5
Barna Galway 248 C4
Barnaderg Galway 249 B5
Barnesmore Donegal 246 B2
Barraduff Kerry 250 B4
Barran Cavan 246 C3
Batterstown Meath 252 B3
Bawnboy Cavan 246 C3
Bealin Westmeath 249 C7
Bealnablath Cork 251 C5
Beaufort Kerry 250 B3
Beech Hill Down 247 C6
Beelaha Clare 250 A3
Belclare Galway 249 C5
Belcoo Fermanagh 246 C3
Belderg Mayo 248 A3
Belfast Antrim 247 B7
Belgooly Cork 251 C6
Bellacorick Mayo 248 A3
Bellaghy Londonderry 247 B5
Bellahy Sligo 249 B5
Bellanagare Roscommon 249 B6
Bellanaleck Fermanagh 246 C3
Bellanamore Donegal 246 B2
Bellananagh Cavan 246 D4
Bellavary Mayo 248 B4
Belleek Donegal 246 C2
Belleek Armagh 247 C6
Belleville Galway 249 C5
Belmullet Mayo 248 A3
Beltra Mayo 248 B4
Beltra Sligo 246 C1
Belturbet Cavan 246 C4
Benburb Tyrone 247 C5
Bennettsbridge Kilkenny 252 C2
Beragh Tyrone 246 B4
Bessbrook Armagh 247 C6
Bettystown Meath 252 A4
Beville Mayo 248 A4
Birdhill Tipperary 251 A6
Birr Offaly 249 C7
Black Rock Louth 247 D6
Blackrock Dublin 252 B4
Blackwater Wexford 252 D4
Blanchardstown Dublin 252 B4
Blaney Fermanagh 246 C3
Blarney Cork 251 C5
Blessington Wicklow 252 B3
Bodyke Clare 249 D5
Boggaun Leitrim 246 C2
Boherahuca Offaly 249 C7
Boherboy Cork 250 B4
Boherlahan Tipperary 251 A7
Boho Fermanagh 246 C3
Bohola Mayo 248 B4
Bolea Londonderry 247 A5
Boley Kildare 252 B3
Borris Carlow 252 C3
Borris-in-Ossory Laois 249 D7
Borrisokane Tipperary 249 D6
Borrisoleigh Tipperary 251 A7
Bouladuff Tipperary 251 A7
Boyle Roscommon 249 B6
Bracklin Cavan 247 D5
Bracknagh Offaly 252 B2
Brandon Kerry 250 B2
Bray Wicklow 252 B4
Breaghva Clare 250 A3
Breedoge Roscommon 249 B6
Breenagh Donegal 246 B3
Brideswell Roscommon 249 C6
Bridge End Donegal 246 A4
Bridgetown Wexford 252 D3
Brittas Dublin 252 B4
Broadford Clare 251 A5
Broadford Limerick 251 B5
Broadway Wexford 252 D4
Brookeborough Fermanagh 246 C4
Broomfield Monaghan 247 C5
Broughderg Tyrone 247 B5
Broughshane Antrim 247 B6
Bruff Limerick 251 B5
Bruree Limerick 251 B5
Buggan Fermanagh 246 C3
Bullaun Galway 249 C5
Bunahowen Mayo 248 A3
Bunalunn Cork 250 C4
Bunaw Kerry 250 C3
Bunbeg Donegal 246 A2
Bunbrosna Westmeath 252 A2
Bunclody Wexford 252 C3
Buncrana Donegal 246 A4
Bundoran Donegal 246 C2
Bunmahon Waterford 252 D2
Bunnaglass Galway 249 C5
Bunnanaddan Sligo 246 C1
Bunnyconnellan Mayo 248 A4
Bunratty Clare 251 A5
Burnfoot Cork 251 B5
Burnfoot Donegal 246 A4
Burren Clare 248 C4
Burren Down 247 C6
Burtonport Donegal 246 B2
Bushmills Antrim 247 A5
Butler's Bridge Cavan 246 C4
Butlerstown Cork 251 C5
Buttevant Cork 251 B5
Bweeng Cork 251 B5

C

Cabinteely Dublin 252 B4
Cabragh Tyrone 247 C5
Cadamstown Offaly 249 C7
Caher Clare 249 D5
Caher Galway 248 C4
Caher Tipperary 251 B7
Caherciveen Kerry 250 C2
Caherconlish Limerick 251 A6
Caherdaniel Kerry 250 C2
Cahermore Cork 250 C2
Cahermurphy Clare 250 A4
Caledon Tyrone 247 C5
Callan Kilkenny 252 C2
Callow Galway 248 C2
Callow Mayo 248 B4
Calta Galway 249 C6
Camlough Armagh 247 C6
Camolin Wexford 252 C4
Camp Kerry 250 B3
Campile Wexford 252 D3
Camross Wexford 252 D3
Canningstown Cavan 246 D4
Cappagh Cork 251 B6
Cappagh Galway 249 C6
Cappagh White Tipperary 251 A6
Cappamore Limerick 251 A6
Cappeen Cork 251 C5
Cappoquin Waterford 251 B7
Carbury Kildare 252 B3
Carlanstown Meath 247 D5
Carlingford Louth 247 C6
Carlow Carlow 252 C3
Carna Galway 248 C3
Carnaross Meath 252 A3
Carncastle Antrim 247 B7
Carndonagh Donegal 246 A4
Carnew Wicklow 252 C4
Carney Sligo 246 C1
Carnlough Antrim 247 B7
Carracastle Mayo 249 B5
Carragh Kildare 252 B3
Carran Clare 248 C4
Carraroe Galway 248 C3
Carrick Donegal 246 B1
Carrick-on-Shannon Roscommon 249 B6
Carrick-on-Suir Tipperary 252 D2
Carrickart Donegal 246 A3
Carrickbeg Waterford 252 D2
Carrickboy Longford 249 B7
Carrickfergus Antrim 247 B7
Carrickmacross Monaghan 247 D5
Carrickmore Tyrone 246 B4
Carrigaholt Clare 250 A3
Carrigahorig Tipperary 249 C6
Carrigaline Cork 251 C6
Carrigallen Leitrim 249 B7
Carriganimmy Cork 250 C4
Carrigfadda Cork 250 C4
Carrigkerry Limerick 250 B4
Carrignavar Cork 251 C6
Carrigtohill Cork 251 C6
Carrowbehy Roscommon 249 B5
Carrowkeel Donegal 246 A3
Carrowkeel Donegal 246 A4
Carrowkeel Galway 249 C6
Carrowkennedy Mayo 248 B3
Carrowreagh Antrim 247 A6
Carrowreilly Sligo 246 C1
Carrowroe Longford 249 B7
Carryduff Down 247 B7
Cashel Galway 248 C3
Cashel Tipperary 251 A7
Castlebar Mayo 248 B4
Castlebellingham Louth 247 D6
Castleblakeney Galway 249 C6
Castleblaney Monaghan 247 C5
Castlebridge Wexford 252 D4
Castlecomer Kilkenny 252 C2
Castleconnell Limerick 251 A6
Castlecor Cork 251 B5
Castledawson Londonderry 247 B5
Castlederg Tyrone 246 B3
Castledermot Kildare 252 C3
Castlefinn Donegal 246 B3
Castlegregory Kerry 250 B2
Castlehill Mayo 248 A3
Castleisland Kerry 250 B4
Castlelyons Cork 251 B6
Castlemaine Kerry 250 B3
Castlemartyr Cork 251 C6
Castleplunket Roscommon 249 B6
Castlepollard Westmeath 252 A2
Castlerea Roscommon 249 B6
Castlerock Londonderry 247 A5
Castletown Laois 252 C2
Castletown Meath 247 D5
Castletown Bearhaven Cork 250 C3
Castletown Geoghegan Westmeath 252 B2
Castletownroche Cork 251 B6
Castletownshend Cork 250 C4
Castlewellan Down 247 C7
Causeway Kerry 250 B3
Cavan Cavan 246 D4
Cavangarden Donegal 246 B2
Celbridge Kildare 252 B3
Chanonrock Louth 247 D5
Charlemont Armagh 247 C5
Charlestown Mayo 249 B5
Charleville Cork 251 B5
Chasel Mayo 248 B3
Church Hill Donegal 246 B3
Church Hill Fermanagh 246 C3
Churchtown Cork 251 C6
Churchtown Wexford 252 D4
Clabby Fermanagh 246 C4
Clady Tyrone 246 B3
Clady Milltown Armagh 247 C5
Clanabogan Tyrone 246 B4
Clane Kildare 252 B3
Clara Offaly 249 C7
Clarahill Laois 252 B2
Clarecastle Clare 251 A5
Clareen Offaly 249 C7
Claregalway Galway 249 C5
Claremorris Mayo 249 B5
Claretuam Galway 249 C5
Clarina Limerick 251 A5
Clarinbridge Galway 249 C5
Clash Cork 251 C6
Clashmore Waterford 251 B7
Claudy Londonderry 246 B4
Cleady Kerry 250 C3
Cleggan Galway 248 B2
Clifden Galway 248 C2
Cliffony Sligo 246 C2
Clogh Kilkenny 252 C2
Clogh Antrim 247 B6
Cloghan Donegal 246 B3
Cloghan Offaly 249 C7
Cloghan Westmeath 252 A2
Cloghane Kerry 250 B2
Clogheaneely Donegal 246 A2
Cloghboy Donegal 246 B1
Clogheen Tipperary 251 B7
Clogher Roscommon 249 B6
Clogher Tyrone 246 C4
Clogher Head Louth 247 D6
Cloghjordan Tipperary 249 D6
Cloghran Dublin 252 B4
Cloghy Down 247 C8
Clomantagh Kilkenny 252 C2
Clonakilty Cork 251 C5
Clonaslee Laois 249 C7
Clonbulloge Offaly 252 B2
Clonbur Galway 248 B4
Cloncurry Kildare 252 B3
Clondalkin Dublin 252 B4
Clonea Waterford 252 D2
Clonee Meath 252 B4
Cloneen Tipperary 251 B7
Clonelly Fermanagh 246 B3
Clones Monaghan 246 C4
Cloney Kildare 252 B2
Clonfert Galway 249 C6
Clonlee Mayo 249 B5
Clonmacnoise Offaly 249 C7
Clonmany Donegal 246 A4
Clonmel Tipperary 251 B7
Clonmellon Westmeath 252 A2
Clonmore Carlow 252 C3
Clonmore Offaly 252 B2
Clonmore Tipperary 251 A7
Clonord Meath 252 B2
Clonroche Wexford 252 D3
Clontarf Dublin 252 B4
Cloodara Longford 249 B7
Clooncool Sligo 249 A5
Cloonart Longford 249 B7
Cloonbannin Cork 250 B4
Cloonboo Galway 248 C4
Cloone Leitrim 249 B7
Cloonfad Roscommon 249 B5
Cloonkeen Kerry 250 C4
Cloonlara Clare 251 A5
Cloonlogh Sligo 249 B6
Cloonmore Mayo 249 B5
Clorbern Galway 249 B5
Clough Down 247 C7
Cloyne Cork 251 C6
Coachford Cork 251 C5
Coagh Tyrone 247 B5
Coalisland Tyrone 247 B5
Cóbh Cork 251 C6
Colehill Longford 249 B7
Coleraine Londonderry 247 A5
Collinstown Westmeath 252 A2
Collon Louth 247 D6
Collooney Sligo 246 C2
Comber Down 247 B7
Commeen Donegal 246 B3
Cong Mayo 248 B4
Conlig Down 247 B7
Conna Cork 251 B6
Connagh Galway 249 D6
Connonagh Cork 250 C4
Connor Antrim 247 B6
Convoy Donegal 246 B3
Cookstown Tyrone 247 B5
Coola Sligo 246 C2
Coolaney Sligo 246 C1
Coolbaun Tipperary 249 D6
Coolderg Galway 249 B5
Coole Westmeath 252 A2
Coolgreany Wexford 252 C4
Coolmore Donegal 246 B2
Coolrain Laois 249 D7
Cooneen Fermanagh 246 C4
Cooraclare Clare 250 A4
Cootehill Cavan 246 C4
Corbally Laois 252 C2
Corbally Sligo 248 A4
Cordal Kerry 250 B4
Corgary Tyrone 246 B3
Cork Cork 251 C6
Corlea Longford 249 B7
Corlogh Mayo 248 A2
Cornafulla Roscommon 249 C7
Cornamona Galway 248 B4
Cornanagh Mayo 248 B4
Cornhaw Cavan 246 C3
Corranny Fermanagh 246 C4
Corrawalleen Leitrim 246 C3
Corrigeenroe Roscommon 246 C2
Corrofin Clare 248 D4
Corvally Monaghan 247 D5
Corvoy Monaghan 247 C5
Costelloe Galway 248 C3
Courtmacsherry Cork 251 C5
Courtown Wexford 252 C4
Craanford Wexford 252 C4
Craigavon Armagh 247 C6
Cranagh Tyrone 246 B4
Crataloe Limerick 250 B4
Craughwell Galway 249 C5
Creaghanroe Monaghan 247 C5
Creegh Clare 250 A4
Creeragh Mayo 248 A4
Creeslough Donegal 246 A3
Creeve Tyrone 247 B5
Creeves Limerick 250 A4
Creggan Tyrone 246 B4
Cregganbaun Mayo 248 B3
Creggs Galway 249 B6
Crindle Londonderry 247 A5
Crinkill Offaly 249 C7
Croagh Limerick 250 B4
Crockets Town Mayo 248 A4
Croghan Offaly 252 B2
Croghan Roscommon 249 B6
Crolly Donegal 246 A2
Crookedwood Westmeath 252 A2
Crookhaven Cork 250 D3
Crookstown Cork 251 C5
Croom Limerick 251 A5
Cross Barry Cork 251 C5
Cross Keys Meath 252 A3
Crossakiel Meath 252 A2
Crossdoney Cavan 246 D4
Crossgar Down 247 C7
Crosshaven Cork 251 C6
Crossmaglen Armagh 247 C5
Crossmolina Mayo 248 A4
Crumlin Dublin 252 B4
Crumlin Antrim 247 B6
Crusheen Clare 249 D5
Culdaff Donegal 246 A4
Cullaville Armagh 247 C5
Cullen Tipperary 251 A6
Cullinane Antrim 247 B6
Cullion Tyrone 246 B4
Cullyhanna Armagh 247 C5
Curraglass Cork 251 B6
Curry Sligo 249 B5
Curryglass Cork 250 C3
Cushendall Antrim 247 A6
Cushendun Antrim 247 A6
Cushina Offaly 252 B2

D

Dacklin Roscommon 249 B6
Daingean Offaly 252 B2
Dalkey Dublin 252 B4
Dalystown Galway 249 C6
Damerstown Kilkenny 252 C2
Darkley Armagh 247 C5
Darragh Clare 250 A4
Deelish Cork 250 C4
Delvin Westmeath 252 A2
Derry Sligo 246 C2
Derrybeg Donegal 246 A2
Derryboy Down 247 C7
Derrybrien Galway 249 C5
Derrycoosh Mayo 248 B4
Derrygonnelly Fermanagh 246 C3
Derrygorry Monaghan 246 C4
Derrygrogan Offaly 252 B2
Derrykeighan Antrim 247 A5
Derrylin Fermanagh 246 C3
Derrymore Kerry 250 B3
Derrynacreeve Cavan 246 C3
Derrynane Kerry 250 C2
Derryrush Galway 248 C3
Derrytrasna Armagh 247 B6
Derry = Londonderry Londonderry 246 B4
Dervock Antrim 247 A6
Desertmartin Londonderry 247 B5
Diamond Down 247 C6
Dingle Kerry 250 B2
Dirtagh Londonderry 247 A5
Doagh Antrim 247 B6
Dolla Tipperary 251 A6
Donabate Dublin 252 B4
Donadea Kildare 252 B3
Donagh Fermanagh 246 C4
Donaghadee Down 247 B7
Donaghmore Laois 249 D7
Donaghmore Tyrone 247 B5
Donard Wicklow 252 B3
Donegal Donegal 246 B2
Doneraile Cork 251 B5
Donohill Tipperary 251 A6
Donore Meath 252 A4
Donoughmore Cork 251 C5
Dooagh Mayo 248 B2
Doocharry Donegal 246 B2
Doogary Cavan 246 C3
Doogort Mayo 248 A2
Dooish Tyrone 246 B4
Doolin Clare 248 C4
Doon Limerick 251 A6
Doonaha Clare 250 A3
Doonbeg Clare 250 A3
Douglas Cork 251 C6
Downhill Londonderry 247 A5
Downies Donegal 246 A3
Downpatrick Down 247 C7
Dowra Cavan 246 C2
Drangan Tipperary 251 A7
Draperstown Londonderry 247 B5
Dreenagh Kerry 250 B3
Drimoleague Cork 250 C4
Drinagh Cork 250 C4
Dripsey Cork 251 C5
Drogheda Louth 252 A4
Dromahair Leitrim 246 C2
Dromara Down 247 C6
Dromard Sligo 246 C1
Dromcolliher Limerick 251 B5
Dromin Louth 247 D6
Dromina Cork 251 B5
Dromineer Tipperary 249 D6
Dromiskin Louth 247 D6
Dromkeen Limerick 251 A6
Dromod Leitrim 249 B7
Dromore Down 247 C6
Dromore Tyrone 246 B4
Dromore West Sligo 249 A5
Drum Monaghan 246 C4
Drumaduff Londonderry 247 B5
Drumahoe Londonderry 246 B4
Drumakilly Tyrone 246 B4
Drumbad Longford 249 B7
Drumbadmeen Fermanagh 246 C3
Drumbear Monaghan 247 C5
Drumbeg Donegal 246 B3
Drumbeg Down 247 B7
Drumbilla Louth 247 C6
Drumbo Monaghan 247 D5
Drumcard Fermanagh 246 C3
Drumcliff Sligo 246 C1
Drumcondra Dublin 252 B4
Drumcondra Meath 247 D5
Drumcoo Monaghan 246 C4
Drumcree Westmeath 252 A2
Drumdallagh Antrim 247 A6
Drumfin Sligo 246 C2
Drumfree Donegal 246 A4
Drumkeeran Leitrim 246 C2
Drumlegagh Tyrone 246 B4
Drumlish Longford 249 B7
Drumnacross Donegal 246 B3
Drumquin Tyrone 246 B4
Drumramer Londonderry 247 A5
Drumsallan Armagh 247 C5
Drumsaragh Londonderry 247 B5
Drumshanbo Leitrim 246 C2
Drumskinny Fermanagh 246 B3
Drumsna Leitrim 249 B6
Drumsurn Londonderry 247 A5
Dublin Dublin 252 B4
Duleek Meath 252 A4
Dun Laoghaire Dublin 252 B4
Dunaff Donegal 246 A4
Dunboyne Meath 252 B4
Duncormick Wexford 252 D3
Dundalk Louth 247 C6
Dunderrow Cork 251 C5
Dunderry Meath 252 A3
Dundonald Down 247 B7
Dundrod Antrim 247 B6
Dundrum Dublin 252 B4
Dundrum Tipperary 251 A6
Dundrum Down 247 C7
Dunfanaghy Donegal 246 A3
Dungannon Tyrone 247 B5
Dungarvan Waterford 251 B7
Dungiven Londonderry 247 B5
Dunglow Donegal 246 B2
Dungourney Cork 251 C6
Dunheeda Meath 247 D5
Dunkerrin Offaly 249 D7
Dunkineely Donegal 246 B2
Dunlavin Wicklow 252 B3
Dunleer Louth 247 D6
Dunloy Antrim 247 A6
Dunmanway Cork 250 C4
Dunmore Galway 249 B5
Dunmore East Waterford 252 D3
Dunmurry Antrim 247 B6
Dunnamanagh Tyrone 246 B4
Dunsany Meath 252 A3
Dunshaughlin Meath 252 A3
Durrow Laois 252 C2
Durrow Abbey Offaly 249 C7
Durrus Cork 250 C3
Dyan Tyrone 247 C5
Dysart Westmeath 252 B2

E

Eargantea Londonderry 247 A5
Earlstown Galway 249 C6
Easky Sligo 249 A5
Eden Antrim 247 B7
Edenaveagh Fermanagh 246 B3
Edenderry Offaly 252 B2
Ederny Fermanagh 246 B3
Edgeworthstown Longford 249 B7
Edmondstown Louth 247 D5
Eglinton Londonderry 246 A4
Eglish Tyrone 247 C5
Eighter Cavan 246 D4
Ellistrin Donegal 246 B3
Elphin Roscommon 249 B6
Emly Tipperary 251 B6
Emmoo Roscommon 249 B6
Emyvale Monaghan 247 C5
Enfield Meath 252 B3
Ennis Clare 251 A5
Enniscorthy Wexford 252 C3
Enniskean Cork 251 C5
Enniskerry Wicklow 252 B4
Enniskillen Fermanagh 246 C3
Ennistimon Clare 248 D4
Errill Laois 251 A7
Essexford Monaghan 247 D5
Eyrecourt Galway 249 C6

F

Falcarragh Donegal 246 A2
Fallmore Mayo 248 A2
Fardrum Westmeath 249 C7
Farranfore Kerry 250 B3
Feakle Clare 249 D5
Fedamore Limerick 251 A5
Feeard Clare 250 A3
Feenhanagh Limerick 251 B5
Feeny Londonderry 246 B4
Fenagh Leitrim 246 C3
Fenit Kerry 250 B3
Fennagh Carlow 252 C3
Ferbane Offaly 249 C7
Fermoy Cork 251 B6
Ferns Wexford 252 C4
Fethard Tipperary 251 B7
Fethard Wexford 252 D3
Fiddown Kilkenny 252 D2
Fincarn Londonderry 247 B5
Finglas Dublin 252 B4
Finnea Westmeath 246 D4
Finnis Down 247 C6
Fintona Tyrone 246 C4
Fintown Donegal 246 B2
Finvoy Antrim 247 A6
Five Alley Offaly 249 C7
Fivemiletown Tyrone 246 C4
Flagmount Clare 249 C5
Fontstown Kildare 252 B3
Ford Wexford 252 C4
Fordstown Meath 252 A3
Fore Westmeath 252 A2
Forgney Longford 249 B7
Forkill Armagh 247 C6
Foulkesmill Wexford 252 D3
Fountain Cross Clare 250 A4
Four Mile House Roscommon 249 B6
Foxford Mayo 248 B4
Foygh Longford 249 B7
Foynes Limerick 250 A4
Frankville Down 247 C7
Freemount Cork 251 B5
Frenchpark Roscommon 249 B6
Freshford Kilkenny 252 C2
Fuerty Roscommon 249 B6
Fybagh Kerry 250 B3

G

Galbally Limerick 251 B6
Galmoy Kilkenny 251 A7
Galway Galway 248 C4
Garbally Galway 249 C6
Garrane Cork 250 C4
Garrison Fermanagh 246 C2
Garristown Dublin 252 A4
Garryvoe Cork 251 C6
Garvagh Londonderry 247 B5
Garvaghy Down 247 C6
Garvaghy Tyrone 246 C4
Garvary Fermanagh 246 C3
Gattabaun Kilkenny 252 C2
Gay Brook Westmeath 252 B2
Geashill Offaly 252 B2
Gilford Down 247 C6
Glandore Cork 250 C4
Glanworth Cork 251 B6
Glasdrumman Down 247 C7
Glaslough Monaghan 247 C5
Glasnevin Dublin 252 B4
Glassan Westmeath 249 C7
Glastry Down 247 C8
Glen Donegal 246 A3
Glen Fermanagh 246 C2
Glenade Leitrim 246 C2
Glenamoy Mayo 248 A3
Glenariff Antrim 247 A6
Glenarm Antrim 247 B7
Glenavy Antrim 247 B6
Glenbeigh Kerry 250 B3

Glencar Kerry 250 B3
Glencolumbkille Donegal 246 B1
Glendalough Wicklow 252 B4
Glendree Clare 249 D5
Glenealy Wicklow 252 C4
Gleneely Donegal 246 A4
Glenfarn Leitrim 246 C3
Glenfesk Kerry 250 B4
Glengarriff Cork 250 C3
Glengavlen Cavan 246 C3
Glengormly Antrim 247 B7
Glennamaddy Galway 249 B5
Glenoe Antrim 247 B7
Glenstal Abbey Limerick 251 A6
Glentane Galway 249 C5
Glenties Donegal 246 B2
Glenville Cork 251 B6
Glin Limerick 250 A4
Glinsk Galway 249 B6
Glinsk Galway 248 C3
Glynn Carlow 252 C3
Glynn Antrim 247 B7
Golden Tipperary 251 B7
Goleen Cork 250 D3
Goresbridge Kilkenny 252 C3
Gorey Wexford 252 C4
Gormanstown Meath 252 A4
Gort Galway 249 C5
Gortahork Donegal 246 A2
Gorteen Galway 249 B5
Gorteen Galway 249 C5
Gorteen Sligo 249 B5
Gorteen Waterford 251 B7
Gorteeng Galway 249 C6
Gortin Tyrone 246 B4
Gortnacross Londonderry 247 B5
Gortroe Cork 251 B5
Gortymadden Galway 249 C6
Gowlaun Galway 248 B3
Gowran Kilkenny 252 C2
Graghil Mayo 248 A3
Graigue Laois 252 C3
Graiguenamanagh Kilkenny 252 C3
Granard Longford 246 D4
Grange Kilkenny 252 C2
Grange Roscommon 249 B6
Grange Sligo 246 C1
Grangebellew Louth 247 D6
Granville Tyrone 247 C5
Greencastle Donegal 247 A5
Greencastle Down 247 C6
Greencastle Tyrone 246 B4
Greenisland Antrim 247 B7
Greenore Louth 247 C6
Greevagh Sligo 246 C2
Greyabbey Down 247 B7
Greysteel Londonderry 246 A4
Greystones Wicklow 252 B4
Groomsport Down 247 B7
Gubaveeny Cavan 246 C3
Gudderstown Louth 247 D5
Gulladuff Londonderry 247 B5
Gweedore Donegal 246 A2
Gwessalia Mayo 248 A3

H

Hacketstown Carlow 252 C3
Hamiltownbawn Armagh 247 C5
Headford Galway 248 C4
Herbertstown Limerick 251 A6
Hillsborough Down 247 C6
Hilltown Down 247 C6
Hollymount Mayo 248 B4
Hollywood Wicklow 252 B3
Holycross Limerick 251 A5
Holycross Tipperary 251 A7
Holywood Down 247 B7
Horseleap Offaly 249 C7
Horseleap Crossroads Galway 249 C5
Hospital Limerick 251 B6
Howth Dublin 252 B4
Hurlers Cross Clare 251 A5

I

Inagh Clare 250 A4
Inch Cork 251 C7
Inch Donegal 246 A4
Inch Kerry 250 B3
Inchigeelagh Cork 250 C4
Inishannon Cork 251 C5
Inishcrone Sligo 248 A4
Inishkeen Monaghan 247 C5
Inishrush Londonderry 247 B5
Inistioge Kilkenny 252 D2
Inver Donegal 246 B2
Inveran Galway 248 C4
Irvinestown Fermanagh 246 C3
Islandtown Antrim 247 B6

J

Johnstown Kilkenny 251 A7
Johnstown Bridge Kildare 252 B3
Julianstown Meath 252 A4

K

Kanturk Cork 251 B5
Katesbridge Down 247 C6
Keadow Roscommon 246 C2
Keady Armagh 247 C5
Kealkill Cork 250 C4
Keel Mayo 248 B2
Keenagh Longford 249 B7
Kells Kilkenny 252 C2
Kells Meath 252 A3
Kells Antrim 247 B6
Kellystown Louth 247 D6
Kenmare Kerry 250 C3
Kentstown Meath 252 A3
Kesh Fermanagh 246 B3
Keshcarrigan Leitrim 246 C3
Kilamery Kilkenny 252 D2
Kilbaha Clare 250 A3
Kilbeggan Westmeath 252 B2
Kilbeheny Limerick 251 B6
Kilbennan Church Galway 249 B5
Kilberry Meath 252 A3
Kilbrickan Galway 248 C3
Kilbride Wicklow 252 C4
Kilbrien Waterford 251 B7
Kilbrittain Cork 251 C5
Kilcar Donegal 246 B1
Kilchreest Galway 249 C5
Kilclooney Donegal 246 B2
Kilcock Kildare 252 B3
Kilcoe Cork 250 C4
Kilcogy Cavan 246 D4
Kilcolgan Galway 249 C5
Kilconly Galway 248 B4
Kilconnell Galway 249 C6
Kilcoo Down 247 C6
Kilcoole Wicklow 252 B4
Kilcormac Offaly 249 C7
Kilcornan Limerick 251 A5
Kilcrohane Cork 250 C3
Kilcullen Kildare 252 B3
Kilcurry Louth 247 C6
Kildalkey Meath 252 A3
Kildare Kildare 252 B3
Kildavin Carlow 252 C3
Kildimo Limerick 251 A5
Kildorrery Cork 251 B6
Kilfane Kilkenny 252 C2
Kilfeakle Tipperary 251 B6
Kilfearagh Clare 250 A3
Kilfenora Clare 248 D4
Kilfinnane Limerick 251 B6
Kilflynn Kerry 250 B3
Kilgarrif Galway 248 C4
Kilgarvan Kerry 250 C4
Kilglass Galway 249 C6
Kilglass Sligo 248 A4
Kilgobnet Kerry 250 B3
Kilgolagh Cavan 246 D4
Kilkea Kildare 252 C3
Kilkee Clare 250 A3
Kilkeel Down 247 C6
Kilkelly Mayo 249 B5
Kilkenny Kilkenny 252 C2
Kilkerrin Galway 249 B5
Kilkieran Galway 248 C3
Kilkinlea Kerry 250 B4
Kilkishen Clare 251 A5
Kill Kildare 252 B3
Kill Waterford 252 D2
Killadangan Mayo 248 B3
Killadeas Fermanagh 246 C3
Killadoon Mayo 248 B3
Killadysert Clare 250 A4
Killala Mayo 248 A4
Killaloe Clare 251 A6
Killaloo Londonderry 246 B4
Killane Offaly 252 B2
Killarbran Fermanagh 246 C4
Killarga Leitrim 246 C2
Killargue Leitrim 246 C2
Killarney Kerry 250 B3
Killashandra Cavan 246 C3
Killashee Longford 249 B7
Killavally Mayo 248 B4
Killavullen Cork 251 B5
Killeagh Cork 251 C7
Killeen Tipperary 249 C7
Killeen Tyrone 247 B5
Killeevan Monaghan 246 C4
Killeglan Roscommon 249 C6
Killeigh Offaly 252 B2
Killen Tyrone 246 B3
Killenagh Wexford 252 C4
Killenaule Tipperary 251 A7
Killerig Carlow 252 C3
Killeter Tyrone 246 B3
Killimor Galway 249 C6
Killinaboy Clare 248 D4
Killinaspick Kilkenny 252 D2
Killiney Dublin 252 B4
Killinick Wexford 252 D4
Killorglin Kerry 250 B3
Killough Down 247 C7
Killowen Down 247 C6
Killsaran Louth 247 D6
Killtullagh Galway 249 C5
Killucan Westmeath 252 A2
Killurin Wexford 252 D3
Killybegs Donegal 246 B2
Killyfassy Cavan 246 D4
Killygordon Donegal 246 B3
Killykergan Londonderry 247 A5
Killylea Armagh 247 C5
Killyleagh Down 247 C7
Killyon Offaly 249 C7
Kilmacow Kilkenny 252 D2
Kilmacrenan Donegal 246 A3
Kilmacthomas Waterford 252 D2
Kilmaganny Kilkenny 252 D2
Kilmaine Mayo 248 B4
Kilmaley Clare 250 A4
Kilmallock Limerick 251 B5
Kilmanagh Kilkenny 252 C2
Kilmeadan Waterford 252 D2
Kilmeage Kildare 252 B3
Kilmeedy Limerick 251 B5
Kilmichael Cork 250 C4
Kilmihil Clare 250 A4
Kilmore Wexford 252 D3
Kilmore Quay Wexford 252 D3
Kilmuckridge Wexford 252 C4
Kilmurry Clare 250 A4
Kilmurry Clare 251 A5
Kilmurvy Galway 248 C3
Kilnaleck Cavan 246 D4
Kilnaskea Fermanagh 246 C3
Kilrea Londonderry 247 B5
Kilreekil Galway 249 C6
Kilronan Galway 248 C3
Kilronane Cork 250 C4
Kilross Tipperary 251 B6
Kilrush Clare 250 A4
Kilsallagh Galway 249 B5
Kilshanny Clare 248 D4
Kilsheelan Tipperary 251 B7
Kiltamagh Mayo 248 B4
Kiltartan Galway 249 C5
Kiltealy Wexford 252 C3
Kilteel Kildare 252 B3
Kilteely Limerick 251 A6
Kiltegan Wicklow 252 C3
Kiltiernan Dublin 252 B4
Kiltoom Roscommon 249 C6
Kiltormer Galway 249 C6
Kiltyclogher Leitrim 246 C2
Kilworth Cork 251 B6
Kinalag Galway 249 B5
Kinawley Fermanagh 246 C3
Kincaslough Donegal 246 A2
Kindrum Donegal 246 A3
Kingarrow Donegal 246 B2
Kingscourt Cavan 247 D5
Kinlough Leitrim 246 C2
Kinnegad Westmeath 252 B2
Kinnitty Offaly 249 C7
Kinsale Cork 251 C5
Kinvarra Galway 249 C5
Kircubbin Down 247 C7
Kishkeam Cork 250 B4
Knock Clare 250 A4
Knock Mayo 249 B5
Knockaderry Limerick 251 B5
Knockagree Cork 250 B4
Knockalina Mayo 248 A3
Knockalough Clare 250 A4
Knockananna Wicklow 252 C4
Knockatallan Monaghan 246 C4
Knockbrit Tipperary 251 B7
Knockcroghery Roscommon 249 B6
Knockfold Donegal 246 A2
Knocklofty Tipperary 251 B7
Knocklong Limerick 251 B6
Knocktopher Kilkenny 252 D2
Kylesa Galway 248 C3

L

Laban Galway 249 C5
Labasheeda Clare 250 A4
Labby Londonderry 247 B5
Lack Fermanagh 246 B3
Lackamore Tipperary 251 A6
Ladysbridge Cork 251 C6
Laghtgeorge Galway 249 C5
Laghy Donegal 246 B2
Lahard Cavan 249 B7
Lahardaun Mayo 248 A4
Lakyle Clare 250 A4
Lanesborough Longford 249 B7
Laracor Meath 252 A3
Laragh Wicklow 252 B4
Largan Mayo 248 A3
Largy Donegal 246 B1
Larne Antrim 247 B7
Lattin Tipperary 251 B6
Lauragh Kerry 250 C3
Laurencetown Galway 249 C6
Lavey Cavan 246 D4
Lawrencetown Down 247 C6
Laytown Meath 252 A4
Leabgarrow Donegal 246 B2
Leap Cork 250 C4
Leckanarainey Leitrim 246 C2
Leckaun Leitrim 246 C2
Leckemy Donegal 246 A4
Leenaun Galway 248 B3
Legoniel Antrim 247 B7
Lehinch Clare 248 D4
Leighlinbridge Carlow 252 C3
Leitrim Leitrim 249 B6
Leixlip Kildare 252 B4
Lemanaghan Offaly 249 C7
Lemybrien Waterford 251 B7
Lerrig Kerry 250 B3
Letterbreen Fermanagh 246 C3
Letterfrack Galway 248 B3
Letterkenny Donegal 246 B3
Lettermacaward Donegal 246 B2
Lettermore Galway 248 C3
Lettermullan Galway 248 C3
Lifford Donegal 246 B4
Ligfordrum Tyrone 246 B4
Limavady Londonderry 247 A5
Limerick Limerick 251 A5
Limerick Junction Tipperary 251 B6
Lisacul Roscommon 249 B5
Lisbane Down 247 B7
Lisbellaw Fermanagh 246 C3
Lisburn Antrim 247 B6
Liscannor Clare 248 D4
Liscarroll Cork 251 B5
Lisdoonvarna Clare 248 C4
Lisgall Monaghan 247 C5
Lisgarode Tipperary 249 D6
Lisheen Clare 250 A4
Lislap Tyrone 246 B4
Lislea Armagh 247 C6
Lismore Waterford 251 B7
Lisnacree Down 247 C6
Lisnagry Limerick 251 A5
Lisnamusk Londonderry 247 B5
Lisnarrick Fermanagh 246 C3
Lisnaskea Fermanagh 246 C4
Lisnaveane Monaghan 246 C4
Lispole Kerry 250 B2
Lisronagh Tipperary 251 B7
Lissatinnig Bridge Kerry 250 C3
Lisselton Kerry 250 B3
Lissinagroagh Leitrim 246 C2
Lissycasey Clare 250 A4
Listerlin Kilkenny 252 D2
Listowel Kerry 250 B4
Littleton Tipperary 251 A7
Lixnaw Kerry 250 B3
Lobinstown Meath 247 D5
Loghill Limerick 250 A4
Londonderry = Derry Londonderry 246 B4
Longford Longford 249 B7
Longwood Meath 252 B3
Loughall Armagh 247 C5
Loughanavally Westmeath 249 C7
Loughanure Donegal 246 B2
Loughbrickland Down 247 C6
Loughglinn Roscommon 249 B5
Loughguile Antrim 247 A6
Loughmoe Tipperary 251 A7
Loughran Antrim 247 A6
Loughrea Galway 249 C5
Louisburgh Mayo 248 B3
Louth Louth 247 D5
Lucan Dublin 252 B4
Lugatemple Mayo 248 B4
Lukeswell Kilkenny 252 D2
Lurgan Armagh 247 C6
Lurgangreen Louth 247 D6
Lusk Dublin 252 A4
Lyracrumpane Kerry 250 B4

M

Maam Cross Galway 248 C3
Maas Donegal 246 B2
Mackan Fermanagh 246 C3
Macosquin Londonderry 247 A5
Macroom Cork 251 C5
Maghera Londonderry 247 B5
Magherafelt Londonderry 247 B5
Magheragall Antrim 247 B6
Magheraveely Fermanagh 246 C4
Maghery Donegal 246 B2
Maghery Armagh 247 B5
Maguiresbridge Fermanagh 246 C4
Malahide Dublin 252 B4
Malin Donegal 246 A4
Malin More Donegal 246 B1
Mallaranny Mayo 248 B3
Mallow Cork 251 B5
Manfieldstown Louth 247 D6
Manorhamilton Leitrim 246 C2
Manselstown Tipperary 251 A7
Manulla Mayo 248 B4
Markethill Armagh 247 C5
Maulyneill Kerry 250 C3
Maum Galway 248 B3
Maylough Galway 249 C5
Maynooth Kildare 252 B3
Mayo Mayo 248 B4
Mayo Bridge Down 247 C6
Meenaneary Donegal 246 B1
Meigh Armagh 247 C6
Mell Louth 252 A4
Menlough Galway 248 C4
Middletown Armagh 247 C5
Midleton Cork 251 C6
Milestone Tipperary 251 A6
Milford Cork 251 B5
Milford Donegal 246 A3
Millbrook Meath 252 A2
Millford Armagh 247 C5
Millisle Down 247 B7
Millstreet Cork 250 B4
Millstreet Waterford 251 B7
Milltown Cavan 246 C4
Milltown Galway 249 B5
Milltown Kerry 250 B2
Milltown Kerry 250 B3
Milltown Monaghan 247 C5
Milltown Antrim 247 B7
Milltown Londonderry 247 A5
Milltown Malbay Clare 250 A4
Miltown Kildare 252 B3
Mitchelstown Cork 251 B6
Moate Westmeath 249 C7
Modreeny Tipperary 249 D6
Mohill Leitrim 249 B7
Moira Down 247 C6
Monaghan Monaghan 247 C5
Monasterevin Kildare 252 B2
Moneygall Offaly 249 D7
Moneyglass Antrim 247 B6
Moneymore Londonderry 247 B5
Moneyneany Londonderry 247 B5
Monivea Galway 249 C5
Monkstown Cork 251 C6
Mooncoin Kilkenny 252 D2
Moone Kildare 252 C3
Moorfields Antrim 247 B6
Mornington Meath 252 A4
Moss-side Antrim 247 A6
Mossley Antrim 247 B7
Mount Bellew Bridge Galway 249 C6
Mount Ida Down 247 C6
Mount Nugent Cavan 246 D4
Mount Talbot Roscommon 249 B6
Mountcharles Donegal 246 B2
Mountfield Tyrone 246 B4
Mountjoy Tyrone 246 B4
Mountmellick Laois 252 B2
Mountnorris Armagh 247 C6
Mountrath Laois 252 B2
Mountshannon Clare 249 D6
Moville Donegal 246 A4
Moy Tyrone 247 C5
Moyad Down 247 C6
Moyard Galway 248 B2
Moyasta Clare 250 A3
Moycullen Galway 248 C4
Moymore Clare 251 A5
Moynalty Meath 247 D5
Moyne Longford 249 B7
Moyne Tipperary 251 A7
Moyroughly Westmeath 249 C7
Moyvally Kildare 252 B3
Moyvore Westmeath 249 B7
Muckross Kerry 250 B4
Muff Donegal 246 A4
Muine Bheag Carlow 252 C3
Muineagh Donegal 246 A3
Mullagh Cavan 247 D5
Mullagh Galway 249 C6
Mullagh Meath 252 B3
Mullaghnaneane Sligo 246 C1
Mullan Fermanagh 246 C3
Mullans Town Tyrone 246 B4
Mullanys Cross Sligo 249 A5
Mullarts Antrim 247 A6
Mulldonagh Londonderry 246 B4
Mullinahone Tipperary 252 C1
Mullinavat Kilkenny 252 D2
Mullingar Westmeath 252 A2
Mullughmore Sligo 246 C2
Mungret Limerick 251 A5
Murrogh Clare 248 C4
Myshall Carlow 252 C3

N

Naas Kildare 252 B3
Nad Cork 251 B5
Naran Donegal 246 B2
Naul Dublin 252 A4
Navan Meath 252 A3
Neale Mayo 248 B4
Nenagh Tipperary 251 A6
New Birmingham Tipperary 251 A7
New Buildings Londonderry 246 B4
New Chapel Cross Kerry 250 C2
New Inn Cavan 246 D4
New Inn Galway 249 C6
New Inn Laois 252 B2
New Ross Wexford 252 D3
Newbliss Monaghan 246 C4
Newbridge Galway 249 B6
Newbridge Kildare 252 B3
Newbridge Limerick 251 A5
Newcastle Tipperary 251 B7
Newcastle Wicklow 252 B4
Newcastle Down 247 C7
Newcastle West Limerick 250 B4
Newinn Tipperary 251 B7
Newmarket Cork 251 B5
Newmarket-on-Fergus Clare 251 A5
Newmills Donegal 246 B3
Newport Mayo 248 B3
Newport Tipperary 251 A6
Newry Down 247 C6
Newtown Laois 252 C2
Newtown Longford 249 B7
Newtown Tipperary 251 B6
Newtown Crommelin Antrim 247 B6
Newtown Cunningham Donegal 246 B3
Newtown Forbes Longford 249 B7
Newtown Gore Leitrim 246 C3
Newtown Hamilton Armagh 247 C5
Newtown Monasterboice Louth 247 D6
Newtown Mount Kennedy Wicklow 252 B4
Newtown Sands Kerry 250 A4
Newtownabbey Antrim 247 B7
Newtownards Down 247 B7
Newtownbreda Down 247 B7
Newtownbutler Fermanagh 246 C4
Newtownshandrum Cork 251 B5
Newtownstewart Tyrone 246 B4
Ninemilehouse Tipperary 252 D2
Nobber Meath 247 D5
Nohaval Cork 251 C6
Nurney Carlow 252 C3
Nutts Corner Antrim 247 B6

O

O'Briensbridge Clare 251 A6
Oghill Londonderry 246 B4
Oilgate Wexford 252 D3
Old Ross Wexford 252 D3
Oldcastle Meath 246 D4
Oldleighlin Carlow 252 C2
Oldtown Laois 252 C2
Omagh Tyrone 246 B4
Omeath Louth 247 C6
Oola Limerick 251 A6
Oran Roscommon 249 B6
Oranmore Galway 249 C5
Oristown Meath 252 A3
Oughterard Galway 248 C4

P

Pallas Green Limerick 251 A6
Pallaskenry Limerick 251 A5
Park Galway 249 C5
Park Londonderry 246 B4
Parknasilla Kerry 250 C3
Parkview Antrim 247 B7
Partry Mayo 248 B4
Passage East Waterford 252 D3
Passage West Cork 251 C6
Patrickswell Limerick 251 A5
Paulstown Kilkenny 252 C2
Peterswell Galway 249 C5
Pettigo Donegal 246 B3
Piltown Kilkenny 252 D2
Pluck Donegal 246 B3
Plumbridge Tyrone 246 B4
Pollremon Galway 249 B5
Pomeroy Tyrone 247 B5
Pontoon Mayo 248 B4
Portacloy Mayo 248 A3
Portadown Armagh 247 C6
Portaferry Down 247 C7
Portarlington Offaly 252 B2
Portavogie Down 247 C8
Portballintrae Antrim 247 A5
Portglenone Antrim 247 B6
Portlaoise Laois 252 B2
Portlaw Waterford 252 D2
Portmagee Kerry 250 C2
Portmarnock Dublin 252 B4
Portrane Dublin 252 B4
Portroe Tipperary 249 D6
Portrush Antrim 247 A5
Portsalon Donegal 246 A3
Portstewart Londonderry 247 A5
Portumna Galway 249 C6
Poyntz Pass Armagh 247 C6
Prosperous Kildare 252 B3
Puckaun Tipperary 249 D6

Q

Quarryfield Sligo 246 C1
Quilty Clare 250 A4
Quin Clare 251 A5

R

Rahan Offaly 249 C7
Rahara Roscommon 249 B6
Raharney Westmeath 252 A2
Raheen Tipperary 251 B7
Rampark Louth 247 C6
Randalstown Antrim 247 B6
Raphoe Donegal 246 B3
Rasharkin Antrim 247 B6
Rath Offaly 249 C7
Rathangan Kildare 252 B3
Ratharney Longford 249 B7
Rathclogh Tipperary 251 A7
Rathconrath Westmeath 249 B7
Rathcool Cork 251 B5
Rathcoole Dublin 252 B4
Rathcor Louth 247 D6
Rathcormack Cork 251 B6
Rathdowney Laois 251 A7
Rathdrum Wicklow 252 C4
Rathduff Cork 251 B5
Rathfriland Down 247 C6
Rathgormuck Waterford 252 D2
Rathkeale Limerick 251 A5
Rathkenny Meath 252 A3
Rathlacken Mayo 248 A4
Rathmelton Donegal 246 A3
Rathmolyon Meath 252 B3
Rathmore Kerry 250 B4
Rathmore Kildare 252 B3
Rathmore Longford 249 B7
Rathmullan Donegal 246 A3
Rathnew Wicklow 252 C4
Rathnure Wexford 252 D3
Rathowen Westmeath 249 B7
Rathvilla Offaly 252 B2
Rathvilly Carlow 252 C3
Ratoath Meath 252 A4
Ravensdale Louth 247 C6
Rear Cross Tipperary 251 A6
Recess Galway 248 C3
Red Castle Donegal 246 A4
Reens Limerick 251 A5
Rhode Offaly 252 B2
Rich Hill Armagh 247 C5
Ringaskiddy Cork 251 C6
Ringsend Londonderry 247 A5
Ringville Waterford 251 B7
Riverchapel Wexford 252 C4
Riverstick Cork 251 C6
Riverstown Cork 251 C6
Riverstown Sligo 246 C2
Robertstown Kildare 252 B3
Rochfortbridge Westmeath 252 B2
Rockchapel Cork 250 B4
Rockcorry Monaghan 246 C4
Rockhill Limerick 251 B5
Rockmills Cork 251 B6
Roosky Leitrim 249 B7
Roscommon Roscommon 249 B6
Roscrea Tipperary 249 D7
Rosegreen Tipperary 251 B7
Rosenallis Laois 252 B2
Rosmult Tipperary 251 A7
Ross Carbery Cork 250 C4
Rossaveel Galway 248 C3
Rosscahill Galway 248 C4
Rosses Point Sligo 246 C1
Rossinver Leitrim 246 C2
Rosslare Wexford 252 D4
Rosslare Harbour Wexford 252 D4
Rosslea Fermanagh 246 C4
Rossnowlagh Donegal 246 B2
Rostellan Cork 251 C6
Rostrevor Down 247 C6
Rosturk Mayo 248 B3
Roundstone Galway 248 C3
Roundwood Wicklow 252 B4
Rousky Tyrone 246 B4
Ruan Clare 249 D5
Rush Dublin 252 A4

S

Saggart Dublin 252 B4
Saintfield Down 247 C7
Sallahig Kerry 250 C2
Sallins Kildare 252 B3
Sally Gap Wicklow 252 B4
Sallybrook Cork 251 C6
Salterstown Louth 247 D6
Salthill Galway 248 C4
Saltpans Donegal 246 A3
Scarriff Clare 249 D5
Scartaglin Kerry 250 B4
Scarva Down 247 C6
Scogh Kilkenny 252 D2
Scotch Corner Monaghan 247 C5
Scotstown Monaghan 246 C4
Scraghy Tyrone 246 B3
Scramoge Roscommon 249 B6
Screeb Galway 248 C3
Screggan Offaly 249 C7
Scribbagh Fermanagh 246 C2
Seskinore Tyrone 246 B4
Shanagolden Limerick 250 A4
Shankill Roscommon 249 B6
Shanlaragh Cork 250 C4
Shannonbridge Offaly 249 C6
Shannow Cavan 246 D4
Shanovogh Clare 250 A4
Shantonagh Monaghan 247 C5
Sharavogue Offaly 249 C7
Shercock Cavan 247 D5
Shillelagh Wicklow 252 C3
Shinrone Offaly 249 D7
Shrigley Down 247 C7
Shrule Mayo 248 B4
Silvermines Tipperary 251 A6
Silverstream Monaghan 247 C5
Single Street Donegal 246 C2
Sion Mills Tyrone 246 B4
Six Crosses Kerry 250 B3
Sixmilebridge Clare 251 A5
Sixmilecross Tyrone 246 B4
Skeagh Westmeath 249 B7
Skerries Dublin 252 A4
Skibbereen Cork 250 C4
Skull Cork 250 C3
Slane Meath 252 A3
Sligo Sligo 246 C2
Slisgarrow Fermanagh 246 C3
Smithborough Monaghan 246 C4
Sneem Kerry 250 C3
Spa Kerry 250 B3
Spancelhill Clare 251 A5
Speenoge Donegal 246 A4
Sperrin Tyrone 246 B4
Spiddle Galway 248 C4
Springfield Fermanagh 246 C3
Square Down 247 C6
Srahmore Mayo 248 A3
Srahnalong Mayo 248 B4
St. Johnstown Donegal 246 B4
Stewartstown Tyrone 247 B5
Stillorgan Dublin 252 B4
Stonyford Kilkenny 252 C2
Strabane Tyrone 246 B4
Stradbally Kerry 250 B2
Stradbally Laois 252 B2
Stradbally Waterford 252 D2
Strade Friary Mayo 248 B4
Stradone Cavan 246 D4
Straffan Kildare 252 B3
Strandhill Sligo 246 C1
Strangford Down 247 C7
Stranorlar Donegal 246 B3
Streamstown Galway 248 B2
Strokestown Roscommon 249 B6
Stroove Donegal 247 A5
Summerhill Meath 252 B3
Swan Laois 252 C2
Swanlinbar Cavan 246 C3
Swatragh Londonderry 247 B5
Swinford Mayo 249 B5
Swords Dublin 252 B4

T

Taghmon Wexford 252 D3
Tallaght Dublin 252 B4
Tallanstown Louth 247 D5
Tallow Waterford 251 B6
Tallowbridge Waterford 251 B6
Tandragee Armagh 247 C6
Tang Westmeath 249 B7
Tara Meath 252 A3
Tarbert Kerry 250 A4
Taur Cork 250 B4
Tawnyinah Mayo 249 B5
Tedavnet Monaghan 246 C4
Teeshan Antrim 247 B6
Templeboy Sligo 249 A5
Templederry Tipperary 251 A6
Templemore Tipperary 251 A7
Templenoe Kerry 250 C3
Templepatrick Antrim 247 B6
Templetouhy Tipperary 251 A7
Tempo Fermanagh 246 C4
Termon Cavan 246 C3
Termon Donegal 246 A3
Termonfeckin Louth 247 D6
Terryglass Tipperary 249 C6
The Downs Westmeath 252 A2
The Loup Londonderry 247 B5
The Sheddings Antrim 247 B6
The Temple Down 247 C7
Thomas Street Roscommon 249 C6
Thomastown Kilkenny 252 C2
Thurles Tipperary 251 A7
Timahoe Kildare 252 B3
Timahoe Laois 252 C2
Timoleague Cork 251 C5
Timolin Kildare 252 C3
Tinahely Wicklow 252 C4
Tintern Abbey Wexford 252 D3
Tipperary Tipperary 251 B6
Tobercurry Sligo 249 A5
Tobermoney Down 247 C7
Tobermore Londonderry 247 B5
Toberroe Galway 249 C5
Togher Cork 250 C4
Togher Louth 247 D6
Toomakeady Mayo 248 B4
Toombeola Galway 248 C3
Toome Antrim 247 B6
Toomyvara Tipperary 251 A6
Toormore Cork 250 C3
Tralee Kerry 250 B3
Tramore Waterford 252 D2
Trillick Tyrone 246 C4
Trim Meath 252 A3
Tuam Galway 249 B5
Tuamgraney Clare 249 D5
Tubber Galway 249 C5
Tulla Clare 251 A5
Tullaghan Leitrim 246 C2
Tullaghoge Tyrone 247 B5
Tullaghought Kilkenny 252 D2
Tullagower Clare 250 A4
Tullamore Offaly 252 B2
Tullaroan Kilkenny 252 C2
Tullow Carlow 252 C3
Tully Roscommon 249 B6
Tully Cross Galway 248 B3
Tullybeg Galway 249 B5
Tullycrossmearan Fermanagh 246 C3
Tullymacreeve Armagh 247 C6
Tullyverry Londonderry 246 A4
Tullyvin Cavan 246 C4
Tulsk Roscommon 249 B6
Tummery Tyrone 246 C3
Turloughmore Galway 249 C5
Turreen Longford 249 B7
Twomileborris Tipperary 251 A7
Tynagh Galway 249 C6
Tynan Armagh 247 C5
Tyrrellspass Westmeath 252 B2

U

Upperchurch Tipperary 251 A6
Urlingford Kilkenny 251 A7

V

Ventry Kerry 250 B2
Vicarstown Laois 252 B2
Virginia Cavan 246 D4

W

Waddington Wexford 252 D3
Ward Dublin 252 B4
Waringstown Down 247 C6
Warrenpoint Down 247 C6
Waterford Waterford 252 D2
Watergrasshill Cork 251 B6
Waterside Londonderry 246 B4
Waterville Kerry 250 C2
Wellingtonbridge Wexford 252 D3
Westport Mayo 248 B3
Wexford Wexford 252 D4
Wheathill Fermanagh 246 C3
White Castle Donegal 246 A4
Whitecross Armagh 247 C6
Whitegate Clare 249 D6
Whitegate Cork 251 C6
Whitehead Antrim 247 B7
Whitehill Fermanagh 246 C3
Wicklow Wicklow 252 C4
Williamstown Galway 249 B5
Windgap Kilkenny 252 D2
Woodenbridge Wicklow 252 C4
Woodford Galway 249 C6
Woodlawn Galway 249 C6
Woodtown Meath 247 D5

Y

Youghal Cork 251 C7

How to use the index

Example

Adlestrop Glos **38** B2

- B2 – grid square
- 38 – page number
- Glos – county or unitary authority

Places of special interest are highlighted in magenta

Abbreviations used in the index

Index to road maps of Britain

Aberdeen	Aberdeen City
Aberds	Aberdeenshire
Ald	Alderney
Anglesey	Isle of Anglesey
Angus	Angus
Argyll	Argyll and Bute
Bath	Bath and North East Somerset
Beds	Bedfordshire
Bl Gwent	Blaenau Gwent
Blkburn	Blackburn with Darwen
Blkpool	Blackpool
Bmouth	Bournemouth
Borders	Scottish Borders
Brack	Bracknell
Bridgend	Bridgend
Brighton	City of Brighton and Hove
Bristol	City and County of Bristol
Bucks	Buckinghamshire
Caerph	Caerphilly
Cambs	Cambridgeshire
Cardiff	Cardiff
Carms	Carmarthenshire
Ceredig	Ceredigion
Ches	Cheshire
Clack	Clackmannanshire
Conwy	Conwy
Corn	Cornwall
Cumb	Cumbria
Darl	Darlington
Denb	Denbighshire
Derby	City of Derby
Derbys	Derbyshire
Devon	Devon
Dorset	Dorset
Dumfries	Dumfries and Galloway
Dundee	Dundee City
Durham	Durham
E Ayrs	East Ayrshire
E Dunb	East Dunbartonshire
E Loth	East Lothian
E Renf	East Renfrewshire
E Sus	East Sussex
E Yorks	East Riding of Yorkshire
Edin	City of Edinburgh
Essex	Essex
Falk	Falkirk
Fife	Fife
Flint	Flintshire
Glasgow	City of Glasgow
Glos	Gloucestershire
Gtr Man	Greater Manchester
Guern	Guernsey
Gwyn	Gwynedd
Halton	Halton
Hants	Hampshire
Hereford	Herefordshire
Herts	Hertfordshire
Highld	Highland
Hrtlpl	Hartlepool
Hull	Hull
I o M	Isle of Man
I o W	Isle of Wight
Invclyd	Inverclyde
Jersey	Jersey
Kent	Kent
Lancs	Lancashire
Leicester	City of Leicester
Leics	Leicestershire
Lincs	Lincolnshire
London	Greater London
Luton	Luton
M Keynes	Milton Keynes
M Tydf	Merthyr Tydfil
M'bro	Middlesbrough
Medway	Medway
Mers	Merseyside
Midloth	Midlothian
Mon	Monmouthshire
Moray	Moray
N Ayrs	North Ayrshire
N Lincs	North Lincolnshire
N Lnrk	North Lanarkshire
N Som	North Somerset
N Yorks	North Yorkshire
NE Lincs	North East Lincolnshire
Neath	Neath Port Talbot
Newport	City and County of Newport
Norf	Norfolk
Northants	Northamptonshire
Northumb	Northumberland
Nottingham	City of Nottingham
Notts	Nottinghamshire
Orkney	Orkney
Oxon	Oxfordshire
P'boro	Peterborough
Pembs	Pembrokeshire
Perth	Perth and Kinross
Plym	Plymouth
Poole	Poole
Powys	Powys
Ptsmth	Portsmouth
Reading	Reading
Redcar	Redcar and Cleveland
Renfs	Renfrewshire
Rhondda	Rhondda Cynon Taff
Rutland	Rutland
S Ayrs	South Ayrshire
S Glos	South Gloucestershire
S Lnrk	South Lanarkshire
S Yorks	South Yorkshire
Scilly	Scilly
Shetland	Shetland
Shrops	Shropshire
Slough	Slough
Som	Somerset
Soton	Southampton
Staffs	Staffordshire
Sthend	Southend-on-Sea
Stirl	Stirling
Stockton	Stockton-on-Tees
Stoke	Stoke-on-Trent
Suff	Suffolk
Sur	Surrey
Swansea	Swansea
T & W	Tyne and Wear
Telford	Telford and Wrekin
Thamesdown	Thamesdown
Thurrock	Thurrock
Torbay	Torbay
Torf	Torfaen
V Glam	The Vale of Glamorgan
W Berks	West Berkshire
W Dunb	West Dunbartonshire
W Isles	Western Isles
W Loth	West Lothian
W Mid	West Midlands
W Sus	West Sussex
W Yorks	West Yorkshire
Warks	Warwickshire
Warr	Warrington
Wilts	Wiltshire
Windsor	Windsor and Maidenhead
Wokingham	Wokingham
Worcs	Worcestershire
Wrex	Wrexham
York	City of York

A

Ab Kettleby Leics 64 B4
Ab Lench Worcs 50 D5
Abbas Combe Som 12 B5
Abberley Worcs 50 C2
Abberton Essex 43 C6
Abberton Worcs 50 D4
Abberwick Northumb 117 C7
Abbess Roding Essex 42 C1
Abbey Devon 11 C6
Abbey-cwm-hir Powys 48 B2
Abbey Dore Hereford 49 F5
Abbey Field Essex 43 B5
Abbey Hulton Stoke 75 E6
Abbey St Bathans Borders 124 C3
Abbey Town Cumb 107 D8
Abbey Village Lancs 86 B4
Abbey Wood London 29 B5
Abbeydale S Yorks 88 F4
Abbeystead Lancs 93 D5
Abbots Bickington Devon 9 C5
Abbots Bromley Staffs 62 B4
Abbots Langley Herts 40 D3
Abbots Leigh N Som 23 B7
Abbots Morton Worcs 50 D5
Abbots Ripton Cambs 54 B3
Abbots Salford Warks 51 D5
Abbotsbury Dorset 12 F3
Abbotsbury Sub Tropical Gardens Dorset 12 F3
Abbotsford House Borders 123 F8
Abbotsham Devon 9 B6
Abbotskerswell Devon 7 C6
Abbotsley Cambs 54 D3
Abbotswood Hants 14 B4
Abbotts Ann Hants 25 E8
Abcott Shrops 49 B5
Abdon Shrops 61 F5
Aber Ceredig 46 E3
Aber-Arad Carms 46 F2
Aber-banc Ceredig 46 E2
Aber Cowarch Gwyn 59 C5
Aber-Giâr Carms 46 E4
Aber-gwynfi Neath 34 E2
Aber-Hirnant Gwyn 72 F3
Aber-nant Rhondda 34 D3
Aber-Rhiwlech Gwyn 59 B6
Aber-Village Powys 35 B5
Aberaeron Ceredig 46 C3
Aberaman Rhondda 34 D4
Aberangell Gwyn 58 C5
Aberarder Highld 147 F7
Aberarder House Highld 148 B2
Aberarder Lodge Highld 147 F8
Aberargie Perth 134 C3
Aberarth Ceredig 46 C3
Aberavon Neath 33 E8
Aberbeeg Bl Gwent 35 D6
Abercanaid M Tydf 34 D4
Abercarn Caerph 35 E6
Abercastle Pembs 44 B3
Abercegir Powys 58 D5
Aberchirder Aberds 160 C3
Aberconwy House, Conwy Conwy 83 D7
Abercraf Powys 34 C2
Abercrombie Fife 135 D7
Abercych Pembs 45 E4
Abercynafon Powys 34 C4
Abercynon Rhondda 34 E4
Aberdalgie Perth 134 B2
Aberdâr = Aberdare Rhondda 34 D3
Aberdare = Aberdâr Rhondda 34 D3
Aberdaron Gwyn 70 E2
Aberdaugleddau = Milford Haven Pembs 44 E4
Aberdeen Aberdeen 151 D8
Aberdeen Airport Aberdeen 151 C7
Aberdesach Gwyn 82 F4
Aberdour Fife 134 F3
Aberdovey Gwyn 58 E3
Aberdulais Neath 34 D1
Aberedw Powys 48 E2
Abereiddy Pembs 44 B2
Abererch Gwyn 70 D4
Aberfan M Tydf 34 D4
Aberfeldy Perth 141 E5
Aberffraw Anglesey 82 E3
Aberffrwd Ceredig 47 B5
Aberford W Yorks 95 F7
Aberfoyle Stirl 132 D4
Abergavenny = Y Fenni Mon 35 C6
Abergele Conwy 72 B3
Abergorlech Carms 46 F4
Abergwaun = Fishguard Pembs 44 B4
Abergwesyn Powys 47 D7
Abergwili Carms 33 B5
Abergwynant Gwyn 58 C3
Abergwyngregyn Gwyn 83 D6
Abergynolwyn Gwyn 58 D3
Aberhonddu = Brecon Powys 34 B4
Aberhosan Powys 58 E5
Aberkenfig Bridgend 34 F2
Aberlady E Loth 135 F6
Aberlemno Angus 143 D5
Aberllefenni Gwyn 58 D4
Abermagwr Ceredig 47 B5
Abermaw = Barmouth Gwyn 58 C3
Abermeurig Ceredig 46 D4
Abermule Powys 59 E8
Abernaint Powys 59 B8
Abernant Carms 32 B4
Abernethy Perth 134 C3
Abernyte Perth 142 F2
Aberpennar = Mountain Ash Rhondda 34 E4
Aberporth Ceredig 45 D4
Abersoch Gwyn 70 E4
Abersychan Torf 35 D6
Abertawe = Swansea Swansea 33 E7
Aberteifi = Cardigan Ceredig 45 E3
Aberthin V Glam 22 B2
Abertillery = Abertyleri Bl Gwent 35 D6
Abertridwr Caerph 35 F5
Abertridwr Powys 59 C7
Abertyleri = Abertillery Bl Gwent 35 D6
Abertysswg Caerph 35 D5
Aberuthven Perth 133 C8
Aberyscir Powys 34 B3
Aberystwyth Ceredig 58 F2
Abhainn Suidhe W Isles 173 H3
Abingdon Oxon 38 E4
Abinger Common Sur 28 E2
Abinger Hammer Sur 27 E8
Abington S Lnrk 114 B2
Abington Piggotts Cambs 54 E4
Ablington Glos 37 D8
Ablington Wilts 25 E6
Abney Derbys 75 B8
Aboyne Aberds 150 E4
Abram Gtr Man 86 D4
Abriachan Highld 157 F6
Abridge Essex 41 E7
Abronhill N Lnrk 121 B7
Abson S Glos 24 B2
Abthorpe Northants 52 E4
Abune-the-Hill Orkney 176 D1
Aby Lincs 79 B7
Acaster Malbis York 95 E8
Acaster Selby N Yorks 95 E8
Accrington Lancs 87 B5
Acha Argyll 136 C2
Acha Mor W Isles 172 F6
Achabraid Argyll 128 B3
Achachork Highld 152 E5
Achafolla Argyll 130 D3
Achagary Highld 168 D2
Achahoish Argyll 128 C2
Achalader Perth 141 E8
Achallader Argyll 139 E7
Ach'an Todhair Highld 138 B4
Achanalt Highld 156 C3
Achanamara Argyll 128 B2
Achandunie Highld 157 B7
Achany Highld 164 D2
Achaphubuil Highld 138 B4
Acharacle Highld 137 B7
Acharn Highld 137 C8
Acharn Perth 140 E4
Acharole Highld 169 D7
Achath Aberds 151 C6
Achavanich Highld 169 E6
Achavraat Highld 158 E3
Achddu Carms 33 D5
Achduart Highld 162 D4
Achentoul Highld 168 F3
Achfary Highld 166 F4
Achgarve Highld 162 E2
Achiemore Highld 167 C5
Achiemore Highld 168 D3
A'Chill Highld 144 C2
Achiltibuie Highld 162 D4
Achina Highld 168 C2
Achinduich Highld 164 D2
Achinduin Argyll 130 B4
Achingills Highld 169 C6
Achintee Highld 139 B5
Achintee Highld 155 F5
Achintraid Highld 155 G4
Achlean Highld 148 E4
Achleck Argyll 137 D5
Achluachrach Highld 147 F5
Achlyness Highld 166 D4
Achmelvich Highld 162 B4
Achmore Highld 155 G4
Achmore Stirl 140 F2
Achnaba Argyll 130 B5
Achnaba Argyll 128 B4
Achnabat Highld 157 F6
Achnacarnin Highld 166 F2
Achnacarry Highld 146 F4
Achnacloich Argyll 131 B5
Achnacloich Highld 145 C5
Achnaconeran Highld 147 C7
Achnacraig Argyll 137 D5
Achnacroish Argyll 138 E2
Achnadrish Argyll 137 C5
Achnafalnich Argyll 131 C8
Achnagarron Highld 157 C7
Achnaha Highld 137 B5
Achnahanat Highld 164 E2
Achnahannet Highld 149 B5
Achnairn Highld 164 C2
Achnaluachrach Highld 164 D3
Achnasaul Highld 146 F4
Achnasheen Highld 156 D2
Achosnich Highld 137 B5
Achranich Highld 137 D8
Achreamie Highld 168 C5
Achriabhach Highld 139 C5
Achriesgill Highld 166 D4
Achrimsdale Highld 165 D6
Achtoty Highld 167 C8
Achurch Northants 65 F7
Achuvoldrach Highld 167 D7
Achvaich Highld 164 E4
Achvarasdal Highld 168 C4
Ackergill Highld 169 D8
Acklam M'bro 102 C2
Acklam N Yorks 96 C3
Ackleton Shrops 61 E7
Acklington Northumb 117 D8
Ackton W Yorks 88 B5
Ackworth Moor Top W Yorks 88 C5
Acle Norf 69 C7
Acock's Green W Mid 62 F5
Acol Kent 31 C7
Acomb Northumb 110 C2
Acomb York 95 D8
Aconbury Hereford 49 F7
Acre Lancs 87 B5
Acre Street W Sus 15 E8
Acrefair Wrex 73 E6
Acton Ches 74 D3
Acton Dorset 13 G7
Acton London 41 F5
Acton Shrops 60 F3
Acton Suff 56 E2
Acton Wrex 73 D7
Acton Beauchamp Hereford 49 D8
Acton Bridge Ches 74 B2
Acton Burnell Shrops 60 D5
Acton Green Hereford 49 D8
Acton Pigott Shrops 60 D5
Acton Round Shrops 61 E6
Acton Scott Shrops 60 F4
Acton Trussell Staffs 62 C3
Acton Turville S Glos 37 F5
Adbaston Staffs 61 B7
Adber Dorset 12 B3
Adderley Shrops 74 E3
Adderstone Northumb 125 F7
Addiewell W Loth 122 C2
Addingham W Yorks 94 E3
Addington Bucks 39 B7
Addington London 28 C4
Addington Kent 29 D7
Addinston Borders 123 D8
Addiscombe London 28 C4
Addlestone Sur 27 C8
Addlethorpe Lincs 79 C8
Adel W Yorks 95 F5
Adeney Telford 61 C7
Adfa Powys 59 D7
Adforton Hereford 49 B6
Adisham Kent 31 D6
Adlestrop Glos 38 B2
Adlingfleet E Yorks 90 B2
Adlington Lancs 86 C4
Admaston Staffs 62 B4
Admaston Telford 61 C6
Admington Warks 51 E7
Adstock Bucks 52 F5
Adstone Northants 52 D3
Adversane W Sus 16 B4
Advie Highld 158 F5
Adwalton W Yorks 88 B3
Adwell Oxon 39 E6
Adwick le Street S Yorks 89 D6
Adwick upon Dearne S Yorks 89 D5
Adziel Aberds 161 C6
Ae Village Dumfries 114 F2
Affleck Aberds 151 B7
Affpuddle Dorset 13 E6
Affric Lodge Highld 146 B4
Afon-wen Flint 72 B5
Afton I o W 14 F4
Agglethorpe N Yorks 101 F5
Agneash I o M 84 D4
Aigburth Mers 85 F4
Aiginis W Isles 172 E7
Aike E Yorks 97 E6
Aikerness Orkney 176 A3
Aikers Orkney 176 G3
Aiketgate Cumb 108 E4
Aikton Cumb 108 D2
Ailey Hereford 48 E5
Ailstone Warks 51 D7
Ailsworth P'boro 65 E8
Ainderby Quernhow N Yorks 102 F1
Ainderby Steeple N Yorks 101 E8
Aingers Green Essex 43 B7
Ainsdale Mers 85 C4
Ainsdale-on-Sea Mers 85 C4
Ainstable Cumb 108 E5
Ainsworth Gtr Man 87 C5
Ainthorpe N Yorks 103 D5
Aintree Mers 85 E4
Aintree Racecourse Mers 85 E8
Aird Argyll 130 E3
Aird Dumfries 104 C4
Aird Highld 154 C3
Aird W Isles 172 E8
Aird a Mhachair W Isles 170 F3
Aird a'Mhulaidh W Isles 173 G4
Aird Asaig W Isles 173 H4
Aird Dhail W Isles 172 B7
Aird Mhidhinis W Isles 171 K3
Aird Mhighe W Isles 173 J4
Aird Mhighe W Isles 173 K3
Aird Mhor W Isles 171 K3
Aird of Sleat Highld 145 C5
Aird Thunga W Isles 172 E7
Aird Uig W Isles 172 E3
Airdens Highld 164 E3
Airdrie N Lnrk 121 C7
Airdtorrisdale Highld 167 C8
Airidh a Bhruaich W Isles 172 G5
Airieland Dumfries 106 D4
Airmyn E Yorks 89 B8
Airntully Perth 141 F7
Airor Highld 145 C7
Airth Falk 133 F7
Airton N Yorks 94 D2
Airyhassen Dumfries 105 E7
Aisby Lincs 90 E2
Aisby Lincs 78 F3
Aisgernis W Isles 171 H3
Aiskew N Yorks 101 F7
Aislaby N Yorks 103 D5
Aislaby N Yorks 103 D6
Aislaby Stockton 102 C2
Aisthorpe Lincs 78 A2
Aith Orkney 176 E1
Aith Shetland 175 H5
Aith Shetland 174 D8
Aithsetter Shetland 175 K6
Aitkenhead S Ayrs 112 D3
Aitnoch Highld 158 F3
Akeld Northumb 117 B5
Akeley Bucks 52 F5
Akenham Suff 56 E5
Albaston Corn 6 B2
Alberbury Shrops 60 C3
Albert Dock, Liverpool Mers 85 F8
Albourne W Sus 17 C6
Albrighton Shrops 60 C4
Albrighton Shrops 62 D2
Alburgh Norf 69 F5
Albury Herts 41 B7
Albury Sur 27 E8
Albury End Herts 41 B7
Alby Hill Norf 81 D7
Alcaig Highld 157 D6
Alcaston Shrops 60 F4
Alcester Warks 51 D5
Alciston E Sus 18 E2
Alcombe Som 21 E8
Alcombe Wilts 24 C3
Alconbury Cambs 54 B2
Alconbury Weston Cambs 54 B2
Aldbar Castle Angus 143 D5
Aldborough Norf 81 D7
Aldborough N Yorks 95 C7
Aldbourne Wilts 25 B7
Aldbrough E Yorks 97 F8
Aldbrough St John N Yorks 101 C7
Aldbury Herts 40 C2
Aldcliffe Lancs 92 C4
Aldclune Perth 141 C6
Aldeburgh Suff 57 D8
Aldeby Norf 69 E7
Aldenham Herts 40 E4
Alderbury Wilts 14 B2
Aldercar Derbys 76 E4
Alderford Norf 68 C4
Alderholt Dorset 14 C2
Alderley Glos 36 E4
Alderley Edge Ches 74 B5
Aldermaston W Berks 26 C3
Aldermaston Wharf W Berks 26 C4
Alderminster Warks 51 E7
Alderney Airport Ald 16
Alder's End Hereford 49 E8
Aldersey Green Ches 73 D8
Aldershot Hants 27 D6
Alderton Glos 50 F5
Alderton Northants 52 E5
Alderton Shrops 60 B4
Alderton Suff 57 E7
Alderton Wilts 37 F5
Alderwasley Derbys 76 D3
Aldfield N Yorks 95 C5
Aldford Ches 73 D8
Aldham Essex 43 B5
Aldham Suff 56 E4
Aldie Highld 164 F4
Aldingbourne W Sus 16 D3
Aldingham Cumb 92 B2
Aldington Kent 19 B7
Aldington Worcs 51 E5
Aldington Frith Kent 19 B7
Aldochlay Argyll 132 E2
Aldreth Cambs 54 B5
Aldridge W Mid 62 D4
Aldringham Suff 57 C8
Aldsworth Glos 38 C1
Aldunie Moray 150 B2
Aldwark Derbys 76 D2
Aldwark N Yorks 95 C7
Aldwick W Sus 16 E3
Aldwincle Northants 65 F7
Aldworth W Berks 26 B3
Alexandria W Dunb 120 B3
Alfardisworthy Devon 8 C4
Alfington Devon 11 E6
Alfold Sur 27 F8
Alfold Bars W Sus 27 F8
Alfold Crossways Sur 27 F8
Alford Aberds 150 C4
Alford Lincs 79 B7
Alford Som 23 F8
Alfreton Derbys 76 D4
Alfrick Worcs 50 D2
Alfrick Pound Worcs 50 D2
Alfriston E Sus 18 E2
Algaltraig Argyll 129 C5
Algarkirk Lincs 79 F5
Alhampton Som 23 F8
Aline Lodge W Isles 173 G4
Alisary Highld 145 F7
Alkborough N Lincs 90 B2
Alkerton Oxon 51 E8
Alkham Kent 31 E6
Alkington Shrops 74 F2
Alkmonton Derbys 75 F8
All Cannings Wilts 25 C5
All Saints Church, Godshill I o W 15 F6
All Saints South Elmham Suff 69 F6
All Stretton Shrops 60 E4
Alladale Lodge Highld 163 F8
Allaleigh Devon 7 D6
Allanaquoich Aberds 149 E7
Allangrange Mains Highld 157 D7
Allanton Borders 124 D4
Allanton N Lnrk 121 D8
Allathasdal W Isles 171 K2
Allendale Town Northumb 109 D8
Allenheads Northumb 109 E8
Allens Green Herts 41 C7
Allensford Durham 110 D3
Allensmore Hereford 49 F6
Allenton Derby 76 F3
Aller Som 12 B2
Allerby Cumb 107 F7
Allerford Som 21 E8
Allerston N Yorks 103 F6
Allerthorpe E Yorks 96 E3
Allerton Mers 86 F2
Allerton W Yorks 94 F4
Allerton Bywater W Yorks 88 B5
Allerton Mauleverer N Yorks 95 D7
Allesley W Mid 63 F7
Allestree Derby 76 F3
Allet Corn 3 B6
Allexton Leics 64 D5
Allgreave Ches 75 C6
Allhallows Medway 30 B2
Allhallows-on-Sea Medway 30 B2
Alligin Shuas Highld 154 E4
Allimore Green Staffs 62 C2
Allington Lincs 77 E8
Allington Wilts 25 F7
Allington Wilts 25 C5
Allithwaite Cumb 92 B3
Alloa Clack 133 E7
Allonby Cumb 107 E7
Alloway S Ayrs 112 C3
Allt Carms 33 D6
Allt na h-Airbhe Highld 163 E5
Allt-nan-sùgh Highld 146 B2
Alltchaorunn Highld 139 D5
Alltforgan Powys 59 B6
Alltmawr Powys 48 E2
Alltnacaillich Highld 167 E6
Alltsigh Highld 147 C7
Alltwalis Carms 46 F3
Alltwen Neath 33 D8
Alltyblaca Ceredig 46 E4
Allwood Green Suff 56 B4
Almeley Hereford 48 D5
Almer Dorset 13 E7
Almholme S Yorks 89 D6
Almington Staffs 74 F4
Alminstone Cross Devon 8 B5
Almondbank Perth 134 B2
Almondbury W Yorks 88 C2
Almondsbury S Glos 36 F3
Alne N Yorks 95 C7
Alness Highld 157 C7
Alnham Northumb 117 C5
Alnmouth Northumb 117 C8
Alnwick Northumb 117 C7
Alperton London 40 F4
Alphamstone Essex 56 F2
Alpheton Suff 56 D2
Alphington Devon 10 E4
Alport Derbys 76 C2
Alpraham Ches 74 D2
Alresford Essex 43 B6
Alrewas Staffs 63 C5
Alsager Ches 74 D4
Alsagers Bank Staffs 74 E5
Alsop en le Dale Derbys 75 D8
Alston Cumb 109 E7
Alston Devon 11 D8
Alstone Glos 50 F4
Alstonefield Staffs 75 D8
Alswear Devon 10 B2
Altandhu Highld 162 C3
Altanduin Highld 165 B5
Altarnun Corn 8 F4
Altass Highld 164 D1
Alterwall Highld 169 C7
Altham Lancs 93 F7
Althorne Essex 43 E5
Althorp House, Great Brington Northants 52 C4
Althorpe N Lincs 90 D2
Alticry Dumfries 105 D6
Altnabreac Station Highld 168 E5
Altnacealgach Hotel Highld 163 C6
Altnacraig Argyll 130 C4
Altnafeadh Highld 139 D6
Altnaharra Highld 167 F7
Altofts W Yorks 88 B4
Alton Derbys 76 C3
Alton Hants 26 F5
Alton Staffs 75 E7
Alton Pancras Dorset 12 D5
Alton Priors Wilts 25 C6
Alton Towers Staffs 75 E7
Altrincham Gtr Man 87 F5
Altrua Highld 146 F5
Altskeith Stirl 132 D3
Altyre Ho. Moray 158 D4
Alva Clack 133 E7
Alvanley Ches 73 B8
Alvaston Derby 76 F3
Alvechurch Worcs 50 B5
Alvecote Warks 63 D6
Alvediston Wilts 13 B7
Alveley Shrops 61 F7
Alverdiscott Devon 9 B7
Alverstoke Hants 15 E7
Alverstone I o W 15 F6
Alverton Notts 77 E7
Alves Moray 158 C5
Alvescot Oxon 38 D2
Alveston S Glos 36 F3
Alveston Warks 51 D7
Alvie Highld 148 D4
Alvingham Lincs 91 E7
Alvington Glos 36 D3
Alwalton Cambs 65 E8
Alweston Dorset 12 C4
Alwinton Northumb 116 D5
Alwoodley W Yorks 95 E5
Alyth Perth 142 E2
Am Baile W Isles 171 J3
Am Buth Argyll 130 C4
Amatnatua Highld 164 E1
Amber Hill Lincs 78 E5
Ambergate Derbys 76 D3
Amberley Glos 37 D5
Amberley W Sus 16 C4
Amble Northumb 117 D8
Amblecote W Mid 62 F2
Ambler Thorn W Yorks 87 B8
Ambleside Cumb 99 D5
Ambleston Pembs 44 C5
Ambrosden Oxon 39 C6
Amcotts N Lincs 90 C2
American Adventure, Ilkeston Derbys 76 E4
American Air Museum, Duxford Cambs 55 E5
Amersham Bucks 40 E2
Amerton Working Farm, Stowe-by-Chartley Staffs 62 B3
Amesbury Wilts 25 E6
Amington Staffs 63 D6
Amisfield Dumfries 114 F2
Amlwch Anglesey 82 B4
Amlwch Port Anglesey 82 B4
Ammanford = Rhydaman Carms 33 C7
Amod Argyll 118 C4
Amotherby N Yorks 96 B3
Ampfield Hants 14 B5
Ampleforth N Yorks 95 B8
Ampney Crucis Glos 37 D7
Ampney St Mary Glos 37 D7
Ampney St Peter Glos 37 D7
Amport Hants 25 E7
Ampthill Beds 53 F8
Ampton Suff 56 B2
Amroth Pembs 32 D2
Amulree Perth 141 F5
An Caol Highld 155 E2
An Cnoc W Isles 172 E7
An Gleann Ur W Isles 172 E7
An t-Ob = Leverburgh W Isles 173 K3
Anagach Highld 149 B6
Anaheilt Highld 138 C2
Anancaun Highld 154 D6
Ancaster Lincs 78 E2
Anchor Shrops 59 F8
Anchorsholme Blkpool 92 E3
Ancroft Northumb 125 E5
Ancrum Borders 116 B2
Anderby Lincs 79 B8
Anderson Dorset 13 E6
Anderton Ches 74 B3
Andover Hants 25 E8
Andover Down Hants 25 E8
Andoversford Glos 37 C7
Andreas I o M 84 C4
Anfield Mers 85 E4
Angersleigh Som 11 C6

Angle Pembs 44 E3
Angmering W Sus 16 D4
Angram N Yorks 95 E8
Angram N Yorks 100 E3
Anie Stirl 132 C4
Ankerville Highld 158 B2
Anlaby E Yorks 90 B4
Anmer Norf 80 E3
Anna Valley Hants 25 E8
Annan Dumfries 107 C8
Annat Argyll 131 C6
Annat Highld 155 E4
Annbank S Ayrs 112 B4
Anne Hathaway's Cottage, Stratford-upon-Avon Warks 51 D6
Annesley Notts 76 D5
Annesley Woodhouse Notts 76 D4
Annfield Plain Durham 110 D4
Annifirth Shetland 175 J3
Annitsford T & W 111 B5
Annscroft Shrops 60 D4
Ansdell Lancs 85 B4
Ansford Som 23 F8
Ansley Warks 63 E6
Anslow Staffs 63 B6
Anslow Gate Staffs 63 B5
Anstey Herts 54 F5
Anstey Leics 64 D2
Anstruther Easter Fife 135 D7
Anstruther Wester Fife 135 D7
Ansty Hants 26 E5
Ansty Warks 63 F7
Ansty Wilts 13 B7
Ansty W Sus 17 B6
Anthill Common Hants 15 C7
Anthorn Cumb 107 D8
Antingham Norf 81 D8
Anton's Gowt Lincs 79 E5
Antonshill Falk 133 F7
Antony Corn 5 D8
Anwick Lincs 78 D4
Anwoth Dumfries 106 D2
Aoradh Argyll 126 C2
Apes Hall Cambs 67 E5
Apethorpe Northants 65 E7
Apeton Staffs 62 C2
Apley Lincs 78 B4
Apperknowle Derbys 76 B3
Apperley Glos 37 B5
Apperley Bridge W Yorks 94 F4
Appersett N Yorks 100 E3
Appin Argyll 138 E3
Appin House Argyll 138 E3
Appleby N Lincs 90 C3
Appleby-in-Westmorland Cumb 100 B1
Appleby Magna Leics 63 D7
Appleby Parva Leics 63 D7
Applecross Highld 155 F3
Applecross Ho. Highld 155 F3
Appledore Devon 20 F3
Appledore Devon 11 C5
Appledore Kent 19 C6
Appledore Heath Kent 19 B6
Appleford Oxon 39 E5
Applegarthtown Dumfries 114 F4
Appleshaw Hants 25 E8
Applethwaite Cumb 98 B4
Appleton Halton 86 F3
Appleton Oxon 38 D4
Appleton-le-Moors N Yorks 103 F5
Appleton-le-Street N Yorks 96 B3
Appleton Roebuck N Yorks 95 E8
Appleton Thorn Warr 86 F4
Appleton Wiske N Yorks 102 D1
Appletreehall Borders 115 C8
Appletreewick N Yorks 94 C3
Appley Som 11 B5
Appley Bridge Lancs 86 D3
Apse Heath I o W 15 F6
Apsley End Beds 54 F2
Apuldram W Sus 16 D2
Aquhythie Aberds 151 C6
Arabella Highld 158 B2
Arbeadie Aberds 151 E5
Arbeia Roman Fort and Museum T & W 111 C6
Arberth = Narberth Pembs 32 C2
Arbirlot Angus 143 E6
Arboll Highld 165 F5
Arborfield Wokingham 27 C5
Arborfield Cross Wokingham 27 C5
Arborfield Garrison Wokingham 27 C5
Arbour-thorne S Yorks 88 F4
Arbroath Angus 143 E6
Arbuthnott Aberds 143 B7
Archiestown Moray 159 E6
Arclid Ches 74 C4
Ard-dhubh Highld 155 F3
Ardachu Highld 164 D3
Ardalanish Argyll 136 G4
Ardanaiseig Argyll 131 C6
Ardaneaskan Highld 155 G4
Ardanstur Argyll 130 D4
Ardargie House Hotel Perth 134 C2
Ardarroch Highld 155 G4
Ardbeg Argyll 126 E4
Ardbeg Argyll 129 B6
Ardbeg Distillery, Port Ellen Argyll 126 E4
Ardcharnich Highld 163 F5
Ardchiavaig Argyll 136 G4
Ardchullarie More Stirl 132 C4
Ardchyle Stirl 132 B4
Arddleen Powys 60 C2
Ardechvie Highld 146 E4
Ardeley Herts 41 B6
Ardelve Highld 155 H4
Arden Argyll 132 F2
Ardens Grafton Warks 51 D6
Ardentinny Argyll 129 B6
Ardentraive Argyll 129 C5
Ardeonaig Stirl 140 F3
Ardersier Highld 157 D8
Ardessie Highld 162 F4
Ardfern Argyll 130 E4
Ardgartan Argyll 131 E8
Ardgay Highld 164 E2
Ardgour Highld 138 C4
Ardheslaig Highld 154 E3
Ardiecow Moray 160 B2
Ardindrean Highld 163 F5
Ardingly W Sus 17 B7
Ardington Oxon 38 F4
Ardlair Aberds 150 B4
Ardlamont Ho. Argyll 128 D4
Ardleigh Essex 43 B6
Ardler Perth 142 E2
Ardley Oxon 39 B5
Ardlui Argyll 132 C2
Ardlussa Argyll 127 D4
Ardmair Highld 163 E5
Ardmay Argyll 131 E8
Ardminish Argyll 118 B3
Ardmolich Highld 145 F7
Ardmore Argyll 130 C3
Ardmore Highld 166 D4
Ardmore Highld 164 F4
Ardnacross Argyll 137 D6
Ardnadam Argyll 129 C6
Ardnagrask Highld 157 E6
Ardnarff Highld 155 G4
Ardnastang Highld 138 C2
Ardnave Argyll 126 B2
Ardno Argyll 131 E7
Ardo Aberds 160 E5
Ardo Ho. Aberds 151 B8
Ardoch Perth 141 F7
Ardochy House Highld 146 D5
Ardoyne Aberds 151 B5
Ardpatrick Argyll 128 D2
Ardpatrick Ho. Argyll 128 E2
Ardpeaton Argyll 129 B7
Ardrishaig Argyll 128 B3
Ardross Fife 135 D7
Ardross Highld 157 B7
Ardross Castle Highld 157 B7
Ardrossan N Ayrs 120 E2
Ardshealach Highld 137 B7
Ardsley S Yorks 88 D4
Ardslignish Highld 137 B6
Ardtalla Argyll 126 D4
Ardtalnaig Perth 140 F4
Ardtoe Highld 145 F6
Ardtrostan Perth 133 B5
Arduaine Argyll 130 D3
Ardullie Highld 157 C6
Ardvasar Highld 145 C6
Ardvorlich Perth 132 B5
Ardwell Dumfries 104 E5
Ardwell Mains Dumfries 104 E5
Ardwick Gtr Man 87 E6
Areley Kings Worcs 50 B3
Arford Hants 27 F6
Argoed Caerph 35 E5
Argoed Mill Powys 47 C8
Argyll & Sutherland Highlanders Museum (See Stirling Castle) Stirl 133 E6
Arichamish Argyll 130 E5
Arichastlich Argyll 131 B8
Aridhglas Argyll 136 F4
Arileod Argyll 136 C2
Arinacrinachd Highld 154 E3
Arinagour Argyll 136 C3
Arion Orkney 176 E1
Arisaig Highld 145 E6
Ariundle Highld 138 C2
Arkendale N Yorks 95 C6
Arkesden Essex 55 F5
Arkholme Lancs 93 B5
Arkle Town N Yorks 101 D5
Arkley London 41 E5
Arksey S Yorks 89 D6
Arkwright Town Derbys 76 B4
Arle Glos 37 B6
Arlecdon Cumb 98 C2
Arlesey Beds 54 F2
Arleston Telford 61 C6
Arley Ches 86 F4
Arlingham Glos 36 C4
Arlington Devon 20 E5
Arlington E Sus 18 E2
Arlington Glos 37 D8
Arlington Court Devon 20 E5
Armadale Highld 168 C2
Armadale W Loth 122 C2
Armadale Castle Highld 145 C6
Armathwaite Cumb 108 E5
Arminghall Norf 69 D5
Armitage Staffs 62 C4
Armley W Yorks 95 F5
Armscote Warks 51 E7
Armthorpe S Yorks 89 D7
Arnabost Argyll 136 C3
Arncliffe N Yorks 94 B2
Arncroach Fife 135 D7
Arne Dorset 13 F7
Arnesby Leics 64 E3
Arngask Perth 134 C3
Arnisdale Highld 145 B8
Arnish Highld 152 E6
Arniston Engine Midloth 123 C6
Arnol W Isles 172 D6
Arnold E Yorks 97 E7
Arnold Notts 77 E5
Arnolfini Gallery Bristol 23 B7
Arnprior Stirl 132 E5
Arnside Cumb 92 B4
Aros Mains Argyll 137 D6
Arowry Wrex 73 F8
Arpafeelie Highld 157 D7
Arrad Foot Cumb 99 F5
Arram E Yorks 97 E6
Arrathorne N Yorks 101 E7
Arreton I o W 15 F6
Arrington Cambs 54 D4
Arrivain Argyll 131 B8
Arrochar Argyll 131 E8
Arrow Warks 51 D5
Arthington W Yorks 95 E5
Arthingworth Northants 64 F4
Arthog Gwyn 58 C3
Arthrath Aberds 161 E6
Arthurstone Perth 142 E2
Artrochie Aberds 161 E7
Arundel W Sus 16 D4
Arundel Castle W Sus 16 D4
Aryhoulan Highld 138 C4
Asby Cumb 98 B2
Ascog Argyll 129 D6
Ascot Windsor 27 C7
Ascot Racecourse Windsor 27 C7
Ascott Warks 51 F8
Ascott-under-Wychwood Oxon 38 C3
Asenby N Yorks 95 B6
Asfordby Leics 64 C4
Asfordby Hill Leics 64 C4
Asgarby Lincs 78 E4
Asgarby Lincs 79 C6
Ash Kent 29 C6
Ash Kent 31 D6
Ash Som 12 B2
Ash Sur 27 D6
Ash Bullayne Devon 10 D2
Ash Green Warks 63 F7
Ash Magna Shrops 74 F2
Ash Mill Devon 10 B2
Ash Priors Som 11 B6
Ash Street Suff 56 E4
Ash Thomas Devon 10 C5
Ash Vale Sur 27 D6
Ashampstead W Berks 26 B3
Ashbocking Suff 57 D5
Ashbourne Derbys 75 E8
Ashbrittle Som 11 B5
Ashburton Devon 7 C5
Ashbury Devon 9 E7
Ashbury Oxon 38 F2
Ashby N Lincs 90 D3
Ashby by Partney Lincs 79 C7
Ashby cum Fenby NE Lincs 91 D6
Ashby de la Launde Lincs 78 D3
Ashby-de-la-Zouch Leics 63 C7
Ashby Folville Leics 64 C4
Ashby Magna Leics 64 E2
Ashby Parva Leics 64 F2
Ashby Puerorum Lincs 79 B6
Ashby St Ledgers Northants 52 C3
Ashby St Mary Norf 69 D6
Ashchurch Glos 50 F4
Ashcombe Devon 7 B7
Ashcott Som 23 F6
Ashdon Essex 55 E6
Ashe Hants 26 E3
Asheldham Essex 43 D5
Ashen Essex 55 E8
Ashendon Bucks 39 C7
Ashfield Carms 33 B7
Ashfield Stirl 133 D6
Ashfield Suff 57 C6
Ashfield Green Suff 57 B6
Ashfold Crossways W Sus 17 B6
Ashford Devon 20 F4
Ashford Hants 14 C2
Ashford Kent 30 E4
Ashford Sur 27 B8
Ashford Bowdler Shrops 49 B7
Ashford Carbonell Shrops 49 B7
Ashford Hill Hants 26 C3
Ashford in the Water Derbys 75 C8
Ashgill S Lnrk 121 E7
Ashill Devon 11 C5
Ashill Norf 67 D8
Ashill Som 11 C8
Ashingdon Essex 42 E4
Ashington Northumb 117 F8
Ashington Som 12 B3
Ashington W Sus 16 C5
Ashintully Castle Perth 141 C8
Ashkirk Borders 115 B7
Ashlett Hants 15 D5
Ashleworth Glos 37 B5
Ashley Cambs 55 C7
Ashley Ches 87 F5
Ashley Devon 9 C8
Ashley Dorset 14 D2
Ashley Glos 37 E6
Ashley Hants 14 E3
Ashley Hants 25 F8
Ashley Northants 64 E4
Ashley Staffs 74 F4
Ashley Green Bucks 40 D2
Ashley Heath Dorset 14 D2
Ashley Heath Staffs 74 F4
Ashmanhaugh Norf 69 B6
Ashmansworth Hants 26 D2
Ashmansworthy Devon 8 C5
Ashmore Dorset 13 C7
Ashorne Warks 51 D8
Ashover Derbys 76 C3
Ashow Warks 51 B8
Ashprington Devon 7 D6
Ashreigney Devon 9 C8
Ashtead Sur 28 D2
Ashton Ches 74 C2
Ashton Corn 2 D5
Ashton Hants 15 C6
Ashton Hereford 49 C7
Ashton Invclyd 129 C7
Ashton Northants 53 E5
Ashton Northants 65 F7
Ashton Common Wilts 24 D3
Ashton-In-Makerfield Gtr Man 86 E3
Ashton Keynes Wilts 37 E7
Ashton under Hill Worcs 50 F4
Ashton-under-Lyne Gtr Man 87 E7
Ashton upon Mersey Gtr Man 87 E5
Ashurst Hants 14 C4
Ashurst Kent 18 B2
Ashurst W Sus 17 C5
Ashurstwood W Sus 28 F5
Ashwater Devon 9 E5
Ashwell Herts 54 F3
Ashwell Rutland 65 C5
Ashwell Som 11 C8
Ashwellthorpe Norf 68 E4
Ashwick Som 23 E8
Ashwicken Norf 67 C7
Ashybank Borders 115 C8
Askam in Furness Cumb 92 B2
Askern S Yorks 89 C6
Askerswell Dorset 12 E3
Askett Bucks 39 D8
Askham Cumb 99 B7
Askham Notts 77 B7
Askham Bryan York 95 E8
Askham Richard York 95 E8
Asknish Argyll 128 A4
Askrigg N Yorks 100 E4
Askwith N Yorks 94 E4
Aslackby Lincs 78 F3
Aslacton Norf 68 E4
Aslockton Notts 77 F7
Asloun Aberds 150 C4
Aspatria Cumb 107 E8
Aspenden Herts 41 B6
Asperton Lincs 79 F5
Aspley Guise Beds 53 F7
Aspley Heath Beds 53 F7
Aspull Gtr Man 86 D4
Asselby E Yorks 89 B8
Asserby Lincs 79 B7
Assington Suff 56 F3
Assynt Ho. Highld 157 C6
Astbury Ches 74 C5
Astcote Northants 52 D4
Asterley Shrops 60 D3
Asterton Shrops 60 E3
Asthall Oxon 38 C2
Asthall Leigh Oxon 38 C3
Astley Shrops 60 C5
Astley Warks 63 F7
Astley Worcs 50 C2
Astley Abbotts Shrops 61 E7
Astley Bridge Gtr Man 86 C5
Astley Cross Worcs 50 C3
Astley Green Gtr Man 86 E5
Aston Ches 74 E3
Aston Ches 74 B2
Aston Derbys 88 F2
Aston Hereford 49 B6
Aston Herts 41 B5
Aston Oxon 38 D3
Aston Shrops 60 B5
Aston Staffs 74 E4
Aston S Yorks 89 F5
Aston Telford 61 D6
Aston W Mid 62 F4
Aston Wokingham 39 F7
Aston Abbotts Bucks 39 B8
Aston Botterell Shrops 61 F6
Aston-By-Stone Staffs 75 F6
Aston Cantlow Warks 51 D6
Aston Clinton Bucks 40 C1
Aston Crews Hereford 36 B3
Aston Cross Glos 50 F4
Aston End Herts 41 B5
Aston Eyre Shrops 61 E6
Aston Fields Worcs 50 C4
Aston Flamville Leics 63 E8
Aston Ingham Hereford 36 B3
Aston juxta Mondrum Ches 74 D3
Aston le Walls Northants 52 D2
Aston Magna Glos 51 F6
Aston Munslow Shrops 60 F5
Aston on Clun Shrops 60 F3
Aston-on-Trent Derbys 63 B8
Aston Rogers Shrops 60 D3
Aston Rowant Oxon 39 E7
Aston Sandford Bucks 39 D7
Aston Somerville Worcs 50 F5
Aston Subedge Glos 51 E6
Aston Tirrold Oxon 39 F5
Aston Upthorpe Oxon 39 F5
Astrop Northants 52 F3
Astwick Beds 54 F3
Astwood M Keynes 53 E7
Astwood Worcs 50 D3
Astwood Bank Worcs 50 C5
Aswarby Lincs 78 F3
Aswardby Lincs 79 B6
Atch Lench Worcs 50 D5
Atcham Shrops 60 D5
Athelhampton Dorset 13 E5
Athelington Suff 57 B6
Athelney Som 11 B8
Athelstaneford E Loth 123 B8
Atherington Devon 9 B7
Atherstone Warks 63 E7
Atherstone on Stour Warks 51 D7
Atherton Gtr Man 86 D4
Atley Hill N Yorks 101 D7
Atlow Derbys 76 E2
Attadale Highld 155 G5
Attadale Ho. Highld 155 G5
Attenborough Notts 76 F5
Atterby Lincs 90 E3
Attercliffe S Yorks 88 F4
Attleborough Norf 68 E3
Attleborough Warks 63 E7
Attlebridge Norf 68 C4
Atwick E Yorks 97 D7
Atworth Wilts 24 C3
Aubourn Lincs 78 C2
Auchagallon N Ayrs 119 C5
Auchallater Aberds 149 F7
Aucharnie Aberds 160 D3
Auchattie Aberds 151 E5
Auchavan Angus 142 C1
Auchbreck Moray 149 B8
Auchenback E Renf 120 D5
Auchenbainzie Dumfries 113 E8
Auchenblae Aberds 143 B7
Auchenbrack Dumfries 113 E7
Auchenbreck Argyll 129 B5
Auchencairn Dumfries 106 D4
Auchencairn Dumfries 114 F2
Auchencairn N Ayrs 119 D7
Auchencrosh S Ayrs 104 B5
Auchencrow Borders 124 C4
Auchendinny Midloth 123 C5
Auchengray S Lnrk 122 D2
Auchenhalrig Moray 159 C7
Auchenheath S Lnrk 121 E8
Auchenlochan Argyll 128 C4
Auchenmalg Dumfries 105 D6
Auchensoul S Ayrs 112 E2
Auchentiber N Ayrs 120 E3
Auchertyre Highld 155 H4
Auchgourish Highld 148 C5
Auchincarroch W Dunb 132 F3
Auchindrain Argyll 131 E6
Auchindrean Highld 163 F5
Auchininna Aberds 160 D3
Auchinleck E Ayrs 113 B5
Auchinloch N Lnrk 121 B6
Auchinroath Moray 159 D6
Auchintoul Aberds 150 C4
Auchiries Aberds 161 E7
Auchlee Aberds 151 E7
Auchleven Aberds 150 B5
Auchlochan S Lnrk 121 F8
Auchlossan Aberds 150 D4
Auchlunies Aberds 151 E7
Auchlyne Stirl 132 B4
Auchmacoy Aberds 161 E6
Auchmair Moray 150 B2
Auchmantle Dumfries 105 C5
Auchmillan E Ayrs 112 B5
Auchmithie Angus 143 E6
Auchmuirbridge Fife 134 D4
Auchmull Angus 143 B5
Auchnacree Angus 142 C4
Auchnagallin Highld 158 F4
Auchnagatt Aberds 161 D6
Auchnaha Argyll 128 B4
Auchnashelloch Perth 133 C6
Aucholzie Aberds 150 E2
Auchrannie Angus 142 D2
Auchroisk Highld 149 B6
Auchronie Angus 150 F3
Auchterarder Perth 133 C8
Auchteraw Highld 147 D6
Auchterderran Fife 134 E4
Auchterhouse Angus 142 F3
Auchtermuchty Fife 134 C4
Auchterneed Highld 157 D5
Auchtertool Fife 134 E4
Auchtertyre Moray 159 D5
Auchtubh Stirl 132 B4
Auckengill Highld 169 C8
Auckley S Yorks 89 D7
Audenshaw Gtr Man 87 E7
Audlem Ches 74 E3
Audley Staffs 74 D4
Audley End Essex 56 F2
Audley End House Essex 55 F6
Auds Aberds 160 B3
Aughton E Yorks 96 F3
Aughton Lancs 85 D4
Aughton Lancs 93 C5
Aughton S Yorks 89 F5
Aughton Wilts 25 D7
Aughton Park Lancs 86 D2
Auldearn Highld 158 D3
Aulden Hereford 49 D6
Auldgirth Dumfries 114 F2
Auldhame E Loth 135 F7
Auldhouse S Lnrk 121 D6
Ault a'chruinn Highld 146 B2
Aultanrynie Highld 166 F5
Aultbea Highld 162 F2
Aultdearg Highld 156 C3
Aultgrishan Highld 154 B3
Aultguish Inn Highld 156 B4
Aultibea Highld 165 B7
Aultiphurst Highld 168 C3
Aultmore Moray 159 D8
Aultnagoire Highld 147 B8
Aultnamain Inn Highld 164 F3
Aultnaslat Highld 146 D4
Aulton Aberds 150 B5
Aundorach Highld 149 C5
Aunsby Lincs 78 F3
Auquhorthies Aberds 151 B7
Aust S Glos 36 F2
Austendike Lincs 66 B2
Austerfield S Yorks 89 E7
Austrey Warks 63 D6
Austwick N Yorks 93 C7
Authorpe Lincs 91 F8
Authorpe Row Lincs 79 B8
Avebury Wilts 25 C6
Aveley Thurrock 42 F1
Avening Glos 37 E5
Averham Notts 77 D7
Aveton Gifford Devon 6 E4
Avielochan Highld 148 C5
Aviemore Highld 148 C4
Avington Hants 26 F3
Avington W Berks 25 C8
Avoch Highld 157 D8
Avon Hants 14 E2
Avon Dassett Warks 52 E2
Avonbridge Falk 122 B2
Avonmouth Bristol 23 B7
Avonwick Devon 6 D5
Awbridge Hants 14 B4
Awhirk Dumfries 104 D4
Awkley S Glos 36 F2
Awliscombe Devon 11 D6
Awre Glos 36 D4
Awsworth Notts 76 E4
Axbridge Som 23 D6
Axford Hants 26 E4
Axford Wilts 25 B7
Axminster Devon 11 E7
Axmouth Devon 11 E7
Axton Flint 85 F2
Aycliff Kent 31 E7
Aycliffe Durham 101 B7
Aydon Northumb 110 C3
Aylburton Glos 36 D3
Ayle Northumb 109 E7
Aylesbeare Devon 10 E5
Aylesbury Bucks 39 C8
Aylesby NE Lincs 91 D6
Aylesford Kent 29 D8
Aylesham Kent 31 D6
Aylestone Leicester 64 D2
Aylmerton Norf 81 D7
Aylsham Norf 81 E7
Aylton Hereford 49 F8
Aymestrey Hereford 49 C6
Aynho Northants 52 F3
Ayot St Lawrence Herts 40 C4
Ayot St Peter Herts 41 C5
Ayr S Ayrs 112 B3
Ayr Racecourse S Ayrs 112 B3
Aysgarth N Yorks 101 F5
Ayside Cumb 99 F5
Ayston Rutland 65 D5
Aythorpe Roding Essex 42 C1
Ayton Borders 124 C5
Aywick Shetland 174 E7
Azerley N Yorks 95 B5

B

Babbacombe Torbay 7 C7
Babbinswood Shrops 73 F7
Babcary Som 12 B3
Babel Carms 47 F7
Babell Flint 73 B5
Babraham Cambs 55 D6
Babworth Notts 89 F7
Bac W Isles 172 D7
Bachau Anglesey 82 C4
Back of Keppoch Highld 145 E6
Back Rogerton E Ayrs 113 B5
Backaland Orkney 176 C4
Backaskaill Orkney 176 A3
Backbarrow Cumb 99 F5
Backe Carms 32 C3
Backfolds Aberds 161 C7
Backford Ches 73 B8
Backford Cross Ches 73 B7
Backhill Aberds 160 E4
Backhill Aberds 161 E7
Backhill of Clackriach Aberds 161 D6
Backhill of Fortree Aberds 161 D6
Backhill of Trustach Aberds 150 E5
Backies Highld 165 D5
Backlass Highld 169 D7
Backwell N Som 23 C6
Backworth T & W 111 B6
Bacon End Essex 42 C2
Baconsthorpe Norf 81 D7
Bacton Hereford 49 F5
Bacton Norf 81 D9
Bacton Suff 56 C4
Bacton Green Suff 56 C4
Bacup Lancs 87 B6
Badachro Highld 154 C3
Badanloch Lodge Highld 168 F2
Badavanich Highld 156 D2
Badbury Thamesdown 38 F1
Badby Northants 52 D3
Badcall Highld 166 D4
Badcaul Highld 162 E4
Baddeley Green Stoke 75 D6
Baddesley Clinton Warks 51 B7
Baddesley Clinton Hall Warks 51 B7
Baddesley Ensor Warks 63 E6
Baddidarach Highld 162 B4
Baddoch Aberds 149 F7
Baddock Highld 157 D8
Badenscoth Aberds 160 E4
Badenyon Aberds 150 C2
Badger Shrops 61 E7
Badger's Mount Kent 29 C5
Badgeworth Glos 37 C6
Badgworth Som 23 D5
Badicaul Highld 155 H3
Badingham Suff 57 C7
Badlesmere Kent 30 D4
Badlipster Highld 169 E7
Badluarach Highld 162 E3
Badminton S Glos 37 F5
Badnaban Highld 162 B4
Badninish Highld 164 E4
Badrallach Highld 162 E4
Badsey Worcs 51 E5
Badshot Lea Sur 27 E6
Badsworth W Yorks 89 C5
Badwell Ash Suff 56 C3
Bae Colwyn = Colwyn Bay Conwy 83 D8
Bag Enderby Lincs 79 B6
Bagby N Yorks 102 F2
Bagendon Glos 37 D7
Bagh a Chaisteil = Castlebay W Isles 171 L2
Bagh Mor W Isles 170 E4
Bagh Shiarabhagh W Isles 171 K3
Baghasdal W Isles 171 J3
Bagillt Flint 73 B6
Baginton Warks 51 B8
Baglan Neath 33 E8
Bagley Shrops 60 B4
Bagnall Staffs 75 D6
Bagnor W Berks 26 C2
Bagshot Sur 27 C7
Bagshot Wilts 25 C8
Bagthorpe Norf 80 D3
Bagthorpe Notts 76 D4
Bagworth Leics 63 D8
Bagwy Llydiart Hereford 35 B8
Bail Àrd Bhuirgh W Isles 172 C7
Bail Uachdraich W Isles 170 D4
Baildon W Yorks 94 F4
Baile W Isles 173 K2
Baile a Mhanaich W Isles 170 E3
Baile Ailein W Isles 172 F5
Baile an Truiseil W Isles 172 C6
Baile Boidheach Argyll 128 C2
Baile Glas W Isles 170 E4
Baile Mhartainn W Isles 170 C3
Baile Mhic Phail W Isles 170 C4
Baile Mor Argyll 136 F3
Baile Mor W Isles 170 D3
Baile na Creige W Isles 171 K2
Baile nan Cailleach W Isles 170 E3
Baile Raghaill W Isles 170 C3
Bailebeag Highld 147 C8
Baileyhead Cumb 108 B5
Bailiesward Aberds 159 F8
Baillieston Glasgow 121 C6
Bail'lochdrach W Isles 170 E4
Bail'Ur Tholastaidh W Isles 172 D8
Bainbridge N Yorks 100 E4
Bainsford Falk 133 F7
Bainshole Aberds 160 E3
Bainton E Yorks 97 D5
Bainton P'boro 65 D7
Bairnkine Borders 116 C2
Baker Street Thurrock 42 F2
Baker's End Herts 41 C6
Bakewell Derbys 76 C2
Bala = Y Bala Gwyn 72 F3
Balachuirn Highld 153 E6
Balavil Highld 148 D3
Balbeg Highld 147 B7
Balbeg Highld 157 F5
Balbeggie Perth 134 B3
Balbithan Aberds 151 C6
Balbithan Ho. Aberds 151 C7
Balblair Highld 157 C8
Balblair Highld 164 E2
Balby S Yorks 89 D6
Balchladich Highld 166 F2
Balchraggan Highld 157 F6
Balchraggan Highld 157 E6
Balchrick Highld 166 D3
Balchrystie Fife 135 D6
Balcladaich Highld 147 B5
Balcombe W Sus 28 F4
Balcombe Lane W Sus 28 F4
Balcomie Fife 135 C8
Balcurvie Fife 134 D5
Baldersby N Yorks 95 B6
Baldersby St James N Yorks 95 B6
Balderstone Lancs 93 F6
Balderton Ches 73 C7
Balderton Notts 77 D8
Baldhu Corn 3 B6
Baldinnie Fife 135 C6
Baldock Herts 54 F3
Baldovie Dundee 142 F4
Baldrine I o M 84 D4
Baldslow E Sus 18 D4
Baldwin I o M 84 D3
Baldwinholme Cumb 108 D3
Baldwin's Gate Staffs 74 E4
Bale Norf 81 D6
Balearn Aberds 161 C7
Balemartine Argyll 136 F1
Balephuil Argyll 136 F1
Balerno Edin 122 C4
Balevullin Argyll 136 F1
Balfield Angus 143 C5
Balfour Orkney 176 E3
Balfron Stirl 132 F4
Balfron Station Stirl 132 F4
Balgaveny Aberds 160 D3
Balgavies Angus 143 D5
Balgonar Fife 134 E2
Balgove Aberds 160 E5
Balgowan Highld 148 E2
Balgown Highld 152 C4
Balgrochan E Dunb 121 B6
Balgy Highld 155 E4
Balhaldie Stirl 133 D7
Balhalgardy Aberds 151 B6
Balham London 28 B3
Balhary Perth 142 E2
Baliasta Shetland 174 C8
Baligill Highld 168 C3
Balintore Angus 142 D2
Balintore Highld 158 B2
Balintraid Highld 157 B8
Balk N Yorks 102 F2
Balkeerie Angus 142 E3
Balkemback Angus 142 F3
Balkholme E Yorks 89 B8
Balkissock S Ayrs 104 A5
Ball Shrops 60 B3
Ball Haye Green Staffs 75 D6
Ball Hill Hants 26 C2
Ballabeg I o M 84 E2
Ballacannel I o M 84 D4
Ballachulish Highld 138 D4
Ballajora I o M 84 C4
Ballaleigh I o M 84 D3
Ballamodha I o M 84 E2
Ballantrae S Ayrs 104 A4
Ballaquine I o M 84 D4
Ballards Gore Essex 43 E5
Ballasalla I o M 84 C3
Ballasalla I o M 84 E2
Ballater Aberds 150 E2
Ballaugh I o M 84 C3
Ballaveare I o M 84 E3
Ballcorach Moray 149 B7
Ballechin Perth 141 D6
Balleigh Highld 164 F4
Ballencrieff E Loth 123 B7
Ballentoul Perth 141 C5
Ballidon Derbys 76 D2
Balliemore Argyll 129 B5
Balliemore Argyll 130 C4
Ballikinrain Stirl 132 F4
Ballimeanoch Argyll 131 D6
Ballimore Argyll 128 B4
Ballimore Stirl 132 C4
Ballinaby Argyll 126 C2
Ballindean Perth 134 B4
Ballingdon Suff 56 E2
Ballinger Common Bucks 40 D2
Ballingham Hereford 49 F7
Ballingry Fife 134 E3
Ballinlick Perth 141 E6
Ballinluig Perth 141 D6
Ballintuim Perth 141 D8
Balloch Angus 142 D3
Balloch Highld 157 E8
Balloch N Lnrk 121 B7
Balloch W Dunb 132 F2
Ballochan Aberds 150 E4
Ballochford Moray 159 F7
Ballochmorrie S Ayrs 112 F2
Balls Cross W Sus 16 B3
Balls Green Essex 43 B6
Ballygown Argyll 137 D5
Ballygrant Argyll 126 C3
Ballyhaugh Argyll 136 C2
Balmacara Highld 155 H4
Balmacara Square Highld 155 H4
Balmaclellan Dumfries 106 B3
Balmacneil Perth 141 D6
Balmacqueen Highld 152 B5
Balmae Dumfries 106 E3
Balmaha Stirl 132 E3
Balmalcolm Fife 134 D5
Balmeanach Highld 153 E6
Balmedie Aberds 151 C8
Balmer Heath Shrops 73 F8
Balmerino Fife 135 B5
Balmerlawn Hants 14 D4
Balmichael N Ayrs 119 C6
Balmirmer Angus 143 F5
Balmoral Castle and Gardens Aberds 149 E8
Balmore Highld 153 E3
Balmore Highld 156 F4
Balmore Highld 158 E2
Balmore Perth 141 D6
Balmule Fife 134 F4
Balmullo Fife 135 B6
Balmungie Highld 157 D8
Balnaboth Angus 142 C3
Balnabruaich Highld 157 C8
Balnabruich Highld 165 B8
Balnacoil Highld 165 C5
Balnacra Highld 155 F5
Balnafoich Highld 157 F7
Balnagall Highld 165 F5
Balnaguard Perth 141 D6
Balnahard Argyll 127 C2
Balnahard Argyll 137 E5
Balnain Highld 157 F5
Balnakeil Highld 167 C5
Balnaknock Highld 152 C5
Balnapaling Highld 157 C8
Balne N Yorks 89 C6
Balochroy Argyll 128 E2
Balone Fife 135 C6
Balornock Glasgow 121 C6
Balquharn Perth 141 F7
Balquhidder Stirl 132 B4
Balsall W Mid 51 B7
Balsall Common W Mid 51 B7
Balsall Heath W Mid 62 F4
Balscott Oxon 51 E8
Balsham Cambs 55 D6
Baltasound Shetland 174 C8

Balterley Staffs 74 D4
Baltersan Dumfries 105 C8
Balthangie Aberds 160 C5
Baltonsborough Som 23 F7
Balvaird Highld 157 D6
Balvicar Argyll 130 D3
Balvraid Highld 145 B8
Balvraid Highld 158 F2
Bamber Bridge Lancs 86 B3
Bambers Green Essex 42 B1
Bamburgh Northumb 125 F7
Bamburgh Castle Northumb 125 F7
Bamff Perth 142 D2
Bamford Derbys 88 F3
Bamford Gtr Man 87 C6
Bampton Cumb 99 C7
Bampton Devon 10 B4
Bampton Oxon 38 D3
Bampton Grange Cumb 99 C7
Banavie Highld 139 B5
Banbury Oxon 52 E2
Bancffosfelen Carms 33 C5
Banchory Aberds 151 E5
Banchory-Devenick Aberds 151 D8
Bancycapel Carms 33 C5
Bancyfelin Carms 32 C4
Bancyffordd Carms 46 F3
Bandirran Perth 142 F2
Banff Aberds 160 B3
Bangor Gwyn 83 D5
Bangor-is-y-coed Wrex 73 E7
Bangor on Dee Racecourse Wrex 73 E7
Banham Norf 68 F3
Banham Zoo, Diss Norf 68 F3
Bank Hants 14 D3
Bank Newton N Yorks 94 D2
Bank Street Worcs 49 C8
Bankend Dumfries 107 C7
Bankfoot Perth 141 F7
Bankglen E Ayrs 113 C6
Bankhead Aberdeen 151 C7
Bankhead Aberds 151 D5
Banknock Falk 121 B7
Banks Cumb 109 C5
Banks Lancs 85 B4
Bankshill Dumfries 114 F4
Banningham Norf 81 E8
Banniskirk Ho. Highld 169 D6
Bannister Green Essex 42 B2
Bannockburn Stirl 133 E7
Banstead Sur 28 D3
Bantham Devon 6 E4
Banton N Lnrk 121 B7
Banwell N Som 23 D5
Banyard's Green Suff 57 B6
Bapchild Kent 30 C3
Bar Hill Cambs 54 C4
Barabhas W Isles 172 D6
Barabhas Iarach W Isles 172 D6
Barabhas Uarach W Isles 172 C6
Barachandroman Argyll 130 C2
Barassie S Ayrs 120 F3
Baravullin Argyll 130 B4
Barbaraville Highld 157 B8
Barber Booth Derbys 88 F2
Barbieston S Ayrs 112 C4
Barbon Cumb 99 F8
Barbridge Ches 74 D3
Barbrook Devon 21 E6
Barby Northants 52 B3
Barcaldine Argyll 138 E3
Barcaldine Sea Life Centre Argyll 130 A5
Barcheston Warks 51 F7
Barcombe E Sus 17 C8
Barcombe Cross E Sus 17 C8
Barden N Yorks 101 E6
Barden Scale N Yorks 94 D3
Bardennoch Dumfries 113 E5
Bardfield Saling Essex 42 B2
Bardister Shetland 174 F5
Bardney Lincs 78 C4
Bardon Leics 63 C8
Bardon Mill Northumb 109 C7
Bardowie E Dunb 121 B5
Bardrainney Invclyd 120 B3
Bardsea Cumb 92 B3
Bardsey W Yorks 95 E6
Bardwell Suff 56 B3
Bare Lancs 92 C4
Barfad Argyll 128 D3
Barford Norf 68 D4
Barford Warks 51 C7
Barford St John Oxon 52 F2
Barford St Martin Wilts 25 F5
Barford St Michael Oxon 52 F2
Barfreston Kent 31 D6
Bargod = Bargoed Caerph 35 E5
Bargoed = Bargod Caerph 35 E5
Bargrennan Dumfries 105 B7
Barham Cambs 54 B2
Barham Kent 31 D6
Barham Suff 56 D5
Barharrow Dumfries 106 D3
Barhill Dumfries 106 C5
Barholm Lincs 65 C7
Barkby Leics 64 D3
Barkestone-le-Vale Leics 77 F7
Barkham Wokingham 27 C5
Barking London 41 F7
Barking Suff 56 D4
Barking Tye Suff 56 D4
Barkingside London 41 F7
Barkisland W Yorks 87 C8
Barkston Lincs 78 E2
Barkston N Yorks 95 F7
Barkway Herts 54 F4
Barlaston Staffs 75 F5
Barlavington W Sus 16 C3
Barlborough Derbys 76 B4
Barlby N Yorks 96 F2
Barlestone Leics 63 D8
Barley Herts 54 F4
Barley Lancs 93 E8
Barley Mow T & W 111 D5
Barleythorpe Rutland 64 D5
Barling Essex 43 F5
Barlow Derbys 76 B3
Barlow N Yorks 89 B7
Barlow T & W 110 C4
Barmby Moor E Yorks 96 E3
Barmby on the Marsh E Yorks 89 B7
Barmer Norf 80 D4
Barmoor Castle Northumb 125 F5
Barmoor Lane End Northumb 125 F6
Barmouth = Abermaw Gwyn 58 C3
Barmpton Darl 101 C8
Barmston E Yorks 97 D7
Barnack P'boro 65 D7
Barnacle Warks 63 F7
Barnard Castle Durham 101 C5
Barnard Gate Oxon 38 C4
Barnardiston Suff 55 E8
Barnbarroch Dumfries 106 D5
Barnburgh S Yorks 89 D5
Barnby Suff 69 F7
Barnby Dun S Yorks 89 D7
Barnby in the Willows Notts 77 D8
Barnby Moor Notts 89 F7
Barnes Street Kent 29 E7
Barnet London 41 E5
Barnetby le Wold N Lincs 90 D4
Barney Norf 81 D5
Barnham Suff 56 B2
Barnham W Sus 16 D3
Barnham Broom Norf 68 D3
Barnhead Angus 143 D6
Barnhill Ches 73 D8
Barnhill Dundee 142 F4
Barnhill Moray 158 D5
Barnhills Dumfries 104 B3
Barningham Durham 101 C5
Barningham Suff 56 B3
Barnoldby le Beck NE Lincs 91 D6
Barnoldswick Lancs 93 E8
Barns Green W Sus 16 B5
Barnsley Glos 37 D7
Barnsley S Yorks 88 D4
Barnstaple Devon 20 F4
Barnston Essex 42 C2
Barnston Mers 85 F3
Barnstone Notts 77 F7
Barnt Green Worcs 50 B5
Barnton Ches 74 B3
Barnton Edin 122 B4
Barnwell All Saints Northants 65 F7
Barnwell St Andrew Northants 65 F7
Barnwood Glos 37 C5
Barochreal Argyll 130 C4
Barons Cross Hereford 49 D6
Barr S Ayrs 112 E2
Barra Airport W Isles 171 K2
Barra Castle Aberds 151 B6
Barrachan Dumfries 105 E7
Barrack Aberds 161 D5
Barraglom W Isles 172 E4
Barrahormid Argyll 128 B2
Barran Argyll 130 C4
Barrapol Argyll 136 F1
Barras Aberds 151 F7
Barras Cumb 100 C3
Barrasford Northumb 110 B2
Barravullin Argyll 130 E4
Barregarrow I o M 84 D3
Barrhead E Renf 120 D4
Barrhill S Ayrs 112 F2
Barrington Cambs 54 E4
Barrington Som 11 C8
Barripper Corn 2 C5
Barrmill N Ayrs 120 D3
Barrock Highld 169 B7
Barrock Ho. Highld 169 C7
Barrow Lancs 93 F7
Barrow Rutland 65 C5
Barrow Suff 55 C8
Barrow Green Kent 30 C3
Barrow Gurney N Som 23 C7
Barrow Haven N Lincs 90 B4
Barrow-in-Furness Cumb 92 C2
Barrow Island Cumb 92 C1
Barrow Nook Lancs 86 D2
Barrow Street Wilts 24 F3
Barrow upon Humber N Lincs 90 B4
Barrow upon Soar Leics 64 C2
Barrow upon Trent Derbys 63 B7
Barroway Drove Norf 67 D5
Barrowburn Northumb 116 C4
Barrowby Lincs 77 F8
Barrowcliff N Yorks 103 F8
Barrowden Rutland 65 D6
Barrowford Lancs 93 F8
Barrows Green Ches 74 D3
Barrows Green Cumb 99 F7
Barrow's Green Mers 86 F3
Barry Angus 143 F5
Barry = Y Barri V Glam 22 C3
Barry Island V Glam 22 C3
Barsby Leics 64 C3
Barsham Suff 69 F6
Barston W Mid 51 B7
Bartestree Hereford 49 E7
Barthol Chapel Aberds 160 E5
Barthomley Ches 74 D4
Bartley Hants 14 C4
Bartley Green W Mid 62 F4
Bartlow Cambs 55 E6
Barton Cambs 54 D5
Barton Ches 73 D8
Barton Glos 37 B8
Barton Lancs 85 D4
Barton Lancs 92 F5
Barton N Yorks 101 D7
Barton Oxon 39 D5
Barton Torbay 7 C7
Barton Warks 51 D6
Barton Bendish Norf 67 D7
Barton Hartshorn Bucks 52 F4
Barton in Fabis Notts 76 F5
Barton in the Beans Leics 63 D7
Barton-le-Clay Beds 53 F8
Barton-le-Street N Yorks 96 B3
Barton-le-Willows N Yorks 96 C3
Barton Mills Suff 55 B8
Barton on Sea Hants 14 E3
Barton on the Heath Warks 51 F7
Barton St David Som 23 F7
Barton Seagrave Northants 53 B6
Barton Stacey Hants 26 E2
Barton Turf Norf 69 B6
Barton-under-Needwood Staffs 63 C5
Barton-upon-Humber N Lincs 90 B4
Barton Waterside N Lincs 90 B4
Barugh S Yorks 88 D4
Barway Cambs 55 B6
Barwell Leics 63 E8
Barwick Herts 41 C6
Barwick Som 12 C3
Barwick in Elmet W Yorks 95 F6
Baschurch Shrops 60 B4
Bascote Warks 52 C2
Basford Green Staffs 75 D6
Bashall Eaves Lancs 93 E6
Bashley Hants 14 E3
Basildon Essex 42 F3
Basingstoke Hants 26 D4
Baslow Derbys 76 B2
Bason Bridge Som 22 E5
Bassaleg Newport 35 F6
Bassenthwaite Cumb 108 F2
Bassett Soton 14 C5
Bassingbourn Cambs 54 E4
Bassingfield Notts 77 F6
Bassingham Lincs 78 C2
Bassingthorpe Lincs 65 B6
Basta Shetland 174 D7
Baston Lincs 65 C8
Bastwick Norf 69 C7
Baswick Steer E Yorks 97 E6
Batchworth Heath Herts 40 E3
Batcombe Dorset 12 D4
Batcombe Som 23 F8
Bate Heath Ches 74 B3
Bateman's, Burwash E Sus 18 C3
Batford Herts 40 C4
Bath Bath 24 C2
Bath Abbey Bath 24 C2
Bath Racecourse Bath 24 C2
Bathampton Bath 24 C2
Bathealton Som 11 B5
Batheaston Bath 24 C2
Bathford Bath 24 C2
Bathgate W Loth 122 C2
Bathley Notts 77 D7
Bathpool Corn 5 B7
Bathpool Som 11 B7
Bathville W Loth 122 C2
Batley W Yorks 88 B3
Batsford Glos 51 F6
Battersby N Yorks 102 D3
Battersea London 28 B3
Battisborough Cross Devon 6 E3
Battisford Suff 56 D4
Battisford Tye Suff 56 D4
Battle E Sus 18 D4
Battle Powys 48 F2
Battle Abbey E Sus 18 D4
Battledown Glos 37 B6
Battlefield Shrops 60 C5
Battlesbridge Essex 42 E3
Battlesden Beds 40 B2
Battlesea Green Suff 57 B6
Battleton Som 10 B4
Battram Leics 63 D8
Battramsley Hants 14 E4
Baughton Worcs 50 E3
Baughurst Hants 26 D3
Baulking Oxon 38 E3
Baumber Lincs 78 B5
Baunton Glos 37 D7
Baverstock Wilts 24 F5
Bawburgh Norf 68 D4
Bawdeswell Norf 81 E6
Bawdrip Som 22 F5
Bawdsey Suff 57 E7
Bawtry S Yorks 89 E7
Baxenden Lancs 87 B5
Baxterley Warks 63 E6
Baybridge Hants 15 B6
Baycliff Cumb 92 B2
Baydon Wilts 25 B7
Bayford Herts 41 D6
Bayford Som 12 B5
Bayles Cumb 109 E7
Baylham Suff 56 D5
Baynard's Green Oxon 39 B5
Bayston Hill Shrops 60 D4
Baythorn End Essex 55 E8
Bayton Worcs 49 B8
Beach Highld 138 D1
Beachampton Bucks 53 F5
Beachamwell Norf 67 D7
Beachans Moray 158 E4
Beacharr Argyll 118 B3
Beachborough Kent 19 B8
Beachley Glos 36 E2
Beacon Devon 11 D6
Beacon End Essex 43 B5
Beacon Hill Sur 27 F6
Beacon's Bottom Bucks 39 E7
Beaconsfield Bucks 40 F2
Beacrabhaic W Isles 173 J4
Beadlam N Yorks 102 F4
Beadlow Beds 54 F2
Beadnell Northumb 117 B8
Beaford Devon 9 C7
Beal Northumb 125 E6
Beal N Yorks 89 B6
Beale Park, Goring W Berks 26 B4
Beamhurst Staffs 75 F7
Beaminster Dorset 12 D2
Beamish Durham 110 D5
Beamish Open Air Museum, Stanley Durham 110 D5
Beamsley N Yorks 94 D3
Bean Kent 29 B6
Beanacre Wilts 24 C4
Beanley Northumb 117 C6
Beaquoy Orkney 176 D2
Bear Cross Bmouth 13 E8
Beardwood Blkburn 86 B4
Beare Green Sur 28 E2
Bearley Warks 51 C6
Bearnus Argyll 136 D4
Bearpark Durham 110 E5
Bearsbridge Northumb 109 D7
Bearsden E Dunb 120 B5
Bearsted Kent 29 D8
Bearstone Shrops 74 F4
Bearwood Hereford 49 D5
Bearwood Poole 13 E8
Bearwood W Mid 62 F4
Beattock Dumfries 114 D3
Beauchamp Roding Essex 42 C1
Beauchief S Yorks 88 F4
Beaufort Bl Gwent 35 C5
Beaufort Castle Highld 157 E6
Beaulieu Hants 14 D4
Beauly Highld 157 E6
Beaumaris Anglesey 83 D6
Beaumaris Castle Anglesey 83 D6
Beaumont Cumb 108 D3
Beaumont Essex 43 B7
Beaumont Hill Darl 101 C7
Beausale Warks 51 B7
Beauworth Hants 15 B6
Beaworthy Devon 9 E6
Beazley End Essex 42 B3
Bebington Mers 85 F4
Bebside Northumb 117 F8
Beccles Suff 69 E7
Becconsall Lancs 86 B2
Beck Foot Cumb 99 E8
Beck Hole N Yorks 103 D6
Beck Row Suff 55 B7
Beck Side Cumb 98 F4
Beckbury Shrops 61 D7
Beckenham London 28 C4
Beckermet Cumb 98 D2
Beckfoot Cumb 98 D3
Beckfoot Cumb 107 E7
Beckford Worcs 50 F4
Beckhampton Wilts 25 C5
Beckingham Lincs 77 D8
Beckingham Notts 89 F8
Beckington Som 24 D3
Beckley E Sus 19 C5
Beckley Hants 14 E3
Beckley Oxon 39 C5
Beckton London 41 F7
Beckwithshaw N Yorks 95 D5
Becontree London 41 F7
Bed-y-coedwr Gwyn 71 E8
Bedale N Yorks 101 F7
Bedburn Durham 110 F4
Bedchester Dorset 13 C6
Beddau Rhondda 34 F4
Beddgelert Gwyn 71 C6
Beddingham E Sus 17 D8
Beddington London 28 C4
Bedfield Suff 57 C6
Bedford Beds 53 D8
Bedham W Sus 16 B4
Bedhampton Hants 15 D8
Bedingfield Suff 57 C5
Bedlam N Yorks 95 C5
Bedlington Northumb 117 F8
Bedlington Station Northumb 117 F8
Bedlinog M Tydf 34 D4
Bedminster Bristol 23 B7
Bedmond Herts 40 D3
Bednall Staffs 62 C3
Bedrule Borders 116 C2
Bedstone Shrops 49 B5
Bedwas Caerph 35 F5
Bedworth Warks 63 F7
Bedworth Heath Warks 63 F7
Beeby Leics 64 D3
Beech Hants 26 F4
Beech Staffs 75 F5
Beech Hill Gtr Man 86 D3
Beech Hill W Berks 26 C4
Beechingstoke Wilts 25 D5
Beedon W Berks 26 B2
Beeford E Yorks 97 D7
Beeley Derbys 76 C2
Beelsby NE Lincs 91 D6
Beenham W Berks 26 C3
Beeny Corn 8 E3
Beer Devon 11 F7
Beer Hackett Dorset 12 C3
Beercrocombe Som 11 B8
Beesands Devon 7 E6
Beesby Lincs 91 F8
Beeson Devon 7 E6
Beeston Beds 54 E2
Beeston Ches 74 D2
Beeston Norf 68 C2
Beeston Notts 76 F5
Beeston W Yorks 95 F5
Beeston Castle Ches 74 D2
Beeston Regis Norf 81 C7
Beeswing Dumfries 107 C5
Beetham Cumb 92 B4
Beetley Norf 68 C2
Begbroke Oxon 38 C4
Begelly Pembs 32 D2
Beggar's Bush Powys 48 C4
Beguildy Powys 48 B3
Beighton Norf 69 D6
Beighton S Yorks 88 F5
Beighton Hill Derbys 76 D2
Beith N Ayrs 120 D3
Bekesbourne Kent 31 D5
Bekonscot Model Village, Beaconsfield Bucks 40 C2
Belaugh Norf 69 C5
Belbroughton Worcs 50 B4
Belchamp Otten Essex 56 E2
Belchamp St Paul Essex 55 E8
Belchamp Walter Essex 56 E2
Belchford Lincs 79 B5
Belford Northumb 125 F7
Belhaven E Loth 124 B2
Belhelvie Aberds 151 C8
Belhinnie Aberds 150 B3
Bell Bar Herts 41 D5
Bell Busk N Yorks 94 D2
Bell End Worcs 50 B4
Bell o'th'Hill Ches 74 E2
Bellabeg Aberds 150 C2
Bellamore S Ayrs 112 F2
Bellanoch Argyll 128 A2
Bellaty Angus 142 D2
Belleau Lincs 79 B7
Bellehiglash Moray 159 F5
Bellerby N Yorks 101 E6
Bellever Devon 6 B4
Belliehill Angus 143 C5
Bellingdon Bucks 40 D2
Bellingham Northumb 116 F4
Belloch Argyll 118 C3
Bellochantuy Argyll 118 C3
Bells Yew Green E Sus 18 B3
Bellsbank E Ayrs 112 D4
Bellshill N Lnrk 121 C7
Bellshill Northumb 125 F7
Bellspool Borders 122 F4
Bellsquarry W Loth 122 C3
Belmaduthy Highld 157 D7
Belmesthorpe Rutland 65 C7
Belmont Blkburn 86 C4
Belmont London 28 C3
Belmont S Ayrs 112 B3
Belmont Shetland 174 C7
Belnacraig Aberds 150 C2
Belowda Corn 4 C4
Belper Derbys 76 E3
Belper Lane End Derbys 76 E3
Belsay Northumb 110 B4
Belsay Hall Northumb 110 B3
Belses Borders 115 B8
Belsford Devon 7 D5
Belstead Suff 56 E5
Belston S Ayrs 112 B3
Belstone Devon 9 E8
Belthorn Lancs 86 B5
Beltinge Kent 31 C5
Beltoft N Lincs 90 D2
Belton Leics 63 B8
Belton Lincs 78 F2
Belton N Lincs 89 D8
Belton Norf 69 D7
Belton House, Grantham Lincs 78 F2
Belton in Rutland Rutland 64 D5
Beltring Kent 29 E7
Belts of Collonach Aberds 151 E5
Belvedere London 29 B5
Belvoir Leics 77 F8
Belvoir Leics 77 F8
Bembridge I o W 15 F7
Bemersyde Borders 123 F8
Bemerton Wilts 25 F6
Bempton E Yorks 97 B7
Ben Alder Lodge Highld 140 B2
Ben Armine Lodge Highld 164 C4
Ben Casgro W Isles 172 F7
Benacre Suff 69 F8
Benbecula Airport W Isles 170 E3
Benbuie Dumfries 113 E7
Benderloch Argyll 130 B5
Bendronaig Lodge Highld 155 G6
Benenden Kent 18 B5
Benfield Dumfries 105 C7
Bengate Norf 69 B6
Bengeworth Worcs 50 E5
Benhall Green Suff 57 C7
Benhall Street Suff 57 C7
Benholm Aberds 143 C8
Beningbrough N Yorks 95 D8
Beningbrough Hall N Yorks 95 D8
Benington Herts 41 B5
Benington Lincs 79 E6
Benllech Anglesey 82 C5
Benmore Argyll 129 B6
Benmore Stirl 132 B3
Benmore Lodge Highld 163 C7
Bennacott Corn 8 E4
Bennan N Ayrs 119 D6
Benniworth Lincs 91 F6
Benover Kent 29 E8
Bensham T & W 110 C5
Benslie N Ayrs 120 E3
Benson Oxon 39 E6
Bent Aberds 143 B6
Bent Gate Lancs 87 B5
Benthall Northumb 117 B8
Benthall Shrops 61 D6
Bentham Glos 37 C6
Benthoul Aberdeen 151 D7
Bentlawnt Shrops 60 D3
Bentley E Yorks 97 F6
Bentley Hants 27 E5
Bentley Suff 56 F5
Bentley S Yorks 89 D6
Bentley Warks 63 E6
Bentley Worcs 50 C4
Bentley Heath W Mid 51 B6
Benton Devon 21 F5
Bentpath Dumfries 115 E6
Bents W Loth 122 C2
Bentworth Hants 26 E4
Benvie Dundee 142 F3
Benwick Cambs 66 E3
Beoley Worcs 51 C5
Beoraidbeg Highld 145 D6
Bepton W Sus 16 C2
Berden Essex 41 B7
Bere Alston Devon 6 C2
Bere Ferrers Devon 6 C2
Bere Regis Dorset 13 E6
Berepper Corn 3 D5
Bergh Apton Norf 69 D6
Berinsfield Oxon 39 E5
Berkeley Glos 36 E3
Berkhamsted Herts 40 D2
Berkley Som 24 E3
Berkswell W Mid 51 B7
Bermondsey London 28 B4
Bernera Highld 155 H4
Bernice Argyll 129 A6
Bernisdale Highld 152 D5
Berrick Salome Oxon 39 E6
Berriedale Highld 165 B8
Berrier Cumb 99 B5
Berriew Powys 59 D8
Berrington Northumb 125 E6
Berrington Shrops 60 D5
Berrow Som 22 D5
Berrow Green Worcs 50 D2
Berry Down Cross Devon 20 E4
Berry Hill Glos 36 C2
Berry Hill Pembs 45 E2
Berry Pomeroy Devon 7 C6
Berryhillock Moray 160 B2
Berrynarbor Devon 20 E4
Bersham Wrex 73 E7
Berstane Orkney 176 E3
Berwick E Sus 18 E2
Berwick Bassett Wilts 25 B5
Berwick Hill Northumb 110 B4
Berwick St James Wilts 25 F5
Berwick St John Wilts 13 B7
Berwick St Leonard Wilts 24 F4
Berwick-upon-Tweed Northumb 125 D5
Bescar Lancs 85 C4
Besford Worcs 50 E4
Bessacarr S Yorks 89 D7
Bessels Leigh Oxon 38 D4
Bessingby E Yorks 97 C7
Bessingham Norf 81 D7
Bestbeech Hill E Sus 18 B3
Besthorpe Norf 68 E3
Besthorpe Notts 77 C8
Bestwood Nottingham 77 E5
Bestwood Village Notts 77 E5
Beswick E Yorks 97 E6
Betchworth Sur 28 E3
Beth Shalom Holocaust Centre, Laxton Notts 77 C7
Bethania Ceredig 46 C4
Bethania Gwyn 83 F6
Bethania Gwyn 71 C8
Bethel Anglesey 82 D3
Bethel Gwyn 82 E5
Bethel Gwyn 72 F3
Bethersden Kent 30 E3
Bethesda Gwyn 83 E6
Bethesda Pembs 32 C1
Bethlehem Carms 33 B7
Bethnal Green London 41 F6
Betley Staffs 74 E4
Betsham Kent 29 B7
Betteshanger Kent 31 D7
Bettiscombe Dorset 11 E8
Bettisfield Wrex 73 F8
Betton Shrops 60 D3
Betton Shrops 74 F3
Bettws Bridgend 34 F3
Bettws Newport 35 E6
Bettws Cedewain Powys 59 E8
Bettws Gwerfil Goch Denb 72 E4
Bettws Ifan Ceredig 46 E2
Bettws Newydd Mon 35 D7
Bettws-y-crwyn Shrops 60 F2
Bettyhill Highld 168 C2
Betws Carms 33 C7
Betws Bledrws Ceredig 46 D4
Betws-Garmon Gwyn 82 F5
Betws-y-Coed Conwy 83 F7
Betws-yn-Rhos Conwy 72 B3
Beulah Ceredig 45 E4
Beulah Powys 47 D8
Bevendean Brighton 17 D7
Bevercotes Notts 77 B6
Beverley E Yorks 97 F6
Beverley Minster E Yorks 97 F6
Beverley Racecourse E Yorks 97 E6
Beverston Glos 37 E5
Bevington Glos 36 E3
Bewaldeth Cumb 108 F2
Bewcastle Cumb 109 B5
Bewdley Worcs 50 B2
Bewerley N Yorks 94 C4
Bewholme E Yorks 97 D7
Bexhill E Sus 18 E4
Bexley London 29 B5
Bexleyheath London 29 B5
Bexwell Norf 67 D6
Beyton Suff 56 C3
Bhaltos W Isles 172 E3
Bhatarsaigh W Isles 171 L2
Bibury Glos 37 D8
Bicester Oxon 39 B5
Bickenhall Som 11 C7
Bickenhill W Mid 63 F5
Bicker Lincs 78 F5
Bickershaw Gtr Man 86 D4
Bickerstaffe Lancs 86 D2
Bickerton Ches 74 D2
Bickerton N Yorks 95 D7
Bickington Devon 7 B5
Bickington Devon 20 F4
Bickleigh Devon 6 C3
Bickleigh Devon 10 D4
Bickleton Devon 20 F4
Bickley London 28 C5
Bickley Moss Ches 74 E2
Bicknacre Essex 42 D3
Bicknoller Som 22 F3
Bicknor Kent 30 D2
Bickton Hants 14 C2
Bicton Shrops 60 C4
Bicton Shrops 60 F2
Bicton Park Gardens Devon 11 F5
Bidborough Kent 29 E6
Biddenden Kent 19 B5
Biddenham Beds 53 E8
Biddestone Wilts 24 B3
Biddisham Som 23 D5
Biddlesden Bucks 52 E4
Biddlestone Northumb 117 D5
Biddulph Staffs 75 D5
Biddulph Moor Staffs 75 D6
Bideford Devon 9 B6
Bidford-on-Avon Warks 51 D6
Bidston Mers 85 E3
Bielby E Yorks 96 E3
Bieldside Aberdeen 151 D7
Bierley I o W 15 G6
Bierley W Yorks 94 F4
Bierton Bucks 39 C8
Big Pit National Mining Museum, Blaenavon Torf 35 D6
Big Sand Highld 154 C3
Bigbury Devon 6 E4
Bigbury on Sea Devon 6 E4
Bigby Lincs 90 D4
Biggar Cumb 92 C1
Biggar S Lnrk 122 F3
Biggin Derbys 75 D8
Biggin Derbys 76 E2
Biggin N Yorks 95 F8
Biggin Hill London 28 D5
Biggings Shetland 175 G3
Biggleswade Beds 54 E2
Bighouse Highld 168 C3
Bighton Hants 26 F4
Bignor W Sus 16 C3
Bigton Shetland 175 L5
Bilberry Corn 4 C5
Bilborough Nottingham 76 E5
Bilbrook Som 22 E2
Bilbrough N Yorks 95 E8
Bilbster Highld 169 D7
Bildershaw Durham 101 B7
Bildeston Suff 56 E3
Billericay Essex 42 E2
Billesdon Leics 64 D4
Billesley Warks 51 D6
Billingborough Lincs 78 F4
Billinge Mers 86 D3
Billingford Norf 81 E6
Billingham Stockton 102 B2
Billinghay Lincs 78 D4
Billingley S Yorks 88 D5
Billingshurst W Sus 16 B4
Billingsley Shrops 61 F7
Billington Beds 40 B2
Billington Lancs 93 F7
Billockby Norf 69 C7
Billown Motor Racing Circuit I o M 84 F2
Billy Row Durham 110 F4
Bilsborrow Lancs 92 F5
Bilsby Lincs 79 B7
Bilsham W Sus 16 D3
Bilsington Kent 19 B7
Bilson Green Glos 36 C3
Bilsthorpe Notts 77 C6
Bilsthorpe Moor Notts 77 D6
Bilston Midloth 123 C5
Bilston W Mid 62 E3
Bilstone Leics 63 D7
Bilting Kent 30 E4
Bilton E Yorks 97 F7
Bilton Northumb 117 C8
Bilton Warks 52 B2
Bilton in Ainsty N Yorks 95 E7
Bimbister Orkney 176 E2
Binbrook Lincs 91 E6
Binchester Blocks Durham 110 F5
Bincombe Dorset 12 F4
Bindal Highld 165 F6
Binegar Som 23 E8
Binfield Brack 27 B6
Binfield Heath Oxon 26 B5
Bingfield Northumb 110 B2
Bingham Notts 77 F7
Bingley W Yorks 94 F4
Bings Heath Shrops 60 C5
Binham Norf 81 D5
Binley Hants 26 D2
Binley W Mid 51 B8
Binley Woods Warks 51 B8
Binniehill Falk 121 B8
Binsoe N Yorks 94 B5
Binstead I o W 15 E6
Binsted Hants 27 E5
Binton Warks 51 D6
Bintree Norf 81 E6
Binweston Shrops 60 D3
Birch Essex 43 C5
Birch Gtr Man 87 D6
Birch Green Essex 43 C5
Birch Heath Ches 74 C2
Birch Hill Ches 74 B2
Birch Vale Derbys 87 F8
Bircham Newton Norf 80 D3
Bircham Tofts Norf 80 D3
Birchanger Essex 41 B8
Birchencliffe W Yorks 88 C2
Bircher Hereford 49 C6
Birchfield Highld 149 B5
Birchgrove Cardiff 22 B3
Birchgrove Swansea 33 E8
Birchington Kent 31 C6
Birchmoor Warks 63 D6
Birchover Derbys 76 C2
Birchwood Lincs 78 C2
Birchwood Warr 86 E4
Bircotes Notts 89 E7
Birdbrook Essex 55 E8
Birdforth N Yorks 95 B7
Birdham W Sus 16 E2
Birdholme Derbys 76 C3
Birdingbury Warks 52 C2
Birdland Park, Bourton-on-the-Water Glos 38 B1
Birdlip Glos 37 C6
Birds Edge W Yorks 88 D3
Birdsall N Yorks 96 C4
Birdsgreen Shrops 61 F7
Birdsmoor Gate Dorset 11 D8
Birdston E Dunb 121 B6
Birdwell S Yorks 88 D4
Birdwood Glos 36 C4
Birdworld and Underwaterworld, Farnham Hants 27 E6
Birgham Borders 124 F3
Birkby N Yorks 101 D8
Birkdale Mers 85 C4
Birkenhead Mers 85 F4
Birkenhills Aberds 160 D4
Birkenshaw N Lnrk 121 C6
Birkenshaw W Yorks 88 B3
Birkhall Aberds 150 E2
Birkhill Angus 142 F3
Birkhill Dumfries 114 C5
Birkholme Lincs 65 B6
Birkin N Yorks 89 B6
Birley Hereford 49 D6
Birling Kent 29 C7
Birling Northumb 117 D8
Birling Gap E Sus 18 F2
Birlingham Worcs 50 E4
Birmingham W Mid 62 F4
Birmingham Botanical Gardens W Mid 62 F4
Birmingham International Airport W Mid 63 F5
Birmingham Museum and Art Gallery W Mid 62 F4
Birmingham Museum of Science and Technology W Mid 62 F4
Birnam Perth 141 E7
Birse Aberds 150 E4
Birsemore Aberds 150 E4
Birstall Leics 64 D2
Birstall W Yorks 88 B3
Birstwith N Yorks 94 D5
Birthorpe Lincs 78 F4
Birtley Hereford 49 C5
Birtley Northumb 109 B8
Birtley T & W 111 D5
Birts Street Worcs 50 F2
Bisbrooke Rutland 65 E5
Biscathorpe Lincs 91 F6
Biscot Luton 40 B3
Bish Mill Devon 10 B2
Bisham Windsor 39 F8
Bishampton Worcs 50 D4
Bishop Auckland Durham 101 B7
Bishop Burton E Yorks 97 F5
Bishop Middleham Durham 111 F6
Bishop Monkton N Yorks 95 C6
Bishop Norton Lincs 90 E3
Bishop Sutton Bath 23 D7
Bishop Thornton N Yorks 95 C5

Bishop Wilton E Yorks 96 D3
Bishopbridge Lincs 90 E4
Bishopbriggs E Dunb 121 C6
Bishopmill Moray 159 C6
Bishops Cannings Wilts 24 C5
Bishop's Castle Shrops 60 F3
Bishop's Caundle Dorset 12 C4
Bishop's Cleeve Glos 37 B6
Bishops Frome Hereford 49 E8
Bishop's Green Essex 42 C2
Bishop's Hull Som 11 B7
Bishop's Itchington Warks 51 D8
Bishops Lydeard Som 11 B6
Bishops Nympton Devon 10 B2
Bishop's Offley Staffs 61 B7
Bishop's Stortford Herts 41 B7
Bishop's Sutton Hants 26 F4
Bishop's Tachbrook Warks 51 C8
Bishops Tawton Devon 20 F4
Bishop's Waltham Hants 15 C6
Bishop's Wood Staffs 62 D2
Bishopsbourne Kent 31 D5
Bishopsteignton Devon 7 B7
Bishopstoke Hants 15 C5
Bishopston Swansea 33 F6
Bishopstone Bucks 39 C8
Bishopstone E Sus 17 D8
Bishopstone Hereford 49 E6
Bishopstone Thamesdown 38 F2
Bishopstone Wilts 13 B8
Bishopstrow Wilts 24 E3
Bishopswood Som 11 C7
Bishopsworth Bristol 23 C7
Bishopthorpe York 95 E8
Bishopton Darl 102 B1
Bishopton Dumfries 105 E8
Bishopton N Yorks 95 B6
Bishopton Renfs 120 B4
Bishopton Warks 51 D6
Bishton Newport 35 F7
Bisley Glos 37 D6
Bisley Sur 27 D7
Bispham Blkpool 92 E3
Bispham Green Lancs 86 C2
Bissoe Corn 3 B6
Bisterne Close Hants 14 D3
Bitchfield Lincs 65 B6
Bittadon Devon 20 E4
Bittaford Devon 6 D4
Bittering Norf 68 C2
Bitterley Shrops 49 B7
Bitterne Soton 15 C5
Bitteswell Leics 64 F2
Bitton S Glos 23 C8
Bix Oxon 39 F7
Bixter Shetland 175 H5
Blaby Leics 64 E2
Black Bourton Oxon 38 D2
Black Callerton T & W 110 C4
Black Clauchrie S Ayrs 112 F2
Black Corries Lodge Highld 139 D6
Black Crofts Argyll 130 B5
Black Dog Devon 10 D3
Black Heddon Northumb 110 B3
Black Lane Gtr Man 87 D5
Black Marsh Shrops 60 E3
Black Mount Argyll 139 E6
Black Notley Essex 42 B3
Black Pill Swansea 33 E7
Black Tar Pembs 44 E4
Black Torrington Devon 9 D6
Blackacre Dumfries 114 E3
Blackadder West Borders 124 D4
Blackawton Devon 7 D6
Blackborough Devon 11 D5
Blackborough End Norf 67 C6
Blackboys E Sus 18 C2
Blackbrook Derbys 76 E3
Blackbrook Mers 86 E3
Blackbrook Staffs 74 F4
Blackburn Aberds 160 E2
Blackburn Aberds 151 C7
Blackburn Blkburn 86 B4
Blackburn W Loth 122 C2
Blackcraig Dumfries 113 F7
Blackden Heath Ches 74 B4
Blackdog Aberds 151 C8
Blackfell T & W 111 D5
Blackfield Hants 14 D5
Blackford Cumb 108 C3
Blackford Perth 133 D7
Blackford Som 23 E6
Blackford Som 12 B4
Blackfordby Leics 63 C7
Blackgang I o W 15 G5
Blackgang Chine Fantasy I o W 15 G5
Blackhall Colliery Durham 111 F7
Blackhall Mill T & W 110 D4
Blackhall Rocks Durham 111 F7
Blackham E Sus 29 F5
Blackhaugh Borders 123 F7
Blackheath Essex 43 B6
Blackheath Suff 57 B8
Blackheath Sur 27 E8
Blackheath W Mid 62 F3
Blackhill Aberds 161 D7
Blackhill Aberds 161 C7
Blackhill Highld 152 D4
Blackhills Highld 158 D3
Blackhills Moray 159 D6
Blackhorse S Glos 23 B8
Blackland Wilts 24 C5
Blacklaw Aberds 160 C3
Blackley Gtr Man 87 D6
Blacklunans Perth 142 C1
Blackmill Bridgend 34 F3
Blackmoor Hants 27 F5
Blackmoor Gate Devon 21 E5
Blackmore Essex 42 D2
Blackmore End Essex 55 F8
Blackmore End Herts 40 C4
Blackness Falk 122 B3
Blacknest Hants 27 E5
Blacko Lancs 93 E8
Blackpool Blkpool 92 F3
Blackpool Devon 7 E6
Blackpool Pembs 32 C1
Blackpool Airport Lancs 92 F3
Blackpool Gate Cumb 108 B5
Blackpool Pleasure Beach Blkpool 92 F3
Blackpool Sea Life Centre Blkpool 92 F3
Blackpool Tower Blkpool 92 F3
Blackpool Zoo Park Blkpool 92 F3
Blackridge W Loth 121 C8
Blackrock Argyll 126 C3
Blackrock Mon 35 C6
Blackrod Gtr Man 86 C4
Blackshaw Dumfries 107 C7
Blackshaw Head W Yorks 87 B7
Blacksmith's Green Suff 56 C5
Blackstone W Sus 17 C6
Blackthorn Oxon 39 C6
Blackthorpe Suff 56 C3
Blacktoft E Yorks 90 B2
Blacktop Aberdeen 151 D7
Blacktown Newport 35 F6
Blackwall Tunnel London 41 F6
Blackwater Corn 3 B6
Blackwater Hants 27 D6
Blackwater I o W 15 F6
Blackwaterfoot N Ayrs 119 D5
Blackwell Darl 101 C7
Blackwell Derbys 75 B8
Blackwell Derbys 76 D4
Blackwell Warks 51 E7
Blackwell Worcs 50 B4
Blackwell W Sus 28 F4
Blackwood S Lnrk 121 E7
Blackwood = Coed Duon Caerph 35 E5
Blackwood Hill Staffs 75 D6
Blacon Ches 73 C7
Bladnoch Dumfries 105 D8
Bladon Oxon 38 C4
Blaen-gwynfi Neath 34 E2
Blaen-waun Carms 32 B3
Blaen-y-coed Carms 32 B4
Blaen-y-Cwm Denb 72 F4
Blaen-y-cwm Gwyn 71 E8
Blaen-y-cwm Powys 59 B7
Blaenannerch Ceredig 45 E4
Blaenau Ffestiniog Gwyn 71 C8
Blaenavon Torf 35 D6
Blaenawey Mon 35 C6
Blaencelyn Ceredig 46 D2
Blaendyryn Powys 47 F8
Blaenffos Pembs 45 F3
Blaengarw Bridgend 34 E3
Blaengwrach Neath 34 D2
Blaenpennal Ceredig 46 C5
Blaenplwyf Ceredig 46 B4
Blaenporth Ceredig 45 E4
Blaenrhondda Rhondda 34 D3
Blaenycwm Ceredig 47 B7
Blagdon N Som 23 D7
Blagdon Torbay 7 C6
Blagdon Hill Som 11 C7
Blagill Cumb 109 E7
Blaguegate Lancs 86 D2
Blaich Highld 138 B4
Blain Highld 137 B7
Blaina Bl Gwent 35 D6
Blair Atholl Perth 141 C5
Blair Castle, Blair Atholl Perth 141 C5
Blair Drummond Stirl 133 E6
Blair Drummond Safari Park, Dunblane Stirl 133 E6
Blairbeg N Ayrs 119 C7
Blairdaff Aberds 151 C5
Blairglas Argyll 129 B8
Blairgowrie Perth 142 E1
Blairhall Fife 134 F2
Blairingone Perth 133 E8
Blairland N Ayrs 120 E3
Blairlogie Stirl 133 E7
Blairlomond Argyll 131 F7
Blairmore Argyll 129 B6
Blairnamarrow Moray 149 C8
Blairquhosh Stirl 132 F4
Blair's Ferry Argyll 128 D4
Blairskaith E Dunb 121 B5
Blaisdon Glos 36 C4
Blakebrook Worcs 50 B3
Blakedown Worcs 50 B3
Blakelaw Borders 124 F3
Blakeley Staffs 62 E2
Blakeley Lane Staffs 75 E6
Blakemere Hereford 49 E5
Blakeney Glos 36 D3
Blakeney Norf 81 C6
Blakeney Point NNR Norf 81 C6
Blakenhall Ches 74 E4
Blakenhall W Mid 62 E3
Blakeshall Worcs 62 F2
Blakesley Northants 52 D4
Blanchland Northumb 110 D2
Bland Hill N Yorks 94 D5
Blandford Forum Dorset 13 D6
Blandford St Mary Dorset 13 D6
Blanefield Stirl 121 B5
Blankney Lincs 78 C3
Blantyre S Lnrk 121 D6
Blar a'Chaorainn Highld 139 C5
Blaran Argyll 130 D4
Blarghour Argyll 131 D5
Blarmachfoldach Highld 138 C4
Blarnalearoch Highld 163 E5
Blashford Hants 14 D2
Blaston Leics 64 E5
Blatherwycke Northants 65 E6
Blawith Cumb 98 F4
Blaxhall Suff 57 D7
Blaxton S Yorks 89 D7
Blaydon T & W 110 C4
Bleadon N Som 22 D5
Bleak Hey Nook Gtr Man 87 D8
Blean Kent 30 C5
Bleasby Lincs 90 F5
Bleasby Notts 77 E7
Bleasdale Lancs 93 E5
Bleatarn Cumb 100 C2
Blebocraigs Fife 135 C6
Bleddfa Powys 48 C4
Bledington Glos 38 B2
Bledlow Bucks 39 D7
Bledlow Ridge Bucks 39 E7
Blegbie E Loth 123 C7
Blencarn Cumb 109 F6
Blencogo Cumb 107 E8
Blendworth Hants 15 C8
Blenheim Palace, Woodstock Oxon 38 C4
Blenheim Park Norf 80 D4
Blennerhasset Cumb 107 E8
Blervie Castle Moray 158 D4
Bletchingdon Oxon 39 C5
Bletchingley Sur 28 D4
Bletchley M Keynes 53 F6
Bletchley Shrops 74 F3
Bletherston Pembs 32 B1
Bletsoe Beds 53 D8
Blewbury Oxon 39 F5
Blickling Norf 81 E7
Blickling Hall, Aylsham Norf 81 E7
Blidworth Notts 77 D5
Blindburn Northumb 116 C4
Blindcrake Cumb 107 F8
Blindley Heath Sur 28 E4
Blisland Corn 5 B6
Bliss Gate Worcs 50 B2
Blissford Hants 14 C2
Blisworth Northants 52 D5
Blithbury Staffs 62 B4
Blitterlees Cumb 107 D8
Blockley Glos 51 F6
Blofield Norf 69 D6
Blofield Heath Norf 69 C6
Blo'Norton Norf 56 B4
Bloomfield Borders 115 B8
Blore Staffs 75 E8
Blount's Green Staffs 75 F7
Blowick Mers 85 C4
Bloxham Oxon 52 F2
Bloxholm Lincs 78 D3
Bloxwich W Mid 62 D3
Bloxworth Dorset 13 E6
Blubberhouses N Yorks 94 D4
Blue Anchor Som 22 E2
Blue Anchor Swansea 33 E6
Blue Planet Aquarium Ches 73 B8
Blue Row Essex 43 C6
Blundeston Suff 69 E8
Blunham Beds 54 D2
Blunsdon St Andrew Thamesdown 37 F8
Bluntington Worcs 50 B3
Bluntisham Cambs 54 B4
Blunts Corn 5 C8
Blyborough Lincs 90 E3
Blyford Suff 57 B8
Blymhill Staffs 62 C2
Blyth Notts 89 F7
Blyth Northumb 117 F9
Blyth Bridge Borders 122 E4
Blythburgh Suff 57 B8
Blythe Borders 123 E8
Blythe Bridge Staffs 75 E6
Blyton Lincs 90 E2
Boarhills Fife 135 C7
Boarhunt Hants 15 D7
Boars Head Gtr Man 86 D3
Boars Hill Oxon 38 D4
Boarshead E Sus 18 B2
Boarstall Bucks 39 C6
Boasley Cross Devon 9 E6
Boat of Garten Highld 148 C5
Boath Highld 157 B6
Bobbing Kent 30 C2
Bobbington Staffs 62 E2
Bobbingworth Essex 41 D8
Bocaddon Corn 5 D6
Bochastle Stirl 132 D5
Bocking Essex 42 B3
Bocking Churchstreet Essex 42 B3
Boddam Aberds 161 D8
Boddam Shetland 175 M5
Boddington Glos 37 B5
Bodedern Anglesey 82 C3
Bodelwyddan Denb 72 B4
Bodenham Hereford 49 D7
Bodenham Wilts 14 B2
Bodenham Arboretum and Earth Centre Worcs 62 F2
Bodenham Moor Hereford 49 D7
Bodermid Gwyn 70 E2
Bodewryd Anglesey 82 B3
Bodfari Denb 72 B4
Bodffordd Anglesey 82 D4
Bodham Norf 81 C7
Bodiam E Sus 18 C4
Bodiam Castle E Sus 18 C4
Bodicote Oxon 52 F2
Bodieve Corn 4 B4
Bodinnick Corn 5 D6
Bodle Street Green E Sus 18 D3
Bodmin Corn 5 C5
Bodnant Garden, Colwyn Bay Conwy 83 D8
Bodney Norf 67 E8
Bodorgan Anglesey 82 E3
Bodsham Kent 30 E5
Boduan Gwyn 70 D4
Bodymoor Heath Warks 63 E5
Bogallan Highld 157 D7
Bogbrae Aberds 161 E7
Bogend Borders 124 E3
Bogend S Ayrs 120 F3
Boghall W Loth 122 C2
Boghead S Lnrk 121 E7
Bogmoor Moray 159 C7
Bogniebrae Aberds 160 D2
Bognor Regis W Sus 16 E3
Bograxie Aberds 151 C6
Bogside N Lnrk 121 D8
Bogton Aberds 160 C3
Bogue Dumfries 113 F6
Bohenie Highld 147 F5
Bohortha Corn 3 C7
Bohuntine Highld 147 F5
Boirseam W Isles 173 K3
Bojewyan Corn 2 C2
Bolam Durham 101 B6
Bolam Northumb 117 F6
Bolberry Devon 6 F4
Bold Heath Mers 86 F3
Boldon T & W 111 C6
Boldon Colliery T & W 111 C6
Boldre Hants 14 E4
Boldron Durham 101 C5
Bole Notts 89 F8
Bolehill Derbys 76 D2
Boleside Borders 123 F7
Bolham Devon 10 C4
Bolham Water Devon 11 C6
Bolingey Corn 4 D2
Bollington Ches 75 B6
Bollington Cross Ches 75 B6
Bolney W Sus 17 B6
Bolnhurst Beds 53 D8
Bolshan Angus 143 D6
Bolsover Derbys 76 B4
Bolsterstone S Yorks 88 E3
Bolstone Hereford 49 F7
Boltby N Yorks 102 F2
Bolter End Bucks 39 E7
Bolton Cumb 99 B8
Bolton E Loth 123 B8
Bolton E Yorks 96 D3
Bolton Gtr Man 86 D5
Bolton Northumb 117 C7
Bolton Abbey N Yorks 94 D3
Bolton Abbey, Skipton N Yorks 94 D3
Bolton Bridge N Yorks 94 D3
Bolton-by-Bowland Lancs 93 E7
Bolton Castle, Leyburn N Yorks 101 E5
Bolton le Sands Lancs 92 C4
Bolton Low Houses Cumb 108 E2
Bolton-on-Swale N Yorks 101 E7
Bolton Percy N Yorks 95 E8
Bolton Town End Lancs 92 C4
Bolton upon Dearne S Yorks 89 D5
Boltonfellend Cumb 108 C4
Boltongate Cumb 108 E2
Bolventor Corn 5 B6
Bomere Heath Shrops 60 C4
Bon-y-maen Swansea 33 E7
Bonar Bridge Highld 164 E3
Bonawe Argyll 131 B6
Bonby N Lincs 90 C4
Boncath Pembs 45 F4
Bonchester Bridge Borders 115 C8
Bonchurch I o W 15 G6
Bondleigh Devon 9 D8
Bonehill Devon 6 B5
Bonehill Staffs 63 D5
Bo'ness Falk 133 F8
Bonhill W Dunb 120 B3
Boningale Shrops 62 D2
Bonjedward Borders 116 B2
Bonkle N Lnrk 121 D8
Bonnavoulin Highld 137 C6
Bonnington Edin 122 C4
Bonnington Kent 19 B7
Bonnybank Fife 135 D5
Bonnybridge Falk 133 F7
Bonnykelly Aberds 161 C5
Bonnyrigg and Lasswade Midloth 123 C6
Bonnyton Aberds 160 E3
Bonnyton Angus 142 F3
Bonnyton Angus 143 D6
Bonsall Derbys 76 D2
Bonskeid House Perth 141 C5
Bont Mon 35 C7
Bont-Dolgadfan Powys 59 D5
Bont-goch Ceredig 58 F3
Bont-newydd Conwy 72 B4
Bont Newydd Gwyn 71 C8
Bont Newydd Gwyn 71 E8
Bontddu Gwyn 58 C3
Bonthorpe Lincs 79 B7
Bontnewydd Ceredig 46 C5
Bontnewydd Gwyn 82 F4
Bontuchel Denb 72 D4
Bonvilston V Glam 22 B2
Booker Bucks 39 E8
Boon Borders 123 E8
Boosbeck Redcar 102 C4
Boot Cumb 98 D3
Boot Street Suff 57 E6
Booth W Yorks 87 B8
Booth Wood W Yorks 87 C8
Boothby Graffoe Lincs 78 D2
Boothby Pagnell Lincs 78 F2
Boothen Stoke 75 E5
Boothferry E Yorks 89 B8
Boothville Northants 53 C5
Bootle Cumb 98 F3
Bootle Mers 85 E4
Booton Norf 81 E7
Boquhan Stirl 132 F4
Boraston Shrops 49 B8
Borden Kent 30 C2
Borden W Sus 16 B2
Bordley N Yorks 94 C2
Bordon Hants 27 F6
Bordon Camp Hants 27 F5
Boreham Essex 42 D3
Boreham Wilts 24 E3
Boreham Street E Sus 18 D3
Borehamwood Herts 40 E4
Boreland Dumfries 114 E4
Boreland Stirl 140 F2
Borgh W Isles 171 K2
Borgh W Isles 173 K2
Borghastan W Isles 172 D5
Borgie Highld 167 D8
Borgue Dumfries 106 E3
Borgue Highld 165 B8
Borley Essex 56 E2
Bornais W Isles 171 H3
Bornesketaig Highld 152 B4
Borness Dumfries 106 E3
Borough Green Kent 29 D7
Boroughbridge N Yorks 95 C6
Borras Head Wrex 73 D7
Borreraig Highld 152 D2
Borrobol Lodge Highld 165 B5
Borrowash Derbys 76 F4
Borrowby N Yorks 102 F2
Borrowdale Cumb 98 C4
Borrowfield Aberds 151 E7
Borth Ceredig 58 E3
Borth-y-Gest Gwyn 71 D6
Borthertoft Lincs 79 E5
Borthwickbrae Borders 115 C7
Borthwickshiels Borders 115 C7
Borve Highld 152 E5
Borve Lodge W Isles 173 J3
Borwick Lancs 92 B5
Bosavern Corn 2 C2
Bosbury Hereford 49 E8
Boscastle Corn 8 E3
Boscombe Bmouth 14 E2
Boscombe Wilts 25 F7
Boscoppa Corn 4 D5
Bosham W Sus 16 D2
Bosherston Pembs 44 F4
Boskenna Corn 2 D3
Bosley Ches 75 C6
Bossall N Yorks 96 C3
Bossiney Corn 8 F2
Bossingham Kent 31 E5
Bossington Som 21 E7
Bostock Green Ches 74 C3
Boston Lincs 79 E6
Boston Long Hedges Lincs 79 E6
Boston Spa W Yorks 95 E7
Boston West Lincs 79 E5
Boswinger Corn 3 B8
Botallack Corn 2 C2
Botany Bay London 41 E5
Botcherby Cumb 108 D4
Botcheston Leics 63 D8
Botesdale Suff 56 B4
Bothal Northumb 117 F8
Bothamsall Notts 77 B6
Bothel Cumb 107 F8
Bothenhampton Dorset 12 E2
Bothwell S Lnrk 121 D7
Botley Bucks 40 D2
Botley Hants 15 C6
Botley Oxon 38 D4
Botolph Claydon Bucks 39 B7
Botolphs W Sus 17 D5
Bottacks Highld 157 C5
Bottesford Leics 77 F8
Bottesford N Lincs 90 D2
Bottisham Cambs 55 C6
Bottlesford Wilts 25 D6
Bottom Boat W Yorks 88 B4
Bottom House Staffs 75 D7
Bottom of Hutton Lancs 86 B2
Bottom o'th'Moor Gtr Man 86 C4
Bottomcraig Fife 135 B5
Botusfleming Corn 6 C2
Botwnnog Gwyn 70 D3
Bough Beech Kent 29 E5
Boughrood Powys 48 F3
Boughspring Glos 36 E2
Boughton Norf 67 D6
Boughton Notts 77 C6
Boughton Northants 53 C5
Boughton Aluph Kent 30 E4
Boughton Lees Kent 30 E4
Boughton Malherbe Kent 30 E2
Boughton Monchelsea Kent 29 D8
Boughton Street Kent 30 D4
Boulby Redcar 103 C5
Boulden Shrops 60 F5
Boulmer Northumb 117 C8
Boulston Pembs 44 D4
Boultenstone Aberds 150 C3
Boultham Lincs 78 C2
Bourn Cambs 54 D4
Bourne Lincs 65 B7
Bourne End Beds 53 E7
Bourne End Bucks 40 F1
Bourne End Herts 40 D3
Bournemouth Bmouth 13 E8
Bournemouth International Airport Dorset 14 E2
Bournes Green Glos 37 D6
Bournes Green Sthend 43 F5
Bournheath Worcs 50 B4
Bournmoor Durham 111 D6
Bournville W Mid 62 F4
Bourton Dorset 24 F2
Bourton N Som 23 C5
Bourton Oxon 38 F2
Bourton Shrops 61 E5
Bourton on Dunsmore Warks 52 B2
Bourton on the Hill Glos 51 F6
Bourton-on-the-Water Glos 38 B1
Bousd Argyll 136 B3
Boustead Hill Cumb 108 D2
Bouth Cumb 99 F5
Bouthwaite N Yorks 94 B4
Boveney Bucks 27 B7
Boverton V Glam 21 C8
Bovey Tracey Devon 7 B6
Bovingdon Herts 40 D3
Bovingdon Green Bucks 39 F8
Bovingdon Green Herts 40 D3
Bovinger Essex 41 D8
Bovington Camp Dorset 13 F6
Bow Borders 123 E7
Bow Devon 10 D2
Bow Orkney 176 G2
Bow Brickhill M Keynes 53 F7
Bow of Fife Fife 134 C5
Bow Street Ceredig 58 F3
Bowbank Durham 100 B4
Bowburn Durham 111 F6
Bowcombe I o W 15 F5
Bowd Devon 11 E6
Bowden Borders 123 F8
Bowden Devon 7 E6
Bowden Hill Wilts 24 C4
Bowderdale Cumb 100 D1
Bowdon Gtr Man 87 F5
Bower Northumb 116 F3
Bower Hinton Som 12 C2
Bowerchalke Wilts 13 B8
Bowerhill Wilts 24 C4
Bowermadden Highld 169 C7
Bowers Gifford Essex 42 F3
Bowershall Fife 134 E2
Bowertower Highld 169 C7
Bowes Durham 100 C4
Bowgreave Lancs 92 E4
Bowgreen Gtr Man 87 F5
Bowhill Borders 115 B7
Bowhouse Dumfries 107 C7
Bowland Bridge Cumb 99 F6
Bowley Hereford 49 D7
Bowlhead Green Sur 27 F7
Bowling W Dunb 120 B4
Bowling W Yorks 94 F4
Bowling Bank Wrex 73 E7
Bowling Green Worcs 50 D3
Bowmanstead Cumb 99 E5
Bowmore Argyll 126 D3
Bowness-on-Solway Cumb 108 C2
Bowness-on-Windermere Cumb 99 E6
Bowood House and Gardens, Calne Wilts 24 C4
Bowsden Northumb 125 E5
Bowside Lodge Highld 168 C3
Bowston Cumb 99 E6
Bowthorpe Norf 68 D4
Box Glos 37 D5
Box Wilts 24 C3
Box End Beds 53 E8
Boxbush Glos 36 C4
Boxford Suff 56 E3
Boxford W Berks 26 B2
Boxgrove W Sus 16 D3
Boxley Kent 29 D8
Boxmoor Herts 40 D3
Boxted Essex 56 F4
Boxted Suff 56 D2
Boxted Cross Essex 56 F4
Boxted Heath Essex 56 F4
Boxworth Cambs 54 C4
Boxworth End Cambs 54 C4
Boyden Gate Kent 31 C6
Boylestone Derbys 75 F8
Boyndie Aberds 160 B3
Boynton E Yorks 97 C7
Boysack Angus 143 E6
Boyton Corn 8 E5
Boyton Suff 57 E7
Boyton Wilts 24 F4
Boyton Cross Essex 42 D2
Boyton End Suff 55 E8
Bozeat Northants 53 D7
Braaid I o M 84 E3
Braal Castle Highld 169 C6
Brabling Green Suff 57 C6
Brabourne Kent 30 E4
Brabourne Lees Kent 30 E4
Brabster Highld 169 C8
Bracadale Highld 153 F4
Bracara Highld 145 D7
Braceborough Lincs 65 C7
Bracebridge Lincs 78 C2
Bracebridge Heath Lincs 78 C2
Bracebridge Low Fields Lincs 78 C2
Braceby Lincs 78 F3
Bracewell Lancs 93 E8
Brackenfield Derbys 76 D3
Brackenthwaite Cumb 108 E2
Brackenthwaite N Yorks 95 D5
Bracklesham W Sus 16 E2
Brackletter Highld 146 F4
Brackley Argyll 118 B4
Brackley Northants 52 F3
Brackloch Highld 163 B5
Bracknell Brack 27 C6
Braco Perth 133 D7
Bracobrae Moray 160 C2
Bracon Ash Norf 68 E4
Bracorina Highld 145 D7
Bradbourne Derbys 76 D2
Bradbury Durham 101 B8
Bradda I o M 84 F1
Bradden Northants 52 E4
Braddock Corn 5 C6
Bradeley Stoke 75 D5
Bradenham Bucks 39 E8
Bradenham Norf 68 D2
Bradenstoke Wilts 24 B5
Bradfield Essex 56 F5
Bradfield Norf 81 D8
Bradfield W Berks 26 B4
Bradfield Combust Suff 56 D2
Bradfield Green Ches 74 D3
Bradfield Heath Essex 43 B7
Bradfield St Clare Suff 56 D3
Bradfield St George Suff 56 C3
Bradford Corn 5 B6
Bradford Derbys 76 C2
Bradford Devon 9 D6
Bradford Northumb 125 F7
Bradford W Yorks 94 F4
Bradford Abbas Dorset 12 C3
Bradford Cathedral W Yorks 94 F4
Bradford Industrial Museum W Yorks 94 F4
Bradford Leigh Wilts 24 C3
Bradford-on-Avon Wilts 24 C3
Bradford on Tone Som 11 B6
Bradford Peverell Dorset 12 E4
Brading I o W 15 F7
Bradley Derbys 76 E2
Bradley Hants 26 E4
Bradley NE Lincs 91 D6
Bradley Staffs 62 C2
Bradley W Mid 62 E3
Bradley W Yorks 88 B2
Bradley Green Worcs 50 C4
Bradley in the Moors Staffs 75 E7
Bradlow Hereford 50 F2
Bradmore Notts 77 F5
Bradmore W Mid 62 E2
Bradninch Devon 10 D5
Bradnop Staffs 75 D7
Bradpole Dorset 12 E2
Bradshaw Gtr Man 86 C5
Bradshaw W Yorks 87 C8
Bradstone Devon 9 F5
Bradwall Green Ches 74 C4
Bradway S Yorks 88 F4
Bradwell Derbys 88 F2
Bradwell Essex 42 B4
Bradwell M Keynes 53 F6
Bradwell Norf 69 D8
Bradwell Staffs 74 E5
Bradwell Grove Oxon 38 D2
Bradwell on Sea Essex 43 D6
Bradwell Waterside Essex 43 D5
Bradworthy Devon 8 C5
Bradworthy Cross Devon 8 C5
Brae Dumfries 107 B5
Brae Highld 154 B4
Brae Highld 163 D8
Brae Shetland 174 G5
Brae of Achnahaird Highld 162 C4
Brae Roy Lodge Highld 147 E6
Braeantra Highld 157 B6
Braedownie Angus 142 B2
Braefield Highld 156 F5
Braegrum Perth 134 B2
Braehead Dumfries 105 D8
Braehead Orkney 176 F4
Braehead Orkney 176 B3
Braehead S Lnrk 121 F8
Braehead S Lnrk 122 D2
Braehead of Lunan Angus 143 D6
Braehoulland Shetland 174 F4
Braehungie Highld 169 F6
Braelangwell Lodge Highld 164 E2
Braemar Aberds 149 E7
Braemore Highld 169 F5
Braemore Highld 156 B2
Braes of Enzie Moray 159 D7
Braeside Invclyd 129 C7
Braeswick Orkney 176 C5
Braewick Shetland 175 H5
Brafferton Darl 101 B7
Brafferton N Yorks 95 B7
Brafield-on-the-Green Northants 53 D6
Bragar W Isles 172 D5
Bragbury End Herts 41 B5
Bragleenmore Argyll 130 C5
Braichmelyn Gwyn 83 E6
Braid Edin 122 C5
Braides Lancs 92 D4
Braidley N Yorks 101 F5
Braidwood S Lnrk 121 E8
Braigo Argyll 126 C2
Brailsford Derbys 76 E2
Brainshaugh Northumb 117 D8
Braintree Essex 42 B3
Braiseworth Suff 56 B5
Braishfield Hants 14 B4
Braithwaite Cumb 98 B4
Braithwaite S Yorks 89 C7
Braithwaite W Yorks 94 E3
Braithwell S Yorks 89 E6
Bramber W Sus 17 C5
Bramcote Notts 76 F5
Bramcote Warks 63 F8
Bramdean Hants 15 B7
Bramerton Norf 69 D5
Bramfield Herts 41 C5
Bramfield Suff 57 B7
Bramford Suff 56 E5
Bramhall Gtr Man 87 F6
Bramham W Yorks 95 E7
Bramhope W Yorks 95 E5
Bramley Hants 26 D4
Bramley Sur 27 E8
Bramley S Yorks 89 E5
Bramley W Yorks 94 F5
Bramling Kent 31 D6
Brampford Speke Devon 10 E4
Brampton Cambs 54 B3
Brampton Cumb 100 B1
Brampton Cumb 108 C5
Brampton Derbys 76 B3
Brampton Hereford 49 F6
Brampton Lincs 77 B8
Brampton Norf 81 E8
Brampton Suff 69 F7
Brampton S Yorks 88 D5
Brampton Abbotts Hereford 36 B3
Brampton Ash Northants 64 F4
Brampton Bryan Hereford 49 B5
Brampton en le Morthen S Yorks 89 F5
Bramshall Staffs 75 F7
Bramshaw Hants 14 C3
Bramshill Hants 26 C5
Bramshott Hants 27 F6
Bran End Essex 42 B2
Branault Highld 137 B6
Brancaster Norf 80 C3
Brancaster Staithe Norf 80 C3
Brancepeth Durham 110 F5
Branch End Northumb 110 C3
Branchill Moray 158 D4
Brand Green Glos 36 B4
Branderburgh Moray 159 B6
Brandesburton E Yorks 97 E7
Brandeston Suff 57 C6
Brandhill Shrops 49 B6
Brandis Corner Devon 9 D6
Brandiston Norf 81 E7
Brandon Durham 110 F5
Brandon Lincs 78 E2
Brandon Northumb 117 C6
Brandon Suff 67 F7
Brandon Warks 52 B2
Brandon Bank Norf 67 F6
Brandon Creek Norf 67 E6
Brandon Parva Norf 68 D3
Brands Hatch Motor Racing Circuit Kent 29 C6
Brandsby N Yorks 95 B8
Brandy Wharf Lincs 90 E4
Brane Corn 2 D3
Branksome Poole 13 E8
Branksome Park Poole 13 E8
Bransby Lincs 77 B8
Branscombe Devon 11 F6
Bransford Worcs 50 D2
Bransgore Hants 14 E2
Branshill Clack 133 E7
Bransholme Hull 97 F7
Branson's Cross Worcs 51 B5
Branston Leics 64 B5
Branston Lincs 78 C3
Branston Staffs 63 B6
Branston Booths Lincs 78 C3
Branstone I o W 15 F6
Bransty Cumb 98 C1
Brant Broughton Lincs 78 D2
Brantham Suff 56 F5
Branthwaite Cumb 98 B2
Branthwaite Cumb 108 F2
Brantingham E Yorks 90 B3
Branton Northumb 117 C6
Branton S Yorks 89 D7
Branxholm Park Borders 115 C7
Branxholme Borders 115 C7
Branxton Northumb 124 F4
Brassey Green Ches 74 C2
Brassington Derbys 76 D2
Brasted Kent 29 D5
Brasted Chart Kent 29 D5
Brathens Aberds 151 E5
Bratoft Lincs 79 C7
Brattleby Lincs 90 F3
Bratton Telford 61 C6
Bratton Wilts 24 D4

Bratton Clovelly Devon 9 E6
Bratton Fleming Devon 20 F5
Bratton Seymour Som 12 B4
Braughing Herts 41 B6
Braunston Northants 52 C3
Braunston-in-Rutland Rutland 64 D5
Braunstone Town Leics 64 D2
Braunton Devon 20 F3
Brawby N Yorks 96 B3
Brawl Highld 168 C3
Brawlbin Highld 169 D5
Bray Windsor 27 B7
Bray Shop Corn 5 B8
Bray Wick Windsor 27 B6
Braybrooke Northants 64 F4
Braye Ald 16
Brayford Devon 21 F5
Braystones Cumb 98 D2
Braythorn N Yorks 94 E5
Brayton N Yorks 95 F9
Brazacott Corn 8 E4
Breach Kent 30 C2
Breachacha Castle Argyll 136 C2
Breachwood Green Herts 40 B4
Breacleit W Isles 172 E4
Breaden Heath Shrops 73 F8
Breadsall Derbys 76 F3
Breadstone Glos 36 D4
Breage Corn 2 D5
Breakachy Highld 157 E5
Bream Glos 36 D3
Breamore Hants 14 C2
Brean Som 22 D4
Breanais W Isles 172 F2
Brearton N Yorks 95 C6
Breasclete W Isles 172 E5
Breaston Derbys 76 F4
Brechfa Carms 46 F4
Brechin Angus 143 C5
Breck of Cruan Orkney 176 E2
Breckan Orkney 176 F1
Breckrey Highld 152 C6
Brecon = Aberhonddu Powys 34 B4
Brecon Beacons Mountain Centre Powys 34 B3
Bredbury Gtr Man 87 E7
Brede E Sus 18 D5
Bredenbury Hereford 49 D8
Bredfield Suff 57 D6
Bredgar Kent 30 C2
Bredhurst Kent 29 C8
Bredicot Worcs 50 D4
Bredon Worcs 50 F4
Bredon's Norton Worcs 50 F4
Bredwardine Hereford 48 E5
Breedon on the Hill Leics 63 B8
Breibhig W Isles 171 L2
Breibhig W Isles 172 E7
Breich W Loth 122 C2
Breightmet Gtr Man 86 D5
Breighton E Yorks 96 F3
Breinton Hereford 49 F6
Breinton Common Hereford 49 E6
Breiwick Shetland 175 J6
Bremhill Wilts 24 B4
Bremirehoull Shetland 175 L6
Brenchley Kent 29 E7
Brendon Devon 21 E6
Brenkley T & W 110 B5
Brent Eleigh Suff 56 E3
Brent Knoll Som 22 D5
Brent Pelham Herts 54 F5
Brentford London 28 B2
Brentingby Leics 64 C4
Brentwood Essex 42 E1
Brenzett Kent 19 C7
Brereton Staffs 62 C4
Brereton Green Ches 74 C4
Brereton Heath Ches 74 C5
Bressingham Norf 68 F3
Bretby Derbys 63 B6
Bretford Warks 52 B2
Bretforton Worcs 51 E5
Bretherdale Head Cumb 99 D7
Bretherton Lancs 86 B2
Brettabister Shetland 175 H6
Brettenham Norf 68 F2
Brettenham Suff 56 D3
Bretton Derbys 76 B2
Bretton Flint 73 C7
Brewer Street Sur 28 D4
Brewlands Bridge Angus 142 C1
Brewood Staffs 62 D2
Briach Moray 158 D4
Briants Puddle Dorset 13 E6
Brick End Essex 42 B1
Brickendon Herts 41 D6
Bricket Wood Herts 40 D4
Bricklehampton Worcs 50 E4
Bride I o M 84 B4
Bridekirk Cumb 107 F8
Bridell Pembs 45 E3
Bridestowe Devon 9 F7
Brideswell Aberds 160 E2
Bridford Devon 10 F3
Bridfordmills Devon 10 F3
Bridge Kent 31 D5
Bridge End Lincs 78 F4
Bridge Green Essex 55 F5
Bridge Hewick N Yorks 95 B6
Bridge of Alford Aberds 150 C4
Bridge of Allan Stirl 133 E6
Bridge of Avon Moray 159 F5
Bridge of Awe Argyll 131 C6
Bridge of Balgie Perth 140 E2
Bridge of Cally Perth 141 D8
Bridge of Canny Aberds 151 E5
Bridge of Craigisla Angus 142 D2
Bridge of Dee Dumfries 106 D4
Bridge of Don Aberdeen 151 C8
Bridge of Dun Angus 143 D6
Bridge of Dye Aberds 151 F5
Bridge of Earn Perth 134 C3
Bridge of Ericht Perth 140 D2
Bridge of Feugh Aberds 151 E6
Bridge of Forss Highld 168 C5
Bridge of Gairn Aberds 150 E2
Bridge of Gaur Perth 140 D2
Bridge of Muchalls Aberds 151 E7
Bridge of Oich Highld 147 D6
Bridge of Orchy Argyll 131 B8
Bridge of Waith Orkney 176 E1
Bridge of Walls Shetland 175 H4
Bridge of Weir Renfs 120 C3
Bridge Sollers Hereford 49 E6
Bridge Street Suff 56 E2
Bridge Trafford Ches 73 B8
Bridge Yate S Glos 23 B8
Bridgefoot Angus 142 F3
Bridgefoot Cumb 98 B2
Bridgehampton Som 12 B3
Bridgehill Durham 110 D3
Bridgemary Hants 15 D6
Bridgemont Derbys 87 F8
Bridgend Aberds 160 E2
Bridgend Aberds 150 C4
Bridgend Angus 143 C5
Bridgend Argyll 128 A3
Bridgend Argyll 126 C3
Bridgend Argyll 118 C4
Bridgend Cumb 99 C5
Bridgend Fife 135 C5
Bridgend Moray 159 F7
Bridgend N Lnrk 121 B6
Bridgend Pembs 45 E3
Bridgend W Loth 122 B3
Bridgend = Pen-y-bont ar Ogwr Bridgend 21 B8
Bridgend of Lintrathen Angus 142 D2
Bridgerule Devon 8 D4
Bridges Shrops 60 E3
Bridgeton Glasgow 121 C6
Bridgetown Corn 8 F5
Bridgetown Som 21 F8
Bridgham Norf 68 F2
Bridgnorth Shrops 61 E7
Bridgnorth Cliff Railway Shrops 61 E7
Bridgtown Staffs 62 D3
Bridgwater Som 22 F5
Bridlington E Yorks 97 C7
Bridport Dorset 12 E2
Bridstow Hereford 36 B2
Brierfield Lancs 93 F8
Brierley Glos 36 C3
Brierley Hereford 49 D6
Brierley S Yorks 88 C5
Brierley Hill W Mid 62 F3
Briery Hill Bl Gwent 35 D5
Brig o'Turk Stirl 132 D4
Brigg N Lincs 90 D4
Briggswath N Yorks 103 D6
Brigham Cumb 107 F7
Brigham E Yorks 97 D6
Brighouse W Yorks 88 B2
Brighstone I o W 14 F5
Brightgate Derbys 76 D2
Brighthampton Oxon 38 D3
Brightling E Sus 18 C3
Brightlingsea Essex 43 C6
Brighton Brighton 17 D7
Brighton Corn 4 D4
Brighton Hill Hants 26 E4
Brighton Museum and Art Gallery Brighton 17 D7
Brighton Racecourse Brighton 17 D7
Brighton Sea Life Centre Brighton 17 D7
Brightons Falk 122 B2
Brightwalton W Berks 26 B2
Brightwell Suff 57 E6
Brightwell Baldwin Oxon 39 E6
Brightwell cum Sotwell Oxon 39 E5
Brignall Durham 101 C5
Brigsley NE Lincs 91 D6
Brigsteer Cumb 99 F6
Brigstock Northants 65 F6
Brill Bucks 39 C6
Brilley Hereford 48 E4
Brimaston Pembs 44 C4
Brimfield Hereford 49 C7
Brimington Derbys 76 B4
Brimley Devon 7 B5
Brimpsfield Glos 37 C6
Brimpton W Berks 26 C3
Brims Orkney 176 H1
Brimscombe Glos 37 D5
Brimstage Mers 85 F4
Brinacory Highld 145 D7
Brind E Yorks 96 F3
Brindister Shetland 175 H4
Brindister Shetland 175 K6
Brindle Lancs 86 B4
Brindley Ford Staffs 75 D5
Brineton Staffs 62 C2
Bringhurst Leics 64 E5
Brington Cambs 53 B8
Brinian Orkney 176 D3
Briningham Norf 81 D6
Brinkhill Lincs 79 B6
Brinkley Cambs 55 D7
Brinklow Warks 52 B2
Brinkworth Wilts 37 F7
Brinmore Highld 148 B2
Brinscall Lancs 86 B4
Brinsea N Som 23 C6
Brinsley Notts 76 E4
Brinsop Hereford 49 E6
Brinsworth S Yorks 88 F5
Brinton Norf 81 D6
Brisco Cumb 108 D4
Brisley Norf 81 E5
Brislington Bristol 23 B8
Bristol Bristol 23 B7
Bristol City Museum and Art Gallery Bristol 23 B7
Bristol International Airport N Som 23 C7
Bristol Zoo Bristol 23 B7
Briston Norf 81 D6
Britannia Lancs 87 B6
Britford Wilts 14 B2
Brithdir Gwyn 58 C4
British Legion Village Kent 29 D8
British Museum London 41 F5
Briton Ferry Neath 33 E8
Britwell Salome Oxon 39 E6
Brixham Torbay 7 D7
Brixton Devon 6 D3
Brixton London 28 B4
Brixton Deverill Wilts 24 F3
Brixworth Northants 52 B5
Brize Norton Oxon 38 D3
Broad Blunsdon Thamesdown 38 E1
Broad Campden Glos 51 F6
Broad Chalke Wilts 13 B8
Broad Green Beds 53 E7
Broad Green Essex 42 B4
Broad Green Worcs 50 D2
Broad Haven Pembs 44 D3
Broad Heath Worcs 49 C8
Broad Hill Cambs 55 B6
Broad Hinton Wilts 25 B6
Broad Laying Hants 26 C2
Broad Marston Worcs 51 E6
Broad Oak Carms 33 B6
Broad Oak Cumb 98 E3
Broad Oak Dorset 12 E2
Broad Oak Dorset 13 C5
Broad Oak E Sus 18 D5
Broad Oak E Sus 18 C3
Broad Oak Hereford 36 B1
Broad Oak Mers 86 E3
Broad Street Kent 30 D2
Broad Street Green Essex 42 D4
Broad Town Wilts 25 B5
Broadbottom Gtr Man 87 E7
Broadbridge W Sus 16 D2
Broadbridge Heath W Sus 28 F2
Broadclyst Devon 10 E4
Broadfield Gtr Man 87 C6
Broadfield Lancs 86 B3
Broadfield Pembs 32 D2
Broadfield W Sus 28 F3
Broadford Highld 155 H2
Broadford Bridge W Sus 16 B4
Broadhaugh Borders 115 D7
Broadhaven Highld 169 D8
Broadheath Gtr Man 87 F5
Broadhembury Devon 11 D6
Broadhempston Devon 7 C6
Broadholme Derbys 76 E3
Broadholme Lincs 77 B8
Broadland Row E Sus 18 D5
Broadlay Carms 32 D4
Broadley Lancs 87 C6
Broadley Moray 159 C7
Broadley Common Essex 41 D7
Broadmayne Dorset 12 F5
Broadmeadows Borders 123 F7
Broadmere Hants 26 E4
Broadmoor Pembs 32 D1
Broadoak Kent 31 C5
Broadrashes Moray 159 D8
Broadsea Aberds 161 B6
Broadstairs Kent 31 C7
Broadstone Poole 13 E8
Broadstone Shrops 60 F5
Broadtown Lane Wilts 25 B5
Broadview Gardens, Hadlow Kent 29 E7
Broadwas Worcs 50 D2
Broadwater Herts 41 B5
Broadwater W Sus 17 D5
Broadway Carms 32 D3
Broadway Pembs 44 D3
Broadway Som 11 C8
Broadway Suff 57 B7
Broadway Worcs 51 F5
Broadwell Glos 38 B2
Broadwell Glos 36 C2
Broadwell Oxon 38 D2
Broadwell Warks 52 C2
Broadwell House Northumb 110 D2
Broadwey Dorset 12 F4
Broadwindsor Dorset 12 D2
Broadwood Kelly Devon 9 D8
Broadwoodwidger Devon 9 F6
Brobury Hereford 48 E5
Brochel Highld 152 E6
Brochloch Dumfries 113 E5
Brochroy Argyll 131 B6
Brockamin Worcs 50 D2
Brockbridge Hants 15 C7
Brockdam Northumb 117 B7
Brockdish Norf 57 B6
Brockenhurst Hants 14 D4
Brocketsbrae S Lnrk 121 F8
Brockford Street Suff 56 C5
Brockhall Northants 52 C4
Brockham Sur 28 E2
Brockhampton Glos 37 B7
Brockhampton Hereford 49 F7
Brockhole -National Park Visitor Centre, Windermere Cumb 99 D5
Brockholes W Yorks 88 C2
Brockhurst Derbys 76 C3
Brockhurst Hants 15 D7
Brocklebank Cumb 108 E3
Brocklesby Lincs 90 C5
Brockley N Som 23 C6
Brockley Green Suff 56 D2
Brockleymoor Cumb 108 F4
Brockton Shrops 60 F3
Brockton Shrops 61 E5
Brockton Shrops 60 D3
Brockton Shrops 61 D7
Brockton Telford 61 C7
Brockweir Glos 36 D2
Brockwood Hants 15 B7
Brockworth Glos 37 C5
Brocton Staffs 62 C3
Brodick N Ayrs 119 C7
Brodick Castle N Ayrs 119 C7
Brodsworth S Yorks 89 D6
Brogaig Highld 152 C5
Brogborough Beds 53 F7
Broken Cross Ches 74 B3
Broken Cross Ches 75 B5
Brokenborough Wilts 37 F6
Bromborough Mers 85 F4
Brome Suff 56 B5
Brome Street Suff 57 B5
Bromeswell Suff 57 D7
Bromfield Cumb 107 E8
Bromfield Shrops 49 B6
Bromham Beds 53 D8
Bromham Wilts 24 C4
Bromley London 28 C5
Bromley W Mid 62 F3
Bromley Common London 28 C5
Bromley Green Kent 19 B6
Brompton Medway 29 C8
Brompton N Yorks 102 E1
Brompton N Yorks 103 F7
Brompton-on-Swale N Yorks 101 E7
Brompton Ralph Som 22 F2
Brompton Regis Som 21 F8
Bromsash Hereford 36 B3
Bromsberrow Heath Glos 50 F2
Bromsgrove Worcs 50 B4
Bromyard Hereford 49 D8
Bromyard Downs Hereford 49 D8
Bronaber Gwyn 71 D8
Brongest Ceredig 46 E2
Bronington Wrex 73 F8
Bronllys Powys 48 F3
Bronnant Ceredig 46 C5
Bronte Parsonage Museum, Keighley W Yorks 94 F3
Bronwydd Arms Carms 33 B5
Bronydd Powys 48 E4
Bronygarth Shrops 73 F6
Brook Carms 32 D3
Brook Hants 14 C3
Brook Hants 14 B4
Brook I o W 14 F4
Brook Kent 30 E4
Brook Sur 27 F7
Brook Sur 27 E8
Brook End Beds 53 C8
Brook Hill Hants 14 C3
Brook Street Kent 29 E6
Brook Street Kent 19 B6
Brook Street W Sus 17 B7
Brooke Norf 69 E5
Brooke Rutland 64 D5
Brookenby Lincs 91 E6
Brookend Glos 36 E2
Brookfield Renfs 120 C4
Brookhouse Lancs 92 C5
Brookhouse Green Ches 74 C5
Brookland Kent 19 C6
Brooklands Dumfries 106 B5
Brooklands Gtr Man 87 E5
Brooklands Shrops 74 E2
Brookmans Park Herts 41 D5
Brooks Powys 59 E8
Brooks Green W Sus 16 B5
Brookthorpe Glos 37 C5
Brookville Norf 67 E7
Brookwood Sur 27 D7
Broom Beds 54 E2
Broom S Yorks 88 E5
Broom Warks 51 D5
Broom Worcs 50 B4
Broom Green Norf 81 E5
Broom Hill Dorset 13 D8
Broome Norf 69 E6
Broome Shrops 60 F4
Broome Park Northumb 117 C7
Broomedge Warr 86 F5
Broomer's Corner W Sus 16 B5
Broomfield Aberds 161 E6
Broomfield Essex 42 C3
Broomfield Kent 30 D2
Broomfield Kent 31 C5
Broomfield Som 22 F4
Broomfleet E Yorks 90 B2
Broomhall Ches 74 E3
Broomhall Windsor 27 C7
Broomhaugh Northumb 110 C3
Broomhill Norf 67 D6
Broomhill Northumb 117 D8
Broomhill S Yorks 88 D5
Broomholm Norf 81 D9
Broomley Northumb 110 C3
Broompark Durham 110 E5
Broom's Green Hereford 50 F2
Broomy Lodge Hants 14 C3
Brora Highld 165 D6
Broseley Shrops 61 D6
Brotherhouse Bar Lincs 66 C2
Brotherstone Borders 124 F2
Brotherton N Yorks 89 B5
Brotton Redcar 102 C4
Broubster Highld 168 C5
Brough Cumb 100 C2
Brough Derbys 88 F2
Brough E Yorks 90 B3
Brough Highld 169 B7
Brough Notts 77 D8
Brough Orkney 176 E2
Brough Shetland 174 F6
Brough Shetland 174 G7
Brough Shetland 174 F7
Brough Shetland 175 J7
Brough Shetland 175 H6
Brough Lodge Shetland 174 D7
Brough Sowerby Cumb 100 C2
Broughall Shrops 74 E2
Broughton Borders 122 F4
Broughton Cambs 54 B3
Broughton Flint 73 C7
Broughton Hants 25 F8
Broughton Lancs 92 F5
Broughton M Keynes 53 E6
Broughton N Lincs 90 D3
Broughton Northants 53 B6
Broughton N Yorks 94 D2
Broughton N Yorks 96 B3
Broughton Orkney 176 B3
Broughton Oxon 52 F2
Broughton V Glam 21 B8
Broughton Astley Leics 64 E2
Broughton Beck Cumb 98 F4
Broughton Common Wilts 24 C3
Broughton Gifford Wilts 24 C3
Broughton Hackett Worcs 50 D4
Broughton in Furness Cumb 98 F4
Broughton Mills Cumb 98 E4
Broughton Moor Cumb 107 F7
Broughton Park Gtr Man 87 D6
Broughton Poggs Oxon 38 D2
Broughtown Orkney 176 B5
Broughty Ferry Dundee 142 F4
Browhouses Dumfries 108 C2
Browland Shetland 175 H4
Brown Candover Hants 26 F3
Brown Edge Lancs 85 C4
Brown Edge Staffs 75 D6
Brown Heath Ches 73 C8
Brownhill Aberds 161 D5
Brownhill Aberds 160 D3
Brownhill Blkburn 93 F6
Brownhill Shrops 60 B4
Brownhills Fife 135 C7
Brownhills W Mid 62 D4
Brownlow Ches 74 C5
Brownlow Heath Ches 74 C5
Brownmuir Aberds 143 B7
Brown's End Glos 50 F2
Brownshill Glos 37 D5
Brownston Devon 6 D4
Brownyside Northumb 117 B7
Broxa N Yorks 103 E7
Broxbourne Herts 41 D6
Broxburn E Loth 124 B2
Broxburn W Loth 122 B3
Broxholme Lincs 78 B2
Broxted Essex 42 B1
Broxton Ches 73 D8
Broxwood Hereford 49 D5
Broyle Side E Sus 17 C8
Brù W Isles 172 D6
Bruairnis W Isles 171 K3
Bruan Highld 169 F8
Bruar Lodge Perth 141 B5
Brucehill W Dunb 120 B3
Bruera Ches 73 C8
Bruern Abbey Oxon 38 B2
Bruichladdich Argyll 126 C2
Bruisyard Suff 57 C7
Brumby N Lincs 90 D2
Brund Staffs 75 C8
Brundall Norf 69 D6
Brundish Suff 57 C6
Brundish Street Suff 57 B6
Brunery Highld 145 F7
Brunshaw Lancs 93 F8
Brunswick Village T & W 110 B5
Bruntcliffe W Yorks 88 B3
Bruntingthorpe Leics 64 E3
Brunton Fife 134 B5
Brunton Northumb 117 B8
Brunton Wilts 25 D7
Brushford Devon 9 D8
Brushford Som 10 B4
Bruton Som 23 F8
Bryanston Dorset 13 D6
Brydekirk Dumfries 107 B8
Bryher Scilly 2 E3
Brymbo Wrex 73 D6
Brympton Som 12 C3
Bryn Carms 33 D6
Bryn Gtr Man 86 D3
Bryn Neath 34 E2
Bryn Shrops 60 F2
Bryn-coch Neath 33 E8
Bryn Du Anglesey 82 D3
Bryn Gates Gtr Man 86 D3
Bryn-glas Conwy 83 E8
Bryn Golau Rhondda 34 F3
Bryn-Iwan Carms 46 F2
Bryn-mawr Gwyn 70 D3
Bryn-nantllech Conwy 72 C3
Bryn-penarth Powys 59 D8
Bryn Rhyd-yr-Arian Conwy 72 C3
Bryn Saith Marchog Denb 72 D4
Bryn Sion Gwyn 59 C5
Bryn-y-gwenin Mon 35 C7
Bryn-y-maen Conwy 83 D8
Bryn-yr-eryr Gwyn 70 C4
Brynamman Carms 33 C8
Brynberian Pembs 45 F3
Brynbryddan Neath 34 E1
Brynbuga = Usk Mon 35 D7
Bryncae Rhondda 34 F3
Bryncethin Bridgend 34 F3
Bryncir Gwyn 71 C5
Bryncroes Gwyn 70 D3
Bryncrug Gwyn 58 D3
Bryneglwys Denb 72 E5
Brynford Flint 73 B5
Bryngwran Anglesey 82 D3
Bryngwyn Ceredig 45 E4
Bryngwyn Mon 35 D7
Bryngwyn Powys 48 E3
Brynhenllan Pembs 45 F2
Brynhoffnant Ceredig 46 D2
Brynithel Bl Gwent 35 D6
Brynmawr Bl Gwent 35 C5
Brynmenyn Bridgend 34 F3
Brynmill Swansea 33 E7
Brynna Rhondda 34 F3
Brynrefail Anglesey 82 C4
Brynrefail Gwyn 83 E5
Brynsadler Rhondda 34 F4
Brynsiencyn Anglesey 82 E4
Brynteg Anglesey 82 C4
Brynteg Ceredig 46 E3
Buaile nam Bodach W Isles 171 K3
Bualintur Highld 153 G5
Buarthmeini Gwyn 72 F2
Bubbenhall Warks 51 B8
Bubwith E Yorks 96 F3
Buccleuch Borders 115 C6
Buchanhaven Aberds 161 D8
Buchanty Perth 133 B8
Buchlyvie Stirl 132 E4
Buckabank Cumb 108 E3
Buckden Cambs 54 C2
Buckden N Yorks 94 B2
Buckenham Norf 69 D6
Buckerell Devon 11 D6
Buckfast Devon 6 C5
Buckfast Abbey, Buckfastleigh Devon 6 C5
Buckfastleigh Devon 6 C5
Buckhaven Fife 135 E5
Buckholm Borders 123 F7
Buckholt Mon 36 C2
Buckhorn Weston Dorset 13 B5
Buckhurst Hill Essex 41 E7
Buckie Moray 159 C8
Buckies Highld 169 C6
Buckingham Bucks 52 F4
Buckingham Palace London 28 B3
Buckland Bucks 40 C1
Buckland Devon 6 E4
Buckland Glos 51 F5
Buckland Hants 14 E4
Buckland Herts 54 F4
Buckland Kent 31 E7
Buckland Oxon 38 E3
Buckland Sur 28 D3
Buckland Abbey Devon 6 C2
Buckland Brewer Devon 9 B6
Buckland Common Bucks 40 D2
Buckland Dinham Som 24 D2
Buckland Filleigh Devon 9 D6
Buckland in the Moor Devon 6 B5
Buckland Monachorum Devon 6 C2
Buckland Newton Dorset 12 D4
Buckland St Mary Som 11 C7
Bucklebury W Berks 26 B3
Bucklegate Lincs 79 F6
Bucklerheads Angus 142 F4
Bucklers Hard Hants 14 E5
Bucklesham Suff 57 E6
Buckley = Bwcle Flint 73 C6
Bucklow Hill Ches 86 F5
Buckminster Leics 65 B5
Bucknall Lincs 78 C4
Bucknall Stoke 75 E6
Bucknell Oxon 39 B5
Bucknell Shrops 49 B5
Buckpool Moray 159 C8
Buck's Cross Devon 8 B5
Bucks Green W Sus 27 F8
Bucks Horn Oak Hants 27 E6
Buck's Mills Devon 9 B5
Bucksburn Aberdeen 151 D7
Buckskin Hants 26 D4
Buckton E Yorks 97 B7
Buckton Hereford 49 B5
Buckton Northumb 125 F6
Buckworth Cambs 54 B2
Budbrooke Warks 51 C7
Budby Notts 77 C6
Budd's Titson Corn 8 D4
Bude Corn 8 D4
Budlake Devon 10 E4
Budle Northumb 125 F7
Budleigh Salterton Devon 11 F5
Budock Water Corn 3 C6
Buerton Ches 74 E3
Buffler's Holt Bucks 52 F4
Bugbrooke Northants 52 D4
Buglawton Ches 75 C5
Bugle Corn 4 D5
Bugley Wilts 24 E3
Bugthorpe E Yorks 96 D3
Buildwas Shrops 61 D6
Builth Road Powys 48 D2
Builth Wells = Llanfair-ym-Muallt Powys 48 D2
Buirgh W Isles 173 J3
Bulby Lincs 65 B7
Bulcote Notts 77 E6
Buldoo Highld 168 C4
Bulford Wilts 25 E6
Bulford Camp Wilts 25 E6
Bulkeley Ches 74 D2
Bulkington Warks 63 F7
Bulkington Wilts 24 D4
Bulkworthy Devon 9 C5
Bull Hill Hants 14 E4
Bullamoor N Yorks 102 E1
Bullbridge Derbys 76 D3
Bullbrook Brack 27 C6
Bulley Glos 36 C4
Bullgill Cumb 107 F7
Bullington Hants 26 E2
Bullington Lincs 78 B3
Bull's Green Herts 41 C5
Bullwood Argyll 129 C6
Bulmer Essex 56 E2
Bulmer N Yorks 96 C2
Bulmer Tye Essex 56 F2
Bulphan Thurrock 42 F2
Bulverhythe E Sus 18 E4
Bulwark Aberds 161 D6
Bulwell Nottingham 76 E5
Bulwick Northants 65 E6
Bumble's Green Essex 41 D7
Bun Abhainn Eadarra W Isles 173 H4
Bun a'Mhuillin W Isles 171 J3
Bun Loyne Highld 146 D5
Bunacaimb Highld 145 E6
Bunarkaig Highld 146 F4
Bunbury Ches 74 D2
Bunbury Heath Ches 74 D2
Bunchrew Highld 157 E7
Bundalloch Highld 155 H4
Buness Shetland 174 C8
Bunessan Argyll 136 F4
Bungay Suff 69 F6
Bunker's Hill Lincs 78 B2
Bunker's Hill Lincs 79 D5
Bunkers Hill Oxon 38 C4
Bunloit Highld 147 B8
Bunnahabhain Argyll 126 B4
Bunny Notts 64 B2
Buntait Highld 156 F4
Buntingford Herts 41 B6
Bunwell Norf 68 E4
Burbage Derbys 75 B7
Burbage Leics 63 E8
Burbage Wilts 25 C7
Burchett's Green Windsor 39 F8
Burcombe Wilts 25 F5
Burcot Oxon 39 E5
Burcott Bucks 40 B1
Burdon T & W 111 D6
Bures Suff 56 F3
Bures Green Suff 56 F3
Burford Ches 74 D3
Burford Oxon 38 C2
Burford Shrops 49 C7
Burg Argyll 136 D4
Burgar Orkney 176 D2
Burgate Hants 14 C2
Burgate Suff 56 B4
Burgess Hill W Sus 17 C7
Burgh Suff 57 D6
Burgh-by-Sands Cumb 108 D3
Burgh Castle Norf 69 D7
Burgh Heath Sur 28 D3
Burgh le Marsh Lincs 79 C8
Burgh Muir Aberds 151 B6
Burgh next Aylsham Norf 81 E8
Burgh on Bain Lincs 91 F6
Burgh St Margaret Norf 69 C7
Burgh St Peter Norf 69 E7
Burghclere Hants 26 C2
Burghead Moray 158 C5
Burghfield W Berks 26 C4
Burghfield Common W Berks 26 C4
Burghfield Hill W Berks 26 C4
Burghill Hereford 49 E6
Burghwallis S Yorks 89 C6
Burham Kent 29 C8
Buriton Hants 15 B8
Burland Ches 74 D3
Burlawn Corn 4 B4
Burleigh Brack 27 C6
Burlescombe Devon 11 C5
Burleston Dorset 13 E5
Burley Hants 14 D3
Burley Rutland 65 C5
Burley W Yorks 95 F5
Burley Gate Hereford 49 E7
Burley in Wharfedale W Yorks 94 E4
Burley Lodge Hants 14 D3
Burley Street Hants 14 D3
Burleydam Ches 74 E3
Burlingjobb Powys 48 D4
Burlow E Sus 18 D2
Burlton Shrops 60 B4
Burmarsh Kent 19 B7
Burmington Warks 51 F7
Burn N Yorks 89 B6
Burn of Cambus Stirl 133 D6
Burnaston Derbys 76 F2
Burnbank S Lnrk 121 D7
Burnby E Yorks 96 E4
Burncross S Yorks 88 E4
Burneside Cumb 99 E7
Burness Orkney 176 B5
Burneston N Yorks 101 F8
Burnett Bath 23 C8
Burnfoot Borders 115 C7
Burnfoot Borders 115 C8
Burnfoot E Ayrs 112 D4
Burnfoot Perth 133 D8
Burnham Bucks 40 F2
Burnham N Lincs 90 C4
Burnham Deepdale Norf 80 C4
Burnham Green Herts 41 C5
Burnham Market Norf 80 C4
Burnham Norton Norf 80 C4
Burnham-on-Crouch Essex 43 E5
Burnham-on-Sea Som 22 E5
Burnham Overy Staithe Norf 80 C4
Burnham Overy Town Norf 80 C4
Burnham Thorpe Norf 80 C4
Burnhead Dumfries 113 E8
Burnhead S Ayrs 112 D2
Burnhervie Aberds 151 C6
Burnhill Green Staffs 61 D7
Burnhope Durham 110 E4
Burnhouse N Ayrs 120 D3
Burniston N Yorks 103 E8
Burnlee W Yorks 88 D2
Burnley Lancs 93 F8
Burnley Lane Lancs 93 F8
Burnmouth Borders 125 C5
Burnopfield Durham 110 D4
Burnsall N Yorks 94 C3
Burnside Angus 143 D5
Burnside E Ayrs 113 C5
Burnside Fife 134 D3
Burnside Shetland 174 F4
Burnside S Lnrk 121 C6
Burnside W Loth 122 B3
Burnside of Duntrune Angus 142 F4
Burnswark Dumfries 107 B8
Burnt Heath Derbys 76 B2
Burnt Houses Durham 101 B6
Burnt Yates N Yorks 95 C5
Burntcommon Sur 27 D8
Burnthouse Corn 3 C6
Burntisland Fife 134 F4
Burnton E Ayrs 112 D4
Burntwood Staffs 62 D4
Burnwynd Edin 122 C4
Burpham Sur 27 D8
Burpham W Sus 16 D4
Burradon Northumb 117 D5
Burradon T & W 111 B5
Burrafirth Shetland 174 B8
Burraland Shetland 174 F5
Burraland Shetland 175 J4
Burras Corn 3 C5
Burravoe Shetland 174 G5
Burravoe Shetland 174 F7
Burray Village Orkney 176 G3
Burrells Cumb 100 C1
Burrelton Perth 142 F2
Burridge Devon 20 F4
Burridge Hants 15 C6
Burrill N Yorks 101 F7
Burringham N Lincs 90 D2
Burrington Devon 9 C8
Burrington Hereford 49 B6
Burrington N Som 23 D6
Burrough Green Cambs 55 D7
Burrough on the Hill Leics 64 C4
Burrow-bridge Som 11 B8
Burrowhill Sur 27 C7
Burry Swansea 33 E5
Burry Green Swansea 33 E5
Burry Port = Porth Tywyn Carms 33 D5
Burscough Lancs 86 C2
Burscough Bridge Lancs 86 C2
Bursea E Yorks 96 F4
Burshill E Yorks 97 E6
Bursledon Hants 15 D5
Burslem Stoke 75 E5
Burstall Suff 56 E4
Burstock Dorset 12 D2
Burston Norf 68 F4
Burston Staffs 75 F6
Burstow Sur 28 E4
Burstwick E Yorks 91 B6
Burtersett N Yorks 100 F3
Burtle Som 23 E5
Burton Ches 73 B7
Burton Ches 74 C2
Burton Dorset 14 E2
Burton Lincs 78 B2
Burton Northumb 125 F7
Burton Pembs 44 E4
Burton Som 22 E3
Burton Wilts 24 B3
Burton Agnes E Yorks 97 C7
Burton Bradstock Dorset 12 F2
Burton Dassett Warks 51 D8

Burton Fleming E Yorks 97 B6
Burton Green W Mid 51 B7
Burton Green Wrex 73 D7
Burton Hastings Warks 63 E8
Burton-in-Kendal Cumb 92 B5
Burton in Lonsdale N Yorks 93 B6
Burton Joyce Notts 77 E6
Burton Latimer Northants 53 B7
Burton Lazars Leics 64 C4
Burton-le-Coggles Lincs 65 B6
Burton Leonard N Yorks 95 C6
Burton on the Wolds Leics 64 B2
Burton Overy Leics 64 E3
Burton Pedwardine Lincs 78 E4
Burton Pidsea E Yorks 97 F8
Burton Salmon N Yorks 89 B5
Burton Stather N Lincs 90 C2
Burton upon Stather N Lincs 90 C2
Burton upon Trent Staffs 63 B6
Burtonwood Warr 86 E3
Burwardsley Ches 74 D2
Burwarton Shrops 61 F6
Burwash E Sus 18 C3
Burwash Common E Sus 18 C3
Burwash Weald E Sus 18 C3
Burwell Cambs 55 C6
Burwell Lincs 79 B6
Burwen Anglesey 82 B4
Burwick Orkney 176 H3
Bury Cambs 66 F2
Bury Gtr Man 87 C6
Bury Som 10 B4
Bury W Sus 16 C4
Bury Green Herts 41 B7
Bury St Edmunds Suff 56 C2
Burythorpe N Yorks 96 C3
Busby E Renf 121 D5
Buscot Oxon 38 E2
Bush Bank Hereford 49 D6
Bush Crathie Aberds 149 E8
Bush Green Norf 68 F5
Bushbury W Mid 62 D3
Bushby Leics 64 D3
Bushey Herts 40 E4
Bushey Heath Herts 40 E4
Bushley Worcs 50 F3
Bushton Wilts 25 B5
Buslingthorpe Lincs 90 F4
Busta Shetland 174 G5
Butcher's Cross E Sus 18 C2
Butcher's Pasture Essex 42 B2
Butcombe N Som 23 C7
Butetown Cardiff 22 B3
Butleigh Som 23 F7
Butleigh Wootton Som 23 F7
Butler's Cross Bucks 39 D8
Butler's End Warks 63 F6
Butlers Marston Warks 51 E8
Butley Suff 57 D7
Butley High Corner Suff 57 E7
Butt Green Ches 74 D3
Butterburn Cumb 109 B6
Buttercrambe N Yorks 96 D3
Butterknowle Durham 101 B6
Butterleigh Devon 10 D4
Buttermere Cumb 98 C3
Buttermere Wilts 25 C8
Buttershaw W Yorks 88 B2
Butterstone Perth 141 E7
Butterton Staffs 75 D7
Butterwick Durham 102 B1
Butterwick Lincs 79 E6
Butterwick N Yorks 96 B3
Butterwick N Yorks 97 B5
Buttington Powys 60 D2
Buttonoak Shrops 50 B2
Butt's Green Hants 14 B4
Buttsash Hants 14 D5
Buxhall Suff 56 D4
Buxhall Fen Street Suff 56 D4
Buxley Borders 124 D4
Buxted E Sus 17 B8
Buxton Derbys 75 B7
Buxton Norf 81 E8
Buxworth Derbys 87 F8
Bwcle = Buckley Flint 73 C6
Bwlch Powys 35 B5
Bwlch-Llan Ceredig 46 D4
Bwlch-y-cibau Powys 59 C8
Bwlch-y-fadfa Ceredig 46 E3
Bwlch-y-ffridd Powys 59 E7
Bwlch-y-sarnau Powys 48 B2
Bwlchgwyn Wrex 73 D6
Bwlchnewydd Carms 32 B4
Bwlchtocyn Gwyn 70 E4
Bwlchyddar Powys 59 B8
Bwlchygroes Pembs 45 F4
Byermoor T & W 110 D4
Byers Green Durham 110 F5
Byfield Northants 52 D3
Byfleet Sur 27 C8
Byford Hereford 49 E5
Bygrave Herts 54 F3
Byker T & W 111 C5
Bylchau Conwy 72 C3
Byley Ches 74 C4
Bynea Carms 33 E6
Byrness Northumb 116 D3
Bythorn Cambs 53 B8
Byton Hereford 49 C5
Byworth W Sus 16 B3

C

Cabharstadh W Isles 172 F6
Cablea Perth 141 F6
Cabourne Lincs 90 D5
Cabrach Argyll 127 F2
Cabrach Moray 150 B2
Cabrich Highld 157 E6
Cabus Lancs 92 E4
Cackle Street E Sus 17 B8
Cadbury Devon 10 D4
Cadbury Barton Devon 9 C8
Cadbury World, Bournville W Mid 62 F4
Cadder E Dunb 121 B6
Caddington Beds 40 C3
Caddonfoot Borders 123 F7
Cade Street E Sus 18 C3
Cadeby Leics 63 D8
Cadeby S Yorks 89 D6
Cadeleigh Devon 10 D4
Cadgwith Corn 3 E6
Cadham Fife 134 D4
Cadishead Gtr Man 86 E5
Cadle Swansea 33 E7
Cadley Lancs 92 F5
Cadley Wilts 25 D7
Cadley Wilts 25 C7
Cadmore End Bucks 39 E7
Cadnam Hants 14 C3
Cadney N Lincs 90 D4
Cadole Flint 73 C6
Cadoxton V Glam 22 C3
Cadoxton-Juxta-Neath Neath 34 E1
Cadshaw Blkburn 86 C5
Cadwell Park Motor Racing Circuit Lincs 91 F6
Cadzow S Lnrk 121 D7
Caeathro Gwyn 82 E4
Caehopkin Powys 34 C2
Caenby Lincs 90 F4
Caenby Corner Lincs 90 F3
Caer-bryn Carms 33 C6
Caer Llan Mon 36 D1
Caerau Bridgend 34 E2
Caerau Cardiff 22 B3
Caerdeon Gwyn 58 C3
Caerdydd = Cardiff Cardiff 22 B3
Caerfarchell Pembs 44 C2
Caerffili = Caerphilly Caerph 35 F5
Caerfyrddin = Carmarthen Carms 33 B5
Caergeiliog Anglesey 82 D3
Caergwrle Flint 73 D7
Caergybi = Holyhead Anglesey 82 C2
Caerleon = Caerllion Newport 35 E7
Caerllion = Caerleon Newport 35 E7
Caernarfon Gwyn 82 E4
Caernarfon Castle Gwyn 82 E4
Caerphilly = Caerffili Caerph 35 F5
Caersws Powys 59 E7
Caerwedros Ceredig 46 D2
Caerwent Mon 36 E1
Caerwych Gwyn 71 D7
Caerwys Flint 72 B5
Caethle Gwyn 58 E3
Caim Anglesey 83 C6
Caio Carms 47 F5
Cairinis W Isles 170 D4
Cairisiadar W Isles 172 E3
Cairminis W Isles 173 K3
Cairnbaan Argyll 128 A3
Cairnbanno Ho. Aberds 160 D5
Cairnborrow Aberds 159 E8
Cairnbrogie Aberds 151 B7
Cairnbulg Castle Aberds 161 B7
Cairncross Angus 142 B4
Cairncross Borders 124 C4
Cairndow Argyll 131 D7
Cairness Aberds 161 B7
Cairneyhill Fife 134 F2
Cairnfield Ho. Moray 159 C8
Cairngaan Dumfries 104 F5
Cairngarroch Dumfries 104 E4
Cairnhill Aberds 160 E3
Cairnie Aberds 159 E8
Cairnie Aberds 151 D7
Cairnorrie Aberds 161 D5
Cairnpark Aberds 151 C7
Cairnryan Dumfries 104 C4
Cairnton Orkney 176 F2
Caister-on-Sea Norf 69 C8
Caistor Lincs 90 D5
Caistor St Edmund Norf 68 D5
Caistron Northumb 117 D5
Caitha Bowland Borders 123 E7
Caithness Glass, Perth Perth 134 B2
Calais Street Suff 56 F3
Calanais W Isles 172 E5
Calbost W Isles 172 G7
Calbourne I o W 14 F5
Calceby Lincs 79 B6
Calcot Row W Berks 26 B4
Calcott Kent 31 C5
Caldback Shetland 174 C8
Caldbeck Cumb 108 F3
Caldbergh N Yorks 101 F5
Caldecote Cambs 54 D4
Caldecote Cambs 65 F8
Caldecote Herts 54 F3
Caldecote Northants 52 D4
Caldecott Northants 53 C7
Caldecott Oxon 38 E4
Caldecott Rutland 65 E5
Calder Bridge Cumb 98 D2
Calder Hall Cumb 98 D2
Calder Mains Highld 169 D5
Calder Vale Lancs 92 E5
Calderbank N Lnrk 121 C7
Calderbrook Gtr Man 87 C7
Caldercruix N Lnrk 121 C8
Caldermill S Lnrk 121 E6
Calderwood S Lnrk 121 D6
Caldhame Angus 142 E4
Caldicot Mon 36 F1
Caldwell Derbys 63 C6
Caldwell N Yorks 101 C6
Caldy Mers 85 F3
Caledrhydiau Ceredig 46 D3
Calfsound Orkney 176 C4
Calgary Argyll 136 C4
Califer Moray 158 D4
California Falk 122 B2
California Norf 69 C8
Calke Derbys 63 B7
Callakille Highld 155 E2
Callaly Northumb 117 D6
Callander Stirl 132 D5
Callaughton Shrops 61 E6
Callestick Corn 4 D2
Calligarry Highld 145 C6
Callington Corn 5 C8
Callow Hereford 49 F6
Callow End Worcs 50 E3
Callow Hill Wilts 37 F7
Callow Hill Worcs 50 B2
Callows Grave Worcs 49 C7
Calmore Hants 14 C4
Calmsden Glos 37 D7
Calne Wilts 24 B5
Calow Derbys 76 B4
Calshot Hants 15 D5
Calstock Corn 6 C2
Calstone Wellington Wilts 24 C5
Calthorpe Norf 81 D7
Calthwaite Cumb 108 E4
Calton N Yorks 94 D2
Calton Staffs 75 D8
Calveley Ches 74 D2
Calver Derbys 76 B2
Calver Hill Hereford 49 E5
Calverhall Shrops 74 F3
Calverleigh Devon 10 C4
Calverley W Yorks 94 F5
Calvert Bucks 39 B6
Calverton M Keynes 53 F5
Calverton Notts 77 E6
Calvine Perth 141 C5
Calvo Cumb 107 D8
Cam Glos 36 E4
Camas-luinie Highld 146 B2
Camasnacroise Highld 138 D2
Camastianavaig Highld 153 F6
Camasunary Highld 153 H6
Camault Muir Highld 157 E6
Camb Shetland 174 D7
Camber E Sus 19 D6
Camberley Sur 27 C6
Camberwell London 28 B4
Camblesforth N Yorks 89 B7
Cambo Northumb 117 F6
Cambois Northumb 117 F9
Camborne Corn 3 B5
Cambourne Cambs 54 D4
Cambridge Cambs 55 D5
Cambridge Glos 36 D4
Cambridge Airport Cambs 55 D5
Cambridge Town Sthend 43 F5
Cambus Clack 133 E7
Cambusavie Farm Highld 164 E4
Cambusbarron Stirl 133 E6
Cambuskenneth Stirl 133 E7
Cambuslang S Lnrk 121 C6
Cambusmore Lodge Highld 164 E4
Camden London 41 F5
Camelford Corn 8 F3
Camelot Theme Park, Chorley Lancs 86 C3
Camelsdale W Sus 27 F6
Camerory Highld 158 F4
Camer's Green Worcs 50 F2
Camerton Bath 23 D8
Camerton Cumb 107 F7
Camerton E Yorks 91 B6
Camghouran Perth 140 D2
Cammachmore Aberds 151 E8
Cammeringham Lincs 90 F3
Camore Highld 164 E4
Camp Hill Warks 63 E7
Campbeltown Argyll 118 D4
Campbeltown Airport Argyll 118 D3
Camperdown T & W 111 B5
Campmuir Perth 142 F2
Campsall S Yorks 89 C6
Campsey Ash Suff 57 D7
Campton Beds 54 F2
Camptown Borders 116 C2
Camrose Pembs 44 C4
Camserney Perth 141 E5
Camster Highld 169 E7
Camuschoirk Highld 138 C1
Camuscross Highld 145 B6
Camusnagaul Highld 138 B4
Camusnagaul Highld 162 F4
Camusrory Highld 145 D8
Camusteel Highld 155 F3
Camusterrach Highld 155 F3
Camusvrachan Perth 140 E3
Canada Hants 14 C3
Canadia E Sus 18 D4
Canal Side S Yorks 89 C7
Candacraig Ho. Aberds 150 C2
Candlesby Lincs 79 C7
Candy Mill S Lnrk 122 E3
Cane End Oxon 26 B4
Canewdon Essex 42 E4
Canford Bottom Dorset 13 D8
Canford Cliffs Poole 13 F8
Canford Magna Poole 13 E8
Canham's Green Suff 56 C4
Canholes Derbys 75 B7
Canisbay Highld 169 B8
Cann Dorset 13 B6
Cann Common Dorset 13 B6
Cannard's Grave Som 23 E8
Cannich Highld 156 F4
Cannington Som 22 F4
Cannock Staffs 62 D3
Cannock Wood Staffs 62 C4
Canon Bridge Hereford 49 E6
Canon Frome Hereford 49 E8
Canon Pyon Hereford 49 E6
Canonbie Dumfries 108 B3
Canons Ashby Northants 52 D3
Canonstown Corn 2 C4
Canterbury Kent 30 D5
Canterbury Cathedral Kent 30 D5
Canterbury Tales Kent 30 D5
Cantley Norf 69 D6
Cantley S Yorks 89 D7
Cantlop Shrops 60 D5
Canton Cardiff 22 B3
Cantraybruich Highld 157 E8
Cantraydoune Highld 157 E8
Cantraywood Highld 157 E8
Cantsfield Lancs 93 B6
Canvey Island Essex 42 F3
Canwick Lincs 78 C2
Canworthy Water Corn 8 E4
Caol Highld 139 B5
Caol Ila Argyll 126 B4
Caolas Argyll 136 F2
Caolas Scalpaigh W Isles 173 J5
Caolas Stocinis W Isles 173 J4
Capel Sur 28 E2
Capel Bangor Ceredig 58 F3
Capel Betws Lleucu Ceredig 46 D5
Capel Carmel Gwyn 70 E2
Capel Coch Anglesey 82 C4
Capel Curig Conwy 83 F7
Capel Cynon Ceredig 46 E2
Capel Dewi Ceredig 46 E3
Capel Dewi Ceredig 58 F3
Capel Dewi Carms 33 B5
Capel Garmon Conwy 83 F8
Capel-gwyn Anglesey 82 D3
Capel Gwyn Carms 33 B5
Capel Gwynfe Carms 33 B8
Capel Hendre Carms 33 C6
Capel Hermon Gwyn 71 E8
Capel Isaac Carms 33 B6
Capel Iwan Carms 45 F4
Capel le Ferne Kent 31 F6
Capel Llanilltern Cardiff 34 F4
Capel Mawr Anglesey 82 D4
Capel St Andrew Suff 57 E7
Capel St Mary Suff 56 F4
Capel Seion Ceredig 46 B5
Capel Tygwydd Ceredig 45 E4
Capel Uchaf Gwyn 70 C5
Capel-y-graig Gwyn 82 E5
Capelulo Conwy 83 D7
Capenhurst Ches 73 B7
Capernwray Lancs 92 B5
Capheaton Northumb 117 F6
Cappercleuch Borders 115 B5
Capplegill Dumfries 114 D4
Capton Devon 7 D6
Caputh Perth 141 F7
Car Colston Notts 77 E7
Carbis Bay Corn 2 C4
Carbost Highld 153 F4
Carbost Highld 152 E5
Carbrook S Yorks 88 F4
Carbrooke Norf 68 D2
Carburton Notts 77 B6
Carcant Borders 123 D6
Carcary Angus 143 D6
Carclaze Corn 4 D5
Carcroft S Yorks 89 C6
Cardenden Fife 134 E4
Cardeston Shrops 60 C3
Cardiff = Caerdydd Cardiff 22 B3
Cardiff Bay Barrage Cardiff 22 B3
Cardiff Castle Cardiff 22 B3
Cardiff International Airport V Glam 22 C2
Cardigan = Aberteifi Ceredig 45 E3
Cardington Beds 53 E8
Cardington Shrops 60 E5
Cardinham Corn 5 C6
Cardonald Glasgow 120 C5
Cardow Moray 159 E5
Cardrona Borders 123 F6
Cardross Argyll 120 B3
Cardurnock Cumb 107 D8
Careby Lincs 65 C7
Careston Castle Angus 143 D5
Carew Pembs 32 D1
Carew Cheriton Pembs 32 D1
Carew Newton Pembs 32 D1
Carey Hereford 49 F7
Carfrae E Loth 123 C8
Cargenbridge Dumfries 107 B6
Cargill Perth 142 F1
Cargo Cumb 108 D3
Cargreen Corn 6 C2
Carham Northumb 124 F4
Carhampton Som 22 E2
Carharrack Corn 3 B6
Carie Perth 140 F3
Carie Perth 140 D3
Carines Corn 4 D2
Carisbrooke I o W 15 F5
Carisbrooke Castle I o W 15 F5
Cark Cumb 92 B3
Carlabhagh W Isles 172 D5
Carland Cross Corn 4 D3
Carlby Lincs 65 C7
Carlecotes S Yorks 88 D2
Carlesmoor N Yorks 94 B4
Carleton Cumb 99 B7
Carleton Cumb 108 D4
Carleton Lancs 92 F3
Carleton N Yorks 94 E2
Carleton Forehoe Norf 68 D3
Carleton Rode Norf 68 E4
Carlin How Redcar 103 C5
Carlingcott Bath 23 D8
Carlisle Cumb 108 D4
Carlisle Airport Cumb 108 C4
Carlisle Cathedral Cumb 108 D3
Carlisle Racecourse Cumb 108 D3
Carlops Borders 122 D4
Carlton Beds 53 D7
Carlton Cambs 55 D7
Carlton Leics 63 D7
Carlton Notts 77 E6
Carlton N Yorks 102 F4
Carlton N Yorks 89 B7
Carlton N Yorks 101 F5
Carlton N Yorks 101 C6
Carlton Stockton 102 B1
Carlton Suff 57 C7
Carlton S Yorks 88 C4
Carlton W Yorks 88 B4
Carlton Colville Suff 69 F8
Carlton Curlieu Leics 64 E3
Carlton Husthwaite N Yorks 95 B7
Carlton in Cleveland N Yorks 102 D3
Carlton in Lindrick Notts 89 F6
Carlton le Moorland Lincs 78 D2
Carlton Miniott N Yorks 102 F1
Carlton on Trent Notts 77 C7
Carlton Scroop Lincs 78 E2
Carluke S Lnrk 121 D8
Carmarthen = Caerfyrddin Carms 33 B5
Carmel Anglesey 82 C3
Carmel Carms 33 C6
Carmel Flint 73 B5
Carmel Guern 16
Carmel Gwyn 82 F4
Carmont Aberds 151 F7
Carmunnock Glasgow 121 D6
Carmyle Glasgow 121 C6
Carmyllie Angus 143 E5
Carn-gorm Highld 146 B2
Carnaby E Yorks 97 C7
Carnach Highld 162 E4
Carnach Highld 146 B3
Carnach W Isles 173 J5
Carnachy Highld 168 D2
Càrnais W Isles 172 E3
Carnbee Fife 135 D7
Carnbo Perth 134 D2
Carnbrea Corn 3 B5
Carnduff S Lnrk 121 E6
Carnduncan Argyll 126 C2
Carne Corn 3 C8
Carnforth Lancs 92 B4
Carnhedryn Pembs 44 C3
Carnhell Green Corn 2 C5
Carnkie Corn 3 C6
Carnkie Corn 3 C5
Carno Powys 59 E6
Carnoch Highld 156 F4
Carnoch Highld 156 D3
Carnock Fife 134 F2
Carnon Downs Corn 3 B6
Carnousie Aberds 160 C3
Carnoustie Angus 143 F5
Carnwath S Lnrk 122 E2
Carnyorth Corn 2 C2
Carperby N Yorks 101 F5
Carpley Green N Yorks 100 F4
Carr S Yorks 89 E6
Carr Hill T & W 111 C5
Carradale Argyll 118 C5
Carragraich W Isles 173 J4
Carrbridge Highld 148 B5
Carrefour Selous Jersey 17
Carreg-wen Pembs 45 E4
Carreglefn Anglesey 82 C3
Carrick Argyll 128 B4
Carrick Fife 135 B6
Carrick Castle Argyll 129 A6
Carrick Ho. Orkney 176 C4
Carriden Falk 134 F2
Carrington Gtr Man 86 E5
Carrington Lincs 79 D6
Carrington Midloth 123 C6
Carrog Conwy 71 C8
Carrog Denb 72 E5
Carron Falk 133 F7
Carron Moray 159 E6
Carron Bridge N Lnrk 133 F6
Carronbridge Dumfries 113 E8
Carrshield Northumb 109 E8
Carrutherstown Dumfries 107 B8
Carrville Durham 111 E6
Carsaig Argyll 137 F6
Carsaig Argyll 128 B2
Carscreugh Dumfries 105 D6
Carse Gray Angus 142 D4
Carse Ho. Argyll 128 D2
Carsegowan Dumfries 105 D8
Carseriggan Dumfries 105 C7
Carsethorn Dumfries 107 D6
Carshalton London 28 C3
Carsington Derbys 76 D2
Carskiey Argyll 118 F3
Carsluith Dumfries 105 D8
Carsphairn Dumfries 113 E5
Carstairs S Lnrk 122 E2
Carstairs Junction S Lnrk 122 E2
Carswell Marsh Oxon 38 E3
Carter's Clay Hants 14 B4
Carterton Oxon 38 D2
Carterway Heads Northumb 110 D3
Carthew Corn 4 D5
Carthorpe N Yorks 101 F8
Cartington Northumb 117 D6
Cartland S Lnrk 121 E8
Cartmel Cumb 92 B3
Cartmel Fell Cumb 99 F6
Cartmel Racecourse Cumb 92 B3
Carway Carms 33 D5
Cary Fitzpaine Som 12 B3
Cas-gwent = Chepstow Mon 36 E2
Cascob Powys 48 C4
Cashlie Perth 140 E1
Cashmere Visitor Centre, Elgin Moray 159 E6
Cashmoor Dorset 13 C7
Casnewydd = Newport Newport 35 F7
Cassey Compton Glos 37 C7
Cassington Oxon 38 C4
Cassop Durham 111 F6
Castell Denb 72 C5
Castell Coch Cardiff 35 F5
Castell-Howell Ceredig 46 E3
Castell-Nedd = Neath Neath 33 E8
Castell Newydd Emlyn = Newcastle Emlyn Carms 46 E2
Castell-y-bwch Torf 35 E6
Castellau Rhondda 34 F4
Casterton Cumb 93 B6
Castle Acre Norf 67 C8
Castle Ashby Northants 53 D6
Castle Bolton N Yorks 101 E5
Castle Bromwich W Mid 62 F5
Castle Bytham Lincs 65 C6
Castle Caereinion Powys 59 D8
Castle Camps Cambs 55 E7
Castle Carrock Cumb 108 D5
Castle Cary Som 23 F8
Castle Combe Wilts 24 B3
Castle Combe Motor Racing Circuit Wilts 24 B3
Castle Donington Leics 63 B8
Castle Douglas Dumfries 106 C4
Castle Drogo, Exeter Devon 10 E2
Castle Eaton Thamesdown 37 E8
Castle Eden Durham 111 F7
Castle Forbes Aberds 150 C5
Castle Frome Hereford 49 E8
Castle Green Sur 27 C7
Castle Gresley Derbys 63 C6
Castle Heaton Northumb 124 E5
Castle Hedingham Essex 55 F8
Castle Hill Kent 29 E7
Castle Howard, Malton N Yorks 96 B3
Castle Huntly Perth 134 B5
Castle Kennedy Dumfries 104 D5
Castle O'er Dumfries 115 E5
Castle Pulverbatch Shrops 60 D4
Castle Rising Norf 67 B6
Castle Stuart Highld 157 E8
Castlebay = Bagh a Chaisteil W Isles 171 L2
Castlebythe Pembs 32 B1
Castlecary N Lnrk 121 B7
Castlecraig Highld 158 C2
Castlefairn Dumfries 113 F7
Castleford W Yorks 88 B5
Castlehill Borders 122 F5
Castlehill Highld 169 C6
Castlehill W Dunb 120 B3
Castlemaddy Dumfries 113 F5
Castlemartin Pembs 44 F4
Castlemilk Dumfries 107 B8
Castlemilk Glasgow 121 D6
Castlemorris Pembs 44 B4
Castlemorton Worcs 50 F2
Castleside Durham 110 E3
Castlethorpe M Keynes 53 E6
Castleton Angus 142 E3
Castleton Argyll 128 B3
Castleton Derbys 88 F2
Castleton Gtr Man 87 C6
Castleton Newport 35 F6
Castleton N Yorks 102 D4
Castletown Ches 73 D8
Castletown Highld 169 C6
Castletown Highld 157 E8
Castletown I o M 84 F2
Castletown T & W 111 D6
Castleweary Borders 115 D7
Castley N Yorks 95 E5
Caston Norf 68 E2
Castor P'boro 65 E8
Catacol N Ayrs 119 B6
Catbrain S Glos 36 F2
Catbrook Mon 36 D2
Catchall Corn 2 D3
Catchems Corner W Mid 51 B7
Catchgate Durham 110 D4
Catcleugh Northumb 116 D3
Catcliffe S Yorks 88 F5
Catcott Som 23 F5
Caterham Sur 28 D4
Catfield Norf 69 B6
Catfirth Shetland 175 H6
Catford London 28 B4
Catforth Lancs 92 F4
Cathays Cardiff 22 B3
Cathcart Glasgow 121 C5
Cathedine Powys 35 B5
Catherington Hants 15 C7
Catherton Shrops 49 B8
Catlodge Highld 148 E2
Catlowdy Cumb 108 B4
Catmore W Berks 38 F4
Caton Lancs 92 C5
Caton Green Lancs 92 C5
Catrine E Ayrs 113 B5
Cat's Ash Newport 35 E7
Catsfield E Sus 18 D4
Catshill Worcs 50 B4
Cattal N Yorks 95 D7
Cattawade Suff 56 F5
Catterall Lancs 92 E4
Catterick N Yorks 101 E7
Catterick Bridge N Yorks 101 E7
Catterick Garrison N Yorks 101 E6
Catterick Racecourse N Yorks 101 E7
Catterlen Cumb 108 F4
Catterline Aberds 143 B8
Catterton N Yorks 95 E8
Catthorpe Leics 52 B3
Cattistock Dorset 12 E3
Catton Northumb 109 D8
Catton N Yorks 95 B6
Catwick E Yorks 97 E7
Catworth Cambs 53 B8
Caudlesprings Norf 68 D2
Caudwell's Mill, Matlock Derbys 76 C2
Caulcott Oxon 39 B5
Cauldcots Angus 143 E6
Cauldhame Stirl 132 E5
Cauldmill Borders 115 C8
Cauldon Staffs 75 E7
Caulkerbush Dumfries 107 D6
Caulside Dumfries 115 F7
Caunsall Worcs 62 F2
Caunton Notts 77 D7
Causeway End Dumfries 105 C8
Causeway Foot W Yorks 94 F3
Causeway-head Stirl 133 E6
Causewayend S Lnrk 122 F3
Causewayhead Cumb 107 D8
Causey Park Bridge Northumb 117 E7
Causeyend Aberds 151 C8
Cautley Cumb 100 E1
Cavendish Suff 56 E2
Cavendish Bridge Leics 63 B8
Cavenham Suff 55 C8
Caversfield Oxon 39 B5
Caversham Reading 26 B5
Caverswall Staffs 75 E6
Cavil E Yorks 96 F3
Cawdor Highld 158 D2
Cawdor Castle and Gardens Highld 158 E2
Cawkwell Lincs 79 B5
Cawood N Yorks 95 F8
Cawsand Corn 6 D2
Cawston Norf 81 E7
Cawthorne S Yorks 88 D3
Cawthorpe Lincs 65 B7
Cawton N Yorks 96 B2
Caxton Cambs 54 D4
Caynham Shrops 49 B7
Caythorpe Lincs 78 E2
Caythorpe Notts 77 E6
Cayton N Yorks 103 F8
Ceann a Bhaigh W Isles 170 D3
Ceann a Deas Loch Baghasdail W Isles 171 J3
Ceann Shiphoirt W Isles 172 G5
Ceann Tarabhaigh W Isles 172 G5
Ceannacroc Lodge Highld 146 C5
Cearsiadair W Isles 172 F6
Cefn Berain Conwy 72 C3
Cefn-brith Conwy 72 D3
Cefn Canol Powys 73 F6
Cefn-coch Conwy 83 E8
Cefn Coch Powys 59 B8
Cefn-coed-y-cymmer M Tydf 34 D4
Cefn Cribbwr Bridgend 34 F2
Cefn Cross Bridgend 34 F2
Cefn-ddwysarn Gwyn 72 F3
Cefn Einion Shrops 60 F2
Cefn-gorwydd Powys 47 E8
Cefn-mawr Wrex 73 E6
Cefn-y-bedd Flint 73 D7
Cefn-y-pant Carms 32 B2
Cefneithin Carms 33 C6
Cei-bach Ceredig 46 D3
Ceinewydd = New Quay Ceredig 46 D2
Ceint Anglesey 82 D4
Cellan Ceredig 46 E5
Cellarhead Staffs 75 E6
Cemaes Anglesey 82 B3
Cemmaes Powys 58 D5
Cemmaes Road Powys 58 D5
Cenarth Carms 45 E4
Cenin Gwyn 71 C5
Central Invclyd 129 C7
Ceos W Isles 172 F6
Ceres Fife 135 C6
Cerne Abbas Dorset 12 D4
Cerney Wick Glos 37 E7
Cerrigceinwen Anglesey 82 D4
Cerrigydrudion Conwy 72 E3
Cessford Borders 116 B3
Ceunant Gwyn 82 E5
Chaceley Glos 50 F3
Chacewater Corn 3 B6
Chackmore Bucks 52 F4
Chacombe Northants 52 E2
Chad Valley W Mid 62 F4
Chadderton Gtr Man 87 D7
Chadderton Fold Gtr Man 87 D6
Chaddesden Derby 76 F3
Chaddesley Corbett Worcs 50 B3
Chaddleworth W Berks 26 B2
Chadlington Oxon 38 B3
Chadshunt Warks 51 D8
Chadwell Leics 64 B4
Chadwell St Mary Thurrock 29 B7
Chadwick End W Mid 51 B7
Chadwick Green Mers 86 E3
Chaffcombe Som 11 C8
Chagford Devon 10 F2
Chailey E Sus 17 C7
Chain Bridge Lincs 79 E6
Chainbridge Cambs 66 D4
Chainhurst Kent 29 E8
Chalbury Dorset 13 D8
Chalbury Common Dorset 13 D8
Chaldon Sur 28 D4
Chaldon Herring or East Chaldon Dorset 13 F5
Chale I o W 15 G5
Chale Green I o W 15 G5
Chalfont Common Bucks 40 E3
Chalfont St Giles Bucks 40 E2
Chalfont St Peter Bucks 40 E3
Chalford Glos 37 D5
Chalgrove Oxon 39 E6
Chalk Kent 29 B7
Challacombe Devon 21 E5
Challoch Dumfries 105 C7
Challock Kent 30 D4
Chalton Beds 40 B3
Chalton Hants 15 C8
Chalvington E Sus 18 E2
Chancery Ceredig 46 B4
Chandler's Ford Hants 14 B5
Channel Tunnel Kent 19 B8
Channerwick Shetland 175 L6
Chantry Som 24 E2
Chantry Suff 56 E5
Chapel Fife 134 E4
Chapel Allerton Som 23 D6
Chapel Allerton W Yorks 95 F6
Chapel Amble Corn 4 B4
Chapel Brampton Northants 52 C5
Chapel Chorlton Staffs 74 F5
Chapel-en-le-Frith Derbys 87 F8
Chapel End Warks 63 E7
Chapel Green Warks 63 F6
Chapel Green Warks 52 C2
Chapel Haddlesey N Yorks 89 B6
Chapel Head Cambs 66 F3
Chapel Hill Aberds 161 E7
Chapel Hill Lincs 78 D5
Chapel Hill Mon 36 E2
Chapel Hill N Yorks 95 E6
Chapel Lawn Shrops 48 B5
Chapel-le-Dale N Yorks 93 B7
Chapel Milton Derbys 87 F8
Chapel of Garioch Aberds 151 B6
Chapel Row W Berks 26 C3
Chapel St Leonards Lincs 79 B8
Chapel Stile Cumb 99 D5
Chapelgate Lincs 66 B4
Chapelhall N Lnrk 121 C7
Chapelhill Dumfries 114 E3
Chapelhill Highld 158 B2
Chapelhill N Ayrs 120 E2
Chapelhill Perth 134 B4
Chapelhill Perth 141 F7
Chapelknowe Dumfries 108 B3
Chapelton Angus 143 E6
Chapelton Devon 9 B7
Chapelton Highld 148 C5
Chapelton S Lnrk 121 E6
Chapeltown Blkburn 86 C5
Chapeltown Moray 149 B8
Chapeltown S Yorks 88 E4
Chapmans Well Devon 9 E5
Chapmanslade Wilts 24 E3
Chapmore End Herts 41 C6
Chappel Essex 42 B4
Chard Som 11 D8
Chardstock Devon 11 D8
Charfield S Glos 36 E4
Charford Worcs 50 C4
Charing Kent 30 E3
Charing Cross Dorset 14 C2

Charing Heath Kent 30 E3
Charingworth Glos 51 F7
Charlbury Oxon 38 C3
Charlcombe Bath 24 C2
Charlecote Warks 51 D7
Charlecote Park, Wellesbourne Warks 51 D7
Charles Devon 21 F5
Charles Manning's Amusement Park, Felixstowe Suff 57 F6
Charles Tye Suff 56 D4
Charlesfield Dumfries 107 C8
Charleston Angus 142 E3
Charleston Renfs 120 C4
Charlestown Aberdeen 151 D8
Charlestown Corn 4 D5
Charlestown Derbys 87 E8
Charlestown Dorset 12 G4
Charlestown Fife 134 F2
Charlestown Gtr Man 87 D6
Charlestown Highld 157 E7
Charlestown Highld 154 C4
Charlestown W Yorks 87 B7
Charlestown of Aberlour Moray 159 E6
Charlesworth Derbys 87 E8
Charleton Devon 7 E5
Charlton London 28 B5
Charlton Hants 25 E8
Charlton Herts 40 B4
Charlton Northants 52 F3
Charlton Northumb 116 F4
Charlton Som 23 D8
Charlton Telford 61 C5
Charlton Wilts 13 B7
Charlton Wilts 25 D6
Charlton Wilts 37 F6
Charlton Worcs 50 E5
Charlton W Sus 16 C2
Charlton Abbots Glos 37 B7
Charlton Adam Som 12 B3
Charlton-All-Saints Wilts 14 B2
Charlton Down Dorset 12 E4
Charlton Horethorne Som 12 B4
Charlton Kings Glos 37 B6
Charlton Mackerell Som 12 B3
Charlton Marshall Dorset 13 D6
Charlton Musgrove Som 12 B5
Charlton on Otmoor Oxon 39 C5
Charltons Redcar 102 C4
Charlwood Sur 28 E3
Charlynch Som 22 F4
Charminster Dorset 12 E4
Charmouth Dorset 11 E8
Charndon Bucks 39 B6
Charney Bassett Oxon 38 E3
Charnock Richard Lancs 86 C3
Charsfield Suff 57 D6
Chart Corner Kent 29 D8
Chart Sutton Kent 30 E2
Charter Alley Hants 26 D3
Charterhouse Som 23 D6
Charterville Allotments Oxon 38 C3
Chartham Kent 30 D5
Chartham Hatch Kent 30 D5
Chartridge Bucks 40 D2
Chartwell, Westerham Kent 29 D5
Charvil Wokingham 27 B5
Charwelton Northants 52 D3
Chasetown Staffs 62 D4
Chastleton Oxon 38 B2
Chasty Devon 8 D5
Chatburn Lancs 93 E7
Chatcull Staffs 74 F4
Chatham Medway 29 C8
Chathill Northumb 117 B7
Chatsworth, Bakewell Derbys 76 B2
Chattenden Medway 29 B8
Chatteris Cambs 66 F3
Chattisham Suff 56 E4
Chatto Borders 116 C3
Chatton Northumb 117 B6
Chawleigh Devon 10 C2
Chawley Oxon 38 D4
Chawston Beds 54 D2
Chawton Hants 26 F5
Cheadle Gtr Man 87 F6
Cheadle Staffs 75 E7
Cheadle Heath Gtr Man 87 F6
Cheadle Hulme Gtr Man 87 F6
Cheam London 28 C3
Cheapside Sur 27 D8
Chearsley Bucks 39 C7
Chebsey Staffs 62 B2
Checkendon Oxon 39 F6
Checkley Ches 74 E4
Checkley Hereford 49 F7
Checkley Staffs 75 F7
Chedburgh Suff 55 D8
Cheddar Som 23 D6
Cheddar Showcaves and Gorge Som 23 D6
Cheddington Bucks 40 C2
Cheddleton Staffs 75 D6
Cheddon Fitzpaine Som 11 B7
Chedglow Wilts 37 E6
Chedgrave Norf 69 E6
Chedington Dorset 12 D2
Chediston Suff 57 B7
Chedworth Glos 37 C7
Chedworth Roman Villa Glos 37 C7
Chedzoy Som 22 F5
Cheeklaw Borders 124 D3
Cheeseman's Green Kent 19 B7
Cheglinch Devon 20 E4
Cheldon Devon 10 C2
Chelford Ches 74 B5
Chell Heath Stoke 75 D5
Chellaston Derby 76 F3
Chellington Beds 53 D7
Chelmarsh Shrops 61 F7
Chelmer Village Essex 42 D3
Chelmondiston Suff 57 F6
Chelmorton Derbys 75 C8
Chelmsford Essex 42 D3
Chelsea London 28 B3
Chelsfield London 29 C5
Chelsworth Suff 56 E3
Cheltenham Glos 37 B6
Cheltenham Racecourse Glos 37 B6
Chelveston Northants 53 C7
Chelvey N Som 23 C6
Chelwood Bath 23 C8
Chelwood Common E Sus 17 B8
Chelwood Gate E Sus 17 B8
Chelworth Wilts 37 E6
Chelworth Green Wilts 37 E7
Chemistry Shrops 74 E2
Chenies Bucks 40 E3
Cheny Longville Shrops 60 F4
Chepstow = Cas-gwent Mon 36 E2
Chepstow Racecourse Mon 36 E2
Chequerfield W Yorks 89 B5
Cherhill Wilts 24 B5
Cherington Glos 37 E6
Cherington Warks 51 F7
Cheriton Devon 21 E6
Cheriton Hants 15 B6
Cheriton Kent 19 B8
Cheriton Swansea 33 E5
Cheriton Bishop Devon 10 E2
Cheriton Fitzpaine Devon 10 D3
Cheriton or Stackpole Elidor Pembs 44 F4
Cherrington Telford 61 B6
Cherry Burton E Yorks 97 E5
Cherry Hinton Cambs 55 D5
Cherry Orchard Worcs 50 D3
Cherry Willingham Lincs 78 B3
Cherrybank Perth 134 B3
Chertsey Sur 27 C8
Cheselbourne Dorset 13 E5
Chesham Bucks 40 D2
Chesham Bois Bucks 40 E2
Cheshire Candle Workshops, Burwardsley Ches 74 D2
Cheshunt Herts 41 D6
Cheslyn Hay Staffs 62 D3
Chessington London 28 C2
Chessington World of Adventures London 28 C2
Chester Ches 73 C8
Chester Cathedral Ches 73 C7
Chester-Le-Street Durham 111 D5
Chester Moor Durham 111 E5
Chester Racecourse Ches 73 C7
Chester Zoo Ches 73 B8
Chesterblade Som 23 E8
Chesterfield Derbys 76 B3
Chesters Borders 116 C2
Chesters Borders 116 B2
Chesters Roman Fort Northumb 110 B2
Chesterton Cambs 65 E8
Chesterton Cambs 55 C5
Chesterton Glos 37 D7
Chesterton Oxon 39 B5
Chesterton Shrops 61 E7
Chesterton Staffs 74 E5
Chesterton Warks 51 D8
Chesterwood Northumb 109 C8
Chestfield Kent 30 C5
Cheston Devon 6 D4
Cheswardine Shrops 61 B7
Cheswick Northumb 125 E6
Chetnole Dorset 12 D4
Chettiscombe Devon 10 C4
Chettisham Cambs 66 F5
Chettle Dorset 13 C7
Chetton Shrops 61 E6
Chetwode Bucks 39 B6
Chetwynd Aston Telford 61 C7
Cheveley Cambs 55 C7
Chevening Kent 29 D5
Chevington Suff 55 D8
Chevithorne Devon 10 C4
Chew Magna Bath 23 C7
Chew Stoke Bath 23 C7
Chewton Keynsham Bath 23 C8
Chewton Mendip Som 23 D7
Chicheley M Keynes 53 E7
Chichester W Sus 16 D2
Chichester Cathedral W Sus 16 D2
Chickerell Dorset 12 F4
Chicklade Wilts 24 F4
Chicksgrove Wilts 24 F4
Chidden Hants 15 C7
Chiddingfold Sur 27 F7
Chiddingly E Sus 18 D2
Chiddingstone Kent 29 E5
Chiddingstone Causeway Kent 29 E6
Chiddingstone Hoath Kent 29 E5
Chideock Dorset 12 E2
Chidham W Sus 15 D8
Chidswell W Yorks 88 B3
Chieveley W Berks 26 B2
Chignall St James Essex 42 D2
Chignall Smealy Essex 42 C2
Chigwell Essex 41 E7
Chigwell Row Essex 41 E7
Chilbolton Hants 25 F8
Chilcomb Hants 15 B6
Chilcombe Dorset 12 E3
Chilcompton Som 23 D8
Chilcote Leics 63 C6
Child Okeford Dorset 13 C6
Childer Thornton Ches 73 B7
Childrey Oxon 38 F3
Child's Ercall Shrops 61 B6
Childswickham Worcs 51 F5
Childwall Mers 86 F2
Childwick Green Herts 40 C4
Chilfrome Dorset 12 E3
Chilgrove W Sus 16 C2
Chilham Kent 30 D4
Chilhampton Wilts 25 F5
Chilla Devon 9 D6
Chillaton Devon 9 F6
Chillenden Kent 31 D6
Chillerton I o W 15 F5
Chillesford Suff 57 D7
Chillingham Northumb 117 B6
Chillington Devon 7 E5
Chillington Som 11 C8
Chilmark Wilts 24 F4
Chilson Oxon 38 C3
Chilsworthy Corn 6 B2
Chilsworthy Devon 8 D5
Chilthorne Domer Som 12 C3
Chiltington E Sus 17 C7
Chilton Bucks 39 C6
Chilton Durham 101 B7
Chilton Oxon 38 F4
Chilton Cantelo Som 12 B3
Chilton Foliat Wilts 25 B8
Chilton Lane Durham 111 F6
Chilton Polden Som 23 F5
Chilton Street Suff 55 E8
Chilton Trinity Som 22 F4
Chilvers Coton Warks 63 E7
Chilwell Notts 76 F5
Chilworth Hants 14 C5
Chilworth Sur 27 E8
Chimney Oxon 38 D3
Chineham Hants 26 D4
Chingford London 41 E6
Chinley Derbys 87 F8
Chinley Head Derbys 87 F8
Chinnor Oxon 39 D7
Chipnall Shrops 74 F4
Chippenhall Green Suff 57 B6
Chippenham Cambs 55 C7
Chippenham Wilts 24 B4
Chipperfield Herts 40 D3
Chipping Herts 54 F4
Chipping Lancs 93 E6
Chipping Campden Glos 51 F6
Chipping Hill Essex 42 C4
Chipping Norton Oxon 38 B3
Chipping Ongar Essex 42 D1
Chipping Sodbury S Glos 36 F4
Chipping Warden Northants 52 E2
Chipstable Som 10 B5
Chipstead Kent 29 D5
Chipstead Sur 28 D3
Chirbury Shrops 60 E2
Chirk = Y Waun Wrex 73 F6
Chirk Bank Shrops 73 F6
Chirk Castle Wrex 73 F6
Chirmorrie S Ayrs 105 B6
Chirnside Borders 124 D4
Chirnsidebridge Borders 124 D4
Chirton Wilts 25 D5
Chisbury Wilts 25 C7
Chiselborough Som 12 C2
Chiseldon Thamesdown 25 B6
Chiserley W Yorks 87 B8
Chislehampton Oxon 39 E5
Chislehurst London 28 B5
Chislet Kent 31 C6
Chiswell Green Herts 40 D4
Chiswick London 28 B3
Chiswick End Cambs 54 E4
Chisworth Derbys 87 E7
Chithurst W Sus 16 B2
Chittering Cambs 55 B5
Chitterne Wilts 24 E4
Chittlehamholt Devon 9 B8
Chittlehampton Devon 9 B8
Chittoe Wilts 24 C4
Chivenor Devon 20 F4
Chobham Sur 27 C7
Choicelee Borders 124 D3
Cholderton Wilts 25 E7
Cholesbury Bucks 40 D2
Chollerford Northumb 110 B2
Chollerton Northumb 110 B2
Cholmondeston Ches 74 C3
Cholsey Oxon 39 F5
Cholstrey Hereford 49 D6
Chop Gate N Yorks 102 E3
Choppington Northumb 117 F8
Chopwell T & W 110 D4
Chorley Ches 74 D2
Chorley Lancs 86 C3
Chorley Shrops 61 F6
Chorley Staffs 62 C4
Chorleywood Herts 40 E3
Chorlton cum Hardy Gtr Man 87 E6
Chorlton Lane Ches 73 E8
Choulton Shrops 60 F3
Chowdene T & W 111 D5
Chowley Ches 73 D8
Chrishall Essex 54 F5
Christ Church Oxford Oxon 39 D5
Christchurch Cambs 66 E4
Christchurch Dorset 14 E2
Christchurch Glos 36 C2
Christchurch Newport 35 F7
Christchurch Priory Dorset 14 E2
Christian Malford Wilts 24 B4
Christleton Ches 73 C8
Christmas Common Oxon 39 E7
Christon N Som 23 D5
Christon Bank Northumb 117 B8
Christow Devon 10 F3
Chryston N Lnrk 121 B6
Chudleigh Devon 7 B6
Chudleigh Knighton Devon 7 B6
Chulmleigh Devon 9 C8
Chunal Derbys 87 E8
Church Lancs 86 B5
Church Aston Telford 61 C7
Church Brampton Northants 52 C5
Church Broughton Derbys 76 F2
Church Crookham Hants 27 D6
Church Eaton Staffs 62 C2
Church End Beds 40 B2
Church End Beds 54 F2
Church End Beds 53 F7
Church End Cambs 66 F2
Church End Cambs 66 D3
Church End E Yorks 97 D6
Church End Essex 55 E6
Church End Essex 42 B3
Church End Hants 26 D4
Church End Lincs 78 F5
Church End Warks 63 E6
Church End Warks 63 E6
Church End Wilts 24 B5
Church Enstone Oxon 38 B3
Church Fenton N Yorks 95 F8
Church Green Devon 11 E6
Church Green Norf 68 E3
Church Gresley Derbys 63 C6
Church Hanborough Oxon 38 C4
Church Hill Ches 74 C3
Church Houses N Yorks 102 E4
Church Knowle Dorset 13 F7
Church Laneham Notts 77 B8
Church Langton Leics 64 E4
Church Lawford Warks 52 B2
Church Lawton Ches 74 D5
Church Leigh Staffs 75 F7
Church Lench Worcs 50 D5
Church Mayfield Staffs 75 E8
Church Minshull Ches 74 C3
Church Norton W Sus 16 E2
Church Preen Shrops 60 E5
Church Pulverbatch Shrops 60 D4
Church Stoke Powys 60 E2
Church Stowe Northants 52 D4
Church Street Kent 29 B8
Church Stretton Shrops 60 E4
Church Town N Lincs 89 D8
Church Town Sur 28 D4
Church Village Rhondda 34 F4
Church Warsop Notts 77 C5
Churcham Glos 36 C4
Churchbank Shrops 48 B4
Churchbridge Staffs 62 D3
Churchdown Glos 37 C5
Churchend Essex 42 B2
Churchend Essex 43 E6
Churchend S Glos 36 E4
Churchfield W Mid 62 E4
Churchgate Street Essex 41 C7
Churchill Devon 20 E4
Churchill Devon 11 D8
Churchill N Som 23 D6
Churchill Oxon 38 B2
Churchill Worcs 50 B3
Churchill Worcs 50 D4
Churchinford Som 11 C7
Churchover Warks 64 F2
Churchstanton Som 11 C6
Churchstow Devon 6 E5
Churchtown Derbys 76 C2
Churchtown I o M 84 C4
Churchtown Lancs 92 E4
Churchtown Mers 85 C4
Churnsike Lodge Northumb 109 B6
Churston Ferrers Torbay 7 D7
Churt Sur 27 F6
Churton Ches 73 D8
Churwell W Yorks 88 B3
Chute Standen Wilts 25 D8
Chwilog Gwyn 70 D5
Chyandour Corn 2 C3
Cilan Uchaf Gwyn 70 E3
Cilcain Flint 73 C5
Cilcennin Ceredig 46 C4
Cilfor Gwyn 71 D7
Cilfrew Neath 34 D1
Cilfynydd Rhondda 34 E4
Cilgerran Pembs 45 E3
Cilgwyn Carms 33 B8
Cilgwyn Gwyn 82 F4
Cilgwyn Pembs 45 F2
Ciliau Aeron Ceredig 46 D3
Cill Donnain W Isles 171 H3
Cille Bhrighde W Isles 171 J3
Cille Pheadair W Isles 171 J3
Cilmery Powys 48 D2
Cilsan Carms 33 B6
Ciltalgarth Gwyn 72 E2
Cilwendeg Pembs 45 F4
Cilybebyll Neath 33 D8
Cilycwm Carms 47 F6
Cimla Neath 34 E1
Cinderford Glos 36 C3
Cippyn Pembs 45 E3
Circebost W Isles 172 E4
Cirencester Glos 37 D7
Ciribhig W Isles 172 D4
City Powys 60 F2
City Dulas Anglesey 82 C4
City of London = London, City of London 41 F6
Clachaig Argyll 129 B6
Clachan Argyll 128 E2
Clachan Argyll 130 D3
Clachan Argyll 138 E2
Clachan Argyll 131 D7
Clachan Highld 153 F6
Clachan W Isles 170 F3
Clachan na Luib W Isles 170 D4
Clachan of Campsie E Dunb 121 B6
Clachan of Glendaruel Argyll 128 B4
Clachan-Seil Argyll 130 D3
Clachan Strachur Argyll 131 E6
Clachaneasy Dumfries 105 B7
Clachanmore Dumfries 104 E4
Clachbreck Argyll 128 C2
Clachnabrain Angus 142 C3
Clachtoll Highld 162 B4
Clackmannan Clack 133 E8
Clacton-on-Sea Essex 43 C7
Cladach Chireboist W Isles 170 D3
Claddach-knockline W Isles 170 D3
Cladich Argyll 131 C6
Claggan Highld 137 D7
Claggan Highld 139 B5
Claigan Highld 152 D3
Claines Worcs 50 D3
Clandown Bath 23 D8
Clanfield Hants 15 C7
Clanfield Oxon 38 D2
Clanville Hants 25 E8
Claonaig Argyll 128 E3
Claonel Highld 164 D2
Clap Hill Kent 19 B7
Clapgate Dorset 13 D8
Clapgate Herts 41 B7
Clapham Beds 53 D8
Clapham London 28 B3
Clapham N Yorks 93 C7
Clapham W Sus 16 D4
Clappers Borders 124 D5
Clappersgate Cumb 99 D5
Clapton Som 12 D2
Clapton-in-Gordano N Som 23 B6
Clapton-on-the-Hill Glos 38 C1
Clapworthy Devon 9 B8
Clara Vale T & W 110 C4
Clarach Ceredig 58 F3
Clarbeston Pembs 32 B1
Clarbeston Road Pembs 32 B1
Clarborough Notts 89 F8
Clardon Highld 169 C6
Clare Suff 55 E8
Clarebrand Dumfries 106 C4
Claremont Landscape Garden, Esher Sur 28 C2
Clarencefield Dumfries 107 C7
Clarilaw Borders 115 C8
Clark's Green Sur 28 F2
Clarkston E Renf 121 D5
Clashandorran Highld 157 E6
Clashcoig Highld 164 E3
Clashindarroch Aberds 159 F8
Clashmore Highld 166 F2
Clashmore Highld 164 F4
Clashnessie Highld 166 F2
Clashnoir Moray 149 B8
Clate Shetland 175 G7
Clathy Perth 133 C8
Clatt Aberds 150 B4
Clatter Powys 59 E6
Clatterford I o W 15 F5
Clatterin Bridge Aberds 143 B6
Clatworthy Som 22 F2
Claughton Lancs 92 E5
Claughton Lancs 93 C5
Claughton Mers 85 F4
Claverdon Warks 51 C6
Claverham N Som 23 C6
Clavering Essex 55 F5
Claverley Shrops 61 E7
Claverton Bath 24 C2
Clawdd-newydd Denb 72 D4
Clawthorpe Cumb 92 B5
Clawton Devon 9 E5
Claxby Lincs 90 E5
Claxby Lincs 79 B7
Claxton Norf 69 D6
Claxton N Yorks 96 C2
Clay Common Suff 69 F7
Clay Coton Northants 52 B3
Clay Cross Derbys 76 C3
Clay Hill W Berks 26 B3
Clay Lake Lincs 66 B2
Claybokie Aberds 149 E6
Claybrooke Magna Leics 63 F8
Claybrooke Parva Leics 63 F8
Claydon Oxon 52 D2
Claydon Suff 56 D5
Claygate Dumfries 108 B3
Claygate Kent 29 E8
Claygate Sur 28 C2
Claygate Cross Kent 29 D7
Clayhanger Devon 10 B5
Clayhanger W Mid 62 D4
Clayhidon Devon 11 C6
Clayhill E Sus 18 C5
Clayhill Hants 14 D4
Clayock Highld 169 D6
Claypole Lincs 77 E8
Clayton Staffs 75 E5
Clayton S Yorks 89 D5
Clayton W Sus 17 C6
Clayton W Yorks 94 F4
Clayton Green Lancs 86 B3
Clayton-le-Moors Lancs 93 F7
Clayton-le-Woods Lancs 86 B3
Clayton West W Yorks 88 C3
Clayworth Notts 89 F8
Cleadale Highld 144 E4
Cleadon T & W 111 C6
Clearbrook Devon 6 C3
Clearwell Glos 36 D2
Cleasby N Yorks 101 C7
Cleat Orkney 176 H3
Cleatlam Durham 101 C6
Cleator Cumb 98 C2
Cleator Moor Cumb 98 C2
Clebrig Highld 167 F7
Cleckheaton W Yorks 88 B2
Clee St Margaret Shrops 61 F5
Cleedownton Shrops 61 F5
Cleehill Shrops 49 B7
Cleethorpes NE Lincs 91 D7
Cleeton St Mary Shrops 49 B8
Cleeve N Som 23 C6
Cleeve Hill Glos 37 B6
Cleeve Prior Worcs 51 E5
Clegyrnant Powys 59 D6
Clehonger Hereford 49 F6
Cleish Perth 134 E2
Cleland N Lnrk 121 D8
Clench Common Wilts 25 C6
Clenchwarton Norf 67 B5
Clent Worcs 50 B4
Cleobury Mortimer Shrops 49 B8
Cleobury North Shrops 61 F6
Cleongart Argyll 118 C3
Clephanton Highld 158 D2
Clerklands Borders 115 B8
Clestrain Orkney 176 F2
Cleuch Head Borders 115 C8
Cleughbrae Dumfries 107 B7
Clevancy Wilts 25 B5
Clevedon N Som 23 B6
Cleveley Oxon 38 B3
Cleveleys Lancs 92 E3
Cleverton Wilts 37 F6
Clevis Bridgend 21 B7
Clewer Som 23 D6
Cley next the Sea Norf 81 C6
Cliaid W Isles 171 K2
Cliasmol W Isles 173 H3
Cliburn Cumb 99 B7
Click Mill Orkney 176 D2
Cliddesden Hants 26 E4
Cliff End E Sus 19 D5
Cliffburn Angus 143 E6
Cliffe Medway 29 B8
Cliffe N Yorks 96 F2
Cliffe Woods Medway 29 B8
Clifford Hereford 48 E4
Clifford W Yorks 95 E7
Clifford Chambers Warks 51 D6
Clifford's Mesne Glos 36 B4
Cliffsend Kent 31 C7
Clifton Beds 54 F2
Clifton Bristol 23 B7
Clifton Cumb 99 B7
Clifton Derbys 75 E8
Clifton Lancs 92 F4
Clifton Nottingham 77 F5
Clifton Northumb 117 F8
Clifton N Yorks 94 E4
Clifton Oxon 52 F2
Clifton Stirl 139 F7
Clifton S Yorks 89 E6
Clifton Worcs 50 E3
Clifton York 95 D8
Clifton Campville Staffs 63 C6
Clifton Green Gtr Man 87 D5
Clifton Hampden Oxon 39 E5
Clifton Reynes M Keynes 53 D7
Clifton upon Dunsmore Warks 52 B3
Clifton upon Teme Worcs 50 C2
Cliftoncote Borders 116 B4
Cliftonville Kent 31 B7
Climaen gwyn Neath 33 D8
Climping W Sus 16 D4
Climpy S Lnrk 122 D2
Clink Som 24 E2
Clint N Yorks 95 D5
Clint Green Norf 68 C3
Clintmains Borders 124 F2
Cliobh W Isles 172 E3
Clippesby Norf 69 C7
Clipsham Rutland 65 C6
Clipston Northants 64 F4
Clipstone Notts 77 C5
Clitheroe Lancs 93 E7
Cliuthar W Isles 173 J4
Clive Shrops 60 B5
Clivocast Shetland 174 C8
Clixby Lincs 90 D5
Clocaenog Denb 72 D4
Clochan Moray 159 C8
Clock Face Mers 86 E3
Clockmill Borders 124 D3
Cloddiau Powys 60 D2
Clodock Hereford 35 B7
Clola Aberds 161 D7
Clophill Beds 53 F8
Clopton Northants 65 F7
Clopton Suff 57 D6
Clopton Corner Suff 57 D6
Clopton Green Suff 55 D8
Close Clark I o M 84 E2
Closeburn Dumfries 113 E8
Closworth Som 12 C3
Clothall Herts 54 F3
Clotton Ches 74 C2
Clough Foot W Yorks 87 B7
Cloughton N Yorks 103 E8
Cloughton Newlands N Yorks 103 E8
Clousta Shetland 175 H5
Clouston Orkney 176 E1
Clova Aberds 150 B3
Clova Angus 142 B3
Clove Lodge Durham 100 C4
Clovelly Devon 8 B5
Clovelly Village Devon 8 B5
Clovenfords Borders 123 F7
Clovenstone Aberds 151 C6
Clovullin Highld 138 C4
Clow Bridge Lancs 87 B6
Clowne Derbys 76 B4
Clows Top Worcs 50 B2
Cloy Wrex 73 E7
Cluanie Inn Highld 146 C3
Cluanie Lodge Highld 146 C3
Clun Shrops 60 F3
Clunbury Shrops 60 F3
Clunderwen Carms 32 C2
Clune Highld 148 B3
Clunes Highld 146 F5
Clungunford Shrops 49 B5
Clunie Aberds 160 C3
Clunie Perth 141 E8
Clunton Shrops 60 F3
Cluny Fife 134 E4
Cluny Castle Highld 148 E2
Clutton Bath 23 D8
Clutton Ches 73 D8
Clwt-grugoer Conwy 72 C3
Clwt-y-bont Gwyn 83 E5
Clydach Mon 35 C6
Clydach Swansea 33 D7
Clydach Vale Rhondda 34 E3
Clydebank W Dunb 120 B4
Clydey Pembs 45 F4
Clyffe Pypard Wilts 25 B5
Clynder Argyll 129 B7
Clyne Neath 34 D2
Clynelish Highld 165 D5
Clynnog-fawr Gwyn 82 F4
Clyro Powys 48 E4
Clyst Honiton Devon 10 E4
Clyst Hydon Devon 10 D5
Clyst St George Devon 10 F4
Clyst St Lawrence Devon 10 D5
Clyst St Mary Devon 10 E4
Cnoc Amhlaigh W Isles 172 E8
Cnwch-coch Ceredig 47 B5
Coachford Aberds 159 E8
Coad's Green Corn 5 B7
Coal Aston Derbys 76 B3
Coalbrookdale Telford 61 D6
Coalbrookvale Bl Gwent 35 D5
Coalburn S Lnrk 121 F8
Coalburns T & W 110 C4
Coalcleugh Northumb 109 E8
Coaley Glos 36 D4
Coalhall E Ayrs 112 C4
Coalhill Essex 42 E3
Coalpit Heath S Glos 36 F3
Coalport Telford 61 D6
Coalsnaughton Clack 133 E8
Coaltown of Balgonie Fife 134 E4
Coaltown of Wemyss Fife 134 E5
Coalville Leics 63 C8
Coalway Glos 36 C2
Coat Som 12 B2
Coatbridge N Lnrk 121 C7
Coatdyke N Lnrk 121 C7
Coate Thamesdown 38 F1
Coate Wilts 24 C5
Coates Cambs 66 E3
Coates Glos 37 D6
Coates Lancs 93 E8
Coates Notts 90 F2
Coates W Sus 16 C3
Coatham Redcar 102 B3
Coatham Mundeville Darl 101 B7
Coatsgate Dumfries 114 D3
Cobbaton Devon 9 B8
Cobbler's Green Norf 69 E5
Coberley Glos 37 C6
Cobham Kent 29 C7
Cobham Sur 28 C2
Cobholm Island Norf 69 D8
Cobleland Stirl 132 E4
Cobnash Hereford 49 C6
Coburty Aberds 161 B6
Cock Bank Wrex 73 E7
Cock Bridge Aberds 149 D8
Cock Clarks Essex 42 D4
Cockayne N Yorks 102 E4
Cockayne Hatley Cambs 54 E3
Cockburnspath Borders 124 B3
Cockenzie and Port Seton E Loth 123 B7
Cockerham Lancs 92 D4
Cockermouth Cumb 107 F8
Cockernhoe Green Herts 40 B4
Cockfield Durham 101 B6
Cockfield Suff 56 D3
Cockfosters London 41 E5
Cocking W Sus 16 C2
Cockington Torbay 7 C6
Cocklake Som 23 E6
Cockley Beck Cumb 98 D4
Cockley Cley Norf 67 D7
Cockshutt Shrops 60 B4
Cockthorpe Norf 81 C5
Cockwood Devon 10 F4
Cockyard Hereford 49 F6
Codda Corn 5 B6
Coddenham Suff 56 D5
Coddington Ches 73 D8
Coddington Hereford 50 E2
Coddington Notts 77 D8
Codford St Mary Wilts 24 F4
Codford St Peter Wilts 24 F4
Codicote Herts 41 C5
Codmore Hill W Sus 16 B4
Codnor Derbys 76 E4
Codrington S Glos 24 B2
Codsall Staffs 62 D2
Codsall Wood Staffs 62 D2
Coed Duon = Blackwood Caerph 35 E5
Coed Mawr Gwyn 83 D5
Coed Morgan Mon 35 C7
Coed-Talon Flint 73 D6
Coed-y-bryn Ceredig 46 E2
Coed-y-paen Mon 35 E7
Coed-yr-ynys Powys 35 B5
Coed Ystumgwern Gwyn 71 E6
Coedely Rhondda 34 F4
Coedkernew Newport 35 F6
Coedpoeth Wrex 73 D6
Coedway Powys 60 C3
Coelbren Powys 34 C2
Coffinswell Devon 7 C6
Cofton Hackett Worcs 50 B5
Cogan V Glam 22 B3
Cogenhoe Northants 53 C6
Cogges Oxon 38 D3
Coggeshall Essex 42 B4
Coggeshall Hamlet Essex 42 B4
Coggins Mill E Sus 18 C2
Coig Peighinnean W Isles 172 B8
Coig Peighinnean Bhuirgh W Isles 172 C7
Coignafearn Lodge Highld 148 C2
Coilacriech Aberds 150 E2
Coilantogle Stirl 132 D4
Coilleag W Isles 171 J3
Coillore Highld 153 F4
Coity Bridgend 34 F3
Col W Isles 172 D7
Col Uarach W Isles 172 E7
Colaboll Highld 164 C2
Colan Corn 4 C3
Colaton Raleigh Devon 11 F5
Colbost Highld 152 E3
Colburn N Yorks 101 E6
Colby Cumb 100 B1
Colby I o M 84 E2
Colby Norf 81 D8
Colchester Essex 43 B6
Colchester Zoo Essex 43 B5
Colcot V Glam 22 C3
Cold Ash W Berks 26 C3
Cold Ashby Northants 52 B4
Cold Ashton S Glos 24 B2
Cold Aston Glos 37 C8
Cold Blow Pembs 32 C2
Cold Brayfield M Keynes 53 D7
Cold Hanworth Lincs 90 F4
Cold Harbour Lincs 78 F2
Cold Hatton Telford 61 B6
Cold Hesledon Durham 111 E7
Cold Higham Northants 52 D4
Cold Kirby N Yorks 102 F3
Cold Newton Leics 64 D4
Cold Northcott Corn 8 F4
Cold Norton Essex 42 D4
Cold Overton Leics 64 C5
Coldbackie Highld 167 D8
Coldbeck Cumb 100 D2
Coldblow London 29 B6
Coldean Brighton 17 D7
Coldeast Devon 7 B6
Colden W Yorks 87 B7
Colden Common Hants 15 B5
Coldfair Green Suff 57 C8
Coldham Cambs 66 D4
Coldharbour Glos 36 D2
Coldharbour Kent 29 D6
Coldharbour Sur 28 E2
Coldingham Borders 124 C5
Coldrain Perth 134 D2
Coldred Kent 31 E6
Coldridge Devon 9 D8
Coldstream Angus 142 F3
Coldstream Borders 124 F4
Coldwaltham W Sus 16 C4
Coldwells Aberds 161 D8
Coldwells Croft Aberds 150 B4
Coldyeld Shrops 60 E3
Cole Som 23 F8
Cole Green Herts 41 C5
Cole Henley Hants 26 D2
Colebatch Shrops 60 F3

Colebrook Devon 10 D5
Colebrooke Devon 10 E2
Coleby Lincs 78 C2
Coleby N Lincs 90 C2
Coleford Devon 10 D2
Coleford Glos 36 C2
Coleford Som 23 E8
Colehill Dorset 13 D8
Coleman's Hatch E Sus 29 F5
Colemere Shrops 73 F8
Colemore Hants 26 F5
Coleorton Leics 63 C8
Colerne Wilts 24 B3
Cole's Green Suff 57 C6
Coles Green Suff 56 E4
Colesbourne Glos 37 C6
Colesden Beds 54 D2
Coleshill Bucks 40 E2
Coleshill Oxon 38 E2
Coleshill Warks 63 F6
Colestocks Devon 11 D5
Colgate W Sus 28 F3
Colgrain Argyll 129 B8
Colinsburgh Fife 135 D6
Colinton Edin 122 C5
Colintraive Argyll 129 C5
Colkirk Norf 80 E5
Collace Perth 142 F2
Collafirth Shetland 174 G6
Collaton St Mary Torbay 7 D6
College Milton S Lnrk 121 D6
Collessie Fife 134 C4
Collier Row London 41 E8
Collier Street Kent 29 E8
Collier's End Herts 41 B6
Collier's Green Kent 18 B4
Colliery Row T & W 111 E6
Collieston Aberds 161 F7
Collin Dumfries 107 B7
Collingbourne Ducis Wilts 25 D7
Collingbourne Kingston Wilts 25 D7
Collingham Notts 77 C8
Collingham W Yorks 95 E6
Collington Hereford 49 C8
Collingtree Northants 53 D5
Collins Green Warr 86 E3
Colliston Angus 143 E6
Collycroft Warks 63 F7
Collynie Aberds 160 E5
Collyweston Northants 65 D6
Colmonell S Ayrs 104 A5
Colmworth Beds 54 D2
Coln Rogers Glos 37 D7
Coln St Aldwyn's Glos 37 D8
Coln St Dennis Glos 37 C7
Colnabaichin Aberds 149 D8
Colnbrook Slough 27 B8
Colne Cambs 54 B4
Colne Lancs 93 E8
Colne Edge Lancs 93 E8
Colne Engaine Essex 56 F2
Colney Norf 68 D4
Colney Heath Herts 41 D5
Colney Street Herts 40 D4
Colpy Aberds 160 E3
Colquhar Borders 123 E6
Colsterdale N Yorks 101 F6
Colsterworth Lincs 65 B6
Colston Bassett Notts 77 F6
Coltfield Moray 158 C5
Colthouse Cumb 99 E5
Coltishall Norf 69 C5
Coltness N Lnrk 121 D8
Colton Cumb 99 F5
Colton Norf 68 D4
Colton N Yorks 95 E8
Colton Staffs 62 B4
Colton W Yorks 95 F6
Colva Powys 48 D4
Colvend Dumfries 107 D5
Colvister Shetland 174 D7
Colwall Green Hereford 50 E2
Colwall Stone Hereford 50 E2
Colwell Northumb 110 B2
Colwich Staffs 62 B4
Colwick Notts 77 E6
Colwinston V Glam 21 B8
Colworth W Sus 16 D3
Colwyn Bay = Bae Colwyn Conwy 83 D8
Colyford Devon 11 E7
Colyton Devon 11 E7
Combe Hereford 48 C5
Combe Oxon 38 C4
Combe W Berks 25 C8
Combe Common Sur 27 F7
Combe Down Bath 24 C2
Combe Florey Som 22 F3
Combe Hay Bath 24 D2
Combe Martin Devon 20 E4
Combe Moor Hereford 49 C5
Combe Raleigh Devon 11 D6
Combe St Nicholas Som 11 C8
Combeinteignhead Devon 7 B7
Comberbach Ches 74 B3
Comberton Cambs 54 D4
Comberton Hereford 49 C6
Combpyne Devon 11 E7
Combridge Staffs 75 F7
Combrook Warks 51 D8
Combs Derbys 75 B7
Combs Suff 56 D4
Combs Ford Suff 56 D4
Combwich Som 22 E4
Comers Aberds 151 D5
Comins Coch Ceredig 58 F3
Commercial End Cambs 55 C6
Commins Capel Betws Ceredig 46 D5
Commins Coch Powys 58 D5
Common Edge Blkpool 92 F3
Common Side Derbys 76 B3
Commondale N Yorks 102 C4
Commonmoor Corn 5 C7
Commonside Ches 74 B2
Compstall Gtr Man 87 E7
Compton Devon 7 C6
Compton Hants 15 B5
Compton Sur 27 E6
Compton Sur 27 E7
Compton W Berks 26 B3
Compton Wilts 25 D6
Compton W Sus 15 C8
Compton Abbas Dorset 13 C6
Compton Abdale Glos 37 C7
Compton Acres Poole 13 F8
Compton Bassett Wilts 24 B5
Compton Beauchamp Oxon 38 F2
Compton Bishop Som 23 D5
Compton Chamberlayne Wilts 13 B8
Compton Dando Bath 23 C8
Compton Dundon Som 23 F6
Compton Martin Bath 23 D7
Compton Pauncefoot Som 12 B4
Compton Valence Dorset 12 E3
Comrie Fife 134 F2
Comrie Perth 133 B6
Conaglen House Highld 138 C4
Conchra Argyll 129 B5
Concraigie Perth 141 E8
Conder Green Lancs 92 D4
Conderton Worcs 50 F4
Condicote Glos 38 B1
Condorrat N Lnrk 121 B7
Condover Shrops 60 D4
Coney Weston Suff 56 B3
Coneyhurst W Sus 16 B5
Coneysthorpe N Yorks 96 B3
Coneythorpe N Yorks 95 D6
Conford Hants 27 F6
Congash Highld 149 B6
Congdon's Shop Corn 5 B7
Congerstone Leics 63 D7
Congham Norf 80 E3
Congl-y-wal Gwyn 71 C8
Congleton Ches 75 C5
Congresbury N Som 23 C6
Congreve Staffs 62 C3
Conicavel Moray 158 D3
Coningsby Lincs 78 D5
Conington Cambs 65 F8
Conington Cambs 54 C4
Conisbrough S Yorks 89 E6
Conisby Argyll 126 C2
Conisholme Lincs 91 E8
Coniston Cumb 99 E5
Coniston E Yorks 97 F7
Coniston Cold N Yorks 94 D2
Conistone N Yorks 94 C2
Connah's Quay Flint 73 C6
Connel Argyll 130 B5
Connel Park E Ayrs 113 C6
Connor Downs Corn 2 C4
Conon Bridge Highld 157 D6
Conon House Highld 157 D6
Cononley N Yorks 94 E2
Conordan Highld 153 F6
Consall Staffs 75 E6
Consett Durham 110 D4
Constable Burton N Yorks 101 E6
Constantine Corn 3 D6
Constantine Bay Corn 4 B3
Contin Highld 157 D5
Contlaw Aberdeen 151 D7
Conwy Conwy 83 D7
Conwy Castle Conwy 83 D7
Conyer Kent 30 C3
Conyers Green Suff 56 C2
Cooden E Sus 18 E4
Cooil I o M 84 E3
Cookbury Devon 9 D6
Cookham Windsor 40 F1
Cookham Dean Windsor 40 F1
Cookham Rise Windsor 40 F1
Cookhill Worcs 51 D5
Cookley Suff 57 B7
Cookley Worcs 62 F2
Cookley Green Oxon 39 E6
Cookney Aberds 151 E7
Cookridge W Yorks 95 E5
Cooksbridge E Sus 17 C8
Cooksmill Green Essex 42 D2
Coolham W Sus 16 B5
Cooling Medway 29 B8
Coombe Corn 8 C4
Coombe Corn 4 D4
Coombe Hants 15 B7
Coombe Wilts 25 D6
Coombe Bissett Wilts 14 B2
Coombe Hill Glos 37 B5
Coombe Keynes Dorset 13 F6
Coombes W Sus 17 D5
Coopersale Common Essex 41 D7
Cootham W Sus 16 C4
Copdock Suff 56 E5
Copford Green Essex 43 B5
Copgrove N Yorks 95 C6
Copister Shetland 174 F6
Cople Beds 54 E2
Copley Durham 101 B5
Coplow Dale Derbys 75 B8
Copmanthorpe York 95 E8
Coppathorne Corn 8 D4
Coppenhall Staffs 62 C3
Coppenhall Moss Ches 74 D4
Copperhouse Corn 2 C4
Coppingford Cambs 65 F8
Copplestone Devon 10 D2
Coppull Lancs 86 C3
Coppull Moor Lancs 86 C3
Copsale W Sus 17 B5
Copshaw Holm = Newcastleton Borders 115 F7
Copster Green Lancs 93 F6
Copston Magna Warks 63 F8
Copt Heath W Mid 51 B6
Copt Hewick N Yorks 95 B6
Copt Oak Leics 63 C8
Copthorne Shrops 60 C4
Copthorne W Sus 28 F4
Copy's Green Norf 80 D5
Copythorne Hants 14 C4
Corbets Tey London 42 F1
Corbridge Northumb 110 C2
Corby Northants 65 F5
Corby Glen Lincs 65 B6
Cordon N Ayrs 119 C7
Coreley Shrops 49 B8
Cores End Bucks 40 F2
Corfe Som 11 C7
Corfe Castle Dorset 13 F7
Corfe Castle Dorset 13 F7
Corfe Mullen Dorset 13 E7
Corfton Shrops 60 F4
Corgarff Aberds 149 D8
Corhampton Hants 15 B7
Corlae Dumfries 113 E6
Corley Warks 63 F7
Corley Ash Warks 63 F6
Corley Moor Warks 63 F6
Cornaa I o M 84 D4
Cornabus Argyll 126 E3
Cornel Conwy 83 E7
Corner Row Lancs 92 F4
Corney Cumb 98 E3
Cornforth Durham 111 F6
Cornhill Aberds 160 C2
Cornhill-on-Tweed Northumb 124 F4
Cornholme W Yorks 87 B7
Cornish Cyder Farm, Truro Corn 4 D2
Cornish Hall End Essex 55 F7
Cornquoy Orkney 176 G4
Cornsay Durham 110 E4
Cornsay Colliery Durham 110 E4
Corntown Highld 157 D6
Corntown V Glam 21 B8
Cornwell Oxon 38 B2
Cornwood Devon 6 D4
Cornworthy Devon 7 D6
Corpach Highld 138 B4
Corpusty Norf 81 D7
Corran Highld 138 C4
Corran Highld 145 C8
Corranbuie Argyll 128 D3
Corrany I o M 84 D4
Corrie N Ayrs 119 B7
Corrie Common Dumfries 114 F5
Corriecravie N Ayrs 119 D6
Corriemoillie Highld 156 C4
Corriemulzie Lodge Highld 163 E7
Corrievarkie Lodge Perth 140 B2
Corrievorrie Highld 148 B3
Corrimony Highld 156 F4
Corringham Lincs 90 E2
Corringham Thurrock 42 F3
Corris Gwyn 58 D4
Corris Uchaf Gwyn 58 D4
Corrour Shooting Lodge Highld 139 C8
Corrow Argyll 131 E7
Corry Highld 155 H2
Corry of Ardnagrask Highld 157 E6
Corrykinloch Highld 163 B7
Corrymuckloch Perth 141 F5
Corrynachenchy Argyll 137 D7
Cors-y-Gedol Gwyn 71 E6
Corsback Highld 169 B7
Corscombe Dorset 12 D3
Corse Aberds 160 D3
Corse Glos 36 B4
Corse Lawn Worcs 50 F3
Corse of Kinnoir Aberds 160 D2
Corsewall Dumfries 104 C4
Corsham Wilts 24 B3
Corsindae Aberds 151 D5
Corsley Wilts 24 E3
Corsley Heath Wilts 24 E3
Corsock Dumfries 106 B4
Corston Bath 23 C8
Corston Wilts 37 F6
Corstorphine Edin 122 B4
Cortachy Angus 142 D3
Corton Suff 69 E8
Corton Wilts 24 E4
Corton Denham Som 12 B4
Coruanan Lodge Highld 138 C4
Corunna W Isles 170 D4
Corwen Denb 72 E4
Coryton Devon 9 F6
Coryton Thurrock 42 F3
Cosby Leics 64 E2
Coseley W Mid 62 E3
Cosgrove Northants 53 E5
Cosham Ptsmth 15 D7
Cosheston Pembs 32 D1
Cossall Notts 76 E4
Cossington Leics 64 C3
Cossington Som 23 E5
Costa Orkney 176 D2
Costessey Norf 68 C4
Costock Notts 64 B2
Coston Leics 64 B5
Cote Oxon 38 D3
Cotebrook Ches 74 C2
Cotehele House Corn 6 C2
Cotehill Cumb 108 D4
Cotes Cumb 99 F6
Cotes Leics 64 B2
Cotes Staffs 74 F5
Cotesbach Leics 64 F2
Cotgrave Notts 77 F6
Cothall Aberds 151 C7
Cotham Notts 77 E7
Cothelstone Som 22 F3
Cotherstone Durham 101 C5
Cothill Oxon 38 E4
Cotleigh Devon 11 D7
Cotmanhay Derbys 76 E4
Cotmaton Devon 11 F6
Coton Cambs 54 D5
Coton Northants 52 B4
Coton Staffs 62 B2
Coton Staffs 75 F6
Coton Clanford Staffs 62 B2
Coton Hill Shrops 60 C4
Coton Hill Staffs 75 F6
Coton in the Elms Derbys 63 C6
Cotswold Wild Life Park, Burford Oxon 38 D2
Cott Devon 7 C5
Cottam E Yorks 97 C5
Cottam Lancs 92 F5
Cottam Notts 77 B8
Cottartown Highld 158 F4
Cottenham Cambs 54 C5
Cotterdale N Yorks 100 E3
Cottered Herts 41 B6
Cotteridge W Mid 50 B5
Cotterstock Northants 65 E7
Cottesbrooke Northants 52 B5
Cottesmore Rutland 65 C6
Cotteylands Devon 10 C4
Cottingham E Yorks 97 F6
Cottingham Northants 64 E5
Cottingley W Yorks 94 F4
Cottisford Oxon 52 F3
Cotton Staffs 75 E7
Cotton Suff 56 C4
Cotton End Beds 53 E8
Cottown Aberds 150 B4
Cottown Aberds 151 C6
Cottown Aberds 160 D5
Cotwalton Staffs 75 F6
Couch's Mill Corn 5 D6
Coughton Hereford 36 B2
Coughton Warks 51 C5
Coulaghailtro Argyll 128 D2
Coulags Highld 155 F5
Coulby Newham M'bro 102 C3
Coulderton Cumb 98 D1
Coulin Highld 155 E6
Coull Aberds 150 D4
Coull Argyll 126 C2
Coulport Argyll 129 B7
Coulsdon London 28 D3
Coulston Wilts 24 D4
Coulter S Lnrk 122 F3
Coulton N Yorks 96 B2
Cound Shrops 61 D5
Coundon Durham 101 B7
Coundon W Mid 63 F7
Coundon Grange Durham 101 B7
Countersett N Yorks 100 F4
Countess Wilts 25 E6
Countess Wear Devon 10 F4
Countesthorpe Leics 64 E2
Countisbury Devon 21 E6
County Oak W Sus 28 F3
Coup Green Lancs 86 B3
Coupar Angus Perth 142 E2
Coupland Northumb 124 F5
Cour Argyll 118 B5
Courance Dumfries 114 E3
Court-at-Street Kent 19 B7
Court Henry Carms 33 B6
Courteenhall Northants 53 D5
Courtsend Essex 43 E6
Courtway Som 22 F4
Cousland Midloth 123 C6
Cousley Wood E Sus 18 B3
Cove Argyll 129 B7
Cove Borders 124 B3
Cove Devon 10 C4
Cove Hants 27 D6
Cove Highld 162 E2
Cove Bay Aberdeen 151 D8
Cove Bottom Suff 57 B8
Covehithe Suff 69 F8
Coven Staffs 62 D3
Coveney Cambs 66 F4
Covenham St Bartholomew Lincs 91 E7
Covenham St Mary Lincs 91 E7
Coventry W Mid 51 B8
Coventry Airport Warks 51 B8
Coventry Cathedral W Mid 51 B8
Coverack Corn 3 E6
Coverham N Yorks 101 F6
Covesea Moray 159 B5
Covington Cambs 53 B8
Covington S Lnrk 122 F2
Cow Ark Lancs 93 E6
Cowan Bridge Lancs 93 B6
Cowbeech E Sus 18 D3
Cowbit Lincs 66 C2
Cowbridge Lincs 79 E6
Cowbridge Som 21 E8
Cowbridge = Y Bont-Faen V Glam 21 B8
Cowdale Derbys 75 B7
Cowden Kent 29 E5
Cowdenbeath Fife 134 E3
Cowdenburn Borders 122 D5
Cowers Lane Derbys 76 E3
Cowes I o W 15 E5
Cowesby N Yorks 102 F2
Cowfold W Sus 17 B6
Cowgill Cumb 100 F2
Cowie Aberds 151 F7
Cowie Stirl 133 F7
Cowley Devon 10 E4
Cowley Glos 37 C6
Cowley London 40 F3
Cowley Oxon 39 D5
Cowleymoor Devon 10 C4
Cowling Lancs 86 C3
Cowling N Yorks 94 E2
Cowling N Yorks 101 F7
Cowlinge Suff 55 D8
Cowpe Lancs 87 B6
Cowpen Northumb 117 F8
Cowpen Bewley Stockton 102 B2
Cowplain Hants 15 C7
Cowshill Durham 109 E8
Cowstrandburn Fife 134 E2
Cowthorpe N Yorks 95 D7
Cox Common Suff 69 F6
Cox Green Windsor 27 B6
Cox Moor Notts 76 D5
Coxbank Ches 74 E3
Coxbench Derbys 76 E3
Coxford Norf 80 E4
Coxford Soton 14 C4
Coxheath Kent 29 D8
Coxhill Kent 31 E6
Coxhoe Durham 111 F6
Coxley Som 23 E7
Coxwold N Yorks 95 B8
Coychurch Bridgend 21 B8
Coylton S Ayrs 112 B4
Coylumbridge Highld 148 C5
Coynach Aberds 150 D3
Coynachie Aberds 159 F8
Coytrahen Bridgend 34 F2
Crabadon Devon 7 D5
Crabbs Cross Worcs 50 C5
Crabtree W Sus 17 B6
Crackenthorpe Cumb 100 B1
Crackington Haven Corn 8 E3
Crackley Warks 51 B7
Crackleybank Shrops 61 C7
Crackpot N Yorks 100 E4
Cracoe N Yorks 94 C2
Craddock Devon 11 C5
Cradhlastadh W Isles 172 E3
Cradley Hereford 50 E2
Cradley Heath W Mid 62 F3
Crafthole Corn 5 D8
Cragg Vale W Yorks 87 B8
Craggan Highld 149 B6
Craggie Highld 165 C5
Craggie Highld 157 F8
Craghead Durham 110 D5
Crai Powys 34 B2
Craibstone Moray 159 D8
Craichie Angus 143 E5
Craig Dumfries 106 B3
Craig Dumfries 106 C3
Craig Highld 155 F6
Craig Castle Aberds 150 B3
Craig-cefn-parc Swansea 33 D7
Craig Penllyn V Glam 21 B8
Craig-y-don Conwy 83 C7
Craig-y-nos Powys 34 C2
Craiganor Lodge Perth 140 D3
Craigdam Aberds 160 E5
Craigdarroch Dumfries 113 E7
Craigdarroch Highld 156 D5
Craigdhu Highld 156 E5
Craigearn Aberds 151 C6
Craigellachie Moray 159 E6
Craigencross Dumfries 104 C4
Craigend Perth 134 B3
Craigend Stirl 133 F6
Craigendive Argyll 129 B5
Craigendoran Argyll 129 B8
Craigends Renfs 120 C4
Craigens Argyll 126 C2
Craigens E Ayrs 113 C5
Craighat Stirl 132 F3
Craighead Fife 135 D8
Craighlaw Mains Dumfries 105 C7
Craighouse Argyll 127 F3
Craigie Aberds 151 C8
Craigie Dundee 142 F4
Craigie Perth 134 B3
Craigie Perth 141 E8
Craigie S Ayrs 120 F4
Craigiefield Orkney 176 E3
Craigielaw E Loth 123 B7
Craiglockhart Edin 122 B5
Craigmalloch E Ayrs 112 E4
Craigmaud Aberds 161 C5
Craigmillar Edin 123 B5
Craigmore Argyll 129 D6
Craignant Shrops 73 F6
Craigneuk N Lnrk 121 D7
Craigneuk N Lnrk 121 C7
Craignure Argyll 130 B3
Craigo Angus 143 C6
Craigow Perth 134 D2
Craigrothie Fife 135 C5
Craigroy Moray 158 D5
Craigruie Stirl 132 B3
Craigston Castle Aberds 160 C4
Craigton Aberdeen 151 D7
Craigton Angus 142 D3
Craigton Angus 143 F5
Craigton Highld 164 E3
Craigtown Highld 168 D3
Craik Borders 115 D6
Crail Fife 135 D8
Crailing Borders 116 B2
Crailinghall Borders 116 B2
Craiselound N Lincs 89 E8
Crakehill N Yorks 95 B7
Crakemarsh Staffs 75 F7
Crambe N Yorks 96 C3
Cramlington Northumb 111 B5
Cramond Edin 122 B4
Cramond Bridge Edin 122 B4
Cranage Ches 74 C4
Cranberry Staffs 74 F5
Cranborne Dorset 13 C8
Cranbourne Brack 27 B7
Cranbrook Kent 18 B4
Cranbrook Common Kent 18 B4
Crane Moor S Yorks 88 D4
Crane's Corner Norf 68 C2
Cranfield Beds 53 E7
Cranford London 28 B2
Cranford St Andrew Northants 53 B7
Cranford St John Northants 53 B7
Cranham Glos 37 C5
Cranham London 42 F1
Crank Mers 86 E3
Crank Wood Gtr Man 86 D4
Cranleigh Sur 27 F8
Cranley Suff 57 B5
Cranmer Green Suff 56 B4
Cranmore I o W 14 F4
Cranna Aberds 160 C3
Crannich Argyll 137 D6
Crannoch Moray 159 D8
Cranoe Leics 64 E4
Cransford Suff 57 C7
Cranshaws Borders 124 C2
Cranstal I o M 84 B4
Crantock Corn 4 C2
Cranwell Lincs 78 E3
Cranwich Norf 67 E7
Cranworth Norf 68 D2
Craobh Haven Argyll 130 E3
Crapstone Devon 6 C3
Crarae Argyll 131 F5
Crask Inn Highld 164 B2
Crask of Aigas Highld 157 E5
Craskins Aberds 150 D4
Craster Northumb 117 C8
Craswall Hereford 48 F4
Cratfield Suff 57 B7
Crathes Aberds 151 E6
Crathes Castle and Gardens Aberds 151 E6
Crathie Aberds 149 E8
Crathie Highld 147 E8
Crathorne N Yorks 102 D2
Craven Arms Shrops 60 F4
Crawcrook T & W 110 C4
Crawford Lancs 86 D2
Crawford S Lnrk 114 B2
Crawfordjohn S Lnrk 113 B8
Crawick Dumfries 113 C7
Crawley Hants 26 F2
Crawley Oxon 38 C3
Crawley W Sus 28 F3
Crawley Down W Sus 28 F4
Crawleyside Durham 110 E2
Crawshawbooth Lancs 87 B6
Crawton Aberds 143 B8
Cray N Yorks 94 B2
Cray Perth 141 C8
Crayford London 29 B6
Crayke N Yorks 95 B8
Crays Hill Essex 42 E3
Cray's Pond Oxon 39 F6
Creacombe Devon 10 C3
Creag Ghoraidh W Isles 170 F3
Creagan Argyll 138 E3
Creaguaineach Lodge Highld 139 C7
Creaksea Essex 43 E5
Creaton Northants 52 B5
Creca Dumfries 108 B2
Credenhill Hereford 49 E6
Crediton Devon 10 D3
Creebridge Dumfries 105 C8
Creech Heathfield Som 11 B7
Creech St Michael Som 11 B7
Creed Corn 3 B8
Creekmouth London 41 F7
Creeting Bottoms Suff 56 D5
Creeting St Mary Suff 56 D4
Creeton Lincs 65 B7
Creetown Dumfries 105 D8
Creg-ny-Baa I o M 84 D3
Creggans Argyll 131 E6
Cregneash I o M 84 F1
Cregrina Powys 48 D3
Creich Fife 134 B5
Creigiau Cardiff 34 F4
Cremyll Corn 6 D2
Creslow Bucks 39 B8
Cressage Shrops 61 D5
Cressbrook Derbys 75 B8
Cresselly Pembs 32 D1
Cressing Essex 42 B3
Cresswell Northumb 117 E8
Cresswell Staffs 75 F6
Cresswell Quay Pembs 32 D1
Creswell Derbys 76 B5
Cretingham Suff 57 C6
Cretshengan Argyll 128 D2
Crewe Ches 73 D8
Crewe Ches 74 D4
Crewgreen Powys 60 C3
Crewkerne Som 12 D2
Crianlarich Stirl 132 B2
Cribyn Ceredig 46 D4
Criccieth Gwyn 71 D5
Crich Derbys 76 D3
Crichie Aberds 161 D6
Crichton Midloth 123 C6
Crick Mon 36 E1
Crick Northants 52 B3
Crickadarn Powys 48 E2
Cricket Malherbie Som 11 C8
Cricket St Thomas Som 11 D8
Crickheath Shrops 60 B2
Crickhowell Powys 35 C6
Cricklade Wilts 37 E8
Cricklewood London 41 F5
Cridling Stubbs N Yorks 89 B6
Crieff Perth 133 B7
Crieff Visitors' Centre Perth 133 B7
Criggion Powys 60 C2
Crigglestone W Yorks 88 C4
Crimond Aberds 161 C7
Crimonmogate Aberds 161 C7
Crimplesham Norf 67 D6
Crinan Argyll 128 A2
Cringleford Norf 68 D4
Cringles W Yorks 94 E3
Crinow Pembs 32 C2
Cripplesease Corn 2 C4
Cripplestyle Dorset 13 C8
Cripp's Corner E Sus 18 C4
Croasdale Cumb 98 C2
Crock Street Som 11 C8
Crockenhill Kent 29 C6
Crockernwell Devon 10 E2
Crockerton Wilts 24 E3
Crocketford or Ninemile Bar Dumfries 106 B5
Crockey Hill York 96 E2
Crockham Hill Kent 28 D5
Crockleford Heath Essex 43 B6
Crockness Orkney 176 G2
Croes-goch Pembs 44 B3
Croes-lan Ceredig 46 E2
Croes-y-mwyalch Torf 35 E7
Croeserw Neath 34 E2
Croesor Gwyn 71 C7
Croesyceiliog Carms 33 C5
Croesyceiliog Torf 35 E7
Croesywaun Gwyn 82 F5
Croft Leics 64 E2
Croft Lincs 79 C8
Croft Pembs 45 E3
Croft Warr 86 E4
Croft Motor Racing Circuit N Yorks 101 D7
Croft-on-Tees N Yorks 101 D7
Croftamie Stirl 132 F3
Croftmalloch W Loth 122 C2
Crofton Wilts 25 C7
Crofton W Yorks 88 C4
Crofts of Benachielt Highld 169 F6
Crofts of Haddo Aberds 160 E5
Crofts of Inverthernie Aberds 160 D4
Crofts of Meikle Ardo Aberds 161 D5
Crofty Swansea 33 E6
Croggan Argyll 130 C3
Croglin Cumb 109 E5
Croich Highld 164 E1
Crois Dughaill W Isles 171 H3
Cromarty Highld 157 C8
Cromblet Aberds 160 E4
Cromdale Highld 149 B6
Cromer Herts 41 B5
Cromer Norf 81 C8
Cromford Derbys 76 D2
Cromhall S Glos 36 E3
Cromhall Common S Glos 36 F3
Cromor W Isles 172 F7
Cromra Highld 147 E8
Cromwell Notts 77 C7
Cronberry E Ayrs 113 B6
Crondall Hants 27 E5
Cronk-y-Voddy I o M 84 D3
Cronton Mers 86 F2
Crook Cumb 99 E6
Crook Durham 110 F4
Crook of Devon Perth 134 D2
Crookedholm E Ayrs 120 F4
Crookes S Yorks 88 F4
Crookham Northumb 124 F5
Crookham W Berks 26 C3
Crookham Village Hants 27 D5
Crookhaugh Borders 114 B4
Crookhouse Borders 116 B3
Crooklands Cumb 99 F7
Croome Park, Pershore Worcs 50 E3
Cropredy Oxon 52 E2
Cropston Leics 64 C2
Cropthorne Worcs 50 E4
Cropton N Yorks 103 F5
Cropwell Bishop Notts 77 F6
Cropwell Butler Notts 77 F6
Cros W Isles 172 B8
Crosbost W Isles 172 F6
Crosby Cumb 107 F7
Crosby I o M 84 E3
Crosby N Lincs 90 C2
Crosby Garrett Cumb 100 D2
Crosby Ravensworth Cumb 99 C8
Crosby Villa Cumb 107 F7
Croscombe Som 23 E7
Cross Som 23 D6
Cross Ash Mon 35 C8
Cross-at-Hand Kent 29 E8
Cross Green Devon 9 F5
Cross Green Suff 56 D3
Cross Green Suff 56 D2
Cross Green Warks 51 D8
Cross Hands Carms 33 C6
Cross-hands Carms 32 B2
Cross Hands Pembs 32 C1
Cross Hill Derbys 76 E4
Cross Houses Shrops 60 D5
Cross in Hand E Sus 18 C2
Cross in Hand Leics 64 F2
Cross Inn Ceredig 46 D2
Cross Inn Ceredig 46 C4
Cross Inn Rhondda 34 F4
Cross Keys Kent 29 D6
Cross Lane Head Shrops 61 E7
Cross Lanes Corn 3 D5
Cross Lanes N Yorks 95 C8
Cross Lanes Wrex 73 E7
Cross Oak Powys 35 B5
Cross of Jackston Aberds 160 E4
Cross o'th'hands Derbys 76 E2
Cross Street Suff 57 B5
Crossaig Argyll 118 A5
Crossal Highld 153 F5
Crossapol Argyll 136 F1
Crossburn Falk 121 B8
Crossbush W Sus 16 D4
Crosscanonby Cumb 107 F7
Crossdale Street Norf 81 D8
Crossens Mers 85 C4
Crossflatts W Yorks 94 E4
Crossford Fife 134 F2
Crossford S Lnrk 121 E8
Crossgate Lincs 66 B2
Crossgatehall E Loth 123 C6
Crossgates Fife 134 F3
Crossgates Powys 48 C2
Crossgill Lancs 93 C5
Crosshill E Ayrs 112 B4
Crosshill Fife 134 E3
Crosshill S Ayrs 112 D3
Crosshouse E Ayrs 120 F3
Crossings Cumb 108 B5
Crosskeys Caerph 35 E6
Crosskirk Highld 168 B5
Crosslanes Shrops 60 C3
Crosslee Borders 115 C6
Crosslee Renfs 120 C4
Crossmichael Dumfries 106 C4
Crossmoor Lancs 92 F4
Crossroads Aberds 151 E6
Crossroads E Ayrs 120 F4
Crossway Hereford 49 F8
Crossway Mon 35 C8
Crossway Powys 48 D2
Crossway Green Worcs 50 C3
Crossways Dorset 13 F5
Crosswell Pembs 45 F3
Crosswood Ceredig 47 B5
Crosthwaite Cumb 99 E6
Croston Lancs 86 C2
Crostwick Norf 69 C5
Crostwight Norf 69 B6
Crothair W Isles 172 E4
Crouch Kent 29 D7
Crouch Hill Dorset 12 C5
Crouch House Green Kent 28 E5
Croucheston Wilts 13 B8
Croughton Northants 52 F3
Crovie Aberds 160 B5
Crow Edge S Yorks 88 D2
Crow Hill Hereford 36 B3
Crowan Corn 2 C5
Crowborough E Sus 18 B2
Crowcombe Som 22 F3
Crowdecote Derbys 75 C8
Crowden Derbys 87 E8
Crowell Oxon 39 E7
Crowfield Northants 52 E4
Crowfield Suff 56 D5
Crowhurst E Sus 18 D4
Crowhurst Sur 28 E4
Crowhurst Lane End Sur 28 E4
Crowland Lincs 66 C2
Crowlas Corn 2 C4
Crowle N Lincs 89 C8
Crowle Worcs 50 D4
Crowmarsh Gifford Oxon 39 F6
Crown Corner Suff 57 B6
Crownhill Plym 6 D2
Crownland Suff 56 C4
Crownthorpe Norf 68 D3
Crowntown Corn 2 C5
Crows-an-wra Corn 2 D2
Crowshill Norf 68 D2
Crowsnest Shrops 60 D3
Crowthorne Brack 27 C6
Crowton Ches 74 B2
Croxall Staffs 63 C5
Croxby Lincs 91 E5
Croxdale Durham 111 F5
Croxden Staffs 75 F7
Croxley Green Herts 40 E3
Croxton Cambs 54 C3
Croxton N Lincs 90 C4
Croxton Norf 67 F8
Croxton Staffs 74 F4
Croxton Kerrial Leics 64 B5
Croxtonbank Staffs 74 F4
Croy Highld 157 E8
Croy N Lnrk 121 B7
Croyde Devon 20 F3
Croydon Cambs 54 E4
Croydon London 28 C4
Crubenmore Lodge Highld 148 E2
Cruckmeole Shrops 60 D4
Cruckton Shrops 60 C4
Cruden Bay Aberds 161 E7
Crudgington Telford 61 C6
Crudwell Wilts 37 E6
Crug Powys 48 B3
Crugmeer Corn 4 B4

Crugybar Carms 47 F5
Crulabhig W Isles 172 E4
Crumlin = Crymlyn Caerph 35 E6
Crumpsall Gtr Man 87 D6
Crundale Kent 30 E4
Crundale Pembs 44 D4
Cruwys Morchard Devon 10 C3
Crux Easton Hants 26 D2
Crwbin Carms 33 C5
Crya Orkney 176 F2
Cryers Hill Bucks 40 E1
Crymlyn Gwyn 83 D6
Crymlyn = Crumlin Caerph 35 E6
Crymych Pembs 45 F3
Crynant Neath 34 D1
Crynfryn Ceredig 46 C4
Crystal Palace National Sports Centre London 28 B4
Cuaig Highld 154 E3
Cuan Argyll 130 D3
Cubbington Warks 51 C8
Cubeck N Yorks 100 F4
Cubert Corn 4 D2
Cubley S Yorks 88 D3
Cubley Common Derbys 75 F8
Cublington Bucks 39 B8
Cublington Hereford 49 F6
Cuckfield W Sus 17 B7
Cucklington Som 13 B5
Cuckney Notts 77 B5
Cuckoo Hill Notts 89 E8
Cuddesdon Oxon 39 D6
Cuddington Bucks 39 C7
Cuddington Ches 74 B3
Cuddington Heath Ches 73 E8
Cuddy Hill Lancs 92 F4
Cudham London 28 D5
Cudliptown Devon 6 B3
Cudworth Som 11 C8
Cudworth S Yorks 88 D4
Cuffley Herts 41 D6
Cuiashader W Isles 172 C8
Cuidhir W Isles 171 K2
Cuidhtinis W Isles 173 K3
Culbo Highld 157 C7
Culbokie Highld 157 D7
Culburnie Highld 157 E5
Culcabock Highld 157 E7
Culcairn Highld 157 C7
Culcharry Highld 158 D2
Culcheth Warr 86 E4
Culdrain Aberds 160 E2
Culduie Highld 155 F3
Culford Suff 56 B2
Culgaith Cumb 99 B8
Culham Oxon 39 E5
Culkein Highld 166 F2
Culkein Drumbeg Highld 166 F3
Culkerton Glos 37 E6
Cullachie Highld 149 B5
Cullen Moray 160 B2
Cullercoats T & W 111 B6
Cullicudden Highld 157 C7
Cullingworth W Yorks 94 F3
Cullipool Argyll 130 D3
Cullivoe Shetland 174 C7
Culloch Perth 133 C6
Culloden Highld 157 E8
Culloden Battlefield, Inverness Highld 157 E8
Cullompton Devon 10 D5
Culmaily Highld 165 E5
Culmazie Dumfries 105 D7
Culmington Shrops 60 F4
Culmstock Devon 11 C6
Culnacraig Highld 162 D4
Culnaknock Highld 152 C6
Culpho Suff 57 E6
Culrain Highld 164 E2
Culross Fife 133 F8
Culroy S Ayrs 112 C3
Culsh Aberds 161 D5
Culsh Aberds 150 E2
Culshabbin Dumfries 105 D7
Culswick Shetland 175 J4
Cultercullen Aberds 151 B8
Cults Aberdeen 151 D7
Cults Aberds 160 E2
Cults Dumfries 105 E8
Culverstone Green Kent 29 C7
Culverthorpe Lincs 78 E3
Culworth Northants 52 E3
Culzean Castle, Maybole S Ayrs 112 D2
Culzie Lodge Highld 157 B6
Cumbernauld N Lnrk 121 B7
Cumbernauld Village N Lnrk 121 B7
Cumberworth Lincs 79 B8
Cuminestown Aberds 160 C5
Cumlewick Shetland 175 L6
Cummersdale Cumb 108 D3
Cummertrees Dumfries 107 C8
Cummingston Moray 158 C5
Cumnock E Ayrs 113 B5
Cumnor Oxon 38 D4
Cumrew Cumb 108 D5
Cumwhinton Cumb 108 D4
Cumwhitton Cumb 108 D5
Cundall N Yorks 95 B7
Cunninghamhead N Ayrs 120 E3
Cunnister Shetland 174 D7
Cupar Fife 135 C5
Cupar Muir Fife 135 C5
Cupernham Hants 14 B4
Curbar Derbys 76 B2
Curbridge Hants 15 C6
Curbridge Oxon 38 D3
Curdridge Hants 15 C6
Curdworth Warks 63 E5
Curland Som 11 C7
Curlew Green Suff 57 C7
Currarie S Ayrs 112 E1
Curridge W Berks 26 B2
Currie Edin 122 C4
Curry Mallet Som 11 B8
Curry Rivel Som 11 B8
Curtisden Green Kent 29 E8
Curtisknowle Devon 6 D5
Cury Corn 3 D5
Cushnie Aberds 160 B4
Cushuish Som 22 F3
Cusop Hereford 48 E4
Cutcloy Dumfries 105 F8
Cutcombe Som 21 F8
Cutgate Gtr Man 87 C6
Cutiau Gwyn 58 C3
Cutlers Green Essex 55 F6
Cutnall Green Worcs 50 C3
Cutsdean Glos 51 F5
Cutthorpe Derbys 76 B3
Cutts Shetland 175 K6
Cutty Sark, Greenwich London 28 B4
Cuxham Oxon 39 E6
Cuxton Medway 29 C8
Cuxwold Lincs 91 D5
Cwm Bl Gwent 35 D5
Cwm Denb 72 B4
Cwm Swansea 33 E7
Cwm-byr Carms 46 F5
Cwm-Cewydd Gwyn 59 C5
Cwm-cou Ceredig 45 E4
Cwm-Dulais Swansea 33 D7
Cwm-felin-fach Caerph 35 E5
Cwm Ffrwd-oer Torf 35 D6
Cwm-hesgen Gwyn 71 E8
Cwm-hwnt Rhondda 34 D3
Cwm Irfon Powys 47 E7
Cwm-Llinau Powys 58 D5
Cwm-mawr Carms 33 C6
Cwm-parc Rhondda 34 E3
Cwm Penmachno Conwy 71 C8
Cwm-y-glo Carms 33 C6
Cwm-y-glo Gwyn 82 E5
Cwmafan Neath 34 E1
Cwmaman Rhondda 34 E4
Cwmann Carms 46 E4
Cwmavon Torf 35 D6
Cwmbach Carms 32 B3
Cwmbach Carms 33 D5
Cwmbach Powys 48 D2
Cwmbach Powys 48 F3
Cwmbâch Rhondda 34 D4
Cwmbelan Powys 59 F6
Cwmbran = Cwmbrân Torf 35 E6
Cwmbrân = Cwmbran Torf 35 E6
Cwmbrwyno Ceredig 58 F4
Cwmcarn Caerph 35 E6
Cwmcarvan Mon 36 D1
Cwmcych Pembs 45 F4
Cwmdare Rhondda 34 D3
Cwmderwen Powys 59 D6
Cwmdu Carms 46 F5
Cwmdu Powys 35 B5
Cwmdu Swansea 33 E7
Cwmduad Carms 46 F2
Cwmdwr Carms 47 F6
Cwmfelin Bridgend 34 F2
Cwmfelin M Tydf 34 D4
Cwmfelin Boeth Carms 32 C2
Cwmfelin Mynach Carms 32 B3
Cwmffrwd Carms 33 C5
Cwmgiedd Powys 34 C1
Cwmgors Neath 33 C8
Cwmgwili Carms 33 C6
Cwmgwrach Neath 34 D2
Cwmhiraeth Carms 46 F2
Cwmifor Carms 33 B7
Cwmisfael Carms 33 C5
Cwmllynfell Neath 33 C8
Cwmorgan Carms 45 F4
Cwmpengraig Carms 46 F2
Cwmrhos Powys 35 B5
Cwmsychpant Ceredig 46 E3
Cwmtillery Bl Gwent 35 D6
Cwmwysg Powys 34 B2
Cwmyoy Mon 35 B6
Cwmystwyth Ceredig 47 B6
Cwrt Gwyn 58 D3
Cwrt-newydd Ceredig 46 E3
Cwrt-y-cadno Carms 47 E5
Cwrt-y-gollen Powys 35 C6
Cydweli = Kidwelly Carms 33 D5
Cyffordd Llandudno = Llandudno Junction Conwy 83 D7
Cyffylliog Denb 72 D4
Cyfronydd Powys 59 D8
Cymer Neath 34 E2
Cyncoed Cardiff 35 F5
Cynghordy Carms 47 E7
Cynheidre Carms 33 D5
Cynwyd Denb 72 E4
Cynwyl Elfed Carms 32 B4
Cywarch Gwyn 59 C5

D

Dacre Cumb 99 B6
Dacre N Yorks 94 C4
Dacre Banks N Yorks 94 C4
Daddry Shield Durham 109 F8
Dadford Bucks 52 F4
Dadlington Leics 63 E8
Dafarn Faig Gwyn 71 C5
Dafen Carms 33 D6
Daffy Green Norf 68 D2
Dagenham London 41 F7
Daglingworth Glos 37 D6
Dagnall Bucks 40 C2
Dail Beag W Isles 172 D5
Dail bho Dheas W Isles 172 B7
Dail bho Thuath W Isles 172 B7
Dail Mor W Isles 172 D5
Daill Argyll 126 C3
Dailly S Ayrs 112 D2
Dairsie or Osnaburgh Fife 135 C6
Daisy Hill Gtr Man 86 D4
Dalabrog W Isles 171 H3
Dalavich Argyll 131 D5
Dalbeattie Dumfries 106 C5
Dalblair E Ayrs 113 C6
Dalbog Angus 143 B5
Dalbury Derbys 76 F2
Dalby I o M 84 E2
Dalby N Yorks 96 B2
Dalchalloch Perth 140 C4
Dalchalm Highld 165 D6
Dalchenna Argyll 131 E6
Dalchirach Moray 159 F5
Dalchork Highld 164 C2
Dalchreichart Highld 147 C5
Dalchruin Perth 133 C6
Dalderby Lincs 78 C5
Dale Pembs 44 E3
Dale Abbey Derbys 76 F4
Dale Head Cumb 99 C6
Dale of Walls Shetland 175 H3
Dalelia Highld 137 B8
Daless Highld 158 F2
Dalfaber Highld 148 C5
Dalgarven N Ayrs 120 E2
Dalgety Bay Fife 134 F3
Dalginross Perth 133 B6
Dalguise Perth 141 E6
Dalhalvaig Highld 168 D3
Dalham Suff 55 C8
Dalinlongart Argyll 129 B6
Dalkeith Midloth 123 C6
Dallam Warr 86 E3
Dallas Moray 158 D5
Dalleagles E Ayrs 113 C5
Dallinghoo Suff 57 D6
Dallington E Sus 18 D3
Dallington Northants 52 C5
Dallow N Yorks 94 B4
Dalmadilly Aberds 151 C6
Dalmally Argyll 131 C7
Dalmarnock Glasgow 121 C6
Dalmary Stirl 132 E4
Dalmellington E Ayrs 112 D4
Dalmeny Edin 122 B4
Dalmigavie Highld 148 C3
Dalmigavie Lodge Highld 148 B3
Dalmore Highld 157 C7
Dalmuir W Dunb 120 B4
Dalnabreck Highld 137 B7
Dalnacardoch Lodge Perth 140 B4
Dalnacroich Highld 156 D4
Dalnaglar Castle Perth 141 C8
Dalnahaitnach Highld 148 B4
Dalnaspidal Lodge Perth 140 B3
Dalnavaid Perth 141 C7
Dalnavie Highld 157 B7
Dalnawillan Lodge Highld 168 E5
Dalness Highld 139 D5
Dalnessie Highld 164 C3
Dalqueich Perth 134 D2
Dalreavoch Highld 164 D4
Dalry N Ayrs 120 E2
Dalrymple E Ayrs 112 C3
Dalserf S Lnrk 121 D8
Dalston Cumb 108 D3
Dalswinton Dumfries 114 F2
Dalton Dumfries 107 B8
Dalton Lancs 86 D2
Dalton Northumb 110 D2
Dalton Northumb 110 B4
Dalton N Yorks 95 B7
Dalton N Yorks 101 D6
Dalton S Yorks 89 E5
Dalton-in-Furness Cumb 92 B2
Dalton-le-Dale Durham 111 E7
Dalton-on-Tees N Yorks 101 D7
Dalton Piercy Hrtlpl 111 F7
Dalveich Stirl 132 B5
Dalvina Lodge Highld 167 E8
Dalwhinnie Highld 148 F2
Dalwood Devon 11 D7
Dalwyne S Ayrs 112 E3
Dam Green Norf 68 F3
Dam Side Lancs 92 E4
Damerham Hants 14 C2
Damgate Norf 69 D7
Damnaglaur Dumfries 104 F5
Damside Borders 122 E4
Danbury Essex 42 D3
Danby N Yorks 103 D5
Danby Wiske N Yorks 101 E8
Dandaleith Moray 159 E6
Danderhall Midloth 123 C6
Dane End Herts 41 B6
Danebridge Ches 75 C6
Danehill E Sus 17 B8
Danemoor Green Norf 68 D3
Danesford Shrops 61 E7
Daneshill Hants 26 D4
Dangerous Corner Lancs 86 C3
Danskine E Loth 123 C8
Darcy Lever Gtr Man 86 D5
Darenth Kent 29 B6
Daresbury Halton 86 F3
Darfield S Yorks 88 D5
Darfoulds Notts 77 B5
Dargate Kent 30 C4
Darite Corn 5 C7
Darlaston W Mid 62 E3
Darley N Yorks 94 D5
Darley Bridge Derbys 76 C2
Darley Head N Yorks 94 D4
Darley Moor Motor Racing Circuit Derbys 75 E8
Darlingscott Warks 51 E7
Darlington Darl 101 C7
Darliston Shrops 74 F2
Darlton Notts 77 B7
Darnall S Yorks 88 F4
Darnick Borders 123 F8
Darowen Powys 58 D5
Darra Aberds 160 D4
Darracott Devon 20 F3
Darras Hall Northumb 110 B4
Darrington W Yorks 89 B5
Darsham Suff 57 C8
Dartford Kent 29 B6
Dartford Crossing Kent 29 B6
Dartington Devon 7 C5
Dartington Cider Press Centre Devon 7 C5
Dartington Crystal Devon 9 C6
Dartmeet Devon 6 B4
Dartmouth Devon 7 D6
Darton S Yorks 88 D4
Darvel E Ayrs 121 F5
Darwell Hole E Sus 18 D3
Darwen Blkburn 86 B4
Datchet Windsor 27 B7
Datchworth Herts 41 C5
Datchworth Green Herts 41 C5
Daubhill Gtr Man 86 D5
Daugh of Kinermony Moray 159 E6
Dauntsey Wilts 37 F6
Dava Moray 158 F4
Davenham Ches 74 B3
Davenport Green Ches 74 B5
Daventry Northants 52 C3
David's Well Powys 48 B2
Davidson's Mains Edin 122 B5
Davidstow Corn 8 F3
Davington Dumfries 115 D5
Daviot Aberds 151 B6
Daviot Highld 157 F8
Davoch of Grange Moray 159 D8
Davyhulme Gtr Man 87 E5
Dawley Telford 61 D6
Dawlish Devon 7 B7
Dawlish Warren Devon 7 B7
Dawn Conwy 83 D8
Daws Heath Essex 42 F4
Daw's House Corn 8 F5
Dawsmere Lincs 79 F7
Dayhills Staffs 75 F6
Daylesford Glos 38 B2
Ddôl-Cownwy Powys 59 C7
Ddrydwy Anglesey 82 D3
Deadwater Northumb 116 E2
Deaf Hill Durham 111 F6
Deal Kent 31 D7
Deal Hall Essex 43 E6
Dean Cumb 98 B2
Dean Devon 6 C5
Dean Devon 20 E4
Dean Dorset 13 C7
Dean Hants 15 C6
Dean Som 23 E8
Dean Prior Devon 6 C5
Dean Row Ches 87 F6
Deanburnhaugh Borders 115 C6
Deane Gtr Man 86 D4
Deane Hants 26 D3
Deanich Lodge Highld 163 F7
Deanland Dorset 13 C7
Deans W Loth 122 C3
Deanscales Cumb 98 B2
Deanshanger Northants 53 F5
Deanston Stirl 133 D6
Dearham Cumb 107 F7
Debach Suff 57 D6
Debden Essex 55 F6
Debden Essex 41 E7
Debden Cross Essex 55 F6
Debenham Suff 57 C5
Dechmont W Loth 122 B3
Deddington Oxon 52 F2
Dedham Essex 56 F4
Dedham Heath Essex 56 F4
Deebank Aberds 151 E5
Deene Northants 65 E6
Deenethorpe Northants 65 E6
Deep Sea World, North Queensferry Fife 134 F3
Deepcar S Yorks 88 E3
Deepcut Sur 27 D7
Deepdale Cumb 100 F2
Deeping Gate Lincs 65 D8
Deeping St James Lincs 65 D8
Deeping St Nicholas Lincs 66 C2
Deerhill Moray 159 D8
Deerhurst Glos 37 B5
Deerness Orkney 176 F4
Defford Worcs 50 E4
Defynnog Powys 34 B3
Deganwy Conwy 83 D7
Deighton N Yorks 102 D1
Deighton W Yorks 88 C2
Deighton York 96 E2
Deiniolen Gwyn 83 E5
Delabole Corn 8 F2
Delamere Ches 74 C2
Delfrigs Aberds 151 B8
Dell Lodge Highld 149 C6
Delliefure Highld 158 F4
Delnabo Moray 149 C7
Delnadamph Aberds 149 D8
Delph Gtr Man 87 D7
Delves Durham 110 E4
Delvine Perth 141 E8
Dembleby Lincs 78 F3
Denaby Main S Yorks 89 E5
Denbigh = Dinbych Denb 72 C4
Denbury Devon 7 C6
Denby Derbys 76 E3
Denby Dale W Yorks 88 D3
Denchworth Oxon 38 E3
Dendron Cumb 92 B2
Denel End Beds 53 F8
Denend Aberds 160 E3
Denford Northants 53 B7
Dengie Essex 43 D5
Denham Bucks 40 F3
Denham Suff 55 C8
Denham Suff 57 B5
Denham Green Bucks 40 F3
Denham Street Suff 57 B5
Denhead Aberds 161 C6
Denhead Fife 135 C6
Denhead of Arbilot Angus 143 E5
Denhead of Gray Dundee 142 F3
Denholm Borders 115 C8
Denholme W Yorks 94 F3
Denholme Clough W Yorks 94 F3
Denio Gwyn 70 D4
Denmead Hants 15 C7
Denmore Aberdeen 151 C8
Denmoss Aberds 160 D3
Dennington Suff 57 C6
Denny Falk 133 F7
Denny Lodge Hants 14 D4
Dennyloanhead Falk 133 F7
Denshaw Gtr Man 87 C7
Denside Aberds 151 E7
Densole Kent 31 E6
Denston Suff 55 D8
Denstone Staffs 75 E8
Dent Cumb 100 F2
Denton Cambs 65 F8
Denton Darl 101 C7
Denton E Sus 17 D8
Denton Gtr Man 87 E7
Denton Kent 31 E6
Denton Lincs 77 F8
Denton Norf 69 F5
Denton Northants 53 D6
Denton N Yorks 94 E4
Denton Oxon 39 D5
Denton's Green Mers 86 E2
Denver Norf 67 D6
Denwick Northumb 117 C8
Deopham Norf 68 D3
Deopham Green Norf 68 E3
Depden Suff 55 D8
Depden Green Suff 55 D8
Deptford London 28 B4
Deptford Wilts 24 F5
Derby Derby 76 F3
Derbyhaven I o M 84 F2
Dereham Norf 68 C2
Deri Caerph 35 D5
Derril Devon 8 D5
Derringstone Kent 31 E6
Derrington Staffs 62 B2
Derriton Devon 8 D5
Derry Hill Wilts 24 B4
Derryguaig Argyll 137 E5
Derrythorpe N Lincs 90 D2
Dersingham Norf 80 D2
Dervaig Argyll 137 C5
Derwen Denb 72 D4
Derwenlas Powys 58 E4
Desborough Northants 64 F5
Desford Leics 63 D8
Detchant Northumb 125 F6
Detling Kent 29 D8
Deuddwr Powys 60 C2
Devauden Mon 36 E1
Devil's Bridge Ceredig 47 B6
Devizes Wilts 24 C5
Devol Invclyd 120 B3
Devon & Exeter Racecourse Devon 10 F4
Devonport Plym 6 D2
Devonside Clack 133 E8
Devoran Corn 3 C6
Dewar Borders 123 E6
Dewlish Dorset 13 E5
Dewsbury W Yorks 88 B3
Dewsbury Moor W Yorks 88 B3
Dewshall Court Hereford 49 F6
Dhoon I o M 84 D4
Dhoor I o M 84 C4
Dhowin I o M 84 B4
Dial Post W Sus 17 C5
Dibden Hants 14 D5
Dibden Purlieu Hants 14 D5
Dickleburgh Norf 68 F4
Didbrook Glos 51 F5
Didcot Oxon 39 F5
Diddington Cambs 54 C2
Diddlebury Shrops 60 F5
Didley Hereford 49 F6
Didling W Sus 16 C2
Didmarton Glos 37 F5
Didsbury Gtr Man 87 E6
Didworthy Devon 6 C4
Digby Lincs 78 D3
Digg Highld 152 C5
Diggerland, Cullompton Devon 10 D5
Diggerland, Langley Park Durham 110 E5
Diggle Gtr Man 87 D8
Digmoor Lancs 86 D2
Digswell Park Herts 41 C5
Dihewyd Ceredig 46 D3
Dilham Norf 69 B6
Dilhorne Staffs 75 E6
Dillarburn S Lnrk 121 E8
Dillington Cambs 54 C2
Dilston Northumb 110 C2
Dilton Marsh Wilts 24 E3
Dilwyn Hereford 49 D6
Dinas Carms 45 F4
Dinas Gwyn 70 D3
Dinas Cross Pembs 45 F2
Dinas Dinlle Gwyn 82 F4
Dinas-Mawddwy Gwyn 59 C5
Dinas Powys V Glam 22 B3
Dinbych = Denbigh Denb 72 C4
Dinbych-y-Pysgod = Tenby Pembs 32 D2
Dinder Som 23 E7
Dinedor Hereford 49 F7
Dingestow Mon 36 C1
Dingle Mers 85 F4
Dingleden Kent 18 B5
Dingley Northants 64 F4
Dingwall Highld 157 D6
Dinlabyre Borders 115 E8
Dinmael Conwy 72 E4
Dinnet Aberds 150 E3
Dinnington Som 12 C2
Dinnington S Yorks 89 F6
Dinnington T & W 110 B5
Dinorwic Gwyn 83 E5
Dinton Bucks 39 C7
Dinton Wilts 24 F5
Dinwoodie Mains Dumfries 114 E4
Dinworthy Devon 8 C5
Dippen N Ayrs 119 D7
Dippenhall Sur 27 E6
Dipple Moray 159 D7
Dipple S Ayrs 112 D2
Diptford Devon 6 D5
Dipton Durham 110 D4
Dirdhu Highld 149 B6
Dirleton E Loth 135 F7
Dirt Pot Northumb 109 E8
Discoed Powys 48 C4
Discovery Point Dundee 135 B6
Diseworth Leics 63 B8
Dishes Orkney 176 D5
Dishforth N Yorks 95 B6
Disley Ches 87 F7
Diss Norf 56 B5
Disserth Powys 48 D2
Distington Cumb 98 B2
Ditchampton Wilts 25 F5
Ditcheat Som 23 F8
Ditchingham Norf 69 E6
Ditchling E Sus 17 C7
Ditherington Shrops 60 C5
Dittisham Devon 7 D6
Ditton Halton 86 F2
Ditton Kent 29 D8
Ditton Green Cambs 55 D7
Ditton Priors Shrops 61 F6
Divach Highld 147 B7
Divlyn Carms 47 F6
Dixton Glos 50 F4
Dixton Mon 36 C2
Dobcross Gtr Man 87 D7
Dobwalls Corn 5 C7
Doc Penfro = Pembroke Dock Pembs 44 E4
Doccombe Devon 10 F2
Dochfour Ho. Highld 157 F7
Dochgarroch Highld 157 E7
Docking Norf 80 D3
Docklow Hereford 49 D7
Dockray Cumb 99 B5
Dockroyd W Yorks 94 F3
Dodburn Borders 115 D7
Doddinghurst Essex 42 E1
Doddington Cambs 66 E3
Doddington Kent 30 D3
Doddington Lincs 78 B2
Doddington Northumb 125 F5
Doddington Shrops 49 B8
Doddiscombsleigh Devon 10 F3
Dodford Northants 52 C4
Dodford Worcs 50 B4
Dodington S Glos 24 A2
Dodleston Ches 73 C7
Dods Leigh Staffs 75 F7
Dodworth S Yorks 88 D4
Doe Green Warr 86 F3
Doe Lea Derbys 76 C4
Dog Village Devon 10 E4
Dogdyke Lincs 78 D5
Dogmersfield Hants 27 D5
Dogridge Wilts 37 F7
Dogsthorpe P'boro 65 D8
Dol-fôr Powys 58 D5
Dôl-y-Bont Ceredig 58 F3
Dol-y-cannau Powys 48 E4
Dolanog Powys 59 C7
Dolau Powys 48 C3
Dolau Rhondda 34 F3
Dolbenmaen Gwyn 71 C6
Dolfach Powys 59 D6
Dolfor Powys 59 F8
Dolgarrog Conwy 83 E7
Dolgellau Gwyn 58 C4
Dolgran Carms 46 F3
Dolhendre Gwyn 72 F2
Doll Highld 165 D5
Dollar Clack 133 E8
Dolley Green Powys 48 C4
Dollwen Ceredig 58 F3
Dolphin Flint 73 B5
Dolphinholme Lancs 92 D5
Dolphinton S Lnrk 122 E4
Dolton Devon 9 C7
Dolwen Conwy 83 D8
Dolwen Powys 59 D6
Dolwyd Conwy 83 D8
Dolwyddelan Conwy 83 F7
Dolyhir Powys 48 D4
Doncaster S Yorks 89 D6
Doncaster Racecourse S Yorks 89 D7
Dones Green Ches 74 B3
Donhead St Andrew Wilts 13 B7
Donhead St Mary Wilts 13 B7
Donibristle Fife 134 F3
Donington Lincs 78 F5
Donington on Bain Lincs 91 F6
Donington Park Motor Racing Circuit Leics 63 B8
Donington South Ing Lincs 78 F5
Donisthorpe Leics 63 C7
Donkey Town Sur 27 C7
Donnington Glos 38 B1
Donnington Hereford 50 F2
Donnington Shrops 61 D5
Donnington Telford 61 C7
Donnington W Berks 26 C2
Donnington W Sus 16 D2
Donnington Wood Telford 61 C7
Donyatt Som 11 C8
Doonfoot S Ayrs 112 C3
Dorback Lodge Highld 149 C6
Dorchester Dorset 12 E4
Dorchester Oxon 39 E5
Dorchester Abbey, Wallingford Oxon 39 E5
Dordon Warks 63 D6
Dore S Yorks 88 F4
Dores Highld 157 F6
Dorking Sur 28 E2
Dormansland Sur 28 E5
Dormanstown Redcar 102 B3
Dormington Hereford 49 E7
Dormston Worcs 50 D4
Dornal S Ayrs 105 B6
Dorney Bucks 27 B7
Dornie Highld 155 H4
Dornoch Highld 164 F4
Dornock Dumfries 108 C2
Dorrery Highld 169 D5
Dorridge W Mid 51 B6
Dorrington Lincs 78 D3
Dorrington Shrops 60 D4
Dorsington Warks 51 E6
Dorstone Hereford 48 E5
Dorton Bucks 39 C6
Dorusduain Highld 146 B2
Dosthill Staffs 63 E6
Dottery Dorset 12 E2
Doublebois Corn 5 C6
Dougarie N Ayrs 119 C5
Doughton Glos 37 E5
Douglas I o M 84 E3
Douglas S Lnrk 121 F8
Douglas & Angus Dundee 142 F4
Douglas Water S Lnrk 121 F8
Douglas West S Lnrk 121 F8
Douglastown Angus 142 E4
Doulting Som 23 E8
Dounby Orkney 176 D1
Doune Highld 163 D8
Doune Stirl 133 D6
Doune Park Aberds 160 B4
Douneside Aberds 150 D3
Dounie Highld 164 E2
Dounreay Highld 168 C4
Dousland Devon 6 C3
Dovaston Shrops 60 B3
Dove Cottage and Wordsworth Museum Cumb 99 D5
Dove Holes Derbys 75 B7
Dovenby Cumb 107 F7
Dover Kent 31 E7
Dover Castle Kent 31 E7
Dovercourt Essex 57 F6
Doverdale Worcs 50 C3
Doveridge Derbys 75 F8
Doversgreen Sur 28 E3
Dowally Perth 141 E7
Dowbridge Lancs 92 F4
Dowdeswell Glos 37 C6
Dowlais M Tydf 34 D4
Dowland Devon 9 C7
Dowlish Wake Som 11 C8
Down Ampney Glos 37 E8
Down Hatherley Glos 37 B5
Down St Mary Devon 10 D2
Down Thomas Devon 6 D3
Downcraig Ferry N Ayrs 129 E6
Downderry Corn 5 D8
Downe London 28 C5
Downend I o W 15 F6
Downend S Glos 23 B8
Downend W Berks 26 B2
Downfield Dundee 142 F3
Downgate Corn 5 B8
Downham Essex 42 E3
Downham Lancs 93 E7
Downham Northumb 124 F4
Downham Market Norf 67 D6
Downhead Som 23 E8
Downhill Perth 141 F7
Downhill T & W 111 D6
Downholland Cross Lancs 85 D4
Downholme N Yorks 101 E6
Downies Aberds 151 E8
Downley Bucks 39 E8
Downside Som 23 E8
Downside Sur 28 D2
Downton Hants 14 E3
Downton Wilts 14 B2
Downton on the Rock Hereford 49 B6
Dowsby Lincs 65 B8
Dowsdale Lincs 66 C2
Dowthwaitehead Cumb 99 B5
Doxey Staffs 62 B3
Doxford Northumb 117 B7
Doxford Park T & W 111 D6
Doynton S Glos 24 B2
Draffan S Lnrk 121 E7
Dragonby N Lincs 90 C3
Drakeland Corner Devon 6 D3
Drakemyre N Ayrs 120 D2
Drake's Broughton Worcs 50 E4
Drakes Cross Worcs 51 B5
Drakewalls Corn 6 B2
Draughton Northants 53 B5
Draughton N Yorks 94 D3
Drax N Yorks 89 B7
Draycote Warks 52 B2
Draycott Derbys 76 F4
Draycott Glos 51 F6
Draycott Som 23 D6
Draycott in the Clay Staffs 63 B5
Draycott in the Moors Staffs 75 E6
Drayford Devon 10 C2
Drayton Leics 64 E5
Drayton Lincs 78 F5
Drayton Norf 68 C4
Drayton Oxon 52 E2
Drayton Oxon 38 E4
Drayton Ptsmth 15 D7
Drayton Som 12 B2
Drayton Worcs 50 B4
Drayton Bassett Staffs 63 D5
Drayton Beauchamp Bucks 40 C2
Drayton Manor Park, Tamworth Staffs 63 D5
Drayton Parslow Bucks 39 B8
Drayton St Leonard Oxon 39 E5
Dre-fach Ceredig 46 E4
Dre-fach Carms 33 C7
Dreamland Theme Park, Margate Kent 31 B7
Drebley N Yorks 94 D3
Dreemskerry I o M 84 C4
Dreenhill Pembs 44 D4
Drefach Carms 46 F2
Drefach Carms 33 C6
Drefelin Carms 46 F2
Dreghorn N Ayrs 120 F3
Drellingore Kent 31 E6
Drem E Loth 123 B8
Dresden Stoke 75 E6
Dreumasdal W Isles 170 G3
Drewsteignton Devon 10 E2
Driby Lincs 79 B6
Driffield E Yorks 97 D6
Driffield Glos 37 E7
Drigg Cumb 98 E2
Drighlington W Yorks 88 B3
Drimnin Highld 137 C6
Drimpton Dorset 12 D2
Drimsynie Argyll 131 E7
Drinisiadar W Isles 173 J4
Drinkstone Suff 56 C3
Drinkstone Green Suff 56 C3
Drishaig Argyll 131 D7
Drissaig Argyll 130 D5
Drochil Borders 122 E4
Drointon Staffs 62 B4
Droitwich Spa Worcs 50 C3
Droman Highld 166 D3
Dron Perth 134 C3
Dronfield Derbys 76 B3
Dronfield Woodhouse Derbys 76 B3
Drongan E Ayrs 112 C4
Dronley Angus 142 F3
Droxford Hants 15 C7
Droylsden Gtr Man 87 E7
Druid Denb 72 E4
Druidston Pembs 44 D3
Druimarbin Highld 138 B4
Druimavuic Argyll 138 E4
Druimdrishaig Argyll 128 C2
Druimindarroch Highld 145 E6
Druimyeon More Argyll 118 A3
Drum Argyll 128 C4
Drum Perth 134 D2
Drumbeg Highld 166 F3
Drumblade Aberds 160 D2
Drumblair Aberds 160 D3
Drumbuie Dumfries 113 F5
Drumbuie Highld 155 G3
Drumburgh Cumb 108 D2
Drumburn Dumfries 107 C6
Drumchapel Glasgow 120 B5
Drumchardine Highld 157 E6
Drumchork Highld 162 F2
Drumclog S Lnrk 121 F6
Drumderfit Highld 157 D7
Drumeldrie Fife 135 D6
Drumelzier Borders 122 F4
Drumfearn Highld 145 B6
Drumgask Highld 148 E2
Drumgley Angus 142 D4
Drumguish Highld 148 E3
Drumin Moray 159 F5
Drumlasie Aberds 150 D5
Drumlemble Argyll 118 E3
Drumligair Aberds 151 C8
Drumlithie Aberds 151 F6

Drummoddie Dumfries 105 E7
Drummond Highld 157 C7
Drummore Dumfries 104 F5
Drummuir Moray 159 E7
Drummuir Castle Moray 159 E7
Drumnadrochit Highld 147 B8
Drumnagorrach Moray 160 C2
Drumoak Aberds 151 E6
Drumpark Dumfries 107 A5
Drumphail Dumfries 105 C6
Drumrash Dumfries 106 B3
Drumrunie Highld 163 D5
Drums Aberds 151 B8
Drumsallie Highld 138 B3
Drumstinchall Dumfries 107 D5
Drumsturdy Angus 142 F4
Drumtochty Castle Aberds 143 B6
Drumtroddan Dumfries 105 E7
Drumuie Highld 152 E5
Drumuillie Highld 148 B5
Drumvaich Stirl 133 D5
Drumwhindle Aberds 161 E6
Drunkendub Angus 143 E6
Drury Flint 73 C6
Drury Square Norf 68 C2
Drusillas Park, Polegate E Sus 18 E2
Dry Doddington Lincs 77 E8
Dry Drayton Cambs 54 C4
Drybeck Cumb 100 C1
Drybridge Moray 159 C8
Drybridge N Ayrs 120 F3
Drybrook Glos 36 C3
Dryburgh Borders 123 F8
Dryhope Borders 115 B5
Drylaw Edin 122 B5
Drym Corn 2 C5
Drymen Stirl 132 F3
Drymuir Aberds 161 D6
Drynoch Highld 153 F5
Dryslwyn Carms 33 B6
Dryton Shrops 61 D5
Dubford Aberds 160 B5
Dubton Angus 143 D5
Duchally Highld 163 C7
Duchlage Argyll 129 B8
Duck Corner Suff 57 E7
Duckington Ches 73 D8
Ducklington Oxon 38 D3
Duckmanton Derbys 76 B4
Duck's Cross Beds 54 D2
Duddenhoe End Essex 55 F5
Duddingston Edin 123 B5
Duddington Northants 65 D6
Duddleswell E Sus 17 B8
Duddo Northum 124 E5
Duddon Ches 74 C2
Duddon Bridge Cumb 98 F4
Dudleston Shrops 73 F7
Dudleston Heath Shrops 73 F7
Dudley T & W 111 B5
Dudley W Mid 62 E3
Dudley Port W Mid 62 E3
Dudley Zoological Gardens W Mid 62 E3
Duffield Derbys 76 E3
Duffryn Newport 35 F6
Duffryn Neath 34 E2
Dufftown Moray 159 F7
Duffus Moray 159 C5
Dufton Cumb 100 B1
Duggleby N Yorks 96 C4
Duirinish Highld 155 G3
Duisdalemore Highld 145 B7
Duisky Highld 138 B4
Dukestown Bl Gwent 35 C5
Dukinfield Gtr Man 87 E7
Dulas Anglesey 82 C4
Dulcote Som 23 E7
Dulford Devon 11 D5
Dull Perth 141 E5
Dullatur N Lnrk 121 B7
Dullingham Cambs 55 D7
Dulnain Bridge Highld 149 B5
Duloe Beds 54 C2
Duloe Corn 5 D7
Dulsie Highld 158 E3
Dulverton Som 10 B4
Dulwich London 28 B4
Dumbarton W Dunb 120 B3
Dumbleton Glos 50 F5
Dumcrieff Dumfries 114 D4
Dumfries Dumfries 107 B6
Dumgoyne Stirl 132 F4
Dummer Hants 26 E3
Dumpford W Sus 16 B2
Dumpton Kent 31 C7
Dun Angus 143 D6
Dun Charlabhaigh W Isles 172 D4
Dunain Ho. Highld 157 E7
Dunalastair Perth 140 D4
Dunan Highld 153 G6
Dunans Argyll 129 A5
Dunball Som 22 E5
Dunbar E Loth 124 B2
Dunbeath Highld 165 B8
Dunbeg Argyll 130 B4
Dunblane Stirl 133 D6
Dunbog Fife 134 C4
Duncanston Aberds 150 B4
Duncanston Highld 157 D6
Dunchurch Warks 52 B2
Duncote Northants 52 D4
Duncow Dumfries 114 F2
Duncraggan Stirl 132 D4
Duncrievie Perth 134 D3
Duncton W Sus 16 C3
Dundas Ho. Orkney 176 H3
Dundee Dundee 142 F4
Dundee Airport Dundee 135 B5
Dundeugh Dumfries 113 F5
Dundon Som 23 F6
Dundonald S Ayrs 120 F3
Dundonnell Highld 162 F4
Dundonnell Hotel Highld 162 F4
Dundonnell House Highld 163 F5
Dundraw Cumb 108 E2
Dundreggan Highld 147 C6
Dundreggan Lodge Highld 147 C6
Dundrennan Dumfries 106 E4
Dundry N Som 23 C7
Dunecht Aberds 151 D6
Dunfermline Fife 134 F2
Dunfield Glos 37 E8
Dunford Bridge S Yorks 88 D2
Dungworth S Yorks 88 F3
Dunham Notts 77 B8
Dunham Massey Gtr Man 86 F5
Dunham-on-the-Hill Ches 73 B8
Dunham Town Gtr Man 86 F5
Dunhampton Worcs 50 C3
Dunholme Lincs 78 B3
Dunino Fife 135 C7
Dunipace Falk 133 F7
Dunira Perth 133 B6
Dunkeld Perth 141 E7
Dunkerton Bath 24 D2
Dunkeswell Devon 11 D6
Dunkeswick N Yorks 95 E6
Dunkirk Kent 30 D4
Dunkirk Norf 81 E8
Dunk's Green Kent 29 D7
Dunlappie Angus 143 C5
Dunley Hants 26 D2
Dunley Worcs 50 C2
Dunlichity Lodge Highld 157 F7
Dunlop E Ayrs 120 E4
Dunmaglass Lodge Highld 147 B8
Dunmore Argyll 128 D2
Dunmore Falk 133 F7
Dunnet Highld 169 B7
Dunnichen Angus 143 E5
Dunninald Angus 143 D7
Dunning Perth 134 C2
Dunnington E Yorks 97 D7
Dunnington Warks 51 D5
Dunnington York 96 D2
Dunnockshaw Lancs 87 B6
Dunollie Argyll 130 B4
Dunoon Argyll 129 C6
Dunragit Dumfries 105 D5
Dunrobin Castle Museum & Gardens Highld 165 D5
Dunrostan Argyll 128 B2
Duns Borders 124 D3
Duns Tew Oxon 38 B4
Dunsby Lincs 65 B8
Dunscore Dumfries 113 F8
Dunscroft S Yorks 89 D7
Dunsdale Redcar 102 C4
Dunsden Green Oxon 26 B5
Dunsfold Sur 27 F8
Dunsford Devon 10 F3
Dunshalt Fife 134 C4
Dunshillock Aberds 161 D6
Dunskey Ho. Dumfries 104 D4
Dunsley N Yorks 103 C6
Dunsmore Bucks 40 D1
Dunsop Bridge Lancs 93 D6
Dunstable Beds 40 B3
Dunstall Staffs 63 B5
Dunstall Common Worcs 50 E3
Dunstall Green Suff 55 C8
Dunstan Northum 117 C8
Dunstan Steads Northum 117 B8
Dunster Som 21 E8
Dunster Castle, Minehead Som 21 E8
Dunston Lincs 78 C3
Dunston Norf 68 D5
Dunston Staffs 62 C3
Dunston T & W 110 C5
Dunsville S Yorks 89 D7
Dunswell E Yorks 97 F6
Dunsyre S Lnrk 122 E3
Dunterton Devon 5 B8
Duntisbourne Abbots Glos 37 D6
Duntisbourne Leer Glos 37 D6
Duntisbourne Rouse Glos 37 D6
Duntish Dorset 12 D4
Duntocher W Dunb 120 B4
Dunton Beds 54 E3
Dunton Bucks 39 B8
Dunton Norf 80 D4
Dunton Bassett Leics 64 E2
Dunton Green Kent 29 D6
Dunton Wayletts Essex 42 E2
Duntulm Highld 152 B5
Dunure S Ayrs 112 C2
Dunvant Swansea 33 E6
Dunvegan Highld 152 E3
Dunvegan Castle Highld 152 E3
Dunwich Suff 57 B8
Dunwood Staffs 75 D6
Dupplin Castle Perth 134 C2
Durdar Cumb 108 D4
Durgates E Sus 18 B3
Durham Durham 111 E5
Durham Cathedral Durham 111 E5
Durham Tees Valley Airport Stockton 102 C1
Durisdeer Dumfries 113 D8
Durisdeermill Dumfries 113 D8
Durkar W Yorks 88 C4
Durleigh Som 22 F4
Durley Hants 15 C6
Durley Wilts 25 C7
Durnamuck Highld 162 E4
Durness Highld 167 C6
Durno Aberds 151 B6
Duror Highld 138 D3
Durran Argyll 131 E5
Durran Highld 169 C6
Durrington Wilts 25 E6
Durrington W Sus 16 D5
Dursley Glos 36 E4
Durston Som 11 B7
Durweston Dorset 13 D6
Dury Shetland 175 G6
Duston Northants 52 C5
Duthil Highld 148 B5
Dutlas Powys 48 B4
Duton Hill Essex 42 B2
Dutson Corn 8 F5
Dutton Ches 74 B2
Duxford Cambs 55 E5
Duxford Oxon 38 E3
Duxford Airfield (Imperial War Museum), Sawston Cambs 55 E5
Dwygyfylchi Conwy 83 D7
Dwyran Anglesey 82 E4
Dyce Aberdeen 151 C7
Dye House Northumb 110 D2
Dyffryn Bridgend 34 E2
Dyffryn Carms 32 B4
Dyffryn Pembs 44 B4
Dyffryn Ardudwy Gwyn 71 E6
Dyffryn Castell Ceredig 58 F4
Dyffryn Ceidrych Carms 33 B8
Dyffryn Cellwen Neath 34 D2
Dyke Lincs 65 B8
Dyke Moray 158 D3
Dykehead Angus 142 C3
Dykehead N Lnrk 121 D8
Dykehead Stirl 132 E4
Dykelands Aberds 143 C7
Dykends Angus 142 D2
Dykeside Aberds 160 D4
Dykesmains N Ayrs 120 E2
Dylife Powys 59 E5
Dymchurch Kent 19 C7
Dymock Glos 50 F2
Dyrham S Glos 24 B2
Dyrham Park S Glos 24 B2
Dysart Fife 134 E5
Dyserth Denb 72 B4

E

Eachwick Northumb 110 B4
Eadar Dha Fhadhail W Isles 172 E3
Eagland Hill Lancs 92 E4
Eagle Lincs 77 C8
Eagle Barnsdale Lincs 77 C8
Eagle Moor Lincs 77 C8
Eaglescliffe Stockton 102 C2
Eaglesfield Cumb 98 B2
Eaglesfield Dumfries 108 B2
Eaglesham E Renf 121 D5
Eaglethorpe Northants 65 E7
Eairy I o M 84 E2
Eakley Lanes M Keynes 53 D6
Eakring Notts 77 C6
Ealand N Lincs 89 C8
Ealing London 40 F4
Eals Northumb 109 D6
Eamont Bridge Cumb 99 B7
Earby Lancs 94 E2
Earcroft Blkburn 86 B4
Eardington Shrops 61 E7
Eardisland Hereford 49 D6
Eardisley Hereford 48 E5
Eardiston Shrops 60 B3
Eardiston Worcs 49 C8
Earith Cambs 54 B4
Earl Shilton Leics 63 E8
Earl Soham Suff 57 C6
Earl Sterndale Derbys 75 C7
Earl Stonham Suff 56 D5
Earle Northumb 117 B5
Earley Wokingham 27 B5
Earlham Norf 68 D5
Earlish Highld 152 C4
Earls Barton Northants 53 C6
Earls Colne Essex 42 B4
Earl's Croome Worcs 50 E3
Earl's Green Suff 56 C4
Earlsdon W Mid 51 B8
Earlsferry Fife 135 E6
Earlsfield Lincs 78 F2
Earlsford Aberds 160 E5
Earlsheaton W Yorks 88 B3
Earlsmill Moray 158 D3
Earlston Borders 123 F8
Earlston E Ayrs 120 F4
Earlswood Mon 36 E1
Earlswood Sur 28 E3
Earlswood Warks 51 B6
Earnley W Sus 16 E2
Earsairidh W Isles 171 L3
Earsdon T & W 111 B6
Earsham Norf 69 F6
Earswick York 96 D2
Eartham W Sus 16 D3
Easby N Yorks 102 D3
Easby N Yorks 101 D6
Easdale Argyll 130 D3
Easebourne W Sus 16 B2
Easenhall Warks 52 B2
Eashing Sur 27 E7
Easington Bucks 39 C6
Easington Durham 111 E7
Easington E Yorks 91 C7
Easington Northumb 125 F7
Easington Oxon 52 F2
Easington Oxon 39 E6
Easington Redcar 103 C5
Easington Colliery Durham 111 E7
Easington Lane T & W 111 E6
Easingwold N Yorks 95 C8
Easole Street Kent 31 D6
Eassie Angus 142 E3
East Aberthaw V Glam 22 C2
East Adderbury Oxon 52 F2
East Allington Devon 7 E5
East Anstey Devon 10 B3
East Appleton N Yorks 101 E7
East Ardsley W Yorks 88 B4
East Ashling W Sus 16 D2
East Auchronie Aberds 151 D7
East Ayton N Yorks 103 F7
East Bank Bl Gwent 35 D6
East Barkwith Lincs 91 F5
East Barming Kent 29 D8
East Barnby N Yorks 103 C6
East Barnet London 41 E5
East Barns E Loth 124 B3
East Barsham Norf 80 D5
East Beckham Norf 81 D7
East Bedfont London 27 B8
East Bergholt Suff 56 F4
East Bilney Norf 68 C2
East Blatchington E Sus 17 D8
East Boldre Hants 14 D4
East Brent Som 22 D5
East Bridgford Notts 77 E6
East Buckland Devon 21 F5
East Budleigh Devon 11 F5
East Burrafirth Shetland 175 H5
East Burton Dorset 13 F6
East Butsfield Durham 110 E4
East Butterwick N Lincs 90 D2
East Cairnbeg Aberds 143 B7
East Calder W Loth 122 C3
East Carleton Norf 68 D4
East Carlton Northants 64 F5
East Carlton W Yorks 94 E5
East Chaldon Dorset 13 F5
East Challow Oxon 38 F3
East Chiltington E Sus 17 C7
East Chinnock Som 12 C2
East Chisenbury Wilts 25 D6
East Clandon Sur 27 D8
East Claydon Bucks 39 B7
East Clyne Highld 165 D6
East Coker Som 12 C3
East Combe Som 22 F3
East Common N Yorks 96 F2
East Compton Som 23 E8
East Cottingwith E Yorks 96 E3
East Cowes I o W 15 E6
East Cowick E Yorks 89 B7
East Cowton N Yorks 101 D8
East Cramlington Northumb 111 B5
East Cranmore Som 23 E8
East Creech Dorset 13 F7
East Croachy Highld 148 B2
East Croftmore Highld 149 C5
East Curthwaite Cumb 108 E3
East Dean E Sus 18 F2
East Dean Hants 14 B3
East Dean W Sus 16 C3
East Down Devon 20 E5
East Drayton Notts 77 B7
East Ella Hull 90 B4
East End Dorset 13 E7
East End E Yorks 91 B6
East End Hants 14 E4
East End Hants 15 B7
East End Hants 26 C2
East End Herts 41 B7
East End Kent 18 B5
East End N Som 23 B6
East End Oxon 38 C3
East Farleigh Kent 29 D8
East Farndon Northants 64 F4
East Ferry Lincs 90 E2
East Fortune E Loth 123 B8
East Garston W Berks 25 B8
East Ginge Oxon 38 F4
East Goscote Leics 64 C3
East Grafton Wilts 25 C7
East Grimstead Wilts 14 B3
East Grinstead W Sus 28 F4
East Guldeford E Sus 19 C6
East Haddon Northants 52 C4
East Hagbourne Oxon 39 F5
East Halton N Lincs 90 C5
East Ham London 41 F7
East Hanney Oxon 38 E4
East Hanningfield Essex 42 D3
East Hardwick W Yorks 89 C5
East Harling Norf 68 F2
East Harlsey N Yorks 102 E2
East Harnham Wilts 14 B2
East Harptree Bath 23 D7
East Hartford Northumb 111 B5
East Harting W Sus 15 C8
East Hatley Cambs 54 D3
East Hauxwell N Yorks 101 E6
East Haven Angus 143 F5
East Heckington Lincs 78 E4
East Hedleyhope Durham 110 E4
East Hendred Oxon 38 F4
East Herrington T & W 111 D6
East Heslerton N Yorks 96 B5
East Hoathly E Sus 18 D2
East Horrington Som 23 E7
East Horsley Sur 27 D8
East Horton Northumb 125 F6
East Huntspill Som 22 E5
East Hyde Beds 40 C4
East Ilkerton Devon 21 E6
East Ilsley W Berks 38 F4
East Keal Lincs 79 C6
East Kennett Wilts 25 C6
East Keswick W Yorks 95 E6
East Kilbride S Lnrk 121 D6
East Kirkby Lincs 79 C6
East Knapton N Yorks 96 B4
East Knighton Dorset 13 F6
East Knoyle Wilts 24 F3
East Kyloe Northumb 125 F6
East Lambrook Som 12 C2
East Lamington Highld 157 B8
East Langdon Kent 31 E7
East Langton Leics 64 E4
East Langwell Highld 164 D4
East Lavant W Sus 16 D2
East Lavington W Sus 16 C3
East Layton N Yorks 101 D6
East Leake Notts 64 B2
East Learmouth Northumb 124 F4
East Leigh Devon 9 D8
East Lexham Norf 67 C8
East Lilburn Northumb 117 B6
East Linton E Loth 123 B8
East Liss Hants 15 B8
East Looe Corn 5 D7
East Lound N Lincs 89 E8
East Lulworth Dorset 13 F6
East Lutton N Yorks 96 C5
East Lydford Som 23 F7
East Mains Aberds 151 E5
East Malling Kent 29 D8
East March Angus 142 F4
East Marden W Sus 16 C2
East Markham Notts 77 B7
East Marton N Yorks 94 D2
East Meon Hants 15 B7
East Mere Devon 10 C4
East Mersea Essex 43 C6
East Mey Highld 169 B8
East Molesey Sur 28 C2
East Morden Dorset 13 E7
East Morton W Yorks 94 E3
East Ness N Yorks 96 B2
East Newton E Yorks 97 F8
East Norton Leics 64 D4
East Nynehead Som 11 B6
East Oakley Hants 26 D3
East Ogwell Devon 7 B6
East Orchard Dorset 13 C6
East Ord Northumb 125 D5
East Panson Devon 9 E5
East Peckham Kent 29 E7
East Pennard Som 23 F7
East Perry Cambs 54 C2
East Portlemouth Devon 6 F5
East Prawle Devon 7 F5
East Preston W Sus 16 D4
East Putford Devon 9 C5
East Quantoxhead Som 22 E3
East Rainton T & W 111 E6
East Ravendale NE Lincs 91 E6
East Raynham Norf 80 E4
East Rhidorroch Lodge Highld 163 E6
East Rigton W Yorks 95 E6
East Rounton N Yorks 102 D2
East Row N Yorks 103 C6
East Rudham Norf 80 E4
East Runton Norf 81 C7
East Ruston Norf 69 B6
East Saltoun E Loth 123 C7
East Sleekburn Northumb 117 F8
East Somerton Norf 69 C7
East Stockwith Lincs 89 E8
East Stoke Dorset 13 F6
East Stoke Notts 77 E7
East Stour Dorset 13 B6
East Stourmouth Kent 31 C6
East Stowford Devon 9 B8
East Stratton Hants 26 F3
East Studdal Kent 31 E7
East Suisnish Highld 153 F6
East Taphouse Corn 5 C6
East-the-Water Devon 9 B6
East Thirston Northumb 117 E7
East Tilbury Thurrock 29 B7
East Tisted Hants 26 F5
East Torrington Lincs 90 F5
East Tuddenham Norf 68 C3
East Tytherley Hants 14 B3
East Tytherton Wilts 24 B4
East Village Devon 10 D3
East Wall Shrops 60 E5
East Walton Norf 67 C7
East Wellow Hants 14 B4
East Wemyss Fife 134 E5
East Whitburn W Loth 122 C2
East Williamston Pembs 32 D1
East Winch Norf 67 C6
East Winterslow Wilts 25 F7
East Wittering W Sus 15 E8
East Witton N Yorks 101 F6
East Woodburn Northumb 116 F5
East Woodhay Hants 26 C2
East Worldham Hants 26 F5
East Worlington Devon 10 C2
East Worthing W Sus 17 D5
Eastbourne E Sus 18 F3
Eastbridge Suff 57 C8
Eastburn W Yorks 94 E3
Eastbury Herts 40 E3
Eastbury W Berks 25 B8
Eastby N Yorks 94 D3
Eastchurch Kent 30 B3
Eastcombe Glos 37 D5
Eastcote London 40 F4
Eastcote Northants 52 D4
Eastcote W Mid 51 B6
Eastcott Corn 8 C4
Eastcott Wilts 24 D5
Eastcourt Wilts 37 E6
Eastcourt Wilts 25 C7
Easter Ardross Highld 157 B7
Easter Balmoral Aberds 149 E8
Easter Boleskine Highld 147 B8
Easter Compton S Glos 36 F2
Easter Cringate Stirl 133 F6
Easter Davoch Aberds 150 D3
Easter Earshaig Dumfries 114 D3
Easter Fearn Highld 164 F3
Easter Galcantray Highld 158 E2
Easter Howgate Midloth 122 C5
Easter Howlaws Borders 124 E3
Easter Kinkell Highld 157 D6
Easter Lednathie Angus 142 C3
Easter Milton Highld 158 D3
Easter Moniack Highld 157 E6
Easter Ord Aberds 151 D7
Easter Quarff Shetland 175 K6
Easter Rhynd Perth 134 C3
Easter Row Stirl 133 E6
Easter Silverford Aberds 160 B4
Easter Skeld Shetland 175 J5
Easter Whyntie Aberds 160 B3
Eastergate W Sus 16 D3
Easterhouse Glasgow 121 C6
Eastern Green W Mid 63 F6
Easterton Wilts 24 D5
Eastertown Som 22 D5
Eastertown of Auchleuchries Aberds 161 E7
Eastfield N Lnrk 121 C8
Eastfield N Yorks 103 F8
Eastfield Hall Northumb 117 D8
Eastgate Durham 110 F2
Eastgate Norf 81 E7
Eastham Mers 85 F4
Eastham Ferry Mers 85 F4
Easthampstead Brack 27 C6
Eastheath Wokingham 27 C6
Easthope Shrops 61 E5
Easthorpe Essex 43 B5
Easthorpe Leics 77 F8
Easthorpe Notts 77 D7
Easthouses Midloth 123 C6
Eastington Devon 10 D2
Eastington Glos 36 D4
Eastington Glos 37 C8
Eastleach Martin Glos 38 D2
Eastleach Turville Glos 38 D1
Eastleigh Devon 9 B6
Eastleigh Hants 14 C5
Eastling Kent 30 D3
Eastmoor Derbys 76 B3
Eastmoor Norf 67 D7
Eastney Ptsmth 15 E7
Eastnor Hereford 50 F2
Eastoft N Lincs 90 C2
Eastoke Hants 15 E8
Easton Cambs 54 B2
Easton Cumb 108 D2
Easton Cumb 108 B4
Easton Devon 10 F2
Easton Dorset 12 G4
Easton Hants 26 F3
Easton Lincs 65 B6
Easton Norf 68 C4
Easton Som 23 E7
Easton Suff 57 D6
Easton Wilts 24 B3
Easton Grey Wilts 37 F5
Easton-in-Gordano N Som 23 B7
Easton Maudit Northants 53 D6
Easton on the Hill Northants 65 D7
Easton Royal Wilts 25 C7
Eastpark Dumfries 107 C7
Eastrea Cambs 66 E2
Eastriggs Dumfries 108 C2
Eastrington E Yorks 89 B8
Eastry Kent 31 D7
Eastville Bristol 23 B8
Eastville Lincs 79 D7
Eastwell Leics 64 B4
Eastwick Herts 41 C7
Eastwick Shetland 174 F5
Eastwood Notts 76 E4
Eastwood Sthend 42 F4
Eastwood W Yorks 87 B7
Eathorpe Warks 51 C8
Eaton Ches 74 C2
Eaton Ches 75 C5
Eaton Leics 64 B4
Eaton Norf 68 D5
Eaton Notts 77 B7
Eaton Oxon 38 D4
Eaton Shrops 60 F3
Eaton Shrops 60 F5
Eaton Bishop Hereford 49 F6
Eaton Bray Beds 40 B2
Eaton Constantine Shrops 61 D5
Eaton Green Beds 40 B2
Eaton Hastings Oxon 38 E2
Eaton on Tern Shrops 61 B6
Eaton Socon Cambs 54 D2
Eavestone N Yorks 94 C5
Ebberston N Yorks 103 F6
Ebbesbourne Wake Wilts 13 B7
Ebbw Vale = Glyn Ebwy Bl Gwent 35 D5
Ebchester Durham 110 D4
Ebford Devon 10 F4
Ebley Glos 37 D5
Ebnal Ches 73 E8
Ebrington Glos 51 E6
Ecchinswell Hants 26 D2
Ecclaw Borders 124 C3
Ecclefechan Dumfries 107 B8
Eccles Borders 124 E3
Eccles Gtr Man 87 E5
Eccles Kent 29 C8
Eccles on Sea Norf 69 B7
Eccles Road Norf 68 E3
Ecclesall S Yorks 88 F4
Ecclesfield S Yorks 88 E4
Ecclesgreig Aberds 143 C7
Eccleshall Staffs 62 B2
Eccleshill W Yorks 94 F4
Ecclesmachan W Loth 122 B3
Eccleston Ches 73 C8
Eccleston Lancs 86 C3
Eccleston Mers 86 E2
Eccleston Park Mers 86 E2
Eccup W Yorks 95 E5
Echt Aberds 151 D6
Eckford Borders 116 B3
Eckington Derbys 76 B4
Eckington Worcs 50 E4
Ecton Northants 53 C6
Edale Derbys 88 F2
Edburton W Sus 17 C6
Edderside Cumb 107 E7
Edderton Highld 164 F4
Eddistone Devon 8 B4
Eddleston Borders 122 E5
Eden Camp Museum, Malton N Yorks 96 B3
Eden Park London 28 C4
Edenbridge Kent 28 E5
Edenfield Lancs 87 C5
Edenhall Cumb 109 F5
Edenham Lincs 65 B7
Edensor Derbys 76 C2
Edentaggart Argyll 129 A8
Edenthorpe S Yorks 89 D7
Edentown Cumb 108 D3
Ederline Argyll 130 E4
Edern Gwyn 70 D3
Edgarley Som 23 F7
Edgbaston W Mid 62 F4
Edgcott Bucks 39 B6
Edgcott Som 21 F7
Edge Shrops 60 D3
Edge End Glos 36 C2
Edge Green Ches 73 D8
Edge Hill Mers 85 F4
Edgebolton Shrops 61 B5
Edgefield Norf 81 D6
Edgefield Street Norf 81 D6
Edgeside Lancs 87 B6
Edgeworth Glos 37 D6
Edgmond Telford 61 C7
Edgmond Marsh Telford 61 B7
Edgton Shrops 60 F3
Edgware London 40 E4
Edgworth Blkburn 86 C5
Edinample Stirl 132 B4
Edinbane Highld 152 D4
Edinburgh Edin 123 B5
Edinburgh Airport Edin 122 B4
Edinburgh Castle Edin 123 B5
Edinburgh Crystal Visitor Centre, Penicuik Midloth 122 C5
Edinburgh Zoo Edin 122 B5
Edingale Staffs 63 C6
Edingight Ho. Moray 160 C2
Edingley Notts 77 D6
Edingthorpe Norf 69 A6
Edingthorpe Green Norf 69 A6
Edington Som 23 F5
Edington Wilts 24 D4
Edintore Moray 159 E8
Edith Weston Rutland 65 D6
Edithmead Som 22 E5
Edlesborough Bucks 40 C2
Edlingham Northumb 117 D7
Edlington Lincs 78 B5
Edmondsham Dorset 13 C8
Edmondsley Durham 110 E5
Edmondthorpe Leics 65 C5
Edmonstone Orkney 176 D4
Edmonton London 41 E6
Edmundbyers Durham 110 D3
Ednam Borders 124 F3
Ednaston Derbys 76 E2
Edradynate Perth 141 D5
Edrom Borders 124 D4
Edstaston Shrops 74 F2
Edstone Warks 51 C6
Edvin Loach Hereford 49 D8
Edwalton Notts 77 F5
Edwardstone Suff 56 E3
Edwinsford Carms 46 F5
Edwinstowe Notts 77 C6
Edworth Beds 54 E3
Edwyn Ralph Hereford 49 D8
Edzell Angus 143 C5
Efail Isaf Rhondda 34 F4
Efailnewydd Gwyn 70 D4
Efailwen Carms 32 B2
Efenechtyd Denb 72 D5
Effingham Sur 28 D2
Effirth Shetland 175 H5
Efford Devon 10 D3
Egdon Worcs 50 D4
Egerton Gtr Man 86 C5
Egerton Kent 30 E3
Egerton Forstal Kent 30 E2
Eggborough N Yorks 89 B6
Eggbuckland Plym 6 D3
Eggington Beds 40 B2
Egginton Derbys 63 B6
Egglescliffe Stockton 102 C2
Eggleston Durham 100 B4
Egham Sur 27 B8
Egleton Rutland 65 D5
Eglingham Northumb 117 C7
Egloshayle Corn 4 B5
Egloskerry Corn 8 F4
Eglwys-Brewis V Glam 22 C2
Eglwys Cross Wrex 73 E8
Eglwys Fach Ceredig 58 E3
Eglwysbach Conwy 83 D8
Eglwyswen Pembs 45 F3
Eglwyswrw Pembs 45 F3
Egmanton Notts 77 C7
Egremont Cumb 98 C2
Egremont Mers 85 E4
Egton N Yorks 103 D6
Egton Bridge N Yorks 103 D6
Eight Ash Green Essex 43 B5
Eignaig Highld 138 E1
Eil Highld 148 C4
Eilanreach Highld 145 B8
Eilean Darach Highld 163 F5
Eileanach Lodge Highld 157 C6
Einacleite W Isles 172 F4
Eisgean W Isles 173 G6
Eisingrug Gwyn 71 D7
Elan Village Powys 47 C8
Elberton S Glos 36 F3
Elburton Plym 6 D3
Elcho Perth 134 B3
Elcombe Thamesdown 37 F8
Eldernell Cambs 66 E3
Eldersfield Worcs 50 F3
Elderslie Renfs 120 C4
Eldon Durham 101 B7
Eldrick S Ayrs 112 F2
Eldroth N Yorks 93 C7
Eldwick W Yorks 94 E4
Elfhowe Cumb 99 E6
Elford Northumb 125 F7
Elford Staffs 63 C5
Elgin Moray 159 C6
Elgol Highld 153 H6
Elham Kent 31 E5
Elie Fife 135 D6
Elim Anglesey 82 C3
Eling Hants 14 C4
Elishader Highld 152 C6
Elishaw Northumb 116 E4
Elkesley Notts 77 B6
Elkstone Glos 37 C6
Ellan Highld 148 B4
Elland W Yorks 88 B2
Ellary Argyll 128 C2
Ellastone Staffs 75 E8
Ellemford Borders 124 C3
Ellenbrook I o M 84 E3
Ellenhall Staffs 62 B2
Ellen's Green Sur 27 F8
Ellerbeck N Yorks 102 E2
Ellerburn N Yorks 103 F6
Ellerby N Yorks 103 C5
Ellerdine Heath Telford 61 B6
Ellerhayes Devon 10 D4
Elleric Argyll 138 E4
Ellerker E Yorks 90 B3
Ellerton E Yorks 96 F3
Ellerton Shrops 61 B7
Ellesborough Bucks 39 D8
Ellesmere Shrops 73 F8
Ellesmere Port Ches 73 B8
Ellingham Norf 69 E6
Ellingham Northumb 117 B7
Ellingstring N Yorks 101 F6
Ellington Cambs 54 B2
Ellington Northumb 117 E8
Elliot Angus 143 F6
Ellisfield Hants 26 E4
Ellistown Leics 63 C8
Ellon Aberds 161 E6
Ellonby Cumb 108 F4
Ellough Suff 69 F7
Elloughton E Yorks 90 B3
Ellwood Glos 36 D2
Elm Cambs 66 D4
Elm Hill Dorset 13 B6
Elm Park London 41 F8
Elmbridge Worcs 50 C4
Elmdon Essex 55 F5
Elmdon W Mid 63 F5
Elmdon Heath W Mid 63 F5
Elmers End London 28 C4
Elmesthorpe Leics 63 E8
Elmfield I o W 15 E7
Elmhurst Staffs 62 C5
Elmley Castle Worcs 50 E4
Elmley Lovett Worcs 50 C3
Elmore Glos 36 C4
Elmore Back Glos 36 C4
Elmscott Devon 8 B4
Elmsett Suff 56 E4
Elmstead Market Essex 43 B6
Elmsted Kent 30 E5
Elmstone Kent 31 C6
Elmstone Hardwicke Glos 37 B6
Elmswell E Yorks 97 D5
Elmswell Suff 56 C3
Elmton Derbys 76 B5
Elphin Highld 163 C6
Elphinstone E Loth 123 B6
Elrick Aberds 151 D7
Elrig Dumfries 105 E7

Elsdon Northumb 117 E5
Elsecar S Yorks 88 E4
Elsenham Essex 41 B8
Elsfield Oxon 39 C5
Elsham N Lincs 90 C4
Elsing Norf 68 C3
Elslack N Yorks 94 E2
Elson Shrops 73 F7
Elsrickle S Lnrk 122 E3
Elstead Sur 27 E7
Elsted W Sus 16 C2
Elsthorpe Lincs 65 B7
Elstob Durham 101 B8
Elston Notts 77 E7
Elston Wilts 25 E5
Elstone Devon 9 C8
Elstow Beds 53 E8
Elstree Herts 40 E4
Elstronwick E Yorks 97 F8
Elswick Lancs 92 F4
Elsworth Cambs 54 C4
Elterwater Cumb 99 D5
Eltham London 28 B5
Eltisley Cambs 54 D3
Elton Cambs 65 E7
Elton Ches 73 B8
Elton Derbys 76 C2
Elton Glos 36 C4
Elton Hereford 49 B6
Elton Notts 77 F7
Elton Stockton 102 C2
Elton Green Ches 73 B8
Elvanfoot S Lnrk 114 C2
Elvaston Derbys 76 F4
Elveden Suff 56 B2
Elvingston E Loth 123 B7
Elvington Kent 31 D6
Elvington York 96 E2
Elwick Hrtlpl 111 F7
Elwick Northumb 125 F7
Elworth Ches 74 C4
Elworthy Som 22 F2
Ely Cambs 66 F5
Ely Cardiff 22 B3
Ely Cathedral and Museum Cambs 66 F5
Emberton M Keynes 53 E6
Embleton Cumb 107 F8
Embleton Northumb 117 B8
Embo Highld 165 E5
Embo Street Highld 165 E5
Emborough Som 23 D8
Embsay N Yorks 94 D3
Emery Down Hants 14 D3
Emley W Yorks 88 C3
Emmbrook Wokingham 27 C5
Emmer Green Reading 26 B5
Emmington Oxon 39 D7
Emneth Norf 66 D4
Emneth Hungate Norf 66 D5
Empingham Rutland 65 D6
Empshott Hants 27 F5
Emstrey Shrops 60 C5
Emsworth Hants 15 D8
Enborne W Berks 26 C2
Enchmarsh Shrops 60 E5
Enderby Leics 64 E2
Endmoor Cumb 99 F7
Endon Staffs 75 D6
Endon Bank Staffs 75 D6
Enfield London 41 E6
Enfield Wash London 41 E6
Enford Wilts 25 D6
Engamoor Shetland 175 H4
Engine Common S Glos 36 F3
Englefield W Berks 26 B4
Englefield Green Sur 27 B7
Englesea-brook Ches 74 D4
English Bicknor Glos 36 C2
English Frankton Shrops 60 B4
Englishcombe Bath 24 C2
Enham Alamein Hants 25 E8
Enmore Som 22 F4
Ennerdale Bridge Cumb 98 C2
Enoch Dumfries 113 D8
Enochdhu Perth 141 C7
Ensay Argyll 136 D4
Ensbury Bmouth 13 E8
Ensdon Shrops 60 C4
Ensis Devon 9 B7
Enstone Oxon 38 B3
Enterkinfoot Dumfries 113 D8
Enterpen N Yorks 102 D2
Enville Staffs 62 F2
Eolaigearraidh W Isles 171 K3
Eorabus Argyll 136 F4
Eòropaidh W Isles 172 B8
Epperstone Notts 77 E6
Epping Essex 41 D7
Epping Green Essex 41 D7
Epping Green Herts 41 D5
Epping Upland Essex 41 D7
Eppleby N Yorks 101 C6
Eppleworth E Yorks 97 F6
Epsom Sur 28 C3
Epsom Racecourse Sur 28 D3
Epwell Oxon 51 E8
Epworth N Lincs 89 D8
Epworth Turbary N Lincs 89 D8
Erbistock Wrex 73 E7
Erbusaig Highld 155 H3
Erchless Castle Highld 156 E5
Erddig Wrex 73 E7
Erdington W Mid 62 E5
Eredine Argyll 131 E5
Eriboll Highld 167 D6
Ericstane Dumfries 114 C3
Eridge Green E Sus 18 B2
Erines Argyll 128 C3
Eriswell Suff 55 B8
Erith London 29 B6
Erlestoke Wilts 24 D4
Ermine Lincs 78 B2
Ermington Devon 6 D4
Erpingham Norf 81 D7
Errogie Highld 147 B8
Errol Perth 134 B4
Erskine Renfs 120 B4
Erskine Bridge Renfs 120 B4
Ervie Dumfries 104 C4
Erwarton Suff 57 F6
Erwood Powys 48 E2
Eryholme N Yorks 101 D8
Eryrys Denb 73 D6
Escomb Durham 101 B6
Escrick N Yorks 96 E2
Esgairdawe Carms 46 E5
Esgairgeiliog Powys 58 D4
Esh Durham 110 E4
Esh Winning Durham 110 E4
Esher Sur 28 C2
Esholt W Yorks 94 E4
Eshott Northumb 117 E8
Eshton N Yorks 94 D2
Esk Valley N Yorks 103 D6
Eskadale Highld 157 F5
Eskbank Midloth 123 C6
Eskdale Green Cumb 98 D3
Eskdalemuir Dumfries 115 E5
Eske E Yorks 97 E6
Eskham Lincs 91 E7
Esprick Lancs 92 F4
Essendine Rutland 65 C7
Essendon Herts 41 D5
Essich Highld 157 F7
Essington Staffs 62 D3
Esslemont Aberds 151 B8
Eston Redcar 102 C3
Eswick Shetland 175 H6
Etal Northumb 124 F5
Etchilhampton Wilts 24 C5
Etchingham E Sus 18 C4
Etchinghill Kent 19 B8
Etchinghill Staffs 62 C4
Ethie Castle Angus 143 E6
Ethie Mains Angus 143 E6
Etling Green Norf 68 C3
Eton Windsor 27 B7
Eton Wick Windsor 27 B7
Etteridge Highld 148 E2
Ettersgill Durham 100 B3
Ettingshall W Mid 62 E3
Ettington Warks 51 E7
Etton E Yorks 97 E5
Etton P'boro 65 D8
Ettrick Borders 115 C5
Ettrickbridge Borders 115 B6
Ettrickhill Borders 115 C5
Etwall Derbys 76 F2
Eureka!, Halifax W Yorks 87 B8
Euston Suff 56 B2
Euximoor Drove Cambs 66 E4
Euxton Lancs 86 C3
Evanstown Bridgend 34 F3
Evanton Highld 157 C7
Evedon Lincs 78 E3
Evelix Highld 164 E4
Evenjobb Powys 48 C4
Evenley Northants 52 F3
Evenlode Glos 38 B2
Evenwood Durham 101 B6
Evenwood Gate Durham 101 B6
Everbay Orkney 176 D5
Evercreech Som 23 F8
Everdon Northants 52 D3
Everingham E Yorks 96 E4
Everleigh Wilts 25 D7
Everley N Yorks 103 F7
Eversholt Beds 53 F7
Evershot Dorset 12 D3
Eversley Hants 27 C5
Eversley Cross Hants 27 C5
Everthorpe E Yorks 96 F5
Everton Beds 54 D3
Everton Hants 14 E3
Everton Mers 85 E4
Everton Notts 89 E7
Evertown Dumfries 108 B3
Evesbatch Hereford 49 E8
Evesham Worcs 50 E5
Evington Leicester 64 D3
Ewden Village S Yorks 88 E3
Ewell Sur 28 C3
Ewell Minnis Kent 31 E6
Ewelme Oxon 39 E6
Ewen Glos 37 E7
Ewenny V Glam 21 B8
Ewerby Lincs 78 E4
Ewerby Thorpe Lincs 78 E4
Ewes Dumfries 115 E6
Ewesley Northumb 117 E6
Ewhurst Sur 27 E8
Ewhurst Green E Sus 18 C4
Ewhurst Green Sur 27 F8
Ewloe Flint 73 C7
Ewloe Green Flint 73 C6
Ewood Blkburn 86 B4
Eworthy Devon 9 E6
Ewshot Hants 27 E6
Ewyas Harold Hereford 35 B7
Exbourne Devon 9 D8
Exbury Hants 14 E5
Exbury Gardens, Fawley Hants 14 E5
Exebridge Som 10 B4
Exelby N Yorks 101 F7
Exeter Devon 10 E4
Exeter Cathedral Devon 10 E4
Exeter International Airport Devon 10 E4
Exford Som 21 F7
Exhall Warks 51 D6
Exley Head W Yorks 94 F3
Exminster Devon 10 F4
Exmouth Devon 10 F5
Exnaboe Shetland 175 M5
Exning Suff 55 C7
Explosion, Gosport Hants 15 D7
Exton Devon 10 F4
Exton Hants 15 B7
Exton Rutland 65 C6
Exton Som 21 F8
Exwick Devon 10 E4
Eyam Derbys 76 B2
Eydon Northants 52 D3
Eye Hereford 49 C6
Eye P'boro 66 D2
Eye Suff 56 B5
Eye Green P'boro 66 D2
Eyemouth Borders 124 C5
Eyeworth Beds 54 E3
Eyhorne Street Kent 30 D2
Eyke Suff 57 D7
Eynesbury Cambs 54 D2
Eynort Highld 153 G4
Eynsford Kent 29 C6
Eynsham Oxon 38 D4
Eype Dorset 12 E2
Eyre Highld 152 D5
Eyre Highld 153 F6
Eythorne Kent 31 E6
Eyton Hereford 49 C6
Eyton Shrops 60 F3
Eyton Wrex 73 E7
Eyton upon the Weald Moors Telford 61 C6

F

Faccombe Hants 25 D8
Faceby N Yorks 102 D2
Facit Lancs 87 C6
Faddiley Ches 74 D2
Fadmoor N Yorks 102 F4
Faerdre Swansea 33 D7
Failand N Som 23 B7
Failford S Ayrs 112 B4
Failsworth Gtr Man 87 D6
Fain Highld 156 B2
Fair Green Norf 67 C6
Fair Hill Cumb 108 F5
Fair Oak Hants 15 C5
Fair Oak Green Hants 26 C4
Fairbourne Gwyn 58 C3
Fairburn N Yorks 89 B5
Fairfield Derbys 75 B7
Fairfield Stockton 102 C2
Fairfield Worcs 50 E5
Fairfield Worcs 50 B4
Fairford Glos 38 D1
Fairhaven Lancs 85 B4
Fairlie N Ayrs 129 E7
Fairlight E Sus 19 D5
Fairlight Cove E Sus 19 D5
Fairmile Devon 11 E5
Fairmilehead Edin 122 C5
Fairoak Staffs 74 F4
Fairseat Kent 29 C7
Fairstead Essex 42 C3
Fairstead Norf 67 C6
Fairwarp E Sus 17 B8
Fairy Cottage I o M 84 D4
Fairy Cross Devon 9 B6
Fakenham Norf 80 E5
Fakenham Magna Suff 56 B3
Fakenham Racecourse Norf 80 E5
Fala Midloth 123 C7
Fala Dam Midloth 123 C7
Falahill Borders 123 D6
Falcon Hereford 49 F8
Faldingworth Lincs 90 F4
Falfield S Glos 36 E3
Falkenham Suff 57 F6
Falkirk Falk 121 B8
Falkland Fife 134 D4
Falkland Palace Fife 134 D4
Falla Borders 116 C3
Fallgate Derbys 76 C3
Fallin Stirl 133 E7
Fallowfield Gtr Man 87 E6
Fallsidehill Borders 124 E2
Falmer E Sus 17 D7
Falmouth Corn 3 C7
Falsgrave N Yorks 103 F8
Falstone Northumb 116 F3
Fanagmore Highld 166 E3
Fangdale Beck N Yorks 102 E3
Fangfoss E Yorks 96 D3
Fankerton Falk 133 F6
Fanmore Argyll 137 D5
Fannich Lodge Highld 156 C3
Fans Borders 124 E2
Far Bank S Yorks 89 C7
Far Bletchley M Keynes 53 F6
Far Cotton Northants 52 D5
Far Forest Worcs 50 B2
Far Laund Derbys 76 E3
Far Sawrey Cumb 99 E5
Farcet Cambs 66 E2
Farden Shrops 49 B7
Fareham Hants 15 D6
Farewell Staffs 62 C4
Farforth Lincs 79 B6
Faringdon Oxon 38 E2
Farington Lancs 86 B3
Farlam Cumb 109 D5
Farlary Highld 164 D4
Farleigh N Som 23 C6
Farleigh Sur 28 C4
Farleigh Hungerford Som 24 D3
Farleigh Wallop Hants 26 E4
Farlesthorpe Lincs 79 B7
Farleton Cumb 99 F7
Farleton Lancs 93 C5
Farley Shrops 60 D3
Farley Staffs 75 E7
Farley Wilts 14 B3
Farley Green Sur 27 E8
Farley Hill Luton 40 B3
Farley Hill Wokingham 26 C5
Farleys End Glos 36 C4
Farlington N Yorks 96 C2
Farlow Shrops 61 F6
Farmborough Bath 23 C8
Farmcote Glos 37 B7
Farmcote Shrops 61 E7
Farmington Glos 37 C8
Farmoor Oxon 38 D4
Farmtown Moray 160 C2
Farnborough London 28 C5
Farnborough Hants 27 D6
Farnborough Warks 52 E2
Farnborough W Berks 38 F4
Farnborough Green Hants 27 D6
Farncombe Sur 27 E7
Farndish Beds 53 C7
Farndon Ches 73 D8
Farndon Notts 77 D7
Farnell Angus 143 D6
Farnham Dorset 13 C7
Farnham Essex 41 B7
Farnham N Yorks 95 C6
Farnham Suff 57 C7
Farnham Sur 27 E6
Farnham Common Bucks 40 F2
Farnham Green Essex 41 B7
Farnham Royal Bucks 40 F2
Farnhill N Yorks 94 E3
Farningham Kent 29 C6
Farnley N Yorks 94 E5
Farnley W Yorks 95 F5
Farnley Tyas W Yorks 88 C2
Farnsfield Notts 77 D6
Farnworth Gtr Man 86 D5
Farnworth Halton 86 F3
Farr Highld 157 F7
Farr Highld 148 D4
Farr Highld 168 C2
Farr House Highld 157 F7
Farringdon Devon 10 E5
Farrington Gurney Bath 23 D8
Farsley W Yorks 94 F5
Farthinghoe Northants 52 F3
Farthingloe Kent 31 E6
Farthingstone Northants 52 D4
Fartown W Yorks 88 C2
Farway Devon 11 E6
Fasag Highld 154 E4
Fascadale Highld 137 A6
Faslane Port Argyll 129 B7
Fasnacloich Argyll 138 E4
Fasnakyle Ho. Highld 147 B6
Fassfern Highld 138 B4
Fatfield T & W 111 D6
Fattahead Aberds 160 C3
Faugh Cumb 108 D5
Fauldhouse W Loth 122 C2
Faulkbourne Essex 42 C3
Faulkland Som 24 D2
Fauls Shrops 74 F2
Faversham Kent 30 C4
Favillar Moray 159 F6
Fawdington N Yorks 95 B7
Fawfieldhead Staffs 75 C7
Fawkham Green Kent 29 C6
Fawler Oxon 38 C3
Fawley Bucks 39 F7
Fawley Hants 15 D5
Fawley W Berks 38 F3
Fawley Chapel Hereford 36 B2
Faxfleet E Yorks 90 B2
Faygate W Sus 28 F3
Fazakerley Mers 85 E4
Fazeley Staffs 63 D6
Fearby N Yorks 101 F6
Fearn Highld 158 B2
Fearn Lodge Highld 164 F3
Fearn Station Highld 158 B2
Fearnan Perth 140 E4
Fearnbeg Highld 154 E3
Fearnhead Warr 86 E4
Fearnmore Highld 154 D3
Featherstone Staffs 62 D3
Featherstone W Yorks 88 B5
Featherwood Northumb 116 D4
Feckenham Worcs 50 C5
Feering Essex 42 B4
Feetham N Yorks 100 E4
Feizor N Yorks 93 C7
Felbridge Sur 28 F4
Felbrigg Norf 81 D8
Felcourt Sur 28 E4
Felden Herts 40 D3
Felin-Crai Powys 34 B2
Felindre Ceredig 46 D4
Felindre Carms 33 B6
Felindre Carms 47 F5
Felindre Carms 33 B8
Felindre Carms 46 F2
Felindre Powys 59 F8
Felindre Swansea 33 D7
Felindre Farchog Pembs 45 F3
Felinfach Ceredig 46 D4
Felinfach Powys 48 F2
Felinfoel Carms 33 D6
Felingwm isaf Carms 33 B6
Felingwm uchaf Carms 33 B6
Felinwynt Ceredig 45 D4
Felixkirk N Yorks 102 F2
Felixstowe Suff 57 F6
Felixstowe Ferry Suff 57 F7
Felkington Northumb 124 E5
Felkirk W Yorks 88 C4
Fell Side Cumb 108 F3
Felling T & W 111 C5
Felmersham Beds 53 D7
Felmingham Norf 81 E8
Felpham W Sus 16 E3
Felsham Suff 56 D3
Felsted Essex 42 B2
Feltham London 28 B2
Felthorpe Norf 68 C4
Felton Hereford 49 E7
Felton Northumb 117 D7
Felton N Som 23 C7
Felton Butler Shrops 60 C3
Feltwell Norf 67 E7
Fen Ditton Cambs 55 C5
Fen Drayton Cambs 54 C4
Fen End W Mid 51 B7
Fen Side Lincs 79 D6
Fenay Bridge W Yorks 88 C2
Fence Lancs 93 F8
Fence Houses T & W 111 D6
Fengate Norf 81 E7
Fengate P'boro 66 E2
Fenham Northumb 125 E6
Fenhouses Lincs 79 E5
Feniscliffe Blkburn 86 B4
Feniscowles Blkburn 86 B4
Feniton Devon 11 E6
Fenlake Beds 53 E8
Fenny Bentley Derbys 75 D8
Fenny Bridges Devon 11 E6
Fenny Compton Warks 52 D2
Fenny Drayton Leics 63 E7
Fenny Stratford M Keynes 53 F6
Fenrother Northumb 117 E7
Fenstanton Cambs 54 C4
Fenton Cambs 54 B4
Fenton Lincs 77 D8
Fenton Lincs 77 B8
Fenton Stoke 75 E5
Fenton Barns E Loth 135 F7
Fenton Town Northumb 125 F5
Fenwick E Ayrs 120 E4
Fenwick Northumb 110 B3
Fenwick Northumb 125 E6
Fenwick S Yorks 89 C6
Feochaig Argyll 118 E4
Feock Corn 3 C7
Feolin Ferry Argyll 127 F2
Ferens Art Gallery, Hull Hull 90 B4
Ferindonald Highld 145 C6
Feriniquarrie Highld 152 D2
Ferlochan Argyll 138 E3
Fern Angus 142 C4
Ferndale Rhondda 34 E4
Ferndown Dorset 13 D8
Ferness Highld 158 E3
Ferney Green Cumb 99 E6
Fernham Oxon 38 E2
Fernhill Heath Worcs 50 D3
Fernhurst W Sus 16 B2
Fernie Fife 134 C5
Ferniegair S Lnrk 121 D7
Fernilea Highld 153 F4
Fernilee Derbys 75 B7
Ferrensby N Yorks 95 C6
Ferring W Sus 16 D4
Ferry Hill Cambs 66 F3
Ferry Point Highld 164 F4
Ferrybridge W Yorks 89 B5
Ferryden Angus 143 D7
Ferryhill Aberdeen 151 D8
Ferryhill Durham 111 F5
Ferryhill Station Durham 111 F6
Ferryside Carms 32 C4
Fersfield Norf 68 F3
Fersit Highld 139 B7
Ferwig Ceredig 45 E3
Feshiebridge Highld 148 D4
Festival Park Visitor Centre, Ebbw Vale Bl Gwent 35 D5
Fetcham Sur 28 D2
Fetlar Airport Shetland 174 D8
Fetterangus Aberds 161 C6
Fettercairn Aberds 143 B6
Fettes Highld 157 D6
Fewcott Oxon 39 B5
Fewston N Yorks 94 D4
Ffair-Rhos Ceredig 47 C6
Ffairfach Carms 33 B7
Ffaldybrenin Carms 46 E5
Ffarmers Carms 47 E5
Ffawyddog Powys 35 C6
Ffestiniog Railway, Porthmadog Gwyn 71 C7
Fforest Carms 33 D6
Fforest-fâch Swansea 33 E7
Ffos-y-ffin Ceredig 46 C3
Ffostrasol Ceredig 46 E2
Ffridd-Uchaf Gwyn 83 F5
Ffrith Flint 73 D6
Ffrwd Gwyn 82 F4
Ffynnon ddrain Carms 33 B5
Ffynnon-oer Ceredig 46 D4
Ffynnongroyw Flint 85 F2
Fidden Argyll 136 F4
Fiddes Aberds 151 F7
Fiddington Glos 50 F4
Fiddington Som 22 E4
Fiddleford Dorset 13 C6
Fiddlers Hamlet Essex 41 D7
Field Staffs 75 F7
Field Broughton Cumb 99 F5
Field Dalling Norf 81 D6
Field Head Leics 63 D8
Fifehead Magdalen Dorset 13 B5
Fifehead Neville Dorset 13 C5
Fifield Oxon 38 C2
Fifield Wilts 25 D6
Fifield Windsor 27 B7
Fifield Bavant Wilts 13 B8
Figheldean Wilts 25 E6
Filands Wilts 37 F6
Filby Norf 69 C7
Filey N Yorks 97 A7
Filgrave M Keynes 53 E6
Filkins Oxon 38 D2
Filleigh Devon 9 B8
Filleigh Devon 10 C2
Fillingham Lincs 90 F3
Fillongley Warks 63 F6
Filton S Glos 23 B8
Fimber E Yorks 96 C4
Finavon Angus 142 D4
Finchairn Argyll 130 E5
Fincham Norf 67 D6
Finchampstead Wokingham 27 C5
Finchdean Hants 15 C8
Finchingfield Essex 55 F7
Finchley London 41 E5
Findern Derbys 76 F3
Findhorn Moray 158 C4
Findhorn Bridge Highld 148 B4
Findo Gask Perth 134 B2
Findochty Moray 159 C8
Findon Aberds 151 E8
Findon W Sus 16 D5
Findon Mains Highld 157 C7
Findrack Ho. Aberds 150 D5
Finedon Northants 53 B7
Fingal Street Suff 57 C6
Fingask Aberds 151 B6
Fingerpost Worcs 50 B2
Fingest Bucks 39 E7
Finghall N Yorks 101 F6
Fingland Cumb 108 D2
Fingland Dumfries 113 C7
Finglesham Kent 31 D7
Fingringhoe Essex 43 B6
Finlarig Stirl 140 F2
Finmere Oxon 52 F4
Finnart Perth 140 D2
Finningham Suff 56 C4
Finningley S Yorks 89 E7
Finnygaud Aberds 160 C2
Finsbury London 41 F6
Finstall Worcs 50 C4
Finsthwaite Cumb 99 F5
Finstock Oxon 38 C3
Finstown Orkney 176 E2
Fintry Aberds 160 C4
Fintry Dundee 142 F4
Fintry Stirl 132 F5
Finzean Aberds 150 E5
Fionnphort Argyll 136 F4
Fionnsbhagh W Isles 173 K3
Fir Tree Durham 110 F4
Firbeck S Yorks 89 F6
Firby N Yorks 101 F7
Firby N Yorks 96 C3
Firgrove Gtr Man 87 C7
Firsby Lincs 79 C7
Firsdown Wilts 25 F7
First Coast Highld 162 E3
Fishbourne I o W 15 E6
Fishbourne W Sus 16 D2
Fishbourne Palace W Sus 16 D2
Fishburn Durham 111 F6
Fishcross Clack 133 E7
Fisher Place Cumb 99 C5
Fisherford Aberds 160 E3
Fisher's Pond Hants 15 B5
Fisherstreet W Sus 27 F7
Fisherton Highld 157 D8
Fisherton S Ayrs 112 C2
Fishguard = Abergwaun Pembs 44 B4
Fishlake S Yorks 89 C7
Fishleigh Barton Devon 9 B7
Fishponds Bristol 23 B8
Fishpool Glos 36 B3
Fishtoft Lincs 79 E6
Fishtoft Drove Lincs 79 E6
Fishtown of Usan Angus 143 D7
Fishwick Borders 124 D5
Fiskavaig Highld 153 F4
Fiskerton Lincs 78 B3
Fiskerton Notts 77 D7
Fitling E Yorks 97 F8
Fittleton Wilts 25 E6
Fittleworth W Sus 16 C4
Fitton End Cambs 66 C4
Fitz Shrops 60 C4
Fitzhead Som 11 B6
Fitzwilliam W Yorks 88 C5
Fitzwilliam Museum, Cambridge Cambs 54 D5
Fiunary Highld 137 D7
Five Acres Glos 36 C2
Five Ashes E Sus 18 C2
Five Oak Green Kent 29 E7
Five Oaks Jersey 17
Five Oaks W Sus 16 B4
Five Roads Carms 33 D5
Fivecrosses Ches 74 B2
Fivehead Som 11 B8
Flack's Green Essex 42 C3
Flackwell Heath Bucks 40 F1
Fladbury Worcs 50 E4
Fladdabister Shetland 175 K6
Flagg Derbys 75 C8
Flambards Experience, Helston Corn 3 D5
Flamborough E Yorks 97 B8
Flamingo Land, Pickering N Yorks 96 B3
Flamstead Herts 40 C3
Flamstead End Herts 41 D6
Flansham W Sus 16 D3
Flanshaw W Yorks 88 B4
Flasby N Yorks 94 D2
Flash Staffs 75 C7
Flashader Highld 152 D4
Flask Inn N Yorks 103 D7
Flaunden Herts 40 D3
Flawborough Notts 77 E7
Flawith N Yorks 95 C7
Flax Bourton N Som 23 C7
Flaxby N Yorks 95 D6
Flaxholme Derbys 76 E3
Flaxley Glos 36 C3
Flaxpool Som 22 F3
Flaxton N Yorks 96 C2
Fleckney Leics 64 E3
Flecknoe Warks 52 C3
Fledborough Notts 77 B8
Fleet Hants 27 D6
Fleet Hants 15 D8
Fleet Lincs 66 B3
Fleet Air Arm Museum, Yeovil Som 12 B3
Fleet Hargate Lincs 66 B3
Fleetham Northumb 117 B7
Fleetlands Hants 15 D6
Fleetville Herts 40 D4
Fleetwood Lancs 92 E3
Flemingston V Glam 22 B2
Flemington S Lnrk 121 D6
Flempton Suff 56 C2
Fleoideabhagh W Isles 173 K3
Fletchertown Cumb 108 E2
Fletching E Sus 17 B8
Flexbury Corn 8 D4
Flexford Sur 27 E7
Flimby Cumb 107 F7
Flimwell E Sus 18 B4
Flint = Y Fflint Flint 73 B6
Flint Mountain Flint 73 B6
Flintham Notts 77 E7
Flinton E Yorks 97 F8
Flintsham Hereford 48 D5
Flitcham Norf 80 E3
Flitton Beds 53 F8
Flitwick Beds 53 F8
Flixborough N Lincs 90 C2
Flixborough Stather N Lincs 90 C2
Flixton Gtr Man 86 E5
Flixton N Yorks 97 B6
Flixton Suff 69 F6
Flockton W Yorks 88 C3
Flodaigh W Isles 170 E4
Flodden Northumb 124 F5
Flodigarry Highld 152 B5
Flood's Ferry Cambs 66 E3
Flookburgh Cumb 92 B3
Florden Norf 68 E4
Flore Northants 52 C4
Flotterton Northumb 117 D5
Flowton Suff 56 E4
Flush House W Yorks 88 D2
Flushing Aberds 161 D7
Flushing Corn 3 C7
Flyford Flavell Worcs 50 D4
Foals Green Suff 57 B6
Fobbing Thurrock 42 F3
Fochabers Moray 159 D7
Fochriw Caerph 35 D5
Fockerby N Lincs 90 C2
Fodderletter Moray 149 B7
Fodderty Highld 157 D6
Foel Powys 59 C6
Foel-gastell Carms 33 C6
Foffarty Angus 142 E4
Foggathorpe E Yorks 96 F3
Fogo Borders 124 E3
Fogorig Borders 124 E3
Foindle Highld 166 E3
Folda Angus 142 C1
Fole Staffs 75 F7
Foleshill W Mid 63 F7
Folke Dorset 12 C4
Folkestone Kent 31 F6
Folkestone Racecourse Kent 19 B8
Folkingham Lincs 78 F3
Folkington E Sus 18 E2
Folksworth Cambs 65 F8
Folkton N Yorks 97 B6
Folla Rule Aberds 160 E4
Follifoot N Yorks 95 D6
Folly Gate Devon 9 E7
Fonthill Bishop Wilts 24 F4
Fonthill Gifford Wilts 24 F4
Fontmell Magna Dorset 13 C6
Fontwell W Sus 16 D3
Fontwell Park Racecourse W Sus 16 D3
Foolow Derbys 75 B8
Foots Cray London 29 B5
Forbestown Aberds 150 C2
Force Mills Cumb 99 E5
Forcett N Yorks 101 C6
Ford Argyll 130 E4
Ford Bucks 39 D7
Ford Devon 9 B6
Ford Glos 37 B7
Ford Northumb 124 F5
Ford Shrops 60 C4
Ford Staffs 75 D7
Ford Wilts 24 B3
Ford W Sus 16 D3
Ford End Essex 42 C2
Ford Street Som 11 C6
Fordcombe Kent 29 E6
Fordell Fife 134 F3
Forden Powys 60 D2
Forder Green Devon 7 C5
Fordham Cambs 55 B7
Fordham Essex 43 B5
Fordham Norf 67 E6
Fordhouses W Mid 62 D3
Fordingbridge Hants 14 C2
Fordon E Yorks 97 B6
Fordoun Aberds 143 B7
Ford's Green Suff 56 C4
Fordstreet Essex 43 B5
Fordwells Oxon 38 C3
Fordwich Kent 31 D5
Fordyce Aberds 160 B2
Forebridge Staffs 62 B3
Forest Durham 109 F8
Forest Becks Lancs 93 D7
Forest Gate London 41 F7
Forest Green Sur 28 E2
Forest Hall Cumb 99 D7
Forest Head Cumb 109 D5
Forest Hill Oxon 39 D5
Forest Lane Head N Yorks 95 D6
Forest Lodge Argyll 139 E6
Forest Lodge Highld 149 C6
Forest Lodge Perth 141 B6
Forest Mill Clack 133 E8
Forest Row E Sus 28 F5
Forest Town Notts 77 C5
Forestburn Gate Northumb 117 E6
Foresterseat Moray 159 D5
Forestside W Sus 15 C8
Forfar Angus 142 D4
Forgandenny Perth 134 C2
Forge Powys 58 E4
Forge Side Torf 35 D6
Forgewood N Lnrk 121 D7
Forgie Moray 159 D7
Forglen Ho. Aberds 160 C3
Formby Mers 85 D4
Forncett End Norf 68 E4
Forncett St Mary Norf 68 E4
Forncett St Peter Norf 68 E4
Forneth Perth 141 E7
Fornham All Saints Suff 56 C2
Fornham St Martin Suff 56 C2
Forres Moray 158 D4
Forrest Lodge Dumfries 113 F5
Forrestfield N Lnrk 121 C8
Forsbrook Staffs 75 E6
Forse Highld 169 F7
Forse Ho. Highld 169 F7
Forsinain Highld 168 E4
Forsinard Highld 168 E3
Forsinard Station Highld 168 E3
Forston Dorset 12 E4
Fort Augustus Highld 147 D6
Fort George Guern 16
Fort George Highld 157 D8
Fort Victoria Country Park & Marine Aquarium I o W 14 F4
Fort William Highld 139 B5
Forteviot Perth 134 C2
Forth S Lnrk 122 D2
Forth Road Bridge Fife 122 B4
Forthampton Glos 50 F3
Fortingall Perth 140 E4
Forton Hants 26 E2
Forton Lancs 92 D4
Forton Shrops 60 C4
Forton Som 11 D8
Forton Staffs 61 B7
Forton Heath Shrops 60 C4
Fortrie Aberds 160 D3
Fortrose Highld 157 D8
Fortuneswell Dorset 12 G4
Forty Green Bucks 40 E2
Forty Hill London 41 E6
Forward Green Suff 56 D4
Fosbury Wilts 25 D8
Fosdyke Lincs 79 F6
Foss Perth 140 D4
Foss Cross Glos 37 D7
Fossebridge Glos 37 C7
Foster Street Essex 41 D7
Fosterhouses S Yorks 89 C7
Foston Derbys 75 F8
Foston Lincs 77 E8
Foston N Yorks 96 C2
Foston on the Wolds E Yorks 97 D7
Fotherby Lincs 91 E7
Fotheringhay Northants 65 E7
Foubister Orkney 176 F4
Foul Mile E Sus 18 D3
Foulby W Yorks 88 C4
Foulden Borders 124 D5
Foulden Norf 67 E7
Foulis Castle Highld 157 C6
Foulridge Lancs 93 E8
Foulsham Norf 81 E6
Fountainhall Borders 123 E7
Fountains Abbey, Ripon N Yorks 95 C5
Four Ashes Staffs 62 F2
Four Ashes Suff 56 B4
Four Crosses Powys 59 D7
Four Crosses Powys 60 C2
Four Crosses Wrex 73 D6
Four Elms Kent 29 E5
Four Forks Som 22 F4
Four Gotes Cambs 66 C4
Four Lane Ends Ches 74 C2
Four Lanes Corn 3 C5
Four Marks Hants 26 F4
Four Mile Bridge Anglesey 82 D2
Four Oaks E Sus 19 C5
Four Oaks W Mid 63 F6
Four Oaks W Mid 62 E5
Four Roads Carms 33 D5
Four Roads I o M 84 F2
Four Throws Kent 18 C4
Fourlane Ends Derbys 76 D3
Fourlanes End Ches 74 D5
Fourpenny Highld 165 E5
Fourstones Northumb 109 C8
Fovant Wilts 13 B8
Foveran Aberds 151 B8
Fowey Corn 5 D6

Fowley Common Warr 86 E4
Fowlis Angus 142 F3
Fowlis Wester Perth 133 B8
Fowlmere Cambs 54 E5
Fownhope Hereford 49 F7
Fox Corner Sur 27 D7
Fox Lane Hants 27 D6
Fox Street Essex 43 B6
Foxbar Renfs 120 C4
Foxcombe Hill Oxon 38 D4
Foxdale I o M 84 E2
Foxearth Essex 56 E2
Foxfield Cumb 98 F4
Foxham Wilts 24 B4
Foxhole Corn 4 D4
Foxhole Swansea 33 E7
Foxholes N Yorks 97 B6
Foxhunt Green E Sus 18 D2
Foxley Norf 81 E6
Foxley Wilts 37 F5
Foxt Staffs 75 E7
Foxton Cambs 54 E5
Foxton Durham 102 B1
Foxton Leics 64 E4
Foxton Canal Locks Leics 64 F3
Foxup N Yorks 93 B8
Foxwist Green Ches 74 C3
Foxwood Shrops 49 B8
Foy Hereford 36 B2
Foyers Highld 147 B7
Fraddam Corn 2 C4
Fraddon Corn 4 D4
Fradley Staffs 63 C5
Fradswell Staffs 75 F6
Fraisthorpe E Yorks 97 C7
Framfield E Sus 17 B8
Framingham Earl Norf 69 D5
Framingham Pigot Norf 69 D5
Framlingham Suff 57 C6
Framlington Castle Suff 57 C6
Frampton Dorset 12 E4
Frampton Lincs 79 F6
Frampton Cotterell S Glos 36 F3
Frampton Mansell Glos 37 D6
Frampton on Severn Glos 36 D4
Frampton West End Lincs 79 E5
Framsden Suff 57 D5
Framwellgate Moor Durham 111 E5
Franche Worcs 50 B3
Frankby Mers 85 F3
Frankley Worcs 62 F3
Frank's Bridge Powys 48 D3
Frankton Warks 52 B2
Frant E Sus 18 B2
Fraserburgh Aberds 161 B6
Frating Green Essex 43 B6
Fratton Ptsmth 15 E7
Freathy Corn 5 D8
Freckenham Suff 55 B7
Freckleton Lancs 86 B2
Freeby Leics 64 B5
Freehay Staffs 75 E7
Freeland Oxon 38 C4
Freeport Hornsea Outlet Village E Yorks 97 E7
Freester Shetland 175 H6
Freethorpe Norf 69 D7
Freiston Lincs 79 E6
Fremington Devon 20 F4
Fremington N Yorks 101 E5
Frenchay S Glos 23 B8
Frenchbeer Devon 9 F8
Frenich Stirl 132 D3
Frensham Sur 27 E6
Fresgoe Highld 168 C4
Freshfield Mers 85 D3
Freshford Bath 24 C2
Freshwater I o W 14 F4
Freshwater Bay I o W 14 F4
Freshwater East Pembs 32 E1
Fressingfield Suff 57 B6
Freston Suff 57 F5
Freswick Highld 169 C8
Fretherne Glos 36 D4
Frettenham Norf 68 C5
Freuchie Fife 134 D4
Freuchies Angus 142 C2
Freystrop Pembs 44 D4
Friar's Gate E Sus 29 F5
Friarton Perth 134 B3
Friday Bridge Cambs 66 D4
Friday Street E Sus 18 E3
Fridaythorpe E Yorks 96 D4
Friern Barnet London 41 E5
Friesland Argyll 136 C2
Friesthorpe Lincs 90 F4
Frieston Lincs 78 E2
Frieth Bucks 39 E7
Frilford Oxon 38 E4
Frilsham W Berks 26 B3
Frimley Sur 27 D6
Frimley Green Sur 27 D6
Frindsbury Medway 29 B8
Fring Norf 80 D3
Fringford Oxon 39 B6
Frinsted Kent 30 D2
Frinton-on-Sea Essex 43 B8
Friockheim Angus 143 E5
Friog Gwyn 58 C3
Frisby on the Wreake Leics 64 C3
Friskney Lincs 79 D7
Friskney Eaudike Lincs 79 D7
Friskney Tofts Lincs 79 D7
Friston E Sus 18 F2
Friston Suff 57 C8
Fritchley Derbys 76 D3
Frith Bank Lincs 79 E6
Frith Common Worcs 49 C8
Fritham Hants 14 C3
Frithelstock Devon 9 C6
Frithelstock Stone Devon 9 C6
Frithville Lincs 79 D6
Frittenden Kent 30 E2
Frittiscombe Devon 7 E6
Fritton Norf 68 E5
Fritton Norf 69 D7
Fritwell Oxon 39 B5
Frizinghall W Yorks 94 F4
Frizington Cumb 98 C2
Frocester Glos 36 D4
Frodesley Shrops 60 D5
Frodingham N Lincs 90 C2
Frodsham Ches 74 B2
Frogden Borders 116 B3
Froggatt Derbys 76 B2
Froghall Staffs 75 E7
Frogmore Devon 7 E5
Frogmore Hants 27 D6
Frognall Lincs 65 C8
Frogshail Norf 81 D8
Frolesworth Leics 64 E2
Frome Som 24 E2
Frome St Quintin Dorset 12 D3
Fromes Hill Hereford 49 E8
Fron Denb 72 C4
Fron Gwyn 82 F5
Fron Gwyn 70 D4
Fron Powys 48 C2
Fron Powys 60 D2
Fron Powys 59 E8
Froncysyllte Wrex 73 E6
Frongoch Gwyn 72 F3
Frostenden Suff 69 F7
Frosterley Durham 110 F3
Frotoft Orkney 176 D3
Froxfield Wilts 25 C7
Froxfield Green Hants 15 B8
Froyle Hants 27 E5
Fryerning Essex 42 D2
Fryton N Yorks 96 B2
Fulbeck Lincs 78 D2
Fulbourn Cambs 55 D6
Fulbrook Oxon 38 C2
Fulford Som 11 B7
Fulford Staffs 75 F6
Fulford York 96 E2
Fulham London 28 B3
Fulking W Sus 17 C6
Full Sutton E Yorks 96 D3
Fullarton Glasgow 121 C6
Fullarton N Ayrs 120 F3
Fuller Street Essex 42 C3
Fuller's Moor Ches 73 D8
Fullerton Hants 25 F8
Fulletby Lincs 79 B5
Fullwood E Ayrs 120 D4
Fulmer Bucks 40 F2
Fulmodestone Norf 81 D5
Fulnetby Lincs 78 B3
Fulstow Lincs 91 E7
Fulwell T & W 111 D6
Fulwood Lancs 92 F5
Fulwood S Yorks 88 F4
Fundenhall Norf 68 E4
Fundenhall Street Norf 68 E4
Funtington W Sus 15 D8
Funtley Hants 15 D6
Funtullich Perth 133 B6
Funzie Shetland 174 D8
Furley Devon 11 D7
Furnace Argyll 131 E6
Furnace Carms 33 D6
Furnace End Warks 63 E6
Furneaux Pelham Herts 41 B7
Furness Vale Derbys 87 F8
Furze Platt Windsor 40 F1
Furzehill Devon 21 E6
Fyfett Som 11 C7
Fyfield Essex 42 D1
Fyfield Glos 38 D2
Fyfield Hants 25 E7
Fyfield Oxon 38 E4
Fyfield Wilts 25 C6
Fylingthorpe N Yorks 103 D7
Fyvie Aberds 160 E4

G

Gabhsann bho Dheas W Isles 172 C7
Gabhsann bho Thuath W Isles 172 C7
Gablon Highld 164 E4
Gabroc Hill E Ayrs 120 D4
Gaddesby Leics 64 C3
Gadebridge Herts 40 D3
Gaer Powys 35 B5
Gaerllwyd Mon 35 E8
Gaerwen Anglesey 82 D4
Gagingwell Oxon 38 B4
Gaick Lodge Highld 148 F3
Gailey Staffs 62 C3
Gainford Durham 101 C6
Gainsborough Lincs 90 E2
Gainsborough Suff 57 E5
Gainsford End Essex 55 F8
Gairloch Highld 154 C4
Gairlochy Highld 146 F4
Gairney Bank Perth 134 E3
Gairnshiel Lodge Aberds 149 D8
Gaisgill Cumb 99 D8
Gaitsgill Cumb 108 E3
Galashiels Borders 123 F7
Galgate Lancs 92 D4
Galhampton Som 12 B4
Gallaberry Dumfries 114 F2
Gallachoille Argyll 128 B2
Gallanach Argyll 130 C4
Gallanach Argyll 136 B3
Gallantry Bank Ches 74 D2
Gallatown Fife 134 E4
Galley Common Warks 63 E7
Galley Hill Cambs 54 C4
Galleyend Essex 42 D3
Galleywood Essex 42 D3
Gallin Perth 140 E2
Gallowfauld Angus 142 E4
Gallows Green Staffs 75 E7
Galltair Highld 155 H4
Galmisdale Highld 144 E4
Galmpton Devon 6 E4
Galmpton Torbay 7 D6
Galphay N Yorks 95 B5
Galston E Ayrs 120 F5
Galtrigill Highld 152 D2
Gamblesby Cumb 109 F6
Gamesley Derbys 87 E8
Gamlingay Cambs 54 D3
Gammersgill N Yorks 101 F5
Gamston Notts 77 B7
Ganarew Hereford 36 C2
Ganavan Argyll 130 B4
Gang Corn 5 C8
Ganllwyd Gwyn 71 E8
Gannochy Angus 143 B5
Gannochy Perth 134 B3
Gansclet Highld 169 E8
Ganstead E Yorks 97 F7
Ganthorpe N Yorks 96 B2
Ganton N Yorks 97 B5
Garbat Highld 156 C5
Garbhallt Argyll 131 F6
Garboldisham Norf 68 F3
Garden City Flint 73 C7
Garden Village Wrex 73 D7
Garden Village W Yorks 95 F7
Gardenstown Aberds 160 B4
Garderhouse Shetland 175 J5
Gardham E Yorks 97 E5
Gardin Shetland 174 G6
Gare Hill Som 24 E2
Garelochhead Argyll 129 A7
Garford Oxon 38 E4
Garforth W Yorks 95 F7
Gargrave N Yorks 94 D2
Gargunnock Stirl 133 E6
Garlic Street Norf 68 F5
Garlieston Dumfries 105 E8
Garlinge Green Kent 30 D5
Garlogie Aberds 151 D6
Garmond Aberds 160 C5
Garmony Argyll 137 D7
Garmouth Moray 159 C7
Garn-yr-erw Torf 35 C6
Garnant Carms 33 C7
Garndiffaith Torf 35 D6
Garndolbenmaen Gwyn 71 C5
Garnedd Conwy 83 F7
Garnett Bridge Cumb 99 E7
Garnfadryn Gwyn 70 D3
Garnkirk N Lnrk 121 C6
Garnlydan Bl Gwent 35 C5
Garnswllt Swansea 33 D7
Garrabost W Isles 172 E8
Garraron Argyll 130 E4
Garras Corn 3 D6
Garreg Gwyn 71 C7
Garrick Perth 133 C7
Garrigill Cumb 109 E7
Garriston N Yorks 101 E6
Garroch Dumfries 113 F5
Garrogie Lodge Highld 147 C8
Garros Highld 152 C5
Garrow Perth 141 E5
Garryhorn Dumfries 113 E5
Garsdale Cumb 100 F2
Garsdale Head Cumb 100 E2
Garsdon Wilts 37 F6
Garshall Green Staffs 75 F6
Garsington Oxon 39 D5
Garstang Lancs 92 E4
Garston Mers 86 F2
Garswood Mers 86 E3
Gartcosh N Lnrk 121 C6
Garth Bridgend 34 E2
Garth Gwyn 83 D5
Garth Powys 47 E8
Garth Shetland 175 H4
Garth Wrex 73 E6
Garth Row Cumb 99 E7
Garthamlock Glasgow 121 C6
Garthbrengy Powys 48 F2
Garthdee Aberdeen 151 D8
Gartheli Ceredig 46 D4
Garthmyl Powys 59 E8
Garthorpe Leics 64 B5
Garthorpe N Lincs 90 C2
Gartly Aberds 160 E2
Gartmore Stirl 132 E4
Gartnagrenach Argyll 128 E2
Gartness N Lnrk 121 C7
Gartness Stirl 132 F4
Gartocharn W Dunb 132 F3
Garton E Yorks 97 F8
Garton-on-the-Wolds E Yorks 97 D5
Gartsherrie N Lnrk 121 C7
Gartymore Highld 165 C7
Garvald E Loth 123 B8
Garvamore Highld 147 E8
Garvard Argyll 127 C1
Garvault Hotel Highld 168 F2
Garve Highld 156 C4
Garvestone Norf 68 D3
Garvock Aberds 143 B7
Garvock Invclyd 129 C7
Garway Hereford 36 B1
Garway Hill Hereford 35 B8
Gaskan Highld 138 B1
Gastard Wilts 24 C3
Gasthorpe Norf 68 F2
Gatcombe I o W 15 F5
Gate Burton Lincs 90 F2
Gate Helmsley N Yorks 96 D2
Gateacre Mers 86 F2
Gatebeck Cumb 99 F7
Gateford Notts 89 F6
Gateforth N Yorks 89 B6
Gatehead E Ayrs 120 F3
Gatehouse Northumb 116 F3
Gatehouse of Fleet Dumfries 106 D3
Gatelawbridge Dumfries 114 E2
Gateley Norf 81 E5
Gatenby N Yorks 101 F8
Gateshead T & W 111 C5
Gateshead International Stadium T & W 111 C5
Gatesheath Ches 73 C8
Gateside Aberds 150 C5
Gateside Angus 142 E4
Gateside E Renf 120 D4
Gateside Fife 134 D3
Gateside N Ayrs 120 D3
Gathurst Gtr Man 86 D3
Gatley Gtr Man 87 F6
Gattonside Borders 123 F8
Gaufron Powys 47 C8
Gaulby Leics 64 D3
Gauldry Fife 135 B5
Gaunt's Common Dorset 13 D8
Gautby Lincs 78 B4
Gavinton Borders 124 D3
Gawber S Yorks 88 D4
Gawcott Bucks 52 F4
Gawsworth Ches 75 C5
Gawthorpe W Yorks 88 B3
Gawthrop Cumb 100 F1
Gawthwaite Cumb 98 F4
Gay Street W Sus 16 B4
Gaydon Warks 51 D8
Gayfield Orkney 176 A3
Gayhurst M Keynes 53 E6
Gayle N Yorks 100 F3
Gayles N Yorks 101 D6
Gayton Mers 85 F3
Gayton Norf 67 C7
Gayton Northants 52 D5
Gayton Staffs 62 B3
Gayton le Marsh Lincs 91 F8
Gayton le Wold Lincs 91 F6
Gayton Thorpe Norf 67 C7
Gaywood Norf 67 B6
Gazeley Suff 55 C8
Geanies House Highld 158 B2
Gearraidh Bhailteas W Isles 171 H3
Gearraidh Bhaird W Isles 172 F6
Gearraidh na h-Aibhne W Isles 172 E5
Gearraidh na Monadh W Isles 171 J3
Geary Highld 152 C3
Geddes House Highld 158 D2
Gedding Suff 56 D3
Geddington Northants 65 F5
Gedintailor Highld 153 F6
Gedling Notts 77 E6
Gedney Lincs 66 B4
Gedney Broadgate Lincs 66 B4
Gedney Drove End Lincs 66 B4
Gedney Dyke Lincs 66 B4
Gedney Hill Lincs 66 C3
Gee Cross Gtr Man 87 E7
Geilston Argyll 120 B3
Geirinis W Isles 170 F3
Geise Highld 169 C6
Geisiadar W Isles 172 E4
Geldeston Norf 69 E6
Gell Conwy 83 E8
Gelli Pembs 32 C1
Gelli Rhondda 34 E3
Gellideg M Tydf 34 D4
Gellifor Denb 72 C5
Gelligaer Caerph 35 E5
Gellilydan Gwyn 71 D7
Gellinudd Neath 33 D8
Gellyburn Perth 141 F7
Gellywen Carms 32 B3
Gelston Dumfries 106 D4
Gelston Lincs 78 E2
Gembling E Yorks 97 D7
Gentleshaw Staffs 62 C4
Geocrab W Isles 173 J4
George Green Bucks 40 F3
George Nympton Devon 10 B2
George Town Bl Gwent 35 D5
Georgefield Dumfries 115 E5
Georgeham Devon 20 F3
Gerlan Gwyn 83 E6
Germansweek Devon 9 E6
Germoe Corn 2 D4
Gerrans Corn 3 C7
Gerrards Cross Bucks 40 F3
Gestingthorpe Essex 56 F2
Geuffordd Powys 60 C2
Gib Hill Ches 74 B3
Gibbet Hill Warks 64 F2
Gibbshill Dumfries 106 B4
Gidea Park London 41 F8
Gidleigh Devon 9 F8
Giffnock E Renf 121 D5
Gifford E Loth 123 C8
Giffordland N Ayrs 120 E2
Giffordtown Fife 134 C4
Giggleswick N Yorks 93 C8
Gilberdyke E Yorks 90 B2
Gilchriston E Loth 123 C7
Gilcrux Cumb 107 F8
Gildersome W Yorks 88 B3
Gildingwells S Yorks 89 F6
Gileston V Glam 22 C2
Gilfach Caerph 35 E5
Gilfach Goch Rhondda 34 F3
Gilfachrheda Ceredig 46 D3
Gillamoor N Yorks 102 F4
Gillar's Green Mers 86 E2
Gillen Highld 152 D3
Gilling East N Yorks 96 B2
Gilling West N Yorks 101 D6
Gillingham Dorset 13 B6
Gillingham Medway 29 C8
Gillingham Norf 69 E7
Gillock Highld 169 D7
Gillow Heath Staffs 75 D5
Gills Highld 169 B8
Gill's Green Kent 18 B4
Gilmanscleuch Borders 115 B6
Gilmerton Edin 123 C5
Gilmerton Perth 133 B7
Gilmonby Durham 100 C4
Gilmorton Leics 64 F2
Gilmourton S Lnrk 121 E6
Gilsland Cumb 109 C6
Gilsland Spa Cumb 109 C6
Gilston Borders 123 D7
Gilston Herts 41 C7
Gilwern Mon 35 C6
Gimingham Norf 81 D8
Giosla W Isles 172 F4
Gipping Suff 56 C4
Gipsey Bridge Lincs 79 E5
Girdle Toll N Ayrs 120 E3
Girlsta Shetland 175 H6
Girsby N Yorks 102 D1
Girtford Beds 54 D2
Girthon Dumfries 106 D3
Girton Cambs 54 C5
Girton Notts 77 C8
Girvan S Ayrs 112 E1
Gisburn Lancs 93 E8
Gisleham Suff 69 F8
Gislingham Suff 56 B4
Gissing Norf 68 F4
Gittisham Devon 11 E6
Gladestry Powys 48 D4
Gladsmuir E Loth 123 B7
Glais Swansea 33 D8
Glaisdale N Yorks 103 D5
Glame Highld 153 E6
Glamis Angus 142 E3
Glamis Castle Angus 142 E3
Glan Adda Gwyn 83 D5
Glan-Conwy Conwy 83 F8
Glan Conwy Conwy 83 D8
Glan-Duar Carms 46 E4
Glan-Dwyfach Gwyn 71 C5
Glan Gors Anglesey 82 D4
Glan-rhyd Gwyn 82 F4
Glan-traeth Anglesey 82 D2
Glan-y-don Flint 73 B5
Glan-y-nant Powys 59 F6
Glan-y-wern Gwyn 71 D7
Glan-yr-afon Anglesey 83 C6
Glan-yr-afon Gwyn 72 E3
Glan-yr-afon Gwyn 72 E4
Glanaman Carms 33 C7
Glandford Norf 81 C6
Glandwr Pembs 32 B2
Glandy Cross Carms 32 B2
Glandyfi Ceredig 58 E3
Glangrwyney Powys 35 C6
Glanmule Powys 59 E8
Glanrafon Ceredig 58 F3
Glanrhyd Gwyn 70 D3
Glanrhyd Pembs 45 E3
Glanton Northumb 117 C6
Glanton Pike Northumb 117 C6
Glanvilles Wootton Dorset 12 D4
Glapthorn Northants 65 E7
Glapwell Derbys 76 C4
Glas-allt Shiel Aberds 149 F8
Glasbury Powys 48 F3
Glaschoil Highld 158 F4
Glascoed Denb 72 B3
Glascoed Mon 35 D7
Glascoed Powys 59 C8
Glascorrie Aberds 150 E2
Glascote Staffs 63 D6
Glascwm Powys 48 D3
Glasdrum Argyll 138 E4
Glasfryn Conwy 72 D3
Glasgow Glasgow 121 C5
Glasgow Airport Renfs 120 C4
Glasgow Art Gallery & Museum Glasgow 121 C5
Glasgow Botanic Gardens Glasgow 121 C5
Glasgow Cathedral Glasgow 121 C6
Glasgow Prestwick International Airport S Ayrs 112 B3
Glashvin Highld 152 C5
Glasinfryn Gwyn 83 E5
Glasnacardoch Highld 145 D6
Glasnakille Highld 153 H6
Glasphein Highld 152 E2
Glaspwll Powys 58 E4
Glassburn Highld 156 F4
Glasserton Dumfries 105 F8
Glassford S Lnrk 121 E7
Glasshouse Hill Glos 36 B4
Glasshouses N Yorks 94 C4
Glasslie Fife 134 D4
Glasson Cumb 108 C2
Glasson Lancs 92 D4
Glassonby Cumb 109 F5
Glasterlaw Angus 143 D5
Glaston Rutland 65 D5
Glastonbury Som 23 F7
Glastonbury Abbey Som 23 F6
Glatton Cambs 65 F8
Glazebrook Warr 86 E4
Glazebury Warr 86 E4
Glazeley Shrops 61 F7
Gleadless S Yorks 88 F4
Gleadsmoss Ches 74 C5
Gleann Tholàstaidh W Isles 172 D8
Gleaston Cumb 92 B2
Gleiniant Powys 59 E6
Glemsford Suff 56 E2
Glen Dumfries 106 D2
Glen Dumfries 106 B5
Glen Auldyn I o M 84 C4
Glen Bernisdale Highld 152 E5
Glen Ho. Borders 123 F5
Glen Mona I o M 84 D4
Glen Nevis House Highld 139 B5
Glen Parva Leics 64 E2
Glen Sluain Argyll 131 F6
Glen Tanar House Aberds 150 E3
Glen Trool Lodge Dumfries 112 F4
Glen Village Falk 121 B8
Glen Vine I o M 84 E3
Glenamachrie Argyll 130 C5
Glenbarr Argyll 118 C3
Glenbeg Highld 137 B6
Glenbeg Highld 149 B6
Glenbervie Aberds 151 F6
Glenboig N Lnrk 121 C7
Glenborrodale Highld 137 B7
Glenbranter Argyll 131 F7
Glenbreck Borders 114 B3
Glenbrein Lodge Highld 147 C7
Glenbrittle House Highld 153 G5
Glenbuchat Lodge Aberds 150 C2
Glenbuck E Ayrs 113 B7
Glenburn Renfs 120 C4
Glencalvie Lodge Highld 164 F1
Glencanisp Lodge Highld 163 B5
Glencaple Dumfries 107 C6
Glencarron Lodge Highld 155 E6
Glencarse Perth 134 B3
Glencassley Castle Highld 163 D8
Glenceitlein Highld 139 E5
Glencoe Highld 138 D4
Glencraig Fife 134 E3
Glencripesdale Highld 137 C7
Glencrosh Dumfries 113 F7
Glendavan Ho. Aberds 150 D3
Glendevon Perth 133 D8
Glendoe Lodge Highld 147 D7
Glendoebeg Highld 147 D7
Glendoick Perth 134 B4
Glendoll Lodge Angus 142 B2
Glendoune S Ayrs 112 E1
Glenduckie Fife 134 C4
Glendye Lodge Aberds 150 F5
Gleneagles Hotel Perth 133 C8
Gleneagles House Perth 133 D8
Glenegedale Argyll 126 D3
Glenelg Highld 145 B8
Glenernie Moray 158 E4
Glenfarg Perth 134 C3
Glenfarquhar Lodge Aberds 151 F6
Glenferness House Highld 158 E3
Glenfeshie Lodge Highld 148 E4
Glenfiddich Distillery, Dufftown Moray 159 E7
Glenfield Leics 64 D2
Glenfinnan Highld 145 E8
Glenfoot Perth 134 C3
Glenfyne Lodge Argyll 131 D8
Glengap Dumfries 106 D3
Glengarnock N Ayrs 120 D3
Glengorm Castle Argyll 137 C5
Glengrasco Highld 153 E5
Glenhead Farm Angus 142 C2
Glenhoul Dumfries 113 F6
Glenhurich Highld 138 C2
Glenkerry Borders 115 C5
Glenkiln Dumfries 106 B5
Glenkindie Aberds 150 C3
Glenlatterach Moray 159 D5
Glenlee Dumfries 113 F6
Glenlichorn Perth 133 C6
Glenlivet Moray 149 B7
Glenlochsie Perth 141 B7
Glenloig N Ayrs 119 C6
Glenluce Dumfries 105 D6
Glenmallan Argyll 131 F8
Glenmarksie Highld 156 D4
Glenmassan Argyll 129 B6
Glenmavis N Lnrk 121 C7
Glenmaye I o M 84 E2
Glenmidge Dumfries 113 F8
Glenmore Argyll 130 D4
Glenmore Highld 153 E5
Glenmore Lodge Highld 149 D5
Glenmoy Angus 142 C4
Glenogil Angus 142 C4
Glenprosen Lodge Angus 142 C2
Glenprosen Village Angus 142 C3
Glenquiech Angus 142 C4
Glenreasdell Mains Argyll 128 E3
Glenree N Ayrs 119 D6
Glenridding Cumb 99 C5
Glenrossal Highld 164 D1
Glenrothes Fife 134 D4
Glensanda Highld 138 E2
Glensaugh Aberds 143 B6
Glenshero Lodge Highld 147 E8
Glenstockadale Dumfries 104 C4
Glenstriven Argyll 129 C5
Glentaggart S Lnrk 113 B8
Glentham Lincs 90 E4
Glentirranmuir Stirl 133 E5
Glenton Aberds 150 B5
Glentress Borders 123 F5
Glentromie Lodge Highld 148 E3
Glentrool Village Dumfries 105 B7
Glentruan I o M 84 B4
Glentruim House Highld 148 E2
Glenturret Distillery, Crieff Perth 133 B7
Glentworth Lincs 90 F3
Glenuig Highld 145 F6
Glenurquhart Highld 157 C8
Glespin S Lnrk 113 B8
Gletness Shetland 175 H6
Glewstone Hereford 36 B2
Glinton P'boro 65 D8
Glooston Leics 64 E4
Glororum Northumb 125 F7
Glossop Derbys 87 E8
Gloster Hill Northumb 117 D8
Gloucester Glos 37 C5
Gloucester Cathedral Glos 37 C5
Gloucestershire Airport Glos 37 B5
Gloup Shetland 174 C7
Glusburn N Yorks 94 E3
Glutt Lodge Highld 168 F4
Glutton Bridge Derbys 75 C7
Glympton Oxon 38 B4
Glyn-Ceiriog Wrex 73 F6
Glyn-cywarch Gwyn 71 D7
Glyn Ebwy = Ebbw Vale Bl Gwent 35 D5
Glyn-Neath = Glynedd Neath 34 D2
Glynarthen Ceredig 46 E2
Glynbrochan Powys 59 F6
Glyncoch Rhondda 34 E4
Glyncorrwg Neath 34 E2
Glynde E Sus 17 D8
Glyndebourne E Sus 17 C8
Glyndyfrdwy Denb 72 E5
Glynedd = Glyn-Neath Neath 34 D2
Glynogwr Bridgend 34 F3
Glyntaff Rhondda 34 F4
Glyntawe Powys 34 C2
Gnosall Staffs 62 B2
Gnosall Heath Staffs 62 B2
Goadby Leics 64 E4
Goadby Marwood Leics 64 B4
Goat Lees Kent 30 E4
Goatacre Wilts 24 B5
Goathill Dorset 12 C4
Goathland N Yorks 103 D6
Goathurst Som 22 F4
Gobernuisgach Lodge Highld 167 E6
Gobhaig W Isles 173 H3
Gobowen Shrops 73 F7
Godalming Sur 27 E7
Godley Gtr Man 87 E7
Godmanchester Cambs 54 B3
Godmanstone Dorset 12 E4
Godmersham Kent 30 D4
Godney Som 23 E6
Godolphin Cross Corn 2 C5
Godre'r-graig Neath 34 D1
Godshill Hants 14 C2
Godshill I o W 15 F6
Godstone Sur 28 D4
Godstone Farm Sur 28 D4
Godwinscroft Hants 14 E2
Goetre Mon 35 D7
Goferydd Anglesey 82 C2
Goff's Oak Herts 41 D6
Gogar Edin 122 B4
Goginan Ceredig 58 F3
Golan Gwyn 71 C6
Golant Corn 5 D6
Golberdon Corn 5 B8
Golborne Gtr Man 86 E4
Golcar W Yorks 88 C2
Gold Hill Norf 66 E5
Goldcliff Newport 35 F7
Golden Cross E Sus 18 D2
Golden Green Kent 29 E7
Golden Grove Carms 33 C6
Golden Hill Hants 14 E3
Golden Pot Hants 26 E5
Golden Valley Glos 37 B6
Goldenhill Stoke 75 D5
Golders Green London 41 F5
Goldhanger Essex 43 D5
Golding Shrops 60 D5
Goldington Beds 53 D8
Goldsborough N Yorks 95 D6
Goldsborough N Yorks 103 C6
Goldsithney Corn 2 C4
Goldsworthy Devon 9 B5
Goldthorpe S Yorks 89 D5
Gollanfield Highld 158 D2
Golspie Highld 165 D5
Golval Highld 168 C3
Gomeldon Wilts 25 F6
Gomersal W Yorks 88 B3
Gomshall Sur 27 E8
Gonalston Notts 77 E6
Gonfirth Shetland 175 G5
Good Easter Essex 42 C2
Gooderstone Norf 67 D7
Goodleigh Devon 20 F5
Goodmanham E Yorks 96 E4
Goodnestone Kent 30 C4
Goodnestone Kent 31 D6
Goodrich Hereford 36 C2
Goodrington Torbay 7 D6
Goodshaw Lancs 87 B6
Goodwick = Wdig Pembs 44 B4
Goodwood Racecourse W Sus 16 C2
Goodworth Clatford Hants 25 E8
Goole E Yorks 89 B8
Goonbell Corn 3 B6
Goonhavern Corn 4 D2
Goose Eye W Yorks 94 E3
Goose Green Gtr Man 86 D3
Goose Green Norf 68 F4
Goose Green W Sus 16 C5
Gooseham Corn 8 C4
Goosey Oxon 38 E3
Goosnargh Lancs 93 F5
Goostrey Ches 74 B4
Gorcott Hill Warks 51 C5
Gord Shetland 175 L6
Gordon Borders 124 E2
Gordonbush Highld 165 D5
Gordonsburgh Moray 159 C8
Gordonstoun Moray 159 C5
Gordonstown Aberds 160 C2
Gordonstown Aberds 160 E4
Gore Kent 31 D7
Gore Cross Wilts 24 D5
Gore Pit Essex 42 C4
Gorebridge Midloth 123 C6
Gorefield Cambs 66 C4
Gorey Jersey 17
Gorgie Edin 122 B5
Goring Oxon 39 F6
Goring-by-Sea W Sus 16 D5
Goring Heath Oxon 26 B4
Gorleston-on-Sea Norf 69 D8
Gornalwood W Mid 62 E3
Gorrachie Aberds 160 C4
Gorran Churchtown Corn 3 B8
Gorran Haven Corn 3 B9
Gorrenberry Borders 115 E7
Gors Ceredig 46 B5
Gorse Hill Thamesdown 38 F1
Gorsedd Flint 73 B5
Gorseinon Swansea 33 E6
Gorseness Orkney 176 E3
Gorsgoch Ceredig 46 D3
Gorslas Carms 33 C6
Gorsley Glos 36 B3
Gorstan Highld 156 C4
Gorstanvorran Highld 138 B2
Gorsteyhill Staffs 74 D4
Gorsty Hill Staffs 62 B5
Gortantaoid Argyll 126 B3
Gorton Gtr Man 87 E6
Gosbeck Suff 57 D5
Gosberton Lincs 78 F5
Gosberton Clough Lincs 65 B8
Gosfield Essex 42 B3
Gosford Hereford 49 C7
Gosforth Cumb 98 D2
Gosforth T & W 110 C5
Gosmore Herts 40 B4
Gosport Hants 15 E7
Gossabrough Shetland 174 E7
Gossington Glos 36 D4
Goswick Northumb 125 E6
Gotham Notts 76 F5
Gotherington Glos 37 B6
Gott Shetland 175 J6
Goudhurst Kent 18 B4
Goulceby Lincs 79 B5
Gourdas Aberds 160 D4
Gourdon Aberds 143 B8
Gourock Invclyd 129 C7
Govan Glasgow 121 C5
Govanhill Glasgow 121 C5
Goveton Devon 7 E5
Govilon Mon 35 C6
Gowanhill Aberds 161 B7
Gowdall E Yorks 89 B7
Gowerton Swansea 33 E6
Gowkhall Fife 134 F2
Gowthorpe E Yorks 96 D3
Goxhill E Yorks 97 E7
Goxhill N Lincs 90 B5
Goxhill Haven N Lincs 90 B5
Goybre Neath 34 F1
Grabhair W Isles 172 G6
Graby Lincs 65 B7
Grade Corn 3 E6
Graffham W Sus 16 C3
Grafham Cambs 54 C2
Grafham Sur 27 E8
Grafton Hereford 49 F6
Grafton N Yorks 95 C7
Grafton Oxon 38 D2
Grafton Shrops 60 C4
Grafton Worcs 49 C7
Grafton Flyford Worcs 50 D4
Grafton Regis Northants 53 E5
Grafton Underwood Northants 65 F6
Grafty Green Kent 30 E2
Graianrhyd Denb 73 D6
Graig Conwy 83 D8
Graig Denb 72 B4
Graig-fechan Denb 72 D5
Grain Medway 30 B2
Grainsby Lincs 91 E6

Grainthorpe Lincs 91 E7
Grampound Corn 3 B8
Grampound Road Corn 4 D4
Gramsdal W Isles 170 E4
Granborough Bucks 39 B7
Granby Notts 77 F7
Grandborough Warks 52 C2
Grandtully Perth 141 D6
Grange Cumb 98 C4
Grange E Ayrs 120 F4
Grange Medway 29 C8
Grange Mers 85 F3
Grange Perth 134 B4
Grange Crossroads Moray 159 D8
Grange Hall Moray 158 C4
Grange Hill Essex 41 E7
Grange Moor W Yorks 88 C3
Grange of Lindores Fife 134 C4
Grange-over-Sands Cumb 92 B4
Grange Villa Durham 110 D5
Grangemill Derbys 76 D2
Grangemouth Falk 133 F8
Grangepans Falk 134 F2
Grangetown Cardiff 22 B3
Grangetown Redcar 102 B3
Granish Highld 148 C5
Gransmoor E Yorks 97 D7
Granston Pembs 44 B3
Grantchester Cambs 54 D5
Grantham Lincs 78 F2
Grantley N Yorks 94 C5
Grantlodge Aberds 151 C6
Granton Dumfries 114 D3
Granton Edin 122 B5
Grantown-on-Spey Highld 149 B6
Grantshouse Borders 124 C4
Grappenhall Warr 86 F4
Grasby Lincs 90 D4
Grasmere Cumb 99 D5
Grasscroft Gtr Man 87 D7
Grassendale Mers 85 F4
Grassholme Durham 100 B4
Grassington N Yorks 94 C3
Grassmoor Derbys 76 C4
Grassthorpe Notts 77 C7
Grateley Hants 25 E7
Gratwich Staffs 75 F7
Graveley Cambs 54 C3
Graveley Herts 41 B5
Gravelly Hill W Mid 62 E5
Gravels Shrops 60 D3
Graven Shetland 174 F6
Graveney Kent 30 C4
Gravesend Kent 29 B7
Grayingham Lincs 90 E3
Grayrigg Cumb 99 E7
Grays Thurrock 29 B7
Grayshott Hants 27 F6
Grayswood Sur 27 F7
Graythorp Hrtlpl 102 B3
Grazeley Wokingham 26 C4
Greasbrough S Yorks 88 E5
Greasby Mers 85 F3
Great Abington Cambs 55 E6
Great Addington Northants 53 B7
Great Alne Warks 51 D6
Great Altcar Lancs 85 D4
Great Amwell Herts 41 C6
Great Asby Cumb 100 C1
Great Ashfield Suff 56 C3
Great Ayton N Yorks 102 C3
Great Baddow Essex 42 D3
Great Bardfield Essex 55 F7
Great Barford Beds 54 D2
Great Barr W Mid 62 E4
Great Barrington Glos 38 C2
Great Barrow Ches 73 C8
Great Barton Suff 56 C2
Great Barugh N Yorks 96 B3
Great Bavington Northumb 117 F5
Great Bealings Suff 57 E6
Great Bedwyn Wilts 25 C7
Great Bentley Essex 43 B7
Great Billing Northants 53 C6
Great Bircham Norf 80 D3
Great Blakenham Suff 56 D5
Great Blencow Cumb 108 F4
Great Bolas Telford 61 B6
Great Bookham Sur 28 D2
Great Bourton Oxon 52 E2
Great Bowden Leics 64 F4
Great Bradley Suff 55 D7
Great Braxted Essex 42 C4
Great Bricett Suff 56 D4
Great Brickhill Bucks 53 F7
Great Bridge W Mid 62 E3
Great Bridgeford Staffs 62 B2
Great Brington Northants 52 C4
Great Bromley Essex 43 B6
Great Broughton Cumb 107 F7
Great Broughton N Yorks 102 D3
Great Budworth Ches 74 B3
Great Burdon Darl 101 C8
Great Burgh Sur 28 D3
Great Burstead Essex 42 E2
Great Busby N Yorks 102 D3
Great Canfield Essex 42 C1
Great Carlton Lincs 91 F8
Great Casterton Rutland 65 D7
Great Chart Kent 30 E3
Great Chatwell Staffs 61 C7
Great Chesterford Essex 55 E6
Great Cheverell Wilts 24 D4
Great Chishill Cambs 54 F5
Great Clacton Essex 43 C7
Great Cliff W Yorks 88 C4
Great Clifton Cumb 98 B2
Great Coates NE Lincs 91 D6
Great Comberton Worcs 50 E4
Great Corby Cumb 108 D4
Great Cornard Suff 56 E2
Great Cowden E Yorks 97 E8
Great Coxwell Oxon 38 E2
Great Crakehall N Yorks 101 E7
Great Cransley Northants 53 B6
Great Cressingham Norf 67 D8
Great Crosby Mers 85 E4
Great Cubley Derbys 75 F8
Great Dalby Leics 64 C4
Great Denham Beds 53 E8
Great Doddington Northants 53 C6
Great Dunham Norf 67 C8
Great Dunmow Essex 42 B2
Great Durnford Wilts 25 F6
Great Easton Essex 42 B2
Great Easton Leics 64 E5
Great Eccleston Lancs 92 E4
Great Edstone N Yorks 103 F5
Great Ellingham Norf 68 E3
Great Elm Som 24 E2
Great Eversden Cambs 54 D4
Great Fencote N Yorks 101 E7
Great Finborough Suff 56 D4
Great Fransham Norf 67 C8
Great Gaddesden Herts 40 C3
Great Gidding Cambs 65 F8
Great Givendale E Yorks 96 D4
Great Glemham Suff 57 C7
Great Glen Leics 64 E3
Great Gonerby Lincs 77 F8
Great Gransden Cambs 54 D3
Great Green Norf 69 F5
Great Green Suff 56 D3
Great Habton N Yorks 96 B3
Great Hale Lincs 78 E4
Great Hallingbury Essex 41 C8
Great Hampden Bucks 39 D8
Great Harrowden Northants 53 B6
Great Harwood Lancs 93 F7
Great Haseley Oxon 39 D6
Great Hatfield E Yorks 97 E7
Great Haywood Staffs 62 B4
Great Heath W Mid 63 F7
Great Heck N Yorks 89 B6
Great Henny Essex 56 F2
Great Hinton Wilts 24 D4
Great Hockham Norf 68 E2
Great Holland Essex 43 C8
Great Horkesley Essex 56 F3
Great Hormead Herts 41 B6
Great Horton W Yorks 94 F4
Great Horwood Bucks 53 F5
Great Houghton Northants 53 D5
Great Houghton S Yorks 88 D5
Great Hucklow Derbys 75 B8
Great Kelk E Yorks 97 D7
Great Kimble Bucks 39 D8
Great Kingshill Bucks 40 E1
Great Langton N Yorks 101 E7
Great Leighs Essex 42 C3
Great Lever Gtr Man 86 D5
Great Limber Lincs 90 D5
Great Linford M Keynes 53 E6
Great Livermere Suff 56 B2
Great Longstone Derbys 76 B2
Great Lumley Durham 111 E5
Great Lyth Shrops 60 D4
Great Malvern Worcs 50 E2
Great Maplestead Essex 56 F2
Great Marton Blkpool 92 F3
Great Massingham Norf 80 E3
Great Melton Norf 68 D4
Great Milton Oxon 39 D6
Great Missenden Bucks 40 D1
Great Mitton Lancs 93 F7
Great Mongeham Kent 31 D7
Great Moulton Norf 68 E4
Great Munden Herts 41 B6
Great Musgrave Cumb 100 C2
Great Ness Shrops 60 C3
Great Notley Essex 42 B3
Great Oakley Essex 43 B7
Great Oakley Northants 65 F5
Great Offley Herts 40 B4
Great Orme Tramway, Llandudno Conwy 83 C7
Great Ormside Cumb 100 C2
Great Orton Cumb 108 D3
Great Ouseburn N Yorks 95 C7
Great Oxendon Northants 64 F4
Great Oxney Green Essex 42 D2
Great Palgrave Norf 67 C8
Great Parndon Essex 41 D7
Great Paxton Cambs 54 C3
Great Plumpton Lancs 92 F3
Great Plumstead Norf 69 C6
Great Ponton Lincs 78 F2
Great Preston W Yorks 88 B5
Great Raveley Cambs 66 F2
Great Rissington Glos 38 C1
Great Rollright Oxon 51 F8
Great Ryburgh Norf 81 E5
Great Ryle Northumb 117 C6
Great Ryton Shrops 60 D4
Great Saling Essex 42 B3
Great Salkeld Cumb 109 F5
Great Sampford Essex 55 F7
Great Sankey Warr 86 F3
Great Saxham Suff 55 C8
Great Shefford W Berks 25 B8
Great Shelford Cambs 55 D5
Great Smeaton N Yorks 101 D8
Great Snoring Norf 80 D5
Great Somerford Wilts 37 F6
Great Stainton Darl 101 B8
Great Stambridge Essex 42 E4
Great Staughton Cambs 54 C2
Great Steeping Lincs 79 C7
Great Stonar Kent 31 D7
Great Strickland Cumb 99 B7
Great Stukeley Cambs 54 B3
Great Sturton Lincs 78 B5
Great Sutton Ches 73 B7
Great Sutton Shrops 60 F5
Great Swinburne Northumb 110 B2
Great Tew Oxon 38 B3
Great Tey Essex 42 B4
Great Thurkleby N Yorks 95 B7
Great Thurlow Suff 55 D7
Great Torrington Devon 9 C6
Great Tosson Northumb 117 D6
Great Totham Essex 42 C4
Great Totham Essex 42 C4
Great Tows Lincs 91 E6
Great Urswick Cumb 92 B2
Great Wakering Essex 43 F5
Great Waldingfield Suff 56 E3
Great Walsingham Norf 80 D5
Great Waltham Essex 42 C2
Great Warley Essex 42 E1
Great Washbourne Glos 50 F4
Great Weldon Northants 65 F6
Great Welnetham Suff 56 D2
Great Wenham Suff 56 F4
Great Whittington Northumb 110 B3
Great Wigborough Essex 43 C5
Great Wilbraham Cambs 55 D6
Great Wishford Wilts 25 F5
Great Witcombe Glos 37 C6
Great Witley Worcs 50 C2
Great Wolford Warks 51 F7
Great Wratting Suff 55 E7
Great Wymondley Herts 41 B5
Great Wyrley Staffs 62 D3
Great Wytheford Shrops 61 C5
Great Yarmouth Norf 69 D8
Great Yarmouth Sea Life Centre Norf 69 D8
Great Yeldham Essex 55 F8
Greater Doward Hereford 36 C2
Greatford Lincs 65 C7
Greatgate Staffs 75 E7
Greatham Hants 27 F5
Greatham Hrtlpl 102 B2
Greatham W Sus 16 C4
Greatstone on Sea Kent 19 C7
Greatworth Northants 52 E3
Greave Lancs 87 B6
Greeba I o M 84 D3
Green Denb 72 C4
Green End Beds 54 D2
Green Hammerton N Yorks 95 D7
Green Lane Powys 59 E8
Green Ore Som 23 D7
Green St Green London 29 C5
Green Street Herts 40 E4
Greenbank Shetland 174 C7
Greenburn W Loth 122 C2
Greendikes Northumb 117 B6
Greenfield Beds 53 F8
Greenfield Flint 73 B5
Greenfield Gtr Man 87 D7
Greenfield Highld 146 D5
Greenfield Oxon 39 E7
Greenford London 40 F4
Greengairs N Lnrk 121 B7
Greenham W Berks 26 C2
Greenhaugh Northumb 116 F3
Greenhead Northumb 109 C6
Greenhill Falk 121 B8
Greenhill London 40 F4
Greenhill Kent 31 C5
Greenhill Leics 63 C8
Greenhills N Ayrs 120 D3
Greenhithe Kent 29 B6
Greenholm E Ayrs 120 F5
Greenholme Cumb 99 D7
Greenhouse Borders 115 B8
Greenhow Hill N Yorks 94 C4
Greenigoe Orkney 176 F3
Greenland Highld 169 C7
Greenlands Bucks 39 F7
Greenlaw Aberds 160 C3
Greenlaw Borders 124 E3
Greenlea Dumfries 107 B7
Greenloaning Perth 133 D7
Greenmeadow Community Farm, Pontnewydd Torf 35 E6
Greenmount Gtr Man 87 C5
Greenmow Shetland 175 L6
Greenock Invclyd 129 C7
Greenock West Invclyd 129 C7
Greenodd Cumb 99 F5
Greenrow Cumb 107 D8
Greens Norton Northants 52 E4
Greenside T & W 110 C4
Greensidehill Northumb 117 C5
Greenstead Green Essex 42 B4
Greensted Essex 41 D8
Greensted Church, Chipping Ongar Essex 41 D8
Greenwich London 28 B4
Greet Glos 50 F5
Greete Shrops 49 B7
Greetham Lincs 79 B6
Greetham Rutland 65 C6
Greetland W Yorks 87 B8
Gregg Hall Cumb 99 E6
Gregson Lane Lancs 86 B3
Greinetobht W Isles 170 C4
Greinton Som 23 F6
Gremista Shetland 175 J6
Grenaby I o M 84 E2
Grendon Northants 53 C6
Grendon Warks 63 D6
Grendon Common Warks 63 E6
Grendon Green Hereford 49 D7
Grendon Underwood Bucks 39 B6
Grenofen Devon 6 B2
Grenoside S Yorks 88 E4
Greosabhagh W Isles 173 J4
Gresford Wrex 73 D7
Gresham Norf 81 D7
Greshornish Highld 152 D4
Gressenhall Norf 68 C2
Gressingham Lancs 93 C5
Gresty Green Ches 74 D4
Greta Bridge Durham 101 C5
Gretna Dumfries 108 C3
Gretna Green Dumfries 108 C3
Gretton Glos 50 F5
Gretton Northants 65 E5
Gretton Shrops 60 E5
Grewelthorpe N Yorks 94 B5
Grey Green N Lincs 89 D8
Greygarth N Yorks 94 B4
Greynor Carms 33 D6
Greysouthen Cumb 98 B2
Greystoke Cumb 108 F4
Greystone Angus 143 E5
Greystone Dumfries 107 B6
Greywell Hants 26 D5
Griais W Isles 172 D7
Grianan W Isles 172 E7
Gribthorpe E Yorks 96 F3
Gridley Corner Devon 9 E5
Griff Warks 63 F7
Griffithstown Torf 35 E6
Grimbister Orkney 176 E2
Grimblethorpe Lincs 91 F6
Grimeford Village Lancs 86 C4
Grimethorpe S Yorks 88 D5
Griminis W Isles 170 E3
Grimister Shetland 174 D6
Grimley Worcs 50 C3
Grimness Orkney 176 G3
Grimoldby Lincs 91 F7
Grimpo Shrops 60 B3
Grimsargh Lancs 93 F5
Grimsbury Oxon 52 E2
Grimsby NE Lincs 91 C6
Grimscote Northants 52 D4
Grimscott Corn 8 D4
Grimsthorpe Lincs 65 B7
Grimston E Yorks 97 F8
Grimston Leics 64 B3
Grimston Norf 80 E3
Grimston York 96 D2
Grimstone Dorset 12 E4
Grinacombe Moor Devon 9 E6
Grindale E Yorks 97 B7
Grindigar Orkney 176 F4
Grindiscol Shetland 175 K6
Grindle Shrops 61 D7
Grindleford Derbys 76 B2
Grindleton Lancs 93 E7
Grindley Staffs 62 B4
Grindley Brook Shrops 74 E2
Grindlow Derbys 75 B8
Grindon Northumb 124 E5
Grindon Staffs 75 D7
Grindonmoor Gate Staffs 75 D7
Gringley on the Hill Notts 89 E8
Grinsdale Cumb 108 D3
Grinshill Shrops 60 B5
Grinton N Yorks 101 E5
Griomsidar W Isles 172 F6
Grishipoll Argyll 136 C2
Grisling Common E Sus 17 B8
Gristhorpe N Yorks 103 F8
Griston Norf 68 E2
Gritley Orkney 176 F4
Grittenham Wilts 37 F7
Grittleton Wilts 37 F5
Grizebeck Cumb 98 F4
Grizedale Cumb 99 E5
Grobister Orkney 176 D5
Groby Leics 64 D2
Groes Conwy 72 C4
Groes Neath 34 F1
Groes-faen Rhondda 34 F4
Groes-lwyd Powys 60 C2
Groesffordd Marli Denb 72 B4
Groeslon Gwyn 82 E5
Groeslon Gwyn 82 F4
Grogport Argyll 118 B5
Gromford Suff 57 D7
Gronant Flint 72 A4
Groombridge E Sus 18 B2
Grosmont Mon 35 B8
Grosmont N Yorks 103 D6
Grosvenor Museum, Chester Ches 73 C8
Groton Suff 56 E3
Groudle Glen Railway I o M 84 E4
Grougfoot Falk 122 B3
Grouville Jersey 17
Grove Dorset 12 G5
Grove Kent 31 C6
Grove Notts 77 B7
Grove Oxon 38 E4
Grove Park London 28 B5
Grove Vale W Mid 62 E4
Grovesend Swansea 33 D6
Grudie Highld 156 C4
Gruids Highld 164 D2
Gruinard House Highld 162 E3
Grula Highld 153 G4
Gruline Argyll 137 D6
Grunasound Shetland 175 K5
Grundisburgh Suff 57 D6
Grunsagill Lancs 93 D7
Gruting Shetland 175 J4
Grutness Shetland 175 N6
Gualachulain Highld 139 E5
Gualin Ho. Highld 166 D5
Guardbridge Fife 135 C6
Guarlford Worcs 50 E3
Guay Perth 141 E7
Guernsey Airport Guern 16
Guestling Green E Sus 19 D5
Guestling Thorn E Sus 18 D5
Guestwick Norf 81 E6
Guestwick Green Norf 81 E6
Guide Blkburn 86 B5
Guide Post Northumb 117 F8
Guilden Morden Cambs 54 E3
Guilden Sutton Ches 73 C8
Guildford Sur 27 E7
Guildtown Perth 141 F8
Guilsborough Northants 52 B4
Guilsfield Powys 60 C2
Guilton Kent 31 D6
Guineaford Devon 20 F4
Guisborough Redcar 102 C4
Guiseley W Yorks 94 E4
Guist Norf 81 E5
Guith Orkney 176 C4
Guiting Power Glos 37 B7
Gulberwick Shetland 175 K6
Gullane E Loth 135 F6
Gulval Corn 2 C3
Gulworthy Devon 6 B2
Gumfreston Pembs 32 D2
Gumley Leics 64 E3
Gummow's Shop Corn 4 D3
Gun Hill E Sus 18 D2
Gunby E Yorks 96 F3
Gunby Lincs 65 B6
Gundleton Hants 26 F4
Gunn Devon 20 F5
Gunnerside N Yorks 100 E4
Gunnerton Northumb 110 B2
Gunness N Lincs 90 C2
Gunnislake Corn 6 B2
Gunnista Shetland 175 J7
Gunthorpe Norf 81 D6
Gunthorpe Notts 77 E6
Gunthorpe P'boro 65 D8
Gunville I o W 15 F5
Gunwalloe Corn 3 D5
Gurnard I o W 15 E5
Gurnett Ches 75 B6
Gurney Slade Som 23 E8
Gurnos Powys 34 D1
Gussage All Saints Dorset 13 C8
Gussage St Michael Dorset 13 C7
Guston Kent 31 E7
Gutcher Shetland 174 D7
Guthrie Angus 143 D5
Guyhirn Cambs 66 D3
Guyhirn Gull Cambs 66 D3
Guy's Head Lincs 66 B4
Guy's Marsh Dorset 13 B6
Guyzance Northumb 117 D8
Gwaenysgor Flint 72 A4
Gwalchmai Anglesey 82 D3
Gwaun-Cae-Gurwen Neath 33 C8
Gwaun-Leision Neath 33 C8
Gwbert Ceredig 45 E3
Gweek Corn 3 D6
Gwehelog Mon 35 D7
Gwenddwr Powys 48 E2
Gwennap Corn 3 C6
Gwenter Corn 3 E6
Gwernaffield Flint 73 C6
Gwernesney Mon 35 D8
Gwernogle Carms 46 F4
Gwernymynydd Flint 73 C6
Gwersyllt Wrex 73 D7
Gwespyr Flint 85 F2
Gwithian Corn 2 B4
Gwredog Anglesey 82 C4
Gwyddelwern Denb 72 E4
Gwyddgrug Carms 46 F3
Gwydyr Uchaf Conwy 83 E7
Gwynfryn Wrex 73 D6
Gwystre Powys 48 C2
Gwytherin Conwy 83 E8
Gyfelia Wrex 73 E7
Gyffin Conwy 83 D7
Gyre Orkney 176 F2
Gyrn-goch Gwyn 70 C5

H

Habberley Shrops 60 D3
Habergham Lancs 93 F8
Habrough NE Lincs 90 C5
Haceby Lincs 78 F3
Hacheston Suff 57 D7
Hackbridge London 28 C3
Hackenthorpe S Yorks 88 F5
Hackford Norf 68 D3
Hackforth N Yorks 101 E7
Hackland Orkney 176 D2
Hackleton Northants 53 D6
Hackness N Yorks 103 E7
Hackness Orkney 176 G2
Hackney London 41 F6
Hackthorn Lincs 90 F3
Hackthorpe Cumb 99 B7
Haconby Lincs 65 B8
Hacton London 41 F8
Hadden Borders 124 F3
Haddenham Bucks 39 D7
Haddenham Cambs 55 B5
Haddington E Loth 123 B8
Haddington Lincs 78 C2
Haddiscoe Norf 69 E7
Haddon Cambs 65 E8
Haddon Ches 75 C6
Haddon Hall Derbys 76 C2
Hade Edge W Yorks 88 D2
Hademore Staffs 63 D5
Hadfield Derbys 87 E8
Hadham Cross Herts 41 C7
Hadham Ford Herts 41 B7
Hadleigh Essex 42 F4
Hadleigh Suff 56 E4
Hadley Telford 61 C6
Hadley End Staffs 62 B5
Hadlow Kent 29 E7
Hadlow Down E Sus 18 C2
Hadnall Shrops 60 C5
Hadstock Essex 55 E6
Hady Derbys 76 B3
Hadzor Worcs 50 C4
Haffenden Quarter Kent 30 E2
Hafod-Dinbych Conwy 83 F8
Hafod-Iom Conwy 83 D8
Haggate Lancs 93 F8
Haggbeck Cumb 108 B4
Haggerston Northumb 125 E6
Haggrister Shetland 174 F5
Hagley Hereford 49 E7
Hagley Worcs 62 F3
Hagworthingham Lincs 79 C6
Haigh Gtr Man 86 D4
Haigh S Yorks 88 C3
Haigh Moor W Yorks 88 B3
Haighton Green Lancs 93 F5
Hail Weston Cambs 54 C2
Haile Cumb 98 D2
Hailes Glos 50 F5
Hailey Herts 41 C6
Hailey Oxon 38 C3
Hailsham E Sus 18 E2
Haimer Highld 169 C6
Hainault London 41 E7
Hainford Norf 68 C5
Hainton Lincs 91 F5
Hairmyres S Lnrk 121 D6
Haisthorpe E Yorks 97 C7
Hakin Pembs 44 E3
Halam Notts 77 D6
Halbeath Fife 134 F3
Halberton Devon 10 C5
Halcro Highld 169 C7
Hale Gtr Man 87 F5
Hale Halton 86 F2
Hale Hants 14 C2
Hale Bank Halton 86 F2
Hale Street Kent 29 E7
Halebarns Gtr Man 87 F5
Hales Norf 69 E6
Hales Staffs 74 F4
Hales Place Kent 30 D5
Halesfield Telford 61 D7
Halesgate Lincs 66 B3
Halesowen W Mid 62 F3
Halesworth Suff 57 B7
Halewood Mers 86 F2
Halford Shrops 60 F4
Halford Warks 51 E7
Halfpenny Furze Carms 32 C3
Halfpenny Green Staffs 62 E2
Halfway Carms 46 F5
Halfway Carms 47 F7
Halfway W Berks 26 C2
Halfway Bridge W Sus 16 B3
Halfway House Shrops 60 C3
Halfway Houses Kent 30 B3
Halifax W Yorks 87 B8
Halket E Ayrs 120 D4
Halkirk Highld 169 D6
Halkyn Flint 73 B6
Hall Dunnerdale Cumb 98 E4
Hall Green W Mid 62 F5
Hall Green W Yorks 88 C4
Hall Grove Herts 41 C5
Hall of Tankerness Orkney 176 F4
Hall of the Forest Shrops 60 F2
Halland E Sus 18 D2
Hallaton Leics 64 E4
Hallatrow Bath 23 D8
Hallbankgate Cumb 109 D5
Hallen S Glos 36 F2
Halliburton Borders 124 E2
Hallin Highld 152 D3
Halling Medway 29 C8
Hallington Lincs 91 F7
Hallington Northumb 110 B2
Halliwell Gtr Man 86 C5
Halloughton Notts 77 D6
Hallow Worcs 50 D3
Hallrule Borders 115 C8
Halls E Loth 124 B2
Hall's Green Herts 41 B5
Hallsands Devon 7 F6
Hallthwaites Cumb 98 F3
Hallworthy Corn 8 F3
Hallyburton House Perth 142 F2
Hallyne Borders 122 E4
Halmer End Staffs 74 E4
Halmore Glos 36 D3
Halmyre Mains Borders 122 E4
Halnaker W Sus 16 D3
Halsall Lancs 85 C4
Halse Northants 52 E3
Halse Som 11 B6
Halsetown Corn 2 C4
Halsham E Yorks 91 B6
Halsinger Devon 20 F4
Halstead Essex 56 F2
Halstead Kent 29 C5
Halstead Leics 64 D4
Halstock Dorset 12 D3
Haltham Lincs 78 C5
Haltoft End Lincs 79 E6
Halton Bucks 40 C1
Halton Halton 86 F3
Halton Lancs 92 C5
Halton Northumb 110 C2
Halton Wrex 73 F7
Halton W Yorks 95 F6
Halton East N Yorks 94 D3
Halton Gill N Yorks 93 B8
Halton Holegate Lincs 79 C7
Halton Lea Gate Northumb 109 D6
Halton West N Yorks 93 D8
Haltwhistle Northumb 109 C7
Halvergate Norf 69 D7
Halwell Devon 7 D5
Halwill Devon 9 E6
Halwill Junction Devon 9 D6
Ham Devon 11 D7
Ham Glos 36 E3
Ham London 28 B2
Ham Highld 169 B7
Ham Kent 31 D7
Ham Shetland 175 K1
Ham Wilts 25 C8
Ham Common Dorset 13 B6
Ham Green Hereford 50 E2
Ham Green Kent 19 C5
Ham Green Kent 30 C2
Ham Green N Som 23 B7
Ham Green Worcs 50 C5
Ham Street Som 23 F7
Hamble-le-Rice Hants 15 D5
Hambleden Bucks 39 F7
Hambledon Hants 15 C7
Hambledon Sur 27 F7
Hambleton Lancs 92 E3
Hambleton N Yorks 95 F8
Hambridge Som 11 B8
Hambrook S Glos 23 B8
Hambrook W Sus 15 D8
Hameringham Lincs 79 C6
Hamerton Cambs 54 B2
Hametoun Shetland 175 K1
Hamilton S Lnrk 121 D7
Hamilton Park Racecourse S Lnrk 121 D7
Hammer W Sus 27 F6
Hammerpot W Sus 16 D4
Hammersmith London 28 B3
Hammerwich Staffs 62 D4
Hammerwood E Sus 28 F5
Hammond Street Herts 41 D6
Hammoon Dorset 13 C6
Hamnavoe Shetland 174 E4
Hamnavoe Shetland 175 K5
Hamnavoe Shetland 174 E6
Hamnavoe Shetland 174 F6
Hampden National Stadium Glasgow 121 C5
Hampden Park E Sus 18 E3
Hamperden End Essex 55 F6
Hampnett Glos 37 C7
Hampole S Yorks 89 C6
Hampreston Dorset 13 E8
Hampstead London 41 F5
Hampstead Norreys W Berks 26 B3
Hampsthwaite N Yorks 95 D5
Hampton London 28 C2
Hampton Shrops 61 F7
Hampton Worcs 50 E5
Hampton Bishop Hereford 49 F7
Hampton Court Palace, Teddington London 28 C2
Hampton Heath Ches 73 E8
Hampton in Arden W Mid 63 F6
Hampton Loade Shrops 61 F7
Hampton Lovett Worcs 50 C3
Hampton Lucy Warks 51 D7
Hampton on the Hill Warks 51 C7
Hampton Poyle Oxon 39 C5
Hamrow Norf 80 E5
Hamsey E Sus 17 C8
Hamsey Green Sur 28 D4
Hamstall Ridware Staffs 62 C5
Hamstead I o W 14 E5
Hamstead W Mid 62 E4
Hamstead Marshall W Berks 26 C2
Hamsterley Durham 110 F4
Hamsterley Durham 110 D4
Hamstreet Kent 19 B7
Hamworthy Poole 13 E7
Hanbury Staffs 63 B5
Hanbury Worcs 50 C4
Hanbury Woodend Staffs 63 B5
Hanby Lincs 78 F3
Hanchurch Staffs 74 E5
Handbridge Ches 73 C8
Handcross W Sus 17 B6
Handforth Ches 87 F6
Handley Ches 73 D8
Handsacre Staffs 62 C4
Handsworth S Yorks 88 F5
Handsworth W Mid 62 E4
Handy Cross Devon 9 B6
Hanford Stoke 75 E5
Hanging Langford Wilts 24 F5
Hangleton W Sus 16 D4
Hanham S Glos 23 B8
Hankelow Ches 74 E3
Hankerton Wilts 37 E6
Hankham E Sus 18 E3
Hanley Stoke 75 E5
Hanley Castle Worcs 50 E3
Hanley Child Worcs 49 C8
Hanley Swan Worcs 50 E3
Hanley William Worcs 49 C8
Hanlith N Yorks 94 C2
Hanmer Wrex 73 F8
Hannah Lincs 79 B8
Hannington Hants 26 D3
Hannington Northants 53 B6
Hannington Thamesdown 38 E1
Hannington Wick Thamesdown 38 E1
Hansel Village S Ayrs 120 F3
Hanslope M Keynes 53 E6
Hanthorpe Lincs 65 B7
Hanwell London 40 F4
Hanwell Oxon 52 E2
Hanwood Shrops 60 D4
Hanworth London 28 B2
Hanworth Norf 81 D7
Happendon S Lnrk 121 F8
Happisburgh Norf 69 A6
Happisburgh Common Norf 69 B6
Hapsford Ches 73 B8
Hapton Lancs 93 F7
Hapton Norf 68 E4
Harberton Devon 7 D5
Harbertonford Devon 7 D5
Harbledown Kent 30 D5
Harborne W Mid 62 F4
Harborough Magna Warks 52 B2
Harbottle Northumb 117 D5
Harbour Park, Littlehampton W Sus 16 D4
Harbury Warks 51 D8
Harby Leics 77 F7
Harby Notts 77 B8
Harcombe Devon 11 E6
Harden W Mid 62 D4
Harden W Yorks 94 F3
Hardenhuish Wilts 24 B4
Hardgate Aberds 151 D6
Hardham W Sus 16 C4
Hardingham Norf 68 D3
Hardingstone Northants 53 D5
Hardington Som 24 D2
Hardington Mandeville Som 12 C3
Hardington Marsh Som 12 D3
Hardley Hants 14 D5
Hardley Street Norf 69 D6
Hardmead M Keynes 53 E7
Hardrow N Yorks 100 E3
Hardstoft Derbys 76 C4
Hardway Hants 15 D7
Hardway Som 24 F2
Hardwick Bucks 39 C8
Hardwick Cambs 54 D4
Hardwick Norf 67 C6
Hardwick Norf 68 F5
Hardwick Notts 77 B6
Hardwick Northants 53 C6
Hardwick Oxon 38 D3
Hardwick Oxon 39 B5
Hardwick W Mid 62 E4
Hardwick Hall Derbys 76 C4
Hardwicke Glos 36 C4
Hardwicke Glos 37 B6
Hardwicke Hereford 48 E4
Hardy's Green Essex 43 B5
Hare Green Essex 43 B6
Hare Hatch Wokingham 27 B6
Hare Street Herts 41 B6
Hareby Lincs 79 C6
Hareden Lancs 93 D6
Harefield London 40 E3
Harehills W Yorks 95 F6
Harehope Northumb 117 B6
Haresceugh Cumb 109 E6
Harescombe Glos 37 C5
Haresfield Glos 37 C5
Hareshaw N Lnrk 121 C8
Hareshaw Head Northumb 116 F4
Harewood W Yorks 95 E6
Harewood End Hereford 36 B2
Harewood House, Wetherby W Yorks 95 E6
Harford Carms 46 E5
Harford Devon 6 D4
Hargate Norf 68 E4
Hargatewall Derbys 75 B8
Hargrave Ches 73 C8
Hargrave Northants 53 B8
Hargrave Suff 55 D8
Harker Cumb 108 C3

Harkland Shetland 174 E6
Harkstead Suff 57 F5
Harlaston Staffs 63 C6
Harlaw Ho. Aberds 151 B6
Harlaxton Lincs 77 F8
Harle Syke Lancs 93 F8
Harlech Gwyn 71 D6
Harlech Castle Gwyn 71 D6
Harlequin Notts 77 F6
Harlescott Shrops 60 C5
Harlesden London 41 F5
Harleston Devon 7 E5
Harleston Norf 68 F5
Harleston Suff 56 D4
Harlestone Northants 52 C5
Harley Shrops 61 D5
Harley S Yorks 88 E4
Harleyholm S Lnrk 122 F2
Harlington Beds 53 F8
Harlington London 27 B8
Harlington S Yorks 89 D5
Harlosh Highld 153 E3
Harlow Essex 41 C7
Harlow Carr RHS Garden, Harrogate N Yorks 95 D5
Harlow Hill Northumb 110 C3
Harlow Hill N Yorks 95 D5
Harlthorpe E Yorks 96 F3
Harlton Cambs 54 D4
Harman's Cross Dorset 13 F7
Harmby N Yorks 101 F6
Harmer Green Herts 41 C5
Harmer Hill Shrops 60 B4
Harmondsworth London 27 B8
Harmston Lincs 78 C2
Harnham Northumb 110 B3
Harnhill Glos 37 D7
Harold Hill London 41 E8
Harold Wood London 41 E8
Haroldston West Pembs 44 D3
Haroldswick Shetland 174 B8
Harome N Yorks 102 F4
Harpenden Herts 40 C4
Harpford Devon 11 E5
Harpham E Yorks 97 C6
Harpley Norf 80 E3
Harpley Worcs 49 C8
Harpole Northants 52 C4
Harpsdale Highld 169 D6
Harpsden Oxon 39 F7
Harpswell Lincs 90 F3
Harpur Hill Derbys 75 B7
Harpurhey Gtr Man 87 D6
Harraby Cumb 108 D4
Harrapool Highld 155 H2
Harrier Shetland 175 J1
Harrietfield Perth 133 B8
Harrietsham Kent 30 D2
Harrington Cumb 98 B1
Harrington Lincs 79 B6
Harrington Northants 64 F4
Harringworth Northants 65 E6
Harris Highld 144 D3
Harris Museum, Preston Lancs 86 B3
Harrogate N Yorks 95 D6
Harrold Beds 53 D7
Harrow London 40 F4
Harrow on the Hill London 40 F4
Harrow Street Suff 56 F3
Harrow Weald London 40 E4
Harrowbarrow Corn 5 C8
Harrowden Beds 53 E8
Harrowgate Hill Darl 101 C7
Harston Cambs 54 D5
Harston Leics 77 F8
Harswell E Yorks 96 E4
Hart Hrtlpl 111 F7
Hart Common Gtr Man 86 D4
Hart Hill Luton 40 B4
Hart Station Hrtlpl 111 F7
Hartburn Northumb 117 F6
Hartburn Stockton 102 C2
Hartest Suff 56 D2
Hartfield E Sus 29 F5
Hartford Cambs 54 B3
Hartford Ches 74 B3
Hartford End Essex 42 C2
Hartfordbridge Hants 27 D5
Hartforth N Yorks 101 D6
Harthill Ches 74 D2
Harthill N Lnrk 122 C2
Harthill S Yorks 89 F5
Hartington Derbys 75 C8
Hartland Devon 8 B4
Hartlebury Worcs 50 B3
Hartlepool Hrtlpl 111 F8
Hartlepool's Maritime Experience Hrtlpl 111 F8
Hartley Cumb 100 D2
Hartley Kent 29 C7
Hartley Kent 18 B4
Hartley Northumb 111 B6
Hartley Westpall Hants 26 D4
Hartley Wintney Hants 27 D5
Hartlip Kent 30 C2
Hartoft End N Yorks 103 E5
Harton N Yorks 96 C3
Harton Shrops 60 F4
Harton T & W 111 C6
Hartpury Glos 36 B4
Hartshead W Yorks 88 B2
Hartshill Warks 63 E7
Hartshorne Derbys 63 B7
Hartsop Cumb 99 C6
Hartwell Northants 53 D5
Hartwood N Lnrk 121 D8
Harvieston Stirl 132 F4
Harvington Worcs 51 E5
Harvington Cross Worcs 51 E5
Harwell Oxon 38 F4
Harwich Essex 57 F6
Harwood Durham 109 F8
Harwood Gtr Man 86 C5
Harwood Dale N Yorks 103 E7
Harworth Notts 89 E7
Hasbury W Mid 62 F3
Hascombe Sur 27 E7
Haselbech Northants 52 B5
Haselbury Plucknett Som 12 C2
Haseley Warks 51 C7
Haselor Warks 51 D6
Hasfield Glos 37 B5
Hasguard Pembs 44 E3
Haskayne Lancs 85 D4
Hasketon Suff 57 D6
Hasland Derbys 76 C3
Haslemere Sur 27 F7
Haslingden Lancs 87 B5
Haslingfield Cambs 54 D5
Haslington Ches 74 D4
Hassall Ches 74 D4
Hassall Green Ches 74 D4
Hassell Street Kent 30 E4
Hassendean Borders 115 B8
Hassingham Norf 69 D6
Hassocks W Sus 17 C6
Hassop Derbys 76 B2
Hastigrow Highld 169 C7
Hastingleigh Kent 30 E4
Hastings E Sus 18 E5
Hastings Castle E Sus 18 D5
Hastings Sea Life Centre E Sus 18 E5
Hastingwood Essex 41 D7
Hastoe Herts 40 D2
Haswell Durham 111 E6
Haswell Plough Durham 111 E6
Hatch Beds 54 E2
Hatch Hants 26 D4
Hatch Wilts 13 B7
Hatch Beauchamp Som 11 B8
Hatch End London 40 E4
Hatch Green Som 11 C8
Hatchet Gate Hants 14 D4
Hatching Green Herts 40 C4
Hatchmere Ches 74 B2
Hatcliffe NE Lincs 91 D6
Hatfield Hereford 49 D7
Hatfield Herts 41 D5
Hatfield S Yorks 89 D7
Hatfield Worcs 50 D3
Hatfield Broad Oak Essex 41 C8
Hatfield Garden Village Herts 41 D5
Hatfield Heath Essex 41 C8
Hatfield House Herts 41 D5
Hatfield Hyde Herts 41 C5
Hatfield Peverel Essex 42 C3
Hatfield Woodhouse S Yorks 89 D7
Hatford Oxon 38 E3
Hatherden Hants 25 D8
Hatherleigh Devon 9 D7
Hathern Leics 63 B8
Hatherop Glos 38 D1
Hathersage Derbys 88 F3
Hathershaw Gtr Man 87 D7
Hatherton Ches 74 E3
Hatherton Staffs 62 C3
Hatley St George Cambs 54 D3
Hatt Corn 5 C8
Hattingley Hants 26 F4
Hatton Aberds 161 E7
Hatton Derbys 63 B6
Hatton Lincs 78 B4
Hatton Shrops 60 E4
Hatton Warks 51 C7
Hatton Warr 86 F3
Hatton Castle Aberds 160 D4
Hatton Country World Warks 51 C7
Hatton Heath Ches 73 C8
Hatton of Fintray Aberds 151 C7
Hattoncrook Aberds 151 B7
Haugh E Ayrs 112 B4
Haugh Gtr Man 87 C7
Haugh Lincs 79 B7
Haugh Head Northumb 117 B6
Haugh of Glass Moray 159 F8
Haugh of Urr Dumfries 106 C5
Haugham Lincs 91 F7
Haughley Suff 56 C4
Haughley Green Suff 56 C4
Haughs of Clinterty Aberdeen 151 C7
Haughton Notts 77 B6
Haughton Shrops 61 E6
Haughton Shrops 60 B3
Haughton Shrops 61 C5
Haughton Shrops 61 D7
Haughton Staffs 62 B2
Haughton Castle Northumb 110 B2
Haughton Green Gtr Man 87 E7
Haughton Le Skerne Darl 101 C8
Haughton Moss Ches 74 D2
Haultwick Herts 41 B6
Haunn Argyll 136 D4
Haunn W Isles 171 J3
Haunton Staffs 63 C6
Hauxley Northumb 117 D8
Hauxton Cambs 54 D5
Havant Hants 15 D8
Haven Hereford 49 D6
Haven Bank Lincs 78 D5
Haven Side E Yorks 91 B5
Havenstreet I o W 15 E6
Havercroft W Yorks 88 C4
Haverfordwest = Hwlffordd Pembs 44 D4
Haverhill Suff 55 E7
Haverigg Cumb 92 B1
Havering-atte-Bower London 41 E8
Haveringland Norf 81 E7
Haversham M Keynes 53 E6
Haverthwaite Cumb 99 F5
Haverton Hill Stockton 102 B2
Hawarden = Penarlâg Flint 73 C7
Hawcoat Cumb 92 B2
Hawen Ceredig 46 E2
Hawes N Yorks 100 F3
Hawes Side Blkpool 92 F3
Hawes'Green Norf 68 E5
Hawford Worcs 50 C3
Hawick Borders 115 C8
Hawk Green Gtr Man 87 F7
Hawkchurch Devon 11 D8
Hawkedon Suff 55 D8
Hawkenbury Kent 30 E2
Hawkenbury Kent 18 B2
Hawkeridge Wilts 24 D3
Hawkerland Devon 11 F5
Hawkes End W Mid 63 F7
Hawkesbury S Glos 36 F4
Hawkesbury Warks 63 F7
Hawkesbury Upton S Glos 36 F4
Hawkhill Northumb 117 C8
Hawkhurst Kent 18 B4
Hawkinge Kent 31 F6
Hawkley Hants 15 B8
Hawkridge Som 21 F7
Hawkshead Cumb 99 E5
Hawkshead Hill Cumb 99 E5
Hawksland S Lnrk 121 F8
Hawkswick N Yorks 94 B2
Hawksworth Notts 77 E7
Hawksworth W Yorks 94 E4
Hawksworth W Yorks 95 F5
Hawkwell Essex 42 E4
Hawley Hants 27 D6
Hawley Kent 29 B6
Hawling Glos 37 B7
Hawnby N Yorks 102 F3
Haworth W Yorks 94 F3
Hawstead Suff 56 D2
Hawthorn Durham 111 E7
Hawthorn Rhondda 35 F5
Hawthorn Wilts 24 C3
Hawthorn Hill Brack 27 B6
Hawthorn Hill Lincs 78 D5
Hawthorpe Lincs 65 B7
Hawton Notts 77 D7
Haxby York 96 D2
Haxey N Lincs 89 D8
Hay Green Norf 66 C5
Hay-on-Wye = Y Gelli Gandryll Powys 48 E4
Hay Street Herts 41 B6
Haydock Mers 86 E3
Haydock Park Racecourse Mers 86 E3
Haydon Dorset 12 C4
Haydon Bridge Northumb 109 C8
Haydon Wick Thamesdown 37 F8
Haye Corn 5 C8
Hayes London 28 C5
Hayes London 40 F4
Hayfield Derbys 87 F8
Hayfield Fife 134 E4
Hayhill E Ayrs 112 C4
Hayhillock Angus 143 E5
Hayle Corn 2 C4
Haynes Beds 53 E8
Haynes Church End Beds 53 E8
Hayscastle Pembs 44 C3
Hayscastle Cross Pembs 44 C4
Hayshead Angus 143 E6
Hayton Aberdeen 151 D8
Hayton Cumb 107 E8
Hayton Cumb 108 D5
Hayton E Yorks 96 E4
Hayton Notts 89 F8
Hayton's Bent Shrops 60 F5
Haytor Vale Devon 7 B5
Haywards Heath W Sus 17 B7
Haywood S Yorks 89 C6
Haywood Oaks Notts 77 D6
Hazel Grove Gtr Man 87 F7
Hazel Street Kent 18 B3
Hazelbank S Lnrk 121 E8
Hazelbury Bryan Dorset 12 D5
Hazeley Hants 26 D5
Hazelhurst Gtr Man 87 D7
Hazelslade Staffs 62 C4
Hazelton Glos 37 C7
Hazelton Walls Fife 134 B5
Hazelwood Derbys 76 E3
Hazlemere Bucks 40 E1
Hazlerigg T & W 110 B5
Hazlewood N Yorks 94 D3
Hazon Northumb 117 D7
Heacham Norf 80 D2
Head of Muir Falk 133 F7
Headbourne Worthy Hants 26 F2
Headbrook Hereford 48 D5
Headcorn Kent 30 E2
Headingley W Yorks 95 F5
Headington Oxon 39 D5
Headlam Durham 101 C6
Headless Cross Worcs 50 C5
Headley Hants 26 C3
Headley Hants 27 F6
Headley Sur 28 D3
Headon Notts 77 B7
Heads S Lnrk 121 E7
Heads Nook Cumb 108 D4
Heage Derbys 76 D3
Healaugh N Yorks 95 E7
Healaugh N Yorks 101 E5
Heald Green Gtr Man 87 F6
Heale Devon 20 E5
Heale Som 23 E8
Healey Gtr Man 87 C6
Healey Northumb 110 D3
Healey N Yorks 101 F6
Healing NE Lincs 91 C6
Heamoor Corn 2 C3
Heanish Argyll 136 F2
Heanor Derbys 76 E4
Heanton Punchardon Devon 20 F4
Heapham Lincs 90 F2
Heart of the National Forest Leics 63 C7
Hearthstane Borders 114 B4
Heasley Mill Devon 21 F6
Heast Highld 145 B6
Heath Cardiff 22 B3
Heath Derbys 76 C4
Heath and Reach Beds 40 B2
Heath End Hants 26 C3
Heath End Sur 27 E6
Heath End Warks 51 C7
Heath Hayes Staffs 62 C4
Heath Hill Shrops 61 C7
Heath House Som 23 E6
Heath Town W Mid 62 E3
Heathcote Derbys 75 C8
Heather Leics 63 C7
Heatherfield Highld 153 E5
Heathfield Devon 7 B6
Heathfield E Sus 18 C2
Heathfield Som 11 B6
Heathhall Dumfries 107 B6
Heathstock Devon 11 D7
Heathton Shrops 62 E2
Heatley Warr 86 F5
Heaton Lancs 92 C4
Heaton Staffs 75 C6
Heaton T & W 111 C5
Heaton W Yorks 94 F4
Heaton Moor Gtr Man 87 E6
Heaverham Kent 29 D6
Heaviley Gtr Man 87 F7
Heavitree Devon 10 E4
Hebburn T & W 111 C6
Hebden N Yorks 94 C3
Hebden Bridge W Yorks 87 B7
Hebron Anglesey 82 C4
Hebron Carms 32 B2
Hebron Northumb 117 F7
Heck Dumfries 114 F3
Heckfield Hants 26 C5
Heckfield Green Suff 57 B5
Heckfordbridge Essex 43 B5
Heckington Lincs 78 E4
Heckmondwike W Yorks 88 B3
Heddington Wilts 24 C4
Heddle Orkney 176 E2
Heddon-on-the-Wall Northumb 110 C4
Hedenham Norf 69 E6
Hedge End Hants 15 C5
Hedgerley Bucks 40 F2
Hedging Som 11 B8
Hedley on the Hill Northumb 110 D3
Hednesford Staffs 62 C4
Hedon E Yorks 91 B5
Hedsor Bucks 40 F2
Hedworth T & W 111 C6
Heeley City Farm, Sheffield S Yorks 88 F4
Hegdon Hill Hereford 49 D7
Heggerscales Cumb 100 C3
Heglibister Shetland 175 H5
Heighington Darl 101 B7
Heighington Lincs 78 C3
Heights of Brae Highld 157 C6
Heights of Kinlochewe Highld 154 D6
Heilam Highld 167 C6
Heiton Borders 124 F3
Hele Devon 20 E4
Hele Devon 10 D4
Helensburgh Argyll 129 B7
Helford Corn 3 D6
Helford Passage Corn 3 D6
Helhoughton Norf 80 E4
Helions Bumpstead Essex 55 E7
Hellaby S Yorks 89 E6
Helland Corn 5 B5
Hellesdon Norf 68 C5
Hellidon Northants 52 D3
Hellifield N Yorks 93 D8
Hellingly E Sus 18 D2
Hellington Norf 69 D6
Hellister Shetland 175 J5
Helm Northumb 117 E7
Helmdon Northants 52 E3
Helmingham Suff 57 D5
Helmington Row Durham 110 F4
Helmsdale Highld 165 C7
Helmshore Lancs 87 B5
Helmsley N Yorks 102 F4
Helperby N Yorks 95 C7
Helperthorpe N Yorks 97 B5
Helpringham Lincs 78 E4
Helpston P'boro 65 D8
Helsby Ches 73 B8
Helsey Lincs 79 B8
Helston Corn 3 D5
Helstone Corn 8 F2
Helton Cumb 99 B7
Helwith Bridge N Yorks 93 C8
Hemblington Norf 69 C6
Hemel Hempstead Herts 40 D3
Hemingbrough N Yorks 96 F2
Hemingby Lincs 78 B5
Hemingford Abbots Cambs 54 B3
Hemingford Grey Cambs 54 B3
Hemingstone Suff 57 D5
Hemington Leics 63 B8
Hemington Northants 65 F7
Hemington Som 24 D2
Hemley Suff 57 E6
Hemlington M'bro 102 C3
Hemp Green Suff 57 C7
Hempholme E Yorks 97 D6
Hempnall Norf 68 E5
Hempnall Green Norf 68 E5
Hempriggs House Highld 169 E8
Hempstead Essex 55 F7
Hempstead Medway 29 C8
Hempstead Norf 81 D7
Hempstead Norf 69 B7
Hempsted Glos 37 C5
Hempton Norf 80 E5
Hempton Oxon 52 F2
Hemsby Norf 69 C7
Hemswell Lincs 90 E3
Hemswell Cliff Lincs 90 F3
Hemsworth W Yorks 88 C5
Hemyock Devon 11 C6
Hen-feddau fawr Pembs 45 F4
Henbury Bristol 23 B7
Henbury Ches 75 B5
Hendon London 41 F5
Hendon T & W 111 D7
Hendre Flint 73 C5
Hendre-ddu Conwy 83 E8
Hendreforgan Rhondda 34 F3
Hendy Carms 33 D6
Heneglwys Anglesey 82 D4
Henfield W Sus 17 C6
Henford Devon 9 E5
Henghurst Kent 19 B6
Hengoed Caerph 35 E5
Hengoed Powys 48 D4
Hengoed Shrops 73 F6
Hengrave Suff 56 C2
Henham Essex 41 B8
Heniarth Powys 59 D8
Henlade Som 11 B7
Henley Shrops 49 B7
Henley Som 23 F6
Henley Suff 57 D5
Henley W Sus 16 B2
Henley-in-Arden Warks 51 C6
Henley-on-Thames Oxon 39 F7
Henley's Down E Sus 18 D4
Henllan Ceredig 46 E2
Henllan Denb 72 C4
Henllan Amgoed Carms 32 B2
Henllys Torf 35 E6
Henlow Beds 54 F2
Hennock Devon 10 F3
Henny Street Essex 56 F2
Henryd Conwy 83 D7
Henry's Moat Pembs 32 B1
Hensall N Yorks 89 B6
Henshaw Northumb 109 C7
Hensingham Cumb 98 C1
Henstead Suff 69 F7
Henstridge Som 12 C5
Henstridge Ash Som 12 B5
Henstridge Marsh Som 12 B5
Henton Oxon 39 D7
Henton Som 23 E6
Henwood Corn 5 B7
Heogan Shetland 175 J6
Heol-las Swansea 33 E7
Heol Senni Powys 34 B3
Heol-y-Cyw Bridgend 34 F3
Hepburn Northumb 117 B6
Hepple Northumb 117 D5
Hepscott Northumb 117 F8
Heptonstall W Yorks 87 B7
Hepworth Suff 56 B3
Hepworth W Yorks 88 D2
Herbrandston Pembs 44 E3
Hereford Hereford 49 E7
Hereford Cathedral Hereford 49 F7
Hereford Racecourse Hereford 49 E7
Heriot Borders 123 D6
Heritage Motor Centre, Gaydon Warks 51 D8
Hermiston Edin 122 B4
Hermitage Borders 115 E8
Hermitage Dorset 12 D4
Hermitage W Berks 26 B3
Hermitage W Sus 15 D8
Hermon Anglesey 82 E3
Hermon Carms 46 F2
Hermon Carms 33 B7
Hermon Pembs 45 F4
Herne Kent 31 C5
Herne Bay Kent 31 C5
Herner Devon 9 B7
Hernhill Kent 30 C4
Herodsfoot Corn 5 C7
Herongate Essex 42 E2
Heronsford S Ayrs 104 A5
Herriard Hants 26 E4
Herringfleet Suff 69 E7
Herringswell Suff 55 B8
Hersden Kent 31 C6
Hersham Corn 8 D4
Hersham Sur 28 C2
Herstmonceux E Sus 18 D3
Herston Orkney 176 G3
Hertford Herts 41 C6
Hertford Heath Herts 41 C6
Hertingfordbury Herts 41 C6
Hesket Newmarket Cumb 108 F3
Hesketh Bank Lancs 86 B2
Hesketh Lane Lancs 93 E6
Heskin Green Lancs 86 C3
Hesleden Durham 111 F7
Hesleyside Northumb 116 F4
Heslington York 96 D2
Hessay York 95 D8
Hessenford Corn 5 D8
Hessett Suff 56 C3
Hessle E Yorks 90 B4
Hest Bank Lancs 92 C4
Heston London 28 B2
Hestwall Orkney 176 E1
Heswall Mers 85 F3
Hethe Oxon 39 B5
Hethersett Norf 68 D4
Hethersgill Cumb 108 C4
Hethpool Northumb 116 B4
Hett Durham 111 F5
Hetton N Yorks 94 D2
Hetton-le-Hole T & W 111 E6
Hetton Steads Northumb 125 F6
Heugh Northumb 110 B3
Heugh-head Aberds 150 C2
Heveningham Suff 57 B7
Hever Kent 29 E5
Hever Castle and Gardens Kent 29 E5
Heversham Cumb 99 F6
Hevingham Norf 81 E7
Hewas Water Corn 3 B8
Hewelsfield Glos 36 D2
Hewish N Som 23 C6
Hewish Som 12 D2
Heworth York 96 D2
Hexham Northumb 110 C2
Hexham Abbey Northumb 110 C2
Hexham Racecourse Northumb 110 C2
Hextable Kent 29 B6
Hexton Herts 54 F2
Hexworthy Devon 6 B4
Hey Lancs 93 E8
Heybridge Essex 42 E2
Heybridge Essex 42 D4
Heybridge Basin Essex 42 D4
Heybrook Bay Devon 6 E3
Heydon Cambs 54 E5
Heydon Norf 81 E7
Heydour Lincs 78 F3
Heylipol Argyll 136 F1
Heylor Shetland 174 E4
Heysham Lancs 92 C4
Heyshott W Sus 16 C2
Heyside Gtr Man 87 D7
Heytesbury Wilts 24 E4
Heythrop Oxon 38 B3
Heywood Gtr Man 87 C6
Heywood Wilts 24 D3
Hibaldstow N Lincs 90 D3
Hickleton S Yorks 89 D5
Hickling Norf 69 B7
Hickling Notts 64 B3
Hickling Green Norf 69 B7
Hickling Heath Norf 69 B7
Hickstead W Sus 17 B6
Hidcote Boyce Glos 51 E6
Hidcote Manor Garden, Moreton-in-Marsh Glos 51 E6
High Ackworth W Yorks 88 C5
High Angerton Northumb 117 F6
High Bankhill Cumb 109 E5
High Barnes T & W 111 D6
High Beach Essex 41 E7
High Bentham N Yorks 93 C6
High Bickington Devon 9 B8
High Birkwith N Yorks 93 B7
High Blantyre S Lnrk 121 D6
High Bonnybridge Falk 121 B8
High Bradfield S Yorks 88 E3
High Bray Devon 21 F5
High Brooms Kent 29 E6
High Bullen Devon 9 B7
High Buston Northumb 117 D8
High Callerton Northumb 110 B4
High Catton E Yorks 96 D3
High Cogges Oxon 38 D3
High Coniscliffe Darl 101 C7
High Cross Hants 15 B8
High Cross Herts 41 C6
High Easter Essex 42 C2
High Eggborough N Yorks 89 B6
High Ellington N Yorks 101 F6
High Ercall Telford 61 C5
High Etherley Durham 101 B6
High Garrett Essex 42 B3
High Grange Durham 110 F4
High Green Norf 68 D4
High Green S Yorks 88 E4
High Green Worcs 50 E3
High Halden Kent 19 B5
High Halstow Medway 29 B8
High Ham Som 23 F6
High Harrington Cumb 98 B2
High Hatton Shrops 61 B6
High Hawsker N Yorks 103 D7
High Hesket Cumb 108 E4
High Hesleden Durham 111 F7
High Hoyland S Yorks 88 C3
High Hunsley E Yorks 97 F5
High Hurstwood E Sus 17 B8
High Hutton N Yorks 96 C3
High Ireby Cumb 108 F2
High Kelling Norf 81 C7
High Kilburn N Yorks 95 B8
High Lands Durham 101 B6
High Lane Gtr Man 87 F7
High Lane Hereford 49 C8
High Laver Essex 41 D8
High Legh Ches 86 F5
High Leven Stockton 102 C2
High Littleton Bath 23 D8
High Lorton Cumb 98 B3
High Marishes N Yorks 96 B4
High Marnham Notts 77 B8
High Melton S Yorks 89 D6
High Mickley Northumb 110 C3
High Mindork Dumfries 105 D7
High Moorland Visitor Centre, Princetown Devon 6 B3
High Newton Cumb 99 F6
High Newton-by-the-Sea Northumb 117 B8
High Nibthwaite Cumb 98 F4
High Offley Staffs 61 B7
High Ongar Essex 42 D1
High Onn Staffs 62 C2
High Roding Essex 42 C2
High Row Cumb 108 F3
High Salvington W Sus 16 D5
High Sellafield Cumb 98 D2
High Shaw N Yorks 100 E3
High Spen T & W 110 D4
High Stoop Durham 110 E4
High Street Corn 4 D4
High Street Kent 18 B4
High Street Suff 57 D8
High Street Suff 57 B8
High Street Suff 56 E2
High Street Green Suff 56 D4
High Throston Hrtlpl 111 F7
High Toynton Lincs 79 C5
High Trewhitt Northumb 117 D6
High Valleyfield Fife 134 F2
High Westwood Durham 110 D4
High Wray Cumb 99 E5
High Wych Herts 41 C7
High Wycombe Bucks 40 E1
Higham Derbys 76 D3
Higham Kent 29 B8
Higham Lancs 93 F8
Higham Suff 56 F4
Higham Suff 55 C8
Higham Dykes Northumb 110 B4
Higham Ferrers Northants 53 C7
Higham Gobion Beds 54 F2
Higham on the Hill Leics 63 E7
Higham Wood Kent 29 E6
Highampton Devon 9 D6
Highbridge Highld 146 F4
Highbridge Som 22 E5
Highbrook W Sus 28 F4
Highburton W Yorks 88 C2
Highbury Som 23 E8
Highclere Hants 26 C2
Highcliffe Dorset 14 E3
Higher Ansty Dorset 13 D5
Higher Ashton Devon 10 F3
Higher Ballam Lancs 92 F3
Higher Bartle Lancs 92 F5
Higher Boscaswell Corn 2 C2
Higher Burwardsley Ches 74 D2
Higher Clovelly Devon 8 B5
Higher End Gtr Man 86 D3
Higher Kinnerton Flint 73 C7
Higher Penwortham Lancs 86 B3
Higher Town Scilly 2 E4
Higher Walreddon Devon 6 B2
Higher Walton Lancs 86 B3
Higher Walton Warr 86 F3
Higher Wheelton Lancs 86 B4
Higher Whitley Ches 86 F4
Higher Wincham Ches 74 B3
Higher Wych Ches 73 E8
Highfield E Yorks 96 F3
Highfield Gtr Man 86 D5
Highfield N Ayrs 120 D3
Highfield Oxon 39 B5
Highfield S Yorks 88 F4
Highfield T & W 110 D4
Highfields Cambs 54 D4
Highfields Northumb 125 D5
Highgate London 41 F5
Highland Folk Museum, Aultlairie Highld 148 E3
Highland Folk Museum, Kingussie Highld 148 D3
Highlane Ches 75 C5
Highlane Derbys 88 F5
Highlaws Cumb 107 E8
Highleadon Glos 36 B4
Highleigh W Sus 16 E2
Highley Shrops 61 F7
Highmoor Cross Oxon 39 F7
Highmoor Hill Mon 36 F1
Highnam Glos 36 C4
Highnam Green Glos 36 B4
Highsted Kent 30 C3
Highstreet Green Essex 55 F8
Hightae Dumfries 107 B7
Hightown Ches 75 C5
Hightown Mers 85 D4
Hightown Green Suff 56 D3
Highway Wilts 24 B5
Highweek Devon 7 B6
Highworth Thamesdown 38 E2
Hilborough Norf 67 D8
Hilcote Derbys 76 D4
Hilcott Wilts 25 D6
Hilden Park Kent 29 E6
Hildenborough Kent 29 E6
Hildersham Cambs 55 E6
Hilderstone Staffs 75 F6
Hilderthorpe E Yorks 97 C7
Hilfield Dorset 12 D4
Hilgay Norf 67 E6
Hill Pembs 32 D2
Hill S Glos 36 E3
Hill W Mid 62 E5
Hill Brow W Sus 15 B8
Hill Dale Lancs 86 C2
Hill Dyke Lincs 79 E6
Hill End Durham 110 F3
Hill End Fife 134 E2
Hill End N Yorks 94 D3
Hill Head Hants 15 D6
Hill Head Northumb 110 C2
Hill Mountain Pembs 44 E4
Hill of Beath Fife 134 E3
Hill of Fearn Highld 158 B2
Hill of Mountblairy Aberds 160 C3
Hill Ridware Staffs 62 C4
Hill Top Durham 100 B4
Hill Top Hants 14 D5
Hill Top W Mid 62 E3
Hill Top W Yorks 88 C4
Hill Top, Sawrey Cumb 99 E5
Hill View Dorset 13 E7
Hillam N Yorks 89 B6
Hillbeck Cumb 100 C2
Hillborough Kent 31 C6
Hillbrae Aberds 151 B6
Hillbrae Aberds 160 D3
Hillbutts Dorset 13 D7
Hillclifflane Derbys 76 E2
Hillcommon Som 11 B6
Hillend Fife 134 F3
Hillerton Devon 10 E2
Hillesden Bucks 39 B6
Hillesley Glos 36 F4
Hillfarance Som 11 B6
Hillhead Aberds 160 E2
Hillhead Devon 7 D7
Hillhead S Ayrs 112 C4
Hillhead of Auchentumb Aberds 161 C6
Hillhead of Cocklaw Aberds 161 D7
Hillhouse Borders 123 D8
Hilliclay Highld 169 C6
Hillier Gardens and Arboretum Hants 14 B4
Hillingdon London 40 F3
Hillington Glasgow 120 C5
Hillington Norf 80 E3
Hillmorton Warks 52 B3
Hillockhead Aberds 150 C3
Hillockhead Aberds 150 D2
Hillside Aberds 151 E8
Hillside Angus 143 C7
Hillside Mers 85 C4
Hillside Orkney 176 G3
Hillside Shetland 175 G6
Hillswick Shetland 174 F4
Hillway I o W 15 F7
Hillwell Shetland 175 M5
Hilmarton Wilts 24 B5
Hilperton Wilts 24 D3
Hilsea Ptsmth 15 D7
Hilston E Yorks 97 F8
Hilton Aberds 161 E6
Hilton Cambs 54 C3
Hilton Cumb 100 B2
Hilton Derbys 76 F2
Hilton Dorset 13 D5
Hilton Durham 101 B6
Hilton Highld 164 F4
Hilton Shrops 61 E7
Hilton Stockton 102 C2
Hilton of Cadboll Highld 158 B2
Himbleton Worcs 50 D4
Himley Staffs 62 E2
Hincaster Cumb 99 F7
Hinckley Leics 63 E8
Hinderclay Suff 56 B4
Hinderton Ches 73 B7
Hinderwell N Yorks 103 C5
Hindford Shrops 73 F7
Hindhead Sur 27 F6
Hindley Gtr Man 86 D4
Hindley Green Gtr Man 86 D4
Hindlip Worcs 50 D3
Hindolveston Norf 81 E6
Hindon Wilts 24 F4
Hindringham Norf 81 D5
Hingham Norf 68 D3
Hinstock Shrops 61 B6
Hintlesham Suff 56 E4
Hinton Hants 14 E3
Hinton Hereford 48 F5
Hinton Northants 52 D3
Hinton Shrops 60 D4
Hinton S Glos 24 B2
Hinton Ampner Hants 15 B6
Hinton Blewett Bath 23 D7
Hinton Charterhouse Bath 24 D2
Hinton-in-the-Hedges Northants 52 F3
Hinton Martell Dorset 13 D8
Hinton on the Green Worcs 50 E5
Hinton Parva Thamesdown 38 F2

Hinton St George Som 12 C2
Hinton St Mary Dorset 13 C5
Hinton Waldrist Oxon 38 E3
Hints Shrops 49 B8
Hints Staffs 63 D5
Hinwick Beds 53 C7
Hinxhill Kent 30 E4
Hinxton Cambs 55 E5
Hinxworth Herts 54 E3
Hipperholme W Yorks 88 B2
Hipswell N Yorks 101 E6
Hirael Gwyn 83 D5
Hiraeth Carms 32 B2
Hirn Aberds 151 D6
Hirnant Powys 59 B7
Hirst N Lnrk 121 C8
Hirst Northumb 117 F8
Hirst Courtney N Yorks 89 B7
Hirwaen Denb 72 C5
Hirwaun Rhondda 34 D3
Hiscott Devon 9 B7
Histon Cambs 54 C5
Hitcham Suff 56 D3
Hitchin Herts 40 B4
Hither Green London 28 B4
Hittisleigh Devon 10 E2
Hive E Yorks 96 F4
Hixon Staffs 62 B4
HMS Victory Ptsmth 15 D7
HMY Britannia Edin 123 B5
Hoaden Kent 31 D6
Hoaldalbert Mon 35 B7
Hoar Cross Staffs 62 B5
Hoarwithy Hereford 36 B2
Hoath Kent 31 C6
Hobarris Shrops 48 B5
Hobbister Orkney 176 F2
Hobkirk Borders 115 C8
Hobson Durham 110 D4
Hoby Leics 64 C3
Hockering Norf 68 C3
Hockerton Notts 77 D7
Hockley Essex 42 E4
Hockley Heath W Mid 51 B6
Hockliffe Beds 40 B2
Hockwold cum Wilton Norf 67 F7
Hockworthy Devon 10 C5
Hoddesdon Herts 41 D6
Hoddlesden Blkburn 86 B5
Hoddom Mains Dumfries 107 B8
Hoddomcross Dumfries 107 B8
Hodgeston Pembs 32 E1
Hodley Powys 59 E8
Hodnet Shrops 61 B6
Hodthorpe Derbys 76 B5
Hoe Hants 15 C6
Hoe Norf 68 C2
Hoe Gate Hants 15 C7
Hoff Cumb 100 C1
Hog Patch Sur 27 E6
Hoggard's Green Suff 56 D2
Hoggeston Bucks 39 B8
Hogha Gearraidh W Isles 170 C3
Hoghton Lancs 86 B4
Hognaston Derbys 76 D2
Hogsthorpe Lincs 79 B8
Holbeach Lincs 66 B3
Holbeach Bank Lincs 66 B3
Holbeach Clough Lincs 66 B3
Holbeach Drove Lincs 66 C3
Holbeach Hurn Lincs 66 B3
Holbeach St Johns Lincs 66 C3
Holbeach St Marks Lincs 79 F6
Holbeach St Matthew Lincs 79 F7
Holbeck Notts 76 B5
Holbeck W Yorks 95 F5
Holbeck Woodhouse Notts 76 B5
Holberrow Green Worcs 50 D5
Holbeton Devon 6 D4
Holborn London 41 F6
Holbrook Derbys 76 E3
Holbrook Suff 57 F5
Holbrook S Yorks 88 F5
Holburn Northumb 125 F6
Holbury Hants 14 D5
Holcombe Devon 7 B7
Holcombe Som 23 E8
Holcombe Rogus Devon 11 C5
Holcot Northants 53 C5
Holden Lancs 93 E7
Holdenby Northants 52 C4
Holdenhurst Bmouth 14 E2
Holdgate Shrops 61 F5
Holdingham Lincs 78 E3
Holditch Dorset 11 D8
Hole-in-the-Wall Hereford 36 B3
Holefield Borders 124 F4
Holehouses Ches 74 B4
Holemoor Devon 9 D6
Holestane Dumfries 113 E8
Holford Som 22 E3
Holgate York 95 D8
Holker Cumb 92 B3
Holkham Norf 80 C4
Hollacombe Devon 9 D5
Holland Orkney 176 A3
Holland Orkney 176 D5
Holland Fen Lincs 78 E5
Holland-on-Sea Essex 43 C8
Hollandstoun Orkney 176 A6
Hollee Dumfries 108 C2
Hollesley Suff 57 E7
Hollicombe Torbay 7 C6
Hollingbourne Kent 30 D2
Hollington Derbys 76 F2
Hollington E Sus 18 D4
Hollington Staffs 75 F7
Hollington Grove Derbys 76 F2
Hollingworth Gtr Man 87 E8
Hollins Gtr Man 87 D6
Hollins Green Warr 86 E4
Hollins Lane Lancs 92 D4
Hollinsclough Staffs 75 C7
Hollinwood Gtr Man 87 D7
Hollinwood Shrops 74 F2
Hollocombe Devon 9 C8
Hollow Meadows S Yorks 88 F3
Holloway Derbys 76 D3
Hollowell Northants 52 B4
Holly End Norf 66 D4
Holly Green Worcs 50 E3
Hollybush Caerph 35 D5
Hollybush E Ayrs 112 C3
Hollybush Worcs 50 F2
Hollym E Yorks 91 B7
Hollywood Worcs 51 B5
Holmbridge W Yorks 88 D2
Holmbury St Mary Sur 28 E2
Holmbush Corn 4 D5
Holmcroft Staffs 62 B3
Holme Cambs 65 F8
Holme Cumb 92 B5
Holme Notts 77 D8
Holme N Yorks 102 F1
Holme W Yorks 88 D2
Holme Chapel Lancs 87 B6
Holme Green N Yorks 95 E8
Holme Hale Norf 67 D8
Holme Lacy Hereford 49 F7
Holme Marsh Hereford 48 D5
Holme next the Sea Norf 80 C3
Holme-on-Spalding-Moor E Yorks 96 F4
Holme on the Wolds E Yorks 97 E5
Holme Pierrepont Notts 77 F6
Holme St Cuthbert Cumb 107 E8
Holme Wood W Yorks 94 F4
Holmer Hereford 49 E7
Holmer Green Bucks 40 E2
Holmes Chapel Ches 74 C4
Holmesfield Derbys 76 B3
Holmeswood Lancs 86 C2
Holmewood Derbys 76 C4
Holmfirth W Yorks 88 D2
Holmhead Dumfries 113 F7
Holmhead E Ayrs 113 B5
Holmisdale Highld 152 E2
Holmpton E Yorks 91 B7
Holmrook Cumb 98 E2
Holmsgarth Shetland 175 J6
Holmwrangle Cumb 108 E5
Holne Devon 6 C5
Holnest Dorset 12 D4
Holsworthy Devon 8 D5
Holsworthy Beacon Devon 9 D5
Holt Dorset 13 D8
Holt Norf 81 D6
Holt Wilts 24 C3
Holt Worcs 50 C3
Holt Wrex 73 D8
Holt End Hants 26 F4
Holt End Worcs 51 C5
Holt Fleet Worcs 50 C3
Holt Heath Worcs 50 C3
Holt Park W Yorks 95 E5
Holtby York 96 D2
Holton Oxon 39 D6
Holton Som 12 B4
Holton Suff 57 B7
Holton cum Beckering Lincs 90 F5
Holton Heath Dorset 13 E7
Holton le Clay Lincs 91 D6
Holton le Moor Lincs 90 E4
Holton St Mary Suff 56 F4
Holwell Dorset 12 C5
Holwell Herts 54 F2
Holwell Leics 64 B4
Holwell Oxon 38 D2
Holwick Durham 100 B4
Holworth Dorset 13 F5
Holy Cross Worcs 50 B4
Holy Island Northumb 125 E7
Holybourne Hants 26 E5
Holyhead = Caergybi Anglesey 82 C2
Holymoorside Derbys 76 C3
Holyport Windsor 27 B6
Holystone Northumb 117 D5
Holytown N Lnrk 121 C7
Holywell Cambs 54 B4
Holywell Corn 4 D2
Holywell Dorset 12 D3
Holywell E Sus 18 F2
Holywell Northumb 111 B6
Holywell = Treffynnon Flint 73 B5
Holywell Bay Fun Park, Newquay Corn 4 D2
Holywell Green W Yorks 87 C8
Holywell Lake Som 11 B6
Holywell Row Suff 55 B8
Holywood Dumfries 114 F2
Hom Green Hereford 36 B2
Homer Shrops 61 D6
Homersfield Suff 69 F5
Homington Wilts 14 B2
Honey Hill Kent 30 C5
Honey Street Wilts 25 C6
Honey Tye Suff 56 F3
Honeyborough Pembs 44 E4
Honeybourne Worcs 51 E6
Honeychurch Devon 9 D8
Honiley Warks 51 B7
Honing Norf 69 B6
Honingham Norf 68 C4
Honington Lincs 78 E2
Honington Suff 56 B3
Honington Warks 51 E7
Honiton Devon 11 D6
Honley W Yorks 88 C2
Hoo Green Ches 86 F5
Hoo St Werburgh Medway 29 B8
Hood Green S Yorks 88 D4
Hooe E Sus 18 E3
Hooe Plym 6 D3
Hooe Common E Sus 18 D3
Hook E Yorks 89 B8
Hook London 28 C2
Hook Hants 26 D5
Hook Pembs 44 D4
Hook Wilts 37 F7
Hook Green Kent 18 B3
Hook Green Kent 29 C7
Hook Norton Oxon 51 F8
Hooke Dorset 12 E3
Hookgate Staffs 74 F4
Hookway Devon 10 E3
Hookwood Sur 28 E3
Hoole Ches 73 C8
Hooley Sur 28 D3
Hooton Ches 73 B7
Hooton Levitt S Yorks 89 E6
Hooton Pagnell S Yorks 89 D5
Hooton Roberts S Yorks 89 E5
Hop Pole Lincs 65 C8
Hope Derbys 88 F2
Hope Devon 6 F4
Hope Highld 167 D6
Hope Powys 60 D2
Hope Shrops 60 D3
Hope Staffs 75 D8
Hope = Yr Hôb Flint 73 D7
Hope Bagot Shrops 49 B7
Hope Bowdler Shrops 60 E4
Hope End Green Essex 42 B1
Hope Green Ches 87 F7
Hope Mansell Hereford 36 C3
Hope under Dinmore Hereford 49 D7
Hopeman Moray 158 C5
Hope's Green Essex 42 F3
Hopesay Shrops 60 F3
Hopley's Green Hereford 48 D5
Hopperton N Yorks 95 D7
Hopstone Shrops 61 E7
Hopton Shrops 60 B3
Hopton Shrops 61 B5
Hopton Staffs 62 B3
Hopton Suff 56 B3
Hopton Cangeford Shrops 60 F5
Hopton Castle Shrops 49 B5
Hopton on Sea Norf 69 D8
Hopton Wafers Shrops 49 B8
Hoptonheath Shrops 49 B5
Hopwas Staffs 63 D5
Hopwood Gtr Man 87 D6
Hopwood Worcs 50 B5
Horam E Sus 18 D2
Horbling Lincs 78 F4
Horbury W Yorks 88 C3
Horcott Glos 38 D1
Horden Durham 111 E7
Horderley Shrops 60 F4
Hordle Hants 14 E3
Hordley Shrops 73 F7
Horeb Ceredig 46 E2
Horeb Carms 33 D5
Horeb Carms 33 B6
Horfield Bristol 23 B8
Horham Suff 57 B6
Horkesley Heath Essex 43 B5
Horkstow N Lincs 90 C3
Horley Oxon 52 E2
Horley Sur 28 E3
Hornblotton Green Som 23 F7
Hornby Lancs 93 C5
Hornby N Yorks 101 E7
Hornby N Yorks 102 D1
Horncastle Lincs 79 C5
Hornchurch London 41 F8
Horncliffe Northumb 124 E5
Horndean Borders 124 E4
Horndean Hants 15 C8
Horndon Devon 6 B3
Horndon on the Hill Thurrock 42 F2
Horne Sur 28 E4
Horniehaugh Angus 142 C4
Horning Norf 69 C6
Horninghold Leics 64 E5
Horninglow Staffs 63 B6
Horningsea Cambs 55 C5
Horningsham Wilts 24 E3
Horningtoft Norf 80 E5
Horns Corner Kent 18 C4
Horns Cross Devon 9 B5
Horns Cross E Sus 18 C5
Hornsby Cumb 108 D5
Hornsea E Yorks 97 E8
Hornsea Bridge E Yorks 97 E8
Hornsey London 41 F6
Hornton Oxon 51 E8
Horrabridge Devon 6 C3
Horringer Suff 56 C2
Horringford I o W 15 F6
Horse Bridge Staffs 75 D6
Horsebridge Devon 6 B2
Horsebridge Hants 25 F8
Horsebrook Staffs 62 C2
Horsehay Telford 61 D6
Horseheath Cambs 55 E7
Horsehouse N Yorks 101 F5
Horsell Sur 27 D7
Horseman's Green Wrex 73 E8
Horseway Cambs 66 F4
Horsey Norf 69 B7
Horsford Norf 68 C4
Horsforth W Yorks 94 F5
Horsham W Sus 28 F2
Horsham Worcs 50 D2
Horsham St Faith Norf 68 C5
Horsington Lincs 78 C4
Horsington Som 12 B5
Horsley Derbys 76 E3
Horsley Glos 37 E5
Horsley Northumb 110 C3
Horsley Northumb 116 E4
Horsley Cross Essex 43 B7
Horsley Woodhouse Derbys 76 E3
Horsleycross Street Essex 43 B7
Horsleyhill Borders 115 C8
Horsleyhope Durham 110 E3
Horsmonden Kent 29 E7
Horspath Oxon 39 D5
Horstead Norf 69 C5
Horsted Keynes W Sus 17 B7
Horton Bucks 40 C2
Horton Dorset 13 D8
Horton Lancs 93 D8
Horton Northants 53 D6
Horton Shrops 60 B4
Horton S Glos 36 F4
Horton Som 11 C8
Horton Staffs 75 D6
Horton Swansea 33 F5
Horton Wilts 25 C5
Horton Windsor 27 B8
Horton-cum-Studley Oxon 39 C5
Horton Green Ches 73 E8
Horton Heath Hants 15 C5
Horton in Ribblesdale N Yorks 93 B8
Horton Kirby Kent 29 C6
Hortonlane Shrops 60 C4
Horwich Gtr Man 86 C4
Horwich End Derbys 87 F8
Horwood Devon 9 B7
Hose Leics 64 B4
Hoselaw Borders 124 F4
Hoses Cumb 98 E4
Hosh Perth 133 B7
Hosta W Isles 170 C3
Hoswick Shetland 175 L6
Hotham E Yorks 96 F4
Hothfield Kent 30 E3
Hoton Leics 64 B2
Houbie Shetland 174 D8
Houdston S Ayrs 112 E1
Hough Ches 74 D4
Hough Ches 75 B5
Hough Green Halton 86 F2
Hough-on-the-Hill Lincs 78 E2
Hougham Lincs 77 E8
Houghton Cambs 54 B3
Houghton Cumb 108 D4
Houghton Hants 25 F8
Houghton Pembs 44 E4
Houghton W Sus 16 C4
Houghton Conquest Beds 53 E8
Houghton Green E Sus 19 C6
Houghton Green Warr 86 E4
Houghton-le-Side Darl 101 B7
Houghton-Le-Spring T & W 111 E6
Houghton on the Hill Leics 64 D3
Houghton Regis Beds 40 B3
Houghton St Giles Norf 80 D5
Houlland Shetland 175 H5
Houlland Shetland 174 F7
Houlsyke N Yorks 103 D5
Hound Hants 15 D5
Hound Green Hants 26 D5
Houndslow Borders 124 E2
Houndwood Borders 124 C4
Hounslow London 28 B2
Hounslow Green Essex 42 C2
Housay Shetland 174 F8
House of Daviot Highld 157 E8
House of Glenmuick Aberds 150 E2
Housesteads Roman Fort Northumb 109 C7
Housetter Shetland 174 E5
Houss Shetland 175 K5
Houston Renfs 120 C4
Houstry Highld 169 F6
Houton Orkney 176 F2
Hove Brighton 17 D6
Hoveringham Notts 77 E6
Hoveton Norf 69 C6
Hovingham N Yorks 96 B2
How Cumb 108 D5
How Caple Hereford 49 F8
How End Beds 53 E8
How Green Kent 29 E5
Howbrook S Yorks 88 E4
Howden Borders 116 B2
Howden E Yorks 89 B8
Howden-le-Wear Durham 110 F4
Howe Highld 169 C8
Howe Norf 69 D5
Howe N Yorks 101 F8
Howe Bridge Gtr Man 86 D4
Howe Green Essex 42 D3
Howe of Teuchar Aberds 160 D4
Howe Street Essex 42 C2
Howe Street Essex 55 F7
Howell Lincs 78 E4
Howey Powys 48 D2
Howgate Midloth 122 D5
Howick Northumb 117 C8
Howle Durham 101 B5
Howle Telford 61 B6
Howlett End Essex 55 F6
Howley Som 11 D7
Hownam Borders 116 C3
Hownam Mains Borders 116 B3
Howpasley Borders 115 D6
Howsham N Lincs 90 D4
Howsham N Yorks 96 C3
Howslack Dumfries 114 D3
Howtel Northumb 124 F4
Howton Hereford 35 B8
Howtown Cumb 99 C6
Howwood Renfs 120 C3
Hoxne Suff 57 B5
Hoy Orkney 176 F1
Hoylake Mers 85 F3
Hoyland S Yorks 88 D4
Hoylandswaine S Yorks 88 D3
Hubberholme N Yorks 94 B2
Hubbert's Bridge Lincs 79 E5
Huby N Yorks 95 E5
Huby N Yorks 95 C8
Hucclecote Glos 37 C5
Hucking Kent 30 D2
Hucknall Notts 76 E5
Huddersfield W Yorks 88 C2
Huddington Worcs 50 D4
Hudswell N Yorks 101 D6
Huggate E Yorks 96 D4
Hugglescote Leics 63 C8
Hugh Town Scilly 2 E4
Hughenden Valley Bucks 40 E1
Hughley Shrops 61 E5
Huish Devon 9 C7
Huish Wilts 25 C6
Huish Champflower Som 11 B5
Huish Episcopi Som 12 B2
Huisinis W Isles 173 G2
Hulcott Bucks 40 C1
Hulland Derbys 76 E2
Hulland Ward Derbys 76 E2
Hullavington Wilts 37 F5
Hullbridge Essex 42 E4
Hulme Gtr Man 87 E6
Hulme End Staffs 75 D8
Hulme Walfield Ches 74 C5
Hulver Street Suff 69 F7
Hulverstone I o W 14 F4
Humber Hereford 49 D7
Humber Bridge E Yorks 90 B4
Humberside International Airport N Lincs 90 C4
Humberston NE Lincs 91 D7
Humbie E Loth 123 C7
Humbleton E Yorks 97 F8
Humbleton Northumb 117 B5
Humby Lincs 78 F3
Hume Borders 124 E3
Humshaugh Northumb 110 B2
Huna Highld 169 B8
Huncoat Lancs 93 F7
Huncote Leics 64 E2
Hundalee Borders 116 C2
Hunderthwaite Durham 100 B4
Hundle Houses Lincs 79 D5
Hundleby Lincs 79 C6
Hundleton Pembs 44 E4
Hundon Suff 55 E8
Hundred Acres Hants 15 C6
Hundred End Lancs 86 B2
Hundred House Powys 48 D3
Hungarton Leics 64 D3
Hungerford Hants 14 C2
Hungerford W Berks 25 C8
Hungerford Newtown W Berks 25 B8
Hungerton Lincs 65 B5
Hungladder Highld 152 B4
Hunmanby N Yorks 97 B6
Hunmanby Moor N Yorks 97 B7
Hunningham Warks 51 C8
Hunny Hill I o W 15 F5
Hunsdon Herts 41 C7
Hunsingore N Yorks 95 D7
Hunslet W Yorks 95 F6
Hunsonby Cumb 109 F5
Hunspow Highld 169 B7
Hunstanton Norf 80 C2
Hunstanworth Durham 110 E2
Hunsterson Ches 74 E3
Hunston Suff 56 C3
Hunston W Sus 16 D2
Hunstrete Bath 23 C8
Hunt End Worcs 50 C5
Hunter's Quay Argyll 129 C6
Hunthill Lodge Angus 142 B4
Hunting-tower Perth 134 B2
Huntingdon Cambs 54 B3
Huntingdon Racecourse Cambs 54 B3
Huntingfield Suff 57 B7
Huntingford Dorset 24 F3
Huntington E Loth 123 B7
Huntington Hereford 48 D4
Huntington Staffs 62 C3
Huntington York 96 D2
Huntley Glos 36 C4
Huntly Aberds 160 E2
Huntlywood Borders 124 E2
Hunton Kent 29 E8
Hunton N Yorks 101 E6
Hunt's Corner Norf 68 F3
Hunt's Cross Mers 86 F2
Huntsham Devon 10 B5
Huntspill Som 22 E5
Huntworth Som 22 F5
Hunwick Durham 110 F4
Hunworth Norf 81 D6
Hurdsfield Ches 75 B6
Hurley Warks 63 E6
Hurley Windsor 39 F8
Hurlford E Ayrs 120 F4
Hurliness Orkney 176 H1
Hurn Dorset 14 E2
Hurn's End Lincs 79 E7
Hursley Hants 14 B5
Hurst N Yorks 101 D5
Hurst Som 12 C2
Hurst Wokingham 27 B5
Hurst Green E Sus 18 C4
Hurst Green Lancs 93 F6
Hurst Wickham W Sus 17 C6
Hurstbourne Priors Hants 26 E2
Hurstbourne Tarrant Hants 25 D8
Hurstpierpoint W Sus 17 C6
Hurstway Common Hereford 48 E4
Hurstwood Lancs 93 F8
Hurtmore Sur 27 E7
Hurworth Place Darl 101 D7
Hury Durham 100 C4
Husabost Highld 152 D3
Husbands Bosworth Leics 64 F3
Husborne Crawley Beds 53 F7
Husthwaite N Yorks 95 B8
Hutchwns Bridgend 21 B7
Huthwaite Notts 76 D4
Huttoft Lincs 79 B8
Hutton Borders 124 D5
Hutton Cumb 99 B6
Hutton E Yorks 97 D6
Hutton Essex 42 E2
Hutton Lancs 86 B2
Hutton N Som 22 D5
Hutton Buscel N Yorks 103 F7
Hutton Conyers N Yorks 95 B6
Hutton Cranswick E Yorks 97 D6
Hutton End Cumb 108 F4
Hutton Gate Redcar 102 C3
Hutton Henry Durham 111 F7
Hutton-le-Hole N Yorks 103 E5
Hutton Magna Durham 101 C6
Hutton Roof Cumb 108 F3
Hutton Roof Cumb 93 B5
Hutton Rudby N Yorks 102 D2
Hutton Sessay N Yorks 95 B7
Hutton Village Redcar 102 C3
Hutton Wandesley N Yorks 95 D8
Huxley Ches 74 C2
Huxter Shetland 175 H5
Huxter Shetland 175 G7
Huxton Borders 124 C4
Huyton Mers 86 E2
Hwlffordd = Haverfordwest Pembs 44 D4
Hycemoor Cumb 98 F2
Hyde Glos 37 D5
Hyde Gtr Man 87 E7
Hyde Hants 14 C2
Hyde Heath Bucks 40 D2
Hyde Park S Yorks 89 D6
Hydestile Sur 27 E7
Hylton Castle T & W 111 D6
Hyndford Bridge S Lnrk 122 E2
Hynish Argyll 136 G1
Hyssington Powys 60 E3
Hythe Hants 14 D5
Hythe Kent 19 B8
Hythe End Windsor 27 B8
Hythie Aberds 161 C7

I

Ibberton Dorset 13 D5
Ible Derbys 76 D2
Ibsley Hants 14 D2
Ibstock Leics 63 C8
Ibstone Bucks 39 E7
Ibthorpe Hants 25 D8
Ibworth Hants 26 D3
Ichrachan Argyll 131 B6
Ickburgh Norf 67 E8
Ickenham London 40 F3
Ickford Bucks 39 D6
Ickham Kent 31 D6
Ickleford Herts 54 F2
Icklesham E Sus 19 D5
Ickleton Cambs 55 E5
Icklingham Suff 55 B8
Ickwell Green Beds 54 E2
Icomb Glos 38 B2
Idbury Oxon 38 C2
Iddesleigh Devon 9 D7
Ide Devon 10 E3
Ide Hill Kent 29 D5
Ideford Devon 7 B6
Iden E Sus 19 C6
Iden Green Kent 18 B5
Iden Green Kent 18 B4
Idle W Yorks 94 F4
Idlicote Warks 51 E7
Idmiston Wilts 25 F6
Idole Carms 33 C5
Idridgehay Derbys 76 E2
Idrigill Highld 152 C4
Idstone Oxon 38 F2
Idvies Angus 143 E5
Iffley Oxon 39 D5
Ifield W Sus 28 F3
Ifold W Sus 27 F8
Iford E Sus 17 D8
Ifton Heath Shrops 73 F7
Ightfield Shrops 74 F2
Ightham Kent 29 D6
Ightham Mote, Sevenoaks Kent 29 D6
Iken Suff 57 D8
Ilam Staffs 75 D8
Ilchester Som 12 B3
Ilderton Northumb 117 B6
Ilford London 41 F7
Ilfracombe Devon 20 E4
Ilkeston Derbys 76 E4
Ilketshall St Andrew Suff 69 F6
Ilketshall St Lawrence Suff 69 F6
Ilketshall St Margaret Suff 69 F6
Ilkley W Yorks 94 E4
Illey W Mid 62 F3
Illingworth W Yorks 87 B8
Illogan Corn 3 B5
Illston on the Hill Leics 64 E4
Ilmer Bucks 39 D7
Ilmington Warks 51 E7
Ilminster Som 11 C8
Ilsington Devon 7 B5
Ilston Swansea 33 E6
Ilton N Yorks 94 B4
Ilton Som 11 C8
Imachar N Ayrs 119 B5
Imeraval Argyll 126 E3
Immingham NE Lincs 91 C5
Imperial War Museum London 28 B4
Imperial War Museum North Gtr Man 87 E5
Impington Cambs 54 C5
Ince Ches 73 B8
Ince Blundell Mers 85 D4
Ince in Makerfield Gtr Man 86 D3
Inch of Arnhall Aberds 143 B6
Inchbare Angus 143 C6
Inchberry Moray 159 D7
Inchbraoch Angus 143 D7
Incheril Highld 154 D6
Inchgrundle Angus 142 B4
Inchina Highld 162 E3
Inchinnan Renfs 120 C4
Inchkinloch Highld 167 E7
Inchlaggan Highld 146 D4
Inchlumpie Highld 157 B6
Inchmore Highld 156 E4
Inchnacardoch Hotel Highld 147 C6
Inchnadamph Highld 163 B6
Inchree Highld 138 C4
Inchture Perth 134 B4
Inchyra Perth 134 B3
Indian Queens Corn 4 D4
Inerval Argyll 126 E3
Ingatestone Essex 42 E2
Ingbirchworth S Yorks 88 D3
Ingestre Staffs 62 B3
Ingham Lincs 90 F3
Ingham Norf 69 B6
Ingham Suff 56 B2
Ingham Corner Norf 69 B6
Ingleborough Norf 66 C4
Ingleby Derbys 63 B7
Ingleby Lincs 77 B8
Ingleby Arncliffe N Yorks 102 D2
Ingleby Barwick Stockton 102 C2
Ingleby Greenhow N Yorks 102 D3
Inglemire Hull 97 F6
Inglesbatch Bath 24 C2
Inglesham Thamesdown 38 E2
Ingleton Durham 101 B6
Ingleton N Yorks 93 B6
Inglewhite Lancs 92 E5
Ingliston Edin 122 B4
Ingoe Northumb 110 B3
Ingol Lancs 92 F5
Ingoldisthorpe Norf 80 D2
Ingoldmells Lincs 79 C8
Ingoldsby Lincs 78 F3
Ingon Warks 51 D7
Ingram Northumb 117 C6
Ingrave Essex 42 E2
Ingrow W Yorks 94 F3
Ings Cumb 99 E6
Ingst S Glos 36 F2
Ingworth Norf 81 E7
Inham's End Cambs 66 E2
Inkberrow Worcs 50 D5
Inkpen W Berks 25 C8
Inkstack Highld 169 B7
Inn Cumb 99 D6
Innellan Argyll 129 C6
Innerleithen Borders 123 F6
Innerleven Fife 135 D5
Innermessan Dumfries 104 C4
Innerwick E Loth 124 B3
Innerwick Perth 140 E2
Innis Chonain Argyll 131 C7
Insch Aberds 150 B5
Insh Highld 148 D4
Inshore Highld 166 C5
Inskip Lancs 92 F4
Instoneville S Yorks 89 C6
Instow Devon 20 F3
Intake S Yorks 89 D6
Inver Aberds 149 E8
Inver Highld 165 F5
Inver Perth 141 E7
Inver Mallie Highld 146 F4
Inverailort Highld 145 E7
Inveraldie Angus 142 F4
Inveralligin Highld 154 E4
Inverallochy Aberds 161 B7
Inveran Highld 164 E2
Inveraray Argyll 131 E6
Inveraray Jail Argyll 131 E6
Inverarish Highld 153 F6
Inverarity Angus 142 E4
Inverarnan Stirl 132 C2
Inverasdale Highld 154 B4
Inverbeg Argyll 132 E2
Inverbervie Aberds 143 B8
Inverboyndie Aberds 160 B3
Inverbroom Highld 163 F5
Invercassley Highld 164 D1
Invercauld House Aberds 149 E7
Inverchaolain Argyll 129 C5
Invercharnan Highld 139 E5
Inverchoran Highld 156 D3
Invercreran Argyll 138 E4
Inverdruie Highld 148 C5
Inverebrie Aberds 161 E6
Invereck Argyll 129 B6
Inverernan Ho. Aberds 150 C2
Invereshie House Highld 148 D4
Inveresk E Loth 123 B6
Inverewe Gardens, Gairloch Highld 154 B4
Inverey Aberds 149 F6
Inverfarigaig Highld 147 B8
Invergarry Highld 147 D6
Invergelder Aberds 149 E8
Invergeldie Perth 133 B6
Invergordon Highld 157 C8
Invergowrie Perth 142 F3
Inverguseran Highld 145 C7
Inverhadden Perth 140 D3
Inverharroch Moray 159 F7
Inverherive Stirl 132 B2
Inverie Highld 145 D7
Inverinan Argyll 131 D5
Inverinate Highld 146 B2
Inverkeilor Angus 143 E6
Inverkeithing Fife 134 F3
Inverkeithny Aberds 160 D3
Inverkip Invclyd 129 C7
Inverkirkaig Highld 162 C4
Inverlael Highld 163 F5
Inverlochlarig Stirl 132 C3
Inverlochy Argyll 131 C7
Inverlochy Highld 139 B5
Inverlussa Argyll 127 D4
Invermark Lodge Angus 150 F3
Invermoidart Highld 145 F6
Invermoriston Highld 147 C7
Invernaver Highld 168 C2
Inverneill Argyll 128 B3
Inverness Highld 157 E7
Inverness Airport Highld 157 D8
Invernettie Aberds 161 D8
Invernoaden Argyll 131 F7
Inveroran Hotel Argyll 139 E6
Inverpolly Lodge Highld 162 C4
Inverquharity Angus 142 D4
Inverquhomery Aberds 161 D7
Inverroy Highld 147 F5
Inversanda Highld 138 D3
Invershiel Highld 146 C2
Invershin Highld 164 E2
Inversnaid Hotel Stirl 132 D2
Inverugie Aberds 161 D8
Inveruglas Argyll 132 D2
Inveruglass Highld 148 D4
Inverurie Aberds 151 B6
Invervar Perth 140 E3
Inverythan Aberds 160 D4
Inwardleigh Devon 9 E7
Inworth Essex 42 C4
Iochdar W Isles 170 F3
Iona Abbey and Cathedral Argyll 136 F3
Iping W Sus 16 B2
Ipplepen Devon 7 C6
Ipsden Oxon 39 F6
Ipsley Worcs 51 C5
Ipstones Staffs 75 D7
Ipswich Suff 57 E5
Irby Mers 85 F3
Irby in the Marsh Lincs 79 C7
Irby upon Humber NE Lincs 91 D5
Irchester Northants 53 C7
Ireby Cumb 108 F2
Ireby Lancs 93 B6
Ireland Orkney 176 F2
Ireland Shetland 175 L5
Ireland's Cross Shrops 74 E4
Ireleth Cumb 92 B2
Ireshopeburn Durham 109 F8
Irlam Gtr Man 86 E5
Irnham Lincs 65 B7
Iron Acton S Glos 36 F3
Iron Cross Warks 51 D5
Ironbridge Telford 61 D6
Ironbridge Gorge Museum, Telford Shrops 61 D6
Irongray Dumfries 107 B6
Ironmacannie Dumfries 106 B3
Ironside Aberds 161 C5
Ironville Derbys 76 D4
Irstead Norf 69 B6
Irthington Cumb 108 C4
Irthlingborough Northants 53 B7
Irton N Yorks 103 F8
Irvine N Ayrs 120 F3
Isauld Highld 168 C4
Isbister Orkney 176 D1
Isbister Orkney 176 E2
Isbister Shetland 174 D5

Isbister Shetland 175 G7
Isfield E Sus 17 C8
Isham Northants 53 B6
Islay Airport Argyll 126 D3
Isle Abbotts Som 11 B8
Isle Brewers Som 11 B8
Isle of Man Airport I o M 84 F2
Isle of Man Steam Railway I o M 84 F1
Isle of Whithorn Dumfries 105 F8
Isleham Cambs 55 B7
Isleornsay Highld 145 B7
Islesburgh Shetland 174 G5
Islesteps Dumfries 107 B6
Isleworth London 28 B2
Isley Walton Leics 63 B8
Islibhig W Isles 172 F2
Islington London 41 F6
Islip Northants 53 B7
Islip Oxon 39 C5
Istead Rise Kent 29 C7
Isycoed Wrex 73 D8
Itchen Soton 14 C5
Itchen Abbas Hants 26 F3
Itchen Stoke Hants 26 F3
Itchingfield W Sus 16 B5
Itchington S Glos 36 F3
Itteringham Norf 81 D7
Itton Devon 9 E8
Itton Common Mon 36 E1
Ivegill Cumb 108 E4
Iver Bucks 40 F3
Iver Heath Bucks 40 F3
Iveston Durham 110 D4
Ivinghoe Bucks 40 C2
Ivinghoe Aston Bucks 40 C2
Ivington Hereford 49 D6
Ivington Green Hereford 49 D6
Ivy Chimneys Essex 41 D7
Ivy Cross Dorset 13 B6
Ivy Hatch Kent 29 D6
Ivybridge Devon 6 D4
Ivychurch Kent 19 C7
Iwade Kent 30 C3
Iwerne Courtney or Shroton Dorset 13 C6
Iwerne Minster Dorset 13 C6
Ixworth Suff 56 B3
Ixworth Thorpe Suff 56 B3

J

Jack Hill N Yorks 94 D5
Jack in the Green Devon 10 E5
Jacksdale Notts 76 D4
Jackstown Aberds 160 E4
Jacobstow Corn 8 E3
Jacobstowe Devon 9 D7
Jameston Pembs 32 E1
Jamestown Dumfries 115 E6
Jamestown Highld 157 D5
Jamestown W Dunb 132 F2
Jarlshof Prehistoric Site Shetland 175 M5
Jarrow T & W 111 C6
Jarvis Brook E Sus 18 C2
Jasper's Green Essex 42 B3
Java Argyll 130 B3
Jawcraig Falk 121 B8
Jaywick Essex 43 C7
Jealott's Hill Brack 27 B6
Jedburgh Borders 116 B2
Jeffreyston Pembs 32 D1
Jellyhill E Dunb 121 B6
Jemimaville Highld 157 C8
Jersey Airport Jersey 17
Jersey Farm Herts 40 D4
Jersey Zoo & Wildlife Park Jersey 17
Jesmond T & W 111 C5
Jevington E Sus 18 E2
Jockey End Herts 40 C3
Jodrell Bank Visitor Centre, Holmes Chapel Ches 74 B4
John o'Groats Highld 169 B8
Johnby Cumb 108 F4
John's Cross E Sus 18 C4
Johnshaven Aberds 143 C7
Johnston Pembs 44 D4
Johnstone Renfs 120 C4
Johnstonebridge Dumfries 114 E3
Johnstown Carms 33 C5
Johnstown Wrex 73 E7
Joppa Edin 123 B6
Joppa S Ayrs 112 C4
Jordans Bucks 40 E2
Jordanthorpe S Yorks 88 F4
Jorvik Centre York 96 D2
Judges Lodging, Presteigne Powys 48 C5
Jump S Yorks 88 D4
Jumpers Green Dorset 14 E2
Juniper Green Edin 122 C4
Jurby East I o M 84 C3
Jurby South Motor Racing Circuit I o M 84 C3
Jurby West I o M 84 C3

K

Kaber Cumb 100 C2
Kaimend S Lnrk 122 E2
Kaimes Edin 123 C5
Kalemouth Borders 116 B3
Kames Argyll 128 C4
Kames Argyll 130 D4
Kames E Ayrs 113 B6
Kea Corn 3 B7
Keadby N Lincs 90 C2
Keal Cotes Lincs 79 C6
Kearsley Gtr Man 87 D5
Kearstwick Cumb 99 F8
Kearton N Yorks 100 E4
Kearvaig Highld 166 B4
Keasden N Yorks 93 C7
Keckwick Halton 86 F3
Keddington Lincs 91 F7
Kedington Suff 55 E8
Kedleston Derbys 76 E3
Kedleston Hall Derbys 76 E3
Keelby Lincs 91 C5
Keele Staffs 74 E5
Keeley Green Beds 53 E8
Keeston Pembs 44 D4
Keevil Wilts 24 D4
Kegworth Leics 63 B8
Kehelland Corn 2 B5
Keig Aberds 150 C5
Keighley W Yorks 94 E3
Keighley and Worth Valley Railway W Yorks 94 F3
Keil Highld 138 D3
Keilarsbrae Clack 133 E7
Keilhill Aberds 160 C4
Keillmore Argyll 128 B1
Keillor Perth 142 E2
Keillour Perth 133 B8
Keills Argyll 126 C4
Keils Argyll 127 F3
Keinton Mandeville Som 23 F7
Keir Mill Dumfries 113 E8
Keisby Lincs 65 B7
Keiss Highld 169 C8
Keith Moray 159 D8
Keith Inch Aberds 161 D8
Keithock Angus 143 C6
Kelbrook Lancs 94 E2
Kelby Lincs 78 E3
Keld Cumb 99 C7
Keld N Yorks 100 D3
Keldholme N Yorks 103 F5
Kelfield N Lincs 90 D2
Kelfield N Yorks 95 F8
Kelham Notts 77 D7
Kellan Argyll 137 D6
Kellas Angus 142 F4
Kellas Moray 159 D5
Kellaton Devon 7 F6
Kelleth Cumb 100 D1
Kelleythorpe E Yorks 97 D5
Kelling Norf 81 C6
Kellingley N Yorks 89 B6
Kellington N Yorks 89 B6
Kelloe Durham 111 F6
Kelloholm Dumfries 113 C7
Kelly Devon 9 F5
Kelly Bray Corn 5 B8
Kelmarsh Northants 52 B5
Kelmscot Oxon 38 E2
Kelsale Suff 57 C7
Kelsall Ches 74 C2
Kelsall Hill Ches 74 C2
Kelshall Herts 54 F4
Kelsick Cumb 107 D8
Kelso Borders 124 F3
Kelso Racecourse Borders 124 F3
Kelstedge Derbys 76 C3
Kelstern Lincs 91 E6
Kelston Bath 24 C2
Keltneyburn Perth 140 E4
Kelton Dumfries 107 B6
Kelty Fife 134 E3
Kelvedon Essex 42 C4
Kelvedon Hatch Essex 42 E1
Kelvin S Lnrk 121 D6
Kelvinside Glasgow 121 C5
Kelynack Corn 2 C2
Kemback Fife 135 C6
Kemberton Shrops 61 D7
Kemble Glos 37 E6
Kemerton Worcs 50 F4
Kemeys Commander Mon 35 D7
Kemnay Aberds 151 C6
Kemp Town Brighton 17 D7
Kempley Glos 36 B3
Kemps Green Warks 51 B6
Kempsey Worcs 50 E3
Kempsford Glos 38 E1
Kempshott Hants 26 D4
Kempston Beds 53 E8
Kempston Hardwick Beds 53 E8
Kempton Shrops 60 F3
Kempton Park Racecourse Sur 28 B2
Kemsing Kent 29 D6
Kemsley Kent 30 C3
Kenardington Kent 19 B6
Kenchester Hereford 49 E6
Kencot Oxon 38 D2
Kendal Cumb 99 E7
Kendoon Dumfries 113 F6
Kendray S Yorks 88 D4
Kenfig Bridgend 34 F2
Kenfig Hill Bridgend 34 F2
Kenilworth Warks 51 B7
Kenilworth Castle Warks 51 B7
Kenknock Stirl 140 F1
Kenley London 28 D4
Kenley Shrops 61 D5
Kenmore Highld 154 E3
Kenmore Perth 140 E4
Kenn Devon 10 F4
Kenn N Som 23 C6
Kennacley W Isles 173 J4
Kennacraig Argyll 128 D3
Kennerleigh Devon 10 D3
Kennet Clack 133 E8
Kennethmont Aberds 150 B4
Kennett Cambs 55 C7
Kennford Devon 10 F4
Kenninghall Norf 68 F3
Kenninghall Heath Norf 68 F3
Kennington Kent 30 E4
Kennington Oxon 39 D5
Kennoway Fife 135 D5
Kenny Hill Suff 55 B7
Kennythorpe N Yorks 96 C3
Kenovay Argyll 136 F1
Kensaleyre Highld 152 D5
Kensington London 28 B3
Kensworth Beds 40 C3
Kensworth Common Beds 40 C3
Kent International Airport Kent 31 C7
Kent Street E Sus 18 D4
Kent Street Kent 29 D7
Kent Street W Sus 17 B6
Kentallen Highld 138 D4
Kentchurch Hereford 35 B8
Kentford Suff 55 C8
Kentisbeare Devon 11 D5
Kentisbury Devon 20 E5
Kentisbury Ford Devon 20 E5
Kentmere Cumb 99 D6
Kenton Devon 10 F4
Kenton Suff 57 C5
Kenton T & W 110 C5
Kenton Bankfoot T & W 110 C5
Kentra Highld 137 B7
Kents Bank Cumb 92 B3
Kent's Green Glos 36 B4
Kent's Oak Hants 14 B4
Kenwick Shrops 73 F8
Kenwyn Corn 3 B7
Keoldale Highld 167 C5
Keppanach Highld 138 C4
Keppoch Highld 146 B2
Keprigan Argyll 118 E3
Kepwick N Yorks 102 E2
Kerchesters Borders 124 F3
Keresley W Mid 63 F7
Kernborough Devon 7 E5
Kerne Bridge Hereford 36 C2
Kerris Corn 2 D3
Kerry Powys 59 F8
Kerrycroy Argyll 129 D6
Kerry's Gate Hereford 49 F5
Kerrysdale Highld 154 C4
Kersall Notts 77 C7
Kersey Suff 56 E4
Kershopefoot Cumb 115 F7
Kersoe Worcs 50 F4
Kerswell Devon 11 D5
Kerswell Green Worcs 50 E3
Kesgrave Suff 57 E6
Kessingland Suff 69 F8
Kessingland Beach Suff 69 F8
Kessington E Dunb 121 B5
Kestle Corn 3 B8
Kestle Mill Corn 4 D3
Keston London 28 C5
Keswick Cumb 98 B4
Keswick Norf 68 D5
Keswick Norf 81 D9
Ketley Telford 61 C6
Ketley Bank Telford 61 C6
Ketsby Lincs 79 B6
Kettering Northants 53 B6
Ketteringham Norf 68 D4
Kettins Perth 142 F2
Kettlebaston Suff 56 D3
Kettlebridge Fife 134 D5
Kettleburgh Suff 57 C6
Kettlehill Fife 134 D5
Kettleholm Dumfries 107 B8
Kettleness N Yorks 103 C6
Kettleshume Ches 75 B6
Kettlesing Bottom N Yorks 94 D5
Kettlesing Head N Yorks 94 D5
Kettlestone Norf 81 D5
Kettlethorpe Lincs 77 B8
Kettletoft Orkney 176 C5
Kettlewell N Yorks 94 B2
Ketton Rutland 65 D6
Kew London 28 B2
Kew Br. London 28 B2
Kew Gardens London 28 B2
Kewstoke N Som 22 C5
Kexbrough S Yorks 88 D4
Kexby Lincs 90 F2
Kexby York 96 D3
Key Green Ches 75 C5
Keyham Leics 64 D3
Keyhaven Hants 14 E4
Keyingham E Yorks 91 B6
Keymer W Sus 17 C7
Keynsham Bath 23 C8
Keysoe Beds 53 C8
Keysoe Row Beds 53 C8
Keyston Cambs 53 B8
Keyworth Notts 77 F6
Kibblesworth T & W 110 D5
Kibworth Beauchamp Leics 64 E3
Kibworth Harcourt Leics 64 E3
Kidbrooke London 28 B5
Kiddemore Green Staffs 62 D2
Kidderminster Worcs 50 B3
Kiddington Oxon 38 B4
Kidlington Oxon 38 C4
Kidmore End Oxon 26 B4
Kidsgrove Staffs 74 D5
Kidstones N Yorks 100 F4
Kidwelly = Cydweli Carms 33 D5
Kiel Crofts Argyll 130 B5
Kielder Northumb 116 E2
Kielder Castle Visitor Centre Northumb 116 E2
Kierfield Ho. Orkney 176 E1
Kilbagie Clack 133 F8
Kilbarchan Renfs 120 C4
Kilbeg Highld 145 C6
Kilberry Argyll 128 D2
Kilbirnie N Ayrs 120 D3
Kilbride Argyll 130 C4
Kilbride Argyll 130 C5
Kilbride Highld 153 G6
Kilburn Angus 142 C3
Kilburn Derbys 76 E3
Kilburn London 41 F5
Kilburn N Yorks 95 B8
Kilby Leics 64 E3
Kilchamaig Argyll 128 D3
Kilchattan Argyll 127 C1
Kilchattan Bay Argyll 129 E6
Kilchenzie Argyll 118 D3
Kilcheran Argyll 130 B4
Kilchiaran Argyll 126 C2
Kilchoan Argyll 130 D3
Kilchoan Highld 137 B5
Kilchoman Argyll 126 C2
Kilchrenan Argyll 131 C6
Kilconquhar Fife 135 D6
Kilcot Glos 36 B3
Kilcoy Highld 157 D6
Kilcreggan Argyll 129 B7
Kildale N Yorks 102 D4
Kildalloig Argyll 118 E4
Kildary Highld 157 B8
Kildermorie Lodge Highld 157 B6
Kildonan N Ayrs 119 D7
Kildonan Lodge Highld 165 B6
Kildonnan Highld 144 E4
Kildrummy Aberds 150 C3
Kildwick N Yorks 94 E3
Kilfinan Argyll 128 C4
Kilfinnan Highld 147 E5
Kilgetty Pembs 32 D2
Kilgwrrwg Common Mon 36 E1
Kilham E Yorks 97 C6
Kilham Northumb 124 F4
Kilkenneth Argyll 136 F1
Kilkerran Argyll 118 E4
Kilkhampton Corn 8 C4
Killamarsh Derbys 89 F5
Killay Swansea 33 E7
Killbeg Argyll 137 D7
Killean Argyll 118 B3
Killearn Stirl 132 F4
Killen Highld 157 D7
Killerby Darl 101 C6
Killerton House, Exeter Devon 10 D4
Killichonan Perth 140 D2
Killiechonate Highld 146 F5
Killiechronan Argyll 137 D6
Killiecrankie Perth 141 C6
Killiemor Argyll 137 E5
Killiemore House Argyll 137 F5
Killilan Highld 155 G5
Killimster Highld 169 D8
Killin Stirl 140 F2
Killin Lodge Highld 147 D8
Killinallan Argyll 126 B3
Killinghall N Yorks 95 D5
Killington Cumb 99 F8
Killingworth T & W 111 B5
Killmahumaig Argyll 128 A2
Killochyett Borders 123 E7
Killocraw Argyll 118 C3
Killundine Highld 137 D6
Kilmacolm Invclyd 120 C3
Kilmaha Argyll 130 E5
Kilmahog Stirl 132 D5
Kilmalieu Highld 138 D2
Kilmaluag Highld 152 B5
Kilmany Fife 135 B5
Kilmarie Highld 153 H6
Kilmarnock E Ayrs 120 F4
Kilmaron Castle Fife 135 C5
Kilmartin Argyll 130 F4
Kilmaurs E Ayrs 120 E4
Kilmelford Argyll 130 D4
Kilmeny Argyll 126 C3
Kilmersdon Som 23 D8
Kilmeston Hants 15 B6
Kilmichael Argyll 118 D3
Kilmichael Glassary Argyll 128 A3
Kilmichael of Inverlussa Argyll 128 B2
Kilmington Devon 11 E7
Kilmington Wilts 24 F2
Kilmonivaig Highld 146 F4
Kilmorack Highld 157 E5
Kilmore Argyll 130 C4
Kilmore Highld 145 C6
Kilmory Argyll 128 C2
Kilmory Highld 137 A6
Kilmory Highld 144 C3
Kilmory N Ayrs 119 D6
Kilmuir Highld 152 E3
Kilmuir Highld 157 E7
Kilmuir Highld 157 B8
Kilmuir Highld 152 B4
Kilmun Argyll 129 B6
Kilmun Argyll 130 D5
Kiln Pit Hill Northumb 110 D3
Kilncadzow S Lnrk 121 E8
Kilndown Kent 18 B4
Kilnhurst S Yorks 89 E5
Kilninian Argyll 136 D4
Kilninver Argyll 130 C4
Kilnsea E Yorks 91 C8
Kilnsey N Yorks 94 C2
Kilnwick E Yorks 97 E5
Kilnwick Percy E Yorks 96 D4
Kiloran Argyll 127 C1
Kilpatrick N Ayrs 119 D6
Kilpeck Hereford 49 F6
Kilphedir Highld 165 C6
Kilpin E Yorks 89 B8
Kilpin Pike E Yorks 89 B8
Kilrenny Fife 135 D7
Kilsby Northants 52 B3
Kilspindie Perth 134 B4
Kilsyth N Lnrk 121 B7
Kiltarlity Highld 157 E6
Kilton Notts 77 B5
Kilton Som 22 E3
Kilton Thorpe Redcar 102 C4
Kilvaxter Highld 152 C4
Kilve Som 22 E3
Kilvington Notts 77 E7
Kilwinning N Ayrs 120 E3
Kimberworth S Yorks 88 E5
Kimberley Norf 68 D3
Kimberley Notts 76 E5
Kimble Wick Bucks 39 D8
Kimblesworth Durham 111 E5
Kimbolton Cambs 53 C8
Kimbolton Hereford 49 C7
Kimcote Leics 64 F2
Kimmeridge Dorset 13 G7
Kimmerston Northumb 125 F5
Kimpton Hants 25 E7
Kimpton Herts 40 C4
Kinbrace Highld 168 F3
Kinbuck Stirl 133 D6
Kincaple Fife 135 C6
Kincardine Fife 133 F8
Kincardine Highld 164 F3
Kincardine Bridge Fife 133 F8
Kincardine O'Neil Aberds 150 E4
Kinclaven Perth 142 F1
Kincorth Aberdeen 151 D8
Kincorth Ho. Moray 158 C4
Kincraig Highld 148 D4
Kincraigie Perth 141 E6
Kindallachan Perth 141 E6
Kinderland, Scarborough N Yorks 103 E8
Kineton Glos 37 B7
Kineton Warks 51 D8
Kinfauns Perth 134 B3
King Edward Aberds 160 C4
King Sterndale Derbys 75 B7
Kingairloch Highld 138 D2
Kingarth Argyll 129 E5
Kingcoed Mon 35 D8
Kingerby Lincs 90 E4
Kingham Oxon 38 B2
Kinghorn Fife 134 F4
Kingholm Quay Dumfries 107 B6
Kingie Highld 146 D4
Kinglassie Fife 134 E4
Kingoodie Perth 134 B5
King's Acre Hereford 49 E6
King's Bromley Staffs 62 C5
King's Caple Hereford 36 B2
King's Cliffe Northants 65 E7
Kings College Chapel, Cambridge Cambs 54 D5
King's Coughton Warks 51 D5
King's Heath W Mid 62 F4
Kings Hedges Cambs 55 C5
Kings Langley Herts 40 D3
King's Lynn Norf 67 B6
King's Meaburn Cumb 99 B8
King's Mills Wrex 73 E7
Kings Muir Borders 123 F5
King's Newnham Warks 52 B2
King's Newton Derbys 63 B7
King's Norton Leics 64 D3
King's Norton W Mid 51 B5
King's Nympton Devon 9 C8
King's Pyon Hereford 49 D6
King's Ripton Cambs 54 B3
King's Somborne Hants 25 F8
King's Stag Dorset 12 C5
King's Stanley Glos 37 D5
King's Sutton Northants 52 F2
King's Thorn Hereford 49 F7
King's Walden Herts 40 B4
Kings Worthy Hants 26 F2
Kingsand Corn 6 D2
Kingsbarns Fife 135 C7
Kingsbridge Devon 6 E5
Kingsbridge Som 21 F8
Kingsburgh Highld 152 D4
Kingsbury London 41 F5
Kingsbury Warks 63 E6
Kingsbury Episcopi Som 12 B2
Kingsclere Hants 26 D3
Kingscote Glos 37 E5
Kingscott Devon 9 C7
Kingscross N Ayrs 119 D7
Kingsdon Som 12 B3
Kingsdown Kent 31 E7
Kingseat Fife 134 E3
Kingsey Bucks 39 D7
Kingsfold W Sus 28 F2
Kingsford E Ayrs 120 E4
Kingsford Worcs 62 F2
Kingsforth N Lincs 90 C4
Kingsgate Kent 31 B7
Kingsheanton Devon 20 F4
Kingshouse Hotel Highld 139 D6
Kingside Hill Cumb 107 D8
Kingskerswell Devon 7 C6
Kingskettle Fife 134 D5
Kingsland Anglesey 82 C2
Kingsland Hereford 49 C6
Kingsley Ches 74 B2
Kingsley Hants 27 F5
Kingsley Staffs 75 E7
Kingsley Green W Sus 27 F6
Kingsley Holt Staffs 75 E7
Kingsley Park Northants 53 C5
Kingsmuir Angus 142 E4
Kingsmuir Fife 135 D7
Kingsnorth Kent 19 B7
Kingstanding W Mid 62 E4
Kingsteignton Devon 7 B6
Kingsthorpe Northants 53 C5
Kingston Cambs 54 D4
Kingston Devon 6 E4
Kingston Dorset 13 D5
Kingston Dorset 13 G7
Kingston E Loth 135 F7
Kingston Hants 14 D2
Kingston I o W 15 F5
Kingston Kent 31 D5
Kingston Moray 159 C7
Kingston Bagpuize Oxon 38 E4
Kingston Blount Oxon 39 E7
Kingston by Sea W Sus 17 D6
Kingston Deverill Wilts 24 F3
Kingston Gorse W Sus 16 D4
Kingston Lacy, Wimborne Minster Dorset 13 D7
Kingston Lisle Oxon 38 F3
Kingston Maurward Dorset 12 E5
Kingston near Lewes E Sus 17 D7
Kingston on Soar Notts 64 B2
Kingston Russell Dorset 12 E3
Kingston St Mary Som 11 B7
Kingston Seymour N Som 23 C6
Kingston Upon Hull Hull 90 B4
Kingston upon Thames London 28 C2
Kingston Vale London 28 B3
Kingstone Hereford 49 F6
Kingstone Som 11 C8
Kingstone Staffs 62 B4
Kingstown Cumb 108 D3
Kingswear Devon 7 D6
Kingswells Aberdeen 151 D7
Kingswinford W Mid 62 F2
Kingswood Bucks 39 C6
Kingswood Glos 36 E4
Kingswood Hereford 48 D4
Kingswood Kent 30 D2
Kingswood Powys 60 D2
Kingswood S Glos 23 B8
Kingswood Sur 28 D3
Kingswood Warks 51 B6
Kingthorpe Lincs 78 B4
Kington Hereford 48 D4
Kington Worcs 50 D4
Kington Langley Wilts 24 B4
Kington Magna Dorset 13 B5
Kington St Michael Wilts 24 B4
Kingussie Highld 148 D3
Kingweston Som 23 F7
Kininvie Ho. Moray 159 E7
Kinkell Bridge Perth 133 C8
Kinknockie Aberds 161 D7
Kinlet Shrops 61 F7
Kinloch Fife 134 C4
Kinloch Highld 144 D3
Kinloch Highld 166 F5
Kinloch Highld 145 B6
Kinloch Perth 141 E8
Kinloch Perth 142 E2
Kinloch Hourn Highld 146 D2
Kinloch Laggan Highld 147 F8
Kinloch Lodge Highld 167 D7
Kinloch Rannoch Perth 140 D3
Kinlochan Highld 138 C2
Kinlochard Stirl 132 D3
Kinlochbeoraid Highld 145 E8
Kinlochbervie Highld 166 D4
Kinlocheil Highld 138 B3
Kinlochewe Highld 154 D6
Kinlochleven Highld 139 C5
Kinlochmoidart Highld 145 F7
Kinlochmorar Highld 145 D8
Kinlochmore Highld 139 C5
Kinlochspelve Argyll 130 C2
Kinloid Highld 145 E6
Kinloss Moray 158 C4
Kinmel Bay Conwy 72 A3
Kinmuck Aberds 151 C7
Kinmundy Aberds 151 C7
Kinnadie Aberds 161 D6
Kinnaird Perth 134 B4
Kinnaird Castle Angus 143 D6
Kinneff Aberds 143 B8
Kinnelhead Dumfries 114 D3
Kinnell Angus 143 D6
Kinnerley Shrops 60 B3
Kinnersley Hereford 48 E5
Kinnersley Worcs 50 E3
Kinnerton Powys 48 C4
Kinnesswood Perth 134 D3
Kinninvie Durham 101 B5
Kinnordy Angus 142 D3
Kinoulton Notts 77 F6
Kinross Perth 134 D3
Kinrossie Perth 142 F1
Kinsbourne Green Herts 40 C4
Kinsey Heath Ches 74 E3
Kinsham Hereford 49 C5
Kinsham Worcs 50 F4
Kinsley W Yorks 88 C5
Kinson Bmouth 13 E8
Kintbury W Berks 25 C8
Kintessack Moray 158 C3
Kintillo Perth 134 C3
Kintocher Aberds 150 D4
Kinton Hereford 49 B6
Kinton Shrops 60 C3
Kintore Aberds 151 C6
Kintour Argyll 126 D4
Kintra Argyll 136 F4
Kintra Argyll 126 E3
Kintraw Argyll 130 E4
Kinuachdrachd Argyll 130 F3
Kinveachy Highld 148 C5
Kinver Staffs 62 F2
Kippax W Yorks 95 F7
Kippen Stirl 133 E5
Kippford or Scaur Dumfries 106 D5
Kirbister Orkney 176 F2
Kirbister Orkney 176 D5
Kirbuster Orkney 176 D1
Kirby Bedon Norf 69 D5
Kirby Bellars Leics 64 C4
Kirby Cane Norf 69 E6
Kirby Cross Essex 43 B8
Kirby Grindalythe N Yorks 96 C5
Kirby Hill N Yorks 95 C6
Kirby Hill N Yorks 101 D6
Kirby Knowle N Yorks 102 F2
Kirby-le-Soken Essex 43 B8
Kirby Misperton N Yorks 96 B3
Kirby Muxloe Leics 64 D2
Kirby Overblow N Yorks 95 E6
Kirby Row Norf 69 E6
Kirby Sigston N Yorks 102 E2
Kirby Underdale E Yorks 96 D4
Kirby Wiske N Yorks 102 F1
Kirdford W Sus 16 B4
Kirk Highld 169 D7
Kirk Bramwith S Yorks 89 C7
Kirk Deighton N Yorks 95 D6
Kirk Ella E Yorks 90 B4
Kirk Hallam Derbys 76 E4
Kirk Hammerton N Yorks 95 D7
Kirk Ireton Derbys 76 D2
Kirk Langley Derbys 76 F2
Kirk Merrington Durham 111 F5
Kirk Michael I o M 84 C3
Kirk of Shotts N Lnrk 121 C8
Kirk Sandall S Yorks 89 D7
Kirk Smeaton N Yorks 89 C6
Kirk Yetholm Borders 116 B4
Kirkabister Shetland 175 K6
Kirkandrews Dumfries 106 E3
Kirkandrews upon Eden Cumb 108 D3
Kirkbampton Cumb 108 D3
Kirkbean Dumfries 107 D6
Kirkbride Cumb 108 D2
Kirkbuddo Angus 143 E5
Kirkburn Borders 123 F5
Kirkburn E Yorks 97 D5
Kirkburton W Yorks 88 C2
Kirkby Lincs 90 E4
Kirkby Mers 86 E2
Kirkby N Yorks 102 D3
Kirkby Fleetham N Yorks 101 E7
Kirkby Green Lincs 78 D3
Kirkby In Ashfield Notts 76 D5
Kirkby-in-Furness Cumb 98 F4
Kirkby la Thorpe Lincs 78 E3
Kirkby Lonsdale Cumb 93 B6
Kirkby Malham N Yorks 93 C8
Kirkby Mallory Leics 63 D8
Kirkby Malzeard N Yorks 94 B5
Kirkby Mills N Yorks 103 F5
Kirkby on Bain Lincs 78 C5
Kirkby Stephen Cumb 100 D2
Kirkby Thore Cumb 99 B8
Kirkby Underwood Lincs 65 B7
Kirkby Wharfe N Yorks 95 E8
Kirkbymoorside N Yorks 102 F4
Kirkcaldy Fife 134 E4
Kirkcambeck Cumb 108 C5
Kirkcarswell Dumfries 106 E4
Kirkcolm Dumfries 104 C4
Kirkconnel Dumfries 113 C7
Kirkconnell Dumfries 107 C6
Kirkcowan Dumfries 105 C7
Kirkcudbright Dumfries 106 D3
Kirkdale Mers 85 E4
Kirkfieldbank S Lnrk 121 E8
Kirkgunzeon Dumfries 107 C5
Kirkham Lancs 92 F4
Kirkham N Yorks 96 C3
Kirkhamgate W Yorks 88 B3
Kirkharle Northumb 117 F6
Kirkheaton Northumb 110 B3
Kirkheaton W Yorks 88 C2
Kirkhill Angus 143 C6
Kirkhill Highld 157 E6
Kirkhill Midloth 122 C5
Kirkhill Moray 159 F6
Kirkhope Borders 115 B6
Kirkhouse Borders 123 F6
Kirkiboll Highld 167 D7
Kirkibost Highld 153 H6
Kirkinch Angus 142 E3
Kirkinner Dumfries 105 D8
Kirkintilloch E Dunb 121 B6
Kirkland Cumb 98 C2
Kirkland Cumb 109 F6
Kirkland Dumfries 113 E8
Kirkland Dumfries 113 C7
Kirkleatham Redcar 102 B3
Kirklevington Stockton 102 D2
Kirkley Suff 69 E8
Kirklington Notts 77 D6
Kirklington N Yorks 101 F8
Kirklinton Cumb 108 C4
Kirkliston Edin 122 B4
Kirkmaiden Dumfries 104 F5
Kirkmichael Perth 141 D7
Kirkmichael S Ayrs 112 D3
Kirkmuirhill S Lnrk 121 E7
Kirknewton Northumb 124 F5
Kirknewton W Loth 122 C4
Kirkney Aberds 160 E2
Kirkoswald Cumb 109 E5
Kirkoswald S Ayrs 112 D2
Kirkpatrick Durham Dumfries 106 B4
Kirkpatrick-Fleming Dumfries 108 B2
Kirksanton Cumb 98 F3
Kirkstall W Yorks 95 F5
Kirkstead Lincs 78 C4
Kirkstile Aberds 160 E2
Kirkstyle Highld 169 B8
Kirkton Aberds 150 B5
Kirkton Aberds 160 D3
Kirkton Angus 142 E4
Kirkton Angus 142 F4
Kirkton Borders 115 C8
Kirkton Dumfries 114 F2
Kirkton Fife 135 B5
Kirkton Highld 155 H4
Kirkton Highld 155 F5
Kirkton Highld 164 E4
Kirkton Highld 157 D8
Kirkton Perth 133 C8
Kirkton S Lnrk 114 B2
Kirkton Stirl 132 D4
Kirkton Manor Borders 122 F5
Kirkton of Airlie Angus 142 D3
Kirkton of Auchterhouse Angus 142 F3
Kirkton of Auchterless Aberds 160 D4
Kirkton of Barevan Highld 158 E2
Kirkton of Bourtie Aberds 151 B7
Kirkton of Collace Perth 142 F1
Kirkton of Craig Angus 143 D7
Kirkton of Culsalmond Aberds 160 E3
Kirkton of Durris Aberds 151 E6
Kirkton of Glenbuchat Aberds 150 C2
Kirkton of Glenisla Angus 142 C2
Kirkton of Kingoldrum Angus 142 D3
Kirkton of Largo Fife 135 D6
Kirkton of Lethendy Perth 141 E8
Kirkton of Logie Buchan Aberds 151 B8
Kirkton of Maryculter Aberds 151 E7
Kirkton of Menmuir Angus 143 C5
Kirkton of Monikie Angus 142 F4
Kirkton of Oyne Aberds 151 B5
Kirkton of Rayne Aberds 160 F3
Kirkton of Skene Aberds 151 D7
Kirkton of Tough Aberds 150 C5
Kirktonhill Borders 123 D7
Kirktown Aberds 161 C7
Kirktown of Alvah Aberds 160 B3
Kirktown of Deskford Moray 160 B2
Kirktown of Fetteresso Aberds 151 F7
Kirktown of Mortlach Moray 159 F7
Kirktown of Slains Aberds 161 F7
Kirkurd Borders 122 E4
Kirkwall Orkney 176 E3
Kirkwall Airport Orkney 176 F3
Kirkwhelpington Northumb 117 F5
Kirmington N Lincs 90 C5
Kirmond le Mire Lincs 91 E5
Kirn Argyll 129 C6
Kirriemuir Angus 142 D3
Kirstead Green Norf 69 E5
Kirtlebridge Dumfries 108 B2
Kirtleton Dumfries 115 F5
Kirtling Cambs 55 D7
Kirtling Green Cambs 55 D7
Kirtlington Oxon 38 C4
Kirtomy Highld 168 C2
Kirton Lincs 79 F6
Kirton Notts 77 C6
Kirton Suff 57 F6
Kirton End Lincs 79 E5
Kirton Holme Lincs 79 E5
Kirton in Lindsey N Lincs 90 E3
Kislingbury Northants 52 D4
Kites Hardwick Warks 52 C2
Kittisford Som 11 B5
Kittle Swansea 33 F6
Kitt's Green W Mid 63 F5
Kitt's Moss Gtr Man 87 F6
Kittybrewster Aberdeen 151 D8

Kitwood Hants 26 F4
Kivernoll Hereford 49 F6
Kiveton Park S Yorks 89 F5
Knaith Lincs 90 F2
Knaith Park Lincs 90 F2
Knap Corner Dorset 13 B6
Knaphill Sur 27 D7
Knapp Perth 142 F2
Knapp Som 11 B8
Knapthorpe Notts 77 D7
Knapton Norf 81 D9
Knapton York 95 D8
Knapton Green Hereford 49 D6
Knapwell Cambs 54 C4
Knaresborough N Yorks 95 D6
Knarsdale Northumb 109 D6
Knauchland Moray 160 C2
Knaven Aberds 161 D5
Knayton N Yorks 102 F2
Knebworth Herts 41 B5
Knebworth House, Stevenage Herts 41 B5
Knedlington E Yorks 89 B8
Kneesall Notts 77 C7
Kneesworth Cambs 54 E4
Kneeton Notts 77 E7
Knelston Swansea 33 F5
Knenhall Staffs 75 F6
Knettishall Suff 68 F2
Knightacott Devon 21 F5
Knightcote Warks 51 D8
Knightley Dale Staffs 62 B2
Knighton Devon 6 E3
Knighton Leicester 64 D2
Knighton Staffs 61 B7
Knighton Staffs 74 E4
Knighton = Tref-y-Clawdd Powys 48 B4
Knightshayes Court Devon 10 C4
Knightswood Glasgow 120 C5
Knightwick Worcs 50 D2
Knill Hereford 48 C4
Knipton Leics 77 F8
Knitsley Durham 110 E4
Kniveton Derbys 76 D2
Knock Argyll 137 E6
Knock Cumb 100 B1
Knock Moray 160 C2
Knockally Highld 165 B8
Knockan Highld 163 C6
Knockandhu Moray 149 B8
Knockando Moray 159 E5
Knockando Ho. Moray 159 E6
Knockbain Highld 157 D7
Knockbreck Highld 152 C3
Knockbrex Dumfries 106 E2
Knockdee Highld 169 C6
Knockdolian S Ayrs 104 A5
Knockenkelly N Ayrs 119 D7
Knockentiber E Ayrs 120 F3
Knockespock Ho. Aberds 150 B4
Knockfarrel Highld 157 D6
Knockglass Dumfries 104 D4
Knockhill Motor Racing Circuit Fife 134 E2
Knockholt Kent 29 D5
Knockholt Pound Kent 29 D5
Knockie Lodge Highld 147 C7
Knockin Shrops 60 B3
Knockinlaw E Ayrs 120 F4
Knocklearn Dumfries 106 B4
Knocknaha Argyll 118 E3
ocknain Dumfries 104 C3
ckrome Argyll 127 E3
ksharry I o M 84 D2
dishall Suff 57 C8
le House & Gardens Kent 29 D6
olls Green Ches 74 B5
olton Wrex 73 F7
olton Bryn Wrex 73 F7
nook Wilts 24 E4
ossington Leics 64 D5
nott End-on-Sea Lancs 92 E3
Knotting Beds 53 C8
Knotting Green Beds 53 C8
Knottingley W Yorks 89 B6
Knotts Cumb 99 B6
Knotts Lancs 93 D7
Knotty Ash Mers 86 E2
Knotty Green Bucks 40 E2
Knowbury Shrops 49 B7
Knowe Dumfries 105 B7
Knowehead Dumfries 113 E6
Knowes of Elrick Aberds 160 C3
Knowesgate Northumb 117 F5
Knoweton N Lnrk 121 D7
Knowhead Aberds 161 C6
Knowl Hill Windsor 27 B6
Knowle Bristol 23 B8
Knowle Devon 10 D2
Knowle Devon 11 F5
Knowle Devon 20 F3
Knowle Shrops 49 B7
Knowle W Mid 51 B6
Knowle Green Lancs 93 F6
Knowle Park W Yorks 94 E3
Knowlton Dorset 13 C8
Knowlton Kent 31 D6
Knowsley Mers 86 E2
Knowsley Safari Park Mers 86 E2
Knowstone Devon 10 B3
Knox Bridge Kent 29 E8
Knucklas Powys 48 B4
Knuston Northants 53 C7
Knutsford Ches 74 B4
Knutton Staffs 74 E5
Knypersley Staffs 75 D5
Kuggar Corn 3 E6
Kyle of Lochalsh Highld 155 H3
Kyleakin Highld 155 H3
Kylerhea Highld 155 H3
Kylesknoydart Highld 145 D8
Kylesku Highld 166 F4
Kylesmorar Highld 145 D8
Kylestrome Highld 166 F4
Kyllachy House Highld 148 B3
Kynaston Shrops 60 B3
Kynnersley Telford 61 C6
Kyre Magna Worcs 49 C8

L

La Fontenelle Guern 16
La Planque Guern 16
Labost W Isles 172 D5
Lacasaidh W Isles 172 F6
Lacasdal W Isles 172 E7
Laceby NE Lincs 91 D6
Lacey Green Bucks 39 E8
Lach Dennis Ches 74 B4
Lackford Suff 55 B8
Lacock Wilts 24 C4
Ladbroke Warks 52 D2
Laddingford Kent 29 E7
Lade Bank Lincs 79 D6
Ladock Corn 4 D3
Lady Orkney 176 B5
Ladybank Fife 134 C5
Ladykirk Borders 124 E4
Ladysford Aberds 161 B6
Laga Highld 137 B7
Lagalochan Argyll 130 D4
Lagavulin Argyll 126 E4
Lagg Argyll 127 E3
Lagg N Ayrs 119 D6
Laggan Argyll 126 D2
Laggan Highld 147 E5
Laggan Highld 148 E2
Laggan Highld 145 F7
Laggan S Ayrs 112 F2
Lagganulva Argyll 137 D5
Laide Highld 162 E2
Laigh Fenwick E Ayrs 120 E4
Laigh Glengall S Ayrs 112 C3
Laighmuir E Ayrs 120 E4
Laindon Essex 42 F2
Lair Highld 155 F6
Lairg Highld 164 D2
Lairg Lodge Highld 164 D2
Lairg Muir Highld 164 D2
Lairgmore Highld 157 F6
Laisterdyke W Yorks 94 F4
Laithes Cumb 108 F4
Lake I o W 15 F6
Lake Wilts 25 F6
Lakenham Norf 68 D5
Lakenheath Suff 67 F7
Lakesend Norf 66 E5
Lakeside Cumb 99 F5
Lakeside and Haverthwaite Railway Cumb 99 F5
Laleham Sur 27 C8
Laleston Bridgend 21 B7
Lamarsh Essex 56 F2
Lamas Norf 81 E8
Lambden Borders 124 E3
Lamberhurst Kent 18 B3
Lamberhurst Quarter Kent 18 B3
Lamberton Borders 125 D5
Lambeth London 28 B4
Lambhill Glasgow 121 C5
Lambley Notts 77 E6
Lambley Northumb 109 D6
Lamborough Hill Oxon 38 D4
Lambourn W Berks 25 B8
Lambourne End Essex 41 E7
Lambs Green W Sus 28 F3
Lambston Pembs 44 D4
Lambton T & W 111 D5
Lamerton Devon 6 B2
Lamesley T & W 111 D5
Laminess Orkney 176 C5
Lamington Highld 157 B8
Lamington S Lnrk 122 F2
Lamlash N Ayrs 119 C7
Lamloch Dumfries 112 E5
Lamonby Cumb 108 F4
Lamorna Corn 2 D3
Lamorran Corn 3 B7
Lampardbrook Suff 57 C6
Lampeter = Llanbedr Pont Steffan Ceredig 46 E4
Lampeter Velfrey Pembs 32 C2
Lamphey Pembs 32 D1
Lamplugh Cumb 98 B2
Lamport Northants 53 B5
Lamyatt Som 23 F8
Lana Devon 8 E5
Lanark S Lnrk 121 E8
Lancaster Lancs 92 C4
Lancaster Leisure Park Lancs 92 C4
Lanchester Durham 110 E4
Lancing W Sus 17 D5
Landbeach Cambs 55 C5
Landcross Devon 9 B6
Landerberry Aberds 151 D6
Landford Wilts 14 C3
Landford Manor Wilts 14 B3
Landimore Swansea 33 E5
Landkey Devon 20 F4
Landore Swansea 33 E7
Landrake Corn 5 C8
Land's End Corn 2 D2
Land's End Airport Corn 2 D2
Landscove Devon 7 C5
Landshipping Pembs 32 C1
Landshipping Quay Pembs 32 C1
Landulph Corn 6 C2
Landwade Suff 55 C7
Lane Corn 4 C3
Lane End Bucks 39 E8
Lane End Cumb 98 E3
Lane End Dorset 13 E6
Lane End Hants 15 B6
Lane End I o W 15 F7
Lane End Lancs 93 E8
Lane Ends Lancs 93 F7
Lane Ends Lancs 93 D7
Lane Ends N Yorks 94 E2
Lane Head Derbys 75 B8
Lane Head Durham 101 C6
Lane Head Gtr Man 86 E4
Lane Head W Yorks 88 D2
Lane Side Lancs 87 B5
Laneast Corn 8 F4
Laneham Notts 77 B8
Lanehead Durham 109 E8
Lanehead Northumb 116 F3
Lanercost Cumb 109 C5
Laneshaw Bridge Lancs 94 E2
Lanfach Caerph 35 E6
Langar Notts 77 F7
Langbank Renfs 120 B3
Langbar N Yorks 94 D3
Langburnshiels Borders 115 D8
Langcliffe N Yorks 93 C8
Langdale Highld 167 E8
Langdale End N Yorks 103 E7
Langdon Corn 8 F5
Langdon Beck Durham 109 F8
Langdon Hills Essex 42 F2
Langdyke Fife 134 D5
Langenhoe Essex 43 C6
Langford Beds 54 E2
Langford Devon 10 D5
Langford Essex 42 D4
Langford Notts 77 D8
Langford Oxon 38 D2
Langford Budville Som 11 B6
Langham Essex 56 F4
Langham Norf 81 C6
Langham Rutland 64 C5
Langham Suff 56 C3
Langhaugh Borders 122 F5
Langho Lancs 93 F7
Langholm Dumfries 115 F6
Langleeford Northumb 117 B5
Langley Ches 75 B6
Langley Hants 14 D5
Langley Herts 41 B5
Langley Kent 30 D2
Langley Northumb 109 C8
Langley Slough 27 B8
Langley Warks 51 C6
Langley W Sus 16 B2
Langley Burrell Wilts 24 B4
Langley Common Derbys 76 F2
Langley Heath Kent 30 D2
Langley Lower Green Essex 54 F5
Langley Marsh Som 11 B5
Langley Park Durham 110 E5
Langley Street Norf 69 D6
Langley Upper Green Essex 54 F5
Langney E Sus 18 E3
Langold Notts 89 F6
Langore Corn 8 F5
Langport Som 12 B2
Langrick Lincs 79 E5
Langridge Bath 24 C2
Langridge Ford Devon 9 B7
Langrigg Cumb 107 E8
Langrish Hants 15 B8
Langsett S Yorks 88 D3
Langshaw Borders 123 F8
Langside Perth 133 C6
Langskaill Orkney 176 B3
Langstone Hants 15 D8
Langstone Newport 35 E7
Langthorne N Yorks 101 E7
Langthorpe N Yorks 95 C6
Langthwaite N Yorks 101 D5
Langtoft E Yorks 97 C6
Langtoft Lincs 65 C8
Langton Durham 101 C6
Langton Lincs 78 C5
Langton Lincs 79 B6
Langton N Yorks 96 C3
Langton by Wragby Lincs 78 B4
Langton Green Kent 18 B2
Langton Green Suff 56 B5
Langton Herring Dorset 12 F4
Langton Matravers Dorset 13 G8
Langtree Devon 9 C6
Langwathby Cumb 109 F5
Langwell Ho. Highld 165 B8
Langwell Lodge Highld 163 D5
Langwith Derbys 76 C5
Langwith Junction Derbys 76 C5
Langworth Lincs 78 B3
Lanhydrock House, Bodmin Corn 5 C5
Lanivet Corn 4 C5
Lanlivery Corn 5 D5
Lanner Corn 3 C6
Lanreath Corn 5 D6
Lansallos Corn 5 D6
Lansdown Glos 37 B6
Lanteglos Highway Corn 5 D6
Lanton Borders 116 B2
Lanton Northumb 124 F5
Lapford Devon 10 D2
Laphroaig Argyll 126 E3
Lapley Staffs 62 C2
Lapworth Warks 51 B6
Larachbeg Highld 137 D7
Larbert Falk 133 F7
Larden Green Ches 74 D2
Largie Aberds 160 E3
Largiemore Argyll 128 B4
Largoward Fife 135 D6
Largs N Ayrs 129 E7
Largybeg N Ayrs 119 D7
Largymore N Ayrs 119 D7
Larkfield Invclyd 129 C7
Larkhall S Lnrk 121 D7
Larkhill Wilts 25 E6
Larling Norf 68 F2
Larriston Borders 115 E8
Lartington Durham 101 C5
Lary Aberds 150 D2
Lasham Hants 26 E4
Lashenden Kent 30 E2
Lassington Glos 36 B4
Lassodie Fife 134 E3
Lastingham N Yorks 103 E5
Latcham Som 23 E6
Latchford Herts 41 B6
Latchford Warr 86 F4
Latchingdon Essex 42 D4
Latchley Corn 6 B2
Lately Common Warr 86 E4
Lathbury M Keynes 53 E6
Latheron Highld 169 F6
Latheronwheel Highld 169 F6
Latheronwheel Ho. Highld 169 F6
Lathones Fife 135 D6
Latimer Bucks 40 E3
Latteridge S Glos 36 F3
Lattiford Som 12 B4
Latton Wilts 37 E7
Latton Bush Essex 41 D7
Lauchintilly Aberds 151 C6
Lauder Borders 123 E8
Laugharne Carms 32 C4
Laughterton Lincs 77 B8
Laughton E Sus 18 D2
Laughton Leics 64 F3
Laughton Lincs 78 F3
Laughton Lincs 90 E2
Laughton Common S Yorks 89 F6
Laughton en le Morthen S Yorks 89 F6
Launcells Corn 8 D4
Launceston Corn 8 F5
Launton Oxon 39 B6
Laurencekirk Aberds 143 B7
Laurieston Dumfries 106 C3
Laurieston Falk 122 B2
Lavendon M Keynes 53 D7
Lavenham Suff 56 E3
Laverhay Dumfries 114 E4
Laversdale Cumb 108 C4
Laverstock Wilts 25 F6
Laverstoke Hants 26 E2
Laverton Glos 51 F5
Laverton N Yorks 94 B5
Laverton Som 24 D2
Lavister Wrex 73 D7
Law S Lnrk 121 D8
Lawers Perth 140 F3
Lawers Perth 133 B6
Lawford Essex 56 F4
Lawhitton Corn 9 F5
Lawkland N Yorks 93 C7
Lawley Telford 61 D6
Lawnhead Staffs 62 B2
Lawrenny Pembs 32 D1
Lawshall Suff 56 D2
Lawton Hereford 49 D6
Laxey I o M 84 D4
Laxey Wheel and Mines I o M 84 D4
Laxfield Suff 57 B6
Laxfirth Shetland 175 J6
Laxfirth Shetland 175 H6
Laxford Bridge Highld 166 E4
Laxo Shetland 175 G6
Laxobigging Shetland 174 F6
Laxton E Yorks 89 B8
Laxton Notts 77 C7
Laxton Northants 65 E6
Laycock W Yorks 94 E3
Layer Breton Essex 43 C5
Layer de la Haye Essex 43 C5
Layer Marney Essex 43 C5
Layham Suff 56 E4
Laylands Green W Berks 25 C8
Laytham E Yorks 96 F3
Layton Blkpool 92 F3
Lazenby Redcar 102 B3
Lazonby Cumb 108 F5
Le Planel Guern 16
Le Villocq Guern 16
Lea Derbys 76 D3
Lea Hereford 36 B3
Lea Lincs 90 F2
Lea Shrops 60 F3
Lea Shrops 60 D4
Lea Wilts 37 F6
Lea Marston Warks 63 E6
Lea Town Lancs 92 F4
Leabrooks Derbys 76 D4
Leac a Li W Isles 173 J4
Leachkin Highld 157 E7
Leadburn Midloth 122 D5
Leaden Roding Essex 42 C1
Leadenham Lincs 78 D2
Leadgate Cumb 109 E7
Leadgate Durham 110 D4
Leadgate Northumb 110 D4
Leadhills S Lnrk 113 C8
Leafield Oxon 38 C3
Leagrave Luton 40 B3
Leake N Yorks 102 E2
Leake Commonside Lincs 79 D6
Lealholm N Yorks 103 D5
Lealt Argyll 128 A1
Lealt Highld 152 C6
Leamington Hastings Warks 52 C2
Leamonsley Staffs 62 D5
Leamside Durham 111 E6
Leanaig Highld 157 D6
Leargybreck Argyll 127 E3
Leasgill Cumb 99 F6
Leasingham Lincs 78 E3
Leasingthorne Durham 101 B7
Leasowe Mers 85 E3
Leatherhead Sur 28 D2
Leatherhead Common Sur 28 D2
Leathley N Yorks 94 E5
Leaton Shrops 60 C4
Leaveland Kent 30 D4
Leavening N Yorks 96 C3
Leaves Green London 28 C5
Leazes Durham 110 D4
Lebberston N Yorks 103 F8
Lechlade-on-Thames Glos 38 E2
Leck Lancs 93 B6
Leckford Hants 25 F8
Leckfurin Highld 168 D2
Leckgruinart Argyll 126 C2
Leckhampstead Bucks 52 F5
Leckhampstead W Berks 26 B2
Leckhampstead Thicket W Berks 26 B2
Leckhampton Glos 37 C6
Leckie Highld 154 D6
Leckmelm Highld 163 E5
Leckwith V Glam 22 B3
Leconfield E Yorks 97 E6
Ledaig Argyll 130 B5
Ledburn Bucks 40 B2
Ledbury Hereford 50 F2
Ledcharrie Stirl 132 B4
Ledgemoor Hereford 49 D6
Ledicot Hereford 49 C6
Ledmore Highld 163 C6
Lednagullin Highld 168 C2
Ledsham Ches 73 B7
Ledsham W Yorks 89 B5
Ledston W Yorks 88 B5
Ledston Luck W Yorks 95 F7
Ledwell Oxon 38 B4
Lee Argyll 137 F5
Lee Devon 20 E3
Lee Hants 14 C4
Lee Lancs 93 D5
Lee Shrops 73 F8
Lee Brockhurst Shrops 60 B5
Lee Clump Bucks 40 D2
Lee Mill Devon 6 D4
Lee Moor Devon 6 C3
Lee-on-the-Solent Hants 15 D6
Leeans Shetland 175 J5
Leebotten Shetland 175 L6
Leebotwood Shrops 60 E4
Leece Cumb 92 C2
Leechpool Pembs 44 D4
Leeds Kent 30 D2
Leeds W Yorks 95 F5
Leeds Bradford International Airport W Yorks 94 E5
Leeds Castle Kent 30 D2
Leeds City Art Gallery W Yorks 95 F5
Leedstown Corn 2 C5
Leek Staffs 75 D6
Leek Wootton Warks 51 C7
Leekbrook Staffs 75 D6
Leeming N Yorks 101 F7
Leeming Bar N Yorks 101 E7
Lees Derbys 76 F2
Lees Gtr Man 87 D7
Lees W Yorks 94 F3
Leeswood Flint 73 C6
Legbourne Lincs 91 F7
Legerwood Borders 123 E8
Legoland Windsor 27 B7
Legsby Lincs 90 F5
Leicester Leicester 64 D2
Leicester Forest East Leics 64 D2
Leicester Racecourse Leics 64 D3
Leigh Dorset 12 D4
Leigh Glos 37 B5
Leigh Gtr Man 86 D4
Leigh Kent 29 E6
Leigh Shrops 60 D3
Leigh Sur 28 E3
Leigh Wilts 37 E7
Leigh Worcs 50 D2
Leigh Beck Essex 42 F4
Leigh Common Som 12 B5
Leigh Delamere Wilts 24 B3
Leigh Green Kent 19 B6
Leigh on Sea Sthend 42 F4
Leigh Park Hants 15 D8
Leigh Sinton Worcs 50 D2
Leigh upon Mendip Som 23 E8
Leigh Woods N Som 23 B7
Leighswood W Mid 62 D4
Leighterton Glos 37 E5
Leighton N Yorks 94 B4
Leighton Powys 60 D2
Leighton Shrops 61 D6
Leighton Som 24 E2
Leighton Bromswold Cambs 54 B2
Leighton Buzzard Beds 40 B2
Leinthall Earls Hereford 49 C6
Leinthall Starkes Hereford 49 C6
Leintwardine Hereford 49 B6
Leire Leics 64 E2
Leirinmore Highld 167 C6
Leiston Suff 57 C8
Leitfie Perth 142 E2
Leith Edin 123 B5
Leitholm Borders 124 E3
Lelant Corn 2 C4
Lelley E Yorks 97 F8
Lem Hill Worcs 50 B2
Lemmington Hall Northumb 117 C7
Lempitlaw Borders 124 F3
Lenchwick Worcs 50 E5
Lendalfoot S Ayrs 112 F1
Lendrick Lodge Stirl 132 D4
Lenham Kent 30 D2
Lenham Heath Kent 30 E3
Lennel Borders 124 E4
Lennoxtown E Dunb 121 B6
Lenton Lincs 78 F3
Lenton Nottingham 77 F5
Lentran Highld 157 E6
Lenwade Norf 68 C3
Leny Ho. Stirl 132 D5
Lenzie E Dunb 121 B6
Leoch Angus 142 F3
Leochel-Cushnie Aberds 150 C4
Leominster Hereford 49 D6
Leonard Stanley Glos 37 D5
Leonardslee Gardens W Sus 17 B6
Leorin Argyll 126 E3
Lepe Hants 15 E5
Lephin Highld 152 E2
Lephinchapel Argyll 128 A4
Lephinmore Argyll 128 A4
Leppington N Yorks 96 C3
Lepton W Yorks 88 C3
Lerryn Corn 5 D6
Lerwick Shetland 175 J6
Lerwick (Tingwall) Airport Shetland 175 J6
Lesbury Northumb 117 C8
Leslie Aberds 150 B4
Leslie Fife 134 D4
Lesmahagow S Lnrk 121 F8
Lesnewth Corn 8 E3
Lessendrum Aberds 160 D2
Lessingham Norf 69 B6
Lessonhall Cumb 108 D2
Leswalt Dumfries 104 C4
Letchmore Heath Herts 40 E4
Letchworth Herts 54 F3
Letcombe Bassett Oxon 38 F3
Letcombe Regis Oxon 38 F3
Letham Angus 143 E5
Letham Falk 133 F7
Letham Fife 134 C5
Letham Perth 134 B2
Letham Grange Angus 143 E6
Lethenty Aberds 160 D5
Letheringham Suff 57 D6
Letheringsett Norf 81 D6
Lettaford Devon 10 F2
Lettan Orkney 176 B6
Letterewe Highld 154 C5
Letterfearn Highld 155 H4
Letterfinlay Highld 147 E5
Lettermorar Highld 145 E7
Lettermore Argyll 137 D5
Letters Highld 163 F5
Letterston Pembs 44 C4
Lettoch Highld 149 C6
Lettoch Highld 158 F4
Letton Hereford 48 E5
Letton Hereford 49 B5
Letton Green Norf 68 D2
Letty Green Herts 41 C5
Letwell S Yorks 89 F6
Leuchars Fife 135 B6
Leuchars Ho. Moray 159 C6
Leumrabhagh W Isles 173 G6
Levan Invclyd 129 C7
Levaneap Shetland 175 G6
Levedale Staffs 62 C2
Leven E Yorks 97 E7
Leven Fife 135 D5
Levencorroch N Ayrs 119 D7
Levens Cumb 99 F6
Levens Green Herts 41 B6
Levenshulme Gtr Man 87 E6
Levenwick Shetland 175 L6
Leverburgh = An t-Ob W Isles 173 K3
Leverington Cambs 66 C4
Leverton Lincs 79 E7
Leverton Highgate Lincs 79 E7
Leverton Lucasgate Lincs 79 E7
Leverton Outgate Lincs 79 E7
Levington Suff 57 F6
Levisham N Yorks 103 E6
Levishie Highld 147 C7
Lew Oxon 38 D3
Lewannick Corn 8 F4
Lewdown Devon 9 F6
Lewes E Sus 17 C8
Leweston Pembs 44 C4
Lewisham London 28 B4
Lewiston Highld 147 B8
Lewistown Bridgend 34 F3
Lewknor Oxon 39 E7
Leworthy Devon 8 D5
Leworthy Devon 21 F5
Lewtrenchard Devon 9 F6
Lexden Essex 43 B5
Ley Aberds 150 C4
Ley Corn 5 C6
Leybourne Kent 29 D7
Leyburn N Yorks 101 E6
Leyfields Staffs 63 D6
Leyhill Bucks 40 D2
Leyland Lancs 86 B3
Leylodge Aberds 151 C6
Leymoor W Yorks 88 C2
Leys Aberds 161 C7
Leys Perth 142 F2
Leys Castle Highld 157 E7
Leys of Cossans Angus 142 E3
Leysdown-on-Sea Kent 30 B4
Leysmill Angus 143 E6
Leysters Pole Hereford 49 C7
Leyton London 41 F6
Leytonstone London 41 F6
Lezant Corn 5 B8
Leziate Norf 67 C6
Lhanbryde Moray 159 C6
Liatrie Highld 156 F3
Libanus Powys 34 B3
Libberton S Lnrk 122 E2
Liberton Edin 123 C5
Liceasto W Isles 173 J4
Lichfield Staffs 62 D5
Lichfield Cathedral Staffs 62 C5
Lickey Worcs 50 B4
Lickey End Worcs 50 B4
Lickfold W Sus 16 B3
Liddel Orkney 176 H3
Liddesdale Highld 138 D1
Liddington Thamesdown 38 F2
Lidgate Suff 55 D8
Lidget S Yorks 89 D7
Lidget Green W Yorks 94 F4
Lidgett Notts 77 C6
Lidlington Beds 53 F7
Lidstone Oxon 38 B3
Lieurary Highld 169 C5
Liff Angus 142 F3
Lifton Devon 9 F5
Liftondown Devon 9 F5
Lighthorne Warks 51 D8
Lightwater Sur 27 C7
Lightwater Valley N Yorks 95 B6
Lightwood Stoke 75 E6
Lightwood Green Ches 74 E3
Lightwood Green Wrex 73 E7
Lilbourne Northants 52 B3
Lilburn Tower Northumb 117 B6
Lilleshall Telford 61 C7
Lilley Herts 40 B4
Lilley W Berks 26 B2
Lilliesleaf Borders 115 B8
Lillingstone Dayrell Bucks 52 F5
Lillingstone Lovell Bucks 52 E5
Lillington Dorset 12 C4
Lillington Warks 51 C8
Lilliput Poole 13 E8
Lilstock Som 22 E3
Lilyhurst Shrops 61 C7
Limbury Luton 40 B3
Limebrook Hereford 49 C5
Limefield Gtr Man 87 C6
Limekilnburn S Lnrk 121 D7
Limekilns Fife 134 F2
Limerigg Falk 121 B8
Limerstone I o W 14 F5
Limington Som 12 B3
Limpenhoe Norf 69 D6
Limpley Stoke Wilts 24 C2
Limpsfield Sur 28 D5
Limpsfield Chart Sur 28 D5
Linby Notts 76 D5
Linchmere W Sus 27 F6
Lincluden Dumfries 107 B6
Lincoln Lincs 78 B2
Lincoln Castle Lincs 78 B2
Lincoln Cathedral Lincs 78 B2
Lincomb Worcs 50 C3
Lincombe Devon 6 D5
Lindal in Furness Cumb 92 B2
Lindale Cumb 99 F6
Lindean Borders 123 F7
Lindfield W Sus 17 B7
Lindford Hants 27 F6
Lindifferon Fife 134 C5
Lindisfarne Priory, Holy Island Northumb 125 E7
Lindley W Yorks 88 C2
Lindley Green N Yorks 94 E5
Lindores Fife 134 C4
Lindridge Worcs 49 C8
Lindsell Essex 42 B2
Lindsey Suff 56 E3
Linford Hants 14 D2
Linford Thurrock 29 B7
Lingague I o M 84 E2
Lingards Wood W Yorks 87 C8
Lingbob W Yorks 94 F3
Lingdale Redcar 102 C4
Lingen Hereford 49 C5
Lingfield Sur 28 E4
Lingfield Park Racecourse Sur 28 E4
Lingreabhagh W Isles 173 K3
Lingwood Norf 69 D6
Linicro Highld 152 C4
Linkenholt Hants 25 D8
Linkhill Kent 18 C5
Linkinhorne Corn 5 B8
Linklater Orkney 176 H3
Linksness Orkney 176 F1
Linktown Fife 134 E4
Linley Shrops 60 E3
Linley Green Hereford 49 D8
Linlithgow W Loth 122 B3
Linlithgow Bridge W Loth 122 B2
Linshiels Northumb 116 D4
Linsiadar W Isles 172 E5
Linsidemore Highld 164 E2
Linslade Beds 40 B2
Linstead Parva Suff 57 B7
Linstock Cumb 108 D4
Linthwaite W Yorks 88 C2
Lintlaw Borders 124 D4
Lintmill Moray 160 B2
Linton Borders 116 B3
Linton Cambs 55 E6
Linton Derbys 63 C6
Linton Hereford 36 B3
Linton Kent 29 E8
Linton Northumb 117 E8
Linton N Yorks 94 C2
Linton W Yorks 95 E6
Linton-on-Ouse N Yorks 95 C7
Linwood Hants 14 D2
Linwood Lincs 90 F5
Linwood Renfs 120 C4
Lionacleit W Isles 170 F3
Lional W Isles 172 B8
Liphook Hants 27 F6
Liscard Mers 85 E4
Liscombe Som 21 F7
Liskeard Corn 5 C7
L'Islet Guern 16
Liss Hants 15 B8
Liss Forest Hants 15 B8
Lissett E Yorks 97 D7
Lissington Lincs 90 F5
Lisvane Cardiff 35 F5
Liswerry Newport 35 F7
Litcham Norf 67 C8
Litchborough Northants 52 D4
Litchfield Hants 26 D2
Litherland Mers 85 E4
Litlington Cambs 54 E4
Litlington E Sus 18 E2
Little Abington Cambs 55 E6
Little Addington Northants 53 B7
Little Alne Warks 51 C6
Little Altcar Mers 85 D4
Little Asby Cumb 100 D1
Little Assynt Highld 163 B5
Little Aston Staffs 62 D4
Little Atherfield I o W 15 F5
Little Ayre Orkney 176 G2
Little-ayre Shetland 175 G5
Little Ayton N Yorks 102 C3
Little Baddow Essex 42 D3
Little Badminton S Glos 37 F5
Little Ballinluig Perth 141 D6
Little Bampton Cumb 108 D2
Little Bardfield Essex 55 F7
Little Barford Beds 54 D2
Little Barningham Norf 81 D7
Little Barrington Glos 38 C2
Little Barrow Ches 73 B8
Little Barugh N Yorks 96 B3
Little Bavington Northumb 110 B2
Little Bealings Suff 57 E6
Little Bedwyn Wilts 25 C7
Little Bentley Essex 43 B7
Little Berkhamsted Herts 41 D5
Little Billing Northants 53 C6
Little Birch Hereford 49 F7
Little Blakenham Suff 56 E5
Little Blencow Cumb 108 F4
Little Bollington Ches 86 F5
Little Bookham Sur 28 D2
Little Bowden Leics 64 F4
Little Bradley Suff 55 D7
Little Brampton Shrops 60 F3
Little Brechin Angus 143 C5
Little Brickhill M Keynes 53 F7
Little Brington Northants 52 C4
Little Bromley Essex 43 B6
Little Broughton Cumb 107 F7
Little Budworth Ches 74 C2
Little Burstead Essex 42 E2
Little Bytham Lincs 65 C7
Little Carlton Lincs 91 F7
Little Carlton Notts 77 D7
Little Casterton Rutland 65 D7
Little Cawthorpe Lincs 91 F7
Little Chalfont Bucks 40 E2
Little Chart Kent 30 E3
Little Chesterford Essex 55 E6
Little Cheverell Wilts 24 D4
Little Chishill Cambs 54 F5
Little Clacton Essex 43 C7
Little Clifton Cumb 98 B2
Little Colp Aberds 160 D4
Little Comberton Worcs 50 E4
Little Common E Sus 18 E4
Little Compton Warks 51 F7
Little Cornard Suff 56 F2
Little Cowarne Hereford 49 D8
Little Coxwell Oxon 38 E2
Little Crakehall N Yorks 101 E7
Little Cressingham Norf 67 D8
Little Crosby Mers 85 D4
Little Dalby Leics 64 C4
Little Dawley Telford 61 D6
Little Dens Aberds 161 D7
Little Dewchurch Hereford 49 F7

Little Downham Cambs 66 F5
Little Driffield E Yorks 97 D6
Little Dunham Norf 67 C8
Little Dunkeld Perth 141 F7
Little Dunmow Essex 42 B2
Little Easton Essex 42 B2
Little Eaton Derbys 76 E3
Little Eccleston Lancs 92 E4
Little Ellingham Norf 68 E3
Little End Essex 41 D8
Little Eversden Cambs 54 D4
Little Faringdon Oxon 38 D2
Little Fencote N Yorks 101 E7
Little Fenton N Yorks 95 F8
Little Finborough Suff 56 D4
Little Fransham Norf 68 C2
Little Gaddesden Herts 40 C2
Little Gidding Cambs 65 F8
Little Glemham Suff 57 D7
Little Glenshee Perth 141 F6
Little Gransden Cambs 54 D3
Little Green Som 24 E2
Little Grimsby Lincs 91 E7
Little Gruinard Highld 162 F3
Little Habton N Yorks 96 B3
Little Hadham Herts 41 B7
Little Hale Lincs 78 E4
Little Hallingbury Essex 41 C7
Little Hampden Bucks 40 D1
Little Harrowden Northants 53 B6
Little Haseley Oxon 39 D6
Little Hatfield E Yorks 97 E7
Little Hautbois Norf 81 E8
Little Haven Pembs 44 D3
Little Hay Staffs 62 D5
Little Hayfield Derbys 87 F8
Little Haywood Staffs 62 B4
Little Heath W Mid 63 F7
Little Hereford Hereford 49 C7
Little Horkesley Essex 56 F3
Little Horsted E Sus 17 C8
Little Horton W Yorks 94 F4
Little Horwood Bucks 53 F5
Little Houghton Northants 53 D6
Little Houghton S Yorks 88 D5
Little Hucklow Derbys 75 B8
Little Hulton Gtr Man 86 D5
Little Humber E Yorks 91 B5
Little Hungerford W Berks 26 B3
Little Irchester Northants 53 C7
Little Kimble Bucks 39 D8
Little Kineton Warks 51 D8
Little Kingshill Bucks 40 E1
Little Langdale Cumb 99 D5
Little Langford Wilts 25 F5
Little Laver Essex 41 D8
Little Leigh Ches 74 B3
Little Leighs Essex 42 C3
Little Lever Gtr Man 87 D5
Little London Bucks 39 C6
Little London E Sus 18 D2
Little London Hants 25 E8
Little London Hants 26 D4
Little London Lincs 66 B2
Little London Lincs 66 B4
Little London Norf 81 E7
Little London Powys 59 F7
Little Longstone Derbys 75 B8
Little Lynturk Aberds 150 C4
Little Malvern Worcs 50 E2
Little Maplestead Essex 56 F2
Little Marcle Hereford 49 F8
Little Marlow Bucks 40 F1
Little Marsden Lancs 93 F8
Little Massingham Norf 80 E3
Little Melton Norf 68 D4
Little Mill Mon 35 D7
Little Milton Oxon 39 D6
Little Missenden Bucks 40 E2
Little Musgrave Cumb 100 C2
Little Ness Shrops 60 C4
Little Neston Ches 73 B6
Little Newcastle Pembs 44 C4
Little Newsham Durham 101 C6
Little Oakley Essex 43 B8
Little Oakley Northants 65 F5
Little Orton Cumb 108 D3
Little Ouseburn N Yorks 95 C7
Little Paxton Cambs 54 C2
Little Petherick Corn 4 B4
Little Pitlurg Moray 159 E8
Little Plumpton Lancs 92 F3
Little Plumstead Norf 69 C6
Little Ponton Lincs 78 F2
Little Raveley Cambs 54 B3
Little Reedness E Yorks 90 B2
Little Ribston N Yorks 95 D6
Little Rissington Glos 38 C1
Little Ryburgh Norf 81 E5
Little Ryle Northumb 117 C6
Little Salkeld Cumb 109 F5
Little Sampford Essex 55 F7
Little Sandhurst Brack 27 C6
Little Saxham Suff 55 C8
Little Scatwell Highld 156 D4
Little Sessay N Yorks 95 B7
Little Shelford Cambs 54 D5
Little Singleton Lancs 92 F3
Little Skillymarno Aberds 161 C6
Little Smeaton N Yorks 89 C6
Little Snoring Norf 81 D5
Little Sodbury S Glos 36 F4
Little Somborne Hants 25 F8
Little Somerford Wilts 37 F6
Little Stainforth N Yorks 93 C8
Little Stainton Darl 101 B8
Little Stanney Ches 73 B8
Little Staughton Beds 54 C2
Little Steeping Lincs 79 C7
Little Stoke Staffs 75 F6
Little Stonham Suff 56 C5
Little Stretton Leics 64 D3
Little Stretton Shrops 60 E4
Little Strickland Cumb 99 C7
Little Stukeley Cambs 54 B3
Little Sutton Ches 73 B7
Little Tew Oxon 38 B3
Little Thetford Cambs 55 B6
Little Thirkleby N Yorks 95 B7
Little Thurlow Suff 55 D7
Little Thurrock Thurrock 29 B7
Little Torboll Highld 164 E4
Little Torrington Devon 9 C6
Little Totham Essex 42 C4
Little Toux Aberds 160 C2
Little Town Cumb 98 C4
Little Town Lancs 93 F6
Little Urswick Cumb 92 B2
Little Wakering Essex 43 F5
Little Walden Essex 55 E6
Little Waldingfield Suff 56 E3
Little Walsingham Norf 80 D5
Little Waltham Essex 42 C3
Little Warley Essex 42 E2
Little Weighton E Yorks 97 F5
Little Weldon Northants 65 F6
Little Welnetham Suff 56 C2
Little Wenlock Telford 61 D6
Little Whittingham Green Suff 57 B6
Little Wilbraham Cambs 55 D6
Little Wishford Wilts 25 F5
Little Witley Worcs 50 C2
Little Wittenham Oxon 39 E5
Little Wolford Warks 51 F7
Little Wratting Suff 55 E7
Little Wymington Beds 53 C7
Little Wymondley Herts 41 B5
Little Wyrley Staffs 62 D4
Little Yeldham Essex 55 F8
Littlebeck N Yorks 103 D6
Littleborough Gtr Man 87 C7
Littleborough Notts 90 F2
Littlebourne Kent 31 D6
Littlebredy Dorset 12 F3
Littlebury Essex 55 F6
Littlebury Green Essex 55 F5
Littledean Glos 36 C3
Littleferry Highld 165 E5
Littleham Devon 10 F5
Littleham Devon 9 B6
Littlehampton W Sus 16 D4
Littlehempston Devon 7 C6
Littlehoughton Northumb 117 C8
Littlemill Aberds 150 E2
Littlemill E Ayrs 112 C4
Littlemill Highld 158 D3
Littlemill Northumb 117 C8
Littlemoor Dorset 12 F4
Littlemore Oxon 39 D5
Littleover Derby 76 F3
Littleport Cambs 67 F5
Littlestone on Sea Kent 19 C7
Littlethorpe Leics 64 E2
Littlethorpe N Yorks 95 C6
Littleton Ches 73 C8
Littleton Hants 26 F2
Littleton Perth 142 F2
Littleton Som 23 F6
Littleton Sur 27 C8
Littleton Sur 27 E7
Littleton Drew Wilts 37 F5
Littleton-on-Severn S Glos 36 F2
Littleton Pannell Wilts 24 D5
Littletown Durham 111 E6
Littlewick Green Windsor 27 B6
Littleworth Beds 53 E8
Littleworth Glos 37 D5
Littleworth Oxon 38 E3
Littleworth Staffs 62 C4
Littleworth Worcs 50 D3
Litton Derbys 75 B8
Litton N Yorks 94 B2
Litton Som 23 D7
Litton Cheney Dorset 12 E3
Liurbost W Isles 172 F6
Liverpool Mers 85 E4
Liverpool Cathedral (C of E) Mers 85 F8
Liverpool Cathedral (RC) Mers 85 E8
Liverpool John Lennon Airport Mers 86 F2
Liversedge W Yorks 88 B3
Liverton Devon 7 B6
Liverton Redcar 103 C5
Livingston W Loth 122 C3
Livingston Village W Loth 122 C3
Lixwm Flint 73 B5
Lizard Corn 3 E6
Llaingoch Anglesey 82 C2
Llaithddu Powys 59 F7
Llan Powys 59 D5
Llan Ffestiniog Gwyn 71 C8
Llan-y-pwll Wrex 73 D7
Llanaber Gwyn 58 C3
Llanaelhaearn Gwyn 70 C4
Llanafan Ceredig 47 B5
Llanafan-fawr Powys 47 D8
Llanallgo Anglesey 82 C4
Llanandras = Presteigne Powys 48 C5
Llanarmon Gwyn 70 D5
Llanarmon Dyffryn Ceiriog Wrex 73 F5
Llanarmon-yn-Ial Denb 73 D5
Llanarth Ceredig 46 D3
Llanarth Mon 35 C7
Llanarthne Carms 33 B6
Llanasa Flint 85 F2
Llanbabo Anglesey 82 C3
Llanbadarn Fawr Ceredig 58 F3
Llanbadarn Fynydd Powys 48 B3
Llanbadarn-y-Garreg Powys 48 E3
Llanbadoc Mon 35 E7
Llanbadrig Anglesey 82 B3
Llanbeder Newport 35 E7
Llanbedr Gwyn 71 E6
Llanbedr Powys 48 E3
Llanbedr Powys 35 B6
Llanbedr-Dyffryn-Clwyd Denb 72 D5
Llanbedr Pont Steffan = Lampeter Ceredig 46 E4
Llanbedr-y-cennin Conwy 83 E7
Llanbedrgoch Anglesey 82 C5
Llanbedrog Gwyn 70 D4
Llanberis Gwyn 83 E5
Llanbethêry V Glam 22 C2
Llanbister Powys 48 B3
Llanblethian V Glam 21 B8
Llanboidy Carms 32 B3
Llanbradach Caerph 35 E5
Llanbrynmair Powys 59 D5
Llancarfan V Glam 22 B2
Llancayo Mon 35 D7
Llancloudy Hereford 36 B1
Llancynfelyn Ceredig 58 E3
Llandaff Cardiff 22 B3
Llandanwg Gwyn 71 E6
Llandarcy Neath 33 E8
Llandawke Carms 32 C3
Llanddaniel Fab Anglesey 82 D4
Llanddarog Carms 33 C6
Llanddeiniol Ceredig 46 B4
Llanddeiniolen Gwyn 82 E5
Llandderfel Gwyn 72 F3
Llanddeusant Anglesey 82 C3
Llanddeusant Carms 34 B1
Llanddew Powys 48 F2
Llanddewi Swansea 33 F5
Llanddewi-Brefi Ceredig 47 D5
Llanddewi Rhydderch Mon 35 C7
Llanddewi Velfrey Pembs 32 C2
Llanddewi'r Cwm Powys 48 E2
Llanddoged Conwy 83 E8
Llanddona Anglesey 83 D5
Llanddowror Carms 32 C3
Llanddulas Conwy 72 B3
Llanddwywe Gwyn 71 E6
Llanddyfnan Anglesey 82 D5
Llandefaelog Fach Powys 48 F2
Llandefaelog-tre'r-graig Powys 35 B5
Llandefalle Powys 48 F3
Llandegai Gwyn 83 D5
Llandegfan Anglesey 83 D5
Llandegla Denb 73 D5
Llandegley Powys 48 C3
Llandegveth Mon 35 E7
Llandegwning Gwyn 70 D3
Llandeilo Carms 33 B7
Llandeilo Graban Powys 48 E2
Llandeilo'r Fan Powys 47 F7
Llandeloy Pembs 44 C3
Llandenny Mon 35 D8
Llandevenny Mon 35 F8
Llandewednock Corn 3 E6
Llandewi Ystradenny Powys 48 C3
Llandinabo Hereford 36 B2
Llandinam Powys 59 F7
Llandissilio Pembs 32 B2
Llandogo Mon 36 D2
Llandough V Glam 21 B8
Llandough V Glam 22 B3
Llandovery = Llanymddyfri Carms 47 F6
Llandow V Glam 21 B8
Llandre Ceredig 58 F3
Llandre Carms 47 E5
Llandrillo Denb 72 F4
Llandrillo-yn-Rhos Conwy 83 C8
Llandrindod = Llandrindod Wells Powys 48 C2
Llandrindod Wells = Llandrindod Powys 48 C2
Llandrinio Powys 60 C2
Llandudno Conwy 83 C7
Llandudno Junction = Cyffordd Llandudno Conwy 83 D7
Llandwrog Gwyn 82 F4
Llandybie Carms 33 C7
Llandyfaelog Carms 33 C5
Llandyfan Carms 33 C7
Llandyfriog Ceredig 46 E2
Llandyfrydog Anglesey 82 C4
Llandygwydd Ceredig 45 E4
Llandynan Denb 73 E5
Llandyrnog Denb 72 C5
Llandysilio Powys 60 C2
Llandyssil Powys 59 E8
Llandysul Ceredig 46 E3
Llanedeyrn Cardiff 35 F6
Llanedy Carms 33 D6
Llaneglwys Powys 48 F2
Llanegryn Gwyn 58 D2
Llanegwad Carms 33 B6
Llaneilian Anglesey 82 B4
Llanelian-yn-Rhos Conwy 83 D8
Llanelidan Denb 72 D5
Llanelieu Powys 48 F3
Llanellen Mon 35 C7
Llanelli Carms 33 E6
Llanelli Mon 35 C6
Llanelltyd Gwyn 58 C4
Llanelly Hill Mon 35 C6
Llanelwedd Powys 48 D2
Llanelwy = St Asaph Denb 72 B4
Llanenddwyn Gwyn 71 E6
Llanengan Gwyn 70 E3
Llanerchymedd Anglesey 82 C4
Llanerfyl Powys 59 D7
Llanfachraeth Anglesey 82 C3
Llanfachreth Gwyn 71 E8
Llanfaelog Anglesey 82 D3
Llanfaelrhys Gwyn 70 E3
Llanfaenor Mon 35 C8
Llanfaes Anglesey 83 D6
Llanfaes Powys 34 B4
Llanfaethlu Anglesey 82 C3
Llanfaglan Gwyn 82 E4
Llanfair Gwyn 71 E6
Llanfair-ar-y-bryn Carms 47 F7
Llanfair Caereinion Powys 59 D8
Llanfair Clydogau Ceredig 46 D5
Llanfair-Dyffryn-Clwyd Denb 72 D5
Llanfair-Nant-Gwyn Pembs 45 F3
Llanfair Talhaiarn Conwy 72 B3
Llanfair Waterdine Shrops 48 B4
Llanfair-ym-Muallt = Builth Wells Powys 48 D2
Llanfairfechan Conwy 83 D6
Llanfairpwll-gwyngyll Anglesey 82 D5
Llanfairyneubwll Anglesey 82 D3
Llanfairynghornwy Anglesey 82 B3
Llanfallteg Carms 32 C2
Llanfaredd Powys 48 D2
Llanfarian Ceredig 46 B4
Llanfechain Powys 59 B8
Llanfechan Powys 47 D8
Llanfechell Anglesey 82 B3
Llanfendigaid Gwyn 58 D2
Llanferres Denb 73 C5
Llanfflewyn Anglesey 82 C3
Llanfihangel-ar-arth Carms 46 F3
Llanfihangel-Crucorney Mon 35 B7
Llanfihangel Glyn Myfyr Conwy 72 E3
Llanfihangel Nant Bran Powys 47 F8
Llanfihangel-nant-Melan Powys 48 D3
Llanfihangel Rhydithon Powys 48 C3
Llanfihangel Rogiet Mon 35 F8
Llanfihangel Tal-y-llyn Powys 35 B5
Llanfihangel-uwch-Gwili Carms 33 B5
Llanfihangel-y-Creuddyn Ceredig 47 B5
Llanfihangel-y-pennant Gwyn 71 C6
Llanfihangel-y-pennant Gwyn 58 D3
Llanfihangel-y-traethau Gwyn 71 D6
Llanfihangel-yn-Ngwynfa Powys 59 C7
Llanfihangel yn Nhowyn Anglesey 82 D3
Llanfilo Powys 48 F3
Llanfoist Mon 35 C6
Llanfor Gwyn 72 F3
Llanfrechfa Torf 35 E7
Llanfrothen Gwyn 71 C7
Llanfrynach Powys 34 B4
Llanfwrog Anglesey 82 C3
Llanfwrog Denb 72 D5
Llanfyllin Powys 59 C8
Llanfynydd Carms 33 B6
Llanfynydd Flint 73 D6
Llanfyrnach Pembs 45 F4
Llangadfan Powys 59 C7
Llangadog Carms 33 B8
Llangadwaladr Anglesey 82 E3
Llangadwaladr Powys 73 F5
Llangaffo Anglesey 82 E4
Llangain Carms 32 C4
Llangammarch Wells Powys 47 E8
Llangan V Glam 21 B8
Llangarron Hereford 36 B2
Llangasty Talyllyn Powys 35 B5
Llangathen Carms 33 B6
Llangattock Powys 35 C6
Llangattock Lingoed Mon 35 B7
Llangattock nigh Usk Mon 35 D7
Llangattock-Vibon-Avel Mon 36 C1
Llangedwyn Powys 59 B8
Llangefni Anglesey 82 D4
Llangeinor Bridgend 34 F3
Llangeitho Ceredig 46 D5
Llangeler Carms 46 F2
Llangelynin Gwyn 58 D2
Llangendeirne Carms 33 C5
Llangennech Carms 33 D6
Llangennith Swansea 33 E5
Llangenny Powys 35 C6
Llangernyw Conwy 83 E8
Llangian Gwyn 70 E3
Llanglydwen Carms 32 B2
Llangoed Anglesey 83 D6
Llangoedmor Ceredig 45 E3
Llangollen Denb 73 E6
Llangolman Pembs 32 B2
Llangors Powys 35 B5
Llangovan Mon 36 D1
Llangower Gwyn 72 F3
Llangrannog Ceredig 46 D2
Llangristiolus Anglesey 82 D4
Llangrove Hereford 36 C2
Llangua Mon 35 B7
Llangunllo Powys 48 B4
Llangunnor Carms 33 C5
Llangurig Powys 47 B8
Llangwm Conwy 72 E3
Llangwm Mon 35 D8
Llangwm Pembs 44 E4
Llangwnnadl Gwyn 70 D3
Llangwyfan Denb 72 C5
Llangwyfan-isaf Anglesey 82 E3
Llangwyllog Anglesey 82 D4
Llangwyryfon Ceredig 46 B4
Llangybi Ceredig 46 D5
Llangybi Gwyn 70 C5
Llangybi Mon 35 E7
Llangyfelach Swansea 33 E7
Llangynhafal Denb 72 C5
Llangynidr Powys 35 C5
Llangynin Carms 32 C3
Llangynog Carms 32 C4
Llangynog Powys 59 B7
Llangynwyd Bridgend 34 F2
Llanhamlach Powys 34 B4
Llanharan Rhondda 34 F4
Llanharry Rhondda 34 F4
Llanhennock Mon 35 E7
Llanhiledd = Llanhilleth Bl Gwent 35 D6
Llanhilleth = Llanhiledd Bl Gwent 35 D6
Llanidloes Powys 59 F6
Llaniestyn Gwyn 70 D3
Llanifyny Powys 59 F5
Llanigon Powys 48 F4
Llanilar Ceredig 46 B5
Llanilid Rhondda 34 F3
Llanilltud Fawr = Llantwit Major V Glam 21 C8
Llanishen Cardiff 35 F5
Llanishen Mon 36 D1
Llanllawddog Carms 33 B5
Llanllechid Gwyn 83 E6
Llanllowel Mon 35 E7
Llanllugan Powys 59 D7
Llanllwch Carms 32 C4
Llanllwchaiarn Powys 59 E8
Llanllwni Carms 46 F3
Llanllyfni Gwyn 82 F4
Llanmadoc Swansea 33 E5
Llanmaes V Glam 21 C8
Llanmartin Newport 35 F7
Llanmihangel V Glam 21 B8
Llanmorlais Swansea 33 E6
Llannefydd Conwy 72 B3
Llannon Carms 33 D6
Llannor Gwyn 70 D4
Llanon Ceredig 46 C4
Llanover Mon 35 D7
Llanpumsaint Carms 33 B5
Llanreithan Pembs 44 C3
Llanrhaeadr Denb 72 C4
Llanrhaeadr-ym-Mochnant Powys 59 B8
Llanrhian Pembs 44 B3
Llanrhidian Swansea 33 E5
Llanrhos Conwy 83 C7
Llanrhyddlad Anglesey 82 C3
Llanrhystud Ceredig 46 C4
Llanrosser Hereford 48 F4
Llanrothal Hereford 36 C1
Llanrug Gwyn 82 E5
Llanrumney Cardiff 35 F6
Llanrwst Conwy 83 E8
Llansadurnen Carms 32 C3
Llansadwrn Anglesey 83 D5
Llansadwrn Carms 47 F5
Llansaint Carms 32 D4
Llansamlet Swansea 33 E7
Llansannan Conwy 72 C3
Llansannor V Glam 21 B8
Llansantffraed Ceredig 46 C4
Llansantffraed Powys 35 B5
Llansantffraed Cwmdeuddwr Powys 47 C8
Llansantffraed-in-Elvel Powys 48 D2
Llansantffraid-ym-Mechain Powys 60 B2
Llansawel Carms 46 F5
Llansilin Powys 60 B2
Llansoy Mon 35 D8
Llanspyddid Powys 34 B4
Llanstadwell Pembs 44 E4
Llansteffan Carms 32 C4
Llanstephan Powys 48 E3
Llantarnam Torf 35 E7
Llanteg Pembs 32 C2
Llanthony Mon 35 B6
Llantilio Crossenny Mon 35 C7
Llantilio Pertholey Mon 35 C7
Llantood Pembs 45 E3
Llantrisant Anglesey 82 C3
Llantrisant Mon 35 E7
Llantrisant Rhondda 34 F4
Llantrithyd V Glam 22 B2
Llantwit Fardre Rhondda 34 F4
Llantwit Major = Llanilltud Fawr V Glam 21 C8
Llanuwchllyn Gwyn 72 F2
Llanvaches Newport 35 E8
Llanvair Discoed Mon 35 E8
Llanvapley Mon 35 C7
Llanvetherine Mon 35 C7
Llanveynoe Hereford 48 F5
Llanvihangel Gobion Mon 35 D7
Llanvihangel-Ystern-Llewern Mon 35 C8
Llanwarne Hereford 36 B2
Llanwddyn Powys 59 C7
Llanwenog Ceredig 46 E3
Llanwern Newport 35 F7
Llanwinio Carms 32 B3
Llanwnda Gwyn 82 F4
Llanwnda Pembs 44 B4
Llanwnnen Ceredig 46 E4
Llanwnog Powys 59 E7
Llanwrda Carms 47 F6
Llanwrin Powys 58 D4
Llanwrthwl Powys 47 C8
Llanwrtud = Llanwrtyd Wells Powys 47 E7
Llanwrtyd Powys 47 E7
Llanwrtyd Wells = Llanwrtud Powys 47 E7
Llanwyddelan Powys 59 D7
Llanyblodwel Shrops 60 B2
Llanybri Carms 32 C4
Llanybydder Carms 46 E4
Llanycefn Pembs 32 B1
Llanychaer Pembs 44 B4
Llanycil Gwyn 72 F3
Llanycrwys Carms 46 E5
Llanymawddwy Gwyn 59 C6
Llanymddyfri = Llandovery Carms 47 F6
Llanymynech Powys 60 B2
Llanynghenedl Anglesey 82 C3
Llanynys Denb 72 C5
Llanyre Powys 48 C2
Llanystumdwy Gwyn 71 D5
Llanywern Powys 35 B5
Llawhaden Pembs 32 C1
Llawnt Shrops 73 F6
Llawr Dref Gwyn 70 E3
Llawryglyn Powys 59 E6
Llay Wrex 73 D7
Llechcynfarwy Anglesey 82 C3
Llecheiddior Gwyn 71 C5
Llechfaen Powys 34 B4
Llechryd Caerph 35 D5
Llechryd Ceredig 45 E4
Llechrydau Powys 73 F6
Llechwedd Slate Caverns, Blaenau Ffestiniog Gwyn 71 C8
Lledrod Ceredig 46 B5
Llenmerewig Powys 59 E8
Llethrid Swansea 33 E6
Llidiad Nenog Carms 46 F4
Llidiardau Gwyn 72 F2
Llidiart-y-parc Denb 72 E5
Llithfaen Gwyn 70 C4
Llong Flint 73 C6
Llowes Powys 48 E3
Llundain-fach Ceredig 46 D4
Llwydcoed Rhondda 34 D3
Llwyn Shrops 60 F2
Llwyn-du Mon 35 C6
Llwyn-hendy Carms 33 E6
Llwyn-têg Carms 33 D6
Llwyn-y-brain Carms 32 C2
Llwyn-y-groes Ceredig 46 D4
Llwyncelyn Ceredig 46 D3
Llwyndafydd Ceredig 46 D2
Llwynderw Powys 60 D2
Llwyndyrys Gwyn 70 C4
Llwyngwril Gwyn 58 D2
Llwynmawr Wrex 73 F6
Llwynypia Rhondda 34 E3
Llynclys Shrops 60 B2
Llynfaes Anglesey 82 D4
Llys-y-frân Pembs 32 B1
Llysfaen Conwy 83 D8
Llyswen Powys 48 F3
Llysworney V Glam 21 B8
Llywel Powys 47 F7
Loan Falk 122 B2
Loanend Northumb 124 D5
Loanhead Midloth 123 C5
Loans S Ayrs 120 F3
Loans of Tullich Highld 158 B2
Lobb Devon 20 F3
Loch a Charnain W Isles 170 F4
Loch a'Ghainmhich W Isles 172 F5
Loch Baghasdail = Lochboisdale W Isles 171 J3
Loch Choire Lodge Highld 167 F8
Loch Euphoirt W Isles 170 D4
Loch Head Dumfries 105 E7
Loch Loyal Lodge Highld 167 E8
Loch nam Madadh = Lochmaddy W Isles 170 D5
Loch Ness Monster Exhibition, Drumnadrochit Highld 157 F6
Loch Sgioport W Isles 170 G4
Lochailort Highld 145 E7
Lochaline Highld 137 D7
Lochanhully Highld 148 B5
Lochans Dumfries 104 D4
Locharbriggs Dumfries 114 F2
Lochassynt Lodge Highld 163 B5
Lochavich Ho. Argyll 130 D5
Lochawe Argyll 131 C7
Lochboisdale = Loch Baghasdail W Isles 171 J3
Lochbuie Argyll 137 F7
Lochcarron Highld 155 G4
Lochdhu Highld 168 E5
Lochdochart House Stirl 132 B3
Lochdon Argyll 130 B3
Lochdrum Highld 156 B3
Lochead Argyll 128 C2
Lochearnhead Stirl 132 B4
Lochee Dundee 142 F3
Lochend Highld 157 F6
Lochend Highld 169 C7
Locherben Dumfries 114 E2
Lochfoot Dumfries 107 B5
Lochgair Argyll 128 A4
Lochgarthside Highld 147 C8
Lochgelly Fife 134 E3
Lochgilphead Argyll 128 B3
Lochgoilhead Argyll 131 E8
Lochhill Moray 159 C6
Lochindorb Lodge Highld 158 F3
Lochinver Highld 162 B4
Lochlane Perth 133 B7
Lochluichart Highld 156 C4
Lochmaben Dumfries 114 F3
Lochmaddy = Loch nam Madadh W Isles 170 D5
Lochmore Cottage Highld 169 E5
Lochmore Lodge Highld 166 F4
Lochore Fife 134 E3
Lochportain W Isles 170 C5
Lochranza N Ayrs 119 A6
Lochs Crofts Moray 159 C7
Lochside Aberds 143 C7
Lochside Highld 167 D6
Lochside Highld 168 F3
Lochside Highld 158 D2
Lochslin Highld 165 F5
Lochstack Lodge Highld 166 E4
Lochton Aberds 151 E6
Lochty Angus 143 C5
Lochty Fife 135 D7
Lochty Perth 134 B2
Lochuisge Highld 138 D1
Lochurr Dumfries 113 F7
Lochwinnoch Renfs 120 D3
Lochwood Dumfries 114 E3
Lochyside Highld 139 B5
Lockengate Corn 4 C5
Lockerbie Dumfries 114 F4
Lockeridge Wilts 25 C6
Lockerley Hants 14 B3
Locking N Som 23 D5
Lockinge Oxon 38 F4
Lockington E Yorks 97 E5
Lockington Leics 63 B8
Lockleywood Shrops 61 B6
Locks Heath Hants 15 D6
Lockton N Yorks 103 E6
Lockwood W Yorks 88 C2
Locomotion Museum, Shildon Durham 101 B7
Loddington Leics 64 D4
Loddington Northants 53 B6
Loddiswell Devon 6 E5
Loddon Norf 69 E6
Lode Cambs 55 C6
Loders Dorset 12 E2
Lodsworth W Sus 16 B3
Lofthouse N Yorks 94 B4
Lofthouse W Yorks 88 B4
Loftus Redcar 103 C5
Logan E Ayrs 113 B5
Logan Mains Dumfries 104 E4
Loganlea W Loth 122 C2
Loggerheads Staffs 74 F4
Logie Angus 143 C6
Logie Fife 135 B6
Logie Moray 158 D4
Logie Coldstone Aberds 150 D3
Logie Hill Highld 157 B8
Logie Newton Aberds 160 E3
Logie Pert Angus 143 C6
Logiealmond Lodge Perth 141 F6
Logierait Perth 141 D6
Login Carms 32 B2
Lolworth Cambs 54 C4
Lonbain Highld 155 E2
Londesborough E Yorks 96 E4
London, City of = City of London London 41 F6
London City Airport London 41 F7
London Colney Herts 40 D4
London Gatwick Airport W Sus 28 E3
London Heathrow Airport London 27 B8
London Luton Airport Luton 40 B4
London Stansted Airport Essex 41 B8
London Zoo London 41 F5
Londonderry N Yorks 101 F8
Londonthorpe Lincs 78 F2
Londubh Highld 154 B4
Lonemore Highld 164 F4
Long Ashton N Som 23 B7
Long Bennington Lincs 77 E8
Long Bredy Dorset 12 E3
Long Buckby Northants 52 C4
Long Clawson Leics 64 B4
Long Common Hants 15 C6
Long Compton Staffs 62 B2
Long Compton Warks 51 F7
Long Crendon Bucks 39 D6
Long Crichel Dorset 13 C7
Long Ditton Sur 28 C2
Long Drax N Yorks 89 B7
Long Duckmanton Derbys 76 B4
Long Eaton Derbys 76 F4
Long Green Worcs 50 F3
Long Hanborough Oxon 38 C4
Long Itchington Warks 52 C2
Long Lawford Warks 52 B2
Long Load Som 12 B2
Long Marston Herts 40 C1
Long Marston N Yorks 95 D8
Long Marston Warks 51 E6
Long Marton Cumb 100 B1
Long Melford Suff 56 E2
Long Newnton Glos 37 E6
Long Newton E Loth 123 C8
Long Preston N Yorks 93 D8
Long Riston E Yorks 97 E7
Long Sight Gtr Man 87 D7
Long Stratton Norf 68 E4
Long Street M Keynes 53 E5
Long Sutton Hants 26 E5
Long Sutton Lincs 66 B4
Long Sutton Som 12 B2
Long Thurlow Suff 56 C4
Long Whatton Leics 63 B8
Long Wittenham Oxon 39 E5
Longbar N Ayrs 120 D3
Longbenton T & W 111 C5
Longborough Glos 38 B1
Longbridge Warks 51 C7
Longbridge W Mid 50 B5
Longbridge Deverill Wilts 24 E3
Longburton Dorset 12 C4
Longcliffe Derbys 76 D2
Longcot Oxon 38 E2
Longcroft Falk 121 B7
Longden Shrops 60 D4
Longdon Staffs 62 C4
Longdon Worcs 50 F3
Longdon Green Staffs 62 C4
Longdon on Tern Telford 61 C6
Longdown Devon 10 E3
Longdowns Corn 3 C6
Longfield Kent 29 C7
Longfield Shetland 175 M5
Longford Derbys 76 F2
Longford Glos 37 B5
Longford London 27 B8
Longford Shrops 74 F3
Longford Telford 61 C7
Longford W Mid 63 F7
Longfordlane Derbys 76 F2
Longforgan Perth 134 B5
Longformacus Borders 124 [illegible]
Longframlington Northumb 11[illegible]
Longham Dorset 1[illegible]
Longham Norf 68 [illegible]
Longhaven Aberds 161 [illegible]
Longhill Aberds 161 [illegible]
Longhirst Northumb 117 [illegible]
Longhope Glos 36 C[illegible]
Longhope Orkney 176 [illegible]
Longhorsley Northumb 117 E[illegible]
Longhoughton Northumb 117 C8
Longlane Derbys 76 F2
Longlane W Berks 26 B2
Longleat, Warminster Wilts 24 E3
Longlevens Glos 37 B5
Longley W Yorks 88 D2
Longley Green Worcs 50 D2
Longmanhill Aberds 160 B4
Longmoor Camp Hants 27 F5
Longmorn Moray 159 D6
Longnewton Borders 115 B8
Longnewton Stockton 102 C1
Longney Glos 36 C4
Longniddry E Loth 123 B7
Longnor Shrops 60 D4
Longnor Staffs 75 C7
Longparish Hants 26 E2
Longport Stoke 75 E5
Longridge Lancs 93 F6
Longridge Staffs 62 C3
Longridge W Loth 122 C2
Longriggend N Lnrk 121 B8
Longsdon Staffs 75 D6
Longshaw Gtr Man 86 D3
Longside Aberds 161 D7
Longstanton Cambs 54 C4
Longstock Hants 25 F8
Longstone Pembs 32 D2
Longstowe Cambs 54 D4
Longthorpe P'boro 65 E8
Longthwaite Cumb 99 B6
Longton Lancs 86 B2
Longton Stoke 75 E6
Longtown Cumb 108 C3
Longtown Hereford 35 B7

Longview Mers 86 E2
Longville in the Dale Shrops 60 E5
Longwick Bucks 39 D7
Longwitton Northumb 117 F6
Longwood Shrops 61 D6
Longworth Oxon 38 E3
Longyester E Loth 123 C8
Lonmay Aberds 161 C7
Lonmore Highld 152 E3
Looe Corn 5 D7
Loose Kent 29 D8
Loosley Row Bucks 39 D8
Lopcombe Corner Wilts 25 F7
Lopen Som 12 C2
Loppington Shrops 60 B4
Lopwell Devon 6 C2
Lorbottle Northumb 117 D6
Lorbottle Hall Northumb 117 D6
Lord's Cricket Ground London 41 F5
Lornty Perth 142 E1
Loscoe Derbys 76 E4
Losgaintir W Isles 173 J3
Lossiemouth Moray 159 C6
Lossit Argyll 126 D1
Lostford Shrops 74 F3
Lostock Gralam Ches 74 B3
Lostock Green Ches 74 B3
Lostock Hall Lancs 86 B3
Lostock Junction Gtr Man 86 D4
Lostwithiel Corn 5 D6
Loth Orkney 176 C5
Lothbeg Highld 165 C6
Lothersdale N Yorks 94 E2
Lothmore Highld 165 C6
Loudwater Bucks 40 E2
Loughborough Leics 64 C2
Loughor Swansea 33 E6
Loughton Essex 41 E7
Loughton M Keynes 53 F6
Loughton Shrops 61 F6
Louis Tussaud's Waxworks Blkpool 92 F3
Lound Lincs 65 C7
Lound Notts 89 F7
Lound Suff 69 E8
Lount Leics 63 C7
Louth Lincs 91 F7
Love Clough Lancs 87 B6
Lovedean Hants 15 C7
Lover Wilts 14 B3
Loversall S Yorks 89 E6
Loves Green Essex 42 D2
Lovesome Hill N Yorks 102 E1
Loveston Pembs 32 D1
Lovington Som 23 F7
Low Ackworth W Yorks 89 C5
Low Barlings Lincs 78 B3
Low Bentham N Yorks 93 C6
Low Bradfield S Yorks 88 E3
Low Bradley N Yorks 94 E3
Low Braithwaite Cumb 108 E4
Low Brunton Northumb 110 B2
Low Burnham N Lincs 89 D8
Low Burton N Yorks 101 F7
Low Buston Northumb 117 D8
Low Catton E Yorks 96 D3
Low Clanyard Dumfries 104 F5
Low Coniscliffe Darl 101 C7
Low Crosby Cumb 108 D4
ow Dalby N Yorks 103 F6
Dinsdale Darl 101 C8
Ellington N Yorks 101 F7
w Etherley Durham 101 B6
w Fell T & W 111 D5
ow Fulney Lincs 66 B2
ow Garth N Yorks 103 D5
ow Gate Northumb 110 C2
ow Grantley N Yorks 94 B5
ow Habberley Worcs 50 B3
ow Ham Som 12 B2
ow Hesket Cumb 108 E4
ow Hesleyhurst Northumb 117 E6
Low Hutton N Yorks 96 C3
Low Laithe N Yorks 94 C4
Low Leighton Derbys 87 F8
Low Lorton Cumb 98 B3
Low Marishes N Yorks 96 B4
Low Marnham Notts 77 C8
Low Mill N Yorks 102 E4
Low Moor Lancs 93 E7
Low Moor W Yorks 88 B2
Low Moorsley T & W 111 E6
Low Newton Cumb 99 F6
Low Newton-by-the-Sea Northumb 117 B8
Low Row Cumb 108 F3
Low Row Cumb 109 C5
Low Row N Yorks 100 E4
Low Salchrie Dumfries 104 C4
Low Smerby Argyll 118 D4
Low Torry Fife 134 F2
Low Worsall N Yorks 102 D1
Low Wray Cumb 99 D5
Lowbridge House Cumb 99 D7
Lowca Cumb 98 B1
Lowdham Notts 77 E6
Lowe Shrops 74 F2
Lowe Hill Staffs 75 D6
Lower Aisholt Som 22 F4
Lower Arncott Oxon 39 C6
Lower Ashton Devon 10 F3
Lower Assendon Oxon 39 F7
Lower Badcall Highld 166 E3
Lower Bartle Lancs 92 F4
Lower Basildon W Berks 26 B4
Lower Beeding W Sus 17 B6
Lower Benefield Northants 65 F6
Lower Boddington Northants 52 D2
Lower Brailes Warks 51 F8
Lower Breakish Highld 155 H2
Lower Broadheath Worcs 50 D3
Lower Bullingham Hereford 49 F7
Lower Cam Glos 36 D4
Lower Chapel Powys 48 F2
Lower Chute Wilts 25 D8
Lower Cragabus Argyll 126 E3
Lower Crossings Derbys 87 F8
Lower Cumberworth W Yorks 88 D3
Lower Cwm-twrch Powys 34 C1
Lower Darwen Blkburn 86 B4
Lower Dean Beds 53 C8
Lower Diabaig Highld 154 D3
Lower Dicker E Sus 18 D2
Lower Dinchope Shrops 60 F4
Lower Down Shrops 60 F3
Lower Drift Corn 2 D3
Lower Dunsforth N Yorks 95 C7
Lower Egleton Hereford 49 E8
Lower Elkstone Staffs 75 D7
Lower End Beds 40 B2
Lower Everleigh Wilts 25 D6
Lower Farringdon Hants 26 F5
Lower Foxdale I o M 84 E2
Lower Frankton Shrops 73 F7
Lower Froyle Hants 27 E5
Lower Gledfield Highld 164 E2
Lower Green Norf 81 D5
Lower Hacheston Suff 57 D7
Lower Halistra Highld 152 D3
Lower Halstow Kent 30 C2
Lower Hardres Kent 31 D5
Lower Hawthwaite Cumb 98 F4
Lower Heath Ches 75 C5
Lower Hempriggs Moray 158 C5
Lower Hergest Hereford 48 D4
Lower Heyford Oxon 38 B4
Lower Higham Kent 29 B8
Lower Holbrook Suff 57 F5
Lower Hordley Shrops 60 B3
Lower Horsebridge E Sus 18 D2
Lower Killeyan Argyll 126 E2
Lower Kingswood Sur 28 D3
Lower Kinnerton Ches 73 C7
Lower Langford N Som 23 C6
Lower Largo Fife 135 D6
Lower Leigh Staffs 75 F7
Lower Lemington Glos 51 F7
Lower Lenie Highld 147 B8
Lower Lydbrook Glos 36 C2
Lower Lye Hereford 49 C6
Lower Machen Newport 35 F6
Lower Maes-coed Hereford 48 F5
Lower Mayland Essex 43 D5
Lower Midway Derbys 63 B7
Lower Milovaig Highld 152 D2
Lower Moor Worcs 50 E4
Lower Nazeing Essex 41 D6
Lower Netchwood Shrops 61 E6
Lower Ollach Highld 153 F6
Lower Penarth V Glam 22 B3
Lower Penn Staffs 62 E2
Lower Pennington Hants 14 E4
Lower Peover Ches 74 B4
Lower Pexhill Ches 75 B5
Lower Place Gtr Man 87 C7
Lower Quinton Warks 51 E6
Lower Rochford Worcs 49 C8
Lower Seagry Wilts 37 F6
Lower Shelton Beds 53 E7
Lower Shiplake Oxon 27 B5
Lower Shuckburgh Warks 52 C2
Lower Slaughter Glos 38 B1
Lower Stanton St Quintin Wilts 37 F6
Lower Stoke Medway 30 B2
Lower Stondon Beds 54 F2
Lower Stow Bedon Norf 68 E2
Lower Street Norf 81 D8
Lower Street Norf 69 C6
Lower Strensham Worcs 50 E4
Lower Stretton Warr 86 F4
Lower Sundon Beds 40 B3
Lower Swanwick Hants 15 D5
Lower Swell Glos 38 B1
Lower Tean Staffs 75 F7
Lower Thurlton Norf 69 E7
Lower Tote Highld 152 C6
Lower Town Pembs 44 B4
Lower Tysoe Warks 51 E8
Lower Upham Hants 15 C6
Lower Vexford Som 22 F3
Lower Weare Som 23 D6
Lower Welson Hereford 48 D4
Lower Whitley Ches 74 B3
Lower Wield Hants 26 E4
Lower Winchendon Bucks 39 C7
Lower Withington Ches 74 C5
Lower Woodend Bucks 39 F8
Lower Woodford Wilts 25 F6
Lower Wyche Worcs 50 E2
Lowesby Leics 64 D4
Lowestoft Suff 69 E8
Loweswater Cumb 98 B3
Lowford Hants 15 C5
Lowgill Cumb 99 E8
Lowgill Lancs 93 C6
Lowick Northants 65 F6
Lowick Northumb 125 F6
Lowick Bridge Cumb 98 F4
Lowick Green Cumb 98 F4
Lowlands Torf 35 E6
Lowmoor Row Cumb 99 B8
Lownie Moor Angus 142 E4
Lowsonford Warks 51 C6
Lowther Cumb 99 B7
Lowthorpe E Yorks 97 C6
Lowton Gtr Man 86 E4
Lowton Common Gtr Man 86 E4
Loxbeare Devon 10 C4
Loxhill Sur 27 F8
Loxhore Devon 20 F5
Loxley Warks 51 D7
Loxton N Som 23 D5
Loxwood W Sus 27 F8
Lubcroy Highld 163 D7
Lubenham Leics 64 F4
Luccombe Som 21 E8
Luccombe Village I o W 15 G6
Lucker Northumb 125 F7
Luckett Corn 5 B8
Luckington Wilts 37 F5
Lucklawhill Fife 135 B6
Luckwell Bridge Som 21 F8
Lucton Hereford 49 C6
Ludag W Isles 171 J3
Ludborough Lincs 91 E6
Ludchurch Pembs 32 C2
Luddenden W Yorks 87 B8
Luddenden Foot W Yorks 87 B8
Luddesdown Kent 29 C7
Luddington N Lincs 90 C2
Luddington Warks 51 D6
Luddington in the Brook Northants 65 F8
Lude House Perth 141 C5
Ludford Lincs 91 F6
Ludford Shrops 49 B7
Ludgershall Bucks 39 C6
Ludgershall Wilts 25 D7
Ludgvan Corn 2 C4
Ludham Norf 69 C6
Ludlow Shrops 49 B7
Ludlow Racecourse Shrops 49 B6
Ludwell Wilts 13 B7
Ludworth Durham 111 E6
Luffincott Devon 8 E5
Lugar E Ayrs 113 B5
Lugg Green Hereford 49 C6
Luggate Burn E Loth 124 B2
Luggiebank N Lnrk 121 B7
Lugton E Ayrs 120 D4
Lugwardine Hereford 49 E7
Luib Highld 153 G6
Lulham Hereford 49 E6
Lullenden Sur 28 E5
Lullington Derbys 63 C6
Lullington Som 24 D2
Lulsgate Bottom N Som 23 C7
Lulsley Worcs 50 D2
Lulworth Castle Dorset 13 F6
Lumb W Yorks 87 B8
Lumby N Yorks 95 F7
Lumloch E Dunb 121 C6
Lumphanan Aberds 150 D4
Lumphinnans Fife 134 E3
Lumsdaine Borders 124 C4
Lumsden Aberds 150 B3
Lunan Angus 143 D6
Lunanhead Angus 142 D4
Luncarty Perth 134 B2
Lund E Yorks 97 E5
Lund N Yorks 96 F2
Lund Shetland 174 C7
Lunderton Aberds 161 D8
Lundie Angus 142 F2
Lundie Highld 146 C4
Lundin Links Fife 135 D6
Lunga Argyll 130 E3
Lunna Shetland 174 G6
Lunning Shetland 174 G7
Lunnon Swansea 33 F6
Lunsford's Cross E Sus 18 D4
Lunt Mers 85 D4
Luntley Hereford 49 D5
Luppitt Devon 11 D6
Lupset W Yorks 88 C4
Lupton Cumb 99 F7
Lurgashall W Sus 16 B3
Lusby Lincs 79 C6
Luson Devon 6 E4
Luss Argyll 132 E2
Lussagiven Argyll 127 D4
Lusta Highld 152 D3
Lustleigh Devon 10 F2
Luston Hereford 49 C6
Luthermuir Aberds 143 C6
Luthrie Fife 134 C5
Luton Devon 7 B7
Luton Luton 40 B3
Luton Medway 29 C8
Lutterworth Leics 64 F2
Lutton Devon 6 D3
Lutton Lincs 66 B4
Lutton Northants 65 F8
Lutworthy Devon 10 C2
Luxborough Som 21 F8
Luxulyan Corn 5 D5
Lybster Highld 169 F7
Lydbury North Shrops 60 F3
Lydcott Devon 21 F5
Lydd Kent 19 C7
Lydd on Sea Kent 19 C7
Lydden Kent 31 E6
Lydden Motor Racing Circuit Kent 31 E6
Lyddington Rutland 65 E5
Lyde Green Hants 26 D5
Lydeard St Lawrence Som 22 F3
Lydford Devon 9 F7
Lydford-on-Fosse Som 23 F7
Lydgate W Yorks 87 B7
Lydham Shrops 60 E3
Lydiard Green Wilts 37 F7
Lydiard Millicent Wilts 37 F7
Lydiate Mers 85 D4
Lydlinch Dorset 12 C5
Lydney Glos 36 D3
Lydstep Pembs 32 E1
Lye W Mid 62 F3
Lye Cross N Som 23 C6
Lye Green Bucks 40 D2
Lye Green E Sus 18 B2
Lyford Oxon 38 E3
Lymbridge Green Kent 30 E5
Lyme Park, Disley Ches 87 F7
Lyme Regis Dorset 11 E8
Lyminge Kent 31 E5
Lymington Hants 14 E4
Lyminster W Sus 16 D4
Lymm Warr 86 F4
Lymore Hants 14 E3
Lympne Kent 19 B8
Lympsham Som 22 D5
Lympstone Devon 10 F4
Lynchat Highld 148 D3
Lyndale Ho. Highld 152 D4
Lyndhurst Hants 14 D4
Lyndon Rutland 65 D6
Lyne Sur 27 C8
Lyne Down Hereford 49 F8
Lyne of Gorthleck Highld 147 B8
Lyne of Skene Aberds 151 C6
Lyneal Shrops 73 F8
Lyneham Oxon 38 B2
Lyneham Wilts 24 B5
Lynemore Highld 149 B6
Lynemouth Northumb 117 E8
Lyness Orkney 176 G2
Lyng Norf 68 C3
Lyng Som 11 B8
Lynmouth Devon 21 E6
Lynsted Kent 30 C3
Lynton Devon 21 E6
Lynton & Lynmouth Cliff Railway Devon 21 E6
Lyon's Gate Dorset 12 D4
Lyonshall Hereford 48 D5
Lytchett Matravers Dorset 13 E7
Lytchett Minster Dorset 13 E7
Lyth Highld 169 C7
Lytham Lancs 85 B4
Lytham St Anne's Lancs 85 B4
Lythe N Yorks 103 C6
Lythes Orkney 176 H3

M

Mabe Burnthouse Corn 3 C6
Mabie Dumfries 107 B6
Mablethorpe Lincs 91 F9
Macclesfield Ches 75 B6
Macclesfield Forest Ches 75 B6
Macduff Aberds 160 B4
Mace Green Suff 56 E5
Macharioch Argyll 118 F4
Machen Caerph 35 F6
Machrihanish Argyll 118 D3
Machynlleth Powys 58 D4
Machynys Carms 33 E6
Mackerel's Common W Sus 16 B4
Mackworth Derbys 76 F3
Macmerry E Loth 123 B7
Madame Tussaud's London 41 F5
Madderty Perth 133 B8
Maddiston Falk 122 B2
Madehurst W Sus 16 C3
Madeley Staffs 74 E4
Madeley Telford 61 D6
Madeley Heath Staffs 74 E4
Madeley Park Staffs 74 E4
Madingley Cambs 54 C4
Madley Hereford 49 F6
Madresfield Worcs 50 E3
Madron Corn 2 C3
Maen-y-groes Ceredig 46 D2
Maenaddwyn Anglesey 82 C4
Maenclochog Pembs 32 B1
Maendy V Glam 22 B2
Maentwrog Gwyn 71 C7
Maer Staffs 74 F4
Maerdy Conwy 72 E4
Maerdy Rhondda 34 E3
Maes-Treylow Powys 48 C4
Maesbrook Shrops 60 B2
Maesbury Shrops 60 B3
Maesbury Marsh Shrops 60 B3
Maesgwyn-Isaf Powys 59 C8
Maesgwynne Carms 32 B3
Maeshafn Denb 73 C6
Maesllyn Ceredig 46 E2
Maesmynis Powys 48 E2
Maesteg Bridgend 34 E2
Maestir Ceredig 46 E4
Maesy cwmmer Caerph 35 E5
Maesybont Carms 33 C6
Maesycrugiau Carms 46 E3
Maesymeillion Ceredig 46 E3
Magdalen Laver Essex 41 D8
Maggieknockater Moray 159 E7
Magham Down E Sus 18 D3
Maghull Mers 85 D4
Magna Science Adventure Centre, Rotherham S Yorks 88 E5
Magor Mon 35 F8
Magpie Green Suff 56 B4
Maiden Bradley Wilts 24 F3
Maiden Law Durham 110 E4
Maiden Newton Dorset 12 E3
Maiden Wells Pembs 44 F4
Maidencombe Torbay 7 C7
Maidenhall Suff 57 E5
Maidenhead Windsor 40 F1
Maidens S Ayrs 112 D2
Maiden's Green Brack 27 B6
Maidensgrave Suff 57 E6
Maidenwell Corn 5 B6
Maidenwell Lincs 79 B6
Maidford Northants 52 D4
Maids Moreton Bucks 52 F5
Maidstone Kent 29 D8
Maidwell Northants 52 B5
Mail Shetland 175 L6
Main Powys 59 C8
Maindee Newport 35 F7
Mains of Airies Dumfries 104 C3
Mains of Allardice Aberds 143 B8
Mains of Annochie Aberds 161 D6
Mains of Ardestie Angus 143 F5
Mains of Balhall Angus 143 C5
Mains of Ballindarg Angus 142 D4
Mains of Balnakettle Aberds 143 B6
Mains of Birness Aberds 161 E6
Mains of Burgie Moray 158 D4
Mains of Clunas Highld 158 E2
Mains of Crichie Aberds 161 D6
Mains of Dalvey Highld 158 F5
Mains of Dellavaird Aberds 151 F6
Mains of Drum Aberds 151 E7
Mains of Edingight Moray 160 C2
Mains of Fedderate Aberds 161 D5
Mains of Inkhorn Aberds 161 E6
Mains of Mayen Moray 160 D2
Mains of Melgund Angus 143 D5
Mains of Thornton Aberds 143 B6
Mains of Watten Highld 169 D7
Mainsforth Durham 111 F6
Mainsriddle Dumfries 107 D6
Mainstone Shrops 60 F2
Maisemore Glos 37 B5
Malacleit W Isles 170 C3
Malborough Devon 6 F5
Malcoff Derbys 87 F8
Maldon Essex 42 D4
Malham N Yorks 94 C2
Maligar Highld 152 C5
Mallaig Highld 145 D6
Malleny Mills Edin 122 C4
Malling Stirl 132 D4
Mallory Park Motor Racing Circuit Leics 63 D8
Malltraeth Anglesey 82 E4
Mallwyd Gwyn 59 C5
Malmesbury Wilts 37 F6
Malmsmead Devon 21 E6
Malpas Ches 73 E8
Malpas Corn 3 B7
Malpas Newport 35 E7
Malswick Glos 36 B4
Maltby Stockton 102 C2
Maltby S Yorks 89 E6
Maltby le Marsh Lincs 91 F8
Malting Green Essex 43 B5
Maltman's Hill Kent 30 E3
Malton N Yorks 96 B3
Malvern Link Worcs 50 E2
Malvern Wells Worcs 50 E2
Mamble Worcs 49 B8
Man-moel Caerph 35 D5
Manaccan Corn 3 D6
Manafon Powys 59 D8
Manais W Isles 173 K4
Manar Ho. Aberds 151 B6
Manaton Devon 10 F2
Manby Lincs 91 F7
Mancetter Warks 63 E7
Manchester Gtr Man 87 E6
Manchester Airport Gtr Man 87 F6
Manchester National Velodrome Gtr Man 87 E6
Mancot Flint 73 C7
Mandally Highld 147 D5
Manea Cambs 66 F4
Manfield N Yorks 101 C7
Mangaster Shetland 174 F5
Mangotsfield S Glos 23 B8
Mangurstadh W Isles 172 E3
Mankinholes W Yorks 87 B7
Manley Ches 74 B2
Mannal Argyll 136 F1
Mannerston W Loth 122 B3
Manningford Bohune Wilts 25 D6
Manningford Bruce Wilts 25 D6
Manningham W Yorks 94 F4
Mannings Heath W Sus 17 B6
Mannington Dorset 13 D8
Manningtree Essex 56 F4
Mannofield Aberdeen 151 D8
Manor Estate S Yorks 88 F4
Manor Park London 41 F7
Manorbier Pembs 32 E1
Manordeilo Carms 33 B7
Manorhill Borders 124 F2
Manorowen Pembs 44 B4
Mansel Lacy Hereford 49 E6
Manselfield Swansea 33 F6
Mansell Gamage Hereford 49 E5
Mansergh Cumb 99 F8
Mansfield E Ayrs 113 C6
Mansfield Notts 76 C5
Mansfield Woodhouse Notts 76 C5
Mansriggs Cumb 98 F4
Manston Dorset 13 C6
Manston Kent 31 C7
Manston W Yorks 95 F6
Manswood Dorset 13 D7
Manthorpe Lincs 65 C7
Manthorpe Lincs 78 F2
Manton N Lincs 90 D3
Manton Notts 77 B5
Manton Rutland 65 D5
Manton Wilts 25 C6
Manuden Essex 41 B7
Manx Electric Railway I o M 84 C4
Maperton Som 12 B4
Maple Cross Herts 40 E3
Maplebeck Notts 77 C7
Mapledurham Oxon 26 B4
Mapledurwell Hants 26 D4
Maplehurst W Sus 17 B5
Maplescombe Kent 29 C6
Mapleton Derbys 75 E8
Mapleton E Yorks 97 E8
Mapperley Derbys 76 E4
Mapperley Park Nottingham 77 E5
Mapperton Dorset 12 E3
Mappleborough Green Warks 51 C5
Mappowder Dorset 12 D5
Mar Lodge Aberds 149 E6
Maraig W Isles 173 H4
Marazanvose Corn 4 D3
Marazion Corn 2 C4
Marbhig W Isles 172 G7
Marbury Ches 74 E2
March Cambs 66 E4
March S Lnrk 114 C2
Marcham Oxon 38 E4
Marchamley Shrops 61 B5
Marchington Staffs 75 F8
Marchington Woodlands Staffs 62 B5
Marchroes Gwyn 70 E4
Marchwiel Wrex 73 E7
Marchwood Hants 14 C4
Marcross V Glam 21 C8
Marden Hereford 49 E7
Marden Kent 29 E8
Marden T & W 111 B6
Marden Wilts 25 D5
Marden Beech Kent 29 E8
Marden Thorn Kent 29 E8
Mardy Mon 35 C7
Marefield Leics 64 D4
Mareham le Fen Lincs 79 C5
Mareham on the Hill Lincs 79 C5
Marehay Derbys 76 E3
Marehill W Sus 16 C4
Maresfield E Sus 17 B8
Marfleet Hull 90 B5
Marford Wrex 73 D7
Margam Neath 34 F1
Margaret Marsh Dorset 13 C6
Margaret Roding Essex 42 C1
Margaretting Essex 42 D2
Margate Kent 31 B7
Margnaheglish N Ayrs 119 C7
Margrove Park Redcar 102 C4
Marham Norf 67 C7
Marhamchurch Corn 8 D4
Marholm P'boro 65 D8
Mariandyrys Anglesey 83 C6
Marianglas Anglesey 82 C5
Mariansleigh Devon 10 B2
Marionburgh Aberds 151 D6
Marishader Highld 152 C5
Maritime and Industrial Museum Swansea 33 E7
Marjoriebanks Dumfries 114 F3
Mark Dumfries 104 D5
Mark S Ayrs 104 B4
Mark Som 23 E5
Mark Causeway Som 23 E5
Mark Cross E Sus 17 C8
Mark Cross E Sus 18 B2
Markbeech Kent 29 E5
Markby Lincs 79 B7
Market Bosworth Leics 63 D8
Market Deeping Lincs 65 D8
Market Drayton Shrops 74 F3
Market Harborough Leics 64 F4
Market Lavington Wilts 24 D5
Market Overton Rutland 65 C5
Market Rasen Lincs 90 F5
Market Rasen Racecourse Lincs 90 F5
Market Stainton Lincs 78 B5
Market Warsop Notts 77 C5
Market Weighton E Yorks 96 E4
Market Weston Suff 56 B3
Markethill Perth 142 F2
Markfield Leics 63 C8
Markham Caerph 35 D5
Markham Moor Notts 77 B7
Markinch Fife 134 D4
Markington N Yorks 95 C5
Marks Tey Essex 43 B5
Marksbury Bath 23 C8
Markyate Herts 40 C3
Marland Gtr Man 87 C6
Marlborough Wilts 25 C6
Marlbrook Hereford 49 D7
Marlbrook Worcs 50 B4
Marlcliff Warks 51 D5
Marldon Devon 7 C6
Marlesford Suff 57 D7
Marley Green Ches 74 E2
Marley Hill T & W 110 D5
Marley Mount Hants 14 E3
Marlingford Norf 68 D4
Marloes Pembs 44 E2
Marlow Bucks 39 F8
Marlow Hereford 49 B6
Marlow Bottom Bucks 40 F1
Marlpit Hill Kent 28 E5
Marlpool Derbys 76 E4
Marnhull Dorset 13 C5
Marnoch Aberds 160 C2
Marnock N Lnrk 121 C7
Marple Gtr Man 87 F7
Marple Bridge Gtr Man 87 F7
Marr S Yorks 89 D6
Marrel Highld 165 C7
Marrick N Yorks 101 E5
Marrister Shetland 175 G7
Marros Carms 32 D3
Marsden T & W 111 C6
Marsden W Yorks 87 C8
Marsett N Yorks 100 F4
Marsh Devon 11 C7
Marsh W Yorks 94 F3
Marsh Baldon Oxon 39 E5
Marsh Gibbon Bucks 39 B6
Marsh Green Devon 10 E5
Marsh Green Kent 28 E5
Marsh Green Staffs 75 D5
Marsh Lane Derbys 76 B4
Marsh Street Som 21 E8
Marshall's Heath Herts 40 C4
Marshalsea Dorset 11 D8
Marshalswick Herts 40 D4
Marsham Norf 81 E7
Marshaw Lancs 93 D5
Marshborough Kent 31 D7
Marshbrook Shrops 60 F4
Marshchapel Lincs 91 E7
Marshfield Newport 35 F6
Marshfield S Glos 24 B2
Marshgate Corn 8 E3
Marshland St James Norf 66 D5
Marshside Mers 85 C4
Marshwood Dorset 11 E8
Marske N Yorks 101 D6
Marske-by-the-Sea Redcar 102 B4
Marston Ches 74 B3
Marston Hereford 49 D5
Marston Lincs 77 E8
Marston Oxon 39 D5
Marston Staffs 62 C2
Marston Staffs 62 B3
Marston Warks 63 E6
Marston Wilts 24 D4
Marston Doles Warks 52 D2
Marston Green W Mid 63 F5
Marston Magna Som 12 B3
Marston Meysey Wilts 37 E8
Marston Montgomery Derbys 75 F8
Marston Moretaine Beds 53 E7
Marston on Dove Derbys 63 B6
Marston St Lawrence Northants 52 E3
Marston Stannett Hereford 49 D7
Marston Trussell Northants 64 F3
Marstow Hereford 36 C2
Marsworth Bucks 40 C2
Marten Wilts 25 D7
Marthall Ches 74 B5
Martham Norf 69 C7
Martin Hants 13 C8
Martin Kent 31 E7
Martin Lincs 78 D4
Martin Lincs 78 C5
Martin Dales Lincs 78 C4
Martin Drove End Hants 13 B8
Martin Hussingtree Worcs 50 C3
Martin Mill Kent 31 E7
Martinhoe Devon 21 E5
Martinhoe Cross Devon 21 E5
Martinscroft Warr 86 F4
Martinstown Dorset 12 F4
Martlesham Suff 57 E6
Martlesham Heath Suff 57 E6
Martletwy Pembs 32 C1
Martley Worcs 50 D2
Martock Som 12 C2
Marton Ches 75 C5
Marton E Yorks 97 F7
Marton Lincs 90 F2
Marton M'bro 102 C3
Marton N Yorks 95 C7
Marton N Yorks 103 F5
Marton Shrops 60 D2
Marton Shrops 60 B4
Marton Warks 52 C2
Marton-le-Moor N Yorks 95 B6
Martyr Worthy Hants 26 F3
Martyr's Green Sur 27 D8
Marwell Zoo, Bishop's Waltham Hants 15 B6
Marwick Orkney 176 D1
Marwood Devon 20 F4
Mary Arden's House, Stratford-upon-Avon Warks 51 D6
Mary Rose Ptsmth 15 D7
Mary Tavy Devon 6 B3
Marybank Highld 157 D5
Maryburgh Highld 157 D6
Maryhill Glasgow 121 C5
Marykirk Aberds 143 C6
Marylebone Gtr Man 86 D3
Marypark Moray 159 F5
Maryport Cumb 107 F7
Maryport Dumfries 104 F5
Maryton Angus 143 D6
Marywell Aberds 150 E4
Marywell Aberds 151 E8
Marywell Angus 143 E6
Masham N Yorks 101 F7
Mashbury Essex 42 C2
Masongill N Yorks 93 B6
Masonhill S Ayrs 112 B3
Mastin Moor Derbys 76 B4
Mastrick Aberdeen 151 D7
Matching Essex 41 C8
Matching Green Essex 41 C8
Matching Tye Essex 41 C8
Matfen Northumb 110 B3
Matfield Kent 29 E7
Mathern Mon 36 E2
Mathon Hereford 50 E2
Mathry Pembs 44 B3
Matlaske Norf 81 D7
Matlock Derbys 76 C2
Matlock Bath Derbys 76 D2
Matson Glos 37 C5
Matterdale End Cumb 99 B5
Mattersey Notts 89 F7
Mattersey Thorpe Notts 89 F7
Mattingley Hants 26 D5
Mattishall Norf 68 C3
Mattishall Burgh Norf 68 C3
Mauchline E Ayrs 112 B4
Maud Aberds 161 D6
Maugersbury Glos 38 B2
Maughold I o M 84 C4
Mauld Highld 156 F5
Maulden Beds 53 F8
Maulds Meaburn Cumb 99 C8
Maunby N Yorks 102 F1
Maund Bryan Hereford 49 D7
Maundown Som 11 B5
Mautby Norf 69 C7
Mavis Enderby Lincs 79 C6
Maw Green Ches 74 D4
Mawbray Cumb 107 E7
Mawdesley Lancs 86 C2
Mawdlam Bridgend 34 F2
Mawgan Corn 3 D6
Mawla Corn 3 B6
Mawnan Corn 3 D6
Mawnan Smith Corn 3 D6
Mawsley Northants 53 B6
Maxey P'boro 65 D8
Maxstoke Warks 63 F6
Maxton Borders 124 F2
Maxton Kent 31 E7
Maxwellheugh Borders 124 F3
Maxwelltown Dumfries 107 B6
Maxworthy Corn 8 E4
May Bank Staffs 75 E5
Mayals Swansea 33 E7
Maybole S Ayrs 112 D3
Mayfield E Sus 18 C2
Mayfield Midloth 123 C6
Mayfield Staffs 75 E8
Mayfield W Loth 122 C2
Mayford Sur 27 D7
Mayland Essex 43 D5
Maynard's Green E Sus 18 D2
Maypole Mon 36 C1
Maypole Scilly 2 E4
Maypole Green Essex 43 B5
Maypole Green Norf 69 E7
Maypole Green Suff 57 C6
Maywick Shetland 175 L5
Meadle Bucks 39 D8
Meadowtown Shrops 60 D3
Meaford Staffs 75 F5
Meal Bank Cumb 99 E7
Mealabost W Isles 172 E7
Mealabost Bhuirgh W Isles 172 C7
Mealsgate Cumb 108 E2
Meanwood W Yorks 95 F5
Mearbeck N Yorks 93 C8
Meare Som 23 E6
Meare Green Som 11 B8
Mears Ashby Northants 53 C6
Measham Leics 63 C7
Meath Green Sur 28 E3

Meathop Cumb 99 F6
Meaux E Yorks 97 F6
Meavy Devon 6 C3
Medbourne Leics 64 E4
Medburn Northumb 110 B4
Meddon Devon 8 C4
Meden Vale Notts 77 C5
Medlam Lincs 79 D6
Medmenham Bucks 39 F8
Medomsley Durham 110 D4
Medstead Hants 26 F4
Meer End W Mid 51 B7
Meerbrook Staffs 75 C6
Meers Bridge Lincs 91 F8
Meesden Herts 54 F5
Meeth Devon 9 D7
Meggethead Borders 114 B4
Meidrim Carms 32 B3
Meifod Denb 72 D4
Meifod Powys 59 C8
Meigle N Ayrs 129 D6
Meigle Perth 142 E2
Meikle Earnock S Lnrk 121 D7
Meikle Ferry Highld 164 F4
Meikle Forter Angus 142 C1
Meikle Gluich Highld 164 F3
Meikle Pinkerton E Loth 124 B3
Meikle Strath Aberds 143 B6
Meikle Tarty Aberds 151 B8
Meikle Wartle Aberds 160 E4
Meikleour Perth 142 F1
Meinciau Carms 33 C5
Meir Stoke 75 E6
Meir Heath Staffs 75 E6
Melbourn Cambs 54 E4
Melbourne Derbys 63 B7
Melbourne E Yorks 96 E3
Melbourne S Lnrk 122 E3
Melbury Abbas Dorset 13 B6
Melbury Bubb Dorset 12 D3
Melbury Osmond Dorset 12 D3
Melbury Sampford Dorset 12 D3
Melby Shetland 175 H3
Melchbourne Beds 53 C8
Melcombe Bingham Dorset 13 D5
Melcombe Regis Dorset 12 F4
Meldon Devon 9 E7
Meldon Northumb 117 F7
Meldreth Cambs 54 E4
Meldrum Ho. Aberds 151 B7
Melfort Argyll 130 D4
Melgarve Highld 147 E7
Meliden Denb 72 A4
Melin-y-coed Conwy 83 E8
Melin-y-ddôl Powys 59 D7
Melin-y-grug Powys 59 D7
Melin-y-Wig Denb 72 E4
Melinbyrhedyn Powys 58 E5
Melincourt Neath 34 D2
Melkinthorpe Cumb 99 B7
Melkridge Northumb 109 C7
Melksham Wilts 24 C4
Melldalloch Argyll 128 C4
Melling Lancs 93 B5
Melling Mers 85 D4
Melling Mount Mers 86 D2
Mellis Suff 56 B5
Mellon Charles Highld 162 E2
Mellon Udrigle Highld 162 E2
Mellor Gtr Man 87 F7
Mellor Lancs 93 F6
Mellor Brook Lancs 93 F6
Mells Som 24 E2
Melmerby Cumb 109 F6
Melmerby N Yorks 95 B6
Melmerby N Yorks 101 F5
Melplash Dorset 12 E2
Melrose Borders 123 F8
Melsetter Orkney 176 H1
Melsonby N Yorks 101 D6
Meltham W Yorks 88 C2
Melton Suff 57 D6
Melton Constable Norf 81 D6
Melton Mowbray Leics 64 C4
Melton Ross N Lincs 90 C4
Meltonby E Yorks 96 D3
Melvaig Highld 154 B3
Melverley Shrops 60 C3
Melverley Green Shrops 60 C3
Melvich Highld 168 C3
Membury Devon 11 D7
Memsie Aberds 161 B6
Memus Angus 142 D4
Menabilly Corn 5 D5
Menai Bridge = Porthaethwy Anglesey 83 D5
Mendham Suff 69 F5
Mendlesham Suff 56 C5
Mendlesham Green Suff 56 C4
Menheniot Corn 5 C7
Mennock Dumfries 113 D8
Menston W Yorks 94 E4
Menstrie Clack 133 E7
Menthorpe N Yorks 96 F2
Mentmore Bucks 40 C2
Meoble Highld 145 E7
Meole Brace Shrops 60 C4
Meols Mers 85 E3
Meonstoke Hants 15 C7
Meopham Kent 29 C7
Meopham Station Kent 29 C7
Mepal Cambs 66 F4
Meppershall Beds 54 F2
Merbach Hereford 48 E5
Mere Ches 86 F5
Mere Wilts 24 F3
Mere Brow Lancs 86 C2
Mere Green W Mid 62 E5
Mereclough Lancs 93 F8
Mereside Blkpool 92 F3
Mereworth Kent 29 D7
Mergie Aberds 151 F6
Meriden W Mid 63 F6
Merkadale Highld 153 F4
Merkland Dumfries 106 B4
Merkland S Ayrs 112 E2
Merkland Lodge Highld 163 B8
Merley Poole 13 E8
Merlin's Bridge Pembs 44 D4
Merrington Shrops 60 B4
Merrion Pembs 44 F4
Merriott Som 12 C2
Merrivale Devon 6 B3
Merrow Sur 27 D8
Merrymeet Corn 5 C7
Merseyside Maritime Museum Mers 85 F8
Mersham Kent 19 B7
Merstham Sur 28 D3
Merston W Sus 16 D2
Merstone I o W 15 F6
Merther Corn 3 B7
Merthyr Carms 32 B4
Merthyr Cynog Powys 47 F8
Merthyr-Dyfan V Glam 22 C3
Merthyr Mawr Bridgend 21 B7
Merthyr Tudful = Merthyr Tydfil M Tydf 34 D4
Merthyr Tydfil = Merthyr Tudful M Tydf 34 D4
Merthyr Vale M Tydf 34 E4
Merton Devon 9 C7
Merton London 28 B3
Merton Norf 68 E2
Merton Oxon 39 C5
Mervinslaw Borders 116 C2
Meshaw Devon 10 C2
Messing Essex 42 C4
Messingham N Lincs 90 D2
Metfield Suff 69 F5
Metheringham Lincs 78 C3
Methil Fife 135 E5
Methlem Gwyn 70 D2
Methley W Yorks 88 B4
Methlick Aberds 161 E5
Methven Perth 134 B2
Methwold Norf 67 E7
Methwold Hythe Norf 67 E7
Metroland, Gateshead T & W 110 C5
Mettingham Suff 69 F6
Mevagissey Corn 3 B9
Mewith Head N Yorks 93 C7
Mexborough S Yorks 89 D5
Mey Highld 169 B7
Meysey Hampton Glos 37 E8
Miabhag W Isles 173 J4
Miabhag W Isles 173 H3
Miabhig W Isles 172 E3
Michaelchurch Hereford 36 B2
Michaelchurch Escley Hereford 48 F5
Michaelchurch on Arrow Powys 48 D4
Michaelston-le-Pit V Glam 22 B3
Michaelston-y-Fedw Newport 35 F6
Michaelstow Corn 5 B5
Michealston-super-Ely Cardiff 22 B3
Micheldever Hants 26 F3
Michelmersh Hants 14 B4
Mickfield Suff 56 C5
Mickle Trafford Ches 73 C8
Micklebring S Yorks 89 E6
Mickleby N Yorks 103 C6
Mickleham Sur 28 D2
Mickleover Derby 76 F3
Micklethwaite W Yorks 94 E4
Mickleton Durham 100 B4
Mickleton Glos 51 E6
Mickletown W Yorks 88 B4
Mickley N Yorks 95 B5
Mickley Square Northumb 110 C3
Mid Ardlaw Aberds 161 B6
Mid Auchinlech Invclyd 120 B3
Mid Beltie Aberds 150 D5
Mid Calder W Loth 122 C3
Mid Cloch Forbie Aberds 160 C4
Mid Clyth Highld 169 F7
Mid-Hants Railway (Watercress Line), New Alresford Hants 26 F3
Mid Lavant W Sus 16 D2
Mid Main Highld 156 F5
Mid Urchany Highld 158 E2
Mid Walls Shetland 175 H4
Mid Yell Shetland 174 D7
Midbea Orkney 176 B3
Middle Assendon Oxon 39 F7
Middle Aston Oxon 38 B4
Middle Barton Oxon 38 B4
Middle Cairncake Aberds 160 D5
Middle Claydon Bucks 39 B7
Middle Drums Angus 143 D5
Middle Handley Derbys 76 B4
Middle Littleton Worcs 51 E5
Middle Maes-coed Hereford 48 F5
Middle Mill Pembs 44 C3
Middle Rasen Lincs 90 F4
Middle Rigg Perth 134 D2
Middle Tysoe Warks 51 E8
Middle Wallop Hants 25 F7
Middle Winterslow Wilts 25 F7
Middle Woodford Wilts 25 F6
Middlebie Dumfries 108 B2
Middleforth Green Lancs 86 B3
Middleham N Yorks 101 F6
Middlehope Shrops 60 F4
Middlemarsh Dorset 12 D4
Middlemuir Aberds 151 B8
Middlesbrough M'bro 102 B2
Middleshaw Cumb 99 F7
Middleshaw Dumfries 107 B8
Middlesmoor N Yorks 94 B3
Middlestone Durham 111 F5
Middlestone Moor Durham 110 F5
Middlestown W Yorks 88 C3
Middlethird Borders 124 E2
Middleton Aberds 151 C7
Middleton Argyll 136 F1
Middleton Cumb 99 F8
Middleton Derbys 76 D2
Middleton Derbys 75 C8
Middleton Essex 56 F2
Middleton Gtr Man 87 D6
Middleton Hants 26 E2
Middleton Hereford 49 C7
Middleton Lancs 92 D4
Middleton Midloth 123 D6
Middleton Norf 67 C6
Middleton Northants 64 F5
Middleton Northumb 117 F6
Middleton Northumb 125 F7
Middleton N Yorks 103 F5
Middleton Perth 134 D3
Middleton Perth 141 E8
Middleton Shrops 49 B7
Middleton Shrops 60 E2
Middleton Shrops 60 B3
Middleton Suff 57 C8
Middleton Swansea 33 F5
Middleton Warks 63 E5
Middleton W Yorks 88 B3
Middleton W Yorks 94 E4
Middleton Cheney Northants 52 E2
Middleton Green Staffs 75 F6
Middleton Hall Northumb 117 B5
Middleton-in-Teesdale Durham 100 B4
Middleton Moor Suff 57 C8
Middleton-on-Leven N Yorks 102 D2
Middleton-on-Sea W Sus 16 D3
Middleton on the Hill Hereford 49 C7
Middleton-on-the-Wolds E Yorks 96 E5
Middleton One Row Darl 102 C1
Middleton Priors Shrops 61 E6
Middleton Quernham N Yorks 95 B6
Middleton Railway, Hunslet W Yorks 88 B4
Middleton St George Darl 101 C8
Middleton Scriven Shrops 61 F6
Middleton Stoney Oxon 39 B5
Middleton Tyas N Yorks 101 D7
Middletown Cumb 98 D1
Middletown Powys 60 C3
Middlewich Ches 74 C3
Middlewood Green Suff 56 C4
Middlezoy Som 23 F5
Middridge Durham 101 B7
Midfield Highld 167 C7
Midge Hall Lancs 86 B3
Midgeholme Cumb 109 D6
Midgham W Berks 26 C3
Midgley W Yorks 87 B8
Midgley W Yorks 88 C3
Midhopestones S Yorks 88 E3
Midhurst W Sus 16 B2
Midlem Borders 115 B8
Midmar Aberds 151 D5
Midsomer Norton Bath 23 D8
Midton Invclyd 129 C7
Midtown Highld 167 C7
Midtown Highld 154 B4
Midtown of Buchromb Moray 159 E7
Midville Lincs 79 D6
Midway Ches 87 F7
Migdale Highld 164 E3
Migvie Aberds 150 D3
Milarrochy Stirl 132 E3
Milborne Port Som 12 C4
Milborne St Andrew Dorset 13 E6
Milborne Wick Som 12 B4
Milbourne Northumb 110 B4
Milburn Cumb 100 B1
Milbury Heath S Glos 36 E3
Milcombe Oxon 52 F2
Milden Suff 56 E3
Mildenhall Suff 55 B8
Mildenhall Wilts 25 C7
Mile Cross Norf 68 C5
Mile Elm Wilts 24 C4
Mile End Essex 43 B5
Mile End Glos 36 C2
Mile Oak Brighton 17 D6
Milebrook Powys 48 B5
Milebush Kent 29 E8
Mileham Norf 68 C2
Milesmark Fife 134 F2
Milestones, Basingstoke Hants 26 D4
Milfield Northumb 124 F5
Milford Derbys 76 E3
Milford Devon 8 B4
Milford Powys 59 E7
Milford Staffs 62 B3
Milford Sur 27 E7
Milford Wilts 14 B2
Milford Haven = Aberdaugleddau Pembs 44 E4
Milford on Sea Hants 14 E3
Milkwall Glos 36 D2
Milkwell Wilts 13 B7
Mill Bank W Yorks 87 B8
Mill Common Suff 69 F7
Mill End Bucks 39 F7
Mill End Herts 54 F4
Mill Green Essex 42 D2
Mill Green Norf 68 F4
Mill Green Suff 56 E3
Mill Hill London 41 E5
Mill Lane Hants 27 D5
Mill of Kingoodie Aberds 151 B7
Mill of Muiresk Aberds 160 D3
Mill of Sterin Aberds 150 E2
Mill of Uras Aberds 151 F7
Mill Place N Lincs 90 D3
Mill Side Cumb 99 F6
Mill Street Norf 68 C3
Milland W Sus 16 B2
Millarston Renfs 120 C4
Millbank Aberds 161 D8
Millbank Highld 169 C6
Millbeck Cumb 98 B4
Millbounds Orkney 176 C4
Millbreck Aberds 161 D7
Millbridge Sur 27 E6
Millbrook Beds 53 F8
Millbrook Corn 6 D2
Millbrook Soton 14 C4
Millburn S Ayrs 112 B4
Millcombe Devon 7 E6
Millcorner E Sus 18 C5
Milldale Staffs 75 D8
Millden Lodge Angus 143 B5
Milldens Angus 143 D5
Millennium Stadium Cardiff 22 B3
Millerhill Midloth 123 C6
Miller's Dale Derbys 75 B8
Miller's Green Derbys 76 D2
Millgreen Shrops 61 B6
Millhalf Hereford 48 E4
Millhayes Devon 11 D7
Millhead Lancs 92 B4
Millheugh S Lnrk 121 D7
Millholme Cumb 99 E7
Millhouse Argyll 128 C4
Millhouse Cumb 108 F3
Millhouse Green S Yorks 88 D3
Millhousebridge Dumfries 114 F4
Millhouses S Yorks 88 F4
Millikenpark Renfs 120 C4
Millin Cross Pembs 44 D4
Millington E Yorks 96 D4
Millmeece Staffs 74 F5
Millom Cumb 98 F3
Millook Corn 8 E3
Millpool Corn 5 B6
Millport N Ayrs 129 E6
Millquarter Dumfries 113 F6
Millthorpe Lincs 78 F4
Millthrop Cumb 100 E1
Milltimber Aberdeen 151 D7
Milltown Corn 5 D6
Milltown Derbys 76 C3
Milltown Devon 20 F4
Milltown Dumfries 108 B3
Milltown of Aberdalgie Perth 134 B2
Milltown of Auchindoun Moray 159 E7
Milltown of Craigston Aberds 160 C4
Milltown of Edinvillie Moray 159 E6
Milltown of Kildrummy Aberds 150 C3
Milltown of Rothiemay Moray 160 D2
Milltown of Towie Aberds 150 C3
Milnathort Perth 134 D3
Milner's Heath Ches 73 C8
Milngavie E Dunb 121 B5
Milnrow Gtr Man 87 C7
Milnshaw Lancs 87 B5
Milnthorpe Cumb 99 F6
Milo Carms 33 C6
Milson Shrops 49 B8
Milstead Kent 30 D3
Milston Wilts 25 E6
Milton Angus 142 E3
Milton Cambs 55 C5
Milton Cumb 109 C5
Milton Derbys 63 B7
Milton Dumfries 105 D6
Milton Dumfries 106 B5
Milton Dumfries 113 F8
Milton Highld 156 D4
Milton Highld 157 F5
Milton Highld 157 E6
Milton Highld 169 D8
Milton Highld 157 B8
Milton Moray 160 B2
Milton Notts 77 B7
Milton N Som 22 C5
Milton Oxon 52 F2
Milton Oxon 38 E4
Milton Pembs 32 D1
Milton Perth 133 C8
Milton Ptsmth 15 E7
Milton Stirl 132 D4
Milton Stoke 75 D6
Milton W Dunb 120 B4
Milton Abbas Dorset 13 D6
Milton Abbot Devon 6 B2
Milton Bridge Midloth 122 C5
Milton Bryan Beds 53 F7
Milton Clevedon Som 23 F8
Milton Coldwells Aberds 161 E6
Milton Combe Devon 6 C2
Milton Damerel Devon 9 C5
Milton End Glos 37 D8
Milton Ernest Beds 53 D8
Milton Green Ches 73 D8
Milton Hill Oxon 38 E4
Milton Keynes M Keynes 53 F6
Milton Keynes Village M Keynes 53 F6
Milton Lilbourne Wilts 25 C6
Milton Malsor Northants 52 D5
Milton Morenish Perth 140 F3
Milton of Auchinhove Aberds 150 D4
Milton of Balgonie Fife 134 D5
Milton of Buchanan Stirl 132 E3
Milton of Campfield Aberds 150 D5
Milton of Campsie E Dunb 121 B6
Milton of Corsindae Aberds 151 D5
Milton of Cushnie Aberds 150 C4
Milton of Dalcapon Perth 141 D6
Milton of Edradour Perth 141 D6
Milton of Gollanfield Highld 157 D8
Milton of Lesmore Aberds 150 B3
Milton of Logie Aberds 150 D3
Milton of Murtle Aberdeen 151 D7
Milton of Noth Aberds 150 B4
Milton of Tullich Aberds 150 E2
Milton on Stour Dorset 13 B5
Milton Regis Kent 30 C3
Milton under Wychwood Oxon 38 C2
Miltonduff Moray 159 C5
Miltonhill Moray 158 C4
Miltonise Dumfries 105 B5
Milverton Som 11 B6
Milverton Warks 51 C8
Milwich Staffs 75 F6
Minard Argyll 131 F5
Minchinhampton Glos 37 D5
Mindrum Northumb 124 F4
Minehead Som 21 E8
Minera Wrex 73 D6
Minety Wilts 37 E7
Minffordd Gwyn 71 D6
Minffordd Gwyn 58 C4
Minffordd Gwyn 83 D5
Miningsby Lincs 79 C6
Minions Corn 5 B7
Minishant S Ayrs 112 C3
Minllyn Gwyn 59 C5
Minnes Aberds 151 B8
Minngearraidh W Isles 171 H3
Minnigaff Dumfries 105 C8
Minnonie Aberds 160 B4
Minskip N Yorks 95 C6
Minstead Hants 14 C3
Minsted W Sus 16 B2
Minster Kent 30 B3
Minster Kent 31 C7
Minster Lovell Oxon 38 C3
Minsterley Shrops 60 D3
Minsterworth Glos 36 C4
Minterne Magna Dorset 12 D4
Minting Lincs 78 B4
Mintlaw Aberds 161 D7
Minto Borders 115 B8
Minton Shrops 60 E4
Minwear Pembs 32 C1
Minworth W Mid 63 E5
Mirbister Orkney 176 D2
Mirehouse Cumb 98 C1
Mireland Highld 169 C8
Mirfield W Yorks 88 C3
Miserden Glos 37 D6
Miskin Rhondda 34 F4
Misson Notts 89 E7
Misterton Leics 64 F2
Misterton Notts 89 E8
Misterton Som 12 D2
Mistley Essex 56 F5
Mitcham London 28 C3
Mitchel Troy Mon 36 C1
Mitcheldean Glos 36 C3
Mitchell Corn 4 D3
Mitcheltroy Common Mon 36 D1
Mitford Northumb 117 F7
Mithian Corn 4 D2
Mitton Staffs 62 C2
Mixbury Oxon 52 F4
Moat Cumb 108 B4
Moats Tye Suff 56 D4
Mobberley Ches 74 B4
Mobberley Staffs 75 E7
Moccas Hereford 49 E5
Mochdre Conwy 83 D8
Mochdre Powys 59 F7
Mochrum Dumfries 105 E7
Mockbeggar Hants 14 D2
Mockerkin Cumb 98 B2
Modbury Devon 6 D4
Moddershall Staffs 75 F6
Model Village, Babbacombe Devon 7 C7
Moelfre Anglesey 82 C5
Moelfre Powys 59 B8
Moffat Dumfries 114 D3
Moggerhanger Beds 54 E2
Moira Leics 63 C7
Mol-chlach Highld 153 H5
Molash Kent 30 D4
Mold = Yr Wyddgrug Flint 73 C6
Moldgreen W Yorks 88 C2
Molehill Green Essex 42 B1
Molescroft E Yorks 97 E6
Molesden Northumb 117 F7
Molesworth Cambs 53 B8
Moll Highld 153 F6
Molland Devon 10 B3
Mollington Ches 73 B7
Mollington Oxon 52 E2
Mollinsburn N Lnrk 121 B7
Monachty Ceredig 46 C4
Monachylemore Stirl 132 C3
Monar Lodge Highld 156 E3
Monaughty Powys 48 C4
Monboddo House Aberds 143 B7
Mondynes Aberds 143 B7
Monevechadan Argyll 131 E7
Monewden Suff 57 D6
Moneydie Perth 134 B2
Moniaive Dumfries 113 E7
Monifieth Angus 142 F4
Monikie Angus 142 F4
Monimail Fife 134 C4
Monington Pembs 45 E3
Monk Bretton S Yorks 88 D4
Monk Fryston N Yorks 89 B6
Monk Sherborne Hants 26 D4
Monk Soham Suff 57 C6
Monk Street Essex 42 B2
Monken Hadley London 41 E5
Monkhopton Shrops 61 E6
Monkland Hereford 49 D6
Monkleigh Devon 9 B6
Monknash V Glam 21 B8
Monkokehampton Devon 9 D7
Monks Eleigh Suff 56 E3
Monk's Gate W Sus 17 B6
Monks Heath Ches 74 B5
Monks Kirby Warks 63 F8
Monks Risborough Bucks 39 D8
Monkseaton T & W 111 B6
Monkshill Aberds 160 D4
Monksilver Som 22 F2
Monkspath W Mid 51 B6
Monkswood Mon 35 D7
Monkton Devon 11 D6
Monkton Kent 31 C6
Monkton Pembs 44 E4
Monkton S Ayrs 112 B3
Monkton Combe Bath 24 C2
Monkton Deverill Wilts 24 F3
Monkton Farleigh Wilts 24 C3
Monkton Heathfield Som 11 B7
Monkton Up Wimborne Dorset 13 C8
Monkwearmouth T & W 111 D6
Monkwood Hants 26 F4
Monmouth = Trefynwy Mon 36 C2
Monmouth Cap Mon 35 B7
Monnington on Wye Hereford 49 E5
Monreith Dumfries 105 E7
Monreith Mains Dumfries 105 E7
Mont Saint Guern 16
Montacute Som 12 C2
Montacute House Som 12 C3
Montcoffer Ho. Aberds 160 B3
Montford Argyll 129 D6
Montford Shrops 60 C4
Montford Bridge Shrops 60 C4
Montgarrie Aberds 150 C4
Montgomery = Trefaldwyn Powys 60 E2
Montrave Fife 135 D5
Montrose Angus 143 D7
Montsale Essex 43 E6
Monxton Hants 25 E8
Monyash Derbys 75 C8
Monymusk Aberds 151 C5
Monzie Perth 133 B7
Monzie Castle Perth 133 B7
Moodiesburn N Lnrk 121 B6
Moonzie Fife 134 C5
Moor Allerton W Yorks 95 F5
Moor Crichel Dorset 13 D7
Moor End E Yorks 96 F4
Moor End York 96 D2
Moor Monkton N Yorks 95 D8
Moor of Granary Moray 158 D4
Moor of Ravenstone Dumfries 105 E7
Moor Row Cumb 98 C2
Moor Street Kent 30 C2
Moorby Lincs 79 C5
Moordown Bmouth 13 E8
Moore Halton 86 F3
Moorend Glos 36 D4
Moorends S Yorks 89 C7
Moorgate S Yorks 88 E5
Moorgreen Notts 76 E4
Moorhall Derbys 76 B3
Moorhampton Hereford 49 E5
Moorhead W Yorks 94 F4
Moorhouse Cumb 108 D3
Moorhouse Notts 77 C7
Moorlinch Som 23 F5
Moorsholm Redcar 102 C4
Moorside Gtr Man 87 D7
Moorthorpe W Yorks 89 C5
Moortown Hants 14 D2
Moortown I o W 14 F5
Moortown Lincs 90 E4
Morangie Highld 164 F4
Morar Highld 145 D6
Morborne Cambs 65 E8
Morchard Bishop Devon 10 D2
Morcombelake Dorset 12 E2
Morcott Rutland 65 D6
Morda Shrops 60 B2
Morden Dorset 13 E7
Morden London 28 C3
Mordiford Hereford 49 F7
Mordon Durham 101 B8
More Shrops 60 E3
Morebath Devon 10 B4
Morebattle Borders 116 B3
Morecambe Lancs 92 C4
Morefield Highld 163 E5
Moreleigh Devon 7 D5
Morenish Perth 140 F2
Moresby Cumb 98 B1
Moresby Parks Cumb 98 C1
Morestead Hants 15 B6
Moreton Dorset 13 F6
Moreton Essex 41 D8
Moreton Mers 85 E3
Moreton Oxon 39 D6
Moreton Staffs 61 C7
Moreton Corbet Shrops 61 B5
Moreton-in-Marsh Glos 51 F7
Moreton Jeffries Hereford 49 E8
Moreton Morrell Warks 51 D8
Moreton on Lugg Hereford 49 E7
Moreton Pinkney Northants 52 E3
Moreton Say Shrops 74 F3
Moreton Valence Glos 36 D4
Moretonhampstead Devon 10 F2
Morfa Carms 33 C6
Morfa Carms 33 E6
Morfa Bach Carms 32 C4
Morfa Bychan Gwyn 71 D6
Morfa Dinlle Gwyn 82 F4
Morfa Glas Neath 34 D2
Morfa Nefyn Gwyn 70 C3
Morfydd Denb 72 E5
Morgan's Vale Wilts 14 B2
Moriah Ceredig 46 B5
Morland Cumb 99 B7
Morley Derbys 76 E3
Morley Durham 101 B6
Morley W Yorks 88 B3
Morley Green Ches 87 F6
Morley St Botolph Norf 68 E3
Morningside Edin 122 B5
Morningside N Lnrk 121 D8
Morningthorpe Norf 68 E5
Morpeth Northumb 117 F8
Morphie Aberds 143 C7
Morrey Staffs 62 C5
Morris Green Essex 55 F8
Morriston Swansea 33 E7
Morston Norf 81 C6
Mortehoe Devon 20 E3
Mortimer W Berks 26 C4
Mortimer West End Hants 26 C4
Mortimer's Cross Hereford 49 C6
Mortlake London 28 B3
Morton Cumb 108 D3
Morton Derbys 76 C4
Morton Lincs 65 B7
Morton Lincs 90 E2
Morton Lincs 77 C8
Morton Norf 68 C4
Morton Notts 77 D7
Morton Shrops 60 B2
Morton S Glos 36 E3
Morton Bagot Warks 51 C6
Morton-on-Swale N Yorks 101 E8
Morvah Corn 2 C3
Morval Corn 5 D7
Morvich Highld 146 B2
Morvich Highld 164 D4
Morville Shrops 61 E6
Morville Heath Shrops 61 E6
Morwenstow Corn 8 C4
Mosborough S Yorks 88 F5
Moscow E Ayrs 120 E4
Mosedale Cumb 108 F3
Moseley W Mid 62 F4
Moseley W Mid 62 E3
Moseley Worcs 50 D3
Mosquito Aircraft Museum, London Colney Herts 40 D4
Moss Argyll 136 F1
Moss Highld 137 B7
Moss S Yorks 89 C6
Moss Wrex 73 D7
Moss Bank Mers 86 E3
Moss Edge Lancs 92 E4
Moss End Brack 27 B6
Moss of Barmuckity Moray 159 C6
Moss Pit Staffs 62 B3
Moss-side Highld 158 D2
Moss Side Lancs 92 F3
Mossat Aberds 150 C3
Mossbank Shetland 174 F6
Mossbay Cumb 98 B1
Mossblown S Ayrs 112 B4
Mossbrow Gtr Man 86 F5
Mossburnford Borders 116 C2
Mossdale Dumfries 106 B3
Mossend N Lnrk 121 C7
Mosser Cumb 98 B3
Mossfield Highld 157 B7
Mossgiel E Ayrs 112 B4
Mosside Angus 142 D4
Mossley Ches 75 C5
Mossley Gtr Man 87 D7
Mossley Hill Mers 85 F4
Mosstodloch Moray 159 D7
Mosston Angus 143 E5
Mossy Lea Lancs 86 C3
Mosterton Dorset 12 D2
Moston Gtr Man 87 D6
Moston Shrops 61 B5
Moston Green Ches 74 C4
Mostyn Flint 85 F2
Mostyn Quay Flint 85 F2
Motcombe Dorset 13 B6
Mothecombe Devon 6 E4
Motherby Cumb 99 B6
Motherwell N Lnrk 121 D7
Mottingham London 28 B5
Mottisfont Hants 14 B4
Mottisfont Abbey Garden Hants 14 B4
Mottistone I o W 14 F5
Mottram in Longdendale Gtr Man 87 E7
Mottram St Andrew Ches 75 B5
Mouilpied Guern 16
Mouldsworth Ches 74 B2
Moulin Perth 141 D6
Moulsecoomb Brighton 17 D7
Moulsford Oxon 39 F5
Moulsoe M Keynes 53 E7
Moulton Ches 74 C3
Moulton Lincs 66 B3
Moulton Northants 53 C5
Moulton N Yorks 101 D7
Moulton Suff 55 C7
Moulton V Glam 22 B2
Moulton Chapel Lincs 66 C2
Moulton Eaugate Lincs 66 C3
Moulton St Mary Norf 69 D6
Moulton Seas End Lincs 66 B3
Mounie Castle Aberds 151 B6
Mount Corn 4 D2
Mount Corn 5 C6
Mount Highld 158 E3
Mount Bures Essex 56 F3
Mount Canisp Highld 157 B8
Mount Hawke Corn 3 B6
Mount Pleasant Ches 74 D5
Mount Pleasant Derbys 76 E3
Mount Pleasant Derbys 63 C6
Mount Pleasant Flint 73 B6
Mount Pleasant Hants 14 E3
Mount Pleasant W Yorks 88 B3
Mount Sorrel Wilts 13 B8
Mount Tabor W Yorks 87 B8
Mountain W Yorks 94 F3
Mountain Ash = Aberpennar Rhondda 34 E4
Mountain Cross Borders 122
Mountain Water Pembs 44
Mountbenger Borders 115
Mountfield E Sus 18 C
Mountgerald Highld 157 C
Mountjoy Corn 4 C
Mountnessing Essex 42 E
Mounton Mon 36 E
Mountsorrel Leics 64 C
Mousehole Corn 2 D
Mousen Northumb 125 F7
Mouswald Dumfries 107 B7
Mow Cop Ches 75 D5
Mowhaugh Borders 116 B4
Mowsley Leics 64 F3
Moxley W Mid 62 E3
Moy Highld 147 F7
Moy Highld 157 F8
Moy Hall Highld 157 F8
Moy Ho. Moray 158 C4
Moy Lodge Highld 147 F7
Moyles Court Hants 14 D2
Moylgrove Pembs 45 E3
Muasdale Argyll 118 B3
Much Birch Hereford 49 F7
Much Cowarne Hereford 49 E8
Much Dewchurch Hereford 49 F6
Much Hadham Herts 41 C7
Much Hoole Lancs 86 B2
Much Marcle Hereford 49 F8
Much Wenlock Shrops 61 D6
Muchalls Aberds 151 E8
Muchelney Som 12 B2
Muchlarnick Corn 5 D7
Muchrachd Highld 156 F3
Muckernich Highld 157 D6
Mucking Thurrock 42 F2
Muckleford Dorset 12 E4
Mucklestone Staffs 74 F4
Muckleton Shrops 61 B5
Muckletown Aberds 150 B4
Muckley Corner Staffs 62 D4
Muckton Lincs 91 F7
Mudale Highld 167 F7
Muddiford Devon 20 F4
Mudeford Dorset 14 E2

Mudford Som 12 C3
Mudgley Som 23 E6
Mudgock Stirl 121 B5
Mugeary Highld 153 F5
Mugginton Derbys 76 E2
Muggleswick Durham 110 E3
Muie Highld 164 D3
Muir Aberds 149 F6
Muir of Fairburn Highld 157 D5
Muir of Fowlis Aberds 150 C4
Muir of Ord Highld 157 D6
Muir of Pert Angus 142 F4
Muirden Aberds 160 C4
Muirdrum Angus 143 F5
Muirhead Angus 142 F3
Muirhead Fife 134 D4
Muirhead N Lnrk 121 C6
Muirhead S Ayrs 120 F3
Muirhouselaw Borders 116 B2
Muirhouses Falk 134 F2
Muirkirk E Ayrs 113 B6
Muirmill Stirl 133 F6
Muirshearlich Highld 146 F4
Muirskie Aberds 151 E7
Muirtack Aberds 161 E6
Muirton Highld 157 C8
Muirton Perth 134 B3
Muirton Perth 133 C8
Muirton Mains Highld 157 D5
Muirton of Ardblair Perth 142 E1
Muirton of Ballochy Angus 143 C6
Muiryfold Aberds 160 C4
Muker N Yorks 100 E4
Mulbarton Norf 68 D4
Mulben Moray 159 D7
Mulindry Argyll 126 D3
Mullardoch House Highld 156 F3
Mullion Corn 3 E5
Mullion Cove Corn 3 E5
Mumby Lincs 79 B8
Muncaster Owl Trust World HQ Cumb 98 E3
Munderfield Row Hereford 49 D8
Munderfield Stocks Hereford 49 D8
Mundesley Norf 81 D9
Mundford Norf 67 E8
Mundham Norf 69 E6
Mundon Essex 42 D4
Mundurno Aberdeen 151 C8
Munerigie Highld 147 D5
Muness Shetland 174 C8
Mungasdale Highld 162 E3
Mungrisdale Cumb 108 F3
Munlochy Highld 157 D7
Munsley Hereford 49 E8
Munslow Shrops 60 F5
Murchington Devon 9 F8
Murcott Oxon 39 C5
Murkle Highld 169 C6
Murlaggan Highld 146 E3
Murlaggan Highld 147 F6
Murra Orkney 176 F1
Murrayfield Edin 122 B5
Murrayfield Stadium Edin 123 B5
Murrays Motorcycle Museum I o M 84 D3
Murrow Cambs 66 D3
Mursley Bucks 39 B8
Murthill Angus 142 D4
Murthly Perth 141 F7
Murton Cumb 100 B2
Murton Durham 111 E6
Murton Northumb 125 E5
Murton York 96 D2
Musbury Devon 11 E7
Muscoates N Yorks 102 F4
Musdale Argyll 130 C5
Museum of Childhood, Bethnal Green London 41 F6
Museum of the Broads, Sutton Norf 69 B6
Musselburgh E Loth 123 B6
Musselburgh Racecourse E Loth 123 B6
Muston Leics 77 F8
Muston N Yorks 97 B6
Mustow Green Worcs 50 B3
Mutehill Dumfries 106 E3
Mutford Suff 69 F7
Muthill Perth 133 C7
Mutterton Devon 10 D5
Muxton Telford 61 C7
Mybster Highld 169 D6
Myddfai Carms 34 B1
Myddle Shrops 60 B4
Mydroilyn Ceredig 46 D3
Myerscough Lancs 92 F4
Mylor Bridge Corn 3 C7
Mynachlog-ddu Pembs 45 F3
Myndtown Shrops 60 F3
Mynydd Bach Ceredig 47 B6
Mynydd-bach Mon 36 E1
Mynydd Bodafon Anglesey 82 C4
Mynydd-isa Flint 73 C6
Mynyddygarreg Carms 33 D5
Mynytho Gwyn 70 D4
Myrebird Aberds 151 E6
Myrelandhorn Highld 169 D7
Myreside Perth 134 B4
Myrtle Hill Carms 47 F6
Mytchett Sur 27 D6
Mytholm W Yorks 87 B7
Mytholmroyd W Yorks 87 B8
Myton-on-Swale N Yorks 95 C7
Mytton Shrops 60 C4

N

Na Gearrannan W Isles 172 D4
Naast Highld 154 B4
Naburn York 95 E8
Nackington Kent 31 D5
Nacton Suff 57 E6
Nafferton E Yorks 97 D6
Nailbridge Glos 36 C3
Nailsbourne Som 11 B7
Nailsea N Som 23 B6
Nailstone Leics 63 D8
Nailsworth Glos 37 E5
Nairn Highld 158 D2
Nalderswood Sur 28 E3
Nancegollan Corn 2 C5
Nancledra Corn 2 C3
Nanhoron Gwyn 70 D3
Nannau Gwyn 71 E8
Nannerch Flint 73 C5
Nanpantan Leics 64 C2
Nanpean Corn 4 D4
Nanstallon Corn 4 C5
Nant-ddu Powys 34 C4
Nant-glas Powys 47 C8
Nant Peris Gwyn 83 F6
Nant Uchaf Denb 72 D4
Nant-y-Bai Carms 47 E6
Nant-y-cafn Neath 34 D2
Nant-y-derry Mon 35 D7
Nant-y-ffin Carms 46 F4
Nant-y-moel Bridgend 34 E3
Nant-y-pandy Conwy 83 D6
Nanternis Ceredig 46 D2
Nantgaredig Carms 33 B5
Nantgarw Rhondda 35 F5
Nantglyn Denb 72 C4
Nantgwyn Powys 47 B8
Nantlle Gwyn 82 F5
Nantmawr Shrops 60 B2
Nantmel Powys 48 C2
Nantmor Gwyn 71 C7
Nantwich Ches 74 D3
Nantycaws Carms 33 C5
Nantyffyllon Bridgend 34 E2
Nantyglo Bl Gwent 35 C5
Naphill Bucks 39 E8
Nappa N Yorks 93 D8
Napton on the Hill Warks 52 C2
Narberth = Arberth Pembs 32 C2
Narborough Leics 64 E2
Narborough Norf 67 C7
Nasareth Gwyn 82 F4
Naseby Northants 52 B4
Nash Bucks 53 F5
Nash Hereford 48 C5
Nash Newport 35 F7
Nash Shrops 49 B8
Nash Lee Bucks 39 D8
Nassington Northants 65 E7
Nasty Herts 41 B6
Nateby Cumb 100 D2
Nateby Lancs 92 E4
National Agricultural Centre, Stoneleigh Warks 51 B8
National Botanic Garden of Wales Carms 33 C6
National Cycle Collection, Llandrindod Wells Powys 48 C2
National Exhibition Centre, Birmingham W Mid 63 F5
National Fishing Heritage Centre, Grimsby NE Lincs 91 D6
National Gallery London 41 F5
National Hockey Stadium M Keynes 87 E6
National Ice Centre Nottingham 77 F5
National Maritime Museum London 28 B4
National Maritime Museum, Falmouth Corn 4 F3
National Motor Museum, Beaulieu Hants 14 D4
National Museum of Photography, Bradford W Yorks 94 F4
National Museum of Wales Cardiff 22 B3
National Portrait Gallery (See National Gallery) London 41 F5
National Railway Museum York 95 D8
National Seal Sanctuary, Gweek Corn 3 D6
National Space Science Centre Leics 64 D2
National Squash Centre Gtr Man 87 E6
Natland Cumb 99 F7
Natural History Museum London 28 B3
Natureland Seal Sanctuary, Skegness Lincs 79 C8
Naughton Suff 56 E4
Naunton Glos 37 B8
Naunton Worcs 50 F3
Naunton Beauchamp Worcs 50 D4
Navenby Lincs 78 D2
Navestock Heath Essex 41 E8
Navestock Side Essex 42 E1
Navidale Highld 165 C7
Nawton N Yorks 102 F4
Nayland Suff 56 F3
Nazeing Essex 41 D7
Neacroft Hants 14 E2
Neal's Green Warks 63 F7
Neap Shetland 175 H7
Near Sawrey Cumb 99 E5
Neasham Darl 101 C8
Neath = Castell-Nedd Neath 33 E8
Neath Abbey Neath 33 E8
Neatishead Norf 69 B6
Nebo Anglesey 82 B4
Nebo Ceredig 46 C4
Nebo Conwy 83 F8
Nebo Gwyn 82 F4
Necton Norf 67 D8
Nedd Highld 166 F3
Nedderton Northumb 117 F8
Nedging Tye Suff 56 E4
Needham Norf 68 F5
Needham Market Suff 56 D4
Needingworth Cambs 54 B4
Needwood Staffs 63 B5
Neen Savage Shrops 49 B8
Neen Sollars Shrops 49 B8
Neenton Shrops 61 F6
Nefyn Gwyn 70 C4
Neilston E Renf 120 D4
Neinthirion Powys 59 D6
Neithrop Oxon 52 E2
Nelly Andrews Green Powys 60 D2
Nelson Caerph 35 E5
Nelson Lancs 93 F8
Nelson Village Northumb 111 B5
Nemphlar S Lnrk 121 E8
Nempnett Thrubwell Bath 23 C7
Nene Terrace Lincs 66 D2
Nenthall Cumb 109 E7
Nenthead Cumb 109 E7
Nenthorn Borders 124 F2
Nerabus Argyll 126 D2
Nercwys Flint 73 C6
Nerston S Lnrk 121 D6
Nesbit Northumb 125 F5
Ness Ches 73 B7
Ness Gardens, Connah's Quay Ches 73 B7
Nesscliffe Shrops 60 C3
Neston Ches 73 B6
Neston Wilts 24 C3
Nether Alderley Ches 74 B5
Nether Blainslie Borders 123 E8
Nether Booth Derbys 88 F2
Nether Broughton Leics 64 B3
Nether Burrow Lancs 93 B6
Nether Cerne Dorset 12 E4
Nether Compton Dorset 12 C3
Nether Crimond Aberds 151 B7
Nether Dalgliesh Borders 115 D5
Nether Dallachy Moray 159 C7
Nether Exe Devon 10 D4
Nether Glasslaw Aberds 161 C5
Nether Handwick Angus 142 E3
Nether Haugh S Yorks 88 E5
Nether Heage Derbys 76 D3
Nether Heyford Northants 52 D4
Nether Hindhope Borders 116 C3
Nether Howecleuch S Lnrk 114 C3
Nether Kellet Lancs 92 C5
Nether Kinmundy Aberds 161 D7
Nether Langwith Notts 76 B5
Nether Leask Aberds 161 E7
Nether Lenshie Aberds 160 D3
Nether Monynut Borders 124 C3
Nether Padley Derbys 76 B2
Nether Park Aberds 161 C7
Nether Poppleton York 95 D8
Nether Silton N Yorks 102 E2
Nether Stowey Som 22 F3
Nether Urquhart Fife 134 D3
Nether Wallop Hants 25 F8
Nether Wasdale Cumb 98 D3
Nether Whitacre Warks 63 E6
Nether Worton Oxon 52 F2
Netheravon Wilts 25 E6
Netherbrae Aberds 160 C4
Netherbrough Orkney 176 E2
Netherburn S Lnrk 121 E8
Netherbury Dorset 12 E2
Netherby Cumb 108 B3
Netherby N Yorks 95 E6
Nethercote Warks 52 C3
Nethercott Devon 20 F3
Netherend Glos 36 D2
Netherfield E Sus 18 D4
Netherhampton Wilts 14 B2
Netherlaw Dumfries 106 E4
Netherley Aberds 151 E7
Netherley Mers 86 F2
Nethermill Dumfries 114 F3
Nethermuir Aberds 161 D6
Netherplace E Renf 120 D5
Netherseal Derbys 63 C6
Netherthird E Ayrs 113 C5
Netherthong W Yorks 88 D2
Netherthorpe S Yorks 89 F6
Netherton Angus 143 D5
Netherton Devon 7 B6
Netherton Hants 25 D8
Netherton Mers 85 D4
Netherton Northumb 117 D5
Netherton Oxon 38 E4
Netherton Perth 141 D8
Netherton Stirl 121 B5
Netherton W Mid 62 F3
Netherton Worcs 50 E4
Netherton W Yorks 88 C2
Netherton W Yorks 88 C3
Nethertown Cumb 98 D1
Nethertown Highld 169 B8
Netherwitton Northumb 117 E7
Netherwood E Ayrs 113 B6
Nethy Bridge Highld 149 B6
Netley Hants 15 D5
Netley Marsh Hants 14 C4
Netteswell Essex 41 C7
Nettlebed Oxon 39 F7
Nettlebridge Som 23 E8
Nettlecombe Dorset 12 E3
Nettleden Herts 40 C3
Nettleham Lincs 78 B3
Nettlestead Kent 29 D7
Nettlestead Green Kent 29 D7
Nettlestone I o W 15 E7
Nettlesworth Durham 111 E5
Nettleton Lincs 90 D5
Nettleton Wilts 24 B3
Neuadd Carms 33 B7
Nevendon Essex 42 E3
Nevern Pembs 45 E2
Nevis Range Ski Centre, Torlundy Highld 139 B5
New Abbey Dumfries 107 C6
New Aberdour Aberds 161 B5
New Addington London 28 C4
New Alresford Hants 26 F3
New Alyth Perth 142 E2
New Arley Warks 63 F6
New Ash Green Kent 29 C7
New Barn Kent 29 C7
New Barnetby N Lincs 90 C4
New Barton Northants 53 C6
New Bewick Northumb 117 B6
New-bigging Angus 142 E2
New Bilton Warks 52 B2
New Bolingbroke Lincs 79 D6
New Boultham Lincs 78 B2
New Bradwell M Keynes 53 E6
New Brancepeth Durham 110 E5
New Bridge Wrex 73 E6
New Brighton Flint 73 C6
New Brighton Mers 85 E4
New Brinsley Notts 76 D4
New Broughton Wrex 73 D7
New Buckenham Norf 68 E3
New Byth Aberds 160 C5
New Catton Norf 68 C5
New Cheriton Hants 15 B6
New Costessey Norf 68 C4
New Cowper Cumb 107 E8
New Cross Ceredig 46 B5
New Cross London 28 B4
New Cumnock E Ayrs 113 C6
New Deer Aberds 161 D5
New Delaval Northumb 111 B5
New Duston Northants 52 C5
New Earswick York 96 D2
New Edlington S Yorks 89 E6
New Elgin Moray 159 C6
New Ellerby E Yorks 97 F7
New Eltham London 28 B5
New End Worcs 51 D5
New Farnley W Yorks 94 F5
New Ferry Mers 85 F4
New Fryston W Yorks 89 B5
New Galloway Dumfries 106 B3
New Gilston Fife 135 D6
New Grimsby Scilly 2 E3
New Hainford Norf 68 C5
New Hartley Northumb 111 B6
New Haw Sur 27 C8
New Hedges Pembs 32 D2
New Herrington T & W 111 D6
New Hinksey Oxon 39 D5
New Holkham Norf 80 D4
New Holland N Lincs 90 B4
New Houghton Derbys 76 C4
New Houghton Norf 80 E3
New Houses N Yorks 93 B8
New Humberstone Leicester 64 D3
New Hutton Cumb 99 E7
New Hythe Kent 29 D8
New Inn Carms 46 F3
New Inn Mon 36 D1
New Inn Pembs 45 F2
New Inn Torf 35 E7
New Invention Shrops 48 B4
New Invention W Mid 62 D3
New Kelso Highld 155 F5
New Kingston Notts 64 B2
New Lanark S Lnrk 121 E8
New Lanark Village & Visitor Centre, Lanark S Lnrk 121 E8
New Lane Lancs 86 C2
New Lane End Warr 86 E4
New Leake Lincs 79 D7
New Leeds Aberds 161 C6
New Longton Lancs 86 B3
New Luce Dumfries 105 C5
New Malden London 28 C3
New Marske Redcar 102 B4
New Marton Shrops 73 F7
New Micklefield W Yorks 95 F7
New Mill Aberds 151 F6
New Mill Herts 40 C2
New Mill Wilts 25 C6
New Mill W Yorks 88 D2
New Mills Ches 87 F5
New Mills Corn 4 D3
New Mills Derbys 87 F7
New Mills Powys 59 D7
New Milton Hants 14 E3
New Moat Pembs 32 B1
New Ollerton Notts 77 C6
New Oscott W Mid 62 E4
New Park N Yorks 95 D5
New Pitsligo Aberds 161 C5
New Pleasurewood Hills Leisure Park, Lowestoft Suff 69 E8
New Polzeath Corn 4 B4
New Quay = Ceinewydd Ceredig 46 D2
New Rackheath Norf 69 C5
New Radnor Powys 48 C4
New Rent Cumb 108 F4
New Ridley Northumb 110 D3
New Road Side N Yorks 94 E2
New Romney Kent 19 C7
New Rossington S Yorks 89 E7
New Row Ceredig 47 B6
New Row Lancs 93 F6
New Row N Yorks 102 C4
New Sarum Wilts 25 F6
New Silksworth T & W 111 D6
New Stevenston N Lnrk 121 D7
New Street Staffs 75 D7
New Street Lane Shrops 74 F3
New Swanage Dorset 13 F8
New Totley S Yorks 76 B3
New Town E Loth 123 B7
New Tredegar = Tredegar Newydd Caerph 35 D5
New Trows S Lnrk 121 F8
New Ulva Argyll 128 B2
New Walsoken Cambs 66 D4
New Waltham NE Lincs 91 D6
New Whittington Derbys 76 B3
New Wimpole Cambs 54 E4
New Winton E Loth 123 B7
New Yatt Oxon 38 C3
New York Lincs 78 D5
New York N Yorks 94 C4
Newall W Yorks 94 E4
Newark Orkney 176 B6
Newark P'boro 66 D2
Newark Castle Notts 77 D7
Newark-on-Trent Notts 77 D7
Newarthill N Lnrk 121 D7
Newbarns Cumb 92 B2
Newbattle Midloth 123 C6
Newbiggin Cumb 98 E2
Newbiggin Cumb 92 C2
Newbiggin Cumb 99 B6
Newbiggin Cumb 109 E5
Newbiggin Cumb 99 B8
Newbiggin Durham 100 B4
Newbiggin N Yorks 100 E4
Newbiggin N Yorks 100 F4
Newbiggin-by-the-Sea Northumb 117 F9
Newbiggin-on-Lune Cumb 100 D2
Newbigging Angus 142 F4
Newbigging Angus 142 F4
Newbigging S Lnrk 122 E3
Newbold Derbys 76 B3
Newbold Leics 63 C8
Newbold on Avon Warks 52 B2
Newbold on Stour Warks 51 E7
Newbold Pacey Warks 51 D7
Newbold Verdon Leics 63 D8
Newborough Anglesey 82 E4
Newborough P'boro 66 D2
Newborough Staffs 62 B5
Newbottle Northants 52 F3
Newbottle T & W 111 D6
Newbourne Suff 57 E6
Newbridge Caerph 35 E6
Newbridge Ceredig 46 D4
Newbridge Corn 2 C3
Newbridge Corn 5 C8
Newbridge Dumfries 107 B6
Newbridge Edin 122 B4
Newbridge Hants 14 C3
Newbridge I o W 14 F5
Newbridge Pembs 44 B4
Newbridge Green Worcs 50 F3
Newbridge-on-Usk Mon 35 E7
Newbridge on Wye Powys 48 D2
Newbrough Northumb 109 C8
Newbuildings Devon 10 D2
Newburgh Aberds 151 B8
Newburgh Aberds 161 C6
Newburgh Borders 115 C6
Newburgh Fife 134 C4
Newburgh Lancs 86 C2
Newburn T & W 110 C4
Newbury W Berks 26 C2
Newbury Park London 41 F7
Newbury Racecourse W Berks 26 C2
Newby Cumb 99 B7
Newby Lancs 93 E8
Newby N Yorks 93 B7
Newby N Yorks 102 C3
Newby N Yorks 103 E8
Newby Bridge Cumb 99 F5
Newby East Cumb 108 D4
Newby Hall, Ripon N Yorks 95 C6
Newby West Cumb 108 D3
Newby Wiske N Yorks 102 F1
Newcastle Mon 35 C8
Newcastle Shrops 60 F2
Newcastle Discovery T & W 110 C5
Newcastle Emlyn = Castell Newydd Emlyn Carms 46 E2
Newcastle International Airport T & W 110 B4
Newcastle Racecourse T & W 110 B5
Newcastle-under-Lyme Staffs 74 E5
Newcastle Upon Tyne T & W 110 C5
Newcastleton = Copshaw Holm Borders 115 F7
Newchapel Pembs 45 F4
Newchapel Powys 59 F6
Newchapel Staffs 75 D5
Newchapel Sur 28 E4
Newchurch Carms 32 B4
Newchurch I o W 15 F6
Newchurch Kent 19 B7
Newchurch Lancs 93 F8
Newchurch Mon 36 E1
Newchurch Powys 48 D4
Newchurch Staffs 62 B5
Newcott Devon 11 D7
Newcraighall Edin 123 B6
Newdigate Sur 28 E2
Newell Green Brack 27 B6
Newenden Kent 18 C5
Newent Glos 36 B4
Newerne Glos 36 D3
Newfield Durham 110 F5
Newfield Highld 157 B8
Newford Scilly 2 E4
Newfound Hants 26 D3
Newgale Pembs 44 C3
Newgate Norf 81 C6
Newgate Street Herts 41 D6
Newhall Ches 74 E3
Newhall Derbys 63 B6
Newhall House Highld 157 C7
Newhall Point Highld 157 C8
Newham Northumb 117 B7
Newham Hall Northumb 117 B7
Newhaven Derbys 75 D8
Newhaven Edin 123 B5
Newhaven E Sus 17 D8
Newhey Gtr Man 87 C7
Newholm N Yorks 103 C6
Newhouse N Lnrk 121 C7
Newick E Sus 17 B8
Newingreen Kent 19 B8
Newington Kent 30 C2
Newington Kent 19 B8
Newington Kent 31 C7
Newington Notts 89 E7
Newington Oxon 39 E6
Newington Shrops 60 F4
Newland Glos 36 D2
Newland Hull 97 F6
Newland N Yorks 89 B7
Newland Worcs 50 E2
Newlandrig Midloth 123 C6
Newlands Borders 115 E8
Newlands Highld 157 E8
Newlands Moray 159 D7
Newlands Northumb 110 D3
Newland's Corner Sur 27 E8
Newlands of Geise Highld 169 C5
Newlands of Tynet Moray 159 C7
Newlands Park Anglesey 82 C2
Newlandsmuir S Lnrk 121 D6
Newlot Orkney 176 E4
Newlyn Corn 2 D3
Newmachar Aberds 151 C7
Newmains N Lnrk 121 D8
Newmarket Suff 55 C7
Newmarket W Isles 172 E7
Newmarket Racecourse Suff 55 C7
Newmill Borders 115 C7
Newmill Corn 2 C3
Newmill Moray 159 D8
Newmill of Inshewan Angus 142 C4
Newmills Mon 36 D2
Newmills of Boyne Aberds 160 C2
Newmiln Perth 141 F8
Newmilns E Ayrs 120 F5
Newnham Cambs 54 D5
Newnham Glos 36 C3
Newnham Hants 26 D5
Newnham Herts 54 F3
Newnham Kent 30 D3
Newnham Northants 52 D3
Newnham Bridge Worcs 49 C8
Newpark Fife 135 C6
Newport Devon 20 F4
Newport E Yorks 96 F4
Newport Essex 55 F6
Newport Highld 165 B8
Newport I o W 15 F6
Newport Norf 69 C8
Newport Telford 61 C7
Newport = Casnewydd Newport 35 F7
Newport = Trefdraeth Pembs 45 F2
Newport Museum & Art Gallery Newport 35 F7
Newport-on-Tay Fife 135 B6
Newport Pagnell M Keynes 53 E6
Newpound Common W Sus 16 B4
Newquay Corn 4 C3
Newquay Airport Corn 4 C3
Newquay Sea Life Centre Corn 4 C3
Newsbank Ches 74 C5
Newseat Aberds 160 E4
Newseat Aberds 161 D7
Newsham Northumb 111 B6
Newsham N Yorks 101 C6
Newsham N Yorks 102 F1
Newsholme E Yorks 89 B8
Newsholme Lancs 93 D8
Newsome W Yorks 88 C2
Newstead Borders 123 F8
Newstead Notts 76 D5
Newstead Northumb 117 B7
Newstead Abbey, Kirkby in Ashfield Notts 76 D5
Newthorpe N Yorks 95 F7
Newton Argyll 131 F6
Newton Borders 116 B2
Newton Bridgend 21 B7
Newton Cambs 54 E5
Newton Cambs 66 C4
Newton Cardiff 22 B4
Newton Ches 74 D2
Newton Ches 73 C8
Newton Ches 74 B2
Newton Cumb 92 B2
Newton Derbys 76 D4
Newton Dorset 13 C5
Newton Dumfries 114 E4
Newton Dumfries 108 B2
Newton Gtr Man 87 E7
Newton Hereford 48 F5
Newton Hereford 49 D7
Newton Highld 157 C8
Newton Highld 166 F4
Newton Highld 169 E8
Newton Highld 157 E8
Newton Lancs 92 F4
Newton Lancs 93 D6
Newton Lancs 93 B5
Newton Lincs 78 F3
Newton Moray 159 C5
Newton Norf 67 C8
Newton Notts 77 E6
Newton Northants 65 F5
Newton Northumb 110 C3
Newton Perth 141 F5
Newton S Lnrk 121 C6
Newton S Lnrk 122 F2
Newton Staffs 62 B4
Newton Suff 56 E3
Newton Swansea 33 F7
Newton S Yorks 89 D6
Newton Warks 52 B3
Newton Wilts 14 B3
Newton W Loth 122 B3
Newton Abbot Devon 7 B6
Newton Abbot Racecourse Devon 7 B6
Newton Arlosh Cumb 107 D8
Newton Aycliffe Durham 101 B7
Newton Bewley Hrtlpl 102 B2
Newton Blossomville M Keynes 53 D7
Newton Bromswold Northants 53 C7
Newton Burgoland Leics 63 D7
Newton by Toft Lincs 90 F4
Newton Ferrers Devon 6 E3
Newton Flotman Norf 68 E5
Newton Hall Northumb 110 C3
Newton Harcourt Leics 64 E3
Newton Heath Gtr Man 87 D6
Newton Ho. Aberds 151 B5
Newton Kyme N Yorks 95 E7
Newton-le-Willows Mers 86 E3
Newton-le-Willows N Yorks 101 F7
Newton Longville Bucks 53 F6
Newton Mearns E Renf 120 D5
Newton Morrell N Yorks 101 D7
Newton Mulgrave N Yorks 103 C5
Newton of Ardtoe Highld 145 F6
Newton of Balcanquhal Perth 134 C3
Newton of Falkland Fife 134 D4
Newton on Ayr S Ayrs 112 B3
Newton on Ouse N Yorks 95 D8
Newton-on-Rawcliffe N Yorks 103 E6
Newton-on-the-Moor Northumb 117 D7
Newton on Trent Lincs 77 B8
Newton Park Argyll 129 D6
Newton Poppleford Devon 11 F5
Newton Purcell Oxon 52 F4
Newton Regis Warks 63 D6
Newton Reigny Cumb 108 F4
Newton St Cyres Devon 10 E3
Newton St Faith Norf 68 C5
Newton St Loe Bath 24 C2
Newton St Petrock Devon 9 C6
Newton Solney Derbys 63 B6
Newton Stacey Hants 26 E2
Newton Stewart Dumfries 105 C8
Newton Tony Wilts 25 E7
Newton Tracey Devon 9 B7
Newton under Roseberry Redcar 102 C3
Newton upon Derwent E Yorks 96 E3
Newton Valence Hants 26 F5
Newtonairds Dumfries 113 F8
Newtongrange Midloth 123 C6
Newtonhill Aberds 151 E8
Newtonhill Highld 157 E6
Newtonmill Angus 143 C6
Newtonmore Highld 148 E3
Newtown Argyll 131 E6
Newtown Ches 74 B2
Newtown Corn 3 D6
Newtown Cumb 107 E7
Newtown Cumb 108 C5
Newtown Derbys 87 F7
Newtown Devon 10 B2
Newtown Glos 36 D3
Newtown Glos 50 F4
Newtown Hants 14 C3
Newtown Hants 14 B4
Newtown Hants 15 C7
Newtown Hants 26 C2
Newtown Hants 15 C6
Newtown Hants 15 D5
Newtown Hereford 49 E8
Newtown Highld 147 D6
Newtown I o M 84 E3
Newtown I o W 14 E5
Newtown Northumb 117 D6
Newtown Northumb 117 B6
Newtown Northumb 125 F5
Newtown Poole 13 E8
Newtown Shrops 73 F8
Newtown Staffs 75 C6
Newtown Staffs 75 C7
Newtown Wilts 13 B7
Newtown = Y Drenewydd Powys 59 E8
Newtown Linford Leics 64 D2
Newtown St Boswells Borders 123 F8
Newtown Unthank Leics 63 D8
Newtyle Angus 142 E2
Neyland Pembs 44 E4
Niarbyl I o M 84 E2
Nibley S Glos 36 F3
Nibley Green Glos 36 E4
Nibon Shetland 174 F5
Nicholashayne Devon 11 C6
Nicholaston Swansea 33 F6
Nidd N Yorks 95 C6
Nigg Aberdeen 151 D8
Nigg Highld 158 B2
Nigg Ferry Highld 157 C8
Nightcott Som 10 B3
Nilig Denb 72 D4
Nine Ashes Essex 42 D1
Nine Mile Burn Midloth 122 D4
Nine Wells Pembs 44 C2
Ninebanks Northumb 109 D7
Ninfield E Sus 18 D4
Ningwood I o W 14 F4
Nisbet Borders 116 B2
Nisthouse Orkney 176 E2
Nisthouse Shetland 175 G7
Niton I o W 15 G6
Nitshill Glasgow 120 C5
No Man's Heath Ches 74 E2
No Man's Heath Warks 63 D6
Noak Hill London 41 E8
Noblethorpe S Yorks 88 D3
Nobottle Northants 52 C4
Nocton Lincs 78 C3
Noke Oxon 39 C5
Nolton Pembs 44 D3
Nolton Haven Pembs 44 D3
Nomansland Devon 10 C3
Nomansland Wilts 14 C3
Noneley Shrops 60 B4
Nonikiln Highld 157 B7
Nonington Kent 31 D6
Noonsbrough Shetland 175 H4
Norbreck Blkpool 92 E3
Norbridge Hereford 50 E2
Norbury Ches 74 E2
Norbury Derbys 75 E8
Norbury Shrops 60 E3
Norbury Staffs 61 B7
Nordelph Norf 67 D5
Norden Gtr Man 87 C6
Norden Heath Dorset 13 F7
Nordley Shrops 61 E6
Norham Northumb 124 E5
Norley Ches 74 B2
Norleywood Hants 14 E4
Norman Cross Cambs 65 E8
Normanby N Lincs 90 C2
Normanby N Yorks 103 F5
Normanby Redcar 102 C3
Normanby-by-Spital Lincs 90 F4
Normanby by Stow Lincs 90 F2
Normanby le Wold Lincs 90 E5
Normandy Sur 27 D7
Norman's Bay E Sus 18 E3
Norman's Green Devon 11 D5
Normanstone Suff 69 E8
Normanton Derby 76 F3

Normanton Leics 77 E8
Normanton Lincs 78 E2
Normanton Notts 77 D7
Normanton Rutland 65 D6
Normanton W Yorks 88 B4
Normanton le Heath Leics 63 C7
Normanton on Soar Notts 64 B2
Normanton-on-the-Wolds Notts 77 F6
Normanton on Trent Notts 77 C7
Normoss Lancs 92 F3
Norney Sur 27 E7
Norrington Common Wilts 24 C3
Norris Green Mers 85 E4
Norris Hill Leics 63 C7
North Anston S Yorks 89 F6
North Aston Oxon 38 B4
North Baddesley Hants 14 C4
North Ballachulish Highld 138 C4
North Barrow Som 12 B4
North Barsham Norf 80 D5
North Benfleet Essex 42 F3
North Bersted W Sus 16 D3
North Berwick E Loth 135 F7
North Boarhunt Hants 15 C7
North Bovey Devon 10 F2
North Bradley Wilts 24 D3
North Brentor Devon 9 F6
North Brewham Som 24 F2
North Buckland Devon 20 E3
North Burlingham Norf 69 C6
North Cadbury Som 12 B4
North Cairn Dumfries 104 B3
North Carlton Lincs 78 B2
North Carrine Argyll 118 F3
North Cave E Yorks 96 F4
North Cerney Glos 37 D7
North Charford Wilts 14 C2
North Charlton Northumb 117 B7
North Cheriton Som 12 B4
North Cliff E Yorks 97 E8
North Cliffe E Yorks 96 F4
North Clifton Notts 77 B8
North Cockerington Lincs 91 E7
North Coker Som 12 C3
North Collafirth Shetland 174 E5
North Common E Sus 17 B7
North Connel Argyll 130 B5
North Cornelly Bridgend 34 F2
North Cotes Lincs 91 D7
North Cove Suff 69 F7
North Cowton N Yorks 101 D7
North Crawley M Keynes 53 E7
North Cray London 29 B5
North Creake Norf 80 D4
North Curry Som 11 B8
North Dalton E Yorks 96 D5
North Dawn Orkney 176 F3
North Deighton N Yorks 95 D6
North Duffield N Yorks 96 F2
North Elkington Lincs 91 E6
North Elmham Norf 81 E5
North Elmshall W Yorks 89 C5
North End Bucks 39 B8
North End E Yorks 97 F8
North End Essex 42 C2
North End Hants 26 C2
North End Lincs 78 E5
North End N Som 23 C6
North End Ptsmth 15 D7
North End Som 11 B7
North End W Sus 16 D5
North Erradale Highld 154 B3
North Fambridge Essex 42 E4
North Fearns Highld 153 F6
North Featherstone W Yorks 88 B5
North Ferriby E Yorks 90 B3
North Frodingham E Yorks 97 D7
North Gluss Shetland 174 F5
North Gorley Hants 14 C2
North Green Norf 68 F5
North Green Suff 57 C7
North Greetwell Lincs 78 B3
North Grimston N Yorks 96 C4
North Halley Orkney 176 F4
North Halling Medway 29 C8
North Hayling Hants 15 D8
North Hazelrigg Northumb 125 F6
North Heasley Devon 21 F6
North Heath W Sus 16 B4
North Hill Cambs 55 B5
North Hill Corn 5 B7
North Hinksey Oxon 38 D4
North Holmwood Sur 28 E2
North Howden E Yorks 96 F3
North Huish Devon 6 D5
North Hykeham Lincs 78 C2
North Johnston Pembs 44 D4
North Kelsey Lincs 90 D4
North Kelsey Moor Lincs 90 D4
North Kessock Highld 157 E7
North Killingholme N Lincs 90 C5
North Kilvington N Yorks 102 F2
North Kilworth Leics 64 F3
North Kirkton Aberds 161 C8
North Kiscadale N Ayrs 119 D7
North Kyme Lincs 78 D4
North Lancing W Sus 17 D5
North Lee Bucks 39 D8
North Leigh Oxon 38 C3
North Leverton with Habblesthorpe Notts 89 F8
North Littleton Worcs 51 E5
North Lopham Norf 68 F3
North Luffenham Rutland 65 D6
North Marden W Sus 16 C2
North Marston Bucks 39 B7
North Middleton Midloth 123 D6
North Middleton Northumb 117 B6
North Molton Devon 10 B2
North Moreton Oxon 39 F5
North Mundham W Sus 16 D2
North Muskham Notts 77 D7
North Newbald E Yorks 96 F5
North Newington Oxon 52 F2
North Newnton Wilts 25 D6
North Newton Som 22 F4
North Nibley Glos 36 E4
North Norfolk Railway, Sheringham Norf 81 C7
North Oakley Hants 26 D3
North Ockendon London 42 F1
North Ormesby M'bro 102 B3
North Ormsby Lincs 91 E6
North Otterington N Yorks 102 F1
North Owersby Lincs 90 E4
North Perrott Som 12 D2
North Petherton Som 22 F4
North Petherwin Corn 8 F4
North Pickenham Norf 67 D8
North Piddle Worcs 50 D4
North Poorton Dorset 12 E3
North Port Argyll 131 C6
North Queensferry Fife 134 F3
North Radworthy Devon 21 F6
North Rauceby Lincs 78 E3
North Reston Lincs 91 F7
North Rigton N Yorks 95 E5
North Rode Ches 75 C5
North Roe Shetland 174 E5
North Ronaldsay Airport Orkney 176 A6
North Runcton Norf 67 C6
North Sandwick Shetland 174 D7
North Scale Cumb 92 C1
North Scarle Lincs 77 C8
North Seaton Northumb 117 F8
North Shian Argyll 138 E3
North Shields T & W 111 C6
North Shoebury Sthend 43 F5
North Shore Blkpool 92 F3
North Side Cumb 98 B2
North Side P'boro 66 E2
North Skelton Redcar 102 C4
North Somercotes Lincs 91 E8
North Stainley N Yorks 95 B5
North Stainmore Cumb 100 C3
North Stifford Thurrock 42 F2
North Stoke Bath 24 C2
North Stoke Oxon 39 F6
North Stoke W Sus 16 C4
North Street Hants 26 F4
North Street Kent 30 D4
North Street Medway 30 B2
North Street W Berks 26 B4
North Sunderland Northumb 125 F8
North Tamerton Corn 8 E5
North Tawton Devon 9 D8
North Thoresby Lincs 91 E6
North Tidworth Wilts 25 E7
North Togston Northumb 117 D8
North Tuddenham Norf 68 C3
North Walbottle T & W 110 C4
North Walsham Norf 81 D8
North Waltham Hants 26 E3
North Warnborough Hants 26 D5
North Water Bridge Angus 143 C6
North Watten Highld 169 D7
North Weald Bassett Essex 41 D7
North Wheatley Notts 89 F8
North Whilborough Devon 7 C6
North Wick Bath 23 C7
North Willingham Lincs 91 F5
North Wingfield Derbys 76 C4
North Witham Lincs 65 B6
North Woolwich London 28 B5
North Wootton Dorset 12 C4
North Wootton Norf 67 B6
North Wootton Som 23 E7
North Wraxall Wilts 24 B3
North Wroughton Thamesdown 38 F1
North Yorkshire Moors Railway, Pickering N Yorks 103 F6
Northacre Norf 68 E2
Northallerton N Yorks 102 E1
Northam Devon 9 B6
Northam Soton 14 C5
Northampton Northants 53 C5
Northaw Herts 41 D5
Northbeck Lincs 78 E3
Northborough P'boro 65 D8
Northbourne Kent 31 D7
Northbridge Street E Sus 18 C4
Northchapel W Sus 16 B3
Northchurch Herts 40 D2
Northcott Devon 8 E5
Northdown Kent 31 B7
Northdyke Orkney 176 D1
Northend Bath 24 C2
Northend Bucks 39 E7
Northend Warks 51 D8
Northenden Gtr Man 87 E6
Northfield Aberdeen 151 D8
Northfield Borders 124 C5
Northfield E Yorks 90 B4
Northfield W Mid 50 B5
Northfields Lincs 65 D7
Northfleet Kent 29 B7
Northgate Lincs 65 B8
Northhouse Borders 115 D7
Northiam E Sus 18 C5
Northill Beds 54 E2
Northington Hants 26 F3
Northlands Lincs 79 D6
Northlea Durham 111 D7
Northleach Glos 37 C8
Northleigh Devon 11 E6
Northlew Devon 9 E7
Northmoor Oxon 38 D4
Northmoor Green or Moorland Som 22 F5
Northmuir Angus 142 D3
Northney Hants 15 D8
Northolt London 40 F4
Northop Flint 73 C6
Northop Hall Flint 73 C6
Northorpe Lincs 65 C7
Northorpe Lincs 78 F5
Northorpe Lincs 90 E2
Northover Som 23 F6
Northover Som 12 B3
Northowram W Yorks 88 B2
Northport Dorset 13 F7
Northpunds Shetland 175 L6
Northrepps Norf 81 D8
Northtown Orkney 176 G3
Northumbria Craft Centre, Morpeth Northumb 117 F7
Northway Glos 50 F4
Northwich Ches 74 B3
Northwick S Glos 36 F2
Northwold Norf 67 E7
Northwood Derbys 76 C2
Northwood London 40 E3
Northwood I o W 15 E5
Northwood Kent 31 C7
Northwood Shrops 73 F8
Northwood Green Glos 36 C4
Norton E Sus 17 D8
Norton Glos 37 B5
Norton Halton 86 F3
Norton Herts 54 F3
Norton I o W 14 F4
Norton Mon 35 C8
Norton Notts 77 B5
Norton Northants 52 C4
Norton Powys 48 C5
Norton Shrops 60 F4
Norton Shrops 61 D5
Norton Shrops 61 D7
Norton Stockton 102 B2
Norton Suff 56 C3
Norton S Yorks 89 C6
Norton Wilts 37 F5
Norton Worcs 50 D3
Norton Worcs 50 E5
Norton W Sus 16 E2
Norton W Sus 16 D3
Norton Bavant Wilts 24 E4
Norton Bridge Staffs 75 F5
Norton Canes Staffs 62 D4
Norton Canon Hereford 49 E5
Norton Corner Norf 81 E6
Norton Disney Lincs 77 D8
Norton East Staffs 62 D4
Norton Ferris Wilts 24 F2
Norton Fitzwarren Som 11 B6
Norton Green I o W 14 F4
Norton Hawkfield Bath 23 C7
Norton Heath Essex 42 D2
Norton in Hales Shrops 74 F4
Norton-in-the-Moors Stoke 75 D5
Norton-Juxta-Twycross Leics 63 D7
Norton-le-Clay N Yorks 95 B7
Norton Lindsey Warks 51 C7
Norton Malreward Bath 23 C8
Norton Mandeville Essex 42 D1
Norton-on-Derwent N Yorks 96 B3
Norton St Philip Som 24 D2
Norton sub Hamdon Som 12 C2
Norton Woodseats S Yorks 88 F4
Norwell Notts 77 C7
Norwell Woodhouse Notts 77 C7
Norwich Norf 68 D5
Norwich Castle Museum Norf 68 D5
Norwich Cathedral Norf 68 D5
Norwich International Airport Norf 68 C5
Norwick Shetland 174 B8
Norwood Derbys 89 F5
Norwood Hill Sur 28 E3
Norwoodside Cambs 66 E4
Noseley Leics 64 E4
Noss Shetland 175 M5
Noss Mayo Devon 6 E3
Nosterfield N Yorks 101 F7
Nostie Highld 155 H4
Notgrove Glos 37 B8
Nothe Fort, Weymouth Dorset 12 G4
Nottage Bridgend 21 B7
Nottingham Nottingham 77 F5
Nottingham Castle Museum Nottingham 77 E5
Nottingham East Midlands Airport Leics 63 B8
Nottingham Racecourse Nottingham 77 F6
Nottington Dorset 12 F4
Notton Wilts 24 C4
Notton W Yorks 88 C4
Nounsley Essex 42 C3
Noutard's Green Worcs 50 C2
Novar House Highld 157 C7
Nox Shrops 60 C4
Nuffield Oxon 39 F6
Nun Hills Lancs 87 B6
Nun Monkton N Yorks 95 D8
Nunburnholme E Yorks 96 E4
Nuncargate Notts 76 D5
Nuneaton Warks 63 E7
Nuneham Courtenay Oxon 39 E5
Nunney Som 24 E2
Nunnington N Yorks 96 B2
Nunnykirk Northumb 117 E6
Nunsthorpe NE Lincs 91 D6
Nunthorpe M'bro 102 C3
Nunthorpe York 96 D2
Nunton Wilts 14 B2
Nunwick N Yorks 95 B6
Nupend Glos 36 D4
Nursling Hants 14 C4
Nursted Hants 15 B8
Nutbourne W Sus 16 C4
Nutbourne W Sus 15 D8
Nutfield Sur 28 D4
Nuthall Notts 76 E5
Nuthampstead Herts 54 F5
Nuthurst W Sus 17 B5
Nutley E Sus 17 B8
Nutley Hants 26 E4
Nutwell S Yorks 89 D7
Nybster Highld 169 C8
Nyetimber W Sus 16 E2
Nyewood W Sus 16 B2
Nymans Garden, Crawley W Sus 17 B6
Nymet Rowland Devon 10 D2
Nymet Tracey Devon 10 D2
Nympsfield Glos 37 D5
Nynehead Som 11 B6
Nyton W Sus 16 D3

O

Oad Street Kent 30 C2
Oadby Leics 64 D3
Oak Cross Devon 9 E7
Oakamoor Staffs 75 E7
Oakbank W Loth 122 C3
Oakdale Caerph 35 E5
Oake Som 11 B6
Oaken Staffs 62 D2
Oakenclough Lancs 92 E5
Oakengates Telford 61 C7
Oakenholt Flint 73 B6
Oakenshaw Durham 110 F5
Oakenshaw W Yorks 88 B2
Oakerthorpe Derbys 76 D3
Oakes W Yorks 88 C2
Oakfield Torf 35 E7
Oakford Ceredig 46 D3
Oakford Devon 10 B4
Oakfordbridge Devon 10 B4
Oakgrove Ches 75 C6
Oakham Rutland 65 D5
Oakhanger Hants 27 F5
Oakhill Som 23 E8
Oakhurst Kent 29 D6
Oakington Cambs 54 C5
Oaklands Herts 41 C5
Oaklands Powys 48 D2
Oakle Street Glos 36 C4
Oakley Beds 53 D8
Oakley Bucks 39 C6
Oakley Fife 134 F2
Oakley Hants 26 D3
Oakley Oxon 39 D7
Oakley Poole 13 E8
Oakley Suff 57 B5
Oakley Green Windsor 27 B7
Oakley Park Powys 59 F6
Oakmere Ches 74 C2
Oakridge Glos 37 D6
Oakridge Hants 26 D4
Oaks Shrops 60 D4
Oaks Green Derbys 75 F8
Oaksey Wilts 37 E6
Oakthorpe Leics 63 C7
Oakwood Adventure Park, Narberth Pembs 32 C1
Oakwoodhill Sur 28 F2
Oakworth W Yorks 94 F3
Oape Highld 163 D8
Oare Kent 30 C4
Oare Som 21 E7
Oare W Berks 26 B3
Oare Wilts 25 C6
Oasby Lincs 78 F3
Oathlaw Angus 142 D4
Oatlands N Yorks 95 D6
Oban Argyll 130 C4
Oban Highld 145 E8
Oborne Dorset 12 C4
Obthorpe Lincs 65 C7
Occlestone Green Ches 74 C3
Occold Suff 57 B5
Ocean Beach Amusement Park, Rhyl Denb 72 A3
Ochiltree E Ayrs 112 B5
Ochtermuthill Perth 133 C7
Ochtertyre Perth 133 B7
Ockbrook Derbys 76 F4
Ockham Sur 27 D8
Ockle Highld 137 A6
Ockley Sur 28 F2
Ocle Pychard Hereford 49 E7
Octon E Yorks 97 C6
Octon Cross Roads E Yorks 97 C6
Odcombe Som 12 C3
Odd Down Bath 24 C2
Oddendale Cumb 99 C7
Odder Lincs 78 B2
Oddingley Worcs 50 D4
Oddington Glos 38 B2
Oddington Oxon 39 C5
Odell Beds 53 D7
Odie Orkney 176 D5
Odiham Hants 26 D5
Odstock Wilts 14 B2
Odstone Leics 63 D7
Offchurch Warks 51 C8
Offenham Worcs 51 E5
Offham E Sus 17 C7
Offham Kent 29 D7
Offham W Sus 16 D4
Offord Cluny Cambs 54 C3
Offord Darcy Cambs 54 C3
Offton Suff 56 E4
Offwell Devon 11 E6
Ogbourne Maizey Wilts 25 B6
Ogbourne St Andrew Wilts 25 B6
Ogbourne St George Wilts 25 B7
Ogil Angus 142 C4
Ogle Northumb 110 B4
Ogmore V Glam 21 B7
Ogmore-by-Sea V Glam 21 B7
Ogmore Vale Bridgend 34 E3
Okeford Fitzpaine Dorset 13 C6
Okehampton Devon 9 E7
Okehampton Camp Devon 9 E7
Okraquoy Shetland 175 K6
Old Northants 53 B5
Old Aberdeen Aberdeen 151 D8
Old Alresford Hants 26 F3
Old Arley Warks 63 E6
Old Basford Nottingham 76 E5
Old Basing Hants 26 D4
Old Bewick Northumb 117 B6
Old Blacksmith's Shop Centre, Gretna Green Dumfries 108 C3
Old Bolingbroke Lincs 79 C6
Old Bramhope W Yorks 94 E5
Old Brampton Derbys 76 B3
Old Bridge of Tilt Perth 141 C5
Old Bridge of Urr Dumfries 106 C4
Old Buckenham Norf 68 E3
Old Burghclere Hants 26 D2
Old Byland N Yorks 102 F3
Old Cassop Durham 111 F6
Old Castleton Borders 115 E8
Old Catton Norf 68 C5
Old Clee NE Lincs 91 D6
Old Cleeve Som 22 E2
Old Clipstone Notts 77 C6
Old Colwyn Conwy 83 D8
Old Coulsdon London 28 D4
Old Crombie Aberds 160 C2
Old Dailly S Ayrs 112 E2
Old Dalby Leics 64 B3
Old Deer Aberds 161 D6
Old Denaby S Yorks 89 E5
Old Edlington S Yorks 89 E6
Old Eldon Durham 101 B7
Old Ellerby E Yorks 97 F7
Old Felixstowe Suff 57 F7
Old Fletton P'boro 65 E8
Old Glossop Derbys 87 E8
Old Goole E Yorks 89 B8
Old Hall Powys 59 F6
Old Heath Essex 43 B6
Old Heathfield E Sus 18 C2
Old Hill W Mid 62 F3
Old House, Rochford Essex 42 E4
Old Hunstanton Norf 80 C2
Old Hurst Cambs 54 B3
Old Hutton Cumb 99 F7
Old Kea Corn 3 B7
Old Kilpatrick W Dunb 120 B4
Old Kinnernie Aberds 151 D6
Old Knebworth Herts 41 B5
Old Langho Lancs 93 F7
Old Laxey I o M 84 D4
Old Leake Lincs 79 D7
Old Malton N Yorks 96 B3
Old Micklefield W Yorks 95 F7
Old Milton Hants 14 E3
Old Milverton Warks 51 C7
Old Monkland N Lnrk 121 C7
Old Netley Hants 15 D5
Old Philpstoun W Loth 122 B3
Old Quarrington Durham 111 F6
Old Radnor Powys 48 D4
Old Rattray Aberds 161 C7
Old Rayne Aberds 151 B5
Old Romney Kent 19 C7
Old Sarum, Salisbury Wilts 25 F6
Old Sodbury S Glos 36 F4
Old Somerby Lincs 78 F2
Old Stratford Northants 53 E5
Old Thirsk N Yorks 102 F2
Old Town Cumb 108 E4
Old Town Cumb 99 F7
Old Town Northumb 116 E4
Old Town Scilly 2 E4
Old Trafford Gtr Man 87 E6
Old Tupton Derbys 76 C3
Old Warden Beds 54 E2
Old Weston Cambs 53 B8
Old Whittington Derbys 76 B3
Old Wick Highld 169 D8
Old Windsor Windsor 27 B7
Old Wives Lees Kent 30 D4
Old Woking Sur 27 D8
Old Woodhall Lincs 78 C5
Oldany Highld 166 F3
Oldberrow Warks 51 C6
Oldborough Devon 10 D2
Oldbury Shrops 61 E7
Oldbury Warks 63 E7
Oldbury W Mid 62 F3
Oldbury-on-Severn S Glos 36 E3
Oldbury on the Hill Glos 37 F5
Oldcastle Bridgend 21 B8
Oldcastle Mon 35 B7
Oldcotes Notts 89 F6
Oldfallow Staffs 62 C3
Oldfield Worcs 50 C3
Oldford Som 24 D2
Oldham Gtr Man 87 D7
Oldhamstocks E Loth 124 B3
Oldland S Glos 23 B8
Oldmeldrum Aberds 151 B7
Oldshore Beg Highld 166 D3
Oldshoremore Highld 166 D4
Oldstead N Yorks 102 F3
Oldtown Aberds 150 B4
Oldtown of Ord Aberds 160 C3
Oldway Swansea 33 F6
Oldways End Devon 10 B3
Oldwhat Aberds 161 C5
Olgrinmore Highld 169 D5
Oliver's Battery Hants 15 B5
Ollaberry Shetland 174 E5
Ollerton Ches 74 B4
Ollerton Notts 77 C6
Ollerton Shrops 61 B6
Olmarch Ceredig 46 D5
Olney M Keynes 53 D6
Olrig Ho. Highld 169 C6
Olton W Mid 62 F5
Olveston S Glos 36 F3
Olwen Ceredig 46 E4
Ombersley Worcs 50 C3
Ompton Notts 77 C6
Onchan I o M 84 E3
Onecote Staffs 75 D7
Onen Mon 35 C8
Ongar Hill Norf 67 B5
Ongar Street Hereford 49 C5
Onibury Shrops 49 B6
Onich Highld 138 C4
Onllwyn Neath 34 C2
Onneley Staffs 74 E4
Onslow Village Sur 27 E7
Onthank E Ayrs 120 E4
Openwoodgate Derbys 76 E3
Opinan Highld 162 E2
Opinan Highld 154 C3
Orange Lane Borders 124 E3
Orange Row Norf 66 B5
Orasaigh W Isles 173 G6
Orbliston Moray 159 D7
Orbost Highld 153 E3
Orby Lincs 79 C7
Orchard Hill Devon 9 B6
Orchard Portman Som 11 B7
Orcheston Wilts 25 E5
Orcop Hereford 36 B1
Orcop Hill Hereford 36 B1
Ord Highld 145 B6
Ordhead Aberds 151 C5
Ordie Aberds 150 D3
Ordiequish Moray 159 D7
Ordsall Notts 89 F7
Ore E Sus 18 D5
Oreton Shrops 61 F6
Orford Suff 57 E8
Orford Warr 86 E4
Orgreave Staffs 63 C5
Orlestone Kent 19 B6
Orleton Hereford 49 C6
Orleton Worcs 49 C8
Orlingbury Northants 53 B6
Ormesby Redcar 102 C3
Ormesby St Margaret Norf 69 C7
Ormesby St Michael Norf 69 C7
Ormiclate Castle W Isles 171 G3
Ormiscaig Highld 162 E2
Ormiston E Loth 123 C7
Ormsaigbeg Highld 137 B5
Ormsaigmore Highld 137 B5
Ormsary Argyll 128 C2
Ormsgill Cumb 92 B1
Ormskirk Lancs 86 D2
Orpington London 29 C5
Orrell Gtr Man 86 D3
Orrell Mers 85 E4
Orrisdale I o M 84 C3
Orroland Dumfries 106 E4
Orsett Thurrock 42 F2
Orslow Staffs 62 C2
Orston Notts 77 E7
Orthwaite Cumb 108 F2
Ortner Lancs 92 D5
Orton Cumb 99 D8
Orton Northants 53 B6
Orton Longueville P'boro 65 E8
Orton-on-the-Hill Leics 63 D7
Orton Waterville P'boro 65 E8
Orwell Cambs 54 D4
Osbaldeston Lancs 93 F6
Osbaldwick York 96 D2
Osbaston Shrops 60 B3
Osborne House I o W 15 E6
Osbournby Lincs 78 F3
Oscroft Ches 74 C2
Ose Highld 153 E4
Osgathorpe Leics 63 C8
Osgodby Lincs 90 E4
Osgodby N Yorks 96 F2
Osgodby N Yorks 103 F8
Oskaig Highld 153 F6
Oskamull Argyll 137 D5
Osmaston Derbys 76 E2
Osmaston Derby 76 F3
Osmington Dorset 12 F5
Osmington Mills Dorset 12 F5
Osmotherley N Yorks 102 E2
Ospisdale Highld 164 F4
Ospringe Kent 30 C4
Ossett W Yorks 88 B3
Ossington Notts 77 C7
Ostend Essex 43 E5
Oswaldkirk N Yorks 96 B2
Oswaldtwistle Lancs 86 B5
Oswestry Shrops 60 B2
Otford Kent 29 D6
Otham Kent 29 D8
Othery Som 23 F5
Otley Suff 57 D6
Otley W Yorks 94 E5
Otter Ferry Argyll 128 B4
Otterbourne Hants 15 B5
Otterburn Northumb 116 E4
Otterburn N Yorks 93 D8
Otterburn Camp Northumb 116 E4
Otterham Corn 8 E3
Otterhampton Som 22 E4
Ottershaw Sur 27 C8
Otterswick Shetland 174 E7
Otterton Devon 11 F5
Ottery St Mary Devon 11 E6
Ottinge Kent 31 E5
Ottringham E Yorks 91 B6
Oughterby Cumb 108 D2
Oughtershaw N Yorks 100 F3
Oughterside Cumb 107 E8
Oughtibridge S Yorks 88 E4
Oughtrington Warr 86 F4
Oulston N Yorks 95 B8
Oulton Cumb 108 D2
Oulton Norf 81 E7
Oulton Staffs 75 F6
Oulton Suff 69 E8
Oulton W Yorks 88 B4
Oulton Broad Suff 69 E8
Oulton Park Motor Racing Circuit Ches 74 C2
Oulton Street Norf 81 E7
Oundle Northants 65 F7
Ousby Cumb 109 F6
Ousdale Highld 165 B7
Ousden Suff 55 D8
Ousefleet E Yorks 90 B2
Ouston Durham 111 D5
Ouston Northumb 110 B3
Out Newton E Yorks 91 B7
Out Rawcliffe Lancs 92 E4
Outertown Orkney 176 E1
Outgate Cumb 99 E5
Outhgill Cumb 100 D2
Outlane W Yorks 87 C8
Outwell Norf 66 D5
Outwick Hants 14 C2
Outwood Sur 28 E4
Outwood W Yorks 88 B4
Outwoods Staffs 61 C7
Ovenden W Yorks 87 B8
Ovenscloss Borders 123 F7
Over Cambs 54 B4
Over Ches 74 C3
Over S Glos 36 F2
Over Compton Dorset 12 C3
Over Green W Mid 63 E5
Over Haddon Derbys 76 C2
Over Hulton Gtr Man 86 D4
Over Kellet Lancs 92 B5
Over Kiddington Oxon 38 B4
Over Knutsford Ches 74 B4
Over Monnow Mon 36 C2
Over Norton Oxon 38 B3
Over Peover Ches 74 B4
Over Silton N Yorks 102 E2
Over Stowey Som 22 F3
Over Stratton Som 12 C2
Over Tabley Ches 86 F5
Over Wallop Hants 25 F7
Over Whitacre Warks 63 E6
Over Worton Oxon 38 B4
Overbister Orkney 176 B5
Overbury Worcs 50 F4
Overcombe Dorset 12 F4
Overgreen Derbys 76 B3
Overleigh Som 23 F6
Overley Green Warks 51 D5
Overpool Ches 73 B7
Overscaig Hotel Highld 163 B8
Overseal Derbys 63 C6
Oversland Kent 30 D4
Overstone Northants 53 C6
Overstrand Norf 81 C8
Overthorpe Northants 52 E2
Overton Aberdeen 151 C7
Overton Ches 74 B2
Overton Dumfries 107 C6
Overton Hants 26 E3
Overton Lancs 92 D4
Overton N Yorks 95 D8
Overton Shrops 49 B7
Overton Swansea 33 F5
Overton W Yorks 88 C3
Overton = Owrtyn Wrex 73 E7
Overton Bridge Wrex 73 E7
Overtown N Lnrk 121 D8
Oving Bucks 39 B7
Oving W Sus 16 D3
Ovingdean Brighton 17 D7
Ovingham Northumb 110 C3
Ovington Durham 101 C6
Ovington Essex 55 E8
Ovington Hants 26 F3
Ovington Norf 68 D2
Ovington Northumb 110 C3
Ower Hants 14 C4
Owermoigne Dorset 13 F5
Owlbury Shrops 60 E3
Owler Bar Derbys 76 B2
Owlerton S Yorks 88 F4
Owl's Green Suff 57 C6
Owlswick Bucks 39 D7
Owmby Lincs 90 D4
Owmby-by-Spital Lincs 90 F4
Owrtyn = Overton Wrex 73 E7
Owslebury Hants 15 B6
Owston Leics 64 D4
Owston S Yorks 89 C6
Owston Ferry N Lincs 90 D2
Owstwick E Yorks 97 F8
Owthorne E Yorks 91 B7
Owthorpe Notts 77 F6
Oxborough Norf 67 D7
Oxburgh Hall Norf 67 D7
Oxcombe Lincs 79 B6
Oxen Park Cumb 99 F5
Oxenholme Cumb 99 F7
Oxenhope W Yorks 94 F3
Oxenton Glos 50 F4
Oxenwood Wilts 25 D8
Oxford Oxon 39 D5
Oxford University Botanic Garden Oxon 39 D5
Oxhey Herts 40 E4
Oxhill Warks 51 E8
Oxley W Mid 62 D3
Oxley Green Essex 43 C5
Oxley's Green E Sus 18 C3
Oxnam Borders 116 C2
Oxshott Sur 28 C2
Oxspring S Yorks 88 D3
Oxted Sur 28 D4
Oxton Borders 123 D7
Oxton Notts 77 D6
Oxwich Swansea 33 F5
Oxwick Norf 80 E5
Oykel Bridge Highld 163 D7
Oyne Aberds 151 B5

P

Pabail Iarach W Isles 172 E8
Pabail Uarach W Isles 172 E8
Pace Gate N Yorks 94 D
Packington Leics 63
Padanaram Angus 142
Padbury Bucks 52 F
Paddington London 41 F
Paddlesworth Kent 19 B
Paddock Wood Kent 29 E
Paddockhaugh Moray 159 D6
Paddockhole Dumfries 115 F5
Padfield Derbys 87 E8
Padiham Lancs 93 F7
Padog Conwy 83 F8
Padside N Yorks 94 D4
Padstow Corn 4 B4
Padworth W Berks 26 C4
Page Bank Durham 110 F5
Pagelsham Eastend Essex 43 E5
Pagham W Sus 16 E2
Paglesham Churchend Essex 43 E5
Paibeil W Isles 170 D3
Paible W Isles 173 J3
Paignton Torbay 7 C6
Paignton & Dartmouth Steam Railway Devon 7 C6
Paignton Zoo Devon 7 D6
Pailton Warks 63 F8
Painscastle Powys 48 E3
Painshawfield Northumb 110 C3
Painsthorpe E Yorks 96 D4
Painswick Glos 37 D5
Pairc Shiaboist W Isles 172 D5
Paisley Renfs 120 C4
Pakefield Suff 69 E8
Pakenham Suff 56 C3
Palace House, Beaulieu Hants 14 D4
Palace of Holyroodhouse Edin 123 B5
Pale Gwyn 72 F3
Palestine Hants 25 E7
Paley Street Windsor 27 B6
Palfrey W Mid 62 E4

Palgowan Dumfries 112 F3
Palgrave Suff 56 B5
Pallion T & W 111 D6
Palmarsh Kent 19 B8
Palnackie Dumfries 106 D5
Palnure Dumfries 105 C8
Palterton Derbys 76 C4
Pamber End Hants 26 D4
Pamber Green Hants 26 D4
Pamber Heath Hants 26 C4
Pamphill Dorset 13 D7
Pampisford Cambs 55 E5
Pan Orkney 176 G2
Panbride Angus 143 F5
Pancrasweek Devon 8 D4
Pandy Gwyn 58 D3
Pandy Mon 35 B7
Pandy Powys 59 D6
Pandy Wrex 73 F5
Pandy Tudur Conwy 83 E8
Panfield Essex 42 B3
Pangbourne W Berks 26 B4
Pannal N Yorks 95 D6
Panshanger Herts 41 C5
Pant Shrops 60 B2
Pant-glas Carms 33 B6
Pant-glas Gwyn 71 C5
Pant-glâs Powys 58 E4
Pant-glas Shrops 73 F6
Pant gwyn Carms 33 B6
Pant Mawr Powys 59 F5
Pant-teg Carms 33 B5
Pant-y-Caws Carms 32 B2
Pant-y-dwr Powys 47 B8
Pant-y-ffridd Powys 59 D8
Pant-y-Wacco Flint 72 B5
Pant-yr-awel Bridgend 34 F3
Pantgwyn Ceredig 45 E4
Pantlasau Swansea 33 E7
Panton Lincs 78 B4
Pantperthog Gwyn 58 D4
Pantyffynnon Carms 33 C7
Pantymwyn Flint 73 C5
Panxworth Norf 69 C6
Papa Westray Airport Orkney 176 A3
Papcastle Cumb 107 F8
Papigoe Highld 169 D8
Papil Shetland 175 K5
Papley Orkney 176 G3
Papple E Loth 123 B8
Papplewick Notts 76 D5
Papworth Everard Cambs 54 C3
Papworth St Agnes Cambs 54 C3
Par Corn 5 D5
Paradise Wildlife Park, Broxbourne Herts 41 D6
Parbold Lancs 86 C2
Parbrook Som 23 F7
Parbrook W Sus 16 B4
Parc Gwyn 72 F2
Parc-Seymour Newport 35 E8
Parc-y-rhôs Carms 46 E4
Parcllyn Ceredig 45 D4
Pardshaw Cumb 98 B2
Parham Suff 57 C7
Park Dumfries 114 E2
Park Corner Oxon 39 F6
Park Corner Windsor 40 F1
Park End M'bro 102 C3
Park End Northumb 109 B8
Park Gate Hants 15 D6
Park Hill Notts 77 D6
Park Hill N Yorks 95 C6
Park Rose Pottery and Leisure Park, Bridlington E Yorks 97 C7
Park Street W Sus 28 F2
Parkend Glos 36 D3
Parkeston Essex 57 F6
Parkgate Ches 73 B6
Parkgate Dumfries 114 F3
Parkgate Kent 19 B5
Parkgate Sur 28 E3
Parkham Devon 9 B5
Parkham Ash Devon 9 B5
Parkhill Ho. Aberds 151 C7
Parkhouse Mon 36 D1
Parkhouse Green Derbys 76 C4
Parkhurst I o W 15 E5
Parkmill Swansea 33 F6
Parkneuk Aberds 143 B7
Parkstone Poole 13 E8
Parley Cross Dorset 13 E8
Parracombe Devon 21 E5
Parrog Pembs 45 F2
Parsley Hay Derbys 75 C8
Parson Cross S Yorks 88 E4
Parson Drove Cambs 66 D3
Parsonage Green Essex 42 D3
Parsonby Cumb 107 F8
Parson's Heath Essex 43 B6
Partick Glasgow 121 C5
Partington Gtr Man 86 E5
Partney Lincs 79 C7
Parton Cumb 98 B1
Parton Dumfries 106 B3
Parton Glos 37 B5
Partridge Green W Sus 17 C5
Parwich Derbys 75 D8
Passenham Northants 53 F5
Paston Norf 81 D9
Patchacott Devon 9 E6
Patcham Brighton 17 D7
Patching W Sus 16 D4
Patchole Devon 20 E5
Patchway S Glos 36 F3
Pateley Bridge N Yorks 94 C4
Paternoster Heath Essex 43 C5
Path of Condie Perth 134 C2
Pathe Som 23 F5
Pathhead Aberds 143 C7
Pathhead E Ayrs 113 C6
Pathhead Fife 134 E4
Pathhead Midloth 123 C6
Pathstruie Perth 134 C2
Patmore Heath Herts 41 B7
Patna E Ayrs 112 C4
Patney Wilts 25 D5
Patrick I o M 84 D2
Patrick Brompton N Yorks 101 E7
Patrington E Yorks 91 B7
Patrixbourne Kent 31 D5
Patterdale Cumb 99 C5
Pattingham Staffs 62 E2
Pattishall Northants 52 D4
Pattiswick Green Essex 42 B4
Patton Bridge Cumb 99 E7
Paul Corn 2 D3
Paulerspury Northants 52 E5
Paull E Yorks 91 B5
Paulton Bath 23 D8
Paultons Park, Totton Hants 14 C4
Pavenham Beds 53 D7
Pawlett Som 22 E5
Pawston Northumb 124 F4
Paxford Glos 51 F6
Paxton Borders 124 D5
Payhembury Devon 11 D5
Paythorne Lancs 93 D8
Peacehaven E Sus 17 D8
Peak Dale Derbys 75 B7
Peak Forest Derbys 75 B8
Peakirk P'boro 65 D8
Pearsie Angus 142 D3
Pease Pottage W Sus 28 F3
Peasedown St John Bath 24 D2
Peasemore W Berks 26 B2
Peasenhall Suff 57 C7
Peaslake Sur 27 E8
Peasley Cross Mers 86 E3
Peasmarsh E Sus 19 C5
Peaston E Loth 123 C7
Peastonbank E Loth 123 C7
Peat Inn Fife 135 D6
Peathill Aberds 161 B6
Peatling Magna Leics 64 E2
Peatling Parva Leics 64 F2
Peaton Shrops 60 F5
Peats Corner Suff 57 C5
Pebmarsh Essex 56 F2
Pebworth Worcs 51 E6
Pecket Well W Yorks 87 B7
Peckforton Ches 74 D2
Peckham London 28 B4
Peckleton Leics 63 D8
Pedlinge Kent 19 B8
Pedmore W Mid 62 F3
Pedwell Som 23 F6
Peebles Borders 123 E5
Peel I o M 84 D2
Peel Common Hants 15 D6
Peel Park S Lnrk 121 D6
Peening Quarter Kent 19 C5
Pegsdon Beds 54 F2
Pegswood Northumb 117 F8
Pegwell Kent 31 C7
Peinchorran Highld 153 F6
Peinlich Highld 152 D5
Pelaw T & W 111 C5
Pelcomb Bridge Pembs 44 D4
Pelcomb Cross Pembs 44 D4
Peldon Essex 43 C5
Pellon W Yorks 87 B8
Pelsall W Mid 62 D4
Pelton Durham 111 D5
Pelutho Cumb 107 E8
Pelynt Corn 5 D7
Pemberton Gtr Man 86 D3
Pembrey Carms 33 D5
Pembrey Motor Racing Circuit Carms 33 D5
Pembridge Hereford 49 D5
Pembroke = Penfro Pembs 44 E4
Pembroke Castle Pembs 44 E4
Pembroke Dock = Doc Penfro Pembs 44 E4
Pembury Kent 29 E7
Pen-bont Rhydybeddau Ceredig 58 F3
Pen-clawdd Swansea 33 E6
Pen-ffordd Pembs 32 B1
Pen-groes-oped Mon 35 D7
Pen-llyn Anglesey 82 C3
Pen-lon Anglesey 82 E4
Pen-sarn Gwyn 70 C5
Pen-sarn Gwyn 71 E6
Pen-twyn Mon 36 D2
Pen-y-banc Carms 33 B7
Pen-y-bont Carms 32 B4
Pen-y-bont Gwyn 58 D4
Pen-y-bont Gwyn 71 E7
Pen-y-bont Powys 60 B2
Pen-y-bont ar Ogwr = Bridgend Bridgend 21 B8
Pen-y-bryn Gwyn 58 C3
Pen-y-bryn Pembs 45 E3
Pen-y-cae Powys 34 C2
Pen-y-cae-mawr Mon 35 E8
Pen-y-cefn Flint 72 B5
Pen-y-clawdd Mon 36 D1
Pen-y-coedcae Rhondda 34 F4
Pen-y-fai Bridgend 34 F2
Pen-y-garn Ceredig 58 F3
Pen-y-garn Carms 46 F4
Pen-y-garnedd Anglesey 82 D5
Pen-y-gop Conwy 72 E3
Pen-y-graig Gwyn 70 D2
Pen-y-groes Carms 33 C6
Pen-y-groeslon Gwyn 70 D3
Pen-y-Gwryd Hotel Gwyn 83 F6
Pen-y-stryt Denb 73 D5
Pen-yr-heol Mon 35 C8
Pen-yr-Heolgerrig M Tydf 34 D4
Penallt Mon 36 C2
Penally Pembs 32 E2
Penalt Hereford 36 B2
Penare Corn 3 B8
Penarlâg = Hawarden Flint 73 C7
Penarth V Glam 22 B3
Penbryn Ceredig 45 D4
Pencader Carms 46 F3
Pencaenewydd Gwyn 70 C5
Pencaitland E Loth 123 C7
Pencarnisiog Anglesey 82 D3
Pencarreg Carms 46 E4
Pencelli Powys 34 B4
Pencoed Bridgend 34 F3
Pencombe Hereford 49 D7
Pencoyd Hereford 36 B2
Pencraig Hereford 36 B2
Pencraig Powys 59 B7
Pendeen Corn 2 C2
Pendennis Castle Corn 4 F3
Penderyn Rhondda 34 D3
Pendine Carms 32 D3
Pendlebury Gtr Man 87 D5
Pendleton Lancs 93 F7
Pendock Worcs 50 F2
Pendoggett Corn 4 B5
Pendomer Som 12 C3
Pendoylan V Glam 22 B2
Pendre Bridgend 34 F3
Penegoes Powys 58 D4
Penfro = Pembroke Pembs 44 E4
Pengam Caerph 35 E5
Penge London 28 B4
Pengenffordd Powys 48 F3
Pengorffwysfa Anglesey 82 B4
Pengover Green Corn 5 C7
Penhale Corn 3 E5
Penhale Corn 4 D4
Penhalvaen Corn 3 C6
Penhill Thamesdown 38 F1
Penhow Newport 35 E8
Penhurst E Sus 18 D3
Peniarth Gwyn 58 D3
Penicuik Midloth 122 C5
Peniel Carms 33 B5
Peniel Denb 72 C4
Penifiler Highld 153 E5
Peninver Argyll 118 D4
Penisarwaun Gwyn 83 E5
Penistone S Yorks 88 D3
Penjerrick Corn 3 C6
Penketh Warr 86 F3
Penkill S Ayrs 112 E2
Penkridge Staffs 62 C3
Penley Wrex 73 F8
Penllergaer Swansea 33 E7
Penllyn V Glam 21 B8
Penmachno Conwy 83 F7
Penmaen Swansea 33 F6
Penmaenan Conwy 83 D7
Penmaenmawr Conwy 83 D7
Penmaenpool Gwyn 58 C3
Penmark V Glam 22 C2
Penmarth Corn 3 C6
Penmon Anglesey 83 C6
Penmore Mill Argyll 137 C5
Penmorfa Ceredig 46 D2
Penmorfa Gwyn 71 C6
Penmynydd Anglesey 82 D5
Penn Bucks 40 E2
Penn W Mid 62 E2
Penn Street Bucks 40 E2
Pennal Gwyn 58 D4
Pennan Aberds 160 B5
Pennant Ceredig 46 C4
Pennant Denb 72 F4
Pennant Denb 72 D4
Pennant Powys 59 E5
Pennant Melangell Powys 59 B7
Pennar Pembs 44 E4
Pennard Swansea 33 F6
Pennerley Shrops 60 E3
Pennington Cumb 92 B2
Pennington Gtr Man 86 E4
Pennington Hants 14 E4
Penny Bridge Cumb 99 F5
Pennycross Argyll 137 F6
Pennygate Norf 69 B6
Pennygown Argyll 137 D6
Pennymoor Devon 10 C3
Pennywell T & W 111 D6
Penparc Ceredig 45 E4
Penparc Pembs 44 B3
Penparcau Ceredig 58 F2
Penperlleni Mon 35 D7
Penpillick Corn 5 D5
Penpol Corn 3 C7
Penpoll Corn 5 D6
Penpont Dumfries 113 E8
Penpont Powys 34 B3
Penrherber Carms 45 F4
Penrhiw goch Carms 33 C6
Penrhiw-llan Ceredig 46 E2
Penrhiw-pâl Ceredig 46 E2
Penrhiwceiber Rhondda 34 E4
Penrhos Gwyn 70 D4
Penrhôs Mon 35 C8
Penrhos Powys 34 C1
Penrhosfeilw Anglesey 82 C2
Penrhyn Bay Conwy 83 C8
Penrhyn Castle Gwyn 83 D6
Penrhyn-coch Ceredig 58 F3
Penrhyndeudraeth Gwyn 71 D7
Penrhynside Conwy 83 C8
Penrice Swansea 33 F5
Penrith Cumb 108 F5
Penrose Corn 4 B3
Penruddock Cumb 99 B6
Penryn Corn 3 C6
Pensarn Carms 33 C5
Pensarn Conwy 72 B3
Pensax Worcs 50 C2
Pensby Mers 85 F3
Penselwood Som 24 F2
Pensford Bath 23 C8
Penshaw T & W 111 D6
Penshurst Kent 29 E6
Pensilva Corn 5 C7
Penston E Loth 123 B7
Pentewan Corn 3 B9
Pentir Gwyn 83 E5
Pentire Corn 4 C2
Pentlow Essex 56 E2
Pentney Norf 67 C7
Penton Mewsey Hants 25 E8
Pentraeth Anglesey 82 D5
Pentre Carms 33 C6
Pentre Powys 59 F7
Pentre Powys 60 E2
Pentre Rhondda 34 E3
Pentre Shrops 60 C3
Pentre Wrex 73 E6
Pentre Wrex 72 F5
Pentre-bâch Ceredig 46 E4
Pentre-bach Powys 47 F8
Pentre Berw Anglesey 82 D4
Pentre-bont Conwy 83 F7
Pentre-celyn Denb 72 D5
Pentre-Celyn Powys 59 D5
Pentre-chwyth Swansea 33 E7
Pentre-cwrt Carms 46 F2
Pentre Dolau-Honddu Powys 47 E8
Pentre-dwr Swansea 33 E7
Pentre-galar Pembs 45 F3
Pentre-Gwenlais Carms 33 C7
Pentre Gwynfryn Gwyn 71 E6
Pentre Halkyn Flint 73 B6
Pentre-Isaf Conwy 83 E8
Pentre Llanrhaeadr Denb 72 C4
Pentre-llwyn-llŵyd Powys 47 D8
Pentre-llyn Ceredig 46 B5
Pentre-llyn cymmer Conwy 72 D3
Pentre Meyrick V Glam 21 B8
Pentre-poeth Newport 35 F6
Pentre-rhew Ceredig 47 D5
Pentre-tafarn-y-fedw Conwy 83 E8
Pentre-ty-gwyn Carms 47 F7
Pentrebach M Tydf 34 D4
Pentrebach Swansea 33 D7
Pentrebeirdd Powys 59 C8
Pentrecagal Carms 46 E2
Pentredwr Denb 73 E5
Pentrefelin Ceredig 46 E5
Pentrefelin Carms 33 B6
Pentrefelin Conwy 83 D8
Pentrefelin Gwyn 71 D6
Pentrefoelas Conwy 83 F8
Pentregat Ceredig 46 D2
Pentreheyling Shrops 60 E2
Pentre'r Felin Conwy 83 E8
Pentre'r-felin Powys 47 F8
Pentrich Derbys 76 D3
Pentridge Dorset 13 C8
Pentyrch Cardiff 35 F5
Penuchadre V Glam 21 B7
Penuwch Ceredig 46 C4
Penwithick Corn 4 D5
Penwyllt Powys 34 C2
Penybanc Carms 33 C7
Penybont Powys 48 C3
Penybontfawr Powys 59 B7
Penycae Wrex 73 E6
Penycwm Pembs 44 C3
Penyffordd Flint 73 C7
Penyffridd Gwyn 82 F5
Penygarnedd Powys 59 B8
Penygraig Rhondda 34 E3
Penygroes Gwyn 82 F4
Penygroes Pembs 45 F3
Penyrheol Caerph 35 F5
Penysarn Anglesey 82 B4
Penywaun Rhondda 34 D3
Penzance Corn 2 C3
Penzance Heliport Corn 2 C3
People's Palace Glasgow 121 C6
Peopleton Worcs 50 D4
Peover Heath Ches 74 B4
Peper Harow Sur 27 E7
Perceton N Ayrs 120 E3
Percie Aberds 150 E4
Percyhorner Aberds 161 B6
Periton Som 21 E8
Perivale London 40 F4
Perkinsville Durham 111 D5
Perlethorpe Notts 77 B6
Perranarworthal Corn 3 C6
Perranporth Corn 4 D2
Perranuthnoe Corn 2 D4
Perranzabuloe Corn 4 D2
Perry Barr W Mid 62 E4
Perry Green Herts 41 C7
Perry Green Wilts 37 F6
Perry Street Kent 29 B7
Perryfoot Derbys 88 F2
Pershall Staffs 74 F5
Pershore Worcs 50 E4
Pert Angus 143 C6
Pertenhall Beds 53 C8
Perth Perth 134 B3
Perth Racecourse Perth 134 B3
Perthy Shrops 73 F7
Perton Staffs 62 E2
Pertwood Wilts 24 F3
Peter Tavy Devon 6 B3
Peterborough P'boro 65 E8
Peterborough Cathedral P'boro 65 E8
Peterburn Highld 154 B3
Peterchurch Hereford 48 F5
Peterculter Aberdeen 151 D7
Peterhead Aberds 161 D8
Peterlee Durham 111 E7
Peter's Green Herts 40 C4
Peters Marland Devon 9 C6
Petersfield Hants 15 B8
Peterston super-Ely V Glam 22 B2
Peterstone Wentlooge Newport 35 F6
Peterstow Hereford 36 B2
Petertown Orkney 176 F2
Petham Kent 30 D5
Petrockstow Devon 9 D7
Pett E Sus 19 D5
Pettaugh Suff 57 D5
Petteridge Kent 29 E7
Pettinain S Lnrk 122 E2
Pettistree Suff 57 D6
Petton Devon 10 B5
Petton Shrops 60 B4
Petts Wood London 28 C5
Petty Aberds 160 E4
Pettycur Fife 134 F4
Pettymuick Aberds 151 B8
Petworth W Sus 16 B3
Petworth House W Sus 16 B3
Pevensey E Sus 18 E3
Pevensey Bay E Sus 18 E3
Pewsey Wilts 25 C6
Philham Devon 8 B4
Philiphaugh Borders 115 B7
Phillack Corn 2 C4
Philleigh Corn 3 C7
Philpstoun W Loth 122 B3
Phocle Green Hereford 36 B3
Phoenix Green Hants 27 D5
Pica Cumb 98 B2
Piccotts End Herts 40 D3
Pickering N Yorks 103 F5
Picket Piece Hants 25 E8
Picket Post Hants 14 D2
Pickhill N Yorks 101 F8
Picklescott Shrops 60 E4
Pickletillem Fife 135 B6
Pickmere Ches 74 B3
Pickney Som 11 B6
Pickstock Telford 61 B7
Pickwell Devon 20 E3
Pickwell Leics 64 C4
Pickworth Lincs 78 F3
Pickworth Rutland 65 C6
Picton Ches 73 B8
Picton Flint 85 F2
Picton N Yorks 102 D2
Piddinghoe E Sus 17 D8
Piddington Northants 53 D6
Piddington Oxon 39 C6
Piddlehinton Dorset 12 E5
Piddletrenthide Dorset 12 E5
Pidley Cambs 54 B4
Piece Hall Art Gallery, Halifax W Yorks 87 B8
Piercebridge Darl 101 C7
Pierowall Orkney 176 B3
Pigdon Northumb 117 F7
Pikehall Derbys 75 D8
Pilgrims Hatch Essex 42 E1
Pilham Lincs 90 E2
Pill N Som 23 B7
Pillaton Corn 5 C8
Pillerton Hersey Warks 51 E8
Pillerton Priors Warks 51 E7
Pilleth Powys 48 C4
Pilley Hants 14 E4
Pilley S Yorks 88 D4
Pilling Lancs 92 E4
Pilling Lane Lancs 92 E3
Pillowell Glos 36 D3
Pillwell Dorset 13 C5
Pilning S Glos 36 F2
Pilsbury Derbys 75 C8
Pilsdon Dorset 12 E2
Pilsgate P'boro 65 D7
Pilsley Derbys 76 B2
Pilsley Derbys 76 C4
Pilton Devon 20 F4
Pilton Northants 65 F7
Pilton Rutland 65 D6
Pilton Som 23 E7
Pilton Green Swansea 33 F5
Pimperne Dorset 13 D7
Pinchbeck Lincs 66 B2
Pinchbeck Bars Lincs 65 B8
Pinchbeck West Lincs 66 B2
Pincheon Green S Yorks 89 C7
Pinehurst Thamesdown 38 F1
Pinfold Lancs 85 C4
Pinged Carms 33 D5
Pinhoe Devon 10 E4
Pinkneys Green Windsor 40 F1
Pinley W Mid 51 B8
Pinmill Suff 57 F6
Pinminnoch S Ayrs 112 E1
Pinmore S Ayrs 112 E2
Pinmore Mains S Ayrs 112 E2
Pinner London 40 F4
Pinvin Worcs 50 E4
Pinwherry S Ayrs 112 F1
Pinxton Derbys 76 D4
Pipe and Lyde Hereford 49 E7
Pipe Gate Shrops 74 E4
Piperhill Highld 158 D2
Piper's Pool Corn 8 F4
Pipewell Northants 64 F5
Pippacott Devon 20 F4
Pipton Powys 48 F3
Pirbright Sur 27 D7
Pirnmill N Ayrs 119 B5
Pirton Herts 54 F2
Pirton Worcs 50 E3
Pisgah Ceredig 47 B5
Pisgah Stirl 133 D6
Pishill Oxon 39 F7
Pistyll Gwyn 70 C4
Pitagowan Perth 141 C5
Pitblae Aberds 161 B6
Pitcairngreen Perth 134 B2
Pitcalnie Highld 158 B2
Pitcaple Aberds 151 B6
Pitch Green Bucks 39 D7
Pitch Place Sur 27 D7
Pitchcombe Glos 37 D5
Pitchcott Bucks 39 B7
Pitchford Shrops 60 D5
Pitcombe Som 23 F8
Pitcorthie Fife 135 D7
Pitcox E Loth 124 B2
Pitcur Perth 142 F2
Pitfichie Aberds 151 C5
Pitforthie Aberds 143 B8
Pitgrudy Highld 164 E4
Pitkennedy Angus 143 D5
Pitkevy Fife 134 D4
Pitkierie Fife 135 D7
Pitlessie Fife 134 D5
Pitlochry Perth 141 D6
Pitmachie Aberds 151 B5
Pitmain Highld 148 D3
Pitmedden Aberds 151 B7
Pitminster Som 11 C7
Pitmuies Angus 143 E5
Pitmunie Aberds 151 C5
Pitney Som 12 B2
Pitscottie Fife 135 C6
Pitsea Essex 42 F3
Pitsford Northants 53 C5
Pitsmoor S Yorks 88 F4
Pitstone Bucks 40 C2
Pitstone Green Bucks 40 C2
Pitt Rivers Museum (See University Museum) Oxon 39 D5
Pittendreich Moray 159 C5
Pittentrail Highld 164 D4
Pittenweem Fife 135 D7
Pittington Durham 111 E6
Pittodrie Aberds 151 B5
Pitton Wilts 25 F7
Pittswood Kent 29 E7
Pittulie Aberds 161 B6
Pity Me Durham 111 E5
Pityme Corn 4 B4
Pityoulish Highld 148 C5
Pixey Green Suff 57 B6
Pixham Sur 28 D2
Pixley Hereford 49 F8
Place Newton N Yorks 96 B4
Plaidy Aberds 160 C4
Plains N Lnrk 121 C7
Plaish Shrops 60 E5
Plaistow W Sus 27 F8
Plaitford Hants 14 C3
Plank Lane Gtr Man 86 E4
Plâs Carms 33 B5
Plas-canol Gwyn 58 C2
Plas Gogerddan Ceredig 58 F3
Plas Llwyngwern Powys 58 D4
Plas Mawr, Conwy Conwy 83 D7
Plas Nantyr Wrex 73 F5
Plas-yn-Cefn Denb 72 B4
Plastow Green Hants 26 C3
Platt Kent 29 D7
Platt Bridge Gtr Man 86 D4
Platts Common S Yorks 88 D4
Plawsworth Durham 111 E5
Plaxtol Kent 29 D7
Play Hatch Oxon 26 B5
Playden E Sus 19 C6
Playford Suff 57 E6
Playing Place Corn 3 B7
Playley Green Glos 50 F2
Plealey Shrops 60 D4
Plean Stirl 133 F7
Pleasington Blkburn 86 B4
Pleasley Derbys 76 C5
Pleasure Island Theme Park NE Lincs 91 D7
Pleasureland Mers 85 C8
Pleckgate Blkburn 93 F6
Plemeller Northumb 109 C7
Pleshey Essex 42 C2
Plockton Highld 155 G4
Plocrapol W Isles 173 J4
Ploughfield Hereford 49 E5
Plowden Shrops 60 F3
Ploxgreen Shrops 60 D3
Pluckley Kent 30 E3
Pluckley Thorne Kent 30 E3
Plumbland Cumb 107 F8
Plumley Ches 74 B4
Plumpton Cumb 108 F4
Plumpton E Sus 17 C7
Plumpton Green E Sus 17 C7
Plumpton Head Cumb 108 F5
Plumpton Racecourse E Sus 17 C7
Plumstead London 29 B5
Plumstead Norf 81 D7
Plumtree Notts 77 F6
Plungar Leics 77 F7
Plush Dorset 12 D5
Plwmp Ceredig 46 D2
Plymouth Plym 6 D2
Plymouth City Airport Plym 6 C3
Plympton Plym 6 D3
Plymstock Plym 6 D3
Plymtree Devon 11 D5
Pockley N Yorks 102 F4
Pocklington E Yorks 96 E4
Pode Hole Lincs 66 B2
Podimore Som 12 B3
Podington Beds 53 C7
Podmore Staffs 74 F4
Point Clear Essex 43 C6
Pointon Lincs 78 F4
Pokesdown Bmouth 14 E2
Pol a Charra W Isles 171 J3
Polbae Dumfries 105 B6
Polbain Highld 162 C3
Polbathic Corn 5 D8
Polbeth W Loth 122 C3
Polchar Highld 148 D4
Pole Elm Worcs 50 E3
Polebrook Northants 65 F7
Polegate E Sus 18 E2
Poles Highld 164 E4
Polesden Lacey, Dorking Sur 28 D2
Polesworth Warks 63 D6
Polgigga Corn 2 D2
Polglass Highld 162 D4
Polgooth Corn 4 D4
Poling W Sus 16 D4
Polkerris Corn 5 D5
Polla Highld 167 D5
Pollington E Yorks 89 C7
Polloch Highld 138 C1
Pollok Glasgow 120 C5
Pollok House Glasgow 121 C5
Pollokshields Glasgow 121 C5
Polmassick Corn 3 B8
Polmont Falk 122 B2
Polnessan E Ayrs 112 C4
Polnish Highld 145 E7
Polperro Corn 5 D7
Polruan Corn 5 D6
Polsham Som 23 E7
Polstead Suff 56 F3
Poltalloch Argyll 130 F4
Poltimore Devon 10 E4
Polton Midloth 123 C5
Polwarth Borders 124 D3
Polyphant Corn 8 F4
Polzeath Corn 4 B4
Ponders End London 41 E6
Pondersbridge Cambs 66 E2
Pondtail Hants 27 D6
Ponsanooth Corn 3 C6
Ponsworthy Devon 6 B5
Pont Aber Carms 33 B8
Pont Aber-Geirw Gwyn 71 E8
Pont-ar-gothi Carms 33 B6
Pont ar Hydfer Powys 34 B2
Pont-ar-llechau Carms 33 B8
Pont Cwm Pydew Denb 72 F4
Pont Cyfyng Conwy 83 F7
Pont Cysyllte Wrex 73 E6
Pont Dolydd Prysor Gwyn 71 D8
Pont-faen Powys 47 F8
Pont Fronwydd Gwyn 58 B5
Pont-gareg Pembs 45 E3
Pont-Henri Carms 33 D5
Pont-Llogel Powys 59 C7
Pont Pen-y-benglog Gwyn 83 E6
Pont Rhyd-goch Conwy 83 E6
Pont-Rhyd-sarn Gwyn 59 B5
Pont Rhyd-y-cyff Bridgend 34 F2
Pont-rhyd-y-groes Ceredig 47 B6
Pont-rug Gwyn 82 E5
Pont Senni = Sennybridge Powys 34 B3
Pont-siân Ceredig 46 E3
Pont-y-gwaith Rhondda 34 E4
Pont-y-pant Conwy 83 F7
Pont y Pennant Gwyn 59 B6
Pont-y-Pŵl = Pontypool Torf 35 D6
Pont yclun Rhondda 34 F4
Pont yr Afon-Gam Gwyn 71 C8
Pont-yr-hafod Pembs 44 C4
Pontamman Carms 33 C7
Pontantwn Carms 33 C5
Pontardawe Neath 33 D8
Pontarddulais Swansea 33 D6
Pontarsais Carms 33 B5
Pontblyddyn Flint 73 C6
Pontbren Araeth Carms 33 B7
Pontbren Llwyd Rhondda 34 D3
Pontefract W Yorks 89 B5
Pontefract Racecourse W Yorks 88 B5
Ponteland Northumb 110 B4
Ponterwyd Ceredig 58 F4
Pontesbury Shrops 60 D3
Pontfadog Wrex 73 F6
Pontfaen Pembs 45 F2
Pontgarreg Ceredig 46 D2
Ponthir Torf 35 E7
Ponthirwaun Ceredig 45 E4
Pontllanfraith Caerph 35 E5
Pontlliw Swansea 33 D7
Pontllyfni Gwyn 82 F4
Pontlottyn Caerph 35 D5
Pontneddfechan Powys 34 D3
Pontnewydd Torf 35 E6
Pontrhydfendigaid Ceredig 47 C6
Pontrhydyfen Neath 34 E1
Pontrilas Hereford 35 B7
Pontrobert Powys 59 C8
Ponts Green E Sus 18 D3
Pontshill Hereford 36 B3
Pontsticill M Tydf 34 C4
Pontwgan Conwy 83 D7
Pontyates Carms 33 D5
Pontyberem Carms 33 C6
Pontycymer Bridgend 34 E3
Pontyglasier Pembs 45 F3
Pontypool = Pont-y-Pŵl Torf 35 D6
Pontypridd Rhondda 34 F4
Pontywaun Caerph 35 E6
Pooksgreen Hants 14 C4
Pool Corn 3 B5
Pool W Yorks 94 E5
Pool o'Muckhart Clack 134 D2
Pool Quay Powys 60 C2
Poole Poole 13 E8
Poole Keynes Glos 37 E6
Poolend Staffs 75 D6
Poolewe Highld 154 B4
Pooley Bridge Cumb 99 B6
Poolfold Staffs 75 D5
Poolhill Glos 36 B4
Poolsbrook Derbys 76 B4
Pootings Kent 29 E5
Pope Hill Pembs 44 D4
Popeswood Brack 27 C6
Popham Hants 26 E3
Poplar London 41 F6
Popley Hants 26 D4
Porchester Notts 77 E5
Porchfield I o W 14 E5
Porin Highld 156 D4
Poringland Norf 69 D5
Porkellis Corn 3 C5
Porlock Som 21 E7
Porlock Weir Som 21 E7
Port Ann Argyll 128 B4
Port Appin Argyll 138 E3
Port Arthur Shetland 175 K5
Port Askaig Argyll 126 C4
Port Bannatyne Argyll 129 D5
Port Carlisle Cumb 108 C2
Port Charlotte Argyll 126 D2
Port Clarence Stockton 102 B2
Port Driseach Argyll 128 C4
Port e Vullen I o M 84 C4
Port Ellen Argyll 126 E3
Port Elphinstone Aberds 151 C6
Port Erin I o M 84 F1
Port Erroll Aberds 161 E7
Port-Eynon Swansea 33 F5
Port Gaverne Corn 8 F2
Port Glasgow Invclyd 120 B3
Port Henderson Highld 154 C3
Port Isaac Corn 4 A4
Port Lamont Argyll 129 C5
Port Lion Pembs 44 E4
Port Logan Dumfries 104 E4
Port Mholair W Isles 172 E8
Port Mor Highld 144 F4
Port Mulgrave N Yorks 103 C5
Port Nan Giùran W Isles 172 E8
Port nan Long W Isles 170 C4
Port Nis W Isles 172 B8
Port of Menteith Stirl 132 D4
Port Quin Corn 4 A4
Port Ramsay Argyll 138 E2
Port St Mary I o M 84 F2
Port Sunlight Mers 85 F4
Port Talbot Neath 34 E1
Port Tennant Swansea 33 E7
Port Wemyss Argyll 126 D1
Port William Dumfries 105 E7
Portachoillan Argyll 128 E2
Portavadie Argyll 128 D4
Portbury N Som 23 B7
Portchester Hants 15 D7
Portclair Highld 147 C7
Portencalzie Dumfries 104 B4
Portencross N Ayrs 119 B8
Portesham Dorset 12 F4
Portessie Moray 159 C8
Portfield Gate Pembs 44 D4
Portgate Devon 9 F6
Portgordon Moray 159 C7
Portgower Highld 165 C7
Porth Corn 4 C3
Porth Rhondda 34 E4
Porth Navas Corn 3 D6
Porth Tywyn = Burry Port Carms 33 D5
Porth-y-waen Shrops 60 B2
Porthaethwy = Menai Bridge Anglesey 83 D5
Porthallow Corn 3 D6
Porthallow Corn 5 D7
Porthcawl Bridgend 21 B7
Porthcothan Corn 4 B3
Porthcurno Corn 2 D2
Porthgain Pembs 44 B3
Porthill Shrops 60 C4
Porthkerry V Glam 22 C2
Porthleven Corn 2 D5
Porthllechog Anglesey 82 B4
Porthmadog Gwyn 71 D6
Porthmeor Corn 2 C3
Portholland Corn 3 B8
Porthoustock Corn 3 D7
Porthpean Corn 4 D5
Porthtowan Corn 3 B5
Porthyrhyd Carms 33 C6
Porthyrhyd Carms 47 F6
Portincaple Argyll 129 A7
Portington E Yorks 96 F3
Portinnisherrich Argyll 131 D5
Portinscale Cumb 98 B4
Portishead N Som 23 B6
Portkil Argyll 129 B7
Portknockie Moray 159 C8

Portlethen Aberds 151 E8
Portling Dumfries 107 D5
Portloe Corn 3 C8
Portmahomack Highld 165 F6
Portmeirion Gwyn 71 D6
Portmeirion Village Gwyn 71 D6
Portmellon Corn 3 B9
Portmore Hants 14 E4
Portnacroish Argyll 138 E3
Portnahaven Argyll 126 D1
Portnalong Highld 153 F4
Portnaluchaig Highld 145 E6
Portnancon Highld 167 C6
Portnellan Stirl 132 B3
Portobello Edin 123 B6
Porton Wilts 25 F6
Portpatrick Dumfries 104 D4
Portreath Corn 3 B5
Portree Highld 153 E5
Portscatho Corn 3 C7
Portsea Ptsmth 15 D7
Portskerra Highld 168 C3
Portskewett Mon 36 F2
Portslade Brighton 17 D6
Portslade-by-Sea Brighton 17 D6
Portsmouth Ptsmth 15 D7
Portsmouth W Yorks 87 B7
Portsmouth Sea Life Centre Ptsmth 15 E7
Portsonachan Argyll 131 C6
Portsoy Aberds 160 B2
Portswood Soton 14 C5
Porttanachy Moray 159 C7
Portuairk Highld 137 B5
Portway Hereford 49 F6
Portway Worcs 51 B5
Portwrinkle Corn 5 D8
Poslingford Suff 55 E8
Postbridge Devon 6 B4
Postcombe Oxon 39 E7
Postling Kent 19 B8
Postwick Norf 69 D5
Potholm Dumfries 115 F6
Potsgrove Beds 40 B2
Pott Row Norf 80 E3
Pott Shrigley Ches 75 B6
Potten End Herts 40 D3
Potter Brompton N Yorks 97 B5
Potter Heigham Norf 69 C7
Potter Street Essex 41 D7
Potterhanworth Lincs 78 C3
Potterhanworth Booths Lincs 78 C3
Potteries Museum & Art Gallery, Stoke-on-Trent Stoke 75 E5
Potterne Wilts 24 D4
Potterne Wick Wilts 24 D5
Potternewton W Yorks 95 F6
Potters Bar Herts 41 D5
Potter's Cross Staffs 62 F2
Potterspury Northants 53 E5
Potterton Aberds 151 C8
Potterton W Yorks 95 F7
Potto N Yorks 102 D2
Potton Beds 54 E3
Poughill Corn 8 D4
Poughill Devon 10 D3
Poulshot Wilts 24 D4
Poulton Glos 37 D8
Poulton Mers 85 E4
Poulton-le-Fylde Lancs 92 F3
Pound Bank Worcs 50 B2
Pound Green E Sus 18 C2
Pound Green I o W 14 F4
Pound Green Worcs 50 B2
Pound Hill W Sus 28 F3
Poundfield E Sus 18 B2
Poundland S Ayrs 112 F1
Poundon Bucks 39 B6
Poundsgate Devon 6 B5
Poundstock Corn 8 E4
Powburn Northumb 117 C6
Powderham Devon 10 F4
Powderham Castle Devon 10 F4
Powerstock Dorset 12 E3
Powfoot Dumfries 107 C8
Powick Worcs 50 D3
Powis Castle, Welshpool Powys 60 D2
Powmill Perth 134 E2
Poxwell Dorset 12 F5
Poyle Slough 27 B8
Poynings W Sus 17 C6
Poyntington Dorset 12 C4
Poynton Ches 87 F7
Poynton Green Telford 61 C5
Poystreet Green Suff 56 D3
Praa Sands Corn 2 D4
Pratt's Bottom London 29 C5
Praze Corn 2 C4
Praze-an-Beeble Corn 2 C5
Predannack Wollas Corn 3 E5
Prees Shrops 74 F2
Prees Green Shrops 74 F2
Prees Heath Shrops 74 F2
Prees Higher Heath Shrops 74 F2
Prees Lower Heath Shrops 74 F2
Preesall Lancs 92 E3
Preesgweene Shrops 73 F6
Prenderguest Borders 124 D5
Prendwick Northumb 117 C6
Prengwyn Ceredig 46 E3
Prenteg Gwyn 71 C6
Prenton Mers 85 F4
Prescot Mers 86 E2
Prescott Shrops 60 B4
Pressen Northumb 124 F4
Prestatyn Denb 72 A4
Prestbury Ches 75 B6
Prestbury Glos 37 B6
Presteigne = Llanandras Powys 48 C5
Presthope Shrops 61 E5
Prestleigh Som 23 E8
Preston Borders 124 D3
Preston Brighton 17 D7
Preston Devon 7 B6
Preston Dorset 12 F5
Preston E Loth 123 B8
Preston E Yorks 97 F7
Preston Glos 37 D7
Preston Glos 49 F8
Preston Herts 40 B4
Preston Kent 30 C4
Preston Kent 31 C6
Preston Lancs 86 B3
Preston Northumb 117 B7
Preston Rutland 65 D5
Preston Shrops 60 C5
Preston Suff 56 D3
Preston Wilts 24 B5
Preston Wilts 25 B7
Preston Bagot Warks 51 C6
Preston Bissett Bucks 39 B6
Preston Bowyer Som 11 B6
Preston Brockhurst Shrops 60 B5
Preston Brook Halton 86 F3
Preston Candover Hants 26 E4
Preston Capes Northants 52 D3
Preston Crowmarsh Oxon 39 E6
Preston Gubbals Shrops 60 C4
Preston Hall Museum, Stockton-on-Tees Stockton 102 C2
Preston on Stour Warks 51 E7
Preston on the Hill Halton 86 F3
Preston on Wye Hereford 49 E5
Preston Plucknett Som 12 C3
Preston-under-Scar N Yorks 101 E5
Preston upon the Weald Moors Telford 61 C6
Preston Wynne Hereford 49 E7
Prestonmill Dumfries 107 D6
Prestonpans E Loth 123 B6
Prestwich Gtr Man 87 D6
Prestwick Northumb 110 B4
Prestwick S Ayrs 112 B3
Prestwood Bucks 40 D1
Price Town Bridgend 34 E3
Prickwillow Cambs 67 F5
Priddy Som 23 D7
Priest Hutton Lancs 92 B5
Priest Weston Shrops 60 E2
Priesthaugh Borders 115 D7
Primethorpe Leics 64 E2
Primrose Green Norf 68 C3
Primrose Valley N Yorks 97 B7
Primrosehill Herts 40 D3
Princes Gate Pembs 32 C2
Princes Risborough Bucks 39 D8
Princethorpe Warks 52 B2
Princetown Caerph 35 C5
Princetown Devon 6 B3
Prinknash Abbey, Gloucester Glos 37 C5
Prion Denb 72 C4
Prior Muir Fife 135 C7
Prior Park Northumb 125 D5
Priors Frome Hereford 49 F7
Priors Hardwick Warks 52 D2
Priors Marston Warks 52 D2
Priorslee Telford 61 C7
Priory Church, Lancaster Lancs 92 C4
Priory Wood Hereford 48 E4
Priston Bath 23 C8
Pristow Green Norf 68 F4
Prittlewell Sthend 42 F4
Privett Hants 15 B7
Prixford Devon 20 F4
Probus Corn 3 B7
Proncy Highld 164 E4
Prospect Cumb 107 E8
Prudhoe Northumb 110 C3
Ptarmigan Lodge Stirl 132 D2
Pubil Perth 140 E1
Puckeridge Herts 41 B6
Puckington Som 11 C8
Pucklechurch S Glos 23 B8
Pucknall Hants 14 B4
Puckrup Glos 50 F3
Puddinglake Ches 74 C4
Puddington Ches 73 B7
Puddington Devon 10 C3
Puddledock Norf 68 E3
Puddletown Dorset 13 E5
Pudleston Hereford 49 D7
Pudsey W Yorks 94 F5
Pulborough W Sus 16 C4
Puleston Telford 61 B7
Pulford Ches 73 D7
Pulham Dorset 12 D5
Pulham Market Norf 68 F4
Pulham St Mary Norf 68 F5
Pulloxhill Beds 53 F8
Pumpherston W Loth 122 C3
Pumsaint Carms 47 E5
Puncheston Pembs 32 B1
Puncknowle Dorset 12 F3
Punnett's Town E Sus 18 C3
Purbrook Hants 15 D7
Purewell Dorset 14 E2
Purfleet Thurrock 29 B6
Puriton Som 22 E5
Purleigh Essex 42 D4
Purley London 28 C4
Purley W Berks 26 B4
Purlogue Shrops 48 B4
Purls Bridge Cambs 66 F4
Purse Caundle Dorset 12 C4
Purslow Shrops 60 F3
Purston Jaglin W Yorks 88 C5
Purton Glos 36 D3
Purton Glos 36 D3
Purton Wilts 37 F7
Purton Stoke Wilts 37 E7
Pury End Northants 52 E5
Pusey Oxon 38 E3
Putley Hereford 49 F8
Putney London 28 B3
Putsborough Devon 20 E3
Puttenham Herts 40 C1
Puttenham Sur 27 E7
Puxton N Som 23 C6
Pwll Carms 33 D5
Pwll-glas Denb 72 D5
Pwll-Meyric Mon 36 E2
Pwll-trap Carms 32 C3
Pwll-y-glaw Neath 34 E1
Pwllcrochan Pembs 44 E4
Pwllgloyw Powys 48 F2
Pwllheli Gwyn 70 D4
Pye Corner Newport 35 F7
Pye Green Staffs 62 C3
Pyecombe W Sus 17 C6
Pyewipe NE Lincs 91 C6
Pyle I o W 15 G5
Pyle = Y Pîl Bridgend 34 F2
Pylle Som 23 F8
Pymoor Cambs 66 F4
Pyrford Sur 27 D8
Pyrton Oxon 39 E6
Pytchley Northants 53 B6
Pyworthy Devon 8 D5

Q

Quabbs Shrops 60 F2
Quadring Lincs 78 F5
Quainton Bucks 39 C7
Quarley Hants 25 E7
Quarndon Derbys 76 E3
Quarrier's Homes Invclyd 120 C3
Quarrington Lincs 78 E3
Quarrington Hill Durham 111 F6
Quarry Bank W Mid 62 F3
Quarry Bank Mill, Wilmslow Ches 87 F6
Quarryford E Loth 123 C8
Quarryhill Highld 164 F4
Quarrywood Moray 159 C5
Quarter S Lnrk 121 D7
Quatford Shrops 61 E7
Quatt Shrops 61 F7
Quebec Durham 110 E4
Quedgeley Glos 37 C5
Queen Adelaide Cambs 67 F5
Queen Camel Som 12 B3
Queen Charlton Bath 23 C8
Queen Dart Devon 10 C3
Queen Oak Dorset 24 F2
Queen Street Kent 29 E7
Queen Street Wilts 37 F7
Queenborough Kent 30 B3
Queenhill Worcs 50 F3
Queen's Head Shrops 60 B3
Queen's Park Beds 53 E8
Queen's Park Northants 53 C5
Queen's View Centre, Loch Tummel Perth 141 D5
Queensbury W Yorks 94 F4
Queensferry Edin 122 B4
Queensferry Flint 73 C7
Queenstown Blkpool 92 F3
Queenzieburn N Lnrk 121 B6
Quemerford Wilts 24 C5
Quendale Shetland 175 M5
Quendon Essex 55 F6
Queniborough Leics 64 C3
Quenington Glos 37 D8
Quernmore Lancs 92 D5
Quethiock Corn 5 C8
Quholm Orkney 176 E1
Quicks Green W Berks 26 B3
Quidenham Norf 68 F3
Quidhampton Hants 26 D3
Quidhampton Wilts 25 F6
Quilquox Aberds 161 E6
Quina Brook Shrops 74 F2
Quindry Orkney 176 G3
Quinton Northants 53 D5
Quinton W Mid 62 F3
Quintrell Downs Corn 4 C3
Quixhill Staffs 75 E8
Quoditch Devon 9 E6
Quoig Perth 133 B7
Quorndon Leics 64 C2
Quothquan S Lnrk 122 F2
Quoyloo Orkney 176 D1
Quoyness Orkney 176 F1
Quoys Shetland 174 B8
Quoys Shetland 175 G6

R

Raasay Ho. Highld 153 F6
Rabbit's Cross Kent 29 E8
Raby Mers 73 B7
Rachan Mill Borders 122 F4
Rachub Gwyn 83 E6
Rackenford Devon 10 C3
Rackham W Sus 16 C4
Rackheath Norf 69 C5
Racks Dumfries 107 B7
Rackwick Orkney 176 G1
Rackwick Orkney 176 B3
Radbourne Derbys 76 F2
Radcliffe Gtr Man 87 D5
Radcliffe Northumb 117 D8
Radcliffe on Trent Notts 77 F6
Radclive Bucks 52 F4
Radcot Oxon 38 E2
Raddery Highld 157 D8
Radernie Fife 135 D6
Radford Semele Warks 51 C8
Radipole Dorset 12 F4
Radlett Herts 40 E4
Radley Oxon 39 E5
Radmanthwaite Notts 76 C5
Radmoor Shrops 61 B6
Radmore Green Ches 74 D2
Radnage Bucks 39 E7
Radstock Bath 23 D8
Radstone Northants 52 E3
Radway Warks 51 E8
Radway Green Ches 74 D4
Radwell Beds 53 D8
Radwell Herts 54 F3
Radwinter Essex 55 F7
Radyr Cardiff 35 F5
RAF Museum, Cosford Shrops 61 D7
RAF Museum, Hendon London 41 F5
Rafford Moray 158 D4
Ragdale Leics 64 C3
Raglan Mon 35 D8
Ragley Hall Warks 51 D5
Ragnall Notts 77 B8
Rahane Argyll 129 B7
Rainford Mers 86 D2
Rainford Junction Mers 86 D2
Rainham London 41 F8
Rainham Medway 30 C2
Rainhill Mers 86 E2
Rainhill Stoops Mers 86 E3
Rainow Ches 75 B6
Rainton N Yorks 95 B6
Rainworth Notts 77 D5
Raisbeck Cumb 99 D8
Raise Cumb 109 E7
Rait Perth 134 B4
Raithby Lincs 91 F7
Raithby Lincs 79 C6
Rake W Sus 16 B2
Rakewood Gtr Man 87 C7
Ram Carms 46 E4
Ram Lane Kent 30 E3
Ramasaig Highld 153 E2
Rame Corn 3 C6
Rame Corn 6 E2
Rameldry Mill Bank Fife 134 D5
Ramnageo Shetland 174 C8
Rampisham Dorset 12 D3
Rampside Cumb 92 C2
Rampton Cambs 54 C5
Rampton Notts 77 B7
Ramsbottom Gtr Man 87 C5
Ramsbury Wilts 25 B7
Ramscraigs Highld 165 B8
Ramsdean Hants 15 B8
Ramsdell Hants 26 D3
Ramsden Oxon 38 C3
Ramsden Bellhouse Essex 42 E3
Ramsden Heath Essex 42 E3
Ramsey Cambs 66 F2
Ramsey Essex 57 F6
Ramsey I o M 84 C4
Ramsey Forty Foot Cambs 66 F3
Ramsey Heights Cambs 66 F2
Ramsey Island Essex 43 D5
Ramsey Mereside Cambs 66 F2
Ramsey St Mary's Cambs 66 F2
Ramseycleuch Borders 115 C5
Ramsgate Kent 31 C7
Ramsgill N Yorks 94 B4
Ramshorn Staffs 75 E7
Ramsnest Common Sur 27 F7
Ranais W Isles 172 F7
Ranby Lincs 78 B5
Ranby Notts 89 F7
Rand Lincs 78 B4
Randwick Glos 37 D5
Ranfurly Renfs 120 C3
Rangag Highld 169 E6
Rangemore Staffs 63 B5
Rangeworthy S Glos 36 F3
Rankinston E Ayrs 112 C4
Ranmoor S Yorks 88 F4
Ranmore Common Sur 28 D2
Rannerdale Cumb 98 C3
Rannoch Station Perth 139 D8
Ranochan Highld 145 E8
Ranskill Notts 89 F7
Ranton Staffs 62 B2
Ranworth Norf 69 C6
Raploch Stirl 133 E6
Rapness Orkney 176 B4
Rascal Moor E Yorks 96 F4
Rascarrel Dumfries 106 E4
Rashiereive Aberds 151 B8
Raskelf N Yorks 95 B7
Rassau Bl Gwent 35 C5
Rastrick W Yorks 88 B2
Ratagan Highld 146 C2
Ratby Leics 64 D2
Ratcliffe Culey Leics 63 E7
Ratcliffe on Soar Leics 63 B8
Ratcliffe on the Wreake Leics 64 C3
Rathen Aberds 161 B7
Rathillet Fife 135 B5
Rathmell N Yorks 93 D8
Ratho Edin 122 B4
Ratho Station Edin 122 B4
Rathven Moray 159 C8
Ratley Warks 51 E8
Ratlinghope Shrops 60 E4
Rattar Highld 169 B7
Ratten Row Lancs 92 E4
Rattery Devon 6 C5
Rattlesden Suff 56 D3
Rattray Perth 142 E1
Raughton Head Cumb 108 E3
Raunds Northants 53 B7
Ravenfield S Yorks 89 E5
Ravenglass Cumb 98 E2
Ravenglass and Eskdale Railway & Museum Cumb 98 E2
Raveningham Norf 69 E6
Ravenscar N Yorks 103 D7
Ravenscraig Invclyd 129 C7
Ravensdale I o M 84 C3
Ravensden Beds 53 D8
Ravenseat N Yorks 100 D3
Ravenshead Notts 77 D5
Ravensmoor Ches 74 D3
Ravensthorpe Northants 52 B4
Ravensthorpe W Yorks 88 B3
Ravenstone Leics 63 C8
Ravenstone M Keynes 53 D6
Ravenstonedale Cumb 100 D2
Ravenstown Cumb 92 B3
Ravenstruther S Lnrk 122 E2
Ravensworth N Yorks 101 D6
Raw N Yorks 103 D7
Rawcliffe E Yorks 89 B7
Rawcliffe York 95 D8
Rawcliffe Bridge E Yorks 89 B7
Rawdon W Yorks 94 F5
Rawmarsh S Yorks 88 E5
Rawreth Essex 42 E3
Rawridge Devon 11 D7
Rawtenstall Lancs 87 B6
Raxton Aberds 161 E5
Raydon Suff 56 F4
Raylees Northumb 117 E5
Rayleigh Essex 42 E4
Rayne Essex 42 B3
Rayners Lane London 40 F4
Raynes Park London 28 C3
Reach Cambs 55 C6
Read Lancs 93 F7
Reading Reading 26 B5
Reading Street Kent 19 B6
Reagill Cumb 99 C8
Rearquhar Highld 164 E4
Rearsby Leics 64 C3
Reaster Highld 169 C7
Reawick Shetland 175 J5
Reay Highld 168 C4
Rechullin Highld 154 E4
Reculver Kent 31 C6
Red Dial Cumb 108 E2
Red Hill Worcs 50 D3
Red House Glass Cone, Wordsley W Mid 62 F2
Red Houses Jersey 17
Red Lodge Suff 55 B7
Red Rail Hereford 36 B2
Red Rock Gtr Man 86 D3
Red Roses Carms 32 C3
Red Row Northumb 117 E8
Red Street Staffs 74 D5
Red Wharf Bay Anglesey 82 C5
Redberth Pembs 32 D1
Redbourn Herts 40 C4
Redbourne N Lincs 90 E3
Redbrook Glos 36 C2
Redbrook Wrex 74 E2
Redburn Highld 157 C6
Redburn Highld 158 E3
Redburn Northumb 109 C7
Redcar Redcar 102 B4
Redcar Racecourse Redcar 102 B4
Redcastle Angus 143 D6
Redcastle Highld 157 E6
Redcliff Bay N Som 23 B6
Redding Falk 122 B2
Reddingmuirhead Falk 122 B2
Reddish Gtr Man 87 E6
Redditch Worcs 50 C5
Rede Suff 56 D2
Redenhall Norf 69 F5
Redesdale Camp Northumb 116 E4
Redesmouth Northumb 116 F4
Redford Aberds 143 B7
Redford Angus 143 E5
Redford Durham 110 F3
Redfordgreen Borders 115 C6
Redgorton Perth 134 B2
Redgrave Suff 56 B4
Redhill Aberds 160 E3
Redhill Aberds 151 D6
Redhill N Som 23 C7
Redhill Sur 28 D3
Redhouse Argyll 128 D3
Redhouses Argyll 126 C3
Redisham Suff 69 F7
Redland Bristol 23 B7
Redland Orkney 176 D2
Redlingfield Suff 57 B5
Redlynch Som 23 F9
Redlynch Wilts 14 B3
Redmarley D'Abitot Glos 50 F2
Redmarshall Stockton 102 B1
Redmile Leics 77 F7
Redmire N Yorks 101 E5
Redmoor Corn 5 C5
Rednal Shrops 60 B3
Redpath Borders 123 F8
Redpoint Highld 154 D3
Redruth Corn 3 B5
Redvales Gtr Man 87 D6
Redwick Newport 35 F8
Redwick S Glos 36 F2
Redworth Darl 101 B7
Reed Herts 54 F4
Reedham Norf 69 D7
Reedness E Yorks 89 B8
Reeds Beck Lincs 78 C5
Reepham Lincs 78 B3
Reepham Norf 81 E6
Reeth N Yorks 101 E5
Regaby I o M 84 C4
Regoul Highld 158 D2
Reiff Highld 162 C3
Reigate Sur 28 D3
Reighton N Yorks 97 B7
Reighton Gap N Yorks 97 B7
Reinigeadal W Isles 173 H5
Reiss Highld 169 D8
Rejerrah Corn 4 D2
Releath Corn 3 C5
Relubbus Corn 2 C4
Relugas Moray 158 E3
Remenham Wokingham 39 F7
Remenham Hill Wokingham 39 F7
Remony Perth 140 E4
Rempstone Notts 64 B2
Rendcomb Glos 37 D7
Rendham Suff 57 C7
Rendlesham Suff 57 D7
Renfrew Renfs 120 C5
Renhold Beds 53 D8
Renishaw Derbys 76 B4
Rennington Northumb 117 C8
Renton W Dunb 120 B3
Renwick Cumb 109 E5
Repps Norf 69 C7
Repton Derbys 63 B7
Reraig Highld 155 H4
Rescobie Angus 143 D5
Resipole Highld 137 B8
Resolis Highld 157 C7
Resolven Neath 34 D2
Reston Borders 124 C4
Reswallie Angus 143 D5
Retew Corn 4 D4
Retford Notts 89 F8
Rettendon Essex 42 E3
Rettendon Place Essex 42 E3
Revesby Lincs 79 C5
Revesby Bridge Lincs 79 C6
Rew Street I o W 15 E5
Rewe Devon 10 E4
Reydon Suff 57 B8
Reydon Smear Suff 57 B8
Reymerston Norf 68 D3
Reynalton Pembs 32 D1
Reynoldston Swansea 33 E5
Rezare Corn 5 B8
Rhaeadr Gwy = Rhayader Powys 47 C8
Rhandirmwyn Carms 47 E6
Rhayader = Rhaeadr Gwy Powys 47 C8
Rhedyn Gwyn 70 D3
Rhemore Highld 137 C6
Rhencullen I o M 84 C3
Rhes-y-cae Flint 73 B5
Rhewl Denb 72 C5
Rhewl Denb 73 E5
Rhian Highld 164 C2
Rhicarn Highld 162 B4
Rhiconich Highld 166 D4
Rhicullen Highld 157 B7
Rhidorroch Ho. Highld 163 E5
Rhifail Highld 168 E2
Rhigos Rhondda 34 D3
Rhilochan Highld 164 D4
Rhiroy Highld 163 F5
Rhisga = Risca Caerph 35 E6
Rhiw Gwyn 70 E3
Rhiwabon = Ruabon Wrex 73 E7
Rhiwbina Cardiff 35 F5
Rhiwbryfdir Gwyn 71 C7
Rhiwderin Newport 35 F6
Rhiwlas Gwyn 83 E5
Rhiwlas Gwyn 72 F3
Rhiwlas Powys 73 F5
Rhodes Gtr Man 87 D6
Rhodes Minnis Kent 31 E5
Rhodesia Notts 77 B5
Rhodiad Pembs 44 C2
Rhondda Rhondda 34 E3
Rhonehouse or Kelton Hill Dumfries 106 D4
Rhoose = Y Rhws V Glam 22 C2
Rhôs Carms 46 F2
Rhôs Neath 33 D8
Rhos-fawr Gwyn 70 D4
Rhos-hill Pembs 45 E3
Rhos-on-Sea Conwy 83 C8
Rhos-y-brithdir Powys 59 B8
Rhos-y-garth Ceredig 46 B5
Rhos-y-gwaliau Gwyn 72 F3
Rhos-y-llan Gwyn 70 D3
Rhos-y-Madoc Wrex 73 E7
Rhos-y-meirch Powys 48 C4
Rhosaman Carms 33 C8
Rhosbeirio Anglesey 82 B3
Rhoscefnhir Anglesey 82 D5
Rhoscolyn Anglesey 82 D2
Rhoscrowther Pembs 44 E4
Rhosesmor Flint 73 C6
Rhosgadfan Gwyn 82 F5
Rhosgoch Anglesey 82 C4
Rhosgoch Powys 48 E3
Rhoshirwaun Gwyn 70 E2
Rhoslan Gwyn 71 C5
Rhoslefain Gwyn 58 D2
Rhosllanerchrugog Wrex 73 E6
Rhosmaen Carms 33 B7
Rhosmeirch Anglesey 82 D4
Rhosneigr Anglesey 82 D3
Rhosnesni Wrex 73 D7
Rhosrobin Wrex 73 D7
Rhossili Swansea 33 F5
Rhosson Pembs 44 C2
Rhostryfan Gwyn 82 F4
Rhostyllen Wrex 73 E7
Rhosybol Anglesey 82 C4
RHS Garden, Wisley Sur 27 D8
Rhu Argyll 128 D3
Rhu Argyll 129 B7
Rhuallt Denb 72 B4
Rhuddall Heath Ches 74 C2
Rhuddlan Ceredig 46 E3
Rhuddlan Denb 72 B4
Rhue Highld 162 E4
Rhulen Powys 48 E3
Rhunahaorine Argyll 118 B4
Rhuthun = Ruthin Denb 72 D5
Rhyd Gwyn 71 C7
Rhyd Powys 59 D6
Rhyd-Ddu Gwyn 83 F5
Rhyd-moel-ddu Powys 48 B2
Rhyd-Rosser Ceredig 46 C4
Rhyd-uchaf Gwyn 72 F3
Rhyd-wen Gwyn 58 C4
Rhyd-y-clafdy Gwyn 70 D4
Rhŷd-y-foel Conwy 72 B3
Rhyd-y-fro Neath 33 D8
Rhyd-y-gwin Swansea 33 D7
Rhyd-y-meirch Mon 35 D7
Rhyd-y-meudwy Denb 72 D5
Rhyd-y-pandy Swansea 33 D7
Rhyd-y-sarn Gwyn 71 C7
Rhyd-yr-onen Gwyn 58 D3
Rhydaman = Ammanford Carms 33 C7
Rhydargaeau Carms 33 B5
Rhydcymerau Carms 46 F4
Rhydd Worcs 50 E3
Rhydding Neath 33 E8
Rhydfudr Ceredig 46 C4
Rhydlewis Ceredig 46 E2
Rhydlios Gwyn 70 D2
Rhydlydan Conwy 83 F8
Rhydness Powys 48 E3
Rhydowen Ceredig 46 E3
Rhydspence Hereford 48 E4
Rhydtalog Flint 73 D6
Rhydwyn Anglesey 82 C3
Rhydycroesau Shrops 73 F6
Rhydyfelin Ceredig 46 B4
Rhydyfelin Rhondda 34 F4
Rhydymain Gwyn 58 B5
Rhydymwyn Flint 73 C6
Rhyl = Y Rhyl Denb 72 A4
Rhymney = Rhymni Caerph 35 D5
Rhymni = Rhymney Caerph 35 D5
Rhynd Fife 135 B6
Rhynd Perth 134 B3
Rhynie Aberds 150 B3
Rhynie Highld 158 B2
Ribbesford Worcs 50 B2
Ribblehead N Yorks 93 B7
Ribbleton Lancs 93 F5
Ribchester Lancs 93 F6
Ribigill Highld 167 D7
Riby Lincs 91 D5
Riby Cross Roads Lincs 91 D5
Riccall N Yorks 96 F2
Riccarton E Ayrs 120 F4
Richards Castle Hereford 49 C6
Richings Park Bucks 27 B8
Richmond London 28 B2
Richmond N Yorks 101 D6
Rickarton Aberds 151 F7
Rickinghall Suff 56 B4
Rickleton T & W 111 D5
Rickling Essex 55 F5
Rickmansworth Herts 40 E3
Riddings Cumb 108 B4
Riddings Derbys 76 D4
Riddlecombe Devon 9 C8
Riddlesden W Yorks 94 E3
Riddrie Glasgow 121 C6
Ridge Dorset 13 F7
Ridge Hants 14 C4
Ridge Wilts 24 F4
Ridge Green Sur 28 E4
Ridge Lane Warks 63 E6
Ridgebourne Powys 48 C2
Ridgehill N Som 23 C7
Ridgeway Cross Hereford 50 E2
Ridgewell Essex 55 E8
Ridgewood E Sus 17 C8
Ridgmont Beds 53 F7
Riding Mill Northumb 110 C3
Ridleywood Wrex 73 D8
Ridlington Norf 69 A6
Ridlington Rutland 64 D5
Ridsdale Northumb 116 F5
Riechip Perth 141 E7
Riemore Perth 141 E7
Rienachait Highld 166 F2
Rievaulx N Yorks 102 F3
Rievaulx Abbey N Yorks 102 F3
Rift House Hrtlpl 111 F7
Rigg Dumfries 108 C2
Riggend N Lnrk 121 B7
Rigsby Lincs 79 B7
Rigside S Lnrk 121 F8
Riley Green Lancs 86 B4
Rileyhill Staffs 62 C5
Rilla Mill Corn 5 B7
Rillington N Yorks 96 B4
Rimington Lancs 93 E8
Rimpton Som 12 B4
Rimswell E Yorks 91 B7
Rinaston Pembs 44 C4
Ringasta Shetland 175 M5
Ringford Dumfries 106 D3
Ringinglow S Yorks 88 F3
Ringland Norf 68 C4
Ringles Cross E Sus 17 B8
Ringmer E Sus 17 C8
Ringmore Devon 6 E4
Ringorm Moray 159 E6
Ring's End Cambs 66 D3
Ringsfield Suff 69 F7
Ringsfield Corner Suff 69 F7
Ringshall Herts 40 C2
Ringshall Suff 56 D4
Ringshall Stocks Suff 56 D4
Ringstead Norf 80 C3
Ringstead Northants 53 B7
Ringwood Hants 14 D2
Ringwould Kent 31 E7
Rinmore Aberds 150 C3
Rinnigill Orkney 176 G2
Rinsey Corn 2 D4
Riof W Isles 172 E4
Ripe E Sus 18 D2
Ripley Derbys 76 D3
Ripley Hants 14 E2
Ripley N Yorks 95 C5
Ripley Sur 27 D8
Riplingham E Yorks 97 F5
Ripon N Yorks 95 B6
Ripon Cathedral N Yorks 95 B6
Ripon Racecourse N Yorks 95 C6
Rippingale Lincs 65 B7
Ripple Kent 31 E7
Ripple Worcs 50 F3
Ripponden W Yorks 87 C8
Rireavach Highld 162 E4
Risabus Argyll 126 E3
Risbury Hereford 49 D7
Risby Suff 55 C8
Risca = Rhisga Caerph 35 E6
Rise E Yorks 97 E7
Riseden E Sus 18 B3
Risegate Lincs 66 B2
Riseholme Lincs 78 B2
Riseley Beds 53 C8
Riseley Wokingham 26 C5
Rishangles Suff 57 C5
Rishton Lancs 93 F7
Rishworth W Yorks 87 C8
Rising Bridge Lancs 87 B5
Risley Derbys 76 F4
Risley Warr 86 E4
Risplith N Yorks 94 C5
Rispond Highld 167 C6
Rivar Wilts 25 C8
Rivenhall End Essex 42 C4
River Bank Cambs 55 C6
Riverhead Kent 29 D6
Rivington Lancs 86 C4
Roa Island Cumb 92 C2
Roachill Devon 10 B3
Road Green Norf 69 E5
Roade Northants 53 D5
Roadhead Cumb 108 B5
Roadmeetings S Lnrk 121 E8
Roadside Highld 169 C6
Roadside of Catterline Aberds 143 B8
Roadside of Kinneff Aberds 143 B8
Roadwater Som 22 F2
Roag Highld 153 E3
Roath Cardiff 22 B3
Rob Roy and Trossachs Visitor Centre, Callander Stirl 132 D5
Robert Burns Centre, Dumfries Dumfries 107 B6
Roberton Borders 115 C7
Roberton S Lnrk 114 B2
Robertsbridge E Sus 18 C4
Roberttown W Yorks 88 B2
Robeston Cross Pembs 44 E3
Robeston Wathen Pembs 32 C1
Robin Hood W Yorks 88 B4
Robin Hood Doncaster Sheffield Airport S Yorks 89 E7
Robin Hood's Bay N Yorks 103 D7
Roborough Devon 9 C7
Roborough Devon 6 C3
Roby Mers 86 E2
Roby Mill Lancs 86 D3
Rocester Staffs 75 F8
Roch Pembs 44 C3
Roch Gate Pembs 44 C3
Rochdale Gtr Man 87 C6
Roche Corn 4 C4
Rochester Medway 29 C8
Rochester Northumb 116 E4
Rochester Castle Medway 29 C8
Rochester Cathedral Medway 29 C8
Rochford Essex 42 E4
Rock Corn 4 B4
Rock Northumb 117 B8
Rock Worcs 50 B2
Rock W Sus 16 C5
Rock Ferry Mers 85 F4
Rockbeare Devon 10 E5

Rockbourne Hants 14 C2
Rockcliffe Cumb 108 C3
Rockcliffe Dumfries 107 D5
Rockfield Highld 165 F6
Rockfield Mon 36 C1
Rockford Hants 14 D2
Rockhampton S Glos 36 E3
Rockingham Northants 65 E5
Rockingham Motor Speedway Northants 65 E6
Rockland All Saints Norf 68 E2
Rockland St Mary Norf 69 D6
Rockland St Peter Norf 68 E2
Rockley Wilts 25 B6
Rockwell End Bucks 39 F7
Rockwell Green Som 11 B6
Rodborough Glos 37 D5
Rodbourne Thamesdown 37 F8
Rodbourne Wilts 37 F6
Rodbourne Cheney Thamesdown 37 F8
Rodd Hereford 48 C5
Roddam Northumb 117 B6
Rodden Dorset 12 F4
Rode Som 24 D3
Rode Heath Ches 74 D5
Rodeheath Ches 75 C5
Roden Telford 61 C5
Rodhuish Som 22 F2
Rodington Telford 61 C5
Rodley Glos 36 C4
Rodley W Yorks 94 F5
Rodmarton Glos 37 E6
Rodmell E Sus 17 D8
Rodmersham Kent 30 C3
Rodney Stoke Som 23 D6
Rodsley Derbys 76 E2
Rodway Som 22 F4
Rodwell Dorset 12 G4
Roe Green Herts 54 F4
Roecliffe N Yorks 95 C6
Roehampton London 28 B3
Roesound Shetland 174 G5
Roffey W Sus 28 F2
Rogart Highld 164 D4
Rogart Station Highld 164 D4
Rogate W Sus 16 B2
Rogerstone Newport 35 F6
Roghadal W Isles 173 K3
Rogiet Mon 36 F1
Rogue's Alley Cambs 66 D3
Roke Oxon 39 E6
Roker T & W 111 D7
Rollesby Norf 69 C7
Rolleston Leics 64 D4
Rolleston Notts 77 D7
Rolleston-on-Dove Staffs 63 B6
Rolston E Yorks 97 E8
Rolvenden Kent 18 B5
Rolvenden Layne Kent 19 B5
Romaldkirk Durham 100 B4
Roman Baths & Pump Room, Bath Bath 24 C2
Romanby N Yorks 102 E1
Romannobridge Borders 122 E4
Romansleigh Devon 10 B2
Romford London 41 F8
Romiley Gtr Man 87 E7
Romney, Hythe and Dymchurch Light Railway Kent 19 B8
Romsey Hants 14 B4
Romsey Town Cambs 55 D5
Romsley Shrops 61 F7
Romsley Worcs 50 B4
Ronague I o M 84 E2
Rookhope Durham 110 E2
Rookley I o W 15 F6
Rooks Bridge Som 23 D5
Roos E Yorks 97 F8
Roosebeck Cumb 92 C2
Rootham's Green Beds 54 D2
Rootpark S Lnrk 122 D2
Ropley Hants 26 F4
Ropley Dean Hants 26 F4
Ropsley Lincs 78 F2
Rora Aberds 161 C7
Rorandle Aberds 151 C5
Rorrington Shrops 60 D3
Roscroggan Corn 3 B5
Rose Corn 4 D2
Rose Ash Devon 10 B2
Rose Green W Sus 16 E3
Rose Grove Lancs 93 F8
Rose Hill E Sus 17 C8
Rose Hill Lancs 93 F8
Rose Hill Suff 57 E5
Roseacre Kent 29 D8
Roseacre Lancs 92 F4
Rosebank S Lnrk 121 E8
Rosebrough Northumb 117 B7
Rosebush Pembs 32 B1
Rosecare Corn 8 E3
Rosedale Abbey N Yorks 103 E5
Roseden Northumb 117 B6
Rosefield Highld 158 D2
Rosehall Highld 164 D1
Rosehaugh Mains Highld 157 D7
Rosehearty Aberds 161 B6
Rosehill Shrops 74 F3
Roseisle Moray 158 C5
Roselands E Sus 18 E3
Rosemarket Pembs 44 E4
Rosemarkie Highld 157 D8
Rosemary Lane Devon 11 C6
Rosemount Perth 142 E1
Rosenannon Corn 4 C4
Rosewell Midloth 123 C5
Roseworth Stockton 102 B2
Roseworthy Corn 2 C5
Rosgill Cumb 99 C7
Roshven Highld 145 F7
Roskhill Highld 152 E3
Roskill House Highld 157 D7
Rosley Cumb 108 E3
Roslin Midloth 123 C5
Rosliston Derbys 63 C6
Rosneath Argyll 129 B7
Ross Dumfries 106 E3
Ross Northumb 125 F7
Ross Perth 133 B6
Ross-on-Wye Hereford 36 B3
Rossett Wrex 73 D7
Rossett Green N Yorks 95 D6
Rossie Ochill Perth 134 C2
Rossie Priory Perth 142 F2
Rossington S Yorks 89 E7
Rosskeen Highld 157 C7
Rossland Renfs 120 B4
Roster Highld 169 F7
Rostherne Ches 86 F5
Rosthwaite Cumb 98 C4
Roston Derbys 75 E8
Rosyth Fife 134 F3
Rothbury Northumb 117 D6
Rotherby Leics 64 C3
Rotherfield E Sus 18 C2
Rotherfield Greys Oxon 39 F7
Rotherfield Peppard Oxon 39 F7
Rotherham S Yorks 88 E5
Rothersthorpe Northants 52 D5
Rotherwick Hants 26 D5
Rothes Moray 159 E6
Rothesay Argyll 129 D5
Rothiebrisbane Aberds 160 E4
Rothiemurchus Estate Visitor Centre Highld 148 C5
Rothienorman Aberds 160 E4
Rothiesholm Orkney 176 D5
Rothley Leics 64 C2
Rothley Northumb 117 F6
Rothley Shield East Northumb 117 E6
Rothmaise Aberds 160 E3
Rothwell Lincs 91 E5
Rothwell Northants 64 F5
Rothwell W Yorks 88 B4
Rothwell Haigh W Yorks 88 B4
Rotsea E Yorks 97 D6
Rottal Angus 142 C3
Rotten End Suff 57 C7
Rottingdean Brighton 17 D7
Rottington Cumb 98 C1
Rotunda, Folkestone Kent 31 F6
Roud I o W 15 F6
Rough Close Staffs 75 F6
Rough Common Kent 30 D5
Rougham Norf 80 E4
Rougham Suff 56 C3
Rougham Green Suff 56 C3
Roughburn Highld 147 F6
Roughlee Lancs 93 E8
Roughley W Mid 62 E5
Roughsike Cumb 108 B5
Roughton Lincs 78 C5
Roughton Norf 81 D8
Roughton Shrops 61 E7
Roughton Moor Lincs 78 C5
Roundhay W Yorks 95 F6
Roundstonefoot Dumfries 114 D4
Roundstreet Common W Sus 16 B4
Roundway Wilts 24 C5
Rous Lench Worcs 50 D5
Rousdon Devon 11 E7
Routenburn N Ayrs 129 D6
Routh E Yorks 97 E6
Row Corn 5 B5
Row Cumb 99 F6
Row Heath Essex 43 C7
Rowanburn Dumfries 108 B4
Rowardennan Stirl 132 E2
Rowde Wilts 24 C4
Rowen Conwy 83 D7
Rowfoot Northumb 109 C6
Rowhedge Essex 43 B6
Rowhook W Sus 28 F2
Rowington Warks 51 C7
Rowland Derbys 76 B2
Rowlands Castle Hants 15 C8
Rowlands Gill T & W 110 D4
Rowledge Sur 27 E6
Rowley E Yorks 97 F5
Rowley Shrops 60 D3
Rowley Hill W Yorks 88 C2
Rowley Regis W Mid 62 F3
Rowlstone Hereford 35 B7
Rowly Sur 27 E8
Rowney Green Worcs 50 B5
Rownhams Hants 14 C4
Rowrah Cumb 98 C2
Rowsham Bucks 39 C8
Rowsley Derbys 76 C2
Rowstock Oxon 38 F4
Rowston Lincs 78 D3
Rowton Ches 73 C8
Rowton Shrops 60 C3
Rowton Telford 61 C6
Roxburgh Borders 124 F3
Roxby N Lincs 90 C3
Roxby N Yorks 103 C5
Roxton Beds 54 D2
Roxwell Essex 42 D2
Royal Botanic Gardens Edin 122 B5
Royal Leamington Spa Warks 51 C8
Royal Museum of Scotland Edin 122 B5
Royal Oak Darl 101 B7
Royal Oak Lancs 86 D2
Royal Pavilion, Brighton Brighton 17 D7
Royal Tunbridge Wells Kent 18 B2
Royal Welch Fusiliers Regimental Museum (See Caernarfon Castle) Gwyn 82 E4
Royal Worcester Porcelain, Worcester Worcs 50 D3
Roybridge Highld 147 F5
Roydhouse W Yorks 88 C3
Roydon Essex 41 D7
Roydon Norf 80 E3
Roydon Norf 68 F3
Roydon Hamlet Essex 41 D7
Royston Herts 54 E4
Royston S Yorks 88 C4
Royton Gtr Man 87 D7
Rozel Jersey 17
Ruabon = Rhiwabon Wrex 73 E7
Ruaig Argyll 136 F2
Ruan Lanihorne Corn 3 B7
Ruan Minor Corn 3 E6
Ruarach Highld 146 B2
Ruardean Glos 36 C3
Ruardean Woodside Glos 36 C3
Rubery Worcs 50 B4
Ruckcroft Cumb 108 E5
Ruckhall Common Hereford 49 F6
Ruckinge Kent 19 B7
Ruckland Lincs 79 B6
Ruckley Shrops 60 D5
Rudbaxton Pembs 44 C4
Rudby N Yorks 102 D2
Ruddington Notts 77 F5
Rudford Glos 36 B4
Rudge Shrops 62 E2
Rudge Som 24 D3
Rudgeway S Glos 36 F3
Rudgwick W Sus 27 F8
Rudhall Hereford 36 B3
Rudheath Ches 74 B3
Rudley Green Essex 42 D4
Rudry Caerph 35 F5
Rudston E Yorks 97 C6
Rudyard Staffs 75 D6
Rufford Lancs 86 C2
Rufforth York 95 D8
Rugby Warks 52 B3
Rugeley Staffs 62 C4
Ruglen S Ayrs 112 D2
Ruilick Highld 157 E6
Ruishton Som 11 B7
Ruisigearraidh W Isles 173 K2
Ruislip London 40 F3
Ruislip Common London 40 F3
Rumbling Bridge Perth 134 E2
Rumburgh Suff 69 F6
Rumford Corn 4 B3
Rumney Cardiff 22 B4
Runcorn Halton 86 F3
Runcton W Sus 16 D2
Runcton Holme Norf 67 D6
Rundlestone Devon 6 B3
Runfold Sur 27 E6
Runhall Norf 68 D3
Runham Norf 69 D8
Runham Norf 69 C7
Runnington Som 11 B6
Runsell Green Essex 42 D3
Runswick Bay N Yorks 103 C6
Runwell Essex 42 E3
Ruscombe Wokingham 27 B5
Rush Green London 41 F8
Rush-head Aberds 160 D5
Rushall Hereford 49 F8
Rushall Norf 68 F4
Rushall Wilts 25 D6
Rushall W Mid 62 D4
Rushbrooke Suff 56 C2
Rushbury Shrops 60 E5
Rushden Herts 54 F4
Rushden Northants 53 C7
Rushenden Kent 30 B3
Rushford Norf 68 F2
Rushlake Green E Sus 18 D3
Rushmere Suff 69 F7
Rushmere St Andrew Suff 57 E6
Rushmoor Sur 27 E6
Rushock Worcs 50 B3
Rusholme Gtr Man 87 E6
Rushton Ches 74 C2
Rushton Northants 64 F5
Rushton Shrops 61 D6
Rushton Spencer Staffs 75 C6
Rushwick Worcs 50 D3
Rushyford Durham 101 B7
Ruskie Stirl 132 D5
Ruskington Lincs 78 D3
Rusland Cumb 99 F5
Rusper W Sus 28 F3
Ruspidge Glos 36 C3
Russell's Water Oxon 39 F7
Russel's Green Suff 57 B6
Rusthall Kent 18 B2
Rustington W Sus 16 D4
Ruston N Yorks 103 F7
Ruston Parva E Yorks 97 C6
Ruswarp N Yorks 103 D6
Rutherford Borders 124 F2
Rutherglen S Lnrk 121 C6
Ruthernbridge Corn 4 C5
Ruthin = Rhuthun Denb 72 D5
Ruthin Craft Centre Denb 72 D5
Ruthrieston Aberdeen 151 D8
Ruthven Aberds 160 D2
Ruthven Angus 142 E2
Ruthven Highld 158 F2
Ruthven Highld 148 E3
Ruthven House Angus 142 E3
Ruthvoes Corn 4 C4
Ruthwell Dumfries 107 C7
Ruyton-XI-Towns Shrops 60 B3
Ryal Northumb 110 B3
Ryal Fold Blkburn 86 B4
Ryall Dorset 12 E2
Ryarsh Kent 29 D7
Rydal Cumb 99 D5
Ryde I o W 15 E6
Rye E Sus 19 C6
Rye Foreign E Sus 19 C5
Rye Harbour E Sus 19 D6
Rye Park Herts 41 C6
Rye Street Worcs 50 F2
Ryecroft Gate Staffs 75 C6
Ryehill E Yorks 91 B6
Ryhall Rutland 65 C7
Ryhill W Yorks 88 C4
Ryhope T & W 111 D7
Rylstone N Yorks 94 D2
Ryme Intrinseca Dorset 12 C3
Ryther N Yorks 95 F8
Ryton Glos 50 F2
Ryton N Yorks 96 B3
Ryton Shrops 61 D7
Ryton T & W 110 C4
Ryton-on-Dunsmore Warks 51 B8

S

Sabden Lancs 93 F7
Sacombe Herts 41 C6
Sacriston Durham 110 E5
Sadberge Darl 101 C8
Saddell Argyll 118 C4
Saddington Leics 64 E3
Saddle Bow Norf 67 C6
Saddlescombe W Sus 17 C6
Sadgill Cumb 99 D6
Saffron Walden Essex 55 F6
Sageston Pembs 32 D1
Saham Hills Norf 68 D2
Saham Toney Norf 68 D2
Saighdinis W Isles 170 D4
Saighton Ches 73 C8
St Abbs Borders 124 C5
St Abb's Haven Borders 124 C5
St Agnes Corn 4 D2
St Agnes Scilly 2 F3
St Albans Herts 40 D4
St Alban's Abbey Herts 40 D4
St Allen Corn 4 D3
St Andrews Fife 135 C7
St Andrew's Major V Glam 22 B3
St Anne Ald 16
St Annes Lancs 85 B4
St Ann's Dumfries 114 E3
St Ann's Chapel Corn 6 B2
St Ann's Chapel Devon 6 E4
St Anthony Corn 3 D6
St Anthony's Hill E Sus 18 E3
St Arvans Mon 36 E2
St Asaph = Llanelwy Denb 72 B4
St Athan V Glam 22 C2
St Aubin Jersey 17
St Austell Corn 4 D5
St Bees Cumb 98 C1
St Blazey Corn 5 D5
St Boswells Borders 123 F8
St Brelade Jersey 17
St Breock Corn 4 B4
St Breward Corn 5 B5
St Briavels Glos 36 D2
St Bride's Pembs 44 D3
St Brides Major V Glam 21 B7
St Bride's Netherwent Mon 35 F8
St Brides super Ely V Glam 22 B2
St Brides Wentlooge Newport 35 F6
St Budeaux Plym 6 D2
St Buryan Corn 2 D3
St Catherine Bath 24 B2
St Catherine's Argyll 131 E7
St Clears = Sanclêr Carms 32 C3
St Cleer Corn 5 C7
St Clement Corn 3 B7
St Clements Jersey 17
St Clement's Caves, Hastings E Sus 18 D5
St Clether Corn 8 F4
St Colmac Argyll 129 D5
St Columb Major Corn 4 C4
St Columb Minor Corn 4 C3
St Columb Road Corn 4 D4
St Combs Aberds 161 B7
St Cross South Elmham Suff 69 F5
St Cyrus Aberds 143 C7
St David's Perth 133 B8
St David's = Tyddewi Pembs 44 C2
St Day Corn 3 B6
St Dennis Corn 4 D4
St Devereux Hereford 49 F6
St Dogmaels Pembs 45 E3
St Dogwells Pembs 44 C4
St Dominick Corn 6 C2
St Donat's V Glam 21 C8
St Edith's Wilts 24 C4
St Endellion Corn 4 B4
St Enoder Corn 4 D3
St Erme Corn 4 D3
St Erney Corn 5 D8
St Erth Corn 2 C4
St Ervan Corn 4 B3
St Eval Corn 4 C3
St Ewe Corn 3 B8
St Fagans Cardiff 22 B3
St Fagans Museum of Welsh Life Cardiff 22 B3
St Fergus Aberds 161 C7
St Fillans Perth 133 B5
St Florence Pembs 32 D1
St Genny's Corn 8 E3
St George Conwy 72 B3
St George's V Glam 22 B2
St Germans Corn 5 D8
St Giles Lincs 78 B2
St Giles Cathedral Edin 122 B5
St Giles in the Wood Devon 9 C7
St Giles on the Heath Devon 9 E5
St Harmon Powys 47 B8
St Helen Auckland Durham 101 B6
St Helena Warks 63 D6
St Helen's E Sus 18 D5
St Helens I o W 15 F7
St Helens Mers 86 E3
St Helier London 28 C3
St Helier Jersey 17
St Hilary Corn 2 C4
St Hilary V Glam 22 B2
Saint Hill W Sus 28 F4
St Illtyd Bl Gwent 35 D6
St Ippollitts Herts 40 B4
St Ishmael's Pembs 44 E3
St Issey Corn 4 B4
St Ive Corn 5 C8
St Ives Cambs 54 B4
St Ives Corn 2 B4
St Ives Dorset 14 D2
St James South Elmham Suff 69 F6
St Jidgey Corn 4 C4
St John Corn 6 D2
St John's I o M 84 D2
St John's Jersey 17
St John's Sur 27 D7
St John's Worcs 50 D3
St John's Chapel Durham 109 F8
St John's Fen End Norf 66 C5
St John's Highway Norf 66 C5
St John's Town of Dalry Dumfries 113 F6
St Judes I o M 84 C3
St Just Corn 2 C2
St Just in Roseland Corn 3 C7
St Just In Roseland Corn 4 F3
St Katherine's Aberds 160 E4
St Keverne Corn 3 D6
St Kew Corn 4 B5
St Kew Highway Corn 4 B5
St Keyne Corn 5 C7
St Lawrence Corn 4 C5
St Lawrence Essex 43 D5
St Lawrence I o W 15 G6
St Leonard's Bucks 40 D2
St Leonards Dorset 14 D2
St Leonards E Sus 18 E4
Saint Leonards S Lnrk 121 D6
St Levan Corn 2 D2
St Lythans V Glam 22 B3
St Mabyn Corn 4 B5
St Madoes Perth 134 B3
St Margaret South Elmham Suff 69 F6
St Margaret's Hereford 49 F5
St Margarets Herts 41 C6
St Margaret's at Cliffe Kent 31 E7
St Margaret's Hope Orkney 176 G3
St Mark's I o M 84 E2
St Martin Corn 5 D7
St Martins Corn 3 D6
St Martin's Jersey 17
St Martins Perth 142 F1
St Martin's Shrops 73 F7
St Mary Bourne Hants 26 D2
St Mary Church V Glam 22 B2
St Mary Cray London 29 C5
St Mary Hill V Glam 21 B8
St Mary Hoo Medway 30 B2
St Mary in the Marsh Kent 19 C7
St Mary's Jersey 17
St Mary's Orkney 176 F3
St Mary's Bay Kent 19 C7
St Mary's Church Warks 51 C7
St Maughans Mon 36 C1
St Mawes Corn 3 C7
St Mawgan Corn 4 C3
St Mellion Corn 5 C8
St Mellons Cardiff 35 F6
St Merryn Corn 4 B3
St Mewan Corn 4 D4
St Michael Caerhays Corn 3 B8
St Michael Penkevil Corn 3 B7
St Michael South Elmham Suff 69 F6
St Michael's Kent 19 B5
St Michaels Worcs 49 C7
St Michael's Mount, Penzance Corn 2 D4
St Michael's on Wyre Lancs 92 E4
St Minver Corn 4 B4
St Monans Fife 135 D7
St Neot Corn 5 C6
St Neots Cambs 54 C2
St Newlyn East Corn 4 D3
St Nicholas Pembs 44 B3
St Nicholas V Glam 22 B2
St Nicholas at Wade Kent 31 C6
St Ninians Stirl 133 E6
St Osyth Essex 43 C7
St Osyth Heath Essex 43 C7
St Ouens Jersey 17
St Owens Cross Hereford 36 B2
St Paul's Cathedral London 41 F6
St Paul's Cray London 29 C5
St Paul's Walden Herts 40 B4
St Peter Port Guern 16
St Peter's Jersey 17
St Peter's Kent 31 C7
St Petrox Pembs 44 F4
St Pinnock Corn 5 C7
St Quivox S Ayrs 112 B3
St Ruan Corn 3 E6
St Sampson Guern 16
St Stephen Corn 4 D4
St Stephen's Corn 8 F5
St Stephens Corn 6 D2
St Stephens Herts 40 D4
St Teath Corn 8 F2
St Thomas Devon 10 E4
St Tudy Corn 5 B5
St Twynnells Pembs 44 F4
St Veep Corn 5 D6
St Vigeans Angus 143 E6
St Wenn Corn 4 C4
St Weonards Hereford 36 B1
Saintbury Glos 51 F6
Salcombe Devon 6 F5
Salcombe Regis Devon 11 F6
Salcott Essex 43 C5
Sale Gtr Man 87 E5
Sale Green Worcs 50 D4
Saleby Lincs 79 B7
Salehurst E Sus 18 C4
Salem Ceredig 58 F3
Salem Carms 33 B7
Salen Argyll 137 D6
Salen Highld 137 B7
Salesbury Lancs 93 F6
Salford Beds 53 F7
Salford Gtr Man 87 E6
Salford Oxon 38 B2
Salford Priors Warks 51 D5
Salfords Sur 28 E3
Salhouse Norf 69 C6
Saline Fife 134 E2
Salisbury Wilts 14 B2
Salisbury Cathedral Wilts 14 B2
Salisbury Racecourse Wilts 13 B8
Sallachan Highld 138 C3
Sallachy Highld 155 G5
Sallachy Highld 164 D2
Salle Norf 81 E7
Salmonby Lincs 79 B6
Salmond's Muir Angus 143 F5
Salperton Glos 37 B7
Salph End Beds 53 D8
Salsburgh N Lnrk 121 C8
Salt Staffs 62 B3
Salt End E Yorks 91 B5
Saltaire W Yorks 94 F4
Saltaire 1853 Gallery W Yorks 94 F4
Saltash Corn 6 D2
Saltburn Highld 157 C8
Saltburn-by-the-Sea Redcar 102 B4
Saltby Leics 65 B5
Saltcoats Cumb 98 E2
Saltcoats N Ayrs 120 E2
Saltdean Brighton 17 D7
Salter Lancs 93 C6
Salterforth Lancs 93 E8
Salterswall Ches 74 C3
Saltfleet Lincs 91 E8
Saltfleetby All Saints Lincs 91 E8
Saltfleetby St Clements Lincs 91 E8
Saltfleetby St Peter Lincs 91 F8
Saltford Bath 23 C8
Salthouse Norf 81 C6
Saltmarshe E Yorks 89 B8
Saltney Flint 73 C7
Salton N Yorks 96 B3
Saltwick Northumb 110 B4
Saltwood Kent 19 B8
Salum Argyll 136 F2
Salvington W Sus 16 D5
Salwarpe Worcs 50 C3
Salwayash Dorset 12 E2
Sambourne Warks 51 C5
Sambrook Telford 61 B7
Samhla W Isles 170 D3
Samlesbury Lancs 93 F5
Samlesbury Bottoms Lancs 86 B4
Sammy Miller's Motorcycle Museum Hants 14 E3
Sampford Arundel Som 11 C6
Sampford Brett Som 22 E2
Sampford Courtenay Devon 9 D8
Sampford Peverell Devon 10 C5
Sampford Spiney Devon 6 B3
Sampool Bridge Cumb 99 F6
Samuelston E Loth 123 B7
Sanachan Highld 155 F4
Sanaigmore Argyll 126 B2
Sanclêr = St Clears Carms 32 C3
Sancreed Corn 2 D3
Sancton E Yorks 96 F5
Sand Highld 162 E3
Sand Shetland 175 J5
Sand Hole E Yorks 96 F4
Sand Hutton N Yorks 96 D2
Sandaig Highld 145 C7
Sandal Magna W Yorks 88 C4
Sandale Cumb 108 E2
Sanday Airport Orkney 176 B5
Sandbach Ches 74 C4
Sandbank Argyll 129 B6
Sandbanks Poole 13 F8
Sandend Aberds 160 B2
Sanderstead London 28 C4
Sandfields Glos 37 B6
Sandford Cumb 100 C2
Sandford Devon 10 D3
Sandford Dorset 13 F7
Sandford I o W 15 F6
Sandford N Som 23 D6
Sandford Shrops 74 F2
Sandford S Lnrk 121 E7
Sandford on Thames Oxon 39 D5
Sandford Orcas Dorset 12 B4
Sandford St Martin Oxon 38 B4
Sandfordhill Aberds 161 D8
Sandgate Kent 19 B8
Sandgreen Dumfries 106 D2
Sandhaven Aberds 161 B6
Sandhead Dumfries 104 E4
Sandhills Sur 27 F7
Sandhoe Northumb 110 C2
Sandholme E Yorks 96 F4
Sandholme Lincs 79 F6
Sandhurst Brack 27 C6
Sandhurst Glos 37 B5
Sandhurst Kent 18 C4
Sandhurst Cross Kent 18 C4
Sandhutton N Yorks 102 F1
Sandiacre Derbys 76 F4
Sandilands Lincs 91 F9
Sandilands S Lnrk 121 F8
Sandiway Ches 74 B3
Sandleheath Hants 14 C2
Sandling Kent 29 D8
Sandlow Green Ches 74 C4
Sandness Shetland 175 H3
Sandon Essex 42 D3
Sandon Herts 54 F4
Sandon Staffs 75 F6
Sandown I o W 15 F6
Sandown Park Racecourse Sur 28 C2
Sandplace Corn 5 D7
Sandridge Herts 40 C4
Sandridge Wilts 24 C4
Sandringham Norf 67 B6
Sandsend N Yorks 103 C6
Sandside Ho. Highld 168 C4
Sandsound Shetland 175 J5
Sandtoft N Lincs 89 D8
Sandway Kent 30 D2
Sandwell W Mid 62 F4
Sandwich Kent 31 D7
Sandwick Cumb 99 C6
Sandwick Orkney 176 H3
Sandwick Shetland 175 L6
Sandwith Cumb 98 C1
Sandy Beds 54 E2
Sandy Carms 33 D5
Sandy Bank Lincs 79 D5
Sandy Haven Pembs 44 E3
Sandy Lane Wilts 24 C4
Sandy Lane Wrex 73 E7
Sandycroft Flint 73 C7
Sandyford Dumfries 114 E5
Sandyford Stoke 75 D5
Sandygate I o M 84 C3
Sandyhills Dumfries 107 D5
Sandylands Lancs 92 C4
Sandypark Devon 10 F2
Sandysike Cumb 108 C3
Sangobeg Highld 167 C6
Sangomore Highld 167 C6
Sanna Highld 137 B5
Sanndabhaig W Isles 172 E7
Sanndabhaig W Isles 170 F4
Sannox N Ayrs 119 B7
Sanquhar Dumfries 113 D7
Santa Pod Raceway Beds 53 C7
Santon N Lincs 90 C3
Santon Bridge Cumb 98 D3
Santon Downham Suff 67 F8
Sapcote Leics 63 E8
Sapey Common Hereford 50 C2
Sapiston Suff 56 B3
Sapley Cambs 54 B3
Sapperton Glos 37 D6
Sapperton Lincs 78 F3
Saracen's Head Lincs 66 B3
Sarclet Highld 169 E8
Sardis Carms 33 D6
Sarn Bridgend 34 F3
Sarn Powys 60 E2
Sarn Bach Gwyn 70 E4
Sarn Meyllteyrn Gwyn 70 D3
Sarnau Ceredig 46 D2
Sarnau Carms 32 C4
Sarnau Gwyn 72 F3
Sarnau Powys 48 F2
Sarnau Powys 60 C2
Sarnesfield Hereford 49 D5
Saron Carms 46 F2
Saron Carms 33 C7
Saron Denb 72 C4
Saron Gwyn 82 F4
Saron Gwyn 82 E5
Sarratt Herts 40 E3
Sarre Kent 31 C6
Sarsden Oxon 38 B2
Sarsgrum Highld 167 C5
Satley Durham 110 E4
Satron N Yorks 100 E4
Satterleigh Devon 9 B8
Satterthwaite Cumb 99 E5
Satwell Oxon 39 F7
Sauchen Aberds 151 C5
Saucher Perth 142 F1
Sauchie Clack 133 E7
Sauchieburn Aberds 143 C6
Saughall Ches 73 B7
Saughtree Borders 115 E8
Saul Glos 36 D4
Saundby Notts 89 F8
Saundersfoot Pembs 32 D2
Saunderton Bucks 39 D7
Saunton Devon 20 F3
Sausthorpe Lincs 79 C6
Saval Highld 164 D2
Savary Highld 137 D7
Savile Park W Yorks 87 B8
Sawbridge Warks 52 C3
Sawbridgeworth Herts 41 C7
Sawdon N Yorks 103 F7
Sawley Derbys 76 F4
Sawley Lancs 93 E7
Sawley N Yorks 94 C5
Sawston Cambs 55 E5
Sawtry Cambs 65 F8
Saxby Leics 64 C5
Saxby Lincs 90 F4
Saxby All Saints N Lincs 90 C3
Saxelbye Leics 64 B4
Saxham Street Suff 56 C4
Saxilby Lincs 77 B8
Saxlingham Norf 81 D6
Saxlingham Green Norf 68 E5
Saxlingham Nethergate Norf 68 E5
Saxlingham Thorpe Norf 68 E5
Saxmundham Suff 57 C7
Saxon Street Cambs 55 D7
Saxondale Notts 77 F6
Saxtead Suff 57 C6
Saxtead Green Suff 57 C6
Saxthorpe Norf 81 D7
Saxton N Yorks 95 F7
Sayers Common W Sus 17 C6
Scackleton N Yorks 96 B2
Scadabhagh W Isles 173 J4
Scaftworth Notts 89 E7
Scagglethorpe N Yorks 96 B4
Scaitcliffe Lancs 87 B5
Scalasaig Argyll 127 C1
Scalby E Yorks 90 B2
Scalby N Yorks 103 E8
Scaldwell Northants 53 B5
Scale Houses Cumb 109 E5
Scaleby Cumb 108 C4
Scaleby Hill Cumb 108 C4
Scales Cumb 92 B2
Scales Cumb 99 B5
Scales Lancs 92 F4
Scalford Leics 64 B4
Scaling N Yorks 103 C5
Scallastle Argyll 130 B2
Scalloway Shetland 175 K6
Scalpay W Isles 173 J5
Scalpay Ho. Highld 155 H2
Scalpsie Argyll 129 E5
Scamadale Highld 145 D7
Scamblesby Lincs 79 B5
Scamodale Highld 138 B2
Scampston N Yorks 96 B4
Scampton Lincs 78 B2
Scapa Orkney 176 F3
Scapegoat Hill W Yorks 87 C8
Scar Orkney 176 B5
Scarborough N Yorks 103 F8
Scarborough Sea Life Centre N Yorks 103 E8
Scarcliffe Derbys 76 C4
Scarcroft W Yorks 95 E6
Scarcroft Hill W Yorks 95 E6
Scardroy Highld 156 D3
Scarff Shetland 174 E4
Scarfskerry Highld 169 B7
Scargill Durham 101 C5
Scarinish Argyll 136 F2
Scarisbrick Lancs 85 C4
Scarning Norf 68 C2
Scarrington Notts 77 E7
Scartho NE Lincs 91 D6
Scarwell Orkney 176 D1
Scatness Shetland 175 M5
Scatraig Highld 157 F8
Scawby N Lincs 90 D3
Scawsby S Yorks 89 D6
Scawton N Yorks 102 F3
Scayne's Hill W Sus 17 B7
Scethrog Powys 35 B5
Scholar Green Ches 74 D5
Scholes W Yorks 88 D2
Scholes W Yorks 88 B2
Scholes W Yorks 95 F6
School Green Ches 74 C3
Science & Industry Museum, Manchester Gtr Man 87 E6
Science Centre Glasgow 121 C5
Science Museum London 28 B3
Scleddau Pembs 44 B4
Sco Ruston Norf 81 E8
Scofton Notts 89 F7
Scole Norf 56 B5
Scolpaig W Isles 170 C3
Scone Perth 134 B3
Scone Palace, Perth Perth 134 B3

Sconser Highld 153 F6
Scoonie Fife 135 D5
Scoor Argyll 137 G5
Scopwick Lincs 78 D3
Scoraig Highld 162 E4
Scorborough E Yorks 97 E6
Scorrier Corn 3 B6
Scorton Lancs 92 E5
Scorton N Yorks 101 D7
Scotbheinn W Isles 170 E4
Scotby Cumb 108 D4
Scotch Corner N Yorks 101 D7
Scotforth Lancs 92 D4
Scothern Lincs 78 B3
Scotland Gate Northumb 117 F8
Scotlandwell Perth 134 D3
Scotney Castle Garden Kent 18 B3
Scotsburn Highld 157 B8
Scotscalder Station Highld 169 D5
Scotscraig Fife 135 B6
Scots'Gap Northumb 117 F6
Scotston Aberds 143 B7
Scotston Perth 141 E6
Scotstoun Glasgow 120 C5
Scotstown Highld 138 C2
Scotswood T & W 110 C4
Scottas Highld 145 C7
Scotter Lincs 90 D2
Scotterthorpe Lincs 90 D2
Scottlethorpe Lincs 65 B7
Scotton Lincs 90 E2
Scotton N Yorks 101 E6
Scotton N Yorks 95 D6
Scottow Norf 81 E8
Scoughall E Loth 135 F8
Scoulag Argyll 129 E6
Scoulton Norf 68 D2
Scourie Highld 166 E3
Scourie More Highld 166 E3
Scousburgh Shetland 175 M5
Scrabster Highld 169 B5
Scrafield Lincs 79 C6
Scrainwood Northumb 117 D5
Scrane End Lincs 79 E6
Scraptoft Leics 64 D3
Scratby Norf 69 C8
Scrayingham N Yorks 96 C3
Scredington Lincs 78 E3
Scremby Lincs 79 C7
Scremerston Northumb 125 E6
Screveton Notts 77 E7
Scrivelsby Lincs 79 C5
Scriven N Yorks 95 D6
Scrooby Notts 89 E7
Scropton Derbys 75 F8
Scrub Hill Lincs 78 D5
Scruton N Yorks 101 E7
Sculcoates Hull 97 F6
Sculthorpe Norf 80 D4
Scunthorpe N Lincs 90 C2
Scurlage Swansea 33 F5
Sea Palling Norf 69 B7
Sea Zoo Anglesey 82 E4
Seaborough Dorset 12 D2
Seacombe Mers 85 E4
Seacroft Lincs 79 C8
Seacroft W Yorks 95 F6
Seadyke Lincs 79 F6
Seafield S Ayrs 112 B3
Seafield W Loth 122 C3
Seaford E Sus 17 E8
Seaforth Mers 85 E4
Seagrave Leics 64 C3
Seaham Durham 111 E7
Seahouses Northumb 125 F8
Seal Kent 29 D6
Sealand Flint 73 C7
Seale Sur 27 E6
Seamer N Yorks 102 C2
Seamer N Yorks 103 F8
Seamill N Ayrs 120 E2
Searby Lincs 90 D4
Seasalter Kent 30 C4
Seascale Cumb 98 D2
Seathorne Lincs 79 C8
Seathwaite Cumb 98 E4
Seathwaite Cumb 98 C4
Seatoller Cumb 98 C4
Seaton Corn 5 D8
Seaton Cumb 107 F7
Seaton Devon 11 F7
Seaton Durham 111 D6
Seaton E Yorks 97 E7
Seaton Northumb 111 B6
Seaton Rutland 65 E6
Seaton Burn T & W 110 B5
Seaton Carew Hrtlpl 102 B3
Seaton Delaval Northumb 111 B6
Seaton Ross E Yorks 96 E3
Seaton Sluice Northumb 111 B6
Seatown Aberds 160 B2
Seatown Dorset 12 E2
Seave Green N Yorks 102 D3
Seaview I o W 15 E7
Seaville Cumb 107 D8
Seavington St Mary Som 12 C2
Seavington St Michael Som 12 C2
Sebergham Cumb 108 E3
Seckington Warks 63 D6
Second Coast Highld 162 E3
Sedbergh Cumb 100 E1
Sedbury Glos 36 E2
Sedbusk N Yorks 100 E3
Sedgeberrow Worcs 50 F5
Sedgebrook Lincs 77 F8
Sedgefield Durham 102 B1
Sedgefield Racecourse Durham 101 B8
Sedgeford Norf 80 D3
Sedgehill Wilts 13 B6
Sedgley W Mid 62 E3
Sedgwick Cumb 99 F7
Sedlescombe E Sus 18 D4
Sedlescombe Street E Sus 18 D4
Seend Wilts 24 C4
Seend Cleeve Wilts 24 C4
Seer Green Bucks 40 E2
Seething Norf 69 E6
Sefton Mers 85 D4
Seghill Northumb 111 B5
Seifton Shrops 60 F4
Seighford Staffs 62 B2
Seilebost W Isles 173 J3
Seion Gwyn 82 E5
Seisdon Staffs 62 E2
Seisiadar W Isles 172 E8
Selattyn Shrops 73 F6
Selborne Hants 26 F5
Selby N Yorks 96 F2
Selham W Sus 16 B3
Selhurst London 28 C4
Selkirk Borders 115 B7
Selkirk Glass Borders 115 B7
Sellack Hereford 36 B2
Sellafirth Shetland 174 D7
Sellibister Orkney 176 B6
Sellindge Kent 19 B7
Sellindge Lees Kent 19 B8
Selling Kent 30 D4
Sells Green Wilts 24 C4
Selly Oak W Mid 62 F4
Selmeston E Sus 18 E2
Selsdon London 28 C4
Selsey W Sus 16 E2
Selsfield Common W Sus 28 F4
Selsted Kent 31 E6
Selston Notts 76 D4
Selworthy Som 21 E8
Semblister Shetland 175 H5
Semer Suff 56 E3
Semington Wilts 24 C3
Semley Wilts 13 B6
Send Sur 27 D8
Send Marsh Sur 27 D8
Senghenydd Caerph 35 E5
Sennen Corn 2 D2
Sennen Cove Corn 2 D2
Sennybridge = Pont Senni Powys 34 B3
Serlby Notts 89 F7
Sessay N Yorks 95 B7
Setchey Norf 67 C6
Setley Hants 14 D4
Setter Shetland 175 H5
Setter Shetland 174 E6
Setter Shetland 175 J7
Settiscarth Orkney 176 E2
Settle N Yorks 93 C8
Settrington N Yorks 96 B4
Seven Kings London 41 F7
Seven Sisters Neath 34 D2
Sevenhampton Glos 37 B7
Sevenoaks Kent 29 D6
Sevenoaks Weald Kent 29 D6
Severn Beach S Glos 36 F2
Severn Bridges Visitor Centre S Glos 36 F2
Severn Stoke Worcs 50 E3
Severn Valley Railway Worcs 50 B2
Severnhampton Thamesdown 38 E2
Sevington Kent 30 E4
Sewards End Essex 55 F6
Sewardstone Essex 41 E6
Sewardstonebury Essex 41 E6
Sewerby E Yorks 97 C7
Sewerby Hall and Gardens, Bridlington E Yorks 97 C8
Seworgan Corn 3 C6
Sewstern Leics 65 B5
Sezincote Glos 51 F6
Sgarasta Mhor W Isles 173 J3
Sgiogarstaigh W Isles 172 B8
Shabbington Bucks 39 D6
Shackerstone Leics 63 D7
Shackleford Sur 27 E7
Shade W Yorks 87 B7
Shadforth Durham 111 E6
Shadingfield Suff 69 F7
Shadoxhurst Kent 19 B6
Shadsworth Blkburn 86 B5
Shadwell Norf 68 F2
Shadwell W Yorks 95 F6
Shaftesbury Dorset 13 B6
Shafton S Yorks 88 C4
Shakespeare's Birthplace, Stratford-upon-Avon Warks 51 D6
Shalbourne Wilts 25 C8
Shalcombe I o W 14 F4
Shalden Hants 26 E4
Shaldon Devon 7 B7
Shalfleet I o W 14 F5
Shalford Essex 42 B3
Shalford Sur 27 E8
Shalford Green Essex 42 B3
Shallowford Devon 21 E6
Shalmsford Street Kent 30 D4
Shalstone Bucks 52 F4
Shamley Green Sur 27 E8
Shandon Argyll 129 B7
Shandwick Highld 158 B2
Shangton Leics 64 E4
Shankhouse Northumb 111 B5
Shanklin I o W 15 F6
Shanklin Chine I o W 15 F6
Shanquhar Aberds 160 E2
Shanzie Perth 142 D2
Shap Cumb 99 C7
Shapwick Dorset 13 D7
Shapwick Som 23 F6
Shardlow Derbys 76 F4
Shareshill Staffs 62 D3
Sharlston W Yorks 88 C4
Sharlston Common W Yorks 88 C4
Sharnbrook Beds 53 D7
Sharnford Leics 63 E8
Sharoe Green Lancs 92 F5
Sharow N Yorks 95 B6
Sharp Street Norf 69 B6
Sharpenhoe Beds 53 F8
Sharperton Northumb 117 D5
Sharpness Glos 36 D3
Sharpthorne W Sus 28 F4
Sharrington Norf 81 D6
Shatterford Worcs 61 F7
Shaugh Prior Devon 6 C3
Shavington Ches 74 D4
Shaw Gtr Man 87 D7
Shaw W Berks 26 C2
Shaw Wilts 24 C3
Shaw Green Lancs 86 C3
Shaw Mills N Yorks 95 C5
Shawbury Shrops 61 B5
Shawdon Hall Northumb 117 C6
Shawell Leics 64 F2
Shawford Hants 15 B5
Shawforth Lancs 87 B6
Shawhead Dumfries 107 B5
Shawhill Dumfries 108 C2
Shawton S Lnrk 121 E6
Shawtonhill S Lnrk 121 E6
Shear Cross Wilts 24 E3
Shearington Dumfries 107 C7
Shearsby Leics 64 E3
Shebbear Devon 9 D6
Shebdon Staffs 61 B7
Shebster Highld 168 C5
Sheddens E Renf 121 D5
Shedfield Hants 15 C6
Sheen Staffs 75 C8
Sheepscar W Yorks 95 F6
Sheepscombe Glos 37 C5
Sheepstor Devon 6 C3
Sheepwash Devon 9 D6
Sheepway N Som 23 B6
Sheepy Magna Leics 63 D7
Sheepy Parva Leics 63 D7
Sheering Essex 41 C8
Sheerness Kent 30 B3
Sheet Hants 15 B8
Sheffield S Yorks 88 F4
Sheffield Bottom W Berks 26 C4
Sheffield Green E Sus 17 B8
Sheffield Park, Uckfield E Sus 17 B8
Shefford Beds 54 F2
Shefford Woodlands W Berks 25 B8
Sheigra Highld 166 C3
Sheinton Shrops 61 D6
Shelderton Shrops 49 B6
Sheldon Derbys 75 C8
Sheldon Devon 11 D6
Sheldon W Mid 63 F5
Sheldwich Kent 30 D4
Shelf W Yorks 88 B2
Shelfanger Norf 68 F4
Shelfield Warks 51 C6
Shelfield W Mid 62 D4
Shelford Notts 77 E6
Shellacres Northumb 124 E4
Shelley Essex 42 D1
Shelley Suff 56 F4
Shelley W Yorks 88 C3
Shellingford Oxon 38 E3
Shellow Bowells Essex 42 D2
Shelsley Beauchamp Worcs 50 C2
Shelsley Walsh Worcs 50 C2
Shelthorpe Leics 64 C2
Shelton Beds 53 C8
Shelton Norf 68 E5
Shelton Notts 77 E7
Shelton Shrops 60 C4
Shelton Green Norf 68 E5
Shelve Shrops 60 E3
Shelwick Hereford 49 E7
Shenfield Essex 42 E2
Shenington Oxon 51 E8
Shenley Herts 40 D4
Shenley Brook End M Keynes 53 F6
Shenley Church End M Keynes 53 F6
Shenleybury Herts 40 D4
Shenmore Hereford 49 F5
Shennanton Dumfries 105 C7
Shenstone Staffs 62 D5
Shenstone Worcs 50 B3
Shenton Leics 63 D7
Shenval Highld 147 B7
Shenval Moray 149 B8
Shepeau Stow Lincs 66 C3
Shephall Herts 41 B5
Shepherd's Green Oxon 39 F7
Shepherd's Port Norf 80 D2
Shepherdswell Kent 31 E6
Shepley W Yorks 88 D2
Shepperdine S Glos 36 E3
Shepperton Sur 27 C8
Shepreth Cambs 54 E4
Shepshed Leics 63 C8
Shepton Beauchamp Som 12 C2
Shepton Mallet Som 23 E8
Shepton Montague Som 23 F8
Shepway Kent 29 D8
Sheraton Durham 111 F7
Sherborne Dorset 12 C4
Sherborne Glos 38 C1
Sherborne St John Hants 26 D4
Sherbourne Warks 51 C7
Sherburn Durham 111 E6
Sherburn N Yorks 97 B5
Sherburn Hill Durham 111 E6
Sherburn in Elmet N Yorks 95 F7
Shere Sur 27 E8
Shereford Norf 80 E4
Sherfield English Hants 14 B3
Sherfield on Loddon Hants 26 D4
Sherford Devon 7 E5
Sheriff Hutton N Yorks 96 C2
Sheriffhales Shrops 61 C7
Sheringham Norf 81 C7
Sherington M Keynes 53 E6
Shernal Green Worcs 50 C4
Shernborne Norf 80 D3
Sherrington Wilts 24 F4
Sherston Wilts 37 F5
Sherwood Green Devon 9 B7
Shettleston Glasgow 121 C6
Shevington Gtr Man 86 D3
Shevington Moor Gtr Man 86 C3
Shevington Vale Gtr Man 86 D3
Sheviock Corn 5 D8
Shide I o W 15 F5
Shiel Bridge Highld 146 C2
Shieldaig Highld 155 E4
Shieldaig Highld 154 C4
Shieldhill Dumfries 114 F3
Shieldhill Falk 121 B8
Shieldhill S Lnrk 122 E3
Shielfoot Highld 137 B7
Shielhill Angus 142 D4
Shielhill Invclyd 129 C7
Shifford Oxon 38 D3
Shifnal Shrops 61 D7
Shilbottle Northumb 117 D7
Shildon Durham 101 B7
Shillingford Devon 10 B4
Shillingford Oxon 39 E5
Shillingford St George Devon 10 F4
Shillingstone Dorset 13 C6
Shillington Beds 54 F2
Shillmoor Northumb 116 D4
Shilton Oxon 38 D2
Shilton Warks 63 F8
Shilvington Northumb 117 F7
Shimpling Norf 68 F4
Shimpling Suff 56 D2
Shimpling Street Suff 56 D2
Shincliffe Durham 111 E5
Shiney Row T & W 111 D6
Shinfield Wokingham 26 C5
Shingham Norf 67 D7
Shingle Street Suff 57 E7
Shinner's Bridge Devon 7 C5
Shinness Highld 164 C2
Shipbourne Kent 29 D6
Shipdham Norf 68 D2
Shipham Som 23 D6
Shiphay Torbay 7 C6
Shiplake Oxon 27 B5
Shipley Derbys 76 E4
Shipley Northumb 117 C7
Shipley Shrops 62 E2
Shipley W Sus 16 B5
Shipley W Yorks 94 F4
Shipley Shiels Northumb 116 E3
Shipmeadow Suff 69 F6
Shippea Hill Station Cambs 67 F6
Shippon Oxon 38 E4
Shipston-on-Stour Warks 51 E7
Shipton Glos 37 C7
Shipton N Yorks 95 D8
Shipton Shrops 61 E5
Shipton Bellinger Hants 25 E7
Shipton Gorge Dorset 12 E2
Shipton Green W Sus 16 D2
Shipton Moyne Glos 37 F5
Shipton on Cherwell Oxon 38 C4
Shipton Solers Glos 37 C7
Shipton-under-Wychwood Oxon 38 C2
Shiptonthorpe E Yorks 96 E4
Shirburn Oxon 39 E6
Shirdley Hill Lancs 85 C4
Shire Horse Centre, Stratford-upon-Avon Warks 51 D7
Shirebrook Derbys 76 C5
Shiregreen S Yorks 88 E4
Shirehampton Bristol 23 B7
Shiremoor T & W 111 B6
Shirenewton Mon 36 E1
Shireoaks Notts 89 F6
Shirkoak Kent 19 B6
Shirl Heath Hereford 49 D6
Shirland Derbys 76 D3
Shirley Derbys 76 E2
Shirley London 28 C4
Shirley Soton 14 C5
Shirley W Mid 51 B6
Shirrell Heath Hants 15 C6
Shirwell Devon 20 F4
Shirwell Cross Devon 20 F4
Shiskine N Ayrs 119 D6
Shobdon Hereford 49 C6
Shobnall Staffs 63 B6
Shobrooke Devon 10 D3
Shoby Leics 64 C3
Shocklach Ches 73 E8
Shoeburyness Sthend 43 F5
Sholden Kent 31 D7
Sholing Soton 14 C5
Shoot Hill Shrops 60 C4
Shop Corn 8 C4
Shop Corn 4 B3
Shop Corner Suff 57 F6
Shore Mill Highld 157 C8
Shoreditch London 41 F6
Shoreham Kent 29 C6
Shoreham Airport W Sus 17 D6
Shoreham-By-Sea W Sus 17 D6
Shoresdean Northumb 125 E5
Shoreswood Northumb 124 E5
Shoreton Highld 157 C7
Shorncote Glos 37 E7
Shorne Kent 29 B7
Short Heath W Mid 62 D3
Shortacombe Devon 9 F7
Shortgate E Sus 17 C8
Shortlanesend Corn 3 B7
Shortlees E Ayrs 120 F4
Shortstown Beds 53 E8
Shorwell I o W 15 F5
Shoscombe Bath 24 D2
Shotatton Shrops 60 B3
Shotesham Norf 69 E5
Shotgate Essex 42 E3
Shotley Suff 57 F6
Shotley Bridge Durham 110 D3
Shotley Gate Suff 57 F6
Shotleyfield Northumb 110 D3
Shottenden Kent 30 D4
Shottermill Sur 27 F6
Shottery Warks 51 D6
Shotteswell Warks 52 E2
Shottisham Suff 57 E7
Shottle Derbys 76 E3
Shottlegate Derbys 76 E3
Shotton Durham 111 F7
Shotton Flint 73 C7
Shotton Northumb 124 F4
Shotton Colliery Durham 111 E6
Shotts N Lnrk 121 C8
Shotwick Ches 73 B7
Shouldham Norf 67 D6
Shouldham Thorpe Norf 67 D6
Shoulton Worcs 50 D3
Shover's Green E Sus 18 B3
Shrawardine Shrops 60 C4
Shrawley Worcs 50 C3
Shrewley Common Warks 51 C7
Shrewsbury Shrops 60 C4
Shrewton Wilts 25 E5
Shripney W Sus 16 D3
Shrivenham Oxon 38 F2
Shropham Norf 68 E2
Shrub End Essex 43 B5
Shucknall Hereford 49 E7
Shudy Camps Cambs 55 E7
Shulishadermor Highld 153 E5
Shurdington Glos 37 C6
Shurlock Row Windsor 27 B6
Shurrery Highld 168 D5
Shurrery Lodge Highld 168 D5
Shurton Som 22 E4
Shustoke Warks 63 E6
Shute Devon 11 E7
Shute Devon 10 D3
Shutford Oxon 51 E8
Shuthonger Glos 50 F3
Shutlanger Northants 52 D5
Shuttington Warks 63 D6
Shuttlewood Derbys 76 B4
Siabost bho Dheas W Isles 172 D5
Siabost bho Thuath W Isles 172 D5
Siadar W Isles 172 C6
Siadar Iarach W Isles 172 C6
Siadar Uarach W Isles 172 C6
Sibbaldbie Dumfries 114 F4
Sibbertoft Northants 64 F3
Sibdon Carwood Shrops 60 F4
Sibford Ferris Oxon 51 F8
Sibford Gower Oxon 51 F8
Sible Hedingham Essex 55 F8
Sibsey Lincs 79 D6
Sibson Cambs 65 E7
Sibson Leics 63 D7
Sibthorpe Notts 77 E7
Sibton Suff 57 C7
Sibton Green Suff 57 B7
Sicklesmere Suff 56 C2
Sicklinghall N Yorks 95 E6
Sid Devon 11 F6
Sidbury Devon 11 E6
Sidbury Shrops 61 F6
Sidcot N Som 23 D6
Sidcup London 29 B5
Siddick Cumb 107 F7
Siddington Ches 74 B5
Siddington Glos 37 E7
Sidemoor Worcs 50 B4
Sidestrand Norf 81 D8
Sidford Devon 11 E6
Sidlesham W Sus 16 E2
Sidley E Sus 18 E4
Sidlow Sur 28 E3
Sidmouth Devon 11 F6
Sigford Devon 7 B5
Sigglesthorne E Yorks 97 E7
Sighthill Edin 122 B4
Sigingstone V Glam 21 B8
Signet Oxon 38 C2
Silchester Hants 26 C4
Sildinis W Isles 172 G5
Sileby Leics 64 C2
Silecroft Cumb 98 F3
Silfield Norf 68 E4
Silian Ceredig 46 D4
Silk Willoughby Lincs 78 E3
Silkstone S Yorks 88 D3
Silkstone Common S Yorks 88 D3
Silloth Cumb 107 D8
Sills Northumb 116 D4
Sillyearn Moray 160 C2
Siloh Carms 47 F6
Silpho N Yorks 103 E7
Silsden W Yorks 94 E3
Silsoe Beds 53 F8
Silver End Essex 42 C4
Silverburn Midloth 122 C5
Silverdale Lancs 92 B4
Silverdale Staffs 74 E5
Silvergate Norf 81 E7
Silverhill E Sus 18 D4
Silverley's Green Suff 57 B6
Silverstone Northants 52 E4
Silverstone Motor Racing Circuit Northants 52 E4
Silverton Devon 10 D4
Silvington Shrops 49 B8
Silwick Shetland 175 J4
Simmondley Derbys 87 E8
Simonburn Northumb 109 B8
Simonsbath Som 21 F6
Simonstone Lancs 93 F7
Simprim Borders 124 E4
Simpson M Keynes 53 F6
Simpson Cross Pembs 44 D3
Sinclair's Hill Borders 124 D4
Sinclairston E Ayrs 112 C4
Sinderby N Yorks 101 F8
Sinderhope Northumb 109 D8
Sindlesham Wokingham 27 C5
Singdean Borders 115 D8
Singleborough Bucks 53 F5
Singleton Lancs 92 F3
Singleton W Sus 16 C2
Singlewell Kent 29 B7
Sinkhurst Green Kent 30 E2
Sinnahard Aberds 150 C3
Sinnington N Yorks 103 F5
Sinton Green Worcs 50 C3
Sipson London 27 B8
Sirhowy Bl Gwent 35 C5
Sisland Norf 69 E6
Sissinghurst Kent 18 B4
Sissinghurst, Cranbrook Kent 18 B5
Sisterpath Borders 124 E3
Siston S Glos 23 B8
Sithney Corn 2 D5
Sittingbourne Kent 30 C2
Six Ashes Staffs 61 F7
Six Hills Leics 64 B3
Six Mile Bottom Cambs 55 D6
Sixhills Lincs 91 F5
Sixpenny Handley Dorset 13 C7
Sizewell Suff 57 C8
Skail Highld 168 E2
Skaill Orkney 176 E1
Skaill Orkney 176 C3
Skaill Orkney 176 F4
Skara Brae Orkney 176 E1
Skares E Ayrs 113 C5
Skateraw E Loth 124 B3
Skaw Shetland 174 G7
Skeabost Highld 152 E5
Skeabrae Orkney 176 D1
Skeeby N Yorks 101 D7
Skeffington Leics 64 D4
Skeffling E Yorks 91 C7
Skegby Notts 76 C4
Skegness Lincs 79 C8
Skelberry Shetland 175 M5
Skelbo Highld 164 E4
Skelbrooke S Yorks 89 C6
Skeldyke Lincs 79 F6
Skellingthorpe Lincs 78 B2
Skellister Shetland 175 H6
Skellow S Yorks 89 C6
Skelmanthorpe W Yorks 88 C3
Skelmersdale Lancs 86 D2
Skelmonae Aberds 161 E5
Skelmorlie N Ayrs 129 D6
Skelmuir Aberds 161 D6
Skelpick Highld 168 D2
Skelton Cumb 108 F4
Skelton E Yorks 89 B8
Skelton N Yorks 101 D5
Skelton Redcar 102 C4
Skelton York 95 D8
Skelton-on-Ure N Yorks 95 C6
Skelwick Orkney 176 B3
Skelwith Bridge Cumb 99 D5
Skendleby Lincs 79 C7
Skene Ho. Aberds 151 D6
Skenfrith Mon 36 B1
Skerne E Yorks 97 D6
Skeroblingarry Argyll 118 D4
Skerray Highld 167 C8
Skerton Lancs 92 C4
Sketchley Leics 63 E8
Sketty Swansea 33 E7
Skewen Neath 33 E8
Skewsby N Yorks 96 B2
Skeyton Norf 81 E8
Skiag Bridge Highld 163 B6
Skibo Castle Highld 164 F4
Skidbrooke Lincs 91 E8
Skidbrooke North End Lincs 91 E8
Skidby E Yorks 97 F6
Skilgate Som 10 B4
Skillington Lincs 65 B5
Skinburness Cumb 107 D8
Skinflats Falk 133 F8
Skinidin Highld 152 E3
Skinnet Highld 167 C7
Skinningrove Redcar 103 B5
Skipness Argyll 128 E3
Skippool Lancs 92 E3
Skipsea E Yorks 97 D7
Skipsea Brough E Yorks 97 D7
Skipton N Yorks 94 D2
Skipton-on-Swale N Yorks 95 B6
Skipwith N Yorks 96 F2
Skirbeck Lincs 79 E6
Skirbeck Quarter Lincs 79 E6
Skirlaugh E Yorks 97 F7
Skirling Borders 122 F3
Skirmett Bucks 39 F7
Skirpenbeck E Yorks 96 D3
Skirwith Cumb 109 F6
Skirza Highld 169 C8
Skulamus Highld 155 H2
Skullomie Highld 167 C8
Skyborry Green Shrops 48 B4
Skye of Curr Highld 149 B5
Skyreholme N Yorks 94 C3
Slackhall Derbys 87 F8
Slackhead Moray 159 C8
Slad Glos 37 D5
Slade Devon 20 E4
Slade Pembs 44 D4
Slade Green London 29 B6
Slaggyford Northumb 109 D6
Slaidburn Lancs 93 D7
Slaithwaite W Yorks 87 C8
Slaley Northumb 110 D2
Slamannan Falk 121 B8
Slapton Bucks 40 B2
Slapton Devon 7 E6
Slapton Northants 52 E4
Slatepit Dale Derbys 76 C3
Slattocks Gtr Man 87 D6
Slaugham W Sus 17 B6
Slaughterford Wilts 24 B3
Slawston Leics 64 E4
Sleaford Hants 27 F6
Sleaford Lincs 78 E3
Sleagill Cumb 99 C7
Sleapford Telford 61 C6
Sledge Green Worcs 50 F3
Sledmere E Yorks 96 C5
Sleightholme Durham 100 C4
Sleights N Yorks 103 D6
Slepe Dorset 13 E7
Slickly Highld 169 C7
Sliddery N Ayrs 119 D6
Sligachan Hotel Highld 153 G5
Slimbridge Glos 36 D4
Slimbridge Wildfowl & Wetlands Centre, Frampton on Severn Glos 36 D4
Slindon Staffs 74 F5
Slindon W Sus 16 D3
Slinfold W Sus 28 F2
Sling Gwyn 83 E6
Slingsby N Yorks 96 B2
Slioch Aberds 160 E2
Slip End Beds 40 C3
Slip End Herts 54 F3
Slipton Northants 53 B7
Slitting Mill Staffs 62 C4
Slochd Highld 148 B4
Slockavullin Argyll 130 F4
Sloley Norf 81 E8
Sloothby Lincs 79 B7
Slough Slough 27 B7
Slough Green W Sus 17 B6
Sluggan Highld 148 B4
Slumbay Highld 155 G4
Slyfield Sur 27 D7
Slyne Lancs 92 C4
Smailholm Borders 124 F2
Small Dole W Sus 17 C6
Small Hythe Kent 19 B5
Smallbridge Gtr Man 87 C7
Smallburgh Norf 69 B6
Smallburn Aberds 161 D7
Smallburn E Ayrs 113 B6
Smalley Derbys 76 E4
Smallfield Sur 28 E4
Smallridge Devon 11 D8
Smannell Hants 25 E8
Smardale Cumb 100 D2
Smarden Kent 30 E2
Smarden Bell Kent 30 E2
Smeatharpe Devon 11 C6
Smeeth Kent 19 B7
Smeeton Westerby Leics 64 E3
Smercleit W Isles 171 J3
Smerral Highld 169 F6
Smethwick W Mid 62 F4
Smirisary Highld 145 F6
Smisby Derbys 63 C7
Smith Green Lancs 92 D4
Smithfield Cumb 108 C4
Smithincott Devon 11 C5
Smith's Green Essex 42 B1
Smithstown Highld 154 C3
Smithton Highld 157 E8
Smithy Green Ches 74 B4
Smockington Leics 63 F8
Smoogro Orkney 176 F2
Smythe's Green Essex 43 C5
Snaefell Mountain Railway I o M 84 D4
Snaigow House Perth 141 E7
Snailbeach Shrops 60 D3
Snailwell Cambs 55 C7
Snainton N Yorks 103 F7
Snaith E Yorks 89 B7
Snape N Yorks 101 F7
Snape Suff 57 D7
Snape Green Lancs 85 C4
Snarestone Leics 63 D7
Snarford Lincs 90 F4
Snargate Kent 19 C6
Snave Kent 19 C7
Snead Powys 60 E3
Sneath Common Norf 68 F4
Sneaton N Yorks 103 D6
Sneatonthorpe N Yorks 103 D7
Snelland Lincs 90 F4
Snelston Derbys 75 E8
Snetterton Motor Racing Circuit Norf 68 F3
Snettisham Norf 80 D2
Snibston Discovery Park, Coalville Leics 63 C8
Sniseabhal W Isles 171 G3
Snitter Northumb 117 D6
Snitterby Lincs 90 E3
Snitterfield Warks 51 D7
Snitton Shrops 49 B7
Snodhill Hereford 48 E5
Snodland Kent 29 C7
Snowden Hill S Yorks 88 D3
Snowdon Mountain Railway, Llanberis Gwyn 83 F6
Snowdown Kent 31 D6
Snowshill Glos 51 F5
Snowshill Manor Glos 51 F5
Snydale W Yorks 88 C5
Soar Anglesey 82 D3
Soar Carms 33 B7
Soar Devon 6 F5
Soar-y-Mynydd Ceredig 47 D6
Soberton Hants 15 C7
Soberton Heath Hants 15 C7
Sockbridge Cumb 99 B7
Sockburn Darl 101 D8
Soham Cambs 55 B6
Soham Cotes Cambs 55 B6
Solas W Isles 170 C4
Soldon Cross Devon 8 C5
Soldridge Hants 26 F4
Sole Street Kent 29 C7
Sole Street Kent 30 E4
Solihull W Mid 51 B6
Sollers Dilwyn Hereford 49 D6
Sollers Hope Hereford 49 F8
Sollom Lancs 86 C2
Solva Pembs 44 C2
Somerby Leics 64 C4
Somerby Lincs 90 D4
Somercotes Derbys 76 D4
Somerford Dorset 14 E2
Somerford Keynes Glos 37 E7
Somerley W Sus 16 E2
Somerleyton Suff 69 E7
Somersal Herbert Derbys 75 F8
Somersby Lincs 79 B6
Somersham Cambs 54 B4
Somersham Suff 56 E4
Somerton Oxon 38 B4
Somerton Som 12 B2
Sompting W Sus 17 D5
Sonning Wokingham 27 B5
Sonning Common Oxon 39 F7
Sonning Eye Oxon 27 B5
Sontley Wrex 73 E7
Sopley Hants 14 E2
Sopwell Herts 40 D4
Sopworth Wilts 37 F5
Sorbie Dumfries 105 E8
Sordale Highld 169 C6
Sorisdale Argyll 136 B3
Sorn E Ayrs 113 B5
Sornhill E Ayrs 120 F5
Sortat Highld 169 C7
Sotby Lincs 78 B5
Sots Hole Lincs 78 C4
Sotterley Suff 69 F7
Soudley Shrops 61 B7
Soughton Flint 73 C6
Soulbury Bucks 40 B1
Soulby Cumb 100 C2
Souldern Oxon 52 F3
Souldrop Beds 53 C7
Sound Ches 74 E3
Sound Shetland 175 H5
Sound Shetland 175 J6
Sound Heath Ches 74 E3
Soundwell S Glos 23 B8
Sourhope Borders 116 B4
Sourin Orkney 176 C3
Sourton Devon 9 E7
Soutergate Cumb 98 F4
South Acre Norf 67 C8
South Allington Devon 7 F5
South Alloa Falk 133 E7
South Ambersham W Sus 16 B3
South Anston S Yorks 89 F6
South Ascot Windsor 27 C7
South Ballachulish Highld 138 D4
South Balloch S Ayrs 112 E3
South Bank Redcar 102 B3
South Barrow Som 12 B4
South Beach Gwyn 70 D4
South Benfleet Essex 42 F3
South Bersted W Sus 16 D3
South Brent Devon 6 C4
South Brewham Som 24 F2
South Broomhill Northumb 117 E8
South Burlingham Norf 69 D6
South Cadbury Som 12 B4
South Cairn Dumfries 104 C3
South Carlton Lincs 78 B2
South Cave E Yorks 96 F5

South Cerney Glos 37 E7
South Chard Som 11 D8
South Charlton Northumb 117 B7
South Cheriton Som 12 B4
South Cliffe E Yorks 96 F4
South Clifton Notts 77 B8
South Cockerington Lincs 91 F7
South Cornelly Bridgend 34 F2
South Cove Suff 69 F7
South Creagan Argyll 138 E3
South Creake Norf 80 D4
South Croxton Leics 64 C3
South Croydon London 28 C4
South Dalton E Yorks 97 E5
South Darenth Kent 29 C6
South Duffield N Yorks 96 F2
South Elkington Lincs 91 F6
South Elmsall W Yorks 89 C5
South End Bucks 40 B1
South End Cumb 92 C2
South End N Lincs 90 B5
South Erradale Highld 154 C3
South Fambridge Essex 42 E4
South Fawley W Berks 38 F3
South Ferriby N Lincs 90 B3
South Garth Shetland 174 D7
South Garvan Highld 138 B3
South Glendale W Isles 171 J3
South Godstone Sur 28 E4
South Gorley Hants 14 C2
South Green Essex 42 E2
South Green Kent 30 C2
South-haa Shetland 174 E5
South Ham Hants 26 D4
South Hanningfield Essex 42 E3
South Harting W Sus 15 C8
South Hatfield Herts 41 D5
South Hayling Hants 15 E8
South Hazelrigg Northumb 125 F6
South Heath Bucks 40 D2
South Heighton E Sus 17 D8
South Hetton Durham 111 E6
South Hiendley W Yorks 88 C4
South Hill Corn 5 B8
South Hinksey Oxon 39 D5
South Hole Devon 8 B4
South Holme N Yorks 96 B2
South Holmwood Sur 28 E2
South Hornchurch London 41 F8
South Hykeham Lincs 78 C2
South Hylton T & W 111 D6
South Kelsey Lincs 90 E4
South Kessock Highld 157 E7
South Killingholme N Lincs 91 C5
South Kilvington N Yorks 102 F2
South Kilworth Leics 64 F3
South Kirkby W Yorks 88 C5
South Kirkton Aberds 151 D6
South Kiscadale N Ayrs 119 D7
South Kyme Lincs 78 E4
South Lancing W Sus 17 D5
South Leigh Oxon 38 D3
South Leverton Notts 89 F8
South Littleton Worcs 51 E5
South Lopham Norf 68 F3
South Luffenham Rutland 65 D6
South Malling E Sus 17 C8
South Marston Thamesdown 38 F1
South Middleton Northumb 117 B5
South Milford N Yorks 95 F7
South Millbrex Aberds 160 D5
South Milton Devon 6 E5
South Mimms Herts 41 D5
South Molton Devon 10 B2
South Moreton Oxon 39 F5
South Mundham W Sus 16 D2
South Muskham Notts 77 D7
South Newbald E Yorks 96 F5
South Newington Oxon 52 F2
South Newton Wilts 25 F5
South Normanton Derbys 76 D4
South Norwood London 28 C4
South Nutfield Sur 28 E4
South Ockendon Thurrock 42 F1
South Ormsby Lincs 79 B6
South Otterington N Yorks 102 F1
South Owersby Lincs 90 E4
South Oxhey Herts 40 E4
South Perrott Dorset 12 D2
South Petherton Som 12 C2
South Petherwin Corn 8 F5
South Pickenham Norf 67 D8
South Pool Devon 7 E5
South Port Argyll 131 C6
South Radworthy Devon 21 F6
South Rauceby Lincs 78 E3
South Raynham Norf 80 E4
South Reston Lincs 91 F8
South Runcton Norf 67 D6
South Scarle Notts 77 C8
South Shian Argyll 138 E3
South Shields T & W 111 C6
South Shields Museum T & W 111 C6
South Shore Blkpool 92 F3
South Somercotes Lincs 91 E8
South Stainley N Yorks 95 C6
South Stainmore Cumb 100 C3
South Stifford Thurrock 29 B7
South Stoke Oxon 39 F5
South Stoke W Sus 16 D4
South Street E Sus 17 C7
South Street London 28 D5
South Street Kent 30 C5
South Street Kent 30 D4
South Tawton Devon 9 E8
South Thoresby Lincs 79 B7
South Tidworth Wilts 25 E7
South Town Hants 26 F4
South View Hants 26 D4
South Walsham Norf 69 C6
South Warnborough Hants 26 E5
South Weald Essex 42 E1
South Weston Oxon 39 E7
South Wheatley Corn 8 E4
South Wheatley Notts 89 F8
South Whiteness Shetland 175 J5
South Widcombe Bath 23 D7
South Wigston Leics 64 E2
South Willingham Lincs 91 F5
South Wingfield Derbys 76 D3
South Witham Lincs 65 C6
South Wonston Hants 26 F2
South Woodham Ferrers Essex 42 E4
South Wootton Norf 67 B6
South Wraxall Wilts 24 C3
South Zeal Devon 9 E8
Southall London 40 F4
Southam Glos 37 B6
Southam Warks 52 C2
Southampton Soton 14 C5
Southampton International Airport Hants 15 C5
Southborough Kent 29 E6
Southbourne Bmouth 14 E2
Southbourne W Sus 15 D8
Southburgh Norf 68 D2
Southburn E Yorks 97 D5
Southchurch Sthend 43 F5
Southcott Wilts 25 D6
Southcourt Bucks 39 C8
Southdean Borders 116 D2
Southdene Mers 86 E2
Southease E Sus 17 D8
Southend Argyll 118 F3
Southend W Berks 26 B3
Southend Wilts 25 B6
Southend Airport Essex 42 F4
Southend-on-Sea Sthend 42 F4
Southend Sea Life Centre Essex 42 E4
Southernden Kent 30 E2
Southerndown V Glam 21 B7
Southerness Dumfries 107 D6
Southery Norf 67 E6
Southfield Northumb 111 B5
Southfleet Kent 29 B7
Southgate Ceredig 46 B4
Southgate London 41 E5
Southgate Norf 81 E7
Southgate Swansea 33 F6
Southill Beds 54 E2
Southleigh Devon 11 E7
Southminster Essex 43 E5
Southmoor Oxon 38 E3
Southoe Cambs 54 C2
Southolt Suff 57 C5
Southorpe P'boro 65 D7
Southowram W Yorks 88 B2
Southport Mers 85 C4
Southpunds Shetland 175 L6
Southrepps Norf 81 D8
Southrey Lincs 78 C4
Southrop Glos 38 D1
Southrope Hants 26 E4
Southsea Ptsmth 15 E7
Southstoke Bath 24 C2
Southtown Norf 69 D8
Southtown Orkney 176 G3
Southwaite Cumb 108 E4
Southwark London 28 B4
Southwater W Sus 17 B5
Southwater Street W Sus 17 B5
Southway Som 23 E7
Southwell Dorset 12 G4
Southwell Notts 77 D6
Southwell Minster Notts 77 D7
Southwell Racecourse Notts 77 D7
Southwick Hants 15 D7
Southwick Northants 65 E7
Southwick T & W 111 D6
Southwick Wilts 24 D3
Southwick W Sus 17 D6
Southwold Suff 57 B9
Southwood Norf 69 D6
Southwood Som 23 F7
Soval Lodge W Isles 172 F6
Sowber Gate N Yorks 102 F1
Sowerby N Yorks 102 F2
Sowerby W Yorks 87 B8
Sowerby Bridge W Yorks 87 B8
Sowerby Row Cumb 108 F3
Sowood W Yorks 87 C8
Sowton Devon 10 E4
Soyal Highld 164 E2
Spa Common Norf 81 D8
Spacey Houses N Yorks 95 D6
Spadeadam Farm Cumb 109 B5
Spalding Lincs 66 B2
Spaldington E Yorks 96 F3
Spaldwick Cambs 54 B2
Spalford Notts 77 C8
Spanby Lincs 78 F3
Sparham Norf 68 C3
Spark Bridge Cumb 99 F5
Sparkford Som 12 B4
Sparkhill W Mid 62 F4
Sparkwell Devon 6 D3
Sparrow Green Norf 68 C2
Sparrowpit Derbys 87 F8
Sparsholt Hants 26 F2
Sparsholt Oxon 38 F3
Spartylea Northumb 109 E8
Spaunton N Yorks 103 F5
Spaxton Som 22 F4
Spean Bridge Highld 146 F5
Spear Hill W Sus 16 C5
Speen Bucks 39 E8
Speen W Berks 26 C2
Speeton N Yorks 97 B7
Speke Mers 86 F2
Speke Hall Mers 86 F2
Speldhurst Kent 29 E6
Spellbrook Herts 41 C7
Spelsbury Oxon 38 B3
Spelter Bridgend 34 E2
Spencers Wood Wokingham 26 C5
Spennithorne N Yorks 101 F6
Spennymoor Durham 111 F5
Spetchley Worcs 50 D3
Spetisbury Dorset 13 D7
Spexhall Suff 69 F6
Spey Bay Moray 159 C7
Speybridge Highld 149 B6
Speyview Moray 159 E6
Spilsby Lincs 79 C7
Spindlestone Northumb 125 F7
Spinkhill Derbys 76 B4
Spinningdale Highld 164 F3
Spirit of the West, St Columb Major Corn 4 C4
Spirthill Wilts 24 B4
Spital Hill S Yorks 89 E7
Spital in the Street Lincs 90 F3
Spitfire and Hurricane Memorial, Manston Kent 31 C7
Spithurst E Sus 17 C8
Spittal Dumfries 105 D7
Spittal E Loth 123 B7
Spittal Highld 169 D6
Spittal Northumb 125 D6
Spittal Pembs 44 C4
Spittal Stirl 132 F4
Spittal of Glenmuick Aberds 150 F2
Spittal of Glenshee Perth 141 B8
Spittalfield Perth 141 E8
Spixworth Norf 68 C5
Splayne's Green E Sus 17 B8
Spofforth N Yorks 95 D6
Spon End W Mid 51 B8
Spon Green Flint 73 C6
Spondon Derby 76 F4
Spooner Row Norf 68 E3
Sporle Norf 67 C8
Spott E Loth 124 B2
Spratton Northants 52 B5
Spreakley Sur 27 E6
Spreyton Devon 9 E8
Spridlington Lincs 90 F4
Spring Vale S Yorks 88 D3
Spring Valley I o M 84 E3
Springburn Glasgow 121 C6
Springfield Dumfries 108 C3
Springfield Essex 42 D3
Springfield Fife 134 C5
Springfield Moray 158 D4
Springfield W Mid 62 F4
Springhill Staffs 62 D3
Springholm Dumfries 106 C5
Springkell Dumfries 108 B2
Springside N Ayrs 120 F3
Springthorpe Lincs 90 F2
Springwell T & W 111 D5
Sproatley E Yorks 97 F7
Sproston Green Ches 74 C4
Sprotbrough S Yorks 89 D6
Sproughton Suff 56 E5
Sprouston Borders 124 F3
Sprowston Norf 68 C5
Sproxton Leics 65 B5
Sproxton N Yorks 102 F4
Spurstow Ches 74 D2
Spynie Moray 159 C6
Squires Gate Blkpool 92 F3
Srannda W Isles 173 K3
Sronphadruig Lodge Perth 140 B4
SS Great Britain Bristol 23 B7
Stableford Shrops 61 E7
Stableford Staffs 74 F5
Stacey Bank S Yorks 88 E3
Stackhouse N Yorks 93 C8
Stackpole Pembs 44 F4
Staddiscombe Devon 6 D3
Staddlethorpe E Yorks 90 B2
Stadhampton Oxon 39 E6
Stadhlaigearraidh W Isles 170 G3
Staffield Cumb 108 E5
Staffin Highld 152 C5
Stafford Staffs 62 B3
Stagsden Beds 53 E7
Stainburn Cumb 98 B2
Stainburn N Yorks 94 E5
Stainby Lincs 65 B6
Staincross S Yorks 88 C4
Staindrop Durham 101 B6
Staines Sur 27 B8
Stainfield Lincs 65 B7
Stainfield Lincs 78 B4
Stainforth N Yorks 93 C8
Stainforth S Yorks 89 C7
Staining Lancs 92 F3
Stainland W Yorks 87 C8
Stainsacre N Yorks 103 D7
Stainsby Derbys 76 C4
Stainton Cumb 99 F7
Stainton Cumb 99 B6
Stainton Durham 101 C5
Stainton M'bro 102 C2
Stainton N Yorks 101 E6
Stainton S Yorks 89 E6
Stainton by Langworth Lincs 78 B3
Stainton le Vale Lincs 91 E5
Stainton with Adgarley Cumb 92 B2
Staintondale N Yorks 103 E7
Stair Cumb 98 B4
Stair E Ayrs 112 B4
Stairhaven Dumfries 105 D6
Staithes N Yorks 103 C5
Stake Pool Lancs 92 E4
Stakeford Northumb 117 F8
Stalbridge Dorset 12 C5
Stalbridge Weston Dorset 12 C5
Stalham Norf 69 B6
Stalham Green Norf 69 B6
Stalisfield Green Kent 30 D3
Stalling Busk N Yorks 100 F4
Stallingborough NE Lincs 91 C5
Stalmine Lancs 92 E3
Stalybridge Gtr Man 87 E7
Stambourne Essex 55 F8
Stambourne Green Essex 55 F8
Stamford Lincs 65 D7
Stamford Bridge Ches 73 C8
Stamford Bridge E Yorks 96 D3
Stamfordham Northumb 110 B3
Stanah Cumb 99 C5
Stanborough Herts 41 C5
Stanbridge Beds 40 B2
Stanbridge Dorset 13 D8
Stanbrook Worcs 50 E3
Stanbury W Yorks 94 F3
Stand Gtr Man 87 D5
Stand N Lnrk 121 C7
Standburn Falk 122 B2
Standeford Staffs 62 D3
Standen Kent 30 E2
Standen, East Grinstead W Sus 28 F4
Standford Hants 27 F6
Standingstone Cumb 107 F7
Standish Gtr Man 86 C3
Standlake Oxon 38 D3
Standon Hants 14 B5
Standon Herts 41 B6
Standon Staffs 74 F5
Stane N Lnrk 121 D8
Stanfield Norf 80 E5
Stanford Beds 54 E2
Stanford Kent 19 B8
Stanford Bishop Hereford 49 D8
Stanford Bridge Worcs 50 C2
Stanford Dingley W Berks 26 B3
Stanford in the Vale Oxon 38 E3
Stanford-le-Hope Thurrock 42 F2
Stanford on Avon Northants 52 B3
Stanford on Soar Notts 64 B2
Stanford on Teme Worcs 50 C2
Stanford Rivers Essex 41 D8
Stanfree Derbys 76 B4
Stanghow Redcar 102 C4
Stanground P'boro 66 E2
Stanhoe Norf 80 D4
Stanhope Borders 114 B4
Stanhope Durham 110 F2
Stanion Northants 65 F6
Stanley Derbys 76 E4
Stanley Durham 110 D4
Stanley Lancs 86 D2
Stanley Perth 141 F8
Stanley Staffs 75 D6
Stanley W Yorks 88 B4
Stanley Common Derbys 76 E4
Stanley Gate Lancs 86 D2
Stanley Hill Hereford 49 E8
Stanlow Ches 73 B8
Stanmer Brighton 17 D7
Stanmore London 40 E4
Stanmore Hants 15 B5
Stanmore W Berks 26 B2
Stannergate Dundee 142 F4
Stanningley W Yorks 94 F5
Stannington Northumb 110 B5
Stannington S Yorks 88 F4
Stansbatch Hereford 48 C5
Stansfield Suff 55 D8
Stanstead Suff 56 E2
Stanstead Abbotts Herts 41 C6
Stansted Kent 29 C7
Stansted Mountfitchet Essex 41 B8
Stanton Glos 51 F5
Stanton Mon 35 B7
Stanton Northumb 117 F7
Stanton Staffs 75 E8
Stanton Suff 56 B3
Stanton by Bridge Derbys 63 B7
Stanton-by-Dale Derbys 76 F4
Stanton Drew Bath 23 C7
Stanton Fitzwarren Thamesdown 38 E1
Stanton Harcourt Oxon 38 D4
Stanton Hill Notts 76 C4
Stanton in Peak Derbys 76 C2
Stanton Lacy Shrops 49 B6
Stanton Long Shrops 61 E5
Stanton-on-the-Wolds Notts 77 F6
Stanton Prior Bath 23 C8
Stanton St Bernard Wilts 25 C5
Stanton St John Oxon 39 D5
Stanton St Quintin Wilts 24 B4
Stanton Street Suff 56 C3
Stanton under Bardon Leics 63 C8
Stanton upon Hine Heath Shrops 61 B5
Stanton Wick Bath 23 C8
Stanwardine in the Fields Shrops 60 B4
Stanwardine in the Wood Shrops 60 B4
Stanway Essex 43 B5
Stanway Glos 51 F5
Stanway Green Suff 57 B6
Stanwell Sur 27 B8
Stanwell Moor Sur 27 B8
Stanwick Northants 53 B7
Stanwick-St-John N Yorks 101 C6
Stanwix Cumb 108 D4
Stanydale Shetland 175 H4
Staoinebrig W Isles 171 G3
Stape N Yorks 103 E5
Stapehill Dorset 13 D8
Stapeley Ches 74 E3
Stapeley Water Gardens, Nantwich Ches 74 D3
Stapenhill Staffs 63 B6
Staple Kent 31 D6
Staple Som 22 E3
Staple Cross E Sus 18 C4
Staple Fitzpaine Som 11 C7
Staplefield W Sus 17 B6
Stapleford Cambs 55 D5
Stapleford Herts 41 C6
Stapleford Leics 64 C5
Stapleford Lincs 77 D8
Stapleford Notts 76 F4
Stapleford Wilts 25 F5
Stapleford Abbotts Essex 41 E8
Stapleford Tawney Essex 41 E8
Staplegrove Som 11 B7
Staplehay Som 11 B7
Staplehurst Kent 29 E8
Staplers I o W 15 F6
Stapleton Bristol 23 B8
Stapleton Cumb 108 B5
Stapleton Hereford 48 C5
Stapleton Leics 63 E8
Stapleton N Yorks 101 C7
Stapleton Shrops 60 D4
Stapleton Som 12 B2
Stapley Som 11 C6
Staploe Beds 54 C2
Staplow Hereford 49 E8
Star Fife 134 D5
Star Pembs 45 F4
Star Som 23 D6
Stara Orkney 176 D1
Starbeck N Yorks 95 D6
Starbotton N Yorks 94 B2
Starcross Devon 10 F4
Stareton Warks 51 B8
Starkholmes Derbys 76 D3
Starlings Green Essex 55 F5
Starston Norf 68 F5
Startforth Durham 101 C5
Startley Wilts 37 F6
Stathe Som 11 B8
Stathern Leics 77 F7
Station Town Durham 111 F7
Staughton Green Cambs 54 C2
Staughton Highway Cambs 54 C2
Staunton Glos 36 C2
Staunton Glos 36 B4
Staunton in the Vale Notts 77 E8
Staunton on Arrow Hereford 49 C5
Staunton on Wye Hereford 49 E5
Staveley Cumb 99 F5
Staveley Cumb 99 E6
Staveley Derbys 76 B4
Staveley N Yorks 95 C6
Staverton Devon 7 C5
Staverton Glos 37 B5
Staverton Northants 52 C3
Staverton Wilts 24 C3
Staverton Bridge Glos 37 B5
Stawell Som 23 F5
Staxigoe Highld 169 D8
Staxton N Yorks 97 B6
Staylittle Powys 59 E5
Staynall Lancs 92 E3
Staythorpe Notts 77 D7
Stean N Yorks 94 B3
Stearsby N Yorks 96 B2
Steart Som 22 E4
Stebbing Essex 42 B2
Stebbing Green Essex 42 B2
Stedham W Sus 16 B2
Steele Road Borders 115 E8
Steen's Bridge Hereford 49 D7
Steep Hants 15 B8
Steep Marsh Hants 15 B8
Steeple Dorset 13 F7
Steeple Essex 43 D5
Steeple Ashton Wilts 24 D4
Steeple Aston Oxon 38 B4
Steeple Barton Oxon 38 B4
Steeple Bumpstead Essex 55 E7
Steeple Claydon Bucks 39 B6
Steeple Gidding Cambs 65 F8
Steeple Langford Wilts 24 F5
Steeple Morden Cambs 54 E3
Steeton W Yorks 94 E3
Stein Highld 152 D3
Steinmanhill Aberds 160 D4
Stelling Minnis Kent 30 E5
Stemster Highld 169 C6
Stemster Ho. Highld 169 C6
Stenalees Corn 4 D5
Stenhousemuir Falk 133 F7
Stenigot Lincs 91 F6
Stenness Shetland 174 F4
Stenscholl Highld 152 C5
Stenso Orkney 176 D2
Stenson Derbys 63 B7
Stenton E Loth 124 B2
Stenton Fife 134 E4
Stenwith Lincs 77 F8
Stepaside Pembs 32 D2
Stepping Hill Gtr Man 87 F7
Steppingley Beds 53 F8
Stepps N Lnrk 121 C6
Sterndale Moor Derbys 75 C8
Sternfield Suff 57 C7
Sterridge Devon 20 E4
Stert Wilts 24 D5
Stetchworth Cambs 55 D7
Stevenage Herts 41 B5
Stevenston N Ayrs 120 E2
Steventon Hants 26 E3
Steventon Oxon 38 E4
Stevington Beds 53 D7
Stewartby Beds 53 E8
Stewarton Argyll 118 E3
Stewarton E Ayrs 120 E4
Stewkley Bucks 40 B1
Stewton Lincs 91 F7
Steyne Cross I o W 15 F7
Steyning W Sus 17 C5
Steynton Pembs 44 E4
Stibb Corn 8 C4
Stibb Cross Devon 9 C6
Stibb Green Wilts 25 C7
Stibbard Norf 81 E5
Stibbington Cambs 65 E7
Stichill Borders 124 F3
Sticker Corn 4 D4
Stickford Lincs 79 D6
Sticklepath Devon 9 E8
Stickney Lincs 79 D6
Stiffkey Norf 81 C5
Stifford's Bridge Hereford 50 E2
Stillingfleet N Yorks 95 E8
Stillington N Yorks 95 C8
Stillington Stockton 102 B1
Stilton Cambs 65 F8
Stinchcombe Glos 36 E4
Stinsford Dorset 12 E5
Stirchley Telford 61 D7
Stirkoke Ho. Highld 169 D8
Stirling Aberds 161 D8
Stirling Stirl 133 E6
Stirling Castle Stirl 133 E6
Stisted Essex 42 B3
Stithians Corn 3 C6
Stittenham Highld 157 B7
Stivichall W Mid 51 B8
Stixwould Lincs 78 C4
Stoak Ches 73 B8
Stobieside S Lnrk 121 F6
Stobo Borders 122 F4
Stoborough Dorset 13 F7
Stoborough Green Dorset 13 F7
Stobshiel E Loth 123 C7
Stobswood Northumb 117 E8
Stock Essex 42 E2
Stock Green Worcs 50 D4
Stock Wood Worcs 50 D5
Stockbridge Hants 25 F8
Stockbury Kent 30 C2
Stockcross W Berks 26 C2
Stockdalewath Cumb 108 E3
Stockerston Leics 64 E5
Stockheath Hants 15 D8
Stockiemuir Stirl 132 F4
Stocking Pelham Herts 41 B7
Stockingford Warks 63 E7
Stockland Devon 11 D7
Stockland Bristol Som 22 E4
Stockleigh English Devon 10 D3
Stockleigh Pomeroy Devon 10 D3
Stockley Wilts 24 C5
Stocklinch Som 11 C8
Stockport Gtr Man 87 E6
Stocksbridge S Yorks 88 E3
Stocksfield Northumb 110 C3
Stockton Hereford 49 C7
Stockton Norf 69 E6
Stockton Shrops 60 D2
Stockton Shrops 61 E7
Stockton Warks 52 C2
Stockton Wilts 24 F4
Stockton Heath Warr 86 F4
Stockton-on-Tees Stockton 102 C2
Stockton on Teme Worcs 50 C2
Stockton on the Forest York 96 D2
Stockwood Park Museum, Luton Luton 40 C3
Stodmarsh Kent 31 C6
Stody Norf 81 D6
Stoer Highld 162 B4
Stoford Som 12 C3
Stoford Wilts 25 F5
Stogumber Som 22 F2
Stogursey Som 22 E4
Stoke Devon 8 B4
Stoke Hants 26 D2
Stoke Hants 15 D8
Stoke Medway 30 B2
Stoke Suff 57 E5
Stoke Abbott Dorset 12 D2
Stoke Albany Northants 64 F5
Stoke Ash Suff 56 B5
Stoke Bardolph Notts 77 E6
Stoke Bliss Worcs 49 C8
Stoke Bruerne Northants 52 E5
Stoke by Clare Suff 55 E8
Stoke-by-Nayland Suff 56 F3
Stoke Canon Devon 10 E4
Stoke Charity Hants 26 F2
Stoke Climsland Corn 5 B8
Stoke D'Abernon Sur 28 D2
Stoke Doyle Northants 65 F7
Stoke Dry Rutland 65 E5
Stoke Farthing Wilts 13 B8
Stoke Ferry Norf 67 E7
Stoke Fleming Devon 7 E6
Stoke Gabriel Devon 7 D6
Stoke Gifford S Glos 23 B8
Stoke Golding Leics 63 E7
Stoke Goldington M Keynes 53 E6
Stoke Green Bucks 40 F2
Stoke Hammond Bucks 40 B1
Stoke Heath Shrops 61 B6
Stoke Holy Cross Norf 68 D5
Stoke Lacy Hereford 49 E8
Stoke Lyne Oxon 39 B5
Stoke Mandeville Bucks 39 C8
Stoke Newington London 41 F6
Stoke on Tern Shrops 61 B6
Stoke-on-Trent Stoke 75 E5
Stoke Orchard Glos 37 B6
Stoke Poges Bucks 40 F2
Stoke Prior Hereford 49 D7
Stoke Prior Worcs 50 C4
Stoke Rivers Devon 20 F5
Stoke Rochford Lincs 65 B6
Stoke Row Oxon 39 F6
Stoke St Gregory Som 11 B8
Stoke St Mary Som 11 B7
Stoke St Michael Som 23 E8
Stoke St Milborough Shrops 61 F5
Stoke sub Hamdon Som 12 C2
Stoke Talmage Oxon 39 E6
Stoke Trister Som 12 B5
Stoke Wake Dorset 13 D5
Stokeford Dorset 13 F6
Stokeham Notts 77 B7
Stokeinteignhead Devon 7 B7
Stokenchurch Bucks 39 E7
Stokenham Devon 7 E6
Stokesay Shrops 60 F4
Stokesby Norf 69 C7
Stokesley N Yorks 102 D3
Stolford Som 22 E4
Ston Easton Som 23 D8
Stondon Massey Essex 42 D1
Stone Bucks 39 C7
Stone Glos 36 E3
Stone Kent 19 C6
Stone Kent 29 B6
Stone Staffs 75 F6
Stone S Yorks 89 F6
Stone Worcs 50 B3
Stone Allerton Som 23 D6
Stone Bridge Corner P'boro 66 D2
Stone Chair W Yorks 88 B2
Stone Cross E Sus 18 E3
Stone Cross Kent 31 D7
Stone-edge Batch N Som 23 B6
Stone House Cumb 100 F2
Stone Street Kent 29 D6
Stone Street Suff 56 F3
Stone Street Suff 69 F6
Stonebroom Derbys 76 D4
Stoneferry Hull 97 F7
Stonefield S Lnrk 121 D6
Stonegate E Sus 18 C3
Stonegate N Yorks 103 D5
Stonegrave N Yorks 96 B2
Stonehaugh Northumb 109 B7
Stonehaven Aberds 151 F7
Stonehenge, Amesbury Wilts 25 E6
Stonehouse Glos 37 D5
Stonehouse Northumb 109 D6
Stonehouse S Lnrk 121 E7
Stoneleigh Warks 51 B8
Stonely Cambs 54 C2
Stoner Hill Hants 15 B8
Stone's Green Essex 43 B7
Stonesby Leics 64 B5
Stonesfield Oxon 38 C3
Stonethwaite Cumb 98 C4
Stoney Cross Hants 14 C3
Stoney Middleton Derbys 76 B2
Stoney Stanton Leics 63 E8
Stoney Stoke Som 24 F2
Stoney Stratton Som 23 F8
Stoney Stretton Shrops 60 D3
Stoneybreck Shetland 175 L3
Stoneyburn W Loth 122 C2
Stoneygate Aberds 161 E7
Stoneygate Leicester 64 D3
Stoneyhills Essex 43 E5
Stoneykirk Dumfries 104 D4
Stoneywood Aberdeen 151 C7
Stoneywood Falk 133 F6
Stonganess Shetland 174 C7
Stonham Aspal Suff 56 D5
Stonnall Staffs 62 D4
Stonor Oxon 39 F7
Stonton Wyville Leics 64 E4
Stony Cross Hereford 50 E2
Stony Stratford M Keynes 53 E5
Stonyfield Highld 157 B7
Stoodleigh Devon 10 C4
Stopes S Yorks 88 F3
Stopham W Sus 16 C4
Stopsley Luton 40 B4
Stores Corner Suff 57 E7
Storeton Mers 85 F4
Stornoway W Isles 172 E7
Stornoway Airport W Isles 172 E7
Storridge Hereford 50 E2
Storrington W Sus 16 C4
Storrs Cumb 99 E5
Storth Cumb 99 F6
Storwood E Yorks 96 E3
Stotfield Moray 159 B6
Stotfold Beds 54 F3
Stottesdon Shrops 61 F6
Stoughton Leics 64 D3
Stoughton Sur 27 D7
Stoughton W Sus 16 C2
Stoul Highld 145 D7
Stoulton Worcs 50 E4
Stour Provost Dorset 13 B5
Stour Row Dorset 13 B6
Stourbridge W Mid 62 F3
Stourhead Garden Wilts 24 F2
Stourpaine Dorset 13 D6
Stourport on Severn Worcs 50 B3
Stourton Staffs 62 F2
Stourton Warks 51 F7
Stourton Wilts 24 F2
Stourton Caundle Dorset 12 C5
Stove Orkney 176 C5
Stove Shetland 175 L6
Stoven Suff 69 F7
Stow Borders 123 E7
Stow Lincs 90 F2
Stow Lincs 78 F3
Stow Bardolph Norf 67 D6
Stow Bedon Norf 68 E2
Stow cum Quy Cambs 55 C6
Stow Longa Cambs 54 B2
Stow Maries Essex 42 E4
Stow-on-the-Wold Glos 38 B1
Stowbridge Norf 67 D6
Stowe Shrops 48 B5
Stowe-by-Chartley Staffs 62 B4
Stowe Green Glos 36 D2
Stowe House and Gardens, Buckingham Bucks 52 F4
Stowell Som 12 B4
Stowford Devon 9 F6
Stowlangtoft Suff 56 C3
Stowmarket Suff 56 D4
Stowting Kent 30 E5
Stowupland Suff 56 D4
Straad Argyll 129 D5
Strachan Aberds 151 E5
Stradbroke Suff 57 B6
Stradishall Suff 55 D8
Stradsett Norf 67 D6
Stragglethorpe Lincs 78 D2
Straid S Ayrs 112 E1
Straith Dumfries 113 F8
Straiton Edin 123 C5
Straiton S Ayrs 112 D3
Straloch Aberds 151 B7
Straloch Perth 141 C7
Stramshall Staffs 75 F7
Strang I o M 84 E3
Stranraer Dumfries 104 C4
Stratfield Mortimer W Berks 26 C4
Stratfield Saye Hants 26 C4
Stratfield Turgis Hants 26 D4
Stratford London 41 F6
Stratford Racecourse Warks 51 D6
Stratford St Andrew Suff 57 C7
Stratford St Mary Suff 56 F4
Stratford Sub Castle Wilts 25 F6
Stratford Tony Wilts 13 B8
Stratford-upon-Avon Warks 51 D6
Strath Highld 169 D7
Strath Highld 154 C3
Strathan Highld 146 E2
Strathan Highld 167 C7
Strathan Highld 162 B4
Strathaven S Lnrk 121 E7
Strathblane Stirl 121 B5
Strathcanaird Highld 163 D5
Strathcarron Highld 155 F5
Strathcoil Argyll 130 B2
Strathdon Aberds 150 C2
Strathellie Aberds 161 B7
Strathkinness Fife 135 C6
Strathmashie House Highld 147 E8
Strathmiglo Fife 134 C4
Strathmore Lodge Highld 169 E6
Strathpeffer Highld 157 D5
Strathrannoch Highld 156 B4
Strathtay Perth 141 D6

Strathvaich Lodge Highld 156 B4
Strathwhillan N Ayrs 119 C7
Strathy Highld 168 C3
Strathyre Stirl 132 C4
Stratton Corn 8 D4
Stratton Dorset 12 E4
Stratton Glos 37 D7
Stratton Audley Oxon 39 B6
Stratton on the Fosse Som 23 D8
Stratton St Margaret Thamesdown 38 F1
Stratton St Michael Norf 68 E5
Stratton Strawless Norf 81 E8
Stravithie Fife 135 C7
Streat E Sus 17 C7
Streatham London 28 B4
Streatley Beds 40 B3
Streatley W Berks 39 F5
Street Lancs 92 D5
Street N Yorks 103 D5
Street Som 23 F6
Street Dinas Shrops 73 F7
Street End Kent 30 D5
Street End W Sus 16 E2
Street Gate T & W 110 D5
Street Lydan Wrex 73 F8
Streethay Staffs 62 C5
Streetlam N Yorks 101 E8
Streetly W Mid 62 E4
Streetly End Cambs 55 E7
Strefford Shrops 60 F4
Strelley Notts 76 E5
Strensall York 96 C2
Stretcholt Som 22 E4
Strete Devon 7 E6
Stretford Gtr Man 87 E6
Strethall Essex 55 F5
Stretham Cambs 55 B6
Strettington W Sus 16 D2
Stretton Ches 73 D8
Stretton Derbys 76 C3
Stretton Rutland 65 C6
Stretton Staffs 62 C2
Stretton Staffs 63 B6
Stretton Warr 86 F4
Stretton Grandison Hereford 49 E8
Stretton-on-Dunsmore Warks 52 B2
Stretton-on-Fosse Warks 51 F7
Stretton Sugwas Hereford 49 E6
Stretton under Fosse Warks 63 F8
Stretton Westwood Shrops 61 E5
Strichen Aberds 161 C6
Strines Gtr Man 87 F7
Stringston Som 22 E3
Strixton Northants 53 C7
Stroat Glos 36 E2
Stromeferry Highld 155 G4
Stromemore Highld 155 G4
Stromness Orkney 176 F1
Stronaba Highld 146 F5
Stronachlachar Stirl 132 C3
Stronchreggan Highld 138 B4
Stronchrubie Highld 163 C6
Strone Argyll 129 B6
Strone Highld 147 B8
Strone Highld 146 F4
Strone Invclyd 129 C7
Stronmilchan Argyll 131 C7
Stronsay Airport Orkney 176 D5
Strontian Highld 138 C2
Strood Medway 29 C8
Strood Green Sur 28 E3
Strood Green W Sus 16 B4
Strood Green W Sus 28 F2
Stroud Glos 37 D5
Stroud Hants 15 B8
Stroud Green Essex 42 E4
Stroxton Lincs 78 F2
Struan Highld 153 F4
Struan Perth 141 C5
Strubby Lincs 91 F8
Strumpshaw Norf 69 D6
Strutherhill S Lnrk 121 E7
Struy Highld 156 F4
Stryt-issa Wrex 73 E6
Stuartfield Aberds 161 D6
Stub Place Cumb 98 E2
Stubbington Hants 15 D6
Stubbins Lancs 87 C5
Stubbs Cross Kent 19 B6
Stubb's Green Norf 69 E5
Stubbs Green Norf 69 E6
Stubhampton Dorset 13 C7
Stubton Lincs 77 E8
Stuckgowan Argyll 132 D2
Stuckton Hants 14 C2
Stud Green Windsor 27 B6
Studham Beds 40 C3
Studland Dorset 13 F8
Studley Warks 51 C5
Studley Wilts 24 B4
Studley Roger N Yorks 95 B5
Stump Cross Essex 55 E6
Stuntney Cambs 55 B6
Sturbridge Staffs 74 F5
Sturmer Essex 55 E7
Sturminster Marshall Dorset 13 D7
Sturminster Newton Dorset 13 C5
Sturry Kent 31 C5
Sturton N Lincs 90 D3
Sturton by Stow Lincs 90 F2
Sturton le Steeple Notts 89 F8
Stuston Suff 56 B5
Stutton N Yorks 95 E7
Stutton Suff 57 F5
Styal Ches 87 F6
Styrrup Notts 89 E7
Suainebost W Isles 172 B8
Suardail W Isles 172 E7
Succoth Aberds 159 F8
Succoth Argyll 131 E8
Suckley Worcs 50 D2
Suckquoy Orkney 176 H3
Sudborough Northants 65 F6
Sudbourne Suff 57 D8
Sudbrook Lincs 78 E2
Sudbrook Mon 36 F2
Sudbrooke Lincs 78 B3
Sudbury Derbys 75 F8
Sudbury London 40 F4
Sudbury Suff 56 E2
Suddie Highld 157 D7
Sudeley Castle and Gardens Glos 37 B7
Sudgrove Glos 37 D6
Suffield Norf 81 D8
Suffield N Yorks 103 E7
Sugnall Staffs 74 F4
Suladale Highld 152 D4
Sulaisiadar W Isles 172 E8
Sulby I o M 84 C3
Sulgrave Northants 52 E3
Sulham W Berks 26 B4
Sulhamstead W Berks 26 C4
Sulland Orkney 176 B4
Sullington W Sus 16 C4
Sullom Shetland 174 F5
Sullom Voe Oil Terminal Shetland 174 F5
Sully V Glam 22 C3
Sumburgh Shetland 175 N6
Sumburgh Airport Shetland 175 M5
Summer Bridge N Yorks 94 C5
Summer-house Darl 101 C7
Summercourt Corn 4 D3
Summerfield Norf 80 D3
Summergangs Hull 97 F7
Summerleaze Mon 35 F8
Summerlee Heritage Centre, Coatbridge N Lnrk 121 C7
Summersdale W Sus 16 D2
Summerseat Gtr Man 87 C5
Summertown Oxon 39 D5
Summit Gtr Man 87 D7
Sunbury-on-Thames Sur 28 C2
Sundaywell Dumfries 113 F8
Sunderland Argyll 126 C2
Sunderland Cumb 107 F8
Sunderland T & W 111 D6
Sunderland Bridge Durham 111 F5
Sundhope Borders 115 B6
Sundon Park Luton 40 B3
Sundown Kiddies Adventureland, Rampton Notts 77 B7
Sundridge Kent 29 D5
Sunipol Argyll 136 C4
Sunk Island E Yorks 91 C6
Sunningdale Windsor 27 C7
Sunninghill Windsor 27 C7
Sunningwell Oxon 38 D4
Sunniside Durham 110 F4
Sunniside T & W 110 D5
Sunnyhurst Blkburn 86 B4
Sunnylaw Stirl 133 E6
Sunnyside W Sus 28 F4
Sunton Wilts 25 D7
Surbiton London 28 C2
Surby I o M 84 E2
Surfleet Lincs 66 B2
Surfleet Seas End Lincs 66 B2
Surlingham Norf 69 D6
Sustead Norf 81 D7
Susworth Lincs 90 D2
Sutcombe Devon 8 C5
Suton Norf 68 E3
Sutors of Cromarty Highld 158 C2
Sutterby Lincs 79 B6
Sutterton Lincs 79 F5
Sutton Beds 54 E3
Sutton Cambs 54 B5
Sutton London 28 C3
Sutton Kent 31 E7
Sutton Mers 86 E3
Sutton Norf 69 B6
Sutton Notts 77 F7
Sutton Notts 89 F7
Sutton N Yorks 89 B5
Sutton Oxon 38 D4
Sutton P'boro 65 E7
Sutton Shrops 61 F7
Sutton Shrops 74 F3
Sutton Som 23 F8
Sutton Staffs 61 B7
Sutton Suff 57 E7
Sutton Sur 27 E8
Sutton S Yorks 89 C6
Sutton W Sus 16 C3
Sutton at Hone Kent 29 B6
Sutton Bassett Northants 64 E4
Sutton Benger Wilts 24 B4
Sutton Bonington Notts 64 B2
Sutton Bridge Lincs 66 B4
Sutton Cheney Leics 63 D8
Sutton Coldfield W Mid 62 E5
Sutton Courtenay Oxon 39 E5
Sutton Crosses Lincs 66 B4
Sutton Grange N Yorks 95 B5
Sutton Green Sur 27 D8
Sutton Howgrave N Yorks 95 B6
Sutton In Ashfield Notts 76 D4
Sutton-in-Craven N Yorks 94 E3
Sutton in the Elms Leics 64 E2
Sutton Ings Hull 97 F7
Sutton Lane Ends Ches 75 B6
Sutton Leach Mers 86 E3
Sutton Maddock Shrops 61 D7
Sutton Mallet Som 23 F5
Sutton Mandeville Wilts 13 B7
Sutton Manor Mers 86 E3
Sutton Montis Som 12 B4
Sutton on Hull Hull 97 F7
Sutton on Sea Lincs 91 F9
Sutton-on-the-Forest N Yorks 95 C8
Sutton on the Hill Derbys 76 F2
Sutton on Trent Notts 77 C7
Sutton St Edmund Lincs 66 C3
Sutton St James Lincs 66 C3
Sutton St Nicholas Hereford 49 E7
Sutton Scarsdale Derbys 76 C4
Sutton Scotney Hants 26 F2
Sutton under Brailes Warks 51 F8
Sutton-under-Whitestonecliffe N Yorks 102 F2
Sutton upon Derwent E Yorks 96 E3
Sutton Valence Kent 30 E2
Sutton Veny Wilts 24 E3
Sutton Waldron Dorset 13 C6
Sutton Weaver Ches 74 B2
Sutton Wick Bath 23 D7
Swaby Lincs 79 B6
Swadlincote Derbys 63 C7
Swaffham Norf 67 D8
Swaffham Bulbeck Cambs 55 C6
Swaffham Prior Cambs 55 C6
Swafield Norf 81 D8
Swainby N Yorks 102 D2
Swainshill Hereford 49 E6
Swainsthorpe Norf 68 D5
Swainswick Bath 24 C2
Swalcliffe Oxon 51 F8
Swalecliffe Kent 30 C5
Swallow Lincs 91 D5
Swallowcliffe Wilts 13 B7
Swallowfield Wokingham 26 C5
Swallownest S Yorks 89 F5
Swallows Cross Essex 42 E2
Swan Green Ches 74 B4
Swan Green Suff 57 B6
Swanage Dorset 13 G8
Swanage Railway Dorset 13 G8
Swanbister Orkney 176 F2
Swanbourne Bucks 39 B8
Swanland E Yorks 90 B3
Swanley Kent 29 C6
Swanley Village Kent 29 C6
Swanmore Hants 15 C6
Swannery, Abbotsbury Dorset 12 F3
Swannington Leics 63 C8
Swannington Norf 68 C4
Swanscombe Kent 29 B7
Swansea = Abertawe Swansea 33 E7
Swanton Abbot Norf 81 E8
Swanton Morley Norf 68 C3
Swanton Novers Norf 81 D6
Swanton Street Kent 30 D2
Swanwick Derbys 76 D4
Swanwick Hants 15 D6
Swarby Lincs 78 E3
Swardeston Norf 68 D5
Swarister Shetland 174 E7
Swarkestone Derbys 63 B7
Swarland Northumb 117 D7
Swarland Estate Northumb 117 D7
Swarthmoor Cumb 92 B2
Swathwick Derbys 76 C3
Swaton Lincs 78 F4
Swavesey Cambs 54 C4
Sway Hants 14 E3
Swayfield Lincs 65 B6
Swaythling Soton 14 C5
Sweet Green Worcs 49 C8
Sweetham Devon 10 E3
Sweethouse Corn 5 C5
Sweffling Suff 57 C7
Swepstone Leics 63 C7
Swerford Oxon 51 F8
Swettenham Ches 74 C5
Swetton N Yorks 94 B4
Swffryd Bl Gwent 35 E6
Swiftsden E Sus 18 C4
Swilland Suff 57 D5
Swillington W Yorks 95 F6
Swimbridge Devon 9 B8
Swimbridge Newland Devon 20 F5
Swinbrook Oxon 38 C2
Swinderby Lincs 77 C8
Swindon Glos 37 B6
Swindon Staffs 62 E2
Swindon Thamesdown 38 F1
Swine E Yorks 97 F7
Swinefleet E Yorks 89 B8
Swineshead Beds 53 C8
Swineshead Lincs 78 E5
Swineshead Bridge Lincs 78 E5
Swiney Highld 169 F7
Swinford Leics 52 B3
Swinford Oxon 38 D4
Swingate Notts 76 E5
Swingfield Minnis Kent 31 E6
Swingfield St Kent 31 E6
Swinhoe Northumb 117 B8
Swinhope Lincs 91 E6
Swining Shetland 174 G6
Swinithwaite N Yorks 101 F5
Swinnow Moor W Yorks 94 F5
Swinscoe Staffs 75 E8
Swinside Hall Borders 116 C3
Swinstead Lincs 65 B7
Swinton Borders 124 E4
Swinton Gtr Man 87 D5
Swinton N Yorks 94 B5
Swinton N Yorks 96 B3
Swinton S Yorks 88 E5
Swintonmill Borders 124 E4
Swithland Leics 64 C2
Swordale Highld 157 C6
Swordland Highld 145 D7
Swordly Highld 168 C2
Sworton Heath Ches 86 F4
Swydd-ffynnon Ceredig 47 C5
Swynnerton Staffs 75 F5
Swyre Dorset 12 F3
Sychtyn Powys 59 D6
Syde Glos 37 C6
Sydenham London 28 B4
Sydenham Oxon 39 D7
Sydenham Damerel Devon 6 B2
Syderstone Norf 80 D4
Sydling St Nicholas Dorset 12 E4
Sydmonton Hants 26 D2
Syerston Notts 77 E7
Syke Gtr Man 87 C6
Sykehouse S Yorks 89 C7
Sykes Lancs 93 D6
Syleham Suff 57 B6
Sylen Carms 33 D6
Symbister Shetland 175 G7
Symington S Ayrs 120 F3
Symington S Lnrk 122 F2
Symonds Yat Hereford 36 C2
Symondsbury Dorset 12 E2
Synod Inn Ceredig 46 D3
Syon Park & House London 28 B2
Syre Highld 167 E8
Syreford Glos 37 B7
Syresham Northants 52 E4
Syston Leics 64 C3
Syston Lincs 78 E2
Sytchampton Worcs 50 C3
Sywell Northants 53 C6

T

Taagan Highld 154 D6
Tàbost W Isles 172 B8
Tabost W Isles 172 G6
Tackley Oxon 38 B4
Tacleit W Isles 172 E4
Tacolneston Norf 68 E4
Tadcaster N Yorks 95 E7
Taddington Derbys 75 B8
Taddiport Devon 9 C6
Tadley Hants 26 C4
Tadlow Beds 54 E3
Tadmarton Oxon 51 F8
Tadworth Sur 28 D3
Tafarn-y-gelyn Denb 73 C5
Tafarnau-bach Bl Gwent 35 C5
Taff's Well Rhondda 35 F5
Tafolwern Powys 59 D5
Tai Conwy 83 E7
Tai-bach Powys 59 B8
Tai-mawr Conwy 72 E3
Tai-Ucha Denb 72 D4
Taibach Neath 34 F1
Taigh a Ghearraidh W Isles 170 C3
Tain Highld 164 F4
Tain Highld 169 C7
Tainant Wrex 73 E6
Tainlon Gwyn 82 F4
Tai'r-Bull Powys 34 B3
Tairbeart = Tarbert W Isles 173 H4
Tairgwaith Neath 33 C8
Takeley Essex 42 B1
Takeley Street Essex 41 B8
Tal-sarn Ceredig 46 D4
Tal-y-bont Ceredig 58 F3
Tal-y-Bont Conwy 83 E7
Tal-y-bont Gwyn 83 D6
Tal-y-bont Gwyn 71 E6
Tal-y-cafn Conwy 83 D7
Tal-y-llyn Gwyn 58 D4
Tal-y-wern Powys 58 D5
Talachddu Powys 48 F2
Talacre Flint 85 F2
Talardd Gwyn 59 B5
Talaton Devon 11 E5
Talbenny Pembs 44 D3
Talbot Green Rhondda 34 F4
Talbot Village Poole 13 E8
Tale Devon 11 D5
Talerddig Powys 59 D6
Talgarreg Ceredig 46 D3
Talgarth Powys 48 F3
Talisker Highld 153 F4
Talke Staffs 74 D5
Talkin Cumb 109 D5
Talla Linnfoots Borders 114 B4
Talladale Highld 154 C5
Tallarn Green Wrex 73 E8
Tallentire Cumb 107 F8
Talley Carms 46 F5
Tallington Lincs 65 D7
Talmine Highld 167 C7
Talog Carms 32 B4
Talsarn Carms 34 B1
Talsarnau Gwyn 71 D7
Talskiddy Corn 4 C4
Talwrn Anglesey 82 D4
Talwrn Wrex 73 E6
Talybont-on-Usk Powys 35 B5
Talygarn Rhondda 34 F4
Talyllyn Powys 35 B5
Talysarn Gwyn 82 F4
Talywain Torf 35 D6
Tame Bridge N Yorks 102 D3
Tamerton Foliot Plym 6 C2
Tamworth Staffs 63 D6
Tan Hinon Powys 59 F5
Tan-lan Conwy 83 E7
Tan-lan Gwyn 71 C7
Tan-y-bwlch Gwyn 71 C7
Tan-y-fron Conwy 72 C3
Tan-y-graig Anglesey 82 D5
Tan-y-graig Gwyn 70 D4
Tan-y-groes Ceredig 45 E4
Tan-y-pistyll Powys 59 B7
Tan-yr-allt Gwyn 82 F4
Tandem W Yorks 88 C2
Tanden Kent 19 B6
Tandridge Sur 28 D4
Tanerdy Carms 33 B5
Tanfield Durham 110 D4
Tanfield Lea Durham 110 D4
Tangasdal W Isles 171 L2
Tangiers Pembs 44 D4
Tangley Hants 25 D8
Tanglwst Carms 46 F2
Tangmere W Sus 16 D3
Tangwick Shetland 174 F4
Tank Museum, Bovington Dorset 13 F6
Tankersley S Yorks 88 D4
Tankerton Kent 30 C5
Tannach Highld 169 E8
Tannachie Aberds 151 F6
Tannadice Angus 142 D4
Tannington Suff 57 C6
Tansley Derbys 76 D3
Tansley Knoll Derbys 76 C3
Tansor Northants 65 E7
Tantobie Durham 110 D4
Tanton N Yorks 102 C3
Tanworth-in-Arden Warks 51 B6
Tanygrisiau Gwyn 71 C7
Tanyrhydiau Ceredig 47 C6
Taobh a Chaolais W Isles 171 J3
Taobh a Thuath Loch Aineort W Isles 171 H3
Taobh a Tuath Loch Baghasdail W Isles 171 H3
Taobh a'Ghlinne W Isles 172 G6
Taobh Tuath W Isles 173 K2
Taplow Bucks 40 F2
Tapton Derbys 76 B3
Tarbat Ho. Highld 157 B8
Tarbert Argyll 127 D4
Tarbert Argyll 128 D3
Tarbert Argyll 118 A3
Tarbert = Tairbeart W Isles 173 H4
Tarbet Argyll 132 D2
Tarbet Highld 166 E3
Tarbet Highld 145 D7
Tarbock Green Mers 86 F2
Tarbolton S Ayrs 112 B4
Tarbrax S Lnrk 122 D3
Tardebigge Worcs 50 C5
Tarfside Angus 142 B4
Tarland Aberds 150 D3
Tarleton Lancs 86 B2
Tarlogie Highld 164 F4
Tarlscough Lancs 86 C2
Tarlton Glos 37 E6
Tarnbrook Lancs 93 D5
Tarporley Ches 74 C2
Tarr Som 22 F3
Tarrant Crawford Dorset 13 D7
Tarrant Gunville Dorset 13 C7
Tarrant Hinton Dorset 13 C7
Tarrant Keyneston Dorset 13 D7
Tarrant Launceston Dorset 13 D7
Tarrant Monkton Dorset 13 D7
Tarrant Rawston Dorset 13 D7
Tarrant Rushton Dorset 13 D7
Tarrel Highld 165 F5
Tarring Neville E Sus 17 D8
Tarrington Hereford 49 E8
Tarsappie Perth 134 B3
Tarskavaig Highld 145 C5
Tarves Aberds 161 E5
Tarvie Highld 156 D5
Tarvie Perth 141 C7
Tarvin Ches 73 C8
Tasburgh Norf 68 E5
Tasley Shrops 61 E6
Taston Oxon 38 B3
Tate Gallery London 28 B3
Tate Gallery, Albert Dock Mers 85 F8
Tate Modern London 28 B4
Tate St Ives Corn 2 B4
Tatenhill Staffs 63 B6
Tathall End M Keynes 53 E6
Tatham Lancs 93 C6
Tathwell Lincs 91 F7
Tatling End Bucks 40 F3
Tatsfield Sur 28 D5
Tattenhall Ches 73 D8
Tattenhoe M Keynes 53 F6
Tatterford Norf 80 E4
Tattersett Norf 80 D4
Tattershall Lincs 78 D5
Tattershall Bridge Lincs 78 D4
Tattershall Thorpe Lincs 78 D5
Tattingstone Suff 56 F5
Tatton House, Knutsford Ches 86 F5
Tatworth Som 11 D8
Taunton Som 11 B7
Taunton Racecourse Som 11 B7
Taverham Norf 68 C4
Tavernspite Pembs 32 C2
Tavistock Devon 6 B2
Taw Green Devon 9 E8
Tawstock Devon 9 B7
Taxal Derbys 75 B7
Tay Bridge Dundee 135 B6
Tayinloan Argyll 118 B3
Taymouth Castle Perth 140 E4
Taynish Argyll 128 B2
Taynton Glos 36 B4
Taynton Oxon 38 C2
Taynuilt Argyll 131 B6
Tayport Fife 135 B6
Tayvallich Argyll 128 B2
Tealby Lincs 91 E5
Tealing Angus 142 F4
Teangue Highld 145 C6
Teanna Mhachair W Isles 170 D3
Tebay Cumb 99 D8
Tebworth Beds 40 B2
Tedburn St Mary Devon 10 E3
Teddington Glos 50 F4
Teddington London 28 B2
Tedstone Delamere Hereford 49 D8
Tedstone Wafre Hereford 49 D8
Teeton Northants 52 B4
Teffont Evias Wilts 24 F4
Teffont Magna Wilts 24 F4
Tegryn Pembs 45 F4
Teigh Rutland 65 C5
Teigncombe Devon 9 F8
Teigngrace Devon 7 B6
Teignmouth Devon 7 B7
Telford Telford 61 D6
Telham E Sus 18 D4
Tellisford Som 24 D3
Telscombe E Sus 17 D8
Telscombe Cliffs E Sus 17 D7
Templand Dumfries 114 F3
Temple Corn 5 B6
Temple Glasgow 120 C5
Temple Midloth 123 D6
Temple Balsall W Mid 51 B7
Temple Bar Ceredig 46 D4
Temple Bar Carms 33 C6
Temple Cloud Bath 23 D8
Temple Combe Som 12 B5
Temple Ewell Kent 31 E6
Temple Grafton Warks 51 D6
Temple Guiting Glos 37 B7
Temple Herdewyke Warks 51 D8
Temple Hirst N Yorks 89 B7
Temple Normanton Derbys 76 C4
Temple Sowerby Cumb 99 B8
Templehall Fife 134 E4
Templeton Devon 10 C3
Templeton Pembs 32 C2
Templeton Bridge Devon 10 C3
Templetown Durham 110 D4
Tempsford Beds 54 D2
Ten Mile Bank Norf 67 E6
Tenbury Wells Worcs 49 C7
Tenby = Dinbych-y-Pysgod Pembs 32 D2
Tendring Essex 43 B7
Tendring Green Essex 43 B7
Tenston Orkney 176 E1
Tenterden Kent 19 B5
Terling Essex 42 C3
Ternhill Shrops 74 F3
Terregles Banks Dumfries 107 B6
Terrick Bucks 39 D8
Terrington N Yorks 96 B2
Terrington St Clement Norf 66 C5
Terrington St John Norf 66 C5
Teston Kent 29 D8
Testwood Hants 14 C4
Tetbury Glos 37 E5
Tetbury Upton Glos 37 E5
Tetchill Shrops 73 F7
Tetcott Devon 8 E5
Tetford Lincs 79 B6
Tetney Lincs 91 D7
Tetney Lock Lincs 91 D7
Tetsworth Oxon 39 D6
Tettenhall W Mid 62 E2
Teuchan Aberds 161 E7
Teversal Notts 76 C4
Teversham Cambs 55 D5
Teviothead Borders 115 D7
Tewel Aberds 151 F7
Tewin Herts 41 C5
Tewkesbury Glos 50 F3
Tewkesbury Abbey Glos 50 F3
Teynham Kent 30 C3
Thackthwaite Cumb 98 B3
Thainston Aberds 143 B6
Thakeham W Sus 16 C5
Thame Oxon 39 D7
Thames Ditton Sur 28 C2
Thames Haven Thurrock 42 F3
Thamesmead London 41 F7
Thanington Kent 30 D5
Thankerton S Lnrk 122 F2
Tharston Norf 68 E4
Thatcham W Berks 26 C3
Thatto Heath Mers 86 E3
Thaxted Essex 55 F7
The Aird Highld 152 D5
The All England Jumping Course, Hickstead W Sus 17 C6
The Arms Norf 67 E8
The Bage Hereford 48 E4
The Balloch Perth 133 C7
The Barony Orkney 176 D1
The Bluebell Railway, Sheffield Park E Sus 17 B8
The Bog Shrops 60 E3
The Bourne Sur 27 E6
The Braes Highld 153 F6
The Broad Hereford 49 C6
The Burrell Collection Glasgow 121 C5
The Butts Som 24 E2
The Camp Glos 37 D6
The Camp Herts 40 D4
The Chequer Wrex 73 E8
The City Bucks 39 E7
The Common Wilts 25 F7
The Craigs Highld 164 E1
The Cronk I o M 84 C3
The Dell Suff 69 E7
The Den N Ayrs 120 D3
The Dinosaur Museum, Dorchester Dorset 12 E4
The Eals Northumb 116 F3
The Eaves Glos 36 D3
The Flatt Cumb 109 B5
The Four Alls Shrops 74 F3
The Friars, Aylesford Kent 29 D8
The Garths Shetland 174 B8
The Green Cumb 98 F3
The Green Wilts 24 F3
The Grove Dumfries 107 B6
The Hall Shetland 174 D8
The Haven W Sus 27 F8
The Heath Norf 81 E7
The Heath Suff 56 F5
The Hill Cumb 98 F3
The Howe Cumb 99 F6
The Howe I o M 84 F1
The Hundred Hereford 49 C7
The Lee Bucks 40 D2
The Lhen I o M 84 B3
The Living RainForest W Berks 26 B3
The Long Man of Wilmington E Sus 18 E2
The Lost Gardens of Heligan, Mevagissey Corn 4 E4
The Lowry, Salford Gtr Man 87 E6
The Marsh Powys 60 E3
The Marsh Wilts 37 F7
The Middles Durham 110 D5
The Moor Kent 18 C4
The Moors Centre, Danby N Yorks 103 D5
The Mumbles = Y Mwmbwls Swansea 33 F7
The Murray S Lnrk 121 D6
The National Archives, Kew London 28 B3
The National Tramway Museum, Crich Derbys 76 D3
The Needles Old Battery I o W 14 F3
The Neuk Aberds 151 E6
The Oval Bath 24 C2
The Oval Cricket Ground London 28 B4
The Oxford Story, Oxford Oxon 39 D5
The Pole of Itlaw Aberds 160 C3
The Quarry Glos 36 E4
The Rhos Pembs 32 C1
The Rock Telford 61 D6
The Ryde Herts 41 D5
The Sands Sur 27 E6
The Stocks Kent 19 C6
The Tales of Robin Hood Nottingham 77 E5
The Throat Wokingham 27 C6
The Tutankhamun Exhibition, Dorchester Dorset 12 E4
The Vauld Hereford 49 E7
The Vyne Hants 26 D4
The World of Beatrix Potter, Bowness-on-Windermere Cumb 99 E6
The Wyke Shrops 61 D7
Theakston N Yorks 101 F8
Thealby N Lincs 90 C2
Theale Som 23 E6
Theale W Berks 26 B4
Thearne E Yorks 97 F6
Theberton Suff 57 C8
Theddingworth Leics 64 F3
Theddlethorpe All Saints Lincs 91 F8
Theddlethorpe St Helen Lincs 91 F8
Thelbridge Barton Devon 10 C2
Thelnetham Suff 56 B4
Thelveton Norf 68 F4
Thelwall Warr 86 F4
Themelthorpe Norf 81 E6
Thenford Northants 52 E3
Therfield Herts 54 F4
Thetford Lincs 65 C8
Thetford Norf 67 F8
Theydon Bois Essex 41 E7
Thickwood Wilts 24 B3
Thimbleby Lincs 78 C5
Thimbleby N Yorks 102 E2
Thingwall Mers 85 F3
Thirdpart N Ayrs 119 B8
Thirlby N Yorks 102 F2
Thirlestane Borders 123 E8
Thirn N Yorks 101 F7
Thirsk N Yorks 102 F2
Thirsk Racecourse N Yorks 102 F2
Thirtleby E Yorks 97 F7
Thistleton Lancs 92 F4
Thistleton Rutland 65 C6
Thistley Green Suff 55 B7
Thixendale N Yorks 96 C4
Thockrington Northumb 110 B2
Tholomas Drove Cambs 66 D3
Tholthorpe N Yorks 95 C7
Thomas Chapel Pembs 32 D2
Thomas Close Cumb 108 E4
Thomastown Aberds 160 E2
Thompson Norf 68 E2
Thomshill Moray 159 D6
Thong Kent 29 B7
Thongsbridge W Yorks 88 D2
Thoralby N Yorks 101 F5
Thoresway Lincs 91 E5
Thorganby Lincs 91 E6
Thorganby N Yorks 96 E2
Thorgill N Yorks 103 E5
Thorington Suff 57 B8
Thorington Street Suff 56 F4
Thorlby N Yorks 94 D2
Thorley Herts 41 C7
Thorley Street Herts 41 C7
Thorley Street I o W 14 F4
Thormanby N Yorks 95 B7
Thornaby on Tees Stockton 102 C2
Thornage Norf 81 D6
Thornborough Bucks 52 F5
Thornborough N Yorks 95 B5
Thornbury Devon 9 D6
Thornbury Hereford 49 D8
Thornbury S Glos 36 E3
Thornbury W Yorks 94 F4
Thornby Northants 52 B4
Thorncliffe Staffs 75 D7
Thorncombe Dorset 11 D8
Thorncombe Dorset 13 D6
Thorncombe Street Sur 27 E8
Thorncote Green Beds 54 E2
Thorncross I o W 14 F5
Thorndon Suff 56 C5
Thorndon Cross Devon 9 E7
Thorne S Yorks 89 C7
Thorne St Margaret Som 11 B5
Thorner W Yorks 95 E6
Thorney Notts 77 B8
Thorney P'boro 66 D2
Thorney Crofts E Yorks 91 B6
Thorney Green Suff 56 C4
Thorney Hill Hants 14 E2
Thorney Toll Cambs 66 D3
Thornfalcon Som 11 B7
Thornford Dorset 12 C4
Thorngumbald E Yorks 91 B6
Thornham Norf 80 C3
Thornham Magna Suff 56 B5
Thornham Parva Suff 56 B5
Thornhaugh P'boro 65 D7
Thornhill Caerph 35 F5
Thornhill Cumb 98 D2
Thornhill Derbys 88 F2
Thornhill Dumfries 113 E8
Thornhill Soton 15 C5
Thornhill Stirl 133 E5
Thornhill W Yorks 88 C3
Thornhill Edge W Yorks 88 C3
Thornhill Lees W Yorks 88 C3
Thornholme E Yorks 97 C7
Thornley Durham 110 F4
Thornley Durham 111 F6
Thornliebank E Renf 120 D5
Thorns Suff 55 D8
Thorns Green Ches 87 F5
Thornsett Derbys 87 F8
Thornthwaite Cumb 98 B4
Thornthwaite N Yorks 94 D4
Thornton Angus 142 E3
Thornton Bucks 53 F5
Thornton E Yorks 96 E3
Thornton Fife 134 E4
Thornton Lancs 92 E3
Thornton Leics 63 D8
Thornton Lincs 78 C5
Thornton Mers 85 D4
Thornton M'bro 102 C2
Thornton Northumb 125 E5
Thornton Pembs 44 E4
Thornton W Yorks 94 F4
Thornton Curtis N Lincs 90 C4
Thornton Heath London 28 C4
Thornton Hough Mers 85 F4
Thornton in Craven N Yorks 94 E2
Thornton-le-Beans N Yorks 102 E1

Thornton-le-Clay N Yorks 96 C2
Thornton-le-Dale N Yorks 103 F6
Thornton le Moor Lincs 90 E4
Thornton-le-Moor N Yorks 102 F1
Thornton-le-Moors Ches 73 B8
Thornton-le-Street N Yorks 102 F2
Thornton Rust N Yorks 100 F4
Thornton Steward N Yorks 101 F6
Thornton Watlass N Yorks 101 F7
Thorntonhall S Lnrk 121 D5
Thorntonloch E Loth 124 B3
Thorntonpark Northumb 124 E5
Thornwood Common Essex 41 D7
Thornydykes Borders 124 E2
Thoroton Notts 77 E7
Thorp Arch W Yorks 95 E7
Thorpe Derbys 75 D8
Thorpe E Yorks 97 E5
Thorpe Lincs 91 F8
Thorpe Norf 69 E7
Thorpe Notts 77 E7
Thorpe N Yorks 94 C3
Thorpe Sur 27 C8
Thorpe Abbotts Norf 57 B5
Thorpe Acre Leics 64 B2
Thorpe Arnold Leics 64 B4
Thorpe Audlin W Yorks 89 C5
Thorpe Bassett N Yorks 96 B4
Thorpe Bay Sthend 43 F5
Thorpe by Water Rutland 65 E5
Thorpe Common Suff 57 F6
Thorpe Constantine Staffs 63 D6
Thorpe Culvert Lincs 79 C7
Thorpe End Norf 69 C5
Thorpe Fendykes Lincs 79 C7
Thorpe Green Essex 43 B7
Thorpe Green Suff 56 D3
Thorpe Hesley S Yorks 88 E4
Thorpe in Balne S Yorks 89 C6
Thorpe in the Fallows Lincs 90 F3
Thorpe Langton Leics 64 E4
Thorpe Larches Durham 102 B1
Thorpe-le-Soken Essex 43 B7
Thorpe le Street E Yorks 96 E4
Thorpe Malsor Northants 53 B6
Thorpe Mandeville Northants 52 E3
Thorpe Market Norf 81 D8
Thorpe Marriot Norf 68 C4
Thorpe Morieux Suff 56 D3
Thorpe on the Hill Lincs 78 C2
Thorpe Park, Chertsey Sur 27 C8
Thorpe St Andrew Norf 69 D5
Thorpe St Peter Lincs 79 C7
Thorpe Salvin S Yorks 89 F6
Thorpe Satchville Leics 64 C4
Thorpe Thewles Stockton 102 B2
Thorpe Tilney Lincs 78 D4
Thorpe Underwood N Yorks 95 D7
Thorpe Waterville Northants 65 F7
Thorpe Willoughby N Yorks 95 F8
Thorpeness Suff 57 D8
Thorrington Essex 43 C6
Thorverton Devon 10 D4
Thrandeston Suff 56 B5
Thrapston Northants 53 B7
Thrashbush N Lnrk 121 C7
Threapland Cumb 107 F8
Threapland N Yorks 94 C2
Threapwood Ches 73 E8
Threapwood Staffs 75 E7
Threave Gardens Dumfries 106 C4
Three Ashes Hereford 36 B2
Three Bridges W Sus 28 F3
Three Burrows Corn 3 B6
Three Chimneys Kent 18 B5
Three Cocks Powys 48 F3
Three Counties Showground, Malvern Worcs 50 E2
Three Crosses Swansea 33 E6
Three Cups Corner E Sus 18 C3
Three Holes Norf 66 D5
Three Leg Cross E Sus 18 B3
Three Legged Cross Dorset 13 D8
Three Oaks E Sus 18 D5
Threehammer Common Norf 69 C6
Threekingham Lincs 78 F3
Threemile Cross Wokingham 26 C5
Threemilestone Corn 3 B6
Threemiletown W Loth 122 B3
Threlkeld Cumb 99 B5
Threshfield N Yorks 94 C2
Thrigby Norf 69 C7
Thringarth Durham 100 B4
Thringstone Leics 63 C8
Thrintoft N Yorks 101 E8
Thriplow Cambs 54 E5
Throckenholt Lincs 66 D3
Throcking Herts 54 F4
Throckley T & W 110 C4
Throckmorton Worcs 50 E4
Throphill Northumb 117 F7
Thropton Northumb 117 D6
Throsk Stirl 133 E7
Throwleigh Devon 9 E8
Throwley Kent 30 D3
Thrumpton Notts 76 F5
Thrumster Highld 169 E8
Thrunton Northumb 117 C6
Thrupp Glos 37 D5
Thrupp Oxon 38 C4
Thrushelton Devon 9 F6
Thrussington Leics 64 C3
Thruxton Hants 25 E7
Thruxton Hereford 49 F6
Thruxton Motor Racing Circuit Hants 25 E7
Thrybergh S Yorks 89 E5
Thulston Derbys 76 F4
Thundergay N Ayrs 119 B5
Thundersley Essex 42 F3
Thundridge Herts 41 C6
Thurcaston Leics 64 C2
Thurcroft S Yorks 89 F5
Thurgarton Norf 81 D7
Thurgarton Notts 77 E6
Thurgoland S Yorks 88 D3
Thurlaston Leics 64 E2
Thurlaston Warks 52 B2
Thurlbear Som 11 B7
Thurlby Lincs 65 C8
Thurlby Lincs 78 C2
Thurleigh Beds 53 D8
Thurlestone Devon 6 E4
Thurloxton Som 22 F4
Thurlstone S Yorks 88 D3
Thurlton Norf 69 E7
Thurlwood Ches 74 D5
Thurmaston Leics 64 D3
Thurnby Leics 64 D3
Thurne Norf 69 C7
Thurnham Kent 30 D2
Thurnham Lancs 92 D4
Thurning Norf 81 E6
Thurning Northants 65 F7
Thurnscoe S Yorks 89 D5
Thurnscoe East S Yorks 89 D5
Thursby Cumb 108 D3
Thursford Norf 81 D5
Thursford Collection, Fakenham Norf 81 D5
Thursley Sur 27 F7
Thurso Highld 169 C6
Thurso East Highld 169 C6
Thurstaston Mers 85 F3
Thurston Suff 56 C3
Thurstonfield Cumb 108 D3
Thurstonland W Yorks 88 C2
Thurton Norf 69 D6
Thurvaston Derbys 76 F2
Thuxton Norf 68 D3
Thwaite N Yorks 100 E3
Thwaite Suff 56 C5
Thwaite St Mary Norf 69 E6
Thwaites W Yorks 94 E3
Thwaites Brow W Yorks 94 E3
Thwing E Yorks 97 B6
Tibbermore Perth 134 B2
Tibberton Glos 36 B4
Tibberton Telford 61 B6
Tibberton Worcs 50 D4
Tibenham Norf 68 F4
Tibshelf Derbys 76 C4
Tibthorpe E Yorks 97 D5
Ticehurst E Sus 18 B3
Tichborne Hants 26 F3
Tickencote Rutland 65 D6
Tickenham N Som 23 B6
Tickhill S Yorks 89 E6
Ticklerton Shrops 60 E4
Ticknall Derbys 63 B7
Tickton E Yorks 97 E6
Tidcombe Wilts 25 D7
Tiddington Oxon 39 D6
Tiddington Warks 51 D7
Tidebrook E Sus 18 C3
Tideford Corn 5 D8
Tideford Cross Corn 5 C8
Tidenham Glos 36 E2
Tideswell Derbys 75 B8
Tidmarsh W Berks 26 B4
Tidmington Warks 51 F7
Tidpit Hants 13 C8
Tidworth Wilts 25 E7
Tiers Cross Pembs 44 D4
Tiffield Northants 52 D4
Tifty Aberds 160 D4
Tigerton Angus 143 C5
Tigh-na-Blair Perth 133 C6
Tighnabruaich Argyll 128 C4
Tighnafiline Highld 162 F2
Tigley Devon 7 C5
Tilbrook Cambs 53 C8
Tilbury Thurrock 29 B7
Tilbury Juxta Clare Essex 55 E8
Tile Cross W Mid 63 F5
Tile Hill W Mid 51 B7
Tilehurst Reading 26 B4
Tilford Sur 27 E6
Tilgate W Sus 28 F3
Tilgate Forest Row W Sus 28 F3
Tillathrowie Aberds 159 F8
Tilley Shrops 60 B5
Tillicoultry Clack 133 E8
Tillingham Essex 43 D5
Tillington Hereford 49 E6
Tillington W Sus 16 B3
Tillington Common Hereford 49 E6
Tillyarblet Angus 143 C5
Tillybirloch Aberds 151 D5
Tillycorthie Aberds 151 B8
Tillydrine Aberds 150 E5
Tillyfour Aberds 150 C4
Tillyfourie Aberds 150 C5
Tillygarmond Aberds 150 E5
Tillygreig Aberds 151 B7
Tillykerrie Aberds 151 B7
Tilmanstone Kent 31 D7
Tilney All Saints Norf 67 C5
Tilney High End Norf 67 C5
Tilney St Lawrence Norf 66 C5
Tilshead Wilts 24 E5
Tilstock Shrops 74 F2
Tilston Ches 73 D8
Tilstone Fearnall Ches 74 C2
Tilsworth Beds 40 B2
Tilton on the Hill Leics 64 D4
Timberland Lincs 78 D4
Timbersbrook Ches 75 C5
Timberscombe Som 21 E8
Timble N Yorks 94 D4
Timperley Gtr Man 87 F5
Timsbury Bath 23 D8
Timsbury Hants 14 B4
Timsgearraidh W Isles 172 E3
Timworth Green Suff 56 C2
Tincleton Dorset 13 E5
Tindale Cumb 109 D6
Tingewick Bucks 52 F4
Tingley W Yorks 88 B3
Tingrith Beds 53 F8
Tingwall Orkney 176 D2
Tinhay Devon 9 F5
Tinshill W Yorks 95 F5
Tinsley S Yorks 88 E5
Tintagel Corn 8 F2
Tintagel Castle Corn 8 F2
Tintern Abbey Mon 36 D2
Tintern Parva Mon 36 D2
Tintinhull Som 12 C3
Tintwistle Derbys 87 E8
Tinwald Dumfries 114 F3
Tinwell Rutland 65 D7
Tipperty Aberds 151 B8
Tipsend Norf 66 E5
Tipton W Mid 62 E3
Tipton St John Devon 11 E5
Tiptree Essex 42 C4
Tir-y-dail Carms 33 C7
Tirabad Powys 47 E7
Tiraghoil Argyll 136 F4
Tiree Airport Argyll 136 F1
Tirley Glos 37 B5
Tirphil Caerph 35 D5
Tirril Cumb 99 B7
Tisbury Wilts 13 B7
Tisman's Common W Sus 27 F8
Tissington Derbys 75 D8
Titchberry Devon 8 B4
Titchfield Hants 15 D6
Titchmarsh Northants 53 B8
Titchwell Norf 80 C3
Tithby Notts 77 F6
Titley Hereford 48 C5
Titlington Northumb 117 C7
Titsey Sur 28 D5
Tittensor Staffs 75 F5
Tittleshall Norf 80 E4
Tiverton Ches 74 C2
Tiverton Devon 10 C4
Tivetshall St Margaret Norf 68 F4
Tivetshall St Mary Norf 68 F4
Tividale W Mid 62 E3
Tivy Dale S Yorks 88 D3
Tixall Staffs 62 B3
Tixover Rutland 65 D6
Toab Orkney 176 F4
Toab Shetland 175 M5
Toadmoor Derbys 76 D3
Tobermory Argyll 137 C6
Toberonochy Argyll 130 E3
Tobha Mor W Isles 170 G3
Tobhtarol W Isles 172 E4
Tobson W Isles 172 E4
Tocher Aberds 160 E3
Tockenham Wilts 24 B5
Tockenham Wick Wilts 37 F7
Tockholes Blkburn 86 B4
Tockington S Glos 36 F3
Tockwith N Yorks 95 D7
Todber Dorset 13 B6
Todding Hereford 49 B6
Toddington Beds 40 B3
Toddington Glos 50 F5
Todenham Glos 51 F7
Todhills Cumb 108 C3
Todlachie Aberds 151 C5
Todmorden W Yorks 87 B7
Todrig Borders 115 C7
Todwick S Yorks 89 F5
Toft Cambs 54 D4
Toft Lincs 65 C7
Toft Hill Durham 101 B6
Toft Hill Lincs 78 C5
Toft Monks Norf 69 E7
Toft next Newton Lincs 90 F4
Toftrees Norf 80 E4
Tofts Highld 169 C8
Toftwood Norf 68 C2
Togston Northumb 117 D8
Tokavaig Highld 145 B6
Tokers Green Oxon 26 B5
Tolastadh a Chaolais W Isles 172 E4
Tolastadh bho Thuath W Isles 172 D8
Toll Bar S Yorks 89 D6
Toll End W Mid 62 E3
Toll of Birness Aberds 161 E7
Tolland Som 22 F3
Tollard Royal Wilts 13 C7
Tollbar End W Mid 51 B8
Toller Fratrum Dorset 12 E3
Toller Porcorum Dorset 12 E3
Tollerton Notts 77 F6
Tollerton N Yorks 95 C8
Tollesbury Essex 43 C5
Tolleshunt D'Arcy Essex 43 C5
Tolleshunt Major Essex 43 C5
Tolm W Isles 172 E7
Tolpuddle Dorset 13 E5
Tolvah Highld 148 E4
Tolworth London 28 C2
Tomatin Highld 148 B4
Tombreck Highld 157 F7
Tomchrasky Highld 147 C5
Tomdoun Highld 146 D4
Tomich Highld 147 B6
Tomich Highld 157 B7
Tomich House Highld 157 E6
Tomintoul Aberds 149 E7
Tomintoul Moray 149 C7
Tomnaven Moray 159 F8
Tomnavoulin Moray 149 B8
Ton-Pentre Rhondda 34 E3
Tonbridge Kent 29 E6
Tondu Bridgend 34 F2
Tonfanau Gwyn 58 D2
Tong Shrops 61 D7
Tong W Yorks 94 F5
Tong Norton Shrops 61 D7
Tonge Leics 63 B8
Tongham Sur 27 E6
Tongland Dumfries 106 D3
Tongue Highld 167 D7
Tongue End Lincs 65 C8
Tongwynlais Cardiff 35 F5
Tonna Neath 34 E1
Tonwell Herts 41 C6
Tonypandy Rhondda 34 E3
Tonyrefail Rhondda 34 F4
Toot Baldon Oxon 39 D5
Toot Hill Essex 41 D8
Toothill Hants 14 C4
Top of Hebers Gtr Man 87 D6
Topcliffe N Yorks 95 B7
Topcroft Norf 69 E5
Topcroft Street Norf 69 E5
Toppesfield Essex 55 F8
Toppings Gtr Man 86 C5
Topsham Devon 10 F4
Torbay Torbay 7 D7
Torbeg N Ayrs 119 D6
Torboll Farm Highld 164 E4
Torbrex Stirl 133 E6
Torbryan Devon 7 C6
Torcross Devon 7 E6
Tore Highld 157 D7
Torinturk Argyll 128 D3
Torksey Lincs 77 B8
Torlum W Isles 170 E3
Torlundy Highld 139 B5
Tormarton S Glos 24 B2
Tormisdale Argyll 126 D1
Tormitchell S Ayrs 112 E2
Tormore N Ayrs 119 C5
Tornagrain Highld 157 E8
Tornahaish Aberds 149 D8
Tornaveen Aberds 150 D5
Torness Highld 147 B8
Toronto Durham 110 F4
Torpenhow Cumb 108 F2
Torphichen W Loth 122 B2
Torphins Aberds 150 D5
Torpoint Corn 6 D2
Torquay Torbay 7 C7
Torquhan Borders 123 E7
Torran Argyll 130 E4
Torran Highld 152 E6
Torran Highld 157 B8
Torrance E Dunb 121 B6
Torrans Argyll 137 F5
Torranyard N Ayrs 120 E3
Torre Torbay 7 C7
Torridon Highld 154 E5
Torridon Ho. Highld 154 E4
Torrin Highld 153 G6
Torrisdale Highld 167 C8
Torrisdale-Square Argyll 118 C4
Torrish Highld 165 C6
Torrisholme Lancs 92 C4
Torroble Highld 164 D2
Torry Aberdeen 151 D8
Torry Aberds 159 F8
Torryburn Fife 134 F2
Torterston Aberds 161 D7
Torthorwald Dumfries 107 B7
Tortington W Sus 16 D4
Tortworth S Glos 36 E4
Torvaig Highld 153 E5
Torver Cumb 98 E4
Torwood Falk 133 F7
Torworth Notts 89 F7
Tosberry Devon 8 B4
Toscaig Highld 155 G3
Toseland Cambs 54 C3
Tosside N Yorks 93 D7
Tostock Suff 56 C3
Totaig Highld 152 D3
Totaig Highld 155 H4
Tote Highld 152 E5
Totegan Highld 168 C3
Tothill Lincs 91 F8
Totland I o W 14 F4
Totnes Devon 7 C6
Toton Notts 76 F5
Totronald Argyll 136 C2
Totscore Highld 152 C4
Tottenham London 41 E6
Tottenhill Norf 67 C6
Tottenhill Row Norf 67 C6
Totteridge London 41 E5
Totternhoe Beds 40 B2
Tottington Gtr Man 87 C5
Totton Hants 14 C4
Touchen End Windsor 27 B6
Tournaig Highld 154 B4
Toux Aberds 161 C6
Tovil Kent 29 D8
Tow Law Durham 110 F4
Toward Argyll 129 D6
Towcester Northants 52 E4
Towcester Racecourse Northants 52 E5
Towednack Corn 2 C3
Tower End Norf 67 C6
Tower Knowe Visitor Centre, Kielder Water Northumb 116 F2
Tower of London London 41 F6
Towersey Oxon 39 D7
Towie Aberds 150 C3
Towie Aberds 161 B5
Towiemore Moray 159 E7
Town End Cambs 66 E4
Town End Cumb 99 F6
Town Row E Sus 18 B2
Town Yetholm Borders 116 B4
Townend W Dunb 120 B4
Towngate Lincs 65 C8
Townhead Cumb 108 F5
Townhead Dumfries 106 E3
Townhead S Ayrs 112 D2
Townhead S Yorks 88 D2
Townhead of Greenlaw Dumfries 106 C4
Townhill Fife 134 F3
Townsend Bucks 39 D7
Townsend Herts 40 D4
Townshend Corn 2 C4
Towthorpe York 96 D2
Towton N Yorks 95 F7
Towyn Conwy 72 B3
Toxteth Mers 85 F4
Toynton All Saints Lincs 79 C6
Toynton Fen Side Lincs 79 C6
Toynton St Peter Lincs 79 C7
Toy's Hill Kent 29 D5
Trabboch E Ayrs 112 B4
Traboe Corn 3 D6
Tradespark Highld 158 D2
Tradespark Orkney 176 F3
Trafford Park Gtr Man 87 E5
Trago Mills, Newton Abbot Devon 7 B6
Trallong Powys 34 B3
Tranent E Loth 123 B7
Tranmere Mers 85 F4
Trantlebeg Highld 168 D3
Trantlemore Highld 168 D3
Tranwell Northumb 117 F7
Trapp Carms 33 C7
Traprain E Loth 123 B8
Traquair Borders 123 F6
Trawden Lancs 94 F2
Trawsfynydd Gwyn 71 D8
Tre-Gibbon Rhondda 34 D3
Tre-Taliesin Ceredig 58 E3
Tre-vaughan Carms 32 B4
Tre-wyn Mon 35 B7
Trealaw Rhondda 34 E4
Treales Lancs 92 F4
Trearddur Anglesey 82 D2
Treaslane Highld 152 D4
Trebah Garden, Mawnan Smith Corn 3 D6
Trebanog Rhondda 34 E4
Trebanos Neath 33 D8
Trebartha Corn 5 B7
Trebarwith Corn 8 F2
Trebetherick Corn 4 B4
Treborough Som 22 F2
Trebudannon Corn 4 C3
Trebullett Corn 5 B8
Treburley Corn 5 B8
Trebyan Corn 5 C5
Trecastle Powys 34 B2
Trecenydd Caerph 35 F5
Trecwn Pembs 44 B4
Trecynon Rhondda 34 D3
Tredavoe Corn 2 D3
Treddiog Pembs 44 C3
Tredegar Bl Gwent 35 D5
Tredegar Newydd = New Tredegar Caerph 35 D5
Tredington Glos 37 B6
Tredington Warks 51 E7
Tredinnick Corn 4 B4
Tredomen Powys 48 F3
Tredunnock Mon 35 E7
Tredustan Powys 48 F3
Treen Corn 2 D2
Treeton S Yorks 88 F5
Tref-y-Clawdd = Knighton Powys 48 B4
Trefaldwyn = Montgomery Powys 60 E2
Trefasser Pembs 44 B3
Trefdraeth Anglesey 82 D4
Trefdraeth = Newport Pembs 45 F2
Trefecca Powys 48 F3
Trefechan Ceredig 58 F2
Trefeglwys Powys 59 E6
Trefenter Ceredig 46 C5
Treffgarne Pembs 44 C4
Treffynnon Pembs 44 C3
Treffynnon = Holywell Flint 73 B5
Trefgarn Owen Pembs 44 C3
Trefil Bl Gwent 35 C5
Trefilan Ceredig 46 D4
Trefin Pembs 44 B3
Treflach Shrops 60 B2
Trefnanney Powys 60 C2
Trefnant Denb 72 B4
Trefonen Shrops 60 B2
Trefor Anglesey 82 C3
Trefor Gwyn 70 C4
Treforest Rhondda 34 F4
Trefriw Conwy 83 E7
Trefynwy = Monmouth Mon 36 C2
Tregadillett Corn 8 F4
Tregaian Anglesey 82 D4
Tregare Mon 35 C8
Tregaron Ceredig 47 D5
Tregarth Gwyn 83 E6
Tregeare Corn 8 F4
Tregeiriog Wrex 73 F5
Tregele Anglesey 82 B3
Tregidden Corn 3 D6
Treglemais Pembs 44 C3
Tregole Corn 8 E3
Tregonetha Corn 4 C4
Tregony Corn 3 B8
Tregoss Corn 4 C4
Tregoyd Powys 48 F4
Tregroes Ceredig 46 E3
Tregurrian Corn 4 C3
Tregynon Powys 59 E7
Trehafod Rhondda 34 E4
Treharris M Tydf 34 E4
Treherbert Rhondda 34 E3
Trekenner Corn 5 B8
Treknow Corn 8 F2
Trelan Corn 3 E6
Trelash Corn 8 E3
Trelassick Corn 4 D3
Trelawnyd Flint 72 B4
Trelech Carms 45 F4
Treleddyd-fawr Pembs 44 C2
Trelewis M Tydf 35 E5
Treligga Corn 8 F2
Trelights Corn 4 B4
Trelill Corn 4 B5
Trelissick Corn 3 C7
Trelissick Garden, Feock Corn 4 F3
Trellech Mon 36 D2
Trelleck Grange Mon 36 D1
Trelogan Flint 85 F2
Trelystan Powys 60 D2
Tremadog Gwyn 71 C6
Tremail Corn 8 F3
Tremain Ceredig 45 E4
Tremaine Corn 8 F4
Tremar Corn 5 C7
Trematon Corn 5 D8
Tremeirchion Denb 72 B4
Trenance Corn 4 C3
Trenarren Corn 3 B9
Trench Telford 61 C6
Treneglos Corn 8 F4
Trenewan Corn 5 D6
Trent Dorset 12 C3
Trent Vale Stoke 75 E5
Trentham Stoke 75 E5
Trentham Gardens, Newcastle-under-Lyme Staffs 75 F5
Trentishoe Devon 20 E5
Treoes V Glam 21 B8
Treorchy = Treorci Rhondda 34 E3
Treorci = Treorchy Rhondda 34 E3
Tre'r-ddôl Ceredig 58 E3
Trerule Foot Corn 5 D8
Tresaith Ceredig 45 D4
Tresawle Corn 3 B7
Trescott Staffs 62 E2
Trescowe Corn 2 C4
Tresham Glos 36 E4
Tresillian Corn 3 B7
Tresinwen Pembs 44 A4
Treskinnick Cross Corn 8 E4
Tresmeer Corn 8 F4
Tresparrett Corn 8 E3
Tresparrett Posts Corn 8 E3
Tressait Perth 141 C5
Tresta Shetland 175 H5
Tresta Shetland 174 D8
Treswell Notts 77 B7
Trethosa Corn 4 D4
Trethurgy Corn 4 D5
Tretio Pembs 44 C2
Tretire Hereford 36 B2
Tretower Powys 35 B5
Treuddyn Flint 73 D6
Trevalga Corn 8 F2
Trevalyn Wrex 73 D7
Trevanson Corn 4 B4
Trevarren Corn 4 C4
Trevarrian Corn 4 C3
Trevarrick Corn 3 B8
Trevaughan Carms 32 C2
Treveighan Corn 5 B5
Trevellas Corn 4 D2
Treverva Corn 3 C6
Trevethin Torf 35 D6
Trevigro Corn 5 C8
Treviscoe Corn 4 D4
Trevone Corn 4 B3
Trewarmett Corn 8 F2
Trewassa Corn 8 F3
Trewellard Corn 2 C2
Trewen Corn 8 F4
Trewennack Corn 3 D5
Trewern Powys 60 C2
Trewethern Corn 4 B5
Trewidland Corn 5 D7
Trewint Corn 8 F4
Trewint Corn 8 E3
Trewithian Corn 3 C7
Trewoofe Corn 2 D3
Trewoon Corn 4 D4
Treworga Corn 3 B7
Treworlas Corn 3 C7
Treyarnon Corn 4 B3
Treyford W Sus 16 C2
Trezaise Corn 4 D4
Triangle W Yorks 87 B8
Trickett's Cross Dorset 13 D8
Triffleton Pembs 44 C4
Trimdon Durham 111 F6
Trimdon Colliery Durham 111 F6
Trimdon Grange Durham 111 F6
Trimingham Norf 81 D8
Trimley Lower Street Suff 57 F6
Trimley St Martin Suff 57 F6
Trimley St Mary Suff 57 F6
Trimpley Worcs 50 B2
Trimsaran Carms 33 D5
Trimstone Devon 20 E3
Trinafour Perth 140 C4
Trinant Caerph 35 D6
Tring Herts 40 C2
Tring Wharf Herts 40 C2
Trinity Angus 143 C6
Trinity Jersey 17
Trisant Ceredig 47 B6
Trislaig Highld 138 B4
Trispen Corn 4 D3
Tritlington Northumb 117 E8
Trochry Perth 141 E6
Trodigal Argyll 118 D3
Troed rhiwdalar Powys 47 D8
Troedyraur Ceredig 46 E2
Troedyrhiw M Tydf 34 D4
Tromode I o M 84 E3
Trondavoe Shetland 174 F5
Troon Corn 3 C5
Troon S Ayrs 120 F3
Trosaraidh W Isles 171 J3
Trossachs Hotel Stirl 132 D4
Troston Suff 56 B2
Trottiscliffe Kent 29 C7
Trotton W Sus 16 B2
Troutbeck Cumb 99 D6
Troutbeck Cumb 99 B5
Troutbeck Bridge Cumb 99 D6
Trow Green Glos 36 D2
Trowbridge Wilts 24 D3
Trowell Notts 76 F4
Trowle Common Wilts 24 D3
Trowley Bottom Herts 40 C3
Trows Borders 124 F2
Trowse Newton Norf 68 D5
Trudoxhill Som 24 E2
Trull Som 11 B7
Trumaisgearraidh W Isles 170 C4
Trumpan Highld 152 C3
Trumpet Hereford 49 F8
Trumpington Cambs 54 D5
Trunch Norf 81 D8
Trunnah Lancs 92 E3
Truro Corn 3 B7
Truro Cathedral Corn 4 E3
Trusham Devon 10 F3
Trusley Derbys 76 F2
Trusthorpe Lincs 91 F9
Trysull Staffs 62 E2
Tubney Oxon 38 E4
Tuckenhay Devon 7 D6
Tuckhill Shrops 61 F7
Tuckingmill Corn 3 B5
Tuddenham Suff 55 B8
Tuddenham St Martin Suff 57 E5
Tudeley Kent 29 E7
Tudhoe Durham 111 F5
Tudorville Hereford 36 B2
Tudweiliog Gwyn 70 D3
Tuesley Sur 27 E7
Tuffley Glos 37 C5
Tufton Hants 26 E2
Tufton Pembs 32 B1
Tugby Leics 64 D4
Tugford Shrops 61 F5
Tullibardine Perth 133 C8
Tullibody Clack 133 E7
Tullich Argyll 131 D6
Tullich Highld 148 B2
Tullich Muir Highld 157 B8
Tullie House, Carlisle Cumb 108 D3
Tulliemet Perth 141 D6
Tulloch Aberds 143 B7
Tulloch Aberds 160 E5
Tulloch Perth 134 B2
Tulloch Castle Highld 157 C6
Tullochgorm Argyll 131 F5
Tulloes Angus 143 E5
Tullybannocher Perth 133 B6
Tullybelton Perth 141 F7
Tullyfergus Perth 142 E2
Tullymurdoch Perth 142 D1
Tullynessle Aberds 150 C4
Tumble Carms 33 C6
Tumby Woodside Lincs 79 D5
Tummel Bridge Perth 140 D4
Tunga W Isles 172 E7
Tunstall E Yorks 97 F9
Tunstall Kent 30 C2
Tunstall Lancs 93 B6
Tunstall Norf 69 D7
Tunstall N Yorks 101 E7
Tunstall Stoke 75 D5
Tunstall Suff 57 D7
Tunstall T & W 111 D6
Tunstead Derbys 75 B8
Tunstead Gtr Man 87 D8
Tunstead Norf 81 E8
Tunworth Hants 26 E4
Tupsley Hereford 49 E7
Tupton Derbys 76 C3
Tur Langton Leics 64 E4
Turgis Green Hants 26 D4
Turin Angus 143 D5
Turkdean Glos 37 C8
Turleigh Wilts 24 C3
Turn Lancs 87 C6
Turnastone Hereford 49 F5
Turnberry S Ayrs 112 D2
Turnditch Derbys 76 E2
Turners Hill W Sus 28 F4
Turners Puddle Dorset 13 E6
Turnford Herts 41 D6
Turnhouse Edin 122 B4
Turnworth Dorset 13 D6
Turriff Aberds 160 C4
Turton Bottoms Blkburn 86 C5
Turves Cambs 66 E3
Turvey Beds 53 D7
Turville Bucks 39 E7
Turville Heath Bucks 39 E7
Turweston Bucks 52 F4
Tushielaw Borders 115 C6
Tutbury Staffs 63 B6
Tutnall Worcs 50 B4
Tutshill Glos 36 E2
Tuttington Norf 81 E8
Tutts Clump W Berks 26 B3
Tuxford Notts 77 B7
Twatt Orkney 176 D1
Twatt Shetland 175 H5
Twechar E Dunb 121 B7
Tweedmouth Northumb 125 D5
Tweedsmuir Borders 114 B3
Twelve Heads Corn 3 B6
Twemlow Green Ches 74 C4
Twenty Lincs 65 B8
Twerton Bath 24 C2
Twickenham London 28 B2
Twickenham Stadium London 28 B2
Twigworth Glos 37 B5
Twineham W Sus 17 C6
Twinhoe Bath 24 D2
Twinstead Essex 56 F2
Twinstead Green Essex 56 F2
Twiss Green Warr 86 E4
Twiston Lancs 93 E8
Twitchen Devon 21 F6
Twitchen Shrops 49 B5
Two Bridges Devon 6 B4
Two Dales Derbys 76 C2
Two Mills Ches 73 B7
Twycross Leics 63 D7
Twycross Zoo, Ashby-de-la-Zouch Leics 63 D7
Twyford Bucks 39 B6
Twyford Derbys 63 B7
Twyford Hants 15 B5
Twyford Leics 64 C4
Twyford Lincs 65 B6
Twyford Norf 81 E6
Twyford Wokingham 27 B5
Twyford Common Hereford 49 F7
Twyn-y-Sheriff Mon 35 D8
Twynholm Dumfries 106 D3
Twyning Glos 50 F3
Twyning Green Glos 50 F4
Twynllanan Carms 34 B1
Twynmynydd Carms 33 C7
Twywell Northants 53 B7
Ty-draw Conwy 83 F8
Ty-hen Carms 32 B4
Ty-hen Gwyn 70 D2
Ty-mawr Anglesey 82 C4
Ty Mawr Carms 46 E4
Ty Mawr Cwm Conwy 72 E3
Ty-nant Conwy 72 E3
Ty-nant Gwyn 59 B6
Ty-uchaf Powys 59 B7
Tyberton Hereford 49 F5
Tyburn W Mid 62 E5
Tycroes Carms 33 C7
Tycrwyn Powys 59 C8
Tydd Gote Lincs 66 C4
Tydd St Giles Cambs 66 C4
Tydd St Mary Lincs 66 C4
Tyddewi = St David's Pembs 44 C2
Tyddyn-mawr Gwyn 71 C6
Tye Green Essex 55 F6
Tye Green Essex 42 B3
Tye Green Essex 41 D7
Tyldesley Gtr Man 86 D4
Tyler Hill Kent 30 C5
Tylers Green Bucks 40 E2
Tylorstown Rhondda 34 E4
Tylwch Powys 59 F6
Tyn-y-celyn Wrex 73 F5
Tyn-y-coed Shrops 60 B2
Tyn-y-fedwen Powys 72 F5
Tyn-y-ffridd Powys 72 F5
Tyn-y-graig Powys 48 D2
Ty'n-y-groes Conwy 83 D7
Ty'n-y-maes Gwyn 83 E6
Tyn-y-pwll Anglesey 82 C4
Ty'n-yr-eithin Ceredig 47 C5
Tyncelyn Ceredig 46 C5
Tyndrum Stirl 139 F7
Tyne Tunnel T & W 111 C6
Tyneham Dorset 13 F6
Tynehead Midloth 123 D6
Tynemouth T & W 111 C6
Tynemouth Sea Life Centre T & W 111 B6
Tynewydd Rhondda 34 E3
Tyninghame E Loth 124 B2
Tynron Dumfries 113 E8
Tynygongl Anglesey 82 C5
Tynygraig Ceredig 47 C5

Tŷ'r-felin-isaf Conwy 83 E8
Tyrie Aberds 161 B6
Tyringham M Keynes 53 E6
Tythecott Devon 9 C6
Tythegston Bridgend 21 B7
Tytherington Ches 75 B6
Tytherington S Glos 36 F3
Tytherington Som 24 E2
Tytherington Wilts 24 E4
Tytherleigh Devon 11 D8
Tywardreath Corn 5 D5
Tywyn Conwy 83 D7
Tywyn Gwyn 58 D2

U

Uachdar W Isles 170 E3
Uags Highld 155 G3
Ubbeston Green Suff 57 B7
Ubley Bath 23 D7
Uckerby N Yorks 101 D7
Uckfield E Sus 17 B8
Uckington Glos 37 B6
Uddingston S Lnrk 121 C6
Uddington S Lnrk 121 F8
Udimore E Sus 19 D5
Udny Green Aberds 151 B7
Udny Station Aberds 151 B8
Udston S Lnrk 121 D6
Udstonhead S Lnrk 121 E7
Uffcott Wilts 25 B6
Uffculme Devon 11 C5
Uffington Lincs 65 D7
Uffington Oxon 38 F3
Uffington Shrops 60 C5
Ufford P'boro 65 D7
Ufford Suff 57 D6
Ufton Warks 51 C8
Ufton Nervet W Berks 26 C4
Ugadale Argyll 118 D4
Ugborough Devon 6 D4
Uggeshall Suff 69 F7
Ugglebarnby N Yorks 103 D6
Ughill S Yorks 88 E3
Ugley Essex 41 B8
Ugley Green Essex 41 B8
Ugthorpe N Yorks 103 C5
Uidh W Isles 171 L2
Uig Argyll 129 B6
Uig Highld 152 C4
Uig Highld 152 D2
Uigen W Isles 172 E3
Uigshader Highld 152 E5
Uisken Argyll 136 G4
Ulbster Highld 169 E8
Ulceby Lincs 79 B7
Ulceby N Lincs 90 C5
Ulceby Skitter N Lincs 90 C5
Ulcombe Kent 30 E2
Uldale Cumb 108 F2
Uley Glos 36 E4
Ulgham Northumb 117 E8
Ullapool Highld 163 E5
Ullenhall Warks 51 C6
Ullenwood Glos 37 C6
Ulleskelf N Yorks 95 E8
Ullesthorpe Leics 64 F2
Ulley S Yorks 89 F5
Ullingswick Hereford 49 E7
Ullinish Highld 153 F4
Ullock Cumb 98 B2
Ulnes Walton Lancs 86 C3
Ulpha Cumb 98 E3
Ulrome E Yorks 97 D7
Ulsta Shetland 174 E6
Ulva House Argyll 137 E5
Ulverston Cumb 92 B2
Ulwell Dorset 13 F8
Umberleigh Devon 9 B8
Unapool Highld 166 F4
Unasary W Isles 171 H3
Underbarrow Cumb 99 E6
Undercliffe W Yorks 94 F4
Underhoull Shetland 174 C7
Underriver Kent 29 D6
Underwood Notts 76 D4
Undy Mon 35 F8
Unifirth Shetland 175 H4
Union Cottage Aberds 151 E7
Union Mills I o M 84 E3
Union Street E Sus 18 B4
University Museum, Oxford Oxon 39 D5
Unst Airport Shetland 174 C8
Unstone Derbys 76 B3
Unstone Green Derbys 76 B3
Unthank Cumb 108 F4
Unthank Cumb 109 E6
Unthank End Cumb 108 F4
Up Cerne Dorset 12 D4
Up Exe Devon 10 D4
Up Hatherley Glos 37 B6
Up Holland Lancs 86 D3
Up Marden W Sus 15 C8
Up Nately Hants 26 D4
Up Somborne Hants 25 F8
Up Sydling Dorset 12 D4
Upavon Wilts 25 D6
Upchurch Kent 30 C2
Upcott Hereford 48 D5
Upend Cambs 55 D7
Upgate Norf 68 C4
Uphall W Loth 122 B3
Uphall Station W Loth 122 B3
Upham Devon 10 D3
Upham Hants 15 B6
Uphampton Worcs 50 C3
Uphill N Som 22 D5
Uplawmoor E Renf 120 D4
Upleadon Glos 36 B4
Upleatham Redcar 102 C4
Uplees Kent 30 C3
Uploders Dorset 12 E3
Uplowman Devon 10 C5
Uplyme Devon 11 E8
Upminster London 42 F1
Upnor Medway 29 B8
Upottery Devon 11 D7
Uppark, Petersfield Hants 15 C8
Upper Affcot Shrops 60 F4
Upper Ardchronie Highld 164 F3
Upper Arley Worcs 61 F7
Upper Arncott Oxon 39 C6
Upper Astrop Northants 52 F3
Upper Badcall Highld 166 E3
Upper Basildon W Berks 26 B3
Upper Beeding W Sus 17 C5
Upper Benefield Northants 65 F6
Upper Bighouse Highld 168 D3
Upper Boddington Northants 52 D2
Upper Borth Ceredig 58 F3
Upper Boyndlie Aberds 161 B6
Upper Brailes Warks 51 F8
Upper Breakish Highld 155 H2
Upper Breinton Hereford 49 E6
Upper Broadheath Worcs 50 D3
Upper Broughton Notts 64 B3
Upper Bucklebury W Berks 26 C3
Upper Burnhaugh Aberds 151 E7
Upper Caldecote Beds 54 E2
Upper Catesby Northants 52 D3
Upper Chapel Powys 48 E2
Upper Church Village Rhondda 34 F4
Upper Chute Wilts 25 D7
Upper Clatford Hants 25 E8
Upper Clynnog Gwyn 71 C5
Upper Cumberworth W Yorks 88 D3
Upper Cwm-twrch Powys 34 C1
Upper Cwmbran Torf 35 E6
Upper Dallachy Moray 159 C7
Upper Dean Beds 53 C8
Upper Denby W Yorks 88 D3
Upper Denton Cumb 109 C6
Upper Derraid Highld 158 F4
Upper Dicker E Sus 18 E2
Upper Dovercourt Essex 57 F6
Upper Druimfin Argyll 137 C6
Upper Dunsforth N Yorks 95 C7
Upper Eathie Highld 157 C8
Upper Elkstone Staffs 75 D7
Upper End Derbys 75 B7
Upper Farringdon Hants 26 F5
Upper Framilode Glos 36 C4
Upper Glenfintaig Highld 147 F5
Upper Gornal W Mid 62 E3
Upper Gravenhurst Beds 54 F2
Upper Green Mon 35 C7
Upper Green W Berks 25 C8
Upper Grove Common Hereford 36 B2
Upper Hackney Derbys 76 C2
Upper Hale Sur 27 E6
Upper Halistra Highld 152 D3
Upper Halling Medway 29 C7
Upper Hambleton Rutland 65 D6
Upper Hardres Court Kent 31 D5
Upper Hartfield E Sus 29 F5
Upper Haugh S Yorks 88 E5
Upper Heath Shrops 61 F5
Upper Hellesdon Norf 68 C5
Upper Helmsley N Yorks 96 D2
Upper Hergest Hereford 48 D4
Upper Heyford Northants 52 D4
Upper Heyford Oxon 38 B4
Upper Hill Hereford 49 D6
Upper Hopton W Yorks 88 C2
Upper Horsebridge E Sus 18 D2
Upper Hulme Staffs 75 C7
Upper Inglesham Thamesdown 38 E2
Upper Inverbrough Highld 158 F2
Upper Killay Swansea 33 E6
Upper Knockando Moray 159 E5
Upper Lambourn W Berks 38 F3
Upper Leigh Staffs 75 F7
Upper Lenie Highld 147 B8
Upper Lochton Aberds 151 E5
Upper Longdon Staffs 62 C4
Upper Lybster Highld 169 F7
Upper Lydbrook Glos 36 C3
Upper Maes-coed Hereford 48 F5
Upper Midway Derbys 63 B6
Upper Milovaig Highld 152 E2
Upper Minety Wilts 37 E7
Upper Mitton Worcs 50 B3
Upper North Dean Bucks 39 E8
Upper Obney Perth 141 F7
Upper Ollach Highld 153 F6
Upper Padley Derbys 76 B2
Upper Pollicott Bucks 39 C7
Upper Poppleton York 95 D8
Upper Quinton Warks 51 E6
Upper Ratley Hants 14 B4
Upper Rissington Glos 38 C2
Upper Rochford Worcs 49 C8
Upper Sandaig Highld 145 B7
Upper Sanday Orkney 176 F4
Upper Sapey Hereford 49 C8
Upper Seagry Wilts 37 F6
Upper Shelton Beds 53 E7
Upper Sheringham Norf 81 C7
Upper Skelmorlie N Ayrs 129 D7
Upper Slaughter Glos 38 B1
Upper Soudley Glos 36 C3
Upper Stondon Beds 54 F2
Upper Stowe Northants 52 D4
Upper Stratton Thamesdown 38 F1
Upper Street Hants 14 C2
Upper Street Norf 69 C6
Upper Street Norf 69 C6
Upper Street Suff 56 F5
Upper Strensham Worcs 50 F4
Upper Sundon Beds 40 B3
Upper Swell Glos 38 B1
Upper Tean Staffs 75 F7
Upper Tillyrie Perth 134 D3
Upper Tooting London 28 B3
Upper Tote Highld 152 D6
Upper Town N Som 23 C7
Upper Treverward Shrops 48 B4
Upper Tysoe Warks 51 E8
Upper Upham Wilts 25 B7
Upper Wardington Oxon 52 E2
Upper Weald M Keynes 53 F5
Upper Weedon Northants 52 D4
Upper Wield Hants 26 F4
Upper Winchendon Bucks 39 C7
Upper Witton W Mid 62 E4
Upper Woodend Aberds 151 C5
Upper Woodford Wilts 25 F6
Upper Wootton Hants 26 D3
Upper Wyche Worcs 50 E2
Upperby Cumb 108 D4
Uppermill Gtr Man 87 D7
Uppersound Shetland 175 J6
Upperthong W Yorks 88 D2
Upperthorpe N Lincs 89 D8
Upperton W Sus 16 B3
Uppertown Derbys 76 C3
Uppertown Highld 169 B8
Uppertown Orkney 176 G3
Uppingham Rutland 65 E5
Uppington Shrops 61 D6
Upsall N Yorks 102 F2
Upshire Essex 41 D7
Upstreet Kent 31 C6
Upthorpe Suff 56 B3
Upton Cambs 54 B2
Upton Ches 73 C8
Upton Corn 8 D4
Upton Dorset 12 F5
Upton Dorset 13 E7
Upton Hants 14 C4
Upton Hants 25 D8
Upton Leics 63 E7
Upton Lincs 90 F2
Upton Mers 85 F3
Upton Norf 69 C6
Upton Notts 77 D7
Upton Notts 77 B7
Upton Northants 52 C5
Upton Oxon 39 F5
Upton P'boro 65 D8
Upton Slough 27 B7
Upton Som 10 B4
Upton W Yorks 89 C5
Upton Bishop Hereford 36 B3
Upton Cheyney S Glos 23 C8
Upton Cressett Shrops 61 E6
Upton Cross Corn 5 B7
Upton Grey Hants 26 E4
Upton Hellions Devon 10 D3
Upton House Warks 51 E8
Upton Lovell Wilts 24 E4
Upton Magna Shrops 61 C5
Upton Noble Som 24 F2
Upton Pyne Devon 10 E4
Upton St Leonard's Glos 37 C5
Upton Scudamore Wilts 24 E3
Upton Snodsbury Worcs 50 D4
Upton upon Severn Worcs 50 E3
Upton Warren Worcs 50 C4
Upwaltham W Sus 16 C3
Upware Cambs 55 B6
Upwell Norf 66 D4
Upwey Dorset 12 F4
Upwood Cambs 66 F2
Uradale Shetland 175 K6
Urafirth Shetland 174 F5
Urchfont Wilts 24 D5
Urdimarsh Hereford 49 E7
Ure Shetland 174 F4
Ure Bank N Yorks 95 B6
Urgha W Isles 173 J4
Urishay Common Hereford 48 F5
Urlay Nook Stockton 102 C1
Urmston Gtr Man 87 E5
Urpeth Durham 110 D5
Urquhart Highld 157 D6
Urquhart Moray 159 C6
Urquhart Castle, Drumnadrochit Highld 147 B8
Urra N Yorks 102 D3
Urray Highld 157 D6
Ushaw Moor Durham 110 E5
Usk = Brynbuga Mon 35 D7
Usselby Lincs 90 E4
Usworth T & W 111 D6
Utkinton Ches 74 C2
Utley W Yorks 94 E3
Uton Devon 10 E3
Utterby Lincs 91 E7
Uttoxeter Staffs 75 F7
Uttoxeter Racecourse Staffs 75 F8
Uwchmynydd Gwyn 70 E2
Uxbridge London 40 F3
Uyeasound Shetland 174 C7
Uzmaston Pembs 44 D4

V

Valley Anglesey 82 D2
Valley Truckle Corn 8 F2
Valleyfield Dumfries 106 D3
Valsgarth Shetland 174 B8
Valtos Highld 152 C6
Van Powys 59 F6
Vange Essex 42 F3
Varteg Torf 35 D6
Vatten Highld 153 E3
Vaul Argyll 136 F2
Vaynor M Tydf 34 C4
Veensgarth Shetland 175 J6
Velindre Powys 48 F3
Vellow Som 22 F2
Veness Orkney 176 D4
Venn Green Devon 9 C5
Venn Ottery Devon 11 E5
Vennington Shrops 60 D3
Venny Tedburn Devon 10 E3
Ventnor I o W 15 G6
Ventnor Botanic Garden I o W 15 G6
Vernham Dean Hants 25 D8
Vernham Street Hants 25 D8
Vernolds Common Shrops 60 F4
Verwood Dorset 13 D8
Veryan Corn 3 C8
Vicarage Devon 11 F7
Vickerstown Cumb 92 C1
Victoria Corn 4 C4
Victoria S Yorks 88 D2
Victoria and Albert Museum London 28 B3
Vidlin Shetland 174 G6
Viewpark N Lnrk 121 C7
Vigo Village Kent 29 C7
Vinehall Street E Sus 18 C4
Vine's Cross E Sus 18 D2
Viney Hill Glos 36 D3
Virginia Water Sur 27 C8
Virginstow Devon 9 E5
Vobster Som 24 E2
Voe Shetland 175 G6
Voe Shetland 174 E5
Vowchurch Hereford 49 F5
Voxter Shetland 174 F5
Voy Orkney 176 E1

W

Wackerfield Durham 101 B6
Wacton Norf 68 E4
Wadbister Shetland 175 J6
Wadborough Worcs 50 E4
Waddesdon Bucks 39 C7
Waddesdon Manor, Aylesbury Bucks 39 C7
Waddingham Lincs 90 E3
Waddington Lancs 93 E7
Waddington Lincs 78 C2
Wadebridge Corn 4 B4
Wadeford Som 11 C8
Wadenhoe Northants 65 F7
Wadesmill Herts 41 C6
Wadhurst E Sus 18 B3
Wadshelf Derbys 76 B3
Wadsley S Yorks 88 E4
Wadsley Bridge S Yorks 88 E4
Wadworth S Yorks 89 E6
Waen Denb 72 C5
Waen Denb 72 C3
Waen Fach Powys 60 C2
Waen Goleugoed Denb 72 B4
Wag Highld 165 B7
Wainfleet All Saints Lincs 79 D7
Wainfleet Bank Lincs 79 D7
Wainfleet St Mary Lincs 79 D8
Wainfleet Tofts Lincs 79 D7
Wainhouse Corner Corn 8 E3
Wainscott Medway 29 B8
Wainstalls W Yorks 87 B8
Waitby Cumb 100 D2
Waithe Lincs 91 D6
Wake Lady Green N Yorks 102 E4
Wakefield W Yorks 88 B4
Wakehurst Place Garden, Crawley W Sus 28 F4
Wakerley Northants 65 E6
Wakes Colne Essex 42 B4
Walberswick Suff 57 B8
Walberton W Sus 16 D3
Walbottle T & W 110 C4
Walcot Lincs 78 F3
Walcot N Lincs 90 B2
Walcot Shrops 60 F3
Walcot Telford 61 C5
Walcot Thamesdown 38 F1
Walcot Green Norf 68 F4
Walcote Leics 64 F2
Walcote Warks 51 D6
Walcott Lincs 78 D4
Walcott Norf 69 A6
Walden N Yorks 101 F5
Walden Head N Yorks 100 F4
Walden Stubbs N Yorks 89 C6
Waldersey Cambs 66 D4
Walderslade Medway 29 C8
Walderton W Sus 15 C8
Walditch Dorset 12 E2
Waldley Derbys 75 F8
Waldridge Durham 111 D5
Waldringfield Suff 57 E6
Waldringfield Heath Suff 57 E6
Waldron E Sus 18 D2
Wales S Yorks 89 F5
Walesby Lincs 90 E5
Walesby Notts 77 B6
Walford Hereford 49 B5
Walford Hereford 36 B2
Walford Shrops 60 B4
Walford Heath Shrops 60 C4
Walgherton Ches 74 E3
Walgrave Northants 53 B6
Walhampton Hants 14 E4
Walk Mill Lancs 93 F8
Walkden Gtr Man 86 D5
Walker T & W 111 C5
Walker Art Gallery Mers 85 E8
Walker Barn Ches 75 B6
Walker Fold Lancs 93 E6
Walkerburn Borders 123 F6
Walkeringham Notts 89 E8
Walkerith Lincs 89 E8
Walkern Herts 41 B5
Walker's Green Hereford 49 E7
Walkerville N Yorks 101 E7
Walkford Dorset 14 E3
Walkhampton Devon 6 C3
Walkington E Yorks 97 F5
Walkley S Yorks 88 F4
Walkley Clogs, Hebden Bridge W Yorks 87 B3
Wall Northumb 110 C2
Wall Staffs 62 D5
Wall Bank Shrops 60 E5
Wall Heath W Mid 62 F2
Wall under Heywood Shrops 60 E5
Wallaceton Dumfries 113 F8
Wallacetown S Ayrs 112 D2
Wallacetown S Ayrs 112 B3
Wallands Park E Sus 17 C8
Wallasey Mers 85 E4
Wallcrouch E Sus 18 B3
Wallingford Oxon 39 F6
Wallington London 28 C3
Wallington Hants 15 D6
Wallington Herts 54 F3
Wallington House, Ponteland Northumb 117 F6
Wallis Pembs 32 B1
Walliswood Sur 28 F2
Walls Shetland 175 J4
Wallsend T & W 111 C5
Wallston V Glam 22 B3
Wallyford E Loth 123 B6
Walmer Kent 31 D7
Walmer Bridge Lancs 86 B2
Walmersley Gtr Man 87 C6
Walmley W Mid 62 E5
Walney Island Airport Cumb 92 B1
Walpole Suff 57 B7
Walpole Cross Keys Norf 66 C5
Walpole Highway Norf 66 C5
Walpole Marsh Norf 66 C4
Walpole St Andrew Norf 66 C5
Walpole St Peter Norf 66 C5
Walsall W Mid 62 E4
Walsall Arboretum W Mid 62 E4
Walsall Wood W Mid 62 D4
Walsden W Yorks 87 B7
Walsgrave on Sowe W Mid 63 F7
Walsham le Willows Suff 56 B3
Walshaw Gtr Man 87 C5
Walshford N Yorks 95 D7
Walsoken Cambs 66 C4
Walston S Lnrk 122 E3
Walsworth Herts 54 F3
Walters Ash Bucks 39 E8
Walterston V Glam 22 B2
Walterstone Hereford 35 B7
Waltham Kent 30 E5
Waltham NE Lincs 91 D6
Waltham Abbey Essex 41 D6
Waltham Chase Hants 15 C6
Waltham Cross Herts 41 D6
Waltham on the Wolds Leics 64 B5
Waltham St Lawrence Windsor 27 B6
Walthamstow London 41 F6
Walton Cumb 108 C5
Walton Derbys 76 C3
Walton Leics 64 F2
Walton Mers 85 E4
Walton M Keynes 53 F6
Walton P'boro 65 D8
Walton Powys 48 D4
Walton Som 23 F6
Walton Staffs 75 F5
Walton Suff 57 F6
Walton Telford 61 C5
Walton Warks 51 D7
Walton W Yorks 88 C4
Walton W Yorks 95 E7
Walton Cardiff Glos 50 F4
Walton East Pembs 32 B1
Walton Hall Warr 86 F4
Walton-in-Gordano N Som 23 B6
Walton-le-Dale Lancs 86 B3
Walton-on-Thames Sur 28 C2
Walton on the Hill Staffs 62 B3
Walton on the Hill Sur 28 D3
Walton-on-the-Naze Essex 43 B8
Walton on the Wolds Leics 64 C2
Walton-on-Trent Derbys 63 C6
Walton West Pembs 44 D3
Walwen Flint 73 B6
Walwick Northumb 110 B2
Walworth Darl 101 C7
Walworth Gate Darl 101 B7
Walwyn's Castle Pembs 44 D3
Wambrook Som 11 D7
Wanborough Sur 27 E7
Wanborough Thamesdown 38 F2
Wandsworth London 28 B3
Wangford Suff 57 B8
Wanlockhead Dumfries 113 C8
Wansford E Yorks 97 D6
Wansford P'boro 65 E7
Wanstead London 41 F7
Wanstrow Som 24 E2
Wanswell Glos 36 D3
Wantage Oxon 38 F3
Wapley S Glos 24 B2
Wappenbury Warks 51 C8
Wappenham Northants 52 E4
Warbleton E Sus 18 D3
Warblington Hants 15 D8
Warborough Oxon 39 E5
Warboys Cambs 66 F3
Warbreck Blkpool 92 F3
Warbstow Corn 8 E4
Warburton Gtr Man 86 F5
Warcop Cumb 100 C2
Ward End W Mid 62 F5
Ward Green Suff 56 C4
Warden Kent 30 B4
Warden Northumb 110 C2
Wardhill Orkney 176 D5
Wardington Oxon 52 E2
Wardlaw Borders 115 C5
Wardle Ches 74 D3
Wardle Gtr Man 87 C7
Wardley Rutland 64 D5
Wardlow Derbys 75 B8
Wardy Hill Cambs 66 F4
Ware Herts 41 C6
Ware Kent 31 C6
Wareham Dorset 13 F7
Warehorne Kent 19 B6
Waren Mill Northumb 125 F7
Warenford Northumb 117 B7
Warenton Northumb 125 F7
Wareside Herts 41 C6
Waresley Cambs 54 D3
Waresley Worcs 50 B3
Warfield Brack 27 B6
Warfleet Devon 7 D6
Wargrave Wokingham 27 B5
Warham Norf 80 C5
Warhill Gtr Man 87 E7
Wark Northumb 109 B8
Wark Northumb 124 F4
Warkleigh Devon 9 B8
Warkton Northants 53 B6
Warkworth Northants 52 E2
Warkworth Northumb 117 D8
Warlaby N Yorks 101 E8
Warland W Yorks 87 B7
Warleggan Corn 5 C6
Warlingham Sur 28 D4
Warmfield W Yorks 88 B4
Warmingham Ches 74 C4
Warmington Northants 65 E7
Warmington Warks 52 E2
Warminster Wilts 24 E3
Warmlake Kent 30 D2
Warmley S Glos 23 B8
Warmley Tower S Glos 23 B8
Warmonds Hill Northants 53 C7
Warmsworth S Yorks 89 D6
Warmwell Dorset 13 F5
Warndon Worcs 50 D3
Warnford Hants 15 B7
Warnham W Sus 28 F2
Warninglid W Sus 17 B6
Warren Ches 75 B5
Warren Pembs 44 F4
Warren Heath Suff 57 E6
Warren Row Windsor 39 F8
Warren Street Kent 30 D3
Warrington M Keynes 53 D6
Warrington Warr 86 F4
Warsash Hants 15 D5
Warslow Staffs 75 D7
Warter E Yorks 96 D4
Warthermarske N Yorks 94 B5
Warthill N Yorks 96 D2
Wartling E Sus 18 E3
Wartnaby Leics 64 B4
Warton Lancs 86 B2
Warton Lancs 92 B4
Warton Northumb 117 D6
Warton Warks 63 D6
Warwick Warks 51 C7
Warwick Bridge Cumb 108 D4
Warwick Castle Warks 51 C7
Warwick on Eden Cumb 108 D4
Warwick Racecourse Warks 51 C7
Wasbister Orkney 176 C2
Wasdale Head Cumb 98 D3
Wash Common W Berks 26 C2
Washaway Corn 4 C5
Washbourne Devon 7 D5
Washfield Devon 10 C4
Washfold N Yorks 101 D5
Washford Som 22 E2
Washford Pyne Devon 10 C3
Washingborough Lincs 78 B3
Washington T & W 111 D6
Washington W Sus 16 C5
Wasing W Berks 26 C3
Waskerley Durham 110 E3
Wasperton Warks 51 D7
Wasps Nest Lincs 78 C3
Wass N Yorks 95 B8
Watchet Som 22 E2
Watchfield Oxon 38 E2
Watchfield Som 22 E5
Watchgate Cumb 99 E7
Watchhill Cumb 107 E8
Watcombe Torbay 7 C7
Watendlath Cumb 98 C4
Water Devon 10 F2
Water Lancs 87 B6
Water End E Yorks 96 F3
Water End Herts 40 C3
Water End Herts 41 D5
Water Newton Cambs 65 E8
Water Orton Warks 63 E5
Water Stratford Bucks 52 F4
Water Yeat Cumb 98 F4
Waterbeach Cambs 55 C5
Waterbeck Dumfries 108 B2
Watercress Line (Mid Hants Railway), Alton Hants 26 F4
Waterden Norf 80 D4
Waterfall Staffs 75 D7
Waterfoot E Renf 121 D5
Waterfoot Lancs 87 B6
Waterford Hants 14 E4
Waterford Herts 41 C6
Waterhead Cumb 99 D5
Waterhead Dumfries 114 E4
Waterheads Borders 122 D5
Waterhouses Durham 110 E4
Waterhouses Staffs 75 D7
Wateringbury Kent 29 D7
Waterloo Gtr Man 87 D7
Waterloo Highld 155 H2
Waterloo Mers 85 E4
Waterloo N Lnrk 121 D8
Waterloo Norf 68 C5
Waterloo Perth 141 F7
Waterloo Poole 13 E8
Waterloo Shrops 74 F2
Waterloo Port Gwyn 82 E4
Waterlooville Hants 15 D7
Watermeetings S Lnrk 114 C2
Watermillock Cumb 99 B6
Watermouth Castle, Ilfracombe Devon 20 E4
Waterperry Oxon 39 D6
Waterrow Som 11 B5
Water's Nook Gtr Man 86 D4
Waters Upton Telford 61 C6
Watersfield W Sus 16 C4
Watershed Mill Visitor Centre, Settle N Yorks 93 C8
Waterside Aberds 161 F7
Waterside Blkburn 86 B5
Waterside Cumb 108 E2
Waterside E Ayrs 112 D4
Waterside E Ayrs 120 E4
Waterside E Dunb 121 B6
Waterside E Renf 120 D5
Waterstock Oxon 39 D6
Waterston Pembs 44 E4
Watford Herts 40 E4
Watford Northants 52 C4
Watford Gap W Mid 62 D5
Wath N Yorks 94 C4
Wath N Yorks 95 B6
Wath N Yorks 96 B2
Wath Brow Cumb 98 C2
Wath upon Dearne S Yorks 88 D5
Watley's End S Glos 36 F3
Watlington Norf 67 C6
Watlington Oxon 39 E6
Watnall Notts 76 E5
Watten Highld 169 D7
Wattisfield Suff 56 B4
Wattisham Suff 56 D4
Wattlesborough Heath Shrops 60 C3
Watton E Yorks 97 D6
Watton Norf 68 D2
Watton at Stone Herts 41 C6
Wattston N Lnrk 121 B7
Wattstown Rhondda 34 E4
Wauchan Highld 146 F2
Waulkmill Lodge Orkney 176 F2
Waun Powys 59 D5
Waun-y-clyn Carms 33 D5
Waunarlwydd Swansea 33 E7
Waunclunda Carms 47 F5
Waunfawr Gwyn 82 F5
Waungron Swansea 33 D6
Waunlwyd Bl Gwent 35 D5
Wavendon M Keynes 53 F7
Waverbridge Cumb 108 E2
Waverton Ches 73 C8
Waverton Cumb 108 E2
Wavertree Mers 85 F4
Wawne E Yorks 97 F6
Waxham Norf 69 B7
Waxholme E Yorks 91 B7
Way Kent 31 C7
Way Village Devon 10 C3
Wayfield Medway 29 C8
Wayford Som 12 D2
Waymills Shrops 74 E2
Wayne Green Mon 35 C8
Wdig = Goodwick Pembs 44 B4
Weachyburn Aberds 160 C3
Weald Oxon 38 D3
Weald and Downland Open Air Museum, Chichester W Sus 16 C2
Wealdstone London 40 F4
Weardley W Yorks 95 E5
Weare Som 23 D6
Weare Giffard Devon 9 B6
Wearhead Durham 109 F8
Weasdale Cumb 100 D1
Weasenham All Saints Norf 80 E4
Weasenham St Peter Norf 80 E4
Weatherhill Sur 28 E4
Weaverham Ches 74 B3
Weaverthorpe N Yorks 97 B5
Webheath Worcs 50 C5
Wedderlairs Aberds 161 E5
Wedderlie Borders 124 D2
Weddington Warks 63 E7
Wedgwood Visitor Centre, Barlaston Staffs 75 F6
Wedhampton Wilts 25 D5
Wedmore Som 23 E6
Wednesbury W Mid 62 E3
Wednesfield W Mid 62 D3
Weedon Bucks 39 C8
Weedon Bec Northants 52 D4
Weedon Lois Northants 52 E4
Weeford Staffs 62 D5
Week Devon 10 C2
Week St Mary Corn 8 E4
Weeke Hants 26 F2
Weekley Northants 65 F5
Weel E Yorks 97 F6
Weeley Essex 43 B7
Weeley Heath Essex 43 B7
Weem Perth 141 E5
Weeping Cross Staffs 62 B3
Weethley Gate Warks 51 D5
Weeting Norf 67 F7
Weeting Heath NNR Norf 67 F7
Weeton E Yorks 91 B7
Weeton Lancs 92 F3
Weeton N Yorks 95 E5
Weetwood Hall Northumb 117 B6
Weir Lancs 87 B6
Weir Quay Devon 6 C2
Welborne Norf 68 D3
Welbourn Lincs 78 D2
Welburn N Yorks 96 C3
Welburn N Yorks 102 F4
Welbury N Yorks 102 D1
Welby Lincs 78 F2
Welches Dam Cambs 66 F4
Welcombe Devon 8 C4
Weld Bank Lancs 86 C3
Weldon Northumb 117 E7
Welford Northants 64 F3
Welford W Berks 26 B2
Welford-on-Avon Warks 51 D6
Welham Leics 64 E4
Welham Notts 89 F8
Welham Green Herts 41 D5
Well Hants 27 E5
Well Lincs 79 B7
Well N Yorks 101 F7
Well End Bucks 40 F1
Well Heads W Yorks 94 F3
Well Hill Kent 29 C5
Well Town Devon 10 D4
Welland Worcs 50 E2
Wellbank Angus 142 F4
Welldale Dumfries 107 C8
Wellesbourne Warks 51 D7
Welling London 29 B5
Wellingborough Northants 53 C6
Wellingham Norf 80 E4
Wellingore Lincs 78 D2
Wellington Cumb 98 D2
Wellington Hereford 49 E6
Wellington Som 11 B6
Wellington Telford 61 C6
Wellington Heath Hereford 50 E2
Wellington Hill W Yorks 95 F6
Wellow Bath 24 D2
Wellow I o W 14 F4
Wellow Notts 77 C6
Wellpond Green Herts 41 B7
Wells Som 23 E7
Wells Cathedral Som 23 E7
Wells Green Ches 74 D3
Wells-next-the-Sea Norf 80 C5
Wellsborough Leics 63 D7
Wellswood Torbay 7 C7
Wellwood Fife 134 F2
Welney Norf 66 E5
Welsh Bicknor Hereford 36 C2

Welsh End Shrops 74 F2
Welsh Frankton Shrops 73 F7
Welsh Highland Railway, Caernarfon Gwyn 82 E4
Welsh Highland Railway, Porthmadog Gwyn 71 D6
Welsh Hook Pembs 44 C4
Welsh National Velodrome Newport 35 F7
Welsh Newton Hereford 36 C1
Welsh St Donats V Glam 22 B2
Welshampton Shrops 73 F8
Welshpool = Y Trallwng Powys 60 D2
Welton Cumb 108 E3
Welton E Yorks 90 B3
Welton Lincs 78 B3
Welton Northants 52 C3
Welton Hill Lincs 90 F4
Welton le Marsh Lincs 79 C7
Welton le Wold Lincs 91 F6
Welwick E Yorks 91 B7
Welwyn Herts 41 C5
Welwyn Garden City Herts 41 C5
Wem Shrops 60 B5
Wembdon Som 22 F4
Wembley London 40 F4
Wembley Stadium London 40 F4
Wembury Devon 6 E3
Wembworthy Devon 9 D8
Wemyss Bay Invclyd 129 D6
Wenallt Ceredig 47 B5
Wenallt Gwyn 72 E3
Wendens Ambo Essex 55 F6
Wendlebury Oxon 39 C5
Wendling Norf 68 C2
Wendover Bucks 40 D1
Wendron Corn 3 C5
Wendy Cambs 54 E4
Wenfordbridge Corn 5 B5
Wenhaston Suff 57 B8
Wennington Cambs 54 B3
Wennington London 41 F8
Wennington Lancs 93 B6
Wensley Derbys 76 C2
Wensley N Yorks 101 F5
Wentbridge W Yorks 89 C5
Wentnor Shrops 60 E3
Wentworth Cambs 55 B5
Wentworth S Yorks 88 E4
Wenvoe V Glam 22 B3
Weobley Hereford 49 D6
Weobley Marsh Hereford 49 D6
Wereham Norf 67 D6
Wergs W Mid 62 D2
Wern Powys 59 C6
Wern Powys 60 C2
Wernffrwd Swansea 33 E6
Wernyrheolydd Mon 35 C7
Werrington Corn 8 F5
Werrington P'boro 65 D8
Werrington Staffs 75 E6
Wervin Ches 73 B8
Wesham Lancs 92 F4
Wessington Derbys 76 D3
West Acre Norf 67 C7
West Adderbury Oxon 52 F2
West Allerdean Northumb 125 E5
West Alvington Devon 6 E5
West Amesbury Wilts 25 E6
West Anstey Devon 10 B3
West Ashby Lincs 79 B5
West Ashling W Sus 16 D2
West Ashton Wilts 24 D3
West Auckland Durham 101 B6
West Ayton N Yorks 103 F7
West Bagborough Som 22 F3
West Barkwith Lincs 91 F5
West Barnby N Yorks 103 C6
West Barns E Loth 124 B2
West Barsham Norf 80 D5
West Bay Dorset 12 E2
West Beckham Norf 81 D7
West Bedfont Sur 27 B8
West Benhar N Lnrk 121 C8
West Bergholt Essex 43 B5
West Bexington Dorset 12 F3
West Bilney Norf 67 C7
West Blatchington Brighton 17 D6
West Bowling W Yorks 94 F4
West Bradford Lancs 93 E7
West Bradley Som 23 F7
West Bretton W Yorks 88 C3
West Bridgford Notts 77 F5
West Bromwich W Mid 62 E4
West Buckland Devon 21 F5
West Buckland Som 11 B6
West Burrafirth Shetland 175 H4
West Burton N Yorks 101 F5
West Burton W Sus 16 C3
West Butterwick N Lincs 90 D2
West Byfleet Sur 27 C8
West Caister Norf 69 C8
West Calder W Loth 122 C3
West Camel Som 12 B3
West Challow Oxon 38 F3
West Chelborough Dorset 12 D3
West Chevington Northumb 117 E8
West Chiltington W Sus 16 C4
West Chinnock Som 12 C2
West Chisenbury Wilts 25 D6
West Clandon Sur 27 D8
West Cliffe Kent 31 E7
West Clyne Highld 165 D5
West Clyth Highld 169 F7
West Coker Som 12 C3
West Compton Dorset 12 E3
West Compton Som 23 E7
West Cowick E Yorks 89 B7
West Cranmore Som 23 E8
West Cross Swansea 33 F7
West Cullery Aberds 151 D6
West Curry Corn 8 E4
West Curthwaite Cumb 108 E3
West Darlochan Argyll 118 D3
West Dean Wilts 14 B3
West Dean W Sus 16 C2
West Deeping Lincs 65 D8
West Derby Mers 85 E4
West Dereham Norf 67 D6
West Didsbury Gtr Man 87 E6
West Ditchburn Northumb 117 B7
West Down Devon 20 E4
West Drayton London 27 B8
West Drayton Notts 77 B7
West Ella E Yorks 90 B4
West End Beds 53 D7
West End E Yorks 96 F5
West End E Yorks 97 F7
West End Hants 15 C5
West End Lancs 86 B5
West End Norf 68 D2
West End Norf 69 C8
West End N Som 23 C6
West End N Yorks 94 D4
West End Oxon 38 D4
West End S Lnrk 122 E2
West End Suff 69 F7
West End Sur 27 C7
West End S Yorks 89 D7
West End Wilts 13 B7
West End Wilts 24 B4
West End W Sus 17 C6
West End Green Hants 26 C4
West Farleigh Kent 29 D8
West Felton Shrops 60 B3
West Fenton E Loth 135 F6
West Ferry Dundee 142 F4
West Firle E Sus 17 D8
West Ginge Oxon 38 F4
West Grafton Wilts 25 C7
West Green Hants 26 D5
West Greenskares Aberds 160 B4
West Grimstead Wilts 14 B3
West Grinstead W Sus 17 B5
West Haddlesey N Yorks 89 B6
West Haddon Northants 52 B4
West Hagbourne Oxon 39 F5
West Hagley Worcs 62 F3
West Hall Cumb 109 C5
West Hallam Derbys 76 E4
West Halton N Lincs 90 B3
West Ham London 41 F7
West Handley Derbys 76 B3
West Hanney Oxon 38 E4
West Hanningfield Essex 42 E3
West Hardwick W Yorks 88 C5
West Harnham Wilts 14 B2
West Harptree Bath 23 D7
West Hatch Som 11 B7
West Head Norf 67 D5
West Heath Ches 74 C5
West Heath Hants 27 D6
West Heath Hants 26 D3
West Helmsdale Highld 165 C7
West Hendred Oxon 38 F4
West Heslerton N Yorks 96 B5
West Hill Devon 11 E5
West Hill E Yorks 97 C7
West Hill N Som 23 B6
West Hoathly W Sus 28 F4
West Holme Dorset 13 F6
West Horndon Essex 42 F2
West Horrington Som 23 E7
West Horsley Sur 27 D8
West Horton Northumb 125 F6
West Hougham Kent 31 E6
West Houlland Shetland 175 H4
West-houses Derbys 76 D4
West Huntington York 96 D2
West Hythe Kent 19 B8
West Ilsley W Berks 38 F4
West Itchenor W Sus 15 D8
West Keal Lincs 79 C6
West Kennett Wilts 25 C6
West Kilbride N Ayrs 120 E2
West Kingsdown Kent 29 C6
West Kington Wilts 24 B3
West Kinharrachie Aberds 161 E6
West Kirby Mers 85 F3
West Knapton N Yorks 96 B4
West Knighton Dorset 12 F5
West Knoyle Wilts 24 F3
West Kyloe Northumb 125 E6
West Lambrook Som 12 C2
West Langdon Kent 31 E7
West Langwell Highld 164 D3
West Lavington Wilts 24 D5
West Lavington W Sus 16 B2
West Layton N Yorks 101 D6
West Lea Durham 111 E7
West Leake Notts 64 B2
West Learmouth Northumb 124 F4
West Leigh Devon 9 D8
West Lexham Norf 67 C8
West Lilling N Yorks 96 C2
West Linton Borders 122 D4
West Liss Hants 15 B8
West Littleton S Glos 24 B2
West Looe Corn 5 D7
West Luccombe Som 21 E7
West Lulworth Dorset 13 F6
West Lutton N Yorks 96 C5
West Lydford Som 23 F7
West Lyng Som 11 B8
West Lynn Norf 67 B6
West Malling Kent 29 D7
West Malvern Worcs 50 E2
West Marden W Sus 15 C8
West Marina E Sus 18 E4
West Markham Notts 77 B7
West Marsh NE Lincs 91 C6
West Marton N Yorks 93 D8
West Meon Hants 15 B7
West Mersea Essex 43 C6
West Midlands Safari Park, Kidderminster Worcs 50 B3
West Milton Dorset 12 E3
West Minster Kent 30 B3
West Molesey Sur 28 C2
West Monkton Som 11 B7
West Moors Dorset 13 D8
West Morriston Borders 124 E2
West Muir Angus 143 C5
West Ness N Yorks 96 B2
West Newham Northumb 110 B3
West Newton E Yorks 97 F7
West Newton Norf 67 B6
West Norwood London 28 B4
West Ogwell Devon 7 B6
West Orchard Dorset 13 C6
West Overton Wilts 25 C6
West Park Hrtlpl 111 F7
West Parley Dorset 13 E8
West Peckham Kent 29 D7
West Pelton Durham 110 D5
West Pennard Som 23 F7
West Pentire Corn 4 C2
West Perry Cambs 54 C2
West Putford Devon 9 C5
West Quantoxhead Som 22 E3
West Rainton Durham 111 E6
West Rasen Lincs 90 F4
West Raynham Norf 80 E4
West Retford Notts 89 F7
West Rounton N Yorks 102 D2
West Row Suff 55 B7
West Rudham Norf 80 E4
West Runton Norf 81 C7
West Saltoun E Loth 123 C7
West Sandwick Shetland 174 E6
West Scrafton N Yorks 101 F5
West Sleekburn Northumb 117 F8
West Somerset Railway, Minehead Som 21 E8
West Somerton Norf 69 C7
West Stafford Dorset 12 F5
West Stockwith Notts 89 E8
West Stoke W Sus 16 D2
West Stonesdale N Yorks 100 D3
West Stoughton Som 23 E6
West Stour Dorset 13 B5
West Stourmouth Kent 31 C6
West Stow Suff 56 B2
West Stowell Wilts 25 C6
West Strathan Highld 167 C7
West Stratton Hants 26 E3
West Street Kent 30 D3
West Tanfield N Yorks 95 B5
West Taphouse Corn 5 C6
West Tarbert Argyll 128 D3
West Thirston Northumb 117 E7
West Thorney W Sus 15 D8
West Thurrock Thurrock 29 B6
West Tilbury Thurrock 29 B7
West Tisted Hants 15 B7
West Tofts Norf 67 E8
West Tofts Perth 141 F8
West Torrington Lincs 90 F5
West Town Hants 15 E8
West Town N Som 23 C6
West Tytherley Hants 14 B3
West Tytherton Wilts 24 B4
West Walton Norf 66 C4
West Walton Highway Norf 66 C4
West Wellow Hants 14 C3
West Wemyss Fife 134 E5
West Wick N Som 23 C5
West Wickham Cambs 55 E7
West Wickham London 28 C4
West Williamston Pembs 32 D1
West Willoughby Lincs 78 E2
West Winch Norf 67 C6
West Winterslow Wilts 25 F7
West Wittering W Sus 15 E8
West Witton N Yorks 101 F5
West Woodburn Northumb 116 F4
West Woodhay W Berks 25 C8
West Woodlands Som 24 E2
West Worldham Hants 26 F5
West Worlington Devon 10 C2
West Worthing W Sus 16 D5
West Wratting Cambs 55 D7
West Wycombe Bucks 39 E8
West Wylam Northumb 110 C4
West Yell Shetland 174 E6
Westacott Devon 20 F4
Westbere Kent 31 C5
Westborough Lincs 77 E8
Westbourne Bmouth 13 E8
Westbourne Suff 56 E5
Westbourne W Sus 15 D8
Westbrook W Berks 26 B2
Westbury Bucks 52 F4
Westbury Shrops 60 D3
Westbury Wilts 24 D3
Westbury Leigh Wilts 24 D3
Westbury-on-Severn Glos 36 C4
Westbury on Trym Bristol 23 B7
Westbury-sub-Mendip Som 23 E7
Westby Lancs 92 F3
Westcliff-on-Sea Sthend 42 F4
Westcombe Som 23 F8
Westcote Glos 38 B2
Westcott Bucks 39 C7
Westcott Devon 10 D5
Westcott Sur 28 E2
Westcott Barton Oxon 38 B4
Westdean E Sus 18 F2
Westdene Brighton 17 D6
Wester Aberchalder Highld 147 B8
Wester Balgedie Perth 134 D3
Wester Culbeuchly Aberds 160 B3
Wester Dechmont W Loth 122 C3
Wester Denoon Angus 142 E3
Wester Fintray Aberds 151 C7
Wester Gruinards Highld 164 E2
Wester Lealty Highld 157 B7
Wester Milton Highld 158 D3
Wester Newburn Fife 135 D6
Wester Quarff Shetland 175 K6
Wester Skeld Shetland 175 J4
Westerdale Highld 169 D6
Westerdale N Yorks 102 D4
Westerfield Shetland 175 H5
Westerfield Suff 57 E5
Westergate W Sus 16 D3
Westerham Kent 28 D5
Westerhope T & W 110 C4
Westerleigh S Glos 23 B9
Westerton Angus 143 D6
Westerton Durham 110 F5
Westerton W Sus 16 D2
Westerwick Shetland 175 J4
Westfield Cumb 98 B1
Westfield E Sus 18 D5
Westfield Hereford 50 E2
Westfield Highld 169 C5
Westfield N Lnrk 121 B7
Westfield Norf 68 D2
Westfield W Loth 122 B2
Westfields Dorset 12 D5
Westfields of Rattray Perth 142 E1
Westgate Durham 110 F2
Westgate N Lincs 89 D8
Westgate Norf 81 C5
Westgate on Sea Kent 31 B7
Westhall Aberds 151 B5
Westhall Suff 69 F7
Westham Dorset 12 G4
Westham E Sus 18 E3
Westham Som 23 E6
Westhampnett W Sus 16 D2
Westhay Som 23 E6
Westhead Lancs 86 D2
Westhide Hereford 49 E7
Westhill Aberds 151 D7
Westhill Highld 157 E8
Westhope Hereford 49 D6
Westhope Shrops 60 F4
Westhorpe Lincs 78 F5
Westhorpe Suff 56 C4
Westhoughton Gtr Man 86 D4
Westhouse N Yorks 93 B6
Westhumble Sur 28 D2
Westing Shetland 174 C7
Westlake Devon 6 D4
Westleigh Devon 9 B6
Westleigh Devon 11 C5
Westleigh Gtr Man 86 D4
Westleton Suff 57 C8
Westley Shrops 60 D3
Westley Suff 56 C2
Westley Waterless Cambs 55 D7
Westlington Bucks 39 C7
Westlinton Cumb 108 C3
Westmarsh Kent 31 C6
Westmeston E Sus 17 C7
Westmill Herts 41 B6
Westminster London 28 B4
Westminster Cathedral London 28 B3
Westmuir Angus 142 D3
Westness Orkney 176 D2
Westnewton Cumb 107 E8
Westnewton Northumb 124 F5
Westoe T & W 111 C6
Weston Bath 24 C2
Weston Ches 74 D4
Weston Devon 11 F6
Weston Dorset 12 G4
Weston Halton 86 F3
Weston Hants 15 B8
Weston Herts 54 F3
Weston Lincs 66 B2
Weston Notts 77 C7
Weston Northants 52 E3
Weston N Yorks 94 E4
Weston Shrops 61 E5
Weston Shrops 61 B5
Weston Staffs 62 B3
Weston W Berks 25 B8
Weston Beggard Hereford 49 E7
Weston by Welland Northants 64 E4
Weston Colville Cambs 55 D7
Weston Coyney Stoke 75 E6
Weston Favell Northants 53 C5
Weston Green Cambs 55 D7
Weston Green Norf 68 C4
Weston Heath Shrops 61 C7
Weston Hills Lincs 66 B2
Weston-in-Gordano N Som 23 B6
Weston Jones Staffs 61 B7
Weston Longville Norf 68 C4
Weston Lullingfields Shrops 60 B4
Weston-on-the-Green Oxon 39 C5
Weston-on-Trent Derbys 63 B8
Weston Park Staffs 62 C2
Weston Patrick Hants 26 E4
Weston Rhyn Shrops 73 F6
Weston-Sub-Edge Glos 51 E6
Weston-super-Mare N Som 22 C5
Weston Turville Bucks 40 C1
Weston under Lizard Staffs 62 C2
Weston under Penyard Hereford 36 B3
Weston under Wetherley Warks 51 C8
Weston Underwood Derbys 76 E2
Weston Underwood M Keynes 53 D6
Westonbirt Glos 37 F5
Westonbirt Arboretum, Tetbury Glos 37 F5
Westoncommon Shrops 60 B4
Westoning Beds 53 F8
Westonzoyland Som 23 F5
Westow N Yorks 96 C3
Westport Argyll 118 D3
Westport Som 11 C8
Westray Airport Orkney 176 A3
Westrigg W Loth 122 C2
Westruther Borders 124 E2
Westry Cambs 66 E3
Westville Notts 76 E5
Westward Cumb 108 E2
Westward Ho! Devon 9 B6
Westwell Kent 30 E3
Westwell Oxon 38 D2
Westwell Leacon Kent 30 E3
Westwick Cambs 54 C5
Westwick Durham 101 C5
Westwick Norf 81 E8
Westwood Devon 10 E5
Westwood Wilts 24 D3
Westwoodside N Lincs 89 E8
Wetheral Cumb 108 D4
Wetherby W Yorks 95 E7
Wetherby Racecourse W Yorks 95 E7
Wetherden Suff 56 C4
Wetheringsett Suff 56 C5
Wethersfield Essex 55 F8
Wethersta Shetland 174 G5
Wetherup Street Suff 56 C5
Wetley Rocks Staffs 75 E6
Wettenhall Ches 74 C3
Wetton Staffs 75 D8
Wetwang E Yorks 96 D5
Wetwood Staffs 74 F4
Wexcombe Wilts 25 D7
Wexham Street Bucks 40 F2
Weybourne Norf 81 C7
Weybread Suff 68 F5
Weybridge Sur 27 C8
Weycroft Devon 11 E8
Weydale Highld 169 C6
Weyhill Hants 25 E8
Weymouth Dorset 12 G4
Weymouth Sea Life Park Dorset 12 F4
Whaddon Bucks 53 F6
Whaddon Cambs 54 E4
Whaddon Glos 37 C5
Whaddon Wilts 14 B2
Whale Cumb 99 B7
Whaley Derbys 76 B5
Whaley Bridge Derbys 87 F8
Whaley Thorns Derbys 76 B5
Whaligoe Highld 169 E8
Whalley Lancs 93 F7
Whalsay Airport Shetland 174 G7
Whalton Northumb 117 F7
Wham N Yorks 93 C7
Whaplode Lincs 66 B3
Whaplode Drove Lincs 66 C3
Whaplode St Catherine Lincs 66 B3
Wharfe N Yorks 93 C7
Wharles Lancs 92 F4
Wharncliffe Side S Yorks 88 E3
Wharram le Street N Yorks 96 C4
Wharton Ches 74 C3
Wharton Green Ches 74 C3
Whashton N Yorks 101 D6
Whatcombe Dorset 13 D6
Whatcote Warks 51 E8
Whatfield Suff 56 E4
Whatley Som 11 D8
Whatley Som 24 E2
Whatlington E Sus 18 D4
Whatstandwell Derbys 76 D3
Whatton Notts 77 F7
Whauphill Dumfries 105 E8
Whaw N Yorks 100 D4
Wheatacre Norf 69 E7
Wheatcroft Derbys 76 D3
Wheathampstead Herts 40 C4
Wheathill Shrops 61 F6
Wheatley Devon 10 E4
Wheatley Hants 27 E5
Wheatley Oxon 39 D5
Wheatley S Yorks 89 D6
Wheatley W Yorks 87 B8
Wheatley Hill Durham 111 F6
Wheaton Aston Staffs 62 C2
Wheddon Cross Som 21 F8
Wheedlemont Aberds 150 B3
Wheelerstreet Sur 27 E7
Wheelock Ches 74 D4
Wheelock Heath Ches 74 D4
Wheelton Lancs 86 B4
Wheen Angus 142 B3
Wheldrake York 96 E2
Whelford Glos 38 E1
Whelpley Hill Bucks 40 D2
Whempstead Herts 41 B6
Whenby N Yorks 96 C2
Whepstead Suff 56 D2
Wherstead Suff 57 E5
Wherwell Hants 25 E8
Wheston Derbys 75 B8
Whetsted Kent 29 E7
Whetstone Leics 64 E2
Whicham Cumb 98 F3
Whichford Warks 51 F8
Whickham T & W 110 C5
Whiddon Down Devon 9 E8
Whigstreet Angus 142 E4
Whilton Northants 52 C4
Whim Farm Borders 122 D5
Whimble Devon 9 D5
Whimple Devon 10 E5
Whimpwell Green Norf 69 B6
Whinburgh Norf 68 D3
Whinnieliggate Dumfries 106 D4
Whinnyfold Aberds 161 E7
Whippingham I o W 15 E6
Whipsnade Beds 40 C3
Whipsnade Wild Animal Park, Dunstable Beds 40 C3
Whipton Devon 10 E4
Whirlow S Yorks 88 F4
Whisby Lincs 78 C2
Whissendine Rutland 64 C5
Whissonsett Norf 80 E5
Whistlefield Argyll 129 A6
Whistlefield Argyll 129 A7
Whistley Green Wokingham 27 B5
Whiston Mers 86 E2
Whiston Northants 53 C6
Whiston Staffs 62 C2
Whiston Staffs 75 E7
Whiston S Yorks 88 F5
Whitbeck Cumb 98 F3
Whitbourne Hereford 50 D2
Whitbread Hop Farm, Beltring Kent 29 E7
Whitburn T & W 111 C7
Whitburn W Loth 122 C2
Whitburn Colliery T & W 111 C7
Whitby Ches 73 B7
Whitby N Yorks 103 C6
Whitby Abbey N Yorks 103 C7
Whitbyheath Ches 73 B7
Whitchurch Bath 23 C8
Whitchurch Bucks 39 B7
Whitchurch Cardiff 35 F5
Whitchurch Devon 6 B2
Whitchurch Hants 26 E2
Whitchurch Hereford 36 C2
Whitchurch Oxon 26 B4
Whitchurch Pembs 44 C2
Whitchurch Shrops 74 E2
Whitchurch Canonicorum Dorset 11 E8
Whitchurch Hill Oxon 26 B4
Whitcombe Dorset 12 F5
Whitcott Keysett Shrops 60 F2
White Coppice Lancs 86 C4
White Lackington Dorset 12 E5
White Ladies Aston Worcs 50 D4
White Lund Lancs 92 C4
White Mill Carms 33 B5
White Ness Shetland 175 J5
White Notley Essex 42 C3
White Pit Lincs 79 B6
White Post Notts 77 D6
White Post Farm Centre, Farnsfield Notts 77 D6
White Rocks Hereford 35 B8
White Roding Essex 42 C1
White Waltham Windsor 27 B6
Whiteacen Moray 159 E6
Whiteacre Heath Warks 63 E6
Whitebridge Highld 147 C7
Whitebrook Mon 36 D2
Whiteburn Borders 123 E8
Whitecairn Dumfries 105 D6
Whitecairns Aberds 151 C8
Whitecastle S Lnrk 122 E3
Whitechapel Lancs 93 E5
Whitecleat Orkney 176 F4
Whitecraig E Loth 123 B6
Whitecroft Glos 36 D3
Whitecross Corn 4 B4
Whitecross Falk 122 B2
Whitecross Staffs 62 B2
Whiteface Highld 164 F4
Whitefarland N Ayrs 119 B5
Whitefaulds S Ayrs 112 D2
Whitefield Gtr Man 87 D6
Whitefield Perth 142 F1
Whiteford Aberds 151 B6
Whitegate Ches 74 C3
Whitehall Blkburn 86 B4
Whitehall W Sus 16 B5
Whitehall Village Orkney 176 D5
Whitehaven Cumb 98 C1
Whitehill Hants 27 F5
Whitehills Aberds 160 B3
Whitehills S Lnrk 121 D6
Whitehough Derbys 87 F8
Whitehouse Aberds 150 C5
Whitehouse Argyll 128 D3
Whiteinch Glasgow 120 C5
Whitekirk E Loth 135 F7
Whitelaw S Lnrk 121 E6
Whiteleas T & W 111 C6
Whiteley Bank I o W 15 F6
Whiteley Green Ches 75 B6
Whiteley Village Sur 27 C8
Whitemans Green W Sus 17 B7
Whitemire Moray 158 D3
Whitemoor Corn 4 D4
Whitemore Staffs 75 C5
Whitenap Hants 14 B4
Whiteoak Green Oxon 38 C3
Whiteparish Wilts 14 B3
Whiterashes Aberds 151 B7
Whiterow Highld 169 E8
Whiteshill Glos 37 D5
Whiteside Northumb 109 C7
Whiteside W Loth 122 C2
Whitesmith E Sus 18 D2
Whitestaunton Som 11 C7
Whitestone Devon 10 E3
Whitestone Devon 20 E3
Whitestone Warks 63 F7
Whitestones Aberds 160 C5
Whitestreet Green Suff 56 F3
Whitewall Corner N Yorks 96 B3
Whiteway Glos 37 E5
Whiteway Glos 37 C6
Whitewell Aberds 161 B6
Whitewell Lancs 93 E6
Whitewell Bottom Lancs 87 B6
Whiteworks Devon 6 B4
Whitfield Kent 31 E7
Whitfield Northants 52 F4
Whitfield Northumb 109 D7
Whitfield S Glos 36 E3
Whitford Devon 11 E7
Whitford Flint 72 B5
Whitgift E Yorks 90 B2
Whitgreave Staffs 62 B2
Whithorn Dumfries 105 E8
Whiting Bay N Ayrs 119 D7
Whitington Norf 67 E7
Whitkirk W Yorks 95 F6
Whitland Carms 32 C2
Whitletts S Ayrs 112 B3
Whitley N Yorks 89 B6
Whitley Reading 26 B5
Whitley Wilts 24 C3
Whitley Bay T & W 111 B6
Whitley Chapel Northumb 110 D2
Whitley Lower W Yorks 88 C3
Whitley Row Kent 29 D5
Whitlock's End W Mid 51 B6
Whitminster Glos 36 D4
Whitmore Staffs 74 E5
Whitnage Devon 10 C5
Whitnash Warks 51 C8
Whitney Hereford 48 E4
Whitrigg Cumb 108 F2
Whitrigg Cumb 108 D2
Whitsbury Hants 14 C2
Whitsome Borders 124 D4
Whitson Newport 35 F7
Whitstable Kent 30 C5
Whitstone Corn 8 E4
Whittingham Northumb 117 C6
Whittingslow Shrops 60 F4
Whittington Glos 37 B7
Whittington Lancs 93 B6
Whittington Shrops 73 F7
Whittington Staffs 62 F2
Whittington Staffs 63 D5
Whittington Worcs 50 D3
Whittle-le-Woods Lancs 86 B3
Whittlebury Northants 52 E4
Whittlesey Cambs 66 E2
Whittlesford Cambs 55 E5
Whittlestone Head Blkburn 86 C5
Whitton Borders 116 B3
Whitton N Lincs 90 B3
Whitton Northumb 117 D6
Whitton Powys 48 C4
Whitton Shrops 49 B7
Whitton Stockton 102 B1
Whitton Suff 56 E5
Whittonditch Wilts 25 B7
Whittonstall Northumb 110 D3
Whitway Hants 26 D2
Whitwell Derbys 76 B5
Whitwell Herts 40 B4
Whitwell I o W 15 G6
Whitwell N Yorks 101 E7
Whitwell Rutland 65 D6
Whitwell-on-the-Hill N Yorks 96 C3
Whitwell Street Norf 81 E7
Whitwick Leics 63 C8
Whitwood W Yorks 88 B5
Whitworth Lancs 87 C6
Whixall Shrops 74 F2
Whixley N Yorks 95 D7
Whoberley W Mid 51 B8
Whorlton Durham 101 C6
Whorlton N Yorks 102 D2
Whygate Northumb 109 B7
Whyle Hereford 49 C7
Whyteleafe Sur 28 D4
Wibdon Glos 36 E2
Wibsey W Yorks 88 A2
Wibtoft Leics 63 F8
Wichenford Worcs 50 C2
Wichling Kent 30 D3
Wick Bmouth 14 E2
Wick Devon 11 D6
Wick Highld 169 D8
Wick S Glos 24 B2
Wick Shetland 175 K6
Wick V Glam 21 B8
Wick Wilts 14 B2
Wick Worcs 50 E4
Wick W Sus 16 D4
Wick Airport Highld 169 D8
Wick Hill Wokingham 27 C5
Wick St Lawrence N Som 23 C5
Wicken Cambs 55 B6
Wicken Northants 52 F5
Wicken Bonhunt Essex 55 F5
Wicken Green Village Norf 80 D4
Wickenby Lincs 90 F4
Wickersley S Yorks 89 E5
Wickford Essex 42 E3
Wickham Hants 15 C6
Wickham W Berks 25 B8
Wickham Bishops Essex 42 C4
Wickham Market Suff 57 D7
Wickham St Paul Essex 56 F2
Wickham Skeith Suff 56 C4
Wickham Street Suff 55 D8
Wickham Street Suff 56 C4
Wickhambreux Kent 31 D6
Wickhambrook Suff 55 D8
Wickhamford Worcs 51 E5
Wickhampton Norf 69 D7
Wicklewood Norf 68 D3
Wickmere Norf 81 D7
Wicksteed Park, Kettering Northants 53 B6
Wickwar S Glos 36 F4
Widdington Essex 55 F6
Widdrington Northumb 117 E8
Widdrington Station Northumb 117 E8
Wide Open T & W 110 B5
Widecombe in the Moor Devon 6 B5
Widegates Corn 5 D7
Widemouth Bay Corn 8 D4
Widewall Orkney 176 G3
Widford Essex 42 D2
Widford Herts 41 C7
Widham Wilts 37 F7
Widmer End Bucks 40 E1
Widmerpool Notts 64 B3
Widnes Halton 86 F3
Wigan Gtr Man 86 D3
Wigan Pier Gtr Man 86 D3
Wiggaton Devon 11 E6
Wiggenhall St Germans Norf 67 C5
Wiggenhall St Mary Magdalen Norf 67 C5
Wiggenhall St Mary the Virgin Norf 67 C5
Wigginton Herts 40 C2
Wigginton Oxon 51 F8
Wigginton Staffs 63 D6
Wigginton York 95 D8
Wigglesworth N Yorks 93 D8
Wiggonby Cumb 108 D2
Wiggonholt W Sus 16 C4
Wighill N Yorks 95 E7
Wighton Norf 80 D5
Wigley Hants 14 C4
Wigmore Hereford 49 C6
Wigmore Medway 30 C2
Wigsley Notts 77 B8
Wigsthorpe Northants 65 F7
Wigston Leics 64 E3
Wigthorpe Notts 89 F6
Wigtoft Lincs 79 F5
Wigton Cumb 108 E2
Wigtown Dumfries 105 D8
Wigtwizzle S Yorks 88 E3
Wike W Yorks 95 E6
Wike Well End S Yorks 89 C7
Wilbarston Northants 64 F5
Wilberfoss E Yorks 96 D3
Wilberlee W Yorks 87 C8
Wilburton Cambs 55 B5
Wilby Norf 68 F3
Wilby Northants 53 C6
Wilby Suff 57 B6
Wilcot Wilts 25 C6
Wilcott Shrops 60 C3
Wilcrick Newport 35 F8

Wilday Green Derbys 76 B3
Wildboarclough Ches 75 C6
Wilden Beds 53 D8
Wilden Worcs 50 B3
Wildfowl and Wetland Centre, Martin Mere Lancs 86 C2
Wildhern Hants 25 D8
Wildhill Herts 41 D5
Wildlife & Dinosaur Park, Combe Martin Devon 20 E4
Wildmoor Worcs 50 B4
Wildsworth Lincs 90 E2
Wilford Notts 77 F5
Wilkesley Ches 74 E3
Wilkhaven Highld 165 F6
Wilkieston W Loth 122 C4
Willand Devon 10 C5
Willaston Ches 73 B7
Willaston Ches 74 D3
Willen M Keynes 53 E6
Willenhall W Mid 51 B8
Willenhall W Mid 62 E3
Willerby E Yorks 97 F6
Willerby N Yorks 97 B6
Willersey Glos 51 F6
Willersley Hereford 48 E5
Willesborough Kent 30 E4
Willesborough Lees Kent 30 E4
Willesden London 41 F5
Willett Som 22 F3
Willey Shrops 61 E6
Willey Warks 63 F8
Willey Green Sur 27 D7
Williamscott Oxon 52 E2
Willian Herts 54 F3
Willingale Essex 42 D1
Willingdon E Sus 18 E2
Willingham Cambs 54 B5
Willingham by Stow Lincs 90 F2
Willington Beds 54 E2
Willington Derbys 63 B6
Willington Durham 110 F4
Willington T & W 111 C6
Willington Warks 51 F7
Willington Corner Ches 74 C2
Willisham Tye Suff 56 D4
Willitoft E Yorks 96 F3
Williton Som 22 E2
Willoughbridge Staffs 74 E4
Willoughby Lincs 79 B7
Willoughby Warks 52 C3
Willoughby-on-the-Wolds Notts 64 B3
Willoughby Waterleys Leics 64 E2
Willoughton Lincs 90 E3
Willows Green Essex 42 C3
Willsbridge S Glos 23 B8
Willsworthy Devon 9 F7
Wilmcote Warks 51 D6
Wilmington Devon 11 E7
Wilmington E Sus 18 E2
Wilmington Kent 29 B6
Wilminstone Devon 6 B2
Wilmslow Ches 87 F6
Wilnecote Staffs 63 D6
Wilpshire Lancs 93 F6
Wilsden W Yorks 94 F3
Wilsford Lincs 78 E3
Wilsford Wilts 25 D6
Wilsford Wilts 25 F6
Wilsill N Yorks 94 C4
Wilsley Pound Kent 18 B4
Wilsom Hants 26 F5
Wilson Leics 63 B8
Wilsontown S Lnrk 122 D2
Wilstead Beds 53 E8
Wilsthorpe Lincs 65 C7
Wilstone Herts 40 C2
Wilton Borders 115 C7
Wilton Cumb 98 C2
Wilton N Yorks 103 F6
Wilton Redcar 102 C3
Wilton Wilts 25 F5
Wilton Wilts 25 C7
Wilton House, Salisbury Wilts 25 F6
Wimbish Essex 55 F6
Wimbish Green Essex 55 F7
Wimblebury Staffs 62 C4
Wimbledon London 28 B3
Wimbledon All England Tennis Club London 28 B3
Wimblington Cambs 66 E4
Wimborne Minster Dorset 13 E8
Wimborne Minster Dorset 13 E8
Wimborne St Giles Dorset 13 C8
Wimbotsham Norf 67 D6
Wimpole Hall and Home Farm, Royston Cambs 54 D4
Wimpson Soton 14 C4
Wimpstone Warks 51 E7
Wincanton Som 12 B5
Wincanton Racecourse Som 12 B5
Wincham Ches 74 B3
Winchburgh W Loth 122 B3
Winchcombe Glos 37 B7
Winchelsea E Sus 19 D6
Winchelsea Beach E Sus 19 D6
Winchester Hants 15 B5
Winchester Cathedral Hants 15 B5
Winchet Hill Kent 29 E8
Winchfield Hants 27 D5
Winchmore Hill Bucks 40 E2
Winchmore Hill London 41 E6
Wincle Ches 75 C6
Wincobank S Yorks 88 E4
Windermere Cumb 99 E6
Winderton Warks 51 E8
Windhill Highld 157 E6
Windhouse Shetland 174 D6
Windlehurst Gtr Man 87 F7
Windlesham Sur 27 C7
Windley Derbys 76 E3
Windmill Hill E Sus 18 D3
Windmill Hill Som 11 C8
Windrush Glos 38 C1
Windsor N Lincs 89 C8
Windsor Windsor 27 B7
Windsor Castle Windsor 27 B7
Windsor Racecourse Windsor 27 B7
Windsoredge Glos 37 D5
Windygates Fife 134 D5
Windyknowe W Loth 122 C2
Windywalls Borders 124 F3
Wineham W Sus 17 B6
Winestead E Yorks 91 B6
Winewall Lancs 94 E2
Winfarthing Norf 68 F4
Winford I o W 15 F6
Winford N Som 23 C7
Winforton Hereford 48 E4
Winfrith Newburgh Dorset 13 F6
Wing Bucks 40 B1
Wing Rutland 65 D5
Wingate Durham 111 F7
Wingates Gtr Man 86 D4
Wingates Northumb 117 E7
Wingerworth Derbys 76 C3
Wingfield Beds 40 B2
Wingfield Suff 57 B6
Wingfield Wilts 24 D3
Wingham Kent 31 D6
Wingmore Kent 31 E5
Wingrave Bucks 40 C1
Winkburn Notts 77 D7
Winkfield Brack 27 B7
Winkfield Row Brack 27 B6
Winkhill Staffs 75 D7
Winklebury Hants 26 D4
Winkleigh Devon 9 D8
Winksley N Yorks 95 B5
Winkton Dorset 14 E2
Winlaton T & W 110 C4
Winless Highld 169 D8
Winmarleigh Lancs 92 E4
Winnal Hereford 49 F6
Winnall Hants 15 B5
Winnersh Wokingham 27 B5
Winscales Cumb 98 B2
Winscombe N Som 23 D6
Winsford Ches 74 C3
Winsford Som 21 F8
Winsham Som 11 D8
Winshill Staffs 63 B6
Winskill Cumb 109 F5
Winslade Hants 26 E4
Winsley Wilts 24 C3
Winslow Bucks 39 B7
Winson Glos 37 D7
Winson Green W Mid 62 F4
Winsor Hants 14 C4
Winster Cumb 99 E6
Winster Derbys 76 C2
Winston Durham 101 C6
Winston Suff 57 C5
Winston Green Suff 57 C5
Winstone Glos 37 D6
Winswell Devon 9 C6
Winter Gardens Essex 42 F3
Winterborne Bassett Wilts 25 B6
Winterborne Clenston Dorset 13 D6
Winterborne Herringston Dorset 12 F4
Winterborne Houghton Dorset 13 D6
Winterborne Kingston Dorset 13 E6
Winterborne Monkton Dorset 12 F4
Winterborne Monkton Wilts 25 B6
Winterborne Stickland Dorset 13 D6
Winterborne Whitechurch Dorset 13 D6
Winterborne Zelston Dorset 13 E6
Winterbourne S Glos 36 F3
Winterbourne W Berks 26 B2
Winterbourne Abbas Dorset 12 E4
Winterbourne Dauntsey Wilts 25 F6
Winterbourne Down S Glos 23 B8
Winterbourne Earls Wilts 25 F6
Winterbourne Gunner Wilts 25 F6
Winterbourne Steepleton Dorset 12 F4
Winterbourne Stoke Wilts 25 E5
Winterburn N Yorks 94 D2
Winteringham N Lincs 90 B3
Winterley Ches 74 D4
Wintersett W Yorks 88 C4
Wintershill Hants 15 C6
Winterton N Lincs 90 C3
Winterton-on-Sea Norf 69 C7
Winthorpe Lincs 79 C8
Winthorpe Notts 77 D8
Winton Bmouth 13 E8
Winton Cumb 100 C2
Winton N Yorks 102 E2
Wintringham N Yorks 96 B4
Winwick Cambs 65 F8
Winwick Northants 52 B4
Winwick Warr 86 E4
Wirksworth Derbys 76 D2
Wirksworth Moor Derbys 76 D3
Wirswall Ches 74 E2
Wisbech Cambs 66 D4
Wisbech St Mary Cambs 66 D4
Wisborough Green W Sus 16 B4
Wiseton Notts 89 F8
Wishaw N Lnrk 121 D7
Wishaw Warks 63 E5
Wisley Sur 27 D8
Wispington Lincs 78 B5
Wissenden Kent 30 E3
Wissett Suff 57 B7
Wistanstow Shrops 60 F4
Wistanswick Shrops 61 B6
Wistaston Ches 74 D3
Wistaston Green Ches 74 D3
Wiston Pembs 32 C1
Wiston S Lnrk 122 F2
Wiston W Sus 16 C5
Wistow Cambs 66 F2
Wistow N Yorks 95 F8
Wiswell Lancs 93 F7
Witcham Cambs 66 F4
Witchampton Dorset 13 D7
Witchford Cambs 55 B6
Witham Essex 42 C4
Witham Friary Som 24 E2
Witham on the Hill Lincs 65 C7
Withcall Lincs 91 F6
Withdean Brighton 17 D7
Witherenden Hill E Sus 18 C3
Witheridge Devon 10 C3
Witherley Leics 63 E7
Withern Lincs 91 F8
Withernsea E Yorks 91 B7
Withernwick E Yorks 97 E7
Withersdale Street Suff 69 F5
Withersfield Suff 55 E7
Witherslack Cumb 99 F6
Withiel Corn 4 C4
Withiel Florey Som 21 F8
Withington Glos 37 C7
Withington Gtr Man 87 E6
Withington Hereford 49 E7
Withington Shrops 61 C5
Withington Staffs 75 F7
Withington Green Ches 74 B5
Withleigh Devon 10 C4
Withnell Lancs 86 B4
Withybrook Warks 63 F8
Withycombe Som 22 E2
Withycombe Raleigh Devon 10 F5
Withyham E Sus 29 F5
Withypool Som 21 F7
Witley Sur 27 F7
Witnesham Suff 57 D5
Witney Oxon 38 C3
Wittering P'boro 65 D7
Wittersham Kent 19 C5
Witton Angus 143 B5
Witton Worcs 50 C3
Witton Bridge Norf 69 A6
Witton Gilbert Durham 110 E5
Witton-le-Wear Durham 110 F4
Witton Park Durham 110 F4
Wiveliscombe Som 11 B5
Wivelrod Hants 26 F4
Wivelsfield E Sus 17 B7
Wivelsfield Green E Sus 17 B7
Wivenhoe Essex 43 B6
Wivenhoe Cross Essex 43 B6
Wiveton Norf 81 C6
Wix Essex 43 B7
Wixford Warks 51 D5
Wixhill Shrops 61 B5
Wixoe Suff 55 E8
Woburn Beds 53 F7
Woburn Abbey, Woburn Beds 53 F7
Woburn Sands M Keynes 53 F7
Woburn Wild Animal Kingdom Beds 53 F7
Wokefield Park W Berks 26 C4
Woking Sur 27 D8
Wokingham Wokingham 27 C6
Wolborough Devon 7 B6
Wold Newton E Yorks 97 B6
Wold Newton NE Lincs 91 E6
Woldingham Sur 28 D4
Wolfclyde S Lnrk 122 F3
Wolferton Norf 67 B6
Wolfhill Perth 142 F1
Wolf's Castle Pembs 44 C4
Wolfsdale Pembs 44 C4
Woll Borders 115 B7
Wollaston Northants 53 C7
Wollaston Shrops 60 C3
Wollaton Nottingham 76 F5
Wollaton Hall Nottingham 76 F5
Wollerton Shrops 74 F3
Wollescote W Mid 62 F3
Wolsingham Durham 110 F3
Wolstanton Staffs 75 E5
Wolston Warks 52 B2
Wolvercote Oxon 38 D4
Wolverhampton W Mid 62 E3
Wolverhampton Racecourse W Mid 62 D3
Wolverley Shrops 73 F8
Wolverley Worcs 50 B3
Wolverton Hants 26 D3
Wolverton M Keynes 53 E6
Wolverton Warks 51 C7
Wolverton Common Hants 26 D3
Wolvesnewton Mon 36 E1
Wolvey Warks 63 F8
Wolviston Stockton 102 B2
Wombleton N Yorks 102 F4
Wombourne Staffs 62 E2
Wombwell S Yorks 88 D4
Womenswold Kent 31 D6
Womersley N Yorks 89 C6
Wonastow Mon 36 C1
Wonersh Sur 27 E8
Wonson Devon 9 F8
Wonston Hants 26 F2
Wooburn Bucks 40 F2
Wooburn Green Bucks 40 F2
Wood Dalling Norf 81 E6
Wood End Herts 41 B6
Wood End Warks 51 B6
Wood End Warks 63 E6
Wood Enderby Lincs 79 C5
Wood Field Sur 28 D2
Wood Green London 41 E6
Wood Green Animal Shelter, Godmanchester Cambs 54 C3
Wood Hayes W Mid 62 D3
Wood Lanes Ches 87 F7
Wood Norton Norf 81 E6
Wood Street Norf 69 B6
Wood Street Sur 27 D7
Wood Walton Cambs 66 F2
Woodacott Devon 9 D5
Woodale N Yorks 94 B3
Woodbank Argyll 118 E3
Woodbastwick Norf 69 C6
Woodbeck Notts 77 B7
Woodborough Notts 77 E6
Woodborough Wilts 25 D6
Woodbridge Dorset 12 C5
Woodbridge Suff 57 E6
Woodbury Devon 10 F5
Woodbury Salterton Devon 10 F5
Woodchester Glos 37 D5
Woodchurch Kent 19 B6
Woodchurch Mers 85 F3
Woodcombe Som 21 E8
Woodcote Oxon 39 F6
Woodcott Hants 26 D2
Woodcroft Glos 36 E2
Woodcutts Dorset 13 C7
Woodditton Cambs 55 D7
Woodeaton Oxon 39 C5
Woodend Cumb 98 E3
Woodend Northants 52 E4
Woodend W Sus 16 D2
Woodend Green Northants 52 E4
Woodfalls Wilts 14 B2
Woodfield Oxon 39 B5
Woodfield S Ayrs 112 B3
Woodford Corn 8 C4
Woodford Devon 7 D5
Woodford Glos 36 E3
Woodford London 41 E7
Woodford Gtr Man 87 F6
Woodford Northants 53 B7
Woodford Bridge London 41 E7
Woodford Halse Northants 52 D3
Woodgate Norf 68 C3
Woodgate W Mid 62 F3
Woodgate Worcs 50 C4
Woodgate W Sus 16 D3
Woodgreen Hants 14 C2
Woodhall Herts 41 C5
Woodhall Invclyd 120 B3
Woodhall N Yorks 100 E4
Woodhall Spa Lincs 78 C4
Woodham Sur 27 C8
Woodham Ferrers Essex 42 E3
Woodham Mortimer Essex 42 D4
Woodham Walter Essex 42 D4
Woodhaven Fife 135 B6
Woodhead Aberds 160 E4
Woodhey Gtr Man 87 C5
Woodhill Shrops 61 F7
Woodhorn Northumb 117 F8
Woodhouse Leics 64 C2
Woodhouse N Lincs 89 D8
Woodhouse S Yorks 88 F5
Woodhouse W Yorks 95 F5
Woodhouse W Yorks 88 B4
Woodhouse Eaves Leics 64 C2
Woodhouse Park Gtr Man 87 F6
Woodhouselee Midloth 122 C5
Woodhouselees Dumfries 108 B3
Woodhouses Staffs 63 C5
Woodhurst Cambs 54 B4
Woodingdean Brighton 17 D7
Woodkirk W Yorks 88 B3
Woodland Devon 7 C5
Woodland Durham 101 B5
Woodland Leisure Park, Dartmouth Devon 7 D6
Woodlands Aberds 151 E6
Woodlands Dorset 13 D8
Woodlands Hants 14 C4
Woodlands Highld 157 C6
Woodlands N Yorks 95 D6
Woodlands S Yorks 89 D6
Woodlands Park Windsor 27 B6
Woodlands St Mary W Berks 25 B8
Woodlane Staffs 62 B5
Woodleigh Devon 6 E5
Woodlesford W Yorks 88 B4
Woodley Gtr Man 87 E7
Woodley Wokingham 27 B5
Woodmancote Glos 36 E4
Woodmancote Glos 37 D7
Woodmancote Glos 37 B6
Woodmancote W Sus 15 D8
Woodmancote W Sus 17 C6
Woodmancott Hants 26 E3
Woodmansey E Yorks 97 F6
Woodmansterne Sur 28 D3
Woodminton Wilts 13 B8
Woodnesborough Kent 31 D7
Woodnewton Northants 65 E7
Woodplumpton Lancs 92 F5
Woodrising Norf 68 D2
Wood's Green E Sus 18 B3
Woodseaves Shrops 74 F3
Woodseaves Staffs 61 B7
Woodsend Wilts 25 B7
Woodsetts S Yorks 89 F6
Woodsford Dorset 13 E5
Woodside Aberdeen 151 D8
Woodside Aberds 161 D7
Woodside Brack 27 B7
Woodside Fife 135 D6
Woodside Hants 14 E4
Woodside Herts 41 D5
Woodside Perth 142 F2
Woodside Farm and Wildfowl Park, Luton Beds 40 C3
Woodside of Arbeadie Aberds 151 E6
Woodstock Oxon 38 C4
Woodstock Pembs 32 B1
Woodthorpe Derbys 76 B4
Woodthorpe Leics 64 C2
Woodthorpe Lincs 91 F8
Woodthorpe York 95 E8
Woodton Norf 69 E5
Woodtown Devon 9 B6
Woodtown Devon 9 B6
Woodvale Mers 85 C4
Woodville Derbys 63 C7
Woodyates Dorset 13 C8
Woofferton Shrops 49 C7
Wookey Som 23 E7
Wookey Hole Som 23 E7
Wookey Hole Caves & Papermill, Wells Som 23 E7
Wool Dorset 13 F6
Woolacombe Devon 20 E3
Woolage Green Kent 31 E6
Woolaston Glos 36 E2
Woolavington Som 22 E5
Woolbeding W Sus 16 B2
Wooldale W Yorks 88 D2
Wooler Northumb 117 B5
Woolfardisworthy Devon 8 B5
Woolfardisworthy Devon 10 D3
Woolfords Cottages S Lnrk 122 D3
Woolhampton W Berks 26 C3
Woolhope Hereford 49 F8
Woolhope Cockshoot Hereford 49 F8
Woolland Dorset 13 D5
Woollaton Devon 9 C6
Woolley Bath 24 C2
Woolley Cambs 54 B2
Woolley Corn 8 C4
Woolley Derbys 76 C3
Woolley W Yorks 88 C4
Woolmer Green Herts 41 C5
Woolmere Green Worcs 50 C4
Woolpit Suff 56 C3
Woolscott Warks 52 C2
Woolsington T & W 110 C4
Woolstanwood Ches 74 D3
Woolstaston Shrops 60 E4
Woolsthorpe Lincs 77 F8
Woolsthorpe Lincs 65 B6
Woolston Devon 6 E5
Woolston Shrops 60 F4
Woolston Shrops 60 B3
Woolston Soton 14 C5
Woolston Warr 86 F4
Woolstone M Keynes 53 F6
Woolstone Oxon 38 F2
Woolton Mers 86 F2
Woolton Hill Hants 26 C2
Woolverstone Suff 57 F5
Woolverton Som 24 D2
Woolwich London 28 B5
Woolwich Ferry London 28 B5
Woonton Hereford 49 D5
Wooperton Northumb 117 B6
Woore Shrops 74 E4
Wootten Green Suff 57 B6
Wootton Beds 53 E8
Wootton Hants 14 E3
Wootton Hereford 48 D5
Wootton Kent 31 E6
Wootton N Lincs 90 C4
Wootton Northants 53 D5
Wootton Oxon 38 C4
Wootton Oxon 38 D4
Wootton Shrops 49 B6
Wootton Shrops 60 B3
Wootton Staffs 62 B2
Wootton Staffs 75 E8
Wootton Bassett Wilts 37 F7
Wootton Bridge I o W 15 E6
Wootton Common I o W 15 E6
Wootton Courtenay Som 21 E8
Wootton Fitzpaine Dorset 11 E8
Wootton Green Suff 57 B6
Wootton Rivers Wilts 25 C6
Wootton St Lawrence Hants 26 D3
Wootton Wawen Warks 51 C6
Worcester Worcs 50 D3
Worcester Cathedral Worcs 50 D3
Worcester Park London 28 C3
Worcester Racecourse Worcs 50 D3
Wordsley W Mid 62 F2
Worfield Shrops 61 E7
Work Orkney 176 E3
Workington Cumb 98 B1
Worksop Notts 77 B5
Worlaby N Lincs 90 C4
World of James Herriot N Yorks 102 F2
World's End W Berks 26 B2
Worle N Som 23 C5
Worleston Ches 74 D3
Worlingham Suff 69 F7
Worlington Suff 55 B7
Worlingworth Suff 57 C6
Wormald Green N Yorks 95 C6
Wormbridge Hereford 49 F6
Wormegay Norf 67 C6
Wormelow Tump Hereford 49 F6
Wormhill Derbys 75 B8
Wormingford Essex 56 F3
Worminghall Bucks 39 D6
Wormington Glos 50 F5
Worminster Som 23 E7
Wormit Fife 135 B5
Wormleighton Warks 52 D2
Wormley Herts 41 D6
Wormley Sur 27 F7
Wormley West End Herts 41 D6
Wormshill Kent 30 D2
Wormsley Hereford 49 E6
Worplesdon Sur 27 D7
Worrall S Yorks 88 E4
Worsbrough S Yorks 88 D4
Worsbrough Common S Yorks 88 D4
Worsley Gtr Man 86 D5
Worstead Norf 69 B6
Worsthorne Lancs 93 F8
Worston Lancs 93 E7
Worswell Devon 6 E3
Worth Kent 31 D7
Worth W Sus 28 F4
Worth Matravers Dorset 13 G7
Wortham Suff 56 B4
Worthen Shrops 60 D3
Worthenbury Wrex 73 E8
Worthing Norf 68 C2
Worthing W Sus 16 D5
Worthington Leics 63 B8
Worting Hants 26 D4
Wortley S Yorks 88 E4
Wortley W Yorks 95 F5
Worton N Yorks 100 E4
Worton Wilts 24 D4
Wortwell Norf 69 F5
Wotherton Shrops 60 D2
Wotter Devon 6 C3
Wotton Sur 28 E2
Wotton-under-Edge Glos 36 E4
Wotton Underwood Bucks 39 C6
Woughton on the Green M Keynes 53 F6
Wouldham Kent 29 C8
Wrabness Essex 57 F5
Wrafton Devon 20 F3
Wragby Lincs 78 B4
Wragby W Yorks 88 C5
Wragholme Lincs 91 E7
Wramplingham Norf 68 D4
Wrangbrook W Yorks 89 C5
Wrangham Aberds 160 E3
Wrangle Lincs 79 D7
Wrangle Bank Lincs 79 D7
Wrangle Lowgate Lincs 79 D7
Wrangway Som 11 C6
Wrantage Som 11 B8
Wrawby N Lincs 90 D4
Wraxall Dorset 12 D3
Wraxall N Som 23 B6
Wraxall Som 23 F8
Wray Lancs 93 C6
Wraysbury Windsor 27 B8
Wrayton Lancs 93 B6
Wrea Green Lancs 92 F3
Wreay Cumb 99 B6
Wreay Cumb 108 E4
Wrecclesham Sur 27 E6
Wrecsam = Wrexham Wrex 73 D7
Wrekenton T & W 111 D5
Wrelton N Yorks 103 F5
Wrenbury Ches 74 E2
Wrench Green N Yorks 103 F7
Wreningham Norf 68 E4
Wrentham Suff 69 F7
Wrenthorpe W Yorks 88 B4
Wrentnall Shrops 60 D4
Wressle E Yorks 96 F3
Wressle N Lincs 90 D3
Wrestlingworth Beds 54 E3
Wretham Norf 68 F2
Wretton Norf 67 E6
Wrexham = Wrecsam Wrex 73 D7
Wrexham Industrial Estate Wrex 73 E7
Wribbenhall Worcs 50 B2
Wrightington Bar Lancs 86 C3
Wrinehill Staffs 74 E4
Wrington N Som 23 C6
Writhlington Bath 24 D2
Writtle Essex 42 D2
Wrockwardine Telford 61 C6
Wroot N Lincs 89 D8
Wrotham Kent 29 D7
Wrotham Heath Kent 29 D7
Wroughton Thamesdown 37 F8
Wroxall I o W 15 G6
Wroxall Warks 51 B7
Wroxeter Shrops 61 D5
Wroxham Norf 69 C6
Wroxham Barns, Hoveton Norf 69 B6
Wroxton Oxon 52 E2
Wyaston Derbys 75 E8
Wyberton Lincs 79 E6
Wyboston Beds 54 D2
Wybunbury Ches 74 E4
Wych Cross E Sus 28 F5
Wychbold Worcs 50 C4
Wyck Hants 27 F5
Wyck Rissington Glos 38 B1
Wycoller Lancs 94 F2
Wycomb Leics 64 B4
Wycombe Marsh Bucks 40 E1
Wyddial Herts 54 F4
Wye Kent 30 E4
Wyesham Mon 36 C2
Wyfordby Leics 64 C4
Wyke Dorset 13 B5
Wyke Shrops 61 D6
Wyke Sur 27 D7
Wyke W Yorks 88 B2
Wyke Regis Dorset 12 G4
Wykeham N Yorks 103 F7
Wykeham N Yorks 96 B4
Wyken W Mid 63 F7
Wykey Shrops 60 B3
Wylam Northumb 110 C4
Wylde Green W Mid 62 E5
Wyllie Caerph 35 E5
Wylye Wilts 24 F5
Wymering Ptsmth 15 D7
Wymeswold Leics 64 B3
Wymington Beds 53 C7
Wymondham Leics 65 C5
Wymondham Norf 68 D4
Wyndham Bridgend 34 E3
Wynford Eagle Dorset 12 E3
Wyng Orkney 176 G2
Wynyard Village Stockton 102 B2
Wyre Piddle Worcs 50 E4
Wysall Notts 64 B3
Wythall Worcs 51 B5
Wytham Oxon 38 D4
Wythburn Cumb 99 C5
Wythenshawe Gtr Man 87 F6
Wythop Mill Cumb 98 B3
Wyton Cambs 54 B3
Wyverstone Suff 56 C4
Wyverstone Street Suff 56 C4
Wyville Lincs 65 B5
Wyvis Lodge Highld 157 B5

Y

Y Bala = Bala Gwyn 72 F3
Y Barri = Barry V Glam 22 C3
Y Bont-Faen = Cowbridge V Glam 21 B8
Y Drenewydd = Newtown Powys 59 E8
Y Felinheli Gwyn 82 E5
Y Fenni = Abergavenny Mon 35 C6
Y Fflint = Flint Flint 73 B6
Y Ffôr Gwyn 70 D4
Y-Ffrith Denb 72 A4
Y Gelli Gandryll = Hay-on-Wye Powys 48 E4
Y Mwmbwls = The Mumbles Swansea 33 F7
Y Pîl = Pyle Bridgend 34 F2
Y Rhws = Rhoose V Glam 22 C2
Y Rhyl = Rhyl Denb 72 A4
Y Trallwng = Welshpool Powys 60 D2
Y Waun = Chirk Wrex 73 F6
Yaddlethorpe N Lincs 90 D2
Yafford I o W 14 F5
Yafforth N Yorks 101 E8
Yalding Kent 29 D7
Yanworth Glos 37 C7
Yapham E Yorks 96 D3
Yapton W Sus 16 D3
Yarburgh Lincs 91 E7
Yarcombe Devon 11 D7
Yard Som 22 F2
Yardley W Mid 62 F5
Yardley Gobion Northants 53 E5
Yardley Hastings Northants 53 D6
Yardro Powys 48 D4
Yarkhill Hereford 49 E8
Yarlet Staffs 62 B3
Yarlington Som 12 B4
Yarlside Cumb 92 C2
Yarm Stockton 102 C2
Yarmouth I o W 14 F4
Yarmouth Racecourse Norf 69 C8
Yarnbrook Wilts 24 D3
Yarnfield Staffs 75 F5
Yarnscombe Devon 9 B7
Yarnton Oxon 38 C4
Yarpole Hereford 49 C6
Yarrow Borders 115 B6
Yarrow Feus Borders 115 B6
Yarsop Hereford 49 E6
Yarwell Northants 65 E7
Yate S Glos 36 F4
Yateley Hants 27 C6
Yatesbury Wilts 25 B5
Yattendon W Berks 26 B3
Yatton Hereford 49 C6
Yatton Hereford 49 F8
Yatton N Som 23 C6
Yatton Keynell Wilts 24 B3
Yaverland I o W 15 F7
Yaxham Norf 68 C3
Yaxley Cambs 65 E8
Yaxley Suff 56 B5
Yazor Hereford 49 E6
Yeading London 40 F4
Yeadon W Yorks 94 E5
Yealand Conyers Lancs 92 B5
Yealand Redmayne Lancs 92 B5
Yealmpton Devon 6 D3
Yearby Redcar 102 B4
Yearsley N Yorks 95 B8
Yeaton Shrops 60 C4
Yeaveley Derbys 75 E8
Yedingham N Yorks 96 B4
Yeldon Beds 53 C8
Yelford Oxon 38 D3
Yelland Devon 20 F3
Yelling Cambs 54 C3
Yelvertoft Northants 52 B3
Yelverton Devon 6 C3
Yelverton Norf 69 D5
Yenston Som 12 B5
Yeo Mill Devon 10 B3
Yeoford Devon 10 E2
Yeolmbridge Corn 8 F5
Yeovil Som 12 C3
Yeovil Marsh Som 12 C3
Yeovilton Som 12 B3
Yerbeston Pembs 32 D1
Yesnaby Orkney 176 E1
Yetlington Northumb 117 D6
Yetminster Dorset 12 C3
Yettington Devon 11 F5
Yetts o'Muckhart Clack 134 D2
Yieldshields S Lnrk 121 D8
Yiewsley London 40 F3
Ynys-meudwy Neath 33 D8
Ynysboeth Rhondda 34 E4
Ynysddu Caerph 35 E5
Ynysgyfflog Gwyn 58 C3
Ynyshir Rhondda 34 E4
Ynyslas Ceredig 58 E3
Ynystawe Swansea 33 D7
Ynysybwl Rhondda 34 E4
Yockenthwaite N Yorks 94 B2
Yockleton Shrops 60 C3
Yokefleet E Yorks 90 B2
Yoker Glasgow 120 C5
Yonder Bognie Aberds 160 D2
York York 95 D8
York Castle Museum York 96 D2
York Minster York 96 D2
York Racecourse York 95 E8
York Town Sur 27 C6
Yorkletts Kent 30 C4
Yorkley Glos 36 D3
Yorkshire Museum York 95 D8
Yorkshire Sculpture Park, Wakefield W Yorks 88 C3
Yorton Shrops 60 B5
Youlgreave Derbys 76 C2
Youlstone Devon 8 C4
Youlthorpe E Yorks 96 D3
Youlton N Yorks 95 C7
Young Wood Lincs 78 B4
Young's End Essex 42 C3
Yoxall Staffs 62 C5
Yoxford Suff 57 C7
Yr Hôb = Hope Flint 73 D7
Yr Wyddgrug = Mold Flint 73 C6
Ysbyty-Cynfyn Ceredig 47 B6
Ysbyty Ifan Conwy 72 E2
Ysbyty Ystwyth Ceredig 47 B6
Ysceifiog Flint 73 B5
Yspitty Carms 33 E6
Ystalyfera Neath 34 D1
Ystrad Rhondda 34 E3
Ystrad Aeron Ceredig 46 D4
Ystrad-mynach Caerph 35 E5
Ystradfellte Powys 34 C3
Ystradffin Carms 47 E6
Ystradgynlais Powys 34 C1
Ystradmeurig Ceredig 47 C6
Ystradowen Carms 33 C8
Ystradowen V Glam 22 B2
Ystumtuen Ceredig 47 B6
Ythanbank Aberds 161 E6
Ythanwells Aberds 160 E3
Ythsie Aberds 161 E5

Z

Zeal Monachorum Devon 10 D2
Zeals Wilts 24 F2
Zelah Corn 4 D3
Zennor Corn 2 C3